Advertising & Promotion

AN INTEGRATED MARKETING COMMUNICATIONS PERSPECTIVE

Seventh Canadian Edition

Michael A. Guolla
University of Ottawa

George E. Belch
San Diego State University

Michael A. Belch
San Diego State University

ISBN-13: 978-1-26-006598-5
ISBN-10: 1-26-006598-7

1 2 3 4 5 6 7 8 9 0 M 24 23 22 21 20

Printed and bound in Canada.

Care has been taken to trace ownership of copyright material contained in this text; however, the publisher will welcome any information that enables them to rectify any reference or credit for subsequent editions.

Product Director: Rhondda McNabb
Portfolio Manager: Sara Braithwaite
Marketing Manager: Emily Park
Senior Content Developer: Amy Rydzanicz
Portfolio Associate: Tatiana Sevciuc
Supervising Editor: Janie Deneau
Photo/Permissions Editor: Monika Schurmann
Copy Editor: Laurel Sparrow
Plant Production Coordinator: Heitor Moura
Manufacturing Production Coordinator: Jason Stubner
Cover Design: Dianne Reynolds
Cover Images: © TRphotos/Shutterstock
Interior Design: David Montle, Pixel Hive Studio
Page Layout: SPi Global Inc.
Printer: Marquis

Brief Contents

Preface   x

PART 1
Understanding Integrated Marketing
Communications   2

CHAPTER 1
Integrated Marketing Communications   2

CHAPTER 2
Organizing for IMC: Role of Agencies   30

CHAPTER 3
Consumer Behaviour and Target Audience
Decisions   50

CHAPTER 4
Communication Response Models   74

PART 2
Articulating the Message   100

CHAPTER 5
Objectives for the IMC Plan   100

CHAPTER 6
Brand Positioning Strategy Decisions   124

CHAPTER 7
Creative Strategy Decisions   152

CHAPTER 8
Creative Tactics Decisions   186

CHAPTER 9
Measuring the Effectiveness of the
Promotional Message   212

PART 3
Delivering the Message   232

CHAPTER 10
Media Planning and Budgeting for IMC   232

CHAPTER 11
Broadcast Media   266

CHAPTER 12
Print Media   294

CHAPTER 13
Out-of-Home Media   318

PART 4
Strengthening the Message   340

CHAPTER 14
Sales Promotion   340

CHAPTER 15
Public Relations   372

CHAPTER 16
Direct Marketing   398

CHAPTER 17
Internet Media   418

CHAPTER 18
Social Media   450

PART 5
Advertising and Society   478

CHAPTER 19
Regulatory, Ethical, Social, and Economic
Issues for IMC   478

Endnotes   EN-1

Chapter Sources   S-1

Name and Company Index   IN-1

Subject Index   IN-12

Contents

Preface   x

PART 1
Understanding Integrated Marketing
Communications   2

CHAPTER 1
Integrated Marketing Communications   2

Marketing Communication   4
  Marketing   4
  Communicating Product   5
  Communicating Price   7
  Communicating Distribution   8
  Communicating Value   8
The Promotional Mix   9
  Advertising   9
  Sales Promotion   10
  Public Relations   11
  Direct Marketing   11
  Internet Marketing   12
  Personal Selling   13
  Participants in the Promotional Process   13
Integrated Marketing Communications   15
  IMC: Evolution   15
  IMC: Renewed Perspective   16
  IMC: Audience Contact   16
  IMC: Paid, Owned, Earned   18
Integrated Marketing Communications Planning   19
  Review the Marketing Plan   20
  Assess the Marketing Communications Situation 20
  Determine IMC Plan Objectives   23
  Develop IMC Programs   24
  Implement and Control the IMC Plan   25
IMC Planning: Organization of Text   25
  Understanding Integrated Marketing Communications 25
  Articulating the Message   26
  Delivering the Message   26
  Strengthening the Message   26
  Advertising and Society   27
Learning Objectives Summary   27
Review Questions   28
Applied Questions   28

CHAPTER 2
Organizing for IMC: Role of Agencies   30

Advertising Agencies   32
  Advertising Agency Decision   32
  Advertising Agency Industry   34
  Full-Service Agency   36
Agency Compensation and Evaluation   39
  Commissions From Media   40

  Fee Arrangement   40
  Cost-Plus Agreement   40
  Incentive-Based Compensation   41
  Evaluation of Agencies   41
Specialized Services   42
  Creative Boutiques   42
  Media Buying Services   43
  Sales Promotion Agencies   44
  Public Relations Firms   45
  Direct-Response Agencies   45
  Digital/Interactive Agencies   45
IMC Planning: Agency Relationships   46
  Integrated IMC Services   46
  Agency–Client Responsibility   47
  Agency–Client Relationships   47
Learning Objectives Summary   48
Review Questions   48
Applied Questions   49

CHAPTER 3
Consumer Behaviour and Target Audience
Decisions   50

Consumer Decision-Making Process   52
  Need Recognition   52
  Information Search   53
  Alternative Evaluation   55
  Purchase Decision   57
  Post-Purchase Evaluation   58
  Types of Decision Making   58
  Group Decision Making   59
Target Audience Decision   60
  Marketing Planning Process   60
  Segmentation Variables   61
  Promotional Planning Process   65
  Target Audience Options   66
IMC Planning: Target Audience Profile   70
  Profile for Messages   70
  Profile for Media   71
  Profile for IMC Tools   71
Learning Objectives Summary   71
Review Questions   72
Applied Questions   73

CHAPTER 4
Communication Response Models   74

A Model of the Communication Process   76
  Source   76
  Encoding   77
  Message   77
  Non-Personal Channel   78
  Personal Channel   79

Receiver — 80
Decoding — 80
Noise — 81
Response — 82
Feedback — 82
Summary of the Model — 82

The Receiver's Response — **83**
Traditional Response Hierarchy Models — 83
Implications of the Traditional Response Hierarchy Models — 84
Alternative Response Hierarchy Models — 85
Implications of the Alternative Response Hierarchy Models — 86
Summary of Response Hierarchy Models — 87

The Receiver's Processing of Communication — **88**
Processing of Ad Messages — 88
Cognitive Response Model — 89
Elaboration Likelihood Model — 91
Conclusion of Processing Models — 94

Response Model for Managerial Decision Making — **94**
Processing of Messages — 95
Communication Effects of Messages — 95

IMC Planning: Managerial Decision Making — **96**
Learning Objectives Summary — **97**
Review Questions — **99**
Applied Questions — **99**

PART 2
Articulating the Message — 100

CHAPTER 5
Objectives for the IMC Plan — 100

Objective Setting — **102**
Value of Objectives — 102
Marketing Objectives — 103
Sales Objective Debate — 104
Behavioural Objectives — 105
Communication Objectives — 105

From Communication Response Models to Communication Objectives — **106**
Defining Advertising Goals for Measured Results — 106
Communication Response Model Applications — 107

Setting Behavioural Objectives for IMC — **111**
Trial Purchase Objectives — 111
Repeat-Purchase Objectives — 113
Shopping Objectives — 114
Repeat-Consumption Objectives — 114

Setting Communication Objectives for IMC — **116**
Category Need — 116
Brand Awareness — 117
Brand Attitude — 118
Brand Purchase Intention — 119

IMC Planning: Objectives for Buyer Decision Stages — 120
Learning Objectives Summary — **121**
Review Questions — **122**
Applied Questions — **122**

CHAPTER 6
Brand Positioning Strategy Decisions — 124

Positioning — **126**
Market Positioning Strategy — 126
Brand Positioning Strategy — 127
Brand Positioning Strategy Decision Process — 130

Brand Positioning Strategy Decisions — **133**
Market Definition — 133
Differential Advantage — 135
Target Audience Brand Attitude — 137
Consumer Purchase Motive — 141

Brand Repositioning Strategy — **143**
Importance of Repositioning — 143
Market Definition — 144
Differential Advantage — 145
New Target Audience — 146
Purchase Motivation — 147

IMC Planning: Brand Positioning Extensions — **148**
Multiple Target Audiences — 148
Buyer Decision Stages — 148
Corporate Brands — 149

Learning Objectives Summary — **149**
Review Questions — **150**
Applied Questions — **151**

CHAPTER 7
Creative Strategy Decisions — 152

Advertising Creativity — **154**
Definition of Advertising Creativity — 154
Importance of Advertising Creativity — 156

Planning Creative Strategy — **157**
Creative Challenge — 158
Creative Process — 158
Account Planning — 159
Research in the Creative Process — 159
Creative Brief — 162
Advertising Campaign — 163

Creative Theme — **164**
Origin of Creative Theme — 164
Campaign Slogans — 166
Creative Theme Consistency — 167
Canadian Creative Themes — 168

Message Appeals — **170**
Rational Appeals — 170
Emotional Appeals — 172
Fear Appeals — 174
Humour Appeals — 175
Combined Rational and Emotional Appeals — 176

Source Characteristics — **177**
Source Credibility — 177
Source Attractiveness — 178

IMC Planning: Message and Source Combinations — **183**
Learning Objectives Summary — **184**
Review Questions — **185**
Applied Questions — **185**

CHAPTER 8

Creative Tactics Decisions   186

Creative Execution Style   **187**
Straight Sell   188
Scientific/Technical Evidence   188
Demonstration   188
Comparison   188
Testimonial   189
Slice of Life   189
Animation   189
Personality Symbol   190
Imagery   191
Dramatization   192
Humour   192

Message Structure   **193**
Order of Presentation   193
Conclusion Drawing   194
Message Sidedness   195
Verbal/Visual Balance   196

Design Elements for IMC Tools   **197**
Design for Print Messages   197
Design for Video Messages   200
Design for Audio Messages   202

Planning Model for Creative Tactics   **203**
Tactics for Brand Awareness   203
Tactics for Brand Attitude   204

IMC Planning: Guidelines for Creative Evaluation   **208**
Learning Objectives Summary   **209**
Review Questions   **210**
Applied Questions   **211**

CHAPTER 9

Measuring the Effectiveness of the
Promotional Message   212

Decisions for Measuring Effectiveness   **214**
Why Measure Effectiveness   214
What to Measure   215
Where to Measure   215
How to Measure   216
When to Measure   216

Measuring Effectiveness   **217**
Processing Measures   218
Communication Effects Measures   219

Pretest Measuring   **221**
Concept Test   221
Rough Test   221
Pretest of Finished Print Ad   221
Pretest of Finished Broadcast Ad   222

Post-Test Measuring   **225**
Post-Test of Print Ad   225
Post-Test of Broadcast Ad   227

IMC Planning: Program for Measuring Effectiveness **228**
Criteria for Effective Research   228
Guidelines for Effective Testing   229

Learning Objectives Summary   **230**
Review Questions   **231**
Applied Questions   **231**

PART 3

Delivering the Message   232

CHAPTER 10

Media Planning and Budgeting for IMC   232

Media Planning   **234**
Overview   234
Media Plan   235
Media Planning Challenges   237

Media Strategy Decisions   **239**
The Media Mix   239
Target Audience Coverage   242
Geographic Coverage   243
Scheduling   244
Reach and Frequency   245

Media Tactics Decisions   **250**
Media Vehicle   250
Relative Cost Estimates   252
Blocking Chart   254

Budget Setting   **255**
Overview   255
Theoretical Approaches in Budget Setting   256
Managerial Approaches in Budget Setting   258

IMC Planning: Budget Allocation   **262**
Learning Objectives Summary   **263**
Review Questions   **264**
Applied Questions   **264**

CHAPTER 11

Broadcast Media   266

Television   **268**
Delivery of TV Services   268
Types of TV Advertising   269
Time Periods and Programs   273
Measuring the TV Audience   274
OTT TV Viewing   276

Evaluation of Television   **277**
Strengths of Television   278
Limitations of Television   281

Radio   **286**
Types of Radio Advertising   286
Time Periods   286
Measuring the Radio Audience   287
Audio Streaming   287

Evaluation of Radio   **288**
Strengths of Radio   288
Limitations of Radio   290

IMC Planning: Strategic Use of Broadcast Media   **291**
Television   291
Radio   291

Learning Objectives Summary	292
Review Questions	293
Applied Questions	293

CHAPTER 12
Print Media 294

Magazines	296
Classifications of Magazines	296
Magazine Circulation and Readership	298
Magazine Advertising Rates	299
Evaluation of Magazines	300
Strengths of Magazines	300
Limitations of Magazines	306
Newspapers	307
Types of Newspapers	307
Types of Newspaper Advertising	308
Newspaper Circulation and Readership	309
Newspaper Advertising Rates	310
Evaluation of Newspapers	311
Strengths of Newspapers	311
Limitations of Newspapers	313
IMC Planning: Strategic Use of Print Media	314
Magazines	314
Newspapers	315
Learning Objectives Summary	315
Review Questions	317
Applied Questions	317

CHAPTER 13
Out-of-Home Media 318

Outdoor Media	320
Outdoor Media Options	320
Audience Measurement	324
Strengths of Outdoor Media	325
Limitations of Outdoor Media	327
Transit Media	327
Transit Media Options	328
Strengths of Transit Media	329
Limitations of Transit Media	330
Place-Based Media	330
Place-Based Media Options	331
Strengths of Place-Based Media	335
Limitations of Place-Based Media	335
IMC Planning: Strategic Use of Out-of-Home Media	336
Learning Objectives Summary	336
Review Questions	337
Applied Questions	338

PART 4
Strengthening the Message 340

CHAPTER 14
Sales Promotion 340

Sales Promotion Planning	342
Characteristics of Sales Promotion	342
Types of Sales Promotion	342
Growth of Sales Promotion	343
Sales Promotion Plan	346
Objectives of Consumer Sales Promotion	346
Consumer Sales Promotion Strategy Decisions	347
Consumer Sales Promotion Tactics Decisions	350
Consumer Sales Promotion Strategy Options	351
Sampling	351
Coupons	353
Premiums	355
Promotional Products	356
Contests and Sweepstakes	357
Refunds and Rebates	358
Bonus Packs	359
Price Discount	360
Event Marketing	360
Trade Sales Promotion Strategy Options	361
Objectives of Trade Sales Promotion	361
Trade Allowances	362
Point-of-Purchase Displays	363
Cooperative Advertising	365
Contests and Incentives	365
Sales Training Programs	366
Trade Shows	366
IMC Planning: Strategic Use of Sales Promotion	366
Budget Allocation	367
Creative Themes	367
Media Support	367
Brand Equity	368
Measuring Sales Promotion Effectiveness	368
Learning Objectives Summary	369
Review Questions	370
Applied Questions	370

CHAPTER 15
Public Relations 372

Public Relations	374
Traditional View of PR	374
New Role of PR	374
Publicity	375
Public Relations Plan	376
Situation Analysis	377
Determine Relevant Target Audiences	377
Behavioural Objectives	379
Communication Objectives	379
Strategy	380
Tactics	381
Public Relations Effectiveness	381
News Media Publicity	382
Media Options	382
Strengths of News Media Publicity	383
Limitations of News Media Publicity	384
Corporate Advertising	385
Corporate Reputation	385
Corporate Image Advertising	386

Cause-Related Advertising 387
Sponsorship 388
IMC Planning: Strategic Use of PR **394**
Learning Objectives Summary **395**
Review Questions **396**
Applied Questions **396**

CHAPTER 16
Direct Marketing 398
Direct Marketing **400**
Defining Direct Marketing 400
Developing a Database 400
Direct-Marketing Plan **403**
Target Audiences for Direct Marketing 403
Direct-Marketing Objectives 403
Direct-Response Media 404
Direct-Marketing Effectiveness 408
Loyalty Programs **408**
Purpose of Loyalty Programs 408
Loyalty Program Characteristics 409
Consumer Attitudes and Usage 411
Digital Communication 412
Evaluation of Direct Marketing **413**
Strengths of Direct Marketing 413
Limitations of Direct Marketing 414
IMC Planning: Strategic Use of Direct Marketing **414**
Decision-Making Process 414
Direct Marketing and IMC Tools 415
Learning Objectives Summary **415**
Review Questions **416**
Applied Questions **417**

CHAPTER 17
Internet Media 418
Internet Media Communication **419**
Internet Usage 420
Website Communication 422
Website Strategy 424
Digital Advertising Planning **426**
Overview 426
Digital Advertising Plan 427
Target Audience and Objectives 428
Digital Media Strategy 428
Digital Media Tactics 429
Digital Ad Formats **430**
Display Ads 431
Paid Search Ads 433
Video Ads 434
Audio Ads 437
Classified and Directory Ads 438
Promotional Ads 438
Mobile **438**
Mobile Ads 438
Mobile Device Usage 439

Mobile Apps 441
SMS 442
Measuring Internet Media Effectiveness **444**
Audience Measures 444
Communication Model Measures 444
IMC Planning: Strategic Use of Internet Media **445**
Learning Objectives Summary **447**
Review Questions **448**
Applied Questions **448**

CHAPTER 18
Social Media 450
Social Media Communication **452**
Social Media Classes 452
Social Media Engagement 453
eWOM 453
Social Media Usage 454
Social Networking **456**
Facebook 456
Twitter 460
Content Communities **463**
YouTube 463
Instagram 466
Blogs and Collaborative Projects **468**
Blogs 468
Collaborative Projects 469
Social Media Influence **472**
IMC Planning: Strategic Use of Social Media **473**
Learning Objectives Summary **474**
Review Questions **476**
Applied Questions **476**

PART 5
Advertising and Society 478

CHAPTER 19
Regulatory, Ethical, Social, and Economic
Issues for IMC 478
Advertising Regulation In Canada **480**
Canadian Radio-television and Telecommunications
Commission (CRTC) 480
Competition Act 481
Regulations on Advertising to Children 481
Ad Standards (AS) 482
Ethical Effects of Advertising **487**
Advertising as Untruthful or Deceptive 487
Advertising as Offensive or in Bad Taste 488
Advertising and Children 491
Social Effects of Advertising **492**
Advertising Encourages Materialism 492
Advertising and Persuasion 493
Advertising and Stereotyping 494

Advertising and the Media 496
Advertising and Social Benefit 496
Economic Effects of Advertising **498**
Effects on Consumer Choice 498
Effects on Competition 498
Effects on Product Costs and Prices 499
Summarizing Economic Effects 499
Learning Objectives Summary **501**
Review Questions **502**
Applied Questions **502**

Endnotes **EN-1**

Chapter Sources **S-1**

Name and Company Index **IN-1**

Subject Index **IN-12**

Preface

ADVERTISING AND PROMOTION

Organizations in both the private and public sectors frequently demonstrate that communicating effectively and efficiently with their target audiences is critical to their success. Advertising and other types of promotional messages known as marketing communications are used to sell goods and services, promote causes and individuals, and influence attitudes and behaviour to resolve societal problems. In fact, it would be impossible to find an organization that does not communicate externally to its constituents to achieve its mandate, and marketing communication usually contributes in achieving objectives consistent with what an organization intends to accomplish.

In today's complex world, an organization communicating effectively—the right message to the right audience at the right time—is a critical and difficult task for promotional planners to achieve efficiently. A marketer's audiences are current customers, potential customers, and external stakeholders and all of these groups require a customized message if it is to be accepted. The message design is informational and/or transformational and usually communicated with creativity to convince the audiences. And there are myriad media for message delivery—broadcast (TV networks, specialty TV, radio), print (magazines and newspapers), out-of-home (outdoor, transit, place-based), and Internet (websites, content publishers, social media)—that are strengthened with sales promotions, events, sponsorship, and public relations.

Moreover, the Internet's interactive characteristics strengthen (and possibly weaken) an organization's image or reputation due to consumers' brand-related online activities. Watching brand-related videos, reading brand-related information on social networking sites, commenting on brand-related blogs, and uploading brand-related pictures/images potentially influences an organization's audiences. These activities are prompted directly by a brand's communication, and are also a manifestation of attitudes established over time yet initiated by motives we are only beginning to uncover as marketers. In either case, promotional planners must take a broad and all-encompassing view of marketing communication if they are to be successful in their decision making.

This text introduces students to advertising and promotion with an integrated marketing communications (IMC) perspective. IMC calls for a "big picture" approach to planning promotion programs and coordinating the communication tools described above to positively enhance a brand. To make effective promotional decisions, a promotional planner must decide how the IMC tools will work individually and collectively so that the organization can achieve its goals efficiently.

SEVENTH CANADIAN EDITION ADVANTAGES

This seventh Canadian edition accomplishes the task of showing students how to devise and construct an IMC plan better than any other product on the market. Its numerous advantages include:

- **IMC Perspective**—Advertising and promotion takes an integrated marketing communications perspective to attain communication and behavioural objectives for multiple target audiences. The importance of specific communication and behavioural objectives for each target audience and the importance of unique messages that resonate for each target audience are developed. This approach shows how to establish a unique brand position for each target audience while maintaining the overall market position of the brand.

- **Canadian Practice**—Canadian ads and examples provide a comprehensive look at innovative marketing communications occurring in our country. The text features approximately 500 references from sources such as *Marketing Magazine, Strategy,* the *National Post, The Globe and Mail,* and others to illustrate uniquely Canadian stories so that future promotional planners see what successful marketing communication looks like. The 53 new perspectives and vignettes reflect advertising, media, and digital stories representing approximately 200 new articles.

- **Canadian Data**—Statistical information presented in tables, charts, and figures appears throughout the text. There are about 230 figures, of which a substantial portion describe the Canadian marketing communication environment. Most of these data occur in the media chapters, providing the most thorough coverage of media by anyone's standards.

- **Decision Oriented**—Chapter 1 summarizes a planning framework and identifies the content of an IMC plan. This framework guides the text as parts are organized and given a title that corresponds to the steps in the IMC plan. A distinction is made between the type of decision that an advertiser makes and the information used to formulate the decision. This approach helps students understand the key decisions that are made for a successful IMC plan.

- **Internet Focus**—Internet media use occurs throughout the text where it is most relevant. The majority of the opening vignettes and chapter perspectives highlight the use of websites or other digital tools. A balance between Internet media and other media reinforces the importance of IMC decision making.

- **Mobile**—Marketing communication through mobile technology is a focus in this edition as consumer adoption is ubiquitous. It is featured in chapter openers and vignettes, and considerable usage statistics are presented in the media chapters.

- **Internet Media**—Material on this topic appears throughout the book and the specific chapter coverage is significantly improved from the past edition.

- **Social Media**—A dedicated social media chapter enters the seventh edition as Chapter 18. An application of how it can be used as owned, paid, and earned media to achieve a brand's objectives is developed and the scope of social media is shown with its numerous media classes and vehicles.

- **Current Theory**—Extensive updating of academic references from the *Journal of Advertising* and the *Journal of*

Advertising Research and others was done independently by the Canadian author over the past five editions. The text references about 500 journal articles to provide a resource for further understanding and to demonstrate that the material presented is credible.

- **Visual Balance**—The number of figures and exhibits stands at about 500 visuals. Consideration of grouping a few paragraphs and a visual occurred throughout the whole revision to make the reading more enjoyable and the learning more pleasurable.

ORGANIZATION OF THIS TEXT

The seventh Canadian edition is divided into five parts. In Part 1, "Understanding Integrated Marketing Communications," we provide background in the areas of IMC planning, consumer behaviour, and communication. Chapter 1 provides an overview of advertising and promotion and an IMC planning model shows the steps in the promotional planning process. This model provides a framework for developing the IMC program and is followed throughout the text. In Chapter 2, we describe the role of ad agencies and other firms that deliver promotional services. Chapter 3 explains how managers use an understanding of buyer behaviour to develop effective communication that is directed to specific target audiences. Chapter 4 examines communication models of how consumers respond to advertising messages and other forms of marketing communication.

In Part 2, "Articulating the Message," we consider how firms develop objectives for their IMC programs and how to translate those objectives into meaningful messages. Chapter 5 stresses the importance of setting objectives for advertising and promotion and the different types of marketing, communication, and behavioural objectives. Based on models of consumer responses to marketing communication, this approach is applied for advertising and all other facets of IMC. Chapter 6 explores how advertisers position their brands through effective marketing communication to persuade target audiences. Chapter 7 describes the planning and development of the creative strategy and advertising campaign. In Chapter 8, we illustrate ways to execute the creative strategy and identify criteria for evaluating creative work. Like the objectives chapter, these three chapters are applicable for brand positioning and message development for any aspect of marketing communication. Chapter 9 discusses how to measure the effectiveness of promotional messages of an IMC program.

For Part 3, "Delivering the Message," we explore how to direct the message through media to the target audience in Chapters 10 through 13. Chapter 10 introduces the principles of media planning and strategy, and examines how a media plan is developed for all IMC tools. We have also included in this chapter methods for determining and allocating the promotional budget across all IMC tools. Chapter 11 discusses the strengths and limitations of broadcast media, as well as issues regarding the purchase of radio and TV time and audience measurement. Chapter 12 considers the same issues for the print media (magazines and newspapers). Chapter 13 presents similar material for out-of-home (outdoor, transit, and place-based) and support media (promotional products and product placement).

In Part 4, "Strengthening the Message," we examine other promotional tools with a continued IMC emphasis.

Chapter 14 covers sales promotion, including both consumer promotions and programs targeted to the trade (retailers, wholesalers, and other intermediaries). Chapter 15 reviews the role of public relations in IMC. Chapter 16 looks at direct marketing and the importance of databases that allow companies to communicate directly with target audiences through various media. Chapter 17 describes how Internet media deliver promotional messages. New Chapter 18 describes how social media is an important part of an IMC plan due to its paid, owned, and earned characteristics.

The text concludes with Part 5, "Advertising and Society," which contains Chapter 19 on the regulatory, social, ethical, and economic issues for advertising and promotion.

CHAPTER FEATURES

The following features in each chapter enhance students' understanding of the material as well as their reading enjoyment.

Learning Objectives

Learning objectives are provided at the beginning of each chapter to identify the major areas and points covered in the chapter and to guide the learning effort. The objectives are tagged throughout the chapter and summarized at the conclusion of each chapter.

Chapter Opening Vignettes

Each chapter begins with a new vignette that describes an exciting example of the effective use of integrated marketing communications by a company or ad agency, bringing current industry issues into focus as they pertain to the chapter.

IMC Perspectives

These boxed items feature descriptions of interesting issues related to the chapter material or the practical application of integrated marketing communication. Many of these stories integrate aspects of digital technology, social media, or mobile media, as technology is used universally within marketing as an integral part of all marketing communication.

IMC Planning

Each chapter includes an IMC Planning section illustrating how chapter content relates to integrated marketing communication. It provides guidance on how a manager can use the conceptual material to make better practical decisions.

Learning Objectives Summaries

These synopses provide a quick review of the key topics covered and serve to illustrate how the learning objectives have been achieved. Each summary corresponds exactly to the learning objective at the start of the chapter.

Review and Applied Questions

Questions at the end of each chapter give students an opportunity to test their understanding of the material. These questions can also serve as a basis for class discussion or assignments. The applied questions provide students with the opportunity to apply what they have learned within the chapter. Each numbered review question and applied question corresponds to the similarly numbered learning objective of the chapter.

AWARD-WINNING TECHNOLOGY

McGraw Hill connect®

McGraw-Hill Connect® is an award-winning digital teaching and learning solution that empowers students to achieve better outcomes and enables instructors to improve efficiency with course management. Within Connect, students have access to SmartBook®, McGraw-Hill's adaptive learning and reading resource. SmartBook prompts students with questions based on the material they are studying. By assessing individual answers, SmartBook learns what each student knows and identifies which topics they need to practise, giving each student a personalized learning experience and path to success.

Connect's key features also include analytics and reporting, simple assignment management, smart grading, the opportunity to post your own resources, and the Connect Instructor Library, a repository of additional resources to improve student engagement in and out of the classroom.

Instructor Resources:

- **Instructor's Manual.** The instructor's manual includes chapter overviews, learning objectives, chapter and lecture outlines, teaching suggestions, answers to review and applied questions, and additional discussion questions and answers (not shown in text).
- **PowerPoint® Presentation and Digital Assets.** These incorporate a high-quality photo and art program, including figure slides, product shots, and advertisements.
- **Computerized Test Bank.** This test bank contains over 3,000 questions categorized by topic and level of learning (definitional, conceptual, or application). The instructor-friendly format allows easy selection of questions from any part of the text, boxed materials, and cases. The program allows you to select any of the questions, make changes if desired, or add new questions—and quickly print out a finished set customized to your course.
- **Video Case Studies.** A unique series of contemporary advertising cases is available on Connect.

Application-Based Activities

The Connect Application-Based Activities are highly interactive and automatically graded application- and analysis-based exercises wherein students immerse themselves in a marketing environment, analyze the situation, and apply their knowledge of marketing strategies. Students progress from understanding basic concepts to assessing and solving complex real-world scenarios.

ACKNOWLEDGMENTS

I would like to recognize the cooperation I received from people in the business, advertising, and media communities. The seventh Canadian edition contains new ads, illustrations, charts, and tables published by advertisers and/or their agencies, trade sources, and other advertising and industry organizations. Many individuals provided materials and gave permission to use them. A special thanks to all of you for helping us teach students with up-to-date examples and information. A marketing book cannot exist without the assistance of marketing people!

A successful book like this happens because of the publisher's exceptional work. Talented individuals at McGraw-Hill who contributed made the final product look fantastic. My portfolio manager, Sara Braithwaite, encouraged a complete revision with the goal of making a strong book even better. A special thanks goes to Amy Rydzanicz, my content developer, for her tremendous effort and high expectations to stay on schedule and to produce a meticulously prepared manuscript. I want to acknowledge the exceptional work of Monika Schurmann for obtaining permissions for the Canadian content shown in the figures and exhibits. Because of the need for digital publication rights, the amount of work and communication required for each item ranges from a quick email and simple processing of information to many emails and complex communication. I'd also like to recognize Laurel Sparrow for her splendid copy editing and proofreading skills that improved the text. Thank you to Janie Deneau for managing the production process. Thanks also to other members of the production team for their hard work on this edition.

I began the first edition nearly 20 years ago with paper tear sheets and created the seventh edition with an online publishing tool; indeed technology has advanced beyond what most of us imagined a couple of decades ago. The good news is that I believe the tool helped me adjust sections and material to make an improved text, and it is a tribute to the publisher to move in this new direction.

At the Telfer School of Management of the University of Ottawa, I have taught marketing communication to students for many years. I enjoy seeing students appreciate my teaching and apply their knowledge attained during my advertising course, within other marketing courses, and while working in the marketing field. I hope that learning how to make effective promotion decisions proved useful in their career. To my current students, I hope you like reading the book and achieve success after graduating. To students beyond my classroom, I wish you success as well after reading this material.

On a personal note, the first edition began with three children in our home and as I completed the seventh edition I found myself in a new target audience for advertisers: empty nest household! Yes, just like technology, even I advanced beyond what I imagined a couple of decades ago! All my love and gratitude goes to my wife, Teresa, since I disappeared to my offices for hours on end to produce this seventh edition.

Michael Guolla

ABOUT THE AUTHOR

Michael Guolla is an assistant professor at the Telfer School of Management of the University of Ottawa. He completed his Ph.D. in Business Administration with a concentration in Marketing at the Stephen M. Ross School of Business of the University of Michigan (Ann Arbor) and received his Honours in Business Administration from the Richard Ivey School of Business at the University of Western Ontario. Dr. Guolla has published articles in academic journals, proceedings of scholarly conferences, and management journals.

Effective. Efficient. Easy to Use.

McGraw-Hill Connect is an award-winning digital teaching and learning solution that empowers students to achieve better outcomes and enables instructors to improve course-management efficiency.

Personalized & Adaptive Learning

Connect's integrated SmartBook helps students study more efficiently, highlighting where in the text to focus and asking review questions to give each student a personalized learning experience and path to success.

High-Quality Course Material

Our trusted solutions are designed to help students actively engage in course content and develop critical higher-level thinking skills, while offering you the flexibility to tailor your course to meet your needs.

Analytics & Reporting

Monitor progress and improve focus with Connect's visual and actionable dash-boards. Reporting features empower instructors and students with real-time performance analytics.

Seamless Integration

Link your Learning Management System with Connect for single sign-on and gradebook synchroniza-tion, with all-in-one ease for you and your students.

Impact of Connect on Pass Rates

72.5%

Without Connect

85.2%

With Connect

SMARTBOOK®

NEW SmartBook 2.0 builds on our market-leading adaptive technology with enhanced capabilities and a streamlined interface that deliver a more usable, accessible and mobile learning experience for both students and instructors.

Available on mobile smart devices – with both online and offline access – the ReadAnywhere app lets students study anywhere, anytime.

SUPPORT AT EVERY STEP

McGraw-Hill ensures you are supported every step of the way. From course design and set up, to instructor training, LMS integration and ongoing support, your Digital Success Consultant is there to make your course as effective as possible.

Learn more about Connect at mheducation.ca

CHAPTER ONE

Integrated Marketing Communications

LEARNING OBJECTIVES

LO1 Describe the importance of marketing communication within the marketing mix.

LO2 Identify the tools of the promotional mix—advertising, sales promotion, public relations, direct marketing, Internet marketing, and personal selling—and summarize their purpose.

LO3 Illustrate the concept of integrated marketing communications (IMC) by distinguishing its evolution, renewed perspective, and content.

LO4 Explain the IMC planning process model and express the steps in developing a marketing communication program.

LO5 Identify how the IMC planning process is continued throughout all chapters.

RBC's IMC Goes Younger

RBC is the largest Canadian bank and it expected to stay in that number one position in the future with a $3.2 billion investment in technology, digital products, and online resources to attract 2.5 million consumers by 2023. With new online entrants in the financial services industry and pressure from other major banks, RBC's IMC plan relied on getting the message right and spending the money wisely with a larger marketing team, up 15 percent from three years ago.

According to the chief marketing officer, RBC's strategy took a holistic approach by appealing to the individual customer and the community where they lived. The bank saw its brand promise rooted in improving the human experience, in fact going beyond the customer experience. To achieve its ambitious goal, RBC continued with previously established efforts and rolled out new marketing communication programs across many fronts with a consistent message.

RBC carried on with its Olympic support for the 2018 Winter Games, a program first launched in the late 1940s. Its "Someday" message focused on athletes' personal backgrounds and how RBC supported them along with their communities. With heavy rotation and many stories, RBC notched the highest recall for Olympic ads.

RBC started a new CSR initiative—"Future Launch"—that also related to younger people. RBC expected that its investment of $500 million over 10 years would assist Canadian youth with their job market prospects. The community aspect of this program focused on the belief that better prepared youth would remain and contribute positively where they currently reside. Social media and content creation assisted in delivering the message. To coincide with the "Someday" messages, the first ad launched during the closing ceremonies of the Winter Olympics so that all Canadians could understand the issues youth faced.

On the product side, RBC saw younger consumers as an underserved market in need of greater understanding about insurance. Three scenarios presented situations in which insurance is necessary (travel, children, health issue), and an RBC advisor humorously answered their question. The 30-, 15-, and 6-second formats permitted options for delivery on TV and online. In these executions, the message resonated with the humanistic aspect of RBC's strategy.

To help younger consumers understand how the bank differed from other major banks, RBC recruited Jay Baruchel as the spokesperson in three ads. One message featured RBC's partnership with Petro-Canada to save money on gas while using an RBC card. Another showed Jay interacting with the app and the AI-enabled Nomi financial management tool. The third related Jay's conversation within the MyAdvisor online tool. The somewhat silly tone and jokes by Jay likely appealed to RBC's younger target audience. In fact, pre-tests showed positive results of viewers considering a switch to RBC.

Question:

1. What suggestions do you have for RBC to attract younger consumers?

As the opening vignette illustrates, companies use advertising, websites, direct marketing, sales promotion, public relations, and social media to communicate something about their products, prices, or availability. In fact, finding the right approach for marketing communication is a critical decision for small and large firms, private and public organizations, and those marketing goods, services, or ideas. In response, companies use *integrated marketing communications* to link or connect their promotional tools and communicate with their current and prospective customers. Companies develop their marketing communication plans such that each promotional tool retains its unique communication effect and that the combination of promotional tools contributes to the overall communication effect of the brand or organization.

This first chapter sets the direction for the entire book as it highlights the marketing context for advertising and promotion. First, it describes the importance of marketing communication. It then briefly defines the different promotional or marketing communication tools available for marketers. Next, it illustrates the idea of integrated marketing communications and indicates why it is so important. Finally, it explains the content of an integrated marketing communications (IMC) plan as a way of orienting the perspective and organization of this text.

LO1 Marketing Communication

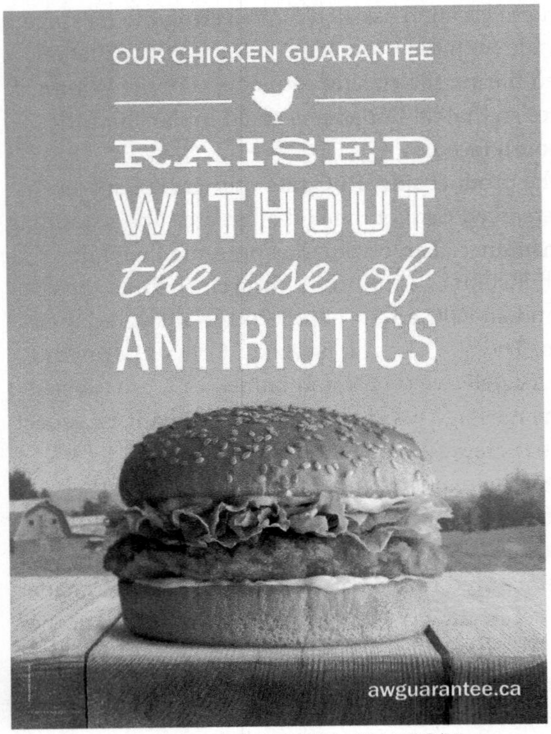
OUR CHICKEN GUARANTEE
RAISED
WITHOUT
the use of
ANTIBIOTICS
awguarantee.ca

Exhibit 1-1 A&W's guarantee potentially reassures consumers that its chicken sandwich is a healthy option for a meal.

Hand-out/A&W RESTAURANTS/Newscom

In this opening section we describe the importance of marketing communication within an organization's overall marketing effort. We review the definition of marketing to understand the importance of marketing communication in delivering value to consumers. We then explore examples of the content of marketing communication plans to illustrate their different purposes.

MARKETING

Historically, the American Marketing Association (AMA), the organization that represents marketing professionals in the United States and Canada, defined marketing as *the process of planning and executing the conception, pricing, promotion, and distribution of ideas, goods, and services to create exchanges that satisfy individual and organizational objectives.*[1] This definition focused on **exchange** as a central concept in marketing and the use of marketing activities to create and sustain relationships with customers.[2] For exchange to occur, there must be two or more parties with something of value to one another, a desire and ability to give up that something to the other party, and a way to *communicate* with each other. Marketing communication facilitates the exchange process by informing consumers of an organization's product and convincing them of its ability to satisfy their needs or wants. **Exhibit 1-1** communicates an important characteristic about A&W's chicken sandwich. Consumers may conclude that this product would be a healthier choice, and better able to meet their dietary needs, than a competitor's sandwich.

The marketing function in an organization facilitates the exchange process by examining the needs and wants of consumers, developing a product that satisfies these needs, offering it at a certain price, making it available through a distribution channel, and developing a marketing communication program. These four Ps—product, price, place (distribution), and promotion (marketing communication)—are elements of the **marketing mix**. The main purpose of the marketing function is to combine these four elements into a marketing program that facilitates the potential for exchange with consumers in the marketplace. The remainder of this section describes how the marketing mix decisions of product, price, and distribution (**Figure 1-1**) are the primary content of marketing communication messages with the ultimate objective of delivering value.

Figure 1-1 Examples of typical marketing decisions

Product Decisions	Price Decisions	Distribution Decisions
Product type	Price level	Channel type
Features or attributes/benefits	Price policy	Channel policy
Corporate name/identification	Discount	Type of intermediary
Brand name/identification	Allowance	Type of location/store
Package design	Flexibility	Service level

COMMUNICATING PRODUCT

Each of the product facets listed in Figure 1-1 is the focus of marketing communication. This section shows how marketing messages communicate the product type, the importance of salient attributes or benefits, and the identity of the brand or organization, in order to assist with brand equity development.

Product Type An organization exists because it offers a product to consumers, generally in exchange for money. This offering may be a physical good (soft drink, pair of jeans, car), a service (banking, air travel, legal assistance), a cause (United Way, March of Dimes), an idea (don't drink and drive), or even a person (professional athlete). TFC soccer player Sebastian Giovinco hired an ad agency to build his personal brand to attract sponsorship deals![3] The product is anything that is marketed and that, when consumed or supported, gives satisfaction to the individual. When we use the term *product* in this book, it refers to any one or a combination of these five product types, which are not always independent. When eating at a restaurant, consumers enjoy the food but also enjoy the service by not having to prepare the meal, or by eating food they may not have the culinary skill to make. Thus, whatever the product type, marketing communication attempts to show how the product offering fulfills a consumer's needs.

Product Attributes/Benefits Every product has fairly objective attributes that characterize what it is; a chocolate bar can have varying types of chocolate (e.g., milk, dark) and different kinds of ingredients (e.g., nuts, wafers). Marketing communication can take the simple role of identifying the composition of a good. For example, ads for Prime Chicken, produced by Maple Leaf Foods, stated in its original message that it was 100 percent all-vegetable-and-grain-fed poultry. Notice how the Surface ad in **Exhibit 1-2** highlights the tablet's performance to change the attitude of laptop users. Moreover, service organizations use marketing communication to educate consumers on their delivery. For instance, WestJet ads demonstrate the personal attentiveness the airline's staff provides to customers, while The Keg Steakhouse ads focus on the ambiance of the restaurant as well as the food.

Consumers typically view a product as an offering of a benefit or a bundle of benefits.[4] Advertising and other marketing communication tools draw attention toward these benefits and make claims about them. Benefits are communicated as functional via the product's attributes, as seen in the above examples. Benefits are also subjectively claimed through the performance of the product (e.g., convenience). Finally, benefits are communicated by feelings or emotions associated with the experiential consumption of a product. These emotions are positive (e.g., contentment) or negative (e.g., fear), and are psychologically based (e.g., pride) or socially based (e.g., jealousy).

Prime Chicken changed its message to show that the convenience of the brand brought families together to create lasting memories, using vignettes of families enjoying their dinner together. The company intended to connect consumers with the brand on an emotional level by highlighting the enjoyment people have with food at dinner time.[5] Thus, managers decide which benefits to emphasize or how to portray the benefits in a message, and come up with a creative way to deliver that message across different time periods. For example, an ad for Western Bulk Transport emphasized the satisfaction experienced by its truck drivers by showing a montage of scenes of one driver when on the job throughout his life. Set to a lovely ballad, the two-minute video emotionally communicates the "Driving for Excellence" slogan.[6]

Brand Identity A brand or corporate name and its identification through its logo, symbol, or trademark represent critical product decisions. Marketers use brand names that communicate the product, such as Air Canada (airline) and Sea-Doo (watercraft). The symbol of every automobile company illustrates the importance of selecting an appropriate visual brand representation. The classic simplicity of the logo for Canadian National Railway is the most celebrated in our country and has been recognized as one of the best in the world.[7] One primary purpose of marketing communication is to present the brand and its identification in favourable locations, situations, or time frames that allow consumers to be aware of the brand and to think or feel more positively toward it. The identification of a trademark in an ad is critical, as evidenced by a legal battle between Victoria's Secret PINK brand and the luxury shirt brand Thomas Pink

Exhibit 1-3 Heineken ensures that its brand identification is prominently displayed.

Figure 1-2 Best Canadian brands

1	TD	6	Bell
2	RBC Financial Group	7	Shoppers Drug Mart
3	Thomson Reuters	8	Rogers
4	Scotiabank	9	Lululemon
5	Tim Hortons	10	Telus

Exhibit 1-4 Showing a product's packaging is a focus of ads.

on the use of the colour in its brand identity.[8] The ad in **Exhibit 1-3** clearly shows the Heineken brand identity with the label on the bottle and similar images on the bottle caps, beer glass, and coaster.

As noted above, brand identity is very important for developing positive consumer responses to the brand, and research firms regularly publish data along these lines. **Figure 1-2** identifies the best Canadian brands as compiled by Interbrand. The list summarizes brands that effectively used advertising and marketing communication to identify the brand in its message which contributed to their ranking.

Brand identity is reinforced by the tagline or slogan appearing in any form of marketing communication. IKEA's slogan, "Long Live the Home," encapsulates the essence of the brand succinctly by connecting the brand name to the products it sells. Executives suggest that the tagline is relevant since it "communicates a brand position or brand benefit." For example, Swiss Chalet returned to a previously successful tagline, "Always so good for so little," after making many changes over the years. Firms that offer many types of goods and services use an audio logo as one way of connecting brand messages across multiple media and IMC tools, much like a visual logo. For example, the Rogers audio logo is heard for many of its services, including wireless and cable. Continuity and consistency in the promotional message across IMC tools—television, radio, wireless, interactive displays, Internet, and podcasts—makes simple reminders of brand identification a key part of the brand experience.

Packaging provides functional benefits such as economy, protection, and storage, which is the main purpose of a marketing communication message at times. However, since a brand's package gives it a distinctive look, its identity is the focal point of a marketing communication message as well. For example, the main point of the perfume ad in **Exhibit 1-4** is to show the packaging of the product since this influences consumer choice. Other characteristics of packaging, like its being fully biodegradable, are a concern for marketers and are the focal marketing communication message. For example, Fredericton-based The Best Deodorant in the World boasts such a package, which is readily mentioned in its public relations.[9]

Brand Equity The culmination of marketing communication messages of product type, product attributes/benefits, and brand identification assists with brand equity, either creating, maintaining, or enhancing this important marketing outcome. **Brand equity** is the differential effect of brand knowledge on consumer responses to the marketing of the brand.[10] By extension, it is an intangible asset added to a product due to the favourable image, impressions of differentiation, or strength of consumer attachment toward a company name, brand name, or trademark. Brand equity provides the company with a competitive advantage by allowing its product to earn greater sales volume and/or higher margins than it could without the name. The watch shown in **Exhibit 1-5** looks really nice, yet the Rolex brand name certainly conveys something greater than a stylish timepiece.

Conceptually, IMC planning and the subsequent marketing communication decisions are expected to strongly generate brand equity.[11] The growing interest in this particular brand effect has led to organizations reporting different ways to view and measure brand equity. **Figure 1-3** highlights the top 10 most valuable Canadian brands as determined by Brand Finance.[12] The differences in this and the earlier table in Figure 1-2 show the challenge in consistently measuring effects like brand equity. In both cases, these organizations use financial data and surveys of consumers of Canadian-based brands. In contrast, Ipsos-Reid uncovers the most influential brands from any country with Canadian survey panelists' attitudes only, and finds Google, Facebook, Apple, Amazon, and Microsoft in its top five.[13] Finally, one issue raised is a trend of weaker top Canadian brands with the decline of noteworthy names over the years.[14]

Beyond brand equity as a strategic initiative, marketers are interested in other aspects with views like brand experience, brand attachment, and brand love. Brand experience involves receiving marketing communication messages, shopping behaviour, product use, and consumption, leading to one view that it includes sensory, affective, intellectual, and behavioural dimensions.[15] Brand attachment is the strength of the bond between a brand and oneself and comprises brand–self connection and brand prominence.[16] Brand love is a more abstract notion reflecting seven more concrete aspects: passion-driven behaviours, self–brand integration, emotional attachment, anticipated separation distress, long-term relationship view, positive attitude, and confidently held attitude.[17]

From these definitions we conclude that marketing communication is important for achieving any brand-based consumer response. While brand equity is currently primary, others are gaining interest, as one research firm published a brand love index to measure a consumer's "intense bonded affection" toward a brand.[18] Measurement of the index indicated that brand love exceeds needs, builds trust, sets trends, shares values, respects consumers, and elevates experiences.[19]

An example of brand love is the Toronto Raptors' "We the North" campaign, which ignited fan passion for the team just before the NBA playoffs began. As a rallying cry for all, the direction for Canada's only basketball team signalled a new era to celebrate a national following of the only team north of the border. A 60-second ad featured Toronto scenes and Raptors game highlights. The imagery gave the team a new identity to go with the planned revision of the logo and uniforms. Moreover, the 86-word spoken copy portrayed the team as distinctively Canadian. The final visual of a black and white flag swaying in the wind flashed "We the North" to go along with the audio of "Let's go Raptors" chanted by the fans. In response, fans waved their own flags publicly and expressed their love in social media.[20] And the love extended to sponsors, with the Raptors signing partnerships with Tangerine bank, Sun Life Financial, Nike, McDonald's, and Drake as a brand ambassador.[21]

COMMUNICATING PRICE

The price of a product, usually expressed in a dollar amount, is a signal of a consumer's economic cost to purchase a product in exchange for receiving its combined benefits. Price planning involves decisions concerning the level, policy, adjustments through discounts or allowances,

Figure 1-3 The top 10 most valuable Canadian brands

Rank 2018	Brand
1	RBC
2	TD
3	Bell
4	Scotiabank
5	Bank of Montreal
6	Rogers
7	TELUS
8	CIBC
9	Brookfield
10	Thomson Reuters

Exhibit 1-6 Ads feature price information as their primary message, as shown in this McDonald's example.

©BirchTree/Alamy Stock Photo

and flexibility when facing competition. Marketing communication plays a role in reinforcing a consumer's belief that the product's benefit or quality accurately reflects the price. One historical study regarding price, product quality, and advertising expenditures concluded that pricing and advertising strategies go together. High relative ad expenditures should accompany premium prices, and low relative ad expenditures should be tailored to low prices.[22]

Price is also a key piece of information conveyed in marketing communication messages. For example, car dealerships and manufacturers focus on price and price discounts in TV and newspaper ads. Internet ads focus on price offers that attempt to influence consumer price beliefs; competitors advertise mortgage rate information in many media and specialized websites like RateHub.ca.[23] The information on websites offering deals is predominantly price related (e.g., RedTag.ca). Research concludes that price comparison advertising plays a key role in consumers' reference price for products when determining the value of a product.[24] Other research finds that communicating price information is critical for influencing consumers who are in the process of deciding to buy a product.[25] Notice that the main purpose of the billboard ad in **Exhibit 1-6** is to communicate that the price of all sizes of soft drinks at McDonald's is only one dollar. The secondary purpose is to identify the brand of soft drinks sold at the quick service restaurant.

COMMUNICATING DISTRIBUTION

Distribution involves the process of making a product available for purchase, use, or consumption. Consumer product companies distribute through **indirect channels** using a network of wholesalers and/or retailers. For example, Samsung distributes its electronic products to retailers. Alternatively, companies use **direct channels** and do not use any channel intermediaries to sell to customers. For example, Bell, Rogers, and Telus have retail outlets to sell their goods and services. The Internet is one obvious direct channel that both Samsung and the telecommunication firms also use. In all these cases, marketing communication provides information as to where, and how, to purchase a product.

For example, sporting goods companies with different quality and price levels might communicate which brands and models are at different types of retailers. Alternatively, different service levels might be available within the distribution network and be the focus of marketing communication. For instance, particular locations for cosmetics products offer customized beautifying services, while others are self-serve. Also, extensive marketing communication occurs to direct consumers through organizational websites for online purchases. As these examples demonstrate, the importance of communicating in a multichannel environment, along with a multimedia universe, makes the development of brand equity within distribution decisions a compelling management task.[26]

COMMUNICATING VALUE

The AMA's earlier definition of marketing highlighted a company's offering via the marketing mix, a useful view for easy reference. More recently, the AMA renewed its definition of marketing as *the activity, set of institutions, and processes for creating, communicating, delivering, and exchanging offerings that have value for customers, clients, partners, and society at large.*[27] The previous elements of the marketing mix remain implied and the importance of value within the exchange is prominent.

The idea of value is elusive across academic disciplines and within managerial usage, however the relative balance or ratio of what consumers "receive" for what they "give" is a view that is well appreciated by researchers and decision makers.[28] From a "give" standpoint, consumers pay for products via the price but also incur time, physical effort, social, and psychological costs while shopping and/or consuming.[29] For example, one could pay a premium price to a travel agent to book a vacation, or one could spend time online searching for the best price; each option clearly has its own unique costs. A final thought on the elusiveness of value emerged with one study's conclusion that consumers value a physical good (e.g., real book) more than its digital equivalent (e.g., ebook)![30]

Thus, marketing communication takes on a significant role to signal to consumers the benefit they will accrue for the total costs they incur to understand how they receive value from a product offering. Consumers' opportunity to shop physically and virtually anywhere, in any way, at any time, opens the door for marketing communication decisions to be among the most important management decisions for an organization so that its customers and potential customers understand a brand's value offering.

LO2 The Promotional Mix

Promotion is the coordination of all initiated efforts from an identified brand or sponsor that uses channels of information and distribution to persuade audiences to buy a product (i.e., good, service, cause, idea, person). While implicit communication occurs through other marketing mix elements, most of an organization's communication with the marketplace occurs as part of a carefully planned and controlled promotional program referred to as the **promotional mix** (**Figure 1-4**). While either *promotion* or *marketing communication* is a suitable term, the latter is commonly used since the tools are often connected. For example, a television commercial can direct viewers to a website, or a brand may use the same type of message in both its radio and print ads. We now define each of the tools and summarize its purpose.

Figure 1-4 Tools of the promotional mix

ADVERTISING

Advertising is defined as a paid form of non-personal communication about an organization, product, service, or idea by an identified sponsor.[31] The *non-personal* component means advertising involves media (e.g., TV, magazine, banner ads on websites) that transmits a message to large groups of individuals. In general, this means there is no immediate feedback from the message recipient; the interactive capability of technology is changing this limitation, but not to the extent that there is feedback in personal communication (salespeople, customer service personnel). The *paid* aspect of this definition means that the space or time for an advertising message is bought from a media organization. Canadian advertisers spend more than $14 billion annually to reach their audiences, and there are several reasons why advertising is part of marketers' promotional mix.

Cost-Efficiency Advertising is a cost-efficient method for communicating with large audiences. For example, during a television season, prime-time network television reached 85 percent of Canadians on a daily basis. The most-watched TV show each week attracts an audience of about 3 million English-speaking viewers. The average top 10 show audience is about 2.4 million viewers, while the average audience for the top 11–20 shows is about 1.7 million viewers.[32] One study quotes media experts who estimate the cost per thousand reached at $25 for a top 10 show and $20 for a top 11–20 show. To reach an audience for Canadian-produced television shows costs $16 per thousand; specialty channel audiences cost $8 per thousand.[33]

Cost-Effectiveness Assuming that a majority of the viewers actually watched a TV ad, paid attention during the airing, and remember something about the message, then advertising is a cost-effective form of marketing communication. In general, advertising is a cost-effective method for allowing potential customers to know something about a brand and have a positive attitude toward the brand prior to, during, or after purchasing a product.

Brand Communication Effects Advertising is valuable because it provides information to consumers and persuades consumers by influencing their attitude toward the brand. Advertising creates a favourable and unique brand image, which is important for companies selling products that are difficult to differentiate on the basis of functional attributes. Brand image is the sum of a consumer's cognitive, affective, and evaluative perceptions of a brand, is a key element of a firm's marketing strategy, and thus provides important direction for advertising decisions.[34] Advertising is also a recommended approach to building brand reputation.[35] Empirical research also finds that advertising directly and indirectly leads to greater firm value due to intangible assets (e.g., brand communication effects).[36]

Brand Interaction Advertising is used to encourage consumers to interact with a brand online. For example, as part of its sponsorship with the Canadian Football League, Belairdirect insurance advertised its contest where consumers would upload a video of themselves in their best "game face" to win a trip to the Grey Cup. The campaign featured three sets

Exhibit 1-7 Business-to-business marketers use advertising to build awareness and brand identity.

Source: General Electric

of ads, contest instructions for digital entry, face-painting tips from CFL players, and answers to common insurance questions. Social media activities motivated media personalities to create their own look as inspiration for potential customers.[37]

Flexible Tool Advertising is a flexible tool used across industries (e.g., cars or soft drinks), market situations (e.g., new product launch or market development for established product), channel members (e.g., consumers or retailers), and target audiences (e.g., new customers or loyal customers). New products entering the Canadian market use some form of advertising, and *Strategy*, a trade publication for ad agencies, annually recognizes outstanding ads. Vaseline Spray and Go ran a series of 15 video ads showing how quickly a woman could moisturize and get dressed. The creatively entertaining demonstration illustrated the key product benefits of ease and speed of application for new customers to understand perfectly.[38]

Multiple Domains Different types of advertising occur in multiple domains. Canadian marketers of goods and services advertise to consumer markets with national or regional brand messages, and in some cases with messages to particular international consumer markets. Alternatively, local retailers and other goods and services providers use advertising for communication purposes to achieve sales objectives. Also, industry associations, like the Dairy Farmers of Canada, advertise extensively to consumer markets as do all levels of government and non-governmental organizations like Canadian Blood Services. Shoppers Drug Mart, Canada's number one pharmaceuticals retailer, advertised to celebrate its 50th anniversary with a "Fabulous 50" campaign featuring its largest media buy ever to support all of its marketing communication. Its "red gift box" messaging and imagery emphasized health, beauty, and convenience.[39]

Business-to-business marketing firms advertise to those who buy or influence the purchase of goods or services for their organization. Professional advertising directed to those with specific designations is found in industries such as health, management, government, and technology. Finally, advertising directed to channel members like wholesalers, distributors, and retailers is found in all industry sectors around the world. **Exhibit 1-7** shows an example of how General Electric communicates its commitment to new water sources through desalination, which may affect business customers and perhaps the general public.

Exhibit 1-8 Dare combines its sales promotion with its advertising.

©Dare Foods Limited

SALES PROMOTION

Sales promotion is defined as marketing activities that provide extra value or incentives to the salesforce, distributors, or the ultimate consumer and can influence their behaviour to stimulate sales. Sales promotion is generally broken into two major categories: consumer-oriented and trade-oriented activities.

Consumer sales promotion is targeted to the ultimate user of a product and includes coupons, samples, premiums, rebates, and contests designed to encourage consumers to make an immediate trial or repeat purchase. Shoppers Drug Mart celebrated its anniversary with a contest offering 50 grand prizes and attracted more than 900,000 entrants. Other promotions encourage consumers to participate in a brand event or to involve themselves with the brand by uploading a video or photo to social media highlighting their consumption. Examples of new types of events include Harley-Davidson's pop-up café for its loyal riders and Molson's "Rooftop Rink" for beer and hockey fans alike. As one might expect, these events gained publicity in news media for additional exposure and from individuals posting their excitement or experience in social media.[40] **Exhibit 1-8** is an example of a coupon offer within an ad that encourages consumers to purchase Dare crackers for holiday entertaining. To facilitate usage, the ad indicates that the packaging offers recipes for serving ideas.

Trade sales promotion is targeted toward marketing intermediaries such as wholesalers, distributors, and retailers. Promotional and merchandising allowances, price deals, sales contests, and trade shows are examples of the promotions designed to encourage the trade to stock and promote a company's products. Some trade promotions benefit consumers since they receive information contained in a display or receive discounted prices that are passed along to them from the retailer. Retail personnel at Shoppers Drug Mart liked the specialized celebration point-of-purchase material so much that they avoided dismantling it even after the party was over.

Exhibit 1-9 TD sponsors events for public relations purposes.

©Roberto Machado Noa/LightRocket via Getty Images

PUBLIC RELATIONS

Public relations (PR) occurs when an organization systematically plans and distributes information in an attempt to control and manage its image. **Public relations** is a corporate communication program designed to enhance a company's reputation and/or earn public understanding and acceptance of a particular issue. A public relations program uses special publications, participation in community activities, fundraising, event sponsorship, and public affairs activities to enhance an organization's image. As expected, the Internet and social media are paramount for enhancing and influencing an organization's reputation in today's digital world.

Organizations make PR an integral part of their predetermined marketing and promotional strategies. Scotiabank and others supported Nuit Blanche, a sunset-to-sunrise, free, contemporary art event. Telus demonstrated its commitment to social causes with a series of online video documentaries produced by its in-house Telus Studios, based in Vancouver. One told the story of adventure seekers using technology to plan their trips to remote mountain lakes and forests.[41] On another front, the company began Telus Wise to assist those who have been bullied while using digital technology. One campaign focused on young people who provided testimonials of their experiences to highlight Telus's commitment and responsibility to eradicate the problem.[42] **Exhibit 1-9** shows a colourful sponsorship by TD that is part of its public relations activities.

Publicity refers to non-personal communications regarding an organization, product, person, or idea not directly paid for by an identified sponsorship. The message reaches the public in the news media as a story or editorial. Like advertising, publicity involves non-personal communication to an audience, but unlike advertising, publicity is not directly paid for by the organization. The organization encourages the media to cover a favourable story by using news releases, press conferences, feature articles, and media.

An advantage of publicity is its credibility; consumers tend to be less skeptical toward favourable information about a product when it comes from a source they perceive as unbiased. For example, movie reviews from film critics may be viewed by moviegoers as an objective evaluation. Another advantage of publicity is its low cost, since the company is not paying for media time or space. While costs in developing public relations items to foster publicity occur, these expenses will be far less than advertising.

DIRECT MARKETING

Direct marketing occurs when organizations communicate directly with target audiences to generate a response and/or a transaction. Direct marketing is used by companies that distribute their products to consumers directly and by companies that distribute their products through traditional distribution channels or their own salesforce. Direct marketing includes telemarketing and call centres, direct mail, mail-order catalogues, Internet-order websites, and direct-response ads in media. Direct marketing is an important component of a firm's marketing communication program since it is connected to other aspects of marketing communication. Direct marketing is used to distribute product samples and promotional products. Extensive direct marketing activities occur with the administration of loyalty programs designed to reward customers who make frequent purchases. Direct marketing can also be used as

Exhibit 1-10 Under Armour sells its products through retail channels and online.

NEW ARRIVALS
We'll keep building the gear. You'll keep getting better.

Source: Under Armour, Inc.

part of a public relations program by sending relevant information. Shoppers Drug Mart revamped its Optimum points program while celebrating its 50th anniversary, which translated into a 20 percent growth in its membership.

In order to communicate directly, companies develop and maintain databases containing contact information (e.g., address, phone number, email), customer profiles, purchase history, and media preferences of present and/or prospective customers, and use this information to target either audience. They use telemarketing to call customers directly and attempt to sell products and services or qualify them as sales leads. Call centres are used to respond to customer inquiries. Marketers send out direct-mail pieces ranging from simple letters to detailed brochures and catalogues, to give potential customers information about their products. Finally, marketers use **direct-response advertising**, whereby a product is promoted through an ad (e.g., broadcast, Internet) that encourages the consumer to purchase directly via the phone or Internet (**Exhibit 1-10**).

INTERNET MARKETING

We are experiencing a dynamic change in marketing through interactive media, delivered via the Internet. **Interactive media** allow for a back-and-forth flow of information where users participate in and modify its form and content instantly. The Internet allows users to receive, alter, and share information and images, experience branded promotional messages, initiate inquiries, respond to questions, and purchase products, making it a multifaceted marketing communication tool for promotional planners. It is also a medium to execute all promotional mix elements beyond advertising. Marketers offer sales promotion incentives such as coupons and contests online, and they use the Internet to conduct direct marketing and public relations activities effectively and efficiently. In fact, a brand can implement a completely digital IMC program that includes advertising, sales promotion, events, public relations, and social media interaction online.

The Internet is an advertising medium since brands pay a fee to place a video ad, various styles of display ads that look like a print ad, or an audio ad virtually anywhere, such as on content publishing websites like TSN or social media sites like Facebook or YouTube. Search engine ads are also "paid media" advertising, as are messages on classified/directory websites. Websites provide current and potential customers with information about the company's products and activities. Other websites entertain or communicate emotionally with their clientele. In either case, these branded websites are much like non-digital marketing collateral material that are "owned media," but the interactive media characteristics of a brand's website alter a consumer's experience considerably.

Social media facilitates interaction and communication among its members to create, share, and exchange information, experiences, perspectives, and media. Social media like Facebook, YouTube, Twitter, and Instagram are means for marketers to reach consumers as each allows a brand to create a group (Facebook) or channel (YouTube) for all kinds of marketing communication activities. Since these types of social media do not charge a brand to set up an account, a brand's presence is much like "owned media" as a brand's personnel (or agency personnel) construct the message and style much like what is found on a brand's website. As seen in Chapter 18, social media players offer additional features for a fee to enhance a brand's marketing communication, thereby moving toward "paid media" that might make the advertising message not necessarily look like advertising from the point of view of a consumer.

The interactive features of social media that facilitate communication among users provide a powerful means of brand influence. Positive communication among users about a brand is referred to as "earned media" by marketing practitioners. This terminology gained stronger notoriety as social media matured, however the idea previously existed in public relations for decades and with managers interested in tracking consumers' verbal word-of-mouth communication. Marketers' online postings stimulate conversations among consumers with the hopes of generating peer or group influence. At other times, brand managers contract special agencies that will financially arrange for an influential blogger to endorse a brand by posting their consumption via a picture or video.[43] So while the blogger's post might look like "earned" media to a consumer, it is in fact "paid" media.

Access to websites, social media, interactive experiences, and all facets of marketing communication is prevalent with mobile media devices like smart phones and tablets. These devices and accompanying applications open the door for marketers to adapt and invent ways of implementing marketing communication. Although consumers access online marketing communication similarly (mobile vs. non-mobile), the portability of receiving brand messages or interacting with a brand, or a peer, makes this a new frontier for IMC planners, who need to consider how existing promotional decisions will be adapted to fit with or influence consumer behaviour. A Starbucks app allows customers to pay for purchases, find locations, obtain nutritional information, and manage their rewards account, all on a smart phone. **Exhibit 1-11** shows an example of a useful shopping app for consumers.

Exhibit 1-11 Shoppers use the ShopSavvy app to compare prices prior to purchase.

Source: ShopSavvy, Inc.

Although the Internet is a popular medium offering media delivery options for marketing communication, the ultimate role of advertising and promotion and the content of the message remain essentially unchanged. According to two noted marketing writers, promotional planners still try to achieve brand communication effects by delivering a relevant message with the ultimate goal of achieving a marketing objective, such as selling more of a product.[44] While feedback on digital message delivery is virtually instantaneous with media like Twitter, considerable planning is required by a promotional manager for initial digital message delivery, much like what has existed for nearly a century since the advent of radio advertising. Supporting this view is research that compares the direct and indirect communication effects of digital and broadcast media.[45]

PERSONAL SELLING

The final promotional mix element is **personal selling**, a form of person-to-person communication in which a seller helps and/or persuades prospective buyers to purchase the company's good or service or to act on an idea. Personal selling involves direct contact between buyer and seller, either face-to-face or through telecommunications. This interaction gives the marketer communication flexibility; the seller can see or hear the potential buyer's reactions and tailor the message to their specific needs or situation. We do not cover personal selling in this book, as decisions pertaining to this topic are the responsibility of a sales manager.

PARTICIPANTS IN THE PROMOTIONAL PROCESS

To understand the context in which promotional decisions are made, we identify the participants of the promotional process (**Figure 1-5**). **Advertisers** have the goods, services, causes, ideas, or persons to be marketed, and provide the funds that pay for advertising. They make the final decisions of the marketing program and the marketing communication

Figure 1-5 Participants in the promotional process

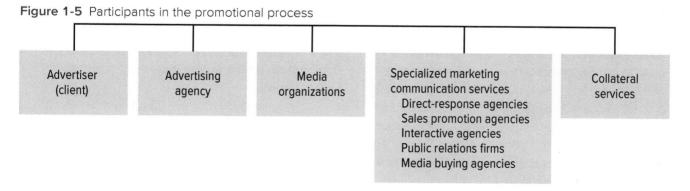

Exhibit 1-12 CityTV promotes its value to advertisers.

©ValeStock/Shutterstock

program. Advertisers may develop the promotional program internally with an ad department or an in-house agency, or work with outside agencies.

Advertising agencies are firms that specialize in the creation, production, and placement of promotional messages, and may provide other services. Advertisers are referred to as **clients** if they work with an ad agency. Large advertisers retain the services of multiple agencies, particularly with multiple products or markets. For example, Schneiders hires different agencies for specific advertising tasks: one for national, one for regional, one for in-store locations, and one for sports locations.[46] An ad agency that is viewed as a partner by the client might assume more responsibility for developing the marketing and promotional programs.

Media organizations provide information or entertainment to their subscribers, viewers, or readers. Media provide an editorial or program content environment for the firm's promotional planner to deliver the marketing communication message. While the media perform functions that help advertisers understand their markets and their customers, a medium's primary objective is to sell its time or space so companies can effectively reach their target audiences (**Exhibit 1-12**). Media companies in Canada have grown significantly through acquisition of different formats and provide considerable integration options for advertisers. For example, Rogers offers customers virtually all media opportunities and its staff has a strong integration orientation when selling packages to clients.[47]

Specialized marketing communication services include agencies for direct marketing (e.g., direct mail), sales promotion (e.g., contests, premium offers, sampling programs), interactive media (e.g., websites, social media activities), public relations (e.g., generate and manage publicity), and media buying (e.g., arrange TV ad placement) who provide services in their areas of expertise. In the case of Schneiders, digital advertising is not done by an agency, but rather an in-house team. **Collateral services** include marketing research, package design, consultants, photographers, printers, video production, and event marketing. These individuals and companies perform specialized functions that the other participants use when planning and executing the IMC plan. **IMC Perspective 1-1** tells the story of Iögo from its launch to its brand refresh; it relied on the services of many organizations listed in Figure 1-5.

IMC PERSPECTIVE 1-1

IMC PLANNING WITH IÖGO

Iögo—the new way to say yogurt—launched in 2012 with much success in the fast growing market despite facing competitors such as Activia, Astro, and Danone, and new trends like 0 percent fat and probiotic yogurt. The manager hoped to duplicate the performance of Activia, launched eight years earlier, with 8 percent market share and 56 percent awareness two years post-launch. The product differentiated from others with a full suite of original

flavours, no artificial colours, and no artificial flavours. As a farmers cooperative based in Quebec, the brand featured a strong heritage that competitors could not copy.

Ads prominently displayed the two dots (known as an umlaut) above the brand name, giving it a distinctive look that consumers readily accepted. Media exposure included TV, out-of-home, and print, and a coupon rounded out the plan with an incentive for trial. After three months, lögo hit 10 percent market share and 74 percent awareness, and other research indicated strong interest and purchase intention.

A few years later, lögo needed a refresh, and the new package design circled the brand with a ribbon of fruit to highlight its signature look with the umlaut. The design also provided colour cues so consumers could understand the product type and format. On the back, the umlaut formed a smile with the fruit, reminiscent of the original ads in the launch.

Ads to announce the change made the umlaut come to life in three scenarios: a therapist with a patient, a hairstylist with a customer, and a couple at breakfast. Each ended with a warm and fuzzy feeling to let viewers see the umlaut as human. An in-store event featured kids pushing grocery carts full of lögo as if they were participating in a fashion show.

Later ads for the protein version showed the umlaut participating in fun activities and then pausing to be energized with the new protein version.

©Torontonian/Alamy Stock Photo

Similar digital and mobile contextual ads targeted active people in snack situations fitting with the target audience aged 25 to 34 who replaced meals with many healthy snacks. Influencer messaging also occurred in social media.

Question:

1. What additional IMC tools could lögo use in its plan and what type of agency would best serve its needs?

LO3 Integrated Marketing Communications

Most large companies understand that the range of promotional tools must be coordinated to communicate effectively and present a consistent image to target audiences. In turn, even smaller-scale marketers have followed suit and moved to a comprehensive perspective of marketing communication. We now illustrate the topic of integrated marketing communications by distinguishing its evolution, renewed perspective, and audience contacts and the use of IMC tools to influence target audiences.

IMC: EVOLUTION

During the 1980s, companies shifted toward **integrated marketing communications (IMC)** as the need for strategic planning and integration of their promotional mix intensified. Marketers subsequently asked their advertising agency to coordinate the use of all promotional tools and employed promotional specialists to develop and implement other parts of their promotional plans. At this point in time, the American Association of Advertising Agencies defined IMC as planning that recognizes the added value of a comprehensive program to evaluate the strategic role of all communication disciplines and to combine them to provide clarity, consistency, and maximum communication impact.[48]

By the 1990s, IMC represented an improvement compared to treating each promotional tool as a virtually separate activity as all agencies contributed to the IMC planning for their clients.[49] IMC became one of the "new-generation" marketing approaches used by companies to better focus their efforts in acquiring, retaining, and developing relationships with customers and other stakeholders.[50] With this change, IMC faced criticism that it reflected a management fad that merely relied on tactical coordination to make all aspects of the promotional mix look and sound alike.[51] Additionally, critics argued that it merely renamed existing ideas and concepts, and questioned its significance for marketing and advertising thought and practice.[52] As IMC evolved, both academics and practitioners saw a renewed perspective.

Hand-out/Air Wick Canada/Newscom

IMC: RENEWED PERSPECTIVE

A renewed understanding views IMC as a strategic business process that identifies the most effective, persuasive brand communication program over time with customers, prospective customers, employees, associates, and other targeted relevant external and internal audiences to build and maintain relationships and achieve financial goals.[53] Marketers see the value of strategically integrating the communication functions by coordinating their marketing communications efforts, minimizing duplication, utilizing the strength of each promotional tool, and developing efficient and effective marketing communications programs. **Exhibit 1-13** shows a marketing effort where IMC planning is paramount for the managers of both brands identified in the promotion: Air Wick and Parks Canada.

IMC is seen by promotional planners as an ongoing strategic business process where a number of relevant target audiences require specific marketing communication programs. This approach reflects the increasing emphasis on accountability and measurement of the *outcomes* of marketing communication programs as well as marketing in general. Thus, a renewed perspective means that IMC has four communication characteristics: unified for consistent message and image, differentiated to multiple customer groups, database-centred for tangible results, and relationship fostering with existing customers.[54]

Marketers and marketing communication agencies embrace IMC within their marketing and business practices. In fact, it is expected that IMC is critically connected to a firm's market and brand orientation.[55] Research reports higher use of IMC leading to higher levels of sales, market share, and profits.[56] Despite this progress, some called IMC an "inside-out" marketing approach that bundles the promotional mix to have one common look.[57] Even with this doubt, the evidence is persuasive: IMC performance predicts market performance in terms of brand and sales performance.[58] And, empirical research shows that strong IMC capability leads to campaign effectiveness and stronger market and financial performance.[59] However, one study concluded that the strategic intent of IMC is warranted, but its implementation falters among promotional specialists due to poor communication, a narrow focus on their own domain, a lack of trust, and weak flexibility for adjusting.[60]

IMC: AUDIENCE CONTACT

A successful IMC program requires having the right combination of promotional tools and a clear purpose for each, and knowing the extent to which each should be used and how to coordinate the ones selected. Marketers use the promotional mix elements to communicate with current and/or prospective customers and other audiences such as employees, suppliers, community, and government. Companies take an *audience contact* or *audience touch-point* perspective by evaluating the potential ways of reaching their target audiences and presenting the brand message favourably to enhance value for the target audience.[61] In terms of customers, for example, marketers identify how their loyal buyers interact with the brand. This contact ranges from seeing or hearing an ad to actually using or experiencing a brand at a company-sponsored event. Moreover, this works with non-customers, such as those loyal to another brand, to whom the company may choose to target its marketing communication. And finally, this audience contact approach is feasible when targeting those who currently do not purchase within the brand's product category.

Figure 1-6 shows how a target audience is in contact with a company or brand. Marketers determine how valuable each contact is for communicating with each target audience and how the IMC tools are combined to form an effective promotional program. This is generally done by starting with one target audience and determining which IMC tools will be most effective in reaching, informing, and persuading them and ultimately influencing their behaviour. This would be repeated if the brand saw the plan requiring additional target audiences. Although consumers may see each of these IMC tools as advertising, the promotional manager takes this audience contact view for planning purposes to ensure that the brand invests in the right set. Adapting this approach to the consumer decision-making process (covered in Chapter 3) and how consumers receive and process ad messages (covered in Chapter 4) provides direction for comprehensive IMC planning.[62]

Figure 1-6 Audience contact via IMC tools

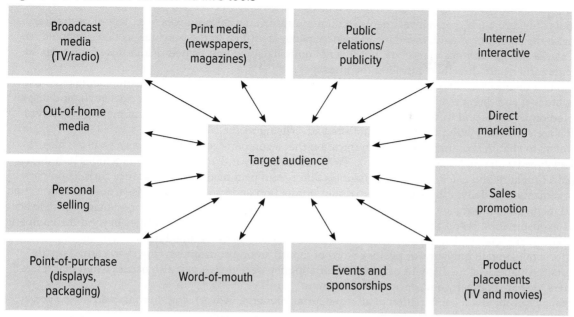

To see this in action, consider how a brand decides what tools to use to communicate with its current customers. For example, banks focus part of their marketing communication efforts on retaining their customers to ensure future profitability. Banks, and other organizations, estimate the *lifetime value* of a customer by calculating the increased revenue and minimized costs of an individual customer over time. The extensive personal and financial information banks collect allows them to serve people's financial needs through financial products (e.g., mortgages) and service (e.g., financial advisers). To assist in their communication, banks build a customer database containing names, geographic and demographic data, purchase patterns, profitability, and credit ratings. Other businesses would include this and other data such as media preferences and psychographic profiles. Marketers use this information to target loyal customers with IMC tools shown above, thereby enhancing the relationship. With so many options, and since their customers are involved so closely with the firm, the need for consistency and coordination becomes critical.[63]

The above scenario is one way companies build on continued purchases from their customers to form long-term bonds. **Relationship marketing** involves creating, maintaining, and enhancing long-term relationships with individual customers for mutual benefit.[64] IMC tools that a bank might evaluate for its customers could include direct marketing (such as email, direct mail, or messages when the customer logs in to do online banking), or special marketing events (like financial seminars), or public relations (including community- and cause-related activities).

In contrast, the bank might evaluate other options to sway customers from competing banks for certain products or services. Advertising in media might be feasible for consumers dissatisfied with their current provider. Social media advertising might be used to alert consumers to consider shopping around when it is mortgage renewal time. As these two points imply, it takes money and/or resources to attract new customers, which makes customer retention a key consideration.

Ubisoft of Montreal presents an application of promotional planning and the concepts in Figure 1-6. Ubisoft is one of the world's largest programming outfits and is responsible for developing big titles like *Assassin's Creed* and *Watch Dogs*. Canadian promotion included TV advertising and the innovative use of IMC tools like video game apps, stunts, events, and sponsorship across all of its brands. Ubisoft faces stiff competition as the industry transforms from niche markets with thousands of developers to a concentrated market of major players like Electronic Arts, Nintendo, and Sony. Planning activities unique to Ubisoft Montreal, compared to Ubisoft US, include its team working on IMC plans for all games, in contrast to dedicated teams for each game. The company's digital marketing reflected this with one Facebook page compared to multiple pages for each game title; this permitted improved awareness and stronger cross-sales of other game brands. This approach grew followers fivefold over the course of 18 months. Social media monitoring and postings moved from external agencies to two internal staff members and ensured a consistent tone and quality of marketing messages.[65]

IMC: PAID, OWNED, EARNED

Each of the IMC tools of Figure 1-6 requires investments in money and/or internal resources (e.g., labour, technology). To see this, we reprise the concepts of paid, owned, and earned media identified in the previous section. It should be noted that earned media is important for marketers, but it is not quite like paid and owned media since brands try to influence what occurs rather than directly controlling the message.

Paid media refers to a media channel of communication a marketer pays for, including advertising media (e.g., television, radio, print, outdoor) and direct mail as well as digital advertising on the Internet such as paid search, and display and video ads located on websites and in social media. In this regard, a considerable proportion of messages received from Internet media are consistent with previously established advertising media.

Owned media refers to channels of marketing communication that a company controls, such as a website, blog, mobile app, and social media channels such as Facebook, Twitter, Instagram, and YouTube. It also includes non-digital communication like a brochure and catalogue. These channels differ from paid media channels since there is no payment to a media organization to deliver the message. No doubt production and support costs arise from communication suppliers as in paid media, and a company likely incurs internal labour and/or technology costs to manage the delivery.

Earned media is exposure for a brand that it did not directly pay for and is generated by entities beyond the company such as media or sharing in social media. In the past, exposure from earned media resulted from a company's plan for public relations, efforts to generate publicity, or positive word of mouth among consumers. However, earned media exposure now occurs through social media with consumers initiating message delivery. It also occurs when marketers encourage consumers to share company and/or brand information.

Effective IMC plans typically use a combination of all three forms of media. Advertising through paid media generates brand awareness and interest efficiently. Media advertising can drive consumers to owned media such as a company's Facebook or Instagram page for brand engagement. Or it might direct consumers to a website where content encourages greater message involvement. Well executed and coordinated paid and owned media efforts serve as a catalyst for generating earned media from consumers who find information or content about a company or brand to be interesting or valuable enough that they want to write about it or share it.

Figure 1-7 extends and applies the paid, owned, and earned media view to IMC tools from Figure 1-6. The top rows show those that existed prior to Internet media, while the bottom rows are the newer digital options. The table demonstrates that the paid, owned, and earned perspective goes beyond media. It also indicates that the rekindled interest in paid, owned, and earned media for the Internet reinforces the point that marketers used the three-media idea for quite some time in all promotional mix elements.

This table illustrates that advertising and other IMC tools follow a paid media perspective; Canada Post delivers the message for brands, organizations receiving sponsorship funds guide a brand's image to its audience, and product placement is a media for ad-like messages within a story. It also shows that IMC tools with an owned media perspective

Figure 1-7 IMC tools across resource source

IMC: Paid	IMC: Owned	IMC: Earned
TV, radio, outdoor	Brochure, catalogue	Publicity via media
Magazine, newspaper	Displays	Journalist reviews
Transit, location, in-store	Sales promotion	Verbal word of mouth
Direct mail	Events, shows	Promotional products
Sponsorship	Public relations	Cause-related support
Product placement	Loyalty program	Public support
Display and video ads in social media	Website, micro-site	Shared videos and pictures
Display and video ads on websites	Social media	Social media messages
Search ads	Mobile app	Shared social media messages
Email	Email	Communities
Audio ads on podcast	Blog, podcast	Ratings, reviews

include options that are directly controlled by the brand (e.g., sales promotion, events, and consumer and trade shows). Earned media occurs beyond PR, publicity, and word of mouth since consumers receive promotional products they display, participate in causes, and support brands publicly in some cases.

As noted, digital paid advertising is pervasive, with more spent on this media than TV advertising; we see companies or brands using all forms of owned digital media, and the growth of social media usage by consumers makes this earned media stand out significantly. It is recognized that the table simplifies the marketing communication situation to some degree, with the breakout of digital media to illustrate a point, however it is still useful to consider for clear promotional decision making and IMC planning.

LO4 Integrated Marketing Communications Planning

IMC planning is a process to conceive, develop, implement, and control the promotional mix elements to communicate effectively with target audiences. An IMC planning process model is shown in **Figure 1-8**. The marketer decides which promotional tools to use, the purpose of each element of the promotional mix, and how to combine them to achieve

Figure 1-8 An integrated marketing communications planning model

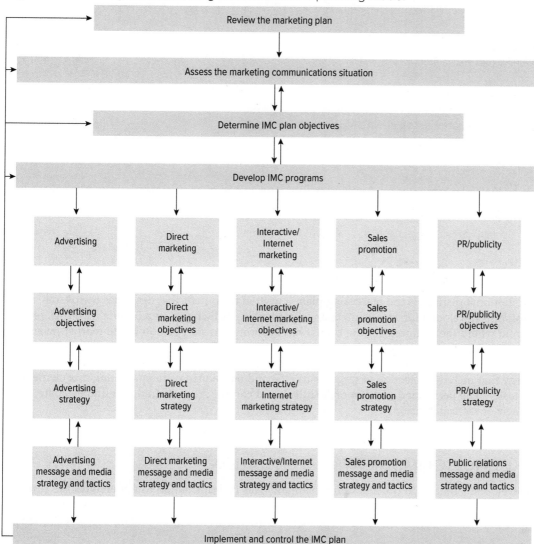

[Continued on next page]

[Figure 1-8 continued]

Review the Marketing Plan
Focus on information and analysis of marketing communications situation
Examine marketing objectives, strategy, and programs
Understand role of promotion within marketing plan

Assess the Marketing Communications Situation

Company analysis   Market analysis
Consumer analysis   Environmental analysis
Competitor analysis

Determine IMC Plan Objectives
Establish IMC communication objectives
Establish IMC behavioural objectives

Develop IMC Programs
For advertising, sales promotion, public relations, direct marketing, and Internet marketing:
   Set specific communication and behavioural objectives for each IMC tool
   Determine budget requirements
   Develop relevant message strategy and tactics
   Select suitable media strategy and tactics
Investigate integration options across all five programs

Implement and Control the IMC Plan
Design all promotional materials internally or with agencies and buy media space/time
Measure promotional program results/effectiveness and make adjustments

IMC objectives. The resulting **IMC plan** provides the framework for managing all of an organization's marketing communications. The remainder of this chapter explains the planning model and describes the steps in developing an IMC program.

REVIEW THE MARKETING PLAN

The starting point for a promotional planner is the **marketing plan**, a written document that describes the overall marketing strategy and programs developed for an organization, a particular product line, or a brand. With this, promotional planners understand where the company (or the brand) has been, its current position in the market, where it intends to go, and how it plans to get there. Marketing plans generally include five parts: situation analysis (market, company, consumer, competition, and environment); marketing objectives that provide a mechanism for measuring performance; marketing strategy that includes selection of target market(s) and decisions for the marketing mix elements; implementation program (tasks to be performed and responsibilities); and control program (monitor and evaluate performance to make strategic or tactical revisions).

ASSESS THE MARKETING COMMUNICATIONS SITUATION

The promotional plan is developed similarly to the marketing plan and uses its information to understand the situation. *Some IMC strategy decisions require specific promotion information to perform detailed analysis for marketing communication decisions.* It is important to note the significance of the preceding sentence. A situation analysis compiles relevant information, and makes conclusions or derives implications from the information. The content generally concerns consumer, competitor, company, market, and environmental information and interpretation, as shown in **Figure 1-9**.

Consumer analysis is a detailed evaluation of consumers' segmentation characteristics (e.g., demographic, psychographic), buying patterns, decision processes, and factors influencing their purchase decisions. Marketing research studies are usually needed to answer these questions. For example, McCain's research for its frozen food products found increased consumer interest toward wholesome or natural foods, which appeared to decrease the sales of frozen food as consumers viewed the latter as less healthy. Consumer beliefs in the freshness and healthfulness of frozen food declined.[66] **IMC Perspective 1-2** documents Chevrolet's "Canadian Dream" campaign, which relied on considerable information about Canadians from research performed by an ad agency.

Competitor analysis examines both direct and indirect competitors. Focus is on the firm's primary competitors' strengths and limitations; segmentation, targeting, and positioning strategies; and promotional strategies and tactics. The size and allocation of competitors' promotional budgets, media strategies, and message strategies should all be considered. In the case of McCain, it faced considerable indirect competition from fresh food used for cooking "from scratch" as input for its new marketing strategy and marketing communication decisions.[67]

Company analysis assesses the relative strengths and limitations of the product; the product's unique selling points, attributes, or benefits; and its packaging, price, and design. This information is important to the creative personnel who develop the brand's advertising message and communicate aspects of the brand. The strengths and limitations of the firm image or brand image impact the way it can advertise and promote itself as well as its products and services. For example, Starbucks has an outstanding image due to the quality of its products and its reputation as a socially responsible company to all stakeholders, which guides the selection of its promotional decisions. Starbucks publishes a

Figure 1-9 Analysis of the marketing communications situation

Consumer analysis
How is the purchase decision made?
Who assumes what role? (e.g., decider, influencer)
What does the consumer buy? What needs must be satisfied?
Why do consumers buy a particular brand?
Where do they go or look to buy the product?
When do they buy? Are there any seasonality factors?
What social, lifestyle, or demographic factors influence the purchase decision?

Competitor analysis
Who are our direct and indirect competitors?
What key benefits and positioning are used by our competitors?
What is our position relative to the competition?
How big are competitors' promotion budgets?
What promotion strategies are competitors using?

Company analysis
What are the product strengths and weaknesses?
How strong is the firm or brand image?
What is the performance of past promotional programs?
What are the firm's promotional capabilities?

Market analysis
What is the size, growth, and profitability of national, regional, and city markets?
Are there changes in product formats, styles, or applications?

Environmental analysis
What current trends or developments affect the promotional program?

CHEVROLET'S "CANADIAN DREAM"

Chevrolet teased Canadians with an unbranded message—"There is a dream we should all know about"—in social media, video media, and out-of-home media for a week or so. Managers for the vehicle brand expected the initial ads would create curiosity and conversation about people's dreams. Then, Chevrolet released a two-minute video documenting a 27-day, cross-country trip that discovered the stories of everyday Canadians. Overall, the managers viewed the campaign as an opportunity to communicate with those unfamiliar with the Chevrolet brand and what it offered.

Inspiration for the campaign originated from the ad agency's research about Canadians that defined the elements of the dream as individual success, caring for others, respect for the system, fairness, and respect for individuals. The storyline captured the experiences of numerous Canadians whom the team met on their journey. Gord drove his Silverado in northwestern Ontario to deliver fresh produce as a food bank volunteer. Carol rode in her Cruze as she created music all the time. A family travelled 80,000 km in one year while going from PEI to Yukon in their Equinox.

The message diverged from past Chevrolet ads that promoted technological innovation in an attempt to spur Canadians out of their indifferent attitude toward a brand firmly established in our country for over 100 years. In fact, the promotional planners saw the campaign as a way for consumers to see themselves in a Chevrolet to fulfill their dreams. While the intention focused on the dream message, its positive reception ignited subsequent ads for individual vehicle brands. Silverado ads profiled the typical driver as being humble, while Spark ads focused on the aspirations of young city consumers.

Exposure of the video message included 30- and 60-second versions, and full 120-second exposure occurred on TV, in the cinemas, on fitness networks, and in Chevrolet's owned social media. The original teaser media continued, along with digital takeovers, display ads, print ads, and point-of-sale promotions.

©Chevrolet/Commonwealth McCann

The campaign fit well within the broader IMC picture. Chevrolet sponsors Participaction and Hockey Canada. For the latter, it created the Good Deed Cup dedicated to a Peewee team that demonstrated significant community involvement. It also sponsored various entertainment events reflecting Canadian dreams. And, the teaser concept worked so well for a relaunch of the Spark a few years ago, it seems that Chevrolet found its niche.

Overall, the campaign posted impressive results: positive attitudes toward the brand on numerous measures, stronger purchase intentions, and 12 percent growth in sales. And, one American commentator gave the two-minute video a thumbs-up, saying, "It manages to skirt jingoistic clichés through its muted/poetic visual style, which achieves an engaging level of realism and grit."

Question:

1. What marketing communication suggestions can be made to grow the "Canadian Dream" campaign?

Global Responsibility Annual Report that describes the company's social, environmental, and economic effects in the communities it serves (**Exhibit 1-14**).

When a firm is devising a new promotional plan, past promotional objectives, budgets, strategies, and tactics of all elements should be reviewed to understand their strengths and limitations. Information from marketing research that tracked the results of previous programs should be examined to determine what promotional decisions should be retained, revised, or withdrawn. In the McCain situation, its past advertising slogan ("It's all good") coincided with ads communicating the brand's wholesome recipes to signal the naturalness of products to consumers. The success of this led to changes during a subsequent campaign. However, it required a big step as research indicated low levels of consumer awareness of McCain's options for frozen potato products beyond the standard french fry.

Market analysis examines a number of factors like market size, growth, and profitability that are investigated nationally, regionally, or locally using a census metropolitan area (CMA) basis. Emerging submarkets may be identified as potential sources of new revenue. Trends with respect to product formats or styles along with new product developments may be relevant. For McCain, the market analysis appeared confusing as one research firm projected the overall Canadian frozen food market declining by 4 percent over the next five years, while another saw the market growing by 2 percent per year.

Despite this, McCain implemented the advertising strategy by communicating different meal occasions for consuming fries, with an emphasis on small households. The change from family focused ads to singles and couples marked a new direction to refocus those consumers' views from their past experiences as children or young adults. The IMC tools used to convey the new approach included TV advertising and in-store promotions. And for the first time, McCain directed its messaging to digital communication to reach younger consumers living in smaller households.

Environmental analysis factors can vary according to industry, but generally concern technology, economic, social, and government/regulatory factors that constrain promotional decisions or offer marketing communication opportunities. Concluding how a brand can address its environmental uncertainty is a planner's priority.

Exhibit 1-14 Starbucks has a strong brand image and reputation as a socially responsible company.

Source: Starbucks

DETERMINE IMC PLAN OBJECTIVES

An important part of this stage of the promotional planning process is establishing relevant and appropriate objectives. In this text, we stress the importance of distinguishing among different types of objectives that are generally decided during the planning of different strategies.

Marketing objectives refer to what is to be accomplished by the overall marketing program. They are stated in terms of sales, market share, or profitability and are determined when the marketing plan is constructed. Precise definition of marketing objectives and their time frame is important to guide what is to be accomplished in the marketing communication plan. With the relaunch of Tourism BC, the government looked to increase tourism revenue by 5 percent over a five-year time period.[68]

Communication objectives refer to what the firm seeks to accomplish with its IMC program. They are stated in terms of the nature of the message to be communicated or what specific communication effects are to be achieved, such as awareness. The promotional planner must think about the process consumers will go through in responding to marketing communications. Tourism BC needed to improve its image as visits there declined while other provinces experienced an increase in tourism.

Behavioural objectives in terms of trial purchase or repeat purchase, among others, may be defined along with the communication objectives. Tourism BC sought to increase the number of visitors from Ontario, presumably many for the first time, to achieve impressive revenue growth. Communication and behavioural objectives should guide the

IMC strategy and each promotional tool. **Exhibit 1-15** shows an ad where the call to action encourages the reader to visit Beau's Internet site.

While determining these objectives, two questions are asked to tentatively set the budget: (1) What will the promotional program cost? and (2) How will these monies be allocated? Ideally, the amount a firm spends on promotion should be determined by what must be accomplished to achieve communication and behavioural objectives. Tourism BC decided to spend $52 million for 2012, down from the $65 million it spent in 2009.

DEVELOP IMC PROGRAMS

As Figure 1-8 shows, each promotional mix element has its own objectives, strategy, message and media strategy and tactics, and budget. For example, the advertising program sets objectives involving the communication of a message or appeal to a target audience. A budget will be determined, providing the advertising manager and the agency with an idea of how much money is available for developing the ad campaign and purchasing media to disseminate the ad message.

Two important aspects of the advertising program are development of the message and the media strategy. Message development, also referred to as *creative strategy,* involves determining the message the advertiser wishes to convey to the target audience. This process, along with the ads that result, is the most fascinating aspect of promotion. The Mini outdoor ad shown in **Exhibit 1-16** creatively displays the vehicle in action to signify an exciting driving experience.

Media strategy involves determining which communication channels will be used to deliver the advertising message to the target audience. Decisions must be made regarding which types of media will be used (e.g., magazine, TV) as well as specific media vehicle selections (e.g., a particular magazine or TV program). This task requires evaluation of the media options' strengths and limitations, costs, and ability to deliver the message effectively to the target audiences. The Mini ad shows an example of how the creative and media decisions are intertwined.

A similar process and set of decisions occur for *all* other elements of the IMC program as objectives are set, an overall strategy is developed, and message and media strategies are determined. If a firm decides to include a sales promotion, it might decide to use a specific message and media strategy and tactics to communicate information about the sales promotion, in addition to whatever advertising decisions that have been recommended.

Furthermore, if a firm considers using multiple tools for its complete plan, it must decide which ones best fit together to solve a particular marketing communication problem. For example, Taco Bell's Canadian national launch (excluding Quebec) of the Doritos Locos Taco attempted to increase same-store sales by 7 percent. The campaign evolved over 12 months with multiple IMC tools and media, resulting in substantial online popularity and higher than expected sales (**Figure 1-10**).[69]

Figure 1-10 Taco Bell: Doritos Locos Taco launch

Budget	$1 million to $2 million
Time Frame	June 2013 to May 2014
Target	Light/medium users
Strategic Message	Eat Your Words
Tactical Message	Ambiguous and mysterious pre-launch teaser messages in social media
Social Media	Fan outreach on Facebook, Instagram, Snapchat, Twitter
Advertising Media	Television
Sales Promotion	Coupon (3 DLTs for $5), invited marketing event
Digital Media	YouTube channel, and pre-roll, micro-site counting down 1 million tacos eaten
Public Relations	Buzzfeed sponsored articles

IMPLEMENT AND CONTROL THE IMC PLAN

Upon making the message and media decisions for each tool, the manager implements the IMC plan. Most large companies hire advertising agencies to plan and produce their messages and to evaluate and purchase the media. Agencies usually work closely with their clients as they develop the ads and select media, because it is the advertiser that ultimately approves (and pays for) the creative work and media plan. The marketer's advertising agency may handle other IMC functions or contract them out to specialist agencies.

An evaluation of how well the IMC plan is meeting communication and behavioural objectives and achieving the brand's marketing objectives is required to know whether corrective steps are necessary. For example, problems with the advertising program may lie in the nature of the message or in a media plan that does not reach the target audience effectively. This final stage of the process is designed to provide managers with continual feedback concerning the effectiveness of the promotional program, which in turn should be used as input into the planning process. As Figure 1-8 shows, information on the results achieved by the promotional program is used in subsequent promotional planning and strategy development.

In conclusion, this final topic—the whole point of IMC planning, and the general idea of marketing communication—relies on information. Much of this information is derived from data, and the current evolution of using such data for decision making is known as *marketing analytics.* The growth and application of this topic is at the forefront of academic research and managerial practice.[70] As such, this book references key analytics where appropriate to see how data is used as information to make effective promotion decisions.

IMC Planning: Organization of Text

This book provides an understanding of advertising and other elements of a firm's promotional mix and shows how they are combined to form a comprehensive marketing communications program with an IMC planning perspective. To implement this idea, we conclude each chapter of the book with an IMC planning section. Its purpose is to relate the chapter material to the content of an IMC plan and illustrate how to make IMC decisions. The final section of this chapter establishes this approach by illustrating how the entire book is organized into five major parts around the IMC planning perspective.

UNDERSTANDING INTEGRATED MARKETING COMMUNICATIONS

Part 1 comprises four chapters that define the topic of the book and provide the context for marketing communication decisions. This initial chapter reviews marketing communication and the promotional mix and how they relate to marketing. The chapter also describes integrated marketing communication and the content of an IMC plan.

We discuss how advertisers work with ad agencies and other firms that provide marketing and promotional services in Chapter 2. Agencies are an important part of the IMC planning process as they assist in the decision making with promotional planners and execute the decisions by creating promotional messages.

To plan, develop, and implement an effective IMC program, those involved must understand consumer behaviour and the communications process. We focus on consumer behaviour and target audience decisions in Chapter 3, and summarize communication response models in Chapter 4. Combined, these two chapters establish a conceptual foundation for developing the subsequent decisions of an IMC plan.

ARTICULATING THE MESSAGE

Part 2 concerns a number of decisions that firms make to put together a persuasive marketing communication message and comprises five chapters. The ideas developed here are applicable for advertising and all other IMC tools. Sales promotion offers include a brand message, as do public relations activities. All brand-initiated communication in Internet media provides a clear message about the brand.

Chapter 5 explains how to set IMC objectives to achieve the desired effects. A general model is explained for setting behavioural and communication objectives that are universally applicable to all parts of an IMC plan.

Chapter 6 reviews the important decisions to construct a brand positioning strategy. This is the heart of marketing communication, where decisions regarding how brands compete with marketing communication messages are determined.

The most exciting aspects of IMC are presented in Chapters 7 and 8, where we illustrate creative strategy and creative tactics decisions that are reflected in the vibrant and exciting ads we all experience in every part of our daily living. Creative illustration of a brand is the pinnacle task of creative specialists and their work is central for building a brand.

Chapter 9 examines how to measure promotional message effectiveness. The research ideas presented in this chapter also set the stage for understanding how to assess the effects of all IMC tools found in later chapters.

DELIVERING THE MESSAGE

Part 3 comprises four chapters and explores the key media strategy, media tactics decisions, and budgeting for IMC, along with the use of six different media.

Chapter 10 provides the technical information for media planning. Media planning is an important advertising decision and this information is also used to implement other IMC tools. Scheduling and determining how many consumers should receive a message and how often is critical with Internet media like all other media. Similarly, the timing and media presentation of promotional offers assist in the success of their execution. The chapter also explores how to construct a budget and allocate the budget for advertising and all IMC tools.

Chapters 11, 12, and 13 describe the use and strengths and limitations of media choices that have been historically labelled as *mass media* (i.e., television, radio, magazines, newspapers, out-of-home). Once again, background on these topics is useful for implementing advertising and for using these media in executing other IMC tools. Much of these mass media are used to direct consumers to different aspects of Internet media. TV and radio messages say "Facebook us" to carry on further communication. These media are also used for presentation of community activities designed to "give back" and foster goodwill among citizens.

STRENGTHENING THE MESSAGE

Our interest turns to the other areas of the promotional mix—sales promotion, public relations, direct marketing, Internet marketing, and social media marketing—in Part 4, "Strengthening the Message." Each tool is explored in its own chapter and related to communication objectives as was done in Part 3.

Chapter 14 investigates consumer and trade sales promotions that are often combined with advertising to influence behaviour and communication. A multitude of options are available for planners to stimulate trial and repeat purchases and to enhance brand equity.

Chapter 15 presents the topic of public relations and related topics of publicity through media and corporate advertising. Using other tools and building a corporate brand through IMC are important topics for fully understanding how to put together a complete IMC plan.

Chapter 16 covers direct marketing and direct-response media used to communicate with this particular IMC tool. Improved technology allows brands to communicate to individuals and vice versa. Methods for advertising and promoting directly are described in this chapter.

Chapter 17 examines the marketing communication and advertising via Internet media. Sections provide guidance for a digital advertising plan and options for different digital ad formats, and apply this direction for mobile.

Chapter 18 reviews social media communication regarding its paid, owned, and earned media characteristics. This point of view is applied for social networking, content communities, blogs, and projects. Social media influence concludes the chapter.

ADVERTISING AND SOCIETY

Part 5 concludes the book with one chapter that examines advertising regulation and the ethical, social, and economic effects of an organization's advertising and promotional program. Advertising is a very public and controversial part of any organization's activities and Chapter 19 explores the complexities of these points. Each topic is relevant at varying points of the earlier chapters and may be read when desired.

Learning Objectives Summary

 Describe the importance of marketing communication within the marketing mix.

Marketing combines four controllable elements, known as the marketing mix, into a comprehensive program that facilitates exchange with a group of customers. The elements of the marketing mix are the product, price, place (distribution), and promotion (market communication). Advertising and other forms of promotion are an integral part of the marketing process in most organizations since these tools communicate the value consumers receive within the exchange. Marketing communication conveys elements of the product through benefit claims and brand identity with the hopes of building brand equity. Providing price and distribution information are two other important roles of marketing communication so that value is perceived by both customers and non-customers.

 Identify the tools of the promotional mix—advertising, sales promotion, public relations, direct marketing, Internet marketing, and personal selling—and summarize their purpose.

Promotion is accomplished through a promotional mix that includes advertising, sales promotion, public relations, direct marketing, Internet marketing, and personal selling. The inherent advantages and disadvantages of each of these promotional mix elements influence the success of the overall marketing program. In developing the promotional program, the manager must decide which tools to use and how to combine them to achieve the organization's objectives. Many organizations assist promotional managers in developing or implementing their plans, including advertising agencies, media organizations, and specialized communication services firms like direct-response agencies, sales promotion agencies, interactive agencies, and public relations firms.

 Illustrate the concept of integrated marketing communications (IMC) by distinguishing its evolution, renewed perspective, and content.

Integrated marketing communications (IMC) is viewed as a strategic and comprehensive planning perspective for all facets of an organization's marketing communication. An IMC perspective starts with the consumer as companies take an *audience contact* perspective by evaluating the potential ways of reaching their target audiences and presenting the brand message favourably. This perspective is critical since audiences receive messages from competing brands across different IMC tools. Long-term customer relationships through relationship marketing strategies to enhance the lifetime value of customers have altered the communication approach of promotional planners. The growth of Internet media

...ital marketing renewed the historic idea of paid, owned, and earned media. An audience contact perspective ...eeing all IMC tools along the notion of paid, owned, and earned provides IMC planners with a clearer direction ...lanning.

Explain the IMC planning process model and express the steps in developing a marketing communication program.

IMC management involves coordinating the promotional mix elements to develop an integrated program of effective marketing communication. The model of the IMC planning process contains five steps: (1) Review the marketing plan; (2) Assess the marketing communications situation; (3) Determine IMC plan objectives; (4) Develop IMC programs; and (5) Implement and control the IMC plan. This model is consistent with a general marketing planning model, but is more specific to the context of marketing communication. It shows that individual marketing communication tools achieve multiple objectives so that the completely integrated plan can build brand equity across multiple target audiences.

Identify how the IMC planning process is continued throughout all chapters.

The IMC planning process is an important perspective that is continually reinforced in every chapter. All chapter material for the rest of the book is presented with an approach to assist in decision making for every step.

Review Questions

1. Why is marketing communication important for communicating value to consumers?

2. How do smart phone brands use each marketing communication tool for communicating messages?

3. What are the reasons why marketers are taking an IMC perspective in their advertising and promotion programs?

4. What parts of the IMC planning model are similar to and different from a marketing planning model?

5. How is the structure of the book consistent with the content of an IMC plan?

Applied Questions

1. Consider how a university or college communicates value in its marketing communication to its prospective students and current students. In what ways are the two approaches similar or different?

2. Identify all the possible marketing communication tools that a favourite brand or performance artist is using. Try to explain why these tools were selected. In what ways did the tools support one another? How did they not support one another? Was each tool effective or ineffective?

3. Find one example where all promotional tools of a brand have the same look and feel, and find another example of a brand where the promotional tools have a different look and feel. Why did these decisions occur, based on relevant situation analysis variables?

4. Why is it important for those who work in the field of advertising and promotion to understand and appreciate all IMC tools, not just the area in which they specialize?

5. How does one of your favourite brands link or integrate its different IMC communication tools? Is it done effectively?

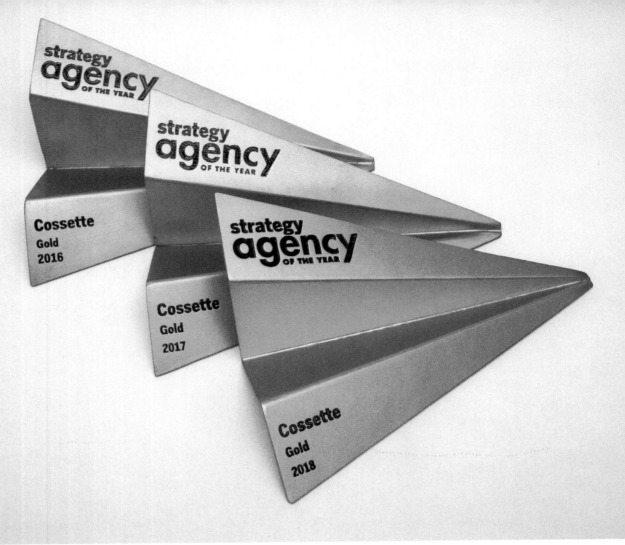

CHAPTER TWO

Organizing for IMC: Role of Agencies

LEARNING OBJECTIVES

LO1 Identify the role of the advertising agency and the services it provides.

LO2 Describe methods for compensating and evaluating advertising agencies.

LO3 Review the functions of specialized marketing communication organizations.

LO4 Evaluate the perspectives on the use of integrated services across agencies or within one agency, and agency–client responsibilities and partnerships.

Cossette Scores a Hat Trick

Cossette received the nod from *Strategy* magazine as Agency of the Year (AOY) for 2016, 2017, and 2018. With excellent work for SickKids Foundation, McDonald's, VIA Rail Canada, Egg Farmers of Canada, and General Mills Canada, the agency has received numerous awards over the past three years including eight Cannes Lions in 2017 for the "SickKids VS" campaign. In 2018, the agency took home 10 Cannes Lions, including the Grand Prix, for its "Follow the Arches" campaign for McDonald's; it was the first Canadian Grand Prix winner since Dove's "Evolution" ad in 2007.

The accolades follow several key changes to the agency, which has made a conscious shift to a more integrated model focused on flexibility and agility since 2015. Under the guidance of CEO Melanie Dunn, there has been a focus on building an ecosystem of creativity and innovation at the agency with the recruitment of inspiring leaders across Canada and global chief creative officers Peter Ignazi and Carlos Moreno, one of the best creative partnerships in the country, to lead and inspire the growing creative team. Cossette has also invested heavily in innovative technologies and full integration, including media. At Cossette, there are no silos and no regional P&Ls. There are full bilingual capabilities and the agency harnesses the power of its regional expertise to offer fully integrated services across Canada.

To support its major clients such as McDonald's, which Cossette has worked with for over 40 years, Cossette created a unique operational model in which a dedicated team with deep knowledge of the brand and product works on McDonald's every day. The team draws on talent from across Cossette and the Vision7 network as needed. In a business where most brand–agency partnerships last only a handful of years, the long-term relationship has resulted in a level of trust that allows the two companies to take risks and reap rewards together.

"Follow the Arches" is a case in point. While the campaign was never briefed, Cossette's deep understanding of McDonald's business challenges resulted in a creative concept that was immediately embraced and recognized for its value to McDonald's Canada as well as its potential value globally.

The Cannes Grand Prix–winning "Follow the Arches" creative uses segments of the iconic golden arches to indicate the location of nearby McDonald's restaurants to drivers (on left, on right, next exit, just missed). The campaign has been made available to McDonald's marketing teams in 120 countries and won dozens of awards for Cossette. The agency also took home a Cannes Effectiveness Lion for its work with SickKids Foundation. The "SickKids VS" campaign represented a revolutionary shift in tone and approach, moving away from typically soft and emotional non-profit marketing and highlighting the fierce side of the patients, families, and staff at the Hospital for Sick Children (SickKids) and the fight that occurs at the hospital each day.

Question:

1. What is significant about these campaigns that allowed Cossette to win awards?

Developing and implementing an IMC program is usually a complex process involving the efforts of individuals from the marketing firm, the advertising agency, and often other types of agencies. Strong relationships with these agencies are important as their expertise in creative planning, media placement, new digital executions, and other activities contributes to successful brand development. Alternatively, brands also work with a full-service marketing communication agency capable of providing all services. This chapter explores how these agencies function, for those who may want to work in the marketing communication agency industry.

The chapter first identifies the characteristics of a full-service agency and its client relationship. It then describes how agencies are compensated and evaluated. Next, the chapter reviews the functions of specialized marketing communication organizations such as creative boutiques; media buying services; direct-response, sales promotion, and interactive agencies; and public relations firms. These organizations are increasingly involved in IMC planning and some are owned by large agencies which they work with considerably. Finally, the chapter evaluates whether marketers are best served by using the integrated services of one large agency or the separate services of multiple marketing communication specialists.

LO1 Advertising Agencies

Different types of advertising agencies make the selection a unique decision for each advertiser. In this section we provide a general overview of advertising agencies; we review the agency decision, highlight the agency industry, and describe the activities of a full-service agency.

ADVERTISING AGENCY DECISION

Marketing decision makers have a choice of whether the organization will have its own in-house agency or whether it will employ an external advertising agency. Interestingly, a trend exists where major corporations employ both approaches and allow collaboration between the two types of agencies.[1] We briefly discuss the relative merits and disadvantages of both options.

In-House Agency An **in-house agency** is an advertising agency that is set up, owned, and operated by the advertiser. Some in-house agencies are essentially advertising departments, but in other companies they are given a separate identity and are responsible for the entire advertising expenditure. Research finds that about half of all companies use an in-house agency and that the likelihood of this occurring decreases with larger advertising budgets but increases with advertising intensity (i.e., advertising/sales ratio), with technological intensity, and for creative industries.[2] Some companies use in-house agencies exclusively, while others combine in-house efforts with those of outside agencies. For example, Vancouver-based Saje sells natural skin care products in over 70 North American stores. The in-house creative team is responsible for website design, social media, events, gifts, paid Instagram ads, location-based ads, community and promotion partnerships, in-store promotional efforts and design.[3]

A reason for using an in-house agency is to reduce advertising and promotion costs, because companies with large advertising budgets pay a substantial amount to outside agencies. An in-house agency can also provide related work—such as sales presentations, package design, and public relations—at a lower cost than outside agencies. One study found that creative and media services were the most likely functions to be performed outside, while merchandising and sales promotion were the most likely to be performed in-house.[4] Time savings, bad experiences with outside agencies, and stronger understanding of the market arising from continuous work on advertising and promotion for the product also support in-house agency use. Companies can maintain tighter control over the process and coordinate promotions with the firm's overall marketing program. A limitation of an in-house agency is that personnel may grow stale while working on the same product line, in comparison to an outside agency where creative specialists design campaigns for a variety of products. Furthermore, changes in an in-house agency could be slow compared to the flexibility of hiring an outside agency.

An example of the above points is seen with Under Armour. Its growth in the athletic shoe and apparel market required the brand to move some in-house advertising to an agency. It hired Droga5 to work for its women's business, and the agency developed award-winning ads including the "I Will What I Want" campaign featuring Gisele Bündchen and ballerina Misty Copeland shown in **Exhibit 2-1**. Droga5 now handles nearly all of Under Armour's advertising for numerous products, although Under Armour retained advertising for football in-house.

Exhibit 2-1 Under Armour uses Droga5 to handle much of its advertising.

Source: Under Armour, Inc.

Advertising Agency Major companies use an advertising agency to assist them in developing, preparing, and executing their promotional programs. An ad agency is a service organization that employs highly skilled personnel and specializes in planning and executing advertising programs for its clients. An advertising agency's staff may include artists, writers, media analysts, researchers, and others with specific skills, knowledge, and experience who can help market the client's products. Agencies may specialize in a particular type of business and use their knowledge of the industry to assist their clients. Alternatively, the agency can draw on the broad range of experience while working on diverse marketing problems for assorted clients and apply this knowledge for new clients.

The Association of Canadian Advertisers offers its members a 10-chapter document that guides the process for selecting a marketing communications partner. The steps of the process include initial consideration, preparation, need identification, search criteria, agency list, pitch, evaluation, financial criteria, final selection, and conclusion. In the end, the client and agency form a partnership where the responsibilities of each are recorded and agreed upon with the intention being to have a positive working relationship. The document also provides forms and examples for advertisers to make records during the selection process.[5]

Sid Lee is an anagram for the agency's original name of *Diesel* to distinguish it from the stylish fashion producer (**Exhibit 2-2**). It is a great example of a Canadian agency with strong client relationships. From its humble start in Montreal 25 years ago when the first owners had no advertising agency experience, Sid Lee ramped up to 550 employees and four more offices located in Toronto, Amsterdam, Paris, and New York. A Canadian advertising agency expanding to the international stage was almost unheard of historically, but Sid Lee proved it to be possible. One international client, Adidas, recognized the talent and hired the agency on as the leader for its worldwide marketing communication. Senior management at Sid Lee attributed their success with clients to the informal work culture, with relaxed dress and no hierarchy. A professional and organizational development program shows new employees the Sid Lee way of doing business. Other clients with strong relationships to Sid Lee include Cirque du Soleil and Absolut.[6]

Exhibit 2-2 Sid Lee is a great Canadian success story as a marketing communication agency.

©Sid Lee

Agency-of-record (AOR) is the term used to describe situations where a client works with a primary agency exclusively. It is the foundation on which the advertising agency business exists—a service provider whose foremost interest is in building the client's brand. Examples of longstanding relationships include Taxi with Telus for 18 years and Marketel with Air Canada for 25 years.[7] Clients periodically put their account up for renewal and allow other agencies to make a sales pitch. Agencies decide how many and which accounts to attract; DDB is very selective on these decisions and its president estimates a 60 percent hit rate.[8] In the case of Taxi and Telus, Telus never opened the account for others to pitch during the whole time but eventually moved on to a new agency in 2014. At times, the AOR subcontracts work to other specialized agencies; however, the AOR retains responsibility given its designation with the client.

Leo Burnett Canada received recognition from *Strategy* with its Agency of the Year (AOY) Award indicating a job well done as an AOR for its clients Always and Ikea. For the agency's "Like a Girl" campaign for P&G's Always brand, the Toronto office teamed up with other offices and recorded video of girls, boys, women, and men reacting to the instructions "Run like a girl" and "Throw like a girl" and answering questions on what these phrases mean. Younger girls ran according to their ability, while teens and young women ran with an exaggerated feeble approach. The difference appeared to highlight the negative connotations of the phrase that young girls learn but are not aware of at a young age. The Always brand sought a unique emotional message for its brand to enhance the confidence of girls as they transitioned to puberty and started to need menstrual products. The video posted on YouTube obtained 76 million views. Post-campaign purchase intent rose from 42 percent to 46 percent overall, and from 40 percent to 60 percent for teens. For Ikea, Leo Burnett explored residents' "house rules" by inviting them in a TV ad to share their rules online; in return, the retailer sent gifts that reflected their story. Rules included mundane things like "We must eat leftovers" and funny things like "There is no laughing when pets walk into screen doors," and the retailer organized the rules online visually by each room. General media advertising communicated the more popular "rules." Ikea also tweeted the "rules" during TV shows and encouraged participation in radio contests. Awareness jumped 10 percent as Ikea compiled almost 27,000 rules as visitors spent 3.5 minutes on the Internet site, giving it a store sales lift of 12 percent.[9]

Exhibit 2-3 TAG Heuer's global campaign features famous people from around the world.

#DontCrackUnderPressure

Source: TAG Heuer

ADVERTISING AGENCY INDUSTRY

The Canadian advertising agency industry features small and mid-sized domestic firms and large international organizations with domestic service providers. The presence of international ad agencies in Canada reflects a global trend of large agencies merged with or acquired by other agencies and support organizations that provide clients with IMC services worldwide. Mid-sized agencies were acquired by or forged alliances with larger agencies because clients wanted an agency with IMC capabilities, and their alignment with larger organizations permitted access to a network of agencies around the world. Currently, most major agencies offer specialized services in areas of interactive communications, direct marketing, PR, and sales promotion so that they can provide their clients with an ever-broader range of IMC services. In fact, a larger multiservice firm is a **marketing communication agency**, making the term "advertising agency" somewhat obsolete for these situations. Larger international marketing communication agencies facilitate global campaigns. For example, the ad in **Exhibit 2-3** by TagHeuer is an example where the message and creative concept resonates in many countries, necessitating an agency with a worldwide presence.

Figure 2-1 summarizes the five major international marketing communication conglomerates and their major divisions.[10] The most significant global player with an original Canadian presence is Vision7 International. Formerly known as Cossette, it retains this brand name among other agencies across multiple services. As expected, two players (Omnicom and Interpublic) are based in New York; each includes famous advertising agencies recognized for their creative talent.

Additionally, the table includes two European conglomerates, WPP and Publicis, which own established American advertising greats Ogilvy and JWT, and BBDO and DDB, respectively. Although Dentsu is based in London, its origin and one main division are Japan-based. A sixth global player not listed, Havas, continues to bring different disciplines together by amalgamating previously acquired agencies under the Havas name.[11] Although a trend toward international holding companies occurred over numerous decades, a study using American data concluded that the advertising services industry concentration levels are consistent with past decades, thereby providing a robust competitive market.[12]

Figure 2-1 Largest international marketing communication firms

WPP	Omnicom	Publicis	Interpublic	Dentsu Aegis
JWT	BBDO	Leo Burnett	Mediabrands	Canat
Hill+Knowlton	DDB	Saatchi & Saatchi	McCann	Dentsu Media
Young & Rubicam	TBWA	Publicis Media	FCB	Isobar
Group M	OMG	Publicis	CMG	DentsuBos
Ogilvy	DAS Group			

Two agencies with strong Canadian roots developed internationally. Taxi won numerous national and international awards and was named agency of the year many times by *Strategy*. Taxi expanded to the United States and Europe and is now a mainstay within WPP as the holding company phased out Young & Rubicam in Canada after 80 years.[13] Sid Lee expanded to the same geographic locations and developed an international presence for Adidas in 100 countries, after Adidas hired the agency as the leader for its worldwide marketing communication. One development featured a mobile app where a shoe photo would direct the user to the closest store with the product available.[14] Zulu Alpha Kilo emulates Taxi and Sid Lee, as a newer agency winning over clients. It is known as a brand transformation agency, handling clients' brands in need of a major strategic or creative shift. It retooled Interac's imagery with the "Be in the Black" campaign to encourage consumers to use their debit card instead of their credit card. **IMC Perspective 2-1** highlights this agency's accomplishments.

As an alternative to larger agencies, small and mid-sized agencies handle local and regional work throughout Canada with great success. For example, C&B Advertising of Calgary works with Travel Alberta and other related tourism clients along with the Calgary Co-op and Big Rock beer.[15] Across the country, these independent agencies offer an opportunity for students to pursue a career in the advertising industry. There are a good number of examples in Canada where agencies are driven by the founders who are the creative leaders for their clients' successful campaigns, and after a great run for a decade or two, a larger agency conglomerate buys out the independent agency. In some cases the agency thrives in its new structure, and in other cases the agency withers without the leadership of the departed founder. A few different arrangements for succession planning emerged in Canada, however, some hot agencies of a few years ago do not live up to the past glory and award-winning work.[16]

The ad agency industry is strong, as demonstrated by international conglomerates employing hundreds of thousands of people and achieving billions of dollars in sales, but digital media giants like Google and Facebook threaten the agency business much like media firms experienced. The two digital firms reached 25 percent of the global ad business in media expenditures, and this dominance opened the opportunity to move toward message development as they hire creative talent.[17]

IMC PERSPECTIVE 2-1

INDIE AGENCY ZULU ALPHA KILO

Zulu Alpha Kilo established a founding principle of operating as an agency differently by serving clients well by solving their marketing communication problems and gaining additional business from that success. It eschewed spec work and did not participate in requests for proposals (RFPs), common industry practices where clients could receive creative work without paying. It also straddled

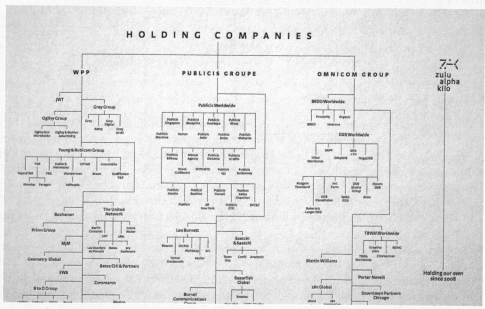

©Zulu Alpha Kilo

[Continued on next page]

the line as to whether the firm operated as an ad agency, design shop, or digital services organization. Nonetheless, its ability to work in many worlds led the agency to great success.

Starting with Bell as its first account in 2008, its roster of clients has grown to include Interac, Harley-Davidson, Cineplex, Labatt, and Whirlpool. Amassing over 1,000 awards, Zulu received *Ad Age*'s Small Agency of the Year Award in 2016, and the publication's International Small Agency of the Year Award in 2017. While no longer particularly small at 100 employees, the innovative indie of Toronto receives call internationally for new business that the agency is very selective in accepting. Ten years later, Bell is completely satisfied with the work since Zulu provided a new visual identity and brand positioning strategy that still remains.

The agency runs smoothly with its employee guidebook, *The Zulu Way*, outlining the guiding principles and long-term mission; its readers instantly transform into "Zuligans" devoted to serving customers better than typical agencies. And, the Zuligans are well treated with innovative employee relations initiatives. Internally, Zulu developed client service capabilities such as the agency's team system. It also opened a content creation and production studio with multiple editing suites, and an audio-recording studio. A new feature is an open concept work space where clients can see the creative work developed.

Examples of its great work include the heartwarming animated stories of *Lily and the Snowman* and *A Balloon for Ben* for Cineplex, a brand that faced the challenge of enticing consumers to the big screen when many desired to watch entertainment on their giant TV at home or their small screen while on the go. For Harley-Davidson and its 100th anniversary, Zulu established a café for first-time bike owners and enthusiasts to enjoy a museum-like display of motorcycle options, and created a documentary shown online and then subsequently on TV. Interac wanted to take on credit cards at point-of-sale transactions and the many creative messages showed Canadians how to stay out of debt by using debit instead of credit. Further description of these cases is seen in IMC examples in later chapters.

What does the future hold for Zulu? There are thoughts of international expansion, additional client growth, and attracting international clients while remaining in Toronto only. One thing is for sure though, the clients will be well served by the Zuligans!

Question:

1. In what new direction would you anticipate this agency moving in the future?

FULL-SERVICE AGENCY

The services offered and functions performed vary depending upon the size of the agency. A **full-service agency** offers its clients a complete range of marketing, communication, and promotion services including planning, performing research, creating the message of the ad campaign, producing the advertising, and selecting media. A full-service agency may also offer non-advertising services, such as strategic market planning, sales promotions, direct marketing, interactive services, public relations and publicity, and package design. The full-service agency has departments led by a director that provide the activities needed to perform the advertising functions and serve the client, as shown in **Figure 2-2**. In this section we summarize these main characteristics.

Account/Client Services Account services, or client services, is the link between the ad agency and its clients. Depending on the size of the client and its advertising budget, one or more account executives serve as liaison. The **account executive** is responsible for understanding the advertiser's marketing and promotions needs and interpreting them to agency personnel. He or she coordinates agency efforts in planning, creating, and producing ads. The account executive also presents agency recommendations and obtains client approval. As the focal point of agency–client relationships, the account executive must know a great deal about the client's business and be able to communicate this to specialists in the agency working on the account. The ideal account executive has a strong marketing background as well as a thorough understanding of all phases of the advertising process.

Figure 2-2 Full-service agency organizational chart

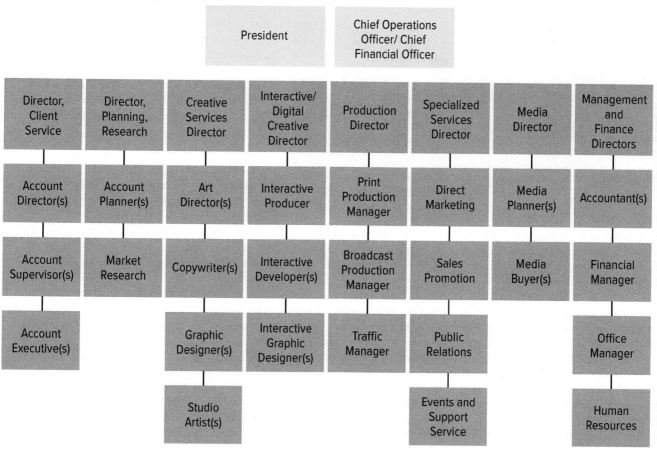

Planning/Research Services Most full-service agencies maintain a research department whose function is to gather, analyze, and interpret information as input for advertising decisions. Both primary research—where a study is designed, executed, and interpreted by the research department—and secondary (previously published) sources of information are relied upon. The research department also acquires studies conducted by independent syndicated research firms or consultants, interprets the findings, and disseminates the information to agency personnel working on that account. The research department may pretest the effectiveness of advertising with copy testing to determine how messages developed by the creative specialists are likely to be interpreted by the receiving audience. John St. is one example of an agency that embraced innovative ways of collecting and analyzing media data to demonstrate IMC effectiveness. For its client Mitsubishi, the agency found stronger responses for email messages versus display ads to those who had visited the company's Internet site.[18]

Research services may be augmented with services performed by account planners, who gather relevant information that is used to develop the creative strategy and other aspects of the IMC campaign. Account planners work with the client and other agency personnel (including the account executives, creative team members, media specialists, and research department personnel) to collect information to better understand the client's target audience and the best ways to communicate with them. They gather and organize information about consumers, competitors, and the market to prepare the **creative brief**, which is a document that the agency's creative department uses to guide the development of advertising ideas and concepts.

Account planners may also be involved in assessing consumers' reactions to the advertising and other elements of the IMC program and providing the creative staff and other agency personnel with feedback regarding performance. Account planning is important because it provides the creative team, and other agency personnel, with insight into consumers and how to use advertising and other IMC tools to communicate with them.[19] However, the account

Exhibit 2-4 The agency Innocean developed creative ads for Hyundai to build the car brand in North America.

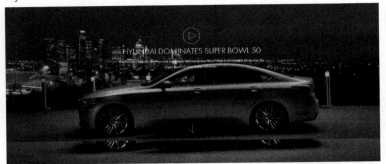

Source: Hyundai Motor America

planning is demanding with the increased number of marketing communication channels. Account planners interact with individuals from all marketing communication disciplines and require expertise in each area. Numbers of senior level planners have grown in Canada significantly, with agencies aligning organizational structure and responsibilities to ensure that optimal strategic planning occurs for all clients.[20]

Creative Services The creative services department is responsible for the creation and execution of advertisements. The individuals who conceive the ideas for the ads and write the headlines, subheads, and body copy (words of an ad message) are known as **copywriters**. They may also be involved in determining the message appeal and/or theme of the ad campaign and prepare a rough initial visual layout of the print ad or television commercial. The creative team at the agency Innocean produced ads that put Hyundai on the map with innovative storylines in their TV ads (**Exhibit 2-4**).

While copywriters are responsible for what the message says, the art director, graphic designers, and studio artist are responsible for how the ad looks. For a print ad, they prepare a **layout**, which is a drawing that shows what the ad will look like and from which the final artwork will be produced. For a TV commercial, the layout is known as a **storyboard**, a sequence of frames or panels that depict the commercial in still form.

Members of the creative department work together to develop ads that are consistent with the creative strategy decisions agreed upon with the client. Writers and artists generally work under the direction of the agency's creative director, who oversees all the advertising produced by the agency. The director sets the creative philosophy of the department and may even become directly involved in creating ads for the agency's largest clients. The creative director's job is quite demanding, even more so with digital media executions that take advantage of interactive media characteristics. Agencies use all sorts of activities to keep their creative skills sharp. Rethink divides its office into teams who receive a fictional creative brief and then deliver a creative concept by the end of the day. Staff also reveal untapped creative talents during "experimental play time" to keep them ready for innovative ideas for future client briefs.[21]

Digital Creative Services Digital creative services share similarity with established creative departments with respect to copywriters and specialists with graphics skills. However, other personnel with computer technology skills are required for programming various interactive features of creative ads found in Internet media vehicles. Moreover, this newer genre of creativity includes an interactive producer to oversee all operations and to coordinate with creative work done in mass media. In order to grow this side of the business, full-service agencies purchase small or mid-sized independent interactive agencies.[22] With its president having a digital background, Zulu Alpha Kilo gravitated toward a higher percentage of its creative work being in this domain.[23]

Production Services The ad is turned over to the production department once the copy, layout, illustrations, and mechanical specifications are completed and approved. Most agencies do not actually produce finished ads; they hire printers, engravers, photographers, typographers, and other suppliers. For broadcast production, the storyboard must be turned into a finished commercial. The production department may supervise the casting of people to appear in the ad, determine the setting for the scenes, and choose an independent production studio. The department may hire an outside director to turn the creative concept into a commercial. Specialists from all departments and client representatives may all participate in production decisions, particularly when large sums of money are involved. To manage this process, a **traffic department**, or traffic manager, coordinates all phases of production to see that the ads are completed on time and that all deadlines for submitting the ads to the media are met.

Media Services The media department of an agency analyzes, selects, and contracts for space or time in the media that will be used to deliver the client's advertising message. The media department is expected to develop a media plan that will reach the target audience and effectively communicate the message. Since most of the client's ad budget is spent on media time and/or space, this department must develop a plan that both communicates with the right audience and is cost-effective and cost-efficient. Due to the potential to place any advertising format (e.g, video, print, audio) in virtually any media space, the global planning system at PHD/Touché revised its approach by organizing by format then media. For example, a video message could be placed out-of-home, on TV, in cinema, on social media, and on different video host sites.[24]

Media specialists must know what audiences the media reach, their rates, and how well they match the client's target audience. The media department reviews information on demographics, magazine and newspaper readership, radio listenership, and consumers' TV and Internet viewing patterns to develop an effective media plan. The media buyer implements the media plan by purchasing the actual time and space. Computerized decision support systems assist in this research, as demonstrated by OMD Canada's installation of the Annalect data management platform which aids in determining the optimal media purchase across all media types.[25] The media department is an important part of the agency business, as large advertisers consolidate their media buying with one or a few agencies to improve media efficiency. An agency's strategic ability to negotiate prices and effectively use the vast array of media vehicles available is as important as its ability to create ads. Full-service agencies see value in offering this service since media companies are competing against agencies by offering creative services.

Specialized Services Large, full-service agencies offer additional marketing services to their clients to assist in other promotional areas. An agency may have a sales promotion department, or merchandising department, that specializes in developing contests, premiums, promotions, point-of-sale materials, and other sales materials. It may have direct-marketing specialists and package designers, as well as a PR/publicity department. Bensimon and Byrne established Narrative PR within the agency, and its creative success makes the PR discipline the lead communication tool for some of its clients' IMC programs. Narrative grew its own client list and now provides leads to the advertising agency component.[26] Agencies have developed interactive media departments to create websites or develop social media and email campaigns for their clients. Internet media growth initiated the opportunity for creative expression of brands and required agencies to organize additional creative departments. However, it is now so common that MEC agency disbanded its digital department on the grounds that personnel with this expertise are part of every client team since most campaigns involve digital and non-digital media.[27] In a completely new direction, Rethink and Sid Lee moved toward design services. Rethink involved itself tremendously with the new look in Freshco grocery stores. Sid Lee opened up its own architecture services as part of its design offering so that a consistent look is presented from both the retail and marketing communication perspectives.[28]

Organizational Structure To provide superior service for its accounts, agencies use the **group system**, in which individuals from each department work together in groups to service particular accounts. In contrast to the **departmental system** discussed thus far, each group is headed by an account executive and includes media planners and buyers; a creative team, which includes copywriters, art directors, artists, and production personnel; and individuals from other departments. The size and composition of the group varies depending on the client's billings and the importance of the account to the agency. For very important accounts, the group members may be assigned exclusively to one client. A group system is preferred because employees become very knowledgeable about the client's business and there is continuity in servicing the account.

 # Agency Compensation and Evaluation

Agencies use a variety of compensation methods depending on the type and amount of service they provide to their clients. We review a number of methods, because there is no one method of compensation to which everyone subscribes. We also examine the related topic of performance evaluation and explore reasons why clients switch agencies.

COMMISSIONS FROM MEDIA

The historical method of compensating agencies is through a **commission system**, where the agency receives a specified commission (usually 15 percent) from the media on any advertising time or space it purchases for its client. This system provides a simple method of determining payments, as shown in the following example.

Assume an agency prepares a full-page magazine ad and arranges to place the ad on the back cover of a magazine at a cost of $100,000. The agency places the order for the space and delivers the ad to the magazine. Once the ad is run, the magazine will bill the agency for $100,000, less the 15 percent ($15,000) commission. The media will also offer a 2 percent cash discount for early payment, which the agency may pass along to the client. The agency will bill the client $100,000 less the 2 percent cash discount on the net amount, or a total of $98,300, as shown in **Figure 2-3**. The $15,000 commission represents the agency's compensation for its services.

Figure 2-3 Example of commission system payment

Media Bills Agency		Agency Bills Advertiser	
Costs for magazine space	$100,000	Costs for magazine space	$100,000
Less 15% commission	−15,000	Less 2% cash discount	−1,700
Cost of media space	$ 85,000	Advertiser pays agency	$ 98,300
Less 2% cash discount	−1,700		
Agency pays media	$ 83,300	Agency income	$ 15,000

Critics of the commission system argue that it encourages agencies to recommend high-priced media to increase their commission level. Another concern is that it ties agency compensation to media costs, allowing the agency to be disproportionately rewarded. Critics have argued that it provides an incentive for agencies to recommend mass-media advertising when other forms of communication might do a better job.[29]

Defenders of the commission system argue that it is easy to administer and it keeps the emphasis in agency competition on non-price factors like advertising quality. Proponents argue that agency services are proportional to the size of the commission, since more time and effort are devoted to the large accounts that generate high revenue for the agency. They also say the system is more flexible than it appears because agencies perform other services for large clients at no extra charge, justifying such actions by the large commission they receive.

Agencies rely less on media commissions for their income as clients expand their IMC programs to include other forms of promotion and use less media advertising. A study of agency compensation conducted by the Association of National Advertisers (ANA) indicates that commission system usage ranged from 5 percent to 15 percent over the past 10 years.[30] Instead, advertisers used a **negotiated commission** system where commissions average 8–10 percent and are based on a sliding scale that becomes lower as clients' media expenditures increase. As the percentage of agency income from media commissions declines, a greater percentage is coming through other methods such as fees and performance incentives.

FEE ARRANGEMENT

There are two types of fee arrangement systems. In the straight or **fixed-fee method**, the agency charges a monthly fee for all of its services and credits to the client any media commissions earned. Agency and client agree on the specific work to be done and the amount the agency will be paid for it. Sometimes agencies are compensated through a **fee–commission combination**, in which the media commissions received by the agency are credited against the fee. If the commissions are less than the agreed-on fee, the client must make up the difference. If the agency does much work for the client in non-commissionable media, the fee may be charged over and above the commissions received.

Both types of fee arrangements require that the agency carefully assess its costs of serving the client for the specified period, or for the project, plus its desired profit margin. To avoid any later disagreement, a fee arrangement should specify exactly what services the agency is expected to perform for the client.

COST-PLUS AGREEMENT

Under a **cost-plus system**, the client agrees to pay the agency a fee based on the costs of its work plus an agreed-on profit margin (often a percentage of total costs). This system requires that the agency keep detailed records of the costs it incurs in working on the client's account. Direct costs (personnel time and out-of-pocket expenses) plus an allocation for overhead and a markup for profits determine the amount the agency bills the client. An agency can add a markup of percentage charges to various services the agency purchases from outside providers (e.g., market research, artwork, printing, photography).

Fee agreements and cost-plus systems are commonly used; the ANA survey reports that fee-based methods usage is at 81 percent.[31] The fee-based system might be advantageous to both the client and the agency, depending on the size of the client, advertising budget, media used, and services required. Clients prefer fee or cost-plus systems because they receive a detailed breakdown of where and how their advertising and promotion dollars were spent. However, these arrangements are challenging for the agency, as they require careful cost accounting to estimate when bidding for an advertiser's business, and allow clients to see their internal cost figures. One complicating factor for agencies is that clients now hire procurement specialists from other industries who put pressure on the costs without fully understanding the advertising process.[32]

INCENTIVE-BASED COMPENSATION

Clients expect accountability from their agencies and link agency compensation to performance through an **incentive-based system**. The idea is that the agency's compensation level depends on how well it meets predetermined performance goals; clear objectives of the promotional plan are compared to the actual measured performance. A summary of this approach in Canada is currently provided to members of the Association of Canadian Advertisers.[33] This is a specific application of a general approach used in many facets of business known as *performance by results* (PBR). PBR in an advertising remuneration process occurs where the advertising agency fee is adjusted by a reward based on the degree of achieving mutually agreed upon objectives between the client and the agency. Overall, the remuneration is part of a system of linking performance, its measurement, and reward within the client–agency relationship. The benefits of the PBR system are:

Greater efficiency and accountability
Achievement of cost efficiencies
Higher productivity
Fewer barriers of self-interest

Stronger mutual understanding
Improved retention of creative talent
Increased agency strategic input
Improved client–agency communication

Three general groups of performance measures are critical in the PBR system: overall business performance, marketing communication effectiveness, and agency process evaluation. Business measures include sales, market share, profitability, and margins. Marketing communication effectiveness measures include brand awareness, brand image ratings, and likability of advertising. This group also includes four objectives that are more behavioural: intent to purchase, trial, repeat purchase, and brand loyalty. The final group, agency process evaluation, concerns the services the agency provides and its overall management process.

Decisions regarding the first two groups are covered in later chapters, however, in general, the relative importance of each measure needs to be investigated for each brand and its marketing situation, and the measures should take into account the role of promotion in the marketing mix and how promotion contributes to business results for the brand and within the product category or industry. The ANA survey finds that over 50 percent of the clients reward agencies with a performance incentive with agency performance reviews, brand awareness, and sales being the highest, which corresponds to one measure from each group. Although the performance incentive added to the fee arrangement is relatively workable for both parties, agencies remain concerned that their compensation is not commensurate for situations when the IMC plan contributes to significant brand profit.[34]

EVALUATION OF AGENCIES

Regular reviews of the agency's performance are necessary. The agency evaluation process usually involves two types of assessments—one that is financial and operational, and another that is more qualitative. The **financial audit** focuses on how the agency conducts its business. It is designed to verify costs and expenses, the number of personnel hours charged to an account, and payments to media and outside suppliers. The **qualitative audit** focuses on the agency's efforts in planning, developing, and implementing the client's advertising programs and considers the results achieved.

Clients may formally evaluate their agency in areas of performance such as account management, creative, planning and research, production, media planning and buying, budget and financial, agency management, direct marketing, interactive marketing, and public relations. Consistent with PBR, advertisers develop formal, systematic evaluation systems, particularly with large ad budgets. Alternatively, agency evaluation might be done on a subjective, informal basis, particularly in smaller companies where ad budgets are low or advertising is not viewed as a critical factor in the firm's marketing performance.

The evaluation process provides valuable feedback to both the agency and the client, such as indicating changes that need to be made by the agency and/or the client to improve performance and make the relationship more productive. Agencies have had very long-lasting relationships with their clients; however, clients may eventually switch agencies for reasons summarized in **Figure 2-4**.[35] If the agency recognizes these warning signs, it can adapt to make sure the client is satisfied. Some of the situations identified are unavoidable, and others are beyond the agency's control. One study reports that a decline of market share in the immediate two quarters precedes an agency firing.[36] So despite doing everything in its power, an agency could feel the effect of weak performance in other marketing mix variables of the client's brand.

Figure 2-4 Common reasons for agencies to lose clients

Performance Quality	The client is dissatisfied with the advertising and/or service.
Declining Sales	Advertising is blamed when the client's sales decline.
Communication	A poor working relationship and weak personal communication exist.
Demands	The client expects service beyond the compensation paid.
Conflict	Rapport is lacking among those working together.
Conflicts of Interest	A change in either business creates an unworkable situation.
Conflicting View	Disagreement arises over the level or method of compensation.
Size Change	Either the agency or the client outgrows the other.
Strategy Change	A client strategy change requires a new agency.
Personnel Change	New personnel prefer to work with established colleagues.
Policy Change	Either party reevaluates the importance of the relationship.

Specialized Services

Companies assign the development and implementation of promotional programs to an advertising agency, but specialized agencies also provide services. Clients work with creative boutiques, media buying services, sales promotion agencies, public relations firms, direct-response agencies, and digital/interactive agencies to execute IMC programs. Labatt works with a few ad agencies for its 60 beer brands, and a specialized agency for other IMC activities like media buying, PR, trade, and experiential.[37] Specialist agencies do their utmost to gain business from full service agencies; for example, the PR agency Veritas placed its glass-encased Growth & Innovation Lab in the centre of its office with the mandate to assist client teams.[38] We review the functions that specialized marketing communication organizations perform for clients.

CREATIVE BOUTIQUES

A **creative boutique** is an agency that provides only creative services. These specialized agencies have creative personnel but offer limited or no services in other areas (e.g., media, research, or account planning). Creative boutiques emerged in response to companies' desire to use only the creative services of an outside agency while managing the other functions internally. While creative boutiques work directly for clients, full-service agencies subcontract work to creative boutiques when they are busy or want to avoid adding full-time employees. Creative boutiques have been formed by members of the creative departments of full-service agencies who leave the firm and take with them clients who want to retain their creative talents.

Other creative boutiques have grown independently with tremendous success on their own. Red Urban is a notable Canadian agency operating as a creative boutique with clients such as VW, Porsche, and Rolling Rock. After seeing the awards won for its VW work, Porsche accepted Red Urban as its creative agency of record with the goal of attracting consumers who had not previously considered buying the sporty brand.[39] One organization refers to itself as this kind of agency; Lg2 Boutique, originally established in Quebec and now expanded to Toronto, has produced award-winning work recognized both nationally and internationally.[40] Other specialized services that are independent like creative boutiques are described in **IMC Perspective 2-2**.

MEDIA BUYING SERVICES

Exhibit 2-5 Initiative is one of the leading media specialist companies.

©Imaginechina/Newscom

Media buying services are independent companies that specialize in the buying of media. The task of purchasing advertising media is complex as specialized media proliferate, so media buying services achieved a niche by specializing in the analysis and purchase of advertising time and space. Agencies and clients usually develop their own media strategies and hire the media buying service to execute them, but the services help advertisers to plan their media strategies. **Exhibit 2-5** is an example of a media placement of an exciting ad in a high traffic area to maximize exposure. Because media buying services purchase large amounts of time and space, they receive large discounts and save money on media purchases for both large and small agencies. Increasingly, this specialized service interacts at the senior level with the ad agency and the client to ensure optimal expenditures to achieve a brand's objectives.[41]

Touché started as a small media boutique 20 years ago in Montreal and, after a series of affiliations (Touché PHD, Touché OMD), it now resides as a key player within the Omnicom Group. *Marketing Magazine* recognized Touché as its Media Agency of the Year with its successful media strategies designed for Canadian Tire. Canadian Tire's "Ice Truck" demonstrated the power of the MotoMaster Eliminator Ultra AGM battery. A team constructed an ice truck around an engine and chassis and inserted the frozen battery (at a temperature of minus 40 degrees Celsius), which showed its capability by starting the engine immediately. Touché arranged for the ad to be launched during the TV broadcast of the Winter Classic, a regular season NHL game played outdoors on or around New Year's Day each year. Touché also placed the ads for airing during the coldest days possible, of course to "feel" the battery's powerful effect when needed most! With digital and social media exposure, the ad achieved a total of 80 million earned media impressions. One execution showed NHL star Jonathan Toews, and others who helped him in his career, coming together to form a Maple Leafs logo in the seats of a hockey arena. Touché's media strategy contribution naturally included the TV broadcast placement, but interestingly, the agency got the TV message placed in people's Facebook newsfeed a few minutes later. Other digital messaging included display ads, YouTube masthead domination, and premium Facebook ad placement. Additional footage of Toews and company became a short documentary shown on CBC and online.[42]

IMC PERSPECTIVE 2-2

CANADIAN INDIE AGENCIES

Canada features numerous independent small and mid-sized agencies from all disciplines and we review a few identified by *Strategy* as up and coming ones with noteworthy success.

No Fixed Address reached 60 employees at its five year anniversary. The agency prides itself on managing simply by minimizing client meetings and providing them with smart, original strategy, great

[Continued on next page]

consumer insights, custom solutions, great ads, and fair compensation. Questrade represented the quality of the agency's work with a campaign that took on established banks in an effort to get consumers to switch to online investing. Central Station resulted from a merger of a design and digital agency with a creative and strategic agency but remains small with a staff of 50. Molson Coors approached the agency for its Mad Jack hybrid beverage (beer/apple cider) and together they worked out a successful plan that included marketing decisions of flavours and packaging in addition to marketing communications that included sampling and messaging.

Cleansheet's view is that a campaign must resonate with the target audience and the employees of the brand advertising. And a great example of the two coming together is the Canadian Tire "We All Play for Canada" campaign, which featured a number of winter scenes with Canadians enjoying outdoor sports and activities. Along with an Internet site, WeAllPlayForCanada.ca, the messaging demonstrated Canadian Tire's commitment to helping all Canadians enjoy playing, no matter what the recreation. CO-OP is a 12-person boutique operation that contracts work to freelancers so it is able to offer customized teams to clients. The growth of this drove the agency to establish an industry awards program for Canada's best freelancers. Demand for continued communication by its clients led the agency to build up its PR skills.

An unusually named indie, send+receive, signifies the communication process of advertising. The agency's primary strength is its flexibility with a staff of eight. It works on a project basis or bills on output and works with any IMC tool to deliver what the client needs. Another key strength is the agency's skill at working with data to help clients understand their marketing communication problems. Jacknife's

©CO-OP

20-person staff focuses on brand development and experiential communication. For example, it designed the branded corporate environment for Nike's Canadian headquarters. According to its founder, the agency works on the intersection of product design, graphic design, packaging, digital and physical environmental experiences.

Majestic's staff of 25 specializes in AR, VR, and AI technology with a focus on both strategic and creative. With in-house capabilities, the agency avoids subcontracting work and controls the whole process for clients. Examples of its work include Maple Leaf Foods and 10 Pepsi brands, for which it created a Man Cave contest and game for a cross-promotion of Ruffles and Budweiser. For Maple Leaf Foods, it overhauled its digital presence completely for websites, mobile, email, and branding. Gravity Partners is an agency with a social media strategy and content focus with its roster of 50 employees. It innovates with the most current digital tools and integrates messages across digital media and TV, out-of-home, and radio.

Question:

1. Which indie is the most appealing for a student's first advertising job?

SALES PROMOTION AGENCIES

Developing and managing sales promotion programs (such as contests and sweepstakes, refunds and rebates, premium and incentive offers) and sampling programs is a complex task. Most companies use a **sales promotion agency** to develop and administer these programs. Some large ad agencies have created their own sales promotion department or acquired a sales promotion firm. However, most sales promotion agencies are independent companies that specialize in providing the services needed to plan, develop, and execute a variety of sales promotion programs.

Sales promotion agencies often work in conjunction with the client's advertising and/or direct-response agencies to coordinate their efforts. Services provided by large sales promotion agencies include promotional planning, creative, research, tie-in coordination, fulfillment, premium design and manufacturing, catalogue production, and contest/sweepstakes management. Sales promotion agencies also develop direct/database marketing to expand their IMC capabilities. Circo de Bakuza, based in Montreal, is one promotional agency specializing in event marketing. It got its start organizing the Just for Laughs festival 10 years ago and has signed clients like Bell, Cirque du Soleil, and UEFA Champions League since then while growing internally.[43] Sales promotion agencies are generally compensated on a fee basis.

PUBLIC RELATIONS FIRMS

Large companies use both an advertising agency and a PR firm. The **public relations firm** develops and implements programs to manage the organization's publicity, image, and affairs with consumers and other relevant publics, including employees, suppliers, shareholders, government, labour groups, citizen action groups, and the general public. The PR firm analyzes the relationships between the client and these diffuse publics, determines how the client's policies and actions relate to and affect these publics, develops PR strategies and programs, implements these programs using public relations tools, and evaluates their effectiveness. The activities of a public relations firm include planning the PR strategy and program, generating publicity, conducting lobbying and public affairs efforts, becoming involved in community activities and events, preparing news releases, performing research, promoting and managing special events, and managing crises.

North Strategic received the inaugural nod from *Strategy* magazine for top PR firm. Started in 2011 by two experienced PR leaders, the small shop expanded to three offices serving major clients like FGL, RBC, Samsung, and Ubisoft. The agency strives creatively by inventing new approaches to generating publicity. For example, it surprised three pitchers of the Toronto Blue Jays with visits from their dads on Father's Day and publicized the event through TV sports channels and digitally. It also prides itself on working directly with senior managers of its client and by offering a unique method for billing based on the project's characteristics.[44] For Samsung, the agency invited media to an interactive fitness class to try out the Galaxy S5 and Gear Fit, a device that works with the wearer's smart phone during a workout. Additional follow-up interviews occurred with fitness leader Tracy Anderson, resulting in 225 featured media stories.[45]

DIRECT-RESPONSE AGENCIES

Direct marketing involves companies communicating with consumers through telemarketing, direct mail, television, the Internet, or any other direct-response media. As this industry has grown, numerous direct-response agencies have evolved that offer companies their specialized skills in both consumer and business markets. Top direct-marketing agencies are subsidiaries of large agency holding companies (refer to Figure 2-1). However, there are also a number of independent direct-marketing agencies including those that serve large companies as well as smaller agencies that handle the needs of local companies.

Direct-response agencies provide a variety of services, including database management, direct mail, research, media services, and creative and production capabilities. A typical direct-response agency is divided into three main departments: account management, creative, and media. Agencies can also have a department whose function is to develop and manage databases for their clients. Database development and management is an important service as companies use database marketing to pinpoint new customers and build relationships and loyalty among existing customers. The account managers work with their clients to plan direct-marketing programs and determine their role in the overall integrated marketing communication process. The creative department consists of copywriters, artists, and producers and is responsible for developing the direct-response message. The media department is concerned with its placement in the most appropriate direct-response media.

DIGITAL/INTERACTIVE AGENCIES

With the growth of the Internet, marketers needed specialized services since interactive marketing programs required expertise in technology, creativity, database marketing, digital media, and customer relationship management. Existing advertising agencies established interactive capabilities, ranging from a few specialists to an entire interactive division, however **digital/interactive agencies** also emerged who specialized in developing interactive marketing tools such as

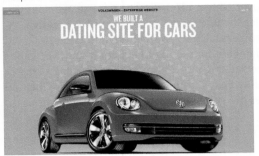

websites, display ads, and social media applications. These agencies specialized and fostered their expertise in designing and developing digital/interactive tools. Currently, interactive agencies range from smaller companies that specialize (e.g., in website design or social media) to full-service interactive agencies that design and implement a complete digital/interactive marketing program through strategic brand consulting, creative and message development, and technical knowledge. **Exhibit 2-6** shows a website image for a car brand that got a lot of mileage with its digital agency.

Both digital/interactive agencies and full-service agencies with digital capabilities are recognized with awards from industry players. *Strategy* recognized one in the latter group for its excellent work as Digital Agency of the Year; Lg2 created a mobile pedometer for its fast-food client Valentine. After a meal, the Walk Off Your Poutine app counted the calories burned using GPS by measuring the speed and distance travelled. Interactive features included messages from Valentine and the option to link one's performance and experiences to Facebook. All told, 50,000 downloaded apps resulted in a total of 5,000 transactions and 300 million steps. Lg2 also installed motion-triggered two-way mirrors in college/university washrooms that projected the story of ghosts of people (played by actors) who had perished after drinking and driving, on behalf of the Quebec government's automotive licensing branch. The agency posted recorded video of the interactive experiences on YouTube for a total of 220,000 views.[46]

As shown with ad agencies, firms bring digital capabilities in-house while using an ad agency. Recipe Unlimited (formerly Cara Operations) owns over a dozen restaurant brands and operates a full digital team of more than 10 staff. Yet it still retains an agency for national advertising for brands like Harvey's and Swiss Chalet. It expanded digital communication to use geo-targeting with apps like The Weather Network for its Bier Market and The Keg restaurants. Innovative creative ads ran in social media for Montana's and Milestones.[47] Similarly, as the subsidiary of a US parent, Golf Town focused its marketing team around digital marketing communication capabilities include web design, web integration, social media, and search.[48] Although GE Appliances works with a few different agencies, it created its own in-house digital team.[49]

LO4 IMC Planning: Agency Relationships

Currently, marketers can choose from a variety of organizations to assist them in planning, developing, and implementing an integrated marketing communication program. Companies must decide whether to use specialized organizations for each marketing communication function or to consolidate them with a large advertising agency that offers all of these services. In this final section, we discuss whether an advertiser would want to use an integrated services agency, assess the agency–client responsibilities for IMC, and summarize the current situation regarding the agency–client relationship in the context of an IMC environment.

INTEGRATED IMC SERVICES

Historically, marketing communication services operated as separate profit centres with each motivated to push its own expertise and pursue its own goals rather than develop truly integrated marketing programs. For example, creative specialists resisted becoming involved in sales promotion or direct marketing and preferred to concentrate on developing magazine ads or television commercials rather than designing coupons or direct-mail pieces. While agencies transitioned to full-service providers, proponents of the "one-stop shop" contend that these past problems are resolved and the individuals in the agencies and subsidiaries are working together.

Integrated services offer clients three benefits. First, clients maintain control of the entire promotional process and achieve greater synergy among the communications program elements. Second, it is more convenient for the client to coordinate all of its marketing efforts—media advertising, direct mail, special events, sales promotions, and public relations—through one agency. Third and finally, an agency with integrated marketing capabilities can create a single image for the client's brand and address everyone, from wholesalers to consumers, with one voice.

Some people feel that an advertising agency offering full services is neither sufficiently staffed to ensure complete integration, nor fully cognizant of multiple target audiences. Advertising agency personnel are trained in particular aspects of the process and are less inclined to consider many marketing variables in their decisions. Furthermore, they tend to consider only the end user or consumer rather than all the parties in the marketing process who are connected to the results of the communication plan. It is recommended that marketers ensure the agencies consider the needs of all (e.g., customer service staff, sales representatives, distributors, and retailers) in their communication plans.

AGENCY–CLIENT RESPONSIBILITY

Surveys of advertisers and agency executives indicated that both groups consider integrated marketing communication important to their organizations' success. However, marketers and agency executives differ on who is in charge of the IMC process. Advertisers prefer to set strategy for and coordinate their campaigns, but agency executives tend to see this as their domain.[50] While agency executives believe their shops are capable of handling the elements an integrated campaign requires, marketers historically preferred to allocate creative services to their advertising agency and use specialized service agencies or in-house departments for other IMC tools.[51] To sum up, agencies view themselves as strategic and execution partners and are offering their clients a full line of services (e.g., interactive and multimedia advertising, database management, direct marketing, public relations, and sales promotion). But, marketers want to set the strategy for their IMC campaigns and seek specialized expertise, more quality and creativity, and greater control and cost efficiency by using multiple providers.

AGENCY–CLIENT RELATIONSHIPS

Recent findings emerged from a survey of agencies and clients conducted by the Association of National Advertisers in the United States (current Canadian data was unavailable). The study investigated the strength of the relationship, the agency's role as a business partner, agency compensation, process management, and other factors. From the perspective of both parties, the relationships are positive, a long-term relationship is viewed strongly, and they trust one another. **Figure 2-5** summarizes five areas in which there is noticeable disagreement between agency and client. In future, both agree on the importance of clients providing a better briefing process and on an agency's understanding of a client's business and situation.[52]

Figure 2-5 Agency–client relationship disagreement

Characteristic	Agency Agreement	Client Agreement
Compensation fairness	40%	72%
Clear assignment brief	27%	58%
Client approval process	36%	54%
Value of procurement	10%	47%
Work well with other agencies	88%	65%

An advertising agency's ability to work with another agency is a function of the growth of other types of agencies; especially digital agencies who recruited creative individuals from advertising agencies to enhance their IMC service delivery. Increasingly, all types of agencies see creative decisions of the message, no matter how they are delivered, as a differentiating factor when a client makes an agency selection. While personnel from any type of agency may publicly say that working with other agencies is positive, specialized agencies are in competition with advertising agencies for clients; as a result some hire a creative director, a job usually seen in advertising agencies only.[53] A recent study summarizes how advertising and PR agencies experienced significant blurring of responsibilities in the age of paid, owned, and earned media.[54]

Finally, a Canadian survey of advertisers showed that 58 percent believed their agency relationship to be "excellent" or "very good," and 72 percent thought their media agency rated as important to their creative agency.[55] On the other hand, a Canadian survey of agencies found that 31 percent of clients expected "more cost effective solutions" and 18 percent expected equally "more strategic insight" and "more integration across marketing disciplines." In addition, agencies expected "clearer and better briefs" and "more realistic budgets."[56]

Learning Objectives Summary

 LO1 **Identify the role of the advertising agency and the services it provides.**

The development, execution, and administration of an advertising and promotion program involves the efforts of many individuals, both within the company and outside it. Firms decide whether they will hire an external advertising agency or use an in-house service to create their ads and purchase media. In-house agencies, while offering the advantages of cost savings, control, and increased coordination, have the disadvantage of less experience and flexibility. Firms using advertising agencies to develop and execute their programs receive a full range of services (including creative, account, marketing, and financial and management services) to resolve their marketing communication issues.

 LO2 **Describe methods for compensating and evaluating advertising agencies.**

Historically, clients compensated agencies through commission systems based on media sales, and fee- and cost-based systems. Increased emphasis on agency accountability led to incentive-based compensation systems that tie agency compensation to performance measures such as sales and market share. Other comprehensive measures include achievement of marketing communication objectives and how the agency operates and delivers services. Agencies are evaluated on both financial and qualitative measures that are formal in certain situations and less formal in others. Upon evaluation, a client may no longer require the service of the agency for performance-related issues. Some clients retain the services of an agency for a relatively long period of time and confer the status of "agency of record."

 LO3 **Review the functions of specialized marketing communication organizations.**

In addition to using ad agencies, marketers use the services of other marketing communication specialists, including creative boutiques and media buying services, direct marketing agencies, sales promotion agencies, public relations firms, and interactive agencies. Contracting out work to a specialized agency potentially enhances the creativity of the overall IMC plan with experts from specific fields. Moreover, while it may be more costly or time-consuming to work with other specialists, these organizations may influence or reach the target audience more precisely, thus yielding a favourable return on investment. A marketer must decide whether to use a different specialist for each promotional function or to have all of its integrated marketing communications done by an advertising agency that offers all of these services under one roof. This latter idea allows an account team to know and control all aspects of the communication.

 LO4 **Evaluate the perspectives on the use of integrated services across agencies or within one agency, and agency–client responsibilities and partnerships.**

Studies have found that most marketers believe it is their responsibility, not the ad agency's, to set strategy for and to coordinate IMC campaigns. The lack of a broad perspective and specialized skills in non-advertising areas is seen as the major barrier to agencies' increased involvement in integrated marketing communications, and individual perspectives of clients and agencies will continue to adapt as the growth of IMC evolves.

Review Questions

1. How are the characteristics of a full-service agency contrasted with the characteristics of specialized marketing communication agencies?

2. Why is compensating with the performance by results approach optimal in comparison with other methods?

3. What are the similar and dissimilar functions of each of the specialized marketing communication agencies?

4. What are the issues of using one full-service agency versus multiple specialized agencies?

Applied Questions

1. The chapter distinguished between full-service and specialized agencies. Using Figure 2-1 as a guide for different agency names based in Canada, examine the websites of different full-service marketing communication agencies. Using the websites as the main source of information, identify which types of services each agency offers.

2. Which type of agency compensation system characterizes an environment where a young advertising graduate would most like to work?

3. Again, using Figure 2-1 as a guide for different agency names based in Canada, examine the websites of different specialized marketing communication agencies. Using the websites as the main source of information, identify which types of services each agency offers.

4. Given the evaluation of different agencies in the above questions, is the use of a full-service agency or the use of multiple specialized agencies the recommended approach for smart phone brands? for breakfast cereal brands? for energy drink brands?

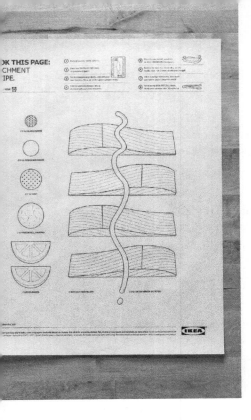
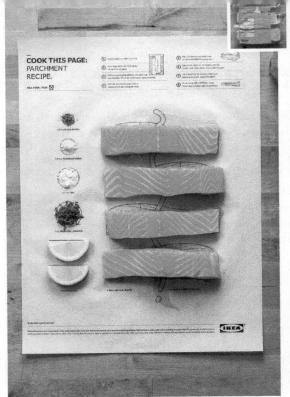

©Ikea/Leo Burnett

CHAPTER THREE

Consumer Behaviour and Target Audience Decisions

LEARNING OBJECTIVES

LO1 Describe the consumer decision-making process and demonstrate how it relates to marketing communication.

LO2 Contrast how the consumer decision-making process varies for different types of purchases.

LO3 Compare the similarities and differences of target market and target audience.

LO4 Identify the options for making a target audience decision for marketing communication.

LO5 Express why a profile of the target audience is important for message, media, and IMC tool decisions.

Ikea's Beautiful Possibilities

Ikea established itself in our country decades ago and its recent marketing communication activities certainly resonated with Canadians to ensure the brand stays at the forefront of consumers' knowledge so that they plan to visit the store when shopping for just about anything for their household. The new "Beautiful Possibilities" campaign promises a direction for the retailer as it has departed from the past "Long Live the Home" campaign.

One amazing innovation gave consumers the chance to "Cook This Page" with a fill-in-the-blanks style of cooking. The instructions drawn on a piece of paper showed consumers where to place the food and ingredients like spices, and then they simply placed the wrapped food in the oven—and voilà—the meal was prepared! The menu offered four items that one could buy at Ikea so the promotion informed consumers about food available for sale in addition to providing a fun way to cook dinner without much effort.

Another innovative creative idea featured a sequel to a commercial 16 years later. One famous ad from 2002 ended with an abandoned lamp on the curb in the rain. A Swedish man approached the scene and said, "Many of you feel bad for this lamp. That is crazy. It has no feelings. And the new one is much better." Directed by Spike Jonze, the ad won the Grand Prix at Cannes. The sequel saw a young girl take the lamp home and put it to good use with a low energy bulb. The same Swedish man entered an outside shot and said, "Many of you feel happy for this lamp. That's not crazy. Reusing things is much better." Execution of the ad followed the original

and respected the creativity of the original's famous director.

From a strategy standpoint, the ad signalled the retailer's plan to publicize its long-standing commitment to the environment. In the past, Ikea went about its environmental business without communicating it to consumers, but the essence of not wasting resources originated from its founder, who eschewed extravagance. Ikea's programs include tree planting, owning wind power generating technology, and a take-it-back program, among others, and these are outlined in its annual sustainability report. One unexpected product taken back was a haunted couch, found in a Craigslist ad; Ikea bought it and featured it on Instagram to communicate its recycling program.

Ikea carried on this "People+Planet" approach with a similar reuse message for its Kallax shelf. After many failed attempts at performing magic acts, a young boy received a gift from his grandfather who rescued a dusty Kallax from the garage and spruced it up for a new magic act that worked while his audience of parents and siblings watched. The holiday message reinforced the idea of multigenerational households, the need to consider repurposing items for gifts rather than buying new, and multicultural Canada.

Question:

1. Does it look like Ikea's new approach for its advertising will encourage consumers to continue shopping at the store?

The opening vignette reveals that effective marketing communication programs require knowledge of consumer behaviour. The resulting insight helps marketers to see how to encourage consumers to buy a product, what to emphasize in communication to specific audiences, where to target the marketing communication, and which types of IMC tools might be used. It is beyond the scope of this text to examine consumer behaviour in depth. However, promotional planners need an understanding of consumer decision making, factors that influence it, and how this knowledge assists in developing promotional strategies and programs.

This chapter describes the consumer decision-making process to demonstrate how marketers use this information for marketing communication decisions. Next, the chapter contrasts how the process varies for different types of consumer decision making. It then identifies the target audience options for marketing communication plans, and expresses the importance of identifying a detailed profile of the target audience.

Consumer Decision-Making Process

Consumer behaviour is defined as the activities people experience when searching for, selecting, purchasing, using, evaluating, and disposing of products to satisfy their needs and desires. The conceptual model in **Figure 3-1** is a framework for understanding the consumer decision-making process. It views the consumer as a problem solver who evaluates alternative brands and determines the degree to which they might satisfy needs. In this section, we describe what occurs at each of the five stages and demonstrate how advertising and promotion is used to influence decision making. For further insight, the section concludes with two additional aspects of the process: types of decision making and group decision making.

Figure 3-1 A model of consumer decision making

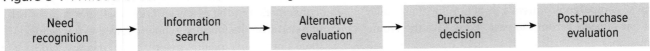

| Need recognition | → | Information search | → | Alternative evaluation | → | Purchase decision | → | Post-purchase evaluation |

This model is an accepted representation of consumer decision making and is useful for managers to plan promotional decisions. Note that the process is not linear as the arrows indicate; consumers backtrack to a previous stage as information is acquired. And there is implied continuity as post-purchase evaluation morphs into prepurchase anticipation at some point, which varies by product category and by individual consumer. In fact, practitioners refer to this as a *journey* since consumers express their thoughts and feelings at all stages across digital and non-digital avenues leading to stronger or weaker levels of brand loyalty.[1] Academic research moved toward this line of thinking as well.[2] Mobile technology allows consumers to experience all stages anywhere and at any time across multiple advertising formats and IMC activities, requiring promotional managers to adapt their plans.[3] One study found that online communication in social media provoked stronger online search for information about a movie prior to its launch than advertising.[4] And, as one expects, mobile shopping apps and non-shopping apps are useful tools for both brands and consumers.[5]

NEED RECOGNITION

The first stage in the consumer decision-making process is **need recognition**, which occurs when the consumer perceives a need and becomes motivated to enter a decision-making process to resolve the felt need. Marketers are required to know the specific needs consumers are attempting to satisfy and how they translate into purchase criteria, since this knowledge allows them to accurately portray the need in promotional messages and place messages in an appropriate location.

Need recognition is caused by a difference between the consumer's *ideal state* and *actual state*. A discrepancy exists between what the consumer desires the situation to be like and what the situation is really like. A goal exists for the consumer, and this goal may be the attainment of a more positive situation from a neutral state. Or, the goal could be a shift from a negative situation, and the consumer wishes to be at a neutral state. A **want** is a felt need that is shaped by a person's knowledge, culture, and personality. Advertised products may satisfy consumer wants rather than basic needs. The Splat ad in **Exhibit 3-1** shows how the brand offers a wide colour palette for consumers to stylishly express themselves.

The sources of need recognition are internal or external, complex or simple, and ones not previously experienced arise from changes in the consumer's current situation. Advertising (i.e., external) helps consumers crystallize their dissatisfaction (i.e., internal) with a currently used brand or realize that a product not currently consumed could enhance their life (i.e., complex). Simple needs are reaffirmed to consumers with visual ads such as the one shown in **Exhibit 3-2**. New needs arise with changes in one's finances or employment status (i.e., situation). For example, graduates from college or university may need a wardrobe change when starting their professional career. Finally, social media facilitates need recognition with consumers seeing "wish lists," "likes," "check-ins," "bought by," and "pinned" depending on the source.[6]

The way a consumer perceives a purchase and drives to resolve it influences the remaining stages of

Exhibit 3-1 Splat offers a variety of hair colours for different consumer wants.

©Developus

the decision process. For example, one consumer may perceive the need to purchase a new watch from a functional perspective and focus on reliable, low-priced alternatives. Another consumer may see the purchase of a watch as part of a fashionable wardrobe and accessories and focus on the design and image. To better understand the reasons underlying consumer purchases, marketers extensively consider **motives**—that is, those factors that compel a consumer to take a particular action.

One approach for understanding consumer motivations is based on the theory of human motivation conceived by psychologist Abraham Maslow.[7] His **hierarchy of needs** theory postulates five levels of human needs, arranged in a hierarchy based on their importance. As shown in **Figure 3-2**, the five needs are (1) *physiological*—the basic level of primary needs for things required to sustain life, such as food, shelter, clothing, and sex; (2) *safety*—the need for security and safety from physical harm; (3) *social*—the desire to have satisfying relationships with others and feel a sense of love, affection, belonging, and acceptance; (4) *esteem*—the need to feel a sense of accomplishment and gain recognition, status, and respect from others; and (5) *self-actualization*—the need for self-fulfillment and a desire to realize one's own potential.

The hierarchy offers a way of designing advertising messages to show consumers how a brand's product can satisfy their need. The Jaguar ad in **Exhibit 3-3** appears to address self-actualization. GoodLife Fitness altered the motive conveyed in ads to self-esteem for consumers who sought a holistic approach to wellness. The testimonial messages revealed the experiences of actual consumers whose life changed significantly. Advertising campaigns can also be designed for multiple consumer segments with different needs.[8] For example, a young single person may want to satisfy social or self-esteem needs in purchasing a car, while a family with children might focus on safety needs. We revisit the topic of motivation in Chapter 6 by presenting consumer purchase motives. A more specific view of motives in the context of consumer decisions is useful for managers to make marketing communication decisions such as brand positioning.

INFORMATION SEARCH

The second stage in the consumer decision-making process is *information search*. Once consumers perceive a need that can be satisfied by the purchase of a product, they begin to search for information needed to make a purchase decision. The initial search effort often consists of reviewing information stored in memory to recall past experiences and/or knowledge regarding purchase alternatives.[9] This information retrieval is referred to as **internal search**. For routine, repetitive purchases, previously acquired information that is stored in memory (such as past performance or outcomes from using a brand) is sufficient for comparing alternatives and making a choice.

Exhibit 3-2 Visual ads remind consumers of their need.

Figure 3-2 Maslow's hierarchy of needs

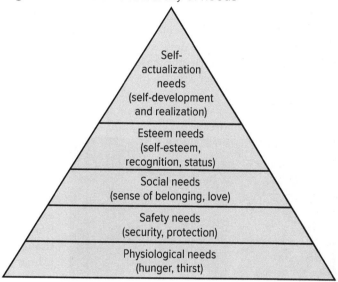

Exhibit 3-3 Jaguar uses an appeal to self-actualization.

Exhibit 3-4 Apps for smart phones and tablets now number in the millions.

If the internal search does not yield enough information, the consumer seeks additional information by an **external search**. External sources of information include:

- *Personal sources* (e.g., friends, relatives, or co-workers, face-to-face or via social media)
- *Marketer-controlled sources* (e.g., advertising, salespeople, displays, Internet)
- *Public sources* (e.g., articles in print media, reports on TV, Internet discussion boards)
- *Personal experience* (e.g., past use, or actually handling, examining, or testing the product)

Determining how many and which sources of external information to use involves the importance of the purchase decision, the effort required to acquire information, the amount of relevant past experience, the degree of perceived risk associated with the purchase, and the time available. For example, the selection of a movie to see at a cinema might entail talking to a friend (digitally or in person), checking movie information online or in a newspaper, or using a mobile app. The fun image in **Exhibit 3-4** is a cute way to visualize how significantly consumers rely on apps for brand information and brand experiences. Use of mobile devices while shopping in stores leads to more time in the store and greater purchases.[10]

A more complex vehicle purchase might rely upon plenty of information sources—perhaps a review of *Road & Track*, *Motor Trend,* or *Consumer Reports;* discussion with family and friends; and a dealer test-drive. The auto industry is the largest digital advertiser as two-thirds of all buyers rely on this media for their vehicle decision. Furthermore, research finds that the time shopping is reduced to four weeks from five weeks, and buyers evaluate four brands versus 2.5 brands.[11] At this point in the purchase decision, the information-providing aspects of advertising are extremely important. In fact, one study concluded that Internet and non-Internet media are important for online purchases, with varying degrees depending on the level of Internet media experience and product type (e.g., utilitarian versus hedonistic). Surprisingly, those with high levels of Internet media experience thought more highly of non-Internet media sources![12] The information and call to action (i.e., website) in the Michelin ad (**Exhibit 3-5**) are likely influential during this stage of consumer decision making for new tires.

Extensive qualitative and quantitative research commissioned by the Advertising Research Foundation (ARF) regarding digital and social media use during the consumer decision-making process reported a number of findings.[13] Consumers in the information search stage are in "active shopping mode" and deliberately seek information (e.g., visit Internet sites, speak with friends, search for product reviews online), although in other stages like pre- or post-purchase, consumers are in "passive shopping mode" where they receive unsolicited information such as advertising and promotion messages or social media postings. The usage level of non-digital media information sources remains strong despite the frequent use of digital information sources, and consumers do not necessarily differentiate among "paid," "owned," and "earned"— newer information sources. Finally, mobile access to digital information sources at all stages of the decision-making process continues to grow.

Instant audio may become an information source in the future with voice assistants (like Alexa, Siri, Cortana, Bixby, and Google Assistant) and smart speakers. While just beginning, brands are

Exhibit 3-5 Michelin stresses its advantages over competitors' tires.

INTRODUCING THE MICHELIN® DEFENDER® TIRE

SAFER. LONGER.

90,000 MILES' OF CONFIDENT DRIVING

The MICHELIN® DEFENDER® tire allows you to stop up to 31 feet shorter[1] and drive up to 21,000 miles longer[2] than a leading competitor[2], and is backed by our 90,000-mile limited warranty.[4] Find out more at **michelinman.com/defender**

1 – Based on internal wet braking test results versus Goodyear® Assurance® ComforTred® Touring tire size 185/65R15. 2 – Based on commissioned third-party wear test results versus Continental® ProContact™ with EcoPlus Technology tire size 215/60R16. 4 – 90,000-mile limited warranty for H- and T-rated tires; 80,000-mile limited warranty for V-rated tires. See michelinman.com for warranty details. Copyright ©2013 Michelin North America, Inc. All rights reserved.

Source: Michelin North America, Inc

investigating what message content is best (functional or experiential), how it will be delivered, and whether the brand will be mentioned first to influence consumer shopping. For example, L'Oréal's use of chatbots is providing information to understand the kinds of questions consumers may ask in future so that the right answer at the right time will be provided.[14]

ALTERNATIVE EVALUATION

After acquiring information, the consumer moves to the **alternative evaluation** stage, where the brands identified as being capable of satisfying the needs that initiated the decision process are compared. The brands identified as purchase options are referred to as the consumer's *evoked set*. Generally a subset of all the brands known to the consumer is included to make this stage manageable. The size of the evoked set varies across consumer segments and

Liya Kebede @ Viva Paris for L'Oréal Paris

depends on factors such as the importance of the purchase and the amount of time and energy the consumer wants to spend comparing alternatives. Effective marketing communication increases the likelihood that a brand will be included in the consumer's evoked set, as seen by the ad in **Exhibit 3-6**.

Once consumers identify their alternatives, they evaluate the brands on specific and important criteria. **Evaluative criteria** are the product attributes used to compare alternative brands. For example, when buying a vehicle, consumers use objective attributes such as price, warranty, and fuel economy as well as subjective attributes such as image and styling. Products are *bundles of attributes* and brands emphasize some over others in their messages. Birks is an established Canadian jewellery retailer that rejuvenated itself to retain its image as a luxury brand by emphasizing that Birks sourced all of its diamonds from Canadian mines, a key attribute considered important to consumers. It associated the Birks brand with Canadian imagery to communicate another valuable attribute.[15]

Consumers tend to view product attributes in terms of their consequences, also known as benefits or *bundles of benefits*. Benefits are specific outcomes that consumers receive when they purchase and/or consume a product. And similar to attributes, consumers view a brand as a bundle of benefits. Marketers distinguish between product attributes and benefits in their ad message claims because consumers assign importance to both when evaluating alternative brands. Moreover, advertisers communicate the link between an attribute and a benefit to enhance consumers' understanding and brand knowledge. Complicating this brand-directed communication, consumers rely on reviews, recommendations, discussion forum comments, blog posts, tweets, and other messages depending on the type of social media.[16] We suggest that ad messages claim three types of benefits for consumers to consider during this stage.

Functional benefits are direct outcomes of product usage that are tangible and objectively related to the purpose of the product. For example, a product placement message during *Amazing Race Canada* stated that the Chevrolet Sonic subcompact car featured 10 air bags; many air bags in a small car exhibit functional utility of enhanced injury prevention for consumers who are in the market for a new small vehicle.

Performance benefits are less tangible and more subjective product usage outcomes based on how the product attributes abstractly affect a consumer. For example, a personal care product may claim in its ad messages that it makes one more attractive. The actual performance of the personal care product experienced by a consumer may or may not be in line with these claims, and this assessment will become internal information that is relied upon during future decisions. The message of the ad in **Exhibit 3-7** implies that using the cosmetic product delivers a beautiful complexion.

Exhibit 3-7 This message implicitly claims a performance benefit.

Source: Estée Lauder Inc

Exhibit 3-8 Levi's communicates a unique experiential benefit.

www.levisthailand.com www.facebook.com/levis

Source: Levi Strauss & Co.

Experiential benefits are related to how a product makes the consumer feel while consuming it. The emotions are individually based, such as feelings of happiness or joy which we see in car ads that show how consumers enjoy driving a particular brand on an open stretch of the highway. Alternatively, the emotions are socially based, such as feelings of pride which we also see in car ads that illustrate a driver passing by an admiring pedestrian. As these two views indicate, ad messages can claim experiential benefits to consumers with little emphasis on the functional or performance benefits. Fashion brands typically use visuals of models or consumers wearing their clothing or accessories. The stylish Levi's ad in **Exhibit 3-8** conveys an experience that will resonate with an audience.

Dove's "Campaign for Real Beauty" illustrates an example where continued advertising maintained the brand in consumers' evoked set and emphasized experiential benefits. At the launch in 2004, the message departed from stereotypical beauty images of women in personal care ads. The first print campaign showed images of everyday women, not models, with questions asking, "Wrinkled or wonderful?" or "Fat or fab?" along with a tick box to answer. A second print campaign supported the initial one with a spotlight on real women. The subsequent "Evolution" video captured the metamorphosis a model experiences for an advertising photo shoot as well as the digital touch-ups thereafter, while the "Onslaught" video showed the sexualized advertising a young girl will experience as she matures. Dove's implied message of natural beauty received numerous awards and resonated with women during the first six years.

Dove then moved the campaign in a different direction with tasks that challenged women to consider their self-perception. The "Sketches" video compared the drawings of an artist from a self-description versus from a friend's description. The "Patches" video revealed women's reaction after they discovered the beauty patch they had worn was a placebo, as many had thought the patch did in fact make them more beautiful. The "Choose Beautiful" video showed the women deciding which door to enter: "Beautiful" or "Average." Critics claimed that these newer messages patronized women and moved away from the original intent of positive experience benefits. Responding to the critics, Dove spokespersons highlighted the 100 million views of the "Patches" video, reminding everyone that Dove continually listens to its customers, and that the company intended to spark a debate about women's relationship with beauty with the recent videos.[17]

IMC Perspective 3-1 illustrates an example where SVEDKA's image and the message delivery worked together and provided a frightening experience for its audience with the intention of making sure that the brand stayed in their evoked set.

IMC PERSPECTIVE 3-1

SVEDKA'S SPOOKY TARGETING

SVEDKA Vodka wanted to absolutely target millennials while they shopped, browsed, chatted, or did whatever else while online. The popular vodka planned to reach these consumers during the run-up to Halloween, a key time to build brand momentum over the final quarter of the year leading to the holidays.

Past campaigns established the brand as a "party amplifier" and achieved strong

Courtesy of Constellation Brands Inc.

awareness to go along with above average category growth. Despite this, managers knew millennials remained a tough audience to maintain continued communication with due to their constant media exposure while online an average of four hours per day.

In keeping with the October timing, SVEDKA tried to scare its target audience with very targeted, "cursed" banner ads based on their browsing history. Banner ads adjusted the message as consumers moved about digitally, including what people posted in social media and being far more invasive than any other banner ad using cookies. But the execution kept consumers aware of the campaign with a transparent display as to what occurred with the data collected to maintain a balance between privacy and entertainment.

SVEDKA created over 70,000 dynamically optimized creative pieces to reach consumers an average of 16 times, targeting across time of day, location, device, or online behaviour. Messages included things like, "I know you like the wrong vodka" and "I saw your costume." To break the curse, consumers visited the SVEDKA website. Results included reaching 74 percent video viewability versus a 70 percent benchmark, and a 7.6-point gain in aided brand awareness versus a 4.6-point benchmark.

Question:
1. Did Svedka cross the line regarding consumers' privacy?

PURCHASE DECISION

At some point during their decision making, the consumer enters the *purchase decision* phase as they stop searching for and evaluating information regarding alternative brands in their evoked set. A purchase decision is not the same as an actual purchase. Once a consumer chooses a brand they intend to buy, they still have to implement the actual purchase decision. Additional concerns may need answering, such as when to buy, where to buy, and how much money to spend. This implies that the purchase decision requires time, particularly for highly involved goods like automobiles and electronics, and complex services such as insurance. Given these circumstances, there is ample opportunity for the actual brand purchase to be different from the initially planned brand purchase. Furthermore, if the additional purchase concerns are not resolved satisfactorily, the consumer may revert to the alternative evaluation stage.

Marketing communication with technology assists in the purchase decision. For example, Adidas implemented a touch-screen interface where consumers can view all of its 8,000-plus shoes. Facial recognition technology customizes the display for males or females, allowing consumers a 3D view of their options. Links to social media provide access to what others thought or felt about the particular model. And if consumers find something they like, the whole system facilitates the transaction much like shopping online at home.[18] As this example shows, marketers continually strive to maintain their loyal consumers, or create innovative ways to entice others to switch brands.

For non-durable products such as consumer packaged goods, the time between the decision and the actual purchase may be short, as it occurs while in the store or while planning at home. Before leaving home, the consumer may make a shopping list that includes specific brand names because the consumer has developed **brand loyalty**—a preference for a particular brand that results in its repeated purchase. In this situation, marketers try to maintain brand loyalty with reminder advertising to keep their brand names in front of consumers; prominent shelf positions and displays in stores; and periodic promotions to deter consumers from switching brands. Market leaders, whose products enjoy strong overall brand images, often use ads that promote the brand (**Exhibit 3-9**).

Internet advertising is used to influence purchase decisions considerably. A consumer may see a banner ad from an alternative brand based on their recent browsing just prior to purchase. Research has shown that a purchase decision is facilitated in social media with consumers seeing price comparison information, experiencing group purchases, reacting to "buy now" messages, and making use of promotions (e.g., coupons).[19]

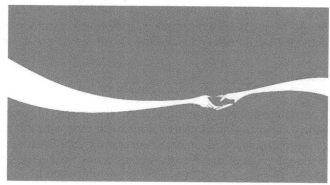

Exhibit 3-9 Ads for market leaders such as Coca-Cola support brand loyalty.

Source: The Coca-Cola Company

Exhibit 3-10 The outcome of consumer choice is clear in this ad for responsible alcohol consumption.

This isn't what they meant by "on-campus accommodation."

— You always have a choice —

For facts about alcohol, visit *healthysask.ca*

Source: Saskatchewan Ministry of Health

POST-PURCHASE EVALUATION

After the purchase decision, the individual consumes or uses the product. Consumers explore a number of activities during this stage to assess the product performance. They may seek out reassurance and opinions from others to confirm the wisdom of their purchase decision. They may be more attentive to the brand's advertising to confirm their decision, or they may look for information that supports their choice in social media, for example. Alternatively, consumers may lower their attitudes or opinions of the unchosen alternative, or deny or distort information that does not support the choice they made.

At some point during the post-purchase evaluation, the consumer will realize they are satisfied or dissatisfied with the product. A leading expert in satisfaction research defined **satisfaction** as a judgment that consumers make with respect to the pleasurable level of consumption-related fulfillment.[20] The notion of fulfillment implies that a consumer's goal has been achieved (i.e., needs met), and that the fulfillment is "judged with reference to a standard." Thus, consumers make a comparison between the consumption outcome and another referent.

Consumers can make different comparisons. One is to compare the level of product performance to the expectations of the product that consumers had prior to purchase. Satisfaction can occur when the consumer's expectations are either met or exceeded, whereas dissatisfaction results when performance is below expectations. Consumers can also compare the product performance to an absolute standard of quality to perceive satisfaction or dissatisfaction. An important aspect of satisfaction is **cognitive dissonance**, a feeling of psychological tension or post-purchase doubt that a consumer experiences after making a purchase choice. **Exhibit 3-10** illustrates advertising of social issues involving consumption decisions with regrettable consequences.

Thus, the post-purchase evaluation process is important because it will likely influence the probability of the consumer purchasing the brand once again. Positive performance means the brand is retained in the evoked set and increases the likelihood it will be repurchased. Unfavourable product outcomes may lead the consumer to form negative attitudes toward the brand, lessening the likelihood that it will be repurchased or even eliminating it from the consumer's evoked set. Beyond repurchase, satisfied consumers may communicate positively about the brand, while dissatisfied consumers may spread negative word-of-mouth information that deters others from purchasing the product or service.

Marketers can influence post-purchase evaluations positively by ensuring that their advertising and other forms of promotion received by consumers prior to and during their shopping do not create unreasonable expectations that their products cannot meet. If consumers see that the advertising claims are consistent with their expectations, they are more likely to have a positive post-purchase evaluation. In addition, markets try to influence a consumer's evaluation with direct communication during this stage.

Companies send follow-up letters or emails and brochures to reassure buyers and reinforce the wisdom of their decision. Companies use toll-free numbers, websites, and social media to allow for consumer feedback. Positive, feel-good images of purchase, consumption, and use are disseminated. Marketers also offer liberal return and refund policies and extended warranties and guarantees to ensure customer satisfaction.

LO2 TYPES OF DECISION MAKING

Consumers do not always experience all five stage of the purchase decision process or proceed in the sequence presented. They may minimize or skip one or more stages if they have previous product experience, or if the decision is of low personal, social, or economic significance. To develop effective promotional decisions, marketers need to understand the types of problem-solving processes their target consumers use to make purchase decisions.[21] One suggested approach classifies consumers into three different types of problem solving.

Consumer purchase decisions based on a habit are known as **routine problem solving** or routine response behaviour. The decision process for low-priced, frequently purchased products consists of recognizing the need, performing a quick internal search, and making the purchase. The consumer spends little time or effort on external search or alternative evaluation due to strong product category and brand knowledge. Marketers use IMC tools to maintain high levels of brand awareness and positive brand attitude, to reinforce the routine for their loyal customers, or to disrupt the routine of non-customers to switch brands.

A more complicated decision-making process characterized by **limited problem solving** or **extended problem solving** occurs when consumers have no product category experience or minimal brand knowledge, or their purchase decision criteria are not determined. In these cases, advertising should provide consumers with detailed information about a brand and how it can satisfy their purchase motives and goals, helping consumers learn what attributes or criteria should be used in making a purchase decision and how the alternatives perform on these dimensions.

GROUP DECISION MAKING

Sometimes consumers are involved in a group situation during their purchases. A group is defined as "two or more individuals who share a set of norms, values, or beliefs and have certain implicitly or explicitly defined relationships to one another such that their behavior is interdependent."[22] One instance of group decision making is when family members act as an individual buying unit during the process. As shown in **Figure 3-3**, family members can assume various roles in the decision-making process for a durable good like a new vehicle.[23] Group interactions can occur at every stage of their decision-making process since members take on different roles throughout.

Figure 3-3 Roles in the family decision-making process

Initiator	Person responsible for starting the purchase decision	Parent identifies the need for a new car
Information provider	Individual who gathers information to be used in making the decision	Teenage car buff finds magazines, dealer brochures, social media images, and user comments
Influencer	Person who exerts influence on the decision criteria	All family members may be involved; criteria may differ or be similar across members
Decider	Someone who actually makes the decision	Possibly one parent alone, or with another family member
Purchaser	Individual performing the physical act of making the purchase	The couple may sign the purchase agreement to have joint ownership
Consumer	Actual user of the product	All are consumers if it is a family car, or mother only for solo use

The planning implications for advertisers focus on how the target audience may vary depending on how the group buying occurs. Messages and media that attempt to persuade one who takes the initiator role could be much different than messages and media for one who assumes the decision-making role. The ad in **Exhibit 3-11** shows how a parent may see the Golf Sportwagon as meeting the needs of all family members during the purchase of a new vehicle.

The roles of the decision-making process provide a unique situation for gift giving where the purchaser is clearly not the consumer. In addition, the purchaser may rely on friends and family members, and seek their opinion to assist in getting the right gift for the occasion. The social approval motives

Exhibit 3-11 The Golf Sportwagon ad shows how all family members' needs may be fulfilled with its purchase.

©Volkswagen Canada

Exhibit 3-12 Roots targets the purchaser in this ad for its handbags.

©Roots

with gift giving could suggest other applications of the roles as well. The ad in **Exhibit 3-12** appeals to a gift giver looking to buy a present for Mother's Day, a birthday, or an anniversary.

LO3 Target Audience Decision

We reviewed the consumer decision-making process since marketers need to understand the behaviour they are attempting to influence through their promotional plans. Marketers try to understand consumers since an IMC plan, IMC program (e.g., advertising campaign), or ad is directed to a target audience. Selection of a single target audience or multiple target audiences is a primary decision prior to other communication decisions such as message, media, or IMC tool, and the decision is derived from the segmentation and target market decisions of the marketing plan. In this section, we therefore review the marketing planning process to understand the context of this important promotional decision. Next, we summarize approaches for segmentation that are used for both target market and target audience selection, and then review the promotional planning process. Finally, we describe an approach for identifying options for the target audience decision.

MARKETING PLANNING PROCESS

The process of developing marketing and promotion decisions is summarized in **Figure 3-4**. The target market is an important focus of marketing effort; it is based on an extensive situation analysis and it provides direction for all marketing decisions, including the promotion decisions identified in Chapter 1. The **target market** is the group of consumers toward which an overall marketing program is directed. This decision is part of three steps: segment the market,

Figure 3-4 Marketing and promotions process model

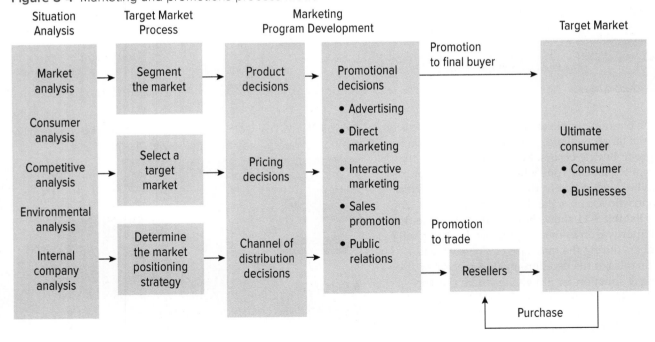

select a target market, and determine the market positioning strategy. The marketing planner identifies the specific needs of groups of people (i.e., segments), selects one or more of these segments as a target, configures a positioning strategy for the selected market segment, and develops a marketing program.

This approach involving segmentation is applicable in marketing for a number of reasons, including changes in the market (consumers are diverse in their needs, attitudes, and lifestyles); increased use of segmentation by competitors; and the fact that managers are trained in segmentation and realize the advantages associated with this strategy. Perhaps the best explanation comes back to the premise that marketing planners must understand consumers as much as possible to design marketing programs that meet consumers' needs most effectively. It should be noted that user profiles of brands seldom deviate and are relatively stable over time.[24]

SEGMENTATION VARIABLES

Figure 3-5 shows five dimensions for segmentation: geographic, demographic, socioeconomic, psychographic, and behaviour. The subsequent segmentation variables in the second column are used for both marketing and marketing communication decisions. A marketing planner might segment the market on the basis of benefits sought and then examine demographic and psychographic characteristics within each benefits sought segment to identify numerous target market options.

Applying this to marketing planning for ski boots, benefits sought based on the level of skiing (low to high quality on responsiveness due to flexibility of the boot's plastic) is a relevant variable for segmentation. The marketing planner could consider age as an additional demographic variable (younger beginners to older beginners) and add varying social classes (lower class to upper class). All this information is combined to provide a complete profile of skier segments across three variables. Thus, more segmentation with three variables in this example provided precise understanding but resulted in fewer consumers in each segment and potential for lower sales. How many segmentation variables are optimal? Which segmentation variable is used first and which others are additionally used? In short, managers use their experience and data to apply the most relevant segmentation variables to their specific marketing decisions to handle these two questions.

A promotional planner, such as one working in an ad agency, faces similar questions when planning an advertising program or other IMC activity, and relies on the same segmentation variables. The decision process is similar, but the actual segmentation variables used can differ noticeably within specific IMC decisions. We review these segmentation variables that are applicable for marketing strategy planners and marketing communication planners as they try to make effective decisions. Note that the application of segmentation variables changes with technology. A new variable is visual segmentation based on people's photo from their online profile, indicating impression management motivated by belonging, self-promotion, and self-expression.[25] Brand sentiment exhibited in social media provides advertisers with detailed data, allowing more precise targeting along consumer belief systems and a little deeper investigation for psychographic segmentation.[26]

Geographic Segmentation In the **geographic segmentation** approach, markets are divided into different geographic units. These units may include nations, provinces, states, counties, or even neighbourhoods. Consumers have different buying habits depending on where they reside. To address this, advertisers use different IMC tools or advertising messages. Internet display ads are delivered geographically since the technology identifies the location of the user. Out-of-home messaging relies extensively on geographic placements. Brands face different penetration levels across markets and alter their sales promotions accordingly to stimulate trial purchases.

Demographic Segmentation Dividing the market on the basis of a demographic variable such as gender, age, marital status, or household size is called **demographic segmentation**. Related socioeconomic variables (such as income, education, and occupation) are viewed as being very similar to demographic ones. While demographic segmentation is a common method, it is important to note that other factors may be the underlying basis for homogeneity and/or consumer behaviour. For example, the Mercedes-Benz promotion putting its A-Class hatchback within a crowded nightclub suggested an age segmentation of young consumers, however the intention focused on the fact that the location had many non–car owners and the luxury brand hoped to entice entry-level buyers.[27]

Thus, an astute promotional planner will identify additional approaches for segmenting and will recognize the limitations of demographics. One critique notably concluded that the use of birth era in marketing and advertising is exploitative, misleading, and condescending since it groups disparate people into one group; this criticism may be relevant for other demographic segmentation variables as well. Interestingly, the definition of Generation X is

Figure 3-5 Examples of market segmentation variables

Main Dimension	Segmentation Variables	Typical Breakdowns
Geographic	Region	West; Central; East
	City size	Under 10,000; 10,000–24,999; 25,000–49,999; 50,000–99,999; 100,000–249,999; 250,000–499,999; 500,000–999,999; 1,000,000 or more
	Metropolitan area	Census Metropolitan Area (CMA); etc.
	Density	Urban; suburban; small town; rural
Demographic	Gender	Male; female
	Age	Under 6 yrs; 6–11 yrs; 12–17 yrs; 18–24 yrs; 25–34 yrs; 35–44 yrs; 45–54 yrs; 55–64 yrs; 65–74 yrs; 75 yrs plus
	Race	Asian; Black; Hispanic; Indian; White/Caucasian; etc.
	Life stage	Infant; preschool; child; youth; collegiate; adult; senior
	Birth era	Baby boomer (1949–1964); Generation X (1965–1980); Generation Y (1981–2000);Generation Z (2001–present)
	Household size	1; 2; 3–4; 5 or more
	Residence tenure	Own home; rent home
	Marital status	Never married; married; separated; divorced; widowed
Socioeconomic	Income	<$15,000; $15,000–$24,999; $25,000–$34,999; $35,000–$49,999; $50,000–$74,999; $75,000+
	Education	Some high school or less; high school graduate; some college or university; university/college graduate; etc.
	Occupation	Managerial; professional; technical; sales; service; administration; farming, forestry, fishing; etc.
Psychographic	Values	Actualizers; fulfilleds; achievers; experiencers; believers; strivers; makers; strugglers
	Lifestyle	Activities; interests; opinions
	Personality	Gregarious; compulsive; introverted; aggressive; ambitious; etc.
	Culture	Ethnic; social; etc.
	Social class	Low middle class; upper middle class; etc.
Behaviour	Brand loyalty	Completely loyal; partially loyal; not loyal
	User status	Non-user; ex-user; first-time user; regular user
	Usage rate	Light, medium, or heavy user
	Situation	Usage or purchase situation
	Benefits sought	Quality; service; price/value; convenience; prestige

inaccurate to a degree. The start of birth era as a segmentation variable originated with the fictional novel *Generation X*, which described the angst of those who were born in the late 1950s and early 1960s (final stage of baby boomers).[28] For now we kept it at the collective misbelief in Figure 3-5, but if a marketing or promotional planner intends to use a demographic variable, it is generally suggested to use it with other variables.

Psychographic Segmentation Dividing the market on the basis of values and lifestyle, personality, culture, and social class is referred to as **psychographic segmentation**. Each of these variables is the basis for segmentation.

Values and Lifestyle The determination of lifestyles is usually based on an analysis of the activities, interests, and opinions (AIOs) of consumers that are obtained via surveys. These lifestyles are then correlated with the consumers' product, brand, and/or media usage. Lifestyle may be the best discriminator between use and non-use of a good or service. Harley-Davidson demonstrated this with a campaign that showed its customer base consisting of virtually every conceivable variable. Its Facebook page boasts over 3 million fans, many of whom are younger and not the stereotypical boomer reliving glory days. The main discerning characteristic is the lifestyle of enjoying motorcycle riding.[29] As another example, notice how the ad for Fluevog in **Exhibit 3-13** reflects the life of the target audience member. Taken from another perspective, our activities, interests, and opinions are reflective of our individual values. We highlight two major approaches that have developed these forms of segmentation with proprietary research methods.

Psychographic segmentation occurred with the advent of the values and lifestyles (VALS) program now offered by Strategic Business Insights. Developed in the late 1970s and refined a decade later, VALS is a method for applying segmentation based on values. The underlying premise of VALS is that psychological traits and demographics are better predictors of behaviour than demographics alone. The VALS approach combines an estimate of the resources the consumer can draw on (education, income, health, energy level, self-confidence, and degree of consumerism) along with their motivation. This is used to identify eight different types of people to understand their consumption behaviour. This U.S. invention is now adapted to other cultures such as Japan, the United Kingdom, and Latin America.

PRIZM$_{NE}$, developed by Claritas, is another American lifestyle segmentation approach that has been adapted for the Canadian market through the two divisions of the research firm Environics (Research Group & Analytics). PRIZM C2 associates the lifestyle questions asked on the survey with demographic data from the federal government's census. The analysis provides 66 different lifestyle segments and 18 social groups based on whether the respondent is a pre-boomer, boomer, or post-boomer. PRIZM C2 claims that the segmentation system is useful for communication decisions like target audience profiling and media planning, and for other marketing strategy decisions for virtually all industries. The data from the different lifestyle segments can also be aligned with other data sources such as media consumption and geography to allow more precise targeting for marketing decisions.

Exhibit 3-14 shows an ad for San Pellegrino asking, "Are you a real foodie?" in the headline. Is a foodie someone who has influence over food trends? Or, is it someone who loves food and always talks about it? Maybe it is someone who eats exotic food or eats in a fashionable restaurant or location? On the other hand, suppose foodies are people who cook at home all the time and use new recipes or food products on a regular basis. Nonetheless, consumers enjoy activities, interests, and opinions surrounding food and this ad hints at a "foodie" lifestyle San Pellegrino used for its campaign. The brand faced weaker brand awareness and diminished dining out sales, so it revamped its "Live in Italy" slogan with this new approach. To reinforce the lifestyle, chefs visited Italy to participate in

Exhibit 3-13 The target audience's lifestyle is reflected in this Fluevog ad.

UNIQUE SOLES
FOR
UNIQUE SOULS
SINCE 1970

JOHN FLUEVOG ♥ OTTAWA
61 WILLIAM ST (BY BEAVERTAILS IN BYWARD MARKET) 613·244·1970
FLUEVOG.COM
©John Fluevog Shoes

Exhibit 3-14 San Pellegrino associates its brand with a foodie lifestyle.

S.PELLEGRINO® is a registered trademark of Sanpellegrino S.p.A., Milano, Italy

San Pellegrino's annual cooking competition. A film crew captured the stories of chefs and their cooking adventure for foodies to savour visually online.[30]

Personality Borrowing from psychological theory, we are interested in consumers' personality traits—the relatively enduring personality characteristics that lead people to respond in a reasonably consistent manner. Characteristics like social orientation (introvert versus extrovert), innovativeness (how much a person likes to try new things), materialism (emphasis placed on product ownership), and self-consciousness (projection of personal image to others) are examples of personality traits used to describe a group of consumers more precisely.[31] Notice how the ad for a pair of John Fluevog shoes in Exhibit 3-13 appeals to potential consumers who view themselves as unique individuals.

Culture An abstract external factor that influences consumer behaviour is **culture**, or the complexity of learned meanings, values, norms, and customs shared by members of a society. Culture guides members of a society in all aspects of their lives, including their consumption behaviour. Marketers must be aware of cultural trends since their influence on consumer behaviour could be useful for segmentation. For example, one global agency employs 300 cultural spotters who identify 60 universal cultural trends occurring.[32] Within a given culture are generally found smaller groups or segments whose beliefs, values, norms, and patterns of behaviour set them apart from the larger cultural group. These **subcultures** may be based on age, geographic, religious, racial, and/or ethnic characteristics. A number of subcultures exist within Canada and they are important to marketers because of their size, growth, purchasing power, and distinct purchasing patterns.

While culture exerts an influence on consumers, it is a challenge for marketers to respond to specific cultural characteristics in different markets. The subtleties of unique cultures require extensive research to understand and appreciate, so marketers must consider the cultural context in which consumer purchase decisions are made and adapt their advertising and promotional programs accordingly. For instance, Nissan devoted a sizable portion of its advertising budget to South Asians when its agency discovered that a car purchase represented an important first step for this group when arriving in Canada. The message concentrated on the in-vehicle technology and all-wheel-drive systems and reached consumers via TV, digital media, and social media to ensure strong top-of-mind awareness. In contrast to this approach, Rogers historically split its advertising resources across "mainstream" and "multicultural" media; however, it considered greater collaboration or integration as the notion of groups of different cultures appeared less relevant.[33] These examples show the need for good research for promotional decision making as cultural effects have varying importance depending on the product category.

Social Class Virtually all societies exhibit a form of stratification whereby individuals are viewed as part of a social category on the basis of criteria important to members of that society. **Social class** refers to relatively homogeneous divisions in a society into which people sharing similar lifestyles, values, norms, interests, and behaviours are grouped. While a number of methods for determining social class exist, class structures in Canada are usually based on occupational status, educational attainment, and income. For example, sociologists generally agree that there are three broad levels of social classes in North America: the upper (14 percent), middle (70 percent), and lower (16 percent) classes.[34]

Social class is an important concept to marketers, since consumers within each social stratum have similar values, lifestyles, and buying behaviour. Thus, the social class groups provide a natural basis for market segmentation.

Exhibit 3-15 This Volvo ad appeals to the upper class.

©Volvo Cars of North America, LLC

Consumers in the different social classes differ in the degree to which they use products and services and in their leisure activities, shopping patterns, and media habits. Marketers respond to these differences through their product and service offerings, the media strategies they use to reach different social classes, and the types of advertising messages they develop. The ad in **Exhibit 3-15** shows how a product attempts to appeal to the upper class in both copy and illustration.

Behaviouristic Segmentation Dividing consumers into groups according to different actions is known as **behaviouristic segmentation**. These actions are measurable and generally observable from a research standpoint. The consumer behaviour that is most critical includes brand loyalty, user status, usage rate, situation, and benefits sought.

Brand Loyalty The degree of loyalty to the brand is a variable used considerably in marketing as programs are developed to retain current customers or attract consumers who purchase other brands. Loyalty status is combined with demographic and/or psychographic criteria to develop profiles of audiences for specific communication. We will have more to say on this idea, because it is a critical variable in designing promotional messages. Its importance is easily seen; current brand users are usually aware of the brand and have considerably stronger product knowledge, and they have some regular or irregular interaction with the brand. For example, loyal users of Nike shoes might be more likely to look at the Nike website to see the latest brands.

User Status In the case of usage, the marketer assumes that non-purchasers of a brand or product who have the same characteristics as purchasers hold greater potential for adoption than non-users with different characteristics. A profile (demographic or psychographic) of the user is developed, which serves as the basis for promotional strategies designed to attract new users. For example, teenagers share certain similarities in their consumption behaviours. Those who do not currently own, say, a smart phone are more likely to be potential buyers than people in other age groups. In this case, the new users may view this purchase decision as a new experience requiring comparison shopping with limited problem-solving activities and are therefore more involved while reading ads or looking at websites or talking to friends online.

Usage Rate Another factor related to the previous two concerns how much of a product category is consumed. Most product categories and most consumers can be classified along the lines of light, medium, or heavy usage. With these groups in mind, and demographic or psychographic variables, advertisers can direct messages more appropriately. For example, men tend to consume fewer cosmetic products than women (yes, men's skin care is a big business), so ads are designed to move the light users to become medium users. Labatt's advertising is trying to increase women's beer purchase rate (which is correlated with usage rate) at 72 percent to the level of men at 89 percent based on the brewer's market research results.[35]

Situation Another way of viewing behaviouristic segmentation is to examine the situation in which consumers plan to use the product or brand since it directly affects their perceptions, preferences, and purchasing behaviours.[36] Two types of **situations** may be relevant: the specific usage situation and the purchase situation. *Usage situation* refers to the circumstance in which the product will be used. For example, purchases made for private consumption may be thought of differently from those that will be obvious to the public. Furthermore, purchases made for oneself versus for others as gifts offer another way to view consumer markets. The *purchase situation* more directly involves the environment operating at the time of the purchase. Time constraints, store environments, and other factors guide consumers' behaviour, which opens the door for inventive ways of segmenting the market.

Benefits Sought In purchasing products, consumers are generally trying to satisfy specific needs and/or wants. They are looking for products that provide specific benefits to satisfy these needs. The grouping of consumers on the basis of attributes sought in a product is known as **benefit segmentation** and is widely used. Consider the purchase of a wristwatch. While some might buy a watch for particular benefits such as accuracy, water resistance, or style, others may seek a different set of benefits. Watches are commonly given as gifts for birthdays, Christmas, and graduation. Certainly the same benefits are considered in the purchase of a gift, but the benefits the purchaser derives are different from those the user will obtain. Ads that portray watches as good gifts stress different criteria to consider in the purchase decision.

PROMOTIONAL PLANNING PROCESS

Promotional planners refer to the segmentation approach used in the marketing plan. For example, the market segmentation may be based on demographics, so the target market could be men aged 18–24 or women aged 25–44. The selection of the target market has direct implications for advertising and promotion. As shown in Chapter 1, specific behavioural and communication objectives are derived and the promotional mix strategies are developed to achieve these objectives. Thus, different objectives may be established, different budgets may be used, and the promotional mix strategies may vary, depending on the market selected. And it is incumbent upon the promotional planner to gather more information or perform additional research to develop a more complete understanding of consumers in the targeted market, as suggested in Chapter 1.

When making decisions, promotional planners focus on a target audience. We make a careful distinction between target market and target audience since an advertising plan or IMC plan is one part of the overall marketing strategy.

This approach is consistent with others regarding the topic of IMC planning.[37] The **target audience** is a group of consumers that a marketing communication program (i.e., advertising) is directed toward. And depending on the circumstances, the target audience decision is applicable for an entire IMC plan, an IMC program like advertising, or a single advertising message.

Conceptually, the target market and target audience are interdependent, but their distinction allows promotional planners to make more effective communication decisions with enhanced precision. The promotional planner must consider key questions. Is the target audience substantial enough to support individualized strategies? Can the target audience be reached with a communication program like advertising? Will a marketing communication program like sales promotion influence a target audience to switch brands? Is the target audience likely to participate in social media activities like creating user-generated content for the brand? As these questions illustrate, promotional planners are involved with determining the delivery of a message to a target audience that is a portion of the target market.

The difference between target audience and target market can also be seen when firms develop promotional programs that fit with an established target market that has a new cohort of consumers every few years. Since its launch in the mid-2000s, Activia's target market appeared to be women over 40 who sought a healthier brand of yogurt as they faced age-related health concerns. To attract new customers a few years later, Activia used the 14-Day Challenge to sway women who were now in the target market as they had gotten older (e.g., previously 35 and now 40). This new group of non–brand users became a target audience to persuade to try the brand to ensure future sales.

As expected, over time, a new cohort of women who did not eat Activia yogurt moved into the target market age range, and became a target audience for an updated campaign. In early 2017, Activia reconfigured the 14-Day Challenge message to eat its yogurt twice daily and to see this as a mindful time-out during a busy day. The English ads featured Dina Pugliese, a 44-year-old TV host, to confirm its target market; the French ads featured Marianne St-Gelais, a 28-year-old Olympic medallist, to stretch the target market age range.[38] Of course, the promotional planners could realize that an alternative target audience exists for Activia, and try to sway lapsed users who are older and in need of additional calcium as they age.

The difference between target audience and target market can also be seen when firms develop selective promotional programs beyond their target market. Promotional planners are concerned with activities like public relations, and the target audience may in fact be part of the general public who are not actual consumers. Alternatively, a promotional planner may be given direction or conclude from the situation analysis that the target audience is virtually identical to the target market. For example, a new brand entering an established product category may have no choice but to switch consumers from a competing brand. We consider how to frame the target audience decision and see which segmentation variable a promotional planner should consider primary.

TARGET AUDIENCE OPTIONS

We turn to the Rossiter and Percy (R&P) perspective of identifying and selecting the target audience for promotional communication.[39] R&P state that the primary and most logical factor for initially defining a target audience is the current behaviour of consumers. This factor is critical since it is customers' individual decisions to purchase a brand that add up to a firm's total sales. Furthermore, this behaviour is a manifestation of a consumer's attitude toward the brand. Thus, in setting the direction for any IMC plan or IMC program (i.e., advertising), the manager must have a clear idea of whether the target audience is customers (brand-loyal customers or favourable brand switchers) or non-customers (new category users, other brand switchers, or other brand loyals). Targeting based on brand loyalty appears to be a sound idea; research firms publish extensive findings indicating the challenges for companies to retain customers.[40] We develop these five options for making the target audience decision for all marketing communication tool decisions.

Brand-Loyal Customers Promotional planners have the opportunity to direct marketing communication to **brand-loyal customers** who regularly buy their firm's products. Marketing strategies (i.e., relationship marketing, discussed in Chapter 1) and communication strategies regularly focus on a firm's current customers to ensure that customers maintain their current purchasing and consumption behaviour. As we noted in Chapter 1, it is generally profitable to maintain a stable core of current customers. From a communication standpoint, it suggests that we do not have to advertise as frequently or we do not require frequent sales promotions. Part of the success with Tide is a stable group of loyal customers to whom the brand still advertises (**Exhibit 3-16**).

Toyota demonstrated the importance of communicating to customers in the wake of its difficulties by having mass media messages, online video messages, specialized communications on safety, and a feel-good ad of customers enjoying the Corolla for decades.[41] While BlackBerry has had ups and downs over time, it recognized the importance of communicating to its current customer base to stay loyal and not defect to other brands.[42] This raises the question as to whether beer company ads should target their loyal customers and ensure future purchases by strengthening the loyalty with relevant messages, or target the remaining customers who claim they are not loyal to a specific beer.

Favourable Brand Switchers The second customer group highlighted by R&P is **favourable brand switchers**. These customers buy the promotional planner's brand but also buy other brands within a given relevant time period for the product category. For certain product categories, consumers habitually purchase from a few favourites or those brands within their evoked set. These types of purchases may occur for many reasons. Consumers face different purchase situations (e.g., own purchase versus gift). Sometimes certain moods influence brand choice. Whatever the motivation or external influencing factor, consumers adjust their purchases accordingly. While a promotional planner would undoubtedly strive to have all customers be truly loyal, favourable brand switchers are an important source of purchases and are loyal to a degree. For these reasons, marketers would like to communicate directly with these consumers so that their brand remains in the evoked set. For example, the Gain ad in **Exhibit 3-17** emphasizes its pleasant aroma to switch consumers back to the brand for their next purchase.

The importance of varying degrees of loyalty within a brand's customer base is a key topic. In a study of the cola market, the authors provide a decision-making framework for measuring varying degrees of customer loyalty and link these customers to varying levels of return on investment. The conclusions suggest that customer groups with different loyalty levels are predicated upon their beliefs toward the brand on the more salient attributes.[43]

The grocery store industry is one faced with considerable switching since it is unlikely that a household shops at one store for all of its food. In the face of competition from discount competitors like Walmart, Loblaw's message of "Crave More" for its PC brand captured the idea of attempting to sway switchers with its food innovations. As part of the switching emphasis, the campaign projected the PC brand as a lifestyle instead of using its historic packaged goods approach. As part of this "foodie" lifestyle, the messages communicated where the food was sourced from and why, since more consumers are interested in such facts.[44]

New Category Users Consumers that are not purchasing within the promotional planner's product category are within the non-customer group and are known as **new category users**. **Exhibit 3-18** shows an ad for the electric Smart car; its most likely target audience is those currently using a gasoline-powered vehicle. Often, people become new category users because of life changes. For example, after graduating from college or university, young adults enter numerous categories partly because they have the income but also because they are at a stage of their life when new or latent needs emerge. Advertisers court this target audience since these consumers are potentially ready to make a purchase. Later on in life, consumers have different needs and move into a product category not previously purchased. RBC launched a series of ads for disability, travel, and life insurance in which the potential customer asks if they need the product. The ads wrapped up with an RBC adviser suggesting they contact the company after humorously showing what could happen without the product.[45]

New category users also appear when brands attempt to attract new customers who might not perceive the product category as relevant for fulfilling their needs. With the decline in eating cereal for breakfast, and with many people skipping breakfast entirely, Mini-Wheats offered a humorous ad featuring the hot-milk man who visited neighbourhoods and got people to try the cereal during cooler winter months. While consumers in this target audience may be lapsed users, the length of time of not eating cereal suggests that the purchase is new enough to see them as new category users.[46] Another example is a campaign for Lotto 6/49 in Quebec that influenced young people who did not buy lottery tickets. The message

Exhibit 3-16 Tide directs ads to its loyal customers.

Source: Tide by Procter & Gamble

Exhibit 3-17 Gain tries to sway consumers back to the brand by reminding them of the scent.

Source: Gain by Procter & Gamble

Charge ahead to Rome.

>> Tell us where we should install charging stations across the country at thesmartcityproject.ca for a chance to win a trip to Rome¹!

The surprisingly quick smart fortwo electric drive from only $26,990* before rebate.

Rebates available!

thesmartcityproject.ca

smart - a Daimler brand

©Mercedes-Benz Canada

demonstrated many low-probability events of serendipity that occur every day to give the non-users an idea that they might win the jackpot.[47]

Other Brand Switchers Another type of consumer that is in the non-customer group is **other brand switchers**. They are like the switchers in the customer group in that they purchase a few different brands within a category. However, from a promotional planner's perspective, they are fundamentally different because they are not purchasing their brand. This is a challenging target audience, as the brand needs to break into consumers' evoked set of the brands that these consumers are currently purchasing. It's a formidable task, but still the focus of a considerable amount of advertising and promotion. The ad in **Exhibit 3-19** tries to encourage people to drink milk instead of other beverages when eating their meals.

Under the leadership of a new senior marketing executive, Leon's Furniture hired on new creative and media agencies for the first time in 20 years to move its marketing communication away from the previous goofy ads and price promotions. While the retailer received considerable loyalty from those aged 45 and older, it needed to alter the attitudes of younger consumers to entice them into the store where they would see the selection and quality and speak with salespeople. In this case, the younger consumers represented other brand switchers since they typically shopped at other furniture retailers in the past, and Leon's new ads convinced them to visit and ultimately switch. Research indicated 16 percent growth in purchase intention after initial promotional efforts.[48] As this example suggests, the key targeting variable is not demographic but rather behavioural.

Other Brand Loyals R&P's final non-customer group for target audience selection is **other brand loyals**. As this label implies, these consumers purchase only one other brand. For example, a Pepsi ad tries to sway a Coke user to its brand. The tourism ad in **Exhibit 3-20** encourages travellers to consider Canada as a destination to visit. In this case, the ad is trying to switch people who travel internationally, not domestically, which indicates a varied application of this target audience option.

It is difficult to say how much in advertising and promotion expenditure is directed to these types of consumers across industries. Logically, it would be very difficult to break strongly held consumer attitudes and behaviours, but it can be done, and Wealthsimple provides another example. It targets dissatisfied 25- to 45-year-old investors who have experienced distrust and confusion with their current financial service provider. Over the course of its first four years, the brand launched three major campaigns with different imagery but a consistent message for the target audience to consider switching brands.[49] Koho, a new financial services brand, followed a similar approach as it tried to sway loyal consumers away from established institutions for everyday banking services.[50] **IMC Perspective 3-2** shows an example of Koodo's campaign to switch consumers from other phone service providers.

Exhibit 3-19 Quebec Milk Producers would like people to drink milk with meals.

Everything's better with milk

©Quebec Milk Producers - AD - 2015

Exhibit 3-20 Travel Alberta and the Canadian Tourism Commission jointly try to attract visitors to Canada.

©Destination Canada

IMC PERSPECTIVE 3-2

KOODO'S SCARY MESSAGE

Koodo launched its "Choose Happy" campaign in 2015 with bright colours to communicate mobile bliss for all of its potential customers. The direct slogan certainly encouraged those dissatisfied with other phone service providers to switch to Koodo. During the first phase, the message increased its subscriber base by 13 percent, even with a lower media budget.

A more recent campaign entitled "Shock Free Data" focused on the fact that almost half of Canadians paid extra fees due to exceeding their monthly mobile data allowance. As part of a $4 million budget, the TV messages retold classic horror movie scenes. Instead of characters meeting their demise through the actions of an evil person, they faced their monthly bill with no additional charges. Without

Your phone bill shouldn't scare you.

Unless you say it like this: phooooooone biiiiiiiiiill.

With Shock-Free® data, you don't get a scary bill. We pause your data so you don't go over your limit.

Choose Happy koodo

©Koodo/Camp Jefferson

[Continued on next page]

any concern and with a shrug of their shoulders, the characters returned to their routine. One scene recreated the famous shower scene from the movie *Psycho*, while the other two showed generic horror movie scenes. Other media included radio, print, out-of-home, Internet display, social media, and paid search.

Post-campaign tracking research showed stronger levels for "transparent pricing" compared to other discount brands like Fido and Virgin, in addition to main player Bell. Koodo posted 74 percent growth in new customers compared to the objective of 15 percent new customers. Ad testing revealed stronger performance on overall brand impression, brand relevance, purchase intent, and call to action.

Question:

1. Why was this message so persuasive in encouraging customers of other brands to switch?

LO5 IMC Planning: Target Audience Profile

According to R&P, after prioritizing the target audience in terms of customer groups, other segmentation variables like lifestyle or demographics are used to develop a complete target audience profile. A complete profile of the target audience beyond the initial behavioural variable is necessary for direction of the remaining decisions in the promotional plan. Creative decisions involving the main message to be communicated require appropriate content so that consumers will attend to and understand the message. Effective media decisions require the promotional planner to match the consumer characteristics of the specific media with a complete target audience profile. Finally, more information about the target audience allows greater precision when assessing and choosing IMC tools to deliver the message. We now explore the planning implications of these three ideas.

PROFILE FOR MESSAGES

In later chapters, we will identify different aspects of constructing the main message a promotional planner would want to develop for its advertising or sales promotion or any other IMC tool like the Internet or public relations. For the message to be completely understood, the content of the message must be consistent with the background or experiences of the intended audience. For example, if the ad uses language or references to a lifestyle that is unfamiliar to the target audience, it is less likely to influence in the direction intended. Thus, a complete profile of the target audience will be useful when finalizing the body copy in a print ad or the scenes in a television commercial.

Companies target a younger demographic, and we may read in the press or in marketing trade publications that a firm is targeting an 18- to 24-year-old demographic. While this may be true, often there is an inherent behavioural variable implied. Sometimes it is more like a new category user, since young adults start to consume new categories of products as they mature. Other times, it is more like favourable brand switchers in an attempt to make these consumers exhibit stronger loyalty. Thus, a communication message has to resonate with the target audience based on their current behaviour, whether they buy the brand or not, and on another variable like demographics.

One clever ad by Tide detergent illustrates this point from the other direction. The ad shows a child, sitting in a highchair, who has just finished eating a bowl of spaghetti. The picture clearly shows the child's face, which is of course very messy. The headline reads, "The day I switched to Tide," and there is no other text in the ad. It appears that this message is targeted toward other brand switchers or other brand loyals who are at a particular stage of the family life cycle. The ad represents the significant decision they undertook to finally stop consuming a current brand and move on to a presumably better brand. Had the ad shown an alternative picture, the additional profile variable would have been considerably different. For instance, the image of a young woman wearing athletic clothing who observes a stain or that the colours of her clothing are fading too quickly suggests an active lifestyle. This illustrates that any marketing segmentation variable can be used to further profile the behavioural variable.

PROFILE FOR MEDIA

Later in this text, we will also identify the different media decisions. For example, the promotional plan television or radio to deliver its message, or the promotional planner might consider newspapers or m titude of other media. Each medium offers avenues that also must be considered. For instance, would planner place the television commercial on a TSN sports event during the day, or on a CTV drama in the evening. detailed profile of the target audience allows the message to be more precisely delivered in a medium that has a higher proportion of the target audience.

Critics contend that the advent of different television channels leading to greater audience fragmentation has caused TV advertising to be less efficient, since an advertiser is required to place a commercial on more than one station to reach a larger audience. In contrast, the detailed target audience profile for media helps a promotional planner move toward greater effectiveness. With the possibility of offering a more customized message to different audiences, promotional planners can have one type of commercial oriented toward younger non-customers on one channel and another message to older current customers on a different channel. Or, with the extensive number of new television channels in languages other than the two official languages, advertisers can provide more customized messages on the respective channels.

Moving toward more interactive media for the purposes of building and maintaining relationships, brands could use certain kinds of media and media vehicles to communicate with different segments based on unique relationship variables that are within the firm's database.[51] This would allow more accurate exposure and more customized messages depending upon where the customer is within the relationship.

PROFILE FOR IMC TOOLS

Similarly, in a later part of the book, we investigate the decisions involved for other IMC tools like sales promotion, public relations, direct marketing, and the Internet. Each of these represents additional avenues for reaching target audiences, and each represents a tool with a greater opportunity for building the brand. Like media, there is also the possibility of more closely aligning the use of a tool with a promotional planner's target audience, provided sufficient profiling is done.

Learning Objectives Summary

 Describe the consumer decision-making process and demonstrate how it relates to marketing communication.

Consumer behaviour is viewed as the process and activities that people experience when searching for, selecting, purchasing, using, evaluating, and disposing of products and services to satisfy their needs and desires. A five-stage model of the consumer decision-making process consists of need recognition, information search, alternative evaluation, purchase, and post-purchase evaluation. Marketing communication influence potentially occurs in every stage as marketers adjust their messages and media along with IMC tools to influence appropriately so that consumers move from one stage to the other.

 Contrast how the consumer decision-making process varies for different types of purchases.

Consumer decision making is classified along a continuum from routine problem solving to extended problem solving. Consumers generally spend more time and effort as they move from routine to extended problem solving. Some types of marketing communication are more relevant than others depending upon the type of behaviour expected. Consumer decision making moves from an individual decision to a group decision, and once again marketing communication must adjust its message, media, or IMC tool accordingly.

LO3 **Compare the similarities and differences of target market and target audience.**

This chapter investigated how promotional planners make a target audience decision for any aspect of an IMC plan. To understand the context of this decision, the chapter examined the role of promotion in the overall marketing process that includes a situation analysis, target market process, and marketing program development, all directed toward a target market. A key aspect pertains to the target marketing process, which includes segmenting the market, selecting a target market, and determining the market positioning strategy, as this process gives direction to the target audience decision. Accordingly, we reviewed how marketing planners and promotional planners segment the market, and explained how each made the target market and target audience decision, respectively.

 LO4 **Identify the options for making a target audience decision for marketing communication.**

 The chapter identified a model to profile a target audience by considering the current purchase behaviour of the target audience with respect to the promotional planner's brand as the primary segmentation variable. Promotional messages can be directed to current customers, such as brand-loyal customers or favourable brand switchers. Alternatively, promotional messages could be targeted to non-customers, like new category users, other brand switchers, or other brand loyals.

LO5 **Express why a profile of the target audience is important for message, media, and IMC tool decisions.**

Finally, the chapter concluded by expressing how other variables more accurately profile the audience in terms of lifestyle or psychographic variables after the initial direction is finalized. This descriptive profile becomes useful for all facets of the promotional plan (i.e., message, media, IMC tools).

Review Questions

1. What are the stages of the consumer decision-making process model? Why are they important for planning marketing communication?

2. How do the stages of the consumer decision-making process model differ with the three types of problem solving?

3. When defining a target audience for marketing communication, why is it a good idea to use consumer behaviour with respect to your brand as the primary variable before using other variables such as demographics or lifestyle?

4. What are the five customer groups? Explain in terms of a beverage product like soft drinks or beer.

5. Why is a complete profile of a target audience important for marketing communication?

Applied Questions

1. Explain the difference between functional, performance, and experiential benefits. Why might the messages recommended in an IMC plan for smart phones focus on each one separately or together?

2. Consider a group purchasing situation you have previously experienced, like going out for the evening. What role did each person play during pre-purchase, purchase and consumption, and post-purchase?

3. In what situations are the target audience and the target market the same? In what situations is the size of the target audience larger or smaller than the target market?

4. Examine the ads in this chapter and identify the target audience each ad is directed toward using the model of five customer groups. Suggest other relevant segmentation variables to further profile the target audience. Also identify a relevant segmentation variable to pinpoint the target market.

5. Which segmentation variables are more useful or appropriate for profiling a target market for an automobile like the Mini? Similarly, which are more useful or appropriate for profiling the target audience for an automobile like the Mini?

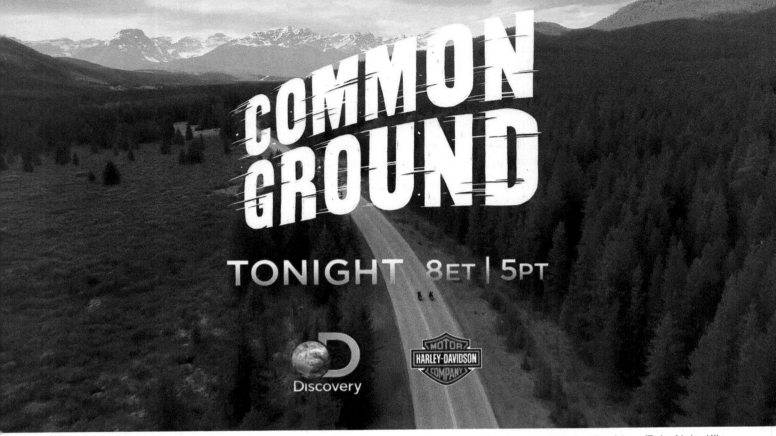

CHAPTER FOUR

Communication Response Models

LEARNING OBJECTIVES

LO1 Explain the elements of the communication process and identify the role of marketing communication.

LO2 Contrast traditional and alternative response hierarchy models and identify their implications for advertising.

LO3 Review the specifics of the receiver's processing of marketing communication.

LO4 Illustrate a response model for managerial decision making.

LO5 Construct ideas on how the knowledge of a response model is used for IMC planning.

Harley-Davidson Rides to 100

To mark its 100th anniversary, Harley-Davidson celebrated Canada's 150th birthday by riding in style. The dual milestone drove the famous motorcycle company to attract a younger and more diverse clientele to the iconic brand by demonstrating that its current customer base extended well beyond the expected 50+-year-old white male rider. Harley-Davidson created "Common Ground," an experience-based promotion in which diverse riders shared their stories. People from New Zealand, Mexico, and India journeyed across Canada with a local Canadian host while a film crew documented the six-day road trip as they all met with Canadians from all walks of life in many towns. The insight that sparked the initiative focused on the belief that individual differences disappear when experiencing new things together.

Livestreaming occurred in paid and owned social media during the tour. From the raw footage, a 12-part story emerged that played in social media and at dealerships. Other promotional activities included promoted tweets about specific models, and a website that relayed additional video, participant biographies, route information, and a link to book a test drive. Other stakeholders were not forgotten: dealers received a supportive tool kit, and media received a press kit to ignite publicity. No doubt potential customers obtained considerable exposure and multiple opportunities to experience the Harley-Davidson message content. Product information, inspiring stories, and continued social media communication contributed to a potential customer receiving an immersive shopping experience while considering a purchase. Research indicated that novice interested riders could require 40 dealership visits prior to purchase.

Communication prior to the travels featured profiles of the local guides in owned social media and through news media, and wild postings in large urban markets. The campaign ran from June to September and hit 47 million media impressions and 7.7 million video views, both well above the anticipated goals. Market share grew 2 percent in the face of a 4 percent decline in market sales. The campaign garnered significant national and international media publicity. The Discovery Channel picked up a one-hour version of the journey and 475,000 viewers watched. The campaign earned numerous national and international creative awards for Harley-Davidson and for its agency, Toronto-based Zulu Alpha Kilo.

To round out its marketing communications around the time of the journey, Zulu Alpha Kilo created pop-up cafés for Harley-Davidson in Toronto, Vancouver, and Montreal. While the brand did sell over 12,000 cups of coffee, the main point of the effort allowed consumers to experience the culture of the brand with historic displays used as decor. After this, the brand asked the agency to design the interior of its new head office. The impressive design established a proper working environment and paid tribute to the legacy of the brand's history. For example, the lobby design recreated images of the original shed where the inventors made the first bike, and meeting rooms reflected classic Canadian rides like British Columbia's Sea to Sky Highway and Ontario's Georgian Bay Loop.

Question:

1. How could brands of other product categories emulate the spirit of Harley-Davidson's promotional and design activities?

An organization's IMC strategy is implemented through the communication tools and messages it sends to current or prospective customers as well as other relevant publics. Organizations communicate with advertisements, websites, press releases, sales promotions, and visual images. Those involved in the planning of an IMC program need to understand how consumers will perceive and interpret their messages and how these reactions will shape consumers' responses to the company and/or its product or service.

This chapter takes a historical perspective to illustrate how academics and practitioners evolved their understanding of how persuasion works in the context of marketing communication. We begin with a model to illustrate the complexity of the communication process. Next, we examine the response process of consumers that is explained by traditional hierarchy response models and alternative hierarchy response models. We then turn to a detailed understanding of the receiver's processing of marketing communication. Finally, we summarize a managerial decision making framework that illustrates a response model taking an IMC planning perspective.

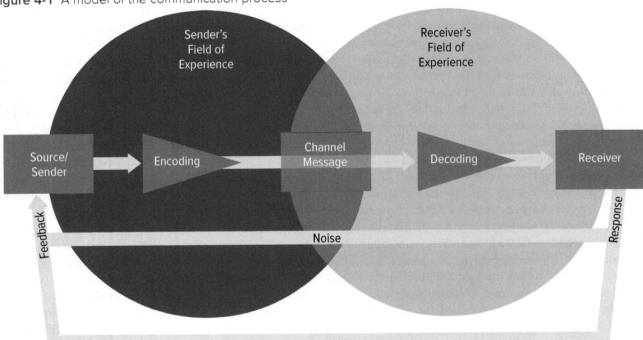 LO1 A Model of the Communication Process

Communication is defined as the passing of information, the exchange of ideas, or the process of establishing a common thought between a sender and a receiver.[1] This definition from communication theory is reflected in **Figure 4-1**. Two major participants in the communication process are the sender and the receiver. Two central elements are the message (what the sender wants to say to the receiver) and the channel (how the sender delivers the message through non-personal or personal means to the receiver). Four other elements of the model are the communication processes: encoding, decoding, response, and feedback. The last element, noise, refers to extraneous factors in the system that interfere with the process and inhibit effective communication.

Figure 4-1 A model of the communication process

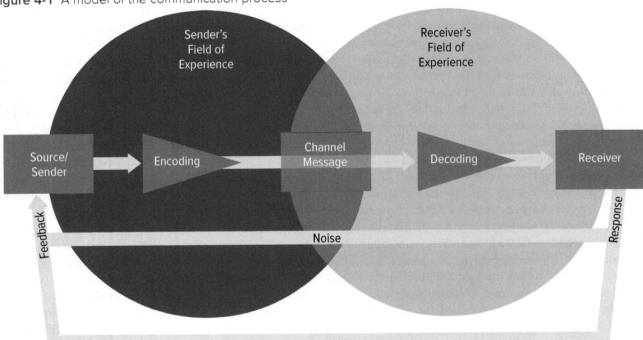

This communication model implies that advertising and marketing communication is a complex process, with success depending on the content of the ad message, the medium selected to deliver the ad, the type of IMC tool used to persuade, and the target audience's interpretation all working together in some manner. Within an ad message, words, pictures, sounds, and symbols may have different meanings to different audiences. Marketers must determine how these different meanings influence consumers' understanding of a brand's ad messages. This point is true for the medium and IMC tool as well. Moreover, the receiver's perception of the source (i.e., brand) of the ad message may also affect successful communication.

SOURCE

The sender, or **source**, of a communication is the person or organization that has information to share with another person or group of people. The source may be an individual (say, a salesperson or hired spokesperson, such as a celebrity who appears in a company's advertisements) or a non-personal entity (such as the brand or organization itself). Because the receiver's perceptions of the source influence how the communication is received, marketers select a communicator that the receiver believes to be knowledgeable and trustworthy or with whom the receiver can identify or relate in some manner. For example, the Citizen Watch Company featured athletes and celebrities as spokespersons in the "Better Starts Now" global campaign for its Eco-Drive watches. **Exhibit 4-1** shows one of the ads from the campaign, featuring singer Kelly Clarkson.

ENCODING

The communication process begins when the source selects words, pictures, symbols, and the like to represent the message that will be delivered to the receiver(s). This process, known as **encoding**, involves putting thoughts, ideas, or information into a form that provides a meaningful message. The sender's ultimate goal is to encode the message in such a way that it will be understood by the receiver. This means using words and pictures that are familiar to the target audience, as demonstrated in the above ad. Companies also have highly recognizable brand symbols that are prominently shown in their ads—such as the McDonald's golden arches, the Nike swoosh, or the Coca-Cola trademark. When these symbols are seen in ads, consumers instantly understand the message that is associated with the brand.

MESSAGE

The encoding process leads to development of a **message** that contains the information or meaning the source intends to convey. The message may be verbal or non-verbal, oral or written, or symbolic. Messages are put into a transmittable form that is appropriate for the channel of communication. In advertising, this may range from simply writing words or copy that will be read as a radio message to producing an expensive television commercial.

Marketers make decisions regarding the message content, structure, and design for optimal communication. **Message content** refers to *what* the message information and/or meaning will communicate. **Message structure/message design** refers to *how* the message is constructed to deliver the information and/or intended meaning. These message decisions are covered in Chapters 7 and 8. The ad in **Exhibit 4-2** illustrates lighthearted *message content* with its religious metaphor contained in the copy. The *message design* of using berries to form the words, a product shot, and the colourful background provides a clear and simple message that Sun-Rype offers a particular flavour.

General Mills turned its *message content* toward socially significant directions for its Cheerios brand. Impetus began with management believing that it should communicate both its brand and what the company cared about. The *message design* involved "The Cheerios Effect," telling the story of how Canadians connect and also showing how the cereal connects: "Take two Os and drop them into a bowl of milk . . . see what happens? They're naturally drawn together. Scientists say the Cheerios Effect is the way small floating objects attract one another. That it has to do with fluid mechanics, surface tension, and buoyancy. We think it's about a lot more." Canadians volunteered their stories, and Cheerios placed them online and on TV. All of the stories showed "The Cheerios Effect," imagery spliced between the scenes of the people in the story. One story featured two gay Caucasian men who adopted a young girl of a different ethnicity. Another story had a couple who fell in love after the woman saw the man in his wheelchair singing in a band on TV. Two cousins—one with hearing limitations—living as sisters were the focus of the third connection story.[2]

Exhibit 4-1 Singer Kelly Clarkson is a source in this ad for Citizen Eco-Drive watches.

Source: Citizen Watch Company of America, Inc.

Exhibit 4-2 The visually appealing message by Sun-Rype invites consumers to try the raspberry flavour.

It's like nectar of the gods. Assuming you worship raspberries.

Exhibit 4-3 The image projected by an ad might communicate more than words.

Source: Coach, Inc.

Note that it is not only the actual words of the message that determines its communication effect, as suggested in the Cheerios example, but rather the impression or image the ad creates. Notice how the Coach ad shown in **Exhibit 4-3** uses pictures to deliver its message. The juxtaposition of the country and city images conveys the dual use of the brand, while the fashionable clothing associated with the stylish bags communicates the classic image of the Coach brand. The meanings of products, brands, and symbols to represent brands, and the story implied about the brand, influence how consumers interpret messages—suggesting that careful consideration of the message content and design is a critical task for promotional planners.[3]

NON-PERSONAL CHANNEL

A method of communication that carries a message without interpersonal contact between sender and receiver is a **non-personal channel**. These channels are generally referred to as the **mass media** or mass communication, since the message is sent to many individuals at one time. For example, a TV commercial broadcast on a prime-time show may be seen by a few million people. Non-personal channels of communication consist of three major types: print (e.g., newspapers, magazines), broadcast (e.g., radio and television), and out-of-home (e.g., outdoor, transit, place-based). Magazines provide a good channel for health messages encouraging people to take action. In the ad in **Exhibit 4-4**, the visual demonstrates the problem of taking asthma medication for too long without any solution and indirectly invites consumers to call the phone number. While these media have existed for decades, innovation flourishes with technology. For example, holograms at events make a spectacular vision for onlookers; Nissan Canada reflected 3-D product images over water to simulate a lake-surface car chase on Canada Day. Laser-guided sound systems emit an audio message when people are within a specific distance or facing a public screen.[4]

Exhibit 4-4 Print media with clever visuals provide an opportunity to convey a message.

Hand-out/Association pulmonaire du Québec/Newscom

Automobile manufacturers continue to use non-personal channels. Subaru targeted its BRZ to young men aged 30–35 who are tech-savvy driving enthusiasts by making it a "hot" new addition to the lineup with a super-slow-motion video showing the heat radiating off the car as it melted everything in the parking garage. It ended with customary close-up shots of its sleek styling and showcased its handling while accelerating with the thrilling sounds of the engine roaring. Combined with the video, Subaru ignited the front cover of *Grid*, a free Toronto city magazine, with a hologram that looked like a regular cover until it was slightly tilted, when it showed an image of the BRZ burning through the page. Other media included ads in national newspapers and magazines showing similar images of the BRZ burning through the pages. A display on the streets of Montreal recreated the video effect with scorched street items like a mailbox and bike rack surrounding the BRZ. Wild postings permitted viewers to "tap or snap" with their smart phone to see a dedicated page for a full description.[5]

The Internet is a non-personal channel with both print and broadcast characteristics. We see display or video ads on websites that publish content, such as TSN for sports information and Facebook or YouTube for social media postings. Thus, the Internet is non-personal as people consume information or entertainment content with no personal contact between them and the company (e.g., source) that disseminates the ad. And interestingly, a company's Internet site is an ad delivered to everyone and anyone, even though we often refer to its information and images as content. For Subaru's BRX, the brand placed its video ad on YouTube and used the same burning imagery in its banner ads.

Alternatively, the Internet is increasingly a form of personal communication, mediated through electronic devices, as consumers can interact with a company's personnel and share information, pictures, and video with other people. Not all digital communication will be non-personal. Proximity- and time-based means of communication occur through data from consumers' smart phones and their use of social media. Finding patterns of routine behaviour, such as buying a daily coffee at one location and time, might be an impetus for targeting people to switch with an incentive or relevant message. Application of these kinds of algorithms produces substantially accurate results. Specialized shopping apps allow consumers to receive personalized information while roaming retail aisles.[6] However, while these methods appear to be directly communicated via technology, they remain non-personal media as there is no person-to-person communication.

PERSONAL CHANNEL

Direct interpersonal (face-to-face) contact with target individuals or groups is the hallmark of a **personal channel** of communication. Salespeople serve as a personal channel of communication when they deliver a sales message to a buyer or potential customer. An advantage is that a customized message can be delivered to the audience, and immediate receiver feedback results in message adjustment from the source. With video and other capabilities of computers and the Internet, face-to-face contact with salespeople and customer service personnel is mediated through technology.

Social channels of communication (such as friends, neighbours, associates, co-workers, and family members) are also personal channels. They represent *word-of-mouth (WOM) communication,* a powerful source of information for consumers that has been researched for decades.[7] For example, a sample of 70 product launches showed that only 10 percent produced 85 percent of the word-of-mouth communication. The majority of it occurred before the launch with traditional media expenditure for distinctive brands in ubiquitous product categories.[8] In turn, companies have always attempted to generate positive WOM for their brands. Knowing that the average consumer listens to what others say about a brand, marketers will target specific groups of influential consumers such as trendsetters or loyal customers with influential messages or promotional incentives.[9]

Consumers communicate about brands within social media and use the Internet's networking features to send links to ads or other brand-related content to whomever they choose. While there is no face-to-face contact in these instances, the interactive capabilities suggest it closely resembles a personal channel. Marketers use this as an opportunity to disseminate a message through the resulting WOM of these newfound personal channels of communication. This social media communication growth spawned research on social networks to understand influential participants within a social network. One finding suggests that one-fifth of a person's contacts actually influence a person's activity level on the site.[10] A second finding suggests that opinion leadership and opinion seeking both contribute to online forwarding and online chatting.[11] Finally, a third result concludes that electronic WOM yields greater shopping time overall and more time considering a recommended product.[12]

Communication in social media like Twitter shares characteristics of a social channel where brand personnel interact with loyal customers. Continued messaging among Dove and its favourite followers who happened to be influential bloggers allowed the brand to recruit these women for a day-long beauty session that resulted in their being part of a cast of dancers in a rendition of *Singing in the Rain* to promote its Nourishing Oil Care line of shampoo shown on TV and Internet media. During their spa day, the women used social media to describe the experience for all to vicariously enjoy the moment.[13]

Advertisers encouraging online word-of-mouth find positive financial results. One study found that post-campaign WOM contributes to profitability through customer lifetime value calculations.[14] Advertising also contributes to WOM with shopping effects with measurable gains for Internet searches and website visits.[15] Although online WOM is important for marketers, other research shows that 90 percent of brand conversations occur offline. Face-to-face interaction accounts for the vast majority (72 percent), phone conversations rank second (18 percent), and only 7 percent takes place through online channels such as email/instant messages, blogs, and chat rooms. And, nearly half the conversations included references to the brand's IMC tools (print and television ads, websites, point-of-sale displays, and promotions).[16]

Additionally, word-of-mouth about a brand's advertising is significantly more likely to involve a recommendation to buy or try a brand when compared to other WOM-induced discussions about brands. One-quarter of all consumer

Exhibit 4-5 A Haiku ad encourages interested homeowners to gather information by phoning or visiting the website.

Exhibit 4-6 This Corona ad allows for different interpretations in decoding.

conversations involve a brand's advertising, with TV ads being most prevalent, and 75 percent of communication occurs face to face.[17] While online and offline WOM appears critical, perhaps for different reasons, the authors of a review of electronic WOM studies conclude that understanding this digital version is paramount with expected future growth. They conclude that there are significant questions to consider: Why do people talk online? Why do people listen online? What happens to the sender? What is the influence on the receiver?[18]

RECEIVER

The **receiver** is the person(s) with whom the sender shares thoughts or information. Generally, receivers are the consumers in the target market or audience who read, hear, and/or see the marketer's message. The target audience may consist of individuals, groups, niche markets, market segments, or a general public or mass audience, as discussed in the previous chapter. The ad in **Exhibit 4-5** targets those interested in learning more about stylish upgrades to their home.

DECODING

Decoding is the process of transforming the sender's message back into thought. This process is heavily influenced by the receiver's frame of reference or **field of experience**, which refers to the experiences, perceptions, attitudes, and values brought to the communication situation. For effective communication to occur, the message decoding process of the receiver must match the encoding of the sender. Simply put, this means the receiver understands and correctly interprets what the source is trying to communicate. **Exhibit 4-6** shows an ad where different ways of decoding might occur.

As Figure 4-1 showed, the source and the receiver each have a frame of reference (the circle around each) that they bring to the communication situation. Effective communication is more likely when there is *common ground* (i.e., overlap of circles) between the two parties. The more knowledge the sender has about the receivers, the better the sender can understand their needs, empathize with them, and communicate effectively.

While this notion of common ground between sender and receiver may sound basic, it causes great difficulty in the advertising communication process. Marketing and advertising people may have different fields of experience from the target audience with whom they must communicate in terms of age, education, and life experiences. Advertisers invest in research to understand the frames of reference of the target audiences and pre-test messages to make sure consumers understand and decode them in the manner the advertiser intended prior to the launch.

VW Canada performed extensive analysis to identify a selective target audience. VW looked at credit data, Internet search metrics, digital display ad results, and dealership data to understand who was most likely to purchase in the next 60 days and who was predisposed to buy.[19] In the end, its creative ads placed cars in unusual situations that tested the audience's ability to understand the message. One consumer discovered the Tiguan in a barn while shopping for a horse, and another consumer picked out a Jetta after placing an order at a butcher shop (**Exhibit 4-7**). For both ads, the consumer immediately said they would buy the car.

IMC Perspective 4-1 presents the story of the No Frills grocery store, which took an unusual approach to communication and certainly let its target audience decode its meaning.

NOISE

Throughout the communication process, the message is subject to extraneous factors that can distort or interfere with its reception. This unplanned distortion or interference is known as **noise**. Errors or problems that occur during message encoding or distractions at the point of reception are examples of noise. Perhaps the foremost distraction is advertising clutter, whereby the receiver is confronted with competing messages. Noise may also occur because the fields of experience of the sender and

Exhibit 4-7 VW creatively communicated how easy it is to buy a VW.

©Volkswagen Canada

IMC PERSPECTIVE 4-1

NO FRILLS

Loblaw started the No Frills brand and store concept in the 1970s amid rising unemployment, inflation, and interest rates. Borrowed from Europe, the new format surprised Canadians accustomed to full service grocery stores. For four decades it retained its low price image, but encroaching competitors like Walmart, Costco, and Food Basics slowly eroded No Frills's position in the discount grocery store category. Somehow the brand had to alter its marketing communication so consumers could see it as more than a place to get good deals.

Research indicated that its patrons' income levels varied considerably; the store's parking lot illustrated this with both pricey and beater cars! In fact, the typical consumer reflected a common attitude of being a good shopper who gained satisfaction from finding deals. The agency designing the campaign decided these consumers needed a name and deemed them "haulers," where *hauler* means "someone who gets a lot, for a lot less."

©No Frills/john st.

The 90-second music video ad showed a hauler in a No Frills store doing handstands on grocery carts while selecting produce, running sideways along the frozen food freezer doors, performing aerial cartwheels, and spinning tubs of detergent on one finger of both hands just like an NBA all-star. It was no doubt a humorous exaggeration, but the message was clear for viewers to decode: No Frills customers are winners! According to the agency creative director, "We bundled up all the pride of getting a great deal, and gave it a name. That is how it feels to be a hauler."

[Continued on next page]

The campaign launched with teaser messages in social media (Instagram @haulhard) with photos of people displaying T-shirts, hoodies, and tote bags. The images looked like fashion photos for a hot new streetwear collection! Ads posted around Toronto appeared like concert messages or album drop hints. Clearly, this part of the campaign gave receivers something to think about as they decoded the message. The music of the ad provided another fun feature as No Frills released a full-length version on iTunes and Spotify.

Self-declared haulers picked up on the social media fun after the ad launch, creating all sorts of additional brand exposure. Results of the campaign included stronger than expected advertising recall and campaign awareness.

Question:
1. Why did the teaser aspect of the campaign work so well?

receiver don't overlap. Lack of common ground may result in improper encoding of the message—using a sign, symbol, or word that is unfamiliar or has a different, unintended meaning for the receiver.

RESPONSE

The receiver's set of reactions after seeing, hearing, or reading the message is known as a **response**. Receivers' responses can be non-observable actions such as storing information in memory. Other responses are emotional, where consumers enjoy or dislike messages they receive. Immediate action such as visiting the brand's Facebook page after seeing an ad is another form of response. Additional responses on social media include retweeting a brand's Twitter message or forwarding a link on Instagram. Resulting communication responses such as stronger awareness of the brand or enhanced attitude to the brand may occur as well. The next section more thoroughly investigates consumers' responses to marketing communication.

FEEDBACK

Marketers are very interested in **feedback**, that part of the receiver's response that is communicated back to the sender. Feedback closes the loop in the communication flow and lets the sender monitor how the intended message is being decoded and received. While the ultimate form of feedback occurs through sales, it is challenging to show a direct relationship between marketing communication and purchase behaviour. So marketers use other methods to obtain feedback, including talking to customers, visiting stores, monitoring participation levels with promotions and within a brand's social media, and visiting Internet sites.

Trends in brand-related consumer-generated content and digital forwarding of ads or stories about products are examples planners view as feedback from their audiences. However, after a few years of running contests or promotional events with user-generated content, brands began to exert control over their messages and appeared more cautious about encouraging further content growth.[20] Research now investigates the qualitative comments posted in social media after viewing consumer-generated ads by mapping the response to understand the message's meaning along cognitive and emotional dimensions.[21] With research-based information similar to this regarding all aspects of a brand's digital communication, advertisers can determine reasons for success or failure in the communication process and make adjustments.

SUMMARY OF THE MODEL

The model has stood the test of time for decades to describe how advertising communicates through traditional media. For the past 15 years, practitioners adapted their marketing communication decisions to digital channels and social media. The practice is now moving toward complete integrated marketing communication as firms are no longer using the term *digital* to identify their strategies and employees.[22] Thus, we conclude that the fundamental tenets of a consistent brand strategy and understanding how that message is delivered through digital avenues are still critical within digital marketing communication.

Furthermore, successful communication is accomplished when the marketer selects an appropriate source, develops an effective message or appeal that is encoded properly, and then selects the channels or media that will best reach the target audience so that the message is effectively decoded and delivered. So whether we are delivering a message on television or through social media, the general communication principles are important to consider for effective decisions. Since these decisions must account for how the target audience will respond to the promotional message, the remainder of this chapter examines the process by which consumers respond to marketing communication.

LO2 The Receiver's Response

Developing effective communication programs involves understanding the response the receiver experiences when a promotional message is delivered through a channel, as shown in Figure 4-1. The receiver may be at any place in the decision-making process (Figure 3-1), and the promotional message is experienced from any IMC tool beyond advertising, like a sales promotion offer, a marketing event, or social media influence. To understand the response, we review two kinds of response hierarchy models—traditional and alternative.

TRADITIONAL RESPONSE HIERARCHY MODELS

Figure 4-2 shows three response models, which are known as hierarchy models since there is a prescribed order the receiver experiences. Each model assumes that an ad message will move consumers through three stages: cognitive (e.g., think), affective (feel), and behavioural (do). While these response models may appear similar with identical stages, they were developed for different reasons, shown by the unique steps within each stage.

The **AIDA model** was developed to represent the steps a salesperson must take a customer through in the personal selling process.[23] The customer's attention is obtained and then their interest in the company's product is aroused. Strong levels of interest should create a stronger emotional response shown as desire. The action step in the AIDA model involves the customer making a purchase commitment. When applying this idea to marketing communication,

Figure 4-2 Models of the response process

Stages	Models		
	AIDA model	Hierarchy of effects model	Information processing model
Cognitive stage	Attention	Awareness	Presentation
			Attention
		Knowledge	Comprehension
Affective stage	Interest	Liking	Yielding
		Preference	
	Desire	Conviction	Retention
Behavioural stage	Action	Purchase	Behaviour

Exhibit 4-8 Second Cup encourages consumers to try its iced coffee.

Exhibit 4-8 Second Cup encourages consumers to try its iced coffee.

©The Second Cup Ltd.

planners might design an ad with one of the stages as a goal. The ad in **Exhibit 4-8** likely sparks a desire to drink one of the iced coffee products from Second Cup on a hot summer day. Brands try to encourage a behaviour other than purchase, such as participation in a contest, like Coca-Cola did with its "Cover" promotion where music-loving youth sang a song by a favourite artist and uploaded the recording (covers.muchmusic.com) to solicit votes to win.[24]

The **hierarchy of effects model** assumes a consumer passes through a series of steps in sequential order from initial awareness of a product to actual purchase.[25] A premise is that advertising effects occur over a period of time. Marketing communication may not lead to immediate behavioural response or purchase; rather, a series of effects must occur, with each step fulfilled before the consumer can move to the next step in the hierarchy. Xbox Kinect advertised and promoted its gaming console and received tremendous participation levels at its demonstration hubs set up in a few major Canadian cities. With celebrities visiting the hubs, the events attracted new users who eventually purchased, leading to stronger trial purchases down the road.[26]

The **information processing model** views the receiver as an information processor of persuasive communication.[27] The persuasion steps a receiver experiences constitute a response hierarchy that is similar to the hierarchy of effects sequence. However, this model includes an additional step: *retention*, or the receiver's ability to remember a portion of the comprehended information that he or she accepts as valid or relevant. This step is important since promotional campaigns are designed to provide information the receiver will use later when making a purchase decision. In this case, the receiver is not motivated to take immediate action. Mobile apps are an example of communicating initially to encourage future purchases. For example, Cineplex's app allows consumers to see schedules, read entertainment news, view movie trailers, and obtain promotional offers.[28] While the initial loading of the app and reading about the brand online did not make an immediate sale, the app certainly facilitates future repeat purchases.

IMPLICATIONS OF THE TRADITIONAL RESPONSE HIERARCHY MODELS

The first significant implication of the hierarchy models of communication response is the usefulness for promotional planners to make specific marketing communication decisions for each *step*. Potential buyers may be at different steps in the hierarchy, so the advertiser will have specific marketing communication issues to resolve. For example, using the hierarchy of effects model, a company introducing an innovative product like the Microsoft Surface may use media advertising to make people aware of the product and its features and benefits (**Exhibit 4-9**). Microsoft provides product information in its ads but also encourages consumers to visit its retail stores and Internet site to learn more about its product. Consumers experiencing these information sources may develop a stronger preference toward the Microsoft Surface, leading to a stronger probability of purchase.

A second implication is that the steps within the hierarchy models are intermediate measures of communication effectiveness that guide the objectives set for communication decisions. For example, research may reveal that one target segment has low awareness of

Exhibit 4-9 Microsoft's Surface tablet is an innovative new product.

Source: Microsoft

the advertiser's brand, and the communication task involves increasing the awareness level for the brand by increasing the number of ads. Another target segment may be aware of the brand and its attributes but have a low level of brand preference, requiring the advertiser to develop a message that addresses the negative feelings.

As shown in Figure 4-2, the three models consistently view the receiver moving through a sequence of three *stages,* even though the specific *steps* within a stage may be defined with variation. Thus, a third implication is that promotional planners could adapt their specific objectives, but maintain consistency in their planning with the same three stages occurring

Figure 4-3 Alternative response hierarchy models

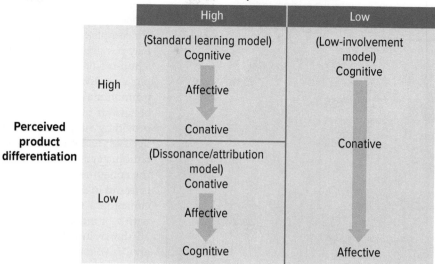

in the same order. The *cognitive stage* represents the receiver's brand knowledge. This stage includes awareness that the brand exists and comprehension about its attributes or benefits. The *affective stage* refers to the receiver's brand feelings (like or dislike). This stage also includes stronger levels of affect such as desire, preference, or conviction. The *behavioural stage* refers to the consumer's action or behaviour toward the brand, such as purchase. While this progression seems logical, research in marketing, social psychology, and communications questioned the cognitive → affective → behavioural sequence, leading to other configurations of the response hierarchy.

ALTERNATIVE RESPONSE HIERARCHY MODELS

Figure 4-3 relates perceived product differentiation and product involvement to illustrate different receiver response processes. Perceived product differentiation is based on whether the receiver views competing *brands* within a product category similarly (b1 vs. b2), or views competing *product categories* similarly (pc1 vs. pc2). Involvement is based on personal relevance with respect to the receiver's individual characteristics (e.g., needs), the marketing stimuli (e.g., message source, message content), situational factors (e.g., time), and potentially social dynamics (e.g., role in group decision).[29] Figure 4-3 identifies the three alternative response hierarchies—standard learning model, dissonance/attribution model, and low-involvement model—which result depending on high or low levels of differentiation and involvement.[30] Promotional planners would presumably alter their marketing communication plans depending on whether their target audience falls into one of the three models.

The **standard learning model** consists of a learn → feel → do sequence. The consumer goes through the same sequence depicted by the traditional response hierarchy models and is an active participant who gathers information. Information and knowledge acquired or *learned* about the brand is the basis for developing affect, or *feelings,* that guide what the consumer will do. High-involvement purchase decisions such as of consumer durable goods (e.g., electronics, cars) are product categories where a standard learning hierarchy response process likely occurs for most consumers. Ads for these products usually provide consumers with important information that is used to evaluate brands and help make a purchase decision (**Exhibit 4-10**). However, for a loyal customer who simply renews the lease or purchases the same brand of car over a few purchase occasions, the decisions are potentially less involving.

Exhibit 4-10 Honda Pilot shows benefits of its model.

Source: American Honda Motor Co., Inc. and Rubin Postaer and Associates

Exhibit 4-11 This ad reinforces the decision to buy an Oral-B toothbrush.

1. Are you brushing too hard?
2. How do you remove the most plaque?
3. How do you reverse gingivitis?
4. How long should you brush?
5. When should you replace your brush head?
6. When should you shift quadrants?
7. What's a quadrant?

Don't know the answers? This toothbrush does.

©Oral B, Procter & Gamble

Exhibit 4-12 Advertising promoting taste quality has helped Heinz dominate the ketchup market.

No one grows Ketchup like Heinz.

©H.J. Heinz Company, used with permission.

The **dissonance/attribution model** indicates a do → feel → learn sequence where consumers first behave, then develop attitudes or feelings as a result of that behaviour. It occurs in situations where consumers choose among alternatives that are similar in quality but are complex and/or may have unknown attributes. The consumer may purchase the product on the basis of a recommendation by a non-media source and then support the decision by developing a positive attitude toward the brand. The main effect of the promotional message is not influencing prior to the initial choice behaviour but rather influencing the choice after the purchase by providing supportive information. Thus, marketing communications decision makers plan advertising efforts for the post-purchase evaluation stage in consumer decision making (Figure 3-1) to reinforce the consumer's confidence in their purchase. Support for this notion is found in research which concluded that advertising can affect consumers' objective sensory interpretation of their experiences with a brand and what they remember about it.[31] For example, the ad shown in **Exhibit 4-11** supports the consumer's decision to buy an Oral-B toothbrush by highlighting how it offers many benefits derived from the questions listed.

The **low-involvement model** shows a learn → do → feel sequence. It characterizes situations when involvement in the purchase decision is low, and there are minimal differences among brand alternatives. The view is based on Krugman's theory explaining television advertising effects.[32] Why does TV advertising produce a strong effect on brand awareness, but little change in consumers' product attitude? In a low-involvement situation, the passive/uninterested consumer does not compare the message with existing beliefs or past experiences. Rather, an ad with repeated exposure results in subtle changes in the consumer's knowledge structure due to non-product information ad characteristics (i.e., brand name, ad theme, slogan/jingle, music, character, symbol) that can initiate a purchase when the consumer enters the decision process.

Advertisers also produce ads with these ad characteristics and simple and distinctive product benefit claims that are repeated, which are more likely to be retained in the receiver's memory and become salient when entering a purchase decision. One supporting study found that under low-involvement conditions, repetition of simple product claims increased consumers' memory of and belief in those claims.[33] For example, Heinz has dominated the ketchup market by repeatedly telling consumers that its brand is the thickest and richest. Heinz has used a variety of advertising campaigns over the years, but they all repeat the message and focus on the consistent quality of the brand (**Exhibit 4-12**).

IMPLICATIONS OF THE ALTERNATIVE RESPONSE HIERARCHY MODELS

The three alternative response hierarchy models show that the standard learning model, similar to the traditional hierarchy models, does not always apply. The notion of a highly involved consumer who is actively processing information and acting on the basis of a well-formed attitude may be inappropriate for particular types of purchases. From a promotional planning perspective, it is important that marketers examine the communication situation and determine which type of response process is most likely to occur. They should analyze involvement levels and product/service differentiation as well as consumers' use of information sources and their levels of product experience. Once the manager has determined which response sequence is most likely to operate, the integrated marketing communications program is designed to influence the response process in favour of the company's product.

Walmart moved to the "Discover Another Side" message in 2015 to improve consumer awareness of its fresh food offerings for produce, meat, and baked goods. IMC tools included enhanced in-store presentation, TV ads, digital banner ads, shareable content in the form of video and recipes, *Walmart Live Better* magazine, a stronger dedication to its 100 percent money back guarantee, and experiential sampling. As noted in its research, 86 percent of all Canadians shop at Walmart at least once per year, but not all purchase fresh foods, a trend that Walmart attempted to change as it continued to make inroads in the grocery market as the fastest growing retailer.[34]

SUMMARY OF RESPONSE HIERARCHY MODELS

The traditional and alternative response hierarchy models show different perspectives on how the receiver of an ad message responds, leading to questions about their feasibility.[35] A comprehensive review concluded that promotional planners have used hierarchy models for 100 years, but there is little support for the sequences proposed.[36] In short, there is no need for a promotional planner to assume one model (e.g., the standard learning model vs. the low-involvement model) is better or more applicable than the other. It is important to conclude that the receiver's response process includes both *cognition* (the "thinking" dimension of a person's response) and *affect* (the "feeling" dimension), however, there is no particular sequence of responses as conceived previously. The implication is that promotional planners should design ads with the intention of eliciting positive brand thoughts and feelings when a receiver processes the brand's message.

IMC Perspective 4-2 describes a new message for Cheerios cereal in which the response of the receiver would be subsequently measured to assess how it contributes positively to the brand. This example and the other Cheerios example reinforce the importance of carefully considering the target audience for communication.

IMC PERSPECTIVE 4-2

CHEERIOS BUZZES WITH CSR ACTIVITIES

Where's Waldo? books provided a fun game for children back in the day. *Where's Buzz the Bee?*, arising from the absence of the mascot formerly on boxes of Honey Nut Cheerios, signalled a serious environmental problem and was definitely not a game. General Mills took a dramatic step when the company removed the beloved character and replaced the image with a blank silhouette. The unusual brand communication drew attention to an issue for consumers in the store, quite possibly leading them to be more involved than initially considered when taking the trip to the store. In fact, General Mills removed its beloved mascot to alert people to the declining bee population.

To advance its corporate social responsibility initiative beyond the alert, General Mills invited consumers to register online to receive free wildflower seeds to be planted and grow the food source for bees. Consumer reaction overwhelmed General Mills as it hit its goal of 35 million seeds in the first

©Joao Paulo Burini/Getty Images

week. It raised the allotment to 110 million seeds, indicating significant message feedback after the initial brand communication. In turn, sales grew 12 percent and the company expanded the successful idea to the United States.

During the second year of the program in Canada, General Mills created a pop-up grocery store showing

[Continued on next page]

life with and without bees. The store featured science-based displays to capture the overwhelming excitement and interest of children. The company partnered with YTV to air bee-related programming during popular shows to further educate children. These two additions augmented a repeat of the previous year's campaign of a TV ad, free wildflower seeds, and Buzz vacating the package.

In the third year, General Mills added another element in the form of a story for children. Paulette Bourgeois, author of the Franklin the Turtle books, published *Bella and Jack Bring Back the Bees,*

which told the exact story behind the CSR activity. General Mills bought and distributed 100,000 copies for free through book retailers. The YTV partnership changed by bringing in the characters from the storybook. Of course, Buzz disappeared once again, and the remaining aspects continued as well. By the end of year three, General Mills estimated distribution at 900 million seeds.

Question:

1. What should General Mills add to the campaign in the fourth year?

The Receiver's Processing of Communication

LO3

Eventually, researchers turned toward studying the thoughts and feelings of the receiver while experiencing a persuasive message. For example, what comes to mind during the 30 seconds an ad is played before a movie at a cinema? When an ad is shown on Instagram, how will the receiver feel for the few seconds (or longer)? This resulted in a more comprehensive understanding of the receiver's response by closely examining the processing of marketing communication, a notable aspect omitted from the hierarchy response models. This section initially reviews the idea of consumer processing of ad messages. It then describes two approaches that adopt this idea: the cognitive response model and the elaboration likelihood model.

PROCESSING OF AD MESSAGES

How humans acquire and use information from external sources is **perception**, which is the way an individual receives, attends to, interprets, and stores information to create a meaningful picture of the world. These four aspects of perception are known as exposure, attention, comprehension, and retention of information. Perception depends on internal factors such as a person's beliefs, experiences, needs, and expectations, and external factors such as the characteristics of a stimulus (e.g., size, colour, intensity) and the context in which it is seen or heard. Applying this to advertising suggests that message and media decisions influence (1) how consumers sense external information (i.e., promotional messages delivered by media), (2) how they attend to different sources of information, (3) how this information is interpreted and given meaning, and (4) how the information is retained, which are all critical aspects of consumers processing ad messages. The number and complexity of marketing stimuli a person is exposed to daily requires filtering, which results in **selective perception**.

Selective exposure occurs as consumers choose whether or not to make themselves available to information. For example, a viewer of a television show may change channels or leave the room during commercial breaks. A non-user of perfume might decide not to open the scented strip to sample the aroma. Or, the smart phone user can decide to simply delete an unwanted email message from an unfamiliar brand. As these examples suggest, consumers' sensation of the exposure is critical. **Sensation** is the immediate, direct response of the senses (taste, smell, sight, touch, hearing) to a stimulus such as an ad, package, brand name, point-of-purchase display, or mobile alert. Marketers try to increase the level of sensory input so that their advertising messages will get noticed and activate a consumer's physiological reactions. For example, the visual elements of an ad must be designed so that consumers sense their existence. This is one reason why many TV ads start with a particular sound effect or visual movement. The ping of an email message from a favourite brand of shoes is also now used for sensation purposes.

Selective attention occurs when the consumer focuses on certain stimuli while excluding others. In terms of advertising, promotional planners use the creative aspects of their ads to gain consumers' attention. The Nike ad in **Exhibit 4-13** would presumably be noticed by most people, with its headline and imposing image. Marketers also place ads in certain time slots or locations so that consumers will notice them more easily. For example, a consumer may pay more attention to a radio ad that is heard while alone at home than to one heard in the presence of friends, at work, or anywhere distractions may be present. Internet advertisers cleverly place their display ads on a page to encourage browsers to attend to their message; however, online ads have the lowest rates for gaining attention. Individuals usually focus on elements of the environment that are relevant to their needs and tune out irrelevant stimuli. In a marketing communication context, two people may perceive the same stimulus (e.g., Internet banner ad, sample offer) in very different ways because they selectively attend to messages differently.

Selective comprehension occurs when consumers interpret information on the basis of their own attitudes, beliefs, motives, and experiences. Often, receivers of ad messages interpret brand claims that support their own position. For example, a comparative ad that disparages a consumer's favourite brand may be seen as biased or untruthful, and its claims may not be accepted. Thus, even

Exhibit 4-13 Nike creates an ad that draws attention.

THE FUTURE WAS YESTERDAY.

JUST DO IT.

Source: NIKE Inc.

if the consumer notices and attends to the advertiser's message, it may not be interpreted in the intended manner. Alternatively, a consumer loyal to a brand who sees an ad for that brand is more likely to agree with the ad claims. Finally, the interpretation and meaning an individual assigns to an incoming stimulus also depends in part on the nature of the stimulus. Consumers more easily comprehend objective ads with a clear and direct message, while the meaning of ambiguous ads is strongly influenced by the consumer's interpretation.

Selective retention means consumers do not remember all the information they see, hear, or read even after attending to and comprehending it. Advertisers attempt to make sure information will be retained in the consumer's memory so that it will be available when it is time to make a purchase. The final stage of the perceptual process involves the storage of the information in short-term or long-term memory. Consumers may make mental notes or focus on part of an advertising message to ensure that they will not forget, thus permitting easy retrieval when the information is needed.

COGNITIVE RESPONSE MODEL

One widely used method for examining consumers' processing of advertising messages is assessment of their **cognitive responses**, the thoughts that occur to them while reading, viewing, and/or hearing a communication.[37] These thoughts are usually measured by having consumers write or verbally report their reactions to a message. The assumption is that these thoughts reflect the recipient's cognitive reactions and shape ultimate acceptance or rejection of the message.

Both academics and advertising practitioners use the cognitive response approach. Its focus has been to determine the types of responses evoked by an advertising message and how these responses relate to attitudes toward the ad, brand attitudes, and purchase intentions. **Figure 4-4** depicts the three categories of cognitive responses—product/message,

Figure 4-4 A model of cognitive response

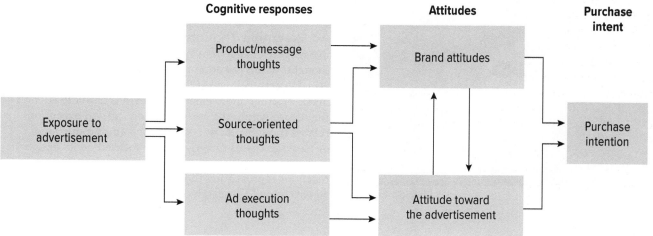

Exhibit 4-14 Consumers generate support arguments in response to ads with extensive copy.

Hand-out/Shred-It/Newscom

source-oriented, and ad execution thoughts—and how they may relate to brand attitude, attitude to ad, and intentions.

Product/Message Thoughts The first category of thoughts comprises those directed at the product or service and/or the claims being made in the communication. Research has focused on two particular types of responses: counterarguments and support arguments.

Counterarguments are thoughts the recipient has that are opposed to the position taken in the message. For example, consider the ad for Shred-It shown in **Exhibit 4-14**. A consumer may express disbelief or disagreement by wondering why they should be concerned about being scammed. Other consumers may generate **support arguments**, or thoughts that affirm the claims conveyed in the message—"Ooohhh . . . I think I'd better take some action to protect my records and documents." Research prior to the launch of a Dove Men+Care ad that encouraged men to take paternity leave garnered virtually 100 percent support arguments from both men and women, despite initial backlash from special interest groups concerned the message infringed on women's rights.[38]

The likelihood of counterarguing is greater when the message makes claims that oppose the receiver's beliefs. For example, a consumer viewing a commercial that attacks a favourite brand is likely to mentally, and potentially verbally, disagree. These counterarguments relate negatively to message acceptance; the more the receiver counterargues, the less likely he or she is to accept the position advocated in the message.[39] Support arguments, on the other hand, relate positively to message acceptance. Thus, the marketer should develop ads or other promotional messages that minimize counterarguing and encourage support arguments.

Source-Oriented Thoughts A second category of cognitive responses shown in Figure 4-4 is directed at the source of the communication. One of the most important types of responses in this category is **source derogations**, or negative thoughts about the spokesperson or organization making the claims. Such thoughts generally lead to a reduction in message acceptance. If consumers find a particular spokesperson annoying or untrustworthy, they are less likely to accept what this source has to say.

Source-related thoughts are not always negative. Receivers who react favourably to the source generate favourable thoughts, or **source bolsters**. In general, most advertisers attempt to hire spokespeople their target audience likes so as to carry this effect over to the message. Considerations involved in choosing an appropriate source or spokesperson will be discussed in Chapter 7. How might consumers react to Gisele Bündchen in this Chanel perfume ad in **Exhibit 4-15**?

Exhibit 4-15 The source in this ad could elicit both types of source thoughts.

©Lou Linwei/Alamy Stock Photo

Ad Execution Thoughts The third category of cognitive responses shown in Figure 4-4 consists of the receiver's thoughts about the ad in terms of creativity, quality of the visual effects, colours, style, layout or design of a print ad, music or other audio element in a video or audio ad, and the scenes within the story of a video ad. **Ad execution-related thoughts** do not concern the ad's product and/or message claims directly but are focused on its design elements. This approach also considered the affective reactions representing the consumer's *feelings* toward the ad execution.[40] Research concluded that these emotional responses are either favourable or unfavourable.[41] Thus, it is acknowledged that the cognitive response model is partially misidentified since it includes affective responses to the design elements of the ad.

Attitude to Brand An important outcome of two categories of cognitive responses is the receiver's attitude toward the brand. Consumers hold attitudes toward a variety of marketing stimuli, including product brands (Cheerios), company brands (Microsoft), product categories (beef, eggs, vegan food), retail stores (Hudson's Bay, Nordstrom), online stores (Amazon), advertising campaigns (Telus), promotional activities (CIBC's Run for the Cure), and individuals (endorser Sidney Crosby).

Initially, researchers viewed attitude as learned predisposition to respond to an object.[42] Decades of investigation led notable researchers to conceive attitude somewhat similarly, by defining attitude as a latent disposition or tendency to respond to an object.[43] They also conclude that attitude is evaluative, ranging from positive to negative. Thus brand attitude in Figure 4-4 is the receiver's overall evaluation of the brand that could lead to favourable behavioural responses for marketers such as purchase intention.

Since ads are typically directed to a target audience, the positive thoughts of the message, source, and execution elements potentially contribute to maintaining a strong brand attitude for loyal customers or establishing an attitude to the brand for non-customers. For example, the former will likely agree with the brand claims in the message and maintain their positive attitude. The latter may see the source as appealing and influencing their view of a brand with which they have no previous consumption experience. The inclusion of brand attitude within the cognitive response model is a significant addition beyond the earlier hierarchy models since it provides advertisers with a clear direction for assessing the effectiveness of their promotional decisions. As the model shows, the direct effects of the advertiser's decisions on brand attitude are assessed.

Attitude to Ad That consumers have affective reactions to ads resulting from cognitive responses to the ad execution is an idea not included in previous response models. **Attitude toward the ad** (A → ad) represents the receivers' favourable or unfavourable feelings toward the ad.[44]

Advertisers are interested in consumers' cognitive responses and affective reactions because these effects may be transferred to the brand itself or directly influence purchase intentions. One study found that people who enjoy a commercial are twice as likely as those who are neutral toward it to be convinced that the brand is the best.[45] Another study found that those with more positive attitudes toward advertising in general attain stronger persuasion levels.[46] In addition, Figure 4-4 shows that the source of the message, such as the spokesperson, can influence the receiver's attitude to the ad as it is akin to an ad execution element.

Consumers' feelings about the ad may be just as important as their attitudes toward the brand (if not more so) in determining an ad's effectiveness.[47] The importance of affective reactions and feelings generated by the ad depends on several factors, among them the nature of the ad and the receiver's processing.[48] Thus, advertisers use emotional ads designed to evoke feelings and affective reactions as the basis of their creative strategy. The success of this strategy depends in part on consumers' involvement with the brand and their likelihood of attending to and processing the message.

Purchase Intention Ultimately, the above attitudinal elements of the cognitive response model influence the receiver's purchase intention toward the brand. **Purchase intention** is a planned self-instruction to actually buy the brand. Extrapolating this idea of purchase intention, managers could view this planned behaviour alternatively like an intention to visit a store, intention to attend a marketing event, or any other worthy consumer behaviour the advertiser would like to influence.

ELABORATION LIKELIHOOD MODEL

Differences in the ways consumers process and respond to persuasive messages are shown in **Figure 4-5**, a revised illustration of the **elaboration likelihood model (ELM)** of persuasion.[49] The ELM explains the process by which persuasive communications (such as ads) lead to persuasion by influencing *attitudes*. According to this model, the attitude formation or change process depends on the amount and nature of *elaboration*, or processing, of relevant information that occurs in response to a persuasive message.

The ELM shows that elaboration likelihood is a function of two elements—motivation, and ability to process the message. *Motivation* to process the message depends on such factors as involvement, personal relevance, and

Figure 4-5 Simplified elaboration likelihood model of persuasion

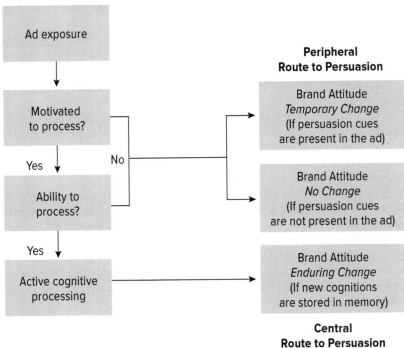

the individual's needs and arousal levels. *Ability* depends on the individual's knowledge, intellectual capacity, and opportunity to process the message.

High elaboration (central route to persuasion) means the receiver carefully evaluates the information or arguments contained in the message. Low elaboration (peripheral route to persuasion) occurs when the receiver does not actively process the information but rather infers conclusions about the position being advocated in the message on the basis of simple positive or negative cues.

Central Route Under the **central route to persuasion**, the receiver is viewed as an active, involved participant in the communication process who has high ability and motivation to attend to, comprehend, and evaluate messages. When central processing of an advertising message occurs, the consumer pays close attention to message content and scrutinizes the message arguments. A high level of cognitive response activity or processing occurs, and the ad's ability to persuade the receiver depends primarily on the receiver's evaluation of the quality of the arguments presented. Predominantly favourable cognitive responses (support arguments and source bolsters) lead to favourable changes in cognitive structure, which lead to positive attitude change, or persuasion. Conversely, if the cognitive processing is predominantly unfavourable and results in counterarguments and/or source derogations, the changes in cognitive structure are unfavourable, resulting in negative attitude change. Attitude change that occurs through central processing is relatively enduring and should resist subsequent efforts to change it. The Siemens ad in **Exhibit 4-16** likely fits with this type of response.

Exhibit 4-16 The central route to persuasion likely occurs with this ad.

Source: Siemens AG

Peripheral Route Under the **peripheral route to persuasion**, the receiver is viewed as lacking the motivation or ability to process information and is not likely to have detailed cognitive processing. Rather than evaluating the information presented in the message, the receiver relies on peripheral cues that may be incidental to the main arguments. The receiver's reaction to the message depends on how he or she evaluates these peripheral cues. As shown in Figure 4-5, the ELM views attitudes resulting from peripheral processing as temporary. Favourable attitudes must be maintained by continual exposure to the peripheral cues, such as through repetitive advertising.

The consumer may use several types of peripheral cues or cognitive shortcuts rather than carefully evaluating the message arguments presented in an advertisement. Favourable attitudes may be formed if the endorser in the ad is viewed as attractive and/or likable, or if the consumer likes certain executional aspects of the ad, such as the way it is made, the music, or the imagery. Notice how the ad in **Exhibit 4-17** contains positive peripheral cues contained in the excellent visual imagery. These cues might help consumers form a positive attitude toward the brand even if they do not process the message portion of the ad.

Explanation for ELM One explanation for how the peripheral route to persuasion works lies in the idea of **classical conditioning**. Classical conditioning assumes that learning is an *associative process* with an already existing relationship between a stimulus and a response. This process is transferred to a **conditioned stimulus** that elicits a **conditioned response** resembling the original unconditioned reaction. Two factors are important for learning to occur through the associative process. The first is *contiguity*, which means the unconditioned stimulus and conditioned stimulus must be close in time and space. The other important principle is *repetition*, or the frequency of the association. The more frequently the unconditioned and conditioned stimuli occur together, the stronger the association between them will be.

Buyers can be conditioned to form favourable impressions of brands through the associative process. Advertisers strive to associate their products and services with perceptions and emotions known to evoke positive reactions from consumers. Products are promoted through image advertising, in which the brand is shown with an unconditioned stimulus that elicits pleasant feelings. When the brand is presented simultaneously with this unconditioned stimulus, the brand itself becomes a conditioned stimulus that elicits the same favourable response. The ad in **Exhibit 4-18** associates the product with the look and sweetness of a lollipop. Extending beyond visual elements of a message, research supports the importance of music in ads to enhance the associative process.[50]

Implications of the ELM The ELM has important implications for marketing communication since the most effective type of message depends on the route to persuasion the target audience follows. If the involvement level of the target audience is high, the message should contain strong arguments that are difficult for the receiver to refute or counterargue. If the involvement level of the target audience is low, peripheral cues such as music or images may be more important than detailed message arguments. For example,

Exhibit 4-17 The colourful imagery in this ad acts as a peripheral cue.

Hand-out/CIBC/Newscom

Exhibit 4-18 Mariah Carey's new perfume associates its product with the look and sweetness of a lollipop.

Source: Mariah Carey Beauty and EA Fragrances Co

Exhibit 4-19 This Casio watch ad emphasizes the cool skateboarder image, rather than price or reliability, likely influencing low-involvement audiences.

©Ovu0ng/Shutterstock

in the Casio ad in **Exhibit 4-19**, the cool skateboarder image and product images dominate the message, leaving someone in a low-involvement target audience group to not consider price or reliability attributes. Therefore, marketers of low-involvement products rely on creative tactics that emphasize peripheral cues and use repetitive advertising to create and maintain favourable attitudes toward their brand.

An interesting test of the ELM showed that the effectiveness of a celebrity endorser in an ad depends on the receiver's involvement level.[51] When involvement was low, a celebrity endorser had a significant effect on attitudes. When the receiver's involvement was high, however, the use of a celebrity had no effect on brand attitudes; the quality of the arguments used in the ad was more important. The explanation given for these findings was that a celebrity may serve as a peripheral cue in the low-involvement situation, allowing the receiver to develop favourable attitudes based on feelings toward the source rather than processing of the message extensively. A highly involved consumer, however, experiences more detailed central processing of the message content. The quality of the message claims becomes more important than the identity of the endorser.

CONCLUSION OF PROCESSING MODELS

These two models demonstrated the usefulness and importance of understanding what the receiver is thinking and feeling when exposed to a persuasive message as part of a brand's marketing communication. The cognitive response model improved our understanding by seeing the effects of message decisions on brand attitude and attitude to the ad. The elaboration likelihood model explained the importance of involvement when receivers processed a message. Combined, these views provided marketers with a better understanding of the receiver's processing of ad messages to form or influence brand attitude.[52]

However, these two models did not account for consumer experience with the product category or the brand. Research showed that product category knowledge and brand *experience* from both purchase and usage strongly influenced how the receiver processed the ad message.[53] Advertising has a differing effect when receiving the message depending on whether the receiver currently uses the *product category* or not, and if a receiver currently uses the *brand* or not. The approach described in the next section resolves this limitation and adheres to the processing improvement established in this section.

Response Model for Managerial Decision Making

We introduced the Rossiter and Percy (R&P) perspective in Chapter 3 when identifying options for the target audience decision. This perspective suggests that promotional planners initially consider the message as being directed to either customers purchasing their brand or non-customers who have not purchased their brand. This managerial view starts with the consumer and is based on the target audience's previous product category experience and degree of brand loyalty.[54] As noted in the previous section, product category and brand experience both influence how an ad message will be processed.

Figure 4-6 shows the initial processing stage, which highlights the immediate responses to any advertising message while receiving the ad exposure. This involves the psychological experiences that occur in the target audience's mind while watching a television commercial, for example. Communication effects refer to the lasting brand impressions that remain with the target audience after the target audience processes the message. This is the target audience's memory of the brand that results after watching the television commercial.

Figure 4-6 Planning for ad processing and communication effects

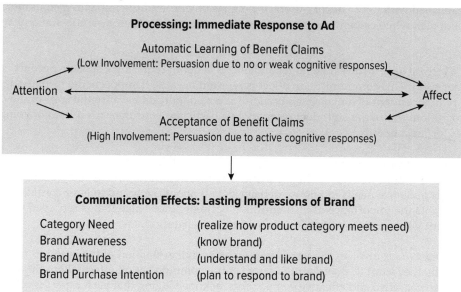

The example of processing and communication effects for a TV ad is readily extended to all methods of marketing communication. Marketing communication professionals and researchers have called for an alternative model that accounts for consumer responses to all aspects of marketing communication.[55] The decision-making orientation of this model with a focus on brand building appears to address these requests. In addition, as we will see in subsequent chapters, the R&P model is applied to formulate objectives (i.e., communication, behavioural) for the target audience, and guide marketing communication decisions (i.e., positioning, creative) for the brand.

PROCESSING OF MESSAGES

This notion of processing is consistent with all the features of the previous models. After attending to the ad, the target audience may have low or high involvement in terms of how much thought regarding the brand's benefit claims is generated while receiving the message. As the ELM indicated, highly involved target audiences are more likely to have active cognitive responses. In addition, affect, or emotional responses, will influence and be generated as a result of these cognitive responses. Furthermore, pleasant or unpleasant emotional responses may occur while attending to the execution variables (e.g., music) of the message, and positive (or negative) emotional responses may focus greater (or less) attention on the message.

The seemingly simultaneous cognitive and emotional responses occurring while attending to a message are consistent with current views of marketing communication and understanding of how the brain works in psychology.[56] Anecdotal evidence of this is seen when one considers reactions to a Super Bowl ad (e.g., TV commercial) where both thinking and feeling something about the brand occurs. Furthermore, the temporal concern of the hierarchical models is diminished by considering the processing stage prior to the communication effects stage.

From an IMC planning perspective, managers need to design brand messages while understanding the target audience's processing. For instance, to attract new customers, the manager may consider brand messages that will support high-involvement processing. And, as we will see in the media chapters and the chapters relating to other communication tools, the manager may consider more involving avenues for delivering the message (e.g., social media).

Alternatively, companies often have programs to both attract and retain customers. This could require promotional planners to strategically evaluate the balance of their messages. Should messages that attempt to generate high involvement be primary or secondary in the overall message strategy? Analytical questions such as this emerge by considering the processing stage as a key precursor to planning for the communication effects stage.

COMMUNICATION EFFECTS OF MESSAGES

Figure 4-6 identifies four **communication effects** that are established more permanently in the target audience's memory. An important distinction of this approach is that there is no assumption of a hierarchy for the communication effects. They are independent of one another, although brand awareness and brand attitude are developed relatively simultaneously in most campaigns. The remaining communication effects can occur prior to, during, or after awareness and attitude are established with new category users or non-customers. And the remaining communication effects may be enhanced in a campaign while current customers maintain or strengthen their awareness of and attitude toward the brand.

Category Need *Category need* involves the target audience's belief in requiring a specific product category to satisfy a particular consumer need. This communication effect is relevant because it supports the primary demand growth of a product category independent of a manager's brand. It is also important because the start of the decision-making process is need recognition, so linking a product category to a particular consumer need is an ongoing marketing communication task for most brands.

Brand Awareness *Brand awareness* involves the target audience's ability to recognize and/or recall the brand within the product category in sufficient detail to make a purchase. This communication effect is a strong form of consumer knowledge as the target audience needs to know extensive details about the brand to have confidence in the purchase selection. It also highlights the importance of distinguishing between knowledge that is retrieved via brand recall and knowledge that is salient when given a prompt or cue via brand recognition.

Brand Attitude *Brand attitude* involves the target audience's overall evaluation of the brand in relation to its ability to satisfy the reason why they want it. Brand attitude is a central communication effect where the target audience's evaluation includes both cognitive and affective components, acknowledging that each aspect is relevant for planning for all purchase situations. Other models represented the entire response process (i.e., cognition, affect, behaviour) as reflecting an attitude that occurred in various orders. This idea of brand attitude does not rely on any hierarchical order of the attitude components.

Brand Purchase Intention *Brand purchase intention* involves the target audience's self-instruction to respond (with shopping behaviour or a purchase) to the brand. A mental activity predicated on the anticipation of participating in a behavioural action specifically directed to the brand is another indicator of the effects of marketing communication.

(LO5) IMC Planning: Managerial Decision Making

We suggest a few conclusions for managers in making advertising and promotion decisions based on the models presented regarding how advertising works in terms of consumer response. After all, academics will continue this investigation while managers still need to make decisions.

First, it appears that managers should consider and plan for both the cognitive and the affective responses of the receiver who is processing advertising or any promotional message. Receivers typically have both cognitive and emotional reactions to the messages they see all around them every day.

Second, managers are concerned with the resulting effects of the advertising or promotional message for a time period after the receiver has received and processed the message. As suggested in the models, managers want to know if their messages are improving awareness or attitudes.

Finally, the primary characteristic that influences communication success appears to be the receiver's previous brand experience. This implies that managers should be cognizant of who exactly is the target of the message. As discussed in Chapter 3, the manager needs a detailed profile of the target audience to have an understanding to gauge communication success. Thus, managers require a decision framework that addresses these points.

The managerial approach suggested at the end of this chapter offers two important IMC planning considerations. First, there is an obvious and clear connection to the target audience's purchase of the promotional manager's particular brand. This is apparent with its reference to the brand in three communication effects. It is also seen in the connection to category need, which addresses the underlying reason why the target audience is motivated to buy the promotional manager's product, and where the target audience understands the brand to fit in the market in relation to brands in other product categories.

Second, the managerial model is applied for all aspects of an IMC program, as shown in **Figure 4-7**.[57] The managerial decisions (i.e., controllable variables), source, message, channel, and receiver (via target audience selection) are assessed in terms of resulting outcomes, exposure, processing, communication effects, and action. For example, ads with iPhone users (i.e., source) taking pictures or listening to music (i.e., message) shown on TV (i.e., channel) are directed to the

Figure 4-7 IMC planning matrix

	Source	Message	Channel	Receiver
Exposure				
Processing				
Communication Effects				
Action				

target audience, who are likely to be users of iPhones. Promotional planners would undoubtedly be interested in four communication results listed for this execution. Furthermore, this logic could be extended for print ads or video-type ads placed on the Internet, either on a website or in social media.

Similarly, the same approach applies for a whole advertising campaign over time. For example, Telus ads with multiple animals (i.e., source) behaving in a way to visually convey a product (i.e., message) across multiple media (i.e., channels) are directed to the target audience, who are likely to be users of other brands (e.g., Bell, Rogers). Across all aspects of this advertising, Telus's promotional planners would concern themselves with all four communication results. Furthermore, this idea is extended to other promotional tools like Telus's public relations activities.

The final implication of this is that all elements of an entire IMC program are planned with a matrix, including any communication via the Internet and any kind of promotional event/activity or sales promotion. Any tool for communication retains the characteristics of the communication model in Figure 4-1. One exception would be a situation where a receiver encounters a brand message from another consumer in social media; however, the other consumer is the sender in this respect, and the planning retains its characteristics. The brand is concerned with how it influenced the consumer who is the sender of the message; this is evident in social media contexts where the brand encourages the development of user-generated content or other forms of marketing communication from ordinary consumers.

The R&P model and the other communication response models will be revisited in the next chapter. Promotional planners use a communication response model to determine the communication objectives for advertising and other promotional tools. It is important to base marketing communication decisions on a model and translate them into specific objectives since promotional planners need clear guidance for the remaining marketing communication decisions.

Learning Objectives Summary

 LO1 Explain the elements of the communication process and identify the role of marketing communication.

The function of all elements of the promotional mix is to communicate, so promotional planners must understand the communication process. This process is complex; successful marketing communication depends on a number of factors, including the nature of the message, the audience's interpretation of it, and the environment in which it is received. For effective communication to occur, the sender encodes a message in such a way that it will be decoded by the receiver in the intended manner. Feedback from the receiver helps the sender determine whether proper decoding has occurred or whether noise has interfered with the communication process.

Contrast traditional and alternative response hierarchy models and identify their implications for advertising.

Promotional planning begins with the receiver or target audience, as marketers must understand how the audience is likely to respond to sources of communication or types of messages. Traditional response hierarchy models provide an initial understanding of this process; however, limitations of these models led to more comprehensive approaches. Alternative response hierarchy models modified past models regarding the target audience's involvement and perceived product differentiation. Different orderings of the traditional response hierarchy include the standard learning, dissonance/attribution, and low-involvement models. The alternative response hierarchy postulated different ordering of cognition, affect, and behaviour depending upon the involvement and differentiation.

 Review the specifics of the receiver's processing of marketing communication.

The cognitive processing of communication revealed two models: the cognitive response approach and the elaboration likelihood model. The former examines the thoughts evoked by a message in terms of product/message thoughts, source-oriented thoughts, and ad execution thoughts and how they shape the receiver's ultimate acceptance or rejection of the communication by influencing brand attitude and attitude to the ad. The elaboration likelihood model of attitude formation and change recognizes two forms of message processing, the central and peripheral routes to persuasion, which are a function of the receiver's motivation and ability to process a message. The model postulates that each route leads to varying degrees of attitude change.

 Illustrate a response model for managerial decision making.

Those responsible for planning the IMC program should learn as much as possible about their target audience and how it may respond to advertising and other forms of marketing communications. A managerial view of the response process provides direction for understanding how promotional planners should determine their brands' communication strategies. Planners should consider the immediate processing stage which includes attentions, cognitive responses, and emotional responses to messages. They should also consider the long-lasting communication effects of category need, brand awareness, brand attitude, and brand purchase intention.

 Construct ideas on how the knowledge of a response model is used for IMC planning.

A useful approach for managers to understand how advertising works is included in this chapter. The model suggests that both cognitive and emotional processing responses are critical during the initial stages of receiving the message, such as while watching a TV ad or seeing an ad paid for by an advertiser in social media. Ads are developed with source and message characteristics to invoke the anticipated cognitive responses and the types of emotions experienced by the target audience. Furthermore, the model identifies lasting brand communication effects that promotional planners should strive to achieve with their ad messages and IMC tools that have source, message, and channel characteristics.

Review Questions

1. Recall the elements of Figure 4-1 and identify them for all aspects of an IMC plan—advertising, sales promotion, direct marketing, public relations, and Internet marketing.

2. Explain why the three response hierarchy models of Figure 4-2 are limited in planning for an IMC campaign.

3. Explain what is meant by a central versus a peripheral route to persuasion, and the factors that would determine when each might be used by consumers in response to an advertisement.

4. What are the key differences between traditional response hierarchy models and the response model shown in Figure 4-6?

5. Why is it important to use a response model that is more applicable to managerial decision making?

Applied Questions

1. Consider ads found in social media like Facebook, Twitter, and YouTube, and assess whether the model in Figure 4-1 is useful for explaining how marketing communication works in these digital contexts.

2. Assume that you are the marketing communications manager for a brand of paper towels. Discuss how the low-involvement hierarchy could be of value in developing an advertising and promotion strategy for this brand.

3. Select an ad that would be processed by a central route to persuasion and one where peripheral processing would occur. Show the ads to several people and ask them to write down the thoughts they have about each ad. Analyze their thoughts using the cognitive and emotional responses discussed in the chapter.

4. Find an example of a print ad and evaluate it using the response model shown in Figure 4-6. Identify the specific types of cognitive and emotional responses that the ad might elicit from consumers and discuss why they might occur.

5. Red Bull has numerous IMC activities, including its TV advertising, events, and promotional activities. Check the Red Bull website and any other online material for background, and use the matrix in Figure 4-7 to validate whether each activity assists in planning for an IMC.

CHAPTER FIVE

Objectives for the IMC Plan

LEARNING OBJECTIVES

LO1 Distinguish among marketing, behavioural, and communication objectives and identify the value of setting each type of objective.

LO2 Describe the historical approaches for setting communication objectives for advertising.

LO3 Evaluate the options for setting behavioural objectives and apply them when constructing a promotional plan.

LO4 Choose among the options for setting communication objectives and apply them when designing IMC recommendations.

LO5 Assemble the best combination of behavioural and communication objectives for each stage of the consumer decision-making process.

Who Is the Real GOAT?

Juicy the goat is the real GOAT (greatest of all time)! The GOAT idea is part of great sports debates about hockey, baseball, football, and basketball. To put a new spin on it, Juicy Fruit gum introduced Juicy the Goat as the real GOAT, who happened to be a real goat—got it? And goats do all sorts of things, such as chew, so the imagery of a goat chewing presented a constant reminder of chewing gum, a consumption habit in decline that impacted Wrigley Canada's bottom line. In the past, Juicy Fruit's promotion focused on the sweet benefit and relied on advertising to spur in-store recognition once a consumer decided to make an impulse purchase within the gum category, or the broader candy product category. Wrigley and other gum brands faced declining sales with fewer new users as younger consumers did not pick up the habit.

Juicy Fruit's partnership with the NBA and the Toronto Raptors provided an opportunity to reach younger consumers who represented potential category users and sway them to become Juicy Fruit customers. And younger consumers seemingly lived in social media, so that appeared a likely avenue, but what would be the message? Enter @Juicy_thegoat to spark a new debate on who is the greatest of all time—the GOAT. NBA fans thrived on competitive online behaviour with debates and fun conversations around the best basketball players, so Juicy entered the fray with a signature chewing action to signal chewing gum.

Juicy became a social media personality with intercepted comments in Twitter and Instagram, cute memes like #goativational, and fun trash-talk commonly experienced by players on the court and fans online. Wrigley also worked with influencers to keep the momentum going digitally. Other brands such as Sportsnet, Nike, Footlocker, and New Era came alongside the NBA stars actively participating. Toward the end of the playoff run for the Raptors, the chewing sensation became the star of a TV ad. Juicy slam dunked the gum brand into the basketball crowd with significant online chatter resulting in a 16 percent sales increase.

And while Juicy placed Wrigley Canada up there in terms of creativity to build strong communication, the gum and candy company had established itself along these creative lines previously. Faced with significant pressure from Wrigley USA, the Canadian division reorganized its marketing department and operations so that it could innovate with its marketing communication. For example, Wrigley gained success with unusual humour in the "Taste the Rainbow" campaign for its Skittles brand of candy. Excel gum created animated characters (e.g., coffee cup, garlic) to represent the reasons why someone would chew gum as a breath freshener. And so Juicy lives within the stable of humorous characters that Wrigley uses to get its messages noticed, and in the second year Juicy promoted a contest on Twitter to keep the momentum going.

Question:

1. Check out Juicy on social media and offer suggestions on how Juicy can maintain GOAT status.

Promotional decision makers see objective setting as an important part of the IMC planning process. The task of setting objectives is complex and difficult and it must be done properly, because specific goals and objectives are the foundation on which all marketing communication decisions are made and provide a standard against which performance is measured. Although the opening vignette seems like a fun idea, the creativity reflects a well thought out plan to achieve specific objectives.

This chapter examines the purpose of objectives and the role they play in the development, implementation, and evaluation of an IMC program. First, we distinguish among marketing, behavioural, and communication objectives. Next, we describe the historical approaches of setting objectives for marketing communication based on the response models discussed in Chapter 4. We then present a comprehensive managerial framework for setting behavioural and communication objectives for each element of the IMC plan and for the overall IMC plan that we refer to in the remaining parts of the book.

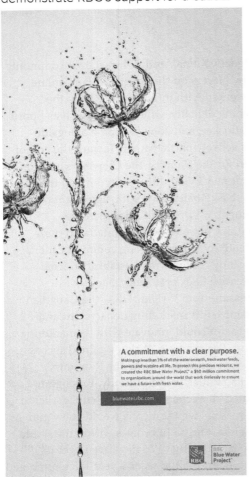

A commitment with a clear purpose.

Making up less than 3% of all the water on earth, fresh water feeds, powers and sustains all life. To protect this precious resource, we created the RBC Blue Water Project,™ a $50 million commitment to organizations around the world that work tirelessly to ensure we have a future with fresh water.

bluewater.rbc.com

RBC Blue Water Project®

©Royal Bank of Canada

LO1 Objective Setting

Setting objectives should be an integral part of the promotional planning process. However, companies fail to set marketing communication objectives or set ones that are inadequate for developing the promotional plan or measuring its effectiveness. This section discusses the value of objectives and distinguishes among marketing, behavioural, and communication objectives for optimal IMC planning.

VALUE OF OBJECTIVES

Perhaps one reason why companies do not set objectives for their IMC programs is an inability to see their value. Advertising and promotional objectives are needed for reasons such as communication function, planning and decision making, and measurement and evaluation.

Communication Function Objectives for the IMC program facilitate coordination among the groups working on the campaign. One notable example is Hellmann's "Real Food Movement," designed to encourage Canadians to enjoy more real, local food. Led by its signature mayonnaise product with its all-natural Canadian ingredients of eggs, canola oil, and vinegar, Hellmann's portrayed its brand as a natural part of everyone's diet. The program featured urban gardens where residents received an allotment to grow fruits and vegetables. Extensive TV, newspaper, digital, direct, and in-store notification invited applicants to the program. Hellmann's worked with a chef who created real food recipes for TV ads and online videos, participated in a broadcast tour, and demonstrated how meal preparation with real food is fun and easy. The "Eat Real. Eat Local." phase featured a "family dinner" video that documented the state of Canada's food delivery system and emphasized the importance of eating local.[1] Promotional personnel involved in the planning and development of the IMC program included client personnel and numerous contracted agencies. All parties coordinated the program together, which required knowledge of what Hellmann's hoped to accomplish through the objectives of its IMC program. As another example, the ad in **Exhibit 5-1** shows that RBC's involvement with the cause was dependent upon all promotional participants' understanding RBC's objectives.

Planning and Decision Making Promotional objectives guide IMC plan development; all phases of a firm's promotional strategy (e.g., budget, creative, and media decisions) should be based on the established objectives. For example, to execute all the programs for its "Real Food Movement" campaign, Hellmann's retained agencies to coordinate public relations activities, digital tools, advertising, and in-store presentations, which all drove traffic to its Internet site. Meaningful objectives certainly helped guide the decision making of all partners that contributed to Hellmann's winning a Canadian Advertising Success Stories (CASSIES) Grand Prix for best overall IMC program. As this example shows, promotional planners face strategic and tactical options in terms of creative themes, media, and budget allocation among promotional mix elements, and their choice should be based on their attainment of promotional objectives.

Measurement and Evaluation Setting objectives provides a benchmark against which the effects of the promotional campaign are measured. In the case of Hellmann's, sales growth averaged 7 percent per year over six years, which culminated in a market share of nearly 50 percent. Consumer belief that Hellmann's contained real and simple ingredients doubled to include nearly 50 percent of the population. As this indicates, good objectives are measurable, and they specify a method and criteria for determining how well the promotional program is working. Most organizations are concerned about the return on promotional investment; comparing actual effects against measurable objectives determines whether the return justifies the expense. With the explosion of digital communication in marketing, established procedures for measuring its effects are still undergoing development. Marketers are still trying to estimate the most appropriate methods and are not fully tracking all digital communication in comparison to established media.[2]

MARKETING OBJECTIVES

Marketing objectives are generally outlined in the firm's marketing plan and are statements of what is to be accomplished by the overall marketing program within a given time period. Marketing objectives are usually defined in terms of specific, measurable outcomes such as sales volume, market share, profit, or return on investment. Good marketing objectives are "smart" as they specifically delineate a target market, provide quantifiable measures, identify achievable and realistic levels of performance, and note the time frame for accomplishing the goal (often one year). For example, a copy-machine company may have as its marketing objective "to increase sales by 10 percent in the small-business segment of the market during the next 12 months."

The selection of the type of marketing objective is a function of market conditions. A company with a high market share may seek to increase its sales volume by stimulating growth in the product category, perhaps by increasing consumption by current users or encouraging non-users to buy the product. A firm in a fast-growing market may have market share as its marketing objective since this reflects that it is growing more quickly than its direct competitors. In mature markets with limited growth, firms tend to focus on profit as the key marketing objective. Finally, a firm that faces unique consumer preferences across various geographic markets (e.g., Ontario versus Quebec) may in fact have a unique marketing objective for each region. The marketing objective guiding the ad in **Exhibit 5-2** may be to increase sales volume since the message attempts to sway consumers to buy while participating in the contest.

Upon reviewing the marketing plan, the promotional planner should understand the marketing objectives, the marketing strategy and tactics, and the importance and purpose of advertising and promotion. Marketing objectives defined in terms of sales, profit, or market share increases are usually not appropriate promotional objectives, however promotional planners may rely on marketing objectives for guiding the content and direction of the marketing communication objectives. Marketing objectives are for the entire marketing program, and achieving them depends on the proper coordination and execution of *all* marketing mix elements, not just promotion. Alternatively, promotional planners usually approach promotion from a communication perspective, where the purpose of advertising and other promotional mix elements is to communicate information or a selling message. **IMC Perspective 5-1** describes the situation facing Mark's where it tries to maximize sales across different target audiences, each with specific communication objectives.

Exhibit 5-2 Guylian Belgian Chocolate encourages consumers to visit its website for the contest with an ultimate goal of increasing sales.

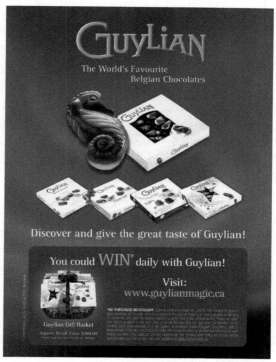

©Guylian

IMC PERSPECTIVE 5-1

MARK'S MAKES ITS ADVERTISING WORK

Mark's was established as Mark's Work Wearhouse in the late 1970s by Mark Blumes to serve the clothing needs of hard-working blue-collar men. Over the past 40 years, a number of changes occurred, including expanding nationwide to 380 stores; starting in-house brands Denver Hayes and Wind River in the early 1990s; selling women's clothing in 1995 but not actively marketing

[Continued on next page]

[IMC Perspective 5-1 continued]

this product line until years later; being sold to Canadian Tire in 2001; shortening the brand name to Mark's in 2010; and expanding its appeal to many audiences thereafter.

Over the past 20 years, the company used various slogans—"Clothes that work," Smart clothes. "Everyday living," and "Ready for this." However, managers sensed that the brand had drifted from the origin of hard-working individuals in its messaging while the store merchandise expanded to include work clothes along with casual clothes and sports clothes (e.g., Columbia).

The campaign launched to resolve this problem reclaimed its historic image and featured a new slogan—"Well worn"—to signify the strength of character of its customers, the style of the work clothes, and the durability of the work clothes. The imagery of the messages conveyed the emotional satisfaction of working hard in physically demanding jobs to alter consumers' views of the retailer. Managers hoped the new message would remain strong with its loyal customers (who typically skewed older), and resonate with younger potential consumers who felt indifferent to the brand.

Delivery of the message occurred on TV, digital video, and out-of-home media. Promotions included pop-up shops in three cities and endorsement from

©Mark's Work Wearhouse

country music star Brett Kissel. Commenting on the initiative, one Mark's executive summed it up well: "We want to talk to the hard-working Canadians who are confident, take pride in their work, value their family, and live life to the fullest through this campaign." Results appeared quite good as Mark's grew sales by 3 percent due to positive communication reactions to the campaign, commentary from social influencers, and publicity from print, radio, and TV.

Question:

1. Why would Mark's focus on the work clothes in its ads when it sells both work clothes and casual clothes?

SALES OBJECTIVE DEBATE

Some managers believe that the only meaningful objective for their promotional program is sales, since the reason why a firm spends money on advertising and promotion is to sell its good or service. Promotional spending represents an investment of a firm's resources that requires an economic justification like any other business decision. Managers generally compare investment options on a common financial basis, such as return on investment (ROI). Their position is that promotional expenditures should produce measurable results, such as increasing sales or the brand's market share, to assess the effectiveness of the investment decision.

One problem with a sales objective for promotion is that poor sales results can be due to other marketing mix variables, including product design or quality, packaging, distribution, or pricing. Advertising can make consumers aware of and interested in the brand, but it can't make them buy it, particularly if it is not readily available or is priced higher than a competing brand. Furthermore, unanticipated or uncontrollable environmental factors can devastate a firm's sales forecast even with a well communicated promotion program.

Another problem with a sales objective is that the effects of advertising occur over an extended period. Advertising has a lagged or **carryover effect**; monies spent on advertising do not necessarily have an immediate impact on sales.[3] Advertising may create awareness, interest, and/or favourable attitudes toward a brand, but these feelings will not result in an actual purchase until the consumer enters the market later. A review of econometric studies that examined the duration of cumulative advertising effects found that for mature, frequently purchased, low-priced products, advertising's effect on sales lasts up to nine months.[4] Models have been developed to account for the carryover effect of advertising and to help determine the long-term effect of advertising on sales.[5]

The counterargument is that a sales objective is appropriate when these two factors are not relevant. If a marketer is certain that other marketing or environmental factors were not influencing sales and that the carryover effect was not occurring, then a sales objective could be plausible. In general, the likelihood of such conditions arising appears quite remote, which necessitates the use of behavioural and communication objectives as the primary approach for promotional planning purposes.

BEHAVIOURAL OBJECTIVES

When a firm sets a brand's sales growth objective (e.g., increase sales by 10 percent), the increased sales can arise from a greater number of purchases from current customers (e.g., brand loyals). Alternatively, higher sales can be gained from new customers who are currently not buying within the product category (i.e., new category users), or those currently buying within the product category but not the firm's brand (e.g., other brand switchers). In all cases, achieving the sales growth is possible; however, the expected behaviour is fundamentally different. In the first case, the sales growth is due to a difference in the repurchase behaviour of current customers. In the latter two cases, the sales growth is due to trial behaviour by non-customers. **Figure 5-1** shows examples of how marketing objectives are attained through variations in the target audience and type of behaviour expected. We will define the behavioural objectives more exactly in a later section. Certainly, other opportunities are made possible by applying the concepts depending upon conclusions from a situation analysis.

Figure 5-1 Marketing objectives, audience, and behaviour

Marketing Objective	Target Audience	Behavioural Objective
Sales volume	New category users	Category and brand trial
Market share	Other brand switchers	Brand trial (switching)
Profit	Brand loyals	Repeat purchase (amount)
Return on investment	Favourable brand switchers	Repeat purchase (rate)

The distinction between repeat purchase versus trial purchase behaviour is critical as it provides direction for the communication objectives, which subsequently provide guidance for message development. For example, increasing the repeat purchasing rate of brand loyals might involve a message reminding these customers of the previous enjoyable consumption experiences, while a message to encourage trial from other brand switchers might require a comparative message to these non-customers showing the benefits of the competing brands. In these cases, the communication objectives are substantially different and are entirely derived from the target audience and the behavioural objective. The ad in **Exhibit 5-3** is likely directed to consumers who have not used a mouthwash previously.

COMMUNICATION OBJECTIVES

Communication objectives are statements of what the marketing communication will accomplish, and are usually based on a consumer response model discussed in Chapter 4. Each of these models identified communication effects a consumer receives from a brand message. Any of these effects are the basis for establishing communication objectives.

For example, brand awareness is an effect that most promotional planners would like to achieve, and they would probably establish a brand awareness objective on three levels. First, an individual print ad is expected

Exhibit 5-3 This ad encourages a trial purchase with its funny message.

Source: J. Walter Thompson Sydney Advertising Agency

Exhibit 5-4 The Mercedes-Benz ad attempts to influence non–hybrid users to consider this technology and brand.

Source: Mercedes-Benz USA

to increase the brand awareness, and the promotional planner will design the message and its presentation so the target audience will recall or recognize the brand when shopping. Second, a specific IMC tool is expected to strengthen brand awareness, and the promotional planner will select one (e.g., event sponsorship) to raise the profile of the brand to those in the target audience. Third and finally, all of the IMC tools within the overall IMC plan should contribute to improving brand awareness. In short, communication objectives are set for each of these aspects of promotional planning: an individual element of an IMC tool, an IMC tool, and the overall IMC plan.

The Mercedes-Benz ad shown in **Exhibit 5-4** illustrates these three considerations with respect to attitudinal communication objectives. An ad for this vehicle would attempt to persuade non-users of hybrid vehicles of its fuel efficiency while reinforcing that it does not compromise on regular vehicle performance. From an advertising campaign standpoint, the communication objective would be to ensure that an overall positive belief was established so that the target audience would visit the website or dealership. Finally, the IMC plan has other IMC tools with the objective of allowing consumers to believe that this brand could fulfill all needs (safety, economy, and performance).

Regardless of whether the communication objectives are for the IMC plan, a particular tool, or a specific ad, objectives should be based on the particular communication tasks required to deliver the appropriate messages to the specific target audience at a relevant point within the target audience's purchase decision-making process and consumption experience.

The promotional planner should see how integrated marketing communication fits into the marketing program and what the firm hopes to achieve through advertising and other promotional elements by reviewing the marketing plan. Managers must be able to translate a general marketing objective into a particular behavioural objective and specific communication objectives.

The importance of setting communication objectives for a promotional plan is seen in Canadian Tire's IMC plan. The ads associated with the Olympic sponsorship, "We All Play for Canada," inspired Canadians as the campaign achieved 55 million media impressions. Advertising tracking measures improved in 2014 over 2013 in terms of prompted recall, brand effects, and message communication. Extensions of the "We All Play for Canada" message included exposure with other sports and a connection to Canadian Tire's Jumpstart program. An important feature of Jumpstart included the "Big Play" where children received tickets to a Team Canada game during the World Junior Championship. With heightened media exposure, awareness reached 95 percent and significant social media activity helped the charity to raise nearly $50,000.[6]

From Communication Response Models to Communication Objectives

LO2

Numerous methods to set communication objectives for advertising, related IMC tools, and complete IMC plans exist. This section describes the DAGMAR model, which established the need for setting advertising objectives based on the communication tasks that advertising would be expected to achieve. Next, this section applies the DAGMAR method to the hierarchy of effects model and the information processing model of Chapter 4 to understand how to set communication objectives.

DEFINING ADVERTISING GOALS FOR MEASURED RESULTS

DAGMAR is the short form for Defining Advertising Goals for Measured Advertising Results, and it is the first model to conclude that communication effects are the logical basis for advertising goals and objectives against which success or failure should be measured.[7] Under this approach, an advertising goal involves a communication task that is specific, measurable, attainable, realistic, and within a time frame. A **communication task**, as opposed to a marketing task, is performed by and attributed to advertising decisions rather than marketing decisions. The communication task should be based on a response model shown in Chapter 4 that outlines specific communication effects. Finally, DAGMAR established the content of a good objective: specify a target audience, state measurable communication tasks, indicate a benchmark starting point, establish the degree of change sought, and identify a time period for accomplishing the objective(s).

Target Audience A well defined target audience may be based on behavioural variables such as customer status (e.g., brand loyal users), usage rate, or benefits sought, as well as descriptive variables such as geography, demographics, and psychographics (on which advertising media selection decisions are based). This step is critical since the communication effect has to be interpreted from the perspective of the intended receiver, as discussed in Chapter 4.

Measurable Tasks The communication task specified in the objective should be a precise statement of what message the advertiser wants to communicate to the target audience. During the planning process, advertisers generally produce a document to describe their basic message that should be specific and clear enough to guide the creative specialists who develop the advertising message. The objective must be measurable to determine whether the intended message has been communicated properly. Other tasks beyond designing a message to influence attitudes are also required, as noted in Chapter 4.

Benchmark To set objectives, one must know the target audience's present level of the response variables (e.g., awareness) with **benchmark measures**, often obtained from a marketing research study. Establishing benchmark measures gives the promotional planner a basis for determining what communication tasks need to be accomplished and for specifying particular objectives. For example, a preliminary study for a brand may reveal that awareness is high but consumer attitudes are negative. The objective for the advertising campaign must then be to change the target audience's attitude toward the brand. In this situation, the promotional planners will likely need to measure existing consumer attitudes with a survey. **Exhibit 5-5** shows an ad for Herbal Essences that is probably attempting to establish a positive attitude toward the brand's new Hydralicious formulation.

Degree of Change Sought Quantitative benchmarks for communications goals and objectives are essential for determining campaign success, as they provide the standard against which the success or failure of a campaign is measured. Advertising planners then determine the degree to which consumers must be changed by the advertising campaign. For example, an ad campaign that projects a 60 percent awareness level for a brand among its target audience from a current 40 percent pre-campaign awareness level indicates a 20 percent improvement from the benchmark.

Exhibit 5-5 A new Herbal Essences shampoo colourfully informs consumers of its moisturizing feature.

©Herbal Essences, Procter & Gamble

Specified Time Period Advertising objectives specify the time period in which they must be accomplished. Appropriate time periods can range from a few days to a year or more. Most ad campaigns specify time periods from a few months to a year, depending on the situation facing the advertiser and the type of response being sought. For example, awareness levels for a brand are created or increased fairly quickly through an intensive media schedule of widespread, repetitive advertising to the target audience. Altering consumers' attitude toward a brand conceivably takes more time for most brands in many product categories.

COMMUNICATION RESPONSE MODEL APPLICATIONS

In developing the response models, their authors suggested how the models could be adopted for setting communication objectives. We present an application of the hierarchy of effects model (Chapter 4) due to its wide use for analyzing the communication response and setting communication objectives. We also present an application of the information processing model (Chapter 4) for measuring

Exhibit 5-6 This cool Vans ad has liking as its communication objective.

Source: Vans, A VF Company

communication effects to illustrate the importance of research in the communication process. Although the previous chapter identified limitations of these hierarchy response models, they are still used in practice and an application is warranted if planners prefer these over the R&P model.

Hierarchy of Effects Model **Figure 5-2** shows the steps in the hierarchy of effects model in the far left column. Consumers are not expected to buy immediately as they proceed through the steps; instead, advertisers provide relevant information and create positive predispositions toward the brand before trial or repurchase behaviour occurs. Figure 5-2 lists examples of relevant messages and types of IMC tools that may be effective for each step. Promotional planners select the right tools for their brand depending on factors uncovered in the situation analysis. For example, **Exhibit 5-6** shows a print ad designed to enhance a strong liking for the Vans brand.

Setting communication objectives with this model is like building a pyramid over time by first accomplishing lower-level objectives, such as awareness and knowledge. Subsequent tasks involve moving consumers who are aware of or knowledgeable about the product to higher levels in the pyramid (**Figure 5-3**). The percentages of prospective customers decline at each pyramid level, indicating that the communication effect did not take hold. For instance, after knowledge hit 70 percent, only 40 percent liked the brand, meaning that 30 percent did not like the brand. An example by American Express shows how to handle this in practice. The brand placed a video message in social media associated with influencers who revealed their passion for travel to build initial consumer awareness. Subsequent video associated with different influencers directly claimed benefits of using the Amex credit card to build the target audience's knowledge. Those watching the second video to completion received messages to drive the receiver to actual sign-up.[8] Note that the percentages in Figure 5-3 are illustrative examples; a tracking study of actual data, proxies based on internal records of customer interactions, or research from a syndicated supplier like Nielsen would be required by a promotional planner.

Figure 5-2 Application of the hierarchy of effects model

Response Stages	Examples of Relevant Messages	Examples of Relevant IMC Tools
Purchase	Value or minimize perceived risk copy	Point-of-purchase display
	Importance of buying now copy	Sales promotion incentive, loyalty program
Conviction	Closing copy	Take-away brochure
	Recapitulate all previous copy	Specialized digital app
Preference	Comparative or argumentative copy	Word-of-mouth communication
	Popularity appeal	Social networking brand fan (e.g., Facebook)
Liking	Imagery copy	Visually appealing media like video or print
	Positive emotional appeals	Blog, radio jingle
Knowledge	Long copy to fully understand offering	Brand's website
	Demonstration copy	Content community (e.g., YouTube)
Awareness	Copy to ensure consumers remember brand	Mass media and digital advertising
	Brand identity imagery such as logo or jingle	Event marketing or sponsorship

The communication effects pyramid guides promotional objective setting. The promotional planner determines where the target audience lies concerning the levels in the pyramid. If brand awareness and knowledge of its features and benefits are low, the communication objective should be to increase them. If these levels of the pyramid are already in place, but liking or preference is low, the advertising goal may be to change the target audience's image of the brand. As the illustrative numbers indicate, the campaign could focus on "liking" since there is a substantial drop in the number of consumers at this level from the previous level. Also, the drop-off from trial to repeat purchase suggests the marketing communication need to focus on continued buying. The varying levels of objectives could be due to factors such as behaviour (e.g., brand loyalty segmentation) or regional differences (e.g., geographic segmentation).

Figure 5-3 Communication effects pyramid

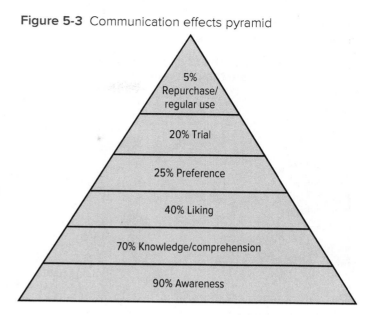

Information Processing Model The information processing model may be an effective framework for setting objectives and evaluating the effects of a promotional campaign. **Figure 5-4** shows the steps of the model from exposure/presentation to purchase behaviour. For example, preliminary research might suggest to promotional planners that the target audience comprehends existing aspects of the brand, but does not accept a newer brand message. Thus, an objective of the marketing communication could be to enhance acceptance.

Also shown in Figure 5-4 are examples of research performed at each step to assess whether the communication effects occurred as planned. This provides the advertiser with data and information regarding the effectiveness of

Figure 5-4 Methods of measuring feedback in the response process

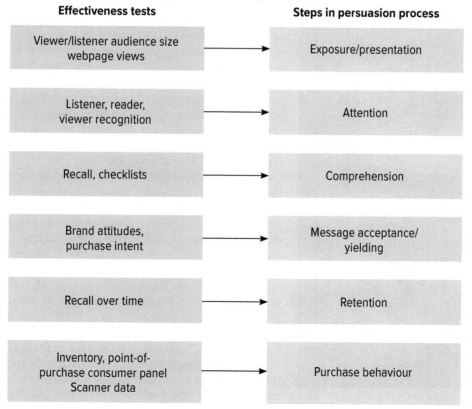

©Fontaine Santé

promotional strategies and tactics designed for each stage of the response process. For example, D'Italiano bread's "Live Large" campaign included a YouTube desktop home-page takeover that featured a livestream of two Italian tenors who took requests from visitors. The exposure measures to assess effectiveness amounted to 23,000 hours of viewing, more than the brand's previous 11 years combined.[9]

Further coverage of the research methods is provided in Chapter 9 to give a general direction for advertising. This understanding is then extended to measuring the effectiveness of individual IMC tools in their respective chapters later in the book. For example, investigating message acceptance is an important criterion for all aspects of marketing communication in which general approaches are applied. However, each media and IMC tool is unique and requires specific investigation. The ad in **Exhibit 5-7** would have multiple measures of effectiveness, such as the number of website visits that occurred in the few weeks following exposure; consumer beliefs regarding attributes of Canadian-made, 100 percent natural, and non-GMO; and the taste benefit claimed.

Application Conclusion Decades of research revealed mixed results when promotional planners applied the communication response model to set communication objectives. One study showed that most advertising agencies did not state appropriate objectives for determining advertising success.[10] A later study found that most advertisers did not set concrete advertising objectives, specify objective tasks, measure results in terms of stages of a hierarchy of effects, or match objectives to evaluation measures.[11] Finally, another later study measured the attitudes of executives, with the majority saying they did not know whether their advertising was working and fewer than 10 percent saying they thought it was working well.[12]

©Raine Vara/Alamy Stock Photo

Clearly, the evidence suggests that an alternative perspective with a stronger managerial point of view is warranted for enhanced adoption. We suggest the Rossiter and Percy (R&P) perspective as a worthy candidate that promotional planners should consider when setting behavioural and communication objectives.[13] We introduced their ideas in Chapter 3 when discussing the guidelines for target audience identification, selection, and profiling, and in Chapter 4 when summarizing communication response models. We include the R&P perspective since it attempts to resolve the limitations of other approaches for objective setting and provides guidelines for creative tactics (i.e., Chapter 8).

The R&P perspective has three distinguishing characteristics. First, it provides guidelines for specific behavioural objectives. The models say something general, like *purchase* or *behaviour*, but promotional planners need to consider *particular kinds* of behaviour and purchases to make a connection to the marketing objectives. Second, it is consistent with the DAGMAR model by making a direct connection between the purchase decision and the communication task required for each target audience. Third, it provides guidelines for communication objectives that are more useful for a manager and the objectives do not rely on a set hierarchy of effects. For example, the Expedia ad in **Exhibit 5-8** targets travellers who are likely at the need recognition stage of their decision making. The ad encourages the target audience to visit the Internet site, thus suggesting a trial purchase of consumers who have not booked travel online or who book with other Internet travel booking sites.

LO3 Setting Behavioural Objectives for IMC

A clear behavioural objective for each target audience needs to be identified, since the individual purchasing behaviours of each customer add up to a firm's overall sales. As suggested earlier, the link between marketing objectives (i.e., sales) and communication objectives (i.e., attitude toward the brand) is behavioural objectives. Advertising and promotion can focus on influencing a particular form of behaviour based on the nature of the advertising message or IMC tool used. We evaluate four options a manager has for setting behavioural objectives: trial purchase, repeat purchase, shopping, and repeat consumption.

TRIAL PURCHASE OBJECTIVES

A trial purchase occurs when a consumer buys a brand not bought by them before. A trial purchase objective is relevant for non-customer groups such as new category users, other brand switchers, and other brand loyals. A trial purchase objective pertaining to the target audience of a promotional planner's brand is contingent upon time, competition, and product category. To account for these three variables, we review four trial objectives: brand trial, brand re-trial, category trial, and brand switching.

Brand Trial A **brand trial purchase** is defined as a consumer's first purchase of a brand. For example, the trial purchase for brands of most everyday products (e.g., soft drinks or snack foods) occurred years ago for most consumers, and it is probably difficult to remember one's first soft drink purchase or the specific brand. However, producers of everyday products like soft drinks continue to have a **brand trial objective** as consumers enter the market when they attain a certain age or have income (i.e., allowance from parents). Generalizing this point, brand managers within all established product categories consider when a substantially large enough group of consumers may enter their market and the manager makes a brand trial objective a priority in the IMC plan. And while brand trial purchases are important for most firms throughout the year to generate sales, they are not necessarily the primary behavioural objective for all campaigns or all communication tools. Naturally, a brand trial objective is paramount for a product launch as there are no consumers buying yet, but a brand trial objective may also be necessary for brand extensions. The message in the Smart car ad in **Exhibit 5-9** suggests that brand trial is a primary objective since it highlights that the electric car does not burn gas. It reassures drivers of gasoline-powered cars that the Smart car is not deficient on speed for city driving.

The variety of campaigns by Boston Pizza suggests that the restaurant looked to build trial. One initiative, "Finger Cooking With Bill," targeted dads who preferred not to cook and emphasized Boston Pizza's online ordering for take-out and delivery. The campaign provided a category-unique message compared to other brands that targeted women, moms, and families. Boston Pizza then launched the "Flatties and Drummies" campaign with a fictional chicken wing critic, Carl Carlson, who humorously and eloquently spoke of Boston Pizza's quality wings. The TV ads, combined with extensive social and Xbox media and promotional items, propelled the brand to win the fictitious Crystal Wingy Award for Best New Wing, much to the chagrin of fooled competitors who wondered why they did not win! The brand changed direction after these fun messages with "We'll Make You a Fan," which associated Boston Pizza to sports and families with images of children, women, and men playing sports and watching sports in the Boston Pizza locations. Citing statistics of high participation levels of children and adults playing sports, the brand looked to a new advertising avenue to build on its professional sports sponsorship of NHL teams and the Toronto Blue Jays.[14]

Exhibit 5-9 Smart strives for a consumer trial purchase of its electric car.

Burn nothing but rubber.

smart

>> Surprisingly quick in the city.

[Dealer Name] [Dealer Address] [Dealer Site]

©Mercedes-Benz Canada

Brand Re-Trial Alternatively, it is quite unlikely that consumers will continue to purchase the same brand of soft drink as their first trial purchase. In fact, people consume more than one brand of soft drink, and for whatever reason stop purchasing their initial brand. Brand managers are faced with this dilemma of trying to

Exhibit 5-10 Coca-Cola desires brand re-trial from lapsed users who gravitated to other soft drinks for a while.

Share a **Coke** with...

Source: The Coca-Cola Company

recapture past customers who have not purchased the brand for a period of time (e.g., perhaps a year). The manager of such a brand would like these past customers to have a new trial experience of the brand. Thus, a **brand re-trial purchase** is defined as a consumer's first purchase of a brand after a time delay. The length of the delay to focus on when setting a **brand re-trial objective** is a decision the promotion manager makes. It depends upon the purchase frequency of the product, among other factors observed from the situation analysis. Brands like Coca-Cola constantly have a brand re-trial objective. The ad in **Exhibit 5-10** shows the promotion that featured people's names on the cans, which likely enticed lapsed consumers who saw their name.

Category Trial Now let's put the trial purchase in another perspective: consider the purchase of a smart phone, which most young adults currently own. The smart phone is a different kind of product and likely a somewhat involved purchase for most consumers. Despite this, phone companies and service providers had trial objectives as they attempted to attract consumers who did not own such technology. While this is obviously a brand trial purchase, it is also something broader. A **category trial purchase** is defined as a consumer's first purchase in a product category that the consumer has not purchased in previously. The ad in **Exhibit 5-11** follows this idea as it attracts users of non-dandruff shampoo to try Head & Shoulders. Marketers of new products, such as the smart phone, have a dual challenge of attaining both a **category trial objective** and brand trial objective. Of course, with significant smart phone adoption levels, a category trial objective is less relevant for marketers, but remains so with market segments with less adoption, such as older consumers perhaps.

Category trial is necessary in mature categories when consumers switch out. For example, bread consumption declined and industry partners addressed bread myths and misconceptions head on. A scientific advisory council was formed and communicates facts promoting the health benefits of bread. The non-profit group meets with dietitians and nutritionists and encourages them (using its science-backed research) to build wheat- and grain-based foods into their clients' meal plans. It has an educational website with healthy recipes and nutritional comparison charts and a social media presence. And now it's looking for funding to go direct to consumers with mass marketing.[15]

Exhibit 5-11 Head & Shoulders wants non-dandruff shampoo users to consider using the product.

there's a very surprising secret to gorgeous hair

©The Advertising Archives/Alamy Stock Photo

Brand Switching A manager may plan for a brand trial or brand re-trial objective when consumers are purchasing another brand. A **brand-switching purchase** is defined as a consumer's purchase toward a brand from another competing brand. A brand-switching purchase occurs whereby the consumer makes a re-trial purchase of a brand and leaves the new favourite and returns to an old favourite. A brand-switching purchase also occurs when the consumer makes a trial purchase of a brand from a competing brand. Thus, a brand trial or brand re-trial objective is more specifically a **brand-switching objective** in certain planning situations.

Pepsi returned to its classic approach to switch Coca-Cola drinkers with its Taste Challenge, a taste test for consumers to demonstrate the brand they prefer while not knowing which brand is which. With a global 10 percent market share versus Coca-Cola's 25 percent, the popular idea launched nearly 40 years ago appeared as a viable alternative to stem the tide, and also keep sales afloat as soft drink consumption declined 18 percent from 2006 to 2010.[16] The S. Pellegrino ad in **Exhibit 5-12** urges current bottled water users to consider a better-tasting alternative.

REPEAT-PURCHASE OBJECTIVES

In the age of relationship marketing and a focus on customer retention, this form of purchase behaviour is critical. A **repeat purchase** is defined as a consumer's continued purchase of a brand within a specified time period. The time factor for a **repeat-purchase objective** is at the discretion of the marketer, and it is contingent upon purchase frequency of the product or other factors derived from the situation analysis. Repeat-purchase objectives are set for loyal customers and those that switch between a brand and its competitors. A repeat-purchase objective pertaining to the target audience of a promotional planner's brand is contingent upon frequency (how often to purchase), amount (how much to purchase), and timing (when to purchase).

Purchase Frequency The first alternative concerns the rate, or how often to purchase the brand. This implies that a marketer may set an objective pertaining to consumers purchasing its brand every week instead of every two weeks. This example shows an option where a manager may want to *increase* the rate of purchase from a half product per week to one product per week. A second managerial option is to *maintain* the rate of purchase. While this is a more conservative objective, it is still a viable option in competitive environments. Finally, a manager may want to *decrease* the rate of purchase. This option may be viable in unique situations of high demand or with products that have potentially negative consequences (i.e., alcohol).

Cineplex's loyalty program—Scene Card—lets enrolled members obtain points for movie ticket purchases that are redeemed for movies or snacks. This program provides managers with an extensive database allowing them to target messages to guide repeat patronage. For example, it can email members with reminders to see an upcoming movie to achieve a purchase frequency objective.[17]

Purchase Amount The amount or how much to purchase on each occasion is the second alternative. As this alternative implies, a marketer may set an objective where consumers purchase two products per occasion versus one per occasion. As above, this option is to *increase* the amount per occasion, but a marketer could still evaluate whether to *maintain* or *decrease* the amount per occasion. The McDonald's ad in **Exhibit 5-13** encourages consumers to purchase multiple food products throughout the day. The extension makes the billboard act as a sundial showing when a consumer could consume each food type.

Brands also have a repeat-purchase objective for customers who habitually consume multiple brands continually (i.e., favourable brand switchers). For instance, across 15 purchases a consumer might buy five from three brands evenly. While this consumer does not purchase a manager's brand for every single occasion, the consumer is a consistent contributor to the firm's sales and a marketer would want to promote appropriately to ensure future repeat purchases. In this case, the brand's manager might offer a sales promotion to encourage a greater amount bought such that the total purchases would grow from five of 15 to perhaps seven of 15.

Purchase Timing The final alternative is the timing, or when to purchase. Certain products are seasonal, have a peak in their sales, or are easily stored. Marketers may have a behavioural objective to influence when consumers

Exhibit 5-12 S. Pellegrino tries to switch over users of other bottled water brands.

S.PELLEGRINO® is a registered trademark of Sanpellegrino S.p.A., Milano, Italy

Exhibit 5-13 McDonald's reminds consumers to purchase multiple food products.

©McGraw-Hill Education/Christopher Kerrigan

will make the purchase. For example, Wendy's restaurant advertises on television in the evening and communicates the fact that its drive-through service stays open late, thus prompting consumers to purchase at a certain time of day. Consistent with the other two alternatives, we can conceive three options: *maintain, accelerate,* and *delay.*

As another example, retailers attempt to influence all three repeat-purchase behaviours while consumers are shopping. Best Buy has an in-store app that provides deeper and richer information than what is found online that consumers obtain prior to the shopping stage. Indigo recommends books to its Plum Rewards members via email and online ads customized for communication when a membership card is swiped at the in-store kiosk. Digital in-store media networks offer specific and detailed video messages when consumers are browsing a product category, much more involved than what is found on 30-second television ads.[18]

SHOPPING OBJECTIVES

Communication is designed to encourage a consumer to progress through the decision-making process more smoothly. For example, most people find it imperative to visit a car dealership prior to buying a car. So the focus of parts of an IMC plan is to have consumers take action that will lead them one step closer to the final destination of a purchase. **Shopping behaviour** is an action consumers take that will lead to a higher probability of purchasing the brand. Many types of shopping behaviour exist, but in general most concern the consumer seeking information (e.g., visiting a website) about the brand or an experience with the brand (e.g., participating in an event, watching a demonstration, consuming a sample).

In Canadian Tire stores, in-aisle devices allow consumers to see its digital catalogue for enhanced shopping. Similarly, Sport Chek innovated with a new digital retail concept with 140 screens, digital tiles built into display tables, tablets attached to clothing racks, and digital displays showing video and still messages. Sport Chek suppliers like Reebok installed customized shoe kiosks that allowed consumers to design their own shoe to be shipped weeks later. CTC saw Sport Chek's innovations as leading the way for similar changes for Canadian Tire retail.[19]

Digital equivalents are prominent as brands encourage website visits, interaction with other customers on Facebook, participation in Twitter, and viewing or posting of video or pictures in content communities. Accordingly, marketers can have many shopping behaviour objectives to know whether enough of the target audience is involved with the brand during the decision-making process. Firms can track the number of sales inquiries, requests for samples, or demonstrations to gauge how well the campaign is performing for the objective. They also can track the digital exposure and participation levels as all the interaction is electronically recorded. The ad in **Exhibit 5-14** directs readers to phone or visit the website for White Oaks Resort and Spa.

Exhibit 5-14 White Oaks directs consumers to its website and provides a phone number.

©White Oaks Resort & Spa, photographer: Jason Dwyer

Another aspect of shopping behaviour is that consumers seek out the opinion of their friends and family, as discussed in the word-of-mouth topic section in Chapter 4. Young people aged 18–24 communicate this way extensively, with virtually 100 percent telling up to four of their friends when they have a positive brand experience.[20] Thus, brands look to achieve specific word-of-mouth objectives as part of their plans, which guides the use of experiential marketing communication or more innovative and exciting digital activities.

REPEAT-CONSUMPTION OBJECTIVES

Thus far we have considered repeat purchase as a behavioural objective. Related to this is repeat consumption as a behavioural objective. **Repeat consumption** is defined as the continued consumption of the brand once purchased. Marketers may have a **repeat-consumption objective** when communicating with their current customers who have previously purchased the brand and have the product at their home or work. This communication has an objective of modifying how often to consume the brand, how much to consume on each occasion, and when to consume.

To give an idea of a repeat-consumption objective in action, we will cite two common approaches. Often, food and drink products advertise through certain television commercials showing consumption visuals that may prompt consumers to snack or have another beverage. For example, dairy industry messages remind consumers to drink milk since it is in people's homes on a regular basis. Also, research suggests that, for these kinds of product categories that have a well established market leader, a consumption intention is a better predictor of advertising success since goods are already in stock and a repeat purchase will not occur until the inventory is depleted.[21] Another approach is to show consumers how to enjoy the product for other uses, or in new or alternative situations. The California almonds ad in **Exhibit 5-15** reinforces continued consumption by showing that the product can provide sustained energy through any activity.

To conclude this section, the types of purchase and consumption behaviour that firms try to influence are varied. A firm with multiple target audiences will quite likely specify the type of behaviour associated with each target audience so that it can develop the most appropriate message and select the most relevant IMC tool. Managers making these subsequent decisions rely on setting clear communication objectives, the topic of the next section. **IMC Perspective 5-2** summarizes a Tourisme Montréal campaign to entice people from Quebec City to visit Montreal. Given the tone of the message, it seems that the agency set a re-trial behavioural objective and picked the right message with advertising.

Exhibit 5-15 California almonds are associated with a situational use to increase repeat consumption.

©Almond Board of California/Mark Katzman, photographer/Andrew Becker, director

IMC PERSPECTIVE 5-2

VISIT MONTREAL

How do you creatively ask your friends over for a visit when they live in another city, province, or country? For Tourisme Montréal, the answer is three simple phrases—"I'm sorry," "I've changed," and "Never grow up"—over the course of a few years.

In 2017, Montreal celebrated its 375th birthday as Canada rejoiced over its 150th birthday, and Tourisme Montréal's marketing communication messages contributed to many visiting the city. A video targeting Toronto showed three people from Montreal apologizing ("I'm sorry") in advance for all the noise that would come from the city as they partied. William Shatner, born and raised in Montreal, delivered a similar video message to people in New York City. Past messages typically communicated activities of particular seasons or emotional

©Tourisme Montréal

creatives to build the city's image, but this time the point focused on getting people to plan a visit knowing that a lot was going on in 2017.

After a busy year, many expected a decline in visitors, so Tourisme Montréal created the "I've

[Continued on next page]

changed" message for the people of Quebec City. This market appeared attractive as it is an easy drive that many would be receptive to taking in the winter of 2018. A direct mail piece sent to 100,000 households read like a letter to a former lover aimed at winning them back with references to Montreal attractions. The message picked up on the friendly rivalry between the cities. Billboards, TV, newspaper, and radio ads, and press kits to journalists fostered publicity and got Quebec City residents talking. The campaign obtained a 34 percent increase in website visits and 138 news stories, and actually improved hotel bookings.

For an encore, Tourisme Montréal switched its message to "Never grow up" to convey the enjoyment people experience no matter what their age. This worked for attracting younger people from Ontario and older people from New York than typically visit. A video, "Fly Over Montréal," captured the spirit of this with footage of a young woman wearing wings and attached to a giant balloon, flying through the city above the Notre-Dame Basilica and other attractions.

Question:

1. How do these messages contribute to getting a trial or repeat visit to Montreal?

LO4 Setting Communication Objectives for IMC

Earlier in this chapter, we saw how communication response models help formulate communication objectives. The R&P approach is similar since it translates these researchers' perspective of communication effects into options for managers to set communication objectives. We review the options for each of the four communication objectives that promotional planners choose from to formulate their IMC plan, which also are applied to one target audience or multiple target audiences.

The options for communication objectives are applied for (1) a specific communication like one print ad or television commercial, (2) a specific campaign like advertising or sponsorship, and (3) a complete IMC program that includes all promotional tools. These communication objectives retain the characteristics set forth earlier for good objective setting (i.e., a specific benchmark with the degree of change sought for a communication task within a specified time period regarding a target audience). Finally, the R&P framework is flexible enough to apply all communication objectives to each stage of the buyer decision-making process for any target audience. We summarize the options for each communication objective.

Exhibit 5-16 The Apple smart watch is shown in a novel usage situation to suggest category need.

©Istvan Balogh/Shutterstock

CATEGORY NEED

Category need pertains to whether the target audience believes that purchasing within a specific product category will fulfill their particular consumer need. Smart phones are a product for which consumers are users or non-users, and phone brands built demand over time by convincing non-users (e.g., owners of a flip phone or no mobile phone) of the benefits of owning a smart phone versus not owning one. This type of message likely differed from the message used to convince a current smart phone user to switch to their brand with improved features. As an example of an ad with a category need objective, notice how the imagery of **Exhibit 5-16** communicates a situation in which the Apple watch would be very useful for consumers who had not considered a smart watch for active recreation previously.

Another type of category need occurs with substitute products, as seen with transportation, for example. When thinking about buying a "car" upon graduation, a student's choice may in fact be a truck or a sport utility vehicle (SUV). In a broad sense, all vehicles are used for transportation, but consumers have particular needs that are ideally satisfied with a specific category of vehicle. For example, a marketer for an SUV brand could communicate a message so that a target audience will feel the need for an SUV more strongly than the need for a sporty sub-compact, which might be the initial product category that young consumers would gravitate toward. In this case, it is a question of which specific yet related category fulfills the target audience's need more completely.

Category Need Is Reminded One obvious example of this is reminder advertising, where the brand is featured in the message and the need for the product is implicitly communicated or clearly illustrated. The reminder option of category need is the focus of campaigns for lapsed users. For example, associations that represent the dairy industry remind Canadians to consume milk and milk products like cheese. Ads typically use imagery of consumption like the photo in **Exhibit 5-17**.

Category Need Is Emphasized The smart phone and vehicle examples show situations where the IMC plan objective is to actively persuade the target audience to believe that a specific product category fulfills their particular consumer need. Emphasizing a category need objective is usually imperative with competing technologies and substitute products. However, market conditions discovered in a situation analysis can sway an established brand toward emphasizing category need in existing markets. With a trend toward healthier eating and drinking being seen, especially among young consumers, Coca-Cola faced declining sales for its pop products. One factor is young people not entering the pop category at all or consuming other beverages along with significant levels of water.[22] Thus, emphasizing category need may be an important step in the famous brand's future, which may explain the inspiration for the "Share a Coke" campaign where loyal drinkers took the message to heart and gave a personalized can to a non–pop drinker who loved seeing their name in the famous Coke font.

BRAND AWARENESS

Brand awareness is the target audience's ability to recognize and/or recall the brand within a specific product category in sufficient detail to make a purchase. Brand awareness is a universal communication objective, which means that every point of communication should contribute to the target audience's understanding and knowledge of the brand, such that the target audience knows the specific product category that the brand competes in when in a position to make a purchase.

There are two types of brand awareness: brand recognition and brand recall. If both are required for the target audience to make a purchase, then a manager plans for two awareness objectives. In setting the *brand awareness* objective, managers should be cognizant of the existing levels of *advertising awareness* for customers and non-customers as the level is typically higher for the former.[23] Further, brand awareness through recall is typically stronger for customers versus non-customers, suggesting that brand awareness is a significant communication task to achieve for non-customers.[24]

Brand Recognition Recognition of the brand at the point of purchase based on past messages is sufficient for brand consideration or purchase. The Corby ad in **Exhibit 5-18**

Exhibit 5-17 Cheese ads remind consumers to purchase by highlighting the textures and taste.

©baibaz/Shutterstock
©baibaz/Shutterstock

Exhibit 5-18 Brand recognition for Corby's product is enhanced in this creative ad.

Hand-out/Corby Spirit and Wine Communications/Newscom

Exhibit 5-19 Huawei establishes a clear brand attitude based on technological innovation.

©Torontonian/Alamy Stock Photo

shows an example where the brand name and logo is prominent, which likely heightens the brand recognition effect. Boldly displaying awards the spirits have won assists consumers in remembering the high quality of the product.

In executing Canadian Tire's IMC plan, management moved toward clear brand identification by focusing on one consistent triangle logo to improve brand recognition (after discovering that the company used over 70 variations). In another activity to support this objective, Canadian Tire retail produced over 30 television commercials, many with the same spokesperson, and identified the brand with a "Canada's store" slogan and consistent logo. The executions focused on families and how Canadian Tire's product fit within the needs of this target audience to associate the brand within the product category.[25]

Brand Recall If the target audience feels the need for a product but needs to remember what brands to consider away from the point of purchase, then recall becomes the focus of the campaign. Brand recall is referred to as unaided brand awareness when measuring. McCain's "It's All Good" campaign increased recall of its brand for its Superfries (from 6 percent to 45 percent) and pizza (from 6 percent to 37 percent).[26]

In defining brand awareness, we must be careful in distinguishing it from advertising awareness, which concerns itself with whether consumers are aware of a brand's television or print ads. While there is a logical connection between the two, they are not identical. For example, Activia established strong effects compared to industry norms with its "Vitality" message for unaided advertising recall (50 percent vs. 18 percent) and aided advertising recall (60 percent vs. 48 percent) levels.[27]

Shoppers Drug Mart's marketing communication tools, loyalty program, beauty magazine, advertising, and various sales promotions reinforce this objective since brand awareness sits at 98 percent. Recall is important, as consumers would decide at home where to shop when in need of personal care, beauty, or other products that the store offers. Of course, recognition is important when consumers are driving by the store and see familiar signage that prompts need recognition for shopping in the product categories offered. Thus, even when a brand attains a strong level of awareness, it continues its effort to retain its strong position—such that Shoppers extended its presence with celebratory zeal with its 50th anniversary communication.[28]

BRAND ATTITUDE

Brand attitude is another universal communication objective. Like brand awareness, every aspect of a firm's IMC program or any particular element, such as a television commercial, should contribute to the overall evaluation of the brand from the perspective of the target audience. A logical conclusion to this point is that there should be no such thing as an "awareness campaign," as every campaign should surely influence brand awareness and an aspect of brand attitude. Since brand attitude is such an important communication objective, prior understanding of the existing brand attitude is a critical guide for each brand attitude objective option.

Exhibit 5-20 Hyundai reminds consumers that its customers are satisfied with vehicle quality.

Source: Hyundai Motor America

Establish Brand Attitude A new target audience that has no awareness and therefore no prior attitude toward the brand generally requires extensive communication so that an attitude is created or established. Huawei is a late entrant to the smart phone market in Canada, and its outdoor ad in **Exhibit 5-19** appears to be establishing a favourable brand attitude based on its technological superiority by the reference to higher intelligence.

Maintain Brand Attitude Advertising is performed so that existing attitude levels will remain constant in order to ensure future sales. Stopping communication is one reason for declining sales that has been seen in examples over time. In contrast, major advertisers (e.g., Coca-Cola) consistently follow this approach to maintain sales. The Hyundai ad in **Exhibit 5-20** reinforces the existing positive attitude its customers would have regarding the quality of its vehicles.

Increase Brand Attitude Target audiences who are familiar with the brand and moderately favourable toward the brand can be influenced. For example, we can increase their brand attitude by getting the target audience to believe that the brand delivers better performance on a particular attribute or benefit. The majority of the consumers who see the Chatime in-store ad are consumers of the brand, and the ad in **Exhibit 5-21** potentially increases their existing favourable attitude by seeing new options to satisfy their variety seeking behaviour with a new taste sensation. The colourful surrounding imagery reinforces the existing belief that the brand offers refreshing beverages.

Modify Brand Attitude Similar to the previous option, if the target audience is moderately favourable, we still seek to improve their attitude. However, we modify the brand attitude if no increase is possible. In this option, marketers use a different point of reference in communicating the benefits. Typically, marketers focus on a new consumer motive for purchasing the brand that the target audience will be receptive toward. Mazda presents an interesting example since its sales are considerably lower than other Japanese brands. It is now pursuing a worldwide emphasis to put the brand in a premium niche, much like BMW did as it grew from humble origins during the 1970s.[29] Its future marketing communication could likely target users of other premium brands for them to switch, or target non-premium brand users to "trade up." In either case, innovative communication will be required to modify existing attitudes. The Coors Light ad in **Exhibit 5-22** attempts to influence attitudes in a new direction beyond its taste while retaining its historic mountain imagery.

Change Brand Attitude Negative or weak positive attitudes toward a brand are difficult to influence, but particular communication situations create the challenge of changing the brand attitude for a target audience. **Exhibit 5-23** highlights a message Samsung directed to those considering or shopping for an iPhone. Presumably, their attitude to Samsung was not strong, so the brand proposed a compelling reason of not lining up to buy an iPhone. With a more positive belief toward the Samsung brand compared to the iPhone, perhaps consumers might be motivated to alter their behaviour.

BRAND PURCHASE INTENTION

There are two fairly simple options for **brand purchase intention**.

Assume Brand Purchase Intention In situations (i.e., low involvement) where the strength of an intention to purchase is consistent (i.e., highly correlated) with brand attitude, a marketer is not required to include this objective.

Generate Brand Purchase Intention In contrast, managers need the target audience to have a plan to purchase a brand in situations of high involvement.

Exhibit 5-21 Chatime establishes the belief that it offers a wider variety of flavours.

©Chatime/CO-OP

Exhibit 5-22 Coors Light offers a new reason to enjoy its beer.

Source: 72andSunny and MillerCoors

Exhibit 5-23 Samsung's comparative ad tried to sway attitudes.

Source: Samsung

LO5 IMC Planning: Objectives for Buyer Decision Stages

In Chapter 3, we presented a model of consumer decision making that showed the stages typically experienced when making a purchase. We outlined several steps: need recognition, information search, alternative evaluation, purchase decision, and post-purchase evaluation. One important role of marketing communication is to guide the target audience through these stages. Marketers require specific communication tools and messages that will resonate with each target audience as they proceed through these stages. We assess this decision-making process for each target audience and make a conclusion as to which communication objectives are most relevant for each stage. **Figure 5-5** illustrates how this works.

Figure 5-5 Assessing the consumer decision-making process

Analysis and Conclusions	Need Recognition	Information Search	Alternative Evaluation	Purchase Decision	Post-Purchase Evaluation
Who? (roles)					
Where? (location)					
When? (time, timing)					
How? (shopping behaviour)					
What? (benefits)					
Why? (motivator)					
Behavioural objectives					
Communication objectives					
Message options					
Communication tool options					

The analysis occurs in the first six rows, where the marketer includes the target audience information and makes a conclusion on the key communication objectives that need to be attained so that the target audience will continue to the next stage. We have addressed these ideas already. The first question (Who?) looks at the key participants in the decision. We highlighted these roles in Chapter 3. The next three questions are descriptors of where, when, and how the shopping behaviour will occur. This is based on market research, managerial experience, flashes of inspiration, and assumptions. Promotional planners are very concerned with the final two points—what are consumers shopping for, and why?

After summarizing these questions, we determine the most relevant behavioural objectives. For example, we may wish to encourage phone inquiries at the information-search stage. Or perhaps we may desire Internet visits to compare brands at the alternative-evaluation stage. Next, we determine which communication objectives ensure that the consumer continues through all stages. For example, what aspect of brand attitude needs to be addressed at the need-recognition stage versus the alternative-evaluation stage? Is recall an awareness objective at the need-recognition stage, and recognition an awareness objective at the purchase-decision stage?

Once this assessment has been done, then the marketer can outline preliminary options concerning the types of messages and communication tools that would be most useful. Returning to the first question above, a marketer may decide to have a fun television commercial (e.g., communication tool option) that emphasizes the emotional attachment (e.g., brand attitude) to the product. It should be noted that, when identifying options, the marketer has not fully committed or recommended that this is exactly the plan, but rather has said that this is the template of analysis for making the final decision.

The rest of this book focuses on how to make IMC plan decisions that are based on the target audience, behaviour objectives, and communication objectives established at the start of the plan. Chapters 6 to 9 focus on the message, while Chapters 10 to 18 focus on the communication tools. As we noted at the start of this chapter, framework become the criteria for making all promotional decisions and measuring their results. Wh. not be able to afford comprehensive studies to assess communication effects, they would benefit from framework because it provides disciplined thinking before investing in promotion.

Learning Objectives Summary

 Distinguish among marketing, behavioural, and communication objectives and identify the value of setting each type of objective.

Objectives guide promotional program development and provide a benchmark against which performance can be measured and evaluated. Objectives serve a communication function for all participants in the planning process and direct all IMC program decision making. Objectives for IMC evolve from the organization's overall marketing plan and are based on the purpose of each promotional mix element within the marketing program. Managers use sales or a related measure such as market share as the basis for setting marketing objectives. Promotional planners believe that the communication role of promotional mix elements is not directly connected with sales-based objectives. They use communication-based objectives like those in the response hierarchy as the basis for setting goals. These models suggest the importance of setting specific behavioural objectives (such as trial or repeat purchase) and appropriate communication objectives to direct the IMC strategy so that it contributes to the attainment of marketing objectives.

 Describe the historical approaches for setting communication objectives for advertising.

Historically, in setting objectives, traditional advertising-based views of marketing communication were emphasized. This originated from an application of response models like DAGMAR and the hierarchy of effects. DAGMAR established the principle that objectives should: specify a target audience; state measurable communication tasks; indicate a benchmark starting point; establish the degree of change sought; and specify a time period for accomplishing the objectives. As an extension of this idea, the principles of the hierarchy of effects model, used in setting advertising objectives, could be applied to other elements in the promotional mix. The hierarchy of effects model suggested that unique promotional tools could be implemented in different stages of the response hierarchy. Managers would determine the location of a particular audience in the hierarchy and make appropriate decisions to move them closer to a trial and repeat purchase.

Adoption of communication models was limited, resulting in the need for a comprehensive managerial framework for setting behavioural and communication objectives for many IMC planning purposes, IMC plans, individual IMC tools (i.e., advertising), and specific elements (i.e., direct mail offer with coupon). Both types of objectives need to be established for any individual communication element, ranging from an activity at a sponsorship event to what is portrayed in a point-of-sale display. In short, all target audience contact points play a role in fulfilling IMC plan objectives and their expenditures can be accountable through achievement of their mandate. A complete plan requires direction through behavioural and communication objectives so that all tools and elements communicate accurately.

 Evaluate the options for setting behavioural objectives and apply them when constructing a promotional plan.

The comprehensive managerial framework identified options for behavioural objectives to guide the achievement of marketing objectives and to direct the formation of communication objectives. Behavioural objectives included brand trial, brand re-trial, brand switching, category trial, repeat purchase, shopping behaviour, and repeat consumption.

...sis of the target audience's decision-making process assists promotional planners in determining what to focus on ... their IMC plan for each IMC tool.

Choose among the options for setting communication objectives and apply them when designing IMC recommendations.

The comprehensive managerial framework also presented many options for setting communication objectives in terms of category need (i.e., omit, remind, emphasize), brand awareness (i.e., recognition and/or recall), brand attitude (i.e., establish, maintain, increase, modify, change), brand purchase intention (assume, generate), and brand purchase facilitation (omit, include). Similar to behavioural objectives, specific communication objectives can be attained for individual IMC tools so that the overall plan achieves each communication objective for a particular target audience. The end result enables managers to construct a multitude of IMC plans.

Assemble the best combination of behavioural and communication objectives for each stage of the consumer decision-making process.

The comprehensive managerial framework was then linked to the buyer decision-making model to show the connection between a consumer's behaviour and a particular brand's objectives. This application implies that, as a consumer's decision making progresses, managers can consider how objectives evolve at each stage in order to adjust the message, media, or IMC tool employed to communicate.

Review Questions

1. Discuss the value of setting objectives for the integrated marketing communications program. What important functions do objectives serve?

2. What are the strengths and weaknesses of using traditional hierarchy models for setting communication objectives?

3. Some claim that promotion is all about communication, so we should focus only on communication objectives and not worry about behavioural objectives. Convince them otherwise.

4. If a firm cannot afford large market research studies to quantitatively assess whether communication objectives have been achieved, why should the firm bother setting communication objectives?

5. A firm is running a campaign with advertising, sales promotion, and public relations. Why might it have different communication objectives for each IMC tool?

Applied Questions

1. In meeting with a client for an energy drink, you are informed that the only goal of advertising and promotion is to generate sales. As an account planner for a marketing communication agency, present reasons why communication objectives must also be considered.

2. Assess what the behavioural objectives would be for each ad in this chapter.

3. Assess what the communication objectives would be for each ad in this chapter.

4. After assessing the objectives for some of the ads of this chapter, check out the brand's Internet site or social media offerings and determine if the objectives are the same or different.

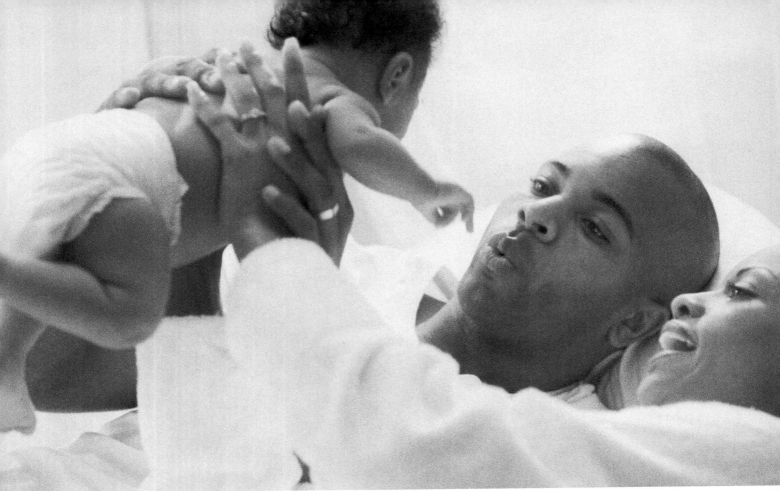

©Francisco Cruz/SuperStock

CHAPTER SIX

Brand Positioning Strategy Decisions

LEARNING OBJECTIVES

LO1 Identify the concepts of market positioning strategy and market position.

LO2 Apply the positioning concept in an advertising context by defining brand positioning strategy and brand position.

LO3 Illustrate how to formulate brand positioning strategy decisions.

LO4 Demonstrate brand repositioning strategy opportunities.

LO5 Interpret brand positioning strategy decisions in other contexts.

Hugs From Huggies

Babies need hugs. They need hugs to regulate their body temperature. They need hugs to strengthen their immune system. And, they need hugs to gain weight. In short, babies need hugs to thrive. But what if Mom had a difficult childbirth and cannot offer enough hugs as she recovers? What about the newborns in intensive care who are separated from their parents? And, do all new parents know about the importance of hugs for babies? These insights provided an opportunity for Huggies to alter its positioning strategy and establish a "No Babies Unhugged" program at hospitals. Could there be a better way of positioning for Huggies than offering hugs?

The brand arranged for highly screened volunteers to visit hospitals and hug babies in situations like the ones described above and teach new parents about babies' need for hugs. The program began in one hospital and then continued in two others initially, with the involvement of the Canadian Association of Pediatric Health Centres. Filming of the activities and testimonials of healthcare professionals provided content for the positioning message. The films appeared on TV, in social media, and on the Huggies website. Further communication included influencers and social media posts, along with display ads. Parents who participated offered their email and became part of a database for direct marketing communication. Other promotions featured samples and standard retail displays and commuication.

The purpose of the campaign from a competitive standpoint focused on Huggies' main rival, Pampers. The two brands continually battle for market share and Huggies wanted a new positioning to go beyond the typical approach of functional claims of protection and absorbency. The program provided consumers a widespread belief in Huggies as being a good brand, and the hugs angle offered a broad emotional association to the brand. Combined, this altered consumer attitudes in a different way than influencing specific attribute beliefs of functionality.

Research results indicated a 10 percent gain in the "better for newborns than other brands" belief, a key measure that signalled a more positive attitude to Huggies. From a behaviour standpoint, a significant number of program sign-ups occurred, and click-through rates of display ads hit well above normal levels. Sales grew 16 percent and market share gained 3 percent in the first year of the program. The made-in-Canada program proved so successful that it was expanded to over 30 other countries!

Question:

1. How can Huggies maintain this brand positioning in future?

As the opening vignette implies, advertising and all IMC tools that occur within a marketing strategy contribute significantly toward the overall positioning of the product to selected target markets, or what is known as a market positioning strategy. However, advertising and each promotional activity has its own unique communication objectives to persuade a particular target audience. In this sense, we can examine how promotional tools and the whole promotional program influence the positioning of a brand to a designated target audience, or what is known as a brand positioning strategy.

Our investigation in this chapter—to understand positioning for both marketing strategy and marketing communication—is consistent with the distinction between target market and target audience (Chapter 3) and the importance of linking communication objectives and strategy with the marketing objectives and strategy (Chapter 5). First, we review market positioning strategy, define brand positioning strategy, and describe the brand positioning strategy decision process. We then define and illustrate the four decisions for developing a comprehensive brand positioning strategy. Finally, we explore opportunities for changing the brand positioning strategy, known as repositioning.

Positioning

In this section, we distinguish between positioning within the marketing strategy and positioning with marketing communication. We highlight the difference between the decision a manager makes in terms of a market positioning strategy directed to a target market and brand positioning strategy directed to a target audience versus the resulting effects known as the market position or the brand position, which represent the beliefs of the target market or target audience respectively. We end the section with an overview of the decision-making process for a brand positioning strategy.

 MARKET POSITIONING STRATEGY

Organizations intending to market their products or services successfully should have a **strategic marketing plan** to identify all marketing decisions and guide the allocation of resources. A strategic marketing plan evolves from an organization's corporate strategy and guides marketing programs and policies. In Chapter 1 we emphasized that promotional planners use the strategic marketing plan as an information source to plan marketing communication decisions. In particular, those creating promotional messages should be familiar with their client's or organization's market positioning strategy since it gives direction for how a brand should be positioned in the promotional program.

A **market positioning strategy** identifies the decision of the market(s) in which the firm competes and the specific elements of the marketing mix that are designed to fulfill the respective needs of the market(s). This view of the positioning decision combines the target market(s) decision with the marketing mix decision that delivers the consumer benefit that is meaningfully distinct from competitors' offerings. For example, Smart cars compete in the electric car market and fulfill a need for those who desire to purchase a vehicle that is beneficial for the environment (**Exhibit 6-1**). With its new Boeing 767 airplanes and new international routes, Air Canada made its marketing strategy more global by competing against big international carriers such as Air France and KLM for the more lucrative international travel market. It shifted a greater portion of its marketing budget in this direction and altered its slogan to "Your world awaits" to signal a much different market positioning.[1] Sephora rejuvenated its presence in the prestige beauty market with its "Teach, Inspire, Play" philosophy. A redesign of the interior revamped its beauty studios, allowed the brand to offer group beauty classes, and permitted user-generated content to be seen on a giant digital screen. The addition of the Sephora Virtual Artist let consumers see the effects of a multitude of products and shades on their face and clearly provided the company with a new market positioning strategy.[2]

A market positioning strategy statement is typically part of a firm's marketing plan for communication purposes. This statement summarizes the decisions within the marketing program—product, price, distribution, service, and marketing communication—and the intended market(s) served. For example, a statement for a brand in the personal computer (PC) industry could focus on the education market (versus home or business) and focus on the university submarket (versus elementary school) with a distinctive offering that meets the needs of faculty replenishing the equipment in the student computer lab. Presumably, the firm used market research and its experience to put together a "package of benefits" or "value offering" that will be acceptable to this particular target market.

Marketing strategy results of sales or market share may be at, above, or below management expectations as reflected by the

Exhibit 6-1 Smart cars compete in the electric car market.

More foot down.
Less footprint.

>> Charge ahead with the surprisingly quick smart fortwo electric drive from only $26,990* before rebate.

Rebate
$3,000
smart discount*

thesmartcityproject.ca

smart – a Daimler brand

©Mercedes-Benz Canada

marketing objectives. These positive or negative results are a function of the reactions of consumers, and can be exactly what the firm intended or quite different. We define this consumer response to be the **market position** of a firm. This distinction signifies that it is not the current or past market positioning strategy decided by the marketing managers, but rather the intended or unintended consumer beliefs caused by the organization's marketing efforts. In the case of Birks jewellery store, the revised store design, modified product line, altered distribution system, and advertising emphasis of Canadian sourced diamonds all resulted in promising sales levels, indicating that it successfully achieved a new market position.[3]

To expand on these ideas, we will use shampoo products as an example. Shampoo is a fragmented market with many brands. Brands compete on product characteristics relating to the purpose of its use, like shining or thickening and anti-dandruff. Popular brands in Canada include Head & Shoulders, Pantene Pro-V, Herbal Essences, Dove, TRESemmé, and salon-based brands. We illustrate this market with a market position diagram, recognizing that alternative interpretations may be feasible (**Figure 6-1**). We graph two axes, cosmetic to therapeutic, and salon exclusive to popular with the mainstream. The salon endpoint represents brands originating from a salon or a brand extensively used by salons.

Given a significant level of product category usage on a regular basis (e.g., daily), it is not surprising to see that virtually every sector of this diagram would have brands competing, via brand name, ad imagery, product performance, packaging, and distribution location. We leave it to the reader to consider where each of the above brands may fit on these or other axes, but offer a couple of observations. Pantene Pro-V implies that professionals use it, with the word *Pro* in the brand name. TRESemmé advertises that professionals use the product as the brand moved to the consumer market after establishing itself in the business market decades ago. Head & Shoulders originally claimed itself to be an anti-dandruff product but now claims benefits regarding how the shampoo makes the user's hair look and feel and has multiple formats and fragrances. Given this information, where do we think Dove and Herbal Essences would be located in this market position diagram?

The market position diagram, also known by the general term *perceptual map*, is a result of market research showing an accumulation of how all the respondents "see" the brands competing. It can also be a summary of how a manager believes consumer perceptions line up if market research is not affordable. The image in **Exhibit 6-2** shows SoBe offering different drink options, with each competing in its own quadrant of a perceptual map for the overall non-alcoholic beverage market. In conclusion, the market position diagram depends entirely upon clearly identifying and accurately defining the criteria for the two axes. Furthermore, multiple diagrams may be necessary if a planner desires to model three axes.

Figure 6-1 Hypothetical illustration of a market position diagram for shampoo brands

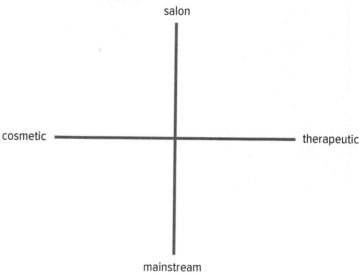

LO2 BRAND POSITIONING STRATEGY

It is tempting to believe that advertising and all other IMC tools define the market positioning strategy, because all these marketing communication exposures are so publicly visible. While this may be true in certain situations, in most cases advertising and IMC

Exhibit 6-2 SoBe competes in various markets with its product line.

Source: SoBe by PepsiCo

Exhibit 6-3 Samsung compares itself to Apple to sway a target audience.

It doesn't take
a genius.
12:45

Source: Samsung

campaigns typically focus on a particular message that helps consumers understand the product in comparison to other brands *within* a specific product market or category. In fact, most ads or IMC tools speak to a very specific target audience, as observed in typical marketing communication done by a bank.

A bank can send a direct-mail piece to current customers (i.e., brand loyals) to obtain mortgage renewals and focus the message on the ease of continuity and the good follow-up service. Or it may run a TV ad with a message of attractive interest rates and specialized options directed to customers from competing banks (i.e., favourable brand switchers). Finally, it may develop a mobile app for young adults who are beginning to buy and use new financial products and services as they mature and earn money (i.e., new category users). The Samsung ad in **Exhibit 6-3** directs its message to a consumer deciding between its product and a recognizable competitor, clearly a specific target audience.

These examples identify different target audiences with different competitive reference points and suggest the need to use the positioning concept appropriately in a marketing communication context that is distinct from positioning in a marketing strategy context. This notion of positioning in marketing communication is the subject of a new direction in the marketing literature.[4] One study confirmed empirical support for this view as specific target audiences responded more positively to ads directed to them versus another target audience.[5]

Advertising practitioners consider positioning to be an important decision in establishing and maintaining a brand. In fact, managing a brand is so critical that the notion of branding is topical with marketers these days; however, the original authors of the positioning concept remind us that branding cannot occur without positioning.[6] This original notion of positioning in an advertising context arose from Jack Trout and Al Ries, who distinguished between a marketer's decisions and the resulting effect in a consumer's knowledge structure.[7] Thus, in this text we use the term **brand positioning strategy** to mean the *intended* image of the product or brand relative to competing brands for a given competitive space as defined by certain product market or category characteristics.

A competitive space is discovered with the market position diagram, as discussed previously. For example, the upper left quadrant is a space where brands like Pantene Pro-V and TRESemmé may be challenging for consumers, and the battle may be on more specific characteristics that relate to desirable hair qualities: volume, thickness, strength, smoothness, shine, and so on. The relevant dimensions of competing within a space allow managers to determine the brand positioning strategy, a key decision prior to determining the most effective selling message of advertising or other IMC tools.

Now consider consumer responses after being exposed to an entire IMC campaign. What do consumers feel and think about the brand after having experienced all of the messages? Do they have positive or negative feelings for the brand? What unique attributes or benefits come to mind when considering the brand? These questions pertain to the reactions consumers have to the marketing communication decisions implemented by the promotional planner. Thus, **brand position** refers to the target audience's overall assessment or image of the brand resulting from brand-related communication that tells the prospective buyer what the brand is, who it is for, and what it offers.[8] The brand V8 successfully altered its brand position over the years with different promotional programs (**Exhibit 6-4**).

Exhibit 6-4 V8 revitalized its image.

V8
V8
V8

Source: V8 by Campbell Soup Company

We need to distinguish between the firm's intended brand image and the actual brand image, since these occur at different points in time and reside in different locations. The brand positioning strategy resides within the overall advertising or IMC plan, while the brand position exists within the target audience. The brand positioning strategy is written annually or perhaps every few years depending on the company's direction. The brand position requires time, perhaps a few years, to take hold in a sufficient number of consumers before the planners will know whether the intended strategy worked. The importance of distinct vocabulary between brand positioning strategy (i.e., plan) and brand position (i.e., result) was implied by Trout and Ries and is consistent with others who have written on this topic.[9]

We turn to our brand position diagram, where brands compete more directly in a competitive space. For this, we turn to the chocolate bar category within the broader chocolate confectionery market that includes stand-up bags of wrapped chocolate, snack boxes, and bagged chocolate/candy. The broader chocolate confectionery market contains more than 100 brands, although there are duplicates with line extensions. Nevertheless, the chocolate bar category provides enough competing brands with varying characteristics such that brands manage their positioning strategy.

Chocolate bar brands actively compete and advertise on certain **salient attributes**. For this, we suggest three possible axes: (1) single-bar format–unique/multi-part format; (2) peanuts, almonds (nut-based)–nougat, caramel; and (3) layered wafers–solid bar. While a three-dimensional brand position diagram is feasible, **Figures 6-2**, **6-3**, and **6-4** show the individual pairs to illustrate the possibilities more easily. Frequently consumed brands are KitKat, Coffee Crisp, Aero, Caramilk, Mars, Reese's Peanut Butter Cups, and Oh Henry!, each of which is placed on these axes accordingly based on its attributes. We suggest that soft-centre bars like Mars and Reese's would be in the middle of the layered wafers–solid bar axis.

Clearly, a brand could consider its distinctive attributes to encourage non-users to gravitate to the product category. The attribute-based brand position diagram helps identify what the competing brands might be and gives direction on how to emphasize the distinctiveness of the attributes. For example, both Reese's and Oh Henry! could target consumers who love peanuts but who do not eat chocolate bars, and specifics of the positioning are clearer if one knows which brand it is up against. Alternatively, the attribute brand position diagrams can assist the managers for the first four bars listed, since they all have a break-apart format. So if one brand tries to switch purchasers away from another brand on this feature, the approach for communicating the break-apart characteristic is estimated more accurately. As these implications show, the brand position diagram visualizes how to consider the options for brand positioning strategy decisions, but this decision can instead be based on benefits, or a combination.

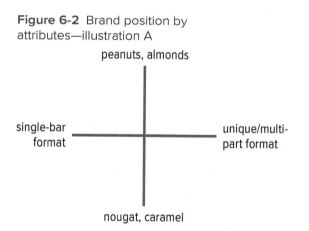

Figure 6-2 Brand position by attributes—illustration A

Figure 6-3 Brand position by attributes—illustration B

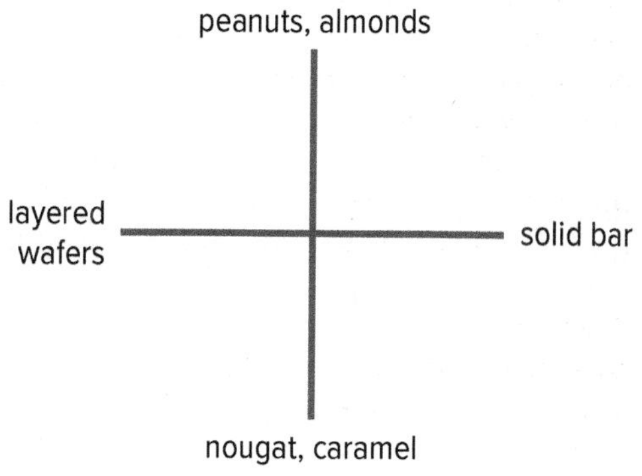

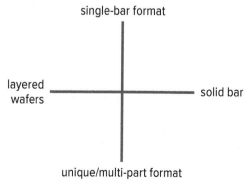

Figure 6-4 Brand position by attributes—illustration C

Figure 6-5 Brand position by benefits—illustration A

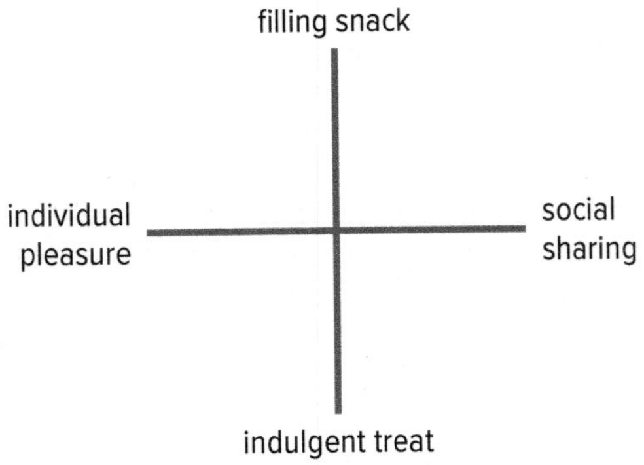

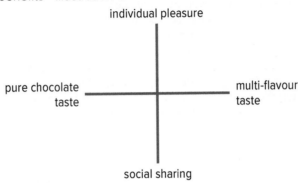

Figure 6-6 Brand position by benefits—illustration B

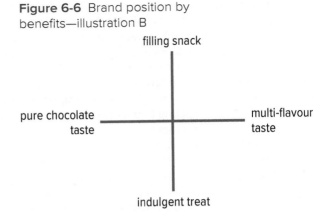

Figure 6-7 Brand position by benefits—illustration C

Chocolate bars also compete on certain **salient benefits**. For these, we again surmise three axes: (1) filling snack–indulgent treat; (2) individual pleasure–social sharing; and (3) pure chocolate taste–multi-flavour taste. The first axis is relatively self-explanatory as brands have competed on these aspects for decades. The individual pleasure–social dimension is relevant for the break-apart bars since the pieces can be shared, thereby signifying an interesting emotional benefit of belongingness along the lines of love for a particular consumer segment. Since one aspect of chocolate bar consumption is the flavour and sensory gratification, whether the resulting taste is mostly chocolate or a mix with others is another aspect brands may emphasize in their messages. Again, these axes are shown as three pairs in **Figures 6-5**, **6-6**, and **6-7**. Readers are encouraged to consider an alternative view and/or place the above brands accordingly to investigate the brand positioning strategy options for each brand.

BRAND POSITIONING STRATEGY DECISION PROCESS

We present a five-step process for making the brand positioning strategy, adapted from other sources.[10] Chapter 1 briefly outlined this process, but here we investigate the actual steps in more detail to fully understand the brand positioning strategy decisions that are presented in the remainder of this chapter. In making the decision, planners will assess whether the brand positioning strategy will be strong enough competitively and whether sufficient financial resources exist to establish the brand position over time.

Develop a Market Partition An approach for defining the market is to make it consistent with how consumers make a purchase decision. It is suggested that promotional planners view the market broadly as a general product category and subsequently divide the market into various subcategories until consumers perceive brands as being relatively similar. The criteria for market partitioning include the type of product, end benefit, usage situation, and brand name. **Figures 6-8** to **6-11** show a partition of the car market for each of these four approaches, and these simple illustrations are expanded or altered to the decision maker's requirements. This task is important for

Figure 6-8 Partition of car market by product type

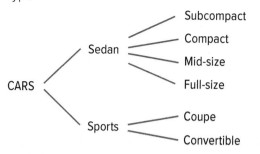

Figure 6-9 Partition of car market by end benefit

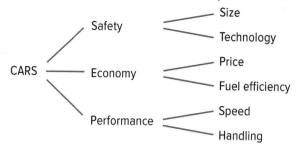

Figure 6-10 Partition of car market by usage situation

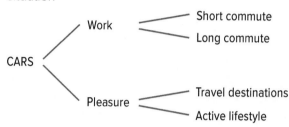

Figure 6-11 Partition of car market by brand

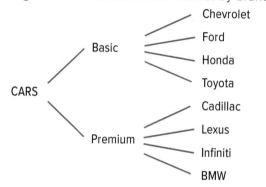

establishing the initial parameters for identifying the most important competitors to determine a unique positioning strategy that is communicated.

Assess Competitors' Position Once we define the competitors through the market partition, we then determine their respective brand positions by assessing consumers' beliefs through new or existing consumer research. Often, survey research is performed to observe how consumers rate the competing brands on the relevant and important attributes and benefits that consumers use when evaluating a brand. The data from these types of surveys are used to formulate the brand position maps shown previously. Preliminary research may be necessary to identify new attributes or benefits that competitors are communicating to establish their brand position.

Assess Brand Position Consumer research for the promotional planner's brand assesses how consumers currently perceive the brand. This research would be compared with the previously determined brand positioning strategy (e.g., last year, or the prior two to four years). If current efforts are not working, it may be time to consider an alternative strategy. Unless there is strong reason to believe a change in positioning is necessary, promotional planners are advised to maintain the current brand positioning strategy.

Determine Brand Positioning Strategy Going through the first three steps provides direction for establishing a brand position; however, planners will be faced with alternatives to select from. **IMC Perspective 6-1** summarizes Nissan's "Conquer All Conditions" campaign in which the promotional planners considered different positioning options within winter driving. As this example suggests, managers perform research or use judgment based on experience to make the final brand positioning strategy decision among identified alternatives.

Implement Brand Positioning Strategy The content of the advertising message, its creative strategy, and creative tactics are formulated once the brand positioning strategy is established. The implementation of other promotional communication tools also requires message and creativity development. For example, prior to launching a public relations or publicity campaign, a marketer would specify the positioning of its brand to its intended target audience before deciding upon the exact content of its message and how to creatively present it.

Monitor Brand Positioning Strategy After implementing a new marketing communication campaign, a promotional planner assesses whether the resulting brand position is consistent with the intended brand positioning strategy. Alternatively, for a continuing marketing communication campaign, monitoring occurs to see how well the brand position is maintained. In either case, tracking studies measure the image of the brand over time, and changes in consumers' perceptions are an input for subsequent planning for future decisions.

IMC PERSPECTIVE 6-1

CONQUER ALL CONDITIONS WITH NISSAN

Nissan hit a winner of new positioning with its "Conquer All Conditions" campaign in Canada. A few years ago, the world's sixth largest automaker languished with 8 percent market share in Canada. The market continued with its trend of consumers switching from cars to sport–utility vehicles (SUVs), but Nissan did not enjoy the ride as did its major competitors Ford, Honda, and Toyota. Although most SUV drivers did not drive their vehicle off-road, they still wanted a safe vehicle for tough driving conditions. In fact, consumer research showed that safety ranked in the top five purchase criteria, up from the top 10–15 range a decade previously. And consumers saw the source of safety as being SUVs with all-wheel drive (AWD). Clearly, safety appeared to be a benefit to position on if Nissan could effectively communicate its capability with AWD.

©Nissan Canada Inc.

The first of six "Conquer All Conditions" scenarios showed a man rescuing others with his Nissan Rogue while they were being attacked by menacing snowmen in the city streets. The Rogue maneuvered around the throng and also crashed into a few, rendering them back to snowflakes. Other Rogue executions over the next few years featured the driver battling scary rocks that came alive, an ugly mud monster, and a return of the snowmen in an epic field of battle. These messages stood in sharp contrast to the global campaign messages shown previously that focused on cargo capacity and styling.

The Nissan Pathfinder went up against a marauding tree, while the Nissan Murano escaped from an icy bridge out to destroy cars. In each of the stories, the Nissan vehicle defeated the monster that symbolized the everyday winter road conditions that Canadians face. All told, the creative ads clearly showed consumers that Nissan defined its competitive space by benefit to tackle its own arch-rivals in the Canadian SUV market.

Brand metrics indicated a successful brand positioning strategy; overall opinion scores and familiarity climbed 40 percent! Market share doubled from 5 percent to 10 percent, just 1 percent below the SUV category leader. Other countries picked up some of the executions, a first for Nissan Canada.

Recent executions carried on with the safety positioning and the idea of conquering a threat. However, the threat appeared as an actual driving risk and was not symbolized by monsters. In this case, the technology point moved away from AWD only, evolving to focus on AWD as part of the Nissan Intelligent Mobility technology features.

Question:

1. Why were the monsters a good symbol to represent the threats of winter driving?

LO3 Brand Positioning Strategy Decisions

The essence of positioning the brand in the context of advertising is to clearly indicate where the brand is competing, with whom it is competing, how it is competing, and finally why consumers will purchase the brand. Each of these questions must be addressed through four decisions within the brand positioning strategy: market definition, differential advantage, target audience brand attitude, and consumer purchase motive.

MARKET DEFINITION

A primary decision for positioning is how the promotional planners define the market and where they intend for the brand to compete with its benefit claims. The market partition illustrations showed that brands compete against other brands on end benefits, brand name, usage situation, and product category. One purpose of advertising is to contribute to developing a perceived advantage over competing brands within the competitive space. Thus, each of these offers tremendous opportunity to communicate benefit claims and establish a perceived differential advantage.

Positioning by End Benefit A common approach to positioning is setting the brand apart from competitors on the basis of its primary end benefit offered; a brand may be positioned on multiple benefits if necessary. The ad for Range Rover in **Exhibit 6-5** exemplifies the driving experience to communicate the performance benefit. Marketers also attempt to identify salient attributes that are important to consumers and are the basis for making a purchase decision. In this case, the positioning focuses on these specific characteristics and the benefits are not directly claimed in the message. Advertisers require good research and reasons for justifying this kind of positioning recommendation, because moving toward a specific attribute or benefit precludes messages regarding other attributes and benefits. One research study concluded that positioning by attributes in an ad message works when the consumer is planning a more immediate purchase, while positioning by benefits in an ad message works when the purchase is more distant in time.[11]

In all of its marketing communication, Roots Canada

Exhibit 6-5 The Range Rover ad captures the driving experience to demonstrate how it competes on performance.

©Lars A. Niki

sticks with the singular focus of being Canadian. All imagery and messaging reflects and reinforces this key attribute about the company. In fact, the brand takes pride in the fact that many of its products are produced in Canada, providing important support for this authentic attribute claim.[12] Alternatively, a pure benefit focus is seen with Reebok Canada's effort as part of the global "Live With Fire" positioning. An ad with NHL stars John Tavares, Matt Duchene, and Maxime Talbot promoted the new Reebok Training collection of footwear and apparel. The direction of the campaign attempted to allow consumers to experience the "passion, intent, and purpose" benefits associated with using the new product line.[13]

The positioning of 5-hour Energy shown in **Exhibit 6-6** is typically based on its attributes (e.g. zero sugar, 4 calories) and sometimes links to benefits (e.g., quick, lasting energy) to these attributes.

While we refer to either attribute or benefit positioning in this discussion, marketers will also make a direct link between a particular attribute and the derived benefit, or they may highlight the attribute and allow the target audience to interpret the benefit. Activia's marketing communication highlighted the unique probiotic culture in its yogurt and the resulting vitality that continued consumption produced, with its interesting ads that featured boxed frames on people's stomachs as they danced and ate the product.[14]

Exhibit 6-6 5-hour Energy communicates its attributes in its ads.

Source: 5-hour ENERGY

©American Express Canada

Positioning by Brand Name

Marketers use an emphasis on quality for a brand positioning strategy with ads that reflect the image of a high-end product where cost, while not irrelevant, is considered secondary to the benefits derived from using a quality brand. Premium or luxury brands tend to use this positioning approach and one might speculate that much of Apple's advertising presumed a positioning by brand name with its innovative quality. Another way of brand name positioning is to focus on the quality offered by the brand at a competitive price (e.g., value-based). For example, Lands' End uses this strategy by suggesting that quality is affordable. Remember that although price is an important consideration, the product quality must be comparable to competing brands for the positioning strategy to be effective. Positioning by brand name also occurs with an emphasis on the importance of the brand, as shown in the American Express ad of **Exhibit 6-7**. The slogan reinforces the positioning and it is a clever revision of the famous "Don't leave home without it," which the brand used for decades.

Samsung is an international electronics brand with new products launched over the past few years—such as a curved-screen TV, smart watch, and wearable tech clothing. As such, its marketing communication moved toward the brand ("I want a Samsung Galaxy") rather than the product category ("I want a smart phone"). One creative example of the success the Canadian division experienced is the work of its agency Cheil, which created the "What's Your Tabitat" video messages shown only on the Internet for the Galaxy 3 Tab. The theme of the three ads spoofed a nature documentary and classified three different tablet users for its three models: *Connecticus,* young socially active users looking for instant access; *Wanderus,* slightly older users on the go; and *Relaxicus,* middle-aged consumers using their tablet at home.

Another aspect of Samsung Canada's messages included a virtual line-up with personal avatars for the new Galaxy S6 smart phone. Targeted to younger consumers, the concept encouraged those interested in moving up higher in the line to post social media messages or pictures that included the hashtag #S6lineup. Banking on research that indicated the importance of social influence as opposed to brand persuasion, Samsung's marketing team took this approach to drive favourable messages. Other communication featured a large digital display of the avatars in Toronto. These and other Canadian advertising initiatives resulted in improved Samsung brand preferences, and market share in Canada reached Samsung's global level.[15]

Positioning by Usage Situation

Another way to communicate a brand position is to associate it with a specific use. One approach is to change the direction of the positioning. For example, alternative Becel advertising emerged after Unilever sold the brand. Past ads communicated the healthy side of using the spreadable margarine, but the new positioning focused on the use of Becel for baking. A heartwarming execution of a low-income family making a gingerbread house coincided with their receiving a home from Habitat for Humanity.[16] Another approach is to expand the situational usage of a product. For example, for its Kit Kat chocolate bars, Nestlé established a "take a break" positioning years ago and returned to it with a new campaign. The launch featured a TV ad showing break situations when people would want to eat a Kit Kat, as well as phone apps that call people automatically and give a fictitious and humorous reason for them to take a break, thus allowing people to get away with a "reason" instead of the truth.[17] Finally, empirical research suggests that marketing communication plays a strong role in consumers' adopting new uses.[18] The ad for DanActive in **Exhibit 6-8** communicates a usage situation positioning by suggesting it is good for breakfast. Imagery of the sun rising in the background adds a visual cue to reinforce morning consumption.

Exhibit 6-8 DanActive encourages breakfast consumption with a usage situation positioning strategy.

©OUTFRONT Media Inc.

Positioning by Product Category Competition for a product also comes from outside the product category and, rather than positioning against another brand, an alternative strategy is to position the brand against another product category. For example, Via Rail positioned itself as an alternative to airplanes, citing cost savings, enjoyment, and other advantages (**Exhibit 6-9**). Craft beers of Ontario made inroads toward the higher-end spirits with their placement in the provincial alcohol retailer. Extensive messaging from the Liquor Control Board of Ontario and the Ontario Craft Brewers Association looked beyond the beer market to carve out a niche and improve sales.[19] This result is all the more remarkable considering the decline of beer sales relative to other alcohol products, moving from 50 percent to 43 percent of all alcohol sales.[20] Dairy Queen, known as

Exhibit 6-9 Via competes with other forms of transportation.

Hand-out/VIA Rail Canada Inc./Newscom

DQ these days, continually faces a message challenge in signalling its market definition, since the brand communicates its outlets as a destination for ice-cream treats while competing with similar kinds of venues, and as a location for eating fast food while competing with the big players like McDonald's. Its slogans over the years—"Fan Food, Not Fast Food," "So Good It's RiDQulous," and "Something Different"—reflect this difficult marketing challenge.[21]

DIFFERENTIAL ADVANTAGE

Brand benefit claims embodied in the positioning and represented in the ads contribute to the differential advantage for a brand. While it is generally expected that a brand positioning strategy should take a differential positioning approach and have a product benefit focus, we highlight situations where brands do not follow this pattern.

Differential Positioning In the previous section, we mentioned the importance of advertising contributing to the perceived differential advantage for the brand. This is true for most brands and the five major Canadian banks try to distance themselves from one another with their advertising.[22] For example, TD Canada Trust implemented its "Banking Can Be This Comfortable" in 1997 and symbolized it with a green leather armchair. TD evolved the idea to other dimensions of consumers' banking experience, such as an intuitive Internet site and stress-free retail environment. The success of this differentiation is seen with its top ranking by Interbrand for two years in a row. The Prada ad in **Exhibit 6-10** is an example where its stylish looking handbags have a prominent focus to differentiate the fashion brand.

One aspect of differential positioning is the degree to which an advertiser will make claims of quality. Academic research on quality in marketing gained ground with more investigative treatments. For example, one study explored the difference between quality and taste, two compelling directions for making claims in messages.[23] Another study concluded that high-quality brands should make quality claims in their ads, but low-quality brands should not try to claim that they are almost as good as leading brands.[24]

Central Positioning Market circumstances allow brands to claim a central position within the product category, quite an alternative direction compared to differential. A central brand positioning strategy is possible when the brand can claim and deliver on the most salient benefits. This is a function of the brand being the market share leader, achieving success in the growth stage of the product life cycle, or having unique characteristics that essentially define the category. For example, Nike's "Just Do It" slogan implies a central position for its ad messages across several product categories. Similarly, one might

Exhibit 6-10 This positioning focuses on the benefit of looking stylish with colourful Prada handbags.

©Lou Linwei/Alamy Stock Photo

Exhibit 6-11 A unique Pepsi ad with soccer star Lionel Messi contributes to a central positioning in the cola product category.

©Danny Clinch for PepsiCo/SIPA/Newscom

conclude that Apple took a central position in its ads that demonstrate key features of its new products over the past two decades.

The ad in **Exhibit 6-11** is an application of a brand potentially claiming a central position in a product category. Pepsi associates its brand identification with legendary soccer star Lionel Messi, implying that its cola product is the best in the world since Messi is arguably the best soccer player in the world. As a prelude to creativity covered in Chapter 7 and Chapter 8, notice how the Pepsi colours are meshed with Messi's legs, giving the impression that Pepsi and Messi are intertwined (one and the same perhaps?). Furthermore, the imagery of a lion in the background plays on his name and any associations with the animal (e.g., king of the jungle) are transferred to the brand as well.

An example with a Canadian focus is the well known house brand for Loblaw, President's Choice, which positions itself as a leader in the generic brand food category with its Insider's Report, product innovation ads, and new cooking shows.[25] SodaStream presents an interesting example of a brand potentially building a central position across campaigns. The in-home soda machine has no real direct competitor, but shows its unique position by defining its market with two product categories. It initially demonstrated how it works, compared its advantage to soft drinks, and explained how to break up with soft drinks. Subsequent ads showed how many plastic bottles that one could avoid recycling by using the machine instead of bottled water and how it would save aquatic life.[26]

Brand Benefit Positioning We have thus far implied that most positioning decisions involve unique and differential benefit claims that the brand can deliver. The market partition and competitive analysis gives promotional planners the opportunity to identify and determine the most important ones to claim in advertising. For example, Advil creatively communicated the strength of its new cold and sinus product with humorous executions that showed a stereotyped strong man demonstrating his power by conquering weight lifting, fighting an adversary, or bending steel rods into the shape of a puppy.[27] A focus on the product such as this is known as a **brand benefit positioning**, although it is generally referred to as a product focus. The Yodel ad shown in **Exhibit 6-12** demonstrates a benefit experienced with the watch technology.

Ads are quite creative and visually stimulating to convince consumers of the brand benefit positioning. Sliced havarti, grated mozzarella, and a block of old cheddar are featured at the end of three amazing cheese ads for Kraft's Cracker Barrel since they are what starts three delicious treats—a steak sandwich, lasagna, and a cheese board.

Exhibit 6-12 Yodel communicates a key benefit for a snowboarder.

Hand-out/YodelTECH Inc./Newscom

Captioned with the slogan, "Start With Cracker Barrel. End With Amazing.", the ads show a close-up of the preparation of each food in reverse order! We start by seeing the juicy steak sandwich, the steaming dish of lasagna, or the elegantly decorated and designed cheese board, and then trace back through each preparation with a reverse recording, until we see that the whole thing started with Cracker Barrel. The video messages shown on TV and online accompanied similar photographs shown in magazines and in social media.

The inspiration for the ads flowed from consumer research. Food preparation represented an expression of love that could be reflected in the ads, and consumers saw cheese as a main ingredient in food preparation. Competitive research indicated that low-priced cheese, and cheese with price promotions, took a growing share of the marketing, giving Kraft the motivation to portray Cracker Barrel as a higher-end brand. To reinforce this, the ads used extensive food imagery with higher quality recording and photography, much like that found on cooking shows or in food magazines, to go along with the imagery found with gourmet brands. The sandwich ad gives testament to the artistic presentation of each individual scene in reverse: biting, cutting in half, baking in the press, lifting the bread, watching greens rising, slicing the steak, cooking the steak, seasoning the steak, unraveling the red pepper, and finally starting with havarti. The ad makes you believe that you are there, eating and preparing the food![28]

User Positioning While a brand benefit or product focus is a useful approach for many product categories and brands, **user positioning** is an alternative where the benefit is expressed personally in the message. In this case, a brand is positioned by association with a particular group of users, as illustrated in the Globe ad of **Exhibit 6-13**. This campaign emphasizes identification or association with skateboard enthusiasts, which may be seen as a reference group or aspiration group.

Exhibit 6-13 Globe positions by product users who are skateboarders.

Source: Globe International Limited

Another perspective for user positioning occurs when a consumer is motivated for individual reasons, and the ads emphasize how the consumer positively feels while consuming the brand. For example, Bombardier moved from a product positioning to a user positioning when its ads changed from just showing the recreational vehicles (snowmobiles, ATVs) to exploring the stories, emotions, and experiences of its customers. The change resulted in positive sales and profits almost immediately.[29] The ad in **Exhibit 6-14** visually expresses the individual experiences of being in the Big Apple and staying at the Hilton.

Going beyond the success of its "Our Food. Your Questions." campaign, McDonald's Canada moved toward a "Welcome to McDonald's" theme. This next step took the story from behind-the-scenes restaurant activities to the front of house where consumers enjoy the food and interact while in the restaurant. While still retaining the "I'm Lovin' It" slogan, the new approach presented the stories of many consumers and heartwarming scenes of consumers within the restaurant. A film crew travelled across the country to 35 locations, interviewed over 450 people, recorded 115 hours of video, and took more than 10,000 photographs. The main ads intended to show how consumers enjoy being at McDonald's and what the restaurant means to Canadians. The shots featured real people, without make-up, in regular light, doing regular restaurant activities.

McDonald's also compiled numerous interview style video messages where Canadians told their stories, some of which appeared in social media. Coinciding with the TV and online video messages, the campaign included extensive out-of-home media showing a photograph of a McDonald's customer, their name, and the location of the photo. The underlying meaning in all of these messages is that McDonald's is a place that Canadians rely on for a variety of reasons, no matter who they are. Whether it is for a simple washroom break, or a new environment after being at the club, or a place to play before a child's nap time, McDonald's is a place to visit and enjoy when not at home or at work.[30]

TARGET AUDIENCE BRAND ATTITUDE

Consumers hold a number of beliefs about a brand, however not all of these beliefs are activated in forming an attitude toward the brand. Beliefs concerning *specific* attributes or benefits that are activated and form the basis of an attitude are referred to as **salient beliefs**. These beliefs are based on salient attributes and salient benefits described earlier in this chapter. Marketers should identify these beliefs and understand how the

Exhibit 6-14 This positioning focuses on the product user.

STAY HILTON. GO TOAST. GO CHILL. GO NY.

STAY HILTON. GO EVERYWHERE.
hilton.com/go

©Hilton Worldwide, Inc.

saliency varies among different target audiences, over time, and across different consumption situations. Marketers can use a model to develop persuasive brand positioning strategies since it guides which attributes and benefits to claim in advertising.

Brand Attitude Model Consumer researchers and marketing practitioners use attitude models to study consumer attitudes.[31] A **multiattribute attitude model** views an attitude object, such as a product or brand, as possessing a number of attributes that provide the basis on which consumers form their attitudes. According to this model, consumers have beliefs about specific brand attributes and attach different levels of importance to these attributes. Using this approach, an attitude toward a particular brand is represented as

$$A_B = \sum_{i=1}^{n} B_i \times E_i$$

where A_B = attitude toward a brand

B_i = beliefs about the brand's performance on attribute i

E_i = importance attached to attribute i

n = number of attributes considered

For example, a consumer may have beliefs (B_i) about certain attributes of brands of toothpaste. One brand may be perceived as having fluoride and thus preventing cavities, tasting good, and helping control tartar buildup, while consumers may believe another brand performs well on other attributes such as freshening breath and whitening teeth. To predict attitudes, one must know how much importance consumers attach to each of these attributes (E_i). For example, parents purchasing toothpaste for their children may prefer a brand that performs well on cavity prevention, a preference that leads to a more favourable attitude toward the first brand. Teenagers and young adults may prefer a brand that freshens their breath and makes their teeth white and thus prefer the second brand.

In the case of Tim Hortons, the iconic Canadian brand competes on five benefits in its coffee marketing: quality (20-minute promise), popularity (Canada's Favourite Coffee), heartwarming emotion (True Stories), promotion (RRRoll Up the Rim to Win), and ethics (Fair Trade). Ads addressing these aspects typically focus on the delivery or importance of these beliefs.[32] As this suggests, this model is applied for attribute- or benefit-based persuasion, depending on the promotional planner's strategic intention.

IMC Perspective 6-2 takes a look at Classico's brand positioning strategy in which the brand compared itself to homemade Italian sauce.

IMC PERSPECTIVE 6-2

CLASSICO'S SAUCE VS. NONNA'S SAUCE

When launched decades ago, Classico owned the prepared pasta sauce category, especially the premium subcategory. Its recent promotional activity relied on price discounts and trade support, and no image advertising occurred for a decade. With the leader not actually leading a market with its messaging, competitors naturally entered the market and threatened Classico's 34 percent market share. Managers viewed the market now as having four distinct subcategories—value, mainstream, premium, and super-premium—with Classico still leading the premium subcategory but now seemingly behind a couple of super-premium entrants.

The brand positioning strategy intended to reclaim the quality beliefs and Italian characteristics so that "authentic epicurean" consumers would see the brand as a very good substitute for homemade sauce when consumers did not have sufficient time to make it from scratch. These consumers would love to cook homemade sauce all the time, but could not during busier weekdays. The brand established a goal of greater repurchases, and improvements in beliefs of "tastes like homemade" and "is a brand for me" for its new ad campaign.

Classico decided to be honest in its message by claiming that its sauce is second to homemade! An ad showed a cook-off contest pitting Classico against a group of Italian nonnas, with the nonnas winning. Their celebration was accompanied by the song "All I Do Is Win," with all sorts of mugging for the camera! This approach worked with a trend of brands making clear and honest brand claims that consumers could accept. Some experts have noted this trend with Canadian consumers and believe it to be working well for many brands, including Classico.

The positioning goal of "tastes more like homemade" grew 32 percent vs. a 5 percent goal, and the goal of "brand for me" rose 19 percent vs. a 5 percent goal, both indicating a strong brand position resulting from the brand positioning strategy decision. Sales and market share improved remarkably from the campaign.

Question:

1. How can Classico maintain its stronger brand position?

©sandoclr/Getty Images

Brand Attitude Persuasion Multiattribute models help marketers diagnose the beliefs that underlie consumers' evaluations of a brand and the importance of specific attributes or benefits. This analysis guides communication strategies, like maintaining attitudes of current customers or changing attitudes of non-customers. A study demonstrated that research examining attribute ratings of customers and non-customers provided important direction for improving the marketing communication strategy for a European telecommunications firm.[33] Thus, a model such as this provides four ways to influence attitudes of target audiences regarding specific brand characteristics to emphasize in ad messages.

Influence Attribute Belief The first strategy is to identify an important attribute or benefit and communicate how well the brand performs on that attribute or benefit. This influence strategy is selected in situations where consumers do not perceive the brand as possessing an important attribute, where the belief strength is low and requires improvement, where belief strength is moderate and needs to be strengthened, and where belief strength is high and needs to be maintained. **Exhibit 6-15** shows a Burt's Bees ad that provides three reasons why beeswax outperforms petroleum in lip balm products. In a number of ads and promotional activities, A&W restaurants communicated its delivery of better ingredients: natural cane sugar in its signature root beer; meat raised without hormones, steroids, or antibiotics; and eggs from vegetarian chickens. Consumers reacted positively as sales grew for nine straight quarters, resulting

Exhibit 6-15 Burt's Bees compares its attribute to its competitor to show how it is better.

Source: Burt's Bees

Exhibit 6-16 The importance of serving a tasteful Italian beverage is highlighted by San Pellegrino.

ENHANCE *your* MOMENTS

★
S.PELLEGRINO
Tastefully Italian

Exhibit 6-17 Mott's highlights the importance of strong bones via its Fruitsations brand.

This delicious snack will go straight to your bones.

NEW MOTT'S FRUITSATIONS:

in market share growth of 1 percent.[34] In the case of CIBC, the use of Percy the penguin in its ads improved its attribute ratings for "consumer-centric" and "personalized," which suggests that consumer attitudes are stronger.[35]

Influence Attribute Importance This second strategy involves getting consumers to attach more importance to the attribute in forming their attitude toward the brand. The importance could be negligible and the advertiser's persuasion makes it become important, or the importance could be at a reasonable level and the advertiser's persuasion makes it even more important. Marketers using this strategy want to increase the importance of an attribute their particular brand has. The print ads for Jergens Ultra Care moisturizer highlight the importance to a woman of regularly applying lotion all over her body. The positioning was intended to demonstrate that moisturizing was as important as all the other beauty activities that women engage in every day. The main message suggested that women "Take Care of What You Wear Every Day" with a visual showing the lotion on a woman's body, and obviously associated a woman's skin with her wardrobe. The positioning was initiated in Quebec, where the brand underachieved significantly compared to other parts of Canada. Research indicated that women from Quebec did not separate beauty and skin care from health. This insight suggested that new users could be attracted to the brand if the ads conveyed the sensuality of moisturized skin. A 50 percent increase in sales in Quebec allowed the brand's positioning to be extended in English rather than continuing with the planned U.S. ads.[36] The ad in **Exhibit 6-16** conveys the importance of serving elegant and tasteful beverages for special occasions.

Add New Attribute Belief The third strategy for influencing consumer attitudes is to add or emphasize a new attribute that consumers can use in evaluating a brand. Marketers do this by focusing on additional benefits or consequences associated with using the brand that have not been communicated previously. Wonder+, a line extension of the famous Wonder bread, needed to communicate that it had the same great taste as the original as well as the nutrition of whole wheat bread. The new brand attempted to influence lapsed users of Wonder bread who thought that white bread was no longer healthy. Yet at the same time, managers knew that the message had to reinforce the attitude of loyal customers. Adding the health benefit worked, with clever imagery of twins eating both types of bread and believing that they both taste the same, yet one is now whole wheat. The positioning of this advertising produced significant gains for all communication effects and sales.[37] **Exhibit 6-17** is an ad for Mott's Fruitsations, with enhanced nutrients for bone health. Most consumers would likely see this as an additional attribute to consider beyond others considered in the past.

Influence Attribute Belief of Competitor Brand A final strategy marketers use is to change consumer beliefs about the attributes of competing brands or product categories. This strategy is associated with a comparative ad, where a marketer directly compares its brand to competitors' on specific product attributes. We see this kind of comparison in food ads. With a better understanding of health, Canadians are concerned with their individual health and food manufacturers responded with emphasis on the ingredients of their products in terms of natural, authentic, and real. These healthier claims spawned growth in direct comparisons on an attribute by attribute basis in many categories.[38]

Finally, an extension of this approach to influence the target audience's brand attitude is not to make claims about *specific* salient attributes and benefits directly, but to make claims about *broad* brand beliefs. For example, public relations initiatives generally try to influence attitudes by showing that the organization is responsible or trusted. Another alternative to the broader belief approach is to influence the target audience's attitude with a *broad* emotion instead of *specific* importance. For example, the Hauler ad of No Frills in Chapter 4 exemplifies this approach, as this user-focus positioning ad does not attempt to influence specific attributes directly but rather shows the exuberance of the loyal shoppers.

CONSUMER PURCHASE MOTIVE

Since positioning involves presenting the brand's benefit claims to a target audience in an ad message, how they are communicated becomes a central decision. This portrayal of benefit claims must communicate the underlying reason why a brand is bought, which is reflected by the consumer purchase motive. Associating the benefit claim with a specific purchase motive influences whether the target audience responds positively to the brand's delivery claim or whether the target audience believes the benefit is important. For example, Campbell's soup tested two positioning strategies that reflected unique motives—a cost-effective way to make dinner vs. saving time to make a meal—and found varied acceptances across regional markets.[39]

Types of Purchase Motives As suggested with the A&W example, consumers could enjoy the better ingredients because the food is tastier or because the food is healthier. Thus, successful attribute positioning requires the right motivation or reason for purchase to be communicated in the ad. Keep in mind that the reasons for the A&W purchase are quite distinct: the sensory enjoyment of the food taste versus the individual accomplishment of eating properly. We highlight these two ideas since they are two of eight consumer purchase motives that guide the brand positioning strategy decision within Rossiter and Percy's managerial framework presented previously. **Figure 6-12** summarizes the motives into two types consistent with psychological theory.

Informational motives are negatively based since the consumer perceives their current consumption situation as a deficit in which the purchase of the product would minimize the shortfall and bring the consumer to a neutral or normal state. The deficit situation is shown with problem and lack of satisfaction in the first four motives. **Exhibit 6-18** suggests an informational motive for non-users. The ad shows six problems that this product resolves to convince those who do not own it to buy it.

Transformational motives imply that consumers perceive their consumption situation as requiring improvement from a neutral

Exhibit 6-18 WD-40 advertises the uses of its product for solving problems.

Courtesy of the WD-40 Company

Figure 6-12 Eight basic consumer purchase motives

Informational Motives	Transformational Motives
Problem removal	Sensory gratification
Problem avoidance	Intellectual stimulation or mastery
Incomplete satisfaction	Social approval
Mixed approach–avoidance	
Normal depletion	

Exhibit 6-19 The enjoyment of wearing a luxury brand like Gucci is visually communicated with a stylish outdoor image.

state. As such, this is a positively oriented motive. The improvement idea is seen in terms of gratification, mastery, and approval. Negatively and positively oriented motives are consistent with psychological theories of motivation and the types of motives are similar to Maslow's theory—however, there is no implied hierarchy. The ad in **Exhibit 6-19** shows how stylish a person looks when wearing a Gucci product, likely signalling an implicit social approval motivation.

Informational Motives Problem-removal motives reflect consumption situations where consumers perceive a problem (for example, dandruff), and seek a product that resolves the problem (anti-dandruff shampoo). Notice how the chewed pencil in the ad of **Exhibit 6-20** conveys the frustration (i.e., emotion) of a small business owner not able to complete the payroll task due to a lack of software; clearly, this is a problem in need of a solution. In contrast, problem avoidance motives occur when consumers anticipate a problem if they do not take pre-emptive action through the purchase of a product.

Insurance advertising typically addresses this as a motive as the messages show the consequences of not having coverage, or not having the right type or amount of coverage. These two examples for removal and avoidance are fairly self-evident; their application to specific brands requires unique executions so that the idea of selling the category does not dominate, causing the brand effects not to be achieved.

Exhibit 6-20 A business owner in need of a solution to the payroll problem may view Intuit favourably.

Payroll doesn't have to be so frustrating.
Unless you like the extra fiber in your diet.

intuit.
Payroll

From the maker of
QuickBooks

Payroll stressing you out? Start using Intuit® Payroll and make it easy on yourself. With a few clicks you can pay employees and file tax forms. Just enter employee hours and Intuit Payroll automatically calculates everything else. And, if you need it, there's live expert support. Saving you time and pencils every month.

Learn more at IntuitPayroll.com

Online Demo | 30-Day FREE Trial | Live Support

Consumers are motivated to switch brands when incomplete satisfaction with their current brand choice leads them to seek a better product. Phone service providers gravitate to this motive in their ads periodically. Telus emphasized its customer service to sway users from Bell and Rogers in its "Expect More" campaign.[40] Koodo demonstrated to frustrated consumers of other brands that they would be satisfied when they "Choose Happy" by switching to Koodo.[41]

Mixed approach–avoidance motives are active for consumers in purchase situations where they enjoy some elements of a product but dislike other parts and are seeking alternative solutions. Van Houtte positions its brand as being a "Master Roaster Since 1919" and the Montreal-based gourmet coffee company released a series of educational videos on its blog and social media vehicles. This historical and anthropological approach lends an air of authenticity to its beans and roasting skills, thereby potentially swaying consumers who may feel that other brands have fewer of these important characteristics.[42]

Consumers regularly require a product because they have none on hand, and so normal depletion as a reason for purchase is an almost-everyday situation; however, it is not a viable option for a primary brand positioning strategy. A message focusing on a reminder purchase when a consumer does not have the product is featured in seasonal purchases. For example, gardening products in the spring and school supplies in the fall are two obvious ad messages we commonly see. In essence, a normal depletion motive is not a long-term strategy; however, it is useful for short-term situations and influencing target audiences at a particular point in time to maximize total sales during a year.

Transformational Motives As the term implies, sensory gratification motives are predicated on the product's providing a positive experience via one of the five senses. The colourful imagery in **Exhibit 6-21** makes consumers want to share in the fun and experience the Canadian Rockies. Clearly, this is a valuable approach for many types of products, but it is important to focus on the right aspect with the right reference point. Newfoundland and Labrador Tourism's "Find Yourself" campaign captured the sensory experience of being in the province through an exquisite portrayal of its landscape and culture. The breathtaking scenery and delightful storylines brought a feeling of being there instantly, providing a prototypical example of communicating transformational motives.[43] The province continued with this style of advertising for many years due to its overwhelming success.

Intellectual stimulation or mastery is an individual motive linked to an element of self-improvement through the purchase of a product or brand. This mastery is driven by an innate human need to explore or learn. The marketing communication agency Sid Lee of Montreal, the global agency of record for Adidas, moved toward this motive in its messaging with the "All In" campaign. The wellness message associated with its sports gear encouraged consumers toward health, fitness, and achievement within the active sports community.[44] Curiously, Kraft Dinner used this kind of motivation to encourage adults to consume the product once again (e.g., lapsed users), with a nostalgic message that reminded them of how much fun they experienced as children when eating the cheesy noodles.[45]

Personal recognition is suggested with the social approval motive, whereby consumers are motivated to purchase certain products or brands because consumers aspire to be accepted in certain social groups. Women's fashion boutique Aritzia eschews traditional advertising, however its extensive use of public relations via influential bloggers, social media conversations, and celebrities wearing its fashions at store events all suggest a subtle connection to social approval. Its prominent placement of a flagship store on Fifth Avenue in New York City carries forth the boutique impression it strives to maintain in the market.[46]

Exhibit 6-21 Travel Alberta conveys the physical enjoyment of skiing in the Rockies.

Hand-out/TRAVEL ALBERTA/Newscom

Brand Repositioning Strategy

Developing a new brand positioning strategy for an established brand is referred to as *repositioning*, and the reasons for the change are discovered in the situation analysis. For example, marketing objectives such as sales or share may be below forecast, or advertising claims from competitors may threaten the current strategy. Repositioning is difficult to achieve because of ingrained consumer understanding of market structure and established brand attitudes. The options for altering the brand positioning strategy typically focus on the four topics previously defined: market definition, differential advantage, target audience, and a salient motive. Each of these is applied subsequently after identifying the communication issue for a number of recent CASSIES winners. Further details of the examples provided in this section are available at Cassies.ca.

IMPORTANCE OF REPOSITIONING

The situational analyses in terms of consumer, competition, company, market, and environment may all signal the need for a brand to move from its existing brand positioning strategy to a new one. This analysis should reveal which of these are most critical and help identify the marketing communication issue the promotional plan will address. **Figure 6-13** summarizes the origin of the repositioning strategy of the CASSIES winners that we now review.

Figure 6-13 Critical analysis guiding repositioning decisions

Competition	Company	Consumer	Market	Environment
Dove	Canadian 67	IKEA	Tetley Herbal Tea	Tourism
McDonald's	Cashmere	Subaru Outback	Reactine	Budweiser
Hospital for Sick Children	Iögo	Oka	TD	Honda

Competition A brand's repositioning is driven from competitive dynamics. Dove's research proved to managers that the brand appeared to be a "latecomer" to the personal care market, in which tremendous innovation had occurred in the preceding years from Procter & Gamble and other entrants like Nivea, Aveeno, and Jergens. While McDonald's invented the concept of a quick-service restaurant chain offering breakfast, it faced increased competition from other coffee shops offering similar breakfast sandwiches that appeared as copies of the original Egg McMuffin. McDonald's looked to invigorate the iconic breakfast sandwich and encourage more frequent purchases with a new repositioning. Toronto's Hospital for Sick Children faced increased competition for fundraising dollars during the Christmas season and required a new approach to encourage donations for its SickKids Foundation.

Company Company-sourced factors are an impetus for repositioning. While in some respects Molson introduced a new brand with Canadian 67, it replaced the previous Canadian Light and required the "re-launched" brand to develop a unique positioning distinct from the popular Coors Light. Kruger Products (formerly Scott Paper) faced a difficult repositioning task when its licence from Kimberly-Clark ran out for the use of the highly successful Cottonelle brand in the bathroom tissue category. This looked even more challenging in the face of competition from Royale and Charmin, not to mention the expected "introduction" of Cottonelle after Kruger had put both the Cashmere and Cottonelle brand names on the packaging and ads for a period of time before the expiration. In a very unusual situation, Ultima Foods needed to completely reposition its marketing communication activities when the company learned that the licensing for its Yoplait brand expired. This required the company to launch a new brand, Iögo, that would have to compete with its own previous brand as the original owners planned to centralize their operations and manage Yoplait's marketing.

Consumer Brands like IKEA and Subaru saw declines in sales as consumers appeared to no longer gravitate to them, while Oka looked to its current customers in Quebec to expand sales. IKEA appeared to be a brand of choice for young consumers setting up their first or first few households, but they tended to move on to other brands once they reached the 35+ age range. Subaru Outback sales declined by over 50 percent during a seven-year time period; it repositioned the brand with its ad suggesting that consumers deserve to be outdoors more. For its home Quebec market, the famous Oka cheese encouraged its current customers to eat the artisan cheese every day for lunch and snacks to spark greater consumption frequency.

Market Tetley saw a substantial decline in the herbal tea market at 2 percent per year with the growth of other types of tea when it repositioned by associating its flavours to different moods a consumer may have prior to consumption, thereby offering the perfect solution. Reactine needed to reposition its brand as the market shifted to increased use of other product formats. TD Bank's research indicated that the demand for mortgages would soften in the important spring season and repositioned its message to new home buyers who might be delaying entry into their first purchase.

Environment The Canadian Tourism Commission and Newfoundland & Labrador Tourism both faced potential further declines in travel to Canada (from other countries) and to the province (from other provinces) during the 2008 recession and slow economic growth that followed, which necessitated new positioning strategies. Budweiser lost its sponsorship contract with the NHL when the league signed with Molson, and needed a new way to link its brand to the hockey fan experience. Honda believed it needed a push in a new direction during the spring so that car shoppers would consider the brand during their shopping for a new car.

MARKET DEFINITION

Markets are partitioned by end benefit, brand name, usage situation, and product category. One possibility for repositioning is that the brand defines its market within a new partition or reconstructs the partition favourably through its messaging so that consumers understand how brands are competing in an entirely different manner. We look at an example for each option derived from **Figure 6-13**.

End Benefit Iögo's launch partly suggests a repositioning by brand name with the slogan "Iögo, a New Way to Say Yogurt," however the ads for its individual brands (such as Zip, Probio, Proteine, Nanö, and Nomad) consistently portray the yogurt as a healthy alternative to existing brands since it has no gelatin or artificial flavours or colours, and contains all natural fruit and milk products (**Exhibit 6-22**).

Brand Name Cashmere's dilemma of repositioning its product with a new brand name suggests it defined the marketing along this partition. The initial communication traced the evolution of the name change from Cottonelle to Cashmere. Subsequent ads connected the brand name of Cashmere to what cashmere material feels like. Maintaining the brand name out front in the positioning proved successful since the brand retained its strength when others might have faltered. In fact, the "new" Cashmere retained its leadership position after a few years and withstood the market entrance of the "new Cottonelle."

Usage Situation Oka cheese tried to extend its growth in Quebec by moving away from a positioning of authentic artisan cheese produced by monks for generations to an entirely modern approach. A series of humorous ads showed the different ways in which the unique cheese could be eaten. In one execution, a man accidentally spills the breakfast he is trying to serve a woman after tripping over a nearby cat. Despite the calamity, the woman finds a piece of Oka cheese on her arm and pleasantly enjoys the taste as she thanks the man for being so thoughtful. Two other executions show people eating the cheese as a snack with a funny little twist in the story.

Exhibit 6-22 Iögo yogurt repositioned itself away from its former brand name, Yoplait.

Hand-out/ULTIMA FOODS/Newscom

Product Category Molson Canadian 67 encouraged those drinking other alcohol, wine, and mixed drinks to switch to the brand due to its much lower calorie content. The brand clearly positioned itself against another category with ads that showed how small other drinks would be if they had 67 calories (**Exhibit 6-23**). This is much different than the positioning of other light beers and the previous Canadian Light positioning that emphasized to current beer drinkers the benefits of drinking a light beer over regular beer. However, Molson Canadian 67 subsequently repositioned the beer once again with its "guyet" ads—humorous messages that showed how the beer fits within a *guy's diet*—thereby suggesting another change of market definition in the direction end-benefit.

DIFFERENTIAL ADVANTAGE

One possibility for repositioning is to move from differential to central or vice versa, or to move from a product focus to a user focus or vice versa. Most often, a brand looks for a differential element to claim in its messaging to carve out its initial positioning, and it is extremely difficult and rare to reposition centrally; nevertheless, it remains an option. It is much more common for brands to examine options on the product/user focus. We look at an example for each option derived from **Figure 6-13**.

Differential McDonald's altered its coffee and used this as a springboard for repositioning its advertising for eating breakfast at the restaurant to those in the habit of eating at other quick-service outlets, notably Tim Hortons, which commanded a strong market share. McDonald's emphasized that its Egg McMuffin contained only 290 calories to

Exhibit 6-23 Drinks with 67 calories would be considerably smaller, unlike Molson Canadian 67 beer.

©Molson Coors Canada

Exhibit 6-24 Steaming cups of coffee appeared in public to entice consumers to McDonald's.

©samdcruz.com

Exhibit 6-25 Dove's ads contrast how women view themselves with how others view them.

Hand-out/DOVE/Newscom

Exhibit 6-26 Subaru Outback ads showed viewers that life outdoors was surprisingly better than sitting at home.

©Subaru

defend its core business. It also claimed superior coffee since the beverage represented the number one drink purchased outside the home. The pairing of coffee and eggs for morning consumption proved to be a key way of communicating its differential advantage. McDonald's used creative ads like the one in **Exhibit 6-24** to defend its breakfast market.

Central While Dove appeared to be a late entrant in the personal care market, the repositioning of the brand with its "Campaign for Real Beauty" attempted to define the market along the lines of "cosmetic beauty" and "real beauty"; the brand would take a central position within the latter definition. Although alternative interpretations may be considered, the public relations and consumer reaction to the campaign indicate it changed the face of the market dramatically and unexpectedly. Continued messaging like the new beauty sketches likely supports this contention (**Exhibit 6-25**).

Brand Benefit Positioning Honda communicated its affordability to consumers who generally believe that the brand's models are priced a little above their budget. Enter the promotional message that concentrated on the flexible payment options to finance a new Honda to those who would not normally consider the brand even though the consumers understood its dependability, quality, and reliability benefits. A series of TV and social media executions showed both perspectives of a pair of neighbours within a friendly rivalry as to how one could possibly afford a Honda.

User Positioning Subaru encouraged its ad viewers to get out more often with its unusual approach of peeling the TV screen back with a crowbar. Follow-up print ads reminded consumers of the unique TV ad with the icon at the top of the page, as seen in **Exhibit 6-26**. An interactive website helped consumers plan their itinerary outdoors to support this user positioning.

NEW TARGET AUDIENCE

As we saw in Chapter 3, organizations target advertising messages both to customers (such as brand loyals and favourable brand switchers) and to non-customers (such as new category users, other brand switchers, and other brand loyals). We illustrate various repositioning strategies for each of these target audiences.

Brand-Loyal Customers Budweiser created Bud Light ads, not to be confused with its Bud Lite beer, in which the main brand associated itself with hockey. The ads visualized the experience of fans watching a hockey game on TV and seeing "their" team score a goal with their own red light flashing nearby just like at a real hockey game. Fans could order their own red light for their home and have it synchronized to flash to replicate the TV ad experience in their own home. Such a promotion and series of ads undoubtedly encouraged loyal Canadian customers to feel stronger affinity for the popular American beer.

Favourable Brand Switcher Customers Ikea's research showed that each household operates in its own way, and its campaign to have its customers continue their patronage once they reach their mid-thirties exemplified this idea. Canadians responded to Ikea's request for #houserules via social media, posting their own version of what was acceptable, such as "No tweeting during dinner" and others that eventually became the message of outdoor ads and messaging in other social media vehicles. The first commercial showed a variety of household compositions and images—all containing Ikea furniture, of course—inviting past customers to send a message, all while discreetly encouraging them to reconsider shopping at Ikea.

New Category Users Mortgage selling involves getting consumers to renew a mortgage periodically (every one to five years), or encouraging people who do not own a home to take the risk and buy one. TD needed a fresh approach for encouraging new home buyers to evaluate the bank as an option for a mortgage, and—more importantly—to actually seriously evaluate purchasing a home for the very first time while the housing market appeared to be softening. Messages across multiple media focused on how TD's mortgage product had features that allowed new users to retain their financial flexibility, a key obstacle that research revealed consumers believed.

Other Brand Loyals Toronto's Hospital for Sick Children responded to the increased competition for fundraising dollars with a superhero theme in its ads that requested donations. The message portrayed children recovering from serious illnesses as everyday superheroes, much like we see in the movies. One execution featured a movie trailer where the actual child featured in the ad attended the movie with the audience giving him a standing ovation as a tribute to his achievement. Extensive media exposure showed different kids with their own effort at fighting off an illness, with an invitation for viewers and readers to contribute financially. The revenue exceeded the previous year's total by 20 percent, indicating that the campaign influenced those who had not contributed in the past.

Other Brand Switchers A primary target audience for promotional messages for touring or travelling to other countries or regions of a country is generally consumers who visited other places and who are looking for new adventures. Nevertheless it is a challenge to get on the consideration list of those shopping around. Both tourism brands mentioned earlier focused their repositioning on potential customers who had travelled extensively elsewhere. The Canadian Tourism Commission targeted Canadians who typically planned to travel abroad but liked to travel to unique locations, so the "Locals Know" campaign revealed a side of Canadian travel not previously evaluated (**Exhibit 6-27**). Similarly, for Newfoundland and Labrador, the target was those who valued the idea of going in a new direction different from their past experiences.

PURCHASE MOTIVATION

A brand repositioning strategy through consumer purchase motivation implies a shift from one type of motive to another. The most significant shift would be moving from an informational motive to a transformational motive or vice versa. We present two examples to show successful repositioning through a new consumer purchase motivation.

Exhibit 6-27 The Canadian Tourism Commission's "Locals Know" campaign reminded Canadians to visit Canada.

©Destination Canada

Problem–Solution Reactine's repositioning changed its motive considerably. Past approaches showed ways in which an allergy sufferer's distress and discomfort with symptoms did not accurately coincide with actual experience. Ads portrayed potential Reactine users in a humorous light without a clear rationale or reason for consumers to use the product category or brand. The repositioning took the problem more seriously and demonstrated the brand solving the problem in a favourable way.

Sensory Gratification Tetley visually conveyed the consumption experience of drinking its herbal tea by connecting the mood of the consumer with the colour of the tea in an innovative use of social media. With the advertising visuals, the senses involved in consumption clearly portrayed the brand in a new light within the product category. Positionings of competitors lack the sensory experience, opening the door for a successful repositioning for Tetley.

(LO5) IMC Planning: Brand Positioning Extensions

From an IMC planning perspective, we can extend or adapt the concepts encompassing the brand positioning strategy decisions in three directions: multiple target audiences, buyer decision stages, and corporate brands. The idea is to work with the general model for the positioning decisions and modify it for different parts of the IMC plan.

MULTIPLE TARGET AUDIENCES

Throughout this chapter, we have examined the brand positioning strategy for a single target audience of end users. Many organizations target multiple audiences for their marketing communication. For example, in Chapter 3 we described different customer and non-customer groups; brands do in fact have the opportunity to invest in marketing communication devoted to each group. This raises the question as to whether the brand should develop exactly the same positioning strategy for each target audience, or whether variation should exist. And if variation is necessary, what aspects of the brand positioning strategy need to be customized? A number of the examples in Chapter 3 implied this issue; however, after describing positioning strategy, we need to return to the opportunity for promotional planners to fully consider their options.

Although promotional planners could consider customizing all four brand positioning strategy decisions, the first two—market definition and differential advantage—would likely remain relatively constant across customer and non-customer groups. The specific messages to influence brand attitude and the purchase motive communicated offer greater opportunity for getting the right message at the right time. One IMC tool to execute this customized brand positioning strategy is the Internet. For example, automobile advertisers might consider consumers who visit websites to gather information while searching for a vehicle as more likely to be brand switchers, and will include messages that position the brand against its strongest competitor on specific benefits and portray those benefits along the lines of the target audience having dissatisfaction with their current brand. While this is just one example, promotional planners can look at all advertising options and all IMC tools for opportunities to deliver a more specific message to a particular target audience that reinforces a particular brand positioning strategy.

Another interpretation for multiple target audiences involves group decision making, another topic introduced in Chapter 3. For example, in traditional family situations an advertiser may attempt one brand positioning strategy for parents and a relatively different one for children. McDonald's has historically employed this approach with child-directed communication featuring Ronald McDonald and other characters, while parents received messages of the special time they could enjoy with their family. Additionally, automobile brands can use print ads to emphasize certain car features that appeal to men in magazines where men represent a higher proportion of the audience, and similarly for women.

BUYER DECISION STAGES

In the IMC planning section of Chapter 5, we noted that marketers could consider message and communication tool options for each stage of the consumer decision-making process. Various message options are discerned from the brand positioning strategy decisions outlined in this chapter. First, promotional planners can decide which part positioning strategy would be most relevant or effective at each stage. Market definition and differential a be more appropriate at the pre-purchase stage or need-recognition stage. For example, the marketing for Canada used television advertising to signal that it competed against two markets: regular compact cars lik Civic, and other smaller sports cars like the BMW 3 Series. It also emphasized its advantage of being small not *too* small.

CORPORATE BRANDS

Thus far we have defined brand positioning strategy and illustrated examples where the brand is at the product level. Corporate brands are also part of integrated marketing communications and are the focus of the public relations topics in Chapter 15. In this context, corporate brands often have varied target audiences, for example investors or members of a particular community.

Given the broader scope of the corporate brand, the initial positioning decision for market definition would concern brand name in most cases. Establishing a differential advantage from a corporate brand entails both differential and central positioning. For example, corporate brand-building activities for Honda suggest that it attempted to establish a central positioning concerning environmental responsibility. This would coincide with its marketing activities of introducing the first hybrid vehicle. Again, the organization-wide communication would imply that most corporate brand positioning would focus on brand benefit positioning over user positioning; however, "green marketing" efforts by companies suggest potential for the latter with an appropriate message that suggests altruistic feelings to the target audience.

All marketing communication decisions are or should be designed to influence target audience attitudes, so corporate brand attitude persuasion is entirely relevant. For example, organizations often involve themselves in sponsorship activities to signal that they are socially responsible, a key attribute to communicate to the general public or to future employees or other stakeholders. Finally, most corporate brand communication is intended along the lines of transformational motives; the clearest examples are television commercials with triumphant music and everlasting positive images.

Learning Objectives Summary

 Identify the concepts of market positioning strategy and market position.

The strategic marketing plan describes all marketing decisions, including promotion and the supporting analysis and justification. It typically includes the market positioning strategy, which summarizes the markets the organization is competing in (i.e., target market) and how the marketing mix fulfills the needs of this market. The resulting consumer perception of where the consumer believes the organization to be competing is known as the market position. Often, market research illuminates where consumers perceive an organization to be with respect to its competitors, which can be graphed on a market position diagram or perceptual map. Promotional planners rely on this document for all decisions, including the overall IMC direction, creative strategy, and creative tactics for advertising or any other IMC tool such as sales promotion, public relations, direct, or Internet.

 Apply the positioning concept in an advertising context by defining brand positioning strategy and brand position.

For many communication problems or opportunities, promotional messages are directed to target audiences. These audiences are a subset of the target market or an entirely different group, depending upon the communications situation.

omotional planners require a detailed profile of the target audience with most appropriate segmentation variables, including whether the target is a customer or non-customer. Advertising or any other promotional message is guided by the brand positioning strategy, which specifies how it is intended to influence its target audience with a given product category or product market. The resulting target audience perception as to what the brand offers is known as the brand position. The flexibility of influencing a target audience's brand position through many IMC tools allows promotional managers to plan for unique brand positions for multiple target audiences.

 ### Illustrate how to formulate brand positioning strategy decisions.

The process for developing a brand positioning strategy in the context of marketing communications is similar to developing a positioning strategy for the overall marketing. However, it differs by evaluating or integrating very micro-level aspects of consumer behaviour in its planning by closely considering the nature of the purchase decision. The direction of the decision is different, with the goal of finding the most appropriate message, media, or IMC tool versus determining optimal product design features.

The brand positioning strategy comprises four decisions: market definition, differential advantage, target audience brand attitude, and consumer purchase motive. The market definition decision allows the promotional planner to consider whether to define the market in which the brand is competing by benefits, brand name, usage situation, or product category. Differential advantage decisions include whether the brand takes a differential or central positioning and whether the brand focuses its positioning on its benefit claims or the user. Target audience attitude decisions consider how the message is expected to persuade existing beliefs to the desired beliefs about the brand. Finally, promotional planners decide what type of purchase motive should be associated with the brand.

 ### Demonstrate brand repositioning strategy opportunities.

In some communication situations—such as new competitors, changing consumer tastes, or poor brand performance—promotional planners need to reposition their brand. The repositioning can follow the same decisions as described above, where the promotional planner can consider an alternative market definition, communicate a new differential advantage, emphasize different benefit claims, or focus on another motivational option. Promotional planners can consider altering one or all four of these decisions to achieve moderate or very significant change in the current brand position.

 ### Interpret brand positioning strategy decisions in other contexts.

A brand positioning strategy can be augmented for any marketing communication purposes. Three relevant ones to consider are multiple target audiences, buyer decision stages, and corporate brand, to name a few. Organizations often face the dual task of communicating to long-time customers and to newer customers, thereby requiring a more specific message for each and therefore raising the possibility of differences in the brand positioning strategy. Similarly, brands may alter their brand positioning strategy by emphasizing different benefits, for example, at varying stages of the consumer decision-making process. Finally, a corporate identity is of paramount importance and the decisions at the brand level are readily interpreted on a broader scale.

Review Questions

1. Describe how the market positioning strategy adopted for a brand would need to be supported by all other elements of the marketing mix.

2. Why is it useful to distinguish between brand positioning strategy and brand position?

3. What problems would a brand encounter if it communicated with an incorrect motive?

4. What factors would lead a marketer to use a repositioning strategy?

5. Why is it important to consider unique brand positioning decisions at each of the buyer decision stages? Is it feasible to implement this approach for all product categories?

Applied Questions

1. Explain how McDonald's market positioning strategy has changed with the new developments in its menu and outlets.

2. Examine the social media presence of a brand and assess whether it clearly identifies a brand positioning strategy.

3. Explain why a central positioning is feasible. Do any brands currently use this approach in their marketing communication?

4. Develop market partition diagrams for beverages. What repositioning options are available for any brand?

5. How can brand positioning decisions be applied to new category users and brand loyal users of smart phones?

CHAPTER SEVEN

Creative Strategy Decisions

LEARNING OBJECTIVES

LO1 Summarize the idea and importance of creativity in an advertising context.

LO2 Describe the creative strategy planning process.

LO3 Identify the approaches used for determining the creative theme that forms the basis of an advertising campaign.

LO4 Summarize the different types of message appeals that advertisers use to persuade their target audience.

LO5 Identify the source or communicator options a marketer has for a promotional message.

LO6 Apply source and message appeal options for different ad executions.

#EatTogether for Wellness

On January 1, 2017, the NHL celebrated its 100th anniversary with the Centennial Classic hockey game between the Toronto Maple Leafs and the Detroit Red Wings. Canadians celebrated 150 years since Confederation with Canada 150. Canada's leading food brand, President's Choice, celebrated with a meaningful initiative by communicating how food brings together people such as family, friends, co-workers, and neighbours.

During the hockey game, a 150-second ad by President's Choice told the story of two women who set up a pot-luck dinner table in the hallway of their apartment building. The two hosts invited their neighbours, who joined with their own food until the hallway was filled with a dozen people. Set to the song "What the World Needs Now Is Love," the non-speaking visual video ad ended with a short written copy ("Nothing brings us together like eating together") and then the brand logo "PC" and slogan "Crave More" and the Canada 150 logo. The impetus for the message of this first film revolved around the company's initial research indicating that 38 percent of Canadians eat dinner together four to six times a week. The extended emotional story kicked off a movement that included in-store eat-together events, a contest, social challenges, and a release of the ad's song during the Grammy Awards.

A revival of #EatTogether occurred with a video message shown in Cineplex theatres and then shown on TV during the World Juniors hockey tournament. The 90-second story focused on the treasured moments a woman experiences when eating with family and friends throughout her life from infancy to adulthood. The story wrapped up with the young woman eating at her desk by herself, as does everyone else in the office. Set to the song "I Got You Babe," this visual video also ended with a short written copy ("We grow up eating together. Why do we stop? This year, let's #EatTogether") and then the brand logo "PC" and slogan "Crave More" closed the ad. Company research conducted after the first film showed that eating in solitude leads to unhappiness, and that two-thirds of people often eat lunch alone, which lent support for this second film. Live and online activities supported the video and an event entitled National Eat Together Day occurred in June. Eight Canadian filmmakers created their own videos, shown in social media leading up to the big event, that told their story of #EatTogether.

To continue the #EatTogether momentum, the third video told the story of all humans who dream to live the life they desire. In this case, the visuals of the 90-second story showed adventurous and pleasurable life experiences. But instead of a catchy song, viewers heard the voice of philosopher Alan Watts reciting part of his "Dreams of Life" speech, along with moving background music. His conclusion coincided with visuals of a family eating together, as Watts stated that we dream to be where we are right now. Once again, the ad ended with a similar closing. President's Choice launched the ad in cinemas, on social media, and on TV during the World Juniors in time for people to adopt #EatTogether in their New Year's resolutions.

Collectively, the three ads represent an example of a trend in advertising where storytelling illustrates consumer behaviour, reflects humanity in a creative and visual manner, and shows a brand's commitment to consumers. All three films garnered critical acclaim and boosted the President's Choice image through 116 million viewings of the films, 18 million people discussing #EatTogether, 450,000 Canadians taking the pledge, and 92 percent having a positive attitude toward eating together. In conclusion, President's Choice's films supporting media, events, and activities contributed significantly by encouraging people to #EatTogether; certainly this is a very positive step for society, and the brand contributed to it significantly.

Question:

1. Why does it make sense for PC to advertise with long, emotional messages to encourage people to #EatTogether?

An important part of an IMC program is the advertising message, the means by which to tell consumers how the product can solve a problem or satisfy desires or achieve goals. Advertising messages create images or associations and establish a brand position as well as transform the experience of buying and/or using a product. Advertising messages play a leading role in the IMC program, and are crucial to the success of the brand's promotional effort. While most students may never design ads, everyone involved in marketing or promotion should understand the strategic decisions that underlie the development of advertising messages.

It is easy to see many ways to convey an advertising message while watching commercials on TV, seeing videos on the Internet, perusing print ads in a magazine, or witnessing advertising in out-of-home locations. Underlying these messages is a **creative strategy** that determines *what* the advertising message will communicate and **creative tactics** for *how* the message will be executed. In this chapter, we focus on three creative strategy decisions. First, we describe approaches for determining the idea of the creative theme, which provides direction for attention-getting, distinctive, and memorable messages. Second, we identify the message appeals that advertisers use to persuade consumers. Third, we focus on the source characteristics that advertisers typically use to alter consumers' attitudes. We summarize the process of planning for creative strategy prior to these decisions. We also apply these latter two points in our IMC planning perspective.

(LO1) Advertising Creativity

Upon determining the direction of the communications program, the advertising agency (or internal ad department) focuses on the appropriate creative approach for communicating a message that reinforces the brand positioning strategy. Good advertising creativity is central to determining the success of a product as it clearly contributes to a strong brand position with its intended target audience. The essence of advertising is its creativity, and we provide a working definition and demonstrate its importance.

DEFINITION OF ADVERTISING CREATIVITY

For students, as well as advertising and marketing practitioners, the most interesting aspect of advertising is the creative side. We are intrigued by a creative ad and admire the consumer insight it reflects as it expresses a unique brand message. A great ad is a joy to behold and an epic to create, with the cost of producing a TV commercial potentially hitting $1 million. Conceiving an ad is such an exciting and enticing activity that a competition searching for the next top ad executive is run each year for university students by the DeGroote School of Business at McMaster University.[1] Companies see money spent on advertising and other forms of marketing communication as good brand investment. They realize that the manner in which the advertising message is developed and executed is critical to the success of the promotion, which in turn can influence the effectiveness of the entire marketing program. For example, BMW's creative messages over time firmly planted the idea of Ultimate Driving Experience in Canada and Ultimate Driving Machine in other countries (**Exhibit 7-1**).

Creativity is a commonly used term in advertising. The people who develop ads are known as creative specialists; they work for ad agencies that develop ad campaigns or for marketers that handle their own advertising without the help of an agency. Perhaps the focus on creativity occurs because people view the specific challenge for those who develop an advertising message as "to be creative." It is their job to turn all of the information regarding product features and benefits, marketing plans, consumer research, and communication objectives into a creative concept that will bring the advertising message to life. This begs the question: What is meant by *creativity* in advertising?

Advertising creativity is the ability to generate fresh, unique, and appropriate ideas that are used as effective solutions to marketing communication issues (e.g., problems or opportunities). To be *appropriate* and *effective*, a creative idea must be relevant to the target audience.[2] Relevance, an important characteristic of creativity, is the quality that lets the ad instantly capture the target audience's attention and generate critical brand associations through specific cognitive and emotional responses.

Exhibit 7-1 Excellent advertising helps create an image for BMW automobiles.

Because one cannot drive a Van Gogh.

The new 7 series.

The ultimate driving machine.

Courtesy of BMW of North America, LLC

The relevance is even more critical when an advertiser takes into account the selective attention of the target audience. Moreover, the creativity has to crystallize the brand so that it is understood by the target audience, who is experiencing selective comprehension when faced with competing promotional messages. Extending this further, the relevance of the creativity to the target audience is critical to establishing an important link to the brand, its benefits, and why the target audience would purchase it. In other words, relevance clearly supports the brand positioning strategy. Reinforcing this view suggests two approaches: *ad to consumer relevance* and *brand to consumer relevance*.[3] *Ad to consumer relevance* involves ad characteristics that are meaningful to the target audience, such as the celebrity spokesperson or imagery. *Brand to consumer relevance* concerns the target audience's personal interest in the product. The message in **Exhibit 7-2** with a striking image is relevant for the target audience for both the ad and the brand.

Appropriate and effective creativity should offer divergence as well, since the message must break through media clutter and attract the target audience's attention. *Divergence* is the extent to which an ad contains novel, different, or unusual characteristics.[4] Advertising creativity is divergent in terms of originality (e.g., rare or surprising ideas that are not common), flexibility (e.g., different ideas), elaboration (e.g., unexpected ideas that become intricate, complicated, or sophisticated), synthesis (e.g., normally unrelated ideas that are combined or connected), and artistic values (e.g., ideas expressed verbally or visually). **Exhibit 7-3** shows an example of divergence in advertising through flexibility and synthesis. The flexibility occurs through the three views of a carpet while the synthesis emerges when relating the three points of view together to understand the concept of value, which is the brand characteristic communicated.

The historic Absolut vodka ads demonstrate relevance and divergence for good creativity. The original creative showed the distinctive shape of the bottle and depicted it with visual puns and witty headlines that played with the Absolut name.[5] The agency and client jointly selected and customized the advertising campaign for the audience of each print magazine. It is recognized as a significant creative campaign, and stood the test of time for over 20 years until sales lagged. A revised creative relied on imagery using the tagline "In an Absolut World" and played off the brand name to illustrate an imagined world where everything is as ideal as Absolut vodka. The creativity challenged consumers to reflect on their world vision to maintain the brand as a cultural icon.[6] Its latest global campaign uses the slogan "Create a better tomorrow, tonight" to appeal to younger consumers who spend time with a close group of friends.[7] The campaign highlighted Absolut's historic distilling practices to provide a sustainability message and featured a contest for creative specialists to design ads. The brand provided a template with the bottle shape and new slogan so the contest ads would be consistent with the original campaign.[8]

Exhibit 7-2 Both the ad and the brand are relevant to the consumer in this visual ad.

Source: Pennzoil and Quaker State by Shell International B.V.

Exhibit 7-3 Advertising divergence by flexibility and synthesis occurs in this HSBC ad.

©The Advertising Archives/Alamy Stock Photo

Exhibit 7-4 This colourful and creative ad captures the attention of people walking by.

©Alistair Laming/Alamy Stock Photo

IMPORTANCE OF ADVERTISING CREATIVITY

Perspectives on what constitutes creativity in advertising differ. At one extreme are people who argue that advertising is creative only if it sells the product. An advertising message's or campaign's impact on sales counts more than whether it is innovative. At the other end of the continuum are those who judge the creativity of an ad in terms of its artistic or aesthetic value and originality. They contend that creative ads can break through the competitive clutter, grab the consumer's attention, and have a positive communication effect. Both perspectives indicate the importance of advertising creativity as it either presents a good public exposure or contributes to a brand positioning strategy and ultimately sales.

The growth of brands has highlighted the importance of advertising creativity leading to renewed investigations.[9] Surveyed executives believe creativity has improved compared to the origin of modern-day advertising during the 1960s.[10] The Leo Burnett agency and *Contagious Magazine* conduct worldwide research to uncover the success of the most creative advertising in traditional and newer evolving media, while others present new or reconfigured ideas to define creativity.[11] In general, creative advertising messages help focus the receiver's attention, allowing deeper processing and stronger recall and recognition.[12]

Perspectives on advertising creativity split along marketing and artistic lines, as shown in one study.[13] Product managers and account executives view ads as promotional tools whose primary purpose is to communicate favourable impressions to the marketplace. They believe a commercial should be evaluated in terms of whether it fulfills the client's marketing and communicative objectives. Alternatively, creative specialists view ads as an expression of their personal aesthetics and an opportunity to communicate their unique creative talent with the hopes of career advancement.

What constitutes creativity in advertising is probably somewhere between the two views. To break through the clutter and make an impression on the target audience, an ad must be unique and entertaining, as demonstrated in **Exhibit 7-4**. Research has shown that a major determinant of whether a commercial will be successful in changing brand preferences is its "likability," or the viewer's overall reaction.[14] Advertising messages that are well designed and executed and generate emotional responses can create positive feelings that are transferred to the product or service being advertised.[15] Creative specialists believe this occurs if they are given considerable latitude in developing advertising messages, but purely creative ads might fail to communicate a relevant product message. In an attempt to resolve this discussion, research findings suggest that very creative advertising messages have additional positive brand communication effects (i.e., brand quality, brand interest) beyond recall and likability.[16]

However, the issue is unclear; one study found that the creative specialists themselves can disagree on the merits of creativity. A survey of art directors and copywriters found that the former are more concerned with visual creativity, while the latter more strongly believe in message delivery.[17] In the age of consumer-generated "advertising" messages, another study found that perceptions of creativity differ among advertising professionals, students, and the general public.[18] Thus, it appears that everyone must keep a balanced perspective on the creativity of advertising messages.

Finally, studies conclude that advertising creativity impacts consumers' cognitive, affective, and behavioural responses to advertising messages.[19] Novel advertising requires consumer processing time, resulting in longer exposure and greater attention. Creative ads draw more attention to the advertised brand, and generate higher levels of recall, greater motivation to process the information, and deeper levels of processing.[20] Creative advertising positively impacts emotional reactions, including attitudes and purchase intentions.[21] Divergence is a particularly important component of advertising creativity; however, clients favour relevance over divergence as they want their agencies to create ads that communicate pertinent information such as specific product features and benefits. Researchers suggest that clients should be less resistant to divergent approaches, and note that there is a fundamental need for divergent thinkers in the ad development process.[22] Considering that most advertising messages are seen and/or heard in a cluttered media environment where marketers must compete for the attention of consumers, it is important that brand managers accept ads that are novel and divergent as well as relevant and meaningful.

IMC Perspective 7-1 describes a couple of very creative Cineplex messages to give consumers a new outlook on the movie chain.

SEE THE BIG PICTURE WITH CINEPLEX

Lily and the Snowman tells the story of a young girl who spends her childhood with a snowman friend who came to life when a beam of light that resembled the light in a cinema shone from the house. They play together in the backyard and make shadow puppets in a light that morphs into what looks like a movie. Eventually spring arrives and the snowman resides in the freezer for safety and returns two more times to enjoy a movie with Lily as she grows into a teen.

Unfortunately, the snowman is forgotten for many years until Lily recalls her wonderful times. She rescues her friend and watches shadow puppets performed by the snowman with her daughter. The ad ends with the message "Make time for what you love," the logo, and the "See the Big Picture" slogan. The featured music was a cover of the Genesis song "Follow You, Follow Me," and was made available for digital download.

The purpose of the campaign originated from Cineplex's having weak brand scores despite near universal awareness. Consumers were flocking to alternative avenues for viewing movies, and the brand needed to recreate the magic of going to the cinema. The emotional enjoyment of seeing the big screen needed to be creatively conveyed, and associating that emotion with spending time with a loved one proved to be a powerful message.

Viewers saw the film at Cineplex theatres and extensively in social media. Cineplex achieved extremely impressive results. It hit 30 million online views and Canadians shared it 620,000 times on Facebook and YouTube. The exposure culminated with increased brand affinity scores of 37 percent. Cineplex's ticket sales grew 25 percent in the month of the film's release.

©Cineplex/Zulu Alpha Kilo

Website visits grew 50 percent and social media following grew in the 30 percent range. The song streamed numerous times and hit the top 50 on the Billboard rankings.

With this momentum, Cineplex extended the "See the Big Picture" theme with another animated film entitled *A Ballon for Ben* one year later. The two-minute tale illuminates a world where movies are encased within brilliant white balloons and tells the story of Ben and his father, who do not enjoy the magic together due to the busyness of life. After witnessing his son's despair, the father lassos the biggest balloon ever for them to watch the movie in the sky. Once again, the film uses an older popular song sung by a new artist and made available online. While Ben's is an entirely different story, the underlying creative theme of sharing something important with a loved one is fully experienced by all. The stories of Lily and Ben demonstrate the importance of creativity once again.

Question:

1. Why does Cineplex want to associate its brand with the idea of love among the family?

Planning Creative Strategy

LO2

Creative specialists use research, creative briefs, strategy statements, communications objectives, and other input and transform it all into an advertising message. Their job is to write copy, design layouts and illustrations, produce video messages, or program interactive digital tools that effectively communicate the central theme on which the campaign or IMC program is based. Rather than simply stating a product's features or benefits, they transform an advertising

Exhibit 7-5 Old Spice rejuvenated its brand with quirky ads that continue to be run.

SMELL LIKE A MAN, MAN.
Old Spice

Old Spice by Procter & Gamble

message into an approach that captures the audience's interest and makes the brand and the ad instantly memorable. In this section, we describe the creative challenge, illustrate the creative process, summarize the job of an account planner, identify forms of research for creative decision making, and summarize the end results—the creative brief and advertising campaign—when planning for creative promotional communication.

CREATIVE CHALLENGE

The job of the creative team is challenging because every marketing situation is different and each campaign or advertisement may require a different creative approach. Numerous guidelines have been developed for creating effective advertising.[23] Creative people follow proven formulas when creating ads because clients can feel uncomfortable with advertising that is too different. An ad executive commented years ago, "Very few clients realize that the reason that their work is so bad is that they are the ones who commandeered it and directed it to be that way. I think that at least 50 percent of an agency's successful work resides in the client."[24] Decades later, empirical research supports this practitioner's point of view.[25]

One agency that has been successful in getting its clients to take risks is Rethink, best known for its excellent creative work for Ikea, WestJet, and A&W. The agency's founders feel that a key element in its success is a steadfast belief in taking risks when most agencies and their clients have been retrenching and becoming more conservative. The agency develops great advertising partly because its clients are willing to take risks and agree with the agency's approach of listening to its client and arriving at a creative solution for the marketing communication problem or opportunity. Empirical research concludes that risk-taking agencies have an orientation to taking risks as a direction from senior management, a creative philosophy to enhance their creative reputation, and an acceptance of working with uncertainty.[26]

Not all agree that advertising has to be risky to be effective. Marketing managers accept advertising that simply communicates product features and benefits and gives the consumer a reason to buy. They see their ad campaigns as investments whose goal is to sell the product rather than to finance the whims of their agency's creative staff. They argue that creative people occasionally lose sight of advertising's bottom line: Does it sell? An Old Spice campaign shown in **Exhibit 7-5** is an example where the ads demonstrated creative flair with quirky executions and contributed to increased sales. Unusual and unique creative approaches continued for many years and established the brand as a popular option to consider purchasing.

CREATIVE PROCESS

Creativity in advertising is a process, and creative success likely occurs when an organized approach is followed. James Webb Young, a former creative vice-president at the J. Walter Thompson agency, proposed the following five-stage approach that still remains a useful reference.[27]

- *Immersion.* Read background information regarding the problem.
- *Digestion.* Work the information over in one's mind.
- *Incubation.* Get away and let ideas develop.
- *Illumination.* See the light or solution with the birth of the idea.
- *Verification.* Study and refine the idea to see if it is a practical solution.

A model of the creative process is valuable to those working in the creative area of advertising, since it offers an organized way to approach an advertising problem. A model like Young's does not say much about how this information will be synthesized and used by the creative specialist, because this part of the process is unique to the individual. An investigation along these lines reveals four individual factors: orientation toward the creative work, approach to the communication problems, mindscribing (i.e., free-flow thinking), and heuristics (i.e., quick creative decision rules).[28] A study of advertising copywriters found that they work without guidance from any formal theories of communication.

However, those interviewed claimed to use similar informal, implicit theories that guide them in creating ads. These theories are based on finding ways to break through the ad clutter, open the consciousness of consumers, and connect with them to deliver the message.[29]

However, advertising creativity is not the exclusive domain of creative specialists, as creative thinking is done by everyone involved when planning creative strategy. Agency people (i.e, account executives, media planners, researchers, account planners) and those on the client side (i.e., marketing and brand managers) must all seek creative solutions to problems encountered in planning, developing, and executing an advertising campaign. It is also important that those working on the client side do not create a relationship with their agencies that inhibits the creative processes required to produce good advertising. Highly skilled creative specialists aspire to work with open-minded clients who are receptive to new ideas, and they note that some of the best creative work developed by agencies does not get used because clients are resistant to taking creative risks unless they are under pressure to perform.[30] Advertising agencies, as well as other IMC specialist organizations, thrive on creativity as it is at the heart of what they do and they must design an environment that fosters the development of creative thinking and creative advertising. **Exhibit 7-6** illustrates a creative ad showing the creative process in car design. Clients must also understand the differences between the perspectives of the creative personnel and marketing and product managers. While the client has ultimate approval of the advertising, the opinions of creative specialists must be respected when advertising ideas and content are evaluated.

Exhibit 7-6 Creativity sparks from any avenue.

Direct from our imagination. **Introducing the all-new Civic.**

HONDA

Source: American Honda Motor Co., Inc. and Rubin Postaer and Associates

ACCOUNT PLANNING

To facilitate the creative process, agencies use **account planning**, which involves conducting research and gathering all relevant information about a client's product or service, brand, and consumers in the target audience. Jon Steel, a former vice-president and director of account planning, has written an excellent book on the process, entitled *Truth, Lies and Advertising: The Art of Account Planning.*[31] He notes that the account planner's job is to provide the key decision makers with all the information they require to make an intelligent decision. According to Steel, "Planners may have to work very hard to influence the way that the advertising turns out, carefully laying out a strategic foundation with the client, handing over tidbits of information to creative people when, in their judgment, that information will have the greatest impact, giving feedback on ideas, and hopefully adding ideas of their own."

Account planning assists creative strategy development by driving the process from the customer's point of view. Planners work with the client as well as other agency personnel, such as the creative team and media specialists, and discuss how their knowledge and information can contribute to creative strategy development. Account planners are usually responsible for all the research (both qualitative and quantitative) conducted during the creative strategy development process. Account planning has evolved considerably such that agencies and clients see it as part of the strategic creative process with a clear understanding of how to evaluate the performance of all personnel involved.[32] In the following section, we examine how research and information can provide input to the creative process of advertising.

RESEARCH IN THE CREATIVE PROCESS

The creative specialist first learns as much as possible about the product, the target audience, the competition, and any other relevant **research**. Much of this information would come from the marketing plan and advertising plan developed by the client. Alternatively, good clients will give proper direction to their agency by constructing a client brief that recapitulates their internal documents and adds additional information that would give the creative specialist an idea as to the direction of the brand positioning strategy. The Institute of Communications and Advertising produces a best

...ent that shows brand managers how to construct a client brief that serves the needs of both parties, ...ging more creative marketing communication.

...us, the creative specialist can acquire additional background information through inventive means:

...d anything related to the product or market.

...Talk to people (e.g., marketing personnel, designers, engineers, consumers).

• Visit stores and malls.

• Use the product or service and become familiar with it.

• Work in and learn about the business.

In addition to background information, creative people use general and product-specific pre-planning input.

General pre-planning input can include books, periodicals, trade publications, scholarly journals, pictures, and clipping services, which gather and organize magazine and newspaper articles on the product, the market, and the competition, including the latter's ads. Another useful general pre-planning input concerns market trends and developments. Information is available from a variety of sources, including local, provincial, and federal governments, secondary research suppliers, and industry trade associations, as well as advertising and media organizations that publish research reports and newsletters. Those involved in developing creative strategy can also gather relevant and timely information by reading the Canadian publication *Strategy,* and American publications like *Adweek* and *Advertising Age.*

Product-specific pre-planning input is information that includes specific studies conducted on how consumers buy and consume the product and/or characteristics of the target audience regarding extensive consumer behaviour variables. This type of research includes both quantitative research and qualitative research.

Quantitative research includes attitude studies, market structure, and positioning studies such as perceptual mapping and psychographic or lifestyle profiles that provide a descriptive understanding of consumer behaviour. As noted in Chapter 3, agencies or affiliated research companies conduct psychographic studies annually and construct detailed psychographic or lifestyle profiles of product or service users. Dove conducted one of the more significant research studies prior to launching the "Campaign for Real Beauty." The research involved personal interviews and sampled women from many countries regarding their attitudes toward beauty with a survey methodology.

Qualitative research includes methods like in-depth interviews, projective techniques, association tests, and focus groups in which consumers are encouraged to bring out associations related to products and brands to provide insight into consumer behaviour. **Figure 7-1** summarizes these methods, which are referred to as motivation research, providing useful information for assessing how and why consumers buy, consume, and use products. Focus groups and in-depth interviews are valuable for gaining insights into consumers' feelings, and projective techniques are often the only way to get around stereotypical or socially desirable responses. Since motivation research studies typically use a low number of participants, a limitation is that findings are not generalizable to the whole population and may reveal idiosyncrasies of a few individuals. Still, it is difficult to ignore motivation research since the resulting consumer insight inspires advertising messages aimed at buyers' deeply rooted feelings, hopes, aspirations, and fears.

Focus groups are a prevalent research tool among the four methods at this stage of the creative process. **Focus groups** are a research method whereby consumers (usually 10 to 12 people) from the target audience are led through a discussion regarding a particular topic. Focus groups give insight as to why and how consumers buy, use, and consume a product, what is important to them in choosing a particular brand, what they like and don't like about products, and

Figure 7-1 Qualitative marketing research methods employed to obtain consumer insight

In-depth interviews	Face-to-face situations in which an interviewer asks a consumer to talk freely in an unstructured interview using specific questions designed to obtain insights into his or her motives, ideas, or opinions
Projective techniques	Efforts designed to gain insights into consumers' values, motives, attitudes, or needs that are difficult to express or identify by having them project these internal states upon some external object
Association tests	A technique in which an individual is asked to respond with the first thing that comes to mind when he or she is presented with a stimulus; the stimulus may be a word, picture, ad, and so on
Focus groups	A small number of people with similar backgrounds and/or interests who are brought together to discuss a particular product, idea, or issue

any special needs they might have that aren't being satisfied. Focus group interviews bring the creative people and others involved in creative strategy development into contact with the customers. Listening to a focus group gives copywriters, art directors, and other creative specialists a better sense of who the target audience is, what the audience is like, and to whom the creatives need to write, design, or direct in creating an advertising message.

Toward the end of the creative process, members of the target audience may evaluate rough creative layouts and indicate what meaning they get from the ad, what they think of its execution, or how the ad makes them feel. This could occur in a focus group session. The creative team gains insight into how a TV commercial communicates its message by having members of the target audience evaluate the ad in storyboard form. A **storyboard** is a series of drawings used to present the visual plan or layout of a proposed commercial. It contains a series of sketches of key frames or scenes along with the copy or audio portion for each scene (**Exhibit 7-7**).

Evaluating a commercial in storyboard form is challenging because the abstract images and words are much different than the finished product consumers usually understand. To make the creative layout more realistic and easier to evaluate, the agency may produce an **animatic**, a video of the storyboard along with an audio soundtrack. Storyboards

Exhibit 7-7 Marketers gain insight into consumers' reactions to a commercial by showing them a storyboard.

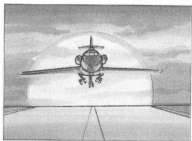

VIDEO: A private Lear jet takes off during sunset as heat vapors rise from runway.

AUDIO: Sound of muffled cocktail music.

VIDEO: Close up of jet racing out of city as night falls over skyline.

AUDIO: Sound of jet engines.

VIDEO: Camera zooms in window to inside of plane. Close up of girl opening bottle of SKYY Blue and blowing mist from bottle.

AUDIO: Refreshing sound of bottle opening.

VIDEO: Camera pans down to woman sitting on modern jet refrigerator as she opens the door and man pulls out two bottles of SKYY Blue.

AUDIO: Sounds of bottles clanking.

VIDEO: Pan continues past couple as they put on a record on jet's high-tech turntable.

AUDIO: Classic cocktail music plays.

VIDEO: Pan continues past woman as she has straw inserted into her bottle.

AUDIO: Cocktail music plays.

VIDEO: Pan continues to close up of man wearing mirrored sunglasses looking out cabin window as clouds and a glimpse of sunlight reflect off sunglasses.

AUDIO: Cocktail music plays.

VIDEO: Man responds by opening another shade to let sunlight in as girl dances in aisle with SKYY Blue.

AUDIO: Cocktail music plays.

VIDEO: Jet zooms over a new city skyline with sun rising in background.

AUDIO: Muffled cocktail music. Jet engines.

Courtesy of Skyy Spirits, LLC

Figure 7-2 Creative brief outline

1. Basic problem or opportunity the advertising must address
2. Target audience(s) and behaviour objective(s)
3. Communication objectives
4. Brand positioning strategy statement
5. Creative strategy (creative theme, message appeal, source characteristic)
6. Supporting information and requirements

and animatics are useful for research purposes as well as for presenting the creative idea to other agency personnel or to the client for discussion and approval. At this stage, the creative team attempts to find the best creative strategy before moving ahead with the actual ad production. The process may conclude with more formal, extensive pretesting of the ad before a final decision is made. Pretesting and related procedures are examined in detail in Chapter 9.

CREATIVE BRIEF

The written **creative brief** specifies the elements of the creative strategy and other relevant information. The creative brief may have other names depending upon the agency, such as creative platform, creative blueprint, creative contract, or copy platform. Essentially, it is a plan that summarizes the entire creative approach that is agreed upon by the creative team and the marketing managers. For example, the creative brief can be written by an agency's account representative or an account planner with input from other specialists from all areas (e.g., creative, media, research, digital, etc.) and approved by the client's marketing communications or brand manager. **Figure 7-2** shows a sample creative brief outline. Just as there are different names for the creative brief, there are variations in the outline and format used and in the level of detail included. The creative brief for the Tacori ad in **Exhibit 7-8** called for a strategy of positioning the 18K925 brand as the ultimate expression of passion, with modern, accessible style and lasting quality.

The first three sections of the creative brief are derived from the marketing plan and prior communication between the creative specialists and brand managers. The planning framework of this text, shown in Chapter 1, also supports all sections of this creative brief illustration. Chapter 1 highlighted the importance of the marketing plan for promotional planning, which should provide sufficient background on the nature of the communication problem or opportunity. Chapter 3 described important aspects of consumer behaviour along with options for target audience selection and guidelines for a target audience profile. Combined, Chapters 4 and 5 explained the usefulness of response models and communication objectives that guide remaining decisions. Chapter 6 indicated different brand positioning options that creative specialists might propose as communication solutions. The rest of this chapter describes the creative strategy decisions that the creative specialists focus on when developing ad executions upon finalizing the creative brief. Creative briefs may include supporting information and requirements that should always appear in order to ensure uniformity across multiple campaign ads.

In the end, the creative brief is a written document so that the creative specialists and all others in the creative process do not experience communication problems that may lead to poor advertising. It should be concise enough that all participants can read it quickly, and yet detailed enough to demonstrate the creativity of the campaign. No doubt this is a significant task, leading to questions of its importance. However, practitioners still believe in its usefulness to produce award-winning ads if the creativity is well communicated.[33] And the creativity should be reflective of the consumer motivation that the brand is trying to influence.[34]

Exhibit 7-8 Tacori's positioning called for 18K925 to be the ultimate expression of passion.

Source: Tacori

ADVERTISING CAMPAIGN

An **advertising campaign** is a set of interrelated and coordinated marketing communication activities that centre on a single theme or idea. A campaign appears in different media and IMC tools across a specified time period. Advertising campaign plans are short-term in nature and, like marketing and IMC plans, are done on an annual basis. However, the campaign themes are usually developed with the intention of being used for a longer time period. Thus far we have referred to creativity as advertising creativity since this is the history and origin of creativity in marketing communication. However, creativity is an important facet in all aspects of promotion, even if there is not accompanying advertising in the campaign. Promotional elements like sponsorship of a good cause will have supporting advertising. And digital communication, whether one classifies it as advertising or advertising-like, contains creativity—big time!

Multiple executions are required in order for a creative message to be considered a campaign. The number of executions will depend on the creative specialists and clients before approval of a campaign occurs, but generally the creative idea driving the message needs at least three executions to tell the story. This notion is based on the "rule of three," where stories or jokes require three episodes for complete understanding; progression occurs as tension is created, built up, and then released with the unfolding of the message. This "rule" is more an observed pattern across many walks of life with respect to communication, rather than scientifically proven; however, it is consistent with how often a consumer needs to receive a message in media planning.

With the ads for Molson Canadian, the "rule" works by telling a story across a few executions over time. Ten years after retiring the "I Am Canadian" campaign, Molson Canadian relaunched it for Canada Day 2013. The 90-second online ad and shortened 30-second TV ad showed a red Canadian fridge in public locations in the United Kingdom, France, and Belgium, with one catch: locals could not open the fridge unless they inserted a Canadian passport into a slot. Eventually a friendly Canadian appeared and opened the door to reveal Molson Canadian beer for everyone. According to a Molson executive, the ad and its red fridge with the white maple leaf symbolized Canadians' national pride (**Exhibit 7-9**). A return of the previous campaign rejuvenated the patriotic culture of the brand, which probably never really ceased, as shown by constant requests for "I Am Canadian" merchandise.

Molson followed up with a three-minute ad during the World Junior Hockey Championship broadcast on Boxing Day six months later. The ad showed two friends travelling from Ottawa to Indonesia with a similar red fridge as a gift to their friend living there who experienced difficulty in seeing hockey games. Success of the red fridge encouraged Molson to keep one in Canada House at the Sochi Olympics in early 2014. Sales improved shortly after the release of these messages and Molson Canadian gained slightly from its 6.4 percent market share while the overall beer category declined in sales.

For Canada Day 2014, the beer fridge would open for Canadians who could sing a passable version of our national anthem. Set at a bar called the Great Canadian Cabin, in Ottawa's Byward Market, Molson's two-minute online video was displayed in multiple social media vehicles. A goal of the holiday messaging was to encourage consumers to believe that "this is the brand of beer to drink on Canada Day," such that it is almost unpatriotic to quaff any other kind of beer on that day. For Canada Day 2015, the beer fridge would open for Canadians who could say the slogan in six languages, with the likely expectation that a group of friends would be teamed up to fulfill the request using Google's speech-to-text recognition software. The new fridge along with the others illustrated a trend of agencies using technology for their clients as part of the creative theme.[35]

Scotiabank began its "Richer Than You Think" campaign in 2006, and included three phases. The first focused on getting a second opinion. The executions for this included three TV ads and two print ads, with supporting digital exposure. A later one in 2009 during the recession addressed people's financial concerns with 11 TV spots conveying a message of "making the most of what you have." A third wave occurred in 2012 when multiple messages looked at how consumers defined richness in their terms, which featured user-generated spots as part of Scotiabank's Richness Project.[36] This example demonstrates the requirement of multiple executions within a campaign, and how a campaign's message evolves.

Exhibit 7-9 Molson's red beer fridge proved to be a winning visual for its campaign.

©Molson Coors Canada

LO3 Creative Theme

Determining the unifying theme of a campaign is a critical decision as it sets the tone for all marketing communication, such as sales promotion or digital applications. Furthermore, the **creative theme** should be a strong idea since it represents the central message of a marketing communication program, reflects the market positioning strategy, and directly communicates the brand positioning strategy to its intended target audience. In this section, we describe four related decisions that comprise the creative theme. First, we identify ways to determine the creative theme. Then, we present the importance of slogans to reinforce brand positioning and/or creative theme. Next, we explore the issue of consistency of the creative theme across parts of the promotional program. We conclude by exploring the importance of unique Canadian creative advertising and its success.

ORIGIN OF CREATIVE THEME

The creative team is provided with the challenge of deciding upon the strong or "big" idea of the creative theme that attracts the consumer's attention, gets a response, and sets the advertiser's product or service apart from the competition. The *big idea* is "that flash of insight that synthesizes the purpose of the strategy, joins the product benefit with consumer desire in a fresh, involving way, brings the subject to life, and makes the reader or audience stop, look, and listen."[37] From another perspective, a theme arises from a story, and advertising creative is much like a storytelling process of the brand, its history, and its meaning that goes beyond the basic communication of product performance.[38] It is difficult to pinpoint the inspiration for a big idea or to teach advertising people how to find one. However, these approaches guide the creative team's search for a creative theme: unique selling proposition, brand image, inherent drama, positioning, and storytelling.

Unique Selling Proposition The concept of the **unique selling proposition (USP)** was developed by Rosser Reeves, former chair of the Ted Bates agency, and is described in his influential book *Reality in Advertising*. Reeves noted three characteristics of unique selling propositions:

1. Each advertisement must make a proposition to the consumer. Not just words, not just product puffery, not just show-window advertising. Each advertisement must say to each reader: "Buy this product and you will get this benefit."

2. The proposition must be one that the competition either cannot or does not offer. It must be unique either in the brand or in the claim.

3. The proposition must be strong enough to move the mass millions, that is, pull over new customers to your brand.[39]

The attribute claim or benefit that forms the basis of the USP should dominate the ad and be emphasized through repetitive advertising. For this approach to work, there must be a unique product or service attribute, benefit, or inherent advantage that is identified in the claim. The approach may require considerable research on the product and consumers, not only to determine the USP but also to document the claim. An example of an ad based on a USP is the ThermaCare message in **Exhibit 7-10** which claims that the product heals effectively.

Brand Image Competing brands in many product and service categories are so similar that it is a challenge to communicate a unique attribute or benefit. For example, packaged goods may be difficult to differentiate on a functional or performance basis and promotional planners look to a more intangible approach to creatively express product uniqueness. The creative theme used to communicate these products is based on the development of a memorable identity for the brand through **image advertising**.

Exhibit 7-10 ThermaCare uses a unique selling proposition.

Source: ThermaCare

David Ogilvy popularized the idea of brand image in his famous book *Confessions of an Advertising Man*. Ogilvy said that with image advertising, "every advertisement should be thought of as a contribution to the complex symbol which is the brand image." He argued that the image or personality of the brand is particularly important when brands are similar. Image advertising is designed to give a brand a unique association and create a certain feeling that is activated when a person consumes the brand. The key to successful image advertising is developing an image that will appeal to product users. For example the Bebe ad in **Exhibit 7-11** gives the fashion brand a distinctive look for its line of clothing.

One method of image development is through literary devices such as metaphor to create the symbolism. A metaphor is concrete (e.g., direct, obvious) or abstract (e.g., indirect, interpretive) and links two dissimilar objects with an analogy made by the receiver. In an ad, this involves both visual and copy elements in which consumers interpret the message by transferring meaning from the metaphor to the brand. Visual metaphor types in advertising can be juxtaposition, replacement, or fusion. Research using this view concluded that ads with a metaphor performed more strongly than those without a metaphor, although different effects emerged for different product types and consumers.[40] Selecting the right metaphor is a challenging decision as consumers have difficulty discovering the references within a metaphor.[41] Simpler metaphors contribute toward higher levels of ad comprehension and ad appreciation compared to ads that do not have metaphors or ads with complex metaphors, giving support for advertisers to consider their usage.[42]

Exhibit 7-11 Bebe uses advertising to build an image as a sexy and stylish brand.

Source: Bebe Stores, Inc.

Inherent Drama Another approach to determining the creative theme is finding the **inherent drama** or characteristic of the product that makes the consumer purchase it. The inherent drama approach expresses the advertising philosophy of Leo Burnett, founder of the Leo Burnett Agency in Chicago. Burnett said inherent drama "is often hard to find but it is always there, and once found it is the most interesting and believable of all advertising appeals."[43] He believed advertising should be based on a foundation of consumer benefits with an emphasis on the dramatic element in expressing those benefits. Academic research generally concludes that inherent drama ads contribute to positive cognitive and emotional responses leading to positive attitudes to both the ad and brand, although there is variation due to type of product on the processing and the level of receiver involvement on the attitudes.[44]

Expression of the drama may take many forms, as the following examples illustrate. Manulife Financial continued the drama of the story in its TV ads by showing the conclusion on its Internet site, which motivated people to visit and spend more time viewing its messages.[45] Sport Chek's "My North"' advertising aligned itself with the NBA's Toronto Raptors with a series of mini-documentaries of nine basketball neighbourhoods in Toronto to portray the brand in a new and dramatic light.[46] With the objective of increasing fundraising dollars, The Hospital for Sick Children in Toronto showed a unique and dramatic story of children's healthcare for 45 days in a row on TV. One execution showed a surgeon repairing a heart defect.[47]

The ad in **Exhibit 7-12** shows one moment of the story of a happy couple celebrating their love for one another. The woman's facial reaction that exudes surprise and happiness, along with her body language, provides a snippet of an emotional event in this dramatic expression of becoming engaged.

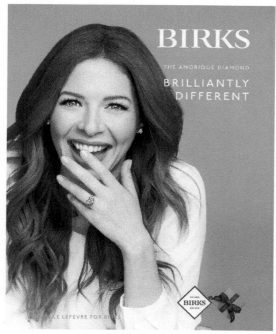

Exhibit 7-12 The emotional expression of the woman conveys a dramatic point in a familiar storyline.

Norman Wong/BIRKS GROUP INC./Newscom

Exhibit 7-13 Positioning Special K's product extension is inspiration for the creative theme.

New
Special K
Nourish® multi-grain flakes with quinoa so you can handle the in-laws for the long (long, long, long) weekend.

REAL GOODNESS TO HELP YOU STAY STRONG.

Special K® FORTIFY.™

Source: Kellogg Co.

Positioning Since advertising helps establish or maintain the brand position, it can also be the source of the creative theme. Positioning is often the basis of a firm's creative strategy when it has multiple brands competing in the same market. For example, Procter & Gamble markets a few brands of laundry detergent—and positions each one differently. Positioning is done for companies as well as for brands. For example, Special K's product extension is healthier with almonds and fruit, and this new positioning shown in **Exhibit 7-13** features a tasty display of the ingredients.

Trout and Ries originally described positioning as the image consumers had of the brand in relation to competing brands in the product or service category, but the concept has been expanded beyond direct competitive positioning.[48] As discussed in Chapter 6, products are positioned on the basis of end benefit, brand name, usage situation, or product category. Any of these can spark a theme that becomes the basis of the creative strategy and results in the brand's occupying a particular place in the minds of the target audience. Since brand positioning can be done on the basis of a distinctive attribute, the positioning and unique selling proposition approaches can overlap.

Storytelling Digital transmission of video provided brands with an opportunity to create longer messages known as *short films* of three to five minutes. For example, BMW released a four-minute video of a promotion entitled "DareTO" which tracked contestants performing adventurous tasks and showcased the vehicles. Canon dropped a five-minute video showing a man travelling in Peru with his Canon camera. The idea of this form of creative is storytelling in which there is a defined sequence of events featuring plot, characters, climax, and outcome. The logic of this idea is that online viewers are drawn to this branded message rather than interrupted by a commercial while consuming media. In some ways, storytelling is a new version of the inherent drama, but with a different point of view of focusing on the people in the many settings instead of strictly a dramatic scene.

Some executions extended storytelling to even longer full-length "brand stories" ranging from 30 to 60 minutes. For example, Harley-Davidson showed an online series of three riders going across Canada on the ubiquitous bike. It was such a compelling story that the Discovery Channel picked it up as a repackaged one-hour show. Companies such as Nike and Red Bull also develop long-form branded content that takes a storytelling approach to be placed in many different digital environments to reach specific audiences.[49] And while these cool videos are great to see, they are still technically advertising since the brands are paying for the production.

CAMPAIGN SLOGANS

The theme for the advertising campaign is usually expressed through a **slogan/tagline** that reduces the key idea into a few words or a brief statement. The advertising slogan should serve as a summation line that succinctly expresses the brand positioning strategy, as well as the message it is trying to deliver to the target audience. The slogan usually appears in every advertisement and is often used in other forms of marketing communications to serve as a reminder of, and to reinforce, the marketer's branding message.

In general, a brand determines its slogan after evaluating options and possibly testing them with consumers prior to campaign launch. Interestingly, BioSteel's slogan shown in **Exhibit 7-14**, #drinkthepink, arose from consumers. Brand imagery and related imagery circulating on social media encouraged consumers to seek

Exhibit 7-14 BioSteel's #drinkthepink is prominent for brand positioning.

BIOSTEEL
READY-TO-DRINK

» DIABETIC & VEGAN FRIENDLY
» SUGAR FREE
» GLUTEN FREE
» CAFFEINE FREE
» LACTOSE FREE
» NO ARTIFICIAL COLOURING OR FLAVOURS
» NO ARTIFICIAL PRESERVATIVES

#DRINK THE PINK

©BioSteel Sports Nutrition Inc.

out BioSteel's innovative high-performance sports drink. Prior to this, personal contacts and word-of-mouth encouraged professional athletes to try it. Sales occurred directly to professional sports teams since athletes requested it after receiving samples and seeing the effects. TV exposure of athletes consuming the product paved the way, and from that and social media, the slogan emerged.[50]

What constitutes a good slogan? All of the following suggestions are not possible for a single slogan, but they offer guidance when making a final decision. Characteristics can pertain to the brand attitude objectives, include a key benefit, differentiate the brand, evoke positive feelings, reflect brand personality, and be believable and likable. Others pertain to brand awareness objectives: be memorable, and recall brand name. Additionally, slogans are oriented strategically, to be campaignable and competitive. Finally, aesthetics are important as slogans should be original, simple, neat/cool, and positive.[51]

Canadian advertisers continually develop slogans, and it is interesting to examine new ones to figure out whether they meet these criteria. WestJet's new slogan ("Love Where You're Going") reinforces its market positioning strategy as a global airline.[52] The slogan also fits well with its brand positioning strategy to switch customers away from Air Canada. Steam Whistle Brewing's new slogan ("Pure Pilsner") defends the brand against imported brands with similar green bottles.[53] The new slogan for Rogers ("Make More Possible") is shown for all of its product lines and resonates with more target groups.[54] Finally, an empirical study that examined six variables concluded that shorter and long-lasting slogans that received high levels of media weight tended to produce higher levels of brand recall.[55]

CREATIVE THEME CONSISTENCY

Consistency in promotional creativity is generally regarded as a key success factor so that the target audience retains the brand position. We explore examples of consistency in the creative theme across time, creative execution, advertising media, promotional tools, and products. The essential point is that when the target audience is exposed to a series of messages across different contexts, the creative theme should not change; thus there is a clear reinforcement of the brand positioning strategy. Deviation of the theme allows the possibility that the target audience will process the message alternatively and arrive at a different interpretation of the brand.

Consistency Across Time Advertising or communication plans are generally done on an annual basis, thus the creative theme is often short-term in nature. However, the creative themes are usually developed with the intention of being used for a longer time period. While marketers might change their campaign themes often, a successful creative theme may last for years. A consistent creative theme across time builds on the established awareness of the brand's current customers by encouraging continued processing of future advertising messages. Moreover, the familiarity of the creative theme is recognizable to a brand's non-customers when they may be entering the product category or considering switching their purchases.

A&W's creative theme during the 2010s featured its commitment to innovation in the mature quick service restaurant market. Its achievements included using meat raised without hormones, steroids, or antibiotics; minimizing waste through less packaging; reformulating its root beer with cane sugar; offering a plant-based burger; and being the first company to offer non-plastic straws. The brand continued with the same spokesperson used since 2001 to ensure consistency with the presentation of this new theme.[56]

Consistency Across Creative Execution As we noted above, an advertising campaign features a series of creative executions over time and it is important that marketers ensure all ads feature a similar "look and feel." Exactly what this entails is a matter of interpretation, but most advertisers and consumers would say they recognize it when they see it. And Telus TV ads of almost 20 years represent the best Canadian example of the most consistent set of messages.

Nature became the canvas for Telus (named Clearnet at the time) when its advertising agency saw the simplicity of animals in its storytelling to deliver the proposition of "the future is friendly." Set to a white background with emotive music, the nature theme and critters help make the brand feel friendly, likable, and approachable. Over time, we saw exotic birds, insects, colourful frogs, and lizards—until Telus took over, and began with a "disco duck" to celebrate the millennium and then moved on to penguins, monkeys, pot-bellied pigs, iguanas, bunnies, meerkats, hedgehogs, and fish, and back to exotic birds once again. The consistency of animals along with the similar creative tactics makes Telus TV ads instantly recognizable with the near uniformity in style. Interestingly, in the latter 2010s, Telus gravitated away from animals only as it emphasized service quality and its commitment to important causes, however the cute critters remained for brand identification.[57]

As a further illustration, **Exhibit 7-15** shows two ads for the Subaru Forester that appeared on the back cover of the same magazine in consecutive months. The consistency is that the vehicle is the same colour and is a focal point of the message. The headline and body copy have the same look. The copy highlights the key features of traction control and cargo capacity, which is supported with the situational visuals.

Exhibit 7-15 Subaru maintains consistency in the creative execution of the two ads with different messages.

©Subaru Canada Inc. - photographer, Chris Gordaneer/Westside Studio

Consistency Across Advertising Media Often a successful creative theme is one that is amenable to more than one medium. For instance, the essence of creativity in a print ad is still captured in a follow-up radio ad. Or, the big idea found in a TV commercial transfers to an outdoor billboard. In both cases, the creativity of the initial media is seen in a supportive medium—one less central to the primary media, yet still important to continue exposing a similar idea to the target audience. Interestingly, this idea is difficult to convey with visual creative themes moving to radio. For a while, listeners heard a "friendly thought" from Telus that differed significantly from the nature theme portrayed in all visual media.

Consistency Across Promotional Tools Using the advertising creative theme across the various promotional tools is an issue to be resolved. The argument for the same look and feel is pervasive. For example, skateboarding brand Vans opened the House of Vans, which gathers boarders together to experience all sorts of creative and cultural activities (e.g., art, tricks, clinics) associated with the lifestyle/sport. The marketing event reinforced the imagery of its historic advertising over time, and yet allowed the brand to evolve with those new to the scene.[58]

Consistency Across Products The use of a consistent theme across all products is seen with Nissan's Legends campaign. Replicating the look of a movie trailer, the ads for the Nissan Rogue and Qashqai show the cars thriving under adverse winter conditions to get passengers safely to their destination. One episode featured fearsome snowmen, while another showed winter attacking the vehicle on a dangerous mountain highway.[59]

CANADIAN CREATIVE THEMES

We present ideas regarding creative themes used in Canadian advertising and promotional communication. We begin with a perspective that supports the importance of unique ways of speaking to Canadian consumers. Since brands may be part of a North American or international marketing strategy, there is a tendency to standardize the message. We highlight success stories as evidence of the importance of Canadian creativity in communication.

Importance of Canadian Creative Themes The need for unique creative advertising is found in the divergence of values between Canadians and Americans. Decades of consumer research by Environics researcher Michael Adams suggests that while the citizens of North America share similar aspects of society, the underlying values are quite distinct.[60] Since this groundbreaking revelation, Adams has continued the research and finds that the types of values are shifting but considerable differences remain.[61]

These unique Canadian values influence the motivation for consumption—Canadians buy products for what they can do for them, not what they say about them. Canadians favour experiences over possessions and are less inclined toward conspicuous consumption. For example, Canadians are more likely to believe that a car is basic transportation rather than a statement of personal style or image. Therefore, certain types of advertising messages are more palatable for Canadians since the underlying reasons for purchase are more accurately reflected in the dialogue of a commercial or the body copy of a print ad produced by Canadian advertisers.

Putting together a creative for Canada sometimes involves obstacles. Canadian managers who market U.S. brands in Canada often feel the pressure to run the same campaign in Canada that is being run in the United States. While this obviously saves on production costs of new ads, the money saving is offset with lower sales due to messages not resonating with Canadian culture. Sometimes firms need to perform specific market research to demonstrate that a unique creative is warranted for the Canadian market. For example, Maytag required an entirely different positioning and creative in Canada when American messages focused on its made-in-the-U.S.A. claims. The Maytag repairman ventured north to shoot new ads that played during *Hockey Night in Canada* with a usage theme for cleaning hockey equipment, among others.[62]

Successful Canadian Creative Themes Historically and recently, insightful and innovative Canadian creative themes have demonstrated effective advertising and promotional communication. We summarize the CASSIES (a trade magazine's awards) and the prestigious Cannes competition, as these are the main competitions that Canadian advertisers currently enter.

CASSIES Awarded by the Institute of Communication Agencies (ICA), the Association of Creative Communications Agencies, and Association des professionels de la communication et du marketing, this recognition is perhaps the most significant in Canada. The CASSIES (Canadian Advertising Success Stories) awards identify Canadian advertising's greatest hits. Initiated in Canada in 1993, the awards are based on a similar idea started during the 1980s in the United Kingdom. Originally awarded every second year from 1993 until 2001, the CASSIES are now an annual event.

The CASSIES recognize advertising and promotional campaigns that document a direct cause and effect relationship between the campaign and communication and business results. Entrants submit the details of their campaign in the form of a business case that summarizes the performance of the brand prior to the campaign and indicates the degree to which the performance has improved. The website, Cassies.ca, provides the complete entry requirements, identifies the winners, and contains the actual case history submitted. Newfoundland and Labrador Tourism showed spectacular and fascinating images of the province in ads across the country in its winning entry (**Exhibit 7-16**).

Exhibit 7-16 A breathtaking image of Gros Morne National Park captivated Canadians in this award-winning campaign.

The world can't weigh you down
when you're standing on top of it.

Considering it took 485,000,000 years to create, it's hardly surprising what you'll find here. Not the least of which is perspective. It tends to happen when you're standing two thousand feet up, seeing things more clearly on the edge of an ancient glacier-carved fjord. A vantage point,

one would think, that could only exist for two reasons: for the view itself, and the inescapable feeling that washes over you. The feeling you get when your troubles seem less significant. And once again, anything's possible.
To find your way here, call Kelly at 1-800-563-6353 or visit NewfoundlandLabrador.com

Newfoundland Labrador

©Newfoundland and Labrador Tourism

Trade Magazines Awards given out annually and sponsored by a trade magazine—*Strategy*—identify the top Canadian creative communication launched each year in a number of categories. Strategy awards recognize topics like creative catalyst, launch strategy, niche strategy, and turnaround strategy to name a few. Another set of awards celebrates the agency of the year and the best design agency of the year, along with specialty awards for PR and digital. A third group pertains to shopper innovation and activation in which significant creativity is developed. Finally, the marketing awards acknowledge an overall winner for best multimedia campaign, a winner for best single ad and campaign across all major media, and awards for nontraditional media, point-of-purchase, and public service announcements.

Cannes On a global level and inspired by the movie industry's more famous Cannes Film Festival, the Cannes Lions International Festival of Creativity is widely considered the most prestigious awards competition for advertising and all types of marketing communication. The Cannes competition receives entries from agencies around the world hoping to win Lions (the name of the award) in major categories—film (television, cinema, and Web film ads), press and poster (print and outdoor ads), cyber advertising (online marketing and ads for websites), media planning/buying, and direct marketing. The competition recently added the Titanium Lion for innovative work across integrated media. Over the years, Canadian advertising agencies' work has performed very well, receiving awards.

LO4 Message Appeals

The **message appeal** refers to the approach used to influence consumers' attitude toward the product, service, or cause. As shown in Chapter 5, we are also concerned with influencing a target audience's attitude toward a brand (e.g., maintain or increase), so an accurate message appeal is important for marketing communication effectiveness. Numerous message appeals are possible, and we summarize five broad appeals: rational, emotional, fear, humour, and combined rational and emotional. In this section, we focus on these appeals as part of a creative strategy and acknowledge that creative advertising may use other appeals.

Exhibit 7-17 A rational appeal is used to promote the success of the Honda Accord.

Source: American Honda Motor Co., Inc. and Rubin Postaer and Associates

RATIONAL APPEALS

Rational appeals focus on the consumer's practical, functional, or utilitarian need for the product or service and emphasize features of a product or service and/or the benefits or reasons for owning or using a particular brand. Rational-based appeals tend to be informative by educating consumers with logical facts, and advertisers using them generally attempt to convince consumers that their product or service has a particular attribute or provides a specific benefit that satisfies their needs. Their objective is to persuade the target audience to buy the brand because it is the best available (e.g., provides a stronger sensory gratification motive) or does a better job of meeting consumers' needs (e.g., addresses an incomplete satisfaction motive). For example, the ad shown in **Exhibit 7-17** uses a rational appeal to communicate the award success of the Honda Accord. We review six typical rational appeals that are commonly understood: feature, comparative, price, news, popularity, and reminder.

Feature Appeal Ads that use a *feature appeal* focus on the dominant traits of the product or service. These ads tend to present the customer with a number of important product attributes or features that will lead to favourable attitudes and are used as the basis for a rational purchase decision. Technical and high-involvement products often use message appeal. **Exhibit 7-18** shows an ad for Red Bull energy drink that focuses on the benefits of its contents.

Comparative Appeal Ads with a *comparative appeal* either directly or indirectly identify competitors and compare the brands (or products) on one or more specific attributes or benefits.[63] A review of a sample of TV ads found that direct and indirect comparisons comprised 5 percent and 20 percent of them respectively, meaning a comparative appeal approximated one-quarter of all ads![64] Studies show that recall is higher for comparative than non-comparative messages, but comparative ads are generally not more effective for brand attitudes or purchase intentions.[65] However, new research found differing effects for current users compared to non-users of a brand and product category. In short, comparative ads are effective for attitudes and purchase intentions for current users.[66]

Based on the research, a few suggestions are possible for managers to consider. Comparative appeals may be useful for new brands, since they allow a market entrant to position itself directly against established brands and to promote its distinctive advantages. Direct comparisons can help position a new brand in consumers' evoked set of brands. Comparative appeals may be useful for low market share brands to sway consumers due to the positive association of an established market leader shown in the message. In contrast, a market leader may avoid use of a comparison ad, having little to gain by featuring competitors' products in its ad. Finally, surveyed practitioners reported strong preference for comparative appeals in situations that fit the market, product, and advertiser.[67]

Price Appeal An ad with a price offer as the dominant point of the message may be known as a *price appeal*. Price appeal advertising is used most often by retailers to announce sales, special offers, or low everyday prices. Fast-food chains have made price an important part of their marketing strategy through promotional deals and "value menus" or lower overall prices. Advertisers for vehicles and electronics use price appeals as part of their IMC strategy as well.

News Appeal When an announcement about the product, service, or company dominates the ad, advertisers are using a *news appeal*. This type of appeal might be used for a new product or to inform consumers of significant modifications, such as a new smart phone model. This appeal works best when a company has important news that it wants to communicate. For example, airlines use news appeals when beginning to offer service to new cities or opening new routes as a way of informing consumers as well as generating media exposure that results in publicity.

Popularity Appeal Ads with a *popularity appeal* stress the popularity of a product or service by pointing out the number of consumers who use the brand, the number who have switched to it, the number of experts who recommend it, or its leadership position in the market. The main point of this advertising appeal is that the wide use of the brand proves its quality or value and other customers should consider using it. The ad shown in **Exhibit 7-19** uses a popularity appeal by noting that TaylorMade drivers are

Exhibit 7-18 Red Bull uses a feature appeal to promote its benefits to students.

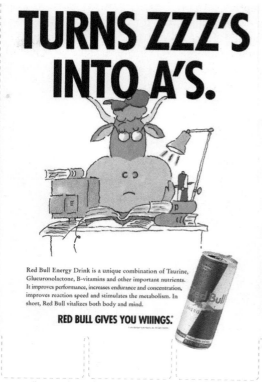

Red Bull Energy Drink is a unique combination of Taurine, Glucuronolactone, B-vitamins and other important nutrients. It improves performance, increases endurance and concentration, improves reaction speed and stimulates the metabolism. In short, Red Bull vitalizes both body and mind.

RED BULL GIVES YOU WIIINGS.

Exhibit 7-19 TaylorMade promotes the popularity of its drivers among golf professionals.

Source: TaylorMade Golf Company, Inc.

Exhibit 7-20 This ad reminds consumers to associate Ecco shoes with happiness.

©Megapress/Alamy Stock Photo

Exhibit 7-21 This Quaker State oil ad demonstrates the pride of long-lasting car ownership.

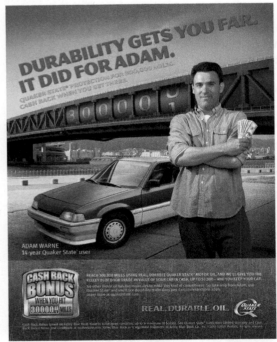

Source: Pennzoil by Shell International B.V.

used the most by PGA Tour professionals. Ads such as this are used to implement TaylorMade's marketing strategy, which focuses on innovation, the technological superiority of its golf equipment, and the popularity and use of its clubs by tour professionals who exert a strong influence on the purchase decisions of amateur golfers.

Reminder Appeal When the objective of the ad is to build or maintain awareness, an advertiser might use a *reminder appeal.* Well known brands and market leaders with frequently used products often use a reminder appeal, which is often referred to as reminder advertising. **Exhibit 7-20** shows a street ad, probably near shoe stores, reminding consumers to smile and to consider Ecco shoes when shopping. Products and services that have a seasonal pattern to their consumption also use reminder advertising, particularly around the appropriate period. For example, marketers of candy products often increase their media budgets and run reminder advertising around Halloween, Valentine's Day, Christmas, and Easter.

EMOTIONAL APPEALS

Emotional appeals relate to the customer's social and/or psychological needs for purchasing a product or service. Consumers' motives for their purchase decisions contain strong emotions, and their feelings about a brand are important when making a purchase decision. The choice between rational and emotional appeal requires careful consideration, to ensure that the advertising resonates with the target audience and evokes relevant processing responses connected to the purchase decision or consumption experience. Advertising appeals to consumers' emotions are useful for brands that are similar to competing brands, since rational differentiation is a difficult communication effect to achieve.[68] For example, the ad in **Exhibit 7-21** portrays the pride a longtime car owner feels after using Quaker State oil for years.

A classic example of emotional appeal is that virtually every single Coca-Cola ad is dedicated to positive emotions associated with drinking the product, and when the beverage brand teamed up with Google to put digital software in dispensing machines that let consumers "buy" a Coke for someone else in the world, the joy spread exponentially.[69] Long versions of brand messages that become mini-films of emotional stories are a trend due to the growth of online video, with examples such as Maddie for Chevrolet, the protective father for VW, and the love story for Cornetto ice cream in the United Kingdom.[70]

The effectiveness of emotion-based appeals is documented in *Brand Immortality.*[71] It examined 880 case studies of successful advertising campaigns submitted for the United Kingdom–based Institute of Practitioners in Advertising Effectiveness Award competition. Analysis compared campaigns that relied primarily on emotional appeals with those that used rational persuasion and information. A key finding is that advertising campaigns with purely emotional content produce nearly double the profit gains of rational content campaigns. One reason why emotional campaigns work so well is that they reduce price sensitivity and strengthen the ability of brands to charge a price premium, which contributes to profitability. Canadian advertisers used emotional appeals to refresh the message for mature products.

Cereal manufacturers faced a declining market and re-launched previously discontinued brands (e.g., Trix) and product extensions (e.g., Special K Protein) with emotional appeals along the lines of nostalgia with the hope of rekindling interest in lapsed users willing to pay high-margin prices.[72] Similarly, Kraft peanut butter experienced a sales decline and tried to rejuvenate the brand to millennials who are not eating the product category with a heartwarming story of a person's life from childhood to adulthood featuring the iconic Kraft teddy bear.[73]

At times ads rely on the concept of *emotional integration*, whereby the message portrays characters in the ad as experiencing an emotional benefit or outcome from using a product or service.[74] Marketers use emotional appeals in hopes that the positive feeling they evoke will transfer to the brand and/or company. Research shows that positive mood states and feelings created by advertising can have a favourable effect on consumers' evaluations of a brand.[75] For example, Air Canada's "Fly the Flag" ad captured the joy of travellers as they arrived at their Canadian and US destinations and were reunited with their family for the holidays. The ad showed heartwarming scenes as some families had been apart for years. Some were overwhelmed with emotion when Air Canada personnel provided free tickets to return more often.[76]

Feelings can serve as the basis for advertising appeals designed to influence consumers on an emotional level, as shown in **Figure 7-3**. Relying on considerable research over time, this taxonomy identifies core negative and positive emotions. Moreover, the table indicates the origin of the emotion, which demonstrates the core subjective meaning of the emotion and the action consequences of someone experiencing the emotion.[77] These additional descriptions of the emotion are important as they give direction as to the content and authenticity of the emotion for planning this emotional message appeal; advertisers that miss the mark on emotional accuracy are quickly rejected.

Each of these core emotions embodies nuances. Contentment might include things like happiness, joy, nostalgia, and sentiment. Elements of pride may be seen in recognition, status, acceptance, and approval. Canadians' feeling of pride toward their county is an emotion resurging in advertising messages for brands such as Tim Hortons and Molson Canadian. With hockey as a backdrop, the ads show Canadians as being more assertive and confident, reflecting

Figure 7-3 Basis for emotional appeals

Negative Emotion	Origin	Action
Anger	Offence against self	Restore justice, hold individuals responsible
Contempt	Other violates role, duty, obligation	Lower the reputation of perpetrator
Disgust	Contact with impure object or action	Push away
Embarrassment	Self has transgressed a social convention	Apologize
Envy	Other is superior to self	Reduce status of other
Fear	Imminent threat to self	Flee, reduce uncertainty
Guilt	Self has violated moral standard regarding harm	Remedy harm
Jealousy	Other threatens source of affection	Protect source of affection from others
Sadness	Irrevocable loss	Acquire new goods
Shame	Self has transgressed aspiration or ideal	Hide, avoid scrutiny

Positive Emotion	Origin	Action
Contentment	Pleasing stimulus	Savouring
Enthusiasm	Reward likely	Goal approach
Love	Perceived commitment	Affection
Sexual desire	Sexual cue or opportunity	Sexual release
Compassion	Undeserved suffering	Pro-social approach
Gratitude	Unexpected gift	Promote reciprocity
Pride	Self-relevant achievement	Status display
Awe	Self is small vs. something vast	Devotion, reverence
Interest	Novel opportunity	Exploration
Amusement	Recognize incongruity	Play
Relief	Cause of distress ends	Signal safety

research that indicates a change in how Canadians perceive themselves.[78] Other emotions appear to combine more than one emotion; for example, excitement is likely part of the first four positive emotions.

Applying these types of emotions, we see ads using lifestyle, humour, and sex appeals that are exciting, entertaining, and arousing. These types of appeals affect the emotions of consumers and put them in a favourable frame of mind just prior to purchase, or affect their brand assessment and influence their overall attitude. Some of these appeals are criticized as being unethical or offensive, and we examine this point in Chapter 18. We review one negative and one positive emotional appeal commonly used in message delivery.

FEAR APPEALS

Fear is an emotional response to a threat that expresses or at least implies danger. Ads sometimes use **fear appeals** to invoke this emotional response and arouse individuals to take steps to remove the threat. Some, like anti-smoking ads, stress physical danger that can occur if behaviours are not altered. Others—like those for deodorant, mouthwash, or dandruff shampoo—threaten disapproval or social rejection.

Before deciding to use a fear appeal–based message strategy, the advertiser should consider how fear operates, what level to use, and how different target audiences may respond. One theory suggests that the relationship between the level of fear in a message and acceptance or persuasion is curvilinear, as shown in **Figure 7-4**.[79] This means that message acceptance increases as the amount of fear rises—to a point. Beyond that point, acceptance decreases as the level of fear rises.

This relationship between fear and persuasion is explained by the fact that fear appeals have both facilitating and inhibiting effects.[80] A low level of fear can have facilitating effects; it attracts attention and interest in the message and may motivate the receiver to act to resolve the threat. Thus, increasing the level of fear in a message from low to moderate can result in increased persuasion. High levels of fear, however, can produce inhibiting effects; the receiver may emotionally block the message by tuning it out, perceiving it selectively, or denying its arguments outright. **Figure 7-4** illustrates how these two countereffects operate to produce the curvilinear relationship between fear and persuasion.

A study by Anand Keller and Block provides support for this perspective on how fear operates.[81] Their study indicated that a communication using a low level of fear may be ineffective because it results in insufficient motivation to elaborate on the harmful consequences of engaging in the destructive behaviour (smoking). However, an appeal arousing high levels of fear was ineffective because it resulted in too much elaboration on the harmful consequences. This led to defensive tendencies such as message avoidance and interfered with processing of recommended solutions to the problem.

Another approach to the curvilinear explanation of fear is the protection motivation model.[82] According to this theory, four cognitive appraisal processes mediate the individual's response to the threat: appraising (1) the information available regarding the severity of the perceived threat, (2) the perceived probability that the threat will occur, (3) the perceived ability of a coping behaviour to remove the threat, and (4) the individual's perceived ability to carry out the coping behaviour. This model suggests that ads using fear appeals should give the target audience information about the severity of the threat, the probability of its occurrence, the effectiveness of a coping response, and the ease with which the response is implemented. For example, the ad shown in **Exhibit 7-22** uses a mild fear appeal for Seagate

Figure 7-4 Relationship between fear levels and message acceptance

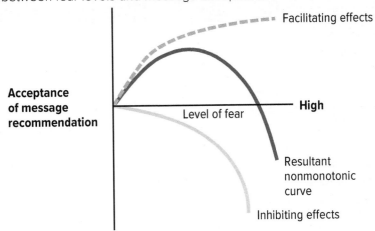

State 1   State 2   State 3   State 4   State 5   State 6

Source: Seagate Techn ..gy LLC

Technology's Replica product designed to back up computer hard drives. The ad uses playful illustrations in a graphic style to communicate what can happen if a computer crashes and all files are lost. The ad offers a solution to the threat by showing the ease of using the Replica product and the resulting peace of mind.

In reviewing research on fear appeals, Herbert Rotfeld has argued that the studies may be confusing different types of threats and the level of potential harm portrayed in the message with fear, which is an emotional response.[83] He concludes that the relationship between the emotional responses of fear or arousal and persuasion is not curvilinear but rather is monotonic and positive, meaning that higher levels of fear do result in greater persuasion. However, Rotfeld notes that not all fear messages are equally effective, because different people fear different things. Thus they will respond differently to the same threat, so the strongest threats are not always the most persuasive. This suggests that marketers using fear appeals must consider the emotional responses generated by the message and how they will affect reactions to the message.

HUMOUR APPEALS

Anecdotally, humorous ads are the most enjoyed of all advertising messages. Humour is usually presented through audio and video messages, as these media lend themselves to the execution of humorous messages. Humour fits with products like food and beverages; however, advertisers use it for personal care products (e.g., Old Spice) that might have used other appeals in the past, which shows that the context and audience dictate the suitability of its use. One recent example of a humour appeal is a Fisherman's Friend cough drop ad showing a story where the captain of a fishing schooner found his lost brothers after a shark coughed them up! Other executions continued the concept of unlikely fish tales. The new campaign continued the use of humour after a successful three-year run of funny ads that ended with the slogan, "Suck it up."[84]

Advertisers use **humour appeals** for good reasons. Humorous messages attract and hold consumers' attention. They enhance effectiveness by putting consumers in a positive mood, increasing their liking of the ad itself and their feeling toward the product or service.[85] A humour appeal draws the receiver into the funny situation and distracts the receiver from counterarguing against the message, which makes the receiver more likely to accept the brand benefit claims.[86] Finally, practitioners and researchers typically use the term *humour appeal*, which corresponds to amusement as the basic emotion, as shown in **Figure 7-3**.

Clearly, there are valid reasons both for and against the use of humour in advertising. Not every product or service lends itself to a humorous approach.[87] A number of studies found that the effectiveness of humour depends on several factors, including the type of product and audience characteristics.[88] For example, humour has been more prevalent and more effective with low-involvement, feeling products than high-involvement, thinking products.[89] An interesting study surveyed the research and creative directors of the top 150 advertising agencies.[90] They specified which communications objectives are facilitated through the appropriate situational use of humour in terms of media, product, and audience factors. The general conclusions of this study are shown in **Figure 7-5**.

Figure 7-5 Advertising executives' experience with humour

Humour can:

Aid in gaining attention.

Assist with comprehension and yielding (i.e., cognitive responses).

Create a positive mood that enhances persuasion (i.e., emotional responses).

Aid name and simple copy registration (i.e., brand awareness).

Not aid persuasion in general (i.e., brand attitude), but does occur.

Generally not encourage consumer action, but does occur.

Enhance persuasion to switch brands.

...vertising for Arrowhead water ...ationally and emotionally.

Born Better.

Every drop of Arrowhead 100% Mountain Spring Water comes from carefully selected mountain springs. When you start with something better, you get something better.
Arrowhead is better.com

ARROWHEAD

Source: Arrowhead by Nestle Waters North America

COMBINED RATIONAL AND EMOTIONAL APPEALS

One decision facing the creative specialist is not whether to choose an emotional or a rational appeal, but rather how to combine the two approaches. Noted copywriters David Ogilvy and Joel Raphaelson eloquently argued years ago that products have both rational thoughts and emotions associated with their use and purchase. One can experience happiness with clean clothes due to a functional product like laundry detergent, and one can find joy in the high-involvement purchase of a new car that requires careful consideration.[91] **Exhibit 7-23** appeals rationally and emotionally with the text of the ad and the compelling visuals.

A unique example of combining rational and emotional appeals is the use of **teaser advertising**. Advertisers introducing a new product or new advertising campaign use teaser advertising, which is designed to build curiosity, interest, and/or excitement about a product or brand by talking about it but not actually showing it. Initial ads for the Chevrolet Spark car claimed that the ultimate mobile device was coming, and the imagery looked like the box of a new phone. After a few weeks of teasing in multiple media, the big launch event revealed the car! It seems the device angle was perfect for young, first-time buyers who would be interested in a subcompact, and it reinforced the technological connectivity features of the new car.[92]

IMC Perspective 7-2 reviews many promotional messages from Interac that feature both emotional and rational appeals to persuade consumers to use their debit card. And we also see how storytelling became part of the appeals.

money to buy a dog; the story has a touching moment when we see the father learning an important money management lesson from his son. And finally, an adventurous 60-second episode revealed a mysterious man who seemingly did not pay for any purchase, as seen through the eyes of a young boy (in fact, the mysterious man paid with virtual payment systems).

Another new film showed a woman's life story unfold in a series of memorable milestone moments, punctuated with beeps from childhood to adulthood. This 2017 message associated all the beeps in life from all sorts of technology to encourage non-users of Interac to begin usage since it was like any other beep in life.

By late 2017, Interac evolved its message to "Own Your World" to ward off new competitors like Google Wallet. The opening message used the metaphor of a bear waking up from hibernation to see all the new technology options Interac offers. He immediately adopts all of them, kind of like the mysterious man, as he shops for organic salmon, gets his claws done at a nail salon, takes a cab, travels, and parties!

©Interac/Zulu Alpha Kilo

Another story in late 2017 illustrated a situation where people typically need cash: donating to a street musician. While playing, he is continually missing out on receiving cash as many people only use their Interac card. So he joins them by setting up a cashless system, much to the delight of many new fans who watch and donate electronically.

Question:

1. Why does a mix of rational and emotional appeal work for Interac?

 # Source Characteristics

The third creative strategy decision is the source of the message appeal. We use the term **source** to mean the person involved in communicating a message appeal, either directly or indirectly. A *direct source* is a spokesperson who delivers a message and/or demonstrates a product or service. An *indirect source* (e.g., a model) doesn't actually deliver a message but draws attention to and/or enhances the appearance of the ad. Some ads use neither a direct nor an indirect source; the source is the brand or organization with the message to communicate. Since most research focuses on individuals as a message source, our examination follows this approach. Companies carefully select individuals to deliver their message appeal due to the costs involved and the fit with their brand positioning strategy. To understand this decision, we rely on a model that identifies three source attributes: credibility, attractiveness, and power.[93] This section applies the first two characteristics to advertising since the compliance effect due to source power is not possible in most promotional communication.

SOURCE CREDIBILITY

Credibility is the extent to which the recipient sees the source as having relevant knowledge, skill, or experience and trusts the source to give unbiased, objective information, implying that there are two important dimensions to credibility: *expertise* and *trustworthiness*. A communicator seen as knowledgeable—someone with expertise—is more persuasive than one with less expertise. But the source also has to be trustworthy—honest, ethical, and believable. The influence of a knowledgeable source will be lessened if audience members think he or she is biased or has underlying personal motives for advocating a position (such as being paid to endorse a product).

One of the most reliable effects found in communications research across many fields of study (including psychology, political science, marketing, and advertising) is that expert and/or trustworthy sources are more persuasive than sources who are less expert or trustworthy.[94] For example in the context of advertising, a couple of early studies examined source credibility effects. One looked at the receiver's cognitive responses while processing the source of the message, as described in Chapter 4.[95] Another studied the attitudinal effects of the source of the message.[96]

Information from a credible source influences beliefs, opinions, attitudes, and/or behaviour through a process known as **internalization**, which occurs when the receiver adopts the opinion of the credible communicator since he or she believes information from this source to be accurate. Once the receiver internalizes an opinion or attitude, it becomes integrated into his or her belief system and may be maintained even after the source of the message is forgotten.

Expertise Because attitudes and opinions developed through an internalization process become part of the individual's belief system, marketers want to use communicators with expertise. Spokespeople are often chosen because of their knowledge of or experience with a particular product or service. Endorsements from individuals or groups recognized as experts, such as doctors or dentists, are also common in advertising (**Exhibit 7-24**). The importance of using expert sources was shown in a study which found that the perceived expertise of celebrity endorsers was more important in explaining purchase intentions than their attractiveness or trustworthiness. One implication is that celebrity spokespeople are most effective when they are knowledgeable, experienced, and qualified to talk about the product they are endorsing.[97]

Trustworthiness While expertise is important, the target audience must also find the source (e.g., celebrities or other figures) to have a trustworthy image. In some cases, ads include actors playing the role of a professional (e.g., medical, technical) giving advice or their opinion to ensure a level of trustworthiness. However, certain brands and product categories may limit this option for selecting a trustworthy spokesperson. In such situations, firms might rely on a customer testimonial so that non-consumers of the category, or non-customers of the brand, might accept the message claims.

One appropriate trustworthy source for an ad message is the company president or chief executive officer who acts as the spokesperson. The use of this source is the ultimate expression of the company's commitment to quality and customer service. Research suggests that the use of this source can improve attitudes and increase the likelihood that consumers will inquire about the company's product or service.[98] Companies are likely to use a top executive in their advertising when they have celebrity value that enhances the firm's image. However, there is a risk if CEO spokespeople become popular and get more attention than their company's product/service or advertising message. Loblaw returned to using its president in advertising, something the retailer originated during the 1970s. The current president, Galen Weston Jr., ranked as the most admired business leader as a company spokesperson.[99] Owners or presidents of medium or small firms and local businesses rely on this approach for source trustworthiness.

Exhibit 7-24 Dove promotes that it is recommended by skin care experts.

DERMATOLOGISTS RECOMMEND DOVE

The Proof is in the Science

Dermatologists recommend Dove 7X more often than Olay®
Dove has our gentlest cleansers AND NutriumMoisture, to moisturize your skin deep down.

Here's what dermatologists are saying...

"I recommend Dove body wash to all of my patients, literally."

— Dr. Indira Misra-Higgins
Beverly Hills, MI

Source: Dove by Unilever

A review of source credibility research in advertising over many decades concluded that a highly credible source exerts the strongest persuasion influence on attitudes when advertisers do the following:[100] (1) Introduce the source at the start, especially if the target audience is highly involved. But, if the receiver is less involved or has a favourable brand attitude, the source can be delayed to the end. (2) State strong arguments quickly, but consider a normal pace for moderate arguments. The ads should consider a fear appeal and implicitly refute counter-arguments at the start of the message.

SOURCE ATTRACTIVENESS

A source characteristic frequently used by advertisers is **attractiveness**, which encompasses similarity, familiarity, and likability.[101] *Similarity* is a supposed resemblance between the source and the receiver of the message. *Likability* is an affection for the source as a result of physical appearance, behaviour, or other personal traits. Even when the sources are not famous, consumers often admire their physical appearance, talent, and/or personality. *Familiarity* refers to knowledge of the source through exposure. We describe these three characteristics and see how they operate via celebrity endorsers and decorative models in this section.

Source attractiveness leads to persuasion through a process of **identification**, whereby the receiver is motivated to seek a relationship with the source and thus adopts similar beliefs, attitudes, preferences, or behaviour. Maintaining this position depends on the source's continued support for the position as well as the receiver's continued identification with the source. If the source changes position, the receiver may also change. Unlike internalization, identification does not usually integrate information from an attractive source into the receiver's belief system. The receiver may maintain the attitudinal position or behaviour only as long as it is supported by the source or the source remains attractive. **Exhibit 7-25** is an ad in which source attractiveness may be a factor for communicating effectively.

Similarity Research findings suggest that people are more likely to be influenced by a message coming from someone with whom they feel a sense of similarity.[102] If the communicator and receiver have similar needs, goals, interests, and lifestyles, the position advocated by the source is better understood and received. Similarity is used to create a situation where the consumer feels empathy for the person shown in a message. In a slice-of-life commercial, the advertiser usually starts by presenting a predicament with the hope of getting the consumer to think, "I can see myself in that situation." This can help establish a bond of similarity between the communicator and the receiver, increasing the source's level of persuasiveness. The President's Choice #EatTogether ads encouraging people to eat their meals with other people are an example of source similarity as the campaign features regular-looking, everyday people with whom the average person can easily identify.

Likability A likable source in an ad message has virtually any characteristics that the advertiser would like to draw attention toward. Presumably, promotional planners select characteristics that reinforce the brand and its intended positioning strategy. For example, marketers of a facial skin care product would select a person who has a good complexion so that this physical characteristic would be noticed and associated with the brand name.

Brands use a source with personality characteristics that emerge in the ad's story to develop the brand personality. Advertisers recently gravitated to telling the story of a person who overcame obstacles in life and eventually thrived. Their accomplishments gave people a reason to like them; consumers respect and admire their achievement.

Brands also use a source who is a member of a reference group to which the receiver aspires and may join in future if they purchase the brand. Mattel presented an alternative view of Barbie in the global "Be Super" campaign that recognized the "super powers" in all girls. For the Canadian launch, girls signed up online to be on the "Super Squad" by demonstrating their super powers—kindness, creativity, or self-expression. Messaging encouraged "Super Squad" girls to be leaders by showing their heroism on a daily basis, and urged other girls to emulate them. A final part of the program featured Mattel donating $15,000 to four girl groups.[103]

Advertisers feature a physically attractive person who serves as a *decorative model* rather than as an active communicator. Research suggests that physically attractive communicators generally have a positive impact and generate more favourable evaluations of both ads and products than less attractive models.[104] The gender appropriateness of the model for the product being advertised and his or her relevance to the product are also important considerations.[105]

Consider the case of Canadian-based Joe Fresh. With a focus on "offering great style at a great price," Loblaw looked to create an iconic value brand with a colourful selection of basic fashionable clothes as it expanded internationally. One creative strategy decision that appears to resonate across all countries is Joe Fresh's employment of world-famous models from many countries. A model recently highlighted in its ads and catalogues was Karlie Kloss. Other prominent models of the past few years included Andrés Velencoso Segura, Liya Kebede, Joan Smalls, and Sean O'Pry, but it is Karlie who became the face of Joe Fresh in much of the imagery. In the past, Karlie Kloss graced the cover of fashion magazines such as *Elle, Vogue,* and *Glamour,* modelled for many high-end designers during their fashion shows, and represented other brands such as Marella, Kurt Geiger, Liu-Jo, L'Oréal, Chanel, and Versace in their advertising.

Exhibit 7-25 Source attractiveness via tennis skill and fame may be persuasive.

Never underestimate the competition.

NikeWomen.com

Source: NIKE Inc.

Exhibit 7-26 Dove's "Campaign for Real Beauty" uses everyday women rather than supermodels in its ads.

campaignforrealbeauty.com 🔊 | *Dove*

Let's face it, firming the thighs of a size 2 supermodel is no challenge. Real women have real curves. And according to women who tried new Dove® Firming, it left their skin feeling firmer in just one week. What better way to celebrate the curves you were born with? New Dove Firming. Lotion, Cream and Body Wash. For beautifully firm skin.

Courtesy of Unilever Home and Personal Care-USA

For the Canadian launch of Karlie Kloss's imagery, Joe Fresh partnered with *Flare* magazine to promote its capsule apparel collection. Subscribers received a special "unzip" cover where they had to open it like an article of clothing to reveal the full cover design that featured Karlie Kloss wearing Joe Fresh fashion. The issue included a four-page feature article about the success of Joe Fresh to go along with the Joe Fresh gatefold ads inside the front cover. Other communication involved publicity on other Rogers media such as TV with programs like *BT* and *CityLine* to go along with digital messaging like #joefreshxflare to direct users to Flare.com and JoeFresh.ca/Flare. With the excitement surrounding Karlie Kloss on the cover, executives expected online communication to peak significantly with the launch of the new fashion collection.[106]

Some models draw attention to the ad but not to the product or message. Studies show that an attractive model facilitates recognition of the ad but does not enhance copy readership or message recall. Thus, advertisers must ensure that the consumer's attention will go beyond the model to the product and advertising message.[107] Marketers must also consider whether the use of highly attractive models might negatively impact advertising effectiveness. Studies have shown that women may experience negative feelings when comparing themselves with beautiful models used in ads and the images of physical perfection they represent.[108]

To address this, Unilever's Dove developed the "Campaign for Real Beauty" (**Exhibit 7-26**), which portrayed typical women and girls in its messages, in contrast to the use of supermodels or decorative models. In essence, Dove relied on source similarity with the use of everyday women; however, their unexpected use in the beauty category quite possibly produced a degree of source likability due to the issues identified above. Thus, while there is often a primary source effect, a strong secondary effect may occur with creative campaigns. The campaign included different types of ads, extensive public relations, and a website (CampaignForRealBeauty.ca) where women discussed beauty-related issues. And, according to experts and the awards it won, the initiative appeared successful from a social standpoint, but less so financially.[109] More recently, the campaign received criticism for its "Patches" and "Choose Beautiful" executions, which showed typical women being misled or manipulated with a condescending or patronizing tone, which may question the viability of the original source effect.[110]

Familiarity Familiarity through exposure from another context can provide a strong source. Essentially, advertisers hope that the characteristics associated with the source in the original context carry over to the brand. This connection is often reinforced with the creative theme of the ad, so the two strategic variables work in tandem. Without question, familiarity often occurs through using famous endorsers, which we discuss subsequently, but it also occurs naturally in other ways. Familiarity is used with prototypical (and sometimes stereotypical) or representative images of a familiar person or persons from a well understood context. For example, familiarity is shown with a common situation that is known to occur within the target audience's use of the product.

Celebrity Endorsers Advertisers understand the value of using spokespeople who are admired: TV and movie stars, athletes, musicians, and other popular public figures. Why do companies spend huge sums to have celebrities appear in their ads and endorse their products? These celebrities are clearly likable due to their professional achievements and anticipated physical attractiveness, and they are generally familiar given their media exposure. While the use of celebrities seems pervasive, they are seen in only about 10 percent of all U.S. TV and print ads. Furthermore, in the case of U.S. magazine ads, celebrities are shown within select product categories (e.g., cosmetics, fashion, food, media) and found in certain magazine vehicles (e.g., sports, teen, women's fashion).[111] Marketers expect that these celebrity characteristics draw consumer attention to advertising messages and favourably influence consumers' feelings, attitudes, and purchase behaviour. A study that summarizes many other studies supports this line of thinking.[112] Notice how a well known former athlete like David Beckham still adds lustre to a high-end brand such as Breitling (**Exhibit 7-27**).

A celebrity endorsement is "an agreement between an individual who enjoys public recognition (celebrity) and an entity (brand) to use the celebrity for the purpose of promoting the entity."[113] This is a broad view in the age of social media influence, as past perspectives saw celebrity endorsers occurring in advertising only. When selecting a celebrity, marketers follow a formal process to avoid problems, and consider the celebrity's congruence with the audience, product/service or brand, overall image, specific source characteristics, profession, popularity, availability, and cost.[114] Two notable Canadian examples of sports celebrities are Marcus Stroman for BioSteel, and Andre De Grasse for Gatorade.[115] Another example is GoDaddy's use of players from the Toronto Raptors who set up their own ecommerce websites; for example, Raptors player Norm Powell stepped up his music career by releasing a single.[116] Four factors for a promotional planner to consider include overshadowing the product, overexposure, the target audience's receptivity, and risk.

Exhibit 7-27 David Beckham is featured in this Breitling ad.

Overshadowing the Product How will the celebrity affect the target audience's processing of the advertising message and their overall attitude toward the brand? Consumers may potentially focus their attention on the celebrity and fail to notice the brand. Advertisers should select a celebrity spokesperson who will attract attention and enhance the brand and its message, not the celebrity. Furthermore, the message should make a clear connection between the celebrity and the brand for a more positive brand attitude effect, otherwise the celebrity effect takes hold more strongly.[117] Canadian actor William Shatner has been Priceline.com's celebrity endorser for 20 years and appears not to overshadow the product. In fact, the U.S. creative expanded internationally with uniquely Canadian creative, proving that the celebrity–brand connection worked.[118]

Overexposure Consumers may be skeptical of endorsements because they know that the celebrities are paid.[119] This problem is particularly pronounced when a celebrity endorses too many brands and becomes overexposed. Advertisers can protect themselves against overexposure with an exclusivity clause limiting the number of products a celebrity can endorse. However, such clauses are usually expensive, and most celebrities agree not to endorse similar products anyway. Celebrities try to earn as much endorsement money as possible, yet they must be careful not to damage their credibility by endorsing too many products. In the case of Stroman, the pitcher also worked for American Express and Lyft besides BioSteel; he represented three different types of brands to manage the overexposure point satisfactorily. De Grasse's other sponsors, clothiers Harry Rosen and Puma, saw his sponsorship as distinct since they sell very different types of clothing.

Target Audience's Receptivity One of the most important considerations in choosing a celebrity endorser is how well the individual matches with and is received by the advertiser's target audience. Consumers who are particularly knowledgeable about a product or service or have strongly established attitudes may be less influenced by a celebrity than those with little knowledge or neutral attitudes. One study found that college-age students were more likely to have a positive attitude toward a product endorsed by a celebrity than were older consumers.[120]

Risk for Advertiser The decision to employ an expensive celebrity spokesperson contains risk; entertainers and athletes who are involved in or accused of unacceptable activities in their personal life or while on the job have unexpected and unpredictable effects on the brand. Allegations against Cristiano Ronaldo (see **Exhibit 7-28**) did

Exhibit 7-28 Allegations against Cristiano Ronaldo caused significant difficulty for his brand sponsors.

DON'T CRACK UNDER PRESSURE

TAGHeuer
SWISS AVANT-GARDE SINCE 1860

AQUARACER CALIBRE 5

Source: Tag Heuer

not result in charges against him, but this is an example of the significant risk advertisers may face. To avoid problems, companies research a celebrity's personal life and background and include a morals clause in the contract allowing the company to terminate the endorsement if controversy arises. However, marketers should remember that adding morals clauses to their endorsement contracts only gets them out of a problem; it does not prevent it from happening. A summary of celebrity endorser studies concluded that the strongest impact on advertising effectiveness was negative information about the celebrity; it had almost twice as strong a negative effect compared to positive effects of source credibility and source attractiveness.[121]

The Meaning of Celebrity Endorsers Advertisers must try to match the product or company's image, the characteristics of the target audience, and the personality of the celebrity.[122] An interesting perspective on celebrity endorsement was developed by Grant McCracken.[123] He argues that credibility and attractiveness don't sufficiently explain how and why celebrity endorsements work and offers a model based on meaning transfer (**Figure 7-6**).

According to this model, a celebrity's effectiveness as an endorser depends on the culturally acquired meanings he or she brings to the endorsement process. Each celebrity contains multiple meanings, including status, class, gender, and age as well as personality and lifestyle. At Stage 1, the characteristics associated with the celebrity from their public exposure in movies and so on extend to their persona. Celebrity endorsers bring their meanings and image into the ad and transfer them to the product they are endorsing in Stage 2. In the final stage, the meanings the celebrity has given to the product are transferred to the consumer. This final stage is complicated and difficult to achieve. The way consumers take possession of the meaning the celebrity has transferred to a product is probably the least understood part of the process.

For example, American Express featured Tina Fey in ads for its Amex EveryDay credit card, which allows users to earn rewards on everyday purchases (**Exhibit 7-29**). The new card was targeted to working mothers who have busy lives.

Figure 7-6 Meaning movement and the endorsement process

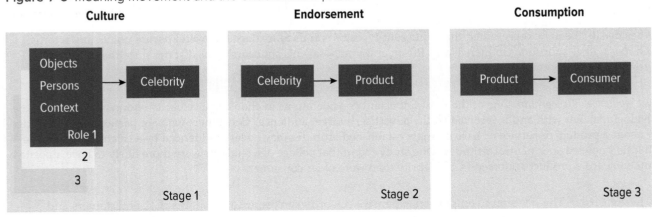

Key: ⟶ = Path of meaning movement

▢ = Stage of meaning movement

The TV messages showed Fey in her trademark witty fashion as a busy, on-the-go working woman and mom, juggling her personal life with work demands. She is an effective endorser since she represents the quintessential do-it-all woman with an endless to-do list but who gets it all done with the help of the product.

The meaning transfer model implies that marketers must first decide on the image or symbolic meanings important to the target audience, and then determine which celebrity best represents the meaning or image to be projected. An advertising campaign must be designed that captures the meaning in the product and moves it to the consumer. Marketing and advertising personnel often rely on intuition in choosing celebrity endorsers for their companies or products, but companies conduct research studies to determine consumers' perceptions of celebrities' meaning. Marketers may also pre-test ads to determine whether they transfer the proper meaning to the product. When celebrity endorsers are used, the marketer should track the campaign's effectiveness by assessing whether the celebrity continues to communicate the proper meaning to the target audience.

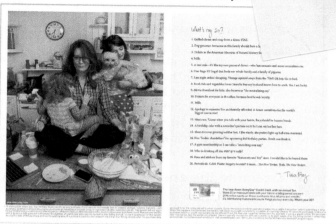

Exhibit 7-29 Tina Fey's image as a comed the humour of this ad for the Amex EveryDa

Source: American Express Company

LO6 IMC Planning: Message and Source Combinations

As noted at the outset of this chapter, the creative strategy comprises decisions regarding the creative theme, message appeal, and source characteristics. In the creative theme section, we noted that promotional planners determine the degree to which there is creative consistency across time, executions, media, promotional tools, and products. In this IMC planning section, we present a table that allows promotional planners to consider various combinations of message and source decisions.

Figure 7-7 summarizes the possible combinations of all message and source decisions. Essentially any ad or IMC tool has one of these 15 combinations. Promotional planners can consider using certain combinations for certain parts of the IMC plan. For example, a brand may select a more credible source with a rational appeal for its print communication, and possibly consider a familiar source with an emotional appeal for its television commercials. As noted in the creative consistency section, Telus has used a different message appeal and source on television and radio. Television ads feature likable critters with emotional appeals, while radio ads feature a trustworthy source with rational appeals.

While a number of combinations exist—and we have shown two examples where brands have adapted the source and message across IMC tools or media—promotional planners can certainly decide to keep the same source and message appeal for all their tools and media.

Figure 7-7 Possible combinations for message and source decisions

	Rational Appeal	Emotional Appeal	Combined Appeal
Credible			
Trustworthy			
Similar			
Likable			
Familiar			

Learning Objectives Summary

LO1 Summarize the idea and importance of creativity in an advertising context.

The creative development and execution of the advertising message are a crucial part of a firm's integrated marketing communications program. The creative specialist or team is responsible for developing an effective way to communicate the marketer's message to both customers and non-customers and reinforce the brand positioning strategy. Creativity is often difficult to articulate, but consumers and advertising people all know it when they see it. The challenge facing the writers, artists, and others who develop ads is to be creative and come up with fresh, unique, and appropriate ideas that can be used as solutions to marketing communication issues that may be problems or opportunities.

LO2 Describe the creative strategy planning process.

Marketers turn to ad agencies to develop, prepare, and implement their creative strategy, since these agencies are specialists in the creative function of advertising. Creativity in advertising is a process of several stages, including preparation, incubation, illumination, and verification. Various sources of information are available to help the creative specialists determine the best creative strategy. Creative strategy is guided by marketing goals and objectives and is based on a number of factors, including the basic problem the advertising must address; the target audience, behavioural, and communication objectives the message seeks to accomplish; and key benefits the advertiser wants to communicate as reflected in the brand positioning strategy. These factors and the creative strategy decisions are generally stated in a copy platform, which is a work plan used to guide development of the ad campaign.

LO3 Identify the approaches used for determining the creative theme that forms the basis of an advertising campaign.

An important part of creative strategy is determining the creative theme of the campaign. Often, a big idea strikes the creative specialist while embarking upon the creative process, which becomes the source of the creative theme. There are approaches to discovering this big idea, including using a unique selling proposition, creating a brand image, looking for inherent drama in the brand, and positioning. In general, the creative theme guides much of the advertising campaign or IMC program. Consistency, originality, and its ability to effectively communicate are three key strengths of a good creative. The creative theme acts as a brand story to give it uniqueness compared to competitors.

LO4 Summarize the different types of message appeals that advertisers use to persuade their target audience.

A message appeal, the second decision of the creative strategy, is the central message used in the ad to elicit cognitive and emotional processing responses and communication effects from the target audience. A message appeal reveals the intended persuasion of the brand. Appeals can be broken into two broad groups—rational and emotional. Rational appeals focus on consumers' practical, functional, or utilitarian need for the product or service. Emotional appeals relate to social and/or psychological reasons for purchasing a product or service. Numerous types of appeals are available to advertisers within each group, and it is important for the client to clearly specify its intended message as accurately as possible.

LO5 Identify the source or communicator options a marketer has for a promotional message.

Selection of the appropriate source or communicator to deliver a message is the third creative strategy decision. The message source is the approach to deliver the message appeal. Three important attributes are source credibility, attractiveness, and power. Marketers enhance message effectiveness by hiring communicators who are experts in a particular area and/or have a trustworthy image. The use of celebrities to deliver advertising messages has become very popular; advertisers hope they will catch the receivers' attention and influence their attitudes or behaviour through an identification process. The chapter discusses the meaning a celebrity brings to the endorsement process and the importance of matching the image of the celebrity with that of the company or brand.

LO6 **Apply source and message appeal options for different ad executions**

The chapter concluded by outlining options for IMC planning and suggesting that different combinat~~ions of source and~~ message appeal could be constructed for different media or different IMC tools. Promotional planners ~~might consider different combi~~nations depending on the context of the media such as TV, print, or social media. Furthermore, promo~~tional planners~~ might consider different combinations for specific IMC tools compared to what is shown in advertising.

Review Questions

1. Television commercials can use unusual creativity that has very little to do with the product being advertised. Explain why creative specialists would recommend such ads and why the brand managers would approve the production and placement.

2. Describe the types of general and product-specific preplanning input one might evaluate when assigned to work on an advertising campaign for a new brand of bottled water.

3. What is your opinion of advertising awards, such as the Cannes Lions, that are based solely on creativity? If you were a marketer looking for an agency, would you take these creative awards into consideration in your agency evaluation process? Why or why not?

4. Assume that a government agency wants to use a fear appeal to encourage college and university students not to drink and drive. Explain how fear appeals might affect persuasion and what factors should be considered in developing the ads.

5. What are source characteristics? What types are there? How do they affect processing of a message and the communication effects of the message?

6. How is it possible that an IMC program could have multiple sources for the message using both rational and emotional appeals?

Applied Questions

1. Find an example of a print ad that is very creative and an ad that is dull and boring. Select each element of the ad and figure out how it is contributing to the creativity or lack of creativity.

2. The chapter outlined a few campaigns; use the Internet to research and identify the most successful Canadian campaign in recent years.

3. Find an example of an ad or campaign that you think reflects one of the approaches used to develop a creative theme, such as unique selling proposition, brand image, inherent drama, or positioning. Discuss how the creative theme is used in this ad or campaign.

4. Describe how a few of the negative emotions conveyed in **Figure 7-3** could be used in a campaign for car insurance. Describe how a few of the positive emotions conveyed in **Figure 7-3** could be used in a campaign for smart phones.

5. Find a celebrity who is currently appearing in ads for a particular company or brand, and use McCracken's meaning transfer model (shown in **Figure 7-6**) to analyze the use of the celebrity as a spokesperson.

6. Actors portraying doctors in ads are often used for rational appeals. In what situation might it make sense to have a doctor for an emotional appeal? What type of emotional appeal would be most logical from **Figure 7-3**?

CHAPTER EIGHT

Creative Tactics Decisions

LEARNING OBJECTIVES

LO1 Analyze the creative execution styles that advertisers use and the situations where they are most appropriate.

LO2 Explain different types of message structures used to develop a promotional message.

LO3 Express design elements involved in the creation of print, video, and audio messages.

LO4 Apply a planning model for making creative tactics decisions.

LO5 Illustrate how clients evaluate the creative work of their agencies and discuss guidelines for the evaluation and approval process.

Gain's Romantic Fragrance

Ty Burrell of *Modern Family* fame starts speaking in a Gain detergent ad with an attention-getting opening: "Don't laugh. This is super serious. I'm in a fragrance ad, people." And so begins the parody of a perfume ad to advertise Gain Flings, the easy-to-use liquid detergent packs.

The creative spark of this execution originated from research that found consumers used candles, moisturizers, and perfumes/colognes for sensory enjoyment of fragrant scents. In contrast, the scent from washed clothes only meant clean, not an enjoyable experience. Further, the majority of consumers in the scent-seeking benefit segment did not view Gain as better than any competitor, despite the brand claiming this for 20 years. And, 8 out of 10 scent seekers reported satisfaction with their current brand.

Ty's ad copy continued: "Living a fantasy. A flash-bulb-filled fragrance fantasy. Because the world of scent isn't about making sense. It's about making sexy faces," with images of Ty being photographed. Indeed, the words and the sequence of scenes re-enacted a stereotypical perfume ad to stand out from all other detergent ads. Ty carried on with similar copy: "It's about running down hallways in slow motion making sexy faces"—while he did in fact run down a hallway showing his sexy face.

As Ty entered a bright, clean room next, he announced, "Searching for an answer only to find more questions. Like, who's this gorgeous guy? And, why does he smell so darn good?" and discovered that he was looking at another version of himself. At this point, viewers realize they are seeing a detergent ad when Ty smells the other Ty! The brief conversation of the two characters reflects a typical selling message for a scented detergent ad. The campaign also featured another parody ad where Ty is on a beach, devastated after breaking up with his sweetheart. And like the other ad, viewers instantly see that it is a spoof and ultimately find out it is a Gain detergent ad. Each ad ended with the slogan, "The Seriously Good Scent," written on the screen.

Both ads aired on TV and ran online, and similar messages occurred on billboards and in magazines. For consistency, the ads emulated the video messages with similar settings and identical wardrobe for Ty. Other digital messages included Twitter and Facebook ads, and influencer promotion. Awareness improved from 61 percent to 71 percent. Consumers associated Gain with scent beliefs much more strongly for three attitudinal questions, and sales nearly doubled in one year.

Question:

1. Why does such an unusual ad execution work for this brand? And why does it work for this product category?

In the previous chapter, we identified and described the three creative strategy decisions. This chapter focuses on the three main creative tactics decisions. It examines execution styles that can be used to develop the ad, the important message structure choices available, and the elements involved in the design and production of effective advertising messages. We also present a framework for guiding the creative tactics decisions. We conclude by presenting guidelines to evaluate the creative recommendations to effectively communicate the brand positioning strategy prior to client approval.

Creative Execution Style

An important creative tactic decision is the **creative execution style**, defined as the way in which a message appeal is presented. While it is obviously important for an ad to have a meaningful message appeal to communicate to the consumer, the manner in which the ad is executed is very critical for achieving processing and communication effects. We identify 11 execution styles commonly seen and provide examples of each. Two or three of these styles are combined to present most message appeals.

Exhibit 8-1 The ad for the Gillette Mach3 uses a straight-sell execution style.

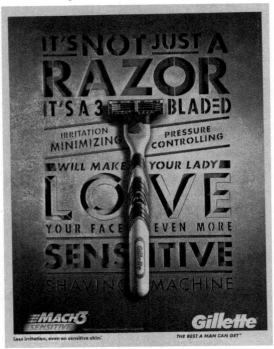

Source: Gillette by Procter & Gamble

Exhibit 8-2 Opti-Free promotes how it is the number one doctor-recommended brand to support the product performance claim.

Source: Alcon, A Novartis Company

STRAIGHT SELL

One creative execution style is the straight sell, which relies on a clear and direct presentation of information. This creative execution style is often used with rational appeals, where the focus of the message is the brand or specific product attributes and/or benefits. Straight-sell executions are seen in print ads where a picture of the product occupies part of the ad, and the factual copy takes up the remaining space. They are used in TV ads, with an announcer generally delivering the sales message while the product/service is shown on the screen. Ads for high-involvement consumer products and business-to-business products use this format. Internet media ads may use a straight sell to encourage consumers to visit a brand's website or social media vehicles. The ad for the Gillette Mach3 shown in **Exhibit 8-1** is an excellent example of a straight-sell execution style.

SCIENTIFIC/TECHNICAL EVIDENCE

In a variation of the straight sell, scientific or technical evidence is presented in the ad. Advertisers cite technical information, results of scientific or laboratory studies, or endorsements by scientific bodies or agencies to support their advertising claims. The ad for Alcon's Opti-Free multipurpose disinfecting solution for contact lens care treatment shown in **Exhibit 8-2** uses this execution style by noting how the product is the number one doctor-recommended brand and how its performance is driven by science.

DEMONSTRATION

Demonstration is designed to illustrate the key advantages of the product by showing it in actual use or in a staged situation. Demonstration executions are effective in convincing consumers of a product's utility or quality and of the benefits of owning or using the brand. Video is particularly well suited for demonstration executions, since the product benefits are shown visually. Although perhaps a little less dramatic, demonstration ads can also work in print. The Varilux progressive lens ad shown in **Exhibit 8-3** uses this style, in print and other media, to demonstrate the superiority of its progressive lenses with W.A.V.E. technology over ordinary progressive lenses by contrasting the clarity of the two images.

COMPARISON

A comparison execution style—direct, indirect, or visual—is an option for advertisers. Direct brand comparisons are advertising executions to communicate a competitive advantage or to position a new or lesser-known brand with industry leaders. For example, some Samsung phone ads directly compared it to the iPhone. Over the years, visual comparison ads for Dove beauty bar versus unidentified competitors like beauty soap, hygiene soap, and natural soap communicated its gentleness. A litmus test for each type of soap showed the others as harsh, leading to dry skin. Although previous research found little support for the effectiveness of comparative ads, one study found positive results for the situation where a challenger brand compares itself to a category leader.[1]

TESTIMONIAL

An advertiser may prefer to have its messages presented by way of a testimonial, where a person praises the product or service on the basis of his or her personal experience with it. Testimonial executions can have ordinary satisfied customers discuss their own experiences with the brand and the benefits of using it. This approach is effective when the person delivering the testimonial is someone with whom the target audience can identify or who has an interesting story to tell. The testimonial must be based on actual use of the product to avoid legal problems, and the spokesperson must be credible. The bicycle rider in **Exhibit 8-4** acts as an indirect testimonial support for the "Ride to Conquer Cancer" fundraising activity. Testimonials are particularly effective when they come from a recognizable or popular person.

SLICE OF LIFE

A widely used advertising format, particularly for packaged-goods products, is the slice-of-life execution. Slice-of-life executions are criticized for being unrealistic and irritating to watch because they are often used to remind consumers of problems of a personal nature (e.g., dandruff, bad breath) and cleaning problems. These ads might be perceived as contrived, silly, phony, or even offensive to consumers. However, advertisers prefer this style for certain marketing communication requirements because they believe it effectively presents a reasonably realistic consumer situation to communicate a product feature or benefit.

Execution is critical in using the technique effectively, as these ads are designed to be dramatizations of a supposedly real-life situation that consumers encounter. Getting viewers to identify with the situation and/or characters depicted is challenging. Since the success of slice-of-life ads depends on how well the actors execute their roles, professional actors are used to achieve credibility and to ensure that the commercial is of high quality. Advertisers with low production budgets may not be able to afford to hire the talent or to pay for the production quality needed to effectively create slice-of-life spots. One alternative gaining ground is the growth of user-generated executions.

Scotiabank tried its hand with this approach as an offshoot of its highly successful "You're Richer Than You Think" ads. In newer executions, the definition of *richer* moved toward how people felt rich in their lives during important life events like having a baby. With a consumer focus, the Scotiabank messages explored the meaning of moments of people's lives that matter to them. Some of these new executions used consumer-generated content across the TV ads, in branch material, and in digital ads. One such execution, entitled "Conversation," concerned the thoughts of parents of a new baby with video shots obtained from a friend of a Scotiabank employee.[2]

ANIMATION

With animation, scenes are drawn by artists or created on the computer, and cartoons, puppets, or other types of fictional

Exhibit 8-3 Varilux demonstrates the superiority of its progressive lenses.

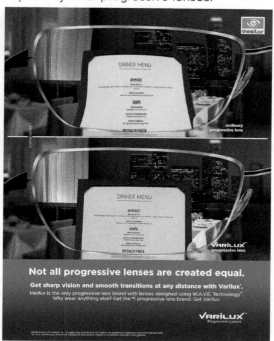

©Varilux by Essilor of America, Inc.

Exhibit 8-4 The image of the rider suggests a testimonial executional style.

©ValeStock/Shutterstock

Source: Chipotle/Cannes Lions International Advertising Festival Winner

characters may be used. Cartoon animation is especially popular for commercials targeted at children for products like toys and cereal; however, we also see it elsewhere. Nike created 100,000 customized animated films, one for each member of its Nike+ community of fitness members. They emailed the finished product, which told the personal story of each individual's training experience. Data derived from the community membership provided the content of the story. Each story showed familiar landmarks from the individual's training regime and encouraged the runner to achieve higher goals for the coming year.[3] Chipotle's ad shown in **Exhibit 8-5** won for best film message at Cannes, quite an achievement for the use of animation!

PERSONALITY SYMBOL

Another advertising execution involves developing a central character or personality symbol that delivers the advertising message. The symbol is associated with the brand and its creativity to enhance brand awareness and contribute to intended brand attitude effects.[4] Shock Top gained notoriety by creating a wisecracking beer tap (**Exhibit 8-6**) for a Super Bowl campaign designed by a Canadian ad agency based in Toronto. Anomaly introduced a personality symbol in the likeness of the Wedgehead image found on the label of Labatt's Shock Top brew. Unsuspecting patrons in Toronto and Montreal interacted with the remote-controlled animatronic creation, who wisecracked his way through many types of conversations. Messages ended with the ironic "It speaks for itself" slogan. Video recordings of the conversations found their way to social media. American executives watched the Canadian success with interest. Looking to expand the brand's awareness beyond 40 percent, they claimed the creative idea for a Super Bowl 50 ad as the brand's first on broadcast TV. The ad featured comedian TJ Millar trading humorous barbs with the Wedgehead character; score another international coup for Canadian ad creatives![5]

The Maytag repairman turned 50 years old in 2017 and the famous appliance brand worked its way through five different actors over that span, sort of like the James Bond character. Although he was originally cast as a goofy, lovable, woebegone, lonely repairman, Maytag updated his image with an attractive and slimmer actor and portrayed him as actively involved in customer service rather than waiting around for a call to fix a broken machine. The executives believed that the character should reflect the brand, preferring a masculine man who looked like he had strength and experience. Finally, the uniform became tailored with a darker blue material and he obtained his own Twitter account.[6]

Exhibit 8-6 Shock Top's Wedgehead represents both animation and a personality symbol.

©Stars and Stripes/Alamy Stock Photo

Closer to home, CIBC introduced Percy the penguin as part of its "Banking That Fits Your Life" campaign. Ads featured Percy and his family for the launch of the Aventura rewards program and then in messages about edeposit to their bank accounts where cheques could be deposited with a digital photograph. In the first message, the ads showed real penguins, while the follow-up ad showed an animated penguin. CIBC planned to use a "real-life" Percy (i.e., a man in a penguin suit) to make visits to events and branch activities. The big Percy launch coincided with the Pan Am Games, in which CIBC acted as a lead partner.[7] An executive at CIBC's ad agency believes that Percy acted as a visual metaphor of the consumer as the penguin's behaviour emulates people's daily routine.[8]

As these examples illustrate, a symbol reflects brand characteristics to reinforce the positioning and is useful within the overall creative strategy. However, eventually changes are made, as we saw in the Maytag example.

In the case of the most interesting man in the world (**Exhibit 8-7**), Dos Equis gave the actor a great send-off into outer space in the final episode before replacing him.

IMAGERY

Some ads contain little or no information about the brand or company and are almost totally visual. These advertisements use imagery executions whereby the ad consists primarily of visual elements such as pictures, illustrations, and/or symbols rather than information. An imagery execution is used when the goal is to encourage consumers to associate the brand with the symbols, characters, and/or situation shown in the ad. Imagery ads are often the basis for emotional appeals that are used to advertise products or services where differentiation based on physical characteristics is difficult.

An imagery execution may be based on **usage imagery** by showing how a brand is used or performs and the situations in which it is used. For example, advertising for trucks and SUVs often shows the vehicles navigating tough terrain or in challenging situations such as towing a heavy load. The San Pellegrino ad shown in **Exhibit 8-8** uses the imagery of an Italian restaurant to convey the usage of its sparkling water.

This type of execution can also be based on **user imagery**, where the focus is on the type of person who uses the brand. Ads for cosmetics often use very attractive models in the hope of getting consumers to associate the model's physical attractiveness with the brand (see **Exhibit 8-9**). Image executions rely heavily on visual elements such as photography, colour, tonality,

Exhibit 8-7 Dos Equis invented "the most interesting man in the world" as part of the brand's identity.

Source: Heineken USA

Exhibit 8-8 San Pellegrino water is enhanced with the Italian restaurant imagery.

S.PELLEGRINO® is a registered trademark of Sanpellegrino S.p.A., Milano, Italy

Exhibit 8-9 This Bebe ad uses an attractive model to create a favourable image for the brand.

Source: Bebe Stores, Inc.

Exhibit 8-10 Hyundai uses a humour execution style to demonstrate the function of its new technology.

Source: Hyundai Motor America

and design to communicate the desired image to the consumer. Marketers who rely on image executions have to be sure that the usage or user imagery with which they associate their brand evokes the right feelings and reactions from the target audience.

DRAMATIZATION

Another execution technique particularly well suited to video is dramatization, where the focus is on telling a short story with the product as the star. Dramatization is akin to a slice-of-life execution, but it uses more excitement and suspense in telling the story. The purpose of using drama is to draw the viewer into the action it portrays. Advocates of drama note that when it is successful, the audience becomes lost in the story and experiences the concerns and feelings of the characters.[9] For instance, an Apple ad with a Christmas theme showed a family enjoying the holiday, playing in the snow, walking, tobogganing, skating, baking, decorating, etc., along with a young teen seemingly not enjoying himself. The message ends with him connecting his phone to the TV and playing a short montage of the day, eliciting smiles and tears from all family members. The ad, which was filmed in Alberta, won a significant creative award in the United States and critics claimed it meant Apple had regained its creative stride.[10]

HUMOUR

Like comparison, humour was discussed in Chapter 7 as a type of message appeal, but this technique can also be used as a way of presenting other message appeals. For example, a humorous ad for the Hyundai Genesis automobile featured actor/comedian Kevin Hart playing an overprotective father who lends his new Genesis—equipped with Hyundai's Blue Link Finder feature—to his daughter's date so he can track the couple. The ad shows Hart spying on the couple to demonstrate the technology (**Exhibit 8-10**). In some ways, this is a rational message appeal as an attribute's function is communicated; however, the execution of the appeal is certainly funny (for most people). Note that the attribute could have been explained with a serious message of safety with a testimonial or dramatization execution style.

Skittles candy used humour as an execution style while going beyond TV or print media. In 2010, Skittles candy advertising showed what would happen were someone to "touch the rainbow," with characters turning anything into Skittles by simply touching it. In 2011, Skittles wanted its consumers to actually experience touching the rainbow by placing and holding their finger on a screen and watching five successive online commercials where their finger had the starring role. In one scene, a cat and a human-like cat licked the finger; other scenes featured a car crashing into the finger, and a woman with a Skittles face complaining about having a finger pointed at her. Communication about the video went to bloggers and was posted on other social media. Within the time frame of the campaign, the ads garnered 6 million views, attained 11,000 fans on the candy's YouTube channel, and were featured extensively on other video outlets and social media. The campaign achieved 60 million media exposures and sales increased by 78 percent. The unique execution attained even greater stature by winning two Gold Lions at Cannes during the summer of 2011 for Film and Cyber.[11]

To understand the difference between the appeal and the execution with respect to humour, one could consider Boston Pizza's campaign with the fictitious Carl Carlson, president of the Flatties and Drummies Association, who expounds about the nibs and nubs of each chicken wing. The execution style uses a personality symbol, and the delivery of the message appeal is all sardonic humour.[12] Taken from a research view, one study concluded that humour with low complexity (e.g., one silly scene) is used within an execution style to garner attention without any direct brand linkage and is not persuasive, while more complex humour (e.g., amusement within the main message) with direct brand linkages is persuasive.[13]

IMC Perspective 8-1 describes a highly unusual execution style used by Doritos shown throughout social media.

#FOR THE BOLD: DORITOS ROSES

Doritos ketchup chips returned for a limited time in 2015 and 2016. In the first year's promotion, the brand launched an app and contest where a person kept their finger on a smart phone continuously. Results appeared acceptable, but the managers wanted a breakout promotion the following year. The launch coincided with Valentine's Day so they decided that a bouquet of Doritos Roses promised to be the ideal gift a woman could give a man! Those interested in ordering visited a website, and deliveries occurred in Toronto, Montreal, and Vancouver. Instructions and a coupon offer allowed others to join in the fun if not living in the distribution area.

The execution lived in social media only. Early on, a launch video used a humorous 1970s-style infomercial to let everyone know of the return. Other digital communication included other fun execution styles. For example, irreverent memes and GIFs placed in social media like Reddit encouraged people to participate in the promotion, leading many to generate their own content such as making a homemade Doritos Rose. Other videos featured animated promotions and unusual instructional guides to encourage people to order.

Social media used included YouTube, Facebook, Twitter, and Instagram, with each involved

©yusia/Shutterstock

with pre-launch, launch, and follow-up phases. Doritos also provided samples to influencers and media outlets. In the end, the managers achieved a breakout plan; sales grew 8 percent, 4.3 million digital views materialized, and there was significant lift in ad recall, love of the Doritos brand, and purchase consideration. Also, the campaign realized worldwide publicity with 56 million media impressions.

Question:

1. What do you suggest for a new execution for Doritos ketchup chips in the future?

 # Message Structure

Marketing communication usually consists of a number of message points that the communicator wants to convey, as advertising messages have an important information provision characteristic. Extensive research has been conducted on how the structure of an advertising message can influence its persuasive effectiveness, including order of presentation, conclusion drawing, message sidedness, and verbal/visual balance. These first three message structure points mostly focus on the written words of a print message or the announcer in a video or audio message, while the last addresses the importance of visuals to deliver the message.

ORDER OF PRESENTATION

One consideration in the design of a persuasive message is the arguments' order of presentation. Should the most important message points be placed at the beginning of the message, in the middle, or at the end? Research on learning and memory generally indicates that items presented first and last are remembered better than those presented in the middle (see **Figure 8-1**).[14] This suggests that a communicator's strongest arguments should be presented early or late in the message but never in the middle.

Figure 8-1 Ad message recall as a function of order of presentation

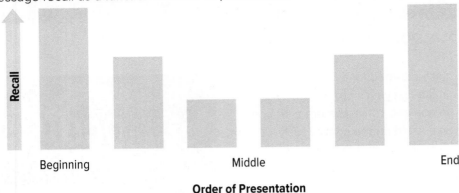

Presenting the strongest arguments at the beginning of the message assumes a **primacy effect** is operating, whereby information presented first is most effective. Putting the strong points at the end assumes a **recency effect**, whereby the last arguments presented are most persuasive. With the advent of multiple media, the presentation of the main message at the end may be to experience the additional messages online. For example, brands encourage Internet site visits at the end of a TV commercial so consumers will obtain additional information. Manulife took this in a different direction by finishing the commercial online. Viewers saw the first 15 seconds on TV as a pre-roll, and then had to see the remainder of the story on the company's Internet site. Consumers stayed on the site three times longer, with 60 percent of the visits arising from online links.[15]

Whether to place the strongest selling points at the beginning or the end of the message depends on several factors. If the target audience is opposed to the communicator's position, presenting strong points first can reduce the level of counterarguing. Putting weak arguments first might lead to such a high level of counterarguing that strong arguments that followed would not be believed. Strong arguments work best at the beginning of the message if the audience is not interested in the topic, so they can arouse interest in the message. When the target audience is predisposed toward the communicator's position or is highly interested in the issue or product, strong arguments can be saved for the end of the message. This may result in a more favourable opinion as well as better retention of the information.

The order of presentation is critical when a long, detailed message with many arguments is being presented. For short communications, such as a 15- or 30-second TV or radio commercial, the order may be less critical. However, many product and service messages are received by consumers with low involvement and minimal interest. Thus, an advertiser may want to present the brand name and key selling points early in the message and repeat them at the end to enhance recall and retention. One study strongly concludes that the brand name should be identified at the start of a TV ad to enhance its persuasive ability.[16]

CONCLUSION DRAWING

Marketing communicators must decide whether their messages should explicitly draw a firm conclusion or allow receivers to draw their own conclusions. Research suggests that, in general, messages with explicit conclusions are more easily understood and effective in influencing attitudes. However, other studies have shown that the effectiveness of conclusion drawing may depend on the target audience, the type of issue or topic, and the nature of the situation.[17]

More highly educated people prefer to draw their own conclusions and may be annoyed at an attempt to explain the obvious or to draw an inference for them. But stating the conclusion may be necessary for a less educated audience, who may not draw any conclusion or may make an incorrect inference from the message. Marketers must also consider the audience's level of involvement in the topic. For highly personal or ego-involving issues, message recipients may want to make up their own minds and resent any attempts by the communicator to draw a conclusion. One study found that open-ended ads (without explicit conclusions) were more effective than closed-ended arguments that did include a specific conclusion—but only for involved audiences.[18]

Whether to draw a conclusion for the audience also depends on the complexity of the topic. Even a highly educated audience may need assistance if its knowledge level in a particular area is low. Does the marketer want the message to trigger immediate action or a more long-term effect? If immediate action is an objective, the message should draw a definite conclusion. When immediate impact is not the objective and repeated exposure will give the audience members opportunities to draw their own conclusions, an open-ended message may be used. Drawing a conclusion in a message may make sure the target audience gets the point the marketer intended. But advertisers believe that letting customers draw their own conclusions reinforces the points being made in the message. The ad for the Hyundai Tucson in **Exhibit 8-11** makes a clear conclusion on how the CUV fulfills the needs of the target audience.

MESSAGE SIDEDNESS

Another message structure decision facing the marketer involves message sidedness. A **one-sided message** mentions only positive attributes or benefits. One-sided messages are most effective when the target audience already holds a favourable opinion about the topic and when the target audience is less educated.[19] A **two-sided message** presents both good and bad points. The logic of a two-sided message is that identifying an attribute or benefit shortcoming enhances credibility, leading to message acceptance. Two-sided messages are more effective when the target audience holds an opposing opinion or is highly educated. A better-educated audience usually knows there are opposing arguments, so a communicator who presents both sides is likely seen as more objective.

A meta-analysis of the research conducted on the effects of one- versus two-sided advertising messages showed that the persuasive impact of message sidedness depends on factors such as the amount and importance of negative information in the ad, attribute quality, placement of the negative information, the correlation between negative and positive attributes, and whether the advertiser discloses negative information voluntarily or because it is required to do so. In particular on the placement point (i.e., presentation order), brand attitudes and purchase intentions are enhanced if the negative information is at the end of the argument.[20]

Most advertisers use one-sided messages since they are concerned about the negative effects of acknowledging a weakness in their brand or don't want to say anything positive about their competitors. However, there are exceptions, such as when advertisers compare brands on several attributes and do not show their product as being the best on every one, or when a company acknowledges its shortcomings and communicates how it has improved. In certain situations, marketers may focus on a negative attribute to enhance product perceptions. W.K. Buckley Limited became a leading brand of cough syrup by using a blunt two-sided slogan: "Buckley's Mixture. It tastes awful. And it works." Ads poked fun at the cough syrup's terrible taste but also claimed that the taste is a reason why the product is effective. In 2011, the Marketing Hall of Legends inducted Frank Buckley (W.K.'s son), the company spokesperson for years.[21] **IMC Perspective 8-2** provides an update on Buckley's advertising, which continues to use a similar executional style and message structure.

A special type of two-sided message is known as a **refutation**. The communicator presents both sides of an issue and then refutes the opposing viewpoint. Since this tends to "inoculate" the target audience against a competitor's counterclaims, refutation is more effective than one-sided messages in making consumers resistant to an opposing message.[22] Refutational messages may be useful when marketers wish to build attitudes that resist change and must defend against attacks or criticism of their products or the company. Market leaders, who are the target of comparative messages, may find that acknowledging competitors' claims and then refuting them can build resistant attitudes.

Exhibit 8-11 This Hyundai Tucson ad makes a direct conclusion.

BREAK FREE.

THE ALL-NEW 2016 *Tucson*

Escape the endless repetition of eat, sleep, work, repeat. Break free from the everyday with a powerful and efficient 1.6 litre Turbocharged engine and all-wheel drive performance*. The all-new 2016 Tucson has arrived; prepare yourself to experience a CUV that will exceed your every expectation. This is the H-Factor.

hyundaicanada.com

©Hyundai Auto Canada Corp.

BUCKLEY'S SUITS STUART

For some reason, Buckley's slogan—"It tastes awful. And it works"—did not translate well to Buckley's pills and capsule formats, which contained no taste or flavour. Consumers could not associate the established effectiveness benefit to the same brand. In addition, consumer awareness of the product extension remained weak.

Buckley's advertising style and honest message has resonated with Canadians since its launch decades ago by Frank Buckley. Stuart the spokesperson took over in more recent times, but he retained the direct and honest message. In fact, Buckley's Tumblr page reflects the consistency with re-purposed print messages such as "The official enemy of winter colds," and "It tastes awful, because there is such a thing as too good to be true." And Buckley's website conveys historic messages like "Feared by more people than ever before" and "Four of the most dreaded words in the English language: Get out the Buckley's!"

Research indicated that loyal Buckley's syrup users often switched to Tylenol or Advil when in need of the portability of a pill/capsule format. As a result, sales and market share remained flat and declined over the years. On the bright side however, loyal customers believed that Buckley's syrup performed better than either competitor, and that Buckley's pills/capsules outperformed competitor pills/capsules. Given these findings, the creative message carried on with Buckley's historic blunt and direct advertising message with a twist.

Hero/Media Bakery

Buckley's dressed its existing Stuart the spokesperson of past ads to look like the branded pill/capsule to plainly show that the alternative format existed. And while Stuart the spokesperson extolled the virtues of the product, he complained about being in the pill suit. Moreover, he strongly encouraged consumers to buy the product so he could stop being in the suit for future ads if sales grew!

Consumers saw the video message on TV for 15 and 30 seconds in both English and French. Six-second pre-roll videos also ran at the same time, leading Google to identify this as an example of how to run short ads. The frequency of the message during cold season resulted in a 15 percent gain in sales vs. 4 percent category sales growth, and a 0.5 percent increase in dollar and units market share.

Question:

1. How would you introduce Stuart in the next ads for Buckley's cough syrup? Would he make mention of getting out of the pill suit?

VERBAL/VISUAL BALANCE

Thus far our discussion has focused on the information, or verbal, portion of the message. However, the nonverbal, visual elements of an ad are very important. Many ads provide minimal amounts of information and rely on visual elements to communicate. Pictures are commonly used in advertising to convey information or reinforce copy or message claims. Advertisers will design ads where the visual image supports the verbal appeal to create a compelling impression. The ad in **Exhibit 8-12** relies on the visual to communicate the ease and nutritional value of the appetizer.

Both the verbal and visual portions of an ad influence the way the advertising message is processed.[23] Consumers may develop images or impressions based on visual elements such as an illustration in an ad or the scenes in a TV commercial. The visual portion of an ad may reduce its persuasiveness, since the processing stimulated by the picture may be less controlled and consequently less favourable than that stimulated by words.[24]

Pictures affect the way consumers process accompanying copy. A study showed that when verbal information was low in imagery value, the use of pictures providing examples increased both immediate and delayed recall of product attributes.[25] However, when the verbal information was already high in imagery value, the addition of pictures did not increase recall. For extremely involved target audiences, a verbal message is effective for persuading consumer attitudes; however, pure text still often requires supporting visuals to heighten motivation.

Advertisers may use a different approach designing ads in which the visual portion is incongruent with or contradicts the verbal information presented. The logic behind this idea is that the use of an unexpected picture or visual image attracts consumers' attention and requires greater mental effort during processing.[26] Studies have shown that the use of a visual that is inconsistent with the verbal content leads to more recall and greater processing of the information presented.[27]

Exhibit 8-12 The images in this Egg Farmers of Ontario ad show how easy it is to make a nutritious appetizer with eggs.

Hand-out/Egg Farmers of Ontario/Newscom

Design Elements for IMC Tools

The design and production of advertising messages involves a number of activities, including writing copy, developing illustrations and other visual elements of the ad, and bringing all of the pieces together to create an effective message. In this section, we examine the verbal and visual elements of an ad and discuss tactical considerations in creating print, video, and audio messages. We use general terminology of print, video, and audio as these basic design elements can be applied to any print, video, or audio media distributed through advertising or other IMC tools.

DESIGN FOR PRINT MESSAGES

The elements of a print message are the headline, the body copy, the visual or illustrations, and the layout. The headline and body copy are the responsibility of the copywriters; artists, often working under the direction of an art director, are responsible for the visual presentation. Art directors also work with the copywriters to develop a layout, or arrangement of the above elements. We briefly examine the three design elements and explain how they are coordinated. These elements pertain to virtually all print messages found in any media.

Headlines The **headline** is the words in the leading position of the ad designed to draw the attention of most people in the target audience and expected to be read first. Headlines are usually set in larger, darker type and are often set apart from the body copy or text portion of the ad to give them prominence. The headline in the UPS ad in **Exhibit 8-13** appeals to small business owners who rely on daily deliveries to operate and serve their customers. The headline attracts attention by using an unlikely premise and draws people into the ad copy which explains how UPS Accent Point locations serve more than 8,000 neighbourhood businesses.

The most important function of a headline is attracting readers' attention and interesting them in the rest of the message. While the visual portion of an ad is obviously important, the headline often shoulders most of the responsibility of attracting readers' attention. Research has shown that the headline is generally the first thing people look at in a print ad, followed by the illustration. In addition to attracting attention, the headline must give the reader good reason to read the copy portion of the ad, which contains more detailed and persuasive information about the product or service. To do this, the headline must put forth the main theme, appeal, or proposition of the ad in a few words. Some print ads contain little if any body copy, so the headline must work with the illustration to communicate the entire advertising message.

Exhibit 8-13 The headline of this UPS ad is designed to attract the attention of small business owners.

I'm glad I missed my delivery. Said no one ever.

Nobody likes to worry about missing a delivery. UPS Access Point™ locations give today's customers the convenience of picking up and dropping off deliveries at more than 8,000 neighbourhood businesses across the country. Just one of the many ways UPS is helping companies solve for today's rising customer expectations. See how we can help you at ups.com/solvers.

ups

united problem solvers™

Source: United Parcel Service of America, Inc.

Exhibit 8-14 The body copy for this ad supports the headline by suggesting a good time at The Keg.

THERE'S NOTHING
MORE CLASSIC
THAN A GOOD TIME

We've always been about good company, great food, and an even better night out. From spontaneous weeknights to birthday celebrations, we'll bring the good times to every get together.

THE KEG
STEAKHOUSE · BAR

kegsteakhouse.com

©Keg Restaurants Ltd.

Headlines also perform a segmentation function by engaging the attention and interest of consumers who are most likely to buy a particular product or service. Advertisers begin the segmentation process by choosing to advertise in certain media vehicles (e.g., fashion magazine, national newspaper, out-of-home). An effective headline goes even further in selecting good prospects for the product by addressing their specific needs, wants, or interests.

Types of Headlines Numerous possibilities exist for headlines. The type used depends on the creative strategy, the particular advertising situation (e.g., product type, media vehicle(s) being used, timeliness), and its relationship to other elements of the ad, such as the illustration or body copy. Headlines are categorized as direct and indirect.

Direct headlines are straightforward and informative in terms of the message they are presenting and the target audience they are directed toward. Common types of direct headlines include those offering a specific benefit, making a promise, or announcing a reason why the reader should be interested in the product or service.

Indirect headlines are not straightforward about identifying the product or service or getting to the point. However, they are often more effective at attracting readers' attention and interest because they provoke curiosity and lure readers into the body copy to learn an answer or get an explanation. Techniques for writing indirect headlines include using questions, provocations, how-to statements, and challenges.

Indirect headlines rely on their ability to generate curiosity or intrigue so as to motivate readers to become involved with the ad and read the body copy to find out the point of the message. This is risky if the headline is not provocative enough to get the readers' interest. Advertisers deal with this problem by using a visual appeal that helps attract attention and offers another reason for reading more of the message.

While ads usually have one headline, it is also common to see print ads containing the main head and one or more secondary heads, or **subheads**. Subheads are usually smaller than the main headline but larger than the body copy. They may appear above or below the main headline or within the body copy. Subheads are often used to enhance the readability of the message by breaking up large amounts of body copy and highlighting key sales points.

Body Copy The main text portion of a print ad is referred to as the **body copy** (or just *copy*). While the body copy is usually the heart of the advertising message, getting the target audience to read it is often difficult. The copywriter faces a dilemma: The body copy must be long enough to communicate the advertiser's message yet short enough to hold readers' interest. **Exhibit 8-14** presents an ad in which the information of the body copy mirrors the headline with extra elaboration.

Body copy content flows from the points made in the headline or subheads, but the specific content depends on the type of advertising appeal and/or execution style being used. For example, straight-sell copy that presents relevant information, product features and benefits, or competitive advantages is often used with the various types of rational appeals discussed earlier in the chapter.

Emotional appeals use narrative copy that tells a story or provides an interesting account of a problem or situation involving the product. Advertising body copy can be written to go along with any message appeal or execution style. Furthermore, copywriters select body copy that is appropriate for the creative strategy (i.e., theme, message appeal, source) and supports the creative tactics like the message structure and other design elements.

One study, the first of its kind, used an eye-tracking methodology to see where readers focused their attention for the most time when reading body copy. The findings suggested that some sentences resulted in greater fixation and more time. Sentences with both attribute and benefit information produced the greatest effect, followed by benefits sentences only, attribute sentences only, concluding "kicker" sentences, introductory sentences, and finally product-relevant neutral sentences.[28]

Visual The third major element of a print ad is the visual. The illustration is a dominant part of a print ad and plays an important role in determining its effectiveness. The visual portion of an ad must attract attention, communicate an idea or image, and work in a synergistic fashion with the headline and body copy to produce an effective message. In some print ads, the visual portion of the ad is essentially the message and thus must convey a strong and meaningful image. The Quebec Milk Producers ad shown in **Exhibit 8-15** contains important visual elements like the delicious treats that are more enjoyable when drinking a cool glass of milk.

Decisions have to be made regarding the visual portion of the ad: what identification marks should be included (brand name, company or trade name, trademarks, logos); whether to use photos or hand-drawn or -painted illustrations; what colours to use (or even perhaps black and white or just a splash of colour); and what the focus of the visual should be. Even the number of pages of visual ads is critical, as in the case of fashion products or automobiles. One study finds that advertisers should use fewer pages (e.g., 4 to 6) versus more pages (e.g., 8 to 10) and insert the ads more frequently.[29] Another study found that comparison ads showing the image of a brand and its competitor should have the sponsored brand's image on the right hand side of the pages.[30] **Exhibit 8-16** shows an ad where the visual is obviously critical to support the copy and the call to action.

Layout While each individual element of a print ad is important, the key factor is how these elements are blended into a finished advertisement. A **layout** is the physical arrangement of the various parts of the ad, including the headline, subheads, body copy, illustrations, and any identifying marks. The layout shows where each part of the ad will be placed and gives guidelines to the people working on the ad. For example, the layout helps the copywriter determine how much space he or she has to work with and how much copy should be written. The layout can also guide the art director in determining the size and type of photos.

Most layouts are standard poster format shown in a portrait orientation, although landscape formats do occur. Sometimes there are vertical or horizontal splits, with the latter being a separation between the visual and body copy. An optimal layout is an artistic expression of the brand as it achieves balance among the space, visuals, and colours.

Exhibit 8-15 The delicious imagery of the treats gives a good reason to enjoy drinking a glass of milk.

©Quebec Milk Producers - AD - 2015

Exhibit 8-16 This ad uses a clever visual image to suggest readers visit the Internet site.

©Jamaica Tourist Board

DESIGN FOR VIDEO MESSAGES

Video messages contain the elements of sight, sound, and motion that are combined to create an unlimited number of advertising appeals and executions. Video messages occur in instances beyond television, as they are seen at theatres, in place-based locations, and online. Historically across much of these media, the viewer does not control the rate at which the message is presented, providing no opportunity to review key points of interest that are not communicated clearly. However, technological change places more control in the hands of viewers, allowing multiple views or skipping messages entirely. Nevertheless, the goal of capturing and maintaining a viewer's attention remains important in creating a video message since receivers may be doing other activities or may be exposed to multiple messages at the same time. The design decisions of these messages include video and audio elements to go along with careful planning of their production.

Video The video elements of a commercial are what the consumer sees on the screen. The visual portion generally dominates the presentation, so it must attract viewers' attention and communicate an idea, message, and/or image. A number of visual elements may have to be coordinated to produce a successful ad. Decisions have to be made regarding the product, the presenter, action sequences, demonstrations, and the like, as well as the setting(s), the talent or characters who will appear in the commercial, and such other factors as lighting, graphics, colour, and identifying symbols.

Video messages are generally expensive due to production personnel, equipment, location fees, video editing, sound recording and mixing, music fees, and talent. Acting talent certainly adds to the cost since good acting is an important characteristic for effective message delivery. Marketers are especially careful in selecting the presenters and actors for a video message, since undesirable associations may be made if viewers recognize the actor from another message. At the heart of the matter is that the brand creates its own identity in the message to ensure brand awareness. While there are exclusivity clauses where actors cannot be in ads for products in the same category, advertisers are concerned about overexposure of the face. However, if one looks closely, one can see many familiar faces across a spectrum of ads.[31]

A longer version of video messages emerged as a new trend due to social media and the sharing of video messages online. Known as microfilm advertising, this message format originates from an identified sponsor; is used to motivate online viewing, discussion, and distribution without further payment; and is intended to persuade. Results of the first ever empirical study concluded that enjoying the story is the only motivator for people to forward the message, however the enjoyment does lead to stronger brand attitude.[32]

Procter & Gamble's feminine hygiene product Always followed the path of Dove with a social message associated with the brand. The three-minute video message featured people's physical response to the instructions "run like a girl" or "throw like a girl" as part of a disguised situation in which the participants believed they were part of a research panel or a casting call for a TV show. Young girls acted accordingly by performing the age-specific skill level, while others imitated stereotypical behaviours that clearly differed from the young girls'. Dubbed a "social experiment" by P&G executives, the creative approach garnered numerous advertising awards such as at Cannes, and continued with another execution one year later.

One motivation for creating a longer video message for online viewing is the belief that consumer segments seek out messages of interest and are more willing to view a longer message if it significantly matters to them. Coupled with the social message, these ads are now more relevant for a growing number of consumers. In the case of Always, 76 percent of women in the targeted 16–24 age range believed the message changed how they viewed the "like a girl" phrase. Over the course of the first year, about 80 million views occurred online, which led the brand to seek greater exposure. P&G created a 30-second version of the "like a girl" message for TV and saw so much potential that it aired it during the Super Bowl broadcast for a cost of $4.5 million to reach 115 million people in the United States, and they reached 9 million people in Canada with a separate media buy.[33]

Related to the longer video trend is a trend of video messages becoming more entertaining with an interesting storyline and visual imagery. One study concluded that the level of entertainment has an inverted U-shaped relationship with purchase intent, and the entertainment influences purchase intent when placed after brand identification but not when placed before it.[34]

A third design trend concerns interactive ads as seen on Microsoft's natural user-interface ads (NUads) placed on its Xbox Live network. An ad is launched by hand, voice, or controller via an ad square on the dashboard and Xbox's 360 Kinect sensor. Subway tested the new format with an ad for its Tuscan Chicken Melt sandwich. Subway provided the ad and Microsoft seamlessly incorporated the ad with the technology so it could be shown on the TV screen. The interactive results allow users to see what others are saying about the ad, while Subway can obtain instant campaign feedback. Subway interactively asked, "Where will you eat your Tuscan Chicken Melt?" with four different options for a response. Results indicated that 37 percent of the viewers explored the interactive feature, and 71 percent of those answered the poll question. One media expert commented that the 37 percent rate looked favourable compared to the 5–10 percent response rates for most digital applications.[35]

Low-budget online digital messages emerged as a fourth trend. Surprisingly, a tactic of recording someone writing something down or doing a simple task has taken off on the Internet. Local businesses that use TV commercials are financially restricted to simple production methods, such as a customer testimonial or demonstration from the owner. With Canada's smaller population relative to the United States, by comparison it is difficult to achieve economies of scale for lavish or high-cost productions. Creative executions and the accompanying video are designed with lower costs in mind. However, quality video everywhere may emerge as digital recording technology costs become more economical in future. Low-budget ads also manifested with user-generated ads. Research suggests that user-generated ads influence brand loyal customers who are not capable of scrutinizing the message and who are given information about the ad creator.[36]

A final trend of video messages using prank jokes to communicate their point occurred. *Just for Laughs* and *Pranked* are two TV shows where someone plays a practical joke on an unsuspecting person. Often set in a real situation, the fun lies in seeing the disbelief during and the relief after the unfolding event. So it is no surprise to see the idea applied to TV commercials and video messages shown online in social media and other media vehicles. One recent example of a prank ad is the effort by the Toronto Humane Society to make people understand that adopting a pet involves a lifetime commitment. The ad showed an easy-to-use app called "Puppy Swap" that let people trade in their older dog for a cute little puppy. At the conclusion, the ad provided statistics about the pet abandonment problem and said people need to consider the choice as a permanent one. Comments on YouTube indicated that the creative indeed pranked the viewers, especially pet owners who ultimately approved of the message. The Humane Society's media relations manager felt that the ad worked since the emotional response to the prank caused viewers to seriously consider the message.

Other brands looked to April Fool's Day to produce another kind of prank ad. In the past, firms distributed joke messages as media releases and gained publicity when news organizations reported the story. Domino's Pizza advertised its edible pizza box, Scope promoted its bacon-flavoured mouthwash, and Cheetos told everyone about its perfume with a snack-food aroma. WestJet received notoriety with its "Kargo Kids" service where parents could enjoy peace and quiet on a flight by packing their children up and checking them along with their baggage. Experts believe brands can pull off the April Fool's Day humour if they have a good relationship with their audience and if the humour fits with the previous real ads.[37]

Audio The audio element of a video message includes voices, music, and the jingle or sound effects.

Voices Voices are used in different ways. They may be heard through the direct presentation of a spokesperson or as a conversation among people appearing in the script. A common method for presenting the audio is through a **voiceover**, where the message is delivered or action on the screen is narrated or described by an announcer who is not visible. Advertisers will use a voice that works with the message and brand as the tone provides a distinctive resonance influencing emotional responses.

Music Music is also an important element that can play a variety of roles.[38] Music acts structurally in an ad, much like grammar in a sentence, and supports the time sequence, motion, repetition, brand identification, and emotion experienced. Music can be a central element as it is used to get attention, break through the advertising clutter, communicate a key selling point, establish an image or position, or add feeling.[39] Music can also create a positive mood that makes the consumer more receptive toward the advertising message.[40] Other research on consumers' cognitive and affective responses to music in advertising found that increased congruity between the music and advertising with respect to variables such as mood, genre, score, image, and tempo contributes to the communication effectiveness of an advertisement by enhancing recall, brand attitude, affective response, and purchase intention.[41]

One new trend is that music houses are placing indie music in ads, following the lead of hit TV shows like *The O.C.*, *Grey's Anatomy*, and *Gossip Girl*. Canadian artist Emilie Mover's song "Made for Each Other" became the key song for the global campaign for Fisher-Price toys. Marketers are looking for a distinctive tone for their ad that is not associated with any other experiences to make the ad more enriching.[42] Hamsters became a hit with the ads for Kia Soul that included popular dance tunes (**Exhibit 8-17**).

Often music is composed specifically for a campaign. Musicians and composers participate early on in the process of developing the ad; alternatively, the creative specialists who produce the ad look for specific types of music to support the visuals. For example, a campaign "Kijiji Raps" showcases emerging rappers who wrote songs that described their experiences using the classifieds directory. Eight ads in two languages entertain viewers on YouTube with the goal of driving visits to the Kijiji site for ad placement and purchases. Each rapper produced their own version and style and Kijiji worked with rap engineers to get the right sound for the brand.[43] Finally, advertisers use **needledrop**, which refers to music that is prefabricated, multipurpose, and highly conventional, much like stock photos used in print ads.[44]

Exhibit 8-17 Music and dancing hamsters are featured in the Kia Soul ad campaign.

Source: Kia Motors America

Jingle Another memorable sound element is a **jingle**, a catchy song about a product or service that delivers the advertising theme and a simple message. For example, "Black's Is Photography" is a jingle that has stood the test of time. Tim Hortons moved to a new jingle, "Always Fresh. Always Tim Hortons," for a while and then picked "It's Time for Tim's." Swiss Chalet reverted to a previous one, "Always So Good for So Little," after trying four different jingles in the past 10 years.[45] Subway garnered lots of mileage with its "Five. Five. Five Dollar. Five Dollar Foot-Long." Sometimes, jingles simply identify a brand and appear at the end of the message. Jingles are often composed by companies that specialize in writing music for advertising. These jingle houses work with the creative team to determine the role music will play in the commercial and the message that needs to be communicated.

Production of Video Messages The elements of a video message are brought together in a **script**, a written version of a message that provides a detailed description of its audio and video content. The audio elements include the copy to be spoken by voices, the music, and sound effects. The video portion includes camera actions and angles, scenes, transitions, and other important descriptions. The script also shows how the video corresponds to the audio portion of the commercial. After establishing the script, the writer and art director produce a storyboard or animatic to present the visual plan (discussed in Chapter 7). Like a layout for a print ad, the storyboard or animatic provides those involved in production and approval with an approximation of what the final ad will look like before moving to the production as shown in **Figure 8-2**. Before these three phases begin, the client usually reviews and approves the creative strategy and tactics of the advertising message.

DESIGN FOR AUDIO MESSAGES

Audio messages are mostly delivered through radio, and that is the context for most of the design guidelines; however, digital opportunities make audio messages more prevalent. For example, audio messages are included in podcasts, and certainly any ad on the Internet (e.g., banner, pop-up) could have an audio equivalent. Imagine listening to an ad while reading the online newspaper. The key elements of an audio message are similar to the audio of video messages, so we concentrate on the verbal and sound elements.

Verbal Historically, radio has been referred to as the theatre of the mind; the voices speaking to us in these audio messages offer a description or story, like the body copy of a print ad, that allows a visual to take hold. The talking can take unique formats—straight announcer, dialogue between two actors, announcer/actor, customer interview—while

Figure 8-2 The three phases of production for commercials

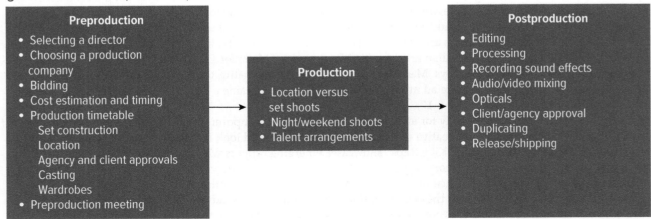

Preproduction
- Selecting a director
- Choosing a production company
- Bidding
- Cost estimation and timing
- Production timetable
  Set construction
  Location
  Agency and client approvals
  Casting
  Wardrobes
- Preproduction meeting

Production
- Location versus set shoots
- Night/weekend shoots
- Talent arrangements

Postproduction
- Editing
- Processing
- Recording sound effects
- Audio/video mixing
- Opticals
- Client/agency approval
- Duplicating
- Release/shipping

following any of the executional styles identified earlier in the chapter. Depending on which format is used, a script is written that will attract attention in the opening, communicate the brand's attributes or benefits, and wrap up with a close that includes a call to action, like a store visit, phone number, or website address. The dialogue of the script is critical, much like the voiceover in a video message, but the illuminating words support the theatre idea to maximize the amount of processing time of the message.

With this in mind, it is often easy to hear silly ideas in radio ads that somehow work because of our natural curiosity to make sense of incongruence. For example, famous actor Gordon Pinsent, who has a perfect radio voice, talked about a new poutine product from NY Fries: "Only the best ingredients coming together for something so perfect, like finding the perfect pair of jeans for your kitten. Little designer ones that sit low on the hips, so that little kitten can work those little designer jeans all sassy-like."[46]

Sound Audio messages naturally rely on sound due to the lack of a visual. Brands employ unique sound effects to allow the visual to take hold in the receiver's mind. Alternatively, the unique voices of the speakers help create a personality to allow the visual to take hold even more. As seen with video messages, music becomes a key component for audio messages on a number of fronts, such as attracting attention or supporting the message and reinforcing the positioning. Moreover, as seen with video messages, jingles become even more critical as they fit with the format of listening to music. Finally, audio logos through music sound effects will start or end audio ads. "Sunwing.ca" is the start of this brand's radio ads, which acts like a print message headline to focus attention, but in this example, it also reinforces brand recall so that people will visit the website. Ads ending with an audio logo are similar to a print message signature, again to reinforce brand awareness.

LO4 Planning Model for Creative Tactics

We highlighted the Rossiter and Percy (R&P) perspective in previous chapters. Another part of their approach concerns recommendations for creative tactics so that communication effects will occur with the target audience after processing the message. The R&P model recommendations for creative tactics contain four distinguishing features: instructions to attain brand awareness, considerations for the type of motivation, suggestions based on the target audience's involvement, and guidelines to generate both cognitive and emotional responses.[47]

TACTICS FOR BRAND AWARENESS

The first R&P model feature is that brand awareness is a necessary precursor to brand attitude. According to R&P, brand awareness is a universal communication objective for all circumstances (i.e., one ad, ad campaign, IMC plan). In this view, all marketing communication should strive to achieve awareness in order to make brand attitude operational. R&P have three instructions for brand awareness:

1. Match the brand stimuli and the type of response behaviour of the target audience so that understanding of the brand in a category is unambiguous.
2. Use a unique brand execution style to connect the brand to the category.
3. Maximize brand contact time in the exposure to reinforce name and category connection.

For awareness to be fully established, the target audience needs to understand the context (brand, behaviour, category), as this illustrates for them how or why the brand exists. If the context is not clear, then the target audience has trouble remembering the brand when it comes time to purchase. A unique execution style helps cut through the clutter. The connection to the category and sufficient exposure is required to make sure that the message is retained. For example, video messages sometimes show the package or brand name for too short a time for target audiences to fully grasp where the brand competes in the market.

We also noted that R&P suggest that awareness is achieved via recognition and/or recall. R&P have two instructions for recognition that require less media frequency as consumers need only to be familiar with the brand stimuli at the point of purchase:

1. The brand package and name should have sufficient exposure in terms of time or size depending on the media.
2. Category need should be mentioned or identified.

The Dasani ad in **Exhibit 8-18** clearly shows the brand name with the large visual of the bottle of water. Its emergence from the plant communicates that the container is made of plant material and is biodegradable, likely to inform those

Exhibit 8-18 The Dasani ad makes use of a visual to clearly identify the brand.

Source: Dasani by The Coca-Cola Company

Exhibit 8-19 This Subway ad uses key brand recall guidelines to encourage new consumers.

©Jeff Morgan 05/Alamy Stock Photo

who stopped consuming the bottled water due to its overreliance on the use of plastic.

Recall also requires high levels of frequency since the brand has to be remembered prior to being at the point of purchase. R&P have six instructions for awareness through recall:

1. The brand and the category need should be connected in the primary benefit claim.
2. The primary benefit claim should be short to be easily understood.
3. Within an exposure, the primary benefit claim should be repeated often.
4. The message should have or imply a clear personal reference.
5. A bizarre or unusual execution style can be used if it is consistent with the brand attitude objective.
6. A jingle or similar "memory" tactic should be included.

We have more specific instructions for recall since this communication reception is a more difficult mental task for consumers. Advertisers have to help their target audience know their brand prior to purchasing. Empirical testing of some of these points for video media concluded that recall is enhanced with brand identification occurring early in the presentation, frequent visual brand identification, and communicating the brand visually and verbally.[48] The ad in **Exhibit 8-19** follows instructions for improving recall. Thus, all three creative tactics decisions must be considered carefully to ensure that the target audience can retrieve the brand name from long-term memory when the need to purchase a product category arises.

TACTICS FOR BRAND ATTITUDE

As explained earlier in the book, brand attitude is a universal communication objective, however the route to influencing consumer attitudes will vary. In this section we present four approaches for influencing attitudes, along with corresponding guidelines for creative tactics.

Brand Attitude Grid The R&P view of consumer attitudes is framed as a planning grid with the dimensions of involvement and motivation. The use of these two concepts is an accurate *practical* representation of attitude for IMC planning.

Low-involvement decision	Low-involvement decision
Informational motivation	Transformational motivation
High-involvement decision	High-involvement decision
Informational motivation	Transformational motivation

The involvement dimension ranges from low involvement to high involvement and is specific to the brand as the target audience makes a purchase decision. R&P interpret involvement as the degree of risk perceived by the target audience (i.e., new category user or loyal customer) in choosing a particular brand for the next purchase occasion. One extension of this idea, not fully developed by R&P, is that the concept can extend to purchase-related shopping behaviour that we discussed in Chapter 5. For example, how much risk does a person buying a car for the first time take in deciding to visit a particular dealer for a test drive?

The motivation dimension is a continuum from negative motive, or informational-based attitude, to positive motive, or transformational-based attitude. The historical interpretation of an informational-based attitude implies that it is based on careful reasoning that results from the cognitive responses that the target audience has while experiencing advertising messages. However, R&P argue that this is too limiting as attitude is based on both cognition and affect. Accordingly, they suggest that creative tactics for this side of the grid should account for the benefit claims (i.e., cognition) and the emotional portrayal of the motive (i.e., affect). Thus, in order for it to be an informational-based attitude, the emphasis of the benefit claim is stronger than the emotional portrayal of the negative motive.

The notion of transformational-based attitude is consistent with image advertising. For example, image advertising is used by travel industry brands so consumers envision the experience or feeling they might have when taking a trip such as a cruise or visiting a particular destination. Image advertising, which is designed to give a company or brand a unique association or personality, is often transformational in nature. It is designed to create a certain feeling or mood that is activated when a consumer uses a particular product or service. For example, the Lambesis agency has created a unique image for Skyy vodka by creating ads that associate the brand with unique consumption moments (see **Exhibit 8-20**).

Just as the informational-based attitude is not purely cognitive, the transformational-based attitude is not purely founded on emotion but includes cognitive elements. Intuitively, this makes a lot of sense as some ads with a very strong fear appeal often leave us thinking. Overall, the emphasis of the emotional portrayal of the consumer motive is stronger than the benefit claim for transformational-based attitude. Providing information in transformational ads is part of the "Fresh Air" campaign for Newfoundland and Labrador. Much of the message involved breathtaking views of the landscape and a humorous way of conveying the clean air one can breathe along the coastline. Another key component included travel logistics and accommodation information.[49]

Exhibit 8-20 Advertising for Skyy vodka uses an intense theme to create a brand image.

Source: Campari America, San Francisco, CA

Brand Attitude Grid Tactics The fourth feature of the R&P model is guidelines for creative tactics to ensure both cognitive and emotional responses that will contribute to both aspects of brand attitude. On the emotional side, we are concerned with how the motive is portrayed in the ad. To consider this, we have three characteristics: its authenticity, or how real it appears to the target audience; whether the target audience likes the ad; and finally, the target audience's reaction to the execution style. On the informational side, we are concerned with the brand's message with respect to the benefit claims. We also have three characteristics to consider: the number, the intensity, and the repetition of the claims.

While the guidelines for all six characteristics may be a function of all three creative tactics decisions, we can make a strong link for certain ones. The authenticity and whether the target audience likes the ad are typically associated with the design elements of the ad. Quite obviously, there is a direct connection between the execution style of the framework and the creative tactics decisions reviewed in this chapter. The benefit claims are mostly a function of the message structure since the latter concerns the details of explaining the product's benefits. It is also a function of the relative balance between a verbal and visual message. We turn our attention to creative tactics guidelines for the four brand attitude cells.

Low Involvement–Informational Creative Tactics Ads designed to influence target audiences' attitudes based on low involvement–informational persuasion should have an obvious benefit claim, as shown in **Exhibit 8-21**. Also, even though a golf club like this

Exhibit 8-21 This ad contains low involvement–informational creative tactics.

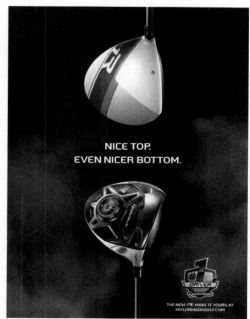

NICE TOP. EVEN NICER BOTTOM.

Source: TaylorMade Golf Company, Inc.

is expensive, the intention is to direct readers to the website for further research at the information gathering stage. Since the intention is to persuade the target audience so that they automatically learn the connection among the brand, its category, and the benefit, consumer acceptance or rejection of the message is not a factor. Further, the emotion demonstrated in the ad and whether the target audience likes the ad are not necessary as the message is intended to make a creative link among the brand, category, and benefit.

Low Involvement–Informational	
Emotional portrayal of motive	
Authenticity	Not necessary
Like ad	Not necessary
Execution style	Unusual, problem–solution format
Benefit claim of brand message	
Number of benefits	One or two, or one clear group
Intensity of benefit claim	State extremely
Repetition of benefit claim	Few required for reminder

Low Involvement–Transformational Creative Tactics Three emotional portrayal guidelines are critical for this type of attitude. These points are consistent with transformational ads described above. For example, the representation of the consumption of the brand in the drama or story of the ad must "ring true" with the target audience such that it is perceived as a very enjoyable ad. This characteristic is demonstrated in the Fluevog shoe ad (**Exhibit 8-22**). In a low-involvement situation, benefit claims are still included but may be indirectly communicated through the story or emotion surrounding the story. Actual acceptance of the benefit claim is not a requirement; however, rejection of the overall message can lead to a reduction in the attitude of the target audience.

Low Involvement–Transformational	
Emotional portrayal of motive	
Authenticity	Key element and is the single benefit
Like ad	Necessary
Execution style	Unique to the brand
Benefit claim of brand message	
Number of benefits	One or two, or one clear group
Intensity of benefit claim	Imply extremely by association
Repetition of benefit claim	Many exposures to build up before trial purchase and reinforce attitude after trial

High Involvement–Informational Creative Tactics This side of the grid illustrates the importance of information, as *high involvement* implies the requirement of considerable and accurate benefit claims. Many benefits can be claimed here, but they must be organized and presented in a manner that respects the current attitude of the target audience. The ad in **Exhibit 8-23** follows the creative guidelines for this attitude. Since this is an informational-based attitude, the emotional portrayal is important but not the primary consideration. Furthermore, the high-involvement characteristic means that the target audience has to accept the benefit claims. Rejection of the benefit claims may not result in any negative change in attitude if the copy respected the prior attitude of the target audience.

Exhibit 8-22 This unique John Fluevog ad captures a particular emotion to encourage store visits.

©John Fluevog Shoes

Exhibit 8-23 Extensive ad copy and the visual support high involvement–informational attitude influence.

The server room can be a cold and lonely place. We can definitely help with the lonely part.

Source: CDW Corporation

High Involvement–Informational	
Emotional portrayal of motive	
Authenticity	Key element early in product life cycle and declines as product reaches later stages
Like ad	Not necessary
Execution style	Unusual
Benefit claim of brand message	
Number of benefits	Overall claim to summarize multiple (no more than seven) benefits
Intensity of benefit claim	Initial attitude is key reference point Very accurate claim; cannot overclaim or underclaim
	Comparative or refutation messages are strong options
Repetition of benefit claim	Many claims within an exposure

High Involvement–Transformational Creative Tactics Persuasion through this type of attitude formation requires strong emphasis on the emotion. A positive attitude toward the ad leads to a positive brand attitude. Likewise, the target audience must relate to the execution style and feel like they identify with the product, as shown in the ad in **Exhibit 8-24**. The end result is that if the target audience rejects the message because the emotion is not accurate, then the persuasion will not work and may even cause significant attitude reduction. The remaining guidelines illustrate that considerable information is required, similar to what is seen for the high involvement–informational attitude. In the case of this ad, it relies on the receiver easily going to social media or calling for more information. Once again, this implies that acceptance of the benefit claims is critical for the attitude to take hold with the target audience.

High Involvement–Transformational	
Emotional portrayal of motive	
Authenticity	Paramount; must reflect lifestyle of target audience
Like ad	Necessary
Execution style	Unique; target audience must identify with product, people, or consumption situation shown
Benefit claim of brand message	
Number of benefits	Acceptable number to provide key information
Intensity of benefit claim	Very accurate claim; may overclaim but do not underclaim
Repetition of benefit claim	Many are required to support informational message

LO5 IMC Planning: Guidelines for Creative Evaluation

While the creative specialists have much responsibility for determining the message appeal and execution style to be used in a campaign, the marketer must evaluate and approve the creative approach before any ads are produced. A number of people may be involved in evaluating the creative recommendation, including the advertising or communications manager, product or brand managers, marketing director or vice-president, representatives from the legal department, and even senior managers if required.

Exhibit 8-24 This ad captures the excitement of skiing and reinforces the mastery idea of an intellectual stimulation motive.

Source: Telluride Ski & Golf Resort

Top management is involved in selecting an ad agency and must approve the theme and creative strategy for the campaign. Evaluation and approval of individual ads proposed by the agency is often the responsibility of advertising and product managers. The account executive and a member of the creative team present the creative concept to the client's advertising and product managers for their approval before beginning production. A careful evaluation should be made before the campaign actually enters production, since this stage requires considerable time and money. Criteria for evaluating the creative approach focus on questions requiring managerial judgment:

- *Is the creative approach aligned with the brand's marketing and advertising objectives?* Advertisers must consider whether the creative strategy and tactics recommended by the agency are consistent with the marketing strategy for the brand and the role that advertising and promotion have been assigned in the overall marketing program (i.e., brand image, marketing positioning strategy).

- *Is the creative approach consistent with the communication objectives?* The creative strategy and tactics must meet the established communication objectives. Creative specialists may lose sight of what the advertising message is supposed to be and come up with an approach that fails to execute the advertising strategy. Individuals responsible for approving the ad should ask the creative specialists to explain how the creative strategy and tactics achieve the creative and communication objectives.

- *Is the creative approach appropriate for the target audience?* Careful consideration should be given to whether ative strategy and tactics recommended will appeal to, be understood by, and communicate effectively v audience. This involves studying all elements of the ad and how the audience will respond to them. Adv not want to approve advertising that they believe will receive a negative reaction from the target audienc

- *Is the creative approach communicating a clear message to the target audience?* While creativity is important in i it is also important that the advertising communicate information regarding attributes, features and benefits, and/or images that motivate consumers to buy the brand.

- *Is the creative approach overwhelming the message?* Creative and entertaining messages may fail to elicit brand responses effectively. Although a creative approach to gain the receiver's attention within advertising clutter may be required, it cannot inhibit message delivery to the target audience.

- *Is the creative approach applicable for the expected media exposure?* Each media vehicle has its own specific climate that results from the nature of its editorial content, the type of reader or viewer it attracts, and the nature of the ads it contains. Consideration should be given to how well the ad fits into the media environment in which it will be shown.

- *Is the creative approach truthful and tasteful?* The ultimate responsibility for determining whether an ad deceives or offends the target audience, or the general public, lies with the client. It is the job of the advertising or brand manager, in conjunction with the firm's legal department, to evaluate the approach against company standards and laws respectively.

The advertising manager, brand manager, or other personnel on the client side can use these guidelines in reviewing, evaluating, and approving the ideas offered by the creative specialists. There may be other factors specific to the firm's advertising and marketing situation. Also, there may be situations where it is acceptable to deviate from the standards the firm usually uses in judging creative output. As we shall see in the next chapter, the client may want to move beyond these subjective criteria and use sophisticated pretesting research employing quantitative and qualitative methods to determine the effectiveness of a particular approach suggested by the creative specialists.

Learning Objectives Summary

 Analyze the creative execution styles that advertisers use and the situations where they are most appropriate.

After the ad campaign's creative strategy is determined, attention turns to the creative tactics that enhance the cognitive and emotional processing of the message. The creative execution style is the way the advertising appeal is presented in the message and is the first of three creative tactics analyzed. This chapter identified execution style techniques; the most appropriate style selected is a matter of balancing uniqueness in the market against effective communication to achieve the stated objectives. A number of standard approaches are available, like straight sell, slice of life, testimonial, drama, humour, and imagery—all of which can be put in TV commercials, print ads, and radio spots and are now developed for online video, banner ads, and podcast sponsorships.

 Explain different types of message structures used to develop a promotional message.

The design of the advertising message is a critical part of the communication process and is the second creative tactic discussed. There are options regarding the message structure, including order of presentation of message arguments, conclusion drawing, message sidedness, refutation, and verbal versus visual traits. How these elements are constructed has important implications for enhancing the processing of the message and whether communication effects are achieved with the target audience. Message structure considerations are important for any form of delivery (i.e., video, print, audio) that may be disseminated via traditional or new media.

 Express design elements involved in the creation of print, video, and audio messages.

Attention was also given to tactical issues involved in creating print, video, and audio messages. The elements of a print ad include headlines, body copy, illustrations, and layout. We also examined the video and audio elements of video messages and considerations involved in the planning and production of commercials. Together, these showed the important design decisions that have to be made to complete the creative approach. Finally, we highlighted a couple of key factors in the development of audio messages. These design elements are relevant for producing print, video, or audio ads that can be delivered through a variety of media.

 Apply a planning model for making creative tactics decisions.

We presented a model for creative specialists and marketers to help them make the appropriate decisions for the creative tactics. It provided general and specific suggestions for brand awareness. The model uses the target audience's attitude as the key factor when deciding upon the correct execution style, message structure, and design. These three characteristics ensure that both cognitive and emotional aspects of processing and attitude formation are addressed in the receiver of the message. The model is like a list to double check and know whether the creative execution results have characteristics that influence the target audience's attitude in the way expected.

 Illustrate how clients evaluate the creative work of their agencies and discuss guidelines for the evaluation and approval process.

Creative specialists are responsible for determining the creative strategy and tactics from the marketer's input. However, the client must review, evaluate, and approve the creative approach before any ads are produced or run. A number of criteria can be used by advertising managers, product or brand managers, and others involved in the promotional process to evaluate the advertising messages before approving final production.

Review Questions

1. Identify the difference between a message appeal and a creative execution style. Why is it important to make this distinction?

2. What is meant by a one-sided versus two-sided message? Discuss reasons why marketers may or may not want to use a two-sided message.

3. Are headlines more important for gaining attention or reinforcing awareness?

4. What are the similarities and differences of creative tactics across the four cells of the brand attitude grid of the R&P planning model?

5. Explain how the guidelines for creative evaluation can be applied to ads seen on the Internet.

Applied Questions

1. Look through ads in other chapters and figure out what execution style is used. Do the same for video ads found online.

2. What are the limitations of constructing standard print-format ads for Facebook and billboards?

3. Brands are experimenting with long-form video messages online. Using the design elements discussed in the chapter, contrast this approach with a standard 30-second TV ad. When would a brand use both within its IMC plan?

4. Find an ad for each of the four cells of the R&P framework for creative tactics. Identify the design elements that match the guidelines for each cell.

5. Apply the guidelines for creative evaluation to a campaign for Telus or Bell or Rogers, and conclude whether it fulfills all the criteria sufficiently.

©Chris Ryan/Age Fotostock

CHAPTER NINE

Measuring the Effectiveness of the Promotional Message

LEARNING OBJECTIVES

LO1 Identify the decisions for measuring promotional message effectiveness.

LO2 Describe what is measured to assess promotional message effectiveness.

LO3 Evaluate pretest approaches for measuring promotional message effectiveness.

LO4 Evaluate post-test approaches for measuring promotional message effectiveness.

LO5 Appraise the requirements of proper effectiveness research.

Ad Effectiveness Measurement

Advertising effectiveness measurement is a topic that confounds promotional planners, market researchers, agency personnel, and brand managers alike. Successful advertising seen in awards presentations like Cannes and CASSIES tends to document the resulting communication effects, behavioural influence, and subsequent impact on marketing objectives like sales or market share in addition to providing evidence of the unique creative approach of the message. However, ad effectiveness measurement is also concerned with research at all stages of the creative process so that advertisers can put together the right message prior to releasing it; managers prefer to avoid wasted media costs or wasted time and effort in the case of messages shown in free social media by testing consumer response ahead of time. The problem of figuring out ad effectiveness has remained over many decades; however the research methods have evolved, uncovering new insights.

One research avenue examines why consumers view online video messages (e.g., ads) and why they share the links. About half of all viewers of an online ad visit the brand's Internet site, with 11 percent forwarding the link, so the question of assessing ad effectiveness for digital messaging is similar to a research question that vexed TV advertisers for decades. The input for these messages ranges from digital communication agencies following established processes, to outsourcing to independent contractors (e.g., Tongal), to do-it-yourself activities (e.g., Blendtec). Right now, researchers are investigating how these different creative inputs are influencing ad effectiveness. Distributing the message follows similar outsourcing and do-it-yourself avenues, both of which are concerned with how long viewers watch the message, since online messages often go beyond the TV norm of 30 seconds.

Consumers receive messages from numerous touchpoints—digital through many devices, broadcast, and print media—to go along with the various promotional efforts including in-store displays. Newer research looks at how all of these media contribute to the overall impact on the target audience, rather than at isolated influences of each. With unique messages arising from each of these media vehicles, researchers are concerned with both the delivery and the message content effects from all of the touchpoints. From a decision-making point of view, the research is integrated into the planning with a three-step process:

1. Attribution involves the combined and independent effects of each touchpoint.
2. Optimization runs what-if scenarios to consider different combinations of media and messages.
3. Allocation involves the instant adjustment of advertising dollars to the right media and message depending on the scenarios investigated.

From a message standpoint, research over the years has shown that more creative ads result in more focused attention while processing and improved communication effects in terms of stronger brand attitudes, however the link to purchase that aggregates to sales remains elusive. New research investigates different dimensions of creativity: originality, elaboration, synthesis, and artistic value. Originality implies "out of the ordinary" messages, uniqueness, and creative ideas departing from stereotypical thinking. Flexibility looks at different ideas, multiple subjects, and shifting ideas. Elaboration has numerous details, intricate ideas, and higher than expected details. Synthesis means unrelated objects, unusual connections, and bringing unusual things together. Artistic value is visually distinctive presentation, ideas that come alive visually, and artistic production. Their conclusions found varying influences of each type and that elaboration has a stronger impact on sales. Moreover, originality tends to be important but it requires another creative characteristic to be fully influential.

Question:

1. What part of advertising effectiveness do these research approaches measure?

Measuring the effectiveness of the promotional program is critical since it allows the marketing manager to assess the performance of specific program elements and provide input into the next period's situation analysis. We are concerned with evaluative research to measure the effectiveness of advertising and promotion and/or to assess various strategies and tactics before implementing them. This is not to be confused with planning research used to develop the promotional program, although the two can (and should) be used together.

In this chapter, we identify the reasons for measuring effectiveness. Next we describe key research decisions for evaluative research. Finally, we evaluate research methods and conclude with our IMC planning perspective to appraise the requirement for effectiveness research. Our primary focus is measuring the effects of advertising, because it is well established and other aspects of marketing communication have an advertisement-like message. Thus, most research techniques can be applied or have been adapted for other IMC tools. We highlight methods of measuring effectiveness for these tools in their respective chapters.

(LO1) Decisions for Measuring Effectiveness

Employees are generally given objectives to accomplish, and their job evaluations are based on achieving these objectives. Advertising and promotion should be held to the same standard where its performance is measured against the objectives established in the promotional plan, as indicated in Chapter 5. In this section we explore a few questions (i.e., why, what, how, where, when) regarding research for measuring advertising effectiveness.

WHY MEASURE EFFECTIVENESS

Avoiding Costly Mistakes Total measured advertising revenue approached $14 billion in 2017, and any brand's advertising budget is often a substantial expenditure. Thus, if a program is not achieving its objectives, the marketing manager needs information to know how or where to spend money more effectively. The opportunity loss due to poor marketing communication is just as important. If the advertising and promotions program is not accomplishing its objectives, the potential gain that could result from an effective program is not realized, thereby minimizing the firm's return on its marketing investment. The alternative to spending money and internal time resources on research is that both could go toward improved ad production or additional media buys. However, imagine the results of a poor campaign that did not motivate the target audience; money would be wasted if the effects could do more harm than good. Spending more money to buy media does not remedy a poor message or substitute for an improper promotional mix.

Evaluating Alternative Strategies Typically, a firm has a number of creative strategies under consideration. Companies test alternative versions of their advertising to determine which ad communicates most effectively. Or the decision may be between two promotional program elements: should money be spent on sponsorship or on advertising? Different participants may try to influence this, however. The sales manager may want to see the impact of promotions on sales, top management may wish to know the impact on corporate image, and those involved in the creative process may wish to assess recall and/or recognition of the ad. However, with the proper design, many or even all of the above might be measured. Since every promotional element is designed to accomplish its own objectives, research can be used to measure its effectiveness in doing so.

Increasing Advertising Efficiency Agency personnel sometimes lose sight of their objectives when focused on the project tasks. They may use technical jargon that not everyone is familiar with. Or the creative department may get too creative or too sophisticated and lose the meaning of the message that needs to be communicated. Conducting research helps companies develop more efficient and effective communications. Clients expect accountability for their promotional programs and pressure agencies to produce. However, an age-old industry issue is that creative specialists do not want their work to be tested. They feel that tests are not true measures of ad creativity and effectiveness: applying measures stifles their creativity, and creative ads are more likely to be successful. So while efficiency is a good argument, difficulties could mitigate some savings.

Determining If Objectives Are Achieved In a well designed IMC plan, specific communication objectives are established. If objectives are attained, new ones are established in the next planning period. An assessment of how program elements led to the attainment of the goals should take place, and/or reasons for less-than-desired achievements must be determined. Research should evaluate whether the strategy delivers the stated objectives and assess the appropriateness of the measures.[1] Although measuring advertising effectiveness potentially faces the challenge of the results being affected by the performance of other marketing mix decisions, promotional planners should still try to determine the specific results of their promotional investments through communication effects.

WHAT TO MEASURE

Creative Strategy Decisions The primary creative strategy decision—the creative theme—can be tested. When a company decides to change its theme or is planning to launch an unusual attention-getting approach, it may want to see the reactions of the target audience prior to investing in the media placement. Similarly, different message appeals can be tested (i.e., rational versus emotional), or different versions of one appeal can be tested. Finally, another important question is whether the spokesperson being used is effective and how the target audience will respond to him or her. A product spokesperson may be an excellent source initially but, owing to a variety of reasons, may lose impact over time in terms of attractiveness or likeability. Thus, all major creative strategy decisions can be tested. IMC Perspective 9-1 summarizes research regarding emotional reactions to creative strategy decisions.

Creative Tactics Decisions Different execution styles displayed on storyboards can be presented to members of the target audience in focus groups for their reaction. The message structure can be looked at, such as reading the body copy in an interview or another method. Specific design elements, such as the music in a television ad or the headline of a print ad, can also be the focus of research. Overall, advertisers use a variety of research methods to test essentially any creative tactic that they are unsure about or that requires confirmation.

Other Promotional Tools The other tools we will discuss in this book have an associated creative or message. Many sales promotions have a visual as well as an advertising-like message that reinforces the brand position. Similarly, firms use many creative tactics to gain the attention of media personnel so that their story will obtain exposure through publicity. Thus, while we have examined the creative in the context of advertising, as we noted previously all the decisions are relevant in the other promotional tools, and as expected the same research is possible if the advertiser believes it to be necessary. We review a few specifics in each of the subsequent chapters to measure the effectiveness of other promotional tools. **Exhibit 9-1** is an ad from a leading market research firm that does effectiveness research and other sorts of market research. Its copy essentially summarizes the point raised thus far.

WHERE TO MEASURE

Laboratory Tests In **laboratory tests**, people go to a particular location and are shown ads and/or commercials. The testers either ask questions about them or measure participants' responses by other methods. The major advantage is that changes in copy, illustration, formats, or colours can be manipulated inexpensively and the differential impact of each assessed to isolate the communication effects of each factor. The major disadvantage is the lack of *realism* that results in **testing bias**. When people go to a lab (even if it has been designed to look like a living room), they may scrutinize the ads more closely than they would at home. A second problem with this lack of realism is that it cannot duplicate the natural viewing situation, complete with the distractions or comforts of home.

Field Tests **Field tests** are evaluations of the ad in natural viewing situations, complete with the realism of noise, distractions, and the comforts of home. Field tests account for the effects of repetition, program content, and the presence of competitive messages. The major disadvantage of field tests is the lack of control. It may be impossible to isolate causes of viewers' evaluations. If atypical events occur during the test, they may bias the results. Field tests usually take more time and money to conduct, so the results are not available to be acted on quickly. Thus, realism is gained at the expense of other important factors.

Exhibit 9-1 This ad promotes the value of performing market research.

Source: GfK

Exhibit 9-2 Online focus groups give advertisers direction on how to improve their message.

Virtual Focus Facility: Observer View

©InsideHeads.com, conducting online focus groups since 1998

HOW TO MEASURE

Most research is classified as either qualitative or quantitative as defined in Chapter 7 when describing research done prior to the development of a campaign. These methods are also used when measuring the effectiveness of the promotional message, although the formats and types of questions are adjusted since the research objectives are different for these two research situations. *Quantitative methods*—such as surveys that ask questions with scaled responses, require a larger sample size, and use statistical analysis—are usually performed *after* launching the campaign. The surveys are executed in a number of different ways (e.g., in person, online, by mail) and done with both electronic and non-electronic data collection.

Qualitative methods such as interviews and focus groups are usually performed *before* launching the campaign.

Participants freely discuss the meanings they get from the ads, consider the relative advantages of alternative messages, and suggest improvements for the creative strategy and tactics decisions. A variety of topics are examined and consumers are free to go into depth in any important areas. The methodology is attractive to marketers since results are easily obtained, directly observable, and immediate. These methods don't require quantitative analysis and are more easily accepted and interpreted by managers. Online focus groups (**Exhibit 9-2**) provide time and cost efficiencies, and their data can be combined with face-to-face focus groups' results.

WHEN TO MEASURE

Pretest Measures taken before the campaign is implemented are known as a **pretest**. A pretest can occur at any point in the creative process before implementation, during the early idea, rough execution, or final version phases. In addition, a pretest could occur at all three of these stages. The advantage of a pretest is that feedback is relatively inexpensive. Any problems with the concept or the way it is to be delivered are identified before large amounts of money are spent in development. Sometimes more than one version of the ad is evaluated to determine which is most likely to be effective. Since a pretest is generally cheaper than making a mistake public without a pretest, it certainly makes sense to pretest. The disadvantage is that mock-ups, storyboards, or animatics may not communicate nearly as effectively as the final ad. The mood-enhancing and/or emotional aspects of the message are very difficult to communicate in this format.

Post-test Measures taken after the campaign is implemented are known as a **post-test** and occur after media exposure of the ad. In contrast to a pretest, a post-test occurs after placing the marketing communication in a media like broadcast or print, or another communication tool if needed. A post-test is designed to (1) determine if the campaign is accomplishing the objectives sought and (2) serve as input into the next period's situation analysis. **IMC Perspective 9-1** summarizes research regarding emotional reactions to creative strategy decisions.

IMC PERSPECTIVE 9-1

AD EFFECTIVENESS MEASUREMENT THROUGH EMOTIONAL RESEARCH

Imagine sitting in an office wondering how consumers would react to new ads shown as storyboards developed by an advertising agency. Or perhaps consider whether the completed print ads should be placed in magazines for the next campaign. For that matter, if managers are wondering about *any* message to be delivered across any or multiple media, how or what evaluation should be implemented to ensure success? Many approaches toward effectiveness tend to measure consumer knowledge in terms of brand recall or recognition, advertising recall or recognition, and rational thoughts connected to the brand. One promising development involves researchers getting a better read on consumer emotions through a variety of methods.

The interest in emotional effects of marketing communication is derived from recent research indicating how intertwined cognition and affect are during human decision making, how and when we process information, and to what extent we remember brand information. At the heart of this is research suggesting that the brain has an intuitive system for making decisions automatically, and another system that rationalizes the intuitive decisions or overrules them so that people will appear more rational. The conclusion of this is that much of decision making is much more emotionally driven than expected, and that our emotional decisions are supported or refuted rationally. From an advertising standpoint, subtle cues in a message can influence emotionally such that consumers automatically prefer aspects of an ad, and quite possibly the brand, as shown in the Chapter 4 models.

Assessing ad effectiveness along the lines of emotional responses is an elusive goal. Typically, consumers have difficulty expressing their emotional attachment to a brand, as they often convey their brand usage in relation to product attributes or benefits. Moreover, self-report measurement through pictorial scales, standard Likert-type scales, and open-ended questions always proves challenging due to validity concerns. Some people express emotions globally while others are more specific, and the very nature of asking about emotions is filtered through the carefully thought out cognitive reply. In short, assessing emotional reactions to ads is a significant measurement issue.

Communication researchers conclude that multiple approaches are warranted. In this case,

©Monkey Business Images/Shutterstock

they suggest three methods to perform data comparisons and make better conclusions so message development can occur. First, in their research they used electrodermal activity, which measures the electrical impulses of the viewer's sympathetic nervous system that are conducted by the perspiration on their skin. Second, they advocate for continuous rating data that viewers indicate with a dial-like joystick throughout the message exposure. The tool allows the respondent to indicate positive or negative feelings easily as they view a message. Third, the standard self-report measures are encouraged for a basis of comparative assessment. Data from their study indicated that all three measurement approaches provided unique and complementary information such that they conclude that one method should not be used, but rather communication planners should consider multiple methods.

Questions:
1. Why are advertisers so concerned with measuring emotions?
2. Should promotional planners measure emotional responses for other IMC tools, such as sales promotions or direct response?

Measuring Effectiveness

Measuring effectiveness requires consideration of the R&P response model summarized in Chapter 4 and subsequently applied in Chapter 5 to form objectives. Measuring effectiveness is required for understanding how a target audience processes the ad message and the communication effects of the ad message.[2] As a reminder, processing included attention, automatic learning of benefit claims, acceptance of benefit claims, and emotional responses, while communication effects included category need, brand awareness, brand attitude, and brand purchase intention. This section provides a general idea of what is measured to assess if the advertising is effective.[3]

A thorough system of measuring effectiveness is followed when all responses are evaluated during pretest research and post-test research. However, in practice, advertisers may focus on one set, or one partial set, of measures. Either qualitative or quantitative approaches are possible for both pretest and post-test research, although most pretest research is with qualitative data collection, and most post-test research uses quantitative data collection. In these cases, open-ended questions are asked to individuals in an interview after message exposure of a mock-up print ad, a storyboard for a TV ad, or the equivalent for an Internet ad for pretest research, and scaled closed-ended questions are asked to a sample of respondents after message exposure from multiple media in a campaign.

PROCESSING MEASURES

Attention Attention is measured by asking the target audience questions such as what aspects of the ad they saw first, what part of the ad held their attention, and what part of the ad distracted them from reading or watching further during a pretest. These questions are most relevant for pretest research. For example, the pretest research for the Classico ad highlighted in IMC Perspective 6-2 reported a score of 78 versus the norm of 65 for the "held my attention" question. Other scores are shown below.[4]

Learning Learning is measured by the respondent's answer to a simple question—"What is the brand message?" A follow-up question asks for the brand name to ensure that the association between the brand and the benefit is comprehended. Note that these measures are relevant for a target audience who do not perceive risk in buying the advertised brand on their next purchase. For a highly involved target audience, acceptance measures are recommended.

Acceptance Acceptance is measured by asking a member of the target audience a question about the thoughts they experienced, which can be categorized as shown with the cognitive response model in Chapter 4. The categories can be quite simple in terms of creative strategy and tactics, or be more specific for each of the decisions (theme, source, and appeal for creative strategy; style, structure, and design for creative tactics). Reading back the cognitive responses to the respondent, a recording of negative, neutral, or positive is associated with each thought. For example, the pretest research for the Classico ad reported a score of 60 versus the norm of 42 for the "makes Classico seem different from other brands in the pasta sauce category" question.

Exhibit 9-3 A pretest of this Dasani ad could focus on the water imagery and other design elements.

Source: Dasani by The Coca-Cola Company

Emotional Response Emotional or affect response to the ad is measured similarly to acceptance. Instead of focusing on thoughts and their assessment, the questions concern the respondent's feelings or emotions toward the ad. Again these responses are categorized broadly with creative strategy and creative tactics, or more specifically with three decisions within each as indicated above. For example, the pretest research for the Classico ad reported a score of 76 versus the norm of 62 for the "enjoyed watching this ad" question.

A pretest of the ad in **Exhibit 9-3** is an example where the researcher would see how the design element of the layout, colours, and imagery affected the processing of the message. Questions addressing the target audience's response to the cascading water and its symbolism would reveal positive or negative thoughts and feelings. One potential research strategy would be a test of the order of the three products, and whether there should be two, three, or four product shots in the image.

Ad Recognition An important processing measure in post-test research is ad recognition. This involves showing a copy of the message and recording if the respondent answers positively. The result is the percentage of people responding yes from the total sample. Note that this is not a measure of brand recognition, but a measure of whether a member of the target audience believes they processed the message. As such, this measure is a result of an effective message and effective media exposure.

Ad Recall Questions to measure ad recall in post-test research involve showing the brand name to the respondent and asking if they remember seeing an ad for the brand. Again, the percentage of people correctly identifying the message is the key result. And, this is not a measure of brand recall, but a measure of where the target audience believes they processed the message without a visual cue other than a brand name. An alternative prompt beyond brand name is to suggest a product category, and then ask what advertising they recall. As one might expect, this is a more challenging mental task and indicates effective message and media decisions.

COMMUNICATION EFFECTS MEASURES

Category Need Category need is measured simply, when the communication objective is to remind, with a question such as how likely the respondent is to buy the product category in future. However, if the category need objective is to sell, the researcher is required to ask three questions pertaining to category need: category purchase intention, benefit beliefs about the category, and category awareness. Since multiple product categories potentially fulfill a need, the research questions treat the category as if it were a brand. Here is an example of a question that measures category need.

> Do you intend to buy a tablet for your social media communication
> needs in the next six months?
>
> Unlikely   1   2   3   4   5   6   7   Likely

Brand Awareness In post-test research, brand awareness must be measured in a specific order, with the brand recall question first and the brand recognition question second. The recall question provides the product category, motivational need, and target audience prompt, and the brands mentioned are recorded. Recall percentages for each brand are tabulated if mentioned. More specific top-of-mind recall is the percentage of respondents who mention a brand first.

> When you think of tablets for social media communication for people like yourself,
> what brands come to mind? (brand recall)

Here is an example of a question for brand recognition, and the recognition percentages for each brand are tabulated if mentioned. More specific top-of-mind recognition is the percentage of respondents who identify a brand first, although this measure is not typically compiled.

> Which of these brands of tablets have you seen before? (brand recognition)

The image in **Exhibit 9-4** is a publicity shot for a Buick ad that starred Emily Ratajkowski and Odell Beckham Jr., who demonstrated his famous one-handed grab of a football by catching a wedding bouquet. Good post-test research would ask brand recall and brand recognition questions like the two proposed above to see if the investment in paying these stars produced stronger awareness of the Buick convertible.

Brand Attitude Multiple questions are asked for a thorough measure of brand attitude. We reviewed in Chapter 6 target audience persuasion strategies for positioning that focused on making benefit claims or making claims of importance. Questions are asked for both of these to measure brand attitude, and variations are possible for the wording and scales, and of course the number of questions. Carrying on with the tablet example, these questions measure the target audience's belief about three attributes, and more are asked depending on the manager's requirements.

Exhibit 9-4 Post-test research could determine if use of celebrities in an ad helped awareness for Buick.

©Buick

Rate the performance of Brand X on the following characteristics.

Screen Resolution	Poor	1	2	3	4	5	6	7	Excellent
Ease of Use	Poor	1	2	3	4	5	6	7	Excellent
Performance	Poor	1	2	3	4	5	6	7	Excellent

How important are the following characteristics for a tablet for social media communication?

Screen Resolution	Not Important	1	2	3	4	5	6	7	Important
Ease of Use	Not Important	1	2	3	4	5	6	7	Important
Performance	Not Important	1	2	3	4	5	6	7	Important

Another set of questions pertains to the overall cognitive belief of the brand. For example, the post-test research for the Nissan campaign highlighted in IMC Perspective 6-1 reported an index score of 116 versus the starting benchmark of 81 for the "overall opinion" question.[5] An example of a similar question one could use for the tablet example is the following:

Overall, how would you rank Brand X for social media communication?

Finally, another set of questions pertains to the overall emotions associated with the brand. Again the wording and scales are adapted to the positioning and creative decisions, but one could use questions such as the following:

What are your overall feelings about Brand X?

I love Brand X	Disagree	1	2	3	4	5	6	7	Agree
Brand X makes me feel great	Disagree	1	2	3	4	5	6	7	Agree
Brand X is my favourite brand	Disagree	1	2	3	4	5	6	7	Agree

When assessing this data, the promotional planner would compare data measured before the campaign with data taken after the campaign to see if there is a positive shift as anticipated from the brand positioning strategy decisions.

Brand Purchase Intention Measuring brand purchase intention requires clarification as to whether "try," "buy," or "use" is the preferred referent. A secondary consideration is the time frame fitting with the type of product such as a durable or a consumable. For example, for a durable, the question would likely start with, "If you were going to buy a car," while for a consumable, the question would likely start with, "The next time you buy a chocolate bar," prior to asking the likelihood of buying etc. Here is a question that could be asked to complete the tablet example.

If you were going to buy a tablet for social media communication, how likely would you be to buy Brand X in the next six months?

Unlikely	1	2	3	4	5	6	7	Likely

In conclusion, the purpose of this section is to indicate how research provides information regarding the effectiveness of ads by showing the kinds of measures advertisers collect to see the link to the objectives established. We reviewed the content of these research questions in the response models of Chapter 4 and applied the models in Chapter 5. One could establish questions based on the other response models reviewed in this text as well. We showed this with the R&P perspective since it clearly demarcates the processing of ad messages and communication effect of ad message, a key limitation of past models. Additionally, showing the questions makes a link to the content of the positioning, creative strategy, and creative tactics chapters since the brand attitude measure should be consistent with the benefit claims of the campaign.

ⓛⓞ3 Pretest Measuring

Pretest measuring may occur at various points throughout the development of an ad or a campaign during the creative process: (1) concept test, (2) rough test, (3) finished print ad, and (4) finished broadcast ad.

CONCEPT TEST

A **concept test** is conducted early in the campaign development process to evaluate the target audience's response to a potential ad or campaign, or alternative advertising strategies. Positioning statements, copy, headlines, and/or illustrations may all be under scrutiny. The material shown, typically in a focus group, is a rough sketch of the ad or a description of a storyboard using words, pictures, or symbols. Reactions and evaluations are sought through qualitative questions that measure message processing as described in the previous section. Another means of gathering opinions of an ad concept is to ask individuals to assess the material shown via questionnaires with rating scales to obtain quantitative data illustrated earlier. Similar testing via the Internet occurs as advertisers show concepts simultaneously to consumers throughout Canada to obtain data that can be analyzed almost instantaneously.

ROUGH TEST

After a concept test, promotional planners consider a **rough test**. Because of the high cost associated with the production of an ad, advertisers spend money testing a rendering of the final ad at early stages of the creative process with slides of the artwork posted on a screen, an animatic, or a photomatic. **Figure 9-1** provides a summary of this terminology. Rough tests must indicate how the finished commercial would perform, and provide accurate information at a reasonable cost. Past studies demonstrated that these testing methods are reliable and the results typically correlate well with the finished ad.[6] Popular tests include comprehension and reaction tests and consumer juries, and again the questions measure message processing and initial communication effects.

A **comprehension and reaction test** assesses whether the message conveys the meaning intended and the cognitive and emotional responses the ad generates. Obviously, the advertiser does not want an ad that evokes a negative reaction or offends someone. Tests of comprehension and reaction employ no one standard procedure and include personal interviews, group interviews, and focus groups.

A **consumer jury** rates a selection of advertising alternatives in terms of different layouts, images, or body copy presented separately. This method uses consumers representative of the target audiences to evaluate the probable success of an ad. Potential viewers look at the ads and give their message processing responses, brand evaluation, and overall ranking of all ads. Each ad is compared to every other ad by all in the jury and the winner is identified based on the votes of everyone on the jury.

PRETEST OF FINISHED PRINT AD

At this stage, researchers test a finished ad but changes occur based on the results since testing the ad in final form typically provides better information. Methods to pretest finished print ads include the portfolio test, readability test, and diagnostic copy test. The tests also work with media with similar display ads (e.g., out-of-home, digital). These tests are a bit limited in that they examine only a portion of the processing of an ad message.

Figure 9-1 Rough testing terminology

Three categories of a rough commercial:

1. Animatic Rough
Succession of drawings/cartoons
Rendered artwork
Still frames
Simulated movement: Panning/zooming of frame/rapid sequence

2. Photomatic Rough
Succession of photographs
Real people/scenery
Still frames
Simulated movements: Panning/zooming of frame/rapid sequence

3. Live-Action Rough
Live motion
Stand-in/nonunion talent
Nonunion crew
Limited props/minimal opticals
Location settings

A **portfolio test** is a laboratory methodology designed to expose a group of respondents to a portfolio consisting of both control and test ads. Respondents are then asked what information they recall from the ads. The assumption is that the ads that yield the highest ad recall are the most effective. Portfolio tests compare alternative ads directly but have two weaknesses. First, factors other than advertising creativity and/or presentation may affect recall. Interest in the product or product category, the fact that respondents know they are participating in a test, or interviewer instructions may account for more differences than the ad itself. Second, ad recognition may be a more useful measure than ad recall for low involvement products.

A **readability test** assesses the communication efficiency of the body copy in a print ad by determining the average number of syllables per 100 words. Human interest, appeal of the material, length of sentences, and familiarity with certain words are also considered and associated with the educational background of target audiences. Test results are compared to previously established norms for different target audiences. The test suggests that copy is best comprehended when sentences are short, words are concrete and familiar, and personal references are drawn. This method eliminates many of the interviewee biases associated with other tests and avoids gross errors in understanding. The norms offer an attractive standard for comparison. However, the copy may become too mechanical, and direct input from the receiver is not available. Without this input, contributing elements like creativity cannot be addressed. Like the portfolio test, this one is limited and should be used with other pretesting methods.

A **diagnostic copy test** is a pretest method using a realistic setting of the respondent's home and collection of multiple communication measures of a finished print ad. Major advertising research firms like Millward-Brown, Ipsos, and G&R provide a copy test service for multiple print-like media in which they track comprehensive measures for a full diagnostic evaluation. Each uses its own vocabulary and consumer response model, but essentially the measures track message processing of cognitive and emotional responses, idea communication, comprehension, believability, and attitudinal measures pertaining to ad attribute ratings, attitude to the ad, brand attribute ratings, and overall brand attitude.

PRETEST OF FINISHED BROADCAST AD

A variety of methods for pretesting finished broadcast ads are available, such as theatre tests, on-air tests, and physiological measures. Research firms who perform TV testing expanded their services for online testing of video messages.

Theatre Test In the past, theatre testing represented a laboratory method for pretesting finished commercials. Participants watched pilots of proposed TV programs with test ads embedded. In some instances, the show is actually being tested, but more commonly a standard program is used so that audience responses can be compared with normative responses established by previous viewers. Variations of this method allow for viewing in more convenient locations (e.g., home, office, mall, hotel), with more consumer-friendly data collection devices so the data can be tabulated in manager-friendly reports.

The closed- and open-ended questions are recorded via a touch-screen system. Key measures include (1) visibility (Will the commercial be remembered?); (2) branding (Will the brand be remembered?); (3) communications (What visuals and messages will be remembered?); (4) brand enhancement (Does the ad promote a positive feeling toward the brand?); and (5) persuasion (Will the commercial inspire non-users to try the product, and will it enhance brand loyalty among existing customers?). The diagnostics include measures of viewers' awareness, comprehension, uniqueness, and involvement of the commercial. The methodology also allows for scene-by-scene analysis, and can be used to test all traditional forms of advertising as well as digital.

On-Air Test Firms conducting theatre tests also may insert the commercials into actual TV programs in certain test markets. Typically, the commercials are in finished form. This is referred to as an on-air test and often includes single-source ad research (described later in this chapter). On-air pretesting of finished commercials offers distinct advantages over lab methods, and the realistic test gives an indication of the ad's success when launched. The most commonly employed metric used in an on-air test is recall—that is, the number of persons able to recall the ad and/or its message. In an examination of real-world advertising tests, one study concludes that recall and persuasion pretests, while often employed, do not fare well in respect to reliability and/or validity. Nevertheless, most of the testing services have offered evidence of both validity and reliability for on-air pretesting of commercials. Research firms claim their pretest and post-test results yield the same recall scores nine out of 10 times—a strong indication of reliability and a good predictor of the effect the ad is likely to have when shown to the population as a whole. Whether the measures used are as strong an indication as the providers say still remains in question.[7]

Physiological Measure An unexpected method of pretesting finished commercials involves measuring physiological responses. These measures indicate the receiver's *involuntary* responses (e.g., heartbeat, reflexes) to the ad, which indicate an aspect of message processing and theoretically eliminate biases associated with the voluntary measures reviewed thus far. Growth of research in this field accounts for the natural and social setting in which advertising exposure occurs.[8] The physiological measures used to test both print and broadcast ads include pupil dilation, galvanic skin response, eye tracking, and brain waves.

Pupil dilation. Research in **pupillometrics** is designed to measure dilation and constriction of the pupils of the eyes in response to stimuli. Dilation is associated with action; constriction involves the body's conservation of energy. Pupil dilation suggests a stronger interest in (or preference for) an ad or implies arousal or attention-getting capabilities. Other attempts to determine the affective (liking or disliking) responses created by ads have met with less success. Because of high costs and methodological problems, the use of pupillometrics has waned, but it can be useful in evaluating certain aspects of advertising.

Galvanic skin response (GSR). Also known as **electrodermal response** (EDR), GSR measures the skin's resistance or conductance to a small amount of current passed between two electrodes. Response to a stimulus activates sweat glands, which in turn increases the conductance of the electrical current. Thus, GSR/EDR activity might reflect a reaction to advertising. A review of research in this area concluded that GSR/EDR (1) is sensitive to affective stimuli, (2) may present a picture of attention, (3) may be useful to measure long-term advertising recall, and (4) is useful in measuring ad effectiveness.[9] Another study concluded that GSR is an effective measure and is useful, yet underused, for measuring affect, or liking, for ads.[10]

Eye tracking. A commonly employed methodology is **eye tracking**, in which viewers see an ad while a sensor aims a beam of infrared light at the eye. The beam follows the movement of the eye and shows the exact spot on which the viewer is focusing. The continuous reading of responses demonstrates which elements of the ad are attracting attention, how long the viewer is focusing on them, and the sequence in which they are being viewed. Fibre optics, digital data processing, and advanced electronics are used to follow eye movements of viewers and/or readers as they process an ad. The research measures what readers see, recall, and comprehend, and provides scan paths of print ads, billboards, commercials, print materials, and Internet sites. Eye tracking can identify strengths and weaknesses in an ad and facilitate adjustments before launching. For example, attractive models or background action may distract the viewer's attention away from the advertised brand. In other instances, colours or illustrations may attract attention and create viewer interest in the ad. Measurement of Internet advertising has adapted many approaches and eye tracking has received considerable usage, as shown in **Exhibit 9-5**.

Brain waves. Electroencephalographic (EEG) measures are taken from the skull to determine electrical frequencies in the brain. EEG research attracted the interest of academic researchers and is now the focus of specialized market research organizations, as shown in **IMC Perspective 9-2**. The electrical impulses are used in three areas of research: alpha waves, hemispheric lateralization, and indirect methods.

- **Alpha activity** refers to the degree of brain activation. People are in an alpha state when they are inactive, resting, or sleeping. The theory is that a person in an alpha state is less likely to be processing information (recall correlates negatively with alpha levels), and that attention and processing require moving from this state. By measuring a subject's alpha level while viewing a commercial, researchers can assess the degree to which attention and processing are likely to occur.

- **Hemispheric lateralization** distinguishes between alpha activity in the left and right sides of the brain. It has been hypothesized that the right side of the brain processes visual stimuli and the left processes verbal stimuli; the right hemisphere responds more to emotional stimuli, while the left responds to logic; and the right determines recognition, while the left assesses recall.[11] If these hypotheses are correct, advertisers could design ads to increase learning and memory by creating stimuli to appeal to each hemisphere. However, some researchers believe the brain does not function laterally, and an ad cannot be designed to appeal to one side or the other.

Exhibit 9-5 Eye tracking is a commonly used research method.

Source: SensoMotoric Instruments (SMI)

- **Indirect methods** use technologies originally designed for the medical field, such as positron emission tomography (PET) and functional magnetic resonance imaging (fMRI). Neuroscientists teamed up with marketers to examine physiological reactions to ads and brands through brain scan imaging. PET tracks changes in metabolism while fMRI tracks blood flow, and both provide an indirect measure of brain activity. By monitoring the brain activity and measuring chemical activity and/or changes in the magnetic fields of the brain, scientists learn how consumers make decisions as well as how they react to commercials.

IMC PERSPECTIVE 9-2

AD EFFECTIVENESS MEASUREMENT THROUGH TECHNOLOGICAL RESEARCH

In the constant quest to determine the effectiveness of advertising, marketers have turned to MRI machines and heart rate monitors, as well as monitored changes in the skin and facial muscles, to examine physiological responses to advertising messages. The use of neurosciences via an electroencephalography (EEG) machine to test commercials is now both an effective and an efficient option for many advertisers. The methodology places a headset with electrode sensors on people and records their brain waves every two milliseconds while they are watching video messages. Resulting data output indicates at which point in the ad the brain is most active. Measurement involves attention, cognitive responses, emotional responses, and encoding to memory that indicates the development of branded communication effects. Brainsights of Toronto and Neurométric of Montreal are two market research firms specializing in the application of this technology and providing guidance to marketers looking to adjust their ads.

An example of a successful application is Brainsights' work with TSN Sportscentre and Molson Coors. The ad tested showed scenes of the on-air personalities bantering about who would win the office fantasy football pool. Encouraging viewers to join the pool appeared to be the most logical objective of the message. The initial version of the ad showed Kate Beirness as the victor with her confident and ambitious approach to go along with her good looks that expectedly would sway the target of 19- to 34-year-old males. However, testing proved otherwise, as viewers preferred Cabbie Richards to win the contest. He came across as an

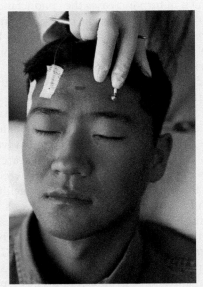

©Keith Brofsky/Getty Images

underdog who worked hard and put together a solid roster of players who unfortunately suffered challenges due to injuries, and he proved to be a more appealing winner. The reasoning suggested that younger viewers had stronger emotional responses to Cabbie since they liked stories of individuals unexpectedly succeeding in the face of obstacles. In contrast, the data indicated that Kate appeared to be an entertaining character in the story, but Cabbie's anguish captured the spirit of the pool more accurately.

There are other applications. Research that looks at whether multinational brands should consider locally produced creative messages or use repurposed global creatives is instructive to find the balance across messages and whether differences may exist in certain product categories. Research into whether viral ads actually influence brand attitude and brand purchase intention is useful as shared video links may be more indicative of the ads being entertaining but doing little for marketing or branding purposes.

In the case of Neurométric, which worked with the dairy cooperative Natrel, the research tested the product name, a billboard message, and the slogan. The English version of the slogan "Make every day more delicious" appeared fine, but the French version used the word "vachement" meaning "really" instead of the equivalent translation of "more" which would be "plus." Research indicated that respondents keyed on the beginning part of the word—"vache," meaning "cow"—so the French ad slogan changed the word to the exact translation of the English slogan. Neurométric's research is now affordable at about $15,000/study and the online execution makes it very convenient for respondents to participate. A simple download of a Java app makes responding to the print messages as easy as completing an online survey.

Question:

1. Express your feelings on whether you would volunteer as a respondent to this kind of research.

Post-Test Measuring

The fact that the ad and/or campaign has been implemented does not mean there is no longer a need for testing. In this section, we discuss methods for post-testing a print ad (e.g, inquiry, recognition, recall) and broadcast ad (day-after-recall, comprehensive, test marketing, single source tracking, tracking), which also have been adapted for other media. Some of the tests are similar to the pretests discussed in the previous section and are provided by the same companies.

POST-TEST OF PRINT AD

Inquiry Tests Marketers use **inquiry tests** to measure advertising effectiveness on the basis of target audience contact that is generated from ads appearing in print media. The inquiry may be the number of coupons returned, phone calls generated, or reader cards completed. Digital inquiries would include emails and social media communication like questions posed on Twitter or Facebook. This is a very simple measure of the ad's or medium's effectiveness; more complex methods may involve (1) running the ad in successive issues of the same medium, (2) running **split-run tests**, in which variations of the ad appear in different copies of the same newspaper or magazine, and/or (3) running the same ad in different media. Each of these methods yields information on different aspects of the strategy. The first measures the cumulative effects of the campaign; the second examines specific elements of the ad or variations on it. The final method measures the effectiveness of the medium rather than the ad itself.

While inquiry tests may yield useful information, weaknesses in this methodology limit its effectiveness. For example, inquiries may not be a true measure of the attention-getting or information-providing aspects of the ad. The reader may be attracted to an ad, read it, and even store the information but not be motivated to inquire at that particular time. Time constraints, lack of a need for the product or service at the time the ad is run, and other factors may limit the number of inquiries. But receiving a small number of inquiries doesn't mean the ad was not effective; attention, attitude change, awareness, and recall of copy points may all have been achieved. At the other extreme, a person with a particular need for the product may respond to any ad for it, regardless of specific qualities of the ad.

Recognition Tests A common post-test of print ads is the **recognition method**, most closely associated with Roper ASW. The Starch Ad Readership Report lets the advertiser assess the impact of an ad in a single issue of a magazine, over time, and/or across different magazines. Starch claims that (1) the pulling power of the ad can be assessed through the control offered, (2) the effectiveness of competitors' ads can be compared through the norms provided, (3) alternative ad executions can be tested, and (4) readership scores are a useful indication of consumers' involvement in the ad or campaign. These scores are processing measures right after looking at a magazine, and include the noted

Exhibit 9-6 A Starch rating scale for an Absolut ad.

ABSOLUT VODKA
Category: Other Alcoholic Beverages
1P4| Page 29

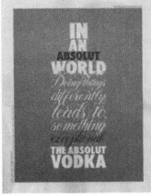

Issue Audience (000): 10,555	Noted	Assoc.	Read Any	Read Most
Advertiser	72%	68%	59%	-
AdMeasure Audience (000)	7,600	7,177	6,227	
Issue Norm (17 Ads)	61%	54%	48%	16%
Issue Index	118	126	123	144
Comparable MRI Starch Adnorm: 1P4 - Other Alcoholic Beverages				
Adnorm (156 Ads)	52%	45%	42%	20%
Adnorm Index	138	151	140	NA

Actions Taken by Those Who Noted the Ad	Any Actions Taken	Purchased the product/ service	Visited their website	Clipped or saved the ad	Contacted company by mail/phone	Looked for the product/ service	Recommended the product to someone	Talked to a doctor about the product (Rx ads only)	Talked to someone about it	None
Advertiser	17%	13%	1%	1%	0%	1%	3%	NA	2%	83%
Category Norm (268 Ads)	43%	12%	6%	4%	1%	12%	8%	NA	15%	57%
Category Index	40	108	17	25	0	8	38	NA	13	146

Brand Disposition	Positively disposed (Net)	My favorite brand	One of several brands I like	Don't use, but it's worth trying	Negatively disposed (Net)	I use it but don't particularly like it	I don't like it	I'm unfamiliar with it
Absolut	67%	6%	42%	19%	33%	5%	14%	13%
Brand Category Norm (268 Ads)	51%	7%	27%	17%	49%	2%	7%	39%
Brand Index	131	86	156	112	67	250	200	33

The brand disposition information is asked at the beginning of the MRI Starch survey, before respondents are asked about specific ads. The brand disposition questions do not reference an ad but rather ask the respondent about the brand itself.

Actions Taken and Brand category norms are created using a fixed average of available data from 10/08 to 12/09.

[=] Ad has fewer than 4 words [-] Ad has fewer than 50 words | Adnorms Grp = Online10CT (10/2008-12/2009) | Run Date: Aug 24, 2010 2:41 PM

Source: GfK MRI

score (percentage of readers who remember seeing the ad), brand-associated score (percentage of readers who recall part of ad identifying the brand), and read most score (percentage of readers who read at least half of the body copy). The theory is that a reader must read and become involved in the ad before the ad can communicate. The degree to which this readership can be shown is a direct indication of effectiveness. An example of a Starch scored ad is shown in **Exhibit 9-6**.

Recall Tests The best-known tests to measure recall of print ads are the Ipsos-ASI Next*Print test and the Gallup & Robinson Magazine Impact Research Service (MIRS). These **recall tests** are similar to those discussed in the section on pretesting broadcast ads, as they attempt to measure recall of specific ads. Magazines are read in people's homes and shortly thereafter three measurement scores are reported: percentage of readers who recall the ad, number of sales points the reader can recall, and brand attitude in terms of purchase reaction.

In addition to having the same interviewer problems as recognition tests, recall tests have other disadvantages. The reader's degree of involvement with the product and/or the distinctiveness of the appeals and visuals may lead to higher-than-accurate recall scores, although in general the method may lead to lower levels of recall than actually exist. Critics contend the test is not strong enough to reflect recall accurately, so many ads may score as less effective than they really are, and advertisers may abandon or modify them needlessly. On the plus side, it is thought that recall tests can assess the ad's impact on memory. Proponents of recall tests say the major concern is not the results themselves but how they are interpreted. Studies have shown that the correlation between recall and recognition is very high for print ads.[12]

POST-TEST OF BROADCAST AD

Day-After Recall (DAR) Tests The DAR test asks questions over the phone to assess whether a respondent could recall seeing an ad on a TV show from the previous day they claimed to have seen. It proved to be a popular method of post-testing in the broadcasting industry for decades, although its use waned because it assessed recall for one exposure on a particular time slot rather than looking at ad recall across multiple exposures. The major advantage of the day-after recall test is that it is a field test, supposedly providing a realistic response. DAR tests also provide norms that give advertisers a standard for comparing how well their ads perform. In addition to recall, a number of different measures of the ad's effectiveness include persuasive and diagnostic measures.

Although popular, day-after recall tests also had problems, including limited samples, high costs, and security issues (ads shown in test markets could be seen by competitors). Furthermore, DAR tests may favour unemotional appeals because respondents verbalize the message in their answers. Thinking messages may be easier to recall than emotional communications, so recall scores for emotional ads may be lower.[13] Other studies concluded that emotional ads may be processed differently from rational ones, and ad agencies developed their own methods of determining emotional response to ads.[14]

Comprehensive Measures As noted in our discussion of pretesting broadcast commercials, a measure of a commercial's effectiveness is gathered and services offer additional measures, including purchase intent and frequency of purchase. Copy testing firms also provide diagnostic measures, which garner viewers' evaluations of the ads, and establish how clearly the creative idea is understood and how well the proposition is communicated. Rational and emotional reactions to the ads are also examined. While each of the measures provides specific input into the effectiveness of a commercial, advertisers are also interested in more than just one specific input.

To assist advertisers in copy testing of their commercials, multiple measures determine (1) the potential of the commercial for impacting sales, (2) how the ad contributes to brand equity, (3) how well it is in line with existing advertising strategies and objectives, and (4) how to optimize effectiveness. Consumers are recruited to evaluate a TV program, with ads embedded into the program as they would be on local prime-time television. Consumers view the recorded program in their home to simulate actual field conditions. Researchers investigate related recall (day-after recall) scores; persuasion scores, including brand preference shifts, purchase intent and frequency, brand equity differentiation, and relevance and communication; and reaction diagnostics to determine what viewers take away from the ad and how creative elements contribute to or distract from advertising effectiveness. Ipsos-ASI's Next*TV test provides a comprehensive approach in which the measures described can be obtained through one testing program **(Exhibit 9-7).**

Test Marketing Companies conduct tests designed to measure their advertising effects in specific test markets before releasing them nationally. The markets chosen are representative of the target audience. For example, a company may test its ads in London, Ontario, Peterborough, Ontario, or Winnipeg, Manitoba, if the demographic and socioeconomic profiles of these cities match the product's market. Many factors may be tested, including reactions to the ads (for example, alternative copy points), the effects of various budget sizes, or special offers. The ads run in finished form in the media where they might normally appear, and effectiveness is measured after the ads run.

The advantage of test marketing of ads is realism. Regular viewing environments are used and the testing effects are minimized. A high degree of control can be attained if the test is designed successfully. The disadvantages of test marketing measures are cost and time. Few firms have the luxury of spending months or years and upwards of a million dollars on such a test. In addition, there is always the fear that competitors may discover and intervene in the research process. Test marketing can provide substantial insight into the effectiveness of advertising if care is taken to minimize the negative aspects of such tests.

Single-Source Tracking More sophisticated approaches are **single-source tracking methods** that track the behaviours of consumers from the television set to the checkout counter. Participants in a

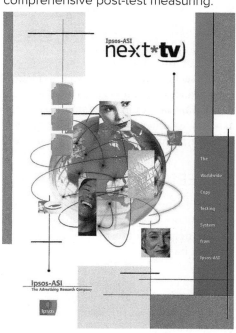

Exhibit 9-7 Ipsos-ASI offers comprehensive post-test measuring.

Source: Ipsos

Exhibit 9-8 Firefly (www.fireflymb.com) was created by Millward Brown to measure brand success through tracking studies.

Source: Firefly Millward Brown

designated area are given a card that identifies their household and gives the research company their demographics. The households are split into matched groups; one group receives an ad while the other does not, or alternative ads are sent to each. Their purchases are recorded from the bar codes of the products bought. Commercial exposures are then correlated with purchase behaviours. The single-source method can be used to post-test ads by tracking the effects of increased ad budgets and different versions of ad copy to see the effects on various dependent measures and sales. Decades after implementation, single-source data fulfilled its claim for effective ad testing.[15]

Tracking Studies A useful and adaptable form of post-testing involves tracking the effects of the ad campaign by taking measurements at regular intervals. **Tracking studies** measure the effects of advertising on awareness, recall, interest, specific copy points, and attitudes toward the ad and/or brand as well as purchase intentions. Personal interviews, phone surveys, mall intercepts, and even mail surveys have been used. Sample sizes typically range from 250 to 500 cases per period (usually quarterly or semiannually). Tracking studies yield perhaps the most valuable information available to the marketing manager for assessing current programs and planning for the future. (See **Exhibit 9-8**.)

Tracking studies can be tailored to each specific campaign and/or situation. A standard set of questions can track effects of the campaign over time. Tracking studies have also been used to measure the differential impact of varying budget sizes, the effects of flighting, and the effects of each medium and all media combined. Finally, when designed properly, tracking studies offer a high degree of reliability and validity.[16] The problems of recall and recognition measures are inherent in tracking studies as well, since many other factors may affect both brand and advertising recall. Despite these limitations, however, tracking studies are a very effective means of assessing the effects of advertising campaigns.

LO5 IMC Planning: Program for Measuring Effectiveness

In this section, we offer prescriptions for managers planning evaluative research. Some time ago, the largest U.S. ad agencies endorsed a set of principles aimed at improving the research used in preparing and testing ads.[17] The nine **PACT (Positioning Advertising Copy Testing)** principles shown in **Figure 9-2** are intended to guide research that assesses whether the ad campaign achieves its objectives. This point of view is consistent with DAGMAR (introduced in Chapter 5) but provides more specific research suggestions.

CRITERIA FOR EFFECTIVE RESEARCH

When testing methods are compared to the criteria established by PACT, it is clear that the principles important to good copy testing can be accomplished. Principle 1 (providing measurements relative to the objectives sought) and Principle 2 (determining at the start how the results will be used) are consistent with DAGMAR (Chapter 5) and are basic advertising management prescriptions along with Principle 6 (providing equivalent test ads). Principles 3, 5, and 7 are in the control of the researcher. Principle 3 (providing multiple measurements) may require a larger budget to make sure additional questions are asked. Likewise, Principle 5 (exposing the test ad more than once) can be accomplished with a proper research design. It might seem that Principle 7 (providing a nonbiasing exposure) would be easy to accomplish, however, lab measures are artificial and vulnerable to testing effects while offering control, while field measures are realistic with less control. Research should likely find a

Figure 9-2 Positioning Advertising Copy Testing (PACT)

1. Provide relevant measurements to the advertising objectives.
2. Agree how the results will be used in advance of each specific test.
3. Provide multiple measures to assess ad performance.
4. Apply a communication response model (reception of stimuli, comprehension, response).
5. Determine whether the advertising stimulus is exposed more than once.
6. Require evaluation of alternative finished ad copy.
7. Ensure controls to avoid biasing effects of the exposure context.
8. Account for sample definition considerations.
9. Demonstrate reliability and validity.

balance by using both types over time. Principle 8 (sample definition) requires sound research methodology; any test should use the target audience to assess an ad's effectiveness. If a study is properly designed, and by that we mean it addresses Principles 1 through 8, it should be both reliable and valid. Principle 9 (concern for reliability and validity) includes two critical distinctions between good and bad research, however most of the measures discussed are lacking in at least one of these criteria.

Principle 4—which states that the research should be guided by a model of human response to communications that encompasses reception, comprehension, and behavioural response—requires careful consideration because it is the principle least addressed by practising researchers. Even though response models (recall Chapter 4 and 5) have existed for many years, few if any common research methods attempt to integrate them into their methodologies. Models that do claim to measure such factors as attitude change or brand preference change have problems that limit their reliability. An effective measure must include a relationship to the communications process.

GUIDELINES FOR EFFECTIVE TESTING

Good tests of advertising effectiveness must address the nine principles established by PACT. One of the easiest ways to accomplish this is by following the decision sequence model in formulating promotional plans.

- *Apply a consumer response model.* Early in this text we reviewed hierarchy of effects models and cognitive response models, which provide an understanding of communication effects that are used to establish communication goals. We also presented Rossiter and Percy's model for understanding the processing stage and setting communication objectives that could also be a basis for measurement.

- *Establish communication objectives.* It is nearly impossible to show the direct impact of advertising on sales. The marketing objectives established for the promotional program are not good measures of communication effectiveness. On the other hand, attainment of communication objectives can be measured and leads to the accomplishment of marketing objectives.

- *Use a pretest and a post-test.* From a cost standpoint—both actual cost outlays and opportunity costs—pretesting makes sense. It may be the difference between success and failure of the campaign or the product. But it should work in conjunction with a post-test, which avoids the limitations of pretests, uses much larger samples, and takes place in more natural settings. Post-testing may be required to determine the ad or campaign effectiveness.

- *Utilize multiple measures.* Attempts to measure the ad effectiveness focus on one dependent variable—perhaps sales, recall, or recognition. As noted earlier in this chapter, advertising has a variety of effects on the consumer, and a thorough assessment of ad effectiveness requires a number of measures.

- *Implement quality research.* It is critical to understand research methodology. What constitutes a good design? Is it valid and reliable? Does it measure what we need it to? There is no shortcut to this criterion, and there is no way to avoid it if you want to measure the effects of advertising.

A major study sponsored by the Advertising Research Foundation (ARF) involving interviews with 12,000 to 15,000 people addressed these issues.[18] While we do not have the space to analyze this study here, note that the research was designed to evaluate measures of copy tests, compare copy testing procedures, and examine the PACT principles. Information on this study has been published in a number of academic and trade journals and by the ARF.

Objectives Summary

the decisions for measuring promotional message effectiveness.

oduced decisions concerning measuring promotional message effectiveness. This information is critical for planning the next period, since program adjustments are based on evaluation of current strategies. We suggest that research measuring the ad effectiveness is important to the promotional program and should be an integral part of the planning process. We indicated that creative strategy decisions, creative tactics decisions, and the messages associated with IMC tools are important for testing. Whether a lab or field test is required should also be determined. While there are many choices for research, a comprehensive, yet expensive, evaluation program would test all message variables with both lab and field methods. Moreover, research could occur prior to a campaign (i.e., pretest) or after the campaign (i.e., post-test).

 Describe what is measured to assess promotional message effectiveness.

The chapter reviewed the types of questions asked in the pretest and post-test approaches used to assess whether an ad or ad campaign is effective in terms of message processing and communication effects. Both of these domains are relevant for both pretest research and post-test research, although the wording and structure changes slightly. Comprehensive research applies a response model that accounts for both processing and communication effects and measures all aspects.

LO3 Evaluate pretest approaches for measuring promotional message effectiveness.

The chapter described research methods that cover the stages of developing a promotional program. Concept tests are used to evaluate initial ideas for creative strategies and promotional messages. Comprehension and reaction tests along with consumer juries appeared useful to testing rough or preliminary examples of print ads and television storyboards. Finished ads are also tested prior to launching the campaign. Investment in these tests reassures managers so that costly media buys can be avoided. We reviewed portfolio tests, readability tests, and dummy advertising vehicles for evaluating completed print ads. Finished broadcast ads can be examined with theatre tests, on-air tests, and physiological measures.

LO4 Evaluate post-test approaches for measuring promotional message effectiveness.

Evaluations after the ads have been launched, known as post-tests, offer greater confirmation of the promotion effectiveness. Print ad post-tests include inquiry tests, recognition tests, and recall tests. Broadcast post-tests include day-after recall tests, comprehensive measures, test marketing, single-source tracking studies, and tracking studies. Single-source research data offer strong potential for improving the effectiveness of ad measures since commercial exposures and reactions may be correlated to actual purchase behaviours.

 Appraise the requirements of proper effectiveness research.

Finally, we reviewed the criteria (defined by PACT) for sound research and suggested ways to accomplish effective studies. It is important to recognize that different measures of effectiveness may lead to different results. Depending on the criteria used, one measure may show that an ad or promotion is effective while another states that it is not. This is why clearly defined objectives, evaluations occurring both before and after the campaigns are implemented, and the use of multiple measures are critical to determining the true effects of an IMC program.

Review Questions

1. Discuss the differences between pretesting and post-testing, and lab testing and field testing.

2. What measures should a marketer use to assess effectiveness for message processing and for communication effects?

3. Why might a firm use theatre testing, on-air tests, and physiological measures to pretest its finished broadcast ads?

4. Why is it useful for an advertiser to do tracking research?

5. Why are the PACT criteria important for testing effectiveness?

Applied Questions

1. Select a popular ad campaign and explain whether it should have tested different creative strategy options or different creative tactics options.

2. Select an ad from the book and describe the questions that should be asked for a post-test for processing and communication effects.

3. Explain why you would or would not want to personally participate in a focus group of a rough ad.

4. Explain why you would or would not want to personally complete a tracking study questionnaire about a major ad campaign (e.g., Telus).

5. For any of the print ads located in the previous chapters, design a testing approach based on the final section of this chapter.

CHAPTER TEN

Media Planning and Budgeting for IMC

LEARNING OBJECTIVES

LO1 Illustrate how a media plan is developed.

LO2 Explain the process and identify the decisions for implementing media strategies.

LO3 Explain the process and identify the decisions for implementing media tactics.

LO4 Distinguish among the theoretical and managerial approaches for media budget setting.

LO5 Apply the methods for allocating the media budget to relevant IMC tools and market situations.

Disruption in Canadian Media

It is no surprise to the average student that the Internet pervades their media consumption; this is true with older Canadians as well. As will be seen in this chapter, Internet media accounted for half of all reported advertising revenue of $13.6 billion in Canada during 2017. The major players like Facebook and Google received approximately half of the $6.8 billion spent on display, video, and search ads. The consequences of this disruption in Canadian media are significant, and organizations and individuals voiced their concerns during 2018.

The significant amount of ad revenue going to foreign-based media organizations meant a drastic reduction of ad revenue going to Canadian media organizations. For example, magazine and newspaper media received about $3 billion less in 2017 compared to a decade ago, almost the exact amount going to the digital giants. Those concerned with this trend focused on the loss of employment of journalists, the erosion of Canadian culture, and the future viability of a healthy media industry in our country.

The details of this situation involve certain financial implications. First, Facebook and Google are not legally required to charge sales tax to Canadians advertising with this media. In theory, these Canadian advertisers are obligated to remit the sales tax but virtually none do. In comparison, Canadians advertising with Canadian media companies are charged sales tax. Interestingly, the federal government spent more on its advertising with Facebook and Google than with Canadian media in 2017, sending money flowing out of the country while communicating with its own citizens.

In response to this issue, the Quebec government required these companies to remit provincial sales tax starting in 2019. Google said it would collect sales taxes if legally required to do so. As part of a worldwide change to sell advertising locally, Facebook announced it would remit sales tax if a Canadian advertiser worked with a local sales agent; however, ads placed with the online self-serve tool would not be charged tax.

The second financial implication is that Canadian advertisers using foreign media to reach Canadians are not permitted to deduct the cost as a expense for established broadcast and print media. However, since the Internet started two decades ago, no federal government amended the law to include digital media. Canada is one of a few OECD countries not having adjusted their laws to address this issue. In response to this issue, a Senate committee suggested the government should revisit the tax law for digital media.

Finally, those voicing their concerns also raised the issue of thousands of journalism jobs lost, especially in smaller towns and cities who lost their local media. Another concern raised is that less revenue going toward news media risks public debate and puts democracy at risk. Perhaps these and the financial consequences might alter the course of media buying in Canada in the future.

Question:

1. How do you as a consumer of media or as a citizen feel about the issues raised?

Planning when, where, and how a message will be delivered is a complex and involved process resulting in a media plan. Its purpose is to identify and justify the decisions that will deliver the message to the target audience cost-efficiently and will communicate the product, brand, and/or service message effectively. This chapter illustrates the media planning process, expresses the development of decisions for media strategy and tactics, and distinguishes approaches of setting and allocating an IMC budget. We include budget setting for IMC in this chapter because of the inherent trade-off between media decisions and financial resources.

Media planning historically occurred within advertising but it is applicable to all IMC tools. For example, advertising media direct visitors to a brand's website or digital alternatives like unique social media vehicles. In fact, much of the media planning process is consistent with delivering digital messages. Communication of a sales promotion generally requires media delivery so consumers are aware of the offer and can act upon it. Public relations campaigns use media planning principles to encourage visits to events or participation in brand activities. Thus, the media planning and budgeting decisions with reference to advertising described in this chapter are directly used for or transferred to other IMC tools.

Media Planning

In this section, we provide an overview of media planning to highlight the context in which messages are delivered, describe the content of a media plan to understand how its content is consistent with other elements of IMC planning, and indicate the challenges with media planning not found in other areas of IMC planning.

OVERVIEW

Media planning is the series of decisions involved in delivering the promotional message to prospective purchasers and/or users of the product or brand. One primary decision is the type of media selected among broadcast (i.e., television, radio), print (i.e., newspaper, magazine), out-of-the-home (i.e., outdoor, transit, place-based), and Internet content publishers and social media. Each offers strengths and limitations that media planners consider in light of the marketing communication problem or opportunity; this is quite a challenge for most planners! In fact, the decisions become more complicated when choosing among alternatives within the same medium, like different television stations or shows and different social media vehicles.

Figure 10-1 illustrates the main options, summarizes the net advertising revenue of recent years, and shows that the total of reported media continued to grow. This table does not include advertising media not reported, meaning that the total is substantially above the levels shown. This snapshot demonstrates the significant shift in revenue away from print to digital that emerged very noticeably in 2010. By way of example, the federal government spent $29.6 million in 2017 with the following allocations in millions: $6.3 TV, $2.6 radio, $2.4 newspaper, $0.5 magazine, $1 out-of-home, and $16.8 Internet for display, social, and search engine.[1] The government's trend to digital continued into 2018 reflecting similar private sector activity.

Academic research of this primary media planning decision examines the optimal expenditure level for each media and the right combination of media since these decisions influence both communication and financial results. A study of the SUV market concluded that national image-oriented messages on TV and print positively influenced brand loyal customers, and tactical promotional messages of the same media positively influenced brand switching consumers.[2] Another study compared the effects of national advertising through broadcast and print media, regional advertising in local TV and local newspapers, and online advertising. It discovered that all three contributed positively to long-term profitability, but each contributed negatively to one another, indicating the importance of planners selecting an optimal allocation among choices.[3] Finally, practical research concluded that multiple media plans achieve stronger communication effects and produce stronger financial results provided there is a unified creative across exposures. This holds true for campaigns directed to all demographic audiences using established broadcast and print media with digital media.[4]

Figure 10-1 Net advertising revenues ($ millions)

Media	2011	2013	2015	2017
Television	3,682	3,537	3,345	3,195
Radio	1,576	1,600	1,576	1,495
Magazine	496	486	434	175
Daily Newspaper	2,216	1,909	1,424	1,001
Community Newspaper	1,211	1,027	881	776
Newspaper (total)	*3,427*	*2,936*	*2,305*	*1,777*
Out-of-Home	484	514	542	624
Internet	2,674	3,418	4,604	6,771
Total	**11,944**	**12,106**	**12,399**	**13,584**

Another factor to consider when selecting media involves the degree to which the effect of each media continues beyond the initial exposure. Thus, the concept of a carryover effect discussed in Chapter 5 is therefore very relevant for initial media planning. One study found that the communication effect of billboard and newspaper ads lasted for 2.2 and 1.4 weeks respectively.[5] Another study established standard carryover effects that managers apply to different types of media. The overall conclusion is that long-term media carryover effects are four times stronger than short-term effects.[6] At the campaign level using multiple media, the carryover effect averages three months.[7] The implication of this for media planning is that the right media expenditures can significantly improve a brand's future results.

Decisions made during the media planning process build on past promotional decisions such as selecting target audiences, establishing objectives, and formulating creative strategies shown in the planning model of Chapter 1 and explained in the first half of this book. The media plan comprises media objectives, media strategy, and media tactics and follows a similar development path as other promotional decisions but focuses on the best way to deliver the message. **Media objectives** are derived from the communication objectives and guide the other two media decisions. **Media strategy** decisions involve the media selected, target audience coverage, geographic coverage, scheduling, and reach and frequency. **Media tactics** decisions concern media vehicles selected, relative cost estimates, specific scheduling points shown in a blocking chart, and any additional execution details. These decisions of the media plan are presented in **Figure 10-2**. Although this template shows a few media for illustrative purposes, the general process is similar for all media.

Media planning occurs for advertising, but it is also a part of other IMC tool decisions. Sales promotions require media expenditure to communicate the offers available or for distribution. Public relations activities use media to communicate corporate activities with respect to sponsorship or community events. A number of media are available for direct marketing. In general, the decisions for media strategy and media tactics are applicable for IMC activities beyond advertising. Finally, media planning faces the challenge of optimizing the attainment of communication and behavioural objectives by allocating a prescribed budget for advertising and IMC tools. In fact, marketing managers are under significant pressure to spend wisely in the promotional domain, as the marketing task has become more financially accountable and firms calculate a return on marketing investment (ROMI).[8]

MEDIA PLAN

The media plan documents the decisions for finding the best way to get the advertiser's message to the market. In a basic sense, the goal of the media plan is to find the combination of media that enables the marketer to communicate the message in the most effective manner to the largest number of the target audience at the lowest cost. In this section, we review the media plan content regarding media objectives, media strategy, and media tactics.

Media Objectives Just as the situation analysis leads to establishment of marketing and communication objectives, it should also lead to specific media objectives. The media objectives are not ends in themselves. Rather, they are derived from and designed to lead to the attainment of communication and behavioural objectives, and contribute to achieving marketing objectives. Media objectives are the goals for the media program and should be limited to those that can be accomplished through media strategies. We now present examples of media objectives that are *derived* from three communication and two behavioural objectives.

Category Need

- Select media to sufficiently demonstrate how the target audience requires the product category.
- Provide sufficient number of exposures to ensure 80 percent of target audience understands the need for the product category.

Brand Awareness

- Select media to provide coverage of 80 percent of the target audience over a six-month period.
- Provide sufficient number of exposures to ensure 60 percent target audience brand recognition.
- Concentrate advertising during the target audience's peak purchasing time.

Brand Attitude

- Select media to ensure that 40 percent of the target audience have favourable beliefs regarding the brand's benefits and have positive emotions associated with the brand.
- Schedule creative executions over six months to heighten emotions associated with the brand and minimize message fatigue.

10-2 Activities involved in developing the media plan

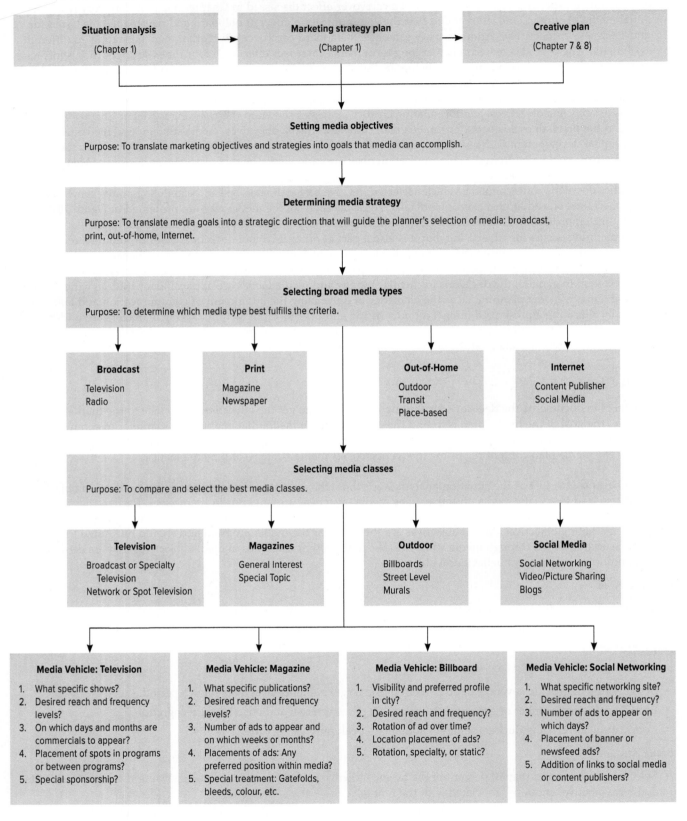

Brand Trial

- Select media to allow immediate purchase of brand.
- Schedule sufficient number of opportunities for target audience brand engagement.

Brand Repeat Purchase

- Select media to remind target audience of brand purchase.
- Provide sufficient advertising throughout the year to minimize target audience switching.

The content and number of media objectives are at the promotional planner's discretion. These examples illustrate the degree to which the link between objectives is not an easy step. The media objectives give direction for the media strategy and tactics decisions. After implementation, marketers need to assess whether or not they were successful. Measures of effectiveness must consider two factors: (1) How well did these strategies achieve the media objectives? (2) How well did this media plan contribute to attaining the overall marketing and communications objectives? If the strategies were successful, they should be used in future plans. If not, their flaws should be analyzed.

Media Strategy As **Figure 10-2** indicates, the primary media strategy decision concerns the use of media, moving from a broad perspective to a more specific one. The **medium** is the general category of available delivery systems, which includes broadcast media (like TV and radio), print media (like newspapers and magazines), out-of-home media (like transit, outdoor, and place-based), and Internet media (like content publishers and social media). **Media type** refers to the individual media within a medium, so TV is a media type, as is radio, and the term is usually shortened to "media." After or during this evaluation, the media planner will consider the relative strengths and limitations of broad **media class** options.

In making the media strategy decisions, a media planner will consider the strategic implications of three concepts. **Reach** is a measure of the number of different audience members exposed at least once to a media vehicle in a given period of time. **Coverage** refers to the potential audience that might receive the message through a vehicle. Coverage relates to potential audience; reach refers to the actual audience delivered. (The importance of this distinction will become clearer later in this chapter.) Finally, **frequency** refers to the number of times the receiver is exposed to the media vehicle in a specified period.

Media Tactics After the general strategic direction of the media plan has been established, the media planner looks to more specific media decisions like the media vehicle. The **media vehicle** is the specific carrier within a media class. For example, *Maclean's* is a print vehicle; *Hockey Night in Canada* is a television vehicle. As described in later chapters, each vehicle has its own characteristics as well as its own relative strengths and limitations. Specific decisions must be made about the value of each in delivering the message.

While making the media vehicle decision, the media planner evaluates the options carefully to maximize coverage, reach, and frequency, and to minimize costs. For example, according to **Figure 10-2**, once print has been established, the media planner has to decide which specific magazine(s) to select. In addition, certain placement factors need to be carefully evaluated. The tactical decisions include relative cost estimates that may lead to refinements in the allocation of the media dollars. Finally, the complete plan is summarized in a blocking chart. The chart may indicate gaps in media coverage or another concern that would lead the media planner to perform additional evaluation prior to completing the media plan.

MEDIA PLANNING CHALLENGES

Since media planning is a series of decisions, a number of challenges contribute to the difficulty of establishing the plan and reduce its effectiveness. These problems include insufficient information, inconsistent terminologies, need for flexibility, role of media planners, and difficulty measuring effectiveness.

Insufficient Information A great deal of information exists about markets and media, but media planners require more than is available. Some data are not measured, either because they cannot be or because measuring them would be too expensive. The timing of measurements is also a problem; audience measures are taken only at specific times of the year for most media. This information is then generalized to succeeding months, so planning decisions are based on past data that may not reflect current behaviours. Think about planning for TV advertising for the fall season. There are no data on the audiences of new shows, and audience information taken on existing programs may not indicate how these programs will do in the fall as most shows eventually lose their audience.

Inconsistent Terminologies Problems arise because of different ways media express their price, and the standards of measurement used to establish these costs are not always consistent. For example, print media may present cost-efficiency data in terms of the cost to reach a thousand people (cost per thousand, or CPM), while broadcast and outdoor media use the cost per ratings point (CPRP). Audience information that is used as a basis for these costs has also been collected by different methods. Finally, terms that actually mean something different (such as *reach* and *coverage*) may be used synonymously, adding to the confusion.

Need for Flexibility Most media plans are written annually so that all participants are well informed and results can be measured against objectives. However, media planners juggle between requiring a document for action and needing flexibility due to changes in the marketing environment. An opportunity to advertise within a new media vehicle might arise and the planner may shift its expenditure from one medium to another. A competitor may spend more money in certain media and the planner decides a change is required to defend against the threat. Preliminary decisions may not be feasibly implemented in terms of medium availability, thus requiring an adjustment. Poor audience size data in a media vehicle may necessitate a movement of money to another.

Role of Media Planners Media planners face expectations from other organizational players. Procurement specialists put extensive pressure on the media decisions in an effort to save money. Clients request media plans prior to contracting services. Decision makers of all the main IMC tools look to media planners to implement decisions instead of being decision-making participants.

Difficulty Measuring Effectiveness Because of the potential inaccuracies of measuring the effectiveness of advertising and promotions, it is also difficult to determine the relative effectiveness of media or media vehicles. While progress has occurred across most media, the media planner must usually balance quantitative data with subjective judgments based on experience when comparing media alternatives. The next section explores how media strategies are developed and ways to increase their effectiveness.

IMC Perspective 10-1 profiles four media agencies that perform the media planning decisions for many clients who are also identified to show how important this kind of agency is for advertisers. *Strategy* recognized each agency with a Media Agency of the Year award.

on winning prompted OMD to run YouTube videos showing how easy winning could be and to show actual winners. OMD led with this media, and then added its usual mix of TV, radio, and out-of-home. OMD believed its senior consultant approach provided a key difference over other media agencies, in-house options, and consulting firms.

Cossette Media, whose clients include Sun Life and Telus, received a bronze award. For Telus, Cossette noted how often teens looked for Wi-Fi when away from home and the agency created a free network in a public location. Upon logging in, the teen was presented with Telus's CSR initiative and invited to take the anti-cyber-bullying pledge. Although, not technically a media buy, the plan took advantage of owned media by virtue of Telus's business. This is an example of Cossette moving to a data focus and the agency believes it

represents the trend of innovation since it recently promoted many younger employees into more senior positions.

And we have a tie for third as PHD also received bronze for its work with clients like BMW and Fountain Tire. This agency believes it moved beyond a traditional media buying firm as it embraced a marketing science approach for its media planning for clients. It is capable in all aspects of digital media and established significant talent to carry on in future. An important differentiator is the agency's use of internal data and research software and its work with other agencies in the Omnicom Media Group in which it belongs.

Question:

1. Explain why a media agency is critical for IMC planning.

Media Strategy Decisions

Having determined what is to be accomplished, media planners consider how to achieve the media objectives by developing and implementing media strategies that consist of five decisions: media mix, target audience coverage, geographic coverage, scheduling, and reach and frequency. This section investigates each of these decisions that are applicable for advertising and media support for other IMC tools.

THE MEDIA MIX

A wide variety of media are available to advertisers in which one or more will be selected. The behavioural and communication objectives, the characteristics of the product or service, the size of the budget, the target audience, and individual preferences are primary factors that determine the combination of media used. While an evaluation of each medium occurs within the perspective of the communication situation a media planner faces, each medium has varying degrees of use across segmentation variables.

The context in which the ad is placed affects viewers' responses, and the creative strategy may require certain media. Therefore, within the media mix a single medium becomes the primary medium where a majority of the budget is spent or the primary effects occur. Because TV and online video provide both sight and sound, they may be more effective in generating emotions than other media. The long-running visual campaign to attract tourists to Newfoundland and Labrador used TV to convey the experience of actually being in the province while viewing. Later, the campaign expanded the delivery online. Magazines may create different responses from newspapers, so we regularly see products in one form of print versus another. In some situations, the media strategy to be pursued may be the driving force behind the creative strategy, as the media and creative departments work closely together to achieve the greatest impact with the audience of the specific media.

As noted at the end of Chapter 5, media planners examine how each medium influences the stages of the consumer decision-making process. For the "All In" campaign for Adidas, the agency viewed its TV and cinema ads and its out-of-home (digital and high impact) as ways of "getting consumers off the couch." The YouTube video and Facebook executions brought all product information together and let consumers enjoy and participate in the "All In" experience. A strong retail presence of display material at Sport Chek and Foot Locker completed the "All In" message.[9]

Figure 10-3 Media and media-usage characteristics

Media Characteristics	Media-Usage Characteristics
Target audience selectivity	Control for selective exposure
Target audience coverage	Attention
Geographic coverage	Creativity for cognitive responses
Scheduling flexibility	Creativity for emotional responses
Reach	Amount of processing time
Frequency	Involvement
Cost efficiency	Clutter
Absolute cost for placement	Media image and production

By employing a media mix, advertisers can add more versatility to their media strategies, since each medium contributes its own distinct advantages. By combining media, marketers can increase coverage, reach, and frequency levels while improving the likelihood of achieving overall communication and marketing goals. Chapters 11, 12, and 13 summarize the characteristics of each medium that make it better or worse for attaining specific communication objectives. We have organized these media and media-usage characteristics as shown in **Figure 10-3**.

A summary of the strengths and limitations of the media reviewed in the next three chapters according to these standard media characteristics and media use characteristics appears in **Figure 10-4**. We continue with these characteristics for direct marketing and Internet marketing in their respective chapters. With competing variables, it becomes clear why media planners spend considerable effort getting the media mix decision right. Finally, keep in mind that these general characteristics guide the media mix decision. Citing them to make a media mix decision is not sufficient. Each strength and limitation needs to be related to the communication situation a specific brand faces, how both types of characteristics will help the brand reach its relevant objectives, and how each medium influences the target audience in the consumer decision-making process. Furthermore, within a given medium there will be variation in the magnitude of the strengths and limitations due to usual examples or the size of the media organization.

Figure 10-4 Strengths and limitations of media characteristics

	Strengths	Limitations
Television	Target audience coverage	Target audience selectivity
	Geographic coverage	Absolute cost
	Scheduling flexibility	Control for selective exposure
	Reach	Amount of processing time
	Frequency	Involvement
	Cost efficiency	Clutter
	Attention	Media image
	Creativity for emotional responses	
	Creativity for cognitive responses	
	Media image	
Radio	Target audience selectivity	Target audience coverage
	Geographic coverage	Control for selective exposure
	Scheduling flexibility	Attention
	Reach	Creativity for emotional responses

	Strengths	Limitations
	Frequency	Amount of processing time
	Cost efficiency	Involvement
	Absolute cost	Clutter
	Creativity for cognitive responses	
	Media image	
Magazines	Target audience selectivity	Target audience coverage
	Geographic coverage	Scheduling flexibility
	Control for selective exposure	Reach
	Attention	Frequency
	Creativity for cognitive responses	Absolute cost
	Creativity for emotional responses	Cost efficiency
	Amount of processing time	Clutter
	Involvement	
	Media image	
Newspapers	Target audience coverage	Target audience selectivity
	Geographic coverage	Control for selective exposure
	Scheduling flexibility	Attention
	Reach	Creativity for emotional responses
	Frequency	Clutter
	Absolute cost	
	Cost efficiency	
	Creativity for cognitive responses	
	Amount of processing time	
	Involvement	
	Media image	
Outdoor	Geographic coverage	Target audience selectivity
	Scheduling flexibility	Target audience coverage
	Reach	Absolute cost
	Frequency	Creativity for cognitive responses
	Cost efficiency	Amount of processing time
	Control for selective exposure	Involvement
	Attention	Clutter
	Creativity for emotional responses	Media image
Transit	Geographic coverage	Target audience selectivity
	Scheduling flexibility	Target audience coverage
	Reach	Attention
	Frequency	Creativity for cognitive responses
	Absolute cost	Creativity for emotional responses
	Cost efficiency	Involvement
	Control for selective exposure	Clutter
	Amount of processing time	Media image

TARGET AUDIENCE COVERAGE

The media planner determines which target audiences should receive the most media emphasis. Developing media strategies involves matching the most appropriate media to this audience by asking, "Through which media and media vehicles can I best get my message to prospective buyers?" The issue here is to get coverage of the audience, as shown in **Figure 10-5**. The optimal goal is full audience coverage, shown in the second pie chart. Business marketing organizations get close to full audience coverage due to the small numbers of customers and potential customers.

More realistically, conditions shown in the third and fourth charts are likely to occur in most marketing situations. In the third chart, the media coverage does not cover the entire target audience, leaving a portion without exposure to the message; this is known as partial coverage. In the fourth chart, the media coverage exceeds the target audience, resulting in overexposure to the message or excessive coverage (also called **waste coverage**). If media coverage reaches people who are not sought as buyers and are not potential users, then it is wasted; waste coverage reaches people who are not potential buyers and/or users. Consumers may not be part of the intended target audience but may still be considered as potential customers—for example, those who buy the product as a gift for someone else.

The promise of online advertising is that Internet media attains full coverage better than other media. However one practitioner with decades of media expertise, including digital, cautioned practitioners that messaging is getting too targeted online. In the interest of expediting short-term sales with direct messages, brands missed the opportunity for long-term brand building.[10]

The goal of the media planner is to extend media coverage to as many members of the target audience as possible while minimizing the amount of waste coverage. The situation usually involves trade-offs. Sometimes one has to live with less coverage than desired; other times, the most effective media expose people not sought. In this instance, waste coverage is justified because the media employed are likely to be the most effective means of delivery available and the cost of the waste coverage is exceeded by the value gained from their use.

The target audience coverage decision relies on primary research and published (secondary) sources. This research can show the number of consumers for a particular product category across demographic variables and their media consumption habits. We review audience information in Chapters 11, 12, and 13, as each medium has its own method.

When examining these data, media planners focus on percentage figures and index numbers versus raw numbers for three reasons: (1) The numbers provided may not be specific enough for their needs. (2) They question the numbers provided because of the data collection methods. (3) The index numbers and percentages provide a comparative view of the market.

Overall, the **index number** is considered a good indicator of the potential of the market. This number is derived from the formula

$$\text{Index} = \frac{\text{Percentage of users in a demographic segment}}{\text{Percentage of population in the same segment}} \times 100$$

An index number over 100 means use of the product is proportionately greater in that segment than in one that is average (100) or below average (less than 100). Depending on the strategy, marketers use this information to target groups consuming the product, or to identify a different group that is using the product less and attempt to develop

Figure 10-5 Marketing coverage possibilities

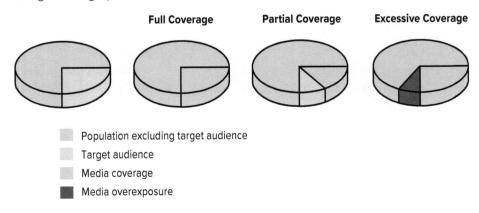

Full Coverage Partial Coverage Excessive Coverage

☐ Population excluding target audience
☐ Target audience
☐ Media coverage
■ Media overexposure

that segment. While the index is helpful, it should not be used alone. Percentages and product usage figures are also needed to get an accurate picture of the market. A very high index for a particular segment doesn't mean it is the only attractive segment to target since the high index may be due to a low denominator (i.e., small proportion of the population in this segment).

Understanding coverage in a multimedia environment is proving difficult for media planners since consumers frequently consume more than one medium at a time. This is a significant trend since coverage historically implied a reasonably close association with exposure and processing of the advertising message. Clearly, the communication is limited even further if other media are competing for the people's attention. However, communication is intensified for an individual brand if viewers go to a social media site after a TV ad prompt, thereby affecting subsequent TV ads for other brands.

One research study regarding media coverage for a beverage product concluded that TV, gift-packs, in-store displays, and outdoor proved to be the right mix since it covered a broad base of category users. It also found that the best coverage for heavy users included public relations, websites, sampling, print, radio, online, and events. Brand growth should avoid media that are associated with heavy category usage. Social media and word-of-mouth proved strong for continued category usage, but not brand growth.[11] These findings imply that both brand and category factors as well as the previous decisions—marketing objectives, target audience, behavioural objectives, and communication objectives—will influence the media mix decision and target audience coverage.

GEOGRAPHIC COVERAGE

The question of where to promote relates to geographic considerations. Should we allocate promotional monies to markets where the brand is already the leader to maintain market share, or does more potential exist in markets where the firm is not doing as well and there is room to grow? In the case of the Canadian Tourism Commission, it directed 10 percent of its $57 million budget toward the United States in 2015 since visiting Canada appeared to give good value because of the weaker Canadian dollar.[12] Perhaps the best answer is that the firm should spend advertising and promotion dollars where they will be the most effective—that is, in those markets where they will achieve the desired objectives. Two useful calculations that marketers examine to make this decision are the Brand Development Index and the Category Development Index.

The **Brand Development Index (BDI)** helps marketers factor the rate of the brand's sales by geographic area into the media decision process.

$$BDI = \frac{\text{Percentage of brand to total Canadian sales in the market}}{\text{Percentage of total Canadian population in the market}} \times 100$$

The BDI compares the percentage of the brand's total sales in a given market area with the percentage of the total population in the market to determine the sales potential for that brand in that geographic area. An example of this calculation is shown in **Figure 10-6**. The higher the index number, the more potential exists for the brand. In the case of this market, the index number indicates a high potential for brand development since it is well above the average of 100. An index number below 100 would indicate a market below average for the brand.

Figure 10-6 Calculating BDI

$$BDI = \frac{\text{Percentage of total brand sales in Ontario}}{\text{Percentage of total Canadian population in Ontario}} \times 100$$
$$= \frac{50\%}{34\%} \times 100$$
$$= 147$$

The **Category Development Index (CDI)** is computed in the same manner as the BDI, except it uses information regarding the product category (as opposed to the brand) in the numerator.

$$CDI = \frac{\text{Percentage of product category total sales in market}}{\text{Percentage of total Canadian population in market}} \times 100$$

The CDI provides information on the potential for development of the total product category rather than specific brands. An example of this calculation is shown in **Figure 10-7**. The marketer analyzes the CDI to find out how well the category is doing in one market relative to how well the category is doing in other markets. Again, the higher the index number, the more product category sales potential exists.

Figure 10-7 Calculating CDI

$$CDI = \frac{\text{Percentage of product category sales in Alberta}}{\text{Percentage of total Canadian population in Alberta}} \times 100$$

$$= \frac{8\%}{11\%} \times 100$$

$$= 73$$

A more insightful promotional strategy is developed when combining the CDI and BDI data. **Figure 10-8** shows four potential combinations where each of the CDI and BDI indices are above and below the average and are designated as high and low. For example, high CDI–high BDI is a situation where the market represents good sales potential for both the product category and the brand. In the opposite quadrant, the low CDI–low BDI shows a situation where a marketer likely decides not to advertise since both indices are below average. The other two quadrants show mixed results since one is low and the other is high, providing the manager with an option of building a strong brand in a weak market or building a weak brand in a strong market.

Figure 10-8 Using BDI and CDI indexes

	High BDI	Low BDI
High CDI	High market share Good market potential	Low market share Good market potential
Low CDI	High market share Monitor for sales decline	Low market share Poor market potential

SCHEDULING

Companies would like to keep their advertising in front of consumers at an appropriate level to maintain their behavioural and communications objectives and support their brand positioning strategy. The primary objective of scheduling is to time promotional efforts to coincide with the highest potential buying times and other important brand-building opportunities. For some products, these times are not easy to identify; for others, they are very obvious. Three scheduling methods available to the media planner—continuity, flighting, and pulsing—are shown in **Figure 10-9**.

Continuity refers to a continuous pattern of advertising, which may mean every day, every week, or every month. The key is that a regular (continuous) pattern is developed without gaps or non-advertising periods. It is important to note that continuity is entirely predicated on the time period. For example, placing an ad in the newspaper every

Figure 10-9 Three methods of promotional scheduling

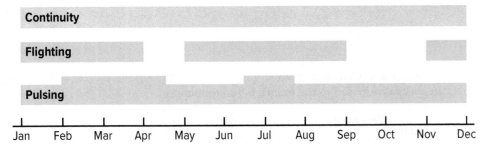

Figure 10-10 Characteristics of scheduling methods

	Advantages	Disadvantages
Continuity	Serves as constant reminder	Higher costs
	Covers entire purchase cycle	Potential for overexposure
	Allows for media priorities (discounts, preferred locations, etc.)	Limited media allocation possible
Flighting	Cost efficiency during purchase cycle	Increased likelihood of wearout
	Allows for inclusion of more than one medium/vehicle with limited budget	Lack of awareness, interest, retention of message during nonscheduled times
	Weighting may offer more exposure and competitive advantage	Vulnerability to competitive efforts during nonscheduled periods
Pulsing	Same as previous two methods	Not required for seasonal/cyclical products

Monday for a whole year is continuous on a weekly basis, but not continuous on a daily basis. Such strategies might be used for advertising for food products, or other products consumed on an ongoing basis without regard for seasonality.

A second method, **flighting**, employs a less regular schedule, with intermittent periods of advertising and non-advertising. In some time periods there are heavier promotional expenditures, and in others there may be no advertising. Snow skis are advertised heavily between October and April; less in May, August, and September; and not at all in June and July. The weekly newspaper placement example could be viewed as flighting on a daily basis since there is no advertising for the other days of the week.

Pulsing is actually a combination of the first two methods. In a pulsing strategy, continuity is maintained, but at certain times promotional efforts are stepped up. In the automobile industry, advertising continues throughout the year but may increase in April (tax refund time), September (when new models are brought out), and the end of the model year. Advantages and disadvantages to each scheduling method are shown in **Figure 10-10**.

As implied above, advertisers decide on the exact days, weeks, or months in which to advertise, so a good media plan provides extensive details on the exact timing of the placement. For example, a brand might want a magazine placement during spring months, TV placement could only occur on weekends, and a planner may decide to place Internet display ads only in the morning. Sport Chek decided to use TV during August to December to coincide with back-to-school, hockey, and holiday gift-giving, and used digital throughout the year.[13]

Another scheduling decision involves the order in which each medium occurs when multiple media are in the plan. Which medium should occur first if TV, magazines, and outdoor are used in the campaign? Alternatively, should all media be placed simultaneously? Media placement constraints remove a planner's ability to completely control this decision, but nevertheless, the order is an important consideration.

REACH AND FREQUENCY

Advertisers usually must trade off reach and frequency because they face budget constraints when trying to attain objectives. They must decide whether to have the message be seen or heard by more people (reach) or by fewer people more often (frequency). This trade-off requires a complex investigation to answer these two questions for any media, and by extension, the whole media plan and the entire IMC plan.

How Much Reach Is Necessary? A universal communication objective is product and/or brand awareness. The more consumers are aware, the more they are likely to consider the brand throughout the decision-making process. Achieving awareness requires reach—that is, exposing the target audience to the message. New brands or products need a very high level of reach since the objective is to make all potential buyers aware. High reach is also desired at later purchase-decision stages since a promotional strategy might use a free sample. An objective of the marketer is to reach a larger number of people with the sample in an attempt to make them learn of the product, use it, and develop a favourable attitude toward it that may lead to an initial brand trial purchase.

Reach is the number of target audience individuals exposed at least once to a media vehicle in a specific time period. Media planners use weekly, monthly, or quarterly time periods that are known as *advertising cycles.* The reach number is usually expressed as a percentage provided the number of target audience individuals is clearly identified.

For example, the most watched TV show each week gets about 3.4 million viewers, according to Numeris, and the population of Canada is about 34 million, according to Statistics Canada as reported in the Media Digest. Thus the reach of an ad placed on this show is approximately 10 percent for the advertising cycle of one week.

$$\text{Reach} = \frac{\text{Number of people watching TV ad}}{\text{Number of people in Canada}} = \frac{3.4 \text{ million}}{34 \text{ million}} = 10\%$$

Reach can be compiled over any time period (i.e., week, month, year), geographically (i.e., city, province), or for any demographic (e.g., women aged 18–35). Reach can also be considered in terms of the stages of the buyer decision-making process and for any other media used for advertising or other IMC tools that have a media plan component. No matter what audience characteristics the media planner works with, the ratio remains as follows:

$$\text{Reach} = \frac{\text{Number of people in target audience exposed to the media vehicle}}{\text{Number of people in target audience}}$$

The concept of reach gets more complex and complicated going beyond the placement of one ad on one TV show. If one ad is placed on one TV show one time, the number of people exposed is the reach (**Figure 10-11A**). In order to achieve high levels of reach, brands use multiple media (e.g., television, Internet). Alternatively, or in addition, brands use multiple media vehicles such as more than one TV station or TV show, or more than one magazine. Thus, it is possible for the target audience to be exposed to an ad more than once with multiple media and multiple media vehicles (**Figure 10-11B**).

The reach of the two shows, as depicted in **Figure 10-11C**, includes a number of people who were reached by both shows. This overlap is referred to as **duplicated reach**. If the ad is placed on two shows, the total number exposed once is **unduplicated reach** (**Figure 10-11D**). Both unduplicated and duplicated reach figures are important. Unduplicated reach indicates potential new exposures, while duplicated reach provides an estimate of frequency since some in the target audience saw the ad multiple times. Media plans should account for both unduplicated reach and duplicated reach, or acknowledge which is used, to provide comprehensive reporting of the media buy.

The amount of reach can be estimated through the information contained in the target audience profile regarding customer group (i.e., loyal users or new category users) and other variables like demographics. Based on this information, media planners would know if the required reach is a niche market requiring a selective 10 percent or a broader audience of moving toward 50 percent, in whatever geographic or timing parameters are decided upon. While reach is an important decision, the duplicated reach resulting in a greater number of exposures for a portion of the target audience leads to the next question: What frequency of exposure is necessary for the ad to be seen and to have a communication effect?

Figure 10-11 Representation of reach and frequency

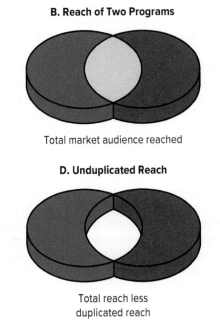

A. Reach of One TV Program

Total market audience reached

B. Reach of Two Programs

Total market audience reached

C. Duplicated Reach

Total market reached
with both shows

D. Unduplicated Reach

Total reach less
duplicated reach

What Frequency Level Is Needed? With respect to media planning, *frequency* carries a particular meaning. **Frequency** is the average number of exposures a target audience individual receives from media vehicles in a specific time period. Frequency is dependent upon how much media target audience individuals consume. It can therefore range substantially, which raises the need to look at average frequency that is derived from a frequency distribution. Continuing with the TV example, ads placed once in each of the top 10 shows in a given week would provide an average frequency of 1.36 (using Numeris data from a randomly selected week).

$$\text{Frequency} = \frac{24 \text{ million exposures across 10 TV shows}}{17.6 \text{ million individuals exposed to ad}} = 1.36 \text{ exposures per person}$$

The 24 million exposures are calculated by adding the numbers of people who watched each show. However, some people watch two or more shows, resulting in fewer people actually exposed to the ad. Thus, the 17.6 million individuals exposed to the ad represent the total number of "unduplicated" viewers for all 10 shows who potentially saw the 24 million exposures.

The 17.6 million is *estimated* by adding the unduplicated viewers for each of the 10 shows. The most watched show was 3.216 million. To that number we add the unduplicated numbers of viewers for all the other nine shows. To calculate unduplicated numbers, we adjust the actual ones downward by a percentage of possible repeat viewers.

The second most watched show reached 2.634 million, resulting in 2.384 million unduplicated viewers [i.e., $2.634 \times (34 - 3.216)/34$]. The percentage of people not watching the first show has an equal chance as those watching the second show. These calculations carry on for each subsequent show so that by the tenth show, the unduplicated audience is reduced; 1.946 million watching the tenth show but only 0.975 million new viewers. These calculations can be done for all media individually and combined across all media, but the general calculation remains as follows:

$$\text{Frequency} = \frac{\text{Total number of exposures}}{\text{Total number of unduplicated individuals exposed to media vehicle}}$$

The example with the Numeris data is calculated with all viewers, but the data could be refined to a specific demographic and/or other variables used to profile the target audience. The general calculation remains the same, but the numbers will change correspondingly to observe the frequency of exposure for the target audience. Furthermore, actually calculating total exposures to estimate average frequency is generally done by computer software as the complexity intensifies exponentially with multiple media vehicles.

The above discussion suggests frequency is the number of times one is exposed to the media vehicle, not necessarily to the ad itself. While one study has estimated that the actual audience for a commercial may be as much as 30 percent lower than that for the program, not all researchers agree.[14] Most advertisers do agree that a 1:1 exposure ratio does not exist. So while the ad may be placed in a certain vehicle, the fact that a consumer has been exposed to that vehicle does not ensure that it has been seen. As a result, the frequency level expressed in the media plan overstates the actual level of exposure to the ad. This overstatement has led some media buyers to refer to the reach of the media vehicle as "opportunities to see" an ad rather than actual exposure to it.

With the calculation of frequency having been defined and illustrated, the question remains of how much frequency is needed within an advertising cycle. Practitioners and academic researchers investigated this question for decades, and **Figure 10-12** summarizes their findings. The conclusion that three exposures within an advertising cycle may be sufficient for communication effects to take hold implies that this average is the minimum; however, anyone in the target

Figure 10-12 The effects of frequency

1. One exposure of an ad to a target group within a purchase cycle has little or no effect.
2. Since one exposure is usually ineffective, the central goal of productive media planning should be to enhance frequency rather than reach.
3. The evidence suggests strongly that an exposure frequency of two within a purchase cycle is an effective level.
4. Beyond three exposures within a brand purchase cycle or over a period of four or even eight weeks, increasing frequency continues to build advertising effectiveness at a decreasing rate but with no evidence of decline.
5. Although there are general principles with respect to frequency of exposure and its relationship to advertising effectiveness, differential effects by brand are equally important.
6. Frequency response principles or generalizations do not vary by medium.
7. The data strongly suggest that wearout is not a function of too much frequency; it is more of a creative or copy problem.

audience who receives only one or two exposures presumably would not be aware of the brand or understand its performance. Therefore, the average exposure level would have to be higher to ensure sufficient communication for all who were exposed to the message. In addition, going beyond three exposures still provides positive effects, as noted in point four. A more recent study concluded that a decline in communication effects did not occur until frequency reached 10.[15]

To understand this situation further, consider a media buy in which 50 percent of the audience is reached one time, 30 percent of the audience is reached five times, and 20 percent of the audience is reached 10 times. The average frequency of this media buy is 4, which is slightly more than the number established as effective. Yet a full 50 percent of the audience receives only one exposure. Presumably a considerable portion of the money spent on advertising has been wasted because so many in the target audience were not exposed to the message.

Determining Effective Reach and Frequency Since marketers have budget constraints, they must decide whether to increase reach at the expense of frequency or increase the frequency of exposure but to a smaller audience. A number of factors influence this decision. For example, a new product or brand introduction will attempt to maximize reach, particularly unduplicated reach, to quickly create a high awareness level. At the same time, for a high-involvement product or one whose benefits are not obvious, a certain level of frequency is needed to achieve effective reach.

Effective reach represents the percentage of a vehicle's audience reached at each effective frequency increment. This concept is based on the assumption that one exposure to an ad may not be enough to convey the desired message. As we saw earlier, no one knows the exact number of exposures necessary for an ad to make an impact, although advertisers have settled on three as the minimum. Effective reach (exposure) is shown in the shaded area in **Figure 10-13** in the range of three to 10 exposures. Fewer than three exposures is considered insufficient reach, while more than 10 is considered overexposure and thus ineffective reach. This exposure level is no guarantee of effective communication; different messages may require more or fewer exposures.

Perhaps the best advice for determining *effective frequency* is offered by Ostrow, who recommended the following:[16] Instead of using **average frequency**, the marketer should decide what minimum frequency goal is needed to reach the advertising objectives effectively and then maximize reach at that frequency level. To determine **minimum effective frequency**, one must consider marketing factors, message factors, and media factors. (See **Figure 10-14**.) While the application of minimum effective frequency occurs in advertising, concern still remains with its use.[17] In contrast, with the growth of more media outlets and enhanced syndicated data, minimum effective frequency within and across combinations of media provides opportunity for more efficient and effective use of media expenditures.[18]

Using Gross Ratings Points A summary indicator that combines the reach (duplicated) and the average frequency during an advertising cycle (e.g., one week, or four weeks) and is commonly used for reference is known as a **gross ratings point (GRP)**. The GRP can best be understood by an equation:

$$1 \text{ GRP} = \text{Reach of } 1\% \times \text{Frequency of } 1$$

Like both reach and frequency, GRP calculations are time dependent so that one can plan, calculate, or purchase a GRP on a weekly or monthly basis. We return to a TV placement example to see how this works. If one ad is placed on a

Figure 10-13 Graph of effective reach

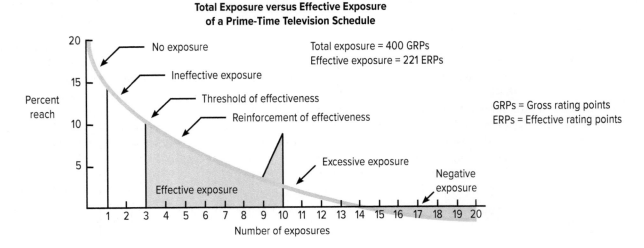

Figure 10-14 Factors important in determining frequency levels

Marketing Factors

- *Brand history.* New brands generally require higher frequency.
- *Brand share.* The higher the brand share, the lower the frequency required.
- *Brand loyalty.* The higher the loyalty, the lower the frequency required.
- *Purchase cycles.* Shorter purchasing cycles require higher frequency to attain awareness.
- *Usage cycle.* Products consumed frequently usually require a higher frequency.
- *Share of voice.* Higher frequency is required with many competitors.
- *Target audience.* The target group's ability to learn and retain messages affects frequency.

Message or Creative Factors

- *Message complexity.* The simpler the message, the less frequency required.
- *Message uniqueness.* The more unique the message, the lower the frequency required.
- *New versus continuing campaigns.* New campaigns require higher frequency.
- *Image versus product sell.* Image ads require higher frequency than product sell ads.
- *Message variation.* A single message requires less frequency; multiple messages require more.
- *Wearout.* Higher frequency may lead to wearout.
- *Advertising units.* Larger units of advertising require less frequency than smaller ones.

Media Factors

- *Clutter.* More frequency is needed to break through when a media has more advertising.
- *Editorial environment.* Less frequency is needed if the ad is consistent with the editorial environment.
- *Attentiveness.* Media vehicles with higher attention levels require less frequency.
- *Scheduling.* Continuous scheduling requires less frequency than does flighting or pulsing.
- *Number of media used.* Fewer media used requires lower frequency.
- *Repeat exposures.* Media that allow for more repeat exposures require less frequency.

top Canadian show with 10 percent reach, then the company has purchased 10 GRPs. If the show happens to be between 60 minutes and three hours (e.g., a sports game), then the number of GRPs could grow to 20 or 30 if the ad is run two or three times, respectively. Of course, this assumes the audience size has remained the same throughout the show.

Extensive amounts of audience data exist and, using computer applications, the planning and scheduling of GRPs is a relatively routine practice. However, most media planners rely on their experience and judgment to complement the quantitative side. GRPs can be calculated for the total population aged 2+, adults 18+, adults 18–34, adults 18–49, or several other measured demographic groups.

Aggregating across multiple shows, media planners can calculate any number of GRPs to achieve their communication objectives. For example, 120 GRPs might be needed in a given week if the planner wants a reach of 30 percent and an average frequency of 4. In this example of 120 GRPs, a media planner would need to run ads on multiple shows and days to achieve these reach and frequency levels.

The purchase of 120 GRPs could mean 60 percent of the audience is exposed twice, or 20 percent of the audience is exposed six times, or 40 percent of the audience is exposed three times, and so on. Thus, for a fixed level of GRPs, there is an inverse relationship between reach and frequency. To know how many GRPs are necessary, the manager chooses the minimum effective frequency and the amount of reach necessary based on the communication and media objectives established from the situation analysis, marketing strategy, and IMC strategy.

The chart in **Figure 10-15** illustrates the trade-off between reach and frequency given a fixed number of GRPs. A purchase of 100 GRPs on one network yields a lower reach—just over 30 percent of the target audience, which translates into a frequency of about 3 ($100 = 33.3 \times 3$). The reach climbs to about 40 percent if two networks are used with a frequency of about 2.5 ($100 = 40 \times 2.5$). The reach then climbs to about 50 percent if three networks are used with a frequency of about 2 ($100 = 50 \times 2$). The increase in reach levels off as the incremental growth of adding more exposure does not affect very many new people in the target audience, and in fact the exposure growth begins to increase the amount of frequency as a greater number within the target audience see the ad more often. For example, at 600 GRPs the reach is 60 percent with a frequency of 10 ($600 = 60 \times 10$).

Figure 10-15 Estimates of reach for network GRPs

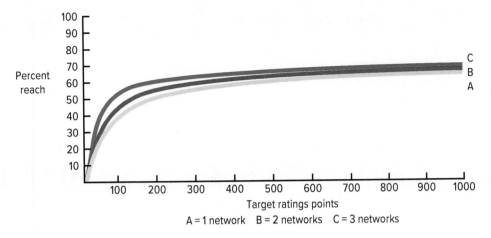

A = 1 network   B = 2 networks   C = 3 networks

LO3 Media Tactics Decisions

Once the initial media strategy has been determined, the marketer addresses three media tactics decisions: media vehicle, relative cost estimates, and blocking chart.

MEDIA VEHICLE

Once the medium or media has been determined, the media planner must consider the most suitable media class and media vehicle. Certain media classes and media vehicles enhance the message because they create a mood that carries over to the communication. The mood is different on each class of TV channels such as sports, comedy, drama, or news. The mood created by magazines like *NUVO, Golf Canada, Canadian Gardening,* and *Style at Home* varies substantially. Each of these special-interest vehicles puts the reader in a particular mood and the promotion of clothing, golf equipment, gardening tools, and home products is affected.

The message may require a specific media and a certain media vehicle to achieve its objectives. Likewise, certain media and vehicles have images that may carry over to the perceptions of messages placed within them. The explanation of these considerations is the **vehicle source effect**, which is defined as the differential impact that the advertising exposure will have on the same audience member if the exposure occurs in one medium versus another.[19] More recent research supported this view and also concluded that "better" advertising content positively influenced attitudes to the media vehicle, thus indicating a symbiotic relationship between advertiser and media vehicle.[20]

Brands look for specific media vehicles when implementing their plans, and Sony's Xperia Ion phone and P&G's Cheer detergent found a good fit with their executions. MTV.ca hosted four episodes of a Sony show that featured artists creating music with unusual items as instruments, all shot with the phone's HD video camera. A little over a half million viewers witnessed the performances and a total of 11 million media impressions ensued. A music video of the band Strange Talk included live links on colourful items (e.g., shirts, leggings); upon clicking, users linked to the Cheer Facebook page to win the item and get a free sample, and received the opportunity to read about the product. Cheer managers looked to young consumers, new users in this category, who wore colourful clothes since that fit with the key benefit claim of the brand. The "Dig It! Get It!" campaign lifted purchase intent by 7 percent and claimed 47,000 new Facebook fans.[21]

An extension of this idea is the development of media engagement, where the media experiences of specific vehicles are identified along the global dimensions: inspiration, trustworthy, life enhancing, social involvement, and personal timeout. The purpose of this more detailed investigation of the media experience is to find a more specific link between the media vehicle and communication and behavioural effects.[22]

Related to the idea of directing messages to customers or non-customers, one author recommends finding a fit between the brand users and the media vehicle selected. Through the use of survey and syndicated data, the researcher concluded that demographic matching of target audience and media vehicle is less effective versus a similarity of brand

and media vehicle users in terms of values. The author suggests that finding media vehicles that brand users are experiencing is possible for most major media.[23]

Once the media vehicle consideration is resolved, the media planner considers other fine-tuning such as the location within a particular medium. In magazines, this could mean the inside front page versus the back page. For TV, it could mean the start or end of a commercial block. Online, the decision could focus on the size of the banner ad or the length of the pre-roll video ad. **IMC Perspective 10-2** identifies award-winning marketing communications where both media strategy and media tactics contributed to their success along with innovation to push the media definition boundary.

IMC PERSPECTIVE 10-2

MEDIA AWARDS WITH A TWIST

The AToMiC awards celebrate the achievements of combined efforts in advertising (A), technology (T), media creativity (M), and content (C). Media, digital, or creative agencies can enter their work for the competition presuming it is AToMiC—meaning the marketing communication is innovative by going against conventional thinking and uses elements in all four areas. We consider notable winners as examples of innovative use of media.

The Canadian Paralympic Committee won the Grand Prix. It encouraged fans to use the "Become a Broadcaster" tool on Facebook and Twitter so that their contacts could see a livestream of any event. The initiative achieved 22,000 events and 990,000 video views for 16,000 hours and fulfilled the objective of ensuring that more Canadians could watch.

When seeking a McDonald's restaurant, consumers usually look for the arches, and that insight paved the way for an out-of-home campaign that reproduced a portion of the arches that acted like directions in messages that said "On your right" or

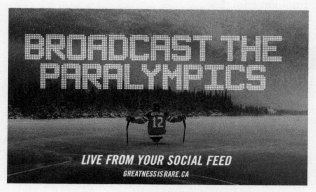

LIVE FROM YOUR SOCIAL FEED
GREATNESSISRARE.CA

©Canadian Paralympic Committee

"Next exit" among others. And speaking of driving and roads, Harley-Davidson created a series of videos showing people's cross-country motorcycle adventures that told a great story of camaraderie.

Fountain Tire identified the most unsafe road in Alberta, and collected data at a gas station along the route. Cars that drove over a mat provided a 3D-mapped sample of their tires to determine their safety. Each driver received a report, and the 31 percent who failed received free tires. Additional data from Waze, Twitter, and the Weather Network shown on digital boards along the road signalled to consumers to get their tires checked. As a result, tire sales increased 8 percent locally.

The spicy sauce, Tabasco, teamed up with a famous chef who transformed the worst-rated take-out food with a few drops of the flavourful liquid. The chef presented the "new" meals at a pop-up restaurant and the agency filmed people's reactions for a two-minute online video that bloggers seeded.

Finally, Tourism Ottawa tried to dispel the belief that Ottawa is a boring city with nothing to do. It invented and launched an ice cream named "Not Vanilla" featuring five flavours that signified tourist attractions. For example, "Rideauculous" picked up on the Rideau Canal as a must-see attraction. The packaging looked boring at first glance, being plain white on the outside, but it was colourful on the inside to symbolize the enjoyment one can have in Ottawa. [You can believe it—it is truthful advertising!]

Question:

1. Which of these media executions appears to be the most innovative?

RELATIVE COST ESTIMATES

The value of any strategy can be determined by how well it delivers the message effectively to the audience with the lowest cost and the least waste. The media planner strives for optimal delivery by balancing costs associated with each of the media strategy decisions. Media planning is inherently a series of trade-offs between reach and frequency or geographic coverage and scheduling, among others. As these trade-offs are investigated and finalized, the media planner estimates and compares costs. Advertising and promotional costs can be categorized in two ways: in terms of absolute cost and relative cost.

The **absolute cost** of the medium or vehicle is the actual total cost required to place the message. For example, magazines quote prices for advertising on a per-page basis. **Relative cost** refers to the relationship between the price paid for advertising time or space and the size of the audience delivered. Relative costs are important because the manager optimizes audience delivery within budget constraints. Since a number of alternatives are available for message delivery, the advertiser evaluates the relative costs associated with these choices. For example, the media planner could compare the relative cost of reaching a member of the target audience in one magazine versus another. This decision can be influenced by the absolute cost of one magazine having a cheaper back page price versus another magazine. As the number of media alternatives rises, the number of comparisons grows considerably, potentially making this a tedious and difficult process. Media planners typically use two calculations—cost per thousand (CPM) and cost per ratings point (CPRP)—to compare both media mix options or media vehicle options.

1. **Cost per thousand (CPM).** Magazines and other media provide cost breakdowns on the basis of cost per thousand people reached. The formula for this computation is

$$CPM = \frac{\text{Cost of ad space (absolute cost)}}{\text{Circulation}} \times 1,000$$

Figure 10-16 provides an example of this computation for two vehicles in the same medium—*Canadian Living* and *Chatelaine*—and shows that *Canadian Living* is a more cost-efficient buy for a comparable full page ad. However, the difference is not substantial enough to influence the decision on which vehicle to select.

Figure 10-16 Cost per thousand computations: *Canadian Living* versus *Chatelaine*

	Canadian Living	Chatelaine
Per-page cost	$52,905	$55,085
Circulation	475,267	440,798
Calculation of CPM	$\frac{\$52,905 \times 1,000}{475,267}$	$\frac{\$55,085 \times 1,000}{440,798}$
CPM	$111.32	$124.97

Like magazines, newspapers use the cost-per-thousand formula to determine relative costs. The sample calculation shown in **Figure 10-17** indicates that the *National Post* costs significantly less to advertise in than does the *Globe and Mail* based on a national advertiser spending $1 million annually.

Figure 10-17 Comparative costs in newspaper advertising

	Globe and Mail	National Post
Cost per page	$56,224	$17,739
Circulation	313,331	188,654
Calculation	$CPM = \frac{\text{Page cost} \times 1,000}{\text{Circulation}}$ $= \frac{\$56,224 \times 1,000}{313,331}$ $= \$179.44$	$\frac{\$17,739 \times 1,000}{188,654}$
CPM	$179.44	$94.03

Some media, such as Internet display ads, quote their prices in terms of CPM. So if a display ad placement has a CPM of $30, the media buyer would select the display ad over these magazine and newspaper examples *if cost efficiency is deemed the only decision criterion.* However, virtually all media placement decisions involve multiple criteria beyond pure cost efficiency. In this case, the sizes of the ads are dramatically different, as other factors would be. A simple paid search result in the United Kingdom for Snickers with a link message consistent with its "Hungry" ad campaign produced a CPM of about $5.[24] While this appears impressive, the message is of low quality with a basic text; however, if the click-through rates to a colourful Internet ad proved strong, the CPM and message quality consideration might look more favourable.

2. **Cost per ratings point (CPRP).** The broadcast media provide a different comparative cost figure, referred to as cost per ratings point or *cost per point (CPP)*, based on the following formula:

$$CPRP = \frac{\text{Cost of commercial time}}{\text{Program rating}}$$

An example of this calculation for a spot ad in a local TV market is shown in **Figure 10-18**. It indicates that Show A would be more cost-effective than Show B or Show C.

Figure 10-18 Comparison of cost per ratings point in a local TV market

	Show A	Show B	Show C
Cost per spot ad	$5,000	$10,000	$16,000
Rating	20	10	40
Calculation	$5,000/20	$10,000/10	$16,000/40
CPRP (CPP)	$250	$1,000	$400

It is difficult to make comparisons across media. What is the broadcast equivalent of cost per thousand? In an attempt to standardize relative costing procedures, the broadcast and newspaper media have begun to provide costs per thousand, using the following formulas:

$$\text{Television: } \frac{\text{Cost of 1 unit of time} \times 1,000}{\text{Program rating}} \qquad \text{Newspapers: } \frac{\text{Cost of ad space} \times 1,000}{\text{Circulation}}$$

While the comparison of media on a cost-per-thousand basis is important, intermedia comparisons can be misleading. The ability of TV to provide both sight and sound, the longevity of magazines, and other characteristics of each medium make direct comparisons difficult. The media planner should use the cost-per-thousand numbers but must also consider the specific characteristics of each medium and each media vehicle in the decision.

The cost per thousand may overestimate or underestimate the actual cost efficiency. Consider a situation where some waste coverage is inevitable because the circulation exceeds the target audience. If the people reached by this message are not potential buyers of the product, then having to pay to reach them results in too low a cost per thousand, as shown in scenario A of **Figure 10-19**. We must use the potential reach to the target audience—the destination sought—rather than the overall circulation figure. A medium with a much higher cost per thousand may be a wiser buy if it is reaching more potential receivers. (Most media buyers rely on **target CPM (TCPM)**, which calculates CPMs based on the target audience, not the overall audience.)

CPM may also underestimate cost efficiency. Sellers of magazine advertising space have argued for years that because more than one person may read an issue, the actual reach is underestimated. They want to use the number of **readers per copy** as the true circulation. This would include a **pass-along rate**, estimating the number of people who read the magazine without buying it. Scenario B in **Figure 10-19** shows how this underestimates cost efficiency. Consider a family in which a father, mother, and two teenagers read each issue of *Maclean's*. While the circulation figure includes only one magazine, in reality there are four potential exposures in this household, increasing the total reach.

While the number of readers per copy makes intuitive sense, it has the potential to be extremely inaccurate. The actual number of times the magazine changes hands is difficult to determine. While research is conducted, pass-along estimates are very subjective and using them to estimate reach is speculative. These figures are regularly provided by the

Figure 10-19 Cost per thousand estimates

Scenario A: Overestimation of Efficiency	
Target audience	18–49
Magazine circulation	400,000
Circulation to target audience	65% (260,000)
Cost per page	$15,600

$$CPM = \frac{\$15,600 \times 1,000}{400,000} = \$39$$

$$CPM\ (actual\ target\ audience) = \frac{\$15,600 \times 1,000}{260,000} = \$60$$

Scenario B: Underestimation of Efficiency	
Target audience	All age groups, male and female
Magazine circulation	400,000
Cost per page	$15,600
Pass-along rate	3

$$CPM\ (based\ on\ readers\ per\ copy) = \frac{Page\ cost \times 1,000}{260,000 + 3(260,000)} = \frac{\$15,600 \times 1,000}{1,040,000} = \$15.00$$

*Assuming pass-along was valid.

media, but managers are selective about using them and rely on their experience to estimate the reach that is greater than published circulation.

A majority of the cost data for media is found with Canadian Advertising Rates and Data (CARD). This subscription service offers extensive information regarding all media. For example, it identifies every media outlet and gives a description of its service and audience. The resource also provides the actual costs of media for computing the media budget. Data regarding some media are not provided (e.g., TV), while some promotional media costs (e.g., coupon book) are included. Students can typically retrieve this information through the library's computer network or the monthly reports kept in the periodical section of their school's library. We will address specific media costs in each of the subsequent media chapters, but as the past several figures indicate, most media are purchased on a per unit basis: page for print, time for broadcast, and some, like Internet display ads, on a CPM basis.

BLOCKING CHART

The media planning process typically concludes with a blocking chart. The **blocking chart** summarizes the media-strategy and media-tactics decisions made thus far, and includes extensive implementation details that guide the media buyers as they attempt to achieve their objectives. An example for Knorr's "What's for Dinner" campaign is shown in **Figure 10-20**.

A blocking chart is typically formatted according to some type of calendar. While it is often done on a weekly basis, a firm with limited communications may organize it monthly. On the other hand, a firm with extensive communications may produce a blocking chart on a daily basis for all or critical parts of its annual media plan. For example, if a firm launches a new product, daily communications during the first few weeks can be critical and specific media exposure is planned in minute detail.

A synopsis of the media choice decisions with respect to television, print, and out-of-home media may also be contained in the blocking chart. In this age of IMC, the blocking chart can also contain elements of other communication tools such as marketing events, public relations, or direct-response tools. In all likelihood, the blocking chart will break these media choices down by different vehicles and different geographic markets.

Figure 10-20 The Knorr blocking chart showing all media and IMC tools

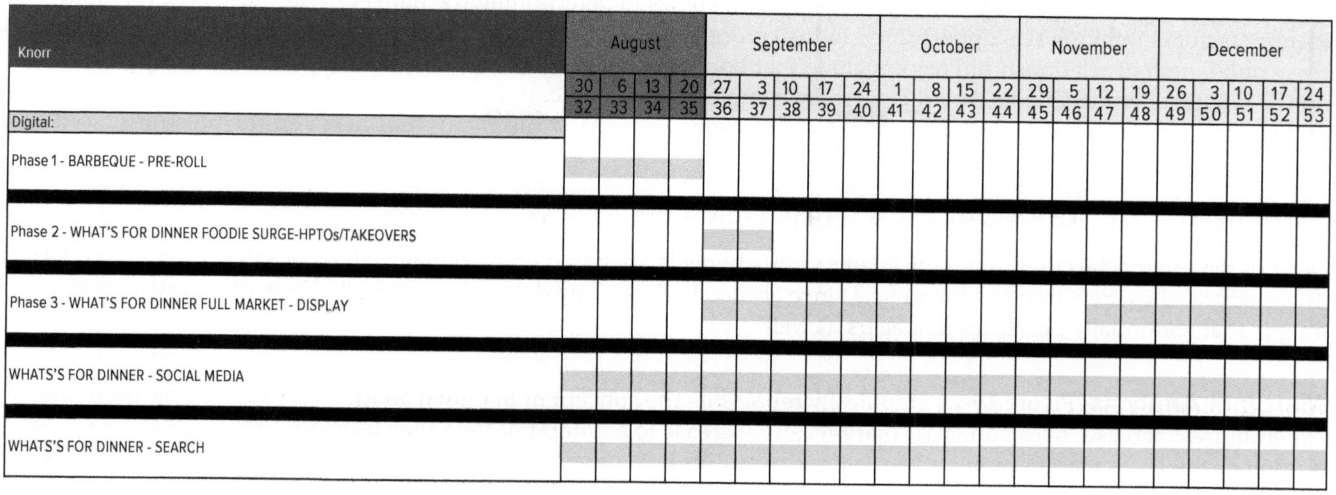

Knorr	August				September					October				November				December				
	30	6	13	20	27	3	10	17	24	1	8	15	22	29	5	12	19	26	3	10	17	24
Digital:	32	33	34	35	36	37	38	39	40	41	42	43	44	45	46	47	48	49	50	51	52	53
Phase 1 - BARBEQUE - PRE-ROLL																						
Phase 2 - WHAT'S FOR DINNER FOODIE SURGE-HPTOs/TAKEOVERS																						
Phase 3 - WHAT'S FOR DINNER FULL MARKET - DISPLAY																						
WHATS'S FOR DINNER - SOCIAL MEDIA																						
WHATS'S FOR DINNER - SEARCH																						

©CASSIES

Another key detail of the blocking chart is showing the relative weight of media expenditures. For example, it could illustrate the number of GRPs per week for each city. Related to this is a clear indication of the reach and frequency of each media decision.

Because the blocking chart concludes the media planning process, the media expenditures have to be included either in summary form or accompanying the blocking chart. This information allows managers to assess the quality of the media plan and to determine whether any adjustments need to be made during the planning time frame.

While we have briefly highlighted the nature of a blocking chart, it may in fact be more than one chart. If a firm is using multiple media across many months and geographic markets, it may have one summary chart and other supporting charts that break the information down into more readable and action-oriented subsections. Remember that a blocking chart is also a communication tool that has to be organized and presented so that all participants are familiar with all decisions.

LO4 Budget Setting

This section begins with an overview of the budget setting process, provides insight into underlying theory with respect to budget setting, discusses how companies budget for promotional efforts, and demonstrates the inherent strengths and weaknesses associated with these theoretical and managerial approaches.

OVERVIEW

Establishing media and communication objectives is an important part of the media planning process; however, the degree to which these objectives are attained is a function of size of the media budget. No organization has an unlimited budget, so objectives must be set with the budget in mind and the budget has to be realistic to achieve any media and communication objectives. However, a longitudinal study with nearly 30 years of data concluded that advertisers consistently overspent in media advertising (e.g., TV, radio, newspaper, magazine, outdoor, Internet) and that the problem worsened over the most recent decade. The data indicated that TV performed the worst by a noticeable amount for just about every year.[25] We discuss budgeting methods even if they are not recommended since it is important to understand all methods that are commonly used by marketers, despite having disadvantages that limit their effectiveness.

In a study of how managers make advertising and promotion budgeting decisions, researchers interviewed 21 managers in eight consumer-product firms and found that the budget-setting process is a perplexing issue and that institutional pressures led to a greater proportion of dollars being spent on sales promotions. The authors concluded that, to successfully develop and implement the budget, managers must (1) employ a comprehensive strategy to guide the process, (2) develop a strategic planning framework that employs an integrated marketing communications philosophy, (3) build in contingency plans, (4) focus on long-term objectives, and (5) consistently evaluate the effectiveness of programs.[26]

Advertising agencies are involved in developing the messages for their clients, but curiously, they are not as involved with the managers of their client organizations when it comes to determining the budget.[27] The authors of this study identify factors inhibiting this opportunity: industry, organizational structure, politics, tradition, compensation system, trust, and length of relationship. They conclude that both agencies and clients could benefit from stronger partnerships on the budget amount. Clients would get a more complete recommendation from communication objectives to message and finally to media purchase, while agencies would better understand the client's business and the pressures faced.

THEORETICAL APPROACHES IN BUDGET SETTING

Most of the approaches used to establish advertising budgets are based on marginal analysis or sales response models. These approaches are viewed as theoretical since academics have long debated the overall effects of advertising on sales, a topic that continually perplexes managers as well.

Marginal Analysis **Figure 10-21** graphically represents the concept of **marginal analysis**. As advertising/promotional expenditures increase, sales and gross margins also increase to a point, but then they level off. Profits are shown to be a result of the gross margin minus advertising expenditures. A marginal analysis theory suggests that a firm would continue to spend advertising/promotional dollars as long as the marginal revenues created by these expenditures exceeded the incremental advertising/promotional costs. As shown on the graph, the optimal expenditure level is the point where marginal costs equal the marginal revenues they generate (point A). If the sum of the advertising/promotional expenditures exceeded the revenues they generated, one would conclude that the appropriations were too high and scale down the budget. If revenues were higher, a higher budget might be in order.

The logic of marginal analysis is weak due to two assumptions. The first is that sales are a direct result of advertising and promotional expenditures and this effect can be measured. In studies using sales as a direct measure, it has been almost impossible to establish the contribution of advertising and promotion.[28] Furthermore, it is generally believed that sales result from the successful attainment of behavioural and communication objectives relevant for the target audience. The second is that advertising and promotion are solely responsible for sales. This assumption ignores the remaining elements of the marketing mix which do contribute to a company's success.

Sales Response Models The sales curve in **Figure 10-21** shows sales levelling off even though advertising and promotion efforts continue to increase. The relationship between advertising and sales has been the topic of much research and discussion designed to determine the shape of the response curve. Almost all advertisers subscribe to one of two models of the advertising/sales response function: the concave-downward response curve or the S-shaped response function.

According to the **concave-downward response curve** (**Figure 10-22A**), the effects of advertising expenditures on sales quickly begin to diminish. Researchers concluded that the effects of advertising budgets follow the microeconomic law of diminishing returns.[29] That is, as the amount of advertising increases, its incremental value decreases. The logic is that those with the greatest potential to buy will likely act on the first (or earliest) exposures, while those less likely to

Figure 10-21 Marginal analysis

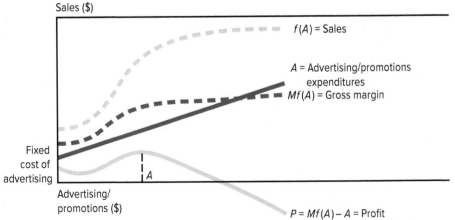

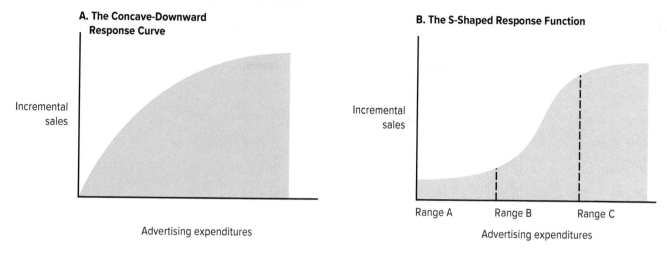

Figure 10-22 Advertising sales/response functions

A. The Concave-Downward Response Curve

Incremental sales

Advertising expenditures

B. The S-Shaped Response Function

Incremental sales

Range A   Range B   Range C

Advertising expenditures

buy are not likely to change as a result of the advertising. For those who may be potential buyers, each additional ad will supply little or no new information that will affect their decision.

According to the **S-shaped response function** (**Figure 10-22B**), the effects of advertising expenditures on sales follow an S-shape. Initial outlays of the advertising budget have little impact (as indicated by the essentially flat sales curve in range A). After a certain budget level has been reached (the beginning of range B), advertising and promotional efforts begin to have an effect, as additional increments of expenditures result in increased sales. This incremental gain continues only to a point, however, because at the beginning of range C additional expenditures begin to return little or nothing in the way of sales. The logic is that advertising takes time before its effects (awareness, etc.) take hold.

Even though marginal analysis and the sales response curves may not apply directly, they give managers insight into a theoretical basis of how the budgeting process should work. Empirical evidence indicates that the models may have validity, however the advertising and sales effects may be reversed as we cannot be sure whether the results actually demonstrate the advertising/sales relationship or vice versa.

A weakness in attempting to use sales as a direct measure of response to advertising is the effect of situational factors as shown in **Figure 10-23**. For a product characterized by emotional buying motives, hidden product qualities, and/or a strong basis for differentiation, advertising would have a noticeable impact on sales. Products characterized as large-dollar purchases and those in the maturity or decline stages of the product life cycle would be less likely to benefit. These factors should be considered in the budget appropriation decision but should not be the sole determinants of where and when to increase or decrease expenditures.

Figure 10-23 Factors influencing advertising budgets

Factor	Relationship of Advertising/Sales	Factor	Relationship of Advertising/Sales
Customer Factors		**Product Factors**	
Industrial products users	—	Basis for differentiation	+
Concentration of users	+	Hidden product qualities	+
Market Factors		Emotional buying motives	+
Stage of product life cycle		Durability	—
Introductory	+	Large dollar purchase	—
Growth	+	Purchase frequency	Curvilinear

[Continued on next page]

[Figure 10-23 continued]

Factor	Relationship of Advertising/Sales	Factor	Relationship of Advertising/Sales
Maturity	—	**Strategy Factors**	
Decline	—	Regional markets	—
Inelastic demand	+	Early stage of brand life cycle	+
Market share	—	High margins in channels	—
Competition		Long channels of distribution	+
Active	+	High prices	+
Concentrated	+	High quality	+
Pioneer in market	—	**Cost Factors**	
		High profit margins	+

Note: + relationship indicates a positive effect of advertising on sales; — relationship indicates little or no effect of advertising on sales.

MANAGERIAL APPROACHES IN BUDGET SETTING

This section reviews practical methods for setting budgets and their relative advantages and disadvantages. We review a few approaches since firms may use more than one and methods vary by the size and sophistication of the firm.[30] Based on this research we indicate its current usage within each description. One approach is **top-down budgeting** because an amount is established at an executive level and then the funds are passed down to the departments (as shown in **Figure 10-24**). Top-down methods include the affordable method, arbitrary allocation, percentage of sales, competitive parity, and return on investment (ROI). A flaw of these methods is that the budget is not linked to the objectives and strategies designed to accomplish them. A more effective method considers the firm's communication objectives and then budgets for the necessary promotional mix strategies to attain these goals. This is known as **bottom-up budgeting** and we review two approaches: the objective and task method and payout planning.

Figure 10-24 Top-down and bottom-up approaches to budget setting

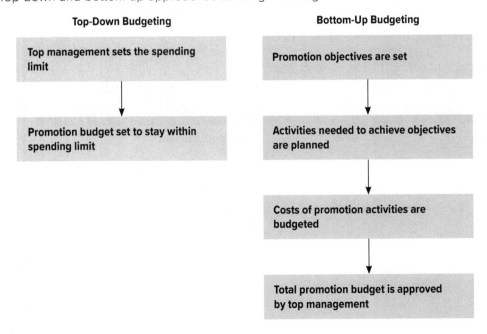

The Affordable Method In the **affordable method**, the firm determines the amount to be spent in production and operations (and so on), and then allocates the remainder to advertising and promotion. The task to be performed by the advertising/promotions function is not considered, and the likelihood of under- or overspending is high, as no guidelines for measuring the effects of budgets are established. In terms of the S-shaped sales response model, the firm is operating in range A. Or the firm may be spending more than necessary, operating in range C. When the market gets tough and sales and/or profits begin to fall, this method can lead to budget cuts at a time when the budget should be increased. This approach is found in small firms due to cash flow concerns and non-market-driven large firms and is used 27 percent of the time.

Arbitrary Allocation An even weaker method method is **arbitrary allocation**, in which virtually no theoretical basis is considered. The budget is determined by management solely on the basis of what is felt to be necessary. The arbitrary allocation approach has no obvious advantages. No systematic thinking has occurred, no objectives have been budgeted for, and the concept and purpose of advertising and promotion have been largely ignored. Other than the fact that the manager believes some monies must be spent on advertising and promotion and then picks a number, there is no good explanation why this approach continues to be used. Yet, about 11 percent of budgets are set this way, and we point out that this method is used—not recommended.

Percentage of Sales Another method used for budget setting, about 10 percent of the time, is the **percentage-of-sales method**, in which the advertising and promotions budget is based on future sales of the product. Management determines the amount by either (1) taking a percentage of the sales dollars or (2) assigning a fixed amount of the unit product cost to promotion and multiplying this amount by the number of units sold. These two methods are shown in **Figure 10-25**.

The percentage-of-sales method offers three advantages. First, the percentage-of-sales method is simple to calculate and easy to implement, as shown in **Figure 10-25**. Second, it is financially safe and keeps ad spending within reasonable limits, as it bases spending on the past year's sales or what the firm expects to sell in the upcoming year. Thus, there will be sufficient monies to cover this budget, with increases in sales leading to budget increases and sales decreases resulting in advertising decreases. Third, this budgeting approach is generally stable. While the budget may vary with increases and decreases in sales, as long as these changes are not drastic, the manager will have a reasonable idea of the parameters of the budget.

However, the percentage-of-sales method has four disadvantages. The first involves the premise on which the budget is established: sales. Letting the level of sales determine the amount of advertising and promotions dollars to be spent reverses the cause-and-effect relationship between advertising and sales. It treats advertising as an expense associated with making a sale, rather than as an investment.

A second problem with this approach is the stability advantage cited earlier, seen from a different view. Stability will occur in the market if all firms use a similar percentage, but what happens if a competitor deviates from this standard percentage? The problem is that this method does not encourage change in the budgeting strategy either internally or from competitors.

Third, the percentage-of-sales method of budgeting may result in severe misappropriation of funds. If advertising and promotion have a role to perform in marketing a product, then allocating more monies to advertising will, as shown in the S-shaped curve, generate incremental sales (to a point). If products with low sales have smaller promotion budgets, this will hinder sales progress. At the other extreme, very successful products may have excess budgets, some of which may be better appropriated elsewhere.

Finally, if the budget is contingent on sales, decreases in sales will lead to decreases in budgets when they most need to be increased. Continuing to cut the advertising and promotion budgets may

Figure 10-25 Alternative methods for computing percentage of sales

Method 1: Straight Percentage of Sales		
Year 1	Total dollar sales	$1,000,000
	Straight % of sales at 10%	$100,000
Year 2	Advertising budget	$100,000
Method 2: Percentage of Unit Cost		
Year 1	Cost per bottle to manufacturer	$4.00
	Unit cost allocated to advertising	$1.00
Year 2	Forecast sales, 100,000 units	
	Advertising budget (100,000 × $1)	$100,000

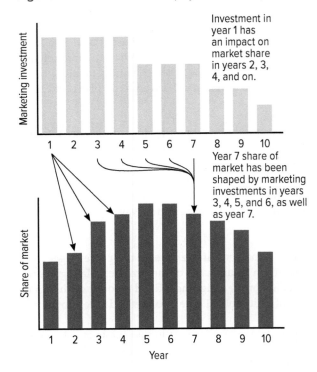

Figure 10-26 Investments pay off in later years

Investment in year 1 has an impact on market share in years 2, 3, 4, and on.

Year 7 share of market has been shaped by marketing investments in years 3, 4, 5, and 6, as well as year 7.

just add impetus to the downward sales trend (**Figure 10-26**). Some argue that more successful companies allocate additional funds during hard times or downturns in the cycle of sales and are rewarded in future years.

A variation on the percentage-of-sales method uses a percentage of projected future sales as a base. This method also uses either a straight percentage of projected sales or a unit cost projection. One advantage of using future sales as a base is that the budget is not based on last year's sales. As the market changes, management must factor the effect of these changes on sales into next year's forecast rather than relying on past data. The resulting budget is more likely to reflect current conditions and be more appropriate. While this appears to be a remedy for the problems discussed, the reality is that problems with forecasting, cyclical growth, and uncontrollable factors limit its effectiveness.

Competitive Parity Firms' having similar advertising expenditures resulting from a competitive analysis occurs 3 percent of the time. Competitors' advertising expenditures are available from market research firms, trade associations, advertising industry periodicals, and media tracking firms. This method is typically used in conjunction with other methods (e.g., percentage of sales).

In the **competitive parity method**, managers establish budget amounts by matching the competition's percentage-of-sales expenditures, essentially taking advantage of the collective wisdom of the industry. It also takes the competition into consideration, which leads to stability in the marketplace by minimizing marketing expenditure battles. If companies know that competitors are unlikely to match their increases in promotional spending, they are less likely to take an aggressive posture to attempt to gain market share.

The competitive parity method has disadvantages. First, it ignores the fact that advertising and promotions are designed to accomplish specific objectives by addressing certain problems and opportunities. Second, it assumes that because firms have similar expenditures, their programs will be equally effective. This assumption ignores the success of creative executions, media allocations, and/or promotion. Third, it ignores advantages of the firm itself—some companies simply make better products than others. A study concluded that a competitive parity strategy must consider the fact that a competitor's advertising can actually benefit one's own firm, and that one competitor's gain is not always the other's loss.[31]

Fourth, there is no guarantee that competitors will continue to pursue their existing strategies. Since competitive parity figures are determined by examination of competitors' previous years' promotional expenditures, changes in market emphasis and/or spending may not be recognized until the competition has already established an advantage. Further, there is no guarantee that a competitor will not increase or decrease its own expenditures, regardless of what other companies do.

Return on Investment (ROI) In the **ROI budgeting method**, advertising and promotions are considered investments, like plant and equipment. This is consistent with the "advertising causes sales" point in the marginal analysis and S-shaped curve approaches; incremental investments in advertising and promotions lead to increases in sales. The key word here is *investment*, as this approach is seen 12 percent of the time. The budgetary appropriation (investment) leads to certain returns; thus advertising and promotion are expected to earn a certain return. While the ROI method appears reasonable, it is a challenge to assess the returns provided by the promotional effort when sales are used as a measure of effectiveness. Thus, while managers are certain to ask how much return they are getting for such expenditures, the question remains unanswered, and ROI remains a virtually unused method of budgeting.

Objective and Task Method Objective setting and budgeting should occur simultaneously rather than sequentially; it is difficult to establish a budget without specific objectives in mind, and setting objectives without regard to how much money is available makes no sense. The **objective and task method** of budget setting consists of three steps: (1) defining the communications objectives to be accomplished, (2) determining the specific strategies and tasks needed

Figure 10-27 The objective and task method

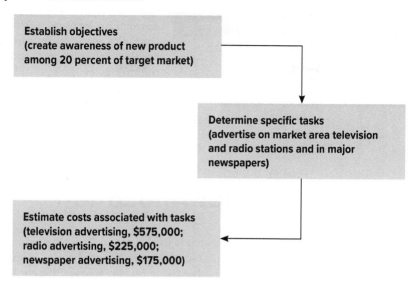

Establish objectives
(create awareness of new product
among 20 percent of target market)

Determine specific tasks
(advertise on market area television
and radio stations and in major
newspapers)

Estimate costs associated with tasks
(television advertising, $575,000;
radio advertising, $225,000;
newspaper advertising, $175,000)

to attain them, and (3) estimating the costs associated with performance of these strategies and tasks (**Figure 10-27**). This method is used 26 percent of the time.

1. *Establish objectives.* A company will have marketing and communication objectives to achieve. After the former are established, the firm determines the specific communication objectives needed to accomplish these goals. Communication objectives must be specific, attainable, and measurable, as well as time limited.

2. *Determine required tasks.* A number of elements are involved in the strategic plan designed to attain the objectives established. These tasks may include advertising in media, sales promotions, and/or other elements of the promotional mix, each with its own role to perform.

3. *Estimate required expenditures.* Buildup analysis requires determining the estimated costs associated with the tasks developed in the previous step. For example, it involves costs for developing awareness through advertising, trial through sampling, and so forth.

As we saw in Chapter 9 on measuring effectiveness, there are ways to determine how well one is attaining established objectives. Performance should be monitored and evaluated in light of the budget appropriated. Money may be better spent on new goals once specific objectives have been attained. For example, if one has achieved the level of consumer awareness sought, the budget should be altered to stress a higher-order objective such as evaluation or trial. As this suggests, the major advantage of the objective and task method is that the budget is driven by the objectives to be attained. The managers closest to the marketing effort will have specific strategies and input into the budget-setting process.

The major disadvantage of this method is the difficulty of determining which tasks will be required and the costs associated with each. For example, specifically what tasks are needed to attain awareness among 50 percent of the target audience? How much will it cost to perform these tasks? While these decisions are easier to determine for certain objectives—for example, estimating the costs of sampling required to stimulate trial in a defined market area—it is not always possible to know exactly what is required and/or how much it will cost to complete the job. This process is easier if there is past experience to use as a guide, with either the existing product or a similar one in the same product category. For this situation, payout planning is offered as an alternative bottom-up approach.

Payout Planning To determine how much to spend, marketers develop a **payout plan** that determines the budget. This is done for a new product introduction or a significant change in the IMC plan, such as brand repositioning strategy. A three-year payout plan is shown in **Figure 10-28**. The first year shows heavier-than-normal advertising and promotion expenditures to stimulate higher levels of awareness and subsequent trial. Promotion expenditures are strong but drop off during years 2 and 3 to maintain communication effects. Different expenditure

Figure 10-28 Example of three-year payout plan ($ millions)

	Year 1	Year 2	Year 3
Product sales	15.0	35.50	60.75
Profit contribution (@ $0.50/case)	7.5	17.75	30.38
Advertising/promotions	15.0	10.50	8.50
Profit (loss)	(7.5)	7.25	21.88
Cumulative profit (loss)	(7.5)	(0.25)	21.63

and revenue calculations provide various "what-if" scenarios before concluding upon an optimal projection. As the figure shows, over time, the brand loses money in year 1, almost breaks even in year 2, and finally shows substantial profits by the end of year 3. When used in conjunction with the objective and task method, payout planning provides a logical approach to budget setting but is seen infrequently, at 3 percent of the time.

IMC Planning: Budget Allocation

Once the overall promotion budget is determined, the next step is to allocate it. The advertising media budget is allocated to broadcast, print, out-of-home, and Internet media, as suggested in the media plan. **Figure 10-29** summarizes examples of how award-winning advertisers allocated their advertising budget across different media, over the time frame of the campaign. In each case, these campaigns primarily used paid advertising to communicate their message, and the brands obtained positive communication and financial results indicating a good allocation across media.

Beyond advertising, firms use a variety of IMC tools (sales promotion, public relations, Internet, and direct marketing) for delivering messages and experiences to their target audiences. Careful consideration of the budget allocation across the tools is a central task for IMC planning to achieve the communication and behavioural objectives. Budweiser's Red Light IMC plan, which occurred over four years, represents an IMC program that allocated its undisclosed budget effectively, given the number of awards received in Canada. It is summarized in **Figure 10-30** and shows that the plan involved five IMC tools. The results indicated that Budweiser improved its association with hockey, strengthened its brand affinity, earned social media impressions versus its main competitor Molson Canadian, and attained a number one market share. All of this suggests a good allocation of the budget across the unique IMC tools.

Figure 10-29 Summary of examples of target and media choices

Brand	Target	Media
Gain	Switchers, non P&G	TV, online video
$5 million	Category users	Magazine, billboard
3 months	Seeking scent benefit	Twitter, Facebook paid ads
Nissan Rogue	Switch SUV users	YouTube, Facebook, Twitter, Instagram
$2 million	Family	Internet video, rich media, HPTO, SEM
6 months	Desiring safety benefit	TV, sponsorship CFL & NFL

Figure 10-30 Summary of Budweiser's Red Light IMC Plan

Sales Promotion	Red Light Premium (pay)	Red Light Glass Premium (free)	Christmas Light Premium (pay)
Event	Zeppelin	Puck Manufacturer	25 Foot Goal Light
Sponsorship	HNIC	TVA, RDS	Sportsnet
Social Media	Facebook	Instagram	Twitter
Advertising	Television	Out-of-home	Cinema
Digital	Google Preferred	YouTube	Seeding video

Learning Objectives Summary

 LO1 Illustrate how a media plan is developed.

Media planning involves delivering the marketing communications message through different channels such as television, radio, print, and out-of-home, among others. Media planning is required for advertising to deliver the creative strategy but also for any other IMC tool. For example, a sales promotion offer might be communicated over the radio; a charity event that a brand sponsors could be found in a local city newspaper; or a transit ad possibly directs commuters to a firm's website.

A media plan is generally the end result of the media planning process, and it contains sections for objectives, strategy decisions, and tactical decisions. The media plan's objectives must be designed to support the overall marketing objectives and help achieve the behavioural and communication objectives determined for each target audience.

The basic task involved in the development of media strategy is to determine the best matching of media to the target audience, given the constraints of the budget. The media planner attempts to balance reach and frequency and to deliver the message to the intended audience with a minimum of waste coverage. Media strategy development has been called more of an art than a science because, while many quantitative data are available, the planner also relies on creativity and non-quantifiable factors.

 LO2 Explain the process and identify the decisions for implementing media strategies.

This chapter discussed five media strategy decisions, including developing a proper media mix, determining target audience coverage, determining geographic coverage, scheduling, and balancing reach and frequency. A summary chart of strengths and limitations of media alternatives was provided. The list provides a starting point for planners who select the right combination of media based on the communication problem or opportunity.

 LO3 Explain the process and identify the decisions for implementing media tactics.

The chapter also looked at tactical decisions that fine-tune the media strategy. The media vehicle plays a key part in the media plan as the media planner carefully matches the viewers, listeners, and readers of the media and the profile of the target audience. Relative cost estimates guide the media planner's final decisions for vehicle selection by finding the most cost-efficient placement. Fine-tuning of scheduling details is finalized with the realization of a blocking chart that summarizes all media decisions and costs across relevant time periods and geographic locations.

 LO4 Distinguish among the theoretical and managerial approaches for media budget setting.

This chapter summarized theoretical and managerial approaches for budget setting. Theoretical methods feature economic models (i.e., marginal analysis, sales response) that attempt to demonstrate the effects of advertising on sales, often without accounting for the effects of other marketing mix variables. Top-down managerial approaches include affordable, arbitrary allocation, percentage of sales, competitive parity, and return on investment. The methods are often viewed as lacking in any theoretical basis while ignoring the role of advertising and promotion in the marketing mix.

Bottom-up managerial approaches include the objective and task method and payout planning. In particular, the objective and task method connects the cost of advertising and promotion to the communication and behavioural objectives expected for the communication program, as opposed to broader marketing objectives expected for the marketing program. While the objective and task method offers an improvement over the top-down approaches, firms continue to use a combination of approaches to make the budget decision.

LO5 Apply the methods for allocating the media budget to relevant IMC tools and market situations.

Once the overall budget has been determined, it is allocated to the individual media for advertising and any other IMC tool requiring expenditures. The money for an individual tool may be allocated to certain markets depending on the level of the brand's current market share. Sometimes markets are developed requiring a boost in expenditures, while other times markets are in a profit mode and less investment may be forthcoming. Some allocation decisions are affected by unique organizational or interorganizational factors that may be tangential to the primary goals of achieving communication objectives.

Review Questions

1. Explain why media planning involves a trade-off between reach and frequency.

2. Describe what is meant by *waste coverage.* The decision must often be made between waste coverage and undercoverage. Give examples when the marketer might have to choose between the two, and when it may be acceptable to live with waste coverage.

3. What is meant by *readers per copy*? How is this different from CPM? Explain the advantages and disadvantages associated with the use of both.

4. Identify the information resources required to calculate the budget using the objective and task method.

5. What factors influence the budget allocation to different media or different IMC tools?

Applied Questions

1. One long-time advertising agency executive noted that media planning is both an art and a science, with a leaning toward art. Explain what this means and provide examples.

2. Visit the websites for two magazines of the same genre and locate their media kits. Compare how each magazine persuades advertisers to select its media vehicle in terms of editorial content, readership information, customized services for advertising placements, and any other unique features.

3. Calculate the CPM for five or six different media vehicles that are interesting or topical.

4. Assume that a new entry-level car brand wants to achieve 30 percent awareness among graduated students aged 21–24. Calculate how much would have to be in the budget to achieve this objective.

5. For an up-and-coming brand of fashionable jeans, a rebranded local night club for dancing, and an established energy drink, identify the most appropriate media budget allocation (in percentages) to create awareness. Do the same for all three brands with respect to IMC tools.

CHAPTER ELEVEN

Broadcast Media

LEARNING OBJECTIVES

LO1 Describe the media of television regarding delivery, types of TV advertising, time periods and programs, audience measurement, and streaming.

LO2 Summarize the strengths and limitations of television as an advertising medium.

LO3 Describe types of radio advertising, time periods, and audience measurement.

LO4 Summarize the strengths and limitations of radio as an advertising medium.

LO5 Apply the media knowledge of TV and radio for strategic IMC decisions.

Broadcast Industry in Transition

People subscribing to services like Netflix—and no longer subscribing to a paid TV service through cable, satellite, or the Internet; or not subscribing to a paid TV service ever; or not watching their paid TV service frequently—have changed the game for all industry players. For broadcasters, there are fewer viewers and consequently less opportunity to charge higher rates to advertisers for revenue growth. For TV service providers, fewer customers means competing with Netflix by offering on-demand options. Since the newer services are not Canadian-based, there are tax implications creating unfair competition, regulatory fee implications for funding Canadian content, and concerns for developing and distributing programming reflecting Canadian culture, and finally, issues regarding the content of the Canadian Broadcasting Act, which governs the industry.

Under the Act, Netflix is exempt from Canadian content quotas and funding requirements that broadcasters like CTV must follow. Accordingly, firms in the industry made proposals to change the Act. BCE (owner of Bell Media, CTC), along with Rogers Communications, proposed that streaming services fund Canadian content like broadcasters are required to, at 30 percent of revenue. These two firms concluded that, without this change, the quality and volume of Canadian content would decline. Netflix appears to have accepted the idea and has struck a deal with the federal government to spend $500 million over five years on original production. Bell proposed that streaming services start contributing at a rate of 20 percent by 2022, and pointed out that the streaming services maintained a built-in price advantage since they did not collect sales tax.

In contrast, Telus, Shaw, Corus, and Quebecor argued for deregulation of the broadcast industry. Corus recommended eliminating foreign investment restrictions, reducing Canadian programming expenditures, and discontinuing the rules limiting local broadcast ownership. Telus suggested phasing out the requirement to pay into the Canadian Media Fund used to create programming, so that our cultural policy goals and industry policy goals would be independent of one another. Quebecor believed the new services should avoid being drawn into old broadcast policies and that the previous regulations should be eliminated for all industry organizations. But organizations involved in production—such as the Canadian Media Producers Association and the Alliance of Canadian Cinema, Television and Radio Artists (ACTRA)—argued for the status quo and that the new services should pay. Some of these points are well taken, as production companies were strongly affected by the drastic changes in the amount of funding for children's programming received from the Canadian Media Fund in recent years.

Despite the upheaval from Netflix, other competitors are entering the market and growing, and Canadian firms have responded by changing their services. For example, Bell Media revitalized its on-demand services with a new brand—Crave instead of CraveTV—and partnerships with new sources of content from Lions Gate and Starz. Rogers moved toward direct access to its sports channel with a subscription. Time will tell where the broadcast industry is in five to ten years, but one thing is for sure: the demand for and consumer interest in video content continues to grow as we watch more and more from new and old systems combined.

Question:

1. Is Canadian content of video entertainment important enough for you to pay for it?

TV is in virtually every Canadian household and is a mainstay in most people's lives. The large number of television viewers are important to the TV networks and stations because they can sell time on popular programs to marketers who want to reach that audience with their advertising messages. Moreover, the qualities that make TV a great medium for information and entertainment also encourage creative ads to influence current and potential customers. Radio is also an integral part of people's lives as it is a constant companion in their cars, at home, and even at work for information and entertainment. Radio listeners are an important audience for marketers, just as TV viewers are.

In this chapter, we describe the types of TV and radio media that advertisers may select within the media strategy, how advertisers buy TV and radio time, and how audiences are measured and evaluated for each medium. We summarize the specific strengths and limitations of each medium. Finally, we explain how advertisers use TV and radio as part of their advertising and media strategies. We follow this structure for TV and then radio.

(LO1) Television

What is to become of TV viewing? One view is that it is thriving, not dying. People's desire to watch TV shows online means that TV shows are very good entertainment, and people are watching TV content on other means of transmission. Nothing replaces the experience of watching live sports on a big screen except actually being there, and the next generation of consumers will likely buy a big-screen TV after leaving a family home that has one.[1] Despite the many viewing options, TV ad revenue remained relatively strong at $3.2 billion in 2017. Academic research concluded that TV advertising results in positive short-term and long-term brand effects.[2] The effectiveness of TV advertising improved over the past few decades, although not every TV campaign is successful.[3] The measurement of TV effectiveness is expected to evolve with multi-screen digital media.[4]

We review many topics to describe TV as an advertising media. Initially we focus on the delivery of TV services. We then review the types of TV advertising. Advertisers purchase TV in time periods and program formats that appeal to various types and sizes of audiences. We also review measures of TV audiences because audience is a critical input for TV advertising decisions. Finally, the implications of viewers watching TV on new services such as Netflix are explored.

DELIVERY OF TV SERVICES

Canadians currently receive TV services at home in more ways than ever, as shown in **Figure 11-1**. The antenna provided initial TV reception through analog airwaves, however reception is now received by digital airwaves and this delivery route hit 7 percent recently. **Cable television** represented a significant development decades ago by delivering TV services through coaxial wire to provide access for remote areas that could not receive broadcast signals, and to distribute American channels more easily and widely. While still leading at 32 percent, its distribution waned with other delivery methods. **Direct broadcast satellite (DBS)** emerged as firms sent TV service from a satellite to homes equipped with a dish and receiver, and its distribution now stands at 17 percent. Fibre optic digital TV service (Internet protocol television, referred to as **IPTV**) hit 19 percent and is distributed by cable operators and telecommunication firms via the Internet. And finally, Canadians receive "TV service" from the Internet directly; this is identified as TV My Way by Media Technology Monitor.

Figure 11-1 How Canadians receive TV services

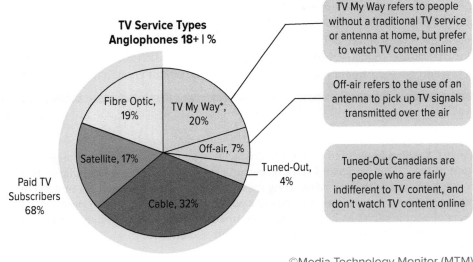

TV Service Types
Anglophones 18+ | %

TV My Way refers to people without a traditional TV service or antenna at home, but prefer to watch TV content online

Off-air refers to the use of an antenna to pick up TV signals transmitted over the air

Tuned-Out Canadians are people who are fairly indifferent to TV content, and don't watch TV content online

Fibre Optic, 19%
TV My Way*, 20%
Satellite, 17%
Off-air, 7%
Tuned-Out, 4%
Paid TV Subscribers 68%
Cable, 32%

©Media Technology Monitor (MTM)

The implication of this data is that conventional TV ads reach 75 percent of Canadians when watching TV at home; 68 percent who pay for a TV service via the three distribution methods; and 7 percent who use an antenna. Those watching TV content online or who are tuned out are exposed to conventional TV ads when away from home and viewing in public (e.g., at a bar) or in private (e.g., when visiting family or friends). TV My Way viewers receive Internet ad messages when watching online programs that may be identical to those shown on TV, or no ads if they are watching a streaming service like Netflix.

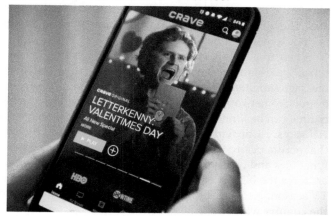

Exhibit 11-1 Crave is an OTT service.

©Graeme Roy/CP Images

To review, TV service subscribers (cable, satellite, IPTV) pay a monthly fee to receive an assortment of channels, including local Canadian and American network affiliates, independent stations, and specialty networks. Other program options that show TV ads are available to viewers and include specialty channels (such as news, music, sports, weather, education, lifestyle, and culture) which broaden advertisers' opportunity to reach viewers. Service providers also offer programming not supported by advertising, like Crave, to those who pay an additional fee. A service like Crave is also sold without buying a paid TV service and is delivered via the Internet similar to independent services, like Netflix, albeit with different content selection (**Exhibit 11-1**). These options are referred to as *over-the-top (OTT)* service and there are many new ones available every year, with specialization emerging in areas such as sports. We review developments of OTT service in a later section after describing conventional television advertising.

TYPES OF TV ADVERTISING

A decision for TV advertisers is how to allocate their media budget to network or local announcements, also known as spot advertising. National advertisers use network schedules to provide complete coverage across the country and supplement this with regional or local purchases to reach markets where additional coverage is desired. Specialty networks offer additional exposure for niche channels; these types of networks show their programming online, giving advertisers another route for exposure. Beyond placing commercials, we periodically see advertisers do sponsorship advertising. In addition, advertisers communicating without running a commercial use product placement within the shows.

National Networks Advertisers disseminate their messages by purchasing airtime from a **television network**. Canada's television industry features six national networks. The Canadian Broadcasting Corporation (CBC) is a Crown corporation of the federal government of Canada, and its network reaches virtually all English-language homes. Radio-Canada is the CBC cousin for the French-language network, reaching viewers in Quebec and other Canadian provinces and territories. The Canadian Television Network (CTV) and Global both operate as a national English-language service in most Canadian provinces. CITY is a semi-national network in more populated cities in larger provinces of Canada. Finally, TVA, a private French-language network, broadcasts to most Quebec households and French-speaking viewers throughout Canada. Regional commercial networks also dot the Canadian landscape, as do provincial networks that do not accept advertising. **Figure 11-2** summarizes viewing statistics for major Canadian networks that accounted for the majority of conventional TV watching during the autumn of 2018. For an average week, 20 million Canadians watch 63,000 hours of CTV, resulting in three hours per week per person.

A network assembles a series of affiliated local TV stations throughout the country or region, known as **affiliates**, to which it supplies programming and services. There are 122 conventional stations in Canada.[5]

Figure 11-2 Weekly hours watched, network TV, fall 2018

Network	Hours (000)	Reach (millions)	Average Hours
CTV	62.8	20.3	3.1
TVA	38.5	5.1	7.5
Global	33.8	10.3	3.3
Radio Canada	24.7	4.8	5.2
CBC	17.4	8.1	2.1
City	10.8	6.1	1.8

These affiliates contractually agree to use programming provided by the networks and to carry the national advertising within the program. The networks share the advertising revenue they receive during these time periods with the affiliates. The affiliates also sell commercial time in non-network periods and during station breaks in the pre-empted periods to both national and local advertisers.

When an advertiser purchases airtime from a national or regional network, the commercial is transmitted through the affiliate station network. Network advertising truly represents a mass medium, since the advertiser broadcasts its message simultaneously through many affiliates. Advertisers interested in reaching many consumers generally buy time from large networks (e.g., CTV) during the evening prime viewing hours when popular programs are aired. Availability of time can be limited as advertisers compete to obtain network advertising. Traditionally, most prime-time commercial spots, particularly on the programs with a sizable viewership, are sold during the buying period in May/June/July that occurs before the TV season begins. Advertisers planning to use prime-time network advertising plan their media schedules and purchase TV time as much as a year in advance. Demands from large clients who are heavy TV advertisers force the biggest agencies to participate in the upfront market. However, TV time is also purchased throughout the TV season. Network TV is purchased on a regional basis, so an advertiser's message can be aired in certain sections of the country with one media purchase.

A network attracts viewers with its programming and acquires the rights to broadcast a particular show from the original production company or the organization responsible for a sport. For example, Rogers Media signed a broadcasting deal worth $5.2 billion over 12 years with the NHL that started in the 2014–2015 season. The deal included the Canadian broadcast and multimedia rights to NHL games in all languages and sub-licensing to the CBC and to TVA for French broadcasting. To make the deal work financially, Rogers Media undertook research to understand how Canadians consume hockey. It needed to attract new viewers who had not watched hockey in the past, such as new Canadians and younger Canadians; both of these groups watched other sports, or other programs, or consumed media content elsewhere. For younger Canadians on a second screen while the game aired, the media brand wanted to get a better read on how to link the game experience with social media activity. In addition, Rogers Media needed to ensure that loyal hockey viewers would transition to the new broadcaster and watch hockey on more nights, or watch two games a night more often since the availability increased.[6]

When using mass media like TV, advertisers are interested in technological adoption for viewing. **Figure 11-3** shows that consumers love TV, as the penetration rates for high-definition TV and high-definition receivers continue to grow, and so does demand for very large televisions! From the actions of TV networks, it appears they do not envision the end of TV either. All major networks are entrenched in the market and owned by major telecommunications firms. Their annual visits to Los Angeles continue with increased intensity as they bid for shows that will attract advertisers. Canadian network TV executives outmaneuver and outbid one another for the top shows as the funnel of good-quality production continues across all the major American producers. A recent trend is that executives look for shows that fit network TV viewer behaviour to enhance the brand building opportunity for advertisers.[7]

Spot advertising refers to commercials shown on local TV stations, with time negotiated and purchased directly from the individual stations or their national station representatives. Spot advertising offers the national advertiser flexibility in adjusting to local market conditions but concentrating messages in areas where market potential is greatest. This ad format is appealing to advertisers with uneven product distribution, limited advertising budgets, test marketing situations, or product introductions in limited markets. National advertisers also use spot advertising through local retailers as part of their cooperative advertising programs and to provide local dealer support. This attractive option is most prevalent in Canada, with about 60 percent of all TV ads.

Figure 11-3 HD screen and HD receiver penetration

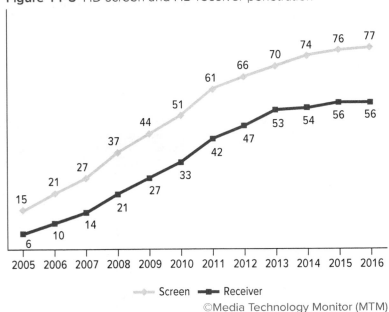

Screen ■ Receiver
©Media Technology Monitor (MTM)

Specialty Networks Canada has an extensive variety of specialty networks and digital specialty networks that advertisers run commercials on to reach specific target audiences. The proliferation of channels influenced the nature of television as an advertising medium since the expanded viewing options led to considerable audience fragmentation. Specialty networks attracted about 50 percent of the viewing audience, and much of this audience growth came from national and regional networks. Note that a good number of these specialty networks are digital only, meaning a viewer requires a subscription service for access. Specialty networks became very popular among consumers, leading advertisers to re-evaluate their media plans and the prices paid for network and affiliate station exposure. Advertising revenue on specialty networks hit $1,233 million in 2017 compared to conventional television ad revenue of $1,804 million.[8]

These advertising revenue figures indicate that advertisers use specialty networks to efficiently reach specific target audiences. Advertising rates on specialty networks are lower than those for the shows on the major networks. This makes TV a viable media option for smaller advertisers with limited budgets and those interested in presenting their commercials to a well defined target audience. Also, specialty network advertisers generally do not have to make the large upfront financial commitments the networks require. In addition to costing less, specialty networks give advertisers flexibility in the types of commercials that are possible. While most network commercials are 30- or 15-second spots, commercials on specialty networks can be longer (e.g., 3 to 30 minutes in length). Finally, specialty network advertising is purchased on a national or a regional basis. Large marketers advertising on specialty networks reach large numbers of viewers across the country with a single media buy. Regional advertising on specialty networks is available but limited.

Figure 11-4 shows Numeris data of the top 12 out of about 40 highly viewed specialty networks that attracted at least 1 million viewers per week for fall 2018. The typical viewer watched TSN an average of 2.4 hours per week and the station reached about 27 percent of Canadians (10 million/36 million) each week. It is the second most watched specialty channel in terms of total hours, just behind the W Network. The reach for another 40 less-viewed specialty channels was below 1 million viewers per week for fall 2018. Note that a weekly viewership of 1 million represents about 3 percent reach based on a population of 36 million. Although specialty networks' share of the TV viewing audience is substantial, the viewers are spread out among the large number of channels available. Collectively, the specialty networks contribute to greater audience fragmentation as the number of viewers who watch any one channel is generally quite low.

Network Advertising Online Both national and specialty networks offer their shows online with commercials embedded within them much like regular television viewing; for example, one can visit CTV's website and watch previously aired programs. The movement of watching "television" programming anytime, anywhere, with any device is expanding TV viewing opportunities and potentially opening up new avenues for advertising as consumers adapt to changing technology. Networks offer mobile apps for viewing on-demand programs or live programs on mobile phones or tablets; for example, one can watch *Hockey Night in Canada* with CBC's sports app and see ads just like when watching the game on the living room big screen. Dynamic advertising occurs in which current ads could be inserted into a downloaded show automatically.[9] Total advertising revenue for online viewing hit $159 million in 2017, 5 percent of the total of $3.2 billion for TV.

Sponsorship Advertising In the early days of TV, an identified corporation produced most programs. Thus, the original concept of a **sponsorship** arrangement occurs when an advertiser produces the content of the program and embeds its own advertising. Today, networks produce the shows, or air shows produced by independent companies. In either case, the network sells the advertising time to a sponsoring advertiser. For example, CTV received major sponsorship expenditures over the years for its Oscars broadcast from L'Oréal, which aired many ads during the program.

Figure 11-4 Weekly hours watched, specialty TV, fall 2018

Specialty	Hours (000)	Reach (000)	Average Hours
Bravo!	11,197	4,743	2.4
Comedy	10,003	4,804	2.1
CP24	10,033	4,557	2.2
Discovery	11,281	6,790	1.7
Food Network	8,888	4.865	1.8
HGTV	12,337	5,695	2.1
History	11,544	5,885	2.0
Showcase	13,462	6,404	2.1
Space	9,567	5,094	1.9
Sportsnet	19,332	8,542	2.3
TSN	24,565	10,114	2.4
W Network	25,639	7,247	3.5

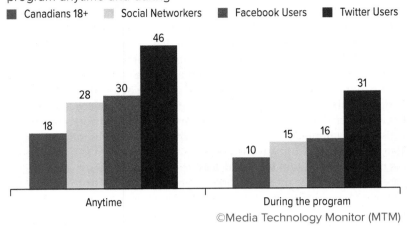

Figure 11-5 Canadians used social media to comment about a TV program anytime and during

■ Canadians 18+   □ Social Networkers   ■ Facebook Users   ■ Twitter Users

©Media Technology Monitor (MTM)

Tetley Tea purchased all the advertising time for the TV premiere of *Pitch Perfect,* but instead of playing its ads, it showed clips of its YouTube sponsored show *MsLabelled* in three 10-minute episodes.[10] A three-year sponsor for *Hockey Night in Canada* is Huawei, which receives logo placement on the studio sets during the pre-game and second intermission and frequent audio statements like "brought to you by Huawei" during the broadcast.[11]

As this demonstrates, today's use of sponsorship has evolved from its original concept, comes in many forms, and is now linked with social media. Sponsorship is seen with synonymous terms "branded entertainment" or "branded content" that is reminiscent of what occurred decades ago. For example, President's Choice cooked up a reality show, *Recipes to Riches,* in which contestants used the branded products to develop their own recipes. The show attracted over 600,000 viewers and reached the number one most watched program on FoodNetwork.ca. With company chairman Galen Weston as a judge, the show offered contestants an opportunity to demonstrate their culinary flair.[12] As for whether the sponsorship approach is identified as branded content or branded entertainment, the commercial intention is expected to be understood by the receiver of the message. However, one industry producer believes the intention of branded content is to sell and differs from branded entertainment with its intention to place the brand in a context that has enduring positive effect with its audience.[13]

Within these sponsored segments, the program itself or the branded component invites viewers to interact with social media through voting, viewing online content, or commenting to friends, giving rise to the idea of social TV. **Figure 11-5** indicates that many Canadians commented about TV programs, including those who are heavy users of "watching TV" on the Internet (i.e., social networkers). A good portion of this communication occurred on shows with hosts, such as sports, entertainment competitions, talk shows, morning programs, and news. **Social TV** is communication among viewers of a TV program through social media channels, and includes communication with the viewer and the TV program. All parties involved—TV programs, advertisers, and viewers—see this as an enrichment of the TV consumption experience and an opportunity for additional brand messages.

A company chooses to sponsor a program since it allows the brand to enhance its image by associating it with the prestige of a high-quality program, and the sponsor has control over the number, placement, and content of its ads. Furthermore, its message can be of any length as long as the total amount of commercial time does not exceed network or station regulations. And the message does not in fact count as an ad if it is in the form of branded entertainment or branded content. Finally, the production of this form of influence may require the production expertise of the media company.

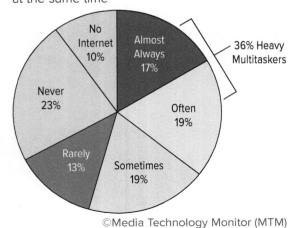

Figure 11-6 Watch TV and access the Internet at the same time

©Media Technology Monitor (MTM)

For example, Canadian Tire partnered with TSN for three years and saw the benefit of being able to access sports stars and teams to produce its branded content pieces that TSN aired and Canadian Tire linked on Twitter and Facebook.[14] As shown in **Figure 11-6**, about one-third of Canadians use the Internet while watching TV, so immediate communication with the brand can occur beyond the TV ad.

Product Placement Some TV programs show a scene in which a brand is featured prominently. For example, *Amazing Race Canada* shows contestants using vehicles made by Chevrolet, a brand partner for seven seasons, and the host communicates the specific brand name and mentions its features. In the past, the competition featured "The BMO Effect Moment of the Race," which picked up on the bank's creative theme and highlighted incidents when contestants assisted other contestants. For a recent season, Dempster's food products became the source of a challenge in which contestants made different dishes.[15]

This form of advertising is known as product placement, but marketers may call it brand placement.[16] **Product placement** occurs when a brand name, a logo, the actual product, or an ad for it is part of an entertainment vehicle like a TV show or movie.[17] We focus on TV here and continue with social media applications (where growth has occurred recently) in Chapter 18, but avoid movies as this is a highly specialized channel not available to many advertisers. However, a study concluded that the maximum rate of return for product placement in movies hit its peak a couple of decades ago, indicating that consumers do not notice the movie placements as much as in the past.[18]

Much of the logic behind product placement is that since the placement is embedded in the script or program setting it cannot be avoided, thereby increasing exposure. For example, HGTV aired a *Home to Win* program with a 10-part series that included stars from other shows from this specialty channel, such as Mike Holmes and Sarah Richardson. The reality-based show takes viewers through the process of designing a dream home, which one of the viewers who enters the contest wins. The renovation stars highlight many brands such as Leon's, KitchenAid, Maytag, Samsung, Tempur-Pedic, Toyota, Benjamin Moore, Moen, and Jeld-Wen as they search for decorating items and design and build the prize winning home.[19] The effects of an example such as this could be tracked with research by Nielsen. Their new methodology examines exposure and standardized brand metrics across media and IMC tools such as TV, on demand video, digital, social, film, and live events.[20] Thus, a brand could plan product placement in all of these domains and track awareness and attitude.

When consumers see their favourite TV star wearing Oakley sunglasses, drinking Gatorade, or driving a Mercedes, this association may lead to a favourable product image. Most of those involved in product placement believe that association with the proper source is critical for success. A product placement done properly has direct relevance for the character or situation and is almost a transformational experience emotionally for the audience member who is paying full attention to the entertainment. **Figure 11-7** summarizes a number of product placement decisions based on the above research. Presumably all of these decisions are appropriate for entertainment shows described previously, including dramas, comedies, and live sports.

Assuming a marketer selected the right TV vehicle, product placement contributes to awareness by its sheer volume of exposure. Product placement appears promising, but its greatest strength may lie in maintaining existing loyalty of current customers who see the product they favour actually consumed by a character in a situation they can relate to. In the past, product placement research concluded that it contributes to brand attitude and awareness and that consumers do not mind the prevalence of product placement.[21]

More recent research found a similar result: a positive attitude toward the product placement segment contributed to a positive attitude to the brand featured in the segment.[22] Another study tested the effects of entertainment, information, and irritation characteristics on product placement value and advertising value. Entertainment and information more strongly predicted advertising value compared to predicting product placement value. However, the irritation factor had a stronger negative prediction to product placement value compared to no link to advertising value. These findings support the media role of product placement that, if not done well, it could potentially cause damage to the brand.[23] Finally, another study compared the recognition and recall effects of a TV ad to a product placement during the same show, and concluded the TV ad yielded stronger ad/product placement recall of the brand.[24]

TIME PERIODS AND PROGRAMS

Another decision in buying TV time is selecting the right time period and program to schedule the advertiser's commercial. The cost of TV advertising time varies depending on the time of day and particular program, since audience size varies as a function of these two factors. As for the particular program, *Hockey Night in Canada* is a popular selection due to the audience size and composition.

TV time periods are divided into **dayparts** which are specific segments of a broadcast day. Advertising rates differ across these dayparts since audience size and demographic composition vary. The dayparts structure varies as well, but the general format is as follows.

Figure 11-7 Product placement decisions

Program Title/Genre	Title of show, associated mood with genre
Screen/Audio Time	Negotiated, dependent on artistic direction
Size/Visibility	Foreground, background
Type of Exposure	Verbal, visual
Type of Execution	Actual, virtual
Brand Relevance	Fit with plot, characters, entertainment
Context	Competing screen images, clutter
Creativity	Portrayal of brand

Prime time occurs seven days a week between 7:00 p.m. and 11:00 p.m. when front-running shows are aired, leading to the largest audiences. Prime time is the most expensive time slot in which to advertise and is typically dominated by national advertisers. Prime time draws about 40 percent of per capita television consumption. On weekdays, prior to prime time (4:00 p.m. to 7:00 p.m.) and after prime time (11:00 p.m. to 2:00 a.m.) are early and late fringe times respectively, with each daypart drawing about 10 percent per capita television consumption, for a total of 20 percent. On weekdays, early morning (6:00 a.m. to 10:00 a.m.), daytime (10:00 a.m. to 4:00 p.m.), and overnight (2:00 a.m. to 6:00 a.m.) dayparts draw about 20 percent of per capita television consumption. Finally, Saturday and Sunday dayparts (2:00 a.m. to 7:00 p.m.) draw the remaining 20 percent.

Audience size and demographic composition also vary depending on the program. For example, *The Big Bang Theory* peaked as a top-ranked show in Canada and regularly drew 4 million viewers each week. Other top 10 shows typically attracted 1.5 million to 2 million viewers. Other top shows for the past few years include *Grey's Anatomy* and *The Amazing Race*. As one might expect, the audiences for these programs are likely quite different and, as indicated in Chapter 10, an advertiser might want to place a message in all these shows to obtain greater reach. Alternatively, an advertiser might want to place a message in many first responder dramas like *Station 19* and *9-1-1* to obtain stronger frequency, since these shows possibly draw overlapping audiences. Data from the audience measurement system would confirm these or other similar conclusions. As this suggests, selecting the right daypart and the show within the daypart is an important decision, and the variation of the types of programs within the dayparts influences other media decisions significantly.

Given the importance of dayparts and programs for advertisers, Canadian TV networks carefully bid on new programs when they come available and decide on their prime time lineup across each day of the week. In fact, each typically planned an overall strategy for the networks for the week and for each individual evening.[25] For example, networks not airing *Monday Night Football* need to consider what shows to air to attract those not interested in the sport or league. Alternatively, networks may want an evening with programs with a broader audience that may be appealing to advertisers. From another view, a network might want to balance its evening programming for different ages, or for males and females. Strategically, a network may want to insert a new program each evening with the intention of drawing loyal followers of one program to stay on the channel to see the next one. And this idea works for specialty channels as well, as demonstrated by the success of *Orphan Black* which followed the successful *Dr. Who* program on the Space Channel. Ultimately for its time slot, the program became the number one among specialty channels, averaging 330,000 viewers.[26]

MEASURING THE TV AUDIENCE

As the preceding indicated, audience measurement is critical to advertisers as well as to the networks and stations. Advertisers want to know the size and characteristics of the audience they are reaching when they purchase time on a particular program. And since the rates they pay are a function of audience size, advertisers want to be sure audience measurements are accurate. Audience size and composition are also important to the network or station, since they determine the amount it can charge for commercial time. Shows are cancelled once they fail to attract enough viewers to make their commercial time attractive to potential advertisers. In this section, we examine how audiences are measured and how advertisers use this information in planning their media schedules.

Audience Measurement Television audiences are measured by Numeris, a not-for-profit broadcast research company based on cooperation among the Canadian Association of Broadcasters, the Association of Canadian Advertisers, and Canadian advertising agencies. Numeris collects TV audience measurement data with two methods: portable people meter (PPM) for national and some local markets, and diary for remaining local markets. **Figure 11-8** summarizes data collected by Numeris regarding the amount of TV watched across different age groups for fall 2018. TV viewing remained strong despite the prevalence of the Internet, although viewership variation exists across demographic groups. At present, there is a drop in hours watched and daily reach for younger adults aged 18–24 versus those aged 25–54, but weekly reach is similar. The substantial viewership for those aged 55+ signals heavier TV viewing for retired people with additional spare time.

Figure 11-8 Weekly hours watched by age, fall 2018

Age	Weekly Hours per Capita	Weekly Reach %	Daily Reach %
Persons 2+	23.3	92.5	79.3
Adults 18+	25.2	93.0	80.7
Adults 18–24	14.2	88.6	67.5
Adults 25–54	17.6	90.3	74.4
Adults 55+	37.9	97.8	92.4

Currently, Numeris's portable people meter collects data nationally and in large local markets: Montreal (French and English), Toronto–Hamilton, Calgary, Edmonton, and Vancouver–Victoria. People in the panel wear a device that automatically records a silent audio signal emitted from programming. In fact, the PPM is capable of receiving the signal from other media such as radio, cinema, or any medium that emits a sound. The device records information regarding station, program, and time. Each evening, the device is placed in a docking station and the data are transferred to Numeris. The method offers numerous measurement benefits over the previous technology: it measures unobtrusively since the person does not interact with the device while recording data; it measures on an individual level instead of on a household or television basis; it measures exposure to multiple media for each individual; and it measures exposure of recorded programming from any technology (e.g., PVR).

Criticism of the PPM emerged as specialty channel executives believed the system worked best for measuring audience sizes for large networks. A decline in viewership for children, teens, and young adults appeared in the data, possibly due to the research method since the device needs to be continually worn and placed in the dock each night; some thought that these two actions might not be happening consistently enough with younger members of the sampling panel. Part of the problem lies in the fact that it is chronically difficult to obtain data from young people, and now the pager does not look as "cool" as it used to when first established. A sleeker and wireless version is under development.[27]

Numeris also uses the diary research method for collecting television audience information in 36 local markets. A booklet for each television owned in the household is sent to a representative sample of households. Numeris gathers viewership information from this sample and then projects this information to the total viewing area. The diary method works as follows. Each person aged two years or older records his or her viewing for one week in the booklet. The recordings are based on 15-minute increments from 6:00 a.m. until 2:00 a.m. Viewers write down station call letters, channel numbers, programs, and who is watching. The booklet also contains a number of basic demographic questions. As expected, the diary method is a substantially weaker measurement system than the PPM; the cost efficiencies and ease of use of the PPM will likely lead to expansion to local markets in future.

Numeris provides an extensive array of services, of which we highlight a few. For total Canada and meter markets, advertisers can track the average weekly audience size by demographic, reception type (e.g., satellite, cable, off-air), and station group (e.g., conventional, specialty). Advertisers can observe reach by province, market, station, time period, and program across numerous demographic variables. Numeris offers resources to members regarding research methodology (e.g., sample size and characteristics, data collection, response rates, panel background, geographic boundaries), TV programming (e.g., program listings, technology adoption and use), and day-after viewership data. The EM Stats Card provides detailed viewing information for each market in terms of cable, satellite, and PVR penetration in addition to other similar macro-level data.

Audience Measures The data collected allow for the calculation of two critical audience measures: program rating and share of audience. A **program rating** is the percentage of people in a geographic area tuned in to a specific program during a specific time period. The program rating is calculated by dividing the number of people tuned to a particular show by the total number of people in the geographic area. A **ratings point** represents 1 percent of all the people tuned to a specific television program and is calculated nationally, regionally, and for each local market. The program rating is the key number for individual stations, networks, and advertisers since the amount of money charged for commercial time is based on it. A 1 percent change in a program's rating during a viewing season can gain or lose substantial dollars in advertising revenue for the media organization or increase or decrease audience size for the advertiser.

Another important audience measurement is the **share of audience**, which is the percentage of people watching TV in a specified time period that are tuned to a specific program. Audience share is always higher than the program rating unless all people are watching television (in which case they would be equal). Share of audience is an important performance metric since it indicates how well a program does with the available viewing audience. For example, late at night the size of the viewing audience drops substantially, so the best way to assess the popularity of a late-night program is to examine the share of the available audience it attracts relative to competing programs. Again, share of audience is calculated nationally and for each local market.

Since the data are recorded on a minute-by-minute basis for the PPM and in 15-minute increments for the diary method, the program ratings and share of audience can be examined over different time intervals. In fact, some believe that the ability of new technology to measure audiences with short time intervals on a minute-by-minute basis will provide unexpected research results regarding TV viewing behaviour in the future.[28] Also, since demographic and other consumer data are recorded, these measures can be investigated in great detail for many target audience profile variables. For example, we saw a breakout of the data in **Figure 11-8** by age. The sheer complexity and extensiveness of the data makes advanced software analysis paramount.

Audience Measurement Reporting The collected television data are analyzed with software applications provided by other organizations. One company, nlogic, is a subsidiary of Numeris and offers numerous solutions for examining the program ratings and share of audience data extensively, by time and by different audience characteristics.

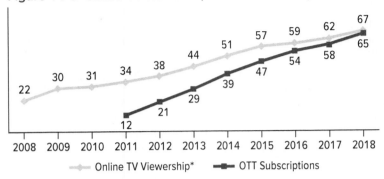

Figure 11-9 Online TV viewership and OTT subscriptions

— Online TV Viewership* — OTT Subscriptions

* Past month.
**OTT services measured include Netflix, CraveTV, Sportsnet Now and Amazon Prime.
©Media Technology Monitor (MTM)

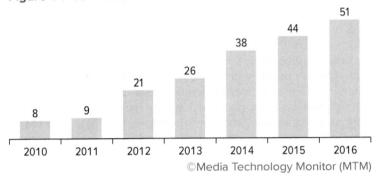

Figure 11-10 Accessed the Internet on a TV

©Media Technology Monitor (MTM)

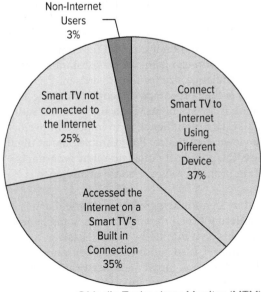

Figure 11-11 Accessing Internet on smart TV

Non-Internet Users 3%

Smart TV not connected to the Internet 25%

Connect Smart TV to Internet Using Different Device 37%

Accessed the Internet on a Smart TV's Built in Connection 35%

©Media Technology Monitor (MTM)

Many other third-party processors exist, as the market for turning data into valuable media planning information is competitive. Some specialize in either diary or meter data, and many offer analysis for both.

Media buying agencies and advertising agencies subscribe to these data and analytic services and use the information for developing media plans for their clients. Advertisers can access some of this aggregate information through ThinkTV, an industry association for television networks, television stations, and firms that sell television advertising time. It offers resources to those in the television industry to demonstrate the value and importance of television as a medium versus competing media (e.g., magazines). It publishes basic facts garnered from the aforementioned sources and conducts primary research through independent market research firms.

OTT TV VIEWING

Earlier we mentioned that viewers see TV programs online in which advertisers spent $159 million in 2017, and see TV programs on over-the-top (OTT) subscription services like Netflix. **Figure 11-9** shows the penetration levels of these types of viewing behaviours, with about two-thirds of Canadians consuming TV programs both ways. The longitudinal data shows steady growth for 10 years, suggesting that the plateau of this innovation diffusion is a few years away. The implication of this is perhaps greater use by advertisers of product placement and social TV communication as more people watch TV programs with fewer TV ads or no TV ads.

Accessing TV programs through online viewership and OTT subscription requires delivery via the Internet. **Figure 11-10** indicates significant growth of Canadians using a TV connected to the Internet to view TV programs for both types of viewing behaviour. The implication of this is that the consumers are dramatically changing their viewing behaviour as broadband Internet becomes more widely distributed.

By fall 2016, smart TV penetration reached 42 percent in Canada. The method of accessing the Internet on TV occurs directly through the smart TV's built-in connection or through another device (e.g., video game console). However, as shown in **Figure 11-11**, one-quarter of smart TV owners do not use the Internet connection option, indicating that complete uptake of online viewing and OTT services is limited for a sizable portion of Canadians.

Figure 11-12 compares OTT subscribers and non-subscribers, indicating that both groups retain high levels of a paid TV service at

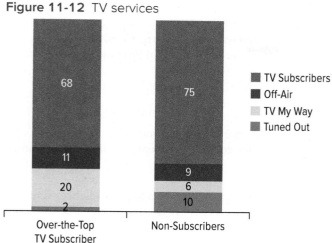

Figure 11-12 TV services

- TV Subscribers
- Off-Air
- TV My Way
- Tuned Out

Over-the-Top TV Subscriber: 68, 11, 20, 2

Non-Subscribers: 75, 9, 6, 10

©Media Technology Monitor (MTM)

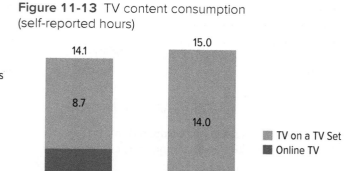

Figure 11-13 TV content consumption (self-reported hours)

- TV on a TV Set
- Online TV

OTT Subscribers: 14.1 (8.7 / 5.4)

Non-Subscribers: 15.0 (14.0 / 1.0)

©Media Technology Monitor (MTM)

68 percent for OTT subscribers and 75 percent for non-subscribers. An OTT subscription is an add-on service for many Canadians; the majority of OTT subscriptions are currently for Netflix at 60 percent. Thus, at any given time, viewers will choose to watch either a paid TV service program or a Netflix program. The implication for networks and advertisers is to improve their TV programs to ensure greater frequency of use or more use per session. Conventional TV executives believe viewer expectations for higher quality programs arose from OTT services and improved TV with serialized prime-time dramas. In the past, complex storylines with continuing week-to-week episodes did not work, but conventional TV picked up on the trend and adjusted.[29]

Figure 11-14 Profile of TV My Way viewers

44% are aged 18–34 vs. 20% average

24% earn $35,000 to $100,000 vs. 20% average

87% subscribe to OTT service vs. 66% average

9 hours of TV watching per week vs. 15 hours average

6.7 hours of OTT watching per week vs. 3.4 hours average

39 hours of Internet use per week vs. 26 hours average

Figure 11-13 further supports the point that OTT services round out a viewer's experience. OTT subscribers report 14 hours of viewing per week with almost nine of those hours consuming programs from their paid TV service. Note that this data is self-reported and it is typically underreported compared to viewership tracked by Numeris for TV and other methods for online viewing. As noted above, TV networks and advertisers would presumably try to maintain the number of hours of paid TV service viewing. Moreover their programming could evolve more to live entertainment like sports or to popular event TV where watching it as it unfolds becomes a viewer priority.

Earlier we mentioned that 20 percent of TV viewers do not use a paid TV service; they watch online only or use an OTT service. Those in the latter group are quite interesting as they represent lead users for new TV technology consumption and TV viewing. **Figure 11-14** provides a snapshot of the profile variables from Media Technology Monitor of anglophone viewers who skew above the average.

The data presented here suggests different futures for conventional TV and opportunities for advertising on TV shows to reach audiences. In addition, as viewers gravitate to OTT services, it remains to be seen whether these services will continue not to show ads as a source of revenue. For example, we may see a series on Netflix or another service begin with a "sponsored by" announcement, much like was seen on live TV in the 1950s.

Evaluation of Television

Television is an ideal advertising medium because of its unique mass media characteristics and its ability to combine visual images, sound, motion, and colour. It presents the advertiser with the opportunity to develop creative and imaginative appeals. And while it seems that some people want to watch TV without commercials, evidence suggests that maybe viewers do not mind them and that TV will survive despite some online brands' predictions that it might not. Witness the anticipation for watching new ads during big TV events, the interest in watching programs that show commercials as the content, the YouTube viewing of TV commercials, and the way people share TV ads with one another via email or social media! Despite the positive features of TV, it has characteristics that limit or prevent its use by advertisers.[30]

STRENGTHS OF TELEVISION

TV has numerous strengths compared to other media, including target audience coverage, geographic coverage, scheduling flexibility, reach, frequency, cost efficiency, attention, creativity for cognitive and emotional responses, and media image.

Target Audience Coverage Marketers selling products and services that appeal to broad target audiences find that TV lets them cover mass markets or large groups of target consumers. Nearly everyone—regardless of age, sex, income, or educational level—watches at least some TV. The average Canadian watches TV 25 hours per week, thereby consuming this medium more than any other. Most people watch on a regular basis: 99 percent of all Canadian households own a TV, and 74 percent have more than one TV. Television advertising makes it possible to ensure that advertisers achieve audience coverage. However, as noted in **Figure 11-1** earlier, coverage for TV content with television ads via paid TV services and antennas is at 75 percent, noticeably lower than previous levels.

Geographic Coverage Advertisers can adjust their media strategies for TV to take advantage of different geographic markets through spot ads in specific market areas. Ads can be scheduled to run repeatedly in more favourable markets. Alternatively, advertisers can obtain national coverage or regional coverage depending upon their marketing objectives. This can be especially useful if promotional planners want to take advantage of information regarding their brand development index or the category development index described in Chapter 10. For example, Oxford Frozen Foods advertised on the Food Network, HGTV, Global, the Cooking Channel, and TSN during major sporting events to communicate the benefits of its wild blueberries. After years of discussing this, managers took the leap to communicate the value of eating the fruit grown in rural Nova Scotia.[31]

Scheduling Flexibility Television has been criticized for being a nonselective medium, since it is difficult to reach a precisely defined target audience through the use of TV advertising. But some selectivity is possible due to variations in the composition of audiences as a result of broadcast time and program content. For example, Saturday morning TV caters to children; Saturday and Sunday afternoon programs are geared to the sports-oriented male; and weekday daytime shows appeal heavily to homemakers. With the growth of specialty channels, advertisers refine their coverage further by appealing to groups with specific interests such as sports, news, history, the arts, or music. The development of specialty channels allowed for selectivity somewhat similar to magazines on these interests.

Reach Television viewing is a closely monitored activity such that the size of the audience for a television program is known fairly quickly. Placement of TV ads on certain combinations of shows allows an advertiser to reach as many in its target audience as it deems necessary. As **Figure 11-15** shows, TV reaches 81 percent of Canadians on a daily basis, and virtually everyone on a weekly basis with 93 percent reach. These statistics indicate that TV is a good media to achieve high reach levels.[32]

In addition, TV continued to reach 65 percent of young adults aged 18–34 on a daily basis and 86 percent on a weekly basis (**Figure 11-16**). Availability of airtime and amount of budget are the main constraints on allowing an advertiser to reach as large an audience as possible.

Frequency Scheduling television permits frequency in concentrated blocks throughout

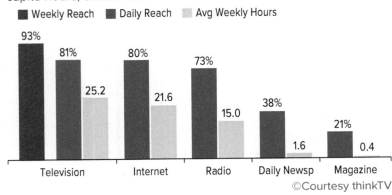

Figure 11-15 Weekly reach/daily reach/average weekly per capita hours, adults 18+

■ Weekly Reach ■ Daily Reach ■ Avg Weekly Hours

©Courtesy thinkTV

a program, evening, week, month, or season. Heightened frequency may be necessary for a new product launch or an effort to obtain switching, while lower levels of frequency may be feasible for advertisers desiring more continuous exposure.

Cost Efficiency Compared to many other media, the cost to reach individuals by television is reasonably affordable. For example, one of the most expensive placements is an ad shown during the Super Bowl costing $130,000, yet with a viewership of 6.5 million, the average cost per thousand (CPM) is about $20, which is on par with basic banner ad rates.[33] Because of its ability to reach large audiences in a cost-efficient manner, TV is a popular medium among companies selling mass-consumption products. Companies with widespread distribution and availability of their products and services use TV to reach the mass market and deliver their advertising messages at a very low cost per thousand. Television is indispensable to large consumer packaged-goods companies and car makers, for example.

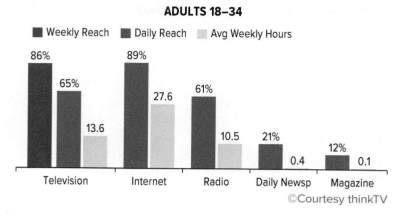

Figure 11-16 Weekly reach/daily reach/average weekly per capita hours, adults 18–34

©Courtesy thinkTV

Attention Television is intrusive in that ads impose themselves on viewers as they watch a program. Unless we make an effort to avoid commercials, most of us are exposed to thousands of them each year. This seemingly continuous exposure implies that viewers devote some attention (i.e., selective attention) to many advertising messages. As discussed in Chapter 4, the low-involvement nature of consumer learning and response processes may mean TV ads have an effect on consumers simply through heavy message repetition and exposure to catchy slogans and jingles. Research suggests that consumers watch their favourite programs with greater attention to the program and subsequently to the embedded television commercial.[34] **Figure 11-17** indicates that most viewers believe they pay attention to TV ads more than other forms of advertising, although we see a different trend with young adults who use other media at higher levels.

Creativity for Cognitive and Emotional Responses Perhaps the greatest advantage of TV is its ability to present the advertising message; the interaction of sight, sound, and motion offers creative flexibility for generating responses that make people both feel and think. Emotionally, TV ads convey a unique image for a brand, develop entertaining appeals that make a dull product appear interesting, give lifelike representation and dramatic insight of consumption, and tell a story about a brand to highlight its features and benefits. For example, the ads for Newfoundland and Labrador tourism showed fjords in Gros Morne National Park and other stunning visuals with beautiful cinematography for many years, and more recently focused on storytelling of the people, activities (e.g., iceberg watching!), and locations across numerous executions.[35] Cognitively, TV ads demonstrate how a product or service works, inform consumers about new brands or products, and allow consumers to see how one product compares to another. For example, about half of all TV ads feature one aspect of comparative advertising.[36]

Exhibit 11-2 shows a couple of shots from an exciting ad for HTC that holds the attention of the target audience for the full 60 seconds. The ad depicted a photography student recording his first fashion shoot while skydiving. HTC deployed the images subsequently in magazine ads to demonstrate the photo quality. The creativity of this novel idea demonstrates how a video story communicates emotionally.

Figure 11-17 Attention to advertising by media

- Watching TV on TV set
- Listening to radio
- Using a social network
- Watching video online on a mobile device
- Using a search engine
- Watching video online on a computer

Q. When do you pay the most attention to advertising?

©Courtesy thinkTV

Exhibit 11-2 A television ad is an effective way to communicate the photo quality of the HTC phone.

©Made by Mother London, www.motherlondon.com

Figure 11-18 Major media comparisons of attitudes, adults 18 to 49

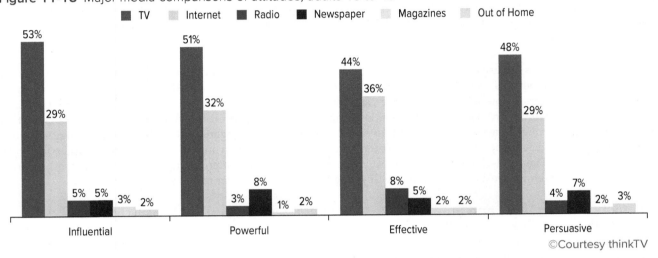

Legend: ■ TV ▨ Internet ■ Radio ■ Newspaper ▨ Magazines ▨ Out of Home

Influential: 53%, 29%, 5%, 5%, 3%, 2%
Powerful: 51%, 32%, 3%, 8%, 1%, 2%
Effective: 44%, 36%, 8%, 5%, 2%, 2%
Persuasive: 48%, 29%, 4%, 7%, 2%, 3%

©Courtesy thinkTV

Media Image Given the prominence television has with its mass-market characteristic, TV advertising often carries a high degree of acceptability. Television is usually viewed favourably due to the higher costs of placement and production, which demonstrates a level of acceptance or establishment for those who advertise with this medium. **Figure 11-18** summarizes data reported by ThinkTV. The evolution of advertisers putting their ads on video hosting sites is a testament to media image.

IMC Perspective 11-1 completes the story of CTV's broadcast of the Super Bowl in Canada. For a couple of years, Canadians could see U.S. ads while watching the game, but we are back to the historic system of simultaneous substitution of Canadian ads.

IMC PERSPECTIVE 11-1

CANADA LOSES U.S. ADS FOR SUPER BOWL

In 2015, the Canadian Radio-television and Telecommunications Commission (CRTC) announced that Canadians would see American ads during the Super Bowl broadcast starting in 2017. CTV, which held the rights, would not be permitted simultaneous substitution (e.g., "simsub") in which Canadian ads replace U.S. ads during the Super Bowl broadcast on their network. While this appeared to be a win for consumers who wanted American ads, it reduced CTV's broadcast rights investment. The purpose of simsub is to provide Canadian broadcasters advertising revenue when they show an

American program on a Canadian network. For example, CTV pays for the rights to broadcast a program in the same time slot as the U.S. broadcast and requires a revenue source for payment in addition to its costs and profits. According to the CRTC, its regulations merely allow broadcasters to request simsub from the television service providers; it is not a regulation that the providers are obligated to follow. However, rarely have Canadians experienced non-simsub broadcasts, so naturally many considered it to be a law.

In the past, American brands could purchase Canadian ad space and show their ads but did not, even though a cost per thousand analysis suggests viability. In the United States, it cost $4.5 million to reach 114 million people, while in Canada it cost $200,000 to reach 8 million, giving a cost per thousand of about $40 and $25 respectively, in favour of the smaller market. For the Canadian broadcaster of the Super Bowl, ad revenue approximated $15 million, with $10 million in broadcasting rights given to the NFL along with production costs, giving the broadcaster a healthy profit. With eyeballs expected to move to a U.S. station to see the ads, one can easily see why Bell Media, the owner of CTV, did not accept the decision and planned to get it overturned. It stood to lose millions, as would Canadian advertising agencies and media buying agencies who supported Bell Media.

Despite this, Canadians watched U.S. ads on the Canadian broadcast of the Super Bowl in 2017, resulting in a decline of viewers from 7.3 million to 4.5 million and a loss of $11 million in ad revenue for Bell Media. In early 2018, just before the Super Bowl, the Supreme Court declined to grant a stay of the CRTC's decision which meant a continuation of U.S. ads on a Canadian broadcast. CTV countered with a contest directed to viewers of the Canadian

©Blend Images/Alamy Stock Photo

broadcast and showed the ads online ahead of the game to entice Canadians to stick with a Canadian channel, but the number of viewers stayed at 4.5 million.

Bell Media pressed on with its efforts and received positive news in the fall of 2018 when a clause within the North American Free Trade Agreement overturned the CRTC decision: "Canada may not accord the Super Bowl program treatment less favourable than the treatment accorded to other programs originating from the United States retransmitted in Canada." Can we make a conclusion about TV and its advertising based on this story, which lasted four years (and through two editions of our advertising book)? First, it demonstrates the importance of TV for live sports and major events shown on TV. For Canadian advertisers, the Super Bowl takes advantage of all of TV's strengths. Second, it confirms the significance of rights within intellectual property, something in decline in the era of digital piracy.

Question:
1. Does this story suggest any other conclusions about Canadian TV broadcasting or Canadian TV advertising?

LIMITATIONS OF TELEVISION

Although television is unsurpassed from a creative perspective, the medium has several limitations that preclude its use by many advertisers. These problems include target audience selectivity, absolute cost, control for selective exposure, processing time, involvement, clutter, and media image.

Target Audience Selectivity Selectivity is available in television through scheduling by day, time, type of program, or program name, but advertisers who are seeking a very specific target audience find the coverage of TV extends beyond their market. Geographic selectivity can be a problem for local advertisers such as retailers, since a station bases its rates on the total market area it reaches, which may be beyond the merchant's trade area. Recent technology to target by household on what TV programming is actually watched is beginning to show stronger selectivity at a lower cost.[37]

Selectivity is possible within a network's portfolio, as Corus Television reaches women with three channels. W Network offers a wide variety of entertainment for women of all ages. Cosmopolitan TV "promises fun, flirty and irreverent entertainment" for women aged 18–34. W Movies is expected to reach women aged 25–54. The flanking strategy of having two niche channels to support the mainstream one is consistent with media vehicle options found with magazines. For example, Transcontinental has *Elle Canada* for women in their twenties, *Canadian Living* and *Homemakers* for women in their thirties and forties, and *More* and *Good Times* for women older than 40.

Absolute Cost Despite the efficiency of TV in reaching large audiences, it is an expensive medium in which to advertise. The high cost of TV stems not only from the expense of buying airtime but also from the costs of producing a quality commercial. More advertisers are using media-driven creative strategies that require production of a variety of commercials, which drive up their costs. Even local ads can be expensive to produce and often are not of high quality. The high costs of producing and airing commercials often price small and medium-sized advertisers out of the market.

Control for Selective Exposure When advertisers buy time on a TV program, they are not purchasing guaranteed exposure but rather the opportunity to communicate a message. There is evidence that the size of the viewing audience shrinks during a commercial break for a variety of obvious reasons and due to zapping and zipping. Multitasking consumers with their phones are distracted from viewing ads as well (**Figure 11-19**).

Zapping refers to changing channels to avoid commercials. An observational study found as much as one-third of program audiences may be lost to zapping when commercials appear.[38] Zapping occurs because commercials are viewed as unbelievable, a poor use of time, and annoying.[39] Research shows that young adults zap more than older adults, and men are more likely to zap than are women.[40] The number of people zapping in and out during breaks was not caused by the type of product being advertised or by characteristics of the ads, but rather to find out what is shown on other channels.[41] Research discovered that zappers recalled fewer brands advertised than non-zappers, and that most of the brands recalled by zappers were placed near the end of the commercial break when viewers returned to a program.[42]

Zipping occurs when customers fast-forward through commercials as they play back a previously recorded program. By 2017, household penetration of PVR technology reached 55 percent and Canadians averaged 3 hours per week of PVR viewing compared to 22 hours of live viewing.[43] One author suggests that data showing how and when viewers avoid commercials provides information to make advertising more relevant and efficient.[44]

Figure 11-19 Percentage of Canadians using their phone while watching TV

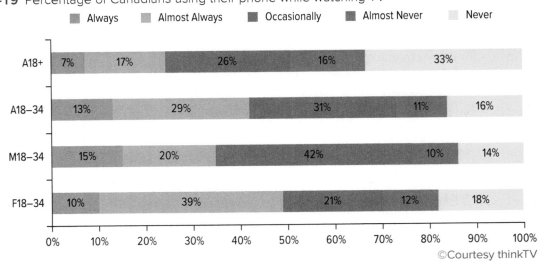

©Courtesy thinkTV

Processing Time TV commercials usually last only 30 or 15 seconds and leave nothing tangible for the viewer to examine or consider. Presumably, consumers do not process much information or have emotional responses beyond the immediate presentation of a few seconds, although this changes with very creative ads that have thoughtful messages or involve consumers with extreme emotions. These two time frames account for about 80 percent of all ads for the past two decades, with the 15-second ad growing somewhat. A 15-second spot typically sells for about two-thirds the price of a 30-second spot. Since these advertisers believe that shorter commercials can deliver a message just as effectively as longer spots, the use of 15-second commercials allows advertisers to run additional spots to reinforce the message through greater frequency, reach a larger audience, or advertise in more purchase cycles.

Involvement The cumulative effect of television's characteristics implies that it is a low-involvement medium. While its invasive messages provide instant exposure and perhaps hold our attention with impressive creative strategies and tactics, the relatively short processing time makes it a less effective media for an advertiser to significantly persuade a target audience. While this assertion of TV appears historically accurate, alternative ideas are emerging. For example, some shows attract a devout cohort of viewers who are so involved with the program that their advertising involvement is equally heightened.[45]

Linking ads with the program content tries to alleviate the low involvement concern. The dissemination of smart TV and the evolution of multitasking viewers as indicated in **Figure 11-20** suggest that TV may overcome some of its involvement limitations. Notice all the activities viewers can engage in to enjoy the show even more. However, viewers directing their attention to two screens at once may not be the best solution for all advertisers and all advertising situations.

Multi-screening is the simultaneous use of multiple screens. Most investigations of this topic concern TV with a smart phone, tablet, or laptop, and the communication effects of TV ads directed to multi-screening viewers appear mixed. One study found that multi-screening led to weaker brand recognition but stronger brand attitude because of less counterarguing since the receiver did not watch the ad message intently.[46] Another study concluded that multi-screening led to stronger brand recognition and brand attitude if participating in a related task on the portable device (such as those shown in **Figure 11-20**) compared to an unrelated task. However, the communication effects for single-screen viewers remained stronger than those for multi-screening viewers.[47] A third study found similar results of stronger communication effects in favour of single-screen viewers versus multi-screening viewers, but the communication effects appeared stronger for emotional messages compared to rational messages for multi-screen viewers.[48]

Clutter The problems of short TV messages are compounded by the fact that the advertiser's message is only one of many spots and other non-programming material seen during a commercial break, so it may have trouble being noticed. One of advertisers' greatest concerns with TV advertising is the potential decline in effectiveness because of

Figure 11-20 Consumer online activities related to program or ads while watching TV

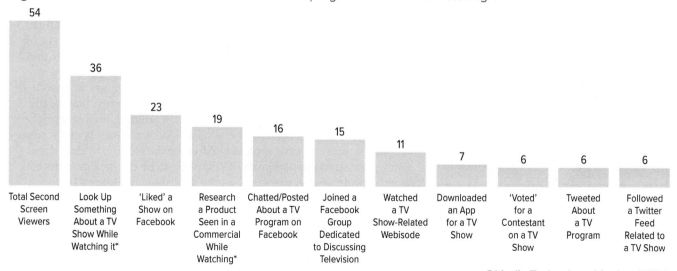

©Media Technology Monitor (MTM)

Figure 11-21 Consumer online activities not related to program or ads while watching TV

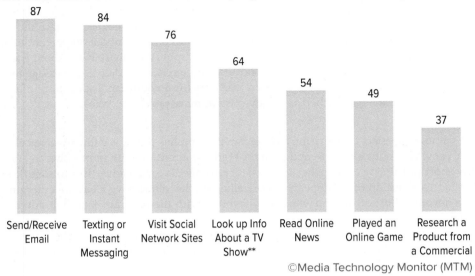

Send/Receive Email	87
Texting or Instant Messaging	84
Visit Social Network Sites	76
Look up Info About a TV Show**	64
Read Online News	54
Played an Online Game	49
Research a Product from a Commercial	37

©Media Technology Monitor (MTM)

such *clutter*, and this clutter expanded considerably with the use of Internet devices while watching TV, as shown in **Figure 11-21**.

Imagine counting the number of commercials, promotions for the news or upcoming programs, or public service announcements that appear during a station break and the concern for clutter becomes obvious. With all of these messages competing for target audiences' attention, it is easy to understand why the viewer comes away confused or even annoyed and unable to remember or properly identify the product or service advertised.

One cause of clutter is the use of shorter commercials and **split-30s**, 30-second spots in which the advertiser promotes two different products with separate messages. The Canadian Radio-television and Telecommunications Commission (CRTC), which regulates television, permits 12 minutes of commercials per hour for specialty channels and an unlimited number of minutes for conventional channels. However, when simulcast Canadian commercials are run, there may be extra time since U.S. TV stations often show more commercial minutes. To fill this time, Canadian stations run ads for other shows, public service announcements, or news/entertainment vignettes. Thus, Canadian viewers sometimes experience a different kind of clutter than their American counterparts.

Figure 11-22 Consumer attitudes toward video-based ads by media, adults 18+

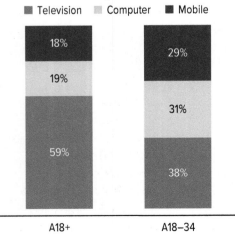

■ Television ■ Computer ■ Mobile

A18+	A18–34
18%	29%
19%	31%
59%	38%

Q. Which types of video advertising are you most likely to watch? Least likely to watch?

©Courtesy thinkTV

Media Image To many critics of advertising, TV commercials illustrate everything that is wrong with the industry. Critics often single out TV commercials because of their pervasiveness and the intrusive nature of the medium. Consumers are seen as defenceless against the barrage of TV ads, since they cannot control the transmission of the message and what appears on their screens. Viewers dislike TV advertising when they believe it to be offensive, uninformative, or shown too frequently, or when they do not like its content.[49] Studies have shown that, of the various forms of advertising, TV commercials generate the highest levels of distrust.[50] Also, concern has been raised about the effects of TV advertising on specific groups, such as children or the elderly.[51] While these historic concerns are legitimate, TV appears to be the best in terms of receiving video-based messages, as the data show in **Figure 11-22**.

IMC Perspective 11-2 discusses issues facing the buyers and sellers of Canadian TV advertising due to the changes noted in the chapter, such as OTT services and a greater digital presence in the delivery of TV services.

COMPLICATIONS IN TV AD BUYING

Pressure from OTT services and other factors caused issues within conventional TV advertising. We review a few discussion points between media buyers and broadcasters.

The first issue concerns smaller audiences as viewers watch video content elsewhere and rising advertising prices as broadcasters cover their fixed costs. One media executive responded that TV still provides the best media value, especially when supported with other media within the company's inventory, such as radio and out-of-home.

The second complaint focused on changing the language of buying TV advertising as it becomes digitally oriented. A broadcaster representative agreed, and promised to communicate more simply in future, but acknowledged that things are changing.

A third problem centred on buyers' view that broadcasters competed too much against digital in selling the merits of TV, such as its ability to achieve strong reach levels or creatively communicate. The same rep suggested that advertisers consider how TV works with digital after the initial broadcast ad.

Fourth, when will industry partners cooperate and allow data from viewers' set-top box to be aligned with Numeris data? One broadcaster absolutely agreed, but cautioned that it will take time due to competing interests and the development of everyone's knowledge base with new technology.

Continuing with broadcasters' interest in a digital approach for TV advertising, the buyers' fifth criticism addressed programmatic buying with respect to whether it transfers from the Internet to TV sufficiently and whether it is an effective approach. Broadcasters responded by saying that programmatic buying is a good start toward automation, but refinement is necessary based on buyers' experience. Further, programmatic buying for niche TV audiences may not be the best allocation for advertisers whose objective is to maximize reach.

As a sixth issue, buyers wondered if broadcasters would measure and communicate audience size for each commercial aired, as is done in other countries. Broadcasters outlined reasons for not moving in this direction: a lack of buyers' request,

©Robert Daly/Caia Image/Glow Images

too many transactions to manage for so many commercial pods, too much complexity, and a concern of data accuracy with small samples.

The relevance of planning by cost-per-thousand (CPM) provided a seventh point of discussion, as CPM in TV did not correspond to CPM in other media. This is not a new point compared to the others, however broadcasters remained committed to CPM as a broad method of understanding the television ad buy and ensuring revenue optimization.

As a backdrop to these issues, broadcasters introduced new methods for selling advertising. Bell launched Data-Enhanced TV, allowing buyers to target based on age, gender, and key performance indicators to increase reach. Rogers Enhanced Data combines audience data from multiple sources to target more precise target audiences. A new Sportsnet app permits advertising sponsorship during events like Blue Jays games.

Corus innovated on a number of fronts. It established the ability to target individual households with ad messages known as addressable advertising. Corus also looked to reducing its commercial pod length for certain shows or days. Corus offered the option for advertisers to insert ads within video-on-demand programs, and looked to implement a system of selling ads more simply, like online media companies.

Question:

1. Which issue appears to be the most contentious between TV advertising buyers and sellers?

LO3 Radio

In contrast to television, radio evolved into a primarily local advertising medium characterized by highly specialized programming appealing to very narrow segments of the population. The pervasiveness of this medium continues as radio advertising revenue hit $1.5 billion in 2017. Although down slightly from a peak of $1.6 billion in 2013, ad revenue bounced between these two levels over the past decade.[52] In this section, we show how buying radio time is mostly similar to buying television time. We also review radio's strengths for advertisers to communicate messages to their current and potential customers, and summarize the inherent limitations that affect its role in the advertiser's media strategy.

TYPES OF RADIO ADVERTISING

The purchase of radio time is similar to that of television; advertisers make either network or spot buys on either AM or FM radio bands.

Network Radio Advertisers purchase time on a radio network (e.g., TSN). Using a network minimizes the amount of negotiation and administrative work needed to get national or regional coverage, and the costs are lower than those for individual stations. However, the number of affiliated stations on the network roster and the types of audiences they reach may vary, so the use of network radio reduces advertisers' flexibility in selecting stations. National advertising revenue topped $517 million in 2017. Syndicated radio operators offer an alternative for radio advertising by offering packages for advertising across their whole network.

Spot Radio National advertisers purchase time on individual stations in various markets. The purchase of spot radio provides greater flexibility in selecting markets, individual stations, and airtime and adjusting the message for local market conditions. Local advertising revenue reached $978 million in 2017. By far the heaviest users of radio are local advertisers; the majority of radio advertising time is purchased from individual stations by local companies. Auto dealers, retailers, restaurants, and financial institutions are among the heaviest users of local radio advertising.

Station Formats The CRTC lists 1,126 stations, with 847 in English, 224 in French, and 103 in other languages. Among these, 725 are commercial stations comprising 104 English AM, 481 English FM, 6 French AM, 93 French FM, 18 other language AM, and 23 other language FM.[53] These numbers tally to 585 English, 99 French, and 41 other language over 128 AM stations and 597 FM stations. Bell, Newcap, and Rogers account for 30 percent of the 725 commercial radio stations. Both network advertising and spot advertising are offered across all these format options.

Radio Streaming Radio stations stream their broadcast online so an Internet listener is exposed to the same ads as the broadcast listener. About one-quarter of all English Canadians listen to a Canadian radio station this way and this level remained constant over the past decade. Streaming of radio stations is skewed more strongly to those who are aged 35–49, have a household income above $100,000, are highly educated, and have children in the household.[54] The majority listen to a local Canadian radio station (62 percent) or one from another Canadian city (26 percent). They stream an average of four hours per week, which is skewed more highly to women and those aged 37 and older.

TIME PERIODS

As with television, the broadcast day for radio is divided into time periods or dayparts. The size of the radio listening audience varies widely across the dayparts, and advertising rates follow accordingly. The largest radio audiences (and thus the highest rates) occur during the early morning and late afternoon drive times. Radio rates also vary according to the number of spots or type of audience plan purchased, the supply of and demand for time available in the local market, and the ratings of the individual station. Rate information is available directly from the stations and is summarized in Canadian Advertising Rates and Data (CARD). Some stations issue grid rate cards. However, many stations do not adhere strictly to rate cards. Their rates are negotiable and depend on factors such as availability, time period, and number of spots purchased. The majority of radio ads are 30 seconds in length; however, stations will book 60-second spots and the majority do not book 15-second spots.

MEASURING THE RADIO AUDIENCE

As noted earlier, Numeris also provides information on radio listenership using the PPM and a diary method similar to television. Surveys are done twice per year in over 130 radio markets. Numeris publishes many reports associated with these surveys. Market reports summarize each radio station's audience by occupation, language, and other important characteristics. Other similar reports with greater aggregation across regions are also published. As seen for television, Numeris provides its members with many supporting documents to understand how to use radio as a communication tool. It also offers many software applications so that advertisers can purchase radio media effectively and efficiently. The three elements in the Numeris reports are similar to those found with TV: the estimated number of people listening, the percentage of listeners in the survey area population, and the percentage of the total estimated listening audience.

These three estimates are further defined by using *quarter-hour* and *cume* figures. The **average quarter-hour (AQH) figure** expresses the average number of people estimated to have listened to a station for a minimum of five minutes during any quarter-hour in a time period. This figure helps to determine the audience and cost of a spot schedule within a particular time period. **Cume** stands for *cumulative audience,* the estimated total number of different people who listened to a station for at least five minutes in a quarter-hour period within a reported daypart. Cume estimates the reach potential of a radio station. The **average quarter-hour rating (AQH RTG)** expresses the estimated number of listeners as a percentage of the survey area population. The **average quarter-hour share (AQH SHR)** is the percentage of the total listening audience tuned to each station. It shows the share of listeners each station captures out of the total listening audience in the survey area.

Audience research data on radio are often limited, particularly compared with TV, magazines, or newspapers. The Numeris audience research measurement mostly focuses on demographics and a handful of lifestyle factors. Most users of radio are local companies that cannot support research on radio listening in their markets. Thus, media planners do not have as much audience information available to guide them in their purchase of radio time as they do with other media. **Figure 11-23** shows an example of breaking down the audience share of listening by location. Another source of general radio listener information is a new industry association, Radio Connects, which summarizes data from various research studies.

AUDIO STREAMING

Audio streaming involves listening to audio entertainment through a number of digital channels: 57 percent of Canadians listen to music on YouTube, with lower levels of listening in free and paid music streaming services (30 percent), online AM/FM radio streams (23 percent), and podcasts (28 percent). The first two account for 70 percent of the listening time across all four channels.[55] Like TV, these online options represent radio station competition for listeners and potentially less advertising revenue. Additionally, these options possibly offer new opportunities for advertisers to deliver messages. **Figure 11-24** indicates that the penetration rate of all online audio streaming in the past month is 68 percent. It is skewed to listeners under 50 living in higher income households with children.

Figure 11-23 Percentage of listening audience by location and demographic

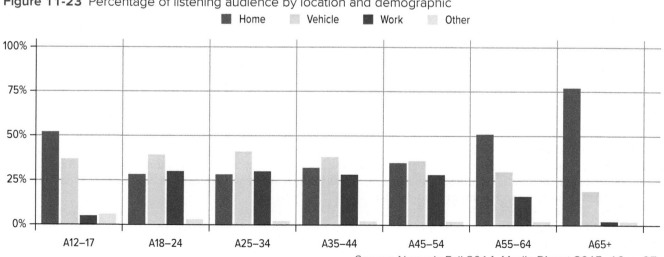

Source: Numeris Fall 2014, Media Digest 2015–16, p. 97.

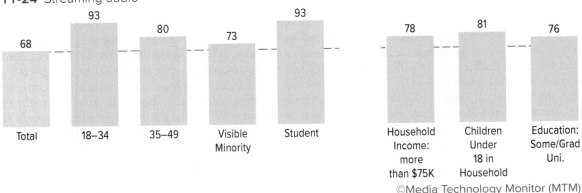

Figure 11-24 Streaming audio

Total	18–34	35–49	Visible Minority	Student
68	93	80	73	93

Household Income: more than $75K	Children Under 18 in Household	Education: Some/Grad Uni.
78	81	76

©Media Technology Monitor (MTM)

LO4 Evaluation of Radio

Radio is an important advertising medium because of its ability to inform consumers of factual information and influence them with rational appeals that often help facilitate their shopping needs. Consumers feel radio keeps them connected: locally with important information, socially with radio personalities, musically with ideas for music not considered, and conveniently with no online search hassles. However, radio does have characteristics that limit its use by advertisers.

STRENGTHS OF RADIO

Radio has many strengths compared to other media, including target audience selectivity, geographic coverage, scheduling flexibility, reach and frequency, cost efficiency and absolute cost, creativity for cognitive responses, and media image.

Target Audience Selectivity One major advantage of radio is the high degree of audience selectivity available through program formats and geographic coverage of numerous stations. Radio lets companies focus their advertising on specialized audiences such as demographic and lifestyle groups with music formats such as easy listening, pop, rock, classical, jazz, country, and news/talk shows, to name a few. Numeris tracks radio listeners across 20 different radio formats, and overlaying radio format listening data with segmentation variables allows advertisers to accurately target their messages. One interesting development is GM's three-month test of tracking drivers' listening habits, with their permission, using the car's Wi-Fi to investigate the possibility of more precise target audience selectivity for advertisers.[56]

Geographic Coverage Radio is essentially a local medium. In this respect, since all listeners can tune in, it offers excellent coverage within its geographic scope. Radio stations become an integral part of many communities, and the program hosts regularly become popular figures. Advertisers use radio stations and personalities to enhance their involvement with a local market and to gain influence with local retailers. Radio also works very effectively in conjunction with place-based/point-of-purchase promotions. Retailers use on-site radio broadcasts combined with special sales or promotions to attract consumers to their stores and get them to make a purchase. Live radio broadcasts are also used in conjunction with event marketing. Recent Numeris research finds greater radio listening in small and medium-sized cities compared to large cities.

Scheduling Flexibility Radio is probably the most flexible of all the advertising media because it has a very short closing period, which means advertisers can change their message almost up to the time it goes on the air. Radio commercials can usually be produced and scheduled on very short notice. Radio advertisers can easily adjust their messages to local market conditions and marketing situations.

Reach and Frequency The low cost of radio means advertisers can build more reach and frequency into their media schedule within a certain budget. They can use different stations to broaden the reach of their messages and multiple spots to ensure adequate frequency. Radio commercials can be produced more quickly than TV spots, and the companies can afford to run them more often. Many national advertisers also recognize the cost efficiency of radio and use it as part of their media strategy. **Figure 11-25** and **Figure 11-26** indicate the degree of reach.

Cost Efficiency and Absolute Cost One of the main strengths of radio as an advertising medium is its low cost. Radio commercials are very inexpensive to produce. They require only a script of the commercial to be read by the radio announcer or a copy of a prerecorded message that can be broadcast by the station. The cost for radio time is also low. The low relative costs of radio make it one of the most efficient of all advertising media, and the low absolute cost means the budget needed for an effective radio campaign is often lower than that for other media.

Creativity for Cognitive Responses The verbal nature of radio ads makes them ideal for long copy to select target audiences who may appreciate greater detailed information for some products. Alternatively, radio ads can also provide more concise brand information in a timely manner. Moreover, both of these factors are highly relevant for those listening in their car, which is a significant percentage of radio listenership. In either case, the informative nature of radio advertising makes it an opportunistic medium to connect with a target audience on a more rational level.

Figure 11-25 Percentage weekly reach by major demographic, by location

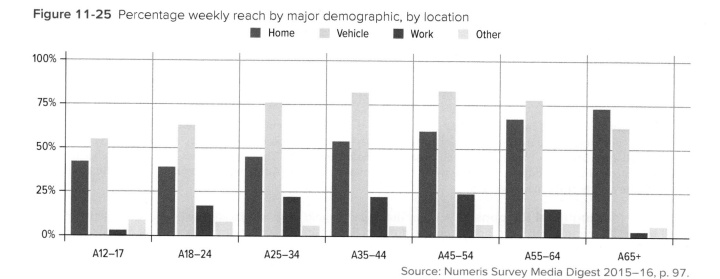

Source: Numeris Survey Media Digest 2015–16, p. 97.

Figure 11-26 Percentage weekly reach and hours tuned by major demographic

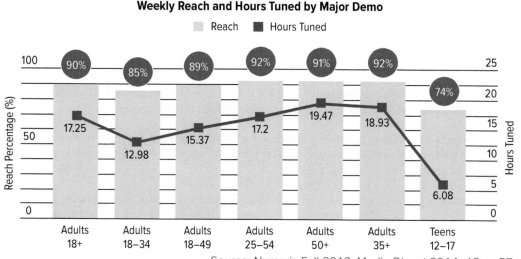

Source: Numeris Fall 2013, Media Digest 2014–15, p. 57.

Media Image Consumers rely on radio for news, weather, and traffic information, not to mention the obvious program content. Radio has a good image in terms of entertainment, relaxation, lifting people's moods, and keeping them up to date on news and gossip. Radio advertising in general has a good media image. For example, almost 50 percent of people report checking the Internet after hearing a radio ad, and appreciating promotion announcements or retail store information.[57]

LIMITATIONS OF RADIO

Several factors limit the effectiveness of radio as an advertising medium, including target audience coverage, control for selective exposure, listener attention, creativity for emotional responses, amount of processing time, involvement, and clutter. The media planner must consider them in determining the role the medium will play in the advertising program.

Target Audience Coverage A problem with radio is the high level of audience fragmentation due to the large number of stations. The percentage of the market tuned to any particular station is usually very small. The top-rated radio station in many major metropolitan areas with a number of AM and FM stations may attract less than 10 percent of the total listening audience. Advertisers that want a broad reach in their radio advertising media schedule have to buy time on a number of stations to cover even a local market. With recent media mergers in Canada, syndicated radio stations now provide advertisers with greater coverage, thus reducing this limitation.

Control for Selective Exposure One environment where radio has a more captive audience is in cars. But getting listeners to expose themselves to commercials can still be difficult. Most people preprogram their car radio and change stations during commercial breaks. One study found large differences between exposure to radio programs and exposure to advertising for listeners in cars. They were exposed to only half of the advertising broadcast and changed stations frequently to avoid commercials.[58]

Listener Attention Another problem that plagues radio is that it is difficult to retain listener attention to commercials. Radio programming, particularly music, is often the background to some other activity and may not receive the listeners' full attention; thus they may miss all or some of the commercials. This is slightly less of a concern because radio is with consumers throughout the day while they do many activities. Advertisers use creativity in radio ads to minimize the effects of listener attention.

Creativity for Emotional Responses A major drawback of radio as an advertising medium is the absence of a visual image. The radio advertiser cannot show the product, demonstrate it, or use any type of visual appeal or information. While the creative options of radio are limited, advertisers take advantage of the absence of a visual element to let consumers create their own picture of what is happening in a radio ad. These messages encourage listeners to use their imagination when processing the words, music, and sound effects.

Radio may reinforce a message received from another media such as television. **Image transfer** occurs where the images of a TV commercial are implanted into a radio spot. First, the advertiser establishes the video image of a TV commercial. Then, a similar—or even the same—audio portion is used in the radio spot. The audio could be the exact same speaker, jingle, or music that occurs in both the TV and the radio executions. Receivers of the radio ad recall the images from the TV commercial as the audio portion is recognized and associated with the TV images. While the idea of image transfer originated with a TV to radio sequence, it can be applied for any visual media to any audio media. For example, a video ad message disseminated in social media could have corresponding audio components in an ad message embedded within a podcast.

Amount of Processing Time A radio commercial is, like a TV ad, a short-lived and fleeting message that is externally paced and does not allow the receiver to control the rate at which it is processed.

Involvement Similar to television, radio is generally considered a low-involvement medium since it is faced with the same characteristics of short processing time and clutter. In fact, it may be seen as being less involving because it has the additional limitation of no visual.

Clutter Clutter is just as much a problem with radio as with other advertising media. Radio stations can play as many minutes of advertising as they like. Most radio stations carry an average of nearly 10 minutes of commercials every hour. During the popular morning and evening rush hours, the amount of commercial time may exceed 12 minutes. Advertisers must create commercials that break through the clutter or use heavy repetition to make sure their messages reach consumers.

LO5 IMC Planning: Strategic Use of Broadcast Media

We continue with our IMC planning sections by relating the use of TV and radio with respect to achieving communication and behavioural objectives in general and in terms of the different stages of the consumer decision-making process for the target audience. This builds on our discussions in earlier chapters and highlights the importance of planning creative and media together.

TELEVISION

The creative opportunities associated with the many types of television advertising allow it to influence many stages of the decision-making process for the target audience. We link the different types of ads with communication objectives and decision-making processes because the integration of television with other media or tools is predicated upon which types of TV ads will be run. For example, the suggestion to combine TV with Internet advertising, an event sponsorship, or perhaps out-of-home media is contingent on how the two media are planned to influence the target audience. As promotional planners decide upon TV as part of their IMC plan, it is critical to consider its communication objectives in relation to the objectives the other tools will contribute.

Promotional managers can plan for ads to influence their target audience at the prepurchase and need recognition stages. These kinds of ads could focus on one key benefit or consumption experience, and identify the brand sufficiently to contribute to awareness. For example, some car ads fit this role quite nicely, like the commercials positioning the Toyota Corolla as a reliable vehicle. The plan included other media to encourage further progress through the decision-making process. In this case, the Corolla utilized newspaper advertising for additional explanation and support of the reliability (e.g., information search), and transit station posters as a reminder for a test drive (e.g., purchase decision). For Corolla, the media selection, including television, planned a particular role for each selection to encourage all aspects of the decision-making process, each with particular attitudinal communication objectives.

Alternatively, marketers could provide a television message with information to influence their target audience while evaluating alternative brands. WestJet ads communicated the enhanced service level compared to its previous discount offering to encourage Air Canada consumers to switch; this message would be critical at the alternative evaluation stage. The many executions showed the variety of customer experiences enhanced by the commitment level of the staff to serve customers in an exemplary manner.

Finally, planners often schedule ads that have more immediate purchase intention or purchase facilitation objectives for the target to take action. An additional type of car ad communicates a promotional event or encourages a dealer visit for a test drive. Virtually all car brands resort to TV ads like this, yet the intensity of the "call to action" and the frequency vary considerably. When these ads are run, car brands typically are not running other types of TV ads but might have instructions to consult the newspaper for additional information. Another example from the social marketing realm is the United Way of Toronto's TV ads that showed a "helping hand" in two different scenarios with a verbal message requesting donations and the Internet address shown visually.

RADIO

While all media are inherently in competition for advertising revenue spent by media planners, radio finds itself with a very significant niche of flexibility that allows it to be in the plans for national brands like Bell and for local advertisers like the pizzeria just around the corner. Moreover, the characteristics of the medium allow planners to integrate radio with virtually any other media or IMC tool.

Whether we are considering a national advertiser like Bell or a local business, often the purchase decision stage is the one where maximum influence occurs. For example, many radio messages have a time frame for encouraging purchase through participation with a price promotion. Retailers use radio extensively for various sales, for instance. Alternatively, other radio messages might remind the target audience of entertainment and leisure activities occurring in the city or province within a time frame requiring more immediate action. In these situations, the key communication objectives attained are brand purchase intention or brand purchase facilitation. As we can see from these points, the scheduling flexibility of radio permits attainment of particular communication objectives or messaging consumers exactly when they are planning to make a purchase decision.

The lower costs associated with radio can contribute to building brand equity or an identifiable positioning through the affordability of repetition. An example of this is the prevalent use of radio by Sleep Country Canada, with owner Christine McGee as the spokesperson. The radio ads give the central positioning as a leading mattress retailer much added frequency beyond its television commercials, thus indicating a natural way to build brands by integrating a consistent message across two broadcast media.

Radio's flexibility and cost implications allow it to support other IMC tools. It can suggest that the target audience visit a brand's Internet site or look for a direct mail piece sent to their home—again, both are action-oriented with a time frame—or with some kind of intention on the part of the receiver of the message.

As noted above with price promotions, many other sales promotions can be communicated through radio, particularly those affiliated with sponsorship. Radio can be a key integrating medium to generate awareness of the other IMC tools for further communication in the target audience's decision making.

Learning Objectives Summary

 Describe the media of television regarding delivery, types of TV advertising, time periods and programs, and audience measurement and streaming.

Television is a system of affiliated stations belonging to a network, as well as individual stations, which broadcast programs and commercial messages. Advertising is done on national or regional network programs or purchased in spots from local stations. The growth of specialized stations offers advertisers niche audiences and stronger selectivity. Television advertising is time dependent rather than space-oriented like print advertising. Advertisers select the program, time, day, week, and month when buying ad time.

Information regarding the size and composition of national and local TV audiences is provided by Numeris Canada. The amount of money a network or station can charge for commercial time on its programs is based on its audience measurement figures. This information is also important to media planners, as it is used to determine the combination of shows needed to attain specific levels of reach and frequency with the advertiser's target audience.

 Summarize the strengths and limitations of television as an advertising medium.

Television is a pervasive medium in most consumers' daily lives and offers advertisers the opportunity to reach vast audiences with very frequent messages. Over the past 60 years, national and local advertisers employed TV as their leading medium. No other medium offers its creative capabilities; the combination of sight, sound, and movement gives the advertiser a vast number of options for presenting a commercial message. As a primary medium for these advertisers, the creative opportunities of television contribute to the brand's awareness and help in establishing or maintaining a brand's position. Television also offers advertisers mass coverage at a low relative cost. Variations in programming and audience composition are helping TV offer scheduling opportunities and some audience selectivity to advertisers.

While television is often viewed as the ultimate advertising medium, it has several limitations, including the high absolute cost of producing and airing commercials, low target audience selectivity, short processing time, extensive clutter, high selective exposure, and distrustful image. Despite these concerns, consumers generally appreciate brands more if they are advertised on television because the expenditure signals a stronger and more reputable brand.

 Describe the types of radio advertising, time periods, and audience measurement.

As with TV, the rate structure for radio advertising time varies with the size of the audience delivered. It differs from television in that purchases are not tied to individual shows or programs. Instead, packages are offered over a period of days, weeks, or months. The primary source of listener information is Numeris. The new PPM technology for television works with radio as well, although the diary method remains for smaller radio markets.

Summarize the strengths and limitations of radio as an advertising medium.

Radio is an entertainment and advertising medium that offers highly specialized programs appealing to narrow segments of the primarily local market. Radio offers strengths in terms of cost efficiency and absolute cost, reach and frequency, target audience selectivity, geographic coverage, scheduling flexibility, creativity for cognitive responses, and media image. The major drawback of radio is its weak creativity owing to the absence of a visual image. The short and fleeting nature of the radio commercial, the highly fragmented nature of the radio audience, low involvement, and clutter are also problems.

 Apply the media knowledge of TV and radio for strategic IMC decisions.

TV and radio still command almost $5 billion in advertising revenue and remain very good media for attaining broad reach and frequency objectives to achieve or maintain brand awareness and establish or reinforce existing brand image perceptions. No doubt these media feel pressure from Internet media and the use of personal devices to watch streaming video services and listen to music; however, creative advertising in these media with the right connections to digital brand exposure makes them a strong part of major brands' advertising.

Review Questions

1. "Television is a mass medium that offers little selectivity to advertisers." Do you agree with this statement? What are the ways selectivity can be achieved through TV advertising?

2. Discuss the strengths of television as an advertising medium and the importance of these factors to major national advertisers and to smaller local companies.

3. Discuss the methods used to measure radio audiences. Do you think the measurement methods used for each are producing reliable and valid estimates of the viewing audiences?

4. What are the strengths and limitations of advertising on radio? What types of advertisers are most likely to use radio?

5. How can TV best be used to work with social media?

Applied Questions

1. Watch a show on TV and make notes on what ads are shown. Find the equivalent show on the network's website and make notes on what ads are shown. What similarities and differences do you notice?

2. Watch TV or listen to the radio and make note of whether the ads direct the receiver to any aspect of digital media (e.g., a social network).

3. Listen to the radio and make notes on what ads are aired. What similarities and differences do you notice in comparison to TV advertising?

4. Listen to a radio station and pay attention to the ads to assess whether any overcome the limitation of a lack of creativity for emotional responses.

5. How can radio best be used to work with social media?

CHAPTER TWELVE

Print Media

LEARNING OBJECTIVES

LO1 Identify the different types of magazines available for advertising, how circulation and readership levels are determined, how audience size and its characteristics are measured, and the factors that influence advertising rates.

LO2 Evaluate the strengths and limitations of magazines as an advertising medium.

LO3 Identify the types of newspapers offered for advertising, how circulation and readership levels are determined, how audience size and its characteristics are measured, and how advertising rates are determined.

LO4 Evaluate the strengths and limitations of newspapers as an advertising medium.

LO5 Apply the media knowledge of magazines and newspapers for strategic IMC decisions.

Creative Print Ads

Despite the decline in advertising revenue devoted to print magazines and print newspapers, advertisers and their agencies continue to put out top quality creative to persuade a target audience. We cite three winners of marketing awards that demonstrated creative use of print media.

Walmart wanted to promote its wide selection of South Asian food to Canadians with this heritage. Many of them already shopped at the discount retailer, but required new awareness of the expanded line-up of food to fulfill their needs. The message remained consistent with Walmart's overall positioning, but the ads customized the offering for this particular target audience with the idea of "Save on a Fave" expressed along with a witty and playful phrase. Examples included, "Save some dough on naan," "Save some chutta on bhutta," "Save some moola on mooli," and "Save some change on chai," to name a few. The numerous print ads also ran in out-of-home transit shelters, and the campaign won for multicultural integrated campaign and multicultural print campaign, showcasing the talent at the Barrett and Welsh agency.

The milk producers of Quebec wanted Canadian consumers to select Quebec cheese over cheese from countries such as Italy, Switzerland, and France. The three ads showed an animated image of a stereotypical person from each of the countries selecting the Quebec cheese over the cheese from their country. The humorous gimmick to show the selection featured their tongue stretched out to the cheese, a noticeable distance away. The short copy said, "Trust your taste," to go along with the brand identification, "Our cheeses. Quebec's Finest." The campaign won for best single print ad and print campaign, a tribute to the agency Lg2.

Carex Mini-Storage conveyed the message of "Small space for your biggest secrets" with fun imagery in an award-winning newspaper campaign. It selected three infamous "secrets" of modern times—Neil Armstrong faked the moon landing, Donald Trump wears a toupee, and Kim Jong Un loves the United States of America. The imagery showed a mini-storage unit with each person surrounded with evidence of their biggest secret. The imagery captured the copy perfectly to demonstrate the need an ordinary consumer would have for a storage solution. This was quite a strong insight for the agency Rethink.

These examples show the power of print media to convey a message with simple copy and the right kind of image to persuade a specific target audience. And the combination of these messages with the strengths of the media provided award winning work for the advertiser and agencies.

Question:

1. What creative strategy and creative tactics are effectively used in these print media award winners?

Thousands of magazines are published in Canada and throughout the world. They appeal to nearly every consumer interest and lifestyle, as well as to thousands of businesses and occupations. The magazine industry has prospered by becoming a highly specialized medium that reaches specific target audiences. Newspapers are a primary advertising medium in terms of both ad revenue and number of advertisers. Newspapers are particularly important as a local advertising medium for retail businesses and are often used by large national advertisers.

The role of print media differs from that of broadcast media because detailed information can be presented that readers may process at their own pace. Print media are not intrusive like radio and TV, and generally require effort on the part of the reader for the advertising message to have a communication effect. For this reason, magazines and newspapers are often referred to as *high-involvement media*.[1] In fact, the three-month reach for magazines is 80 percent, and 73 percent read a print or digital version of newspapers on a weekly basis.[2] This chapter focuses on these two forms of print media as it identifies important information to determine when and how to use magazines and newspapers in the media plan and examines their unique strengths and limitations.

Magazines

Magazines serve the educational, informational, and entertainment needs of a wide range of readers and are a specialized advertising medium. While certain magazines are general mass-appeal publications, most are targeted to a very specific audience. There is a magazine designed to appeal to nearly every type of consumer in terms of demographics, lifestyle, activities, interests, or fascination. Magazines are targeted toward specific industries and professions as well.

Exhibit 12-1 Tourism Australia's ad appeals well in general consumer magazines.

Source: Tourism Australia

Magazine advertising attained $175 million in 2017, down from a peak of $718 million in 2007. In this section, we review different types of magazines, circulation and readership information, and magazine advertising rates to understand how to plan for magazine advertising placement.

CLASSIFICATIONS OF MAGAZINES

To gain perspective on the types of magazines available and the advertisers that use them, consider the way magazines are generally classified. Canadian Advertising Rates and Data (CARD), the primary reference source on periodicals for media planners, divides magazines into four broad categories based on the audience to which they are directed: consumer, ethnic, farm, and business publications. Each category is then further classified according to the magazine's editorial content and audience appeal. We also examine the opportunity of foreign publications.

Consumer Publications Consumer magazines are bought by the general public for information and/or entertainment. CARD divides 674 domestic consumer magazines into classifications with general interest, travel, home/garden, women, and entertainment in the top five circulation as seen in **Figure 12-1**. Consumer magazines are suited to marketers interested in reaching a wide variety of consumers. For example, the ad in **Exhibit 12-1** could be found in general magazines to encourage people to consider Australia as a destination early in their vacation plans.

Figure 12-1 Top editorial category circulation

Rank	Editorial Category	2015 Circulation (000s)		
		Total	English	French
1	General Interest	6,897	5,963	934
2	Travel	5,145	3,843	1,116
3	Home/Garden	4,044	2,928	1,116
4	Women	3,837	3,600	777
5	Entertainment	3,512	1,214	2,289
6	Lifestyle	2,654	2,460	194
7	City & Regional	1,936	1,806	130
8	Food & Beverage	1,709	859	850
9	Business & Finance	1,593	1,461	132
10	Senior/Mature Market	1,409	905	499

Source: Magazines Canada, Consumer Magazine Fact Book 2016, page 10

National advertisers tend to dominate consumer magazine advertising in terms of expenditures in many large circulation magazines. Consumer magazines are important to smaller companies selling products that appeal to specialized markets and reach consumers with special-interest magazines. These publications assemble consumers with similar lifestyles or interests and offer marketers an efficient way to reach these people with little wasted coverage or circulation. For example, a manufacturer of ski equipment (e.g., Salomon) might find *Ski Canada* magazine to be the best vehicle for advertising to serious skiers. Not only are specialty magazines of value to firms interested in reaching a specific market segment, but their editorial content often creates a positive advertising environment for relevant products and services. For example, the TaylorMade ad in **Exhibit 12-2** fits well in a specialty golf magazine for someone at the information search or alternative evaluation stage of their decision-making process.

Exhibit 12-2 TaylorMade ads appeal well in specialty golf magazines.

Source: TaylorMade Golf Company, Inc.

As described in the opening vignette, digital expansion of magazines provides greater overall reach for individual magazine titles. With the transition to another media format, new advertising decisions emerged but many advertising placement decisions in a digital magazine are consistent with a published paper magazine. Magazines with digital presence reported stronger overall readership as duplication levels across the website or app versus the printed version appeared minimal.

The growth of free, customized magazines from retailers on a **controlled-circulation basis** (i.e., free) is an interesting trend. For example, about 500,000 copies of *Food & Drink* are distributed in Ontario liquor stores. Some customized retail magazines are now online; *Chill* is published by The Beer Store in Ontario and is only available in a digital format. Harry Rosen's *Harry* magazine is distributed to the chain's top customers and features many pages of paid advertising from select advertisers like Bugatchi, Versace, Armani, and Hugo Boss.

Ethnic Publications CARD currently lists 113 magazines directed to persons with many backgrounds based on ethnicity. Many are written in English and French, along with other languages such as Arabic, Chinese, Spanish, Punjabi, Greek, Romanian, and Russian. Some of these publications have low circulation figures or do not have an authenticated circulation. Thus, the cost of advertising in these publications is currently very low.

Farm Publications The third major CARD category consists of magazines directed to farmers and their families. About 83 publications are tailored to nearly every possible type of farming or agricultural interest (e.g., *Ontario Milk Producer, Ontario Produce Farmer*). CARD groups farm publications into general, livestock, crops, dairy, and community. A number of farm publications are directed at farmers in specific provinces or regions, such as *Alberta Beef*. Farm publications are not classified with business publications because historically farms were not perceived as businesses.

Business Publications Business publications are magazines or trade journals customized for specific businesses, industries, or occupations. CARD lists 617 business magazines and trade journals, and breaks them into categories that include:

- Magazines directed at specific professional groups, such as *Canadian Lawyer* for lawyers and *Canadian Architect* for architects.

- Industrial magazines directed at businesspeople in manufacturing and production industries—for example, *Process Equipment and Control News* and *Heavy Construction.*

- Trade magazines targeted to wholesalers, dealers, distributors, and retailers, among them *Canadian Grocer.*

- General business magazines aimed at executives in all areas of business, such as *Canadian Business.*

Business publications reach specific types of professional people with particular interests and give them important information relevant to their industry, occupation, and/or career. Business publications are important to advertisers because they provide an efficient means of reaching the specific types of individuals who constitute their target market. Much marketing occurs at the trade and business-to-business level, where one company sells its products or services directly to another.

Foreign Publications Canadian magazines face competition from American consumer magazines that account for about 90 percent of foreign publication sales. These U.S. print vehicles are another means for Canadian advertisers to reach Canadian consumers. Current legislation allows for foreign publications to accept advertising space from Canadian advertisers for magazines sold in Canada. In addition, foreign publications can accept greater amounts of advertising if the majority of editorial content is Canadian.[3]

MAGAZINE CIRCULATION AND READERSHIP

Two important considerations in deciding whether to use a magazine in the advertising media plan are the size and characteristics of the audience it reaches. Media buyers evaluate magazines on the basis of their ability to deliver the advertiser's message to as many people as possible in the target audience. To do this, they consider the circulation of the publication as well as its total readership, and match these figures against their target audience characteristics. Related to these two points, magazines are sold by frequency (weekly, monthly, and bimonthly) and by distribution (subscription, store distribution, digital, or controlled [free]), which can influence the circulation and readership numbers.

Circulation Circulation figures represent the number of individuals who receive a publication through either subscription or store purchase, or on a controlled-circulation basis. Given that circulation figures are the basis for a magazine's advertising rates and one of the primary considerations in selecting a publication for placement, the credibility of circulation figures is important. Most major publications are audited by the Alliance for Audited Media (AAM), a North America–wide organization founded in 1914 and sponsored by advertisers, agencies, and publishers. AAM collects and evaluates information regarding the subscriptions and sales of magazines and newspapers to verify their circulation figures. **Figure 12-2** shows that the majority of all magazines have circulations below 50,000 and only 17 publications have circulations above 500,000.

AAM provides media planners with reliable figures regarding the size and distribution of a magazine's circulation, which helps them evaluate its worth as a media vehicle. The AAM statement also provides detailed circulation information that gives a media planner an indication of the quality of the target audience. For example, it shows how the subscription was sold, the percentage of circulation sold at less than full value, the percentage of circulation sold with an incentive, and the percentage of subscriptions given away. Many advertisers believe that subscribers who pay for a magazine are more likely to read it than are those who get it at a discount or for free. Media buyers are generally skeptical about publications whose circulation figures are not audited and will not advertise in unaudited publications. Circulation data, along with the auditing source, are available from CARD or from the publication itself.

AAM recently added a new category of magazine circulation with the growth of unlimited access programs. Overall digital circulation hit just over 400,000 and represented 6 percent of the overall circulation of nearly 7 million. Planned measurement included the average number of total requests by paid subscribers and average number of times issues were opened, among others. The digital subscription would be counted as a paid subscription, accurately reflecting the media consumption.[4]

Figure 12-2 Circulation distribution

Circulation Size	Number of Titles	Percent of Total Titles	Group Circulation	Percent of Total Circulation
1 million+	5	1.0	7,280,936	16.7
500,000 to 999,999	12	2.5	7,881,160	18.1
250,000 to 499,999	16	3.3	5,794,338	13.3
100,000 to 249,999	71	14.8	10,249,150	23.6
50,000 to 99,999	91	19.0	6,558,505	15.0
Less than 50,000	285	59.3	5,709,764	13.1

Source: Magazines Canada, Consumer Magazine Fact Book 2016, page 11

Readership Advertisers are interested in the number of people a publication reaches as a result of secondary, or pass-along, readership. **Pass-along readership** can occur when the primary subscriber or purchaser gives a magazine to another person or when the publication is read in doctors' waiting rooms or beauty salons, on airplanes, and so forth.

Advertisers generally attach greater value to the primary in-home reader than the pass-along reader or out-of-home reader, as the former generally spends more time with the publication, picks it up more often, and receives greater satisfaction from it. Thus, this reader is more likely to be attentive and responsive to ads. However, the value of pass-along readers should not be ignored since they can expand a magazine's reach.

The **total audience**, or **readership**, of a magazine is calculated by multiplying the **readers per copy** (the total number of primary and pass-along readers) by the circulation of an average issue. For example, a magazine with a circulation of 150,000 and 10 readers per copy has a total audience of 1.5 million. The readers per copy is estimated from market research data. Since it is an estimate, media planners are advised to assess its accuracy when deciding how much actual reach is attained with total readership.

Magazines Canada is an industry association representing hundreds of titles. It provides extensive information services for its members, and promotes magazines to advertisers as worthy media for advertising placement. One may find readership data there or on the websites or media kits of individual magazine titles. A campaign devoted to increasing magazine readership featured a couple in a magazine shop communicating with each other by picking up and showing different magazine covers, a very clever execution! Various magazines offered in-kind media exposure, and a Valentine's Day contest with a vacation as a prize completed the IMC integration of the message.[5]

MAGAZINE ADVERTISING RATES

Magazine rates are primarily a function of circulation; the greater the circulation, the higher the cost of the ad. Ads in controlled-circulation magazines (i.e., free) are generally cheaper than ads in paid circulation magazines. Ad rates for digital magazines are generally sold on a cost-per-thousand (CPM) basis and use combinations of magazine formats and digital advertising formats.

Rates for Print Magazines Advertising space is sold on the basis of space units, such as full-page, half-page, quarter-page, or double-page spread (two facing pages); a greater cost is incurred for ads requiring more space. Rates for magazine ad space vary by the number of times an ad runs and the amount of money spent during a specific period. The more often an advertiser contracts to run an ad, the lower the space charges. Volume discounts are based on the total space purchased within a contract year, measured in dollars or number of insertions. The following table from CARD shows the cost per colour ad (i.e., known as full-page four colour or FP4C) per month by size and the number of times inserted (i.e., ti) for *Ski Canada Magazine,* which publishes four issues per year.[6]

	1 ti	2 ti	3 ti	4 ti
Full page	$5,190	$4,930	$4,411	$4,152
Double page spread	$9,341	$8,874	$7,940	$7,473
2/3 p.	$4,307	$4,092	$3,661	$3,446
1/2 p.	$3,477	$3,303	$2,955	$2,782
1/3 p.	$2,335	$2,219	$1,985	$1,868

Other variables that increase the cost of an ad include its position in the publication, the particular editions (geographic, demographic) chosen, any special mechanical or production requirements, and the number and frequency of insertions. *Ski Canada Magazine* charges an additional 20 percent, 15 percent, and 25 percent for ad placement on inside front cover (IFC), inside back cover (IBC), and outside back cover (OBC), respectively, and charges an extra 10 percent for position requests. The CARD listing for *Ski Canada Magazine* shows an audited paid circulation of about 28,700. The cost per thousand is about $181 for a one-page ad ($5,190/28.7). At three readers per copy, the cost per thousand approaches $60 ($181/3).

Ads can be produced or run using black and white, black and white plus one colour, or four colours. The more colour used in the ad, the greater the expense because of the increased printing costs. Colour ads are so prominent in magazines that many do not even quote a non-colour cost in their CARD listing. Recall and action taken are stronger with colour ads versus non-colour ads. Larger ads produce stronger recall and action taken. For example, a full-page ad can have 20 percent stronger communication effects.[7] Ads placed inside the front cover, inside the back cover, and outside the back cover yield 15 percent, 10 percent, and 20 percent stronger recall than a regularly placed ad.[8]

Rates for Digital Magazines For online advertising, *Ski Canada Magazine* charges a monthly rate for five types of display ads ranging from $300 to $1,600. It cites Google data and claims 45,000 unique visitors per month who view a total of 160,000 pages. The CPM for the most expensive ad purchase is about $35 ($1,600/45) and the least expensive ad purchase is approximately $7 ($300/45). These calculations can be compared to other online titles that sell their ad space on a CPM basis. Note that these rates pertain to a website version of its digital content and CARD does not report a digital magazine for *Ski Canada*. In contrast, *Maclean's* news magazine offers both a print magazine and a digital magazine and charges the same rates for either option. Its rate structure is like other magazines with options for sizes and locations as shown in the *Ski Canada* table reported above. This approach is consistent with other well known titles from other print media owners.

LO2 Evaluation of Magazines

Magazines have a number of strengths and limitations in comparison to other media. We review each of these according to the criteria of Chapter 10. Astute readers will acknowledge that each evaluation represents a generalization across all classifications of magazines. As such, exceptional anomalies may be found, thereby opening the assessment up to debate.

STRENGTHS OF MAGAZINES

Magazines have a number of characteristics that make them attractive for advertisers. Strengths of magazines include their target audience selectivity, geographic coverage, control for selective exposure and attention, creativity for cognitive and emotional responses, amount of processing time and reader involvement, and media image.

Target Audience Selectivity One main advantage of using magazines is their **selectivity**, or ability to reach a specific target audience. Magazines are the most selective of all media except direct communication where the receiver's identity is known (e.g., addressed direct mail). Most magazines are published for readers with very specific reading requirements. The magazines reach all types of consumers and businesses and allow advertisers to target their advertising to groups that are consistent with their segmentation strategies along the lines of demographics, socioeconomics, and lifestyle (e.g., activities and interests). For example, *PhotoLife* is targeted toward camera buffs, while *Exclaim!* appeals to those with an avid interest in music.

One Canadian success story is the lifestyle magazine *Nuvo*, a refined publication (non-paid circulation) catering to the very affluent who appreciate a refined lifestyle of luxury. It claims to be Canada's premier lifestyle magazine with an audited circulation hitting 50,000.[9] Homeowners interested in decoration and renovation ideas can select *Canadian House and Home*, with an audited circulation of 220,000. This is one of Canada's largest special-interest magazines with a paid circulation. A readership of 2.4 million implies 10 readers per copy, resulting in a CPM per reader just under $9, a good balance of selectivity and cost efficiency for advertisers of household decor.[10]

In addition to providing selectivity based on interests, magazines provide advertisers selectivity by other means. *Demographic selectivity*, or the ability to reach specific demographic groups, is available in two ways. First, most magazines are, as a result of editorial content, aimed at fairly well defined demographic segments. *Canadian Living* and *Chatelaine* (**Exhibit 12-3**) are read predominantly by women; *The Hockey News* is read mostly by men. Older consumers can be reached through publications like *FiftyPlus*.

Exhibit 12-3 *Chatelaine* allows for demographic selectivity.

Hand-out/Chatelaine/Newscom

Second, selectivity can be applied effectively by tailoring the message by language since Canada naturally has magazines written in both English and French. Furthermore, publications in other languages permit additional targeting capabilities. *Geographic selectivity* occurs with magazines that offer a *geographic split run* where one region receives one message and another receives a different message.

Two technological developments—selective binding and ink-jet imaging—allow *individual selectivity* so advertisers can deliver personalized messages to targeted audiences. **Selective binding** is a production process that allows a magazine to send different editorial content and/or advertising messages within the same publication issue to groups of subscribers. **Ink-jet imaging** reproduces a message by projecting ink onto paper and makes it possible to personalize an advertising message. These innovations permit advertisers to target their messages more finely and let magazines compete more effectively with direct mail and other direct-marketing vehicles.

Loulou customized its magazine with different versions for Centre à la Mode customers who fit into three groups based on their shopping behaviour as derived from its database: impulsive, thoughtful, and habitual. Eight unique pages of clothing matched the three profiles so that consumers could visit the location with just the right shopping plans. Databases played an important role for Curél in working with *Reader's Digest* and *Selection* magazines, which wrote editorials about dry skin and sent emails using addresses from their subscription lists to those who had indicated having skin concerns. Combined with emails from an Environics list, the communication achieved 190,000 unique visits.[11]

Geographic Coverage One way to achieve specific geographic coverage is to use a vehicle that is targeted toward a particular area—such as city magazines *Toronto Life, Vancouver Magazine,* and *Montréal Scope,* to name a few—which provide residents of these areas with articles concerning lifestyle, events, and the like in these cities and their surrounding metropolitan areas (**Exhibit 12-4**). Toronto enjoyed an expansion of titles much like what occurred 30 years ago due to an energized street scene, new and inexpensive publishing technology, and post-recession optimism.[12]

Another way to achieve selective geographic coverage in magazines is through purchasing ad space in specific geographic editions of national or regional magazines. A number of publications (e.g., *Maclean's, Chatelaine*) divide their circulation into groupings based on regions or major metropolitan areas and offer advertisers the option of concentrating their ads in these editions.

CARD lists the consumer magazines offering geographic editions. Regional advertisers can purchase space in editions that reach only areas where they have distribution, yet still enjoy the prestige of advertising in a major national magazine. National advertisers can use the geographic editions to focus their advertising on areas with the greatest potential or those needing more promotional support. They can also use regional editions to test-market products or alternative promotional campaigns in regions of the country.

Ads in regional editions can also list the names of retailers or distributors, thus encouraging greater local support from the trade. The trend toward regional marketing is increasing the importance of having regional media available to marketers. The availability of regional and demographic editions can also reduce the cost per thousand for reaching desired audiences.

Control for Selective Exposure and Attention With the exception of newspapers, consumers are more receptive to advertising in magazines than in any other medium. Magazines are generally purchased because the information they contain interests the reader, and ads provide additional information that may be of value in making a purchase decision. For example, magazines such as bridal or fashion publications are purchased as much for their advertising as for their editorial content. **Figure 12-3** shows that magazines hold readers' attention better than other media.

Exhibit 12-4 City magazines such as *Toronto Life* offer advertisers high geographic selectivity.

©Toronto Life

Figure 12-3 Consumers' ratings of how well various media hold their attention

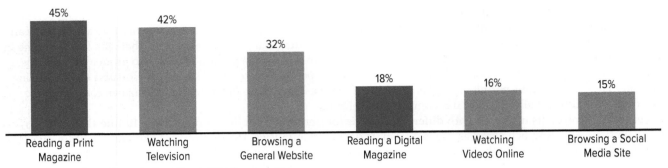

Has my full attention

- 45% — Reading a Print Magazine
- 42% — Watching Television
- 32% — Browsing a General Website
- 18% — Reading a Digital Magazine
- 16% — Watching Videos Online
- 15% — Browsing a Social Media Site

Source: Magazines Canada Fact Book 2015, page 13.

Exhibit 12-5 Airbnb's visual message likely evoked thoughts of visiting Paris and emotions of a wonderful trip.

Paris with a View
★★★★★ Hosted by Alexandre
Book Now

Live there. Even if it's just for a night.

airbnb
Belong Anywhere

Source: Airbnb, Inc.

Creativity for Cognitive and Emotional Responses A valued attribute of magazine advertising is the reproduction quality of the ads. Magazines are generally printed on high-quality paper stock and use printing processes that provide excellent reproduction in black and white or colour. The reproduction quality of most magazines is far superior to that offered by newspapers. Magazines are a visual medium in which a photographic image or illustration is the dominant part of an ad designed to generate emotional reactions like joy or pleasure, or allow receivers to carefully consider the argument put forth in the message. For example, the Airbnb ad shown in **Exhibit 12-5** frames the Eiffel Tower in the apartment window. The target audience envisions being in Paris when receiving the message and presumably experiences all sorts of wonderful thoughts and feelings about visiting Paris. The additional Internet frame might encourage thoughts of posting pictures of a visit for all to appreciate. **Figure 12-4** presents evidence of the emotional importance of magazines.

In addition to their excellent reproduction capabilities, magazines also offer advertisers options in terms of the type, size, and placement of the advertising material. Good magazines offer (often at extra charge) a variety of special opportunities to enhance the creative appeal of the ad such as gatefolds, bleed pages, inserts, and creative space buys.

Gatefolds enable an advertiser to make a striking presentation by using a third page that folds out and gives the ad an extra-large spread. Gatefolds are typically found on the inside cover of

Figure 12-4 Percentage of people experiencing emotion when consuming media

	Print Magazines	Digital Magazines	TV	Radio/Audio	Computer	Mobile	Tablet
Happy	36	39	27	30	22	30	28
Confident	19	30	7	10	8	7	11
Excited	15	23	5	7	5	8	5
Hopeful	17	14	5	6	4	6	7
Interested	25	30	5	4	5	5	9

Source: Magazines Canada Fact Book 2015, p. 50.

large consumer magazines and are especially useful for a new product introduction or new ad creative campaign for the brand. Advertisers use gatefolds to make a very strong impression and gain stronger recall scores.[13] **Bleed pages** are those where the advertisement extends all the way to the edge of the page, with no margin of white space around the ad. Bleeds give the ad an impression of being larger and make a more dramatic impact.

Inserts used in magazines are designed for promotion, and can include recipe booklets, coupons, and even product samples. Cosmetics companies use scented inserts to introduce new fragrances, and others use them to promote products for which scent is important (e.g., deodorants, laundry detergents). Cost-effective technologies enhance the reading of advertising messages through options like anaglyphic images (three-dimensional materials that are viewed with coloured glasses); lenticular (colour) images printed on finely corrugated plastic that seem to move when tilted; and pressure- or heat-sensitive inks that change colour on contact. **Creative space buys** allow advertisers to purchase space units in certain combinations to increase the impact of their media budget.

Magazines work well with other media and promotional tools to contribute to strong responses. Digital technology integration with a print ad is possible; as shown in **Exhibit 12-6**, the Lexus ad becomes animated—the engine revs, the headlights flash, the wheels spin, and the background pulses with colour, all to a musical soundtrack—when placed over an iPad that has a Lexus microsite loaded. *Fashion* magazine helped with the launch of the new Calvin Klein fragrance Beauty by offering a contest via its magazine's website. *Fashion* invited its Twitter and Facebook followers to submit a photo that represented beauty and to explain what beauty meant to them. The communication involved 5,300 readers who commented on the photos and who subsequently received a sample. *Canadian Living* worked with P&G to identify possible leads from the former's reader panel for a Herbal Essences promotion. Participants provided online feedback in social media that proved to be useful content for future testimonial advertising. While these opportunities appear fruitful, research indicated a stronger preference remains for printed magazines for their emotional association.[14]

Exhibit 12-6 This Lexus ad becomes animated when placed over an iPad with a microsite loaded.

©Photographer: John Higginson, Associate Creative Director: Fabio Simoes Pinto/Molly Grubbs, Art Producer: Lisa Matthews. Agency: Team One Advertising

Amount of Processing Time and Reader Involvement A distinctive strength offered by magazines is that they are generally read over several days. TV and radio are characterized by fleeting messages that have a very short life span. Readers devote about 44 minutes to reading a magazine with a high degree of interest.[15] **Figure 12-5** highlights the behavioural effects of the longer processing time and high reader involvement for health care products. Magazines are retained in the home longer than any other media and are referred to on several occasions; nearly 73 percent of consumers retain magazines for future reference.[16] One benefit of the longer life of magazines is that reading occurs at a less hurried pace and there is opportunity to examine ads in considerable detail. This means ads can use longer and more detailed copy, which can be very important for complex products or services. The permanence of magazines also means readers can be exposed to ads on multiple occasions and can pass magazines along to other readers.

Media Image Another positive feature of magazine advertising is the prestige the product or service gains from advertising in publications with a favourable image. Companies whose products rely heavily on perceived quality, reputation, and/or image buy space in prestigious publications with high-quality editorial content whose consumers have a high level of interest in the advertising pages. For example, *Flare* covers young women's fashions in a congruent editorial environment, and a clothing manufacturer may advertise its products in these magazines to enhance the prestige of its lines. *Canadian Geographic* provides an impressive editorial environment that includes high-quality photography. The magazine's upscale readers are likely to have a positive image of the publication that may transfer to the products

Figure 12-5 Behavioural effects of high involvement processing of magazines

Actions Taken (indexed 12 month data)	Magazine Media	Internet	TV	Radio	Newspapers
Visited a pharmaceutical company's website	276	169	112	168	146
Discussed an ad with your doctor	260	99	143	95	149
Asked your doctor for a product sample of a prescription drug	260	109	131	90	126
Discussed an ad with a friend or relative	253	163	148	128	151
Asked your doctor to prescribe a specific drug	234	128	155	119	113
Consulted a pharmacist	231	117	148	107	160
Purchased a nonprescription product	214	109	111	118	135
Used a coupon	210	119	124	144	156
Took medication	190	127	109	137	143
Made an appointment to see doctor	170	108	138	118	144

Source: Magazines Canada, Consumer Magazine Fact Book 2016, page 193

advertised on its pages. Media planners rely on their experiences to assess a magazine's prestige and reader opinion surveys in order to select the best magazine title. Data in **Figure 12-6** indicate how much consumers enjoy advertising in magazines since it is part of the experience and it provides trustworthy information. Similar results occurred for two other measures—"good use of time" and "feel in control"—which suggests a positive media image.

Figure 12-6 Magazines offer a good media image for advertisers

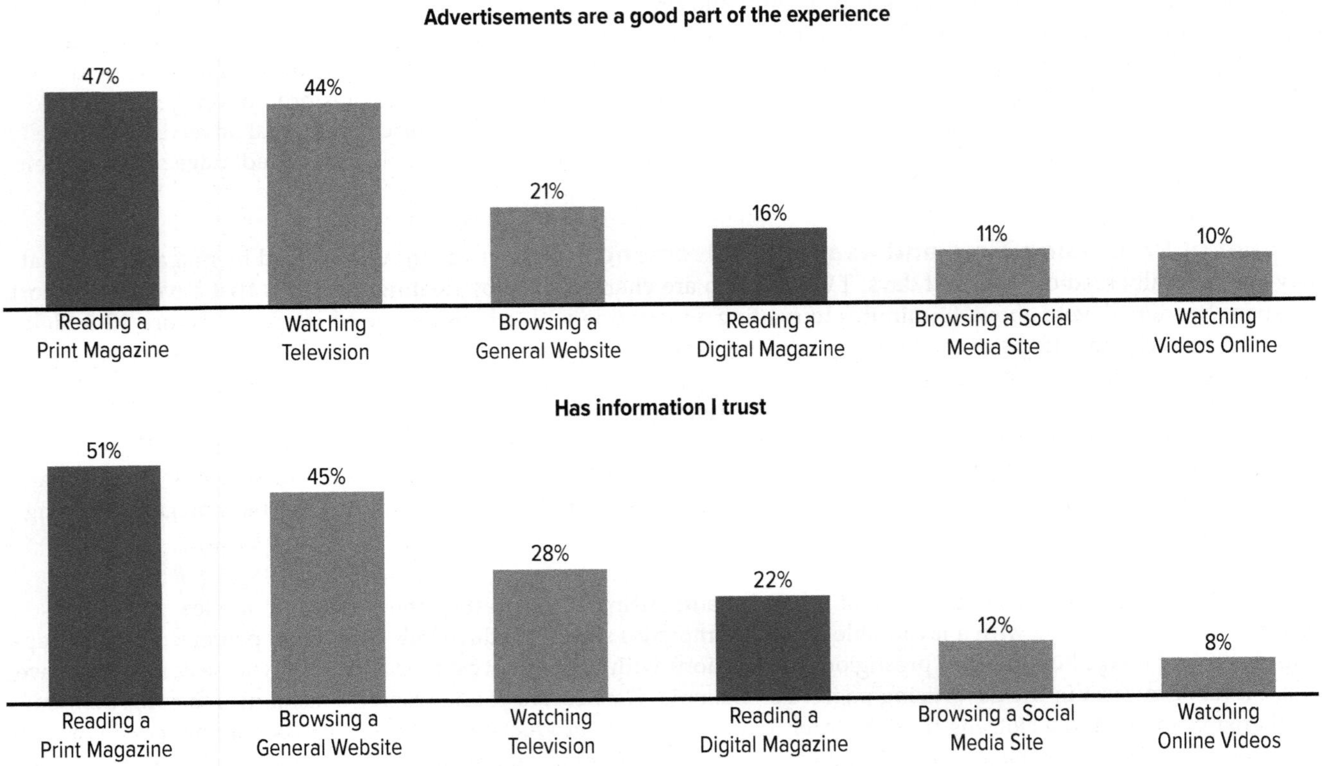

Advertisements are a good part of the experience

Reading a Print Magazine	Watching Television	Browsing a General Website	Reading a Digital Magazine	Browsing a Social Media Site	Watching Videos Online
47%	44%	21%	16%	11%	10%

Has information I trust

Reading a Print Magazine	Browsing a General Website	Watching Television	Reading a Digital Magazine	Browsing a Social Media Site	Watching Online Videos
51%	45%	28%	22%	12%	8%

Source: Magazines Canada Fact Book 2015, pp. 56–59

IMC Perspective 12-1 highlights how consumers love both print and digital magazines, although their usage may differ by type of reader and topic. This example suggests that magazines are evolving along with their readers.

In addition to their relevance, magazine ads are likely to be received favourably by consumers because, unlike broadcast ads, they are nonintrusive and can easily be ignored. The majority of magazine readers welcome ads; only a small percentage have negative attitudes toward magazine advertising. Consumers generally enjoy magazines over other media along many measures such as advertising receptivity, inspirational, trustworthy, life-enhancing, social interaction, and personal timeout. Furthermore, readers believe advertising contributes to the enjoyment of reading a magazine more strongly than other media and they have stronger attitudes to magazine ads versus ads in other media.[17]

LIMITATIONS OF MAGAZINES

Although the strengths offered by magazines are considerable, they have certain drawbacks, too. These include weak target audience coverage, the long lead time required in placing an ad leading to poorer scheduling flexibility, their limited reach and frequency, the absolute cost of advertising and its efficiency, and the problem of clutter.

Target Audience Coverage The flipside of the strength of target audience selectivity is the limitation of magazines in providing extensive target audience coverage. Even though a magazine may draw an audience with a particular interest—for example, hockey with *The Hockey News*—the number of people reading the publication versus the number of people who actually play hockey is substantially disproportionate. The ability to achieve coverage with young adults aged 18–24 is limited as purchase and subscription levels are quite low; however, one study finds that young adults are vastly more receptive to reading print versions of magazines versus digital versions and prefer ads in magazines over digital ads.[18] And one expert sees great opportunity for continued development for magazines—and subsequently advertisers—with the growth of tablets, as long as the content resonates with the young audience.[19]

Scheduling Flexibility Another drawback of magazines is the long lead time needed to place an ad, thus reducing scheduling flexibility. Most major publications have a 30- to 90-day lead time, which means space must be purchased and the ad must be prepared well in advance of the actual publication date. No changes in the art or copy of the ad can be made after the closing date. This long lead time means magazine ads cannot be as timely as other media, such as radio or newspapers, in responding to current events or changing market conditions.

Reach and Frequency Magazines are generally not as effective as other media in offering reach and frequency. While adults in Canada read one or more consumer magazines each month, the percentage of adults reading any individual publication tends to be much smaller. As Figure 12-2 showed, the circulation of 80 percent of all titles is below 100,000. An ad in a magazine with this circulation reaches less than half a percent of all households.

Advertisers seeking broad reach must make media buys in a number of magazines, resulting in greater costs with multiple transactions. For a broad reach strategy, magazines are used in conjunction with other media. Since most magazines are monthly or at best weekly publications, the opportunity for building frequency through the use of the same publication is limited. Using multiple ads in the same issue of a publication is an inefficient way to build frequency, although a product category like fashion finds success with this approach as volume discounts are offered.

Despite these concerns from an individual title's viewpoint, total magazine reach is as impressive as any other media. About 8 out of 10 Canadians (aged 12–64) read magazines within the most recent three months.[20] As for frequency, while magazines cannot compete on this compared to broadcast media, placing an ad in consecutive months (e.g., five or more) provides measurably stronger awareness levels compared to placements for fewer months.[21]

Absolute Cost and Cost Efficiency The cost of advertising in magazines varies according to size of audience reached and selectivity. Advertising in large mass-circulation magazines like *Maclean's* can be very expensive. For example, a full-page, four-colour ad in *Maclean's* national edition (circulation 362,000) had a cost of $37,000. Popular positions such as the back cover cost even more.

Magazines must be considered not only from an absolute cost perspective but also in terms of relative costs. Most magazines emphasize their efficiency in reaching specific target audiences at a low cost per thousand. Media planners generally focus on the relative costs of a publication in reaching their target audience. However, they may recommend a magazine with a high cost per thousand because of its ability to reach a small, specialized market segment. Of course, advertisers with limited budgets will be interested in the absolute costs of space in a magazine and the costs of producing quality ads for these publications. Strong brands or companies with large advertising budgets (e.g., car companies) are regularly in publications where the absolute cost is not a substantial deterrent for ad placement.

Clutter Advertising clutter is not a serious issue for print media, as data show strong communication effects even with a competitor's ad in the same issue.[22] Consumers are more receptive to and tolerant of print advertising and control their exposure to a magazine ad simply by turning the page; however, the many pages of ads in a magazine raise an issue of concern when planning print ad placement. And this issue is a paradox for magazines since successful titles attract more advertising pages, potentially leading to greater clutter. Magazine publishers control clutter by maintaining a reasonable balance of editorial pages to advertising. Advertisers control the clutter with the use of strong visual images, catchy headlines, and other creative techniques to gain a reader's attention. In fact, new creative executions in magazines over many issues minimize ad wearout, another factor contributing to issues of clutter.[23]

 # Newspapers

Newspapers are another form of print media and remain strong in terms of advertising revenue despite a recent and noticeable decline. In 2017, daily newspaper advertising attained $1 billion and community newspapers hit $776 million. Within this total of almost $1.8 billion, online newspaper ad revenue came in at nearly $300 million, but this amount is counted as Internet advertising revenue. Newspapers are an especially important advertising medium for local advertisers, local and national retailers, and national advertisers. In this section, we review different types of newspapers, types of newspaper advertising, newspaper circulation and readership, and finally newspaper advertising rates.

TYPES OF NEWSPAPERS

Newspapers deliver timely information and features that appeal to readers. They provide detailed coverage of news, events, and issues concerning the local area as well as business, sports, and other relevant information and entertainment. The vast majority of newspapers are daily publications. However, community, national, Internet, and special-audience newspapers and supplements offer message delivery options that appeal to advertisers.

Daily Newspapers Daily newspapers, which are published each weekday, are found in cities and larger towns across the country. Some areas have more than one daily paper and are known as competitive markets, while the vast majority of smaller Canadian cities and towns have one publication. In 2016, there were 98 daily newspapers in Canada; of these, 83 were English-language papers and 13 were French-language papers, with an average daily circulation of 5.2 million. Most daily newspapers charge a price (or subscription fee); however, free dailies represent a degree of circulation and advertising revenue. There are 14 free daily newspapers in eight markets under the *Metro* or *24 Hours* or *Epoch Times* banner.[24] **Figure 12-7** provides overview statistics of the number of daily newspapers and markets served. By 2019, daily newspapers reduced to 90 titles (80 paid, 10 free) as Postmedia downsized to 35 titles among a few other changes.[25]

Community Newspapers Most community newspapers publish weekly and originate in small towns where the volume of news and advertising cannot support a daily newspaper. Canada had about 1,100 community newspapers in 2015 with a total circulation of 21 million. Community newspapers also dot the suburbs or neighbourhoods of larger Canadian cities. These papers focus on news, sports, and events relevant to the local area and usually ignore content covered by the city-based daily newspaper. Community newspapers appeal primarily to local advertisers because of their geographic focus and lower absolute cost.

Figure 12-7 Daily newspaper circulation by publisher

Publisher	Number of Titles	Weekly Circulation	Daily Ave. Circulation
Postmedia	44	12,760,000	2,142,000
TorStar	9	5,600,000	965,000
Quebecor	3	3,600,000	558,000
The Globe & Mail	1	2,100,000	350,000
Power Corp.	1	2,100,000	231,000
Group Capitale Medias	7	1,620,000	251,000
TC Media/Metro	9	1,510,000	289,000

National Newspapers Newspapers in Canada with national circulation include the *National Post* and *The Globe and Mail*. Both are daily publications and have editorial content with a national appeal. National newspapers appeal primarily to large national advertisers and to regional advertisers that use specific geographic editions of these publications.

Internet Newspapers Major Canadian daily newspapers, the two national newspapers, and some community newspapers offer an Internet version of their publication. Regular newspapers charge for subscriptions or for individual papers at newsstands, and rely on advertising revenue to support the distribution of editorial content. Internet versions are similar; the publishers experimented with different combinations of fees and ads over the past decade and continue to do so. Newspapers raced to develop apps so readers could consume their media on reading and mobile devices, and this growth of digital media permitted accurate tracking of reader consumption. Consumers are readily adopting digital newspaper editions.

One of the more interesting examples is Montreal's *La Presse*, which moved to digital-only publication and sought to become a non-profit charity after years under the ownership of Power Corporation. The weekday paper became digital-only in 2016 and the Saturday edition followed the same path in 2017, both relying on advertising sales to support free readership. Transitioning to non-profit status became a challenge as the new structure required government approval, but this approach worked well in the United Kingdom for *The Guardian*, which continues to receive donations from readers.[26] After starting, *La Presse* hit 400,000 installed apps and 300,000 weekly readers. Each reader spends more than 30 minutes on weekdays and more than an hour on weekends. The edition is loaded at 5:30 a.m. every day, featuring text, interactive images, videos, photo galleries, and scrolling screens. Interactive ad units provide new ways of communicating with consumers for brand advertising. All ads are hyperlinked to a brand's Internet site.[27]

Special-Audience Newspapers A variety of papers offer specialized editorial content and are published for particular groups, including labour unions, professional organizations, industries, and hobbyists. Many people working in advertising and marketing read *Strategy Magazine*. Specialized newspapers are also published in areas with large foreign-language-speaking ethnic groups. Newspapers targeted at religious and educational groups compose another large class of special-interest papers. A trend has arisen with the establishment of local business newspapers.

Newspaper Supplements Although not a category of newspapers as such, papers include magazine-type supplements. For example, *The Globe and Mail* publishes a glossy *Report on Business* magazine at the end of each month. Newspapers are also in the game of custom publishing magazine supplements for advertisers. This is a relatively new field for this media as titles look to replace lost advertising revenue with classified ads shifting to digital vehicles. In contrast, as noted in the Magazines section, this kind of activity occurred with great frequency in that media, but newspapers struggle with the balance of journalistic integrity and the need to please advertisers. One example is Sunnybrook Hospital's twice-yearly publication, *Sunnybrook Magazine*, put together by *The Globe and Mail*. This publication provides extensive information regarding all of the hospital's activities and is a key tool for generating donations as it is sent to 50,000 *Globe and Mail* subscribers and 30,000 donors.[28]

TYPES OF NEWSPAPER ADVERTISING

The ads appearing in newspapers are divided into different categories: display, classified, special, and sponsorship ads and preprinted inserts. Display ads in printed versions of newspapers represent the majority of the $1.8 billion of ad revenue.

Display Advertising **Display advertising** is found throughout the newspaper and generally uses illustrations, headlines, white space, and other visual devices in addition to the copy text. The two types of display advertising in newspapers are local and national.

Local advertising refers to ads placed by local organizations, businesses, and individuals who want to communicate with consumers in the market area served by the newspaper. Supermarkets and department stores are among the leading local display advertisers, along with numerous other retailers and service operations such as banks and travel agents.

National advertising refers to newspaper display advertising done by marketers of branded products or services that are sold on a national or regional level. These ads are designed to create and maintain demand and to complement the efforts of local retailers that stock and promote the advertiser's products. Major retail chains, auto makers, and airlines are heavy users of newspaper advertising.

Classified Advertising **Classified advertising** provides newspapers with ad revenue; however, online classifieds and search ads completely eroded this to $125 million by 2017 for both types of newspapers from close to $1 billion a decade ago. Text ads for employment, real estate, and selling personal goods and services, etc., moved to a digital equivalent.

Special Ads Special advertisements in newspapers include government and financial reports and public notices of changes in business and personal relationships. Other types include political or special-interest ads promoting a candidate, issue, or cause. Newspapers like *The Globe and Mail* offer opportunities in which, for a few days each week, they will focus on a particular topic (e.g., tax planning, luxury travel, Olympics) that provides interested advertisers with an option to customize messages or focus their spending knowing a certain audience will read featured content.

Sponsorship Ads Another form of special ads in newspapers is sponsorship messages that look very similar to newspaper content and format. The text is laid out in columns with photos in a manner almost indistinguishable from the actual publication. At the top of the ad, a disclaimer indicates to the reader that the message is sponsored by a brand, company, or organization. Given its resemblance to a newspaper article, publishers see this as offering a *content marketing* option to advertisers. For example, *The Globe and Mail* offers its Globe Content Studios to advertisers and Postmedia offers its Content Works to promotional planners. Each works with decision makers to put together a print and digital message for all of its media properties and exposure into social media. In the case of *The Globe and Mail,* the look is different from regular content to indicate that it is promotional in nature, but it is based on the journalistic quality of the regular reporting staff.[29]

Preprinted Inserts **Preprinted inserts** do not appear in the paper itself; they are printed and inserted before delivery. Retailers use inserts such as free-standing inserts (FSI), circulars, catalogues, or brochures in specific circulation zones to reach shoppers in their particular trade areas. "Inserts" advertising revenue is a separate line item in the advertising revenue table and hit $300 million in 2017 for both types of newspapers (see Figure 10-1 in Chapter 10). Canadian Tire spends more than $10 million per year on flyers.[30] While still a significant print option, digital newspapers and other online locations display digital flyers that look exactly like the printed version. One media planner suggested that ads in retail flyers are a good alternative to magazine ads since they offer a low CPM and data indicated that half of all Canadians regularly used a grocery store flyer and readers spend an average of 20 minutes reading flyers.[31]

Digital Ads Newspapers package the ads shown in their print version for their digital publication, and they also accept digital-only campaigns for display ads. Larger media companies embed video ads within their digital edition that are the same as TV ads or unique messages. In 2017, online ads accounted for $280 million in advertising revenue for daily and community newspapers, while mobile ad revenue hit $16 million for daily newspapers.

A significant change for *The Globe and Mail* featured video content for presenting news information. It hit 3 million unique streams per month. An important component included *Globe Now,* a daily news show presented at noon every Monday to Friday featuring 60- to 90-second clips on business, technology, lifestyle, and arts. The show led with a thought piece based on current issues rather than breaking news. Viewers continued to return, with metrics indicating higher repeat visits lasting longer than established norm measures and video pre-roll completion rates hitting 86 percent. These three data points looked favourable to advertisers who targeted affluent and influential audiences. *Globe Now* also offered content to other publisher partners to reach an additional 10 million readers and viewers.[32]

NEWSPAPER CIRCULATION AND READERSHIP

The media planner must understand the size and reader characteristics of the audience reached by a newspaper when considering its value in the media plan. As with other media, advertisers are concerned with the size of the audience reached through a particular vehicle. Thus, the circulation, or number of readers, is an important statistic. And while the audience size is important, advertisers are also interested in the amount of reading occurring and similar reader usage statistics prior to making their decision regarding newspapers.

Circulation The source of information concerning the audience size of newspapers comes from circulation figures available through CARD, discussed earlier in this chapter. The Alliance for Audited Media (AAM) verifies circulation figures for many newspapers, as illustrated in the Magazines media section. Advertisers using a number of papers in their media plan may find CARD to be the most convenient source.

Newspaper circulation figures are generally broken down into three categories: the city zone, the retail trading zone, and all other areas. The **city zone** is a market area composed of the city where the paper is published and contiguous

Figure 12-8 Weekly newspaper readership by access and age groups

	Print	Computer	Phone	Tablet
Adults 18+	51%	56%	68%	51%
Millennials	43%	55%	78%	42%
Age 35–49	39%	61%	77%	55%
Boomers	56%	56%	59%	52%

areas similar in character to the city. The **retail trading zone** is the market outside the city zone whose residents regularly trade with merchants within the city zone. The "all other" category covers all circulation not included in the city or retail trade zones. Sometimes circulation figures are provided only for the primary market, which is the city and retail trade zones combined, and the "all other" area.

Both local and national advertisers consider the circulation patterns across the various categories in evaluating and selecting newspapers.

Readership Circulation figures provide the media planner with the basic data for assessing the value of newspapers and their ability to cover market areas. However, the media planner also wants to match the characteristics of a newspaper's readers with those of the advertiser's target audience. Media planners may seek additional readership information (e.g., demographics), including the number of readers per copy, about a particular newspaper title on its website or within its media kit. For example, the *Globe and Mail* website lists extensive information about its readership. As an example of useful newspaper readership information, **Figure 12-8** shows weekly readership for print and electronic access for four age groups based on research from News Media Canada. The overlap of all these access points provides a weekly reach of almost 90 percent for adults aged 18 and older, and this overall reach does not vary much for the four age groups.

The Canadian Newspaper Association (CNA) and the Canadian Community Newspapers Association (CCNA) jointly execute research for newspaper audience measurement through their joint organization, News Media Canada. Each organization retains its own board of directors and many organizational functions are done as one. CNA promotes the benefits of advertising in newspapers, both daily and community, to advertisers, agencies, media planners, and newspapers themselves through research and information. In the past, News Media Canada performed community newspaper research; however, cost considerations and the infrequency of community newspaper publication required a change in the methodology. The most recent data collection in 2013 surveyed 200 respondents in five regions: Alberta, Saskatchewan, Manitoba, Northern Ontario, and Nova Scotia. The following results demonstrate the significance of community newspapers: 73 percent read a community newspaper (weekend or weekday), females exhibit higher readership at 76 percent, readership is higher with older Canadians, and there is no variation with different income levels.[33]

NEWSPAPER ADVERTISING RATES

Advertisers are faced with a number of options and pricing structures when purchasing newspaper space. The cost of advertising space depends on the circulation, and whether the circulation is controlled (free) or paid. It also depends on factors such as premium charges for colour in a special section, as well as discounts available. National rates can be about 15 percent higher than local rates, to account for agency commission.

Newspaper space is sold by the **agate line** and **column width**. A line (or agate line) is a unit measuring one column wide and 1/14-inch deep. One problem with this unit is that newspapers use columns of varying width, from 6 columns per page to 10 columns per page, which affects the size, shape, and costs of an ad. (Note that these columns are not the actual columns viewed while reading the newspaper.) This results in a complicated production and buying process for national advertisers that purchase space in a number of newspapers.

Advertisers need to know the number of lines and number of columns on a newspaper page in order to calculate the cost of an ad. For example, the following calculation is for the weekday cost of a full-page ad in the national edition of the *National Post*. The paper has 301 lines and 10 columns per page, and the open cost per line is $17.69. (Results of all calculations are rounded to the nearest dollar.)

10 columns × 301 lines × $17.69/line per column = $53,247

This calculation could be done differently with the same result when the entire length of the paper is known (301 lines/14 agate lines per column inch).

10 columns × 21.5 inches × 14 agate lines per column inch × $17.69 per agate line = $53,247

This principle can be used to calculate the cost of ads of various sizes. For example, for an ad that is 5 columns wide and 6 inches deep, the calculation would then be the following:

5 columns × 6 inches × 14 agate lines per column inch × $17.69 per agate line = $7,430

Newspaper rates for local advertisers continue to be based on the column inch, which is 1 inch deep by 1 column wide. Advertising rates for local advertisers are quoted per column inch, and media planners calculate total space costs by multiplying the ad's number of column inches by the cost per inch.

Most newspapers have an **open-rate structure**, which means discounts are available. These discounts are generally based on frequency or bulk purchases of space and depend on the number of column inches purchased in a year. The above calculations used the most expensive cost based on a one-time ad. The maximum discount puts the cost per line at $11.82, about one-third less expensive. A full-page ad would drop from $53,247 to $35,578, a saving of $17,669.

Newspaper space rates also vary with an advertiser's special requests, such as preferred position or colour. The basic rates quoted by a newspaper are **run of paper (ROP)**, which means the paper can place the ad on any page or in any position it desires. While most newspapers try to place an ad in a requested position, the advertiser can ensure a specific section and/or position on a page by paying a higher **preferred position rate**. Colour advertising is also available in many newspapers on an ROP basis or through preprinted inserts or supplements.

With the decline of newspaper advertising revenue, Postmedia signed a three-year advertising payment deal with Mogo, an online financial service targeted to younger adults. Postmedia provided advertising across its 200 media properties in exchange for a percentage of Mogo's revenue and the option to buy shares. The arrangement worked out to $50 million in advertising based on posted ad rates and allowed for a two-year extension.[34] Time will tell if this is a one-time experiment or a new wave of the future for print media and maybe all media.

 # Evaluation of Newspapers

Newspapers have a number of strengths and limitations in comparison to other media. We review each of these according to the criteria of Chapter 10. Newspapers present unique opportunities for ad placement that affect their strengths and limitations, as does the use of national, city, or community publications. Despite this, the generalizations are reasonably consistent no matter the situation.

STRENGTHS OF NEWSPAPERS

Newspapers feature characteristics that make them an attractive option for local and national advertisers. These include target audience coverage, geographic coverage, scheduling flexibility, reach and frequency, absolute cost and cost efficiency, amount of processing time and reader involvement, creativity for cognitive responses, and media image.

Target Audience Coverage Coverage of a specific target audience is argued to be a limitation for the newspaper in comparison to its print cousin, the magazine. However, placement of ads in certain newspaper sections that recur every day (e.g., sports, business, entertainment) or once a week (e.g., food, cars, finance) can be advantageous for marketers.

Geographic Coverage Newspapers offer advertisers targeted geographic or territorial coverage. Advertisers vary their coverage by choosing a paper—or combination of papers—that reaches the areas with the greatest sales potential. National advertisers take advantage of the geographic coverage of newspapers to concentrate their advertising in specific areas they can't reach with other media. For example, more expensive automobile manufacturers advertise in Toronto newspapers that reach the greater Toronto area and beyond with their wide distribution. Companies use newspapers in regional marketing strategies; this lets them feature products on a market-by-market basis, adapt campaigns to local market conditions, and tie in to retailer promotions to foster support from the trade. Local retail advertisers are interested in geographic coverage within a market to concentrate their advertising where most of their current or potential customers are located.

Scheduling Flexibility Newspapers provide flexibility to advertisers in terms of requirements for producing and running the ads. Newspaper ads can be written, laid out, and prepared in a matter of hours. For most dailies, the closing time by which the ad must be received is usually only 48 hours before publication (although closing times for supplements and special ads are longer). The short production time and closing times or dates make newspapers very suitable for responding to current events or presenting timely information to consumers.

Reach and Frequency One of the primary strengths of newspapers is the high degree of market coverage they offer an advertiser; most areas are served by one or two daily newspapers. The extensive penetration of newspapers makes them a truly mass medium and provides advertisers with an excellent opportunity for communicating with all segments of the population. Research shows that newspapers achieve weekly reach of almost 90 percent across print and digital access points. Also, since many newspapers are published and read daily, advertisers build high levels of frequency into the media schedule.

Absolute Cost and Cost Efficiency Newspapers assist small companies through free copywriting and art services. Small advertisers without an agency or advertising department often rely on the newspaper to help them write and produce their ads. Production costs of ads are reasonable since many are simple copy with a standard image or photo-stock visual. The creative flexibility of newspapers in terms of size and format of the ad makes it difficult to exactly conclude the cost implications of this medium. Small and local businesses can run a small ad with a reasonable cost per thousand compared to magazines.

Amount of Processing Time and Reader Involvement Another important feature of newspapers is consumers' level of acceptance for and involvement with papers and the ads they contain. Consumers typically rely on a newspaper because of the advertising it contains; they use retail ads to determine product prices and availability and to see who is having a sale. One aspect of newspapers that is helpful to advertisers is readers' knowledge about particular sections. For example, the food section is popular for recipe and menu ideas as well as for the grocery store ads and promotional offers. The average newspaper reader spends considerable time consuming news, information, and entertainment. **Figure 12-9** gives an idea of how much reading occurs throughout the day for different ways to access the information. As expected, reading via phone devices peaks throughout the day, thereby giving newspapers the opportunity to adjust content and give advertisers direction for targeting.

Creativity for Cognitive Responses Newspapers offer the opportunity for extremely long copy, perhaps a thousand words extolling the attributes and benefits of a product. The option of considerable explanation of a product could be quite important for marketers looking to persuade consumers who are at the information search stage of the decision-making process. Furthermore, newspapers offer numerous creative options as ads can be run in different sizes, shapes, and formats to persuade the reader. Magazine innovations described earlier are adapted to newspapers as well.

Media Image The value of newspaper advertising as a source of information has been shown in several studies. One study found that consumers look forward to ads in newspapers more than in other media. In another study, 80 percent of consumers said newspaper ads were most helpful to them in doing their weekly shopping. Newspaper advertising has also been rated the most believable form of advertising in numerous studies.

IMC Perspective 12-2 reflects on challenges facing newspapers to maintain their journalistic quality and the federal government's response. Despite the difficulties, digital ad revenue grew six consecutive quarters for the *National Post* by mid-2018.[35] It should also be noted that the decline in newspaper ad revenue reversed its course slightly in the United Kingdom. Large advertisers like P&G realized that their budget allocations had become overly dependent on digital media and that their messages placed in media vehicles with inappropriate content did not meet their expectations of quality advertising.[36]

Figure 12-9 Newspaper access types by time of day

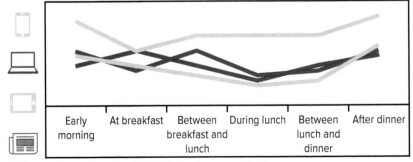

©Newspapers Canada 24-7 Study, January 2016

FINANCIAL CHALLENGES FOR NEWSPAPERS

The downward trajectory of newspapers' advertising revenue continued as the total (including Internet) dropped from $3.7 billion in 2010 to $1.8 billion in 2017. After giving away free journalistic content online for 15 years with no subscription fee and minimal support from Internet advertising revenue at $300 million in 2017, industry players faced an unprofitable situation. As part of the decline, Canada lost about 16,000 journalist positions during the past decade, with 50 percent from print media. Although innovation occurred over the past few years to develop additional revenue, the issues of retaining Canadian journalistic quality, government funding, and alternative methods of revenue growth emerged.

Facebook and Google represented the main source of revenue loss as Canadian advertisers gravitated to digital advertising. These are attractive options for Canadian firms reaching a Canadian target audience, but even more so since the Canadian firm could deduct the ad expense from its revenue and therefore not pay tax on the ad expense. This tax implication is not possible for Canadian brands advertising in established American broadcast and print media.

Thus, digital media provided a significant cost savings while using this type of American media due to the tax law. The historic reason for the tax law encouraged Canadian advertisers to support Canadian media, so the new situation proved to be a significant public policy issue for government officials. The fact that Facebook and Google aggregated the Canadian news without paying for it, and gained ad revenue at the same time, compounded the financial situation for Canadian media who incurred the journalistic cost and did not obtain ad revenue. Talk about a double-whammy!

©Dave and Les Jacobs/Blend Images LLC

In early 2018, federal government officials responded to industry concerns and conceded that granting charitable status for newspapers appeared necessary. Such an arrangement allowed publishers to receive funds and give tax receipts to donors. At the same time, they also granted $10 million to support local newspapers that dwindled in numbers. By the end of 2018, the federal government agreed to the charitable route and offered nearly $600 million over five years to support journalists producing original news content in Canadian print media. Industry members appreciated the direction from the federal government, but the existing situational issue remained unchanged.

Question:
1. Why are digital newspapers a stronger or weaker alternative as an advertising medium compared to other digital alternatives?

LIMITATIONS OF NEWSPAPERS

While newspapers have strengths, they also have limitations that media planners consider as with other media. The limitations of newspapers include their target audience selectivity, control for selective exposure and attention, creativity for emotional responses, and clutter.

Target Audience Selectivity While newspapers offer advertisers geographic selectivity, they are not selective in terms of demographics or lifestyle characteristics. Most newspapers reach broad and very diverse groups of consumers, which makes it difficult for marketers to focus on narrowly defined market segments. For example, manufacturers of fishing rods and reels will find newspapers very inefficient because of the wasted circulation that results from reaching all the newspaper readers who don't fish. Thus, they are more likely to use special-interest magazines. Any newspaper ads for their products will be done through cooperative plans whereby retailers share the costs or spread them over a number of sporting goods featured in the ad.

Control for Selective Exposure and Attention Unlike magazines, which are retained for weeks, a daily newspaper is generally kept for a day. So an ad is unlikely to have much impact beyond its publication date, and repeat exposure is unlikely. Compounding this situation are the amount of time consumers spend with the newspaper and the possibility they may not open sections of the paper. Media planners offset these concerns with a high frequency schedule and advertising in a section where consumers who are in the market for a good or service are likely to look. Other approaches to obtain reader attention include "front page wraps" (actual ads on the first page), "belly bands" (advertising strips surrounding the paper like a belt), and "French doors" (section wraps split down the middle).

Creativity for Emotional Responses A significant limitation of newspapers for advertising is their poor reproduction quality; the coarse paper stock and absence of extensive colour limits the quality of most newspaper ads. Newspapers with wide circulation, such as those owned by Postmedia, improved their reproduction and colour quality with technological advances. One other noteworthy example is the weekend edition of *The Globe and Mail,* which provides high-quality reproduction and colour that approaches magazine quality. Also, advertisers desiring high-quality colour in newspaper ads turn to alternatives such as freestanding inserts or supplements, although they are costly.

Clutter Newspapers suffer from clutter because a substantial amount of the average daily newspaper in Canada is devoted to advertising; an advertiser's message competes with other ads for consumers' attention and interest. Moreover, the creative options in newspapers are limited with black and white ads. Thus, it can be difficult for a newspaper advertiser to break through the clutter without using costly measures such as large space buys or colour.

LO5 IMC Planning: Strategic Use of Print Media

In Chapter 11, we ended with a discussion of the use of broadcast media to achieve strategic IMC objectives. In this IMC planning section, we investigate the use of magazines and newspapers to achieve communication and behavioural objectives at different stages of the target audience's decision-making process.

MAGAZINES

The selectivity and creativity options for magazines allow promotional planners a multitude of opportunities for establishing and maintaining very unique brand positions across all potential target audiences. For example, if research reveals a high proportion of non-users in certain lifestyle publications, the promotional planner can develop print ads with extensive copy to build category need as well as sufficient brand coverage for awareness while communicating the most appropriate brand benefit message for persuasion. Alternatively, research in other publications might indicate strong brand development and a high proportion of current customers, thus allowing the promotional planner the opportunity to use messages that maintain the strong brand equity. This might suggest a more emotional message with enticing visuals for low-involvement processing.

While the decision to offer more customized messages to each audience is met with a certain amount of risk, this is mitigated by the consistency in the creative theme and creative tactics such as the design elements (e.g., layout). This possible scenario for promotional planners suggests that ads directed toward non-users could be developed to influence the prepurchase and need recognition stages, whereas the ads for the customer could attempt to influence the purchase decision stage, as the brand would be encouraging a repeat purchase objective.

Extending this argument geographically is another strategic opportunity for promotional planners. For example, if the brand has a low brand development index in one part of the country, more persuasive switching messages directed to consumers at the purchase decision stage might be considered through regional or city editions. Alternatively, other regional editions could be examined if the brand has a high brand development index and the promotional planner concentrates on brand maintenance messages that focus, for example, on postpurchase satisfaction.

As the use of these key strengths of magazines implies, promotional planners can use magazines to attain virtually any of the communication objectives with any type of target audience and create the unique brand positions desired. Magazines are also strong for attaining purchase intention objectives and shopping objectives; ads generate action or planned action in 50–60 percent of respondents.[37] Magazine ads are useful for prompting Internet searches and website visits, with 26–36 percent of respondents reporting such behaviour.[38] Granted, certain costs are associated with this strategic use of magazines; the promotional planner can schedule the placements over time so as not to break the budget.

These strengths of magazines allow print to work with other media and IMC tools. Visuals can be the same as those from TV commercials to enhance message frequency. Headlines can be consistently used across out-of-home media and print ads. Sales promotions can be added to the message, like coupons or Internet site links to register for samples. Brand-building charity sponsorship or events can be communicated if they especially resonate with the readership audience. In short, magazines offer a degree of potential integration in the IMC plan.

NEWSPAPERS

The strategic use of newspapers is similar to radio in that national and local advertisers design messages with related objectives. National advertisers employ newspapers for brand-building messages they wish to disseminate across the country or in select regions. These ads take a few general forms. One kind of ad builds awareness and benefit beliefs at the prepurchase and need recognition stages due to the broad reach of newspapers. With the majority of Canadian households reading newspapers on a regular basis, brands naturally reach their target audience and those who may not be in the market for such products. Other types of ads contribute at the information search stage for the target audience. The involved nature of the messages that can be creatively communicated in a more rational manner to fit the editorial context permits promotional planners to persuade their audience via high-involvement, informational brand attitude. One limitation with the opportunity is that the number of consumers actually in the market at this stage is smaller, thus making the purchase less cost-efficient. Finally, national advertisers utilize newspapers for disseminating information regarding sales promotions. For example, automobile manufacturers and large retailers are the largest advertisers who communicate their price and other promotions in newspapers to influence consumers at the purchase decision stage.

As noted in the cost implications discussion, newspapers offer local advertisers and small businesses (e.g., retailers, services) a tremendous opportunity for reaching an entire city for a reasonable cost. These advertisers can design ads to meet any communication objectives. A perusal of the local newspaper will identify ads that are clearly trying to build awareness and communicate certain brand benefits. However, the daily/weekly time frame of newspapers reveals that many ads have stronger purchase intention objectives.

Like magazines, newspapers offer good potential for integrating with other media and IMC tools. Television and radio commercials frequently suggest that consumers "see newspaper for details." In this case, the initial ads are influencing the target audience at the need recognition stage and the newspaper is influencing the information search stage. Many public relations activities (such as sponsorship of charity events in the local community) are conveyed in newspapers since they act as a planning resource for things to do in one's city.

Learning Objectives Summary

 LO1 Identify the different types of magazines available for advertising, how circulation and readership levels are determined, how audience size and its characteristics are measured, and the factors that influence advertising rates.

Magazines are a very selective medium and are valuable for reaching specific types of customers and market segments. The four broad categories of magazines are consumer, ethnic, farm, and business publications. Each of these categories can be further classified according to the publication's editorial content and audience appeal. Foreign publications compete with Canadian magazines also.

Circulation and readership are verified with an audit function so advertisers are confident that the number claimed by the individual title is accurate. Extensive information about magazine readers is available.

Advertising space rates in magazines vary according to a number of factors, including the size of the ad, position in the publication, particular editions purchased, use of colour, and number and frequency of insertions. Rates for magazines are compared on the basis of cost per thousand, although other factors such as the editorial content of the publication and its ability to reach specific target audiences must also be considered.

 Evaluate the strengths and limitations of magazines as an advertising medium.

The strengths of magazines include their target audience selectivity, geographic coverage, control for selective exposure and attention, creativity for cognitive and emotional responses, amount of processing time and reader involvement, and media image. Limitations of magazines include their weak target audience coverage, the long lead time required in placing an ad leading to poorer scheduling flexibility, their limited reach and frequency, the absolute cost of advertising and its efficiency, and the problem of clutter.

 Identify the types of newspapers offered for advertising, how circulation and readership levels are determined, how audience size and its characteristics are measured, and how advertising rates are determined.

A variety of newspapers are available for advertisers, including daily, community, national, Internet, and special-audience newspapers and newspaper supplements. Newspapers offer great flexibility regarding the type of ad, including display, classified, special, and inserts. Extensive research is conducted to ensure that the number of readers is accurate. Additional research of newspaper readers provides a detailed profile of their characteristics.

Newspaper ads are sold as a full page or any partial page the advertiser desires. The line and column characteristics of newspapers allow nearly unlimited sizes, although most ads follow conventional sizes of half-page, quarter-page, and so on, with smaller advertisers selecting smaller spaces. Advertising rates are determined by the size of the ad and the circulation.

 Evaluate the strengths and limitations of newspapers as an advertising medium.

Newspapers are a very important medium to local advertisers, especially retailers. Newspapers are a broad-based medium and reach a large percentage of households in a particular area. Newspapers' other advantages include target audience coverage, geographic coverage, scheduling flexibility, reach and frequency, absolute cost and cost efficiency, amount of processing time and reader involvement, creativity for cognitive responses, and media image. Limitations of newspapers include their target audience selectivity, control for selective exposure and attention, creativity for emotional responses, and clutter. The use of special inserts and supplements allows advertisers to overcome these limitations to a degree. However, newspapers face increasing competition from Internet media as the World Wide Web continues to grow as an information resource for consumers.

 Apply the media knowledge of magazines and newspapers for strategic IMC decisions.

Print media are important for IMC plans as their potential for long-form copy, lengthy reading, and selectivity for magazines and coverage for newspapers makes expenditures worthwhile for certain product categories or for when consumers are in the information or purchase decision stage. Given their importance for providing information, print media are readily linked with other media as ads may suggest connection to digital media or follow-up on messages found in broadcast or out-of-home media that have broader coverage.

Review Questions

1. Discuss how circulation figures and readership composition are used in evaluating magazines as part of a media plan and setting advertising rates.

2. Discuss the strengths and limitations of magazines for advertising. How do magazines differ from television and radio as advertising media?

3. Discuss how circulation figures and readership composition are used in evaluating newspapers as part of a media plan and setting advertising rates.

4. Discuss the strengths and limitations of newspapers for advertising. How might the decision to use newspapers in a media plan differ for national versus local advertisers?

5. How do magazines and newspapers help achieve brand behavioural and communication effects?

Applied Questions

1. Explain why advertisers of products such as cosmetics or women's clothing would choose to advertise in magazines such as *Flare, Elle Canada,* or *Chatelaine.*

2. Select an enjoyable print ad from a magazine and apply the earlier text material. Identify the target audience, behavioural objectives, communication objectives, brand positioning strategy, and creative strategy and tactics decisions, and associate these points with the key strengths of magazines as an advertising medium.

3. Explain why advertisers of products such as smart phones or men's clothing would choose to advertise in newspapers such as *The Globe and Mail, Vancouver Sun,* or *Metro.*

4. What differences might one conclude exist between national newspapers and community newspapers regarding the strengths and limitations of newspapers?

5. Identify how newspapers and magazines can be used for each stage of the consumer decision-making process for automobile purchases.

CHAPTER THIRTEEN

Out-of-Home Media

LEARNING OBJECTIVES

LO1 Identify the options within outdoor media for developing an IMC program and audience measurement, and their strengths and limitations.

LO2 Identify the options within transit media for developing an IMC program, and their strengths and limitations.

LO3 Identify the options within place-based media for developing an IMC program, and their strengths and limitations.

LO4 Show how out-of-home media is an important element of IMC planning.

Billboards Go Digital

The growth of digital billboards changed the game for marketers and contributed to the 28 percent increase in advertising revenue for out-of-home media from 2013 to 2017. Media companies installed the first digital billboard over a decade ago. The sheer size and number of billboards attracted advertisers to place their brand messages throughout our cities, and follow-up research unearthed constructive results: 60 percent of Canadian shoppers and 73 percent of smart phone owners noticed digital billboards. Consumers who recall out-of-home ads are more likely to use their device for shopping activities such as finding store locations and researching product information, a boon for those using digital billboards and transit shelter ads.

Key features of digital outdoor media are lower production costs (e.g., no paper for the display), faster installation, improved scheduling flexibility, and increased data provision. The implementation is quick and the message is live immediately. Recent intensification and resulting data improved the ability of marketers to target audiences by location, time of day, and other variables (such as the weather). In fact, the creative message changes as often as an advertiser desires throughout the day. For example, McDonald's implemented the technology on a billboard beside a British Columbia highway, changing the message periodically to focus on a particular beverage depending on the snow conditions.

Digital outdoor media also features wireless near-field communication that works with consumers' mobile devices and offers message customization. An example is JUICE Mobile's proximity network across all outdoor media. Users who are close to a billboard receive an advertising message or promotional offer with an opportunity to accept or decline. The company expects strong consumer adoption as the majority of Canadians are willing to receive a notification on their phone if they perceive it to be an offer of value. The system promises accurate reporting of the numbers of consumers passing by the message and of those accepting the message. Data supports this belief, indicating that the majority of consumers plan to take action after interacting with an outdoor ad.

Astral has expanded its digital billboard business: 10 percent of its 31,000 facings are digitally capable, with plans to double this level. The media company focused on creativity and technology with its advertisers recently. For example, drivers who listened to a Bell Media radio ad for an Infiniti auto subsequently received exposure to an Infiniti digital billboard ad along the side of the highway. Kleenex showed three images of a hand tugging a tissue from a box, indicating three levels of pollen. Beyond the public service announcement, the ad clearly reminded consumers and strengthened brand awareness. RBC alerted consumers about actual airline cancellations and suggested consumers buy travel insurance.

Question:

1. Why are advertisers turning toward mobile messages delivered by digital billboards?

Every time we step out of our home, we encounter media directing an advertising message to us. We see ads while travelling, and many places we go to for leisure have advertising. **Out-of-home media** is pervasive as it delivers advertising messages that we experience while moving throughout our town or city while accomplishing our day-to-day activities. This media generated $624 million in advertising revenue in 2017, which has increased recently with the growth of digital technology.

In this chapter, we review three broad categories of out-of-home media: outdoor, transit, and place-based media. The term *out-of-home media* is adopted because it encompasses media that are located in public spaces. For each out-of-home media, we offer a summary of strengths and limitations; these are generalizations, however, and advertisers can certainly find exceptions as these media continue to flourish and innovate.

LO1 Outdoor Media

Outdoor media are pervasive, and it appears that we are surrounded. However, the amount spent on this medium is but a portion of the $624 million spent on out-of-home media. In contrast, advertising on the Internet is about 10 times larger than out-of-home. Despite this paradox of both large and small scale, the growth of outdoor media options and the medium's contribution to sales may be a key factor in its continued appeal to advertisers. For example, a study showed that outdoor advertising can have a significant effect on sales, particularly when combined with a promotion.[1] We describe outdoor media options, their audience measurement, and their strengths and limitations as an advertising medium.

OUTDOOR MEDIA OPTIONS

Outdoor media options include different formats of large posters, digital media equivalents of posters, and street media (sometimes identified as "street furniture") as shown in **Figure 13-1**. Large posters are the typical big billboard ads one sees when driving. The next column indicates that large posters expanded to digital and video formats with the growth of technology. Street media are ads displayed in a variety of locations and formats within a city or town.

   Posters are billboards in the typical horizontal (e.g., 3 metres by 6 metres) or vertical (e.g., 5 metres by 4 metres) layout. Poster display ads are front-lit for visibility at night and are located in areas with high vehicle traffic volume (see **Exhibit 13-1**). They may be purchased on an individual basis or for a certain level of GRPs in large cities such as Toronto or in smaller markets.

Figure 13-1 Out-of-home media

Large Posters	Digital Media	Street Media
Horizontal/vertical	Horizontal	Street poster
Backlit	Superboard	Transit shelter
Spectacular	Video board	Bench/receptacle
Superboard		Bike rack
Wall mural/banner		Specialty

Backlit posters are generally the same size as standard posters and have a light behind them so that they are clearly illuminated at night (see **Exhibit 13-2**). These units are located at major intersections or high-traffic-volume areas in or near major cities in Canada. Creativity is possible with both types of posters; for example, one located near a subway track featuring a photo of a model advertising hair care products contained an interactive feature where her hair blew as the train arrived. Of course the ad did not actually change, but a video projected upon the billboard gave the effect of visually experiencing the product benefit.[2]

Exhibit 13-1 Example of a poster ad.

©OUTFRONT Media Inc.

Exhibit 13-2 Example of a backlit poster.

©OUTFRONT Media Inc.

Superboards or **spectaculars** are larger displays (two to three times larger) that have a variety of sizes depending upon the media company (see **Exhibit 13-3**). These displays are sold on a per location basis due to their size and the low number of options available in major Canadian markets. *Trivisions* and *permanents* are two specialized forms of bulletins. Trivisions are horizontal or vertical posters with rotating blades that allow three different ads to be shown. Permanents feature unique sizes and formats and are erected in specific locations permanently. Due to the customized nature of permanents, there is considerable latitude for creativity.

One research study found that managers rated billboard visibility and media efficiency as more influential than local presence and tangible results (e.g., sales). The most critical factors for billboard success included name identification, location, readability, and clarity. A secondary set of factors suggested IMC and visuals, while the third group indicated creative and information. This implies that allowing the target audience to clearly read the brand identification at the right place is paramount over the most creative or informative ad.[3] A summary analysis of over 100 studies spanning 80 years concluded that consumers found billboards to be informative, entertaining, irritating, good for the economy, and positive overall.[4] However, a large-scale sales effect study found that billboard ads did not contribute to sales for all brands across numerous product categories.[5]

Murals and **wall banners** are similar to the three above outdoor options but are customized in terms of artistic design. They are sold in a few major markets in Canada (e.g., Toronto, Vancouver) with varying sizes (**Exhibit 13-4**). Murals are hand-painted and therefore more costly and less flexible, with no future use. On the other hand, wall banners are painted vinyl, costing less and having more flexibility for use in another part of the city later. These two options are usually placed in unexpected locations to attract stronger attention and drive subsequent communication effects.

Street-level posters are smaller backlit displays measuring about 2 metres by 1 metre. Media companies offer different formats across the country for street posters and each firm uses a unique name. For example, Astral offers three sizes with the following labels in order of size: street column, signature column, and mega column. **Exhibit 13-5** is an example of a street poster that illuminates at night and is easily visible during the day. Its central location ensures a substantial exposure level.

Transit shelters are specialized locations for street posters, and outdoor media firms provide this option in many cities and towns. Transit shelters are sold and classified as outdoor media instead of transit media because the transit organizations are usually not involved in shelter construction and media selling. The example shown in

Exhibit 13-3 Example of a superboard.

©OUTFRONT Media Inc.

Exhibit 13-4 Murals are part of the outdoor landscape.

©Leonard Zhukovsky/Shutterstock

Exhibit 13-5 Example of a street poster.

©Lukas Davidziuk/Shutterstock

Exhibit 13-6 Example of a transit shelter poster.

©OUTFRONT Media Inc.

Exhibit 13-6 illustrates how creative and colourful messages are placed where people wait for a bus. Some transit stops offer benches as a service and ads are found there as well (thus giving the furniture idea "street cred"). Finally, the latter two on the list of street media show that outdoor advertising appears everywhere, it seems. Astral signed a long-term contract with the City of Toronto to provide 25,000 pieces of furniture (i.e., transit shelters, garbage bins, benches, information pillars) worth $200 million over 20 years, and a cut of the advertising revenue in which the city received $168 million in the first half of the contract.[6]

Other unique *specialty* street media include a whole host of promotional opportunities. One firm, Grassroots, offers many of these shorter-term and seemingly spontaneous forms of street advertising.[7] *Street frames* allow very small posters to be placed in a permanent frame located outside small stores. *Wild postings* are a similar size but are placed in unexpected locations such as building façades, construction site barricades, alleyways, and skate parks, for example. *Projections* shine photos or video in public against buildings. **Mobile signage** occurs with vehicles showing some kind of display or motion ad on vehicles that travel or go to an event. For example, Grassroots set up a promotion for Nordstrom where a floral patterned truck attracted consumers, who received tulips to celebrate spring and, of course, a suggestion to shop at the fashionable retailer.

The major outdoor operators communicate examples of past outdoor campaigns to demonstrate how outdoor media produces awareness and other communication effects. The operators also provide maps to illustrate the locations and other relevant data (e.g., demographics). The aforementioned outdoor options are typically purchased for four weeks and provide anywhere from 25 GRPs to 150 GRPs per day, depending upon the number of displays or showings chosen within a local market. Recall from Chapter 10 that one GRP represents 1 percent of the market exposed to the ad once. Thus, buying 50 GRPs possibly implies that the marketer reaches 50 percent of the market once per day. The costs for placing outdoor advertising are not readily available with CARD any longer; however, the locations and other basic data are still offered.

A study conducted in Europe concluded with suggestions on how to make outdoor advertising effective:[8] These points are consistent with the ideas presented in the message development chapters.

- Clear branding and inclusion of new-product information enhances product recognition.
- Large amounts of text and pictures of people delay product recognition.
- Lengthy, large headlines, information cues, and humour delay brand recognition.
- Short headlines, longer body text, and a product shot enhance the creative appeal.
- Specifying a brand name in the headline or providing price information reduces appeal.

Exhibit 13-7 Advertising at Dundas Square in Toronto.

©rmnoa357/Shutterstock

Figure 13-1 shows that the digital outdoor posters and other digital formats have emerged in Canada, with firms setting up large video display units that have full animation and colour. For example, Dundas Square, near the Eaton Centre in downtown Toronto, features a 12-metre-wide by 9-metre-high full-colour video screen in addition to eight display faces and Canada's largest neon sign, at 18 metres in diameter. With its high-profile location, Dundas Square is ideal for brands looking to extend their reach (**Exhibit 13-7**).

Electronic message signs offer short ads (e.g., 6 to 10 seconds) on a one-minute rotation. As expected, both of these displays are placed in high-traffic locations in a few large urban markets, with various sizes and packages available depending on the media firm. The growth of outdoor video displays is such that the firms offer network services, thereby reaching many viewers across the country.

Application of digital technology for out-of-home media reached new heights with movement on three significant fronts. First, digital signage is a small portion of the facings in Canada, but media companies are moving toward greater penetration. Second, Bluetooth technology used with billboard ads directs messages to the smart phones of passersby. Third, considerable adaptations of Bluetooth and other technology to various types of displays permit enhanced communication. **Figure 13-2** shows data indicating acceptance of digital outdoor ad messages.

As an example of the digital technology in outdoor media, Mark's presented a creative message with digital transit shelters. The image posted a discount corresponding to the temperature—consumers received a 20 percent discount on a day when the temperature hit 20 degrees below zero! Primary media of TV and flyers did not lend themselves to up-to-the-minute approaches for ad execution, and Internet and social media did not build reach and frequency quickly enough, so digital transit shelters offered a useful complement to the existing media strategy. Executives believed the digital message offered brand building communication ability and quick tactical pricing information.[9] Additional innovation in transit shelters features interactive communication with people's phones and is described in **IMC Perspective 13-1**.

Figure 13-2 Consumer responses to digital outdoor ads, % agreement with statements

	Toronto	Montreal	Vancouver
Recall past week of digital ad	56%	47%	50%
Notice digital ad vs. static poster	58%	48%	50%
Digital ads provide useful information	61%	55%	53%
Interest to interact with digital ad	50%	47%	36%

IMC PERSPECTIVE 13-1

TRANSIT SHELTERS GO DIGITAL

Technological advances similar to those we saw earlier with billboards occurred with transit shelters in major Canadian cities; notably, there was a transition to digital message delivery and the opportunity to take advantage of near field communication. Quebecor's outdoor media division made significant advances in developing a digital network among its transit shelters. In time, we may see downtown core and other high-traffic areas using only digital transit shelters as the technology advances and advertisers learn how to customize messages.

Quebecor signed a 20-year deal for the 2,700 advertising faces in Montreal and initially equipped 50 shelters with large screens. The company made a similar deal in Laval and instituted digital technology in some shelters as well. The shelters all featured near field technology and Quebecor planned to add beacons for additional interaction, allowing consumers to receive messages. Other advanced features with Quebecor's transit shelters included a code to scan to receive news, weather, and live bus schedule information, and touch screen and gesture recognition to offer creative message delivery for advertisers.

©Carlos Osorio/Toronto Star via Getty Images

[Continued on next page]

[IMC Perspective 13-1 continued]

Here are a few examples of implementing a campaign with Quebecor transit shelters. Febreze ran a message requesting people to select words and then played corresponding music to create ambiance within the shelter. Another brand displayed a virtual catalogue of winter coats. For Oasis juice, sensors recognized a person going by and spritzed scents to communicate a cooking show. As these examples demonstrate, the new creative messages are possible with this location-based digital technology.

An interesting aspect of Quebecor's roster is its segmentation, with three branded networks based on geographic location in Montreal. DownTown reaches those in the business, entertainment, and cultural locales. HipTown reaches students and transit users in "hip" niches of the city. GoTown reaches drivers on major traffic routes. A similar approach is used for other parts of the metro area and other cities. The advantage of this is changing the message depending on the area; very specific customization can be based on lifestyle, situation, or perhaps customer group.

Quebecor communicates that digital ads are attention-grabbing, interesting, entertaining, and informative to the majority of the respondents. This is especially true as the digital screen shows multiple images over a short period of time to tell a story. It can change throughout the day (one example in the media kit showed a quick service restaurant changing its menu image from morning to evening) or over a few weeks (another example showed teaser ads for two weeks and then the unveiled image two weeks later). Executives see greater opportunities similar to what we see on TV and online, with video messages providing information that contains product placement or brand integration messages.

Question:

1. Why are advertisers turning toward messages delivered by digital transit shelters?

AUDIENCE MEASUREMENT

The Canadian Out of Home Marketing and Measurement Bureau (COMMB) is a national organization comprising members from advertisers, advertising agencies, and out-of-home media firms. To assist all members, COMMB develops and verifies audience measurement methodologies and provides audience data and planning resources. It is also responsible for out-of-home industry marketing communications, government relations, and member services. In the past, two different organizations managed these two broad areas of responsibility. COMMB maintains a national database of all products for outdoor and place-based media firms in order to compile the audience measurement data. The larger firms based on the number of approved products include Astral, OutFront, and Pattison. COMMB publishes circulation and market data for approximately 60,000 out-of-home facings in 270 markets for 42 products from 20 approved media firms.

COMMB's methodology to determine advertising exposure (impressions) of out-of-home media is comprehensive with its unbiased, accurate, and independently collected quantitative data; however, the methodologies for outdoor and place-based are customized to a degree to account for the unique travel patterns associated with viewers of each media type. Important characteristics of the research are the visibility criteria which identify the number of people who have a reliable opportunity to see the message within a standardized distance for each advertising format, the use of sound statistical procedures, the inclusion of market-specific data, and reliable data collection procedures.

For the outdoor research, COMMB begins with data from municipalities for road planning purposes, which is then assessed on how it can be used for measuring the regular traffic flow. This data is adjusted for the visibility criteria, the average number of people in the vehicle, and the number of hours an ad is illuminated. This is augmented with pedestrian data that also meets the visibility criteria in order to calculate the average daily circulation per face. As might be expected, all of this data is examined with advanced mapping technologies to visually represent the volume of people potentially exposed to an advertising message.

These circulations are applied to each poster along a certain part of the road called a link. The numbers are adjusted to account for time-of-day variations throughout the week to arrive at an adjusted circulation. An important refinement of the data is the use of GPS technology that tracks traffic moving into a Census Metropolitan Area (CMA) in Canada's five larger cities, which accounts for commuters who are exposed to advertising messages.

From this data, COMMB calculates the number of people (aged 5+) who have a reasonable opportunity to see an ad and estimates reach and frequency levels with sophisticated mathematical models. Advertisers confidently purchase the advertising space knowing that rigorous standards and exceptional research methodology provide accurate exposure levels. To facilitate their planning, COMMB offers two planning software tools. The COMMB Data Report is a comprehensive system for identifying all of the 80,000 facings with a number of reporting options. The COMMBNavigator® allows planners to select media vehicles to attain reach and frequency levels for various target audience profiles.

STRENGTHS OF OUTDOOR MEDIA

Geographic Coverage Outdoor media can be placed along highways, near stores, or on mobile billboards, almost anywhere that the law permits. Local, regional, or even national markets may be covered.

Scheduling Flexibility As noted earlier, digital technology reduces production times for outdoor advertising and allows for rapid turnaround time and immediate placement. Scheduling of non-digital outdoor advertising is typically done on a monthly basis assuming availability exists.

Reach With proper placement, a broad base of exposure is possible in a given market, with both day and night presence. A 100 GRP **showing** (the percentage of duplicated audience exposed to an outdoor poster daily) could yield exposure to an equivalent of 100 percent of the marketplace daily! This level of coverage is likely to yield high levels of reach. Behavioural responses toward outdoor media are considerable, with extensive reach possibilities as documented in **Figure 13-3**.

Figure 13-3 Behavioural responses to outdoor ads in past six months

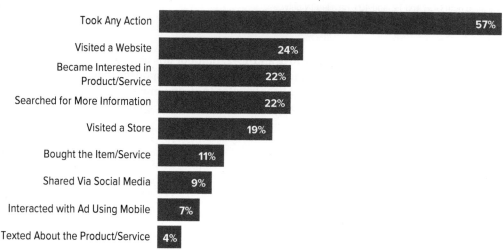

Source: Canadian Out of Home Marketing and Measurement Bureau (COMMB)

Frequency Because purchase cycles for outdoor media are typically for four-week periods, consumers are usually exposed a number of times, resulting in high levels of frequency. The importance of frequency is substantiated with the results of a study shown in **Figure 13-4**.

Cost Efficiency Outdoor ads usually have a very competitive CPM when compared to other media. The average CPM of outdoor ads is less than that of radio, TV, magazines, and newspapers.

Control for Selective Exposure On the one hand, outdoor ads are difficult for consumers to avoid since they are so pervasive. Moreover, a consumer has little control as with television or radio to change the channel or station. On the other hand, consumers can deliberately ignore outdoor ads; however, the high profile of the ads makes this a difficult task at times.

Attention The ads' sheer size, strategic placement, and creative elements of colour make outdoor advertising an attractive medium to draw the attention of the target audience.

Figure 13-4 Out-of-home ads support other media when part of the budget

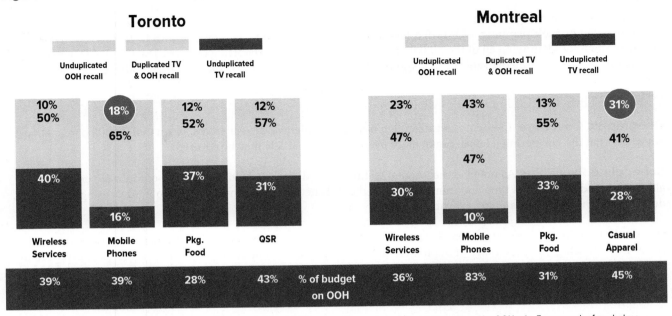

The bar chart shows the unduplicated and duplicated recall of TV and OOH among those who recalled seeing TV and/or OOH ads. For example, for wireless in Toronto: 10% recalled OOH only, 50% recalled both OOH and TV, and 40% recalled TV only.

Source: Canadian Out of Home Marketing and Measurement Bureau (COMMB)

Creativity for Emotional Responses As shown in **Exhibits 13-1** and **13-2**, outdoor ads can be very creative. Large print, colours, and other elements attract attention and tend to generate short emotional responses that connect the target audience to the brand. Presumably this emotional involvement contributes to strong brand building, leading to strong follow-up behaviour for continued shopping due to out-of-home media, as shown in **Figure 13-5**.

Figure 13-5 Behavioural effects of out-of-home advertising

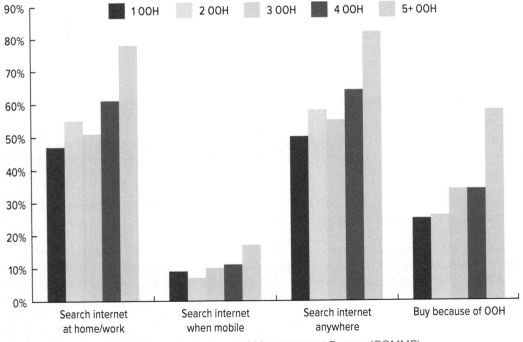

Source: Canadian Out of Home Marketing and Measurement Bureau (COMMB)

LIMITATIONS OF OUTDOOR MEDIA

Target Audience Selectivity
Reaching a specific target audience is challenging due to the broad exposure of outdoor media in general. However, strategic use can overcome this limitation, for example by using reminder ads for a type of product near the retail outlets.

Target Audience Coverage
With the broad base reach of outdoor advertising, it is difficult to ensure that the specific target audience coverage is sufficient. While it is possible to reach an audience with select location placement, in many cases the purchase of outdoor ads results in a high degree of waste coverage. It is not likely that everyone driving past a billboard is part of the target audience.

Absolute Cost A basic level of 25 GRPs per day over four weeks in ten—or even three—major cities is prohibitive for advertisers. For smaller businesses, selecting a few strategic locations in a local market could overcome this limitation. If a firm can afford outdoor media, research suggests that it improves return on investment.

Creativity for Cognitive Responses Lengthy appeals are not physically possible in many instances, and if they were, they would have less likelihood of complete comprehension. Thus, it is expected that outdoor ads suffer from their inability to fully persuade consumers with an involved message.

Amount of Processing Time Because of the speed with which most people pass by outdoor ads, exposure time is short, so messages are limited to a few words and/or an illustration. Despite this concern, there appears to be sufficient processing for consumers to text a response (**Figure 13-6**).

Involvement The overall effect of the short repeated message is that outdoor ads tend to be considered a low-involvement media.

Clutter By their very nature, outdoor ads have competing messages. At any streetscape or location where outdoor ads are featured, it is very likely that other messages will also be vying for consumer attention, as seen in **Exhibit 13-8**.

Media Image Outdoor advertising has suffered image problems and disregard among consumers. This may be in part due to fatigue of the high frequency of exposures that may lead to wearout—people are likely to get tired of seeing the same ad every day.

Figure 13-6 Likelihood* of texting in response to digital OOH advertising by age

- 18–34
- 35+

	Invitation to Special Event	A Promotional Offer	Contest
18–34	36%	38%	31%
35+	26%	28%	26%

*Very/Somewhat likely

Source: Canadian Out of Home Marketing and Measurement Bureau (COMMB)

Exhibit 13-8 Competing messages present a challenge with outdoor media.

©Luciano Mortula/Shutterstock

LO2 Transit Media

Another form of out-of-home media is transit. While similar to outdoor in that it uses posters, digital, and video messages, transit is targeted at the millions of people who are exposed to public transit including buses, trains, subways, streetcars, light rail, and airplanes. Transit ad revenue is a noticeable but small portion of overall out-of-home revenue. We describe transit media options and their strengths and limitations as an advertising medium.

TRANSIT MEDIA OPTIONS

Transit media provide exposure to consumers when travelling on the public transit system. **Figure 13-7** shows that the media options fall into three locations within the transit system: (1) inside and (2) outside the transportation vehicle (e.g., bus, train) and (3) at the transit station. As indicated, there is a degree of similarity with outdoor media and additional options that make transit an attractive media for advertisers to evaluate. To simplify, bus/train refers to all types of vehicles including subway, metro, streetcars, and light rail in which the transit media option is available for advertising.

Figure 13-7 Transit media options

Transit Interior	Transit Exterior	Transit Station
Horizontal card	Horizontal poster	Poster/digital poster
Vertical poster	Superbus/train	Digital video network
Supercard	Bus/train mural	Video matrix wall
Door surround	Bus/train strips	Mural, bulkhead
Ceiling decal	Extension, headliner	Specialty wrap

Interior transit cards are placed horizontally above the seating and positioned in backlit units above windows and along both sides of the bus/train (see **Exhibit 13-9**). A supercard is a larger interior transit card that is much taller to convey more copy or bigger visuals. **Interior door cards** are available in major markets where there is subway-like transit. These vertical posters are placed on both sides of the doors and are about 50 percent larger than the aforementioned interior transit cards. Door surrounds use both types of cards and cover all available space with the brand's message and imagery. Finally, **Exhibit 13-9** also shows the option of putting a decal on the ceiling.

Exhibit 13-9 Example of interior transit ad.

©Pattison Outdoor Advertising

Exhibit 13-10 Example of exterior transit ad.

©Pattison Outdoor Advertising

Exterior posters are placed horizontally on the side and back of a bus/train (see **Exhibit 13-10**). Various sizes are available depending on the media company and the transit vehicles; however, the two most common are "seventies" (0.5 metres by 1.8 metres, but named because the width of 1.8 metres is equal to 70 inches) and "king" (0.75 metres by 3.5 metres), which are seen on buses and so on.

Superbus is an innovation in transit media where an advertiser "owns" the bus/train and places a vinyl wrap of an ad on its entire surface. This is often done for a longer-term contract of a half year or full year because of the application on the bus (see **Exhibit 13-11**). The new TTC streetcars appeared in Toronto with a Volvo wrap to celebrate the Volvo XC90 being voted as truck/utility vehicle of the year for 2016. The longer "Flexity" streetcar allowed for a 30-metre wrap that looked as impressive as a wall mural ad, according to one media expert.[10]

On a less grand scale in a few select markets, smaller bus/train *murals* are applied to the side or tail for a shorter period of time. And in Vancouver, where wireless competition intensified, a few Telus-wrapped buses also offered free Wi-Fi, with riders being directed to the brand's network splash page.[11] *Bus/train strips* are in the shape of the poster but longer, and made of vinyl like the wraps and murals. This is a mid-range option in transit vehicle coverage and cost. Finally, *extensions* add an extra vinyl wrap above the poster (see **Exhibit 13-11**) while the *headliner* is a small strip on the top of the bus running its entire length which can tie in with the poster.

Station posters are of varying sizes and forms, including backlit, directed to those people within a transit station. The most common size is 1 metre by 2 metres. As **Exhibit 13-12** shows, advertisers design attractive station posters to gain attention so that consumers process the message extensively while waiting for a ride or less so while walking to their next destination. As seen with outdoor, transit stations also offer digital posters.

Digital video network is located in the transit stations in major cities. It features digital news centres with video capabilities that deliver news, sports, and weather highlights with video. *Video matrix walls* are multiple video screens compiled into one large screen to display video messages to passersby on station concourses. Elements of communication effectiveness of TV ad messages are relevant for advertisers to consider when evaluating these two options.

Transit stations provide other options in which a brand covers virtually any surface with a message and is the sole sponsor of all points of communication within that station. This includes installing murals and erecting sizable bulkheads wrapped in vinyl. Specialty wraps include different parts of the infrastructure such as walls, pillars, stairs, handrails, escalators, and payment kiosks.

Transit media are sold in select markets on a four-week basis with a certain desired level of GRPs. The range of GRPs is quite varied, going from a low of 5 GRPs to a high of 100 GRPs. Other purchases of transit media are based on the number of showings. For example, if an operator has the rights to 400 buses or subway cars, then an advertiser could typically buy displays in varying numbers (i.e., 25 percent, 50 percent, 75 percent, 100 percent) over a four-week time period. Unlike outdoor advertising, there is no industry association to document circulation or authenticate reach and frequency levels despite their use in pricing of the media purchase.

Finally, transit media viewed while travelling *between* cities and towns presents similar and additional transit options. Free magazines are published by airlines (see **Exhibit 13-13**) and in-flight videos are common on longer flights. For example, Air Canada sells different packages depending on the type of show (e.g., news, movie) and these commercial messages can last up to three minutes. Listening to in-flight radio is a pleasant way to pass the time while flying, and offers another opportunity for advertisers to deliver an audio message beyond standard radio. Ads can be placed on collateral material such as boarding passes, ticket jackets, and meal trays. The design of these media is important; both Air Canada and WestJet put considerable effort into their in-flight magazines to reflect their positioning. Air Canada's looks more like a sophisticated lifestyle magazine with luxurious full-page ads, fitting with its international and business clientele, while WestJet's is a more utilitarian offering with functional travel tips.[12]

STRENGTHS OF TRANSIT MEDIA

Geographic Coverage Transit media provides local advertisers an opportunity to reach a select segment of the population based on where they live or work. For example, the characteristics of people in certain city neighbourhoods will be skewed on segmentation variables like demographics. An ad purchased within a specific location leads to greater exposure for the relevant segmentation variable, providing a more efficient media buy.

Exhibit 13-11 Example of a bus wrap on a streetcar.

©Pattison Outdoor Advertising

Exhibit 13-12 Station posters can be used to attract attention.

©Pattison Outdoor Advertising

Exhibit 13-13 In-flight magazines are available on most carriers.

©enRoute/Bookmark

Scheduling Flexibility The capacity available for transit ads makes it fairly good for placement since ads can be produced quickly and inserted internally or externally, although large station installations require lead time.

Reach Transit media benefits from the absolute number of people exposed. Millions of people ride mass transit every week, providing reach to a substantial number of potential viewers.

Frequency Because our daily routines are standard, those who ride buses, subways, and the like are exposed to the ads repeatedly. If a commuter rode the same subway to work and back every day, in one month the person would have the opportunity to see the ad 20 to 40 times. The locations of station and shelter signs also afford high frequency of exposure.

Absolute Cost and Cost Efficiency Transit media tends to be one of the least expensive media in terms of both absolute and relative costs. An ad on the side of a bus can be purchased for a very reasonable CPM.

Control for Selective Exposure Similar to outdoor media, transit media are quite pervasive for those using the service and consumers have little control over the use of the media. For example, some murals and station domination displays take over the entire visual space.

Amount of Processing Time Long length of exposure to an ad is a potential strength of indoor forms. The audience has nowhere else to go and potentially nothing much to do but look at ads, however people's use of smart phones diminishes this historic strength. The amalgamation of out-of-home media with digital capabilities makes extensive processing possible.

LIMITATIONS OF TRANSIT MEDIA

Target Audience Selectivity While a strength of transit media is the ability to provide exposure to a large number of people, this audience may have certain lifestyle and/or behavioural characteristics that are not true of the target audience as a whole.

Target Audience Coverage While geographic selectivity may be an advantage, not everyone who rides public transit and is exposed to transit media is a potential customer. For products that do not have specific geographic segments, this form of advertising incurs a good deal of waste coverage.

Attention The smaller size and location of interior transit ads make it difficult to use the creative elements to attract attention. The movement of transit vehicles makes it difficult to perceive the message; station advertising mitigates this concern.

Creativity for Emotional and Cognitive Responses It may be difficult to place colourful and attractive ads on cards, thus limiting their emotional content. And while much copy can be provided on inside cards, the short copy on the outside of a bus provides less rational persuasion. Again, for advertisers who can afford transit station options, this is not so much a limitation.

Involvement Like outdoor media, with shorter copy and seemingly fleeting messages, transit ads are generally considered to be low-involvement media.

Clutter Inside ads suffer from clutter of competing ads and outside ads feel the pressure of other street-level ads. Furthermore, the environment is cluttered in another sense as sitting or standing on a crowded subway may not be conducive to reading advertising, let alone experiencing the mood the advertiser would like to create.

Media Image To many advertisers, transit media does not carry the image they would like to represent for their products or services. Thus, advertisers may think having their name on the side of a bus or in a bus does not reflect well on the firm.

 **Place-Based Media**

The variety of out-of-home media continues to increase, and the idea of bringing an advertising medium to consumers wherever they may be underlies the strategy behind place-based media. In this section we summarize the prevalent options, including both print and video messages, and highlight their strengths and limitations.

PLACE-BASED MEDIA OPTIONS

Place-based media are a type of out-of-home media that reaches consumers in numerous locations in a city. **Figure 13-8** shows that advertising messages reach consumers in numerous locations where they enjoy leisure or recreational activities, are entertained, work, study, receive care, and move through public spaces. The locations listed have the highest incidence of place-based media, however media companies and advertisers are always looking for new avenues and it is not surprising to see this form in other locations.

Figure 13-8 Place-based media options

Recreation	Entertainment	Professional	Public
Golf club/ski resort	Restaurant/bar	Office	Shopping mall
Sports field/arena	Arena/stadium	School	Airport
Fitness centre	Cinema	Medical centre	Urban path

Figure 13-9 shows that Canadians are aware of place-based advertising. Many of these media occur indoors (the term *indoor advertising* is also used). The delivery format at these locations can be any combination of the choices described in outdoor and transit media, such as static print-like formats, standard video or a digital equivalent, and in some cases audio. Innovations allow consumers to interact with their hand-held mobile device. Newad, now owned by Astral, specializes in place-based media in restaurants/bars, campuses, arenas, and medical facilities, and offers 40,000 facings in 6,000 locations. It converted many of the facings to digital, and motion sensors allow consumers to interact with the message. Pattison is strong in airport, stadium, and urban pathway opportunities for advertisers. Astral also serves major airports.

Figure 13-9 Awareness of place-based media

	Total %	18–34 %	35+ %
Shopping mall	48	58	45
Outdoor	47	53	45
Airport	28	30	27
Public transit	25	36	21
Restaurant	25	36	20
Medical waiting room	21	23	20
Bar/nightclub	18	28	14
Office elevator	12	16	10
Health/fitness club	9	17	6

Source: Canadian Out of Home Marketing and Measurement Bureau (COMMB)

A number of place-based media are outdoor media brought into a particular environment where people spend a considerable amount of time. Posters, billboards, electronic message signs, and video displays are used in recreation locations such as arenas and venues for golfing, skiing, or fitness. Similarly these media are found in restaurants and bars, professional arenas and sports stadiums, and movie theatres. Advertising with these media in office buildings or similar venues also reaches those who are at work. Firms reach younger consumers on university and college campuses. Digital video networks seen in transit media are found in medical facilities and offices. Shopping locations, airports, and urban pathways feature virtually all options found in outdoor and transit station media, and the location placements are

Figure 13-10 Perceived amount of advertising by indoor medium: percentage having "too much" advertising

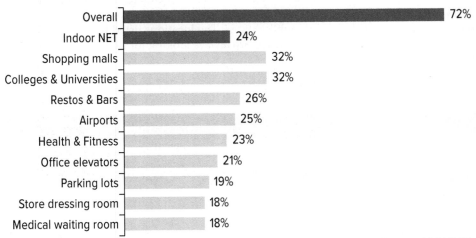

Overall	72%
Indoor NET	24%
Shopping malls	32%
Colleges & Universities	32%
Restos & Bars	26%
Airports	25%
Health & Fitness	23%
Office elevators	21%
Parking lots	19%
Store dressing room	18%
Medical waiting room	18%

Source: Canadian Out of Home Marketing and Measurement Bureau (COMMB)

similar: walls, prominent central areas with heavy traffic, stand-alone displays, and unexpected places (e.g., elevators, escalators, stairs, dressing rooms, washrooms). Despite the prevalence of place-based media, Canadians do not believe it is too much (**Figure 13-10**).

To illustrate place-based media in action, we focus on a few locations from **Figure 13-8**. Prominent ones to consider are shopping areas, movie theatres, and airport terminals, all of which attract high volumes of people and present interesting innovations that are useful to apply to other locations.

Malls and other shopping locations provide many options for advertisers. Posters are frequently used, often backlit like the transit shelter or transit station posters, and located throughout a shopping area. The key feature of the poster in a shopping environment is that the message delivery is close to the actual purchase. These posters are sold in most markets across the country similarly to outdoor posters with individual spot buys and varying levels of GRPs. Firms also sell various sizes of mall posters for branding or interaction purposes. Advertisers use these posters for interaction purposes by including QR codes so consumers can use their smart phone and receive additional information. Video or digital displays are growing in retail locations as well.

An example of video messages occurring out-of-home at a specific location is cinema or movie theatre ads. Since the commercials last 60–90 seconds, advertisers have a unique opportunity to communicate for a longer period of time than with a typical TV ad. In fact, many of the theatre ads are also shown on television, albeit in a shortened format. Cinema ads lead other public video media as they report audience measurement information. Cineplex reported $172 million in media revenue in 2017, comprising cinema advertising and its digital advertising networks in retail locations.[13] Beyond this, Cineplex partnered with Sony Computer Entertainment Canada on the "Cineplex WorldGaming Canadian Tournament Presented by PlayStation." This offered significant advertising opportunities for Sony, which also controlled who sponsored and advertised during the event.[14]

Research on consumer attitudes toward cinema ads in general found a number of sources of negativity in terms of restriction (e.g., less communication, captive, delayed gratification, minimizing escapism) and equity (unfair, time-waster, payment); however, many people enjoy the experience of specific ads (entertaining, liking the ad, involved, ad congruent with movie) as long as it is not shown too many times. It appears that this, like other media, has a tension of both positive and negative reactions.[15] **IMC Perspective 13-2** highlights aspects of Cineplex's advertising media opportunities. This represents an example of all place-based media that offer an abundance of advertising that spans almost all possible delivery formats.

IMC PERSPECTIVE 13-2

SEE ADS AT THE MOVIES

Moviegoers are an attractive market with promising consumption behaviour for advertisers as 59 percent of those aged 14+ went to a cinema in the past 12 months and 47 percent went in the past three months. Higher consumption skews for those aged 14–49. They tend to be well educated with higher incomes, use social media, and combine their movie experience with shopping or eating. Moreover, 62 percent are happy and 29 percent are excited when going to the movies, a mood situation that no other media vehicle can claim.

Cinema ads combined with TV messages produce strong communication numbers, providing strong incentive for advertisers to add this to their mix. With cinemas having a 55-foot screen and superior video and audio capability, it is no wonder that Cineplex's Show Time ads attain 70 percent awareness, 86 percent brand association, and 37 percent positive ad entertainment scores.

Cineplex's Pre-Show numbers attain similar levels, albeit with lower audience size. The Pre-Show features entertainment clips, quizzes, and the like, all supported with ads. Another Pre-Show option is an interactive game called Timeplay in which patrons use their phone to participate. The trivia-like games (based on movies, of course) embed ads or offer branded prizes. A number of customized sponsorship options allow advertisers to develop enjoyable brand messages, providing strong results: 86 percent awareness, 84 percent brand association, and 46 percent positive ad entertainment. Cineplex sees its early traffic increasing so people can play the game before the movie starts.

Cineplex Media offers message delivery opportunities in its theatres beyond on-screen ads. Large digital lobby signage in 140 locations shows movie clips and advertising with 71 percent reach. A total of 438 digital backlit posters similar to those found in digital transit shelters show full-motion HD-quality video ads on a three-minute loop. Digital lobby HD screens located above box offices and concession stands play ads within a 10-minute loop. Cineplex's interactive media zone in 44 theatres presents four high-resolution screens with touch capability and gesture and skeletal tracking. It also allows users to create content for sharing on social media. Services include custom creative support; scheduling flexibility by theatre, city, or national exposure; and processing analytics by capturing a user's experience with a camera.

While waiting in locations throughout the theatre, a movie fan can be one of the 3.9 million *Cineplex Magazine* monthly readers to catch up on the latest about movie stars or upcoming releases.

©GP Images/Getty Images for Warner Brothers Canada

A total of 650,000 free publications regularly garner six readers per copy. Print ads are within the magazine and brands place messages both in print and on-screen, even across all media options depending on frequency requirements. The publication is the third most read magazine in Canada, provides higher reach than other magazines, and gives 70 percent unduplicated reach beyond other popular publications.

Cineplex Media extended its communication to all facets of the movie experience and branched out beyond. It offers massive digital posters with its Oxford Malls Network, which features large HD screens showing ads within its own channel. Its shopping media includes other standards like regular sized digital backlit posters, activation signage, and elevator and escalator wraps in 10 locations. Cineplex Media established TimsTV in over 2,300 coffee outlets for national and regional ad opportunities. Follow-up research demonstrated that the network reached substantial numbers, provided higher brand recall numbers, and enjoyed considerable positive reaction from consumers. A similar TV option is available in 10 major Canadian business centres with its Concourse Network, and the company offers advertising options in Ontario at 20 highway rest stop buildings containing restaurants.

Question:

1. In what way is advertising through Cineplex effective?

Airport terminals have extensive advertising media since they are similar to a mall with shopping concourses and restaurant areas and high volumes of consumers passing by. Pattison lists the following options: gateway TV, many digital choices (carousel, flight information display, interior horizontal poster, matrix wall, pylon, ribbon, showcase, poster, and kiosks), and many non-digital choices (spectacular, poster, and displays) (**Exhibit 13-14**). This shows the pervasiveness of messaging possible in a public space with millions of consumers per year.

An exploratory study of airport terminal advertising reports the following conclusions.[16]

Exhibit 13-14 While picking up luggage, airport travellers viewed an ad encouraging them to consider certain products.

©rmnoa357/Shutterstock

1. Ads are more likely to be processed when in the main concourse or near retail outlets.
2. The situational variable of the person's activity influences their degree of processing.
3. Repetition of a simple message is necessary, but with less frequency.
4. Elements of the ad influence recall and recognition differently, thus necessitating decisions on design and communication objective.
5. Frequent flyers' responses are strong up to a point then taper off after receiving a repetitious message.

Place-based media became experiential as marketers presented their brands in public places. Moving beyond ads, sales promotions, and even digital communication, brands saw the need to allow consumers to participate in a demonstration of product usage to fully enjoy what it has to offer. For example, Nivea opened a temporary pop-up shop in Toronto called Nivea Haus that included interactive skin tests, personalized skin care suggestions, photo shoots, product shots, and an Xbox Kinect game. Nivea designed the experiential effort to communicate how one's skin is an important part of one's physical and emotional well-being. Axe's "Hair Action" campaign featured a Virtual Hair Play Van where men received the touch of a woman as she attended to their hair—all in a virtual simulation, of course. The van visited numerous locations, including campuses and events such as the Warped Tour and Montreal Jazz Festival. Photos of the experience gave the participants the opportunity to upload pictures to their Facebook account where friends could "like" it and give the guy a chance to win a $10,000 prize.[17] **Exhibit 13-15** shows how Budweiser brings the red light to consumers in public locations.

Exhibit 13-15 Budweiser takes its TV imagery to the streets for consumers to see.

©rmnoa357/Shutterstock

As identified earlier with outdoor ads, digital communication within these place-based locations occurs. For example, an Ontario health organization delivered its message to the smart phones of those in medical waiting rooms. People received the ads based on their acceptance of mobile apps for games, news, or maps. And applying this to all of the above locations is certainly possible, however executives feel the message and location context are paramount for acceptance.[18] Finally, portable outdoor-like digital screens for message display can be set up in trade shows, conferences, stores, and marketing events. With Wi-Fi connection, the display analytically tracks consumers' behaviour with respect to the message. The system is fully customizable in various sizes and configurations depending on requirements for the location.[19]

STRENGTHS OF PLACE-BASED MEDIA

Target Audience Selectivity The main purpose of place-based media is to reach a specific target audience or to reach the target audience while closer to the purchase decision in terms of time and space. For example, ads in fitness clubs could contain messages for athletic gear, and mall posters could have ads for brands that are sold in retailers located in the mall. Targeted travel ads directed to those watching World Cup soccer in nationalistic bars provided exceptional selectivity for those desiring to visit their home country.[20]

Absolute Cost and Cost Efficiency The absolute cost and CPM are generally reasonable compared to other media options.

Control for Selective Exposure Since many of these media options have captive or nearly captive audiences, the opportunity for consumers to avoid the ads or direct their attention elsewhere is minimal compared to other media. For example, ads on the walls of restaurants, bars, gyms, etc., will be noticeable by customers enjoying the service.

Attention and Involvement With the above strengths of many place-based media options, the collective conclusion suggests that the target audience may be more involved with the advertising message than similar media in different contexts. The growth of video and digital messages in many locations offers greater opportunity to gain attention, and with a degree of target audience selectivity the creative can be customized with appropriate headlines for print messages.

Creativity for Cognitive and Emotional Responses Because the target and place are intertwined, the message may generate more in-depth cognitive responses or stronger emotional responses. For example, creative lifestyle messages can be prominent in poster ads located in clubs or bars. Large-scale spectaculars have been used to create fantastic visual effects to generate positive feelings. The special mood created in the movie theatre compared to at-home consumption makes the experience richer, and advertisers use theatre ads as an emotional spike that can transfer to the product more readily, especially if the theatre is located next to a mall or store where the product may be sold.

LIMITATIONS OF PLACE-BASED MEDIA

Target Audience and Geographic Coverage The logistical availability of these types of media makes full target audience coverage difficult or quite challenging to implement, and it is nearly impossible to get complete geographic coverage.

Scheduling Flexibility While not a complete or comprehensive limitation, the logistics of changing place-based media, which is done on a monthly basis, put certain restrictions on an advertiser for scheduling a timely message. Placement for cinema ads generally requires eight weeks, and category exclusivity in certain distribution outlets further limits the availability and scheduling ease of this media option.

Reach and Frequency Place-based media plays more of a supporting role to other media since it is very difficult to ensure high levels of either reach or frequency. Exceptions can be considered, but in general media planners will look for other media to maximize these two factors.

Amount of Processing Time For the most part, place-based media suffer from very short messages to target audiences who are likely preoccupied with other tasks. Evidence of strong recall suggests that the processing may be stronger for more creative executions, where additional processing occurs.

Clutter The clutter that consumers perceive while watching television may be similar as the video displays generally play a block of commercials, although this can be lessened in options like cinema ads where one or two video ads could run. Similarly, locations have multiple posters of varying sizes, thus giving a similar clutter experience as reading a newspaper or magazine.

Media Image Place-based media are exposed to consumers when they do not expect a selling message to occur, which may cause displeasure. Consumers appear to be generally accustomed to ads in malls since they are so similar to the store signage.

IMC Planning: Strategic Use of Out-of-Home Media

Previously, the strategic use of out-of-home media seemed like an oxymoron, as it appeared in promotional planners' budgets after money had been allocated to other more "valuable" media. An IMC perspective toward media selection provides a new look at how outdoor, transit, and place-based opportunities achieve communication and behavioural objectives, primarily at the pre-purchase and purchase decision stages.

For the most part, outdoor, transit, and place-based media tend to have two primary objectives. The first is awareness, as these media share common strengths of cost efficiency with extensive reach and frequency levels in the geographic areas in which the media are located or placed. The second is the ability to use clever images and headlines or very short copy messages, which permits these messages to have emotional relevance to help ensure brand recognition or recall. Moreover, these two design elements can be consistent with creative messages from other media to ensure additional message frequency with the intention to build awareness more strongly.

In general, these media are limited in their ability to build category need or influence brand attitudes beyond maintaining the current attitude of the target audience. Many brands will use these media as an inexpensive, yet cost-effective means of communicating simple brand preference messages directed toward current customers or messages to reinforce the general market position of the brand to all potential consumers. Given the limited nature of these media to influence attitudes extensively with short messages, they typically are good for building communication effects at the pre- and post-purchase stages.

Most place-based media typically offer the opportunity for promotional planners to achieve a second objective: brand purchase intention. Since the messages for place-based media are context-dependent in terms of location or time, they can provide the right situational motive to inspire a store visit or more immediate sale. Particular place-based media, like movie theatres, are vehicles for additional exposure of the more traditional broadcast and print media ads and thus permit strong brand positioning strategy opportunities. As noted in the chapter, movie theatres can show longer and more specialized ads that brands may be reluctant to show in a broadcast environment.

Given the broad reach and public nature of these media, often they are more general and have a less clear behavioural objective. However, given that many messages are reinforcing existing attitudes, it appears a substantial number of these ads attempt to influence repeat purchasing. Application of out-of-home messages including connections to mobile hand-held devices suggests greater opportunity for brand switching for trial purchases.

From an integration perspective, out-of-home or transit media provide additional frequency of a creative message that has been placed in broadcast or print media. Typically, we do not see advertisers using these media for executing sales promotions except in poster locations. This medium is also used for public relations activities, and we infrequently observe any connection to direct marketing or Internet applications.

Learning Objectives Summary

LO1 Identify the options within outdoor media for developing an IMC program and audience measurement, and their strengths and limitations.

This chapter introduced three out-of-home media available to marketers: outdoor, transit, and place-based. Within each, there are digital and non-digital options for promotional planners to use to achieve their objectives. The digital capabilities are one reason why out-of-home media ad revenue grew recently. The media options let advertisers creatively express their brand message in a perfect location depending on where people live, work, or play. Outdoor media is all around us in formats such as large posters, interactive digital versions of posters, full video displays, and street media.

Outdoor advertising audience measurement is very strong in Canada. The industry association COMMB established a strong research methodology for ensuring accurate estimates of exposure levels. This research has expanded to place-based media such as those found in restaurants and hotels as well as health and fitness outlets. Documentation for transit audiences is less thorough, although a degree of assessment is possible.

The public nature of outdoor media leads to high numbers of people reached who cannot avoid seeing the messages. This suggests relatively positive cost efficiency that allows advertisers to extend their frequency levels. Also, the options for creativity for emotional responses are significant as one strolls through the city. However, the broad appeal makes selectivity a challenge, absolute costs are high but getting lower with digital, and consumers usually do not spend much time looking at outdoor ads in a cluttered media environment.

 Identify the options within transit media for developing an IMC program, and their strengths and limitations.

Transit media lets advertisers place media inside and outside the bus/train and at the transit stations. The many types of public transit vehicles include buses, trains, subways, metro, light rail, streetcars, and airplanes. The options presented are mostly common across all vehicles, although a few inconsistencies may be found by advertisers. Like outdoor media, digital options have grown over the past decade and advertisers can change their message quite quickly and easily.

Transit media's strengths and limitations are comparable to outdoor, although the cost is substantially lower and to some degree the media image is not as strong. Audience measurement of transit is not overly strong compared to outdoor, but the count of transit users is reasonably well known from sales of monthly passes etc.

 Identify the options within place-based media for developing an IMC program, and their strengths and limitations.

Place-based media are in recreation, entertainment, professional, and public spaces. Much of the format and digital technology seen in outdoor is used in place-based media, although adjustments are made as necessary depending on the size. For example, some of the recreational placements are smaller, to fit in restaurants or fitness facilities. On the other hand, airports feature large-scale digital posters and video displays that rival outdoor ads.

Place-based media allows advertisers to offer creative messages in key locations to reach consumers at the right time for influencing their purchase, thus obtaining strong selectivity. With a reasonable absolute cost and good cost efficiency, advertisers find this an attractive media.

 Show how out-of-home media is an important element of IMC planning.

In many instances, IMC planners require broad exposure levels for the brand name and basic positioning message to be reinforced for many consumers. Out-of-home media is very good at achieving these tasks, and with the development of digital communication, these media are contenders for initiating consumer contact for product information or participation with various kinds of brand experiences or sales promotions. As such, their potential for moving into the realm as a primary medium continually improves over time. Out-of-home is also quite strong at influencing consumers when they are at the purchase decision as the messages are near where they would make a purchase.

Review Questions

1. Explain how out-of-home ads can be creative and foster emotional responses. Why would brands use outdoor ads for this purpose?

2. Who is most influenced by exterior bus/train ads?

3. Why do advertisers consider place-based media to be a good part of their media mix?

4. How do out-of-home media help achieve awareness objectives?

Applied Questions

1. Find a creative outdoor ad and discuss with one of your friends what makes it creative.

2. Travel on a bus/train to school (or elsewhere) and record all the ads that you discover on your trip. Is there a pattern or commonality among the messages?

3. While travelling through a town or city, look for the most unusual place-based ad and decide whether it represents effective advertising.

4. Explain how out-of-home media might be used as part of an IMC program. Take any three of the media discussed in the chapter and explain how they might be used in an IMC program for automobiles, smart phones, and Internet services.

©ZUMA Press, Inc./Alamy Stock Photo

CHAPTER FOURTEEN

Sales Promotion

LEARNING OBJECTIVES

LO1 Explain the role of sales promotion in a company's integrated marketing communications program and examine why it is increasingly important.

LO2 Identify the objectives, strategy, and tactical components of a sales promotion plan.

LO3 Describe consumer sales promotion strategy options and evaluate the factors to consider in using them.

LO4 Describe trade sales promotion strategy options and evaluate the factors to consider in using them.

LO5 Apply key IMC issues related to sales promotion decisions.

Budweiser's Red Light Is a Winner

Budweiser faced a huge problem in 2011 when the National Hockey League not only did not renew its sponsorship, but awarded sponsorship to Molson instead. In addition to no longer having an official association with a prime occasion for drinking beer—watching hockey—the iconic brand witnessed a decline in overall beer consumption and increased craft beer competition. In short, Budweiser needed an innovative idea to associate the brand with hockey. While sponsorship had worked for quite some time, it conveyed neither spontaneous excitement nor Canada's enthusiasm for hockey. The light went on with a red light, and not just any red light, but the red light that illuminates when a goal is scored in a hockey game.

In 2013, Budweiser (along with its agency, Anomaly) invented a physical red goal light synchronized to shine each time a fan's team scored. Sold at a price of $159 plus shipping and handling, the red light connected to a fan's team via Wi-Fi and an app. Extensive media promotion and a sponsorship arrangement with Hockey Night in Canada ensured significant uptake for the premium. After this initial launch, Budweiser upped its game each year (see Figure 10-30). In 2014, Budweiser created the Red Zeppelin, with thousands of red LED lights that shone when Team Canada scored during the Olympic Games. In 2015, Budweiser sent staff carrying red lights as a tribute to a puck manufacturer in Saint-Jérôme, Quebec. In 2016, Budweiser placed goal-synced Red Light Glasses in beer cases and the brand took to the Arctic a large scale red light that also lit when Canadian teams scored goals.

After a few years of the campaign, Budweiser gained 1.6 percent market share over Coors and improved its association with hockey from 37 percent to 43 percent. Additionally, Budweiser built a database after seeking permission to retain customers' information when they downloaded the app; this allowed direct communication and promotion for future promotions. With the success of the campaign, Budweiser expanded it to hockey in the United States and tested the concept for football there as well, and investigated its potential for soccer with a promotion with the FIFA World Cup. That was quite the achievement for the Canadian marketing managers and agency!

In a more recent promotional execution, Budweiser sold $400 red lights that featured Wayne Gretzky's signature and his number, 99. Budweiser used its database of past users for pre-orders. An ad message—"Bring It Home"—coincided with the 2018 Winter Olympics and included famous Canadian hockey players (both female and male) from past years, including Gretzky. Budweiser set up a partnership with the NHL Players Association to celebrate an individual player's first NHL goal. Another partnership with On the Bench featured a couple of social media personalities teaching hockey to a group of neophytes. And finally, tracking the experiences and the reactions of the promotional program on social media continued from day one for all activities.

Question:

1. What next step can Budweiser take with the Red Light promotion?

Advertising alone may not be enough to convince consumers to switch brands, try a new product category, or return to the same brand purchased previously. Companies also use sales promotion methods targeted at both consumers and the wholesalers and retailers that distribute their products to stimulate demand. Most IMC programs include consumer and trade promotions that are coordinated with advertising, direct marketing, and publicity/public relations campaigns as well as salesforce efforts.

This chapter focuses on sales promotion in a firm's IMC program. We explain how marketers use consumer and trade promotions to influence the purchase behaviour of consumers, wholesalers, and retailers. We identify the objectives of sales promotion programs and describe the types of sales promotion tools directed to consumers and trade members. We also consider how sales promotion is integrated with other promotional mix elements, and look at problems that arise when marketers become overly dependent on sales promotion.

LO1 Sales Promotion Planning

Of all the IMC tools available to a promotional planner, sales promotion, with its variety of characteristics and types, allows brands to achieve multiple objectives and provides the opportunity to enhance an IMC plan. We review the characteristics and types of sales promotion in this section and highlight the reasons why sales promotion has grown so tremendously, thus indicating its relative strengths.

CHARACTERISTICS OF SALES PROMOTION

Sales promotion is a direct inducement within an action-focused marketing event that offers an extra value or incentive for the product to the salesforce, distributors, or the ultimate consumer with the primary objective of influencing customer and potential customer behaviour which may include an immediate purchase.[1] This definition indicates two distinguishing features of sales promotion.

First, sales promotion involves an inducement that provides an *extra incentive* to buy. This incentive is usually the key element in a promotional program: It may be purely financial (i.e., coupon, price discount, refund or rebate), emotionally based (i.e., opportunity to enter a contest, premium), value-oriented (e.g., extra amount of product, sample a free product), or experiential (i.e., attend a marketing event). The financial incentive is extrinsic while the intrinsic non-financial incentives are hedonic in nature, demonstrating entertainment, personal exploration, and value expression.[2] One study investigated consumer reactions to online promotions and found slightly stronger recall levels for non-financial offers.[3] Furthermore, sales promotions also reinforce consumers' feelings about themselves, as finding deals is seen as an achievement and a personal reward for being a good shopper, thereby increasing the frequency of purchases.[4]

Second, sales promotion is essentially an *acceleration tool,* designed to speed up the buying process of consumers and maximize sales volume.[5] By providing an extra incentive, sales promotion techniques can motivate consumers to purchase a larger quantity of a brand or shorten the purchase cycle by encouraging consumers to take more immediate action. Sales promotion attempts to maximize sales volume by motivating customers who have not responded to advertising. The ideal sales promotion program generates sales that would not be achieved by other means. However, sales promotion offers may end up being used by current users of a brand rather than attracting new users.

TYPES OF SALES PROMOTION

As shown in **Figure 14-1**, sales promotions are directed to consumers and trade members. Activities involved in **consumer sales promotion** include samples, coupons, premiums, promotional products, contests and sweepstakes, refunds and rebates, bonus packs, price discounts, and event marketing. These promotions are directed at consumers, the end purchasers of goods and services, and are designed to induce them to purchase the marketer's brand. Consumer promotions are also used by retailers to encourage consumers to shop in their particular stores. Sales promotion can also be directed to intermediaries like wholesalers, distributors, and retailers, known as trade members. **Trade sales promotion** includes dealer trade allowances, point-of-purchase displays, cooperative advertising, contests and incentives, sales training programs, trade shows, and potentially other programs designed to motivate organizations in the distribution channel to carry and merchandise a product.

Marketing programs usually include both trade and consumer promotions, since motivating both groups maximizes promotional effectiveness. Programs designed to persuade the trade to stock, merchandise, and promote a manufacturer's products are part of a **promotional push strategy**. The goal of this strategy is to push the product through the channels of distribution with promotional activities. A push strategy tries to convince resellers that they can make a profit on a manufacturer's product and to encourage them to order the merchandise and communicate and promote the brand to their customers. Company sales representatives call on resellers to explain the product, discuss the firm's plans for building demand among ultimate consumers, and describe and offer the trade promotion programs. The company may use **trade advertising**, generally publications that serve the particular industry, to generate reseller interest.

Companies also employ a **promotional pull strategy**, spending money on sales promotion efforts directed to the ultimate consumer with the goal of creating demand among consumers. Effort directed toward the end user encourages

Figure 14-1 Types of sales promotion activities

Consumer Sales Promotions	Trade Sales Promotions
Sampling	Trade allowances
Coupons	Point-of-purchase displays
Premiums	Cooperative advertising
Promotional products	Contests and incentives
Contests/sweepstakes	Sales training programs
Refunds/rebates	Trade shows
Bonus packs	
Price discounts	
Event marketing	

the reseller to stock and promote the product. Thus, stimulating demand at the end-user level pulls the product through the channels of distribution.

Whether to emphasize a push or a pull strategy depends on a number of factors, including the company's trade relations, its promotional budget, and demand for the firm's products. Companies with favourable channel relationships may prefer to use a push strategy and work closely with channel members. A firm with a limited promotional budget may not have the funds for consumer sales promotion and may build distribution and demand by working closely with resellers. When product demand is positive because of its unique benefits, superiority over competing brands, or consumer popularity, a pull strategy may be appropriate.

GROWTH OF SALES PROMOTION

Historically, advertising received the major budget allocation for most consumer-products companies' plans. Over time, the proportion of the marketing budget allocated to sales promotion rose due to increased trade promotion and more attractive and creative consumer promotions. Now, sales promotion takes a strategic role in an IMC program. Factors usually found in a situation analysis influenced this evolution: strategic importance, reaching a specific target audience, promotional sensitivity, declining brand loyalty, brand proliferation, short-term focus, accountability, power of retailers, and competition.

Strategic Importance Previously, sales promotion specialists participated in planning after key strategic branding decisions were made to develop a promotional program that could create a short-term increase in sales. Now, companies include promotional specialists as part of the strategic brand-building team, and promotional agencies offer integrated marketing services and expertise to enhance brand equity (see **Exhibit 14-1**). Critics contend that, if spending more on sales promotion at the expense of advertising continues, brands may lose the equity that advertising helped create. However, not all sales promotion activities detract from the value of a brand, as the next example illustrates.

Nivea coordinated a contest with its pop-up store and other promotional tools to celebrate its 100th anniversary

Exhibit 14-1 Aspen Marketing Services touts its IMC capabilities.

Source: AspenMs.com

Exhibit 14-2 Nivea implemented a comprehensive sales promotion program.

©Vittorio Zunimo Celotto/Stringer/Getty Images

(see **Exhibit 14-2**). "We know from our proprietary research that our consumer is totally interested in educating themselves about skin care," commented one executive. As such, after a visit to the pop-up store and a skin care consultation, consumers received a branded bag containing their after-effects photo, samples, and coupons, and were offered a chance to win a $10,000 "body and soul regimen for two" featuring the services of a beauty and well-being expert, a Nivea skin care expert, a massage therapist, a fashion stylist, a personal trainer, a chef, and a nutritionist. One hundred gift sets rounded out the prize list. Other promotion of the contest included direct mail, national magazine ads in both languages, and a microsite.[6]

Reaching a Specific Target Audience Marketing efforts focus on specific market segments, and firms use sales promotions to reach geographic, demographic, and psychographic audiences. Sales promotion programs can also be targeted to specific user-status groups such as customers or non-customers, as well as non-category users or light versus heavy users. Sales promotion is a primary vehicle for geographic-based programs tied into local flavour, themes, or events.

Promotional Sensitivity Marketers use sales promotion because consumers respond favourably to the incentive. Since the incentive is financial, emotionally based, value-oriented, or experiential, it seems likely that consumers for most goods and services typically look for a little extra, which is consistent with economic theory. Buying a product with a sales promotion is a routine response behaviour for promotion-sensitive consumer segments who only buy when there is a "deal."

Exhibit 14-3 A premium offer is used to provide extra incentive to purchase Lucky Charms.

©The McGraw-Hill Companies/Mark Dierker

Declining Brand Loyalty Consumers are generally willing to buy their preferred brand at full price without any promotional offer. However, consumers can also be loyal coupon users and/or are conditioned to look for deals when they shop. They may switch back and forth among a set of brands they view as essentially equal. These brands are all perceived as being satisfactory and interchangeable, and favourable brand switchers (discussed in Chapter 3) purchase whatever brand is promoted.

Brand Proliferation New brands entering mature product categories may lack significant advantages that an advertising campaign can communicate. Thus, these companies may depend on sales promotion to encourage consumers and trade members to try or to adopt these brands. Marketers also rely on sales promotion to achieve consumer trial of their brand's extensions (**Exhibit 14-3**). Marketers face competitive pressure to obtain shelf space for new products in stores as retailers favour new brands with strong sales promotion support.

Short-Term Focus Marketing plans and reward systems are geared to short-term performance measures of quarterly and yearly market share and sales volume. Critics believe the packaged-goods brand management system has contributed to marketers' increased dependence on sales promotion at the expense of brand building activities. Marketing or brand managers use promotions to help them move products into the retailers' stores at the request of the salespeople, who also face short-term quotas or goals.[7] Managers view consumer and trade promotions as the most dependable way to generate short-term sales, particularly when they are price-related.

Accountability Senior management puts pressure on marketing or brand managers and the salesforce to produce an acceptable return on investment of marketing expenditures. In companies struggling to meet their sales and financial goals, top management is demanding measurable, accountable ways to relate promotional expenditures to sales and profitability. Managers held accountable to producing results use sales promotions since they cause a quick and easily measured jump in sales as compared to advertising, which takes longer to show impact and the effects are more difficult to measure.

Power of Retailers Marketers also feel pressure from the trade as retailers demand sales performance from their brands. Real-time data available from computerized checkout scanners makes it possible for retailers to monitor promotions and track the results generated on a daily basis. With optical checkout scanners and in-store computer systems, retailers estimate how quickly products turn over, which sales promotions are working, and which products make money. Retailers use this information to analyze sales of manufacturers' products and then demand discounts and other promotional support from manufacturers of lagging brands. Companies that fail to comply with retailers' demands for more trade support may have their shelf space reduced or have their product dropped.

Competition Manufacturers rely on trade and consumer promotions to gain or maintain competitive advantage. Exciting, breakthrough creative ideas are difficult to achieve on a regular basis, so there is an over reliance on sales promotion at times. Companies tailor their trade promotions to key retail accounts and develop strategic alliances with retailers that include both trade and consumer promotional programs to achieve differentiation. A major development is **account-specific marketing**, whereby a manufacturer collaborates with an individual retailer to create a customized promotion that accomplishes mutual objectives.

IMC Perspective 14-1 picks up on a few themes described in the section with the context of contests that continue to interest advertisers to attain their objectives.

IMC PERSPECTIVE 14-1

NEW WAYS TO RUN A CONTEST

Contests continued to make gains by brands driven to retain and attract customers and build their equity. The paint brand CIL developed a creative method of communicating its "Beauty on a Small Budget" contest. The message showed a miniature room in need of redecorating to symbolically show consumers they did not have to spend much to give a room a fresh look. A 15-second pre-roll and a one-minute film linked consumers to the brand's Internet site to enter the contest. Participants learned that they would document their redecorating project on social media with a chance to win a $500 gift card from Home Depot and free consultation from a Canadian designer. Sales grew 23 percent and 7.6 million exposures occurred for the online video, leading to significant social media activity.

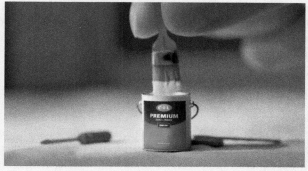

©PPG

Food brands provide another pair of examples where a contest occurred within promotional programs. Taco Bell's contest sent winners to a real-life Texas ranch to introduce its new "Bacon Ranch Naked Chicken Chalupa" product. Interested

[Continued on next page]

contestants entered by tagging three friends in the pinned posts on the brand's social media feeds. Communication included a 6-second pre-roll on YouTube, mid-roll ads on Facebook, and three 15-second videos on Facebook and Instagram. Managers believed this promotion fit the Generation X and young millennial target audience.

Happy Planet branded its contest "Happy Effect," with the winner receiving a trip to Mali that featured a celebration of female farmers. The location and excursion fit with the brand's sourcing of ingredients from small operation farms owned by women in Africa. The target of young enviro-conscious consumers enjoyed the animated message to enter the contest by inputting a promo code found on the cups.

Two travel examples demonstrate how to creatively communicate a contest to build a brand when the prize is a free trip. Air Canada Vacations, a division of Air Canada devoted to selling

packaged vacations, immersed participants in a trip planning game with the assistance of a traveller named Isabella. The "Making Your Dreams Travel" promotional program encouraged young urban dwellers and working adults aged 28–39 to customize their dream trip to Italy as part of their entry, which illustrated how the brand fulfilled their dreams rather than selling an ordinary package.

In another direction, Tourism Yukon and Air Yukon partnered in a contest to fly British Columbia residents to the adjacent territory. Entrants traded two hours of their time for a free two-hour trip to Yukon by posting their offer on social media and the contest's Internet site. Messaging of the contest to direct traffic to the Internet site positioned the trip as an easy weekend getaway.

Question:

1. Why do brand managers see contests as an effective promotional tool?

Sales Promotion Plan

In this section, we examine the content of a sales promotion plan. First, we consider objectives marketers have for sales promotion programs. Next, we illustrate why the sales promotion decisions are strategic options. Finally, we discuss the key tactics that are critical for all sales promotions. We focus on the consumer market to illustrate these ideas. Application to the trade market is readily done once the concept is understood.

OBJECTIVES OF CONSUMER SALES PROMOTION

Marketers plan consumer promotions by conducting a situation analysis and determining the purpose of sales promotion in the IMC program. They decide what the promotion is designed to accomplish and to whom it should be targeted. Setting clearly defined objectives and measurable goals for sales promotion programs is consistent with the planning process of Chapter 1. While the goal is to induce brand purchase, the marketer may have different objectives for new versus established brands or new versus current customers—such as trial purchase, repeat purchase, consumption, and brand equity—that are consistent with the behavioural and communication objectives of Chapter 5.

Trial Purchase An important use of sales promotion is to encourage consumers to try a new product or service. New products introduced to the market may fail due to a lack of promotional support needed to encourage initial brand trial by enough consumers. Also, new versions of existing brands that do not offer additional unique benefits may flounder without promotions that induce trial. Thus, sales promotion is important for new brand introduction strategies; the level of initial trial can be increased through techniques such as samples, coupons, and refund offers (see **Exhibit 14-4**).

A trial purchase objective is also relevant for an established brand that uses a sales promotion to attract non-users of the product category, which can be difficult, as these consumers may not see a need for the product. Sales promotions can appeal to non-users by providing an extra incentive to try the product, but a more common strategy for increasing sales of an established brand is to attract consumers who use a competing brand by giving them an incentive to switch (e.g., sample, coupon).

Repeat Purchase The success of a new brand depends not only on getting initial trial but also on inducing a reasonable percentage of people who try the brand to repurchase it and establish ongoing purchase patterns. Promotional incentives such as coupons or refund offers are included with a sample to encourage repeat purchase after trial. For example, when Peek Freans introduced its Lifestyle Selections brand of cookie, it distributed free samples along with a 50-cent coupon and a contest offer with the winner receiving a trip to Las Vegas. The samples allowed consumers to try the new cookie, while the coupon provided an incentive to purchase it.

Exhibit 14-4 Gillette used a sample and coupon to promote trial.

©The McGraw-Hill Companies, Inc./Mark Dierker

A company can use sales promotion techniques in several ways to retain its current customer base through continued repeat purchases. One way is to load them with the product, taking them out of the market for a certain time. Special price promotions, coupons, or bonus packs can encourage consumers to stock up on the brand. This not only keeps them using the company's brand but also reduces the likelihood they will switch brands in response to a competitor's promotion.

Consumption Marketing managers responsible for established brands competing in mature markets—against established competitors, where consumer purchase patterns are well set—try to ensure continued or increased consumption. Awareness and brand trial of an established brand is generally high after cumulative advertising effects, and sales promotion can generate new interest in an established brand. One way to increase product consumption is by identifying new uses for the brand. Sales promotion tools like recipe books or calendars that show ways of using the product often can accomplish this. Sales promotion also can stimulate consumption of the existing household stock of product. For example, the Bud Red Light, a premium installed in people's homes, shines when their team scores, which possibly reminds loyal drinkers to head to the fridge for another round.

Brand Equity A final objective for consumer promotions is to enhance or support the brand's IMC effort. Although maintaining or building brand equity and image has traditionally been viewed as being accomplished by media advertising, it has also become an important objective for sales promotions. Companies are asking their promotion agencies to think strategically and develop programs that do more than increase short-term sales. They want promotions that require consumer involvement with their brands. Sales promotion techniques such as contests or sweepstakes and premium offers are used to draw attention to an ad, increase involvement with the message and product/service, and help build relationships with consumers. The Peek Freans example demonstrates this since the imagery of the promotion fit the duality of the brand and the trip to Sin City!

CONSUMER SALES PROMOTION STRATEGY DECISIONS

Strategic decisions for sales promotions fall into three broad categories: sales promotion strategy options, application across product lines, and application across geographic markets.

Sales Promotion Strategy Options Our view of sales promotions is that the options identified in **Figure 14-1** are strategic choices for a marketer who selects the most appropriate one(s) that will achieve the behavioural objective for the target audience efficiently and effectively. Two characteristics of sales promotions guide the strategic direction of the sales promotion plan: the degree to which the sales promotion is "franchise building," and whether the incentive of the sales promotion is immediate or delayed.

Franchise-Building Characteristic Sales promotion activities that communicate distinctive brand attributes and contribute to the development and reinforcement of brand identity are **consumer franchise-building (CFB) promotions**.[8] For years, managers viewed franchise or image building as the exclusive realm of advertising, and sales promotion generated short-term sales increases. But now marketers see the image-building potential of sales promotion. Sales promotion efforts cannot make consumers loyal to a brand that is of little value or does not benefit them. But they can make consumers aware of a brand and, by communicating its specific features and benefits, contribute to the development of a favourable brand attitude. Consumer franchise-building promotions are designed to build long-term brand preference and help the company achieve the ultimate goal of full-price purchases that do not depend on a promotional offer. In contrast, **non-franchise-building (non-FB) promotions** are designed to accelerate the purchase decision process and generate an immediate purchase. These activities communicate minimal brand information about its unique features or benefits, so they do not contribute to equity and image building. Price discounts, bonus packs, and rebates or refunds are examples of non-FB sales promotion techniques. Non-FB promotions occur in a firm's promotional mix when market dynamics require switching consumers from competitor brands.

Incentive Characteristic Sales promotions provide consumers with an extra incentive or reward to influence their behaviour, such as repurchasing a brand or switching from a competitor brand. For certain sales promotion tools, the incentive that the consumer receives is immediate, while for others, the reward is delayed and not realized immediately. Using their situation analysis, marketers decide the relative balance between immediate and delayed incentives. The decision is based on the target audience(s) and the intended behavioural objective(s).

The chart in **Figure 14-2** outlines how sales promotion tools accomplish communication and behavioural objectives for franchise building, and identifies whether the incentive is received by the consumer immediately with purchase or delayed. Techniques are listed more than once because they accomplish more than one objective with both immediate and delayed incentives, and with trial and repeat purchase behaviour.

One explanation for how sales promotion incentives work lies in the theory of **operant conditioning**. Individuals act on an aspect of the environment that reinforces behaviour. In a promotion context, if a consumer buys a product with a sales promotion and experiences a positive outcome, the likelihood that the consumer will use this product again increases. If the outcome is not favourable, the likelihood of buying the product again decreases. Two aspects of reinforcement relevant to sales promotion strategies are schedules of reinforcement and shaping.

Different **schedules of reinforcement** result in varying patterns of learning and behaviour. Learning occurs most rapidly under a *continuous reinforcement schedule,* in which every response is rewarded—but the behaviour is likely to cease when the reinforcement stops. This implies promotional offers like earning points in an online branded game should carry on indefinitely so that customers would not switch. Learning occurs more slowly but lasts longer when a *partial or intermittent reinforcement schedule* is used and only some of the individual's responses are rewarded. This implies that an IMC program should have a sales promotion with a partial reinforcement schedule. The firm does not want to offer the incentive every time (continuous reinforcement), because consumers might become dependent on it and stop buying the brand when the incentive is withdrawn.

Reinforcement schedules can also be used to influence consumer behaviour through a process known as **shaping**, the reinforcement of successive acts that lead to a desired behaviour pattern or response.[9] In a promotional context,

Figure 14-2 Consumer sales promotion tools for various objectives

Timing of Incentive	Communication and Behavioural Objectives		
	Trial purchase	Repeat purchase/ Customer loading	Support IMC program/ Build brand equity
Immediate	• Sampling • Instant coupon • In-store coupon • In-store rebate	• Price discount • Bonus pack • In- and on-package free premium	• Event • In- and on-package free premium
Delayed	• Coupon sent by media, mail, scanner, Internet • Mail-in refund and rebate • Free mail-in premium	• In- and on-package coupon • Mail-in refund/rebate	• Self-liquidating premium • Free mail-in premium • Contest, sweepstakes

Figure 14-3 Application of shaping behaviour with sales promotion

Behaviour Change	Sales Promotion
Product trial	Sample and large discount coupon given in-store
Purchase with low financial cost	Wide distribution of good discount coupon
Purchase with moderate cost	Modest discount on-pack coupon for next purchase
Purchase with full cost	No sales promotion

shaping procedures are used as part of the introductory program for new products. **Figure 14-3** provides an example of how samples and discount coupons take a consumer from trial to repeat purchase over four time periods after a new product introduction. Marketers must be careful in their use of shaping procedures: If they drop the incentives too soon, the consumer may not establish the desired behaviour; if they overuse them, the consumer's purchase may become contingent on the incentive rather than the product or service.

Application Across Product Lines Another part of the strategic sales promotion decision is the degree to which each sales promotion is applied to the range of sizes, varieties, models, or products. Overall, there are three important product decisions for sales promotions. (1) Should the sales promotion be run on the entire line, or on individual items? If the individual item option is chosen (i.e., selective application), the next decision point arises: (2) Which specific items should the sales promotion target? The marketer could run a promotion on either the more or the less popular items. Similarly, the marketer could focus on higher or lower price points. Sometimes, a sales promotion is offered on a unique product format or size instead of the regular product. For example, Kellogg's bundled three brands of cereal with plastic in one sales promotion in which each size was not the standard size typically distributed. This raises the remaining strategic issue: (3) Should the sales promotion be run on the "regular" stock or another special version?

Application Across Geographic Markets Sales promotions are run nationally or in select markets. Local or regional market conditions, with respect to consumer demand and competitive intensity, tend to dictate the degree of tailoring of sales promotions for each geographic market. Intuitively, it appears that marketers would be faced with situations where offering unique sales promotions for each geographic market would achieve optimal communication and behavioural effects; however, there are three factors that marketers need to consider. First, a regional focus requires additional managerial commitment in planning and implementation. Second, achieving objectives more specifically may result in greater expense, thus necessitating a cost–benefit analysis. Third and finally, national accounts may not be too receptive, with different types of sales promotions in one province versus another.

IMC Perspective 14-2 illustrates an innovative sales promotion by Coke and Pepsi that contributed to the brands and influenced consumer behaviour.

IMC PERSPECTIVE 14-2

COKE vs PEPSI: THE DIGITAL SUMMER BATTLE

Coke vs. Pepsi battles have swayed cola drinkers from one brand to the other for decades. Recently, the challenge occurred in Canada during two consecutive summers—the most lucrative sales period when 35 percent of market sales occur over the three warmest months of the year. Coke launched the first promotion volley in 2016, while Pepsi responded with a promotion in 2017.

Coke established its "Play a Coke" promotion, where consumers could listen to a Spotify playlist on their phone after pointing the device at the label of a bottle of Coke. Of course, it required a previously downloaded app to execute, but consumers could select from over 180 playlists. For example, labels included themes like "Hug me," "Marry me," "Rally caps on," "Win the boys," and

[Continued on next page]

[IMC Perspective 14-2 continued]

"Summer jams" to build whatever mood the listener preferred.

Coke wanted to increase usage by 2 percent and favourite brand measure by 1.5 percent among teen consumers. The impetus for the promotion originated from research indicating that teens streamed 27,000 hours of music every month. And Coke added another factor—it wanted to go beyond a typical big music experience as it associated the iconic brand with music. The originality of the promotion drew retailers selling Coke who requested their own playlist and prominently displayed the in-store signage. Results proved the campaign successful, with a 9 percent growth in market share and achievement of the two primary objectives.

The following summer, Pepsi desired a higher purchase frequency of single-serve products by young millennial consumers compared to Coke. Research indicated that 78 percent of the target used Snapchat on a daily basis, higher than Facebook or Instagram. Furthermore, 70 percent reported usage of more than six times per day. The "Snap It With Pepsi" promotion allowed consumers to use exclusive on-pack Snapchat lenses to really enjoy summer time. Consumers activated the 20 unique-to-Pepsi lenses by scanning the Snapcode on select bottles. The lenses also became part of the packaging and ad messages.

©Mejini Neskah/Shutterstock

To build excitement, Pepsi's agency created two stunts: one featured a lens with the TV show *ET Canada* in a product placement approach, and the other focused on dropping the Snapcodes in the three largest cities. A teaser message also built curiosity to go along with 15-second online video and out-of-home creatives. Pepsi outperformed Coke by $1 million in sales for the product stock-keeping unit of the promotion. And finally, Pepsi's promotion in Canada became Snapchat's biggest lens activation in the world!!

Question:

1. What are the strengths of these promotions in terms of achieving behavioural and communication objectives?

CONSUMER SALES PROMOTION TACTICS DECISIONS

A coupon is received with a value anywhere from 50¢ to $2.00 for many consumer products, early in the year or later in the year, often or not so often, or from any number of outlets (e.g., direct mail, magazine). As this implies, for each sales promotion option, the marketer makes tactical decisions: value of the incentive, timing, and distribution. We briefly describe each of these in order to put together a comprehensive sales promotion plan.

Value of Incentive Whether the marketer is offering a price discount or a consumer franchise-building sales promotion such as a premium, eventually the marketer has to decide the value of the sales promotion. For example, should the coupon be the equivalent of a 10 percent or a 20 percent discount? This decision is contingent upon the threshold at which consumers will respond to a sales promotion and the number of potential consumer responses; each will contribute to the total cost of the sales promotion. Similarly, if a beer company is offering a premium, a strategic decision has to be made as to the relative value of the premium: for example, a T-shirt worth $10 to $15, or perhaps a "cozy" worth a couple of dollars.

Timing The time element of the sales promotion is important in a few directions that are mutually dependent. A marketer has to decide during which months, weeks, or days the sales promotion will be offered. Seasonal or some other consumption pattern discovered through market research or the situation analysis may guide this choice. In addition, sales promotions are offered for one day, one week, a few weeks, or even a few months. Target audience and behavioural objectives typically guide this duration decision. The frequency of the sales promotion is a final timing consideration. If coupons have been chosen, the marketer needs to decide whether one will be offered every six months or perhaps two every six months. One study that examined the value and timing decisions concluded that the optimal solution for price discounts is a reduction communicated by percentage instead of dollar amount, and infrequent price discount offers to minimize consumers' choosing to wait for a deal.[10]

Distribution For most sales promotions, there is a logistical consideration as to how the promotion will get to the consumer or how the consumer will get to the sales promotion. There are many choices for sales promotions, such as coupons (e.g., direct mail, in-ad), while for others, such as premiums, the choices may be limited. We discuss the distribution options for each sales promotion in the next section, where we describe each sales promotion and its strengths and limitations. Digital distribution of sales promotions emerged in the past decade, with Groupon providing an example of one way for brands to distribute promotions, as shown in **Exhibit 14-5**.

Exhibit 14-5 Groupon provides a method for brands to offer discounts.

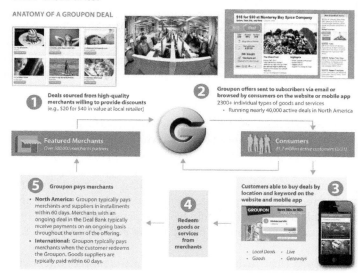

Source: Groupon, Inc.

Consumer Sales Promotion Strategy Options

Promotional planners select from the list of consumer sales promotions identified in **Figure 14-1** to develop a strategic sales promotion plan. Each of the options assists in achieving the behavioural and communication objectives just discussed. We review these options in this section by describing their characteristics, distribution methods, and strengths and limitations.

SAMPLING

Sampling involves procedures whereby consumers are given an amount of a product for no charge to induce trial. Sampling is generally considered an effective way to generate trial and therefore a useful tool with which to introduce a new product, although it is usually the most expensive. Sampling can try to generate trial for an established product; however, it may not induce satisfied users of a competing brand to switch and may simply reward the firm's current customers who would buy the product anyway. One interesting study concluded that giving free apps to users with the expectation of higher levels and greater speed of app adoption through purchase did not occur; the data indicated that a portion of the sample used the free app but delayed their purchase or did not buy at all.[11]

Packaged goods (e.g., food, healthcare) producers are heavy users of sampling since their products meet the three criteria for an effective sampling program. (1) The products are of relatively low unit value, so samples do not cost too much. (2) The products are divisible, which means they break into small sizes that are adequate for demonstrating the brand's features and benefits. (3) The purchase cycle is relatively short, so the consumer will consider an immediate purchase. **Exhibit 14-6** shows a public sampling display to encourage brand activation.

Exhibit 14-6 Cheetos offers samples to consumers to encourage trial.

©Rubens Alarcon/Alamy Stock Photo

Strengths of Sampling In general, managers expect samples to yield strong prospective consumer participation and subsequent trial purchase behaviour. Researchers of in-store food sampling found that it effectively stimulated trial in general, provided an incentive for category users to switch brands, and even encouraged consideration among non-category users.[12] No wonder we see sampling stations set up in Costco! Getting people to try a product is a second benefit of sampling: consumers experience the brand directly, gaining a greater appreciation for its benefits. This is important when a product's features and benefits are difficult to describe through advertising; the subtle features of food, beverage, and cosmetic products are most appreciated when experienced directly.

Limitations of Sampling While samples effectively induce trial, the brand must have unique or superior benefits for a sampling program to be worthwhile. Otherwise, the sampled consumers revert back to other brands and do not become repeat purchasers. The cost of a sampling program is recovered only if the program gets a number of consumers to become regular users of the brand at full retail price.

Another possible limitation to sampling is that the benefits are difficult to gauge immediately, and the learning period required to appreciate the brand may require supplying the consumer with larger amounts of the brand than are affordable. An example would be an expensive skin cream that is promoted as preventing or reducing wrinkles but has to be used for an extended period before any effects are seen.

Sampling Methods One decision for the promotional manager is how to distribute the sample. The sampling method chosen is important not only in terms of costs but also because it influences the type of consumer who receives the sample. The best sampling method gets the product to the best prospects for trial and subsequent repurchase.

Door-to-door sampling, in which the product is delivered directly to the prospect's residence, is used when it is important to control where the sample is delivered. This distribution method is expensive because of labour costs, but it is cost-effective if the marketer has information that defines the target audience and/or if the prospects are located in a well-defined geographic area.

Sampling through media distributes goods through print media delivered to residences. Newspapers use bags with advertising on the outside and the sample is tucked inside with the reading material. Magazines have similar capabilities but for smaller products. Companies use Internet media for consumers to sample their products. Software, information, or entertainment products are easily delivered electronically in the digital age. Samples of physical goods are delivered to consumers who make an online request.

Sampling through the mail is common for small, lightweight, non-perishable products. This gives the marketer control over where and when the product will be distributed. Marketers use information from geodemographic target marketing programs to better direct their sample mailings. Sampling requests obtained from various sources (e.g., phone, Internet, mail) are usually mailed to consumers. The main drawbacks to mail sampling are postal restrictions and costs.

On-package sampling, where a sample of a product is attached to another item, is cost-effective for multi-product firms that attach a sample of a new product to an existing brand's package. A drawback is that the sample will not reach non-users since the sample is distributed to consumers who purchase the primary item.

In-store sampling occurs when demonstrators set up a table or booth, prepare product samples, and pass them out to shoppers. This approach is effective for food products, since consumers taste the item and the demonstrator provides information about the product during consumption. Demonstrators may offer a financial incentive for the sampled item to encourage immediate trial purchase. This sampling method is effective with direct product experience but requires greater investment, extensive planning, and retailer cooperation.

Location sampling allows companies to target consumers who are non-users of a product or users of a competing brand who are working, visiting, or consuming at a specific location. For example, university and college students receive trial-size samples of personal care products while on campus. While similar to in-store sampling, this method provides greater precision in reaching a specific target audience.

Event sampling occurs at temporary venues such as outdoor concerts, sporting events, cultural festivals, and the brand's event marketing activities. As part of the overall IMC program, this distribution method provides a more impressive brand exposure, especially if a brand reaches for the stars! For example, Montreal-based Rouge Maple provided 70 baskets, each containing $300 worth of maple syrup products, to Oscar nominees at the Academy Awards. The cost did not end there, as it also paid a $4,000 participation fee. At the American Music Awards, Halifax-based Miss Foxine Jewellery handed out 150 custom pieces and ultimately doubled its sales after the event due to the notoriety of artists and media personalities receiving the jewellery.[13]

COUPONS

A coupon is a voucher providing a consumer with a discount or free good and it is one of the oldest and most widely used sales promotions. Its characteristics are a function of tactical options: the variability in discount offered (e.g., $0.50, $1.00), time flexibility in terms of offer and expiration (e.g., limited, unlimited), and how it is distributed (e.g., media, direct, package, retailer), allowing it to fit in more than one cell of **Figure 14-2**. Digital distribution of coupons occurred on Internet sites years ago, and new approaches with convenient smart phone apps emerged to go along with the historic media, home, and store delivery. The image in **Exhibit 14-7** illustrates a typical coupon showing a clear savings that might spur a trial purchase and an ad much like a print message that ensures brand communication effects.

Exhibit 14-7 Example of a typical coupon.

Source: Nestlé Purina Petcare

Strengths of Coupons Coupons' strengths make them effective for both new and established products, and for potential and current customers. First, coupons offer a price reduction to consumers who are price-sensitive. Such consumers generally purchase because of coupons, while those who are not as concerned about price buy the brand at full price. Second, coupons reduce the retail price of a product without relying on retailers for cooperation, which can often be a problem. Third, coupons are generally regarded as second only to sampling as a promotional technique for generating trial since they reduce the consumer's perceived risk of buying without prior experience. Fourth, coupons encourage repeat purchase after initial trial as a new product might include a coupon inside the package to encourage a subsequent buy. Fifth, coupons encourage non-users of established products to try a brand and stimulate repeat purchase among current users.

Limitations of Coupons In contrast, there are problems with coupons. First, there is potential that coupons will not achieve their intended objective. Coupons intended to attract new users to an established brand are redeemed by consumers who already use the brand. Rather than attracting new users, coupons reduce the profit margin among consumers who would probably purchase the product anyway. Due to the incentive, conditions, and expiry date, coupons remain less effective than sampling for inducing initial product trial in a short period.

Second, an estimate of how many consumers will use a coupon and when is required. Response to a coupon is rarely immediate; it typically takes anywhere from two to six months to redeem one. A study of coupon redemption patterns found that coupons are redeemed just before the expiration date rather than in the period following the initial coupon drop.[14] Marketers are attempting to expedite redemption by shortening the time period before expiration. The uncertainty in knowing the redemption rate and timing makes for more difficult financial planning for coupons.

Third, coupons have low redemption rates and high costs. Couponing program expenses include the face value of the coupon redeemed plus costs for production, distribution, and handling of the coupons. **Figure 14-4** shows the calculations used to determine the costs of a coupon program using a freestanding insert (FSI) in the newspaper

Figure 14-4 Calculating couponing costs

Cost per Coupon Redeemed: An Illustration	
1. Distribution cost 5,000,000 circulation × $15/M	$75,000
2. Redemptions at 2%	100,000
3. Redemption cost 100,000 redemptions × $1.00 face value	$100,000
4. Retailer handling cost and processor fees 100,000 redemptions × $0.10	$10,000
5. Total program cost (Items 1 + 3 + 4)	$185,000
6. Cost per coupon redeemed (cost divided by redemptions)	$1.85
7. Actual product sold on redemption (misredemption estimated at 10%) 100,000 × 90%	90,000
8. Cost per product moved (program cost divided by amount of product sold)	$2.06

Figure 14-5 Coupon redemption rates (U.S. 2015)

Media	0.5%
Direct mail	4.0%
Instant	18.0%
On-shelf	10.5%
Handout	3.5%
Internet	8.0%

and a coupon with an average face value of one dollar. The marketer should track costs closely to ensure that the promotion is economically feasible.

A final problem with coupon promotions is mistakes during redemption through the wrong product format or incorrect size, or redemption without product purchase. Instances of coupon fraud have occurred at times through store personnel (e.g., redemption by salesclerks in exchange for cash, manager collecting coupons without selling product, etc.).

Coupon Distribution Coupons are disseminated to consumers in a number of ways, including media, direct mail, in/on package, in store, and the Internet. **Figure 14-5** summarizes relevant U.S. coupon redemption rates as Canadian data is unavailable. The average redemption rate for all distribution methods is 2.5 percent. About 320 billion coupons are distributed annually in the United States, which extrapolates to 35 billion in Canada—almost 1,000 coupons per Canadian per year. However, general observation suggests that coupon distribution is more intense in the United States, meaning the 1,000 per person in Canada is too high an estimate.

Freestanding inserts (FSIs) are distributed through newspapers and are used for a number of reasons, including their high-quality four-colour graphics, competitive distribution costs, national same-day circulation, and market selectivity, and the category exclusivity given by the FSI company. Because of their consumer popularity and predictable distribution, coupons distributed in FSIs are also a strong selling point with the retail trade. On the other hand, FSIs suffer from a low redemption rate and their widespread distribution may lead to a clutter problem.

Newspaper and *magazine* distribution of coupons offers a print media alternative. The advantages of newspapers include market selectivity, shorter lead times with timing to the day, cooperative advertising opportunities that can lead to cost efficiencies, and promotional tie-ins with retailers. Other advantages of newspaper-delivered coupons are the broad exposure and consumer receptivity. Magazine distribution takes advantage of the selectivity of the publication to reach specific target audiences, along with enhanced production capabilities and extended copy life in the home. One feature of these print options is that the distribution cost is not a factor if the advertiser was planning to run a print ad in the first place.

Direct-mail coupons are sent by local retailers or through co-op mailings where a packet of coupons for different products is sent to a household. Direct mail coupons have several advantages. First, the mailing is sent to a broad audience or targeted to specific geographic or demographic segments. Second, firms that mail their own coupons through addressed mail can be quite selective about recipients. Third, direct-mail coupons can also be combined with a sample, greatly enhancing communication and behavioural effects. Finally, the above strengths generally give this method a redemption rate higher than FSI. The major disadvantage of direct-mail coupon delivery is the expense relative to other distribution methods. The cost per thousand for distributing coupons through co-op mailings ranges from $10 to $15, and more targeted promotions can cost $20 to $25 or even more. Also, the higher redemption rate of mail-delivered coupons may result from the fact that recipients are already users of the brand who take advantage of the coupons sent directly to them. Some companies produce and distribute their own coupon books, as demonstrated by Procter & Gamble in **Exhibit 14-8**.

An *inside/outside of package* coupon that is redeemable for the next purchase of the same brand is known as a **bounce-back coupon**. Distributing coupons this way has virtually no distribution costs and a much higher redemption rate. Another type is the **cross-ruff coupon**, which is redeemable on the purchase of a different product, usually one made by the same company but occasionally through a tie-in with another manufacturer. A third type is the **instant coupon**, which is attached to the outside of the package so that the consumer can redeem it immediately at the time of purchase.

In-store coupons are distributed to consumers while shopping via tear-off pads, handouts, on-shelf dispensers, and electronic dispensers. These in-store coupons reach consumers when they are ready to make a purchase, increase brand awareness on the shelf, generate impulse buying, encourage product trial, and provide category exclusivity. Extending this idea, coupons are distributed essentially in any place-based location by simply handing them out.

Online distribution also occurs. Couponclick.ca distributes coupons that can be instantly downloaded and printed. Each voucher contains a code tracked to the individual consumer for measurement effectiveness and security purposes. Two websites, Coupons.com and Save.ca, allow consumers to print or receive coupons in the mail, respectively. The famous blue Valpak, distributed to households through the mail system, is available online.

PREMIUMS

A **premium** is an offer of an item of merchandise or service either free or at a low price that is an extra incentive for purchasers. Premiums are usually in a product package, given out at a retail location, or sent to consumers who mail in a request. For example, in/on-package free premiums for cereal products include toys, trading cards, or other items, and Swiss Chalet offers a free chocolate with its holiday meal promotion each December. Marketers seek value-added premiums that reflect the quality of the product and are consistent with its image and positioning in the market and try to avoid gimmicks. A research study concluded that surprising consumers with an unknown gift for an emotion-based purchase produced stronger interest and more positive purchase intentions, but this approach faltered with a cognitive-based purchase.[15] Another research study examined collectible premiums given to consumers who hit certain levels of purchases and numbers of store visits. The results indicated positive results for both sales and visits that benefited both the manufacturer and the retailers, with the results being stronger for those with a propensity to collect.[16]

Exhibit 14-8 P&G produces and distributes its own coupon book.

©The McGraw-Hill Companies, Inc./Mark Dierker

Strengths of Premiums Package-carried premiums are advantageous as they immediately provide an extra incentive to buy the product as a key distinguishing feature. For example, McDonald's is a leader in the restaurant market for giving free premiums with its Happy Meal for children (**Exhibit 14-9**). Interestingly, one disgruntled parent filed a class-action lawsuit against McDonald's, contending that the promotion illegally advertises to children in Quebec.[17]

Thus another key feature is that premiums build or reinforce a brand image and work with cobranding. Premiums also have high impulse value that can lead to frequent purchases. Research concluded that premium usage is a function of deal-proneness, compulsive buying tendency, and variety-seeking tendency.[18]

Another benefit of premiums is their ability to work with the rest of the IMC program effectively to build the brand image. For example, Kraft Canada supported its ad—which told the story of the Kraft peanut butter teddy bear's life with its owner as she grew from a young girl to a woman—by offering a plush version available to buy with the purchase of the product. Kraft opted to promote a higher quality version of the teddy bear, manufactured by Gund, than it had in past iterations of premium offers. The emotional ad warranted a more plush and huggable teddy bear for long-lasting memories, as exhibited in the message.[19]

Finally, premiums can encourage trade support and gain in-store displays for the brand and the premium offer. Coca-Cola's "Share a Coke" campaign featured

Exhibit 14-9 McDonald's Happy Meal uses toys to help attract children.

©urbanbuzz/Alamy Stock Photo

Exhibit 14-10 Consumers and retailers found value in the "Share a Coke" promotion.

©Torontonian/Alamy Stock Photo

various sizes and formats of cans and bottles of its famous beverage adorned with individual names written in the stylized font of the popular brand (**Exhibit 14-10**). In addition to being supported with other IMC activities as noted above, retailers accepted additional units and promoted the initiative with signage to attract customers.[20]

Limitations of Premiums There are limitations associated with the use of premiums. First, there is the cost factor, which results from the premium itself as well as from extra packaging that may be needed. Finding desirable premiums at reasonable costs is a challenge, particularly for adult markets, and using a poor premium that costs less may do more harm than good. A solution to this is to offer **self-liquidating premiums** requiring the consumer to pay a portion or all of the cost of the premium. The marketer usually purchases items used as self-liquidating premiums in large quantities and offers them to consumers at lower-than-retail prices. The goal is not to make a profit on the premium item but rather just to cover costs and offer a value to the consumer. A newer solution is an **embedded premium** where a brand donates money to a worthy social cause for every purchase made by consumers. Research concluded that this sales promotion is an efficient use of marketing dollars and contributes to strengthening the brand.[21] A second limitation is that offers usually require the consumer to send in more than one proof of purchase to receive the premium. This requires effort from the consumer and money for the mailing and does not offer an immediate reinforcement or reward. A third limitation is that the marketer faces the risk of poor acceptance and is left with a supply of items with brand identification (e.g., a logo) that makes them hard to dispose of. Thus, it is important to test consumers' reaction to a premium incentive and determine whether they perceive the offer as valuable. Another option is to use premiums with no brand identification, but that detracts from their consumer franchise-building value.

PROMOTIONAL PRODUCTS

Promotional products are useful and/or symbolic items that are implemented in marketing communication programs as a sales promotion or message vehicle, or a combination of both. Promotional products are essentially a premium, but not typically tied to a purchase as shown in the Happy Meal example. A promotional product is mostly given as a gift to company stakeholders (customers, suppliers, employees, guests) as a thank-you or reward. The items contain brand identification to enhance awareness, maintain brand equity, or strengthen goodwill. Popular items include pens, mugs, glassware, key rings, calendars, and clothing. The variety of promotional products makes it a virtual certainty that a manager can improve attitudes with an item that represents the brand appropriately. The promotional product industry in Canada is substantial (over $2 billion) and the Canadian trade association is known as the Promotional Product Professionals of Canada.

Strengths of Promotional Products When promotional products are distributed directly to target customers, the medium offers a high degree of target audience selectivity and coverage. The communication is distributed to the desired recipient, reducing waste coverage. Most promotional products are designed for consumers to keep for a long time, providing repeat exposures to the advertising message at no additional cost. Promotional products can be expensive in terms of absolute cost (e.g., leather goods), but most are affordable to almost any size organization. While they are costly, the high number of repeat exposures drives the relative cost per exposure downward for respectable cost efficiency.

As the variety of promotional products demonstrates, they offer a high degree of message flexibility contributing to positive cognitive and emotional responses. A message as simple as a logo or as long as is necessary can be distributed through a number of means. Both small and large companies can employ this medium, limited only by their own creativity. With such opportunity, it is possible to use promotional products to achieve particular beliefs about the brand. Because people like gifts and functional products, consumers are grateful to receive them. Attention, processing, and involvement may vary, but all would be considered strengths of promotional products assuming the recipient appreciates the actual item. Certainly the selection of the item in question will heavily influence consumer reaction.

Limitations of Promotional Products An advertiser hoping to expand its market through wider reach would likely find promotional products a weaker choice. While promotional products are distributed essentially anywhere, the cost implications would severely curtail significant geographic distribution for most advertisers. Finally, the lead time required to put together a promotional product message is longer than that for most other media due to supply and printing requirements.

Recipients of promotional products are in complete control of whether they choose to keep or display the item. It is entirely possible that a tremendous investment could receive no or very minimal exposure to the intended target audience. While most forms of promotional products are received as friendly reminders of the brand name, the firm must be careful in choosing the item. The company image may be cheapened by a chintzy or poorly designed advertising form. The more unusual or unique the promotional product, the more value it is likely to have to the receiver.

CONTESTS AND SWEEPSTAKES

Contests and sweepstakes are sales promotions consumers love because of the fun and excitement generated that other promotions lack. For example, a scratch-off card with instant winners is a popular promotional tool as the anticipation of getting a prize stirs up emotions.

A **contest** is a promotion where consumers compete for prizes or money on the basis of skills or ability. The company determines winners by judging the entries or ascertaining which entry comes closest to predetermined criteria. Contests usually provide a purchase incentive by requiring a proof of purchase or an entry form that is available from a dealer or advertisement. Some contests require consumers to read an ad or package or visit a store display to gather information. Marketers must be careful not to make their contests too difficult to enter, as doing so might discourage participation among key prospects in the target audience.

A **sweepstakes** is a promotion where winners are determined purely by chance; it cannot require a proof of purchase as a condition for entry. Entrants need only submit their names for the prize drawing. While there is often an official entry form, handwritten entries must also be permitted. One form of sweepstakes is a **game**, which also has a chance element or odds of winning. Some games occur over a longer period and require more involvement by consumers. Promotions where consumers collect game pieces are popular among retailers and fast-food chains as a way to build store traffic and repeat purchases. For example, McDonald's has used promotions based on the game Monopoly several times.

Tim Hortons' "RRRoll Up the Rim to Win" reached its 30th anniversary in 2016, shortly after the company's 50th anniversary in 2014 (**Exhibit 14-11**). The company made novel changes to keep the momentum going. "RRRoll Up Replay!" allowed consumers to participate online with the chance of winning an additional 250,000 prizes. "RRRoll Up at Home" included purchases made for home brewing as consumers took a photo of their receipt and uploaded it to the contest site for a chance at 10,000 additional prizes.[22] However, by 2019, after unexpectedly weaker sales results, managers foresaw the need for changes in the contest for 2020.[23]

Strengths of Contests/Sweepstakes Sales can be enhanced by trial and repeat purchases through a sweepstakes advertised via in-store ad-pads. For example, Kruger Products (whose brands include Scotties, Cashmere, Sponge Towels, White Swan, and Purex) offered 10 pairs of diamond earrings worth $5,000 a pair in a contest for its Cashmere brand. According to the manager, the earrings fit with the luxury image of the product and proved financially viable.[24] Contests and sweepstakes can involve consumers with a brand by making the promotion product relevant or by connecting the prizes to the lifestyle, needs, or interests of the target audience. For example, Coors Banquet beer established a contest to select the

Exhibit 14-11 Thirty years of "RRRoll Up the Rim to Win" shows the promotion's popularity.

©Lars Hagberg/Alamy Stock Photo

Exhibit 14-12 The imagery and contest fits well with the new Axe Apollo.

Source: Axe by Unilever

best "One Horse Town" in which the winner received a concert featuring live country music. Tied in with the Country Music Television sponsorship and social media, the experience provided a perfect lifestyle match for the premium beer.[25] And some contests are out of this world! The global IMC campaign for the Axe Apollo product line included a contest, as shown in the ad of **Exhibit 14-12**. The prize featured a chance to win a one-hour flight on the Lynx suborbital plane providing a five-minute weightlessness experience before descending back to Earth.

Limitations of Contests/Sweepstakes Sweepstakes and/or contest promotions rarely contribute to consumer franchise building for a product or service and may even detract from it. The sweepstakes or contest often becomes the dominant focus rather than the brand, and little is accomplished other than giving away substantial amounts of money and/or prizes. Promotional experts question the effectiveness of contests and sweepstakes, and numerous legal considerations affect their design and administration.[26] Companies must be careful in designing a contest or sweepstakes and awarding prizes. Most firms use consultants that specialize in the design and administration of contests and sweepstakes to avoid any legal issues, but they may still run into problems with promotions.

A final problem with contests and sweepstakes is participation by professionals or hobbyists who submit entries but have no intention of purchasing the product or service. Because it is illegal to require a purchase as a qualification for a sweepstakes entry, people can enter as many times as they wish. Professional players sometimes enter one sweepstakes several times, depending on the nature of the prizes and the number of entries the promotion attracts. There are even newsletters and websites that inform them of all the contests and sweepstakes being held, the entry dates, estimated probabilities of winning, how to enter, and solutions to any puzzles or other information that might be needed. The presence of these professional entrants not only defeats the purpose of the promotion but also may discourage entries from consumers who think their chances of winning are limited.

Exhibit 14-13 Pennzoil uses a refund offer that is tied to a future purchase.

Source: Pennzoil by Shell International B.V.

REFUNDS AND REBATES

Refunds (also known as rebates) are offers by the manufacturer to return a portion of the product purchase price, usually after the consumer supplies proof of purchase. Consumers are generally very responsive to rebate offers, particularly as the size of the savings increases. Rebates are used by makers of all types of products like packaged goods, appliances, vehicles, and car care items (**Exhibit 14-13**). Consumers may perceive the savings offered through a cash refund as an immediate value that lowers the cost of the item, even though those savings are realized only if the consumer redeems the refund or rebate offer. Redemption rates for refund offers typically range from 1–3 percent for print and point-of-purchase offers to 5 percent for in/on-package offers.

Cash back offers are essentially another way to implement the idea of a refund or a rebate. An interesting approach for implementing a cash back program is taken by the Checkout 51 app, which works as follows. Consumers buy the products that have cash-back offers communicated via the app or Internet site. Afterward, the consumer photographs the receipt to redeem the discount and receives a cheque upon accumulating $20. The app looked promising, as News America Marketing purchased the organization so it could offer a stronger line-up of digital promotional tools.[27] Groupon also expanded its horizons by purchasing SnapSaves. It works similarly to Checkout 51's app, with consumers taking a picture of their receipt and then receiving a cheque in the mail after hitting a threshold. Groupon desired more digital offerings to go along with its initial strategy of discounts and its existing Freebies digital coupons.[28]

Strengths of Refunds/Rebates Marketers use refund offers for all types of behavioural objectives. They are used to induce trial of a new product which encourages users of another brand to switch, or non-category users to try the brand. Refund offers can also encourage repeat purchase since they may require consumers to send in multiple proofs of purchase. The size of the refund offer may even increase as the number of purchases gets larger. Secondly, rebates offer a temporary price reduction in the face of competition to spur consumers who are at the decision stage. The rebate may be perceived as an immediate savings even though consumers do not follow through on the offer. This perception can influence purchase even if the consumer fails to realize the savings, so the marketer can reduce price for much less than if it used a direct price discount that applied to all sales volume. Finally, rebates can influence the timing of a purchase, as seen in vehicle rebates offered toward the end of the model year.

Limitations of Refunds/Rebates Limitations are associated with refunds and rebates since not all consumers are motivated by a refund offer because of the delay and the effort required to obtain the savings (e.g., completing forms and mailing receipts). A study of consumer perceptions found a negative relationship between the use of rebates and the perceived difficulties associated with the redemption process.[29] The study also found that consumers perceive manufacturers as offering rebates to sell products that are not faring well. Non-users of rebates were particularly likely to perceive the redemption process as too complicated and to suspect manufacturers' motives. This implies that companies using rebates must simplify the redemption process and use other promotional elements such as advertising to retain consumer confidence in the brand.

When small refunds are being offered, marketers may find other promotional incentives such as coupons or bonus packs more effective. They must be careful not to overuse rebate offers and confuse consumers about the real price and value of a product or service. Also, consumers can become dependent on rebates and delay their purchases, or purchase only brands for which a rebate is available.

BONUS PACKS

Bonus packs offer the consumer an extra amount of a product at the regular price by providing larger containers or extra units (**Exhibit 14-14**). Bonus packs result in a lower cost per unit for the consumer and provide extra value as well as more product for the money.

Strengths of Bonus Packs There are several advantages to bonus pack promotions. First, they give marketers a direct way to provide extra value without having to get involved with complicated coupons or refund offers. The additional value of a bonus pack is generally obvious to the consumer and can have a strong impact on the purchase decision at the time of purchase. Second, due to the simplicity of the presentation of a percentage of extra quantity, consumers generally prefer a bonus pack over an equivalent price discount.[30] Third, bonus packs can also be an effective defensive manoeuvre against a competitor's promotion or introduction of a new brand. By loading current users with large amounts of its product, a marketer can often remove these consumers from the market and make them less susceptible to a competitor's promotional efforts. Fourth, bonus packs may result in larger purchase orders and favourable display space in the store if relationships with retailers are good.

Exhibit 14-14 Bonus packs provide more value for consumers.

Source: Charmin by Procter & Gamble

Limitations of Bonus Packs A limitation is that bonus packs usually require additional shelf space without providing any extra profit margins for the retailer, so the marketer can encounter problems with bonus packs if trade relationships are not good. A second limitation is that bonus packs may appeal primarily to current users who probably would have purchased the brand anyway, or to promotion-sensitive consumers who may not become loyal to the brand.

PRICE DISCOUNT

Another consumer sales promotion tool is the direct **price discount**, which reduces the price of the brand. Price discounts are offered right on the package through specially marked price packs. Typically, price discounts take 10–25 percent off the regular price, with the reduction coming out of the manufacturer's profit margin, not the retailer's. Keeping the retailer's margin during a price-discount promotion maintains its support and cooperation.

Retailers offer price discounts, and one study found that weak discounts of about 10 percent for non-essential items did not produce the intended results of greater consumer purchases. Instead, retailers should offer a more valuable discount (e.g., 20 percent) or use the lower discount on essential items with high-volume purchases.[31] In a study of premium branded vehicles, a direct price discount increased short-term sales and did not substantially reduce brand image, a common criticism of this type of promotion.[32] Due to the flexible implementation of price discounts within their stores, retailers need to adhere to laws regarding the timing of price discounts. The Competition Bureau periodically investigates retail price discounts, and one case involved major department stores not offering mattresses at a regular price for a substantial period of time before putting them on sale. In the end, both retailers cooperatively provided information to resolve the investigation.[33]

Strengths of Price Discounts Marketers use price-discount promotions for several reasons. First, since price discounts are controlled by the manufacturer, it can make sure the promotional discount reaches the consumer rather than being kept by the trade. Second, price discounts present a readily apparent value (e.g., much like a bonus pack) to shoppers, especially when they have a reference price point for the brand and thus recognize the value of the discount.[34] Third, communication of price discounts at the point of purchase attracts attention and the amount saved influences price comparison and evaluation when shopping. Finally, price-discount promotions encourage consumers to purchase larger quantities, pre-empting competitors' promotions and leading to greater trade support.

Limitations of Price Discounts A limitation is that price-discount promotions may not be favourably received by retailers, since they can create pricing and inventory problems. Another limitation concerns retailer acceptance of packages with a specific price shown, thereby taking price decision-making control away from retailers. Price discounts appeal primarily to regular users instead of attracting non-users, much like bonus packs. Finally, the federal government has regulations regarding the conditions that price-discount labels must meet and the frequency and timing of their use.

Exhibit 14-15 Pepsi established the Dew Tour marketing event.

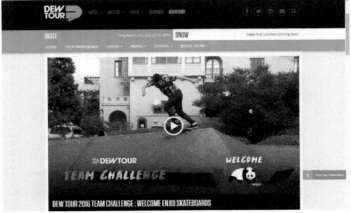

Source: The Enthusiast Network and Mountain Dew

EVENT MARKETING

Event marketing is a promotion where a company or brand is linked to an event or where a themed activity is developed for the purpose of promoting a brand by creating experiences for consumers. For example, Pepsi associated its Mountain Dew brand with various action sports (**Exhibit 14-15**). It is important to make a distinction between *event marketing* and *event sponsorship*, as the two terms are used interchangeably yet refer to different types of promotional activities.

Event marketing allows marketers to develop integrated marketing programs including promotional tools that create experiences for consumers to associate their brand with certain lifestyles. Marketers use events to distribute sales promotions (e.g. sample, promotional product, coupon), communicate product information, or demonstrate the product through consumer experience. Data from one study indicated that stronger brand attitude and brand equity resulted from experiences with marketing events.[35] Some events provide experiential elements associated with the brand with some experimenting with virtual reality. For example, the *Game of Thrones* exhibit at the South by Southwest music festival placed viewers on the 700-foot ice wall of Castle Black.[36]

Event sponsorship is an integrated marketing communications activity where a company develops sponsorship relations with an established event operated by another organization (e.g., concert, art exhibition, cultural activity, social change initiative, sports event). The company provides financial support in return for the right to display a brand name, logo, or advertising message and be identified as a supporter of the event. Part of the confusion between these two promotions arises because brands run event marketing activities as part of their sponsorship of an event. We describe examples of event marketing here and address event sponsorship in Chapter 15 as it relates more closely to public relations activities.

Samsung used an event to demonstrate the capabilities of its virtual reality headset. People used the technology to overcome their life obstacles such as fear of heights or fear of public speaking. Part of this promotion included recording users' experiences for social media storytelling.[37] Other interesting examples include KFC running classes to show consumers how to cook fried chicken and Campbell's having professional chefs demonstrate how its Everyday Gourmet soup could make restaurant-quality meals.[38] Stella Artois established Sensorium in a pop-up dome to create a multi-sensory dining experience in Toronto. It later transitioned the concept internationally to La Savoir featuring the music group The Roots who created a dedicated music video for the event.[39] Finally, BMW partnered with jeweller Isabella Briatico and shoe fashion company Scarpe di Bianco to associate the performance car brand with luxury brands at an event to showcase the products of all three brands.[40]

Trade Sales Promotion Strategy Options

Trade sales promotion strategy options that managers select from to develop a strategic sales promotion plan were identified in Figure 14-1. Each option assists the promotional planner in achieving the objectives with resellers, which are similar to those of consumer sales promotions since the promotion acts as a behavioural incentive. We review objectives and strategic options for trade sales promotions that include trade allowances, point-of-purchase displays, cooperative advertising, contests and incentives, sales training programs, and trade shows.

OBJECTIVES OF TRADE SALES PROMOTION

Like consumer promotions, trade sales promotion programs should be based on well defined objectives and measurable goals. Typical objectives for promotions targeted to marketing intermediaries such as wholesalers and retailers include obtaining distribution for new products, maintaining trade support for established brands, building retail inventories, and encouraging retailers to display established brands. Trade promotions are mostly viewed as non-franchise-building; promotional discounts and allowances given to the trade are passed on to consumers intermittently, and trade promotions forwarded through the channels reach consumers in the form of lower prices or special deals and lead them to buy on the basis of price rather than brand benefits. Like consumer sales promotions, a franchise-building characteristic can be built into the trade promotion program with activities that do not have a price focus.

Obtain Distribution for New Products Trade promotions are often used to encourage retailers to give shelf space to new products. Essentially, this translates into a trial purchase objective like we saw with consumer promotions. Manufacturers recognize that only a limited amount of shelf space is available in supermarkets, drugstores, and other major retail outlets. Thus, they provide retailers with financial incentives to stock new products. While trade discounts or other special price deals are used to encourage retailers and wholesalers to stock a new brand, marketers may use other types of promotions to get them to push the brand. Merchandising allowances can get retailers to display a new product in high-traffic areas of stores, while incentive programs or contests can encourage wholesale or retail store personnel to push a new brand.

Maintain Trade Support for Established Brands Trade promotions are often designed to maintain distribution and trade support for established brands. Clearly, this objective is akin to a repeat purchase objective, which we saw with consumer sales promotion. Brands that are in the mature phase of their product life cycle are vulnerable to losing wholesale and/or retail distribution, particularly if they are not differentiated or face competition from new products. Trade deals induce wholesalers and retailers to continue to carry weaker products because the discounts increase their profit margins. Brands with a smaller market share often rely heavily on trade promotions, since they lack the funds required to differentiate themselves from competitors through media advertising. Even if a brand has a strong market position, trade promotions may be used as part of an overall marketing strategy.

Build Retail Inventories Manufacturers use trade promotions to build the inventory levels of channel members, especially retailers. This is a form of repeat purchasing as brands load retailers with their products. In turn, wholesalers and retailers are more likely to push a product when they have high inventory levels rather than storing it. Building channel members' inventories ensures they will not run out of stock and miss sales opportunities. Manufacturers of seasonal products offer promotional discounts so that retailers will stock up on their products before the peak selling season begins. This enables the manufacturer to smooth out seasonal fluctuations in its production schedule and pass the inventory carrying costs on to retailers or wholesalers. When retailers stock up on a product before the peak selling season, they run special promotions and offer discounts to consumers to reduce excess inventories.

Encourage Retailers to Display Established Brands

Another objective of trade-oriented promotions is to encourage retailers to display and promote an established brand. This could be analogous to increased consumption as seen with consumer sales promotion objectives, since the retailer demonstrates increased commitment. Marketers recognize that purchase decisions are frequently made in the store and promotional displays are an excellent way of generating sales. An important goal is to obtain retail store displays of a product away from its regular shelf location. A typical supermarket has numerous display areas (e.g., end of aisle, checkout counter), and marketers want their products displayed in these areas to increase the probability of shopper exposure. Manufacturers often use multifaceted promotional programs to encourage retailers to promote their products at the retail level. For example, a manufacturer will combine its advertising and consumer sales promotions and offer them at the same time as the trade promotion. For example, **Exhibit 14-16** shows a promotion calendar that WD-40 provides to retailers showing all facets of the IMC plan for the year.

TRADE ALLOWANCES

Probably the most common trade promotion is some form of **trade allowance**, a discount or deal offered to retailers or wholesalers to encourage them to stock, promote, or display the manufacturer's products. Types of allowances offered to retailers include buying allowances, promotional or display allowances, and slotting allowances.

Buying Allowances A buying allowance is a deal or discount offered to resellers in the form of a price reduction on merchandise ordered during a fixed period. These discounts are often in the form of an **off-invoice allowance**, which means a certain per-case amount or percentage is deducted from the invoice. A buying allowance can also take the form of *free goods;* the reseller gets extra cases with the purchase of specific amounts (for example, one free case with every 10 cases purchased).

Exhibit 14-16 Example of WD-40's trade promotion and media support calendar.

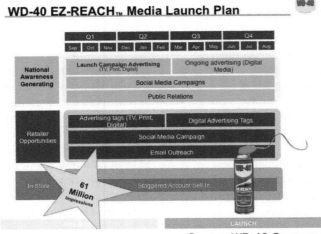

Source: WD-40 Company

Trade Promotional (Display) Allowances Manufacturers give retailers allowances or discounts for performing promotional or merchandising activities in support of their brands. These merchandising allowances are given for providing special displays away from the product's regular shelf position, running in-store promotional programs, or including the product in an ad. The allowances are also directed toward increasing the number of shelf facings and their location. One innovative eye-tracking study found that more shelf facings resulted in greater attention focused on the brand and subsequent sales.[41] The manufacturer generally has guidelines or a contract specifying the activity to be performed to qualify for the promotional allowance. The allowance is usually a fixed amount per case or a percentage deduction from the list price for merchandise ordered during the promotional period. One example is ConAgra's protein snack foods, which obtained significant signage and promotional support in Circle K convenience stores to go along with in-store sampling.[42]

Slotting Allowances Retailers expect a special allowance for agreeing to accept a new product. *Slotting allowances* (also called *stocking allowances, introductory allowances,* or *street money*) are fees retailers charge for providing a slot or position to accommodate the new product. Slotting fees range from a few hundred dollars per store to $50,000 or more for an entire retail chain. Manufacturers that want to get their products on the shelves nationally can face substantial slotting fees. Retailers charge slotting fees because of their power and the limited availability of shelf space in supermarkets relative to the large numbers of products introduced each year. Retailers justify the fees due to the costs of redesigning store shelves, entering product information into computers, finding warehouse space, and briefing store employees.[43] Large manufacturers with popular brands are less likely to pay slotting fees than smaller companies that lack leverage in negotiating with retailers.

A study examined the views of manufacturers, wholesalers, and grocery retailers regarding the use of slotting fees. Their findings suggest that slotting fees shift the risk of new product introductions from retailers to manufacturers and help apportion the supply and demand of new products. They also found that slotting fees lead to higher retail prices, are applied in a discriminatory fashion, and place small marketers at a disadvantage.[44]

Strengths of Trade Allowances Buying allowances are used for several reasons. They are easy to implement and are well accepted—and sometimes expected—by the trade. They are also an effective way to encourage resellers to buy the manufacturer's product, since they will want to take advantage of the discounts being offered during the allowance period. Manufacturers offer trade discounts expecting wholesalers and retailers to pass the price reduction through to consumers, resulting in greater purchases.

Promotional allowances provide brands that sell in retail stores the opportunity to have specialized displays to feature their product. Promotional allowances also permit a brand to obtain a favourable end-of-aisle location or another prominent place where high traffic occurs, thus ensuring greater exposure. Brands would like to reproduce the imagery from their commercials or any other advertising vehicle where brand recognition at the point of sale is required. Extensive and elaborate displays would also reinforce the positioning strategy of the brand and contribute to its overall brand development. Thus, retailers prefer to merchandise a brand that has a consistent and well thought out strategy so that they will not be stuck with inventory unsold due to a lack of in-store communication.

Limitations of Trade Allowances Marketers give retailers these trade allowances so that the savings will be passed through to consumers in the form of lower prices, but companies claim that only one-third of trade promotion discounts actually reach consumers because one-third are lost in inefficiencies and another one-third are pocketed by the trade. Moreover, marketers believe that the trade is taking advantage of their promotional deals and misusing promotional funds.

For example, retailers and wholesalers do **forward buying**, where they stock up on a product at the lower deal or off-invoice price and resell it to consumers after the marketer's promotional period ends. Another common practice is **diverting**, where a retailer or wholesaler takes advantage of the promotional deal and then sells the product purchased at the low price to a store outside its area or to an intermediary that resells it to other stores.

In addition to not passing discounts on to consumers, forward buying and diverting create other problems for manufacturers. They lead to huge swings in demand that cause production scheduling problems and leave manufacturers and retailers always building toward or drawing down from a promotional surge. Marketers also worry that the system leads to frequent price specials, so consumers learn to make purchases on the basis of what's on sale rather than developing any loyalty to their brands.

POINT-OF-PURCHASE DISPLAYS

Point-of-purchase (POP) displays are an important promotional tool because they can help advertisers obtain more effective in-store merchandising of products. In one sense, a display acts as a "medium" since it is an important method of transmitting an advertising-like message when consumers are making a purchase decision. We put *medium* in quotes because often displays do not appear to be typical media; in fact, however, a display shares similar characteristics with place-based media (discussed in Chapter 13). A display is also viewed as a sales promotion since the messages include a sales promotion and most require the participation of retailers and necessitate a payment from the advertiser that is often recorded as a trade promotion expense in the budget.

Figure 14-6 identifies different types of point-of-purchase displays used in different types of stores. **Exhibit 14-17** shows an award-winning POP display to promote the SeaKlear family of pool and spa treatments. The display holds 16 different pool and spa products and the unique octagonal shape allows for 360 degrees of display availability in a relatively small footprint. The display also has large graphic areas to educate consumers regarding specific uses and applications and help them make their purchase decisions.

Figure 14-6 Types of point-of-purchase displays

On-premise sign	Pre-assembled display	Display card	TV display
Window display	Display shipper	Shelf sign	LED board
Modular display rack	Wall display	Stand-up rack	End-of-aisle display

Exhibit 14-17 This award-winning point-of-purchase display assists in merchandising SeaKlear pool and spa treatments.

Source: SeaKlear

The Point of Purchase Advertising Institute (POPAI) is an organization serving marketers and retailers worldwide with research information and examples of successful display innovations. Its main study classifies purchases into four groups, as shown in **Figure 14-7**, with the following breakdown: specifically planned, 24 percent; generally planned, 15 percent; substitutes (i.e., brand switch), 6 percent; and unplanned, 55 percent. The top two reasons provided by respondents on why an unplanned purchase occurred were that they remembered they needed or wanted an item once in the store, and that they took advantage of a sale.[45] These results suggest the importance of displays as they prompt existing beliefs through recognition at the point of purchase.

Strengths of Point-of-Purchase Displays It is easy to see why advertisers use point-of-purchase displays extensively. The main purpose is to reach the target audience while they are making the brand choice, so naturally a message or promotion attempting to influence a decider appears imperative. Indeed, deterministic benefits can be communicated just prior to purchase as these benefits may become salient only during the final choice decision. Innovations in point-of-purchase options—such as video screens at cash registers—attempt to bring the emotion of television commercials to the store environment so that consumers feel the same way just prior to purchasing the product. Since consumers are in the process of shopping, point-of-sale media have a tremendous opportunity for attracting the attention of the target audience. In general, consumers are seeking additional information or sensory experience as they consider the product selection. Coverage objectives also can be achieved by distributing point-of-purchase displays across the country through retail chains. For example, a brand could have displays in virtually all grocery stores at the same time with placement agreed among personnel at a few head offices. A key strength of point-of-sale display is that it is communicating to virtually all people who are considering purchasing in a particular category except those going direct through the Internet or catalogues. It may be difficult to suggest that point-of-purchase displays are universally involving. However, it appears reasonable to suggest that if the target audience has not avoided a certain part of the store and also paid attention to a display, then the potential is strong that the relevant messages will resonate such that a sufficient amount of consideration will be given. And finally, the absolute cost and CPM are generally reasonable compared to other media options.

Limitations of Point-of-Purchase Displays Despite these strengths, point-of-purchase displays have limitations. One source of discontent for a consumer is that the shopping experience may be hindered by numerous promotional messages. Consumers have complete control over where they want to look in a store, how much time they prefer to stay

Figure 14-7 Classification of purchases for POPAI research

Specifically Planned	Purchases the shopper specifically identified by name in a pre-shopping interview and bought.
Generally Planned	Purchases that were referred to generically in a pre-shopping interview and bought on impulse.
Substitutes	Purchases that were specifically identified by name in a pre-shopping interview, but actual purchase reflected a substitute of brand or product.
Unplanned	Purchases that were not mentioned in the pre-shopping interview and bought on impulse.

in one area, and whether they want to look at any form of in-store communication. If an advertiser desires to be there, so does the competition. The clutter consumers feel while watching television or reading a magazine may be felt in the purchase environment. Processing of point-of-sale media requires a consumer's presence in the retail environment. So, except for circumstances where a consumer is entering an establishment repeatedly, the likelihood of an advertiser achieving sufficient frequency through this medium is quite limited. Finally, a marketer is reliant on the retailer, who may not install or set up the display correctly and also requires payment.

COOPERATIVE ADVERTISING

A trade promotion that has consumer effects like point-of-purchase display is **cooperative advertising**, where the cost of advertising is shared by more than one party. There are three types of cooperative advertising. Although the latter two are not exactly trade promotion, they involve the trade at times and are consistent with cooperative advertising.

The most common form of cooperative advertising is **vertical cooperative advertising**, in which a manufacturer pays for a portion of the advertising a retailer runs to promote the manufacturer's product and its availability in the retailer's place of business. Manufacturers generally share the cost of advertising run by the retailer on a percentage basis (usually 50/50) up to a certain limit. Major manufacturers threatened to withdraw this funding to retailers who discounted the manufacturer's brand too substantially. Fierce price competition led retailers to market well-known brands as discounted loss leaders, much to the dismay of the brand managers who felt it significantly cheapened the brand image.[46]

The amount of cooperative advertising the manufacturer pays for is usually based on a percentage of dollar purchases. If a retailer purchases $100,000 of product from a manufacturer, it may receive 3 percent, or $3,000, in cooperative advertising money. Large retail chains often combine their co-op budgets across all of their stores, which gives them a larger sum to work with and more media options.

Cooperative advertising can take several forms. Retailers may advertise a manufacturer's product in a newspaper ad or a flyer insert featuring a number of different products, and the individual manufacturers reimburse the retailer for their portion of the ad. Or the ad may be prepared by the manufacturer and placed in the local media by the retailer. Research supports the value of retail ads like these as advertised products are purchased in greater numbers and dollar amounts.[47]

Horizontal cooperative advertising is advertising sponsored in common by a group of retailers or other organizations providing products or services to the market. For example, automobile dealers who are located near one another often allocate some of their ad budgets to a cooperative advertising fund.

Ingredient-sponsored cooperative advertising is supported by raw materials manufacturers; its objective is to help establish end products that include the company's materials and/or ingredients. A technology company that uses ingredient-sponsored advertising is Qualcomm, which ran a brand-building campaign for its Snapdragon processor that powers smart phones and other mobile devices. The international campaign promoted the features and benefits of the Snapdragon processor and how it contributes to the performance of mobile devices (**Exhibit 14-18**).

CONTESTS AND INCENTIVES

Manufacturers may develop contests or special incentive programs to stimulate greater selling effort and support from reseller management or sales personnel. Contests or incentive programs can be directed toward managers who work for a wholesaler or distributor as well as toward store or department managers at the retail level. Manufacturers often sponsor contests for resellers and use prizes such as trips or valuable merchandise as rewards for meeting sales quotas or other goals.

Manufacturers devise contests or special incentives that are targeted to the sales personnel of the wholesalers, distributors/dealers, or retailers. These trade promotions are typically tied to product sales, new account placements, promotional programs, or merchandising efforts (e.g., displays). These salespeople are an important link in the distribution chain because they are familiar with the market, frequently in touch with the customer (whether it

Exhibit 14-18 Qualcomm uses ingredient-sponsored advertising for its Snapdragon processor.

NO WONDER YOUR PHONE HAS AWESOME POWER AND SPEED. IT'S GOT THE HEART OF A DRAGON.

At the heart of devices you love

Source: Qualcomm

Exhibit 14-19 The International CES is a popular trade show.

©Consumer Electronic Association

be another reseller or the ultimate consumer), and more numerous than the manufacturer's own sales organization. In sales contests, salespeople can win trips or valuable merchandise for meeting certain goals established by the manufacturer. The incentive programs may involve cash payments made directly to the retailer's or wholesaler's sales staff to encourage them to promote and sell a manufacturer's product. These payments are known as **push money** or *spiffs*. For example, an appliance manufacturer may pay a $25 spiff to retail sales personnel for selling a certain model or size.

While contests and incentive programs can generate reseller support, they can also be a source of conflict between retail sales personnel and management. Retailers want to maintain control over the selling activities of their sales staff. They don't want their salespeople devoting an undue amount of effort to trying to win a contest or receive incentives offered by the manufacturer, or becoming too aggressive in pushing products that serve their own interests instead of the product or model that is best for the customer.

SALES TRAINING PROGRAMS

Products sold at the retail level may require knowledgeable salespeople who provide consumers with information about the features and benefits of various brands and models (e.g., cosmetics, appliances, computers). Manufacturers provide assistance to retail salespeople through training sessions so that retail personnel can increase their knowledge of a product line and understand how to sell the manufacturer's product. A manufacturer's salesforce also provides sales training assistance to retail employees. The reps provide ongoing sales training as they come into contact with retail sales staff on a regular basis and can update them on changes in the product line. Sales reps often provide resellers with sales manuals, product brochures, reference manuals, videos, and product-use demonstrations. These selling aids are also presented to customers.

TRADE SHOWS

A forum where manufacturers display their products to current as well as prospective consumers and resellers is a **trade show**. Similar shows are also directed to consumers. According to the Center for Exhibition Industry Research, nearly 107 million people attend over 13,000 trade and consumer shows each year in the United States, Mexico, and Canada, and the number of exhibiting companies reached 1.9 million.[48] Trade shows are a major opportunity to display product lines and interact with customers. They are often attended by important management personnel from large retail chains as well as by distributors and other reseller representatives.

A number of promotional functions are performed at trade shows, including demonstrating products, identifying new prospects, gathering customer and competitive information, and even writing orders for a product. Trade shows are particularly valuable for introducing new products, because resellers are often looking for new merchandise to stock. Shows can also be a source of valuable leads to follow up on through sales calls or direct marketing. The social aspect of trade shows is also important. Companies use them to entertain key customers and to develop and maintain relationships with the trade. An academic study demonstrated that trade shows generate product awareness and interest and can have a measurable economic return.[49] The International Consumer Electronics Show (CES) is a forum for launching all sorts of technological products (**Exhibit 14-19**).

LO5 IMC Planning: Strategic Use of Sales Promotion

When properly planned and executed to work together, advertising and sales promotion provide a persuasive communication effect that is greater than the unique strengths of each promotional mix element operating independently. Successful integration of advertising and sales promotion requires decisions concerning the allocation of the budget to each area, the coordination of the ad and sales promotion creative themes, the brand equity implications of sales promotion, and the measurement of sales promotion effectiveness.

BUDGET ALLOCATION

What percentage of a firm's overall promotional budget should be allocated to advertising versus consumer and trade promotions? The answer may be found within the product life cycle due to different promotional objectives at each stage. Trial is the introductory stage objective requiring more sales promotion; brand positioning through differentiation is the growth stage objective requiring more advertising; and repeat purchasing is the maturity stage objective requiring reminder advertising for brand awareness and brand building sales promotions. Thereafter, periodic consumer sales promotions maintain consumer loyalty, attract new users, and protect against competition, and regular trade promotions maintain shelf space and accommodate retailers' demands for better margins. Some brands never move to the decline stage. In this situation, managers examine the competitive dynamics of new entrants or old foes who attempt to steal share, and allocate based on objectives designed to ward off threats. Longstanding brands remain strong by periodically encouraging new consumer cohorts to try the brand with an optimal allocation, and then retain them with an alternative ratio as new consumers remain loyal.

CREATIVE THEMES

To integrate the advertising and sales promotion programs successfully, the theme of consumer promotions should be tied in with the advertising and positioning theme wherever possible. Sales promotion tools should attempt to communicate a brand's unique attributes or benefits and to reinforce the sales message or campaign theme. In this way, the sales promotion effort contributes to the consumer franchise-building effort for the brand. A fun example of this is the promotion Frosted Flakes executes often during the playoffs as an official partner of the NHL since 2003. In a recent one in 2019, Kellogg's featured the iconic Tony the Tiger in its Gr-r-reatest Playoff Beard contest. Entrants took a selfie with a beard filter and entered online for a chance to win a trip to the Stanley Cup Finals.[50] TV support showed Tony with his pals as they watched a game and announced the contest details humorously. The creative continuity of the personality symbol and the lighthearted message appeal of the promotion made this promotion consistent with past Frosted Flakes messages.

Exhibit 14-20 Dove Men+Care coordinated IMC tools for its launch.

Source: Dove by Unilever

MEDIA SUPPORT

Media support for a sales promotion program should be coordinated with the media of the ad campaign since it is used to deliver sales promotion materials (e.g., coupon, contest entry, premium offer). It is also needed to inform consumers of a promotional offer as well as to create awareness and favourable attitudes toward the brand. By using advertising in conjunction with a sales promotion program, marketers achieve brand communication effects and increase their responsiveness to the promotion. Consumers are more likely to redeem a coupon or respond to a price discount for a brand they know. Using a promotion without prior or concurrent advertising can limit its effectiveness and risk damaging the brand's image. If consumers perceive the brand as being promotion dependent or of lesser quality, they are not likely to develop favourable attitudes and long-term loyalty. Dove's Men+Care launch relied on multiple IMC tools requiring media coordination. **Exhibit 14-20** shows how the brand combined a print ad message with three coupon offers to build communication effects and generate trial. This example required coordination between the sales promotion program managers and media planners, possibly from two different agencies.

BRAND EQUITY

The increasing use of sales promotion led to excessive frequency of the offers or overly valuable economic offers, with both leading to a loss of perceived value. Consumers became accustomed to purchasing a brand because of the promotion rather than basing their decision on a favourable attitude developed over time, and ultimately switched to another brand when the promotional incentive became unavailable. Thus, competitive situations with extensive sales promotion suggest that managers should consider balancing equity-building and non-equity-building promotions during the year. Marketers must consider both the short-term impact of a promotion and its long-term effect on the brand. The ease with which competitors can develop a retaliatory promotion and the likelihood of their doing so should also be considered. Marketers must be careful not to damage the brand franchise with sales promotions or to get the firm involved in a promotional battle that erodes the brand's profit margins and threatens its long-term existence.

One study examined whether price promotions affect pretrial evaluations of a brand.[51] The study found that offering a price promotion is more likely to lower a brand's evaluation when the brand has not been promoted previously compared to when it has been frequently promoted; that price promotions are used as a source of information about a brand to a greater extent when the evaluator is not an expert but does have product or industry knowledge; and that promotions are more likely to result in negative evaluations when they are uncommon in the industry. The findings suggest that marketers must be careful in the use of price promotions as they may inhibit trial of a brand in certain situations.

MEASURING SALES PROMOTION EFFECTIVENESS

The promotional planning framework introduced for advertising in earlier chapters and summarized in Chapter 5 is adapted in **Figure 14-8**. It is also based on past methods to evaluate sales promotion strategies on specific criteria.[52] The table can be applied by a manager considering a promotional program. For any of the sales promotion options listed, the manager decides which method of exposure is optimal, such as in-store, TV, Internet, or social media. In the Frosted Flakes example, Kellogg's executed the promotion online and communicated on TV. Managers choose the surrounding message strategy and tactics to ensure optimal processing of the brand message and the promotional offer. In the Men+Care example, the audience processes the warmth of the family image conveyed and evaluates the discounts offered in the coupon. Subsequently, the content of the Men+Care is expected to contribute to a positive attitude on the part of the decider to consider giving the product as a gift, thus reflecting a trial purchase.

The advertising research methods and measures discussed in Chapter 9 are applied to sales promotions. For example, pre- or post-surveys are used to assess brand awareness or brand attitude (i.e., attribute or benefit beliefs) associated with the sales promotion. Furthermore, assessment of attention, cognitive, and emotional responses of the promotional offer can also be measured with an appropriate method. From a behavioural standpoint, measurement of switching and loyalty is assessed with scanner data. Other aspects of behaviour are measured by counting the number of inquiries or coupon redemptions. Sales promotions communicated and executed online and within social media—such as contest entries or participation with premiums—are readily tracked. Tracking of commentary in social media provides guidance of attitudinal effects of the promotional offer and potential resulting equity effects upon the brand.

Figure 14-8 Framework for planning sales promotion

Sales Promotion	Exposure	Processing	Communication Effects	Behaviour
Sampling				
Coupons				
Premiums				
Promotional products				
Contest/sweepstakes				
Refund/rebates				
Bonus pack				
Price discount				
Events				

Learning Objectives Summary

LO1 **Explain the role of sales promotion in a company's integrated marketing communications program and examine why it is increasingly important.**

Sales promotion is an incentive and an acceleration tool offered as value to any person or organization within the overall marketing system, such as consumers and any trade members like wholesalers and retailers. Marketers allocate promotional dollars to sales promotion to influence purchasing behaviour. Reasons for this shift include the strategic importance of sales promotions, reaching a specific target audience, promotional sensitivity, declining brand loyalty, brand proliferation, short-term focus of managers and accountability of promotional managers, and power of retailers and the competition.

LO2 **Identify the objectives, strategy, and tactical components of a sales promotion plan.**

The objectives of sales promotion focus on brand behaviour such as trial, re-trial, and repeat purchases, or product category trial or re-trial. Sales promotions can be characterized as either consumer franchise-building (CFB) promotions or non-franchise-building (non-FB) promotions. The former contribute to the long-term development and reinforcement of brand identity and image; the latter accelerate the purchase process and generate immediate trial or repeat purchases. Sales promotions incentives can be immediate or delayed to achieve the above behavioural and communication objectives. Tactical considerations for sales promotion include the amount of the incentive, the timing of the promotion in terms of schedule and duration, and the distribution of the sales promotion.

LO3 **Describe consumer sales promotion strategy options and evaluate the factors to consider in using them.**

A number of consumer sales promotion techniques exist, including sampling, coupons, premiums, promotional products, contests/sweepstakes, refunds/rebates, bonus packs, price discounts, and event marketing. Promotional planners select any combination of these tools for their IMC plans to achieve trial and repeat purchasing objectives and execute them with appropriate tactics to reinforce brand communication effects. Each of these promotional tools has both strengths and limitations, so the selection of the right combination reinforces the direction of the plan to influence both customers and non-customers.

LO4 **Describe trade sales promotion strategy options and evaluate the factors to consider in using them.**

The chapter identified trade promotions including trade allowances, point-of-purchase displays, cooperative advertising, contests and incentives, sales training programs, and trade shows. These have different terminology and are similar to consumer sales promotion, but are intended for resellers who are in a similar buying process with more businesslike objectives instead of personal objectives. Strategic and tactical decisions for each sales promotion are as critical here as they are with consumer promotions.

LO5 **Apply key IMC issues related to sales promotion decisions.**

Advertising and sales promotion should be viewed as complementary tools. When planned and executed properly, advertising and sales promotion produce a strong communication and behavioural effect that is greater than the response generated from either promotional mix element alone. To accomplish this, marketers coordinate budgets, creative themes, media support, and target audience reaction. Extensive sales promotion can result in diminished brand equity when marketers become too dependent on the use of sales promotion techniques and sacrifice long-term brand position and image for short-term sales increases. Industries have experienced situations where competitors use promotions extensively and it becomes difficult for any single firm to cut back on promotion without risking a loss in sales. Overuse of sales promotion tools can lower profit margins and threaten the image and even the viability of a brand.

Review Questions

1. What are the differences between consumer and trade sales promotion? Discuss the role of each in a marketer's IMC program.

2. Discuss how sales promotion can be used as an acceleration tool to speed up the sales process and maximize sales volume.

3. Post-secondary educational institutions do not usually use sales promotions. Consider which ones could be used and identify the target audience in which they could be effective.

4. Explain why a brand might devote more of its budget to trade sales promotions than to consumer sales promotions.

5. Explain why it is important for sales promotion to contribute to brand equity. In what circumstances will brand equity enhancement not be a priority?

Applied Questions

1. Explain how the consumer sales promotions identified in **Figure 14-1** can be executed with Internet media.

2. What are the differences between consumer franchise-building and non-franchise-building promotions? Find an example of a promotional offer you believe contributes to the equity of a brand and explain why.

3. Phone service providers do not offer premiums all that often. Identify good ones for different brands.

4. Consider all the trade sales promotions that a sports equipment brand could use and explain how the promotions would be effective or ineffective for increasing sales.

5. Why would a brand use the same imagery from its online advertising at a marketing event?

Mental health
affects us all.

Together, we can all help end
the stigma around mental illness
with these 5 simple ways.

1. Language matters
2. Educate yourself
3. Be kind
4. Listen and ask
5. Talk about it

bell.ca/letstalk

CHAPTER FIFTEEN

Public Relations

LEARNING OBJECTIVES

LO1 Recognize the role of public relations in the promotional mix.

LO2 Explain how to compile a public relations plan.

LO3 Examine how public relations is generated through news media publicity and argue its strengths and limitations.

LO4 Illustrate how public relations is managed through corporate advertising.

LO5 Apply the ideas of public relations within the development of an IMC plan.

Bell Let's Talk Heals

Companies implemented corporate social responsibility (CSR) programs substantially over the past couple of decades. An Ipsos study found that half of all Canadians are "very interested" in causes supported by companies, with poverty and the environment ranked as most important. When asked to name one, the following recall results emerged: Tim Hortons Camp Day, 36 percent; McDonald's McHappy Day, 27 percent; Canadian Tire Jumpstart, 17 percent; Bell Let's Talk, 15 percent; and CIBC Run for the Cure, 10 percent. As this list indicates, a company's CSR program is identified with a specific brand name in addition to the corporate name.

The Bell Let's Talk mental health initiative, launched by Bell in 2010, supports mental health programs. The campaign's message centres on dispelling the stigma surrounding mental illness. Bell invites Canadians to talk about mental health by talking to or texting loved ones, with $0.05 going to the cause for every form of communication. Widespread media support for the cause includes TV, radio, print, in-store, out-of-home, digital, social, video testimonials, online (LetsTalk. Bell.ca), public relations via TV shows, and the Bell Let's Talk Day Special shown on TV. Messages feature notable celebrity spokespersons publicly sharing their personal stories.

In 2018 and 2019, video messages communicated the faces of people affected by mental health issues, revealing that the faces looked like all of us. The implicit message—that sharing one's experience with a loved one or friend is beneficial—signalled hope to remove the stigma surrounding mental illness. New community ambassadors joined the campaign, including comedian and actress Jessica Holmes, musician and author Florence K, and actress Véronique Bannon.

In terms of media, the program increased its use of digital and social media. For example, a Bell Let's Talk geo-filter on Snapchat let people share content and increased Bell's donation beyond the usual methods of call, text, or tweet using #BellLetsTalk on Twitter. This picked up on the success of the previous year where the hashtag was the most used in Canada for the whole year, and it was the most used in the world on Bell Let's Talk Day. The Bell Let's Talk website provided more information, facts on how the money helped people, and resources on how people can get help.

An important part of Bell Let's Talk is the post-secondary student campaign that takes place on campuses across the country. In partnership with educational institutions, hundreds of events occur each year to communicate about mental health, and a video featured a lot of different kinds of stories not seen in past messages. By 2019, total Bell funding reached over $100 million for Canadian mental health programs. According to the chair of Bell Let's Talk (quoted in one of the articles), 40 percent of Canadians participated, 67 percent of those aged 18–24 participated, and 80 percent of Canadians say they are more aware of mental heath issues since the start of the program.

Question:

1. Why is the Bell Let's Talk initiative so effective?

Public relations, publicity, and corporate advertising programs are integral parts of the overall promotional effort that are managed and coordinated with the other parts of the promotional mix. As the Bell Let's Talk example shows, these programs do not usually have specific objectives of product and service promotion, and often involve other methods of reaching their target audiences. Typically, these activities are designed to change attitudes toward an organization or an issue rather than promoting specific products or influencing purchase behaviour directly. However, aspects of these programs assist the marketing of products periodically for firms that adhere to this perspective of public relations. This chapter explores the domain of public relations, its related topic of publicity generated by news media, corporate advertising, the strengths and limitations of each, and the process by which they are planned and implemented.

LO1 Public Relations

What is public relations (PR)? How does it differ from other elements of marketing communication discussed thus far? Perhaps a good starting point is to define what the term *public relations* has traditionally meant, to introduce its new role, and to compare it to publicity.

TRADITIONAL VIEW OF PR

Public relations is a corporate communication program designed to enhance a company's reputation and/or earn public understanding and acceptance of a particular issue. In this definition, public relations requires a series of stages in management: the determination and evaluation of public attitudes, the identification of policies and procedures of an organization with a public interest, and the development and execution of a marketing communication program intended to influence the general public on the issue addressed. An effective public relations program continues over months or even years as it builds public trust between citizens and the organization.

This definition reveals that public relations involves marketing communication activities beyond advertising and promotion that are designed to influence consumers to buy a product. The PR program may also involve promotional program elements previously discussed but use them in a different way. For example, a press release may announce a new product launch or an organizational change, a special event may be organized to create goodwill in the community, and advertising may be used to state the firm's position on an issue. In addition, the *management* aspect means that public relations is not limited to business management but extends to other types of organizations, including government and non-profit institutions.

While the tools of public relations have changed significantly over the past two decades with digital media, practitioners believe the fundamental purpose remains consistent over time with the PR function being required to align corporate communications with the organization's goals. However, the digital media clutter and demand for timely messages puts pressure on PR professionals to deliver top-notch writing with visual storytelling. One avenue where this is especially important is the social media image and presence of the corporate leaders as their personal brand becomes the face of the corporate brand. The changes contribute to the significance of marketing and PR working in tandem.[1]

NEW ROLE OF PR

An increasing number of marketing-oriented companies established new responsibilities for public relations. PR takes on a broader (and more marketing-oriented) perspective, designed to promote the organization as well as its products and/or services. For example, McDonald's continued its efforts at eroding Tim Hortons' hold on the coffee market by sponsoring minor hockey, a long-time sponsorship activity of the leading coffee retailer in the quick service market.[2] Big events like the Rogers Cup allow brands to present their public image (**Exhibit 15-1**).

The way companies and organizations use public relations is viewed as a continuum. On one end of the continuum is the use of PR from a traditional perspective, where it is a non-marketing function whose primary responsibility is to maintain mutually beneficial relationships between the organization and its publics. In this case, customers or potential customers are only part of numerous publics—employees, investors, neighbours, special interest groups, and so on. Marketing and public relations are separate departments; if external agencies are being used, they are separate agencies. At the other end of the continuum, public relations is primarily a marketing

Exhibit 15-1 Rogers offered opportunity for public relations activities.

©ZUMA Press/Alamy Stock Photo

communications function. Public relations reports to marketing and all non-customer relationships are perceived as necessary only in a marketing context.[3] Thus, in these organizations, the PR becomes much closer to a marketing function than a traditional PR function.

Sponsorship is one PR activity that looks more like marketing at times. The Toronto International Film Festival (TIFF) is a non-profit organization and it retains lucrative and satisfied sponsors such as L'Oréal for four years and Visa for 18 years. A recent trend is innovative on-site brand activation to go along with the excitement generated by the movie stars (**Exhibit 15-2**). L'Oréal's beauty team prepped the celebrities, offered tips to fans on social media, and put together a video montage featuring people using the new product line. L'Oréal also set up a location where consumers could use the brand's virtual reality app to test out different make-up looks they could apply on themselves. L'Oréal claimed its sales grow noticeably after a TIFF sponsorship. Visa established the Visa Screening Room at the Elgin Theatre where fans who asked stars questions on Twitter could hear the stars' replies. The theatre featured the Infinite and Infinite Privilege private lounges for cardholders. It also enabled fans to have their photo taken, to be shown later on the giant on-location screen and shared by fans on social media. Finally, Visa opened a story-telling game in its Infinite Story Booth where fans could contribute. Visa expected that consumers would find the experiences unique and hoped the activities would contribute to greater acceptance of its new Infinite line of credit cards.[4]

Thus, in the new role of public relations, strong marketing and PR departments work closely together, blending their talents to provide the best overall image of the firm and its product or service offerings. In fact, marketing and public relations are complementary functions: each makes unique contributions that are mutually supportive to building and maintaining the many relationships essential for achieving organizational goals. This position is consistent with our perspective that public relations is an important part of the IMC process, contributing in its own way but also in a way consistent with marketing goals.

Exhibit 15-2 Prominent sponsors support the Toronto International Film Festival.

©ZUMA Press, Inc./Almay Stock Photo

PUBLICITY

Publicity is the generation of news about a person, good, service, idea, or organization that appears in broadcast or print media, and now on the Internet. In some instances, it seems that publicity and public relations occur at the same time and there is no substantial distinction. For example, Maple Leaf Foods faced the absolute worst experience in its long history when consumers perished or became severely ill after eating its contaminated meat products. In response, CEO Michael McCain took a strong leadership role in reassuring Canadians. Maple Leaf Foods used extensive public relations activities at varying stages of the identification and solution of the problem to address the situation such that consumers were exposed to both publicity (i.e., information coming from news media) and public relations (i.e., information coming from Maple Leaf Foods itself). McCain met with journalists on a regular basis at press conferences and acted as the main spokesperson in corporate advertising messages that communicated the actions the company had undertaken to prevent further problems. Maple Leaf's message reached some Canadians on TV while others viewed it on YouTube. By all accounts, Maple Leaf Foods regained its image as a strong Canadian brand.

In other instances, it seems that publicity is the end result or effect of a public relations effort. Because marketers seek total control over the time and place where information is released, they provide the news media with slick information packages. Print media publications and broadcasters receive material from brands with the intention of getting an editorial story written or communicated. In these cases, the news media presents and endorses the message and likely appears as a credible source in the eyes of consumers who then interpret the message as publicity through news media for the originating organization.

Given these scenarios, there are two significant characteristics that distinguish public relations and publicity: time frame and control. Publicity typically lasts for a short period of time. The communication effect of an article in the newspaper or a story on TV about an organization may last a few weeks. Positive or negative publicity communicated by consumers in social media can recede a few days later. In both cases, the long-term communication effects can be minimal. Publicity arises after an unanticipated positive or negative story emerges from an unexpected source not under the control of or paid by the organization. Organizations try to influence publicity with public relations directed to news media, but they ultimately do not control whether the story will be communicated or not, or its content. Public relations is a concerted program, with several exposures extending over a period of time such as a year, with the intention of establishing lasting communication effects. It is controlled by the firm and designed to provide positive information. Companies or brands use different tools in their public relations plan that we review in a later section.

Negative publicity arising within news media occurs when brands are accurately or inaccurately criticized, possibly by a special interest group. For example, Greenpeace brought to light P&G's use of palm oil in a product and linked the company to issues of deforestation. The consumer products giant immediately responded with a new deforestation policy. Observing this situation, one expert highlighted three steps brands should take: (1) prepare by examining the critic's public communication (e.g., newsletter, website, social media), (2) take corrective action by informing stakeholders with relevant facts, and (3) counterattack if necessary with opinion leaders (e.g., academics, scientists) and a customized message delivered with the most optimal media given the problem.[5]

On the other hand, positive publicity arises and brands take advantage of these unexpected events. For example, while pretending to be an employee working at the drive-through, one loyal Tim Hortons customer proposed to his fiancée, who was ordering. The slick video production placed in social media looked completely professional but the coffee chain's involvement amounted to giving permission for the recording to occur. And in case the romantic side of you was wondering, she said "Yes" with considerable Tim Hortons branding all around the happy couple![6]

In the age of digital communication and social media, organizations and their brands encounter both positive and negative publicity that arises within society. This publicity is not a result of a concerted public relations activity directed to news media, however such publicity may eventually become a news story. An example of this kind of publicity arises from customers' positive and negative experiences, and they decide to share their story with photos and videos in social media. At present, it is unclear whether this kind of online publicity has somewhat similar or much different strengths and limitations as publicity through news media. Certainly, if one believes what an online friend is claiming, it could be seen as credible as news media, or perhaps even more credible.

(LO2) Public Relations Plan

Public relations is an ongoing process requiring formalized policies, procedures, and plans for dealing with problems and taking advantage of opportunities. A PR plan is structured similarly to the plans of other IMC tools. It starts with a situation analysis and includes decisions with respect to target audiences, behavioural objectives, communication objectives, strategy, and tactics. Once the plan is written, marketers should ask themselves the questions in **Figure 15-1** to determine whether their PR plan is complete. These questions are similar to IMC planning guidelines of Chapter 1, but are shown in a PR context for greater specificity. In addition, the PR plan should be integrated into the overall marketing communication program. Given the broad nature of public relations, there are options for each part of the plan.

Figure 15-1 Ten questions for evaluating public relations plans

1. Does the plan reflect the company's business situation?
2. Has the PR program made use of research and background sources?
3. Does the PR program make relevant conclusions from the research?
4. Does the plan include full analysis of recent editorial coverage?
5. Do the PR people understand the brand's strengths and weaknesses?
6. Are the program objectives specific and measurable?
7. Does the program describe the PR activity and its benefits?
8. Does the program describe how its results will be measured?
9. Do the research, objectives, activities, and evaluations tie together?
10. Have PR and marketing communicated during development?

SITUATION ANALYSIS

Elements of the situation analysis from the marketing plan or IMC plan are also in the public relations plan. An additional key piece of information is a current assessment of people's attitudes toward the firm, its product or service, or specific issues beyond those directed at a product or service. Why are firms so concerned with the public's attitudes? One reason is that these attitudes may affect sales of the firm's products. Also, no one wants to be perceived as a bad citizen. Corporations exist in communities where their employees work and live. Negative attitudes carry over to employee morale and may result in a less-than-optimal working environment internally and in the community.

Organizations planning for PR typically survey public attitudes for a few reasons. First, initial public attitudes become the starting point in the development of programs designed to maintain favourable positions or change unfavourable ones. Second, these initial attitudes might signal a significant potential problem, which allows the firm to handle it proactively. Third, it will be much easier for the PR team to gain the support it needs to address this problem. Fourth and finally, optimal communication can occur if the firm understands a problem completely.

DETERMINE RELEVANT TARGET AUDIENCES

The target audiences for public relations efforts vary and, as we saw earlier, each will have unique behavioural and communication objectives. These audiences may be internal or external to the firm. **Internal audiences** are connected to the organization and include the employees of the firm, shareholders and investors, local community members, and suppliers and customers. **External audiences** are those people who are not closely connected with the organization (e.g., the public at large), and may include news media, educators, civic and business organizations, and governments. It may be necessary to communicate with both groups on an ongoing basis for a variety of reasons and it is likely that those who are not in the target audience will in fact receive the message, like we observe with product advertising.

Employees of the Firm Maintaining morale and showcasing the results of employees' efforts are prime objectives of a public relations program. Organizational newsletters, notices on intranet resources, mail/email, and annual reports are methods used to communicate with these groups. Personal methods of communicating may be as formal as an established grievance committee or as informal as an office party. Other social events such as corporate sports teams, picnics, or cause-related or community activities also create goodwill. Home Depot's employees readily supported the company's commitment to helping with youth homelessness with repair projects and development programs. In total, employees devoted 60,000 volunteer hours to 285 projects in one year.[7]

Shareholders and Investors An annual report like the one in **Exhibit 15-3** provides shareholders and investors with financial information regarding the firm. While this is one purpose, annual reports are also a communications channel for informing this audience about why the firm is or is not doing well, future plans, and other information that goes beyond numbers. In addition to current shareholders, potential investors, financial advisers, and lending institutions may be relevant target audiences for annual reports and other related corporate information to keep them abreast of new developments since they offer the potential for new sources of funding. By creating a favourable image and goodwill in the financial community, the firm makes itself attractive to potential share purchasers and investors, leading to investments for working capital and research and development. Other means of communication include meetings, video presentations, direct mail, and digital media.

Community Members People who live and work in the community where a firm is located or doing business are the target of public relations efforts. Such efforts may involve ads informing the

Exhibit 15-3 Annual reports serve a variety of purposes.

DIGITAL INDUSTRIAL

GE 2015 Annual Report

Source: General Electric

Exhibit 15-4 Boston Pizza's community-oriented efforts help children.

Hand-out/Boston Pizza International Inc./Newscom

community of activities that the organization supports, like cleaning up water supplies. Demonstrating to people that the organization is a good citizen with their welfare in mind may also be a reason for communicating to these groups. BMO supported local community soccer when it saw data indicating that the participation level for soccer is 33 percent, double the rate for hockey. The growth of soccer in this country, the link between the Canadians who play soccer and BMO customers, and the fact that the bank is present in most communities motivated BMO to devote 20 percent of its corporate marketing to soccer activities, with 40 percent directed toward sponsorship.[8] For over two decades, Boston Pizza has celebrated Valentine's Day by selling heart-shaped pizza (**Exhibit 15-4**) with proceeds going to worthy causes. Currently, the proceeds go to Boston Pizza Foundation Future Prospects, which donates funds to organizations like Big Brothers Big Sisters, which offers mentoring programs and whose members act as strong role models for children.[9]

Suppliers and Customers An organization wishes to maintain *goodwill* with its suppliers as well as its consuming public. Consumers likely demonstrate loyalty with a company that is socially conscious. For example, "Extraordinary, Authentic Nourishment for All" expressed Campbell Canada's aim to help people alleviate hunger, prepare better meals, and eat nutritious food. The company worked with food banks and donated 1 million pounds of food each year and agreed to provide additional funds, supplies, and personnel support in the future. A new, ambitious undertaking resulted in Campbell's product, Nourish, a complete meal in an easy-open can requiring no heating or water for preparation, and suitable for food banks and disaster relief situations. The product features a protein-rich grain developed by federal government scientists and is the result of committed Campbell's employees who wanted the company to do more for hunger. Campbell's placed ads in multiple media and used public relations to encourage Canadians to participate in the cause by sharing on Facebook, tweeting on Twitter, or watching "The Story of Nourish From Campbell Canada" on YouTube, with each step leading to a donation of one can of Nourish. After five weeks, the campaign achieved a total of 85,000 additional cans donated. Campbell's placed additional funds into the food system with each can sold to consumers, who were also encouraged to buy and donate to food banks.[10]

News Media A critical external audience is the news media, which determine what is read in a newspaper or seen on TV. News media should be informed of a firm's actions because of their power and influence over readers and viewers. Companies issue press releases and communicate to news media through press conferences, interviews, and exclusives. The news media are generally receptive to such information so long as it is handled professionally; reporters are always interested in good stories. Tesla relied on communicating only with news media for consumers to receive news stories about the electric car company for many years as it grew from a startup to selling 25,000 cars globally. One approach included a tour across the United States to feature its network of charging stations, thinking news media would feature the story. Executives expected that regular advertising would be warranted in future as sales grew.[11]

Educators A number of organizations provide educators with information regarding their activities. For example, the Internet site for the Canadian Marketing Association has a very useful public affairs section for marketing and advertising professors, in addition to valuable information for the general public. As noted in the media chapters, Internet sites of many of the media organizations provide resources. Companies like McGraw-Hill (which publishes this text) offer seminars and webcasts to professors regarding interesting trends in education. Activities such as these foster goodwill as well as provide exposure for their mission.

Civic and Business Organizations Local non-profit civic organizations serve as gatekeepers of information. Companies' financial contributions to these groups, speeches at organization functions, and sponsorship are all designed to create goodwill. Corporate executives' service on the boards of non-profit organizations also generates positive public relations. Home Depot's Orange Door Project enlisted the assistance of numerous community groups with expertise on the needs of homeless youth. Home Depot is significantly involved with Volunteer Canada.

Governments Public relations activities attempt to influence government bodies directly at local, provincial, and national levels. Successful lobbying may mean success for a product, such as seen recently for cannabis. Alternatively, regulations detrimental to a firm may require additional financial costs or result in weaker sales. The federal government interacts with food organizations as part of Health Canada's Healthy Eating Strategy. Many of these meetings are initiated by stakeholders who may be affected by proposed government initiatives. For example, organizations met to discuss concerns with the new food guide.[12]

BEHAVIOURAL OBJECTIVES

The framework for behavioural objectives discussed in Chapter 5 is applicable for public relations. Recall that behavioural objectives are trial purchase, repeat purchase, shopping, or consumption. No matter what target audiences are selected in the prior step, an astute marketer will know that it is important to understand the type of behaviour desired as a result of the communication. The idea of a purchase seems incongruous for public relations situations, so the marketer views the target audience's behaviour in other ways to define the objective.

Various PR activities ask citizens to participate by donating money, so a first donation is a "trial purchase" and subsequent donations in following years represent a "repeat purchase." Other PR activities request citizen involvement through volunteering or a related behaviour. While this does not appear to be shopping or consumption, it is akin to these objectives as they are behaviourally oriented but do not involve a financial commitment via donation. The Bell Let's Talk campaign encourages multiple behaviours, including the use of one's phone to make the donation happen. The vast number of possible PR activities suggest managers apply the general framework of behavioural objectives put forth in Chapter 5. Examples shown in this chapter represent insightful suggestions for interpretation.

COMMUNICATION OBJECTIVES

The communication objectives of Chapter 5 can similarly be used for public relations. Communication objectives include category need, brand awareness, brand attitude, and purchase intention. Each of these can be the focus of the public relations plan, although slight modifications are needed. For example, the "brand" may in fact be the corporation itself or a new product that is talked about in a press release. In addition, the notion of a "category" has to be adjusted. Some target audiences want to be affiliated with "good corporate citizens" that are responsible to the community, the environment, or another issue. Often, the "category" will be related to the particular topic or the public relations message content.

Organizations support social causes because the exposure ensures additional awareness for future recall and recognition, and the causes portray the organization favourably and support the beliefs of the owner and employees. For example, Planet Fitness's Judgement Free Generation program tries to alleviate bullying and judgment faced by youth (**Exhibit 15-5**). One recent initiative raised money for Boys and Girls Clubs with custom Snapchat geo-filters that operated when in one of the 26 Canadian locations. The filter communicated the gym's positive judgment-free message and prompted the call to action for a donation.[13]

We started off by highlighting the importance of existing attitudes of the target audiences. Clearly, then, the public relations plan should have a specific section that outlines the attitude change or modification desired. It should also illustrate the key motives addressed and what attributes or benefits of the firm or product the message should focus on. Automobile firms are good examples of

Exhibit 15-5 Planet Fitness is committed to a social cause of no judgment.

©Bernard Weil/Toronto Star via Getty Images

where positive publicity via news media is desired and encouraged. New product launches include media releases and feature interviews for articles appearing in the car section, a weekly feature in national and most large daily newspapers. Further positive press occurs with trade shows that occur in major cities, which typically get coverage resulting in framing initial consumer attitudes about a vehicle model.[14]

STRATEGY

The strategy decisions for public relations are twofold, as we saw with advertising: message and media. The primary message decisions concern the degree to which the message will have a marketing or corporation focus, and the creative associated with the message. We will briefly describe issues related to this decision in this section. Like with advertising, there are a number of options to disseminate the message—news media, advertising media, and events. We will discuss these in more detail in the next major section.

Message Content Public relations activities designed to support marketing objectives are referred to as **marketing public relations (MPR)** functions.[15] Marketing objectives that may be aided by public relations activities include raising awareness, informing and educating, gaining understanding, building trust, giving consumers a reason to buy, and generating consumer acceptance. These points are consistent with the behavioural and communications objective of our framework. Marketing public relations can be used effectively in the following ways: building marketplace excitement before advertising media breaks, creating news about a new advertising or promotional campaign, introducing a product with little or no advertising, providing information to influential opinion leaders, defending products at risk with a message of reassurance, and constructively promoting a product.

IKEA Canada's innovative activities successfully increase media exposure and exemplify marketing public relations. In fact, a key source of zany ideas originated from its consumer surveys—shopping at IKEA was seen as a bit stressful for couples so it hosted relationship seminars on Valentine's Day. IKEA's Relax event noted the fact that Canadians found relaxing to be more naughty than sex. This prompted IKEA to issue instructions for making a restful home along with an "IKEA Adrenaline Index" on the website featuring humorous questions to assess people's stress levels. Store openings and catalogue launches both host ambitious events to ensure the news media cover the story. IKEA sees the value of these activities and invests heavily, with a 50 percent budget increase and each event receiving a $500,000 allotment.[16]

The historical role of public relations is one of communicating a favourable image of the corporation as a whole. The domain of this image or reputation management concerns every facet of how the organization interacts with its social, economic, political, and charitable constituents, in addition to the general public locally, nationally, and internationally. Given the two broad directions of the actual message, marketing versus corporate, an organization has to decide the relative degree of the message's impact over the course of a year or even longer, as public relations tends to have a lasting communication effect. Too much of a focus in either direction and the organization loses the opportunity to communicate fully. As concluded earlier, a balance between using public relations for marketing purposes and corporate purposes appears to be a viable approach for many organizations.

Message Creativity We will discuss the tools for public relations shortly; however, in deciding what message to communicate, the marketer is faced with the decision as to whether the creative strategy of advertising or other IMC tools should be adopted for public relations. On the one hand, there is the argument that all communications should have a common look and feel to them. To counter this, one could argue that unique target audiences with a specific message should have an appropriate associated creative.

Message Delivery In the course of defining public relations and publicity, and explaining the content of a public relations plan, we have generally described two mechanisms for the delivery of the message. News media outlets are available and they have the choice of publishing or not publishing the materials that organizations submit for their consideration. Alternatively, organizations can turn to other options where they control the dissemination of the message through different types of corporate advertising opportunities in which the organization is responsible for the costs, much like regular product advertising we have covered thus far.

During Toyota's major recall, the U.S. division halted sales of the affected models and its advertising response to the negative publicity focused on its reputation for quality. The managing director for Toyota Canada released a four-minute online video that clarified the situation in Canada. Since the problem of the gas pedal sticking affected only one Canadian model, the extensiveness of the problem was not as severe. However, Toyota Canada offered a "voluntary safety improvement campaign," where it replaced the parts on models recalled only in the United States even though the parts on the Canadian versions were manufactured with different materials and would not cause problems. Toyota Canada executives appeared on television news shows. Extensive communication occurred on the company's website, and Toyota directly contacted all owners to explain the solution and how it planned to resolve the problem (**Exhibit 15-6**).[17]

TACTICS

The choice of news media or corporate advertising dictates the types of tactics employed. When using news media, a marketer would need to know how to make a media presentation, whom to contact, how to issue a press release, and what to know about each medium addressed, including TV, radio, newspapers, magazines, and direct-response advertising. In addition, decisions have to be made regarding alternative media such as news conferences, seminars, events, and personal letters, along with insights on how to deal with government and other legislative bodies. Because this information is too extensive to include as a single chapter in this text, we suggest students peruse additional resources for further insight.

Exhibit 15-6 Toyota's brand remains strong after handling its PR challenge.

©JuliusKielaitis/Shutterstock

For corporate advertising, numerous considerations have been addressed in the advertising message chapters (Chapters 7 and 8) and the media chapters (Chapters 10 to 13). We can see an application of this with a recent effort by McDonald's, which publicly emphasized its commitment to Ronald McDonald House Charities (RMHC) Canada to increase people's knowledge of the charity's mission and inspire greater donations. The creative showed how Ronald McDonald Houses provided a place for families to stay while their children received treatment. The storyline showed the point of view of each parent and the child with emotional scenes that evoked heightened empathy. Media included TV, cinema, print, radio, out-of-home and in-store. The combination of paid and donated media yielded 13 million impressions. Both measures improved with a 59 percent lift in understanding and a 72 percent lift in donations.[18]

PUBLIC RELATIONS EFFECTIVENESS

As with the other promotional program elements, it is important to evaluate the effectiveness of the public relations efforts. In addition to determining the contribution of this program element to attaining communications objectives, the evaluation tells management how to assess what has been achieved through public relations activities, measure public relations achievements quantitatively, and judge the quality of public relations achievements and activities.

In measuring the effectiveness of PR, one author suggests three approaches: (1) media content analysis that systematically and objectively identifies the messages appearing in news media and analyzes the content to determine trends and perceptions relevant to the product or brand, (2) survey research that quantitatively assesses consumers' attitudes toward the product or brand, and (3) marketing mix modelling that draws data from multiple sources and integrates them to provide insight into the process.[19] **Figure 15-2** summarizes a number of exposure measures that may be used to assess the effects of PR programs through news media that are consistent with the first step.

Others suggest comprehensive approaches like we have seen with advertising. Walter Lindenmann says three levels of measures are involved: (1) the basic, which measures the actual PR activities undertaken; (2) the intermediate, which

Figure 15-2 Criteria for measuring the effectiveness of PR

A system for measuring the effectiveness of the public relations program has been developed by Lotus HAL. The criteria used in the evaluation process follow:

1. Total number of impressions over time
2. Total number of impressions on the target audience
3. Total number of impressions on specific target audiences
4. Percentage of positive articles over time
5. Percentage of negative articles over time
6. Ratio of positive to negative articles
7. Percentage of positive/negative articles by subject
8. Percentage of positive/negative articles by publication or reporter
9. Percentage of positive/negative articles by target audience

measures audience reception and understanding of the message; and (3) the advanced, which measures the perceptual and behavioural changes that result.[20] As a reminder, this approach is entirely consistent with the exposure, processing, and communications effects model described in Chapter 4. Finally, from another point of view regarding effectiveness, Home Depot did not publicize its Orange Door Project beyond in-store displays and its Internet site, and viewed effectiveness in terms of how well it contributed to eradicating the homelessness problem.

LO3 News Media Publicity

In this section, we discuss how organizations achieve public relations communication objectives through publicity generated through news media. This *news media publicity* is publicity that the firm attempts to control by influencing the news media to report an organization's story to the public. Note that publicity occurs in social media by individuals or non–news media organizations, and companies may try to influence communication in social media, but this discussion concerns publicity through legitimate news media with journalistic standards. In this section, we review ways to reach news media and consider the strengths and limitations of this option. When considering the significance of this assessment, keep in mind that consumers receive the message through all media, which produces varying effects.

MEDIA OPTIONS

A number of options are available for communicating with the news media, including press releases, press conferences, exclusives, and interviews. Of course, this effort could be for naught if the news media decides not to report the information and the message would not reach the intended target audience.

Press Releases One of the most important public entities is the press, and information delivered must be factual, true, and of interest to the medium as well as to its audience. The source of the **press release** can do certain things to improve the likelihood that the "news" will be disseminated, such as ensuring that it reaches the right target audience, making it interesting, and making it easy to pass along. The information in a press release won't be used unless it is of interest to the users of the medium it is sent to, so financial institutions should issue press releases to business trade media and to the editor of the business section of a general-interest newspaper, for example. Press releases are typically a simple one-page text summary of the story a company wishes to be published in news media, along with background and contact information. Digital transmission of these includes a photo and links to other digital resources.

Additional information and presentation material may accompany the press release, making the whole presentation appear to be a complete ad campaign to influence news media. Companies release studies and will provide copies of the report and supporting links to associated data. They may also provide collateral material in both print and digital formats with video and still images. For example, Fairmont Hotels owns many historic properties and views this as an important stewardship. Fairmont released a study indicating the value travellers place on visiting luxury accommodations and its responsibility in maintaining the historical authenticity of its properties. **Exhibit 15-7** shows the cover of the document illustrating the classic architecture. The digital press release included a standard text summary, a short video clip, stunning photos, and other useful information supporting Fairmont's stewardship positioning.[21]

Exhibit 15-7 Fairmont publicly acknowledges its responsibility regarding its historic properties.

©FRHI Hotels & Resorts

Press Conferences We are all familiar with **press conferences** held by political figures. While used less often by organizations and corporations, this delivery can be very effective as scenes of corporate spokespeople may be viewed on television or online. The topic must be of major interest to a specific group before it is likely to gain coverage. Companies call press conferences when they have significant news to announce, such as the introduction of a new product. For example, Uber invited journalists to its Toronto office to describe its Express Pool option for riders to share an Uber with a stranger going in the same direction.[22] Locally, community events, public services, and the like may receive coverage. Professional sports teams use this tool daily to communicate news that interests fans. The development of technology permits remote delivery of press conferences where reporters receive the presentation and participate in the follow-up question and answer session.

Exclusives Although most public relations efforts seek a variety of channels for distribution, an alternative strategy is to offer one particular medium exclusive rights to the story if that medium reaches a substantial number of people in the target audience. Offering an **exclusive** may enhance the likelihood of acceptance, and sometimes the media actually use these exclusives to promote themselves.

Interviews Interviews occur on a variety of news or information shows. Usually, someone will raise specific questions and a spokesperson provided by the firm will answer them. Often, the president or owner will give interviews when there is important news about the firm.

STRENGTHS OF NEWS MEDIA PUBLICITY

Credibility Public relations communication through news media publicity is not perceived in the same light as advertising. Consumers understand that most advertising is directly paid for by the sponsoring organization. Obviously exceptions occur, such as public service announcements heard on the radio, for example. The fact that news media are not compensated for providing the information may lead receivers to consider the information more truthful and credible. For example, an article in a newspaper or magazine discussing the virtues of ibuprofen may be perceived as much more credible than an ad for a particular brand of ibuprofen. And while firms present the media with news releases or press kits and incur a cost, consumers generally perceive the news media source to be reasonably trustworthy with its reporting and journalistic expertise.

Endorsement Information from news media publicity may be perceived as an endorsement by the media vehicle in which it appeared. Automotive awards presented in magazines such as *Motor Trend* carry clout with potential car buyers, and car companies often advertise their achievements. A number of auto manufacturers advertised their high customer satisfaction ratings reported by J.D. Power & Associates, an independent research firm specializing in satisfaction research. Taken together, the credibility and endorsement effects constitute a significantly positive media image.

Cost In both absolute and relative terms, the cost of news media publicity is very low, especially when the possible effects are considered. While a firm can employ public relations agencies and spend millions of dollars, for smaller companies, this form of communication may be the most affordable alternative available. Public relations programs require little more than the time and expenses associated with putting the program together and getting it distributed, yet they still accomplish their objectives.

Avoidance of Clutter Because they are typically perceived as news items, news media publicity messages are not subject to the clutter of ads. A story regarding a new product introduction or breakthrough is treated as a news item and is likely to receive attention.

Reach Specific Audiences Because certain products appeal only to small market segments, it is not feasible to implement advertising and/or promotions to reach them. If the firm does not have the financial capabilities for promotional expenditures, the best way to communicate to these groups is through news media publicity.

Image Building Effective public relations helps to develop a positive image for the organization. The examples discussed thus far have indicated strong image-building capabilities with proactive public relations. News about a product may in itself serve as the subject of an ad.

Frequency Potential Another strength is the frequency of exposure it generates. For example, a successful public relations activity could generate exposure in multiple media (i.e., broadcast, print, Internet).

LIMITATIONS OF NEWS MEDIA PUBLICITY

Brand/Corporate Identification Perhaps the major disadvantage is the potential for not completing the communications process. While these messages break through the clutter of advertising messages, the receiver may not make the connection to the brand or corporate source.

Inconsistent Message News media publicity may also misfire through mismanagement and a lack of coordination with the marketing department. When marketing and PR departments operate independently, there is potential for inconsistent communications or redundancies in efforts.

Timing Timing of news media publicity is not always completely under the control of the marketer. Unless the press thinks the information has very high news value, the timing of the exposure of the press release content to the public is entirely up to the media—if it gets released at all. Thus, the information may be released earlier than desired or too late to achieve communication effects.

Accuracy The information contained in a press release can get lost in translation—that is, it is not always reported the way the provider wishes it to be. As a result, inaccurate information, omissions, or other errors may result.

IMC Perspective 15-1 tracks the publicity surrounding Tim Hortons and summarizes the corporate and marketing strategies announced and the public relations activities the brand responded with during 2018.

IMC PERSPECTIVE 15-1

TIM'S PUBLICITY

In Ontario, 2018 started off with an increase in the minimum wage and some Tim Hortons franchisees adjusted their employee benefits to address the additional costs. News media picked up the story after receiving tips from employees, and protests in front of stores ensued. A statement from the ownership, Restaurant Brands International (RBI), stated, "Team members should never be used to further an agenda or be treated as just an expense." It also pointed out that the issue pertained to a "reckless

©Kristoffer Tripplaar/Alamy Stock Photo

few" franchise owners. And who were these few? That is difficult to answer. But in March 2017, dissatisfied franchisees set up the Great White North Franchisee Association (GWNFA) to address issues with RBI and its owner, Brazil-based 3G Capital. The primary concern centred on a misuse of advertising money franchisees pay to the owner. In addition, GWNFA complained that RBI interfered with the establishment of the association. For both, the GWNFA filed a lawsuit. Other issues focused on how 3G implemented cost-saving measures, a strategy 3G used in the past.

In March, RBI's recently hired president had a mission to improve relations with franchisees and announced a $700 million investment to modernize half of its 3,900 Canadian stores. The president cited that the consumer and competitive situation warranted the change to create a more inviting and comfortable environment and to prepare the stores for future digital transformation. Promising results emerged from 10 test stores and the president believed the new design would attract more customers who would stay longer and spend more. GWNFA responded immediately by criticizing the makeover plans as being too costly and not worth the investment due to high drive-through sales. Ipsos's annual "most influential brands" list placed Tim Hortons out of the top 10, where it had been for the past six years.

In May, the president visited with franchise owners across the country and conceded that the company would communicate better in future, but expressed concern that information about company operations became public with many news stories. The meetings communicated the plans for the redesign, an app, and a new ad campaign, all to enhance the customer experience. However, by June, GWNFA sent a strong letter to the president on behalf of one owner who stood to lose their franchise licence. Publicly, GWNFA conceded that both sides had made mistakes during the conflict, and said it still believed in the Tim Hortons brand and wanted to find a resolution. However, RBI preferred to work with the established franchisee board, in existence since 1983, rather than the newly formed GWNFA. Meanwhile, a U.S. version of GWNFA representing hundreds of franchisees filed a lawsuit against RBI for price gouging and equity theft.

In August, RBI reiterated its view that the advisory board was the only legitimate body to discuss franchisee issues, and the advisory board also refused to acknowledge GWNFA as a recognized association. Tim Hortons announced all-day breakfast and a new loyalty program to boost sales, which had been stagnant. In September, GWNFA stepped up its pressure by citing a second franchisee who had had their licence terminated, and RBI continued to work with the advisory board only. In October, an Ontario Superior Court struck down some of GWNFA's claims in the lawsuit. In November, Tim Hortons announced a new ad campaign designed by Zulu Alpha Kilo to tell the stories of customers, much like the brand did 20 years ago. According to RBI, sharing customer stories is what made the brand strong in the first place.

Question:

1. Did Tim Hortons handle this publicity with the right public relations activities?

 # Corporate Advertising

We use the term **corporate advertising** for marketing communication implemented for the direct benefit of the corporation rather than its products. This approach is selected since it achieves corporate communication objectives, and it is used instead of media publicity since the firm exerts complete control over the message delivery rather than relying on news media acceptance for publicity to occur. Marketers seek attainment of corporate communication objectives by implementing corporate image advertising, cause-related advertising, and sponsorship. Cause-related advertising and sponsorship also occur at the product level, so the corporate/product-level distinction is murky. We cover these three topics in this section, but first we look at the purpose of corporate advertising, namely the management of corporate reputation.

CORPORATE REPUTATION

Earlier in this text we suggested that the communications framework described for advertising is applied to other communication tools, and previously in this chapter we highlighted how it is applied for public relations. We suggest five steps in applying this to corporate advertising to manage corporate reputation. (1) Review the situation in terms of corporate business objectives, competitive positioning, and the desired corporate reputation outcome. (2) Assess current reputation attribute beliefs held by each key stakeholder audience. (3) Identify the target audiences from the stakeholders evaluated, and derive audience-specific behavioural and attitudinal objectives and audience-specific corporate positioning attributes. (4) Decide which corporate reputation-management program will achieve the objective for each audience. (5) Implement reputation-management programs and establish an ongoing plan to measure and monitor corporate reputation.

Figure 15-3 The top 10 companies in the 2019 Leger Most Admired Company Survey

Rank	Company
1	Canadian Tire
2	Google
3	Dollarama
4	Shoppers Drug Mart
5	Sony
6	Kellogg's
7	Microsoft
8	Amazon
9	Samsung
10	Costco Wholesale

©Leger

Exhibit 15-8 Canadian Tire is the most admired company in a 2019 survey.

©kevin brine/Shutterstock

We highlight the issue of *corporate reputation,* a term that is used in public relations to convey the idea of corporate image, since a key outcome of corporate advertising is to influence overall perceptions of the organization. Clearly, the notion of corporate reputation is attitudinal, thus indicating that the general framework suggested in this text can be applied to all IMC tools. Furthermore, all methods described in Chapter 9 (e.g., focus groups, interviews, surveys) are readily applied for measuring corporate advertising effectiveness. News organizations publish polls that ask Canadians their opinion about corporations. **Figure 15-3** summarizes the findings from the 2019 Most Admired Company Survey by the research firm Leger.[23] Retailer Canadian Tire (**Exhibit 15-8**) jumped past Google after the digital giant held the number one position for a few years.

Exhibit 15-9 Toyota uses image advertising.

TODAY
Thinking green

TOMORROW
Planning for blue

TOYOTA
toyota.com/future

Can today's environmental thinking inspire tomorrow's technology? Toyota believes so. Since its launch, the Prius has earned the love of millions of forward-thinking drivers. We estimate our hybrid technology has saved a billion gallons of gas and lowered CO_2 emissions by billions of pounds? It's also paving the way for the next generation of environmental vehicles. Like cars charged at home. Or cars that will run solely on electricity, or consume hydrogen and emit only water. Because when it comes to thinking green, the sky's the limit.

©The Advertising Archives

CORPORATE IMAGE ADVERTISING

One form of corporate advertising is devoted to promoting the organization's overall image. **Corporate image advertising** may accomplish a number of objectives by creating or maintaining an image for the company brand through positioning ads or advocacy ads that specify a firm's perspective on an issue.

Positioning Ads Firms, like products, need to establish a position in the marketplace, and corporate image advertising activities are one way to accomplish this objective. A well positioned product is much more likely to achieve success than is one with a vague image or none at all. The same holds true of the firm. Companies with a strong positive corporate image have an advantage over competitors that may be enhanced when they promote any aspect of their organization or products. As shown in **Exhibit 15-9**, ads are often designed to create an image of the firm in the public mind. The exhibit shows how Toyota is attempting to create an image of itself as an innovator and leader in responsible car manufacturing by explaining how its vehicles emit less carbon dioxide.

Advocacy Ads Firms take positions on social, business, or environmental issues that influence their image and the public's perception. Such **advocacy advertising** is concerned with propagating ideas and elucidating controversial social issues of public importance in a manner that supports the interests of the sponsor. Such messages indirectly promote an image for the company's brand by adopting a position on a particular issue. The ads may be sponsored by a firm or by a trade association and are designed to tell the audience how the firm operates or management's position on the issue. Advocacy ads address the firm's negative publicity and the firm's inability to place a message through public relations channels. They are also used if the firm just wants ideas to be accepted or to have society understand its concerns. Renewable energy producers like Samsung devote a portion of their Internet site to communicating the environmental advantages of wind turbines to fulfill future energy needs. The rationale is to build an understanding of the potential benefits and likely to thwart the efforts of protesters who have health, safety, and economic criticisms (**Exhibit 15-10**).

CAUSE-RELATED ADVERTISING

A method of image building is **cause-related marketing**, in which companies link with charities or non-profit organizations as contributing sponsors. The company benefits from favourable publicity, while the recipient receives much-needed funds or in-kind support. Companies also communicate their involvement, giving rise to the idea of **cause-related advertising**.

A related idea but with a different focus is **corporate social responsibility,** defined as the broad voluntary activities undertaken by a company to operate in an economically, socially, and environmentally sustainable manner. Mountain Equipment Co-Op (**Exhibit 15-11**) is a Canadian leader with social and environmental accountability communicated on its Internet site regarding its products, production, fair trade, materials, and environment. MEC is recognized for its commitment by being the most reputable brand for CSR.[24]

Exhibit 15-10 Citizens protest the development of wind turbines, citing numerous concerns.

©igor kisselev/Shutterstock

Cause-related marketing activities historically took a variety of forms: making outright donations to a non-profit cause, having companies volunteer for the cause, donating materials or supplies, or running public service announcements. Research found that 80 percent of Canadians engage with a cause-related campaign; the same number say they would switch to another brand due to its cause-related activity presuming price and quality parity; and 60 percent want to hear about the cause-related marketing activities through periodic ads.[25] Accordingly, brands look for unique opportunities to facilitate the communication process effectively and efficiently. For example, in 2018, Manulife took over from Becel as the title sponsor of the Heart & Stroke Foundation fundraising activity Ride for Heart. According to the VP of philanthropy and sponsorship, Manulife planned to align the company with healthy living initiatives. Others included Participaction Canada and Montreal's Bixi bike-share program.[26]

Companies become involved in causes that reinforce their brand or corporate mandate by establishing a worthy cause rather than working with an existing organization. For example, an international chocolate brand established the Cadbury's Cocoa Partnership, a 10-year, $80 million program to help cocoa farmers in countries where its beans are purchased. The Canadian division launched a Bicycle Factory program to send bicycles to Ghana, allowing children to travel to school (**Exhibit 15-12**). Cadbury featured promotional activities designed to get Canadian consumers involved; a website allowed consumers to enter the code on its package to "buy" one part for a bike.[27] A later continuation of the program included a light unit that generated its power from the school trips, allowing students to travel and then study in the evening at home where no electricity existed.[28] By 2018, the Bicycle Factory celebrated its 10th anniversary having delivered 30,000 bicycles. Some aspects of the program became refreshed each year, but the essence of it remained consistent because consumers loved it so much.[29]

Exhibit 15-11 MEC is a Canadian leader for CSR.

©Fred Lum/The Globe and Mail/CP Images

Exhibit 15-12 Cadbury's public relations focuses on its Bicycle Factory.

©Mahathir Mohd Yasin/Shutterstock

Exhibit 15-13 Canadian Tire's Jumpstart Day encourages children to play sports.

©Getty Images/iStockphoto

Canadian Tire experienced significant success by positioning its cause-related marketing in a domain that fits its business mandate and consumer basis, creating a beneficial relationship for both sides. Canadian Tire's Jumpstart charity (**Exhibit 15-13**) partnered with the Hockey Canada Foundation (HCF) to launch "The Big Play," an initiative to provide 30,000 children from lower-income families with the opportunity to play minor hockey. The program worked with the World Junior Championship and, in particular, Team Canada. Each player's home town received funding to support five children, for a total of $250,000. A national public service announcement of the program occurred on the Boxing Day launch, with Jumpstart kids being surprised with game tickets! The message encouraged families to visit online to learn more about the program and to get involved. Additional funding occurred for every social media retweet of TSN's "Big Play" highlight. Jumpstart awareness hit 95 percent, website traffic increased 30 percent, and an additional $45,000 fundraising resulted with higher than average social media communication.[30]

While these examples look great, not all cause-related marketing is guaranteed to succeed. Cause-related marketing requires more than just associating with a social issue, since these examples show that it takes time and effort to organize a meaningful activity that will be accepted and gain participation. It is also possible to waste money by associating with a cause that offers little relation to the brand, with firms discovering that their customers and potential customers have little interest in the cause. Finally, the results of cause-related marketing efforts can be hard to quantify. Despite these cautions, one practitioner commented that good cause-related marketing gave people something to do that was simple, rewarding, and interesting.[31]

Figure 15-4 summarizes a handful of successful cause-related marketing programs that the marketing community recognized as innovative examples that exemplified courage over pity in their messages.[32] For each example, we identify the name of the campaign and its key innovation that earned respect. The whole emotional tenor of these messages moved away from historical sadness to uplifting imagery of hope. Many (especially Sick Kids) received publicity through news media, and they all achieved their objectives successfully. Check out the videos for AToMiC Awards.

SPONSORSHIP

Corporate sponsorship of events plays a major role in the public relations plans of organizations. While companies sponsor specific events with primarily traditional public relations objectives in mind, a separate and more marketing-oriented use of sponsorship is prevalent; event sponsorship occurs for product-level brands compared to corporate brands. In either case, the decisions involved are comparable—we turn to these in this section, beginning with a brief overview.

Figure 15-4 Examples of successful cause-related marketing

	Campaign	Innovation
Rethink Breast Cancer	Give-a-Care Collection	Functional gifts
Sick Kids Hospital	Sick Kids VS	Dramatic imagery
Children's Wish Foundation	Do the Levi	Inspirational dance
Canadian Down Syndrome Society	Down Syndrome Answers	Searchable videos

Overview Activities in which a fee is paid in exchange for marketing communication benefits for an organization are known as **event sponsorship**. An organization agrees to sponsor an event since it provides exposure to a selective audience, and potentially a larger audience with television coverage or photos and videos posted in social media. A further benefit is the organization's association with the event, thus providing additional development of its corporate image. Overall, sponsorship offers the potential to achieve multiple objectives: awareness, brand positioning, and trial or repeat purchases through merchandising and promotional offers with the ultimate goal of increasing loyalty and distancing a brand from its competitors.[33]

A survey of managers found that sponsorship contributes to brand differentiation and financial success.[34] Furthermore, academic research conducted in lab experiments and in the field suggests that sponsorship contributes to brand recall and stronger brand attitudes.[35] However, factors like too many sponsors, controversial co-sponsors, poor product association with the event, and weak initial brand attitude can all contribute to less desirable outcomes regarding brand attitude.[36] A longitudinal study of a major sponsor for the United European Football League concluded that awareness measures of recall and recognition grew over time, indicating that brands should view sponsorship as a long-term investment and sign multi-year contracts.[37] Key factors for positive attitudes and loyalty to the sponsoring brand and the sponsored entity include a strategic fit between both partners, a local sponsor, a long contract, and an emotional motive for the brands to become partners.[38] Additionally, a study of pre-event and post-event brand image measures found that image improved due to event image, sponsor–event fit, brand familiarity, and importance of product category of the sponsoring brand.[39] The key message from this snapshot of academic research suggests that sports sponsorship contributes positively to brand communication effects such as awareness, image, attitude, and loyalty provided the execution is implemented well.

An annual survey of Canadian sponsors, sponsorship properties, and agencies provides a snapshot of the industry. In 2017, sponsors spent an average of $9.5 million while sponsorship properties received an average of $4.3 million. Companies devoted 22 percent of their IMC budget on average toward sponsorship over the past 12 years studied. The total amount spent on sponsorship in 2017 hit $3 billion: $2 billion for brand building and $1 billion for activation. The majority of sponsorship is cash (80 percent), while the remainder is for "in kind" goods or services. Sponsors see the most valuable benefits as being digital ads, broadcast ads, exclusivity, and ownership of area. Other benefits seen as less valuable, but still important, included rights to market, hospitality, spokesperson access, and database access.[40]

Sponsorship occurs in six domains, as shown in **Figure 15-5**, and sports sponsorship is the overwhelming leader (Canadian sponsorship ratios are similar). In response to sponsorship growth, industry members began the Sponsorship Marketing Council of Canada to demonstrate sponsorship's communication value by establishing best practices and measurement tools to validate sponsorship investment.[41] The Council annually recognizes the best sponsorship in four categories: arts and culture, sports, causes, and events and festivals. Sponsorship beyond these forms occurs; CIBC is the official financial sponsor of the Greater Toronto Airport Authority and the new UP Express train from Pearson airport to downtown. As part of the deal, CIBC pays for the baggage carts and lets everyone know about it with a decorative sculpture (**Exhibit 15-14**). CIBC also enjoys exclusivity for ATMs, foreign exchange, and specialized hospitality services.[42]

Figure 15-5 Annual sponsorship spending in North America by property ($ billions)

	2002	2006	2009	2012	2015	2018
Sports	$6.43	$ 8.94	$11.28	$13.01	$14.98	$17.05
Entertainment	0.87	1.38	1.64	1.93	2.13	2.40
Festivals, fairs, events	0.83	0.61	0.76	0.83	0.86	0.94
Causes	0.83	1.30	1.51	1.70	1.92	2.14
Arts	0.61	0.74	0.82	0.89	0.86	1.03
Associations	–	0.40	0.50	0.55	0.59	0.64
Total	$9.57	$13.37	$16.51	$18.91	$21.34	$24.20

Exhibit 15-14 CIBC is a sponsor at Toronto's Lester B. Pearson International Airport.

©Jill Morgan/Alamy Stock Photo

Exhibit 15-15 Kraft's Hockeyville celebrates with the NHL.

©Francis Vachon/TCPI/The Canadian Press

One example of a successful sponsorship with many partners is Kraft's Hockeyville. The initiative allowed communities to compete to be named the country's best hockey town, with the winner announced on *Hockey Night in Canada* after online fan voting. Leading up to this, Kraft narrowed down the towns and cities to a final list. The winner received $100,000 in rink upgrades, and the four runners-up received $25,000 each. The promotion continued yearly with sales up noticeably during the eight-week campaign. Several brand measures were strong, like "Kraft has great community spirit," and Kraft "actively cares and supports my community." These results are what Kraft looked for when the promotion began, as its research indicated that most Canadians' lives revolved around the local community centre with a rink for hockey, figure skating, public skating, ringette, and sledge hockey. The assistance to improve the facilities appeared a natural fit for a company that makes family products (**Exhibit 15-15**).[43]

As expected, a number of decisions are associated with event sponsorship, including the type of sponsorship, target audience fit, target audience exposure, and brand positioning. We explore these sponsorship decisions in the context of sports sponsorship for illustrative purposes because it represents the dominant expenditure—$17 billion in North America in 2018. Each idea is readily adapted to other domains, for example, entertainment or arts festivals. Sports sponsorship can be successful with clear objectives, a good positioning strategy, adequate budget, the appropriate sporting vehicle, and key tactical implementation—characteristics we have seen in other types of promotional plans. **IMC Perspective 15-2** describes the growth of Canadian banks sponsoring professional sports in Canada.

IMC PERSPECTIVE 15-2

BANKS LOVE SPORTS SPONSORSHIP

Sports sponsorship deals exist internationally with the Olympics; nationally with the Canadian Football League (CFL), Major League Soccer (MLS), the National Hockey League (NHL), the National Basketball Association (NBA), and Major League Baseball (MLB); and locally with minor hockey, baseball, and soccer, etc. Recent statistics indicate that the Canadian sponsorship industry is worth about

$3 billion, with $1.2 billion going to professional sports. Big banks are a major player in this arena, and we take a look at each.

BMO sponsors teams in the CFL (Montreal Alouettes and Toronto Argonauts [who play at BMO Field]), in MLS (Montreal Impact, Toronto FC, and Vancouver Whitecaps), in the NHL (Chicago Blackhawks, Minnesota Wild, and St. Louis Blues), and in the NBA (Milwaukee Bucks and Chicago Bulls). TD sponsors teams in the NHL (Boston Bruins and Vancouver Canucks), NBA (Boston Celtics), and MLB (Toronto Blue Jays). TD also owns the naming rights to the TD Place in Ottawa and TD Garden in Boston where the Bruins and Celtics play.

Scotiabank has sponsored hockey significantly and earned the reputation as "Canada's hockey bank" over the past decades. It began with a sponsorship of the Ottawa Senators in 2003, and eventually expanded to many other Canadian teams and then to the NHL. The deal permitted the bank to use the NHL logo and all 30 team logos for its ScotiaHockey Visa and debit cards. With Rogers's new TV deal with the NHL, Scotiabank negotiated a six-year broadcast contract for *Scotiabank Wednesday Night Hockey* and is the presenting sponsor of *Rogers Hometown Hockey* and *Hockey Day in Canada*. Scotiabank owns the naming rights to the NHL arenas in Toronto and Calgary. It also sponsors the Toronto Raptors from its new deal with Maple Leaf Sports & Entertainment (MLSE), but uses its subsidiary brand Tangerine. The results are impressive, as executives claimed increased brand familiarity, opinion, and impression to go with higher purchase consideration and likelihood to recommend.

For the most part, RBC and CIBC directed their sponsorship to non-professional sports. RBC

©Gerry Thomas/NHLI via Getty Images

sponsors Hockey Canada, Canadian Olympic Committee, Special Olympics Canada, and RBC Cup. A notable exception for professional sports is its sponsorship of the RBC Canadian Open. CIBC sponsors major junior hockey through the Canadian Hockey League, its three leagues, and the championship Memorial Cup.

The prices for these deals are high. Reports indicate that TD pays the Toronto Blue Jays $20 million per year and Scotiabank agreed to pay MLSE $40 million per year for 20 years. Previously, Air Canada paid $4 million per year to the Leafs. And in the end, it is musical chairs with arena names: the Air Canada Centre changed to Scotiabank Arena, which happens to be the former name of the arena in Ottawa that for seven years now has been called the Canadian Tire Centre.

Question:

1. Why are major Canadian brands investing significantly in sports sponsorship?

Types of Sponsorship Sports sponsorship involves endorsement deals or sponsoring a team, league, event, athlete, or organization, along with stadium naming or broadcast rights. The goal is to associate a brand with its target audience's entertainment consumption or lifestyle, thus enriching the overall brand experience. One innovative partnership is Sun Life's sponsorship of the Toronto Raptors in which the players wear a Sun Life patch on their home jerseys (**Exhibit 15-16**). The sponsorship is part of an initiative for healthy living and the prevention of diabetes.

Working with an athletic sponsorship is similar to sponsorship with a team, but with a few unique issues. Foremost is ensuring a fit between the athlete and the company or brand. Exposure arrangements regarding an athlete's identity (i.e., name, image, and likeness), amount and type of service, and corporate logo placement need to be established. Rounding out the arrangement is the strategic communication use of an athlete in advertising, public relations, or sales

Exhibit 15-16 A Sun Life ad is on the Raptors' jerseys as part of the sponsorship deal.

©EFE News Agency/Alamy Stock Photo

promotion, and conditions for the sponsor to protect its investment (e.g., an ethics clause). A significant sponsorship agreement between Sport Chek and Kyle Lowry of the Raptors was made when the star signed a four-year contract extension. It appeared to be a great match for promoting the retailer in Toronto, especially as the popularity of basketball has exploded in the past few years and in 2019 the Raptors won the NBA Championship.[44]

Brand Positioning Companies are attracted to event sponsorships because effective IMC programs can be built around them and promotional tie-ins can be made to local, regional, national, and even international markets. Companies are finding event sponsorship to be an excellent platform from which to build equity and gain affinity with target audiences, as well as a good public relations tool for the corporation in general.

While the overall market position of the brand may be well established throughout the marketing plan, sports sponsorship permits a brand positioning strategy to a unique and well defined target audience toward which the brand has specific communication and behavioural objectives. For example, a sports sponsorship could enable a brand to establish awareness and new brand associations as it reaches new customers to develop trial purchases.

However, brands should be prepared to spend accordingly in order to achieve their objectives, as the initial sponsorship investment requires additional advertising or sales promotion expenditures. As the foundation is critical, brands should ensure that the rights and benefits of the sports sponsorship allow the brand to achieve its objectives and positioning. For example, sponsorship in hockey can have limits without clearance from its stakeholders (e.g., NHL, NHL Players' Association, and Hockey Canada). Finally, picking the right sponsorship that has the right profile at the right time and a partner that is receptive to making the deal work is paramount for successful implementation.

Target Audience Fit Most companies focus their marketing efforts on specific market segments and are always looking for ways to reach these target audiences. Marketers find that event sponsorship is an effective way to reach specific target audiences based on geographic, demographic, psychographic, and ethnic characteristics. For example, golf tournaments are popular for sponsorship by marketers of luxury automobiles and other upscale products and services. The golf audience is affluent and highly educated, and marketers believe that golfers care passionately about the game, leading them to form emotional attachments to brands they associate with the sport. Alternatively, brands look to similar venues to reach a consistent target audience that fits. For example, Pepsi signed a deal with the NBA and reached the pinnacle of sports sponsorship by owning all four major North American sports leagues: MLB, NFL, NHL, and NBA. Industry observers felt the youthful, pop-culture audience of Pepsi blended well with the fans of all four sports.[45] The Telus World Ski and Snowboard Festival allowed the national telecommunications firm to reach its youth market with its sponsorship investment (**Exhibit 15-17**).

Exhibit 15-17 A competitor on the half-pipe at the Telus Festival.

©Christian Kober 1/Alamy

Target Audience Exposure Marketers are attracted to event sponsorship because it gets their company and/or product names in front of consumers. By choosing the right events for sponsorship, companies can get visibility among their target audience. Clearly this appears to be a key reason why Molson spent its money sponsoring the NHL as it anticipates that hockey watchers are also beer drinkers. Curiously, sponsorship deals raise interesting questions as to the target audience exposure of a sponsorship message, as shown in **Exhibit 15-18**. While exposure is no doubt important, the degree to which the sponsorship is noticed is a concern for managers since most events offer varying exposure levels for different amounts of money invested. Thus, the risk of potential clutter due to the prominence of a major sponsor can inhibit the exposure of secondary sponsors.

An additional exposure issue is the perceived infringement or "ambush" of non-sponsors upon a sponsor's property. In this case, a non-sponsor's marketing communication gives the impression that it is a sponsor through its imagery or promotional activities. This issue arises during the Olympics, and the Canadian Olympic Committee (COC) took exception to North Face's launch of its "International Collection" of clothing that featured the Canadian flag or symbolic references to Sochi or Russia. In addition, North Face ran a contest featuring a trip to Sochi to attend a major international sports competition for the winner. Ultimately, the COC filed a lawsuit against North Face.[46] Similarly, Budweiser continued its Red Light promotion during the Olympics by encouraging Canadians to post a picture of the light in support of Team Canada. Once again the COC took exception to this despite the beer brand's disclaimer that it did not sponsor the Olympics, the COC, or Hockey Canada.[47]

Brand Activities Most sponsored properties include guidelines on what level of marketing the brand's support permits in terms of the number and size of signs, for example. Sponsored properties allow extensive brand activation to occur, while others place significant limitations on the type of brand activities permitted during the exposure. *Brand activation* is a catch-all term that describes various promotional activities—such as sampling, demonstration, and interaction both personally and technologically—that provide interesting experiences for consumers. Essentially, it is marketing communication with a goal of bringing consumers closer to purchase intention while in their decision-making process. For example, Crankworx

Exhibit 15-18 Zurich Insurance saw a connection between its target audience and viewers of beach volleyball.

©Caro/Alamy

is a mountain bike festival held annually in Whistler, British Columbia, that attracts significant sponsorship levels. As shown in **Exhibit 15-19**, Crankworx offers substantial brand activation promotional activities as part of the deal. Its Internet site lists its numerous partners and many exhibitors who showcase their products with clear and colourful brand identification. One study found positive brand communication effects of both anticipating and participating in brand activation experiences at a sponsored event.[48] Another study concluded that the type of activation contributed to consumers' understanding of the brand's message and intention for the sponsorship relationship.[49]

Measuring Sponsorship Effectiveness As we have seen with other communication tools, sponsorship planning follows a general framework of performing a situation analysis with relevant consumer and competitive research, establishing objectives (i.e., marketing, communication, behavioural), developing strategy and tactics, and outlining the criteria and measures of effectiveness to assess whether objectives have been met. A major issue that faces the event sponsorship industry is incomplete research. As marketers become interested in targeted audiences, they will want more evidence that event sponsorship is effective and a good return on their investment.

Despite this concern, the growth in sponsorship investments has led to a corresponding emergence of measuring the effectiveness of sponsorship. While each of these

Exhibit 15-19 Crankworx draws sponsors for its bike events.

©Dan Galic/Alamy

measures has its advantages and disadvantages, we suggest using several in assessing the impact of sponsorship. Essentially, measures of sponsorship effectiveness can be categorized as exposure-based methods or tracking measures:[50]

- *Exposure-based methods.* Exposure-based methods include those that monitor the quantity and nature of the media coverage obtained for the sponsored event and those that estimate direct and indirect audiences. However, media coverage is not the only objective of sponsorship and it should not be considered the sole measure of effectiveness; exposure measures provide no indication of attitude or behavioural change, key measures communicated throughout the text.[51]
- *Tracking measures.* These measures evaluate the awareness, familiarity, and preferences of the target audience based on survey research. A number of empirical studies measured recall of sponsors' ads, awareness of and attitudes toward the sponsors and their products, and brand and corporate images. Moreover, the tracking measures could be done for current customers, potential customers, and the general public before, during, and after the event to get a complete picture of the sponsorship.

Finally, at the conclusion of investigating numerous studies of the persuasion effects of sponsorship, the researcher makes a number of managerial prescriptions based on the findings. Sponsorship content should be visible. An organizer should clearly thank the sponsor at the event; this can be implemented in the media as well. Planners should avoid multiple-sponsor events. The sponsorship should offer true value to the audience, who should perceive it as being distinct from brand advertising.[52]

LO5 IMC Planning: Strategic Use of PR

As discussed in this chapter, public relations activities often communicate infrequently to a broader population and attempt to persuade the target audience on more global or abstract attributes of the company and its brand. With this in mind, public relations generally does not influence the decision-making process because the activities are not sequenced to match the purchase and consumption behaviour of consumers, as they are in advertising or sales promotion. For that matter, it is unlikely that a single public relations activity would coincide exactly with decision making for any other stakeholder that might be a target audience for the organization.

For example, CIBC is the title sponsor for Run for the Cure, an annual event to raise funds for the Canadian Breast Cancer Foundation (**Exhibit 15-20**). The late-September event features considerable lead-up media exposure funded by CIBC; however, this timing does not necessarily fit for all customers and non-customers of CIBC since financial products and services are purchased year-round. Presumably, CIBC expects this sponsorship activity to have a broad, long-term benefit associated with the corporate brand that consumers and all other internal and external stakeholders would retain during the year and until the event returns. After two decades of support, CIBC wanted to stand out from the clutter of charity fundraising events by recording a first-person account of breast cancer treatment. The video contributed to significant increases in post-event attitudinal measures (e.g., inspiring, moving, hopeful).[53] However, the growth of cause-related marketing activities and the resulting data shown in this chapter indicate that programs by major brands may be contributing to stronger overall attitudes.

Advertising and PR often reinforce one another. The launch of a new advertising campaign is helped with additional exposure through news media in the form of announcements in the newspaper, clips shown on television, or information and complete ads posted on the Internet. Sometimes, brands take advantage of favourable publicity and make note of this in their advertising or make it a central theme in a particular message. Alternatively, if the corporation involved itself with sponsorship of arts, a cause, or sports, the advertising can make reference to this for

Exhibit 15-20 CIBC's Run for the Cure draws enthusiastic supporters.

©Photo courtesy of the Canadian Breast Cancer Foundation

regular brand messages beyond advertising messages dedicated to communicating information about the sponsorship. For these reasons, it is no wonder we have seen extensive proliferation of public relations expenditures.

Telus funded $1 million over four years to WWF-Canada by selling Telus-branded pandas, essentially a self-liquidating premium. Media exposure included TV and Internet ads, and additional exposure of the initiative included social media participation (#hometweethome) with $1 donated to the fund for every social media posting to go along with significant media publicity. Overall, impressive participation and website traffic numbers helped Telus be recognized by *Strategy* as a leading cause-related marketing program.[54] Internet sites for corporations are a primary vehicle for communicating basic facts (especially the corporation's social and community interests) and for disseminating common public relations tools. For example, firms regularly put copies of their press releases on their sites and also include video clips of corporate activities like speeches or annual shareholder meetings. The ability of virtually anyone to obtain basic company information through the Internet makes it a desirable tool for firms to project their best image with timely content to ensure strong reputation management. However, the darker side of the Internet appears in the form of unwarranted negative publicity for brands. Even the average person may try to sabotage organizations that have appropriate corporate missions, sell legitimate products, and follow the laws of the land.

Learning Objectives Summary

 Recognize the role of public relations in the promotional mix.

This chapter examined the role of public relations. Public relations is typically accomplished through publicity generated through news media and corporate advertising. We noted that these areas are significant to the marketing communication effort and are usually considered differently from the other promotional elements. The reasons for this special treatment stem from the facts that (1) they are typically not designed to promote a specific product or service, and (2) in many instances it is harder for the consumer to make the connection between the communication and its intent.

PR is often a separate department operating independently of marketing; in others, it is considered a support system. Many large firms have an external public relations agency, just as they have an outside ad agency. Thus, public relations is useful with its traditional responsibilities; however, increasingly more marketing-oriented firms use this tool at the brand or product level for enhanced communication efforts.

 Explain how to compile a public relations plan.

Like all aspects of IMC, a public relations plan begins with a situation analysis, in particular an evaluation of public attitudes to the firm through a survey methodology in order to gauge an accurate reading. Influencing the right audience is another critical element as the organization must decide to communicate with groups such as employees, investors, community members, suppliers, customers, media, educators, and any other relevant societal stakeholder. Objectives need to be set, consistent with the behaviour and communication ideas suggested earlier in this book.

An appeal of sorts is also established for public relations, much like we saw in advertising examples: it is a clear message with a focus that often has creative elements. The delivery of the message can occur through established media channels discussed already, and through the media to generate publicity. Finally, tactical considerations and effective measures need to be established for full implementation.

 Examine how public relations is generated through news media publicity and argue its strengths and limitations.

News about a person, product, service, or organization that appears in broadcast or print media or on the Internet is known as publicity. It can occur through a story a journalist decides to write. In this case, publicity can be positive or negative and the firm is in more of a reactionary mode; preparedness for this scenario is certainly possible and recommended. Alternatively, a firm can seek media coverage for important news by communicating with the media through tools with the planned intention of receiving positive stories. Firms use press releases, press conferences, exclusives, interviews, and community involvement, and may use other creative means to persuade journalists to cover them.

Messages about a company that consumers receive through the media have strengths, including credibility, endorsement, low cost, less clutter, ability to reach specific audiences, image building, and frequency potential. Limitations include whether the brand is actually stronger, and a lack of control leading to an inconsistent message, poor timing, and possible inaccuracy.

 Illustrate how public relations is managed through corporate advertising.

Corporate advertising involves the reputation management of the firm through advertising and promotional activities designed to put the firm in the most favourable public position. *Corporate advertising* is a general term to cover all marketing communication that usually includes image advertising, cause-related advertising, and sponsorship. Corporate advertising can be controversial because sometimes the source of the message is top management, who may have their own intentions and motivations. This element of communication definitely has its place in the promotional mix but should follow the planning suggestions outlined in this chapter in order to be effective.

 Apply the ideas of public relations within the development of an IMC plan.

Public relations is an integral part of an IMC program as PR potentially reaches so many different constituents in the general public and those immediately connected to the organization. Furthermore, public relations both supports and can lead other IMC tools like advertising, sales promotion, and digital communication. As such, the execution of public relations should be carefully planned with objectives, strategies, and tactics much like any other aspect of marketing communication.

Review Questions

1. Identify the key differences between public relations and media publicity. In what ways are the two interdependent?

2. Describe the reasons why firms use public relations in an IMC program. Provide an example of an appropriate use of public relations in this mix.

3. Many companies are now trying to generate as much media publicity as they can. Cite examples, and discuss the advantages and disadvantages associated with this strategy.

4. Companies are now taking the position that their charitable contributions should lead to something in return—for example, sales or increased visibility. Discuss the pros and cons of this position.

5. Explain how public relations activities and media publicity can be executed with Internet media.

Applied Questions

1. Some marketers and PR people believe public relations should replace advertising as the primary tool for introducing new products. Explain why this would or would not be a good plan.

2. Select an organization that you admire and compile notes on the content of its public relations plan based on Internet research.

3. How do music artists take advantage of media publicity? Which strengths do they predominantly use? How do they minimize the limitations of media publicity?

4. Identify the sponsors of different concerts or entertainment activities you have attended and make a conclusion as to why this type of sponsorship may be successful.

5. Explain why a company like RBC would use the tools described in the chapter, including media publicity, corporate image advertising, cause-related advertising, and sponsorship.

©RBC

CHAPTER SIXTEEN

Direct Marketing

LEARNING OBJECTIVES

LO1 Define direct marketing and summarize the importance of a database for direct-marketing communication decisions.

LO2 Express the decisions of a direct-marketing plan.

LO3 Describe the content of a loyalty program.

LO4 Evaluate the strengths and limitations of direct marketing.

LO5 Apply the ideas of direct marketing within the development of an IMC plan.

Loyalty Program Shakeup

PC Plus and Shoppers Optimum morphed into PC Optimum. Air Miles flew in a new direction and revised its loyalty program. RBC and Petro-Canada partnered up to form a linked loyalty program that offers Canadians gas savings as well as additional Petro-Points and RBC Rewards points. RBC Rewards is the bank's own loyalty program where clients can use their points toward everyday things like buying groceries and paying bills to booking travel and everything in between. Canadian Tire wheeled out its rebranded loyalty program—Triangle Rewards. Air Canada and its partners bought back Aeroplan, and then subsequently established a new loyalty program. Esso fueled itself away from Aeroplan to fill up with PC Optimum. Subway relaunched its My Way Rewards. Scene now charges for one of its loyalty program tiers. And a specialty coffee company brewed up Keurig Perks. Whew! What is driving this shakeup of Canadian loyalty programs?

Research suggests that consumers prefer loyalty programs that offer free goods and services (such as PC Optimum and Scotiabank/Cineplex's Scene) over those that offer travel rewards. And here lies the problem, as a couple of the major loyalty programs—Air Miles and Aeroplan—established the programs decades ago with free flights based on member purchases from many retailers. But, over time, consumers and technology changed, giving rise to new expectations and loyalty programs from individual brands rather than a coalition of brands. In a research study on the different programs, the top five attained very similar levels of consumer attitudinal response, motivating many to improve. Any way we look at it, consumers believe in the loyalty program concept, as a vast majority say it influences what, when, and where they purchase.

Air Miles lowered the minimum number of miles required for redemption, made it easier for consumers to use miles for cash purchases, and introduced special offers for consumers using their card regularly. Given the new and revised programs available to members, Air Miles needed to ensure that it provided value to its 200 partners who give Air Miles to their customers. And this is a legitimate concern as the average Canadian is a member in 12 loyalty programs but is active in eight, resulting in a 33 percent dormancy rate. In short, loyalty programs compete against one another for loyalty, and consumers appear to switch among loyalty programs over time if they are not satisfied with the rewards, how to attain the rewards, and how personalized the promotional offers are based on their purchase behaviour.

Research suggests that 81 percent of loyalty program members are willing to have their purchases monitored in exchange for personalized offerings, and 91 percent want to interact with their loyalty program with the latest technology. And some loyalty programs are ahead of others in using the profile data to full advantage for member satisfaction. In particular, younger consumers are quite willing to adopt the methods of loyalty programs.

Question:

1. What would you as a consumer look for in a loyalty program?

Direct marketing includes programs that use direct-response media such as direct mail, catalogues, telephones, TV infomercials, and digital communication. In essence, it uses the media identified thus far and others, but with a behavioural objective that occurs more immediately in addition to communication objectives. We begin with an overview of direct marketing, describing the development of a database and two important uses of database marketing. We then identify key decisions for direct-marketing programs, including target audience, objectives, direct-response media, and effectiveness. A loyalty program is identified as a main direct marketing program and its characteristics and consumer adoption are explored. The chapter concludes with a summary of the strengths and limitations of this marketing tool and an IMC application.

LO1 Direct Marketing

Companies rely on promotional mix elements such as advertising and sales promotion to move their goods and services through intermediaries, but they also market directly to consumers. Advertising and sales promotion manage a brand's image, convey information, and raise awareness. However, communicating directly can generate an immediate behavioural response that makes direct marketing a valuable part of the promotional program. For this section we define the purpose of direct marketing, illustrate how to develop a database, and summarize two implementation uses of a database: targeting and customer relationship management (CRM).

Exhibit 16-1 Bose uses multiple methods to promote its products.

Source: Bose Corporation

DEFINING DIRECT MARKETING

As noted in Chapter 1, **direct marketing** is the interactive use of advertising media to stimulate an immediate behaviour modification in such a way that this behaviour can be tracked, recorded, analyzed, and stored on a database for future retrieval and use.[1] Direct marketing involves marketing research, segmentation, strategic and tactical decisions, and evaluation, as shown in our planning model in Chapter 1. For the execution, direct marketing uses **direct-response media**, including direct mail, telephone, interactive TV, print, the Internet, mobile devices, and other media to reach both customers and prospective customers. Bose Audio markets through stores and online, supporting its efforts through advertising (**Exhibit 16-1**).

The use of direct-response media differs depending on whether the identity of an individual within the target audience is known. For example, direct mail can be addressed, where the person's name and address is on the communication sent to the home (or business) location. In contrast, unaddressed mail reaches homes and is delivered in bulk to selected geographic areas, or to areas determined through the use of another segmentation variable chosen by the promotional planner. In either case, an important element of direct media selected is the development of a database. We briefly examine the content and use of a database for the purpose of marketing communication. This general approach is applicable for all direct-response media described in this chapter and for Internet media discussed in Chapter 17.

DEVELOPING A DATABASE

As noted throughout the text, market segmentation and targeting are critical components of any promotional program. Direct-marketing programs employ these principles significantly since their success is tied to reaching a very specific target audience. Direct marketers use a **database**, a listing of customers and/or potential customers, to identify and profile their target audience. This database is a tool for **database marketing**—the use of specific information about individual customers and/or prospects to implement effective and efficient marketing communication. In this section we look at the content of a database, database use for targeting, and database use for CRM.

Database Content The database contains names, addresses, and postal codes; more sophisticated databases include information on demographics and psychographics, purchase transactions and payments, personal facts, neighbourhood data, and even credit histories (see **Figure 16-1**). With the development of electronic communication, databases may also contain email addresses and consumers' social media identification. For example, Facebook developed an app that automatically generates a contact form that feeds into an advertiser's database.[2] Canada's privacy legislation places limitations on what marketers can do with database information; refer to www.privcom.gc.ca for a complete guide. Companies are very concerned with protecting this data from hackers after significant media stories over the past decade, and are responsible about how they use the data. In fact, one trend is that companies will "de-identify" the data to avoid any potential breaches of privacy.[3]

Organizations compile their own database and regularly update it through transaction information or through past marketing communication activities. Other sources of data include warranty cards, surveys, consumer/trade shows, inbound communication, and Internet browsing behaviour (especially through social media). A key success factor of a customer database is that it must be kept current, purged of old and/or inactive customers, and updated frequently. The **RFM scoring method** is used to see the recency, frequency, and monetary transactions between the company and the customer. Data need to be entered each time there is a transaction so that the company can track how recently purchases have been made, how often they are made, what amounts of money are being spent, and which products and/or services are purchased.

Database marketing has become ubiquitous as companies have established comprehensive databases on existing and potential customers; people are now concerned about their privacy. Direct marketers are concerned as well. The Canadian Marketing Association (CMA) and the Canadian Advertising Foundation (CAF) have asked members to adhere to ethical rules of conduct in their marketing efforts. For example, companies who collect data ask for consent from consumers prior to communicating, and reassure their customers that the data will not be sold to a third party. In contrast, research shows that about half of all Canadians willingly share personal information if they receive pro-

Figure 16-1 Contents of a database for direct marketing

Consumer Database	Business-to-Business Database
Name	Name of company and contact
Address/postal code	Address/postal code
Telephone number	Telephone number
Email, social media coordinates	Email, social media coordinates
Age	Credit history
Gender	Industrial classification
Marital status	Size of business
Family	Revenues
Education	Number of employees
Income	Time in business
Occupation	Source of order/inquiry or referral
Transaction history	Purchase history
Promotion history	Promotion history
Inquiry history	Inquiry history
Unique identifier	Unique identifier

motional offers in return; however two-thirds are uncomfortable about receiving the offers on their smart phone.[4] And another somewhat reassuring point is that managers admit that they have too much data at times and not enough time to analyze the data for their decision making.[5]

There are numerous outside sources of information for buying or renting a database. Census data from Statistics Canada provides information on almost every Canadian household (e.g., size, demographics, income). Canada Post provides information on a postal code level for both household and business locations, and also offers comprehensive mailing lists for rent. Other list service organizations exist, such as Info Canada, which offers numerous types of business and consumer lists that the company builds from many sources. Large market research organizations conduct annual studies of customers and compile the information on total orders placed, types of products purchased, demographics, and purchase satisfaction. Loyalty programs contain significant amounts of information on consumer purchase patterns, and this data is shared with marketing partners. Finally, any company that collects consumer data is a potential source of data for purchase, provided the company disclosed this to its customers.

Database Use for Targeting Marketing decisions require information, and the database compiled for direct marketing purposes provides detailed facts for two managerial concerns in this section. As noted earlier, profiling a target audience with precision provides greater marketing communication effectiveness and efficiency, and CRM practices require considerable data for implementing customized promotional offers. The database permits extensive and advanced statistical analysis to identify specific audiences for which a customized and/or personalized message or promotional offer can be delivered through a direct-response medium. For example, Knorr entered the frozen food category and delivered direct-mail pieces, also containing a coupon, to households according to demographic and purchase behaviour potential along 10 different characteristics. Those most likely to respond included past Knorr consumers of other product categories who were interested in the frozen food category and who had sufficient disposable income to afford a premium product. The various combinations of the 10 characteristics provided opportunities to reach different target audiences ranging from very low to extremely high levels of audience attractiveness. The results indicated a 10 percent response rate, substantially higher than the projected 3 percent. One of the more attractive target audiences attained a response rate of 50 percent.

Exhibit 16-2 Costco mails promotional offers to its members.

Source: Costco Wholesale Corporation

As this Knorr example illustrates, certain consumers are more likely to be potential purchasers than others. By analyzing the characteristics of the database, a marketer like Knorr can target potential audiences that have a stronger likelihood of responding to the offer (e.g., use coupon, trial purchase) and the database serves as the foundation to profile the target audience who will likely make a trial purchase.[6] Finally, this example shows how brands cross-sell by offering new products or related products to customers who have bought in another product category.

Similarly, the database is used to target customers to help encourage repeat purchases. Once an initial purchase occurs, the customer's name and other information may be entered into the database. These people are proven users who offer high potential for repurchase. Magazines, for example, routinely send out subscription renewal letters and/or call subscribers before the expiration date. Companies such as lawn care services and car dealers build a base of customers and contact them when they are "due" to repurchase. These activities are examples where the timing of repeat purchasing is important, as identified in Chapter 5. Costco mails promotions to members regularly to encourage return visits (**Exhibit 16-2**), which likely improves the frequency objective identified in Chapter 5.

Database Use for CRM Another aspect of repeat purchasing occurs through customer relationship management (CRM), where marketers develop and maintain a significant amount of information about their clients. The aim is to establish and maintain a relationship with customers through personalized communication and customized product/ service offerings. CRM relies on software technology and an extensive database specifically designed to implement the management of customer relationships. For example, **Exhibit 16-3** shows a popular brand's loyalty program, a key part of CRM since it provides an incentive for repeat purchase. Loyal buyers are open to receiving regular communication from previously purchased brands; about 60 percent of consumers are interested in personalized promotional offers or product recommendations for items like groceries, entertainment, health/beauty, electronics, and clothing.[7]

Timely communication and appropriate promotional offers that fit with the customer's past purchase behaviour are the hallmark of CRM, for which a database and direct-response media are imperative. One study found that a referral program administered with direct marketing within a banking relationship provided a positive return on investment.[8] The Canadian division for American Express promotes the credit card to its members as a tool for enhanced service with its "Front of the Line" program. It expanded the offering with faster security clearance and taxi service in a sponsorship arrangement with Toronto's Lester B. Pearson International Airport. As part of the package, AMEX sponsored free Wi-Fi and entertainment to all waiting passengers.[9] As this example indicates, a company can identify trends and buying patterns that will help it establish a better relationship with its customers by more effectively meeting their needs through analysis of the data.

Despite this promise, research suggests that up to two-thirds of all organizations did not experience the full benefit of CRM initiatives. Collectively, they spent about $220 billion from 2000 to 2005 and have achieved a return of only $50 billion in the intervening years to date. Criticism focused on the fact that even though companies bought leading-edge call centres, databases, software, hardware, and Internet sites, they did not appropriately adjust how they operated or trained personnel to build these relationships. The researchers suggested that business moved too quickly to expand the program rather than being patient and learning with a smaller base of customers prior to full implementation.[10] In contrast to

Exhibit 16-3 Tims Rewards loyalty program facilitates CRM.

©PurplePanda/Shutterstock

this opinion, one commentator claimed that Nespresso's product introduction strength resided in the "Club," which registered every single customer. Its benefits comprised an online magazine, product alerts, a loaner machine when required, and the opportunity to order capsules for delivery.[11]

LO2 Direct-Marketing Plan

To successfully implement direct-marketing programs, companies must make a number of decisions. As in other marketing programs, they must determine (1) whom to target by using a database; (2) what the program's objectives will be; (3) what direct-response media strategy will be employed; and (4) how to measure direct-marketing effectiveness.

TARGET AUDIENCES FOR DIRECT MARKETING

As the database description suggested, direct marketing is especially useful for targeting current customers. Well managed firms have extensive records of their customers in terms of their purchases and other relevant characteristics, allowing for personalized and customized communication. Alternatively, the database section identified other sources from which to compile a database of non-customers. Businesses expand geographically or along another dimension (e.g., demographic, socioeconomic) where an accurate database and direct marketing could generate trial among prospects. As the earlier Knorr example showed, other segmentation variables accurately profile a target audience for marketing communication.

Thus far we have discussed direct marketing and the use of databases with the idea that the identity of the receiver is known. While this is true, direct marketing is also used with broader media (i.e., television) and with media that allow for delivery without identity (i.e., unaddressed direct mail). In these situations, databases are (or should be) used to identify the most relevant profile variables to ensure the highest response rate possible. A planner can use census data and postal codes to select attractive regions within a vicinity for unaddressed direct mail. Fido (**Exhibit 16-4**) is an example of a brand that could send promotional pieces to postal codes where it has low sales penetration, or to addresses where its database indicates it has no current customer. The high level of brand switching behaviour in the mobile phone service market potentially makes this direct-marketing decision effective and profitable.

A third idea for targeting occurs through profiling current customers and using the information to select prospective customers from an alternative database. Working with Canada Post, the Canadian Cancer Society followed this approach with an experiment. They identified four different groups: (1) profiled postal code and receive mail, (2) profiled postal code and receive no mail, (3) non-profiled postal code and receive mail, and (4) non-profiled postal code and receive no mail. The results found a 13.5 percent higher response rate for profiled segments, with net revenue being 19.2 percent higher.[12]

DIRECT-MARKETING OBJECTIVES

The direct marketer seeks an immediate behavioural response, and behavioural objectives identified in Chapter 5—brand trial, re-trial, switching, or category trial—become more salient. A database of consumers' past purchase history information helps identify those who have not previously purchased the brand. For databases containing current customer purchase history, the direct marketer can attempt to influence the rate, amount, or timing of purchases. Often, direct marketing attempts to bring consumers along in their decision-making process. Thus, shopping behaviour can be an objective through retail visits that manifest in ways such as test driving cars or trying on shoes and clothes, requests for service such as obtaining free estimates, or experiencing other marketing communication.

Exhibit 16-4 A brand like Fido could use direct-response media to entice switching.

©Martin Good/Shutterstock.

The Acura Golf Escape

Your Exclusive Package Includes:

- Resort accommodations for 2 nights
- 25% discount on spa treatments
- Experience Acura, the Preferred vehicle of Pinehurst (available for you to drive at your leisure).
- 3 rounds of championship golf (Pinehurst Nos. 1, 3–8)
- Breakfast and dinner for 2 days
- 1 dozen Titleist® Pro V1 golf balls

Plus One of the Following Free Gifts from Acura:

- Titleist's new high-performance 910 driver (available November 2010)
- A set of 3 Titleist Vokey Design wedges (52-, 56- and 60-degree)
- $300 gift card*

*To take advantage of this exclusive offer, call 1-800-803-0028. Please mention the Acura Golf Escape
and prepare to play on greens that have inspired golf's best.*

FALL SEASON RATES (September 8 – October 23, 2010)	EVERGREEN SEASON RATES (November 7, 2010 – March 16, 2011)	SPRING SEASON RATES (April 1 – 24, 2011)

VALUE SEASON RATES (October 24 – November 6, 2010 & March 17 – 31, 2011)

ACURA
ADVANCE.

Repeat consumption is also an objective with current customers. For example, financial-service firms can use direct marketing to encourage additional visits by customers for yearly financial planning advice. **Exhibit 16-5** shows an ad for a car inviting customers to take a test drive at an exclusive club.

A behavioural response is not the only objective for direct marketing. All communication objectives and how the message and offers influence attitudes are still very relevant for direct marketing. As we noted in Chapter 5, brand objectives (i.e., awareness, attitude) are considerations for all pieces of marketing communication. In fact, direct marketers are very innovative, with clever creative approaches to attract attention and encourage processing the message so that a communication effect occurs even if the receiver declines the call to action. A typical objective of perhaps a 2–3 percent response rate suggests that communication objectives are as valuable here as in other marketing communication tools.

DIRECT-RESPONSE MEDIA

Direct-response media include media like direct mail, catalogue, broadcast, and telemarketing. To help achieve the previously identified objectives, these media generally follow a couple of approaches. In the **one-step approach**, the medium is used directly to obtain an order. For example, TV commercials for products such as workout equipment urge viewers to phone a toll-free number to place an order immediately. The **two-step approach** involves the use of more than one medium. The first effort is designed to screen, or qualify, potential buyers. The second effort generates the response. For example, business marketing companies use telemarketing to screen on the basis of interest, then follow up to interested parties with more information designed to achieve an order or use personal selling to close the sale.

Direct Mail Direct mail advertising revenue by Canada Post hit $1.14 billion in 2016.[13] This amount is 60 percent of the amount spent on Internet display ads for 2016 at $1.91 billion. As an example, the material shown in **Exhibit 16-6** is just one piece that was sent by Jaguar to market its new F Pace automobile, which indicates that high-end brands see considerable value in this direct-response medium. As noted, a successful direct mail program relies on a database that may be a purchased **mailing list** comprising relevant market information regarding geography, demographics, socioeconomics, and lifestyles. Lists are now very selective for improved effectiveness and very current to minimize waste coverage and maximize efficiency. For example, a Canadian company like www.cleanlist.ca offers many different types of lists to acquire, retain, and cross-sell customers and claims it has very current information for all of its lists.

Canada Post has a strong interest in developing the market for direct mail and provides extensive research and service to facilitate this goal, especially for small businesses concerned with reaching their customers and prospects with a low-cost option. Canada Post research shows that:

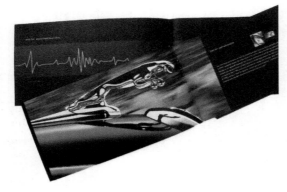

- Receiving mail is meaningful due to the ritual of retrieving and sorting through the mail in the same home location each day. The ritual is more significant in a consumer's life compared to the fluid routine of scanning email or social media messages. In fact, 70 percent are curious to find out what is in their mailbox.

- Direct mail advertising obtains strong exposure levels; 74 percent always or sometimes notice direct mail advertising to go along with the fact that 85 percent will open mail if it looks interesting, and 81 percent read their mail the same day they receive it.

- Direct mail messages contribute to ad recall; 80 percent remember seeing or reading mail sent to them in the past four weeks, and 60 percent say that really good ad mail helps to keep the sender's brand name top of mind.

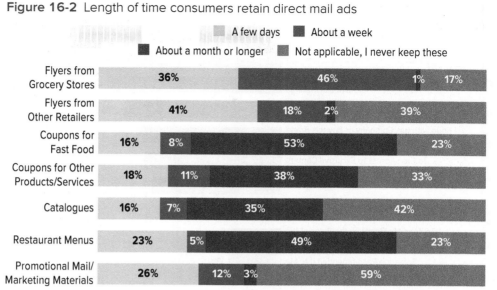

Figure 16-2 Length of time consumers retain direct mail ads

Legend: A few days | About a week | About a month or longer | Not applicable, I never keep these

	A few days	About a week	About a month or longer	Not applicable
Flyers from Grocery Stores	36%	46%	1%	17%
Flyers from Other Retailers	41%	18%	2%	39%
Coupons for Fast Food	16%	8%	53%	23%
Coupons for Other Products/Services	18%	11%	38%	33%
Catalogues	16%	7%	35%	42%
Restaurant Menus	23%	5%	49%	23%
Promotional Mail/Marketing Materials	26%	12%	3%	59%

Source: "Breaking Through the Noise," White Paper published by Canada Post.

- Many direct mail ads remain in the household for a good amount of time, leading to continued exposure and potential action, as **Figure 16-2** indicates.

- Direct ad mail drives behaviour, with 64 percent visiting an Internet site, 47 percent visiting a store, and 54 percent interacting with social media. And surprisingly, Canadians prefer mail over email from businesses marketing their products.[14]

Direct mail works well as the first step in the two-step approach for message delivery. Tourism Yukon's direct mail initiative obtained a 20 percent response rate for website visits versus 5 percent for its online ads presenting the same message. Bear Mountain Resort delivered brochures to two selective markets that encouraged online registration to view its new condominiums and garnered a 37 percent response versus a 14 percent response for past newspaper ads.[15]

Catalogues Certain companies rely solely on catalogue sales. For example, Yves Rocher is a firm that markets botanical beauty care products for women. It expanded into Canada with its small catalogues and sells directly to consumers. Lee Valley Tools of Ottawa began as a mail-order catalogue company years ago, but has branched out to retail stores across the country and online sales.

Companies also use catalogues in conjunction with their retail sales outlets and other promotional tools. For example, Canadian Tire sells directly through catalogues but also uses them to inform consumers of product offerings available in the stores. Canadian Tire revamped its catalogue and presented it online with a much different look than its Internet site. Entitled "The Canadian Way," the virtual presentation featured four sections—living, fixing, playing, and driving—with customized options. Executives saw it as directed toward families with young children with its colour photos and demonstration-like presentation.[16] About 350,000 visitors read more than 4 million pages within the first six months, one-third returned more than one time, and the average time spent lasted six minutes—twice the amount compared to its Internet site; culminating in the retailer winning a bronze in *Strategy*'s Shopper Innovation Award.[17] Moreover, Canadian Tire achieved its best quarterly sales ever by generating 2 percent growth and won a bronze CASSIES award.[18]

IKEA delivers millions of catalogues to Canadian homes each summer, introducing new products, styles, and décor ideas, and the catalogue is a main marketing tool to encourage consumers to visit a retail outlet or the Internet site. The catalogue is a strong brand-building tool to demonstrate how IKEA's products can improve the homes of millions of consumers. With sales lagging slightly, IKEA advertised and promoted the catalogue as a planning vehicle for redecorating when consumers perceived changes in their life.[19] IKEA also developed a mobile app to allow consumers to interact with the catalogue by looking behind closed doors or altering decorative items.[20] IKEA moved into social media communication regarding the catalogue by encouraging consumers to make posts on #IKEAPageForThat. This carried the idea that people used the catalogue much like a fashion magazine for the home.[21]

Email Direct mail on the Internet is essentially an electronic version of regular mail; it is highly targeted, relies heavily on lists, and attempts to reach consumers with specific needs through targeted messages. Consumers can opt to have

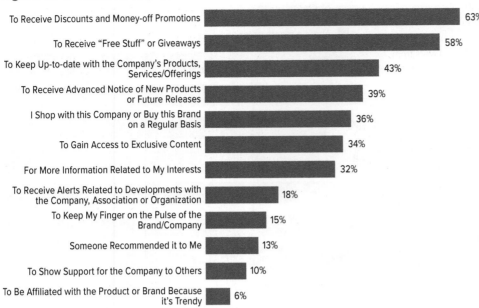

Figure 16-3 Reasons why Canadians receive email messages

Reason	Percentage
To Receive Discounts and Money-off Promotions	63%
To Receive "Free Stuff" or Giveaways	58%
To Keep Up-to-date with the Company's Products, Services/Offerings	43%
To Receive Advanced Notice of New Products or Future Releases	39%
I Shop with this Company or Buy this Brand on a Regular Basis	36%
To Gain Access to Exclusive Content	34%
For More Information Related to My Interests	32%
To Receive Alerts Related to Developments with the Company, Association or Organization	18%
To Keep My Finger on the Pulse of the Brand/Company	15%
Someone Recommended it to Me	13%
To Show Support for the Company to Others	10%
To Be Affiliated with the Product or Brand Because it's Trendy	6%

specific types of email sent to them and other types not sent. **Figure 16-3** summarizes the reasons why Canadian consumers are interested in receiving email messages from companies. One innovative study of a home improvement retailer concluded that seven emails per month is the optimal number to send, and that sending four emails per month yielded 32 percent less lifetime profit and sending ten emails per month yielded 16 percent less lifetime profit.[22]

Consumers also receive unwanted emails, referred to as **spam**. However, legitimate and enlightened marketers accept the practice of permission-based marketing. Canada's anti-spam law requires any organization to obtain the receiver's consent, identify their organization, and provide an unsubscribe option with every electronic communication delivered (for more information, see http://fightspam.gc.ca). The changeover required extensive upgrades in information technology and legal costs for organizations to comply.[23]

Consumers receive email from publication subscriptions and from loyalty programs. A detailed and sophisticated database is developed from consumers agreeing to opt in since they provide segmentation-like information. Best Buy enhanced its Reward Zone loyalty program in an email (with clickable link) where consumers could participate in a contest. Click-through rates hit about 20 percent as Best Buy customized the message for different demographics. Customers normally received monetary reward certificates for qualifying purchases that approximated a 1 percent rebate, and other improvements were gifts like show tickets, free movie rentals, and private shopping events for program members only.[24] Note that the reasons put forth in **Figure 16-3** are oriented for consumer marketing. Email messages also work in a business marketing context. **Exhibit 16-7** illustrates a creative example targeting flooring professionals who rely on strong suppliers.

Exhibit 16-7 An example of a creative message delivered through email.

©Woodchuck Flooring Inc./Full Scoop Marketing

Research investigated two of the behavioural responses to receiving email: visiting the brand's website, and forwarding the email to a friend. In a study for cosmetic and body care products sold in retail stores, more useful permission-based email messages yielded fewer website visits, presumably because the information satisfied consumer requirements. However, more useful, more interesting, and more frequent email messages resulted in more store visits, presumably to examine or buy the product. Consumers perceived useful emails as offering sales promotion information, or information about new products.[25]

In a sample of 1,259 forwarded emails from 34 participants, a study found extraordinary dispersion in the number forwarded during the one-month time frame. One person forwarded 177 messages and two others forwarded more than 100, while three people sent one each. Overall, participants forwarded about 40 percent of the emails received, which ranged from 0 percent to 100 percent.

The implication of finding a "lead sender" for an email forwarding campaign appears critical for success, much like a lead user in a diffusion of innovation. Additional qualitative research in the study finds that participants experienced substantial positive and negative emotional responses when receiving forwarded email.[26]

It is important to note that the pass-along of email is an outcome and not a strategy. It is a manifestation of the cognitive and emotional responses of the receiver to the message. The similarity to a TV ad would be to recall the ad and tell someone about it, or to call out to a family member ("Hey Dad, come check out this ad on TV"). Secondly, email can experience extensive pass-along yet have minimal benefit for the brand since it entails a single exposure of a brand message for many of the receivers, who simply delete it after viewing.

Broadcast Media The majority of direct-marketing broadcast advertising occurs on TV and encompasses direct-response TV spots, infomercials, and home shopping shows, although much of this activity is not as strong as previously.

TV Spots Referred to in the direct-marketing industry as *short-term programs,* these spots include direct-response commercials for products such as health and beauty, fitness, and household goods. In **direct-response advertising**, the product or service is offered and a sales response is solicited through either the one- or two-step approach. Toll-free phone numbers are included so that the receiver can immediately call to order and companies run direct-response television commercials to encourage website visits.

Infomercials An **infomercial** is a commercial that is 3–60 minutes long. Infomercials are usually produced by the advertisers and are designed to be viewed as regular TV shows. As the name implies, *infomercial* is a shorter way of saying *informational commercial* (**Exhibit 16-8**). Relatively speaking, infomercial ad revenue is not significant in Canada. One study compared the communication effects of a one-minute ad, 15-minute infomercial, 30-minute infomercial, and direct experience (i.e., interacting with the product). The authors concluded that infomercials provided results more closely related to direct experience than a one-minute ad, presumably because both messages allow for extensive cognitive and emotional processing for a longer duration.[27]

The decline of Canadian infomercial ad revenue suggests that the video capabilities of the Internet diminished infomercials. Brands place the equivalent of an infomercial on their website, or on video sites like YouTube. Brands now produce long messages of the same length as an infomercial, however the content is more storylike rather than purely informational. These ads are shown both on TV and in Internet media vehicles. For example, Mini (**Exhibit 16-8**) produced a 360 degree virtual reality story, to be used with a smart phone, that provided a cinematic experience of driving the car. We suggest that a long form ad of a brand such as this might be described as a transformational commercial compared to an informational commercial, which is consistent with the two consumer purchase motivations identified in Chapter 6.

Home Shopping The Shopping Channel (TSC) is Canada's broadcast retailer available on all delivery formats (cable, satellite) across the country. It claims a reach of 6.5 million households, viewership of 1.5 million Canadians each week, and a 70:30 female–male ratio. TSC recruits its audience like other channels, via direct mail and email, broadcast ads, print ads, paid Internet search, and social media. The lines of communication get blurred a little as TSC is available in catalogue form and on the Internet.[28]

Telemarketing Communication resulting in sales via the telephone is known as **telemarketing**. There are two types of telemarketing. *Outbound telemarketing* refers to calls made by a company or its sponsor to a potential buyer or client, soliciting the sale of products, services, donations, votes, or any other "value" issue. *Inbound telemarketing* occurs when a company has advertised its toll-free number or its website address—for example, asking the customer to call the number, visit the store, or log on to the website. Both for-profit and charitable organizations have employed this medium effectively in one- and two-step approaches.

Exhibit 16-8 Mini uses an infomercial-like video to attract buyers.

©Adriano Castelli/Shutterstock

The Canadian Marketing Association's Code of Ethics and Standards of Practice provides extensive guidelines for telemarketing, among many other marketing practices, to ensure that Canadians are treated fairly and responsibly using legitimate marketing practices.[29] The federal government offers guidelines for consumers to understand acceptable marketing practices.[30] However, while telemarketing may have a negative media image due to annoying cold-calls, it also receives undeserved negative media image effects when fraudulent and deceptive activities are executed by phoning unsuspecting victims; in this case it is most definitely not telemarketing but rather a crime.

DIRECT-MARKETING EFFECTIVENESS

For direct-marketing programs that do not have an objective of generating an immediate behavioural response, traditional measures of advertising effectiveness can be applied. In those situations requiring a direct response, measuring the effectiveness should include specific behavioural measures in addition to the communication measures. Using the *cost per order (CPO)*, advertisers can evaluate the relative effectiveness of an ad in only a few minutes based on the number of calls generated. By running the same ad on different stations, a direct marketer can determine the relative effectiveness of the medium itself. For example, if the advertiser targets a $5 return per order and a broadcast commercial (production and print) costs $2,500, the ad is considered effective if it generates 500 orders. Similar measures have been developed for print and direct mail ads.

Another measure of effectiveness is **Customer Lifetime Value (CLTV).** CLTV calculates potential profitability the company can generate from a customer associated with the brand over the course of the long-term relationship. The value is used to determine whether or not a customer should be acquired and what service level to provide to existing customers. Companies use CLTV to assist them in assessing future revenues and profit streams from the customer, so that they can focus more on the satisfaction and retention of their more profitable customers. Thus, the company can focus its promotional budget on profitable customers while spending less on those with a lower CLTV score.

(LO3) Loyalty Programs

One significant direct-marketing program is a *loyalty program* designed to reward customers for their repeat purchases. Companies track transactions in a database and provide cash, preferential treatment, goods, or services in return for continued patronage. These programs are common with airlines, car rental companies, hotel chains, and retailers. In this section we explain the purpose of loyalty programs, describe loyalty program characteristics, review consumer attitudes toward and usage of loyalty programs, and discuss digital communication with program members. Numerous other names exist other than *loyalty program,* such as *rewards program, frequency program,* and *continuity program;* however, research we review in this section concluded that the term *loyalty program* is most useful.

Exhibit 16-9 Jones Soda of Vancouver offers a loyalty program.

©Mandel Ngan/AFP/Getty Images

PURPOSE OF LOYALTY PROGRAMS

Loyalty programs are a means of encouraging consumers to buy products or services on a continual basis and an approach for developing strong customer loyalty. Companies realize the importance of customer retention and understand that the key to retaining and growing market share is building relationships with loyal customers. Loyalty programs provide marketers with the opportunity to develop databases containing valuable information on their customers that can be used to better understand their needs, interests, and characteristics as well as to identify and track a company's most valuable customers.

These databases can also be used to target specific programs and offers to customers to increase the amount they purchase and/or to build stronger relationships with them. Careful management of databases is necessary to identify and track valuable customers and their purchase history and to make strategic use of targeted loyalty rewards. For example, Jones Soda's loyalty program is linked with its social media and offers rewards for consumer participation (**Exhibit 16-9**).

The growth of loyalty programs suggests that their implementation now goes beyond a reward mechanism offered by organizations. One view is that a loyalty program is now an important competitive strategic characteristic on which companies differentiate themselves. In short, brands compete on design characteristics since they could be a significant factor in con-

Figure 16-4 Characteristics of a loyalty program

Characteristic	Customer Effect
Objective	Influences purchases (frequency, amount, timing)
Strategy	Program to strengthen brand and customer loyalty
Tactic	Customer formally enrolls as a member
Time Frame	Customer participates continually over time
Incentive	Free products, preferential treatment, financial gain
Frequency	Receives regular communication and offers

sumer decision making. For example, 45 percent believe that a loyalty program could be replaced with a competitor's program. In fact, research suggests that it may be one of the main drivers of consumer satisfaction after overall quality, leading the research company to suggest that loyalty programs may be the fifth "P" in the marketing mix.[31]

Academic studies echo some of this managerial thinking. One study of a convenience store loyalty program found that the program increased the dollar amount of goods purchased by light- and medium-volume purchasers. Heavy-volume consumers did not alter their purchase patterns.[32] Another study found that the monetary, social, and entertainment benefits predicted a more positive view of the loyalty program, which in turn predicted customer brand loyalty, thereby supporting practitioners' view of the effectiveness of loyalty programs.[33] Finally, another study investigated the database of one company's loyalty program and found two segments of customers: one group buying out of habit and another group demonstrating substantial attitudinal brand loyalty. The authors suggest that unique cross-selling offers to each group could yield stronger returns.[34]

LOYALTY PROGRAM CHARACTERISTICS

As the above example suggests, loyalty program characteristics are quite distinct from sales promotions. The most significant point separating a loyalty program from a sales promotion is enrollment. Registration requires information from a consumer which helps build a company's database to track purchases and allow direct communication as described in the first section of this chapter. **Figure 16-4** shows six characteristics of a loyalty program that facilitates long-term customer relationships. The organization of these points is consistent with the structure of promotional decisions described throughout the book.

Research on loyalty programs concluded that this IMC tool influences consumers in three ways.[35] The *points-pressure mechanism* occurs when consumers earn points and then realize they are close to achieving a reward level and make additional purchases to achieve it. The *rewarded-behaviour mechanism* occurs after reward redemption as this process contributes to positive attitudinal and behavioural responses. The *personalized marketing mechanism* occurs with the use of the database marketing activities. The design of the loyalty programs affects each of these mechanisms. Design includes the structure in terms of the time frame and whether the reward is based on frequency or tiered customer groups. Another characteristic is whether the program is a single brand or a partnership. A third design consideration is whether the rewards are monetary vs. non-monetary, or brand vs. non–brand related. Finally, the reward could be immediate or delayed.

The popular Air Miles loyalty program offers an example of these design decisions (**Exhibit 16-10**).

Exhibit 16-10 Air Miles is a popular loyalty program at many different retailers.

©dennizn/Alamy Stock Photo

Air Miles is a partnership approach in which shoppers collect points while buying goods and services at retail locations, online, or in other ways (such as when using a credit card). Air Miles offers tiered customer groups with its gold level for those who collect a certain number of points from a minimum number of brands. Air Miles originally offered non-monetary rewards when consumers redeemed points for goods and services, including air travel. For many items, it would require a time delay to collect points and redeem them. Air Miles currently offers consumers the option of using points collected as cash when making purchases at a point of sale. While a minimal delay is incurred, it is substantially less than before, since the minimum $10 purchase can be made with 95 points, a level someone could accumulate in a month.[36]

Air Miles also retains the characteristics of a loyalty program. It is a major strategic initiative for its participating brands. For example, Shell Canada offers Air Miles and regularly promotes additional offers to encourage repeat visits. Shell recently sent a direct mail piece that contained a card designed to be kept in one's wallet to receive a bonus when buying Shell gas. Air Miles is clearly structured as members enroll, receive a card, and track point totals in their online account. The accumulation of points takes time, and monetary and non-monetary rewards are a strong incentive. Consumers regularly receive direct mail and email notifications of offers to accumulate additional points. Air Miles tested an enhancement of its offerings through a mobile app allowing members to visit a participating retailer's site and earn promotional incentives with more frequent visits.

A number of prescriptions emerged to guide successful implementation of loyalty programs. First, brands use customer information within the database to perform behavioural (level, amount purchased) and attitudinal (brand associations and feeling) segmentation. Second, customized and personalized communication is critical as a one-size-fits-all approach is not useful since the database is established. Third, marketers should consider moving beyond direct mail and email for communication within the loyalty program and augmenting with social media to forge a stronger relationship with consumers. Finally, loyalty programs should communicate ways to earn rewards more immediately through the use of location-based apps.

We take a look at Canadian Tire to see these points applied to its digitally based loyalty program launched in the fall of 2014. Consumers who purchased with their Canadian Tire Options MasterCard, or used their loyalty card or the app, accumulated digital Canadian Tire Money for redemption for purchases online, at Canadian Tire stores, and at retail brands under the corporate umbrella. Previously, the retailer had distributed Canadian Tire Money anonymously for cash purchases, and the new loyalty program worked similarly but with two differences: (1) the program required customers to register, and (2) customers received a payback of 4 percent of sales as a reward if they used the credit card.

Canadian Tire planned promotional offers sent directly to loyalty program members' online account. The smart phone app allowed members to collect, redeem, and manage their Canadian Tire Money and receive bonus offers. Moreover, the app acted as a transaction hub to review transactions and initiate product returns. Executives expected the loyalty program data would provide insight into shoppers' habits and allow the retailer to direct relevant messages to members with personalized and customized communication.[37] After four years and 11 million members signed up, the retailer changed the brand name to Triangle Rewards, and simplified the program.[38]

Another retailer with a huge loyalty program membership is Loblaw, and it got even bigger when it merged two loyalty programs. **IMC Perspective 16-1** highlights the transition from PC Points and Shoppers Optimum to PC Optimum loyalty program.

PC OPTIMUM = PC PLUS + SHOPPERS OPTIMUM

In 2013, Loblaw announced its purchase of Shoppers Drug Mart. Motivated by diversification and more intensive distribution of food products into the health store chain, the executives also eyed the successful Shoppers Optimum loyalty program. It took a few years, but in early 2018 the food retailing giant combined its PC Points program with Shoppers Optimum to form PC Optimum. With duplication across programs, the total number of members approached 18 million consumers across numerous different store formats and banners within the Loblaw empire.

Amalgamating the programs proved relatively straightforward for most consumers even though the accumulation of points and the minimum points for redemption differed. Some consumers experienced lost points, difficulties of merging, and long wait times for help. But as a benefit, the new program retained the best features of both programs, giving consumers an even better deal with weekly personalized offers, points earned, and points-redemption events.

Some features originated from Shoppers as it established itself as Canada's largest retailer loyalty program. For example, Shoppers personalized email messages with an opening rate 10 percent higher than non-personalized messages which yielded stronger purchase levels. This indicated that consumers accepted the exchange of providing their personal information stored in the database for customized offers and incentives, a key learning point that other loyalty programs learned later.

Later, Shoppers Drug Mart launched a digital version that allowed members to receive points and offers via mobile, email, or the web. A new app allowed users to load coupons and other offers directly to their smart phone. The offers remained targeted based on purchase history. Features of the program included the ability to scan a digital Optimum card directly from a mobile device to earn and redeem points, check balance, transfer points, browse flyers, create shopping lists, manage prescriptions, and locate stores.

To implement the merged loyalty program across different Loblaw stores and product categories, it contracted a company with specialized

©Tom Wakeling/Shutterstock

and sophisticated software to allow consumers to interact with the system with the technology of their choosing and to personalize the promotional offers. For example, after getting the system up and running, it tested specific messages and offers to a subset of consumers based on their purchasing behaviour.

Success of the program looked promising as others joined in. Esso withdrew from the independent Aeroplan loyalty program and instead chose to offer PC Optimum points. This represents a significant shake-up in the loyalty program industry as these kinds of programs began with Aeroplan and Air Miles before retailers did it themselves.

Questions:

1. Who would be most attracted to the features of the PC Optimum loyalty program?
2. How competitive is PC Optimum's loyalty program compared to other loyalty programs?

CONSUMER ATTITUDES AND USAGE

Virtually all Canadians are enrolled in a loyalty program; on average, each of us is a member of about 13 programs but we regularly use only seven of them. A number of attitudinal measures demonstrate the appeal of loyalty programs: 79 percent say loyalty programs make them more likely to continue doing business with the brand, 68 percent claim they are more likely to recommend a brand with a good loyalty program, and 65 percent indicate they modify their brand spending to maximize loyalty benefits. The primary motivators for using loyalty programs include that people enjoy participating and that the program meets needs, makes the brand experience better, has appealing rewards, and is consistent with brand expectations.[39]

Overall, about two-thirds are "very" or "somewhat" satisfied with their loyalty program. Functional satisfaction with loyalty programs is strongly associated with the following: appeal of rewards/benefits, ability to reach desired rewards/benefits in a timely manner, number of ways rewards/benefits can be earned, amount accumulated per $1 spent, and the time it takes to receive your redeemed rewards/benefits.[40]

While the success of loyalty programs appears strong, marketers are faced with the continued issue of whether the program merely rewards behaviour that would have occurred anyway since consumers generally sign up for programs with brands that they are already emotionally attached to and have a purchase history with. For example, 30 percent would not be loyal to the brand if the loyalty program did not exist, and 45 percent believe that a loyalty program could be replaced with a competitor's program. Research suggests that hard benefits of financial rewards in terms of discounts, cash, or merchandise are critical; softer rewards with respect to privilege, access, and information are very important for fostering strong loyalty over time. Furthermore, consumers become attached to brands with loyalty programs for regular purchases and are more likely to use the brand once again for infrequent larger purchases.

The experience of being in a loyalty program is also a strong consideration as consumers value seeing the rewards accumulating over time. Furthermore, the experience of "cashing in" for a big-ticket item is seen as an important consumption event that helps strengthen the relationship with the brand. In fact, one-quarter of all Canadians "splurge" with their rewards claim. And this loyalty is seen in the 40 percent of major loyalty program members who have stayed with a program for over 10 years, especially since many "save up" for big-ticket items.

DIGITAL COMMUNICATION

Communicating with existing members and providing promotional offers is a value-enhancing approach to fostering increased use of the loyalty program and greater purchases. While loyalty programs still work with direct mail and email to administer and communicate with members, more are moving toward social media, mobile, and Internet site interactions to permit timely or customized offers. Many of the improvements are designed to provide an experience that is similar to buying and consuming the brand. Industry experts consider the possibility that these channels might permit brands to bring their loyalty programs in-house, away from Air Miles or Aeroplan, while others envision much more personalized and customized offerings, or perhaps profile sites where consumers share their profile to select brands rather than signing up for multiple loyalty cards.[41]

The provincial organization for liquor sales in Quebec, SAQ, introduced its loyalty program, Inspire, with commentators wondering why a monopoly needed to operate such a marketing activity. (By way of comparison, the equivalent organization in Ontario accepted Air Miles.) Initially, the program operated like other loyalty programs—wallet card, phone app, agreement to terms, points system, offer for volume purchases—but afterward the program became customer oriented with digital communication. For example, the app tracked purchases and made suggestions that consumers might enjoy. It also noted their preferences and sent notifications for new or limited-run bottles. The program also produced a customized newsletter, including individualized promotions, for each customer based on their purchases and response to promotional offers.[42]

The Scene card allows its 9 million members to collect reward points by attending movies, using products associated with Scotiabank (e.g., a Scene debit or credit card), buying goods at the concession stand, and ordering tickets in certain ways (e.g., online). Consumers also receive discounts and special promotion offers and contests, and can spend their rewards on free tickets or on restaurants, music, or magazines. Scene augmented its loyalty program by giving more points if members formed online groups and attended movies together. It also offered a mobile app and text alerts for keeping in touch and improving services.[43] Scene augmented its loyalty program by test marketing a paid loyalty tier so that members could acquire points more quickly. For $7 per month, members received points for being registered each month, concession line priority service, movie experience upgrades, discount point use on Wednesdays, and concession upgrades.[44]

Starbucks Rewards gives "stars" to customers with their purchases and offers rewards along three collection levels. At the Welcome level, consumers get a drink for their birthday; at the Green level, consumers can get a free refill with five stars; and at the Gold level, consumers receive free food or drink once they hit 30 stars within a year and obtain status with a gold card. Many tweeted a positive response to the gold card as recognition for their high volume of purchases. A new smart phone app allows consumers to track their stars in a fun way consistent with the brand image. Members can interact with one another

Exhibit 16-11 The Starbucks Rewards program offers consumers useful features with its app.

©BestStockFoto/Shutterstock

for ideas on improving the Starbucks experience.[45] Managers attributed Starbucks' sales growth and increased number of store visits to its rewards program and improved digital communication with its members (see **Exhibit 16-11**). In fact, its rewards program is linked directly with the mobile payment system from the customer's smart phone, and this encouraged stronger mobile payment uptake well ahead of other retailers.[46]

LO4 Evaluation of Direct Marketing

We presented strengths and limitations of direct marketing thus far, but summarize these factors in a concluding section as we have done in previous chapters. Given that direct marketing employs different media, each with its own characteristics, these conclusions are generalizations in which variation can be expected. In addition, the evaluation criteria require adjustment depending on if the direct marketing targets customers or non-customers.

STRENGTHS OF DIRECT MARKETING

Direct marketing has many strengths, including target audience selectivity, target audience coverage, frequency, creativity for cognitive and emotional responses, scheduling flexibility, and costs.

Target Audience Selectivity Marketers can purchase lists of recent product purchasers (e.g., car buyers), and these lists may allow segmentation on the basis of geographic area, occupation, demographics, and job title. Combining this information with the geo-coding capabilities of PRIZM C2 (discussed in Chapter 3), marketers can develop effective segmentation strategies. In fact, a personalized or customized message can be sent in situations where the identity of the person is known. Car owners are mailed letters congratulating them on their new purchase and offering accessories. Computer purchasers are sent software solicitations. With the ability of direct marketing to personalize and customize messages through a relevant direct-response medium, we suggest that fairly strong attention to and involvement with the message occurs in these situations.

Target Audience Coverage Direct marketing lets the advertiser reach a high percentage of the selected target audience and reduces waste coverage. Since the database allows precise target audience profiles, the direct-response medium selected can achieve a strong level of hits. For example, while not everyone drives on highways where there are billboards or pays attention to TV commercials, virtually everyone receives mail. A good list allows for minimal waste, as only those consumers with the highest potential are targeted. For example, a political candidate can direct a message at a very select group of people (those living in a certain postal code, or members of McGill University Alumni or the Royal Vancouver Yacht Club).

Frequency Depending on the medium used, it may be possible to build frequency levels. The program vehicles used for direct-response TV advertising are usually the most inexpensive available, so the marketer can afford to purchase repeat times. Frequency may not be so easily accomplished through the mail, since consumers may be annoyed to receive the same mail repeatedly.

Creativity for Cognitive and Emotional Responses Direct marketing can take on a variety of creative forms. Direct-mail pieces allow for detailed copy that provides a great deal of information. The targeted mailing of DVDs containing product information has increased dramatically, as companies have found this to be a very effective way to provide potential buyers with product information.

Scheduling Flexibility While some media require long-range planning and have long closing dates, direct-response advertising can be much more timely. Direct mail, for example, can be put together very quickly and distributed to the target population. TV programs typically used for direct-response advertising are older, less sought-after programs that are likely to appear on the station's list of available spots. Another common strategy is to purchase available time at the last possible moment to get the best price.

Costs While the CPM for direct mail may be high, its ability to specifically target the audience and eliminate waste coverage reduces the actual CPM. Email costs are generally very affordable. The ads used on TV for infomercials are among the lowest-priced available. A second factor contributing to the cost-efficiency of direct-response advertising is the cost per customer purchasing. Because of the low cost of media, each sale generated is very inexpensive.

LIMITATIONS OF DIRECT MARKETING

As with all things, direct marketing has limitations to balance out its benefits. These include media image, control for selective exposure, and reach.

Media Image Generally, people believe unsolicited mail promotes undesired products, and others dislike being solicited. Likewise, direct-response ads on TV are often low-budget ads for lower-priced products, which contributes to the image that somewhat inferior products are marketed in this way. Some of this image is being overcome by the home shopping channels, which promote very expensive products. Telemarketing is found to be irritating to consumers, as is spam email.

Control for Selective Exposure While target audience selectivity attempts to address this factor, consumers exert tremendous control with respect to direct marketing. It is easy to simply toss a direct-mail piece into one's paper recycling bin. As seen in the discussion for television, consumers can readily zip or zap a direct message, and consumers usually have to actively seek and select an infomercial. In contrast to this point, those who are in fact interested in the offer are expected to devote considerable levels of time to processing the message, irrespective of the limitations of the direct-response media selected.

Reach The selectivity of direct marketing and the cost associated with it suggest that achieving high levels of reach is neither feasible nor even a realistic characteristic of the purpose of this marketing approach. Similarly, the costs associated with complete geographic coverage are expected to be prohibitive in most direct-marketing programs.

(LO5) IMC Planning: Strategic Use of Direct Marketing

Direct marketing is an important component of integrated marketing communication programs of organizations. In some cases it initiates an immediate response, and in other cases it builds the brand by moving the target audience through the decision-making process. In addition, direct-marketing activities support and are supported by other elements of the promotional mix.

DECISION-MAKING PROCESS

As described in this chapter, direct-marketing tools typically persuade immediate consumer action. At this point, it is critical that the promotional manager plan for a specific action in order to select the most appropriate direct-response media. In Chapter 5 we reviewed different types of behavioural objectives for promotional communication, which we will use to develop IMC planning prescriptions. Trial and repeat purchasing objectives suggest that much of direct marketing involves influence at the purchase decision stage.

Trial objectives require a broader-based direct-response medium, much like what is seen in advertising media decisions. Typically, wide-ranging direct-mail pieces targeted by census track allow firms to reach as many potential consumers as possible. In this situation, the database used relies on public sources, and a manager uses unaddressed drop-offs. For more targeted messages, brands rely on the list services and provide addressed mailings. Alternatively, with a database of existing customers, cross-selling of other products is now a trial purchase for the promotional planner's brand in a new product category. This trial purchase may be relatively new and be viewed as a purchase within the product category, thus requiring a direct-response medium providing considerable information.

We mentioned that existing customer databases are used for repeat purchases. Repeat purchasing objectives involve the timing, amount, and rate of consumer purchases. These different options suggest other criteria for evaluating the different direct-media options. For example, repeat purchasing objectives for specific timing might suggest telemarketing if the managers have current databases and permission to call upon the company's current customers. A favourite direct-response medium is bill inserts delivered monthly to enhance frequency and thus improve the amount and rate of purchase. And a natural update of this is digital marketing communication sent with bills accessed online. Thus, the opportunity for promotional planners to match the specific objectives with the right direct-response medium requires full consideration.

Shopping behaviour objectives frequently involve influencing consumers at earlier stages in their decision making. For example, direct-mail pieces may be delivered to encourage need recognition and prompt the target audience to make a sales inquiry at the retail location or over the telephone, or to visit the Internet site for further understanding of the brand during the information search stage. Alternatively, telephone calls can be made to follow up after the sales inquiry to ensure that the brand is seriously considered at the alternative evaluation stage.

DIRECT MARKETING AND IMC TOOLS

Obviously, direct marketing is in itself a form of advertising. Whether through mail, print, or TV, the direct-response offer is an ad. It usually contains a contact number, a form that requests mailing information, or a link to an Internet site. Sometimes the ad supports the direct-selling effort. Direct-response ads or infomercials are also referred to in retail outlet displays.

Public relations activities often employ direct-response techniques. Private companies may use telemarketing activities to solicit funds for charities, or co-sponsor charities that use these and other direct-response techniques to solicit funds. Likewise, corporations and/or organizations engaging in public relations activities may include contact numbers or Internet addresses in their ads or promotional materials.

Telemarketing and direct selling are two methods of personal selling. Non-profit organizations such as charities often use telemarketing to solicit funds. For-profit companies are also using telemarketing with much greater frequency to screen and qualify prospects (which reduces selling costs) and to generate leads. Direct-mail pieces are often used to invite prospective customers to visit auto showrooms to test-drive new cars; the salesperson then assumes responsibility for the selling effort.

Direct mail and email are used to notify consumers of sales promotions like sales events or contests. Ski shops regularly mail announcements of special end-of-season sales. Whistler Ski Resort and Intrawest constantly mail out promotions to their customer database announcing promotional and seasonal vacation packages, room rates, and lift ticket specials. Consumer packaged-goods firm Garnier used both addressed (5 percent redemption) and unaddressed mail (1.5 percent redemption) with extensive profiling to deliver a sample and coupon offer for its Long and Strong brand.[47] Hudson's Bay and other retail outlets call their existing customers to notify them of special sales promotions. In turn, the sales promotion event may support the direct-marketing effort since databases are often built from the names and addresses acquired from a promotion, permitting other direct-marketing follow-up.

Learning Objectives Summary

 Define direct marketing and summarize the importance of a database for direct-marketing communication decisions.

Direct marketing includes a variety of methods and media that seek to obtain an immediate behavioural response from the target audience. Its success is predicated on a database that contains information for each customer or prospect in terms of demographic variables. More thorough databases contain additional variables on purchase history, socioeconomic characteristics, media exposure, and any other relevant segmentation variables the marketer believes to be necessary. Direct marketing is a valuable promotional tool for targeting audiences and for managing CRM activities despite its intrusiveness toward consumers and the challenges and investment requirements of databases.

 Express the decisions of a direct-marketing plan.

Direct marketing involves careful target audience profiling through the use of the database. Direct marketers can target lapsed customers in an attempt to generate re-trial. Alternatively, they can target current customers and try to encourage repeat purchasing of the brand, but with additional products (i.e., cross-selling). Databases garnered through other means can be compiled to develop stronger trial among non-category users or non-brand users. Thus, a critical part of the direct-marketing plan is profiling the target audience and selecting the corresponding objective, since this guides the promotional offer and the selection of the most appropriate direct-response media.

Direct marketing is executed with a variety of direct-response media including direct mail, catalogues, broadcast, telemarketing, and new digital applications. We summarized the former ones in this chapter and examine the latter in the next chapter. These media are used in a specific manner to encourage consumers to take action in terms of a purchase or getting involved with another medium or another IMC tool such as sales promotion.

 Describe the content of a loyalty program.

An important part of a direct-marketing plan is a loyalty program designed to maintain continued repeat purchasing from consumers who enroll and become members. Most of these consumers are behaviourally and attitudinally loyal; however, others join to collect points to earn rewards and might readily switch to an alternative provider if they did not have so much invested in the program. Despite this limitation, consumers are quite satisfied with these programs and Canada has one of the highest participation rates in the world.

 Evaluate the strengths and limitations of direct marketing.

Advantages of direct marketing include target audience selectivity that permits personalization in direct-response media like direct mail leading to stronger attention and involvement, target audience coverage, frequency, creativity for cognitive and emotional responses, scheduling flexibility, and affordable absolute cost and efficiency. At the same time, a number of disadvantages are associated with the use of direct marketing, including media image, control for selective exposure, and reach implying limited geographic scope for some direct-response media.

 Apply the ideas of direct marketing within the development of an IMC plan.

Direct marketing is one activity in marketing where activities are clearly demarcated with respect to targeting potential customers with a message to ensure a trial purchase or targeting existing customers to continue purchasing. The source of information for sending the message and offer is a database of leads or current customers, so the most appropriate approach is possible, unlike with other forms of marketing communication. Direct marketing acts as the delivery mechanism for other IMC tools like sales promotion. As seen in some of the loyalty programs, promotional offers to members can enhance their experience. Similarly, public relations activities can be tied with direct marketing for stronger communication effect or cost efficiencies.

Review Questions

1. Explain how companies use database marketing. How is the information derived from the database used to target audiences?

2. What is the difference between the one- and two-step approaches to direct marketing? Give examples of companies that pursue both methods.

3. Why are loyalty programs considered to be direct-marketing programs rather than sales promotions?

4. One of the disadvantages associated with direct-marketing media is the high cost per exposure. Some marketers feel that this cost is not really as much of a disadvantage as is claimed. Argue for or against this position.

5. How does direct marketing influence each stage of the consumer decision-making process as it works with other IMC tools?

Applied Questions

1. Construct a list of variables that a fashion brand might desire in its database to market to students in college or university.

2. Collect any direct mail delivered to your household and evaluate whether it is effective.

3. Read up online about an interesting loyalty program and apply **Figure 16-4** to identify the characteristics and give an assessment of the program's value.

4. How might a smart phone service improve its marketing communication with the use of direct marketing?

5. Provide examples for both consumer goods and services of how companies might use direct marketing as part of an IMC program.

CHAPTER SEVENTEEN

Internet Media

LEARNING OBJECTIVES

LO1 Describe Internet media usage and explain website communication.

LO2 Review Internet media advertising.

LO3 Identify the advertising formats of Internet media.

LO4 Explore mobile advertising.

LO5 Define measures of Internet media effectiveness.

LO6 Apply the ideas of Internet media within an IMC program.

Internet Media Display Ads

We see display ads every second of the day on content publishers' websites and in social media. At times we may not fully notice them, but advertisers spend money on these ads, which are part of a digital ad plan and part of an overall IMC plan. We review how noteworthy brands use Internet media display ads to achieve communication objectives.

Quesada Burritos wanted to communicate that its Beyond Meat Burrito is 100 percent delicious and not just for vegetarians, as it targeted "flexitarians" looking to add more plant-based options to their diet. The campaign featured owned content in social media, paid search, and in-store ads. It also included Internet media display ads to ensure wider exposure in numerous media vehicles to reach a vast number of new customers.

Leon's intended to position the 110-year-old retailer as a stylish alternative for older millennials who now had competitors to consider such as West Elm, Urban Barn, and EQ3. Its TV ad portrayed a couple showing their new furniture purchases to friends while claiming "Our designer selected the pieces from a boutique called Leon's" in a heavy faux-French accent. The "Surprisingly Stylish" campaign featured owned content in social media, in-store ads, and Internet media display ads to ensure Leon's became part of the target audience's evoked set.

Schick brand of razors sponsors the Toronto Maple Leafs and featured current Leaf Zack Hyman and former Leaf Gary Roberts in its "The Man I AM" campaign designed to portray a diverse view of masculinity. Hyman writes children's books and Roberts is a strong role model for young people, and together the two represented the individuality and authenticity of men who have multiple sides to them, and in these cases, substantially different from the stereotypical tough professional athlete. Interestingly, display ads became useful for a social issue message.

Danone launched a no-sugar-added version to its yogurt product line with new flavours. While still a less sweet taste sensation, the natural fruit purée provided a hint for all to enjoy. The lighthearted TV ad set in an everyday household (complete with a pet dog) associated the yogurt innovation with other famous achievements (landing on the moon). All in the family are in awe as they read the newspaper headline about Danone's new yogurt! The ad targets a younger generation, who are presumably looking for a healthier offering, with digital media and out-of-home media with visuals of fruit exploding from the single-serve package. Once again, display ads supported the campaign with reminder messages to go along with the social media exposure, exciting activations, and PR.

Question:

1. What communications objectives are achieved with a display ad in these examples?

The chapter opener features examples of representative brands and product categories to illustrate that Internet media is part of virtually any large-scale IMC or digital advertising campaign. We view Internet media from a communication perspective that contributes to communication objectives and begins the direct marketing process as well. First we describe Internet media usage and explain website communication. Second, we review the content of a digital advertising plan. Third, we identify the advertising formats that promotional planners place in virtually any location within Internet media. Fourth, we summarize aspects of mobile communication with ad revenue devoted to this route increasing. To conclude, we define the options for measuring Internet media communication effectiveness, and apply the ideas of Internet media within an IMC program.

Internet Media Communication

The **Internet** and the **World Wide Web (WWW)** allow marketers and consumers to conduct transactions for goods and services; however, our focus is to view these digital tools as media for communication and facilitation of the promotional program. In the academic literature, many digital marketing domains are investigated beyond advertising.[1] Our interest is Internet advertising research that examines the effectiveness of Internet media advertising, interactivity, how advertising works, attitude to Internet media ads (including websites), and finally comparisons to other media.[2] As this suggests, the Internet connects consumers—both current customers and potential customers—and marketers seeking or greeting both types of consumers through advertising and other tools. In this section, we describe Canadian Internet media usage and explain the primary purpose of website marketing communication.

INTERNET USAGE

Approximately 90 percent of all Canadians accessed Internet media weekly at any location over the past few years (**Figure 17-1**), according to data provided by Media Technology Monitor (MTM). In addition, after a couple of decades of Internet use, we see similar consistency across demographic groups other than age. Usage proved very consistent provincially, by city/town size and in each major Canadian city. We expect Canadian Internet usage to be close to universal in a few years. Home Internet access hit 92 percent for all Canadian households, and peaked at 99 percent for households with income over $100,000.

On average, Canadians used Internet media 26 hours per week, which varied considerably by age, as shown by MTM's data in **Figure 17-2**. The nearly 40 hours of Internet use per week for the youngest age category translates to 5.5 hours per day, but the measurement includes work use. Other data indicated that weekly use did not vary as significantly by geography (e.g, province, city, community size), income, or education, except for those with very low income and education levels.

Figure 17-3 illustrates smart phone and tablet ownership over the past few years according to MTM. Interestingly, tablet ownership for the youngest age group declined and the use of mobile technology grew for the oldest age group. As noted in Chapter 10, Internet ad revenue is accounted for by online (desktop, laptop) and mobile (smart phone,

Figure 17-1 Weekly Internet use (%) by age group, anglophones 18+

	2014	2016	2018
18–34	97	98	97
35–49	95	96	96
50–64	91	89	90
65+	69	72	74
Total	90	90	90

Figure 17-2 Average number of hours/week of Internet use, anglophones 18+

	2014	2016	2018
18–34	29.5	33.5	38.7
35–49	20.4	24.9	30.6
50–64	15.2	17.5	20.0
65+	8.0	9.4	11.5
Total	19.4	22.3	26.1

Figure 17-3 Percentage of smart phone and tablet ownership by demographic, anglophones 18+

	2014		2016		2018	
	Smart Phone	Tablet	Smart Phone	Tablet	Smart Phone	Tablet
18–34	91	58	96	53	96	49
35–49	81	59	89	68	93	66
50–64	61	48	75	55	79	59
65+	29	32	49	38	52	48
Total	69	51	80	55	82	55

Figure 17-4 Past month Internet activity (%), fall 2018, anglophones 18+

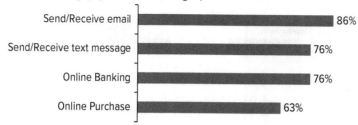

Activity	%
Send/Receive email	86%
Send/Receive text message	76%
Online Banking	76%
Online Purchase	63%

Figure 17-5 Past month Internet entertainment activity (%), anglophones 2018

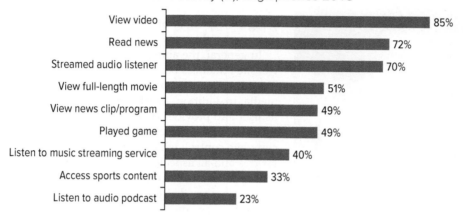

Activity	%
View video	85%
Read news	72%
Streamed audio listener	70%
View full-length movie	51%
View news clip/program	49%
Played game	49%
Listen to music streaming service	40%
Access sports content	33%
Listen to audio podcast	23%

tablet), so understanding technological penetration level is useful for planning purposes. Later in this chapter, we investigate mobile advertising in its own section.

Figure 17-4 summarizes MTM data regarding a few usage activities done online or with mobile devices. These overview statistics indicate that Internet media facilitated many different types of consumer experiences. Taken together with the reach level and time spent consuming, Internet media attained the status of a regular day-to-day media for Canadians, leading to advertisers spending $6.77 billion in advertising for 2017.

Figure 17-5 shows the varying entertainment activities Canadians enjoyed with Internet media according to MTM data. Clearly, the extensive activities Canadians experience on the Internet allow advertisers opportunities to reach specific customer groups, lifestyles, or virtually any marketing segmentation variable. In fact, some opportunities may be *very* good—the Internet spurred greater consumption of news when adding up the total exposure from traditional and digital media as shown in Chapter 12 statistics.

The development of user-generated content—such as product reviews, forum or journal posts, blogs, websites, wikis, audio files, video files, and podcasts—contributes to an enormous amount of word-of-mouth communication. One study documented how certain types of psychographic groups relied on these different Internet media sources of information when making purchase decisions.[3] With these variations within Internet media, we can conclude that some aspects will present advertising opportunities with mass exposure potential like TV, selective reach like magazines, and interactive capabilities unique to Internet media. At present, Procter & Gamble, maker of Crest toothpaste (**Exhibit 17-1**), is one of Canada's leading Internet media advertisers. In fact, how advertisers will allocate the nearly $7 billion in expenditures across the many Internet media vehicles will continue to be an important media decision, much like in past decades with older media.

Exhibit 17-1 Procter & Gamble is one of the largest advertisers in Canada using Internet media.

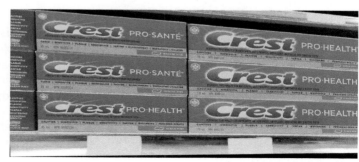

©rmnoa357/Shutterstock

Exhibit 17-2 Red Bull offers many reasons to visit its website.

©arindambanerjee/Shutterstock

WEBSITE COMMUNICATION

Website communication is important to summarize since digital marketing communication directs users to different types of **websites**. One type of website provides factual information to consumers about a company and its products. To attract visitors to the site—and to have them return—requires a combination of creativity, updated information, and the use of digital and other media to direct consumers. A second type of website provides an immersive experience with creative video, striking images, interesting audio, and graphic design; brands create unique messages and digital experiences unlike any previous advertising media. A third type of website facilitates communication and interaction among consumers using the capability of two-way communication features. And, some websites combine two or three of these approaches into one.

In general, the above points imply that the creativity of a brand's website enhances both cognitive and emotional responses much like or even more than the experience with broadcast and print media. In addition, a website is designed to serve the interests of its user and provides strong target audience selectivity. However, the interactive characteristic means consumers retain instant and complete control, which is a limitation advertisers need to overcome for this and all aspects of Internet media. From a communication standpoint, websites typically achieve four broad communication objectives—they develop awareness, disseminate information, build a brand image, and facilitate interaction. These latter three are attitudinal in nature and are consistent with earlier chapters.

Develop Awareness Communicating on a website enhances or creates awareness of an organization as well as its specific product and service offerings. Websites for established products offer additional interactive exposure of the brand in terms of its key messages and typical signature (e.g., logo, slogan, colours). The website for Red Bull creates a fun experience for consumers to enjoy the brand and keep awareness strong. Its brand image is reinforced on its site much like at public events (**Exhibit 17-2**). For small companies with limited budgets, a website is an opportunity to create awareness well beyond what might be achieved through other media. Internet media may not be optimal for awareness in these situations due to its limited reach without other communication to direct consumers to the website; however, these consumers are often in the information search stage of their decision making and are very good prospects for ensuring they do not forget about the brand when making a final decision, or for when they want to buy on their next purchase occasion. To build awareness of its new brands of whiskey, Wiser's created Hold It High, a page on its website where consumers can post a tribute toast to one of their friends. The brand has posted the tributes in outdoor, transit, and radio ads for additional exposure.[4]

Exhibit 17-3 Kraft provides ingredient and nutrition information on its website.

©rmnoa357/Shutterstock

Disseminate Information A primary communication objective for a website is to provide information about a company's products and services. With increased health interest, Canadians rely on food company websites for more in-depth facts than might be seen in other media or at the point of sale. For example, Kraft Canada's website presents ingredient and nutritional information for its salad dressing (**Exhibit 17-3**). In most markets, a website is a necessity since buyers, both consumer and business-to-business, expect that a company will have a site providing them with detailed information about its offerings and where to buy. In fact, considerable current market research indicates that most Canadians "window shop" or browse the Internet for information on goods or services in general, and similar numbers arise for specific activities like getting medical and travel information and banking online. In the public sector, all levels of government use Internet media to provide citizens with a wide range of information on services.

Build a Brand Image Websites are designed to reflect the image a company wants to portray. Interestingly, marketers have had difficulty creating a brand image on the Internet. While some companies have been successful, others have not fared as well and realize that branding and image-creating strategies must be specifically adapted to the medium. Websites also provide a transformational experience, with video, animation, and social media-like tools to make the brand experience truly unique and interactive beyond what consumers experience with other media. Guess is a good example, as it links all of its social media to its website (**Exhibit 17-4**).

A study by the marketing research firm Millward Brown published in the *Journal of Advertising Research* concludes that Internet media is capable of building a brand like other established advertising media, although certain caveats seen elsewhere remain. For example, ensuring that the right message is communicated within the appropriate media vehicle is critical, a key conclusion that we have seen with more established media.[5] Since then, it is clear that Internet sites are a critical component of any brand's ability to project its image to customers, non-customers, and any other stakeholders. A few other great Canadian examples include MAC Cosmetics, Lululemon, Canada Goose, NRML, and Harry Rosen—check them out!

Facilitate Interaction Because Internet media is interactive, it provides strong potential for increased customer involvement and almost immediate feedback. Companies set up websites to interact with an audience on a regular basis, and may use a membership component to obtain personal information with permission and communicate afterward (e.g., email). For example, the Canadian website for Alfa Romeo achieves all three previous objectives and its splash page invites visitors to sign up for a newsletter, obtain a brochure, go to a dealer, or build and price a model (**Exhibit 17-5**). From another perspective, Mazda and its agency JWT created a smart phone app that viewers used in a Cineplex movie theatre to simulate a car test drive. The app synchronized with the big screen video and users tried to match the driving, while the app measured their success. The app ended with an invitation for a real test drive and 9,000 signed up, a 5 percent hit rate. A similar event occurred a year earlier for the Mazda3 that simulated a race car game where participants and winners received concession products or movie tickets. The competition app garnered 6,000 test drive requests.[6]

Exhibit 17-4 The website for Guess builds its brand much like its storefronts.

©Martin Good/Shutterstock

Exhibit 17-5 Alfa Romeo offers many ways for potential customers to interact with the company.

©meunierd/Shutterstock

Exhibit 17-6 Dove uses many transformational features on its website.

©chris brignell/Alamy Stock Photo

Interaction also occurs during the execution of sales promotions. The Coors Light "Search+Rescue" contest required consumers to find 880 "hidden" branded boxes containing prizes (e.g., party invitations, gift cards, sports equipment). Consumers visited the website with an interactive map to find the location. After finding, the lucky contestant tweeted their selfie with the box and then received the skill-testing question from the company to open up their winnings. The promotional event ended with a "Base Camp Party" in nine major cities. Negative publicity ensued when Toronto traffic snarled after police received notice of a "suspicious package" attached to a downtown railing. The company experienced a "human error" when the person placed the box in an incorrect location. The brand took significant precautions and placed the boxes away from transit, schools, and tourist areas, however it scrapped the public placement after the incident.[7]

WEBSITE STRATEGY

Some websites are designed for informational purposes only, while others approach the market with a transformational purpose—providing valuable resources for important life experiences. The website for the Dove brand (**Exhibit 17-6**) is an example having multiple capabilities with an extensive array of text, video, graphics, and photos. Started decades ago as a beauty cream bar differentiated from soap, the brand is placed on other products for women (body wash, hair care, deodorant), similar products for men, and a few for babies. Its main menu offers six selections: Explore Solutions, Products, Baby Dove, Men+Care, Dove Esteem Project, and Dove Stories. Within each menu item, numerous interactive features give product information or communicate details about the experiences of Dove consumers. As this example demonstrates, a website effectively achieves any or all communication objectives, and in fact also achieves different types of behavioural objectives (identified in Chapter 5) for multiple audiences at varying stages of the decision-making process (identified in Chapter 3).

A consumer interacting with a website raises the question of what is meant by *interactivity*. **Interactivity** is the extent to which an actor involved in a communication episode perceives the communication to be reciprocal, responsive, speedy, and characterized by the use of nonverbal information.[8] Applying this idea, a website is *reciprocal* when it offers multiple opportunities for the consumer to act, such as with links, buttons, or connections to other utilities like social media. It is *responsive* if every action produces a relevant and appropriate outcome. Quick response suggests that the website is *speedy*. It is *characterized by the use of nonverbal information* if it makes extensive use of pictures, sounds, and animation. Notably absent from this definition is the notion of control, since it is a media usage characteristic of both interactive media and non-interactive media as described in Chapter 10. Empirical findings supported this definition of interactivity, which was also found to be a strong predictor of attitude to the website and media involvement. Furthermore, preliminary research indicated that more interactive websites generated deeper information processing and message believability, leading to stronger attitudes toward the brand and website.[9]

This attitudinal communication effect is another source of findings where researchers investigate what design factors lead to a consumer's positive attitude toward the website.[10] Additionally, research investigated the impact of attitude to the website on brand attitude or company attitude.[11] This effect has been investigated for both high/low involvement and informational/transformational brand attitudes, previously discussed in Chapter 8.[12] Research also examined the attitudinal effects on purchase intentions.[13] Building on this and consistent with earlier ad research, a paper with two studies investigated design factors for specific cognitive and affective responses to the website, and attitude to the website along with a greater number of behavioural outcomes.[14]

Figure 17-6 summarizes these ideas, which are similar to the models described in Chapter 4. Several of the advertising principles established in other media are investigated with Internet media, and it remains to be seen whether their application will be completely similar or show variation. In the end, however, the notion of Internet advertising is now common terminology. Finally, consumers develop an affinity for or are very loyal to their favourite Internet sites for their information or entertainment needs. More loyal users tend to spend more time at these sites and have much more positive attitudes toward the sites' relevance, content, and features. This is consistent with other media, where people have their favourite TV show or radio station.

Figure 17-6 Model of website advertising effects

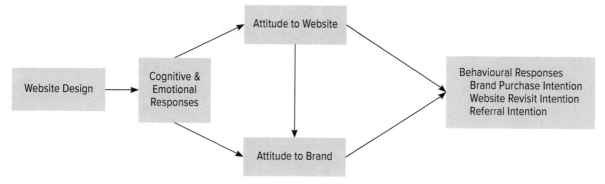

But how do brands motivate consumers to visit their website? While we saw the use of broadcast and print media in earlier chapters to direct viewers, brands also use Internet media advertising. And its growth spawned recognition in the form of Webby Awards. Liberté Blueberry Greek Yogurt used a tablet-based mobile ad, located on the lower part of the page, where users played a game trying to put the blueberries on the banner ad back into the container by tipping and turning the device. Locating the ad at the bottom of the page reinforced the attribute of the berries at the bottom of the container and reinforced the brand's natural positioning. On an automotive shopping website, BMW (**Exhibit 17-7**) created the world's longest banner ad—which expanded when touched by the cursor to reveal a witty story that "people could not put down" as the average time spent with the ad reached three minutes![15]

In addition to Internet media advertising, brands rely on social media for communication and also encourage consumers to visit their social media pages, two topics we examine in the next chapter. For example, Sephora (**Exhibit 17-8**) lists seven different social media sites on its website for visitors to consider checking out. Practitioners refer to each of these IMC tools as "owned" media (e.g., website), "paid" media (e.g., display ad), and "earned" media (e.g., user-generated content). While this handy vocabulary works well to a degree, it does limit the innovativeness and creativity of a plan, as we shall see.

Finally, it is noteworthy to see that Canadian consumers indicated discomfort with Internet media in a survey by Ad Standards (**Figure 17-7**). A poor media image is due to annoying display and video ads, deception, targeting children with subtle advertising messages, data collection without consumers' permission, and crime. Like direct marketing, Internet marketers must respect users' privacy, and IAB issued guidelines to alleviate this concern. In contrast to these Internet media issues, consumers enjoy the abundance of social media experiences and find shopping with Internet media useful for planning all sorts of purchases. In this respect, it is viewed favourably, indicating a paradox: Internet media simultaneously exhibits both a strong and a poor media image.

Exhibit 17-7 BMW is one of many automotive brands using Internet media for advertising.

©Pres Panayotov/Shutterstock

Exhibit 17-8 Sephora provides a consistent image across all social media vehicles.

©Goran Bogicevic/Shutterstock

Figure 17-7 Canadians' comfort with advertising

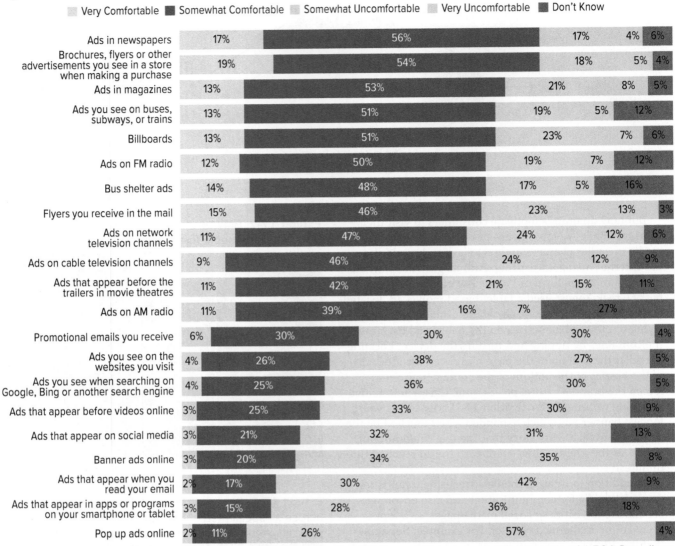

Source: Study conducted in early 2016 by The Gandalf Group with a representative sample of 1,564 Canadians.
©Advertising Standards Canada, Consumer Perspectives on Advertising, 2016.

LO2 **Digital Advertising Planning**

Promotional planners select Internet media for paid advertising messages much like broadcast, print, and out-of-home media. There is a degree of similarity since the delivery of content on an Internet site is supported by fees charged to brands who target the audience of the Internet site. But placing ad messages within Internet media presents a degree of uniqueness due to its interactive characteristic. In this section we review how promotional planners use Internet media for advertising purposes.

OVERVIEW

The Interactive Advertising Bureau (IAB) of Canada estimated that Internet advertising revenue hit $6.77 billion in 2017 (Figure 17-8). Compared to data for other advertising media in 2017, this is higher than the $3.04 billion spent on television, higher than total broadcast at $4.53 billion, and ahead of print at $1.66 billion. Internet advertising revenue accounted for 55 percent of combined top four reported major media revenues in Canada for 2017. Advertising in the

Figure 17-8 Total Canadian Internet advertising revenue ($ millions), over time

	2010	2012	2014	2015	2016	2017
Online (desk/laptop)	2,232	2,925	2,890	2,984	2,942	3,282
Mobile (phone/tablet)	47	160	903	1,620	2,542	3,489
Total (online and mobile)	2,279	3,085	3,793	4,604	5,484	6,771

Source: IAB Canada, Canadian Internet Advertising Revenue Survey, 2017

Figure 17-9 Canadian Internet advertising revenue ($ million), by ad format

	2010	2012	2014	2015	2016	2017
Search	907	1,586	2,052	2,512	2,920	3,364
Display	690	987	1,285	1,559	1,911	2,322
Video	37	92	266	358	481	928
Classified/directory	587	249	171	162	167	145
Email	11	12	19	13	6	12
Total (online & mobile)	2,279	3,085	3,793	4,604	5,484	6,771

Source: IAB Canada, Canadian Internet Advertising Revenue Survey, 2017

Figure 17-10 Canadian Internet advertising revenue ($ million), by ad format and device for 2017

	Online	Mobile	Total
Search	1,594	1,770	3,364
Display	1,147	1,175	2,322
Video	421	507	928

Source: IAB Canada, Canadian Internet Advertising Revenue Survey, 2017

French language declined as a percentage of total Canadian Internet advertising revenue, from 21 percent over 2005–2009 to an average of 19 percent during 2010–2014, and stood at 17 percent for 2017.[16]

Figure 17-8 shows that IAB reports Internet advertising revenue of online ads directed to desktop computers and laptops, and mobile ads directed to phones and tablets. Consumer adoption and use of mobile devices attracted increasing advertising dollars, growing from $160 million in 2012 to $3.5 billion in 2017. In contrast, online ad revenue stabilized at about $2.9 billion for each year during 2012–2016, but picked up slightly thereafter in 2017. Additional proof of the growth of digital advertising is that the federal government spent over 50 percent of its ad budget on Internet media.[17]

Expenditures of advertising formats are shown in **Figure 17-9**. During the early years of mobile advertising (i.e., 2010–2012), the method of estimating advertising revenue by ad format evolved. Thus, the ad revenue breakdown by format for 2010 and 2012 is for online only. The ad revenue breakdown by format during 2013–2017 is for both online and mobile. It is clear that paid advertising on Internet media continued its growth. The trend suggests future growth with video ad messages and it will be interesting to see if search and display have reached their plateau.

Figure 17-10 breaks out the 2017 IAB Canada data by ad format and device. Mobile ad revenue is higher than online ad revenue in total and for each ad format that accounts for 98 percent of all expenditures. The implication of this is significant as consumers receive more ads and receive ads more frequently when they are closer to the point of shopping, either shopping with their mobile device or using their mobile device when active out of home and nearer to retail outlets.

DIGITAL ADVERTISING PLAN

The amount of money spent for online and mobile messages means that a well thought out plan for digital advertising is expected and necessary to achieve objectives and maximize the return on investment. As is done in other chapters, we apply the planning approach of this book. **Figure 1-8** shown in Chapter 1 indicated that a promotional planner follows a planning approach for Internet media to implement an interactive marketing program much like media advertising and other IMC programs covered in the past three chapters.

A brand's digital advertising plan features objectives, strategy, and tactical decisions when delivering messages to its target audience who may be at any point in their decision making, as shown in **Figure 3-1**. In addition, **Figure 3-5** identified segmentation variables within five dimensions (geographic, demographic, socioeconomic, psychographic, and behaviour) as a basis for profiling a target audience. Chapter 3 also highlighted customer and non-customer groups based on brand loyalty as an important variable for planners to consider initially.

TARGET AUDIENCE AND OBJECTIVES

When applying the above for placing advertising messages in Internet media, promotional planners adapt all of the segmentation variables, however, the interactive characteristic provides opportunity for an additional one.[18] **Behavioural targeting** lets advertisers target consumers according to their Internet viewing history. By compiling **click-stream** data and Internet protocol information or **IP address**, advertisers identify segments of potential buyers and direct ads to them. For example, a vehicle brand like Honda or a Honda dealership serves ads to an individual who visited any other automotive brand's website or its own website. Note that behavioural targeting is not entirely consistent with Figure 3-5 since we did not refer to other behavioural segmentation variables such as brand loyalty targeting, user status targeting, or usage rate targeting. And, it is not fully clear whether it is in fact a behaviour like these three behaviours as one has merely clicked a mouse or touched a screen. Nonetheless, this interactive feature provides an additional segmentation variable for a promotional planner developing a digital advertising plan.

The approaches for setting behavioural and communication objectives presented in Chapter 5 are suitable for digital advertising and its intended target audience. Internet media's interactive characteristics require potential adaptation. For example, specific shopping and consumption objectives may be required before directing consumers to a brand's website or social media presence. On the other hand, the primary communication objective of a digital advertising message may be to enhance brand awareness and brand attitude like ads in any other media. Thus, a high proportion of paid digital ads are classified as either messages for developing or maintaining brand communication effects, or messages to influence shopping for online or physical store purchases. And for online purchases, paid digital ads are the first step in the two-step approach of direct marketing identified in Chapter 16. And increasingly, research and technology is linking display ad exposure to sales in physical stores, indicating a stronger direction of digital advertising working within a direct marketing strategy.[19]

In response to concerns about behavioural targeting, other forms of targeting, and advertising fairness, the Digital Advertising Alliance of Canada instituted the AdChoices program in conjunction with similar organizations worldwide. This organization is a self-regulatory body of major advertisers, media companies, and industry organizations (e.g., IAB Canada, Ad Standards). The AdChoices program was implemented such that when consumers see and click the blue triangle icon on ads, they can read information on why the ad is placed on the website they are visiting, choose to opt out of receiving ads from the company listed (generally an ad server), and obtain information about the ad server's privacy policy. After a major privacy incident, IAB Canada released a reminder to its members to participate in the program. Other marketing organizations like the Association of Canadian Advertisers and the Canadian Marketing Association worked with privacy advocates as part of the establishment of the Digital Advertising Alliance of Canada. But the privacy issue remains muddled. On the one hand, consumers are concerned about behavioural targeting, but on the other hand, they realize that their data is in play and that if they get free media, or free service online, then the trade is fair and they are okay with it.[20]

DIGITAL MEDIA STRATEGY

Media strategy and tactics decisions identified in Figure 10-2 occur within a digital advertising plan. Selecting Internet media is a decision within the broader media mix decision, and promotional planners determine the other four decisions of target audience coverage, geographic coverage, scheduling, and reach and frequency within Internet media. Target audience coverage in Internet media is consistent with other media. For example, a brand with a target audience who loves music considers music-related websites for placing ad messages. Geographically, advertisers adjust their brand messages depending upon where the user is located. For example, different versions of ads for a travel website (e.g., Travel Alberta) emerge depending upon where the information seeker is living. And the technological system behind Internet media allows a person living in a city like Ottawa to receive local ads even if they are looking at an American website.

Scheduling decisions occur as well. Ads are scheduled by the time of day, day, week, and month, as seen with TV and radio ad placement. Television viewership composition and frequency vary across the day (e.g., early morning, daytime, prime time). Similarly, radio's audience size and composition varies considerably, especially considering commuters driving to and from work. Internet media advertisers are interested in **time of day scheduling**, much like day parts in broadcast media. Internet media follows a similar pattern, with groups of working people accessing Internet media during the day for business purposes, primarily in the morning. Usage declines during the afternoon and at dinner time and then peaks once again during the evening for leisure purposes.

Finally, reach and frequency decisions occur in Internet media, and they are both easier and more difficult to execute. Traffic counts of website visits make it reasonably easy to know how many people are exposed to an ad message at any point in time. To achieve a reach objective, an advertiser places a message on a sufficient number of websites to achieve its goal. The IP address provides information for when a unique individual visits, thus indicating potential frequency. However, depending on the type of advertising, reach and frequency estimates may prove much trickier in practice.

DIGITAL MEDIA TACTICS

The advertising formats can be placed on virtually any Internet site to target a brand's audience. Promotional planners need guidance on how to structure this decision even though targeting on different Internet media types is similar to targeting in other media types. **Figure 17-11** applies the media terminology of Chapter 10 and compares broadcast and Internet. The Internet is a medium much like broadcast (i.e., TV and radio) is a medium. Since there are two types of broadcast, it is plausible to group Internet media along the same lines. Pre-existing Internet sites that consisted of content publishers and entertainment venues (i.e., early non–social media that continue to exist) provide opportunity for the placement of ads. We also have social media that accept ads as well; however, the membership characteristics, ability for interaction, and facility for contributing user-generated content provide a new way of planning brand messaging.

This implies that ads are placed in a specific media class within social media and a specific media class within content publishers. For example, a social networking Internet site would be a media class within social media. Carrying on, Facebook and LinkedIn would be avenues for placing an ad and would be the equivalent of a media vehicle, much like placing an ad on TSN's broadcast of the Raptors game or on a particular kind and name of radio station. For Internet content publishers, we see Yahoo as a media vehicle within the media class of news and information. However, the targeting capabilities are much different even though the idea of a media vehicle is similar. An advertiser can be very precise on a number of segmentation variables to direct an ad in these social media environments for a particular time frame. In contrast, the TV advertiser reaches an expected group of basketball fans during the game, with certain characteristics based on audience profile data.

We present this perspective to convey the importance and pervasiveness of social media and to understand that the avenues for placing a message via a display ad or within the social media itself offer many vehicles to select from. This is much like what occurs in other aspects of Internet media, like established content publishers such as Yahoo and content publishers from existing print media like *Maclean's* or *The National Post,* and content streamers like CTV. Furthermore, it is an extension of the idea of media vehicles in existing broadcast and print media.

As such, a media vehicle is critical for targeting in any medium, and this is true for any aspect of Internet media since media vehicles assist promotional planners in directing their message to their target audience. Targeting is fundamental to many applications for directing display ads through an ad network or ad exchange to any other Internet site or through a social networking site like Facebook. Advertising on a particular Internet site based on its content is known as **contextual targeting**, and this concept is essentially an extension of the concept of a media vehicle. For example, an advertiser places an airline ad on a travel site, or a golf club ad on a golf site, or even in or near a story about golf on another site. This is much like putting an ad for tools on HGTV during a Mike Holmes renovation show.

In future, ecommerce sites like Amazon are poised as a leading media vehicle for messages. Advertisers would pay for favourable ad placement and size and to appear during consumers' searches. Companies like Procter & Gamble see this as a "digital shelf" much like the shelf space in physical retail stores in which they pay fees for preferred exposure. Advertisers may see this as a viable alternative to paid search expenditures since it is more direct while consumers are actively shopping.[21]

Figure 17-11 Illustration of digital media vehicles

Medium	Internet	Internet	Broadcast	Broadcast
Media type	Content publisher	Social media	Television	Radio
Media class	News and information	Social networking	Sports	Alternative rock
Media vehicle	Yahoo	Facebook	TSN (Raptors)	Live 88.5 (Ottawa)

Digital and Social Media Perspective 17-1 illustrates the extremely creative "Snack Time" campaign in which the digital advertising plan began with paid ad exposure to get the ball rolling in social media. Such a strategy is a reasonable one for brands to consider in the digital plans, and this example nicely ties into the content of this chapter and the subsequent chapter on social media.

DIGITAL AND SOCIAL MEDIA PERSPECTIVE 17-1

"SNACK TIME"

Milk West, which comprises four provincial milk marketing boards in Western Canada (British Columbia, Alberta, Saskatchewan, and Manitoba), faced the problem of declining consumption among teens who often turned to pop or energy drinks. No direct messages to teens had occurred for a few years so top-of-mind awareness did not exist. Research indicated that a typical ad might not resonate with teens so the creative specialists looked in another direction.

Inspired with a situational and differentiated positioning to encourage teens to drink milk with their favourite snacks, since the snacks tasted better with milk versus other drinks, Milk West launched a creative idea proposed by its agency, DDB. The creative involved a series of 30-second animated stories shown on YouTube of Carlton the milk carton and his entourage of snack friends such as Chip, a chocolate chip cookie.

The digital media plan called for promoted YouTube video and YouTube Reserved skippable pre-roll, among other paid digital methods to gain exposure. Additional exposure occurred at theatres during the launch of blockbuster action movies to go along with Carlton USB sticks being handed out. Social media exposure included cartoon posts, .gifs, and text links in Tumblr.

After a couple of years, the campaign had released over 50 videos worth 11 million episode

©Blend Images/Alamy

views and had a YouTube following of 25,000 subscribers. The campaign won at 18 regional, national, and international awards shows. Tracking research showed increased consumption, stronger attitudes ("milk is a fun drink" increased 9 percent), and 30 percent stronger purchase intent. Other measures for emotions, occasions, positioning, and personality showed a 6.5 percent improvement.

This innovative and unbranded creative is akin to branded content telling a story over time with many episodes. The digital media exposure followed paid, owned, and earned channels to get the message to hungry and thirsty teens!

Question:

1. Why was the "Snack Time" campaign so successful?

LO3 Digital Ad Formats

The ad formats identified in Figure 17-9 are described in this section. We begin with display ads that advertisers place on content publishers' websites and in social media. We then review paid search advertising. Together, these two ad formats represent the majority of Internet media advertising. Next we look at video ads that are paid media on content publishers' websites and represent owned media in social media. We wrap up with audio, classified and directory, and promotional ad formats.

DISPLAY ADS

Display advertising revenue hit $2,322 million in 2017, more than tripling since 2010, and accounted for one-third of total Internet advertising ad revenue. The use of display ads originated in print media and so Internet media adaptation is expected. **Display ads** are placed on virtually any Internet site, including social media Internet sites, and within email messages. **Figure 17-12** shows the top four locations where advertisers placed display ads within Internet media. The wide range of Internet sites in terms of type and domain indicates the potential for a degree of target audience selectivity as seen in print media. For example, brands design messages to appeal to the needs and wants of the audience of an entertainment content publisher. In addition, advertisers build reach with frequent scheduling of display ads on particular Internet sites.

Figure 17-13 shows the industries that advertised on the Internet in 2017 by ad revenue, with automotive, retail, financial, telecommunications, packaged goods, and entertainment leading the way with a total of 64 percent. The top advertisers in Canada for 2017 for broadcast, print, and out-of-home included Procter & Gamble ($138 million), Bell ($108 million), General Motors ($102 million), Restaurant Brands International ($88 million), government lotteries ($85 million), Rogers ($76 million), Ford ($75 million), McDonald's ($70 million), Fiat Chrysler ($66 million), and Nissan ($64 million).[22] This breakdown roughly corresponds to the industry ratios of **Figure 17-11**, giving an indication as to which brands use display ads substantially.

Display ads are found in all sorts of Internet media vehicles, and this revenue total includes ads also found in social media outlets like Facebook. Display ads usually have a link embedded allowing users to move to another digital location, usually a brand or company website or a branded page on a social network, and developments allow for different interactive features. Based on a sample of a digital marketing firm's clients, the median click-through rate across 16 industries hit 0.50 percent.[23] Variation exists depending on size, location on page, use of an image, and type of display ad, however the rates do not change significantly over time.

Since display ads are the original marketing communication found in Internet media, academics investigated their effectiveness. Much of this research built on other media studies with an interest in predicting awareness (i.e., recall and recognition), attitude to the brand, attitude to the ad, attitude to the advertising format, purchase intention—all communication and behavioural effects discussed earlier—and click-through rates. One study looked at the effects of forced exposure; that is, whether the user had control to avoid the ad.[24] Other research showed the importance of congruence between the website (i.e., media vehicle) or the search engine keywords inputted and the brand advertised.[25] Additional inquiries studied whether the audience was familiar or unfamiliar with the advertised brand, a key factor in advertising planning that has

Figure 17-12 Ad impressions by type of Internet media

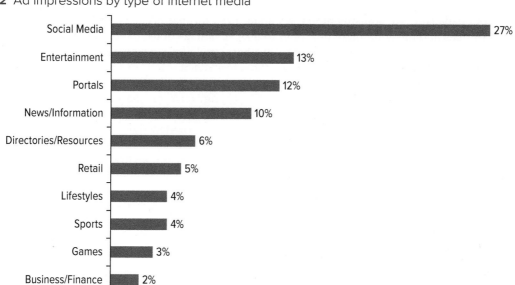

Figure 17-13 Distribution of Canadian Internet ad revenue by major product category, 2017

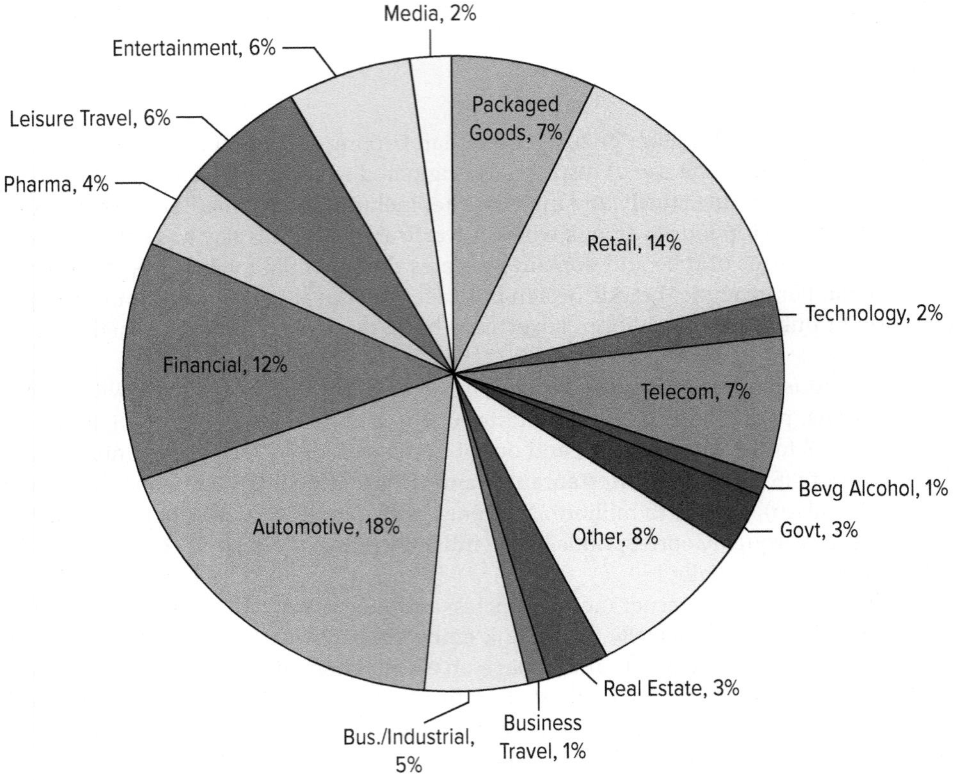

Source: IAB Canada, Canadian Internet Advertising Revenue Survey, 2017

been covered extensively in this book.[26] One research team investigated the effects of differing ad formats.[27] Other research investigated the effects of message content design elements and format of the ads on both communication and behavioural effects.[28] Furthermore, media scheduling and duration of exposure of the display ads replicated findings of advertising from other media. For example, longer exposure and repetition are generally important in achieving desired effects.[29] Research that compared standard display ads to full screen take-over, large display, and splash page wraps yielded stronger brand recognition and recall, and higher ratings for entertainment, education, and brand value.[30]

IAB Canada Display ads follow voluntary industry standardization; the formats and technical requirements are found at IAB.com and IABCanada.com. An adjustment to the standardized formats occurred in 2017 (as in past years) with the deletion of old formats and the addition of new ones to take advantage of technological innovations. Examples of deleted ad formats include pop-up, pop-under, floating, auto/hover/rollover expansions, auto play video with audio, forced countdown, and any flashing animation. If you see these formats, it is likely you are visiting a less reliable website not adhering to IAB guidelines.

The new guidelines concern consumers and advertisers. The change for consumers is known as LEAN (Light, Encrypted, AdChoices, and Non-invasive) and is designed to improve the consumer's experience. The LEAN ad experience is guided by respecting the consumer's primary intention to read or view the publisher's content, allowing the consumer to exert control over the advertising experience, and giving the consumer the choice as to what and how much they want to receive. The change for advertisers is technical, focusing on flexible size ad specifications. The technical adjustment allows for display ads to work for any screen (i.e., size, resolution), ensuring that the intended creative message is shown optimally and loaded quickly.

Based on the above, IAB Canada has made a number of suggestions to follow the guidelines. We summarize a few that are quite relevant and noteworthy, to indicate how the LEAN ad experience is implemented. Rich media with interactive features such as animation, ad expansion, or video play should be user initiated. A close button must be present for ads that may obstruct a publisher's content. Video ads should be 15 seconds long to minimize bandwidth usage and the audio must start as muted.

Display Ad System Ad networks place ads for advertising clients across millions of potential Internet sites that publish content efficiently and effectively. Hundreds of ad networks operate globally, with big names like Google commanding significant market share. The ad network provider obtains ad placement inventory from multiple Internet sites that publish content, forecasts the inventory for the coming time frame (e.g., month), and organizes the inventory across multiple segmentation variables adhering to advertiser requirements. Second, the network negotiates and sells the ad placements to advertising clients. And finally, the network facilitates delivery of the ads from the advertiser to the publisher.

When a network needs to manage its inventory of ads (buying or selling), it turns to an **ad exchange** that operates much like a stock exchange. The publisher provides information and requests an ad from the exchange. The exchange submits the request to advertisers. An advertiser then bids on the ad impression against other advertisers. The ad exchange selects the best bid and sends the ad to the publisher. The publisher completes the process, submitting the ad. The entire process is completed one ad at a time, yet takes milliseconds!

Ad exchanges are beneficial since fewer parties being involved results in less overall commission and greater dollars invested in advertising. Logistically, the whole process is simpler for all parties. The pricing mechanisms offer less risk to the publisher of receiving minimal amounts of money for its space; research suggests publishers stand to make more money. Advertisers know exactly where their ad will appear, thus avoiding any negative media vehicle source effects. This takes care of the problem of ads for wholesome brands with a respectable image appearing in unsavory Internet locations. Finally, the instantaneous bidding permits dynamic allocations of the advertising budget.

The interaction between ad networks and ad exchanges is a feature of the complex system of ad transactions that is known as programmatic buying. Most marketers are unaware of the system, partly out of ignorance and partly because it is contracted to their media agencies. However, the difficulties emerging with the system should get marketers interested in a hurry. Foremost is that the layers of complexity of buyers and sellers within the system disrupt the benefit of knowing where the ads are being placed. Big name brands find their ads on websites that host pirated movies, TV shows, and music. Quality branded products see their ads on websites containing shady content (e.g., violence, hate speech, pornography). In short, the foundation of vehicle source effect has become seriously detrimental.[31]

Although display ads are a worthwhile part of an IMC plan, there exists considerable evidence of substantial fraud due to invalid (non-human) traffic with automated systems. Some example of this fraud include bots driving up ad impressions as they mimic human users, hijack software on a user's device creating fake traffic, injector software placing ads where they do not belong, and sites impersonating legitimate sites. The fraud rate ranged from 3 percent to 37 percent in one study, and other studies confirmed similar levels. The study found that ads with higher CPM showed more severe fraud (e.g., $15 CPM fraud rate is 173 percent higher). Concerned advertisers pushed back with requests for detailed fraud reports and movement to private ad sellers to avoid automatic systems.[32] Other research summarized four challenges of the problem: industry participants intentionally using up advertisers' budgets with poor decisions, inaccurate measurement of ad exposure levels, conflicting interests between buyers and sellers of ads, and ineffective dispute resolution procedures.[33]

PAID SEARCH ADS

A substantial form of Internet advertising is **paid search**, or search engine advertising in which advertisers pay only when a consumer clicks on their ad or link from a search engine page (**Exhibit 17-9**). Other payment methods are available as well. Paid search ads in a link format are primitive display ads received by the searcher who at that point in time has a particular target audience characteristic: "in shopping mode." Visually, link ads are text only and are the most basic form of display ad, containing no visual and no or minimal copy. For example, a Google search ad features a headline, a URL, and two text lines with a 95 character limit. And while search advertising revenue reached $3,364 million in Canada for 2017 and accounted for 50 percent of all Internet advertising revenue, it is almost astounding that so much is spent for such a poor visual and verbal message.

Exhibit 17-9 A familiar student activity is to google it!

©Your Design/Shutterstock

Exhibit 17-10 Google Ads provides links for advertisers to do search engine advertising.

©BigTunaOnline/Shutterstock

In fact, researchers and practitioners caught on to this issue and concluded that the message content of a paid search ad may be a key reason for its low **click-through rate** (CTR). One study suggested that paid search essentially replicated the historic classified ad from print media, and adapted an established method (A/B testing) for advertisers to test different copy to see which resulted in better clicks.[34] Another study investigated four different ways of writing the text message and concluded that message structures with statistical and expert evidence produced higher click-through rates than message structures with causal and basic evidence.[35] Much like decades of advertising research in other media, message content in advertising is important for influencing attitudes and behaviour.

Google is the dominant provider, accounting for the vast majority of Internet searches. Google Ads, a keyword-targeted advertising program, uses short text-only ads to maintain an uncluttered page design and to maximize page loading speed (**Exhibit 17-10**). These text ads are identified, as "ad" appears beside relevant links and the links are separated for clear user distinction. Presentation varies depending on the device (desktop/laptop vs. phone/tablet). Online advertisers compete for the privilege of having their ads displayed with the results of a particular keyword search in a higher position than their competitors' ads. Advertisers pay only when an ad is clicked (called cost per click, or CPC), which in turn takes the viewer to the advertiser's website. Google Ads runs a specialized auction to decide which ads to show on the basis of (1) each advertiser's CPC bid and (2) the advertiser's *quality score,* which is a measure of the *relevance* of how well an ad matches a user's search query. The pricing system is designed to reward more relevant ads and keywords by showing them higher in the search results. Google does this by decreasing the amount that relevant ads must bid per click to beat their competition. This means that Google can display the advertisements that are the most targeted and relevant to a Google user's *search query,* which draws more users and click-throughs and thus generates more revenue for Google.[36] Based on a sample of a digital marketing firm's clients, click-through rates ranged from 2 percent to 5 percent depending on the client's industry.[37]

In an effort to more specifically target customers who may be interested in their offerings, advertisers employ search engine optimization (SEO), the process of improving the volume of traffic driven to one's site by a search engine through unpaid results as opposed to paid inclusions. The belief is that the higher a site appears on the search results list, the more visitors it will receive. SEO considers how search engines work and edits its HTML and coding to increase its relevance to keywords and to remove barriers to the indexing activities of search engines. SEO is an integral part of an Internet marketing strategy of companies and organizations of all sizes.

From a direct marketing standpoint as described in Chapter 16, the search ad represents the first step and a website visit is the second step in the two-step process. When searching, a consumer might type in the brand name they are interested in researching rather than a generic product category; for example, Honda vs. new vehicle. In some respects, this could be seen as user laziness since the person could have typed in the Honda Canada website address. In another respect this is important to an advertiser since the searcher exhibited significant brand recall to initiate the search and it seems to indicate an existing positive brand attitude if they want to read up about the brand. One study that investigated this scenario found support that consumers' existing attitudes and awareness levels guided their Internet search engine activity when in the market for a smart phone or vehicle.[38] Another study found evidence that specific brand searches occurred with higher levels of TV ads, online display ads, advertising expenditures, and multiple media.[39] This highlights the importance of other marketing communication being strong to influence consumers' behaviour when they are shopping.

VIDEO ADS

Video ads on Internet media made great strides, as advertising revenue hit $928 million in 2017, of which $159 million was received by TV stations for on-demand viewing as mentioned in Chapter 11. Video ads are shown on content publisher websites (such as TSN, as noted above) as well as on social media websites (such as YouTube and Facebook). The consumption of video in Internet media is reflective of the growth and potential for video ads.

Figure 17-14 Internet video viewers (weekly), fall 2018, anglophones 18+

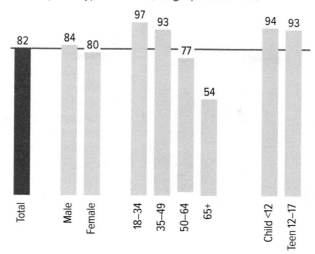

Figure 17-15 Internet video hours viewed (weekly), fall 2018, anglophones

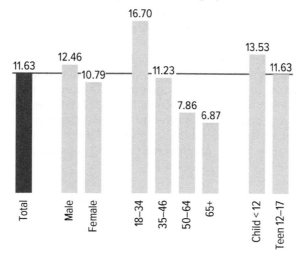

According to MTM data, video streaming penetration on a weekly basis hit 82 percent in 2018 and varies by selected demographics (**Figure 17-14**). Data by income (not shown) skews at or above 82 percent for all income groups except for those earning less than $35,000 per annum. Streaming by device in 2018 showed 61 percent by computer, 60 percent by smart phone, 34 percent by tablet, and 51 percent by Internet-connected TV. This data shifted significantly from 2014, where it was 47 percent by smart phone and 23 percent by Internet-connected TV.

The number of hours of video streaming per person hit 12 hours per week in 2018, double the 4 hours seen in 2011 (**Figure 17-15**) based on MTM data. In comparison, in Chapter 11 we showed that TV viewing hit 25 hours per week with considerable variation for age. Those aged 18–24 watched 14 hours per week while those 55+ watched 38 hours per week. Clearly viewing habits are changing, with technology putting pressure on advertisers to find the right media mix.

The growth of mobile advertising means that brands determine on which device to place a video ad. Recent statistics found that video ad impressions achieved the following distribution: 46 percent for desk/laptop only; 33 percent for desk/laptop and mobile; 12 percent for desk/laptop, mobile, and Internet TV; and 7 percent for mobile only. Fifty-seven percent of the ads lasted 15 seconds and 56 percent featured consumer packaged goods or automotive products. Advertisers purchased 90 percent on a guaranteed CPM basis.[40]

Digital Video Ads: Owned The increased penetration of broadband into households and mobile has increased the use of streaming video advertising messages. The equivalent of traditional television commercials, online commercials are appearing on Internet media vehicles. Some companies create new video messages for the Internet, while others

Exhibit 17-11 Goodlife makes use of video to communicate on its website.

©rmnoa357/Shutterstock

run the same spots they show on TV. Companies have also been successful in blending the two media, showing the commercial on TV and then directing interested viewers to their Internet site if they wish to see it again or to view longer versions. These viewings on a company's Internet site are usually hosted on YouTube or an equivalent video hosting service. Goodlife Fitness (**Exhibit 17-11**) puts training videos on its website that are hosted by Vimeo.

As noted in Chapter 7, storytelling is a newer creative strategy manifested with longer brand video messages. While some advertisers refer to these story messages as branded content or content marketing, the ultimate goal of these messages is to influence a target audience. The message focuses on a company's product and supports its brand positioning strategy from a differential advantage or target audience persuasion perspective, as discussed in Chapter 6. In other situations, the message focuses on its consumers to support a user positioning. For example, Whirlpool created a 2.5-minute mini-documentary, "Sama's Lunchbox," which told the story of a young girl who shared Syrian snacks with her classmates. The heartwarming emotions associated with the video's images eventually gave way to images of Whirlpool appliances in the background. IKEA created a 25-minute film showing many of its products and virtually no people, focusing on the sensory responses consumers experience during consumption.[41]

TV Video Ads: Paid Online video versions of entertainment activities or shows which include ads are also available through Internet media. For instance, as noted in Chapter 11, CTV website visitors watch free TV programs along with embedded commercials, similar to the existing television model. According to MTM data, viewership hit nearly 50 percent in 2014 with similar variation with age and income (**Figure 17-16**). The future of advertising through streamed television shows is a new and promising opportunity for promotional planners, even though the innovation is in the early stages of development for the sender and the receiver. All major TV broadcasters offer varying options for ad placement for the majority of their shows. Much of the targeting potential and fit of audience of a show is now possible via online video.

Digital Video Ads: Paid Looking for even more revenue, YouTube offers the potential to see ads before viewing the intended video. Some have the option for viewers to skip the ad, while others are controlled so the viewer must watch the ad, much like the experience with television. Other media vehicles like news sites offer video ads prior to seeing the intended news video clip. These options are priced using CPM methods to account for instances when viewers do not

Figure 17-16 Internet TV viewers (weekly), fall 2018, anglophones 18+

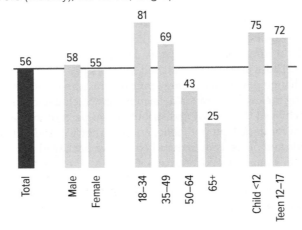

watch the complete message. Future Internet media ad placement may move toward pricing and planning with GRPs like other media as advertisers look toward inter-media comparisons.[42]

Given the growth of video consumption on Internet media, some viewers may feel that online video ads are intrusive. Similar reactions occur with other media when new ad formats are introduced. One study found that more intrusive ads led to skipping, weaker ad recall, weaker ad attitude, and weaker brand attitude. To minimize perceptions of the ads being intrusive, information and humour can be effective.[43]

And much like research in other media, researchers investigate the effects of message creative decisions. For example, one study looked at online video ad length and ad position (pre-, mid-, post-roll) in congruent and non-congruent situations. As found with TV ads, longer online video ads resulted in stronger brand recognition. Mid-roll ads exhibited stronger brand recognition for congruent situations where the ad and the video appeared similar (e.g., both use humour). Pre-roll and post-roll ads exhibited stronger brand recognition for incongruent situations where the ad and video appeared dissimilar (e.g., humour and drama).[44]

One study researched the effects of creative characteristics of pre-roll ads on skipping behaviour. Longer ads encouraged greater skipping. Ads with affect responses such as happiness and sadness elicited greater skipping. Ads with more complex affect responses such as humour, entertainment, and warmth led to less skipping, but four other complex affect responses led to no effect on skipping. And interestingly, ads with standard attention tactics like movement, colour, loudness, uniqueness, and branding led to skipping. The researchers concluded that the attention of someone receiving a pre-roll ad before an Internet video viewing is focused and established because of their goal-driven behaviour of watching the video selected. In contrast, when receiving a TV ad, a viewer is passively watching the show and their attention is less focused.[45] However, another study found that the attention tactics proved effective for congruent ads within the video context, but attention tactics proved less effective with non-congruent ads.[46]

AUDIO ADS

Podcasting **Podcasting** is a medium that uses Internet media to distribute video and audio files for learning or entertainment purposes, and contains ad and sponsorship messages (**Exhibit 17-12**). For $60,000, Volvo sponsored a podcast that was downloaded 150,000 times, while other initial sponsorships garnered $25 per thousand. Metrics for understanding the audience size emerged (e.g., Podtrac.com), as they had with other media. One study investigated podcasting and found an average of 2.4 ads per podcast with an average length of 16 seconds, consistent with a length seen on television and ads shown prior to video clips on news or portal sites. The majority of the ads (i.e., 75 percent) preceded or ended the podcast with a sponsorship message, much like the early days of television in the 1950s. The specificity of the podcast content allowed for very targeted ads (60 percent), such as automobile brands sponsoring a car-care podcast; thus, we see a very strong media vehicle source effect, much like with magazines.[47] It appears that a familiar advertising model with a sponsorship approach will continue to grow; however, the content of a podcast is also a message with possible commercial intent. For example, in order to increase demand for fine wine consumption, a podcast describing the nuances of grapes, vintages, tasting, and so on could act as a means of switching consumers who currently purchase less-than-premium brands. Frank and Oak, a men's online clothing retailer, found success with one- to three-minute podcast ads that described its home try-on program and tracking system. This also worked well with Tumblr since it displayed the imagery of the product line.[48]

Exhibit 17-12 Audiences for podcasts represent a useful audio advertising opportunity.

©Ryan McVay/Getty Images

Audio Streaming A newer form of audio advertising is through streaming services, such as Spotify, which offer a version of the service for free and supported by advertising with audio ads. Essentially, we see the equivalent of radio advertising here but with a degree of unmatched target audience selectivity due to the user's listening habits along with demographics and language spoken. The service also offers display and video ad options shown when the app is launched. For example, users receive ad-free service for 30 minutes after watching a brand's ad, or listen to a sponsored playlist. The costs are reasonable for all options on a CPM basis, but require a basic minimum to be spent per year.[49]

CLASSIFIED AND DIRECTORY ADS

Classified and directory ads are found on Internet sites where consumers search for information when comparison shopping or where consumers are planning a purchase and looking to complete a transaction. One noteworthy example of this is Kijiji; while the average Canadian can post an ad for free to sell used items, Kijiji offers display ad options and paid search capabilities. For the most part, Kijiji sells its ad space on a CPM basis, ranging from $2 to $18. Similarly, Auto Trader lets private sellers post ads for free and generates revenue from auto dealers who try to attract those who are searching for a new car in the free postings. And employment directories like Workopolis charge a set fee for a job posting ad with varying levels of service and exposure. Multiple target audience options are possible with online directories, providing advertisers extensive sophistication over historic newspaper advertising options. In fact, it appeared as if a direct substitution effect from newspaper to online occurred, with online stealing a significant portion of revenue from newspaper for a period of time. However, IAB reported $145 million in ad revenue in 2017, down from a peak of $587 million in 2010. Part of the decline is attributed to measurement adjustments, however it also indicates a general shift in advertising ad revenue to other options.

PROMOTIONAL ADS

Promotional planners offer promotional incentives to consumers (similar to those described in Chapter 14) in various ways within Internet media, typically to encourage continued media consumption. This is not a tracked media as there is generally no distribution cost, although there is a production cost. For example, loyal social media members receive digital treats; loyals are rewarded with related electronic items provided to them—such as ringtones, wallpapers, emoticons, skins, winks, filters, and pictures for instant message services. In this sense, these offers are digital "gifts" to reward behaviour. Another example occurs where various types of points systems allow repeat customers to generate even further rewards—a virtual continuity program for avid Internet media users who are brand loyal. Also, brands offer *advergames*—skill-challenging endeavours that keep customers amused while offering brand messages during play. Another example is the delivery of enhanced content in terms of information or entertainment. Loyal customers are rewarded with exclusive video for their participation, and advertisers provide enhanced levels of information where this is deemed valuable.

 Mobile

Mobile technology presents advertisers with advertising and promotion opportunities. Consumers utilize their mobile device constantly and it becomes a means of continuous two-way communication for brands to influence consumers in their decision-making process (described in Chapter 3).[50] Applying this approach raises questions for promotional planners. How does a mobile message best communicate need recognition? Which mobile approach is optimal for information search? What way is best to stay in touch with consumers post-purchase? Practitioners and academics see mobile as a means of influencing and understanding consumers' shopping behaviour significantly in the future.[51] For example, one study found that consumers reacted positively to a mobile promotion offer for a grocery store product placed elsewhere in the store compared to their present location.[52]

MOBILE ADS

Smart phone penetration reached 82 percent and tablet penetration reached 55 percent of the population in 2017. Mobile ad revenue accounted for messages delivered to either device and topped $3.5 billion in 2017. As seen in **Figure 17-8**, IAB Canada separates its ad revenue statistics by online (desk/laptop) and mobile (phone/tablet). While accessing Internet media via mobile technology differs, IAB Canada tracks advertising expenditures with the same advertising formats—paid search, display, directory, video, email, and gaming. A breakdown of mobile ad revenue data for 2017 showed $1,770 million for paid search, $1,175 million for display, $507 million for video, and $37 million for other. Researchers estimated that up to one-third of all holiday purchases occurred via mobile devices in 2018, indicating the importance of mobile advertising, and many store purchases relied on the use of mobile technology.[53]

Mobile's effectiveness for processing and communication effects raises questions. How could a student pay attention to a smart phone video ad while passing people, dodging cars and cyclists, and avoiding absent-minded professors? Can a small display ad on a smart phone convey the brand sufficiently to build brand awareness? Does a video ad on a smart phone with a much smaller screen influence consumers' attitude the way a TV ad might with a large screen? These questions and others are relevant as brands offer rewards and discounts so that users will view mobile ads. A preliminary study found mobile display ads ineffective for the most part, and only effective for high involvement– utilitarian purchases.[54] Due to the similarity of ad formats, we do not provide information on these topics for mobile. Instead, we present a few specific points regarding mobile device usage, mobile applications, and short message service.

MOBILE DEVICE USAGE

How Canadians use their smart phones is summarized in **Figure 17-17** with MTM data. **Figure 17-18** shows the percentage of Canadians who use various social media on a monthly basis using their smart phone according to MTM data. Data such as these can be used by promotional planners to know how to reach their target audience. Variation in Internet media activities and social media usage reminds us of the importance of applying all media planning principles described in Chapter 10 accordingly. For example, it seems unlikely that a promotional planner would use Snapchat to reach those in the 65+ age bracket!

Figure 17-19 and **Figure 17-20** show similar MTM data as the previous two figures but for tablets. The four figures together indicate that Canadians use each mobile device somewhat differently for communication activities and content sharing. Whether this leads to the potential for adjusting promotional message content or delivery remains to be seen. For example, while at a sports event, most fans would likely have their phone and not their tablet, and a promotional offer might best be sent on Twitter rather than other social media vehicles as people respond to what is happening during the event. A more important consideration for promotional planners may be differences in their promotional plans for online versus mobile. Academic research in this field follows a similar conceptual approach as with established media, and future research will likely evaluate the effects of different technology devices on mobile promotion decisions and their communication effects.[55]

As discussed in Chapter 11, TV broadcasters are interested in social TV where viewers interact with a program with their mobile device, notably through social media. **Figure 17-21** and **Figure 17-22** indicate the kinds of Internet media activities consumers take part in when watching TV. These data indicate opportunities for advertisers with TV programs that may have product placement or sponsorship activities occurring. In particular, live sports regularly encourage consumer feedback or participation in promotional offers while the game is on. For example, during the Raptors'

Figure 17-17 Frequency of Internet media activities (monthly) using smart phones, fall 2018, anglophones 18+

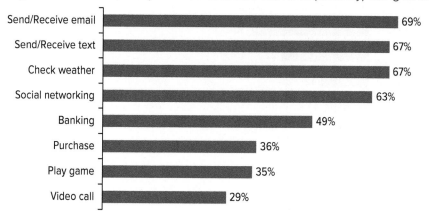

Activity	Percentage
Send/Receive email	69%
Send/Receive text	67%
Check weather	67%
Social networking	63%
Banking	49%
Purchase	36%
Play game	35%
Video call	29%

Figure 17-18 Frequency of social media use (monthly) by smart phone, fall 2018, anglophones 18+

	18–34	35–49	50–64	65+
Facebook	78%	68%	46%	20%
Twitter	24%	22%	12%	4%
Instagram	61%	39%	21%	4%
Snapchat	45%	14%	6%	1%
Pinterest	22%	21%	16%	2%

Figure 17-19 Frequency of Internet media activities (monthly) using tablets, fall 2018, anglophones 18+

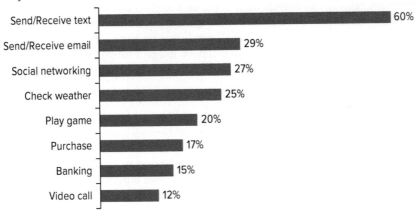

Activity	Percentage
Send/Receive text	60%
Send/Receive email	29%
Social networking	27%
Check weather	25%
Play game	20%
Purchase	17%
Banking	15%
Video call	12%

Figure 17-20 Frequency of social media activities (monthly) using tablets, fall 2018, anglophones 18+

	18–34	35–49	50–64	65+
Facebook	12%	22%	30%	23%
Twitter	2%	4%	5%	4%
Instagram	3%	6%	9%	3%
Pinterest	3%	8%	12%	5%

Figure 17-21 Second screen activities with smart phones, fall 2015, anglophones 18+

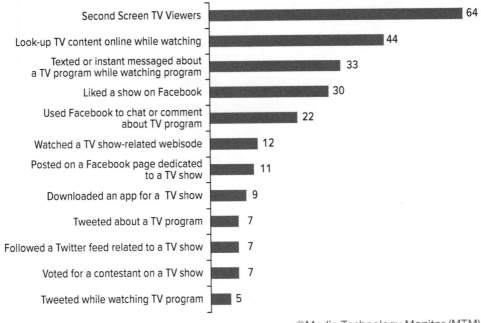

Activity	Value
Second Screen TV Viewers	64
Look-up TV content online while watching	44
Texted or instant messaged about a TV program while watching program	33
Liked a show on Facebook	30
Used Facebook to chat or comment about TV program	22
Watched a TV show-related webisode	12
Posted on a Facebook page dedicated to a TV show	11
Downloaded an app for a TV show	9
Tweeted about a TV program	7
Followed a Twitter feed related to a TV show	7
Voted for a contestant on a TV show	7
Tweeted while watching TV program	5

©Media Technology Monitor (MTM)

playoff drive, the announcers invited viewers to use both Twitter and Snapchat. Similar activities occur with NHL hockey and during the Blue Jays' playoffs. Oreo jumped to the task with instant Twitter messages during the women's gold medal hockey game at the Olympics. After the victory, one tweet proclaimed, "Recipe for gold: 1 part skill, 1 part heart, 1 part awesome comeback." An earlier example when witty and timely Oreo tweets generated 280 million ad impressions after the Super Bowl blackout a few years ago set the stage for the cookie brand to be ready at all times to send out similar messages during big events.[56]

Figure 17-22 Second screen activities with tablets, fall 2015, anglophones 18+

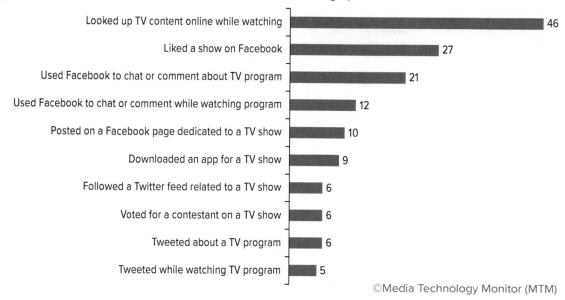

Looked up TV content online while watching — 46
Liked a show on Facebook — 27
Used Facebook to chat or comment about TV program — 21
Used Facebook to chat or comment while watching program — 12
Posted on a Facebook page dedicated to a TV show — 10
Downloaded an app for a TV show — 9
Followed a Twitter feed related to a TV show — 6
Voted for a contestant on a TV show — 6
Tweeted about a TV program — 6
Tweeted while watching TV program — 5

©Media Technology Monitor (MTM)

Figure 17-23 Video streaming on mobile devices (monthly), fall 2018, 18+

		18–34	35–49	50–64	65+
Smart phone	YouTube	78%	64%	31%	13%
	Stream Video	89%	75%	47%	21%
Tablet	YouTube	22%	29%	29%	20%
	Stream Video	30%	38%	39%	29%

Figure 17-23 indicates the pervasiveness of video streaming on mobile devices from MTM data. Clearly, Canadians viewed YouTube a lot, but each age group watched video in other digital media vehicles. The implication of this data is that we can expect growth in video advertising revenue for the foreseeable future. Whether this is at the expense of TV advertising or other Internet media (e.g., display, paid) remains to be seen.

MOBILE APPS

Mobile applications, known as "apps" for short, are small programs downloaded to a mobile device for many purposes. They act as ads since they generally carry brand identification and a brand experience. For example, according to one co-founder of Frank and Oak, "With the app on a phone's home screen you see our logo 20 times a day. That's great marketing for us." In fact, the company finds that consumers with the app (e.g., current customers) tend to buy more.[57]

Fundamentally, the use of a mobile device to participate in marketing communication is not a regular activity for most consumers, but that is changing (as statistics presented in the chapter attest). Advertising and most promotional tools are passive exposures that interrupt people's lives and are for the most part tolerated. However, apps and increasingly interactive digital communication are wonderful from the marketer's point of view since consumers will spend more time processing brand information. However, consumers generally do not share the same perspective, at least not for every brand at all times, as we showed in **Figure 17-7**. But, a signal that things are changing is that Cannes added a Mobile Lion to its prize list in 2012, with the Hospital for Sick Children's app announced as the winner.

Mobile location apps (e.g., Foursquare) are used by marketers and consumers alike. Brands like HarperCollins, Molson, the NHL, and the Toronto International Film Festival used these kinds of apps for advertising and sales promotion purposes to achieve attitudinal and trial objectives. And the apps themselves offer reward points for continued use of the app. Molson established the "Seize the Summer" app with Foursquare where users collected badges for activities accomplished to share on Facebook, which translated to a 20 percent growth in fans. The NHL connected with Foursquare to get fans interested in the game with prizes to be won after collecting badges and demonstrating greater use of hockey's social media.[58]

Companies take advantage of the apps section on Facebook and mobile platforms by offering games with point or badge systems to encourage continued patronage to the site. Brands like Foursquare offer status badges for continued

Figure 17-24 Retail shopping activities via smart phone app and browser

	App	Browser
Made Shopping Lists	18%	6%
Found Store Location	10%	28%
Found Coupon/Deals	9%	15%
Researched Product Features	7%	19%
Checked Product Availability	6%	19%
Compared Product Prices	6%	20%

use of their service.[59] Mobile apps are also a driving force behind the successful implementation of group buying or group discount activities in social media vehicles as well, which suggests that handheld devices will be a main marketing communication tool if consumers desire to interact with brands in this manner.[60] TV broadcasters are developing apps for a second-screen experience for viewers while watching TV shows. Their rationale is to foster enhanced viewer participation in the show's content by commenting on it via social media or enrolling in promotions, and to develop new advertising revenue sources.[61]

Consumers perform many shopping-related activities using apps, as shown in **Figure 17-24**. The mobile characteristics of smart phones make them ideal for consumers to rely on while shopping. Companies can use data like this to configure apps more usefully and design them with key advertising messages. An example of the pervasiveness of shopping-related apps is Poynt, a popular Canadian app that allows users to find restaurants, movies, people, and businesses based on their location. The app allows consumers to book an appointment or reservation, save it in the calendar, and access all the contact information without even exiting the app. The next step appears to be features that will deliver promotional offers to users based on their location and user profile. As it works with data suppliers and other third-party developers, the app is a handy tool for consumers shopping virtually anywhere.[62] One study found that apps provided strong brand effects, and that shopping-related apps led to stronger purchase intentions than experiential brand-building apps.[63] As this indicates once again, advertising researchers continue to use established methods and ad theories to test digital marketing communication.

SMS

Sending a text message is the most common activity when using a smart phone (as shown in **Figure 17-19**), offering a number of opportunities for new communication and promotional offers. Coca-Cola put forth a promotion with under-the-cap personal identification numbers and SMS codes that offered discounts for cellphone bills. In hindsight, the incentive did not completely fit the teen target audience, who usually did not pay their own cellphone bill; however, the new approach gave the soft drink brand strong results for future implementation that included iTunes downloads and a contest to win concert tickets.

Air Miles sends permission-based text alerts customized by transaction activity to encourage shopping at affiliated sponsors; response rates of up to 8 percent have occurred. Opt-in geo-location SMS provides offers to consumers who have not previously visited a store. Additionally, mobile users can now collect reward points via their device with innovative approaches for those interested in continued brand patronage.[64] Consumers can send messages to select what will be viewed in digital display networks in malls and transit stations, or on large screens in public locations.[65]

As the above suggests, these promotional messages have content much like other forms of marketing communication with a particular source and message structure. A study investigated the effects of these variables in an experiment of short messages sent to gamers during a local area network (LAN) party. The source was either a brand or a member of the party, while the message structure was either normal advertising language or shorthand text language, similar to what is sent in short text messages by users on a daily basis.[66] Thus, while this new "medium" is an alternative for sending the message, the principles discussed thus far in terms of positioning and advertising messages remain relevant for understanding attitudinal responses and purchase intentions. Furthermore, while searching with the mobile device occurs as in other computer environments, the GPS feature on smart phones gives retailers and event marketers a greater opportunity to persuade consumers. The coordinates signalled from the device are tracked, allowing brand information to be placed higher in the search.

One study investigated three ways consumers responded to a brand's text message for free music at its website: read text, visit website, and forward message. The messages included a suggestion to forward the offer to friend. The entertainment value of the message positively affected all three responses and the purpose value of the message positively affected the latter two responses. Given the offer and the simplicity of forwarding the message, the results indicated that research participants forwarded the message to all contacts irrespective of whether they were close friends or acquaintances. A result such as this indicates that even for a simple message, its content influences the call to action and resulting behaviour, much like findings from historic direct marketing efforts.[67]

Digital and Social Media Perspective 17-2 shows a few examples of how companies are innovating with apps to communicate with consumers.

MOBILE APP MANIA

Mobile apps perform many communication tasks for advertisers. Earlier we saw how they are integral to the loyalty programs for retailers. And with consumers having a seemingly infinite number of apps on their smart phones these days, brands want to know how best to use them within their digital marketing communication.

Loblaw partnered with Flashfood on an app for consumers interested in buying perishable (and non-perishable) foods like meat, produce, dairy, and baked goods just prior to their "best-before" date. The app appeared to be a good tool to contribute to the grocery retailer's goal of lowering its food wastage 50 percent by 2025. Indeed the worthwhile initiative proved invaluable to society in so many ways and a tribute to good marketing for the brand. A total of 76 percent of the 150,000 app owners use the service weekly.

Other retailers like Walmart and Holt Renfrew evaluated ways to develop apps for consumers. They all agreed that the app should be convenient to use and offer specific utility for it to be worthwhile. At Holt, the app helped consumers be involved in social media like Instagram, which spurred the beginning of a shopping trip. Consumers often showed themselves trying on Holt's outfits on social media, providing another opportunity for clothes brands to communicate. At Walmart, the discount retailer found that many shopping trips began with a mobile web visit.

7-Eleven's app works with its loyalty program and has been augmented with the Pokémon franchise. It developed a special Pokémon promotion for the app with an AR feature to let users find Pokémon characters and gain free goods. Another feature is the ability to get special photo filters with images from the latest Pokémon movie. Posting selfies with the filters gains customers additional loyalty points.

Imagine using your smart phone and scanning a newspaper and seeing a 3D animation of a character come to life! A total of 300,000 readers of two

©Flashfood Inc.

Quebec newspapers used their newspaper app to scan the newspaper and saw an image of Monsieur Fleur from Cirque du Soleil's *Alegría* production. After the visual, the message served an ad link to buy tickets. Users spent an average of 4.5 minutes with the message and traffic to the ticket website increased 30 percent.

Tourism service operators in Newfoundland and Labrador and Canadians in general love the new app to locate icebergs. Every spring, tourists visit the province for glimpses of old ice floating in the ocean. The app offers a number of features so consumers can plan their trip and maximize their experience. The app has increased visits to the website by 60 percent and page views by 80 percent, resulting in 5,000 referrals for the tourist operators.

Question:

1. In what way do these apps achieve communication objectives for the brands?

![LO5] Measuring Internet Media Effectiveness

Understanding how to measure the effectiveness of Internet media is an involved topic requiring perhaps a whole chapter to fully appreciate its complexity, but we will provide a brief overview for direction. As expected, numerous measures, or metrics as they are often known, are electronically recorded with digital communication. These data, and data from other methods similar to those described in Chapter 9, are analyzed to assess whether all facets of marketing communication described in this chapter are effective. Consistent with measurement in other media, we initially comment on audience information measures (demographics, psychographics, and so on) for Internet media. We then apply the communication model adapted through earlier chapters: exposure, processing, communication effects, and action.

AUDIENCE MEASURES

The electronic recording of Internet user behaviour allows advertisers to investigate a multitude of ways of understanding what has been looked at on a website and for how long, along with user characteristics.[68] When Internet media first developed its own audience size measures, concerns with the research methods led to a slower adoption rate by traditional media buyers. In an attempt to respond to criticism of the audience metrics used, as well as to standardize the measures used to gauge effectiveness, the Interactive Advertising Bureau (IAB)—the largest and most influential trade group—formed a task force consisting of global corporations involved in advertising and research. The final reports of the task force are available from IAB.net and contain both American and international guidelines (see also IABCanada.com).

The basic problem facing Internet media concerns a standardized method for determining the size of the audience. The report identified the technical procedures for accurately reporting whether an ad impression has occurred. This answers the fundamental expectation of advertisers as to whether the receiver of the message actually experienced an opportunity to see the ad (i.e., degree of exposure to the message). Another aspect concerns the accepted procedures for auditing the data, much like we see in traditional print media. Another key part of the report included guidelines for presenting data in terms of time of day, week, and month, much like we see in broadcast media. Finally, industry representatives agreed upon substantial guidelines for disclosure of research methodology, again consistent with all major media described in previous chapters. In future, advertisers can look forward to more authentic data to assess the viability of committing increased resources to Internet communication. Firms now use methods similar to those found in other media to measure demographics, psychographics, location and method of Internet access, media usage, and buying habits.

COMMUNICATION MODEL MEASURES

A significant development on this topic is a summary of 197 metrics (shortened from an initial list of 350) for websites, mobile, social media, and email published by the Advertising Research Foundation (ARF).[69] The 197 metrics are catalogued into nine categories: advertising, audience/traffic, site navigation/site performance, media consumption, engagement/interaction, amplification/endorsement, conversion, ecommerce, and ad effectiveness. The metrics are also cross-listed by four marketing stages: capture (86 metrics), connect (90), close (18), and keep (3). Neither of these listing methods is exactly consistent with the communication approach of this book, but the marketing stage view is simpler to consider, with only four marketing stages.

The numbers indicate that the vast majority of the metrics are capture and connect, and for the most part these metrics address exposure, or act as a proxy for processing since they are time-based (e.g., number of minutes on website per visit) or incident-based (e.g., did the viewer watch the complete video). Many of the close metrics address aspects of ecommerce purchases, and some are general measures of conversion of any online behaviour that an advertiser wishes to track. Keep in mind that there are minimal measures of communication effects since these are knowledge-based and attitudinally based, in contrast to the electronic records of people's Internet media consumption. And there are no brand-based measures for trial or repeat purchasing.

Exposure Measures As noted, there are numerous exposure metrics—*How many unique visitors came to our website? How many impressions did our page generate virally? How many times did a person see a specific ad or other piece of content? How many unique people did our video reach?* And, there are many processing measures—*What percentage of people who* *downloaded our app are using it? How long is a specific page viewed? How many of our brochures were downloaded? How many things were pinned from our website?* These selective examples provide an overview of many metrics that can be tracked across all the different communications occurring in Internet media. For a shorter and cheaper investigation, consult a journal article that gives a concise description.[70] While this work is substantial and very useful for promotional planners, concern still remains about fraud, the reliability of the metrics, the poor representation of advertisers within the automatic buying system, and the resiliency of the resolution mechanisms when disputes arise within this complicated system.[71]

Research from a leading digital research firm (Comscore) suggests a number of empirical generalizations that contribute to our understanding of exposure measures. First, prevalent **cookie** deletion overstates unique visits to websites, resulting in an overestimate of reach and an underestimate of frequency. Second, consumer use of multiple devices and the fact that cookies cannot distinguish among multiple users of a device creates even more measurement error. Third, the above two points makes targeting inaccurate, especially for behaviour which averaged 36 percent accuracy. Fourth, approximately one-third of all ads do not provide an opportunity to see since they required scrolling, which did not occur. Finally, the fifth generalization reiterated the previously identified fraud point. In totality, the issues summarized here imply that a substantial part of the $2.3 billion spent for display ads is wasted.[72]

Communication Effects Measures The movement for comprehensive communication effects measurement reveals that the Internet has its own set of criteria for measuring effectiveness and is also borrowing from traditional measures. Companies that provide research information in traditional media now extend their reach to Internet media. Academics publish articles related to measuring communication effectiveness with Internet media, such as consumers' attitudes toward a site or consumers' attitudes to an ad (e.g., banner ads).[73]

A number of companies use traditional measures of recall and retention to test their Internet ads. The same measures have been used to pretest online commercials as well. Survey research, conducted both online and through traditional methods, is employed to determine everything from site usage to attitudes toward a site. Companies now provide information on specific communication measures like brand awareness, message association, brand attitude, and purchase intention.

One of the more extensive attempts to measure the effectiveness of integrating interactive and traditional media is through IAB's *cross-media optimization studies (CMOST)*. These studies are designed to determine the optimal mix of online and offline advertising media vehicles, in terms of frequency, reach, and budget allocation for a given campaign to achieve its marketing goals. Examples of these studies are regularly published on the IAB website. One featured a Tetley Tea campaign using magazines and two expandable rich media ads and a video pre-roll. Results indicated the importance of media with varying communication effects (awareness, message retention, purchase intention) at different stages of the consumer decision-making process, as shown in Chapter 5.[74] What makes these studies important is that they provide insight into (1) the relative contributions of each medium in the mix, (2) the combined contribution of multiple media, (3) optimal media budget allocations, and (4) actionable media mix strategies.

Finally, social media may require its own set of metrics based on its "owned" media characteristics. Reviewing the theoretical and practical literature, authors of one review article conclude with nine guidelines for implementing a measurement system. One significant guideline suggests unique metrics for different social media vehicles and unique metrics within different parts of a given social media vehicle. Another identifies the importance of focusing on the quality of the information rather than the quantity of social media activities.[75] As these two points imply, revised social media metrics will likely give greater insights into attitudinal brand effects.

LO6 IMC Planning: Strategic Use of Internet Media

The text, video, and audio characteristics of Internet media—along with various types of applications (e.g., websites, banner ads, streaming video, sponsorship, promotions, social networks, apps, etc.)—position it as being capable of communicating with customers and non-customers to achieve all communication and behavioural objectives, and to influence consumers at every stage of their decision-making process. The challenge for promotional planners is to select the correct application that fits the target audience and allows for the achievement of the most relevant objective along with the most appropriate message that supports the brand positioning strategy. We suggest that marketers need to think about planning issues similar to those found in other media, like how to break through the clutter and how to deliver messages digitally across a wide spectrum of vehicles.

A second planning issue concerns how Internet media may or may not be better than other media for advertising purposes. Early research investigated whether Internet or TV produced better results and found that Internet appeared stronger for high-involvement purchases only.[76] Other research compared the same ad delivered via print media to Internet media and found similar communication effects; however, ads with promotional messages (i.e., discounts) delivered better in print.[77]

A third planning issue pertains to how Internet media are integrated with other media for advertising purposes. One early study concluded that offline advertising increased awareness and subsequent website visits, while online ads contributed to website visits. Neither affected the brand equity, as the actual visit to the website played more strongly in that regard.[78] Another study found that a combined TV–Internet message performed better in terms of processing and stronger communication effects versus two TV messages or two Internet messages.[79] The conclusions of a print and Internet study recommended that print ads convey clear reasons to motivate readers to visit the website versus merely placing the website address in the ad.[80]

A fourth planning issue is how Internet media are increasingly part of a complete IMC program. Advertising and social media messages are regularly coordinated and integrated. Sales promotions are executions on mobile devices and have supporting messages in ads. Research uncovered a significant communication effect of direct-response media through mobile devices after viewers received advertising or promotional TV messages that prompted continued interaction.[81] The list is endless, as essentially any combination of tools can be used with and within Internet media.

Internet media often work with other IMC tools. Promotional planners using print, broadcast, or out-of-home media would need to investigate the degree to which the advertising campaign in these media would be directly transferred to Internet advertising. This is commonly done and there are many examples. Alternatively, Internet advertising could take a substantially different direction—some microsites, for example, have allowed brands to take a more experiential or informational track and have a substantially different role and message compared to what is more publicly available. Finally, Internet media is consumed with other media, notably TV, and the communication effects of simultaneous brand exposure via a brand's TV ad and social media are promising avenues for future development, especially for heavy multitasking users who tend to be younger.

Internet advertising supports sales promotion activities designed to encourage trial and repeat purchases with banner ads or sponsored search links that direct consumers to contests or price promotional offers. Internet advertising is used successfully for public relations activities, as links to corporate websites are found on relevant Internet sites (e.g., financial information sites) and other mechanisms are available to direct consumers to corporate information to influence appropriate stakeholders. Finally, Internet advertising assists in direct-response marketing as it facilitates communication to the websites for conducting transactions.

Internet media as sales promotion is an opportunity for marketers, as digital content represents a sample for additional purchases or consumption. For example, a musician posting their work in social media provides exposure which may lead to consumers purchasing concert tickets, merchandise, or songs. It may also lead to additional consumption which results in stronger consumer engagement in the performer's social media channels. Brands also develop fun games and activities representing a premium or gift which are consistent with both the brand image and consumer experience as the sales promotion offers additional exposure and meaningful brand experiences.

Internet media as public relations supports considerable advertising for consumer packaged goods and food products. Broadcast and print ads for such products create images and persuade consumers with an appropriate brand positioning strategy. However, consumers may desire more information on usage, or would like to know the exact ingredients in more detail. The Internet site for Becel margarine offers a wonderful array of information for consumers desiring a more involved message about the brand, and acts as a tremendous public relations resource by presenting a comprehensive and honest assessment of the brand.

Internet media for direct-response advertising works very well for Belairdirect. The insurance company's print and radio ads suggest that consumers visit its Internet site to compare quotes from Belairdirect and up to five competitors. In this sense, Internet media function beyond mere communication like a regular informational website, especially considering that for a few years the focus of all the ads has been to encourage a direct response via the Internet.

In short, Internet media is capable of communicating all facets of the IMC program, and all aspects of Internet media can work with any other existing advertising media to achieve a brand's objectives. Careful planning is required like any other promotional decision, but the potential for positive results is limitless.

Learning Objectives Summary

 LO1 **Describe Internet media usage and explain website communication.**

Internet media is relatively common for a vast majority of the population who seemingly do anything and everything online, on a computer or with a mobile device. While older segments of the population rely on these media less than younger groups do, the fact that the average hourly per capita consumption reached significant levels suggests that Internet communication is the most significant media.

Website communication is used for all of communication objectives described in this book. Websites contribute to building brand awareness, disseminating information, building a brand image, and fostering interaction between consumers and the company. The unlimited creativity we have witnessed with websites is remarkable. This creativity has given rise to consumers, practitioners, and academics referring to website communication as website advertising or Internet advertising. They apply existing models to understand how attitudes to the website and brand attitude are influenced by strategic and tactical design elements, much like what occurs with print and broadcast media.

 LO2 **Review Internet media advertising.**

The growth of Internet media in terms of advertising revenue surpassed all other media and is strong for both desktop/laptop access and mobile access on smart phones and tablets. This growth suggests that promotional planners should develop a formal digital advertising plan like any other media. This point is consistent with the planning model in Chapter 1 and media planning in Chapter 10. This chapter applied this material in the context of digital advertising to show that there are very similar decisions in terms of target audience and objectives, media strategy, and media tactics. While the interactive characteristic of Internet media alters the plans to a degree, many of the previous concepts and decisions remain applicable.

Internet media permits targeting across all segmentation variables described in Chapter 3 and, in particular, in terms of behaviour. Targeting occurs through the selection of the right Internet media vehicle. Whether that may be a news or entertainment portal, established media published from print or broadcast, new forms of publications found on the Internet, or many social media such as social networking, social bookmarking, blogging, etc., successful placement of ads in any of these media vehicles requires an understanding of the receivers or participants. Virtually all of these opportunities can provide a profile of their audience so that promotional planners can select the most appropriate target audience characteristics.

 LO3 **Identify the advertising formats of Internet media.**

Advertising formats of Internet media include display ads that involve various types endorsed by IAB Canada. This organization sets guidelines for organizations to communicate effectively and fairly with the new LEAN systems. Paid search ads continue their dominance in terms of advertising revenue. Although search ads are limited in terms of visual presentation compared to other non-video messages, their effectiveness is strong for starting the direct marketing process. Video ads include online commercials on content publishers' websites, commercials within video-on-demand, and video messages placed within all sorts of social media vehicles. Audio ads are a new growth area beyond podcasts with audio streaming services.

 LO4 **Explore mobile advertising.**

The use of mobile devices is surpassing the use of desktop and laptop access to Internet media. Consumers receive all the aforementioned ad formats on their devices. In the case of using a smart phone while away from home, advertisers can reach consumers during the shopping trips or when being entertained with many messages—brand image, promotional incentives, PR, and direct-marketing oriented. The immediacy of promotional communication is significant and is changing how advertisers are communicating with current customers and prospects.

Define measures of Internet media effectiveness.

Like with other media, we concentrated on different measures of effectiveness for each stage of the communication process. Measures are obtained for exposure, processing, and communication effects and behavioural responses. The majority of these are tracked digitally; however, communication effects require direct measurement or a proxy.

 Apply the ideas of Internet media within an IMC program.

Internet media has been the most rapidly adopted medium of our time. It holds great potential for communicating with all groups of consumers, and customers and non-customers alike. Moreover, it is useful for implementing all aspects of the IMC program including sales promotion, public relations, and direct marketing. Other stakeholders are potential audiences as well, making Internet media unlimited in its ability to persuade. However, contrary to popular belief, the Internet is not a standalone medium. Its role in an integrated marketing communications program strengthens the overall program as well as the effectiveness of Internet media itself.

Review Questions

1. How has Internet media threatened other media? How has Internet media assisted other media?

2. What are the similarities and differences in planning for digital advertising vs. TV advertising?

3. Explain the advertising formats that advertisers use with Internet media. Discuss the advantages and disadvantages associated with each.

4. What are the unique characteristics of ads on mobile devices vs. a desktop computer?

5. Describe the ways that marketers measure the effectiveness of their use of Internet media. How do these measures relate to more traditional measures?

6. Discuss the advantages of Internet media. For which types of advertisers is Internet media best suited? Why?

Applied Questions

1. Select a favourite Internet site for a brand and investigate how it achieves the objectives outlined in this chapter.

2. Suggest a digital ad plan for a leading brand for any product category.

3. Visit a number of Internet media vehicles and evaluate the effectiveness of the display ads in terms of creativity, message, and ability to reach the intended target audience.

4. Critically evaluate mobile apps on your smart phone in terms of the brand achieving communication objectives.

5. What measures of marketing communication effectiveness are relevant for each of the four types of social media investigated in this chapter?

6. Select a product of interest and explain how each of the four types of social media described in this chapter can be integrated effectively with other broadcast, print, and out-of-home media.

CHAPTER EIGHTEEN

Social Media

LEARNING OBJECTIVES

LO1 Identify social media communication.

LO2 Review social networking.

LO3 Illustrate content communities.

LO4 Describe blogs and collaborative projects.

LO5 Investigate social media influence.

LO6 Apply the use of social media within an IMC program.

Facebook Faced Issues

Facebook faced a number of issues including a showdown with government officials in the United States and weakened trust from Canadians (34 percent, down from 51 percent) due to privacy concerns resulting from data breaches. A source of its trouble was its fundamental purpose from the viewpoints of the company, governments, and users: Is Facebook a media company supported by advertising, or is Facebook a "platform" for communication among users? In 2012, Facebook took a big step by accepting ads in its news feed after a significant focus on expanding its user base during 2007–2012. A former executive expressed regret that Facebook accepted advertising and suggested it should move to a subscription-based service.

From an advertising perspective, Facebook is a perfect tool since a brand's ad message is directed on a mass scale to millions or billions, or is sent to a selectively targeted audience. For example, Facebook offers tools like "custom audience" and "lookalike" to ensure brands send messages to exactly those whom the brand desires to reach. It established tools and methods for news content publishers to deliver their product through a news feed such that 40 percent of Canadians received their daily news from Facebook. However, as an advertising media vehicle for major brands, Facebook received notice that Procter & Gamble had shifted its $200 million digital ad budget to TV, ecommerce, and streaming services after its research showed that consumers processed a mobile ad in their news feed for only two seconds. Media companies discovered poor ad revenue from Facebook users reading their stories in the news feed and up to 50 percent dropped Facebook as a publishing avenue.

To address public and government concerns, Facebook altered how advertisers communicate to their audiences. The social networking site returned users' news feed to its origin with posts from their friends and family to retain its social networking purpose, to reduce the inflow of posts from brands and news media, and to minimize the amount of fake news transmitted by other entities. In announcing the change, Facebook's CEO expected users would experience fewer hours but higher quality time. Additionally, the company also expected the change would stop the declining consumption of Facebook. One analyst predicted the change would result in less brand exposure but higher quality exposure due to selectivity. However, one advertiser commented that they received diminishing returns on Facebook and planned to consider YouTube instead.

Six months later, Facebook reported less ad revenue growth due to the news feed change, and the CEO suggested that the North American ad revenue market likely hit its limit. To ward off ad revenue decline, Facebook initiated a payment system with discounted or free ads with Facebook receiving fees depending on the number of likes the brand's posting message received. For example, the Canadian federal government paid $5,000 for its Energy Star Canada program after it received 3,611 "likes" as part of its extensive digital ad purchases.

Question:

1. Do these trends suggest a future decline in Facebook paid advertising?

Social media represents a unique form of communication between brands and consumers, and among consumers. Its many different classes and approaches through paid, owned, and earned delivery make social media an important IMC tool for promotional planners, and one for which they need to establish a clear plan before committing money, time, and effort. We begin this chapter by reviewing social media communication in terms of social media classes, social media engagement, eWOM, and social media usage. Next, we review social networking by looking at Facebook and Twitter's paid, owned, and earned characteristics. We then illustrate social media content communities by looking at the same paid, owned, and earned features for YouTube and Instagram. Blogs and collaborative projects are described subsequently. For our final topic, we investigate social media influence exerted by people with an established number of followers who rely on their opinion. To conclude, we apply the ideas of social media within an IMC program.

LO1 Social Media Communication

Without question, the most significant media trend is consumer adoption of social media. Approximately half of all Canadians regularly use social media—media that did not even exist a short while ago. Moreover, they use social media with multiple types of hardware (TVs, personal computers, laptops, smart phones, tablets, and game consoles). In this section we review different classes of social media in which brands plan for paid, owned, and earned media exposure. Other topics covered in this section include social media engagement, eWOM, and social media usage.

SOCIAL MEDIA CLASSES

Social media is an Internet-based application that allows the creation and exchange of user-generated content. From a media planning view for marketing communication decisions, most social media offer paid and owned opportunities to communicate a brand's message, and earned exposure through users' postings (e.g., comments, pictures). To organize our thinking for a social media marketing communication plan, we build on one previous view of social media classes: networking sites (e.g., Facebook), content communities (e.g., YouTube), blogs (e.g., WordPress), collaborative projects (e.g., wikis, social bookmarks, reviews), and virtual worlds.[1] For our purposes, we omit the final one since promotional planners rely on this much less than the others.

Figure 18-1 shows our view of social media with four classes of media for planning messages within social media. The first two are the same as cited above, and we create a broad information class in the third column. The fourth column reflects an emerging idea as we see social media converging on lifestyles, reflecting activities, interests, and opinions, as described in Chapter 3. For example, Trip Advisor focuses completely on travel and it offers many options for user-generated content found in the networking, content, and information classes. Note that organizing a typology of social media classes for promotional planning purposes is a work in progress as companies, consumers, and advertisers adapt to technology. While some classes feature stronger social dynamic characteristics than others, the point remains that social media is a significant media type with multiple classes and many vehicles within each class.

Facebook and LinkedIn are dominant media in social and professional networking, but there are others that an advertiser may select. While messengers are not quite similar, there is consistency with the social and professional realms as people use their contact list. Similarly, YouTube and Instagram are the leaders in video and picture content, however promotional planners might consider alternatives. From a news point of view, a media planner might select Twitter or Buzzfeed for message delivery. Similarly, an advertiser may communicate through information-oriented social media found in wikis, bookmarks, and blogs. In addition, numerous review sites exist as well for an advertiser to locate an optimal target audience for the campaign. As this suggests, the media planning decision for selecting a particular media vehicle within a social media class is consistent with **Figure 10-2**. Finally, lifestyles identified in the fourth column share functional characteristics (e.g., networking, share content, share information) with the others, however the attraction is a specific topic and unique experience for the audience. The significance of this perspective is that promotional planners potentially consider many options for selecting a media class to reach their target audience when constructing a digital ad plan, as described in Chapter 17.

The large number of social media classes and vehicles suggests that there is wide variation among them. From an advertising standpoint, this is a realistic view since each has a distinct audience for advertisers to target. However, at the core, there remain elements of commonality that users experience, which spurred researchers to investigate and define **social media attachment** in terms of eight characteristics.[2]

Connecting—remain linked with others   Advice—learn from others

Nostalgia—remember the past   Affirmation—feel assured/supported

Informed—keep up to date   Enhancement—esteem/actualization

Enjoyment—relaxation/entertainment   Influence—encourage/help others

Figure 18-1 Social media classes for message planning

Networking	Content	Information	Lifestyle
Social	Video	News	Health, Sports
Professional	Picture	Blogs	Music, Travel
Messengers	Live Cast	Collaborative Projects	Food, Gaming

Social media attachment is not difficult to see on a daily basis, as many people are very frequent users of many social media shown in **Figure 18-1**. Given the audience's attachment to a media that did not exist a short while ago, it is important for promotional planners to comprehensively understand their audience's engagement to make effective promotion decisions.

SOCIAL MEDIA ENGAGEMENT

User-generated content is a distinguishing feature of social media, and research expanded this idea and defined *consumers' online brand-related activities (COBRAs)* as consuming, contributing, and creating within social media. These three activities occur in social networking sites, and to varying degrees in other social media classes. Collectively, all three activities represent social media engagement. The examples listed within each activity below are illustrative and are not intended to be the only ones possible.[3]

Consuming includes watching a brand video, listening to brand audio, viewing brand pictures, following brand threads in a forum, reading brand social networking pages, reading product reviews, playing branded games, and downloading branded material (e.g., widgets). This is the lowest level of social media engagement and motivation is based on entertainment (enjoyment, relaxation, escapism) and information (surveillance, knowledge, inspiration, pre-purchase).

Contributing involves rating products, joining a brand social networking page, participating in brand conversations in a forum, and commenting in brand blogs. This is mid-level social media engagement and motivation is based on personal identity (self-expression, self-presentation, self-assurance) and social integration (social interaction, social identity, altruism).

Creating involves behaviours like publishing a brand blog; uploading brand video, audio, or pictures; writing brand articles; and writing product reviews. This is the highest level of social media engagement and motivation is the same as contributing. Clearly, someone who is actually producing brand-related content is showing a high degree of social media engagement, and we suggest that such individuals exhibit substantial brand love or brand attachment as described in Chapter 1, or are very brand-loyal customers.

To some degree all of these COBRAs convey social media engagement, however consumption is relatively passive (such as consuming other media) and there is very little interaction. However, contributing and creating demonstrate complete social media engagement. One initial empirical test of the COBRAs idea found conceptual clarity among the three behaviours, and found support that the behaviours remained distinct from brand equity and brand attitude.[4] Another study building on this view identified activities that constitute social media engagement in the context of luxury brands. The activities are consistent with the initial empirical test and they appear applicable for other product categories.[5]

Like/follow brand	Publish photo of branded product
Comment on brand post/brand ad	Publish photo of self with brand
Like/tag/share brand post	Solicit comments on brand photos
Mention friend in comments	Brand conversations
Tag brand names	Publish shopping stories
Hashtags in posted photos	Modify branded product

Other definitions and measures of engagement exist within the advertising literature that differ remarkably from this list and the items presented above.[6] So when we refer to engagement in this chapter, we are referring to social media engagement only. Thus, we define **social media engagement** as consumer brand-related activities that reflect consuming, contributing, or creating behaviour manifested digitally in social media. Given the vast array of social media vehicles available, the specific consuming, contributing, or creating behaviour toward a brand will vary. However, the COBRAs identified and the above list are a starting point at which promotional planners begin to develop their social media communication plan.

eWOM

Individuals conversing in social media about brands are participating in electronic word-of-mouth communication (eWOM). More formally, **eWOM** refers to positive or negative statements about a brand or company communicated by a potential, actual, or former customer which are made available through Internet media or social media.[7] We initially visited this topic in Chapter 4 when describing personal channels of communication within the communication model and referred to it as *online WOM*, although *eWOM* is emerging as a preferred term. Consumers exchange information on content publishers' websites and in social media such as social networking, content communities, blogs, product review sites, and discussion boards. And eWOM is seen through social media engagement as consumers express their eWOM through consuming, contributing, and creating user-generated content in social media. Communication via eWOM is a digital manifestation of interpersonal WOM that occurred before digital media, but interactive characteristics and user-generated content change the dynamics significantly. In reviewing different social media, we illustrate similar and unique aspects of eWOM that occur.

What is the significance of eWOM? A large-scale review of over 50 studies concluded that the number of eWOM messages contributed to sales very strongly, and that the tone of the eWOM (positive/negative/neutral) contributed to sales almost twice as powerfully. Stronger relationships for both volume and tone occurred for goods with less ability for consumers to try and for privately consumed goods. The implication of this data is that efforts by brands to encourage positive eWOM are worthwhile; if consumers actually put forth positive eWOM, then brands will experience greater sales.[8] A similar review of over 90 studies found the same effect on sales, although the strength did not reach the same level. Nevertheless, the researchers concluded that promotional planners' active management of eWOM appeared warranted.[9]

The selfie is a popular COBRA indicating significant social media engagement and is used for eWOM. In a study comparing individuals who post selfies with a brand/product (known as brand-selfies) versus individuals who post selfies without a brand/product, brand-selfies scored higher on narcissism, materialism, and beliefs that social networking sites offer valuable product information.[10] This illustrates a significant point for advertisers regarding the target audience decision described in Chapter 3. Messages that encourage eWOM could target those with certain personality characteristics and attitudes to social media to achieve a higher probability of positive social media engagement. In addition, we find initial evidence that a hashtag contributes to greater eWOM.[11]

SOCIAL MEDIA USAGE

Figure 18-2 identifies the main social media that Canadians use based on MTM data. The list spans different social media classes and illustrates differences in the percentages of consumers visiting the sites on a monthly basis. Interestingly, growth in social media usage has been fairly consistent over the past few time periods, except for Snapchat. The implication of the usage percentages is that reach is limited for the majority of social media vehicles. This list and the numbers reflect some of the primary ones that we focus on in this chapter.

Figure 18-3 illustrates Canadian usage of social networking over time. This is a reasonable proxy for social media usage in general, and a clear plateau emerged after substantial growth. The implication of this graph is that advertising or communicating through social media remains limited to a degree for maximizing reach.

Figure 18-4 breaks out the overall trend by age groups. As expected, younger age groups (18–34, 35–49) skew higher than the 77 percent average. The growth trend is consistent for all age groups, except for the younger age group, who adopted social media early on. The same point emerges here in that reach is more limited for certain age groups.

Figure 18-5 shows social media use by age from MTM data, and reflects the above trends. We showed this data by smart phone and tablet in Chapter 17, and there is consistency as those in the younger age bracket mostly use social media on their smart phone. A couple of differences emerge in other age brackets, though. Once again, we see a

Figure 18-2 Usage (%) of social media during the past month, anglophones 18+

	2014	2016	2018
Facebook	66	64	68
LinkedIn	24	26	19
Twitter	19	21	19
Pinterest	19	21	22
Instagram	15	24	35
Snapchat	8	14	18
Reddit	6	9	10
Tumblr	6	6	4

Figure 18-3 Social networking usage during the past month, anglophones 18+

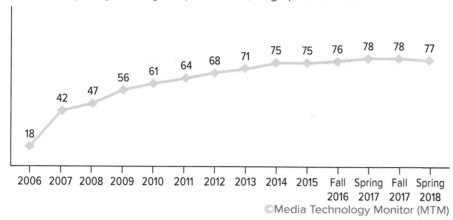

18 42 47 56 61 64 68 71 75 75 76 78 78 77

2006 2007 2008 2009 2010 2011 2012 2013 2014 2015 Fall Spring Fall Spring
2016 2017 2017 2018

©Media Technology Monitor (MTM)

Figure 18-4 Social networking usage during the past month, by age groups, anglophones 18+

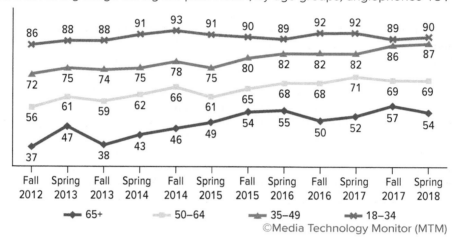

©Media Technology Monitor (MTM)

Figure 18-5 Frequency of social media use (monthly), fall 2018, anglophones 18+

	18–34	35–49	50–64	65+
Facebook	81%	75%	66%	48%
Twitter	26%	23%	18%	10%
Instagram	62%	40%	24%	7%
Snapchat	46%	14%	7%	1%
Pinterest	24%	26%	25%	10%

limitation of social media reaching all age groups, and even within the youngest age group, there is not universal appeal for usage no matter the device. For example, Snapchat is popular but only about half of people aged 18–34 use it on a monthly basis.

Figure 18-6 shows that Canadians use some social media vehicles more than others; it is based on MTM data. This suggests that promotional planners consider unique media decisions for each vehicle. When deciding to recommend the use of social media in an IMC plan, the promotional planner needs to carefully consider whether the plan is addressing paid, owned, or earned characteristics of each vehicle. All three approaches are connected to a degree, but promotional planners want to influence optimally to achieve objectives and should consider how it will work prior to investing time and money. Furthermore, a preliminary study across social media vehicles found different user-generated content. The researchers found user-generated content on YouTube to be akin to self-promotion, on Twitter to be seen as brand information delivery, and on Facebook to be in between these two endpoints of the spectrum.[12] This implies that unique

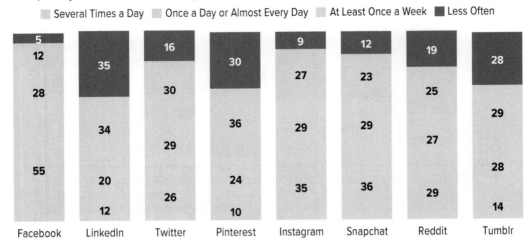

Figure 18-6 Frequency of social media usage, fall 2017, anglophones 18+

Legend: Several Times a Day | Once a Day or Almost Every Day | At Least Once a Week | Less Often

	Facebook	LinkedIn	Twitter	Pinterest	Instagram	Snapchat	Reddit	Tumblr
Less Often	5	35	16	30	9	12	19	28
At Least Once a Week	12	34	30	36	27	23	25	29
Once a Day or Almost Every Day	28	20	29	24	29	29	27	28
Several Times a Day	55	12	26	10	35	36	29	14

COBRAs within a social media vehicle provide a different exposure context, suggesting this as an important media planning consideration.

Paid, owned, and earned approaches for message delivery in social media occur with all major players. Followers subscribe to a Twitter feed of their favourite brand, are exposed to paid messages, and converse with people whom they do not even know. Consumers view a brand's video on YouTube, see ads for the brand on other videos, and forward links to others, comment on videos, or produce a response video. Consumers keep in touch with brands on blogs, see ads alongside the blog, and correspond seemingly as with a beloved friend as they respond to postings. Consumers use a wiki (a social bookmarking page) to creatively express their relationship to a brand, see paid ads, and understand something of a brand from the basic information provided. As all these behaviours imply, consumers digitally involve themselves in several ways with a brand.

The significance of social media and the resulting consumer participation is seen with Mars Canada's campaign with its famous M&Ms candy treat that won a Cannes award. Using Google Street View, Foursquare, Twitter, and Facebook, the brand sent people on a scavenger hunt to locate three oversized red M&M candies hidden in Toronto and captured by Google's cameras. Winners drove away with a red Smart car. While the uniqueness of the adventure is appealing, managers wondered what the significance of looking for the candy meant in terms of brand communication effects.[13] And here is the critical point: with technology at our fingertips—for both planner and consumer alike—which direction should a brand take with social media, and how can it marry the paid, owned, and earned approaches successfully? Furthermore, which social media should it use for which kinds of ad messages, and which IMC tools should a brand work with as usage levels change over time?

LO2 Social Networking

Social media exploded in popularity and social networking sites are a prominent destination for many Canadians who visit on a regular basis, as shown in the past few figures. In fact, social networking users tend to be heavy Internet media consumers (i.e., spend more time, watch more online video, listen to more online audio) compared to non–social networking users. The top social networking sites—Facebook, Twitter, and LinkedIn—attract numerous visitors each month as their users create a personal profile and connect with others to digitally share content. We take a look at Facebook and Twitter by evaluating their use as paid, owned, and earned media since this is a new way in which promotional planners view digital media advertising.[14]

FACEBOOK

About 25 million Canadians (53 percent female and 47 percent male) count on Facebook to meet their social networking needs.[15] As we know, ads are displayed in Facebook in a few locations, which means "paid media" occurs. A brand page in Facebook resembles "owned" media—much like the brand's website, and other "owned" media that

Figure 18-7 Facebook engagement, spring 2018, anglophones 18+

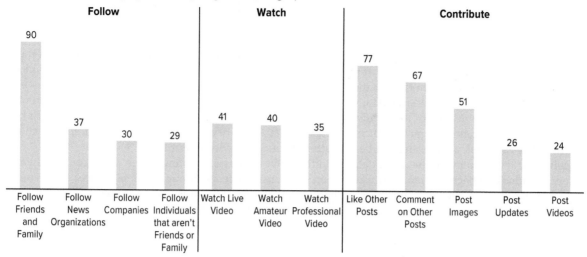

©Media Technology Monitor (MTM)

existed for decades before the Internet that promoted a brand image. Consumers visit a brand page within Facebook, "like" it, and communicate positive and negative consumption experiences in a variety of ways. These activities are COBRAs and indicate user-generated content, a unique feature of social media leading to the designation of "earned" media.

Figure 18-7 summarizes social media engagement activities of Canadians with Facebook. The first two represent consuming, while the third group is labelled exactly as defined by the COBRAs with "Contribute." The data shows that Canadians are quite active with some engagement activities and less so with others. This is important for promotional planners who are designing social media programs to encourage certain activities. For example, if there is a contest that asks consumers to post pictures, we see that only half do so, which might limit the promotion uptake.

How does social networking fit within a media plan? One study compared media advertising, brand messages to Facebook followers, and consumer-to-consumer communication (e.g., eWOM) to see the impact on communication effects and on various stages of consumer decision making. Media advertising contributed strongly to building brand awareness, consumers' information search and alternative evaluation, and purchases. Brand messages in social media contributed to information search and alternative evaluation and purchases. eWOM contributed to preferred attitude and purchases. The implications of this support the points summarized in Chapter 10 regarding media selection to achieve communication effects for each stage of consumer decision making. In general, promotional planners consider the right combination of media (not just one) for their brand, product category, and target audience.[16]

Paid From an advertising standpoint, Facebook is a media vehicle much like a specific magazine or television show. There is placement of an ad message within a content environment (or via a link). These messages are the ads described in Chapter 17, such as a display ad with a link to a brand's website or video messages created by the brand. Facebook also offers other options that are similar and innovative: stories, messenger (which resemble paid search links), carousel, slideshow, and collection. All of these formats are communicated in terms of assisting with online direct marketing activities. While a whole book could be written about Facebook, we highlight a couple of communication similarities to other media, along with its unique features for paid ads (**Exhibit 18-1**).

The targeting abilities of Facebook as a media vehicle make it a very attractive advertising opportunity, allowing for complete choice and substantial precision among all

Exhibit 18-1 Facebook provides information for paid advertising like other media companies.

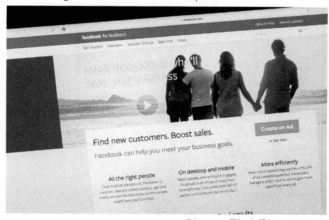

©Ingvar Bjork/Shutterstock

segmentation variables summarized in Chapter 3. For example, Ben and Jerry's wanted to remind ice cream consumers who had savoured the brand in the past to consider eating the seven classic flavours once again. Using data from people's postings and other data, the brand increased sales from this target audience by 8 percent.[17] Facebook provides guidelines on how the targeting and costing operates, and for the most part the steps are similar to what we have seen for other media but with simpler, "point and click" options as opposed to other more involved logistical arrangements.

The ability to target exceedingly precisely on key variables places a premium on this media vehicle, provided people pay attention to the ads. One decision facing advertisers is whether to place a promotional message in a news feed or on the right-hand side; each has different cost implications and click-through rates, but in either case Facebook tracking indicates from which ad the user went to the advertiser's website.[18] However, the news feed is cluttered with both ads and content from friends, making it more difficult to ensure that a step beyond exposure occurred. Empirical research also confirmed that Facebook advertising can be as cluttered a media environment as TV.[19]

And Facebook is trying to make the ads it delivers in the news feed as interesting as the social content a person receives from friends. This becomes more critical as more advertising occurs through mobile devices, but especially for smart phones since there is less screen space for banner ads. The end result is that advertisers now receive fewer impressions but pay higher rates.[20] In particular, Facebook moved into YouTube's territory by offering autoplay video ads arising from the news feed. Canadian Club is one brand accepting the idea and playing its 15-second ads both on TV and digitally, likely with greater emphasis on mobile.[21]

A study evaluating emotional and cognitive assessments of different paid ad formats and forwarded paid ad formats (i.e., earned media) on Facebook demonstrated that users are not thrilled with ads in the social networking site. The results reported a general trend of lower scores for display ads and suggested posts compared to re-promoted messages (e.g., friend like, I like, business pages) found in a user's news feed. While not completely unanimous, the data indicated users liked the forwarded ad messages more for six variables investigated. However, both types of ad formats scored at the midpoint of the scale, suggesting users were not really enthusiastic about either format.[22] Recall that data from ASC in **Figure 17-7** indicated a general lack of liking of Internet media ads and social media ads, so this academic study coincides with practical research as well.

Owned A Facebook brand page is completely unique owned media to communicate with a brand's target audience or the general public. It allows instant connection to exciting brand content, making the whole page a commercial experience in which the user may not even perceive (or may not be concerned about) the advertising due to brand loyalty. This idea of content on a Facebook brand page is not the same as content found in broadcast or print media, where the content is a TV program, a radio show, a newspaper article on a topic like youth unemployment, or a magazine piece on how university and college students can live away from home economically. Much of the content presented by a brand on a Facebook brand page is a form of advertising, or a unique kind of marketing communication depending on the brand and its content.

One study qualitatively evaluated three brand pages over time. The researchers discovered three themes of importance for the followers: content about the fan world, content about the brand, and the brand page community. In summarizing the data, the authors suggest how promotional planners can foster a stronger community on a brand page over time by increasing participation and engagement, introducing topical information (e.g., brand content), identifying communication (e.g., building interaction), and establishing cultural norms (e.g., value of social interaction).[23]

Exhibit 18-2 shows a testimonial message from the Facebook brand page for Big Brothers Big Sisters of Toronto. The Big Brothers Big Sisters organization's 20,700 volunteers provide mentoring services to over 40,000 children and young people in over 1,100 communities across our country. This ad-like message is an example of the communication possible on a brand page that would have a positive influence on those seeking mentor services, volunteers (many likely following the page), and members of the general public interested in volunteering. Inspiring thoughts conveyed in the message would likely fit with the brand page community point mentioned in the above research study.

Exhibit 18-2 An important message from the brand page of Big Brothers Big Sisters of Toronto.

©Big Brothers Big Sisters of Toronto

Facebook's literature is designed to educate businesspeople that a Facebook brand page is unique and yet consistent with advertising elsewhere.[24] The page has a cover photo, a visually attractive brand presentation much like a print ad in a magazine. The profile picture gives a prime location for brands to present their logo or any other identifying image, once again adapting a long-established advertising principle found in other media. The filmstrip-like row of activities that includes apps provides additional promotional experiences. The ability to include brand information or photos in the pinned posts offers extended reading or viewing opportunities, and the experience is akin to reading feature magazine articles about a brand. But the distinction about content made earlier suggests that these posts are more like copy found in catalogues or other collateral material. Communications regarding sales promotions like contests or discounts are certainly familiar as they occur in all other types of media as well.

The content of a brand page is designed to encourage participation with a brand's posting. Research tested the effects of a brand's posting and examined the factors that led to consumers "liking" the posting or commenting on the posting. The results found that high vividness ranging from no visual to photo to video produced higher levels of "likes" for video only, but did not garner more comments. Interactivity produced higher levels of "likes" with contest links, but not for website links, voting links, calls to action, or questions. Information and entertainment value did not produce "likes" or more comments. In contrast, the positional location of the brand post and the positive comments of others produced higher levels of "likes" and more comments.[25]

Followers of a brand page are similar since they demonstrated affinity for the brand, but like any group of consumers, there are likely segments or groups with unique characteristics. To profile followers, one study asked numerous questions pertaining to brand self-expressiveness, brand loyalty, brand love, WOM, motivation for following the brand, and network characteristics. The fascinating result identified four profiles—fanatic, self-expressive, utilitarian, and authentic—which varied on their responses to the questions and which look vaguely like the psychographic profiles described in Chapter 3. The implication of this finding is that organizations should likely consider conducting such a study to understand the profile of followers, who are likely fairly loyal to the brand.[26] If a company found a few different segments within its brand page, it could determine how to communicate with each group with certain posts, events, or promotions.

One interesting study compared the attitudes of three different Facebook users toward a brand page and concluded that current followers exhibited a stronger brand attitude compared to non-followers, indicating that followers are likely aligned toward strong loyalty. In the natural field experiment, some non-followers joined the brand page, as instructed, and they eventually formed a stronger attitude when measured one month later due to actively interacting with others on the social networking site.[27] The implication of this result is that if brands encourage social media engagement on their brand page, they can expect a slightly stronger brand attitude that may contribute to future purchase intentions.

Organizations post on their brand pages to communicate to the followers (i.e., owned) and a follower may forward the message to a friend (i.e., earned). So an interesting question is whether an organization wants to design the post for the follower only, or design it for the follower to forward it (i.e., social media engagement). The previous section identified individual and social motives as the driving reason for social media engagement. One study looked at this with a sample of 10 million brand posts and a sample of users who reposted some of them. In total, 52 percent reposted since it would make them look good and 36 percent reposted since it would make them look intelligent. Emotionally, 47 percent reported reposting because it made them happy and 27 percent said reposting occurred because of excitement. Cognitively, 42 percent viewed the reposting as useful. Variation occurred by product category, but the implication of this study is that if brands want their posts shared, they should focus on exciting and useful messages that enhance the image of their followers![28]

In a comparison of two owned features of Facebook exposure (in-stream, page views) and two earned features of Facebook exposure (likes, user posts), the results indicated that likes and page views drove long-term sales the most. If likes are a proxy for loyalty, then the results highlight the importance of brands delivering accurate messages in their posts, much like any other owned media. Interestingly, news feed messages contributed to a long-term negative effect on sales.[29]

Earned Another important attribute that is distinctive for this social media is the part of the page where fellow Facebookers describe their buying and consumption experiences as a message to consumers. While these messages are not controlled by the advertiser like the initial photos and messages are, their content can be influenced by the brand since they can be reactions to what the brand initially posted. Nevertheless, a degree of brand influence clearly occurs from the social dynamic of people conversing—the extent, however, is open for investigation.

Figure 18-8 reprises the MTM data from **Figure 18-7** by age and for the five contributing aspects of social media engagement. Interestingly, the oldest age group of 65+ is second highest for "comment on other people's post" and is the highest for "like other people's post." Are you surprised? From this data, it seems Facebook is approaching mainstream media status where there is similar behaviour for all ages.

Figure 18-8 Facebook engagement by age, spring 2018, anglophones 18+

	18–34	35–49	50–64	65+
Post image	51%	64%	46%	34%
Comment on other people's post	38%	28%	23%	30%
Like other people's post	28%	20%	15%	29%
Post video	24%	37%	14%	11%
Post update	31%	36%	17%	11%

Kraft Dinner presents a friendly example of a popular brand using Facebook to maintain a fascinating attachment with Canadians. Since the product's name south of the border is Kraft Macaroni and Cheese, KD (as it is known here in Canada) retains its unique identity with home-grown advertising featuring the famous "Gotta Be KD" slogan, invented by a consumer more than 10 years ago during the brand's cross-country promotional tour. Playing on the sense of ownership Canadians feel with KD, the Facebook page presented challenges to consumers—including photobombing with KD, making a KD .gif, putting captions on photos of KD, and "Make It Epic" recipe battles. TV ads with humorous battle scenes between two roommates drove traffic to Facebook. The campaign pumped up its followers from 120,000 to 270,000, an especially impressive result considering the challenges did not reward winners with prizes like most contests. Instead, winners received social media glory as KD victors![30]

TWITTER

Canadian Twitter users amount to 7.5 million, with 46 percent men and 54 percent women. Twitter self-identifies as a "real-time information network" on its Internet site.[31] This contributes to difficulty in classifying it, since "networking" implies it is similar to entities like Facebook, however "real-time information" implies a blog or micro-blog. However, the messages distributed are reasonably similar to the news feed feature on Facebook, so it remains in the social networking domain. The most followed account is video game developer BioWare with 2.8 million followers.

Figure 18-9 summarizes social media engagement activities of Canadians with Twitter. We see lower levels for Twitter compared to Facebook, except for "follow news organizations" which support the classification shown in **Figure 18-1** of Twitter being a news outlet. The new orientation that emerged in the past few years suggests Twitter is best used by brands as a PR tool. On the flip side, Twitter is also featured in notable publicity activities as well. As we saw in Chapter 15, PR and publicity are linked substantially in marketing communication for organizations. Nonetheless, almost half of all Internet users involve themselves with posts showing a strong engagement level.

Figure 18-9 Twitter engagement, spring 2018, anglophones 18+

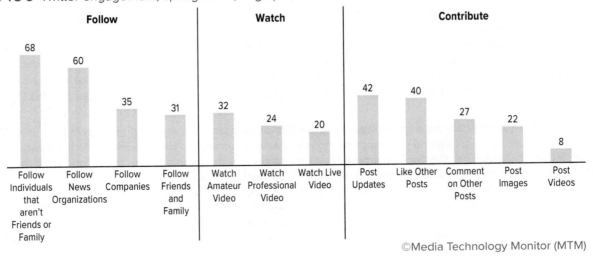

©Media Technology Monitor (MTM)

To some degree, Twitter is entirely free—any brand or person (e.g., performing artist, athlete) can set up an account and send messages to followers, who will ultimately be influenced by such communication. The messages can be simple phrases and, if desired, can include links to whatever digital content the author would like to associate, including video. In this manner, brands can distribute a controlled message to anyone who is following or motivated to seek out the messages, much like other Internet media that is owned. With so many users and so many messages there is considerable clutter, which led to Twitter offering advertising options for fees, and thus moving into a world of paid media.

Paid Twitter's ad products for marketing communication include promoted accounts, promoted tweets, and promoted trends.[32] Promoted accounts are identified by the brand name, like Cirque du Soleil, and are featured in the "Who to follow" account recommendation search engine. Cirque du Soleil wanted to announce tour dates and new shows to potential customers who can find this branded account among others. So this works much like a short link ad from a search engine to encourage repeat exposures to brand messages.

Promoted tweets are brand messages much like specific advertising messages found in other online media where consumers willingly seek brand information (i.e., Internet sites). They are also similar to brand messages placed in non-digital media like magazines. For one promoted tweet, Cirque asked followers to communicate their experience while seeing a show. In this respect, the social media message from a customer (i.e., source of the message) acts as a testimonial so that potential customers vicariously experience the spectacle. The customer testimonial is the unique contribution of social media; this personal content acts as a brand message yet shares similar qualities since there is an identifiable source characteristic regarding similarity (see Chapter 7).

The message often has a link to the Internet site or any other type of digital communication the brand planned. Cirque made use of promoted tweets that include sales promotions for discounted tickets that linked to its Facebook page. Naturally, the links could go to a brand's Internet site, which Gongshow Gear successfully employed, or to a YouTube video for continued brand exposure, like Porsche did for its launch of the 911 model. Promoted trends are listed in a designated trends section on Twitter, which acts as an automated search designed to encourage continued exposure to other messages. Again, this operates much like a link ad from a search engine. For example, Porsche initially established its hashtag in a promoted tweet and then listed the same hashtag in the promoted trends.

Twitter operates like any other media, offering an opportunity for brand exposure for fees. As of early 2013, a promoted trend cost $200,000 per day. Advertisers pay when people follow a promoted account, or when people retweet, reply, favourite, or click on a brand's promoted tweet. The cost for these two ad products is based on a bidding system and ranges from $0.50 to $2.50 per follower for a promoted account and $0.50 to $1.50 per action for a promoted tweet.[33] The minimum price works out to a CPM of $500, a very expensive proposition compared to other media. Like any media company, Twitter offers information and advice for advertising (**Exhibit 18-3**).

Owned From a social marketing standpoint, brands encourage lots of interaction with fun activities like Twestivals, which raise funds for a worthy cause the brand sponsors; TweetUps, where people who follow a brand can meet up and socialize face to face; and Twitter parties, where consumers continually talk about a brand with multiple comments.[34] These and any other follow-up messages from consumers are the height of social media, with user-generated content (e.g., earned media). While these can have positive impact, there is tremendous risk for negative communication as the company loses control, something most brands historically have not desired. But in terms of positives, Ford Canada claimed Twitter success with anecdotal stories of consumers reporting they purchased a Ford after seeing the company's Twitter presence or responses. Furthermore, the brand uses Twitter as a listening post to act upon negative experiences with a direct call once contact information is ascertained. A whole team constantly monitors the account, providing responses 24/7.[35]

However the implementation of Twitter messages remains a concern for brands that are grappling with questions, much like any other media when it first arrived.[36] What message should be sent via Twitter? When should the messages be sent? How frequently should the messages be sent? Molson moved toward posting less frequently but with higher quality images and brand messages due to the value of shared tweets; in contrast,

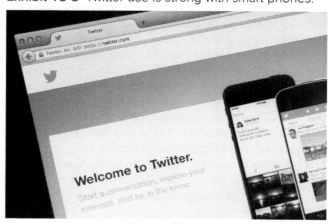

Exhibit 18-3 Twitter use is strong with smart phones.

©dolphfyn / Shutterstock.com

during the World MasterCard Fashion Week, the sponsor tweeted 60 times per day to share the runway photos![37] Where should the brand digitally direct the user via its links? Why is someone motivated to receive our brand's Twitter feed? Companies like Tim Hortons and Harvey's operating in Canada understand that their tone needs to fit with Canadian culture and be humble, sincere, and friendly. Canadian divisions of American brands like Denny's opened a separate Canadian Twitter feed so the message resonated with Canadians.[38] The Canadian Football League worked Twitter into its plan to present the action on the field and the players as part of its Grey Cup communications directed to younger fans less interested in nostalgia.[39]

Finally, who in the organization should be sending the message? PR executives feel strongly that Twitter responses and all social media communication are in their domain, since these professionals are trained and experienced with continual messaging with the press and the public as issues and topics emerge over time. On the other side, digital agencies believe they should be in charge since they have the technical skills and are stronger resources in our technological era.[40]

A number of criticisms and challenges face Twitter despite its appeal. One criticism is the usefulness of the format—a stream of tweets that viewers typically do not backtrack to see, thereby limiting actual exposure. Coupled with this is a problem that messages are cluttered.[41] In terms of concerns, the user base growth is not meeting expectations and a noticeably small portion of users are active tweeters, with the remainder acting as quiet bird-watchers. In addition, the frequency of actually tweeting from the active users is not as strong as hoped for by advertisers looking to invest their budget.[42] To counter these issues, Twitter introduced "conversational" ad formats where consumers answer a branded tweet by touching a ready-made response in which they can also add their own comments. Samsung Canada tested the concept to promote its smart watch Gear S2 and claimed good success by obtaining exposure and responses from 53,000 consumers over four days.[43]

One study experimented with whether a company's own tweets (owned) or influencer retweets increased consumption of a documentary TV program shown on local stations compared to situations where no tweets occurred. It is interesting to consider whether the influencer option is paid or earned, as they are well recognized and paid for the tweets within the experiment. Realistically, the influencers represent paid media since there is a fee paid, akin to brands paying funds to a retailer to administer in-store displays. Alternatively, the recipients of the retweets may not be aware of the fee paid and view this as a non-sponsored message, akin to an earned media message. The data showed that company tweets did in fact increase viewership by 77 percent. Influencer retweets increased consumption by an additional 33 percent, and up to 57 percent when the message included broadcast information, with part of the growth due to the influencers bringing in new followers.[44]

The implication of this study is that brands need to decide on the source of the message, much like we saw with other communication. In this case, the source is the brand or a spokesperson who is remunerated, but the third alternative is that the source is another consumer with no ties to the brand. Additionally, the message appeal is important, as we saw in Chapter 7, and research is investigating whether a promotional message or an experiential message influences consumers' attitudes and their intention to click the message for further reading.[45] As we can see, even a simple tweet has a significant effect and the content and source of the message are important decisions for promotional planners.

Earned What factors drive people to retweet a message? Part of the answer is the actual content of the message and the fit of the content with the sender. Messages that appeal to the person retweeting lead to their actually retweeting. The implication is that brands should design messages for the particular influencers they would like to see retweet the message to pick up on their source effects.[46]

One interesting study examined the content of consumer tweets of four brands within five industries. On average, almost 50 percent of the tweets focused on products, with just under 20 percent for each of service and promotions. The tone of the tweets reached 50 percent for negative, 35 percent for neutral, and 15 percent for positive. Combined, these data suggest that a good number of complaints were about product quality and that consumers used Twitter to announce their dissatisfaction.[47] The implication of this study is that brands need to consider the strategic purpose of their Twitter account, whether it's for proactive brand messaging or reactive post-purchase communication.

Figure 18-10 reprises the MTM data from **Figure 18-9** by age and for the five contributing aspects of social media engagement. Interesting variation occurs for "comment on other people's posts" as there is a dip in the 35–49 age bracket as we move from younger to older. Also curious is the similarity of many social media engagement activities for the 18–34 bracket and the 50–64 bracket. And we see almost the same level for all age brackets for posting tweets. The implication of this is that perhaps Twitter is becoming a bit of a mass media for those who subscribe and many are motivated to participate.

Figure 18-10 Twitter engagement by age, spring 2018, anglophones 18+

	18–34	35–49	50–64	65+
Post image	28%	23%	23%	8%
Comment on other people's post	35%	19%	29%	25%
Like other people's post	49%	37%	48%	21%
Post video	14%	7%	5%	0%
Post tweets	52%	40%	40%	41%

A study of major brands covering almost 20,000 brand tweets discovered that each one resulted in an average of 21 retweets, and 83 percent received at least one retweet. Characteristics that motivated followers to retweet a brand's tweet included links to the brand's website, brand's social network site, photos, and videos, but links to news media had no effect. Product information within the tweet magnified the number of tweets by 11. Interestingly, brand identification, hashtag inclusion, and emotional message content also had no effect. Keep in mind that these factors did not lead to retweets, but they could have had communication effects on the receiver in other ways not measured in the study. The implication of this is that promotional planners design the tweets to influence the receiver to forward the message, or to influence the receiver only.[48]

Content Communities

Content communities exist for users to share video, photo images, and audio media. We concentrate on the first two for this section; there is no documented revenue stream for audio advertising revenue, and video advertising revenue hit $358 million in Canada for 2015. For video, we concentrate on YouTube since it is the industry leader in advertising practices and retains a strong market position.

YOUTUBE

Figure 18-11 summarizes usage statistics from MTM for YouTube indicating that the usage rates are approaching the level of TV. In fact, 80 percent of those aged 18–34 watch YouTube weekly. While the volume is on par with TV for the younger age bracket, the remaining brackets still watch more hours on TV. Like any other Internet site, YouTube generates revenue by selling a variety of display ads and video ads, and also offers in-video overlay display ads and specialized options for homepage ads. These types of ads are available for mobile delivery as well, demonstrating that YouTube is a paid Internet media option. Companies use YouTube for owned media with their branded channels. Social engagement occurs with viral video among other activities.

Paid Streaming ads operate much like TV, showing a message while viewing a content video, with options. True View ads permit viewers to skip the ad after five seconds, and YouTube offers four versions: in-stream ads, in-slate ads, display, and search. Standard in-stream ads occur before, during, or after a video and do not have the skip feature. First Watch plays a brand's ad first no matter what video the viewer watches.

YouTube original channels offer similar media vehicles much like TV. There are a host of genres of shows in terms of sports, comedy, lifestyle, and others. Ads can be selectively placed on any of these channels. Alternatively, advertisers can select placement on regular videos based on profiling characteristics seen in previous media placement.

Figure 18-11 YouTube and Internet video viewing by age, fall 2018, anglophones 18+

	18–34	35–49	50–64	65+
Watch YouTube (monthly)	95%	85%	80%	67%
Internet video (hours/week)	16.7	11.23	7.86	6.87

Figure 18-12 YouTube video view by age, fall 2016, anglophones 18+

	18–34	35–49	50–64	65+
Any video	93%	82%	66%	45%
TV show	38%	22%	10%	5%
Movie	32%	16%	10%	6%
Movie preview	71%	51%	34%	12%

Figure 18-12 shows more detailed viewing data from MTM regarding the above points. For a large part of the younger age bracket, the content watched indicates that YouTube may be a substitute for their TV watching. With the growth of OTT services described in Chapter 10, it is unclear what direction YouTube might take with respect to this viewing trend.

Owned Of course, companies can put video on YouTube as owned media, and this is great for any kind of growing business. Martell Home Builders, a small and enterprising construction startup in Moncton, stumbled upon using YouTube with a video clip of industry tradespeople endorsing the owner to potential customers. With quick distribution of the video link within the real estate industry, Pierre Martell was in business. Subsequent videos describe the customized house building process so well that the owner can now close a sale in two hours, down from eight hours, because the video answers so many preliminary questions.[49]

Brands became very creative with YouTube to establish owned media in different ways. Schick funded a series entitled *MsLabelled* featuring Ella, a young employee working at a fashion magazine with aspirations to be a fashion blogger. Ella came to life with her own accounts on Instagram, Tumblr, and Twitter. The brand saw similarity between Ella's character—who is fun and flirty—and its target audience. Although Schick did not promote its involvement substantially, the company received more visits to its website and strong traffic on Ella's social media.[50] Walmart established a similar idea with *Upstairs Amy* but showed its sponsorship, along with Interac's involvement, during the final minute of a five-minute video in which the viewer received an ad-like message and promotional offers. The captivating storyline enticed viewers to continue watching the episodes; the first received 320,000 views, and the next three averaged 200,000 views after nearly two years (as of 2019, there were 20 episodes online).[51]

YouTube offers the opportunity for channels—designated repositories of whatever videos a brand may want to post for viewers—including ads appearing on TV, on another Internet location, or specifically customized. User channels are cost-free with the same functionality as for any other user. Thus, a YouTube channel retains the idea of owned media for brands desiring to host video messages. Brand channels are cost-free and offer additional avenues for brand identification and enhanced viewer experience. Custom brand channels offer interactive applications, user-generated submission, live streaming, and client services for fees. Even though YouTube has a dominant position, others are interested in gaining a share of a growing market, as seen in **Exhibit 18-4**.

Exhibit 18-4 Popular YouTube faces competition as the market grows.

©dolphfyn/Shutterstock

Earned In some respects, the use of channels on YouTube is a wonderful opportunity for advertisers to initiate further social media communication among their viewers. Skittles' use of YouTube described in Chapter 8 presents ample opportunity for consumers to respond to the brand, much like the sensation with Old Spice a few years ago. And, for some unknown reason, consumers may decide to create tribute ads for brands they love. One enterprising former student created his own "BlackBerry There Then There Now—Z10 Commercial" on YouTube and had picked up nearly 62,000 views by mid-2019. **Figure 18-13** summarizes how Canadian YouTube users are socially engaged by participating in a good number of COBRAs.

Figure 18-13 Usage of YouTube, spring 2015, Canadians 18+

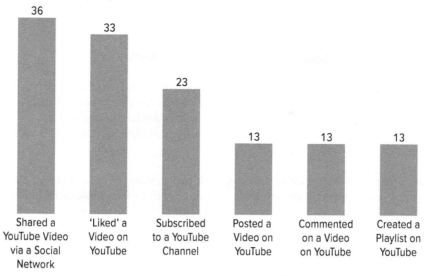

Shared a YouTube Video via a Social Network	36
'Liked' a Video on YouTube	33
Subscribed to a YouTube Channel	23
Posted a Video on YouTube	13
Commented on a Video on YouTube	13
Created a Playlist on YouTube	13

©Media Technology Monitor (MTM)

Figure 18-14 YouTube subscriber statistics

	Ford	Chevrolet	Honda	Toyota	Nissan
2013 subscribers	1,239	2,413	920	751	1,311
2016 subscribers	13,228	21,478	3,547	6,512	8,051
2019 subscribers	130,849	150,287	28,055	23,399	21,242

Major Canadian brand channels for vehicle brands had low subscription rates in 2013, as shown by data recorded over time in **Figure 18-14**, but most of them had achieved significant increase by 2019. However, brands can see razor sharp returns—like Dollar Shave Club, with over 10 million views! And it seems that the old adage—familiar from media before Internet video—is that creativity, no matter where it is located or viewed, gets notoriety. A brand's video message in social media is passed along if it is original and creative, much like we see in all facets of advertising.[52]

In commenting on the success of brand messages on video hosting sites, experts suggest that a positive return on investment is achieved if a clip reaches the 1 million mark. For example, a video that costs $50,000 to produce results in a CPM of $50. This is a different cost comparison based on production since there is no media cost, for now. Canadian advertisers are taking creative risks by placing ads on these sites that they might not normally place on TV. For example, Lululemon posted a video mocking its very own customers in a humorous version of "stuff yogis say" as a take-off on other pop-culture examples.[53] Of course, the 1 million mark only happens if the video link ricochets throughout social media, another example of how the same ad units discussed in Chapter 17 work in social media as well. And the media cost for distribution is free, since ordinary consumers are doing the work that brands would normally pay media companies to do.

Why would someone want to share a video? One study investigated three motives—altruism, affiliation, and distinctiveness—and found reasonable support for this view in their analysis. The key implications suggest that promotional planners should consider how to position the information associated within the link message to resonate with receivers so that they forward the message.[54] Another study investigated the impact on sharing with the following motives: need to belong, individualism, altruism, personal growth, and consumption. The results showed a strong positive effect for individualism and altruism, and a strong negative effect for personal growth.[55]

Beyond the motive of the sender of the video to others, it is critical that the receiver actually likes the video, or has a positive attitude toward it. This is consistent with the attitude to the ad model described in Chapter 4, but in this case the ad is the viral video and researchers found similar results. A positive attitude to the viral video contributed to a more positive brand attitude.[56] Who should receive the viral video? The conclusion of one study is to cast the video out to as many as possible who are relatively similar, have a strong tie to the brand, and have strong influence over others.[57]

INSTAGRAM

About 13 million Canadians visit Instagram regularly (56 percent female and 44 percent male). **Figure 18-15** totals up the content creation of Instagram users with the same data we saw for Facebook and Twitter. On all measures, Instagram users exhibit very strong social media engagement. Instagram leads Facebook on a couple of "follow" activities and is fairly even with Facebook on half of the remaining activities. Like we saw with the other three, Instagram is useful for paid, owned, and earned messages.

Paid Instagram offers numerous avenues for advertising with photo, video, and carousel ads (**Exhibit 18-5**). Many of the targeting features found with Facebook are available here as well since Facebook owns Instagram. And Instagram pushes ads through the news feed similarly, with ads having the same look as the media content. For its Canadian launch, Instagram worked with Hudson's Bay, Target, Sport Chek, Air Canada, and Travel Alberta as the initial advertisers. The advertisers readily accepted this format since most Instagram use occurred on smart phones where display ads cannot work with the smaller screen.[58]

Exhibit 18-5 Instagram photo images provide opportunity for paid media exposure.

©ArthurStock/Shutterstock

Owned The brand development in Instagram appears enormous for different types of advertisers. For example, for experiential products, like travel, entertainment, and so on—essentially, any product category that has a transformational motive—the images contribute to existing positive attitudes or begin to build new ones for non-users. If Canada wanted to foster more travel, what better way than to sprinkle photos or videos in Instagram that people from other countries might see? Mazda posted batches of three to six photos or videos periodically for about four months to communicate the feeling of driving the vehicle and experiencing the brand during a virtual road trip.[59]

Figure 18-15 Instagram engagement, spring 2018, anglophones, 18+

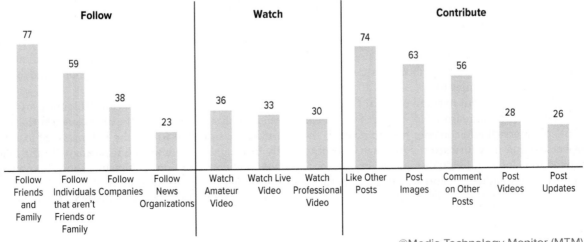

©Media Technology Monitor (MTM)

Businesses selling directly to consumers see Instagram as a creative and visual means to communicate their goods. **Exhibit 18-6** shows an Instagram site for a small business displaying its products. Social media presence like this provides online exposure for small businesses. Also, the beauty of Instagram for companies using Instagram in this way is the content from those who post comments after a photo or video. This illustrates the feedback aspect of the communication model shown in **Figure 4-1**.

Earned **Figure 18-16** shows the social media engagement of Canadians using Instagram across four age groups based on MTM data. We do see a notable skew of social media engagement of younger users for Instagram compared to Facebook. Perhaps in time this may change with greater usage by those in older age brackets. Continuing with the travel example from above, companies in the travel industry could foster user-generated content and encourage photo/video postings of ordinary citizens and create a means for consumers to find them, like a social bookmarking site.

Digital and Social Media Perspective 18-1 illustrates examples of owned media usage of Instagram. These examples suggest the unlimited potential for communicating with existing and potential customers.

Exhibit 18-6 Instagram provides exposure for small businesses.

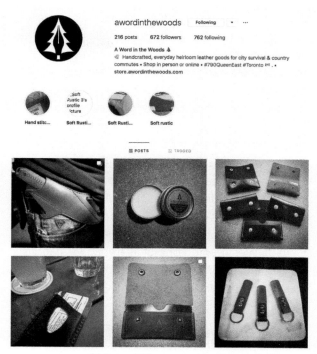

©Michael Zimmermann, @awordinthewoods

Figure 18-16 Instagram engagement by age, spring 2018, anglophones 18+

	18–34	35–49	50–64	65+
Post image	72%	63%	48%	19%
Comment on other people's post	66%	59%	48%	19%
Like other people's post	84%	76%	57%	18%
Post video	38%	32%	10%	10%
Post update	34%	28%	15%	11%

DIGITAL AND SOCIAL MEDIA PERSPECTIVE 18-1

POPULARITY OF INSTAGRAM

Imagine considering plastic surgery and looking for information about procedures. Websites are so 1990s and 2000s, so in the age of social media, why not watch liposuction on Instagram to see how it works? Indeed, one leading specialist shows his practice in all of its gory detail and sees his Instagram page as the new Discovery TV channel for millennials who do not watch television. Since these videos serve an educational purpose, the Canadian Association of Plastic Surgeons is unconcerned about their

©Ira Berger/Alamy Stock Photo

[Continued on next page]

being posted, as long as the information is not misleading or deceptive. Some consumers like the idea so much that they give the doctor permission to share the video recording with other interested consumers, or consent to a live broadcast of the procedure!

Use of video and images in social media is driven by young adults referred to as *the visual generation* who rely less on words and body copy for processing advertising messages. Not only are visuals aesthetically appealing in a brand message, but they are perfect for social media engagement by forwarding links to users' contacts. Interestingly, during National French Fry Day, McDonald's Canada livestreamed one of its french fry stations for 90 minutes and received 750,000 views in Instagram and other social media vehicles. For promotional support, the QSR gave away french fry themed swag on Instagram—the result: gone in 60 minutes—and it enlisted the assistance of a social influencer for added exposure. Taco Bell also used Instagram and live events to successfully launch its Baja Blast drink. Consumers got their hair dyed Baja Blue and, 32 million impressions later, it became the restaurant's number one fountain drink.

However, just when it seems like Instagram is for fast food or other low-involvement products, we find that it is a communication tool for opera stars encouraging young adults to get interested in this entertaining art form. Additionally, opera stars want to develop their career by obtaining work from opera houses, who in turn see the notoriety of the opera stars as a key point for selling tickets.

To encourage the visual generation to visit and shop, Yorkdale Shopping Centre in Toronto installed Insta-worthy places for consumers to snap their pics. Designed by local artists, the fun pop-up environments provide the perfect backdrop for users to glam up their Instagram game. Many arrive at Yorkdale specifically for the new spaces. According to Yorkdale's marketing director, since users tag the location, the initiative has resulted in greater foot traffic.

Question:

1. Why are people motivated to help brands with additional exposure by placing their photos within Instagram?

 # **Blogs and Collaborative Projects**

Social networking and content communities are quite popular and draw considerable interest for brands for paid, owned, and earned approaches. In addition, blogs and collaborative projects are good social media options for brands to evaluate and implement as they are classified as good information resources for consumers. They can ensure greater social media engagement to help brands achieve communication and behavioural objectives to reinforce their brand positioning strategy.

BLOGS

A **blog** (short for *weblog*) is a publication consisting primarily of periodic articles, normally presented in reverse chronological order. Blogs reflect the writings of an individual, a community, a political organization, or a corporation. A blog set up for brand presentation is akin to a website in that it is owned media. Blogs also present the opportunity for ad placement (e.g., paid media). And the ability of consumers to participate with responses and by adding user-generated content permits both positive and negative brand communication. Thus, this social media vehicle is a multifaceted brand communication tool, like other social media. Blog sites where writers set up their own blogs with varying levels of visitor traffic include WordPress, Blogger, and Tumblr.

Companies have experimented with corporate or brand blogs to present a friendly public relations face to the general public and allow some interactions. These can be within the corporate website or standalone. The imagery and tone of blogs provide less formal communication, so companies look to blogs as a way of appearing friendly and opening dialogue. Brands also establish blogs to address issues or ideas related to consumers who are more committed to the brand by virtue of their participation in viewing and interacting with the blog.

Blogs offer advertisers a potential way to reach their target audience at a small cost since they are specialized vehicles for placing display and video ads, as described in the previous section. WordPress does not facilitate the placement of ads; however, Blogger, owned by Google, is associated with its system of ad placements. Individual blogs offer their own media kit for ad prices that are consistent with previous descriptions. For example, BlogTO, a blog about Toronto, offers different banner ad options with a CPM of $10 to $20, along with other customized options.[60] A Vancouver-based blog entitled Scout sells ads to small local businesses on a per placement basis in its "Locals We Recommend" section.[61] Extreme fragmentation occurs, with literally millions of blog media vehicles available in which an advertiser might place its ad. This problem supports the need for digital ad placement firms.

Personal bloggers find themselves as key influencers for consumers while describing their product experiences. For certain consumers, a blogger has a strong source credibility effect. In this respect, bloggers are acting similarly to journalists who feature product stories in newspapers or magazines. Marketers also recognize that mothers who blog are particularly successful in this role, as mothers seem to trust other mothers considerably. Blogs directed to foodies (**Exhibit 18-7**) are popular and provide good opportunity for food companies to influence consumers.

Advertisers also sponsor personal blogs, or an individual blog that is part of a collection of blogs such as the YummyMummyClub.ca. Erica Ehm, a famous media host, documented a trip to Alberta on her blog, including photos taken with a Sony camera. One page of the blog ended with the brand prominently displayed with a sponsorship notice that provided full disclosure of the relationship between the blogger and the brand. Some are critical of this process and suggest that it circumvents the "idea" of a blog, while others are concerned that bloggers do not communicate the advertiser's exact financial contribution. In defence, bloggers cite industries (e.g., fashion, travel) where free goods are routinely passed along for endorsement. We continue this discussion of social media influence in the next section, which encompasses all social media.

Exhibit 18-7 Bloggers post images on their sites and provide opportunity for earned media exposure for brands.

©Stock-Asso/Shutterstock

COLLABORATIVE PROJECTS

This type of social media includes wikis, reviews, and social bookmarking Internet sites. These share a common characteristic of having extensive user-generated content. Wikis permit users to add, remove, or change text-based content, and social bookmarking sites allow users to collect links to Internet sites and rate their quality. The top wiki sites include Wikipedia, Yahoo Answers, About, and Answers. Sites that feature consumer reviews include Yelp and Quora. Some of these sites do not completely reflect wikis, but their format resembles the idea of a collaborative project for the most part since users respond and converse on a multitude of topics.

Wikipedia does not accept advertising and encourages an active debate on its merits.[62] Answers.com offers extensive placement options and provides a comprehensive media kit describing the standard and custom formats; this is similar to other social media and Internet sites that are not social media, as discussed in the advertising section.[63] These kinds of collaborative question and answer sites appear conducive for both positive and negative brand communication effects, as consumers are communicating a testimonial by contributing their consumption experiences, which may or may not resonate with readers.

Top social bookmarking sites are Pinterest and Reddit. What social media vehicles to include on this list demonstrates the difficulty with exact classification given their overlapping features with other social media, however the bookmarking feature is the most noteworthy and these social media vehicles are identified as the main ones. It should be noted that Reddit could fit in the news column and Pinterest could fit in the content column of the social media table in **Figure 18-1**. These examples show the limitation of establishing a clear picture for social media classes for planning messages in social media.

Reddit provides instructions for how would-be advertisers can place ads alongside the content, while others appear not to offer advertising at all. Reddit users are active, with 78 percent creating content overall across many activities

Figure 18-17 Percent of Reddit users that create content, fall 2014, Canadians, 18+

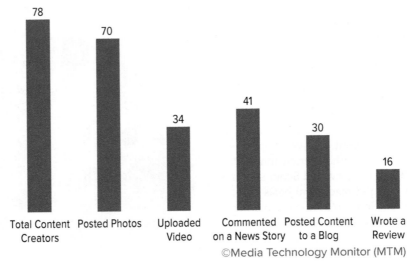

©Media Technology Monitor (MTM)

(Figure 18-17). Seventy-five percent of Reddit users are men; 70 percent are in the age range of 18–34, are active second screen users, and spend many more hours using Internet media than the average Internet users. This data provides further support that each social media vehicle attracts a particular audience like other media. Research into the conversation from the website indicated three psychological traits for Reddit users: individualism, innovation, and fairness.[64]

The user-generated content is quite fascinating from a marketing communication standpoint. For example, extensive lists of bookmarks of Internet sites on a site like Delicious appear very similar to a list of links from a search engine. Additionally, one might construe it as a list of link ads such that the whole site is merely a collection of ads. Alternatively, one could even view it along the same lines as a directory. In either of these cases, the user-generated content appears as if it were advertising of sorts, placed by the advertisers. However, since this "content" was placed by regular people known as "users," this would constitute non-advertising. Of course, all of this gets terribly complicated if the regular person is in fact paid by the advertiser, or its agent, to make the posting.

A site like Pinterest permits all kinds of repurposing of Internet content by users through a simple process of "pinning" images that retain the original link. Eighty percent of Pinterest users are women; 36 percent are in the age range of 18–34, are marginally active second screen users, and spend many more hours using Internet media than the average Internet user. Users spend an average of 16 minutes on the site—versus 3 and 12 minutes for Twitter and Facebook, respectively—and experts see it as a useful social media for expressive and transformational brands.[65] What more could a brand ask than for its customers to select photos from the Internet and comment to show others how great the product is? **Figure 18-18** highlights that 78 percent of Pinterest users create content, with much of that due to posting photos.

Figure 18-18 Percent of Pinterest users that create content, fall 2014, Canadians 18+

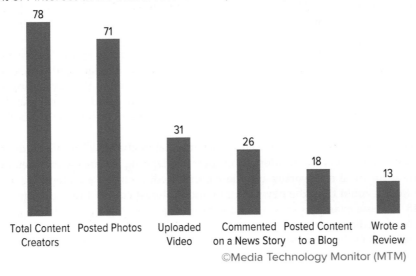

©Media Technology Monitor (MTM)

In its literature to explain how businesses can use this social media, Pinterest cites the example of Sephora, where the retailer noticed that consumers selected pictures from its company Internet site and "pinned" them—which, of course, encouraged others to visit its site.[66] This is another example where "advertising material" became "social media content" as users moved it from one digital location to another. Sephora took advantage of this by adjusting its site with "Pin It" buttons to foster further postings in the social media and sent emails to encourage registered customers to do more pinning. As this suggests, certain aspects of brand messages in social media occur because of consumer initiative, while others are responses to concerted marketing communication efforts by the brand. In either case, Pinterest imagery appears to be a good way to establish owned and earned media (**Exhibit 18-8**).

Digital and Social Media Perspective 18-2 summarizes

Exhibit 18-8 Pinterest photo images provide opportunity for stylish brand expression.

©Bloomua/Shutterstock

a trend of using augmented reality in social media. In particular it highlights how Snapchat is one leader for this emerging way to communicate. Applying the ideas of **Figure 18-1**, Snapchat would likely be listed within the communication social media class despite its strong characteristic for sending pictures. Once again we see difficulty in exactly classifying social media, which offers many innovative opportunities for brands communicating with target audiences.

DIGITAL AND SOCIAL MEDIA PERSPECTIVE 18-2

YOUR REALITY IN AUGMENTED REALITY

Do you like fishing? We're not talking Plenty of Fish, the digital dating site. No, we're talking a "scavenger hunt" within a gamified Snapchat lens in which users find 10 Goldfish Flavor Blasted crackers hidden behind 3-D objects. As you can see, augmented reality (AR) hit social media big time and many brands experimented with fun routes to enhanced social media engagement. Snapchat is a popular alternative, with its lenses that use augmented reality, facial recognition, and visual effects to extend enjoyment by its users. With a skew toward younger people from its 8.5 million users, the messenger service considered its AR a key feature for social media engagement.

For example, Ford brought the showroom to young adults who are less likely to visit. Snapchat's AR allowed users to see a virtual interior/exterior tour of its EcoSport and achieved 1 million views the first day and 3 million views overall. McDonald's also teamed up with Snapchat AR for its promotion.

©Image Press Agency/Alamy Stock Photo

Users scanned a transit shelter ad to view a 3D version of a golden door on which a hand knocks to reveal a $5 coupon for McDelivery via Uber Eats or SkipTheDishes.

IGA employed Facebook's AR for CSR support of the Charles-Bruneau Foundation to raise funds for children with cancer. Five versions of family-friendly temporary tattoos are available and applied to the skin; the AR enlivens the image

[Continued on next page]

[Digital and Social Media Perspective 18-2 continued]

for a virtual experience. The tattoos sold for $2 and other media partners offered exposure in many media. The agency implementing the PR discovered better usage rates with an established AR app since it did not require additional downloads for execution. The simpler convenience of this allowed greater acceptance and stronger fundraising.

In conjunction with the release of a Star Wars movie, Nissan created an AR app experience in the dealerships where consumers saw its cars transform and appear in Star Wars environments with droids, stormtroopers, and other iconic characters

from the movie. The AR allowed consumers to experience Nissan's Intelligent Mobility safety- and driving-assistance-related technologies: ProPILOT assist, automatic emergency braking with pedestrian detection, blind spot warning, rear cross-traffic alert, and intelligent around view monitor. While not executed in social media, the experiences led to considerable social media engagement and news media publicity.

Question:

1. What other goods or services could creatively use AR in social media?

Social Media Influence

Social media is communication among people mediated by technology. It quickly attracted consumers who shop, talk about their purchases, and relate their experiences with branded goods, services, people, and ideas, all of which are the product elements of the marketing mix. Simultaneously, social media opened up communication between consumers and organizations who market products and try to influence their audiences with paid, owned, and earned media exposure. Earned media exposure existed well before social media, but social media opened up many avenues for consumers to communicate positive and negative user-generated content through eWOM as part of their engagement, as highlighted in this chapter.

A social media influencer is one type of consumer who emerged digitally. At first this seemed innocuous. A person claims to be an expert of sorts and offers opinions about products in a blog or displays their consumption conspicuously in photos or videos. They appear like any regular consumer communicating to another consumer. What is wrong with that? However, concern by consumers and regulators arose when social influencers received payment for their public endorsement. According to their view, such a message resembled a paid ad (think TV commercial) where the social media influencer acted as a spokesperson who communicated on behalf of a brand.

For example, the Federal Trade Commission in the United States fined Lord & Taylor, a division of the Hudson's Bay Company, for not disclosing its advertising intent in social media. The fashion retailer paid 50 popular Instagram users and gave them a dress; the users then posted a photo in which they wore the new outfit. The FTC ruled that consumers have a right to know when they are seeing paid advertising.[67] This point is consistent with decades-old media and advertising policies in North America and most countries worldwide. In Canada, the *Competition Act* identifies social media influencer messages as advertising, and in 2015 the Competition Bureau enforced a fine on Bell when an employee wrote a favourable product review without disclosing their employment status; what looked like earned exposure in social media was in fact paid advertising.

Payment to social media influencers is substantial for popular stars; one claimed he could charge a brand $2,000 to $6,000 to share two sponsored photos on his Instagram account.[68] In this case, we see an influencer following guidelines suggested by government regulators and industry self-regulators. As we will see in Chapter 19, Ad Standards (AS) is responsible for administering advertising self-regulation in Canada. AS published disclosure guidelines for advertisers to follow that are consistent with the *Competition Act* and laws and guidelines from the FTC in the United States.[69] The guidelines say that any endorser, reviewer, influencer, or person making a representation must disclose any "material connection" between themselves and the entity (e.g., advertised brand). Material connection refers to money, products, discounts, or gifts. Thus, AS is focused on social media engagement activities where the influencer sends messages with an advertising intent but it is not completely clear to the receiver that it is in fact an ad without the disclosure.

One guideline focuses on the hashtag (which should be #ad, #sponsored, #brandname_ambassador, #brandname_partner), and the hashtag should avoid ambiguous types (like #ambassador, #partner, #spon, #PR, #promo, #collab, #sp) or fabricated misleading ones. The hashtag should be clearly seen and not lost within a long list of hashtags. Disclosures should clearly attract the attention of the receiver no matter the social media placement. In the case of video, disclosure should be at the start, and ideally placed a few times and communicated with video and audio. A blanket disclosure embedded in the profile is not acceptable, and the disclosure should be in close proximity to the main copy and before potential action such as a link. The actual material connection should be communicated, and influencers should not rely on tagging a brand or ambiguous phrases. The report cited above also applies these to specific examples for YouTube, Instagram (gifted product, event, paid collaboration, stories), Snapchat, Twitter, and blogs.

The importance of these guidelines is quite significant. In the cosmetics category, research indicated that shoppers engage with social media to see the latest trends, products, styles, and brands, and specifically key in on influencers who recommend anything along these lines. In addition, direct to consumer brands (e.g., direct marketing) popped up in a number of personal care product categories and they capitalized on social media for exposure, especially with influencers presenting and endorsing their products. Research found that 55 percent of women enjoyed shopping online for cosmetics, and 35 percent read social media reviews before buying in stores.[70]

A Budweiser example illustrates the importance of the guidelines in another way. The company invited influencers to its facilities to learn about its brewing process. Influencers received Blue Jays tickets and a promotional item but no money, and Budweiser did not require any social media posts. The program resulted in 1.1 million impressions from 120 posts. In this case, there is a material connection and the new guidelines expect the influencers to acknowledge it in their posts, although this occurred just prior to the guidelines' release.[71]

Experts estimated the payments to social influencers topped $1 billion in Canada by 2018. To put this into context, this is as much spent on out-of-home and magazine advertising combined, and equal to the amount spent in newspaper advertising during 2017. One company, #paid, acts as a broker between advertisers and social influencers; it seems both sides are learning and rely on outside help at present. It represents about 20,000 social influencers, of which 6,000 are Canadian. A payment formula/system determines the price but the following factors contribute to the tally: number of followers, type of message (post, photo, video, story), and use of the message and influencer in other media (TV, print). Because of its visual characteristic, Instagram is the most sought after social media vehicle and the influencers design the ad so it fits their image and page.[72]

While a social influencer with a large number of followers seems ideal, advertisers succeeded with influencers with smaller numbers (50,000 or less). One agency reported 60 percent higher engagement rates with higher quality responses, and seven times more cost-efficiency. Another one found engagement rates at 11 percent for influencers with 2,000 followers, 3 percent for those with 25,000 followers or fewer, and 2 percent for those with 100,000 plus followers. With this kind of success, advertisers work with many small influencers to maximize reach and target multiple audiences with specific messages rather than one influencer with many followers and one message.[73] This information supports the general point of target audience accuracy being very important for media decisions, much like we have seen in other media for decades.

Finally, we turn to an example of a comprehensive social media influencer plan by Tangerine. The online bank selected three target audiences: up-and-coming adults aged 27–34, parents with young children, and boomers set to retire. Tangerine identified social media influencers for the groups: Bridget Eastgaard (young adults); SavvyMom, UrbanMom, and The Baby Post (parents); and Boomer and Echo (retired). Tangerine's PR agency worked with the company and the influencers to ensure a smooth execution. Tangerine retained final control on technical content, but other than that, the influencers received free rein on their approach. The influencers sent over 200 pieces of content to these three groups to strengthen their financial literacy with approaches such as in-person events, Facebook live sessions, and written and video blogs. A total of 10 million impressions resulted during the two-month campaign.[74]

IMC Planning: Strategic Use of Social Media

Social media engagement is a defining characteristic, making it distinct from placing text, video, and audio ad messages in Internet media. This engagement represents the feedback stage within the communication model shown in **Figure 4-1**. Consumers return ad messages with selfie photos featuring their product usage. They summarize their experience with video messages for all to see. And we cannot forget the power of the written word, as they write about products seemingly everywhere. In short, consumers communicate back to advertisers with social media messages that almost mirror what they received.

While summarizing a few of the major social media players, we see ample opportunity for customers and non-customers to interact with those who deliver messages. As was done with Internet media, we summarize issues promotional planners consider when constructing a social media plan as suggested in **Figure 1-7**. And while social media features considerable consumer feedback which suggests no need for planning, we conclude that social media is too important and too powerful not to make a plan.

The first planning issue is the alignment of target audience and objectives, as we have seen throughout the text. In this case, the challenge for promotional planners is to select the correct social media class that fits the target audience and allows for the achievement of the most relevant objective. The social media classes of **Figure 18-1** are a starting place, along with the six general ones identified in the first section (networking sites, content communities, blogs, collaborative projects, virtual game worlds, and virtual social worlds). In addition, planners decide which social media vehicles need to be selected, as shown in **Figure 10-2**.

A second planning issue concerns how a promotional planner balances the paid, owned, and earned elements of each social media class and social media vehicle. For example, brands use one social media vehicle for paid exposure to ensure exposure for owned social media.

A third planning issue pertains to the type of IMC tool executed within social media. We see examples where social media communicates and delivers a sales promotion (such as the McDonald's coupon). Some social media encourage CSR activities (like the IGA example). And at times, social media is a key tool for managing PR and publicity. Social media is part of direct marketing efforts where businesses use social media as the first step in direct selling.

A fourth planning issue is how social media are part of a complete IMC program to influence consumers in all phases of decision making. Planners might want to consider how Facebook messages through paid, owned, and earned channels might affect need recognition or post-purchase evaluations, for example. Alternatively, monitoring and responding to consumer photos in Instagram provides an understanding of consumer usage and gives opportunity for brands to respond to consumers during consumption.

A fifth planning issue pertains to all the questions associated with social media influencers. Who is the most persuasive social media influencer for a target audience? What task does a brand expect from the social media influencer? How does the social media influencer communicate to followers about a brand? When does the social media influencer communicate? Are there geographic considerations?

A final planning issue is to figure out a way to tap into the resources of the many online connections consumers have through their friends in social media. Social media engagement occurs with communication of users within each social media vehicle and it is likely that the dynamics within various networks influence the message content and delivery.

Learning Objectives Summary

 Identify social media communication.

This chapter demonstrated many ways advertisers communicate in social media. From the perspective of media planning, these domains represent different media classes with specific media vehicles in each. For example, within the video media class, YouTube clearly dominates, but other video hosting sites are available and offer paid, owned, and earned options for communicating. The general idea of this point is relevant to consider for other social media, and promotional planners might also consider the degree of attachment the users experience within the ones selected for communication.

Social media engagement is an important characteristic that advertisers encourage with their IMC plans, and social media engagement occurs independent of any direct effort by motivated consumers. Advertisers are generally interested in the type and amount of social media engagement since it presumably represents a degree of brand affinity leading to positive or negative eWOM.

Finally, social media usage grew significantly for a decade and there is an indication that it reached a plateau to a degree, however there is considerable variation in the usage by age groups, and other segmentation variables not shown in the chapter due to space limitations. Promotional planners would want to investigate this prior to committing resources.

Review social networking.

This chapter reviewed social networking by presenting paid, owned, and earned approaches to communication within Facebook and Twitter. The importance of identifying all three is to remind managers to plan their promotional communication accordingly. For example, if there is a paid ad in Facebook, what would a support message be on the brand page, and what type of communication would a brand deliver depending on the user-generated content that consumers put forth?

 Illustrate content communities.

The chapter took the same approach for YouTube and Instagram as it did for Facebook and Twitter to suggest that promotional planners have numerous decisions to recommend prior to executing their social media communication plan. The chapter also presented social media engagement statistics for all four to provide guidance on the current behaviour to set realistic objectives.

 Describe blogs and collaborative projects.

Blogs and collaborative projects such as wikis and bookmarking sites are another form of social media, although they tend to get less publicity compared to the big four mentioned. However, they too offer a degree of paid, owned, and earned delivery of messages for a target audience. As our social media knowledge evolves, it is likely that these media classes will be reconfigured.

 Investigate social media influence.

Prominent and active users establish a social media persona that elevates them such that others will follow their postings and actually rely on their point of view for their shopping information needs. Known as social media influencers, these people retain brands as clients and charge for positive social media engagements. Some are quite prolific and make a lot of money as brands solicit their partnership. The concept of an influencer in marketing is not new since marketers planned for communication in the past knowing the effects of people within group decision making. What is new is the public nature of social media influencers and the frequency with which consumers receive an ad-like message from a social media influencer.

In response to this newer form of advertising, regulators provided a series of guidelines social media influencers should adhere to for ethical and legal communication. Prominent among the guidelines is the fact that social media influencers should disclose the material remuneration received for their positive brand reviews to avoid fines. Other additional guidelines suggested how the social media influencer should communicate the relationship.

LO6 **Apply the use of social media within an IMC program.**

Social media requires a clear plan like any other aspect of the IMC program, with a target audience and objectives, and a creative message with important tactics. Given the vast number of social media available, a promotional planner would want to establish media strategy and tactic decisions as well. Social media is used for advertising, sales promotion, direct marketing, and PR purposes, so the strategic intent is another planning point for managers to factor into their decisions. Whether paid, owned, or earned characteristics are developed or encouraged is another decision to establish, as is the degree to which a brand involves a social media influencer in the campaign.

Review Questions

1. What is social media engagement? How does social media engagement vary within different social media classes?

2. Identify how Facebook offers paid, owned, and earned media for advertisers.

3. Identify how YouTube offers paid, owned, and earned media for advertisers.

4. In what way is Snapchat a good social media vehicle for earned ad messages?

5. Explain why social media influencers are effective.

6. How does social media fit within an IMC plan?

Applied Questions

1. Select a favourite social media site for a brand and investigate how it achieves the communication objectives.

2. Visit a number of Facebook brand pages and evaluate the effectiveness of the brand posts in terms of creativity, message, and ability to reach the intended target audience.

3. Visit a number of Instagram brand pages and evaluate the effectiveness of the brand posts in terms of creativity. How do they compare to the equivalent in Facebook?

4. Read up about a favourite music artist on Wikipedia. Is it possible to view the content as earned media?

5. See the postings of many social media influencers and evaluate whether they are adhering to the guidelines set by Ad Standards.

6. Select a product of interest and explain how a particular social media vehicle could be effectively used for paid, owned, and earned exposure.

CHAPTER NINETEEN

Regulatory, Ethical, Social, and Economic Issues for IMC

LEARNING OBJECTIVES

LO1 Describe the advertising regulation system in Canada.

LO2 Evaluate the ethical perspectives of advertising.

LO3 Explain the social effects of advertising.

LO4 Examine the economic role of advertising and its effects on consumer choice, competition, and product costs and prices.

No Stopping SickKids VS

SickKids Foundation provided its agency, Cossette, with a tough problem of flattening donations from older donors with a female skew, and research showing that existing ads focused on heart-tugging and emotional messages did not resonate any longer and would not help acquire new donors. They knew they needed to change in anticipation of launching the largest fundraising campaign in SickKids' history the following year. They expected that fundraising growth from younger people and more male donors could occur with a new and surprising message to change people's view of the hospital from a place of illness to a brand with strength and power. In October 2016, The Hospital for Sick Children (SickKids) surprised Toronto and the world with a stunning two-minute video, *SickKids VS: Undeniable,* showing its patients and medical staff fighting against a range of childhood illnesses. In contrast to its award-winning ads in the years leading up to the introduction of VS, the captivating images portrayed children in a startling new light. SickKids changed the old images of sad children in need of help to dynamic images of resilient children overcoming their situation with strength. The video ended with the SickKids VS image, and cut to a super and call to action to support the campaign at fundthefight.ca. The message illustrated a new meaning of sick as a "fierce fighting spirit" which positioned SickKids away from a charity brand to a competitive performance brand like Nike.

The launch occurred on TV during the Toronto Maple Leafs' home opener and a public relations and social media release of the video. A week later, the city received extensive exposure with newspaper ads, streetcar wraps, multiple media in cinemas, paid social media, and Yonge–Dundas Square domination that lasted for a month. Coverage continued for a second month, which included greater out-of-home exposure, a lit-up CN Tower and TORONTO sign with the SickKids blue, and a complete domination of Billy Bishop airport. More informative online films explored a breadth of treatment and the complexity of the hospital. In a couple of months, the campaign raised $58 million with growth from males and younger people. Publicity occurred around the world, with 58 stories in 17 countries to go along with domestic media of nearly 300 stories. The *SickKids VS: Undeniable* spot also went viral, garnering international attention during launch weekend.

The SickKids VS message carried on a year later with another empowering story of children, in *SickKids VS: All In.* This time the images showed the resilient patients preparing to build the new SickKids hospital, with the video ending with the same call to action. This video served to launch a $1.3 billion fundraising campaign, in large part to build a new SickKids—some of its existing buildings were built in 1949. With the success of the first wave, SickKids VS imagery seemed like a logical way to captivate viewers once again to ensure future donations. But the campaign went further by challenging Toronto neighbourhoods to be "all in" with their own way of contributing, just like the imagery of the children in the video. To support this, unique versions of the campaign were placed in each neighbourhood with out-of-home media, and social media stories of SickKids patients geo-targeted to the neighbourhood where they lived. Corporate support ensued, with donations directed to specific fundraising priorities of the hospital. For example, Samsung provided equipment and renovated space for the children to play with electronics.

Question:

1. What are the strengths and potential limitations of these messages?

Not everyone shares the positive view illustrated in this text regarding advertising in today's society. Our perspective looks at advertising and other promotional tools as marketing activities used to convey information to consumers and influence their behaviour in an appropriate manner to facilitate a mutually satisfying exchange. Advertising is a visible business activity and faces scrutiny from scholars, economists, politicians, sociologists, government agencies, social critics, special-interest groups, and consumers, who criticize it from legitimate perspectives.

As such, this text would not be complete without citing the criticisms regarding its ethical, social, and economic effects as well as the defence against these claims. Before we entertain this debate, we review advertising regulations in Canada. The views presented in this chapter reflect judgments of people with different backgrounds, values, and interests. Some students may see nothing wrong with advertising, while others may oppose some ads on moral and ethical grounds. We present arguments on both sides of these issues and allow individuals to draw their own conclusions.

LO1 Advertising Regulation in Canada

Advertising in Canada is subject to both government regulation and self-regulation, and we review both topics in this section. With respect to government regulation, we focus on three relevant domains. The Canadian Radio-television and Telecommunications Commission (CRTC) is responsible for laws and regulations concerning broadcasting and telecommunications, so its role in advertising is relevant. The *Competition Act* regulates misleading or deceptive ads. Finally, the Quebec government has strong regulations with respect to advertising to children. In the other direction, Ad Standards acts as the self-regulation body for the advertising industry. Responsibility for many federal laws regarding the content of advertising messages for specific product categories has been transferred to Ad Standards by the request of the federal government.

CANADIAN RADIO-TELEVISION AND TELECOMMUNICATIONS COMMISSION (CRTC)

The CRTC is an administrative tribunal within the federal government. It is responsible for regulating and supervising Canada's communication system derived from the *CRTC Act,* the *Bell Canada Act,* the *Broadcasting Act,* and the *Telecommunications Act.* The broad objective of these acts ensures that all Canadians receive broadcasting and telecommunications services. Beyond this public service mandate, the CRTC balances the needs of citizens, industries, and interest groups with respect to Canadian content programming, technological considerations, and many communication issues. The CRTC organizes its responsibilities across Phone, Internet, TV & Radio, and Business & Licensing domains. Extensive research occurred recently where the CRTC invited Canadians to offer their opinions. In its current three-year plan, the CRTC planned to focus on three themes: create—by ensuring quality, diverse, and compelling content; connect—by ensuring quality, choice, and innovative communication services; and protect—by ensuring access to safe communication systems.

For the purposes of this chapter, we concentrate on broadcasting since we highlighted telephone (e.g., Chapter 16) and Internet (e.g., Chapter 17) and social media regulatory points (e.g., Chapter 18) previously, and the licensing does not primarily affect IMC decisions directly. The CRTC regulates media organizations (i.e., television, cable distribution, AM and FM radio, pay and specialty television, direct-to-home satellite systems, multipoint distribution systems, subscription television, and pay audio) and is responsible for granting the licences for these media and ensuring that they comply with the *Broadcasting Act.* The CRTC undertakes significant activities to ensure that Canadian content occurs in Canadian media. Its most recent direction is to emphasize quality over quantity. This is beneficial for advertisers trying to reach audiences viewing uniquely Canadian programming. The CRTC is involved significantly in two ad broadcasting topics that are relevant for advertising: advertising time limits and signal substitution.

Advertising Time Limits The CRTC regulates the amount of advertising in a few circumstances. Specialty TV services carry 12 minutes per hour of advertising during the broadcast day, which lasts 18 hours beginning at 6:00 a.m. The CBC radio network is prohibited from advertising except for special sponsorship. CBC Escape Music and CBC 2 are permitted 4 minutes of advertising per hour. Similar 4- and 12-minute limits occur with different community-based services as well. Note that public service announcements, political ads, and "ads" for Canadian TV shows are not counted in this total, nor is product placement or virtual ads placed within shows. Pay TV services have no advertising, while conventional TV and radio stations have no limits.

Signal Substitution Signal substitution occurs when a television service provider temporarily replaces the entire signal of one TV channel with another channel that is showing the same program at the same time. Most times this occurs when a Canadian signal replaces an American signal. This protects the interests of the broadcasters who have paid for the rights to show the program in Canada. It also promotes local broadcasting and content creation by allowing these media to retain their audience. Finally, it keeps advertising revenue within the Canadian market.

While this appears acceptable to many Canadians most of the time, football viewers are not satisfied when U.S. ads are not part of the domestic feed for the Super Bowl. Although some are bought for domestic media, most Canadians resort to seeing the Super Bowl ads online after the game. Other problems occur when a live event (e.g., sport) runs overtime, late programming changes happen, or poor quality occurs. The CRTC reviewed this practice and plans to be more active in resolving the problems and potentially intervening upon media companies.

COMPETITION ACT

The federal *Competition Act* prevents false or misleading advertising. Significantly revised in 1999, most of the act contains civil provisions to ensure compliance with the act rather than to seek punishment. In this situation, the goal is not so much to prove deliberate intent, but rather to remedy the situation with the most appropriate solution, such as a cease-and-desist order. Some criminal provisions still exist for the most serious offences, where false advertising occurred knowingly. Enforcement of the act falls under the jurisdiction of the Competition Bureau of Industry Canada. Some examples of what is not permissible are shown in **Figure 19-1**.[1] In 2009, the *Competition Act* underwent revision with respect to deceptive marketing, items pertaining to pricing, and some other amendments. In particular, the fines for misleading representation in advertising increased substantially for non-criminal offences.[2] Industry people expected strong enforcement and the following example proved them correct.

Figure 19-1 Advertising and marketing law in Canada

Guideline	Advertising Claim	Misleading Content
Cannot make false claims	Buy this vacuum and get a year's supply of vacuum bags absolutely free	There is a $12 administration fee for the vacuum bags
Even if claim is true, do not give false impression	Drive away in a Corvette for just $39,000	The visual display is a version with a sport package and costs $50,000
Avoid double meanings	Number one in the category	Best in sales, but not in quality
Disclaimers should not contradict headlines or body copy	Don't pay a cent until 2022	Fine print says "except for taxes and $750 freight"

The Bureau sought a $30 million fine from Avis and Budget for their misleading advertising regarding price information. The Bureau claimed that each car agency advertised that it charged extra fees on behalf of the government, but the Bureau saw the message as misleading advertising since the extra charges amounted to covering normal business costs. Eight different charges over the course of 10 years for things like air conditioning excise tax, premium location surcharges, and tire management fees raised the price of renting a vehicle significantly above the advertised price. The penalty represented the largest fine the Bureau ever attempted as part of its renewed mandate for improved monitoring for Canadian consumers, and it did not let up, as seen by its next target.[3] In the end, the Bureau received $3 million from each firm plus investigation costs. Another recent target is Ticketmaster for not communicating that the company charged additional fees later in the purchase process.[4]

REGULATIONS ON ADVERTISING TO CHILDREN

Although no federal laws specifically regulate advertising to children, the Broadcast Code for Advertising to Children acts as an important guide to ensure that children are not easily manipulated with exaggerated claims. In contrast, the province of Quebec provides strict regulations. According to the *Consumer Protection Act of Quebec,* it is illegal to direct commercial advertising messages to persons younger than 13 years of age. Specific provisions determine whether or not an ad is directed to children regarding the product, the ad presentation, and the ad time and placement.

To apply the law, the Quebec government provides summary guidelines for advertisers to follow, and it also provides screening services for advertisers if they are uncertain whether an item contravenes the law. The purpose of the guidelines is to ensure that advertisers fully understand and correctly interpret the law. The guidelines precisely describe the types of advertising appeals that are not permitted, clearly define what is meant by a children's TV program, and state exactly the percentage of children in the audience that constitutes a children's TV program. The guidelines include the degree to which messages can be directed toward children depending upon whether the product is exclusively for children (e.g., candy), partially for children (e.g., cereal), or not for children. There are also specific guidelines for public service announcements directed to children, even though there is no commercial message.

Vachon, maker of the Jos Louis and Passion Flakie treats, pushed the limits of these laws. It created a cartoon character named Igor to represent its chocolate-filled, gorilla-shaped muffins. Vachon placed the imagery on CDs, DVDs, and other materials for daycare centres to use when entertaining the children. Vachon tested the laws in three ways—the product, the message, and the time and place—and faced a $44,000 fine. It appears that the Quebec government is getting tougher with not-so-healthy products with the higher incidence of child obesity. However, there are indications that brands of healthier products, or a corporate initiative to encourage children to stay active, might not be as scrutinized. So while there are laws governing advertising to children in Quebec, the consistent application appears murky given the ethical implications.[5]

AD STANDARDS (AS)

AS is a not-for-profit, self-regulatory industry body with a mandate to create and maintain community confidence in advertising.[6] AS represents advertisers, media organizations, and advertising industry suppliers and has more than 200 corporate members. Its Standards Division administers the industry's self-regulatory codes (i.e., Canadian Code of Advertising Standards, Gender Portrayal Guidelines), handles complaints about advertising, and administers any disputes that arise between advertisers. Its Advertising Clearance Division previews advertisements in five industry categories, as well as ads directed toward children, ensuring that advertisers follow applicable legislation, regulatory codes, and industry standards. An example of one of its public service ads is shown in **Exhibit 19-1**. Knowledge of AS varies as its awareness measure fluctuated between 41 percent and 57 percent over the past few years, however Canadians are well aware (82 percent) that advertisers are required to follow rules in presenting their message.[7]

Canadian Code of Advertising Standards The Code, as it is known, describes what is not acceptable advertising. According to AS, "Advertising is defined as any message (the content of which is controlled directly or indirectly by the advertiser) expressed in any language and communicated in any medium to Canadians with the intent to influence their choice, opinion or behaviour." The Code pertains to the content of ads only. It does not limit the promotion of legal products or the demonstration of products for their intended purpose. The intention of the Code is to provide standards so that responsible and effective advertising results without minimizing the right of firms to advertise. It does not supersede any laws or regulations. In early 2016, AS proposed notable revisions to the definition of *advertiser* and *advertisement,* presumably with the growth of digital communication via social media.

The Code provides the criteria to assess whether a complaint is legitimate or not, and AS is very clear in how it uses the Code to resolve complaints. "The context and content of the advertisement and the audience actually, or likely to be, or intended to be, reached by the advertisement, and the medium/media used to deliver the advertisement, are relevant factors in assessing its conformity with the Code." The Code is supported by all member organizations as it sets the standard for advertising with respect to honesty, truth, accuracy, fairness, and propriety. Members are expected to follow the Code both in letter and in spirit and are expected to substantiate any advertised claims when requested. The Code contains 14 clauses:

1. Accuracy & Clarity
2. Disguised Advertising Techniques
3. Price Claims
4. Bait & Switch
5. Guarantees
6. Comparative Advertising
7. Testimonials
8. Professional/Scientific Claims
9. Imitation
10. Safety
11. Superstitions & Fears
12. Advertising to Children
13. Advertising to Minors
14. Unacceptable Depictions & Portrayals

Exhibit 19-1 This ad by Ad Standards communicates its purpose.

Creativity is subjective. **The truth isn't.**

Truth in Advertising Matters. ASC Advertising Standards Canada adstandards.com/psa

©Ad Standards

As part of the 2016 proposed revision, AS suggested revisions for Clauses 1 and 14. Clause 1 changes provided greater clarity on the meaning of *deceptive and misleading ads.* Clause 14 changes identified additional characteristics that could not be the basis of personal discrimination. In 2003, AS updated Clauses 6, 10, and 14 as part of its ongoing mandate to ensure that the Code reflects current practices and fairness. While on the surface the 2003 changes were just a few words for each clause, the meaning permitted a more reasonable and flexible interpretation.

AS Interpretation Guidelines AS released "interpretation guidelines" over the years so that members could understand how AS evaluates ads in terms of specific codes or advertising trends.[8] The first and fourth guidelines concerned Clauses 10 and 14 with respect to humour/fantasy and motor vehicle advertising respectively. Environmental claims and how they are related to Clause 1, the Competition Bureau, and the Canadian Standards Association comprised the third guideline. The second guideline provided extensive documentation on advertising to children pertaining to Clause 12. We reviewed the fifth interpretation guideline with the testimonial endorsement topic in the previous chapter.

As part of the second guideline, AS acts as the administrator for the Canadian Children's Food and Beverage Advertising Initiative (CAI).[9] Canada's largest food and beverage marketers committed to not advertising directly to children under 12 years of age, although some committed to advertising only "better-for-you" products to children. The initiative is in response to the growing obesity problem among children. In doing so, the marketers agreed to five core principles for advertising directed to children under 12 years of age:

1. Devote 100 percent of television, radio, print, and Internet advertising to furthering the goal of promoting healthy dietary choices and/or healthy active living.

2. Incorporate only products that represent healthy dietary choices in interactive games primarily directed to children under 12 years of age.

3. Reduce the use of third-party licensed characters in advertising for products that do not meet the CAI's product criteria.

4. Do not pay for or actively seek to place food and beverage products in program/editorial content of any medium.

5. Do not advertise food or beverage products in elementary schools.

The principles apply to other avenues of communication directed to children under 12, such as micro-sites, early childhood (EC) video/computer games, DVDs, mobile devices, and word-of-mouth. AS monitored the performance of many organizations committed to CAI each year and summarized the results in a publicly available report. Its most recent report concluded that all companies complied with all guidelines in all media and promotional vehicles.[10] Despite this initiative, the industry faced the prospect that the federal government would not permit advertising directed to children for unhealthy food.[11] This potential legislation looked at research concluding that social media influencing messages, product placement, and branded entertainment proved to be quite detrimental to young children who may have difficulty distinguishing between content and advertising.[12]

Gender Portrayal Guidelines The guidelines, based on a previous CRTC task force, attempt to ensure that women and men are portrayed appropriately and equally in advertising. AS presents the guidelines as the direction of areas or topics from which complaints or issues have arisen. There are six overall clauses, pertaining to authority, decision making, sexuality, violence, diversity, and language. For example, some might find the passionate theme of Calvin Klein ads as conveying overt sexuality (**Exhibit 19-2**, **Exhibit 19-3**).

Exhibit 19-2 Calvin Klein ads depict women in sexual poses.

©Sorbis/Shutterstock

When interpreting the guidelines, AS has four suggestions that advertisers should consider. The overall impression of the ad should not violate the spirit of gender equality; there are clauses specifically addressed toward women, as men are at less risk of being negatively portrayed. History and art should not be used as an excuse for violating a clause. Finally, certain products and how they are advertised are amenable to more appropriate media.

Complaint Process The Standards Division handles complaints in three streams. **Consumer complaints** are those from ordinary citizens who believe that an ad is unacceptable. AS receives these complaints directly as well as through government departments and agencies at all levels,

Exhibit 19-3 Calvin Klein ads depict men in sexual poses.

©Lars A. Niki

such as the Better Business Bureau, the CRTC, and the Canadian Broadcast Standards Council. **Special interest group complaints** are those from a demonstrated organization that expresses a unified viewpoint. Complaints from other advertisers are known as **advertiser disputes** or trade disputes. While there are distinct complaint processes for consumers and special interest groups, the general procedures for each have a degree of similarity that we will touch upon. One difference, however, is that AS first determines that the special interest group complaint is not a disguised trade dispute.

The initial complaint is authenticated to make sure that it is, in fact, a consumer or special interest group complaint and not an advertiser dispute. From there, the complaint is evaluated to determine whether it truly violates a Code provision or whether it is not a legitimate complaint. Reasons for a complaint not being legitimate include that the complaint did not identify a specific advertiser, that the ad was no longer current, and that the communication was not advertising. If the complaint is valid, the advertiser is contacted and has an opportunity to respond to the complaint before the Council makes a formal ruling. On the other hand, the advertiser can take an appropriate action to remedy the complaint as part of the response. In these cases, the advertiser would not be identified in the AS complaints report. An advertiser who responds and does not remedy the situation can be identified in the report if the Council upholds the complaint.

While the above general approach existed for many years, and still does, AS instituted a couple of revisions for certain clauses in 2012. For Clauses 10 and 14, AS acts as an intermediary between the complainant and the advertiser so that both can see one another's point of view for resolution prior to the Standards Council involvement. For Clauses 1 and 3, AS administratively resolves these concerns as sometimes they are due to minor human error that can easily be corrected.

For advertiser (or trade) disputes, there is a formal adjudication procedure where each party represents its point of view at a hearing if an initial first-stage resolution is unsuccessful. An appeal of the decision is possible, but eventually there is a resolution if an advertiser is found in violation. As members of AS, they follow the recommendations of AS similar to the consumer and special interest process. However, a situation emerged where for the first time ever an advertiser did not follow AS's decision. Rogers disputed a Bell advertising claim and AS upheld the complaint, suggesting that Bell amend the ad or stop showing it. Bell did not participate in the hearing or comply with the decision since it was not a member and continued running the ad. In turn, and for the first time, AS asked media companies to refrain from airing the ad.[13]

Complaints Report AS publishes a comprehensive annual report that includes the identification of advertisers and the details of all complaints. **Figure 19-2** shows a capsule summary of the past few years. For each statistic, the first data point is the number of complaints, while the second in parentheses is the number of ads those complaints represent.

Figure 19-2 Summary of annual complaints from Ad Standards

	2016		2017		2018	
Number of Complaints (ads)						
Received by AS	1,639	(1,237)	1,808	(864)	2,005	(1,205)
Accepted and reviewed	1,108	(856)	1,172	(832)	1,252	(747)
Raised potential issue	264	(222)	442	(236)	481	(167)
Administratively resolved	178	(171)	224	(164)	125	(104)
Evaluated by Council	86	(51)	218	(72)	356	(63)
Upheld by Council	44	(30)	173	(46)	323	(35)

The ratio of the number of complaints to the number of ads indicates that the number of complaints per ad is fewer than two. This underscores the fact that the content of the complaint is justification for investigating an ad. The source of the most complaints in 2018 occurred with Clause 1 (accuracy and clarity) and Clause 3 (price claims) that combined for 849 complaints, Clause 14 (unacceptable portrayal and depictions) for 322 complaints, and Clause 10 (safety) for 47. Complaints by media showed television (708), out-of-home (473), digital (270), and direct marketing (212).[14] We review ads that achieved notoriety summarized from past reports found at the AS website.

Complaints for Debate　One of the most controversial rulings occurred in 2001. A Ford Motor Company TV ad showed a young female shoving a male store clerk into the hatchback of her car and driving away with him. This ad received nine complaints and the Council upheld them, citing Clause 14 as the ad depicted an abduction, which is an unlawful activity. Ford appealed the decision; however, the Appeal Panel confirmed the original decision. Ford's post-appeal statement makes this example an interesting debate:

> Ford of Canada did not intend to offend any segment of the population in this particular advertisement; rather the aim of the ad was to show the attributes of the Focus. The identical advertisement shown in Quebec (both in English and in French) was determined not to contravene the *Code* by the Consumer Response Council and Appeal Panel in Quebec. Particulars of this complaint were provided to the press by a consumer complainant even though this process is intended to be confidential. Subsequent to the Appeal Decision, Margaret Wente, in a lengthy *Globe and Mail* article dated January 31, 2002, gave strong positive support for the ad. However, in light of the decision of the Ad Standards Appeal Panel, Ford of Canada will withdraw the current English advertisement.[15]

In early 2004, a television ad for an alcohol beverage depicted two women engaging in a passionate kiss. The 113 complaints indicated that the scene was inappropriate for family viewing programming. Council upheld this complaint, stating, "the commercial displayed obvious indifference to conduct or attitudes that offended standards of public decency prevailing among a significant segment of the population." Council concluded that the ad in question did not contravene the Code provided that it was shown later than 9:30 in the evening.

A Kia Canada television commercial caused controversy during 2007 and received 77 complaints from individuals and those in the law-enforcement profession. The advertised vehicle contained two adults "making out," after which the woman returned to a police car wearing an officer's uniform. Council upheld the complaint citing Clause 14(c) and concluded that the ad demeaned female officers in particular and all law-enforcement officials in general. Kia responded to the complaint with the following statement:

> As a responsible advertiser, Kia Canada Inc. [Kia] is aware of Ad Standards guidelines, of which its media service agencies are members, and strives to adhere to the spirit of which they have been written. While not in agreement with the Council's final decision, Kia respects it and the process by which it was achieved. Kia believes it has responded to the subject of the complaints by making revisions to the commercial in question, and in adherence to the Advertising Standards Code.[16]

However, Kia's concern became more public when it ran an edited version of the ad that did not show the woman leaving the car. Instead, words on the screen announced a more suitable ending to the commercial for all audiences. The final scene featured a goat eating in a meadow for 10 seconds while light-hearted music played. We leave the interpretation of this revised ending for interested students to debate![17]

Also in 2007, the council determined that certain Dairy Queen ads showed an unsafe act and reinforced bullying behaviour as the TV ad characters restrained others while eating Dairy Queen ice cream. The response from managers of the brand appears to suggest caution to advertisers with co-branding messages:

> Dairy Queen is all about creating smiles and stories for families and often uses irreverent, off-beat humour in its commercials. The Kit Kat commercial was meant to accentuate in a humorous way how families interact in a playful manner. Although we are not in agreement with the Council's decision, we are respectful of the process.[18]

An ad from Auto Trader, part of an overall campaign that compared buying a used car online to meeting another person with an online dating service, received only six complaints. However, the complaint, the council decision, and the advertiser statement cover new ground:

> In a television commercial, a man and a woman met in a coffee shop for the first time. After exchanging names, the woman asked the man if she could "take a quick peek". The man obliged by lowering his pants so the woman could look at his private parts from various angles. In the audio portion of the commercial the announcer said that "You can do that on Auto Trader—where you can research your car before you buy it."[19]

Exhibit 19-4 An ad from Ad Standards explains how truth in advertising is important.

RUBBER BANDS HAVE FEELINGS TOO

A Screenplay by
Helina Clarke

Creativity is subjective.
The truth isn't.

Truth in Advertising Matters.

ASC Advertising Standards Canada
adstandards.com/psa

©Ad Standards

The complaint alleged that the ad depicted a demeaning portrayal of men and offended standards of public decency. The council agreed with the latter point but concluded that the ad denigrated both men and women. Auto Trader's rebuttal statement took into account the media time frame and media vehicle, two critical points that AS highlighted in previous rulings for more acceptable adult messages. It also concluded that the ad played on *World's Funniest TV Commercials,* shown on TV during prime time, which makes this an interesting case to debate.

We summarized these cases because they illustrate significant milestones during the history of AS decisions. They show disagreement between AS administrators (i.e., Ford), one of the most numerous complaints ever (i.e., alcohol beverage), the most unexpected reaction from an identified advertiser (i.e., Kia), a difficulty with co-branding (i.e., Dairy Queen), and a persuasive rebuttal (i.e., Auto Trader). **Exhibit 19-4** shows an ad from AS to encourage consumer awareness of truth in advertising.

Clearance Process AS provides clearance services for ads for many product categories and ads directed toward children for all jurisdictions except Quebec.

- *Alcohol.* AS adheres to the CRTC *Code for Broadcast Advertising of Alcoholic Beverages.* The CRTC disbanded clearance services in 1997. This code gives 17 precise guidelines on what is not permitted in alcohol ads. Some of the guidelines pertain to not attracting underage drinkers, non-drinkers, or problem drinkers. Many other guidelines focus on the message with respect to the type of consumption motivation, consumption situation, source, and appeal. AS reviews TV and radio ads across the country as well as print and out-of-home ads in British Columbia. AS provides a copy of the guidelines that alcohol distillers follow regarding social responsibility, adult audiences, post-secondary institutions, drinking and driving, consumption, good taste, and a few others. AS provides a designated stream of evaluation for complaints on this topic.

- *Cosmetics.* Health Canada transferred the clearance for cosmetic product ads to AS in 1992, although clearance is not an absolute requirement. AS follows the *Guidelines for Cosmetic Advertising and Labelling Claims.* The most recent version is a joint publication of AS, Health Canada, and the Canadian Cosmetic, Toiletry and Fragrance Association, and was published in 2000. The guidelines list acceptable and unacceptable claims for two types of hair care products, nail products, and five types of skin care products. Another set of guidelines list unacceptable and acceptable claims for toothpaste, deodorant, mouthwash, perfumes/fragrances/colognes, sun-care products, vitamins, and aromatherapy products. Finally, the same is done for different benefit claims, such as anti-wrinkle, healthy ingredients, nourishment, relaxation, respiration, revitalization, therapy/treatment, and lifting.

- *Non-prescription drugs.* Health Canada also transferred the clearance of non-therapeutic aspects of non-prescription drug ads directed toward consumers to AS in 1992. AS ensures that broadcast and print copy comply with Health Canada's *Consumer Drug Advertising Guidelines* and the *Food and Drugs Act and Regulations.* Health Canada has also given AS the responsibility for resolving any complaints of advertising for this category. To facilitate this change, Health Canada has published a document that describes its role, AS's role, and the claims that can be made in ads directed to consumers. Most of the guidelines in this document focus on the need for advertisers to provide factual information about the product's attributes and benefits, and require that the claims be scientifically valid.

- *Ads directed to children.* AS uses the *Broadcast Code for Advertising to Children (Children's Code),* published by the Canadian Association of Broadcasters in cooperation with AS, to assess whether ads directed toward children are appropriate. The Code takes into account the unique characteristics of children to ensure adequate safety and has nine guidelines concerning factual presentation, product prohibitions, avoiding undue pressure, scheduling, source or endorser of the message, price, comparison claims, safety, and social values. The Code also gives seven instructions on clearance procedures, such as when clearance is required or not, when ads can be directed to children, and during which programs ads can be directed to children. AS provides a designated stream of evaluation for complaints on this topic.

- *Food.* AS evaluates broadcast ads with respect to the *Food and Drugs Act and Regulations* and the *Guide to Food Labelling and Advertising.* Its policy guidelines make a distinction between food claims that are exempt from clearance and those that require clearance in four categories: general advertising, occasion–greeting advertising (e.g., Christmas), promotional advertising, and sponsorship advertising. In addition, the AS guidelines for the use of comparative advertising in food commercials outline six principles for appropriate executions of this presentation style. Finally, the AS guidelines on claims based on research and survey data have requirements pertaining to all aspects of the research design (i.e., sample, data collection).

In conclusion, Ad Standards self-regulates advertising in Canada based on Canadian laws. However, as the name indicates, it is responsible only for advertising. Other brand messages arising from more innovative communication tools are not covered by these guidelines. For example, product reviews found on Internet sites or brand evaluations on blogs are not considered advertising, even though the actual effect may be quite similar in terms of awareness or influencing consumer opinion.

LO2 Ethical Effects of Advertising

While many laws and regulations determine what advertisers can and cannot do, not every issue is covered by a rule. Marketers make decisions regarding appropriate and responsible actions on the basis of ethical considerations rather than on what is legal or within industry guidelines. **Ethics** are moral principles and values that govern the actions and decisions of an individual or group. Advertising and promotion are areas where a lapse in ethical standards or judgment can result in actions that are highly visible and often very damaging to a company, so ethical considerations are imperative when planning IMC decisions. We discuss three ways advertising is criticized from an ethical viewpoint: untruthful or deceptive; offensive or in bad taste; and exploitative of certain groups, such as children.

ADVERTISING AS UNTRUTHFUL OR DECEPTIVE

One complaint about advertising is that many ads are misleading or untruthful and deceive consumers. A number of studies have shown a general mistrust of advertising among consumers.[20] A historic study found that consumers felt that less than one-quarter of TV commercials are honest and believable.[21] Another older survey to determine current attitudes toward and confidence in advertising found that consumers generally do not trust advertising, although they tend to feel more confidence in advertising claims when focused on their actual purchase decisions.[22] AS research found that 77 percent of Canadian consumers have a favourable impression of advertising and 62 percent believe advertising assists them in making a purchase decision. And in contrast to the studies mentioned above, two-thirds of Canadians believe that 50 percent or more of the ads they see are truthful.[23]

Advertisers should have a reasonable basis for making a claim about product performance and may be required to provide evidence to support their claims. However, deception can occur more subtly as a result of how consumers perceive the ad and its impact on their beliefs.[24] The difficulty of determining just what constitutes deception, along with the fact that advertisers have the right to use puffery and make subjective claims about their products, tends to complicate the issue. **Puffery** has been legally defined as "advertising or other sales presentations which praise the item to be sold with subjective opinions, superlatives, or exaggerations, vaguely and generally, stating no specific facts."[25] A concern of many critics is the extent to which advertisers are *deliberately* untruthful or misleading, however.

Alcohol advertising is one area where one might conclude that a high degree of puffery has historically existed, with party imagery showing how happy consumers are when associated with a beverage. Sensing a change in consumers prompted Diageo Canada, distiller of Smirnoff vodka, to augment its brand positioning strategy. Researching Canadian consumers led to a Canada-specific focus on common situations in which they consume alcohol: with meals, during house parties, and at cottages, as shown in **Exhibit 19-5**. This represented a departure from club imagery of everyone having the most epic time of their life, which of course only happens occasionally. The impetus for the new strategy focused on the need to introduce the brand to younger drinkers aged 19–24, but also to become a consideration for consumers in the 25–39 age bracket who tend to gravitate away from the party scene as they settle down.

Exhibit 19-5 Consumers enjoy a beverage while socializing at a cottage or on a patio.

©Jacob Lund/Shutterstock

The campaign used TV and print to go with its promoted Twitter messages and hashtag #thisishappening. As all of this implies, this imagery reflected realistic consumption with minimal puffery.[26]

Sometimes advertisers make overtly false or misleading claims, however, these cases usually involve a tiny portion of the billions of dollars spent on advertising. Most advertisers do not design their messages with the intent to mislead or deceive consumers. Not only are such practices unethical, but the culprits would damage their reputation with AS and risk prosecution by government agencies. National advertisers invest large sums of money to develop loyalty to, and enhance the image of, their brands. These companies are not likely to risk hard-won consumer trust and confidence by intentionally deceiving consumers. In the case of Estée Lauder, the CEO apologized when the cosmetics brand realized that it had inadvertently made false ad claims because a small group of employees had changed the testing procedures, thereby making the message incorrect.[27] While many critics of advertising would probably agree that most advertisers are not out to deceive consumers deliberately, they are still concerned that consumers may not be receiving enough information to make an informed choice. They say advertisers usually present only information that is favourable to their position and do not always tell consumers the whole truth about a product or service.

Many believe advertising should be primarily informative in nature and should not be permitted to use puffery or embellished messages. Alternatively, advertisers have the right to present the most favourable case for their products and services and should not be restricted to just objective, verifiable information. Consumers can protect themselves from being persuaded against their will and the industry and government regulations suffice to keep advertisers from misleading consumers.[28] **Figure 19-3** shows the advertising principles of the Association of Canadian Advertisers, which advertisers may use as a guideline in preparing and evaluating their ads.

ADVERTISING AS OFFENSIVE OR IN BAD TASTE

Another consumer criticism of advertising is that ads are offensive, tasteless, irritating, or obnoxious. Studies have found that consumers sometimes feel offended by advertising or that advertising insults their intelligence and that many ads are in poor taste.[29] Consumers can be offended or irritated by advertising in a number of ways, such as product type, fear appeals, sexual appeals, and shock appeals.

Exhibit 19-6 Advertisers for certain products may experience consumer objections.

©McGraw-Hill Education/John Flournoy

Product Type Consumers object when certain products—like personal hygiene products or contraceptives—are advertised at all; however, the objections vary over time. Historically, media did not accept ads for condoms, but they reconsidered with the emergence of AIDS; currently, these ads do not register the same level of concern as in the past. A study of prime-time TV commercials found a strong product class effect (i.e., some personal care products) with respect to the types of ads consumers perceived as distasteful or irritating.[30] Another study found that consumers are more likely to dislike ads for products they do not use and for brands they would not buy.[31] AS's 2018 annual report identified a number of complaints pursued for product categories; non-commercial (540), retail (245), leisure services (232), other services (116), and cars (101). These data suggest that some general categories are more concerning for consumers, although these groupings are very broad compared to individual personal care products. Some products, such as snack foods and sugared

Figure 19-3 Advertising principles of the Association of Canadian Advertisers

1. *Advertisers must behave responsibly.* ACA believes:
   - Industry self-regulation is in the best interests of all Canadians. Self-regulatory policy exists to ensure that Canadians' fundamental rights and social values are not only acknowledged, but also protected.
   - Advertisers already demonstrate their responsibility by endorsing the Canadian Code of Advertising Standards—the principal instrument of self-regulation for the advertising industry in Canada.
   - The Code of Advertising Standards is only one of many industry codes and guidelines. For example, there are guidelines for gender portrayal, advertising to children, and food labelling, to name just a few.

2. *Advertisers have a right to freedom of speech.* Specifically:
   - The ACA does not believe it is reasonable for a government to allow companies to manufacture and sell legal products, and collect taxes, and then restrict them from telling anyone about it.
   - The ACA remains vigilant in ensuring advertisers' commercial freedom of speech.
   - Advertising, including advertising of products we may not like, is an aspect of free speech, and that free speech is one of society's highest values.

3. *Advertisers make an important contribution to the Canadian economy and culture.* Specifically:
   - Advertising is important to the economic and cultural life of Canadians.
   - In all its forms, advertising is estimated to represent an annual $10 billion investment in the Canadian economy.
   - Advertising revenues fuel the Canadian broadcasting system. Advertisers pay for the production and delivery into Canadian homes of programs that entertain, inform, and educate. Advertising also funds newspapers, magazines, and even movies and Internet sites.
   - Commercials reflect our life. They are a powerful tool and means of passing along our values, traditions, and lifestyles to new citizens and the next generation.
   - Locally produced commercials contribute to our sense of identity and promote national unity.

4. *Advertisers support a vibrant, competitive economy.* The ACA believes:
   - An increased reliance on market forces does not mean that a strong and enriched local and Canadian identity cannot be maintained.
   - Our ability to protect culture by limiting access to communications vehicles is becoming increasingly difficult. A prime example is the Internet.
   - In the rapidly changing world of communications, market conditions, not protectionism, should prevail.

beverages, as shown in **Exhibit 19-6**, experience consumer objection for encouraging consumption. However, the development of the Canadian Children's Food and Beverage Advertising Initiative, as noted earlier in this chapter, may reassure consumers that the advertising is more appropriate for healthy living.

Fear Appeals Another way in which advertising can offend consumers is by the type of appeal or the manner of presentation. For example, people object to appeals that exploit consumer anxieties. Fear appeal ads—especially for products such as deodorants, mouthwash, and dandruff shampoos—are criticized for attempting to create anxiety and using a fear of social rejection to sell these products. One writer called out organizations that sell diet programs for using fear messages of body image to young teenagers. In particular, the author criticized one brand for offering teens aged 13–17 a free summer membership to convey the fear message.[32]

Sexual Appeals Advertising appeals receiving the most criticism for being in poor taste are those using sexual appeals and/or nudity. These techniques are often used to gain consumers' attention and may not even be appropriate to the product being advertised. Even if the sexual appeal relates to the product, people may be offended by the nudity or sexual

©Splash News/Newscom

suggestiveness in the advertising message. Another criticism of sexual appeals is that they can demean women or men by depicting them as sex objects, such as with the image shown in **Exhibit 19-7**.

A review of sexual imagery in six mainstream American magazines for the years 1983, 1993, and 2003 across 18 product categories found that use of sexual imagery increased from 15 percent in 1983 to 27 percent in 2003. Most growth occurred in low-involvement product categories of alcohol, entertainment, and beauty, although product categories with the highest use included health/hygiene (38 percent), beauty (36 percent), drugs/medicine (29 percent), and clothing (26 percent).[33] It is difficult to say whether the level grew or declined since the time period investigated.

One significant review of many studies concluded that sexual appeals lead to stronger ad recognition and ad recall, and have no effect on brand recognition or brand recall, no relationship to attitude to the ad, a negative effect on brand attitude, and no effect on purchase intention. These findings support the initial point of this topic that sexual appeals garner attention and significant processing, however their impact on lasting communication effects is not a factor.[34]

It is also difficult to say whether this is similar in Canada or not. However, AS research in 2018 found that just over 50 percent of Canadians believed partial nudity, either male or female, was acceptable or somewhat acceptable. A question asked about the acceptability of sexual themes, images, or innuendo, and acceptability dropped to 46 percent after being at 53 percent in 2013.[35] The other interpretation of this data is that half of all Canadians say nudity and sexual themes are not appropriate, suggesting that possibly individuals' attitudes and opinions vary by their values, religion, age, gender, and education, or perhaps other characteristics. Interestingly, the Vancouver YWCA initiated a program to teach women that they could complain about the sexuality and portrayal of women in advertising to AS, who welcomed the program.[36]

Ethical Perspective 19-1 reviews the story of American Apparel and how the brand believes it has turned away from its sexually suggestive advertising of the past.

ETHICAL PERSPECTIVE 19-1

A NEW DIRECTION FOR AMERICAN APPAREL

American Apparel returned to Canada and internationally with an online store. Its history of ads with women posing suggestively while wearing not very much raised the question of what the now Canadian-owned brand planned for its advertising. At its height, the retailer owned 280 stores worldwide but tumbled into bankruptcy after its founder was charged with sexual harassment and departed the company.

In January 2017, a Montreal-based firm bought the brand's intellectual property rights and minimal physical assets, and planned to run American Apparel as an international online retailer.

©Spencer Platt/Getty Images

It expected to open one test store in Los Angeles to assess the potential for broader expansion. With the news, loyal owners of American Apparel clothing contacted the company, inquiring if they could replace their worn-out favourites, and American Apparel indicated that the new product line remained partly consistent with what had come before, but with lower prices.

When planning the advertising in Canada, the VP of brand marketing reviewed the archived ads and concluded that many fit the brand—fun, irreverent, slightly disruptive, and sexy—but some clearly crossed the line with overly sexual imagery. Despite this, the VP indicated that the brand established a strong photographic style in its ads, and suggested that people should feel empowered in their sexuality and that sexy is acceptable if it is portrayed positively and not uncomfortably.

For its new advertising, American Apparel established an open casting call for its models and selected a range of people with a variety of body shapes and sizes, and many different ethnic and cultural backgrounds. The imagery featured no retouches of the models, but the VP expected the ads retained a degree of tasteful sexiness. According to the VP, American Apparel would only include models aged 21 and up who looked older. In one campaign it showed models aged 30 and up.

American Apparel also established specialty products to show its commitment to diversity. American Apparel hired a public relations agency to build targeted activations and develop influencer marketing in social media. All of the IMC activities promoted American Apparel's positioning strategy of diversity, natural beauty, and body positivity. Despite this renewed direction, one commentator believed American Apparel did not deserve a second chance because of the history of its former owner.

Question:

1. What position do you take on American Apparel's new marketing communication in light of its history?

Shock Appeals Because of advertising clutter, brands continue to use sexual appeals that may offend people but catch the attention of consumers and possibly generate publicity. Heightened emotional intensity occurs with a shock appeal in which marketers use startling or surprising images of nudity or sexual suggestiveness. Shock appeals also show unexpected images or messages about other aspects of society, including religion, politics, family, or work. Advertising experts argue that what underlies the use of shock appeals is the pressure on marketers and their agencies to do anything to attract attention. However, critics argue that the more advertisers use the appeal, the more shocking the ads have to be to achieve this objective. How far advertisers can go with this appeal will probably depend on the public's reaction. When advertisers have gone too far, they are likely to pressure the advertisers to change their ads and the media to stop accepting them. While marketers and ad agencies often acknowledge that their ads push the limits with regard to taste, they also complain about a double standard that exists for advertising versus editorial television program content. They argue that even the most suggestive commercials are bland compared with the content of many television programs.

ADVERTISING AND CHILDREN

One historical review of advertising to children concluded that television is an important source of information for children about products.[37] However, it is a longstanding concern that children, particularly young ones, are especially vulnerable to advertising because they lack the experience and knowledge to understand and critically evaluate the purpose of persuasive advertising appeals. Research has shown that preschool children cannot differentiate between commercials and programs, do not perceive the selling intent of commercials, and cannot distinguish between reality and fantasy.[38] Research has also shown that children need more than a skeptical attitude toward advertising; they must understand how advertising works in order to use their cognitive defences against it effectively.[39] Because of children's limited ability to interpret the selling intent of a message or identify a commercial, some believe that advertising to them is inherently unfair and deceptive and should not be permitted (like we see in Quebec), or should be severely restricted.

At the other extreme is the point that advertising is a part of life and children must learn to deal with it in the **consumer socialization process** of acquiring the skills needed to function in the marketplace.[40] In this respect, existing restrictions may be adequate for controlling advertising directed to children. One study provided support for socialization as it found that adolescents developed skeptical attitudes toward advertising that were learned through interactions with parents and peers. They also found that marketplace knowledge played an important role in adolescents' skepticism toward advertising. Greater knowledge of the marketplace gave teens a basis by which to evaluate ads and made them more likely to recognize the persuasion techniques used by advertisers.[41]

The *Children's Code* and the Canadian Children's Food and Beverage Advertising Initiative discussed earlier recognize the above debate explicitly to find a balance between these two points of view. A study comparing the attitudes of business executives and consumers regarding children's advertising found that marketers of products targeted to children believe advertising to them provides useful information on new products and does not disrupt the parent–child relationship. However, the general public did not have such a favourable opinion. Older consumers and those from households with children had particularly negative attitudes toward children's advertising.[42] Clearly, companies communicating directly to children need to be sensitive to the naïveté of children as consumers to avoid potential conflict with those who believe children should be protected from advertising.

However, this balance becomes even more critical with children using digital media; the issues are increasingly complex, with new ideas for protection and groups making suggestions on how marketers should abide by the spirit of the laws prescribed for existing media. Despite this positive trend, marketers remain intrusive within the everyday lives of children. For example, 90 percent of popular children's Internet sites contain advertising, and many are really advertising disguised as content in the form of games or activities associated with toys, TV characters, or other brand identification. An interpretation guideline of federal laws by Ad Standards is a good start; however, it does not contain guidance for digital sources although the general message is certainly applicable. As well, the Canadian Children's Food and Beverage Advertising Initiative provides strong guidance that includes measures for digital communication, but adherence remains voluntary. Experts in the field expect direction and regulation soon in the aftermath of recent hearings by the Office of the Privacy Commissioner regarding online tracking and behavioural advertising.[43]

In the meantime, it appears reasonable for marketers to consider the following suggestions. (1) Even if there are no guidelines for online, advertisers should just use the broadcast code instructions and the interpretation guidelines for digital since they are readily adaptable. (2) Advertisers should involve parents as much as possible. (3) Advertisers should have an understanding from a moral perspective on blurring the lines between advertising and content since the receiver should always know and understand that advertising has occurred. (4) Advertisers should be respecting children's privacy and treating data in the same way as is done with adults. (5) Advertisers should apply the standard found in other media for online communication. (6) Advertisers should assess whether advertising to children is actually financially viable, as they have no income and do not make purchases.[44]

Despite these suggestions for improvements, advertisers continue to look for ways of influencing children. Another attempt in this direction occurred with the placement of TVs in schools as a pilot project to keep students informed of schedules, events, activities, and student content. To support the cost, the TVs had messages for "good" products such as milk, government, and higher education institutions. Reactions were initially positive, however conflict arose over a planned expansion toward more minutes of advertising per day, with some stakeholders being concerned that this would be the start of messages that many would not welcome in schools. Further, some did question why even "good" advertising messages should be in the school in the first place.[45]

(LO3) Social Effects of Advertising

Concern is expressed over the impact of advertising on society, particularly on values and lifestyles. While a number of factors influence the cultural values, lifestyles, and behaviour of a society, the overwhelming amount of advertising and its prevalence in the mass media lead many critics to argue that advertising plays a major role in influencing and transmitting social values. While there is general agreement that advertising is an important social influence agent, opinions as to the value of its contribution are often negative. Advertising is criticized for encouraging materialism, manipulating consumers to buy things they do not really need, perpetuating stereotypes, and controlling the media.

ADVERTISING ENCOURAGES MATERIALISM

Critics claim advertising has an adverse effect on consumer values by encouraging **materialism**, a preoccupation with material things rather than intellectual or spiritual concerns. Critics contend that an ad like the one shown in **Exhibit 19-8** can promote materialistic values. In summary, they contend that advertising creates needs rather than showing how a product fulfills needs; surrounds consumers with images of the good life, implying material possessions leads to contentment and happiness; and suggests material possessions are symbols of status, success, and accomplishment leading to social acceptance, popularity, or sex appeal.

This criticism of advertising assumes that materialism is undesirable and is sought at the expense of other goals, but some believe materialism is acceptable. For example, some consumers believe their hard work and individual effort and initiative allows for the accumulation of material possessions as evidence of success. Others argue that the acquisition of material possessions has positive economic impact by encouraging greater consumption after basic needs are met. Many believe economic growth is essential and materialism is both a necessity and an inevitable part of this progress. It has also been argued that an emphasis on material possessions does not rule out interest in intellectual, spiritual, or cultural values. Defenders of advertising say consumers can be more interested in higher-order goals when basic needs have been met. For example, a person may buy an expensive stereo system to enjoy music rather than simply to impress someone or acquire a material possession.

Even if we assume materialism is undesirable, there is still the question of whether advertising is responsible for creating and encouraging it. While critics argue that advertising is a major contributing force to materialistic values, others say advertising merely reflects the values of society rather than shaping them.[46] They argue that consumers' values are defined by the society in which they live and are the results of extensive, long-term socialization or acculturation. The argument that advertising is responsible for creating a materialistic and hedonistic society is addressed by Stephen Fox (in his book *The Mirror Makers: A History of American Advertising and Its Creators*), who concludes that advertising reflects society but is labelled a scapegoat.[47] Advertising does contribute to our materialism by portraying products and services as symbols of status, success, and achievement and by encouraging consumption, but as Richard Pollay says, "While it may be true that advertising reflects cultural values, it does so on a very selective basis, echoing and reinforcing certain attitudes, behaviours, and values far more frequently than others."[48]

Exhibit 19-8 Critics argue that advertising contributes to materialistic values.

Rolls-Royce
Like nothing else on earth

©Rolls-Royce Motor Cars NA, LLC

ADVERTISING AND PERSUASION

A common criticism of advertising is that it manipulates and exploits consumers by persuading them to buy things they do not need. Critics say advertising should just provide information useful in making purchase decisions and should not persuade. They view information advertising (which reports price, performance, and other objective criteria) as desirable, but persuasive advertising (which plays on consumers' emotions, anxieties, and psychological needs and desires such as status, self-esteem, and attractiveness) as unacceptable. Persuasive advertising is criticized for fostering discontent among consumers and encouraging them to purchase products and services to solve deeper problems.

Defenders of advertising offer three rebuttals to these criticisms. First, they point out that a substantial amount of advertising is essentially informational in nature. Also, it is difficult to separate desirable informational advertising from undesirable persuasive advertising. Shelby Hunt, in examining the *information–persuasion dichotomy*, points out that advertising that most observers categorize as informative is actually very persuasive, and that the purpose of all advertising is to persuade.[49]

Second, defenders of advertising also take issue with the argument that it should be limited to dealing with basic functional needs. In our society, most lower-level needs recognized in Maslow's hierarchy—such as the needs for food, clothing, and shelter—are satisfied for most people. It is natural to move from basic needs to higher-order ones such as self-esteem and status or self-actualization. Consumers are free to choose the degree to which they attempt to satisfy their desires, and wise advertisers associate their products and services with the satisfaction of higher-order needs.

Exhibit 19-9 With this colourful street ad, Viagra reminds Canadian consumers to talk to their doctor.

Talk to your doctor.

©Marc Bruxelle/Shutterstock

While this is true, fulfillment of lower-level needs continues to benefit from advertising (**Exhibit 19-9**).

Third, this criticism attributes too much power to advertising and assumes consumers have no ability to defend themselves since it ignores the fact that consumers have the freedom to make their own choices when confronted with persuasive advertising. While they readily admit the persuasive intent of their business, advertisers are quick to note that it is extremely difficult to make consumers purchase a product they do not want or for which they do not see a personal benefit. If advertising were as powerful as the critics claim, we would not see products with multimillion-dollar advertising budgets failing in the marketplace. The reality is that consumers do have a choice, and they are not being forced to buy. Consumers ignore ads for products and services they do not really need or that fail to interest them.

ADVERTISING AND STEREOTYPING

Advertising is often accused of creating and perpetuating stereotypes through its portrayal of women and visible minorities.

Women The portrayal of women in advertising is an issue that has received a great deal of attention through the years.[50] Advertising has received much criticism for stereotyping women and failing to recognize the changing role of women in our society. Critics have argued that advertising often depicts women as preoccupied with beauty, household duties, and motherhood, or shows them as decorative objects or sexually provocative figures. The research studies conducted through the years show a consistent picture of gender stereotyping that has varied little over time. Portrayals of adult women in American television and print advertising have emphasized passivity, deference, lack of intelligence and credibility, and punishment for high levels of effort. In contrast, men have been portrayed as constructive, powerful, autonomous, and achieving.[51]

Research on gender stereotyping in advertising targeted to children has found a pattern of results similar to that reported for adults. A study found sex-role stereotyping in television advertising targeted at children in the United States as well as in Australia.[52] Boys are generally shown as being more knowledgeable, active, aggressive, and instrumental than girls. Nonverbal behaviours involving dominance and control are associated more with boys than girls. Advertising directed toward children has also been shown to feature more boys than girls, to position boys in more dominant, active roles, and to use male voiceovers more frequently than female ones.[53]

While stereotyping still exists, advertising's portrayal of women is improving in many areas as advertisers show women realistically. Researchers argue that the transformed social positioning of women in North American society is perhaps the most important social development of this century.[54] They note that, as women have crossed the boundary from the domestic sphere to the professional arena, expectations and representations of women have changed as well. Advertisers depict women in a diversity of roles that reflect their changing place in society. The stereotypical character traits attributed to women have shifted from weak and dependent to strong and autonomous.[55] The ad for Network Solutions shown in **Exhibit 19-10** is an example of how advertisers portray women in their ads.

Exhibit 19-10 Many advertisers now portray women in powerful roles.

My client just added 1 BR and .5 BA. No problem—I'll bring this job home on time.

So why is it so hard to get my own Web site built?

NetworkSolutions.

Source: Network Solutions LLC

Recent academic research has supported this direction. For example, one review of studies from around the world concluded that there has been a positive trend of both women and men away from uniform stereotyped portrayals.[56] A longitudinal study compared ads from 1990–1999 and 2000–2009, and found that women were depicted in non-traditional activities in 16 percent of the earlier ads versus 29 percent of the later ones. The percentage of ads showing a woman as a "housewife" dropped from 12 percent to 6 percent. Men portrayed as authority figures dropped from 31 percent to 17 percent over the two time periods.[57]

Note that the portrayal of women did not elicit overwhelming complaints shown in the 2018 AS annual report, suggesting a positive trend. It received a total of 322 complaints regarding 233 ads associated with Clause 14 (unacceptable depictions and portrayals). Most concerned personal taste or preference, and the Council ultimately upheld 13 complaints for 6 ads, of which the exact portrayal problem is unknown. In comparison, AS received 849 complaints for Clause 1 (accuracy and clarity) and Clause 3 (price claims) combined and upheld 321 complaints for 37 ads. As well, portrayal and depiction problems of advertising are not reflected in the statistics if advertising is amended or withdrawn prior to an AS complaint. The issue of ad images that are criticized for being in public display is raised periodically, and ads such as the one shown in **Exhibit 19-11** may elicit objections or complaints.

Exhibit 19-11 This Triumph lingerie ad may be inappropriate for public display to some consumers.

©Philippe Hays/Alamy Stock Photo

A study by Microsoft and its agency Omnicom concluded that advertisers might want to reconsider how men are portrayed in ads, and their data found that high percentages of men declared themselves to be interested in cooking, nutrition, and personal care and grooming. Men indicated significant involvement in shopping for durables, consumables, and their own clothing, thereby challenging marketers' belief that women made most purchase decisions.[58]

Visible Minorities Several U.S. academic studies in the late 1980s and early 1990s examined the incidence of visible minorities in advertising. A study found that African-Americans appeared in 26 percent of all ads on network TV that used live models but Hispanics appeared in only 6 percent of the commercials with live models. The researchers also found that TV ads in which African-American people appeared were overwhelmingly integrated and that African-American people were likely to have played either minor or background roles in the majority of the ads.[59] Research conducted in 1995 found that 17 percent of prime-time network TV ads featured African-Americans as dominant characters and the majority of commercials featured them in minor roles.[60] One researcher found that ads targeting African-Americans through racially targeted media, especially with race-based products, benefit from featuring African-American models with a dominant presence in the ad.[61]

A study of U.S. prime-time TV commercials found that Asian male and female models are overrepresented in terms of their proportion of the U.S. population (3.6 percent), appearing in 8.4 percent of the commercials. However, Asian models were more likely than members of other minority groups to appear in background roles, and Asian women were rarely depicted in major roles. The study also found that portrayals of Asian-Americans put more emphasis on their work ethic and less on other aspects of their lives.[62]

In Ottawa, one writer criticized the portrayal of East Asian women in transit shelter ads located in the Chinatown area of the city for a casino communicating that it offered an Asian gaming area. The other problem centred on the blatant targeting of the ad message given the high level of gambling addiction in the Chinese community. While making the points, the writer acknowledged a point of view expressed by a reporter who debated the ethics of such a targeting decision by wondering if it exhibited "savvy" or "predatory" ad messaging.[63] Extending the cultural point to a broader issue, it raises a concern about how people of any nationality are portrayed in advertising with respect to specific goods or services that reinforce negative connotations. Certainly it provides a valuable lesson for promotional planners in Canada with its many cultures.

It may be difficult to generalize the academic studies to Canada; however, Canadians are exposed to American ads when watching U.S. television programs that do not simulcast Canadian commercials or when reading American magazines. So, to a degree, Canadian consumers will experience and perceive an imbalance through U.S. exposure. However to counter this, one recent study of 2,000 ads shown in prime time on CBC, Global, and CTV found that 79 percent of the characters in the ads were Caucasian, and a corresponding 21 percent were non-Caucasian. In the 2011 census, about 6.25 million Canadians identified themselves as visible minorities, about 19 percent of the population of 33.5 million. Thus, based on this one sample, we can see a roughly equal representation.[64] And the outcomes of Cheerios ads that showed an interracial couple in the United States and Canada are revealing. The American ads shown during 2013 and 2014 received racist commentary in social media; however, an interracial couple shown in a Canadian Cheerios ad execution aired three years earlier produced no racial commentary, and therefore seeing the U.S. ad did not surprise the Canadian executives as being unexpected.[65] Despite this, Canadian outdoor equipment and clothing companies received criticism regarding a lack of diversity in their ads. MEC took the message seriously and quickly responded by announcing in an open letter that the retailer would alter its ads in future.[66]

ADVERTISING AND THE MEDIA

The fact that advertising plays such an important role in financing the media has led to concern that advertisers may influence or even control the media. It is well documented that *economic censorship* occurs, whereby the media avoid certain topics or even present biased news coverage in acquiescence to advertiser demands.[67] Having the media in Canada supported by advertising means we can enjoy them for free or for a fraction of what they would cost without advertising. The alternative to an advertiser-supported media system is support by users through higher subscription costs for the print media and a fee or pay-per-view system with TV. Although not perfect, our system of advertising-supported media provides the best option for receiving information and entertainment, however the points on both sides of the issue have merit.

Critics charge that the media's dependence on advertisers' support makes them susceptible to influence, including exerting control over the editorial content of magazines and newspapers; biasing editorial opinions to favour the position of an advertiser; limiting coverage of a controversial story that might reflect negatively on a company; and influencing the program content of television. A survey of 147 daily newspapers found that more than 90 percent of editors have been pressured by advertisers and more than one-third of them said advertisers had succeeded in influencing news at their papers.[68] Thus, a newspaper may be reluctant to print an unfavourable story about a local business upon whose advertising it depends. For TV, programming decisions are made largely on the basis of what shows will attract the most viewers and thus be most desirable to advertisers. Critics say this results in lower-quality television as educational, cultural, and informative programming is sacrificed for shows that get high ratings and appeal to the mass markets.

Media executives cite two reasons why advertisers do not exert undue influence over the media. First, it is in the media's best interest not to be influenced by advertisers. To retain public confidence, media must report the news fairly and accurately without showing bias or attempting to avoid controversial issues. The vast array of topics media cover and their investigative reporting is evidence of their objectivity. Second, media executives note that an advertiser needs the media more than the media need any individual advertiser, particularly when the medium has a large audience or does a good job of reaching a specific market segment. Many publications and stations have a very broad base of advertising support and can afford to lose an advertiser that attempts to exert too much influence.

Exhibit 19-12 The Alberta Gaming and Liquor Commission encourages people to drink responsibly.

©Alberta Gaming And Liquor Commission

ADVERTISING AND SOCIAL BENEFIT

It is important to note that advertising contributes to activities that provide tremendous social benefit in a number of ways. Companies use advertising in their sponsorship or cause-related activities that encourage participation to help raise money for important causes. For example, communicating to the thousands who participated in Manulife's Ride for Heart efforts would not be possible without advertising—and, more importantly, would not occur without the existing advertising industry and infrastructure.

Organizations dealing with social problems, such as alcohol-impaired driving, use advertising to influence attitudes and behaviour. **Exhibit 19-12** identifies one organization that uses advertising and other marketing communication tools to achieve these objectives. The messages try to persuade at-risk individuals not to engage in the behaviour and to take precautions if they do. One study reviewing the effects of mass media campaigns found a 13 percent decline in alcohol-related crashes and concluded that the social benefit of the advertising clearly outweighed the cost of the advertising.[69] Furthermore, advertising attempts to influence social norms by giving friends and family the courage to intervene.

The Canadian National Institute for the Blind celebrated its 100th anniversary. It changed the brand name to CNIB Foundation and instituted a yellow and black colour motif that is more easily seen by those with partial vision. A new initiative—"Phone It Forward"—asked Canadians to donate their old smart phones to be refurbished and loaded with apps to assist those with vision loss as they navigated through life. As expected, the non-profit organization benefited with advertising to communicate the request to Canadians.[70]

Ethical Perspective 19-2 describes the marketing communication of Rethink Breast Cancer, a leading breast cancer awareness organization. Its success is built on the existing advertising infrastructure and the commitment of advertising professionals. And the examples show that creative messages and media flourish in the non-profit sector. There are numerous examples such as this where advertising and other promotions and the advertising industry contribute to social benefit.

ETHICAL PERSPECTIVE 19-2

SOCIAL BENEFIT OF RETHINK BREAST CANCER

Advertising provides considerable benefit in many facets of society despite criticism it faces across multiple domains. Critics claim that advertising contributes to obesity since it encourages people to eat too much non-nutritious food, encourages consumers to drink alcohol excessively leading to a myriad of problems, or sways people to buy goods that they do not really need. Despite the potential for this possibly occurring, advertising and the system of advertising effectively contribute positively to significant issues, as we see with Rethink Breast Cancer.

©Rethink Breast Cancer

Research indicated that women with breast cancer did not enjoy being treated like a "sick person" while receiving treatment. Enter Give-A-Care, a product line for young women with breast cancer that actually understands young women with breast cancer. The 22-item product list (sold online at Giveacare.ca), priced from $4 to $100, included lemon candies to get rid of the metallic taste of chemo, and an easy-to-use zip-front hoodie for after surgery. Witty remarks written on each item and on the online description provided a hint of the recovery experience. All donated products provided a profit margin that provided financial support for Rethink Breast Cancer to fulfill its mission of

supporting young people affected by breast cancer. Agency Lg2 donated creative and management time to the cause.

The collection represented a substantial change from its previous campaigns such as, "Live.Laugh. Learn.," a YouTube series providing educational information for women living with breast cancer, as well as "Your Man Reminder," a video series and app that in a bold and novel way encouraged women to check themselves regularly. However, across all three campaigns, a clear direction of innovation in the message and media prevailed to communicate their mission effectively.

[Continued on next page]

[Ethical Perspective 19-2 continued]

More recently, Rethink Breast Cancer targeted teenagers who received misinformation about breast cancer through social media, causing substantial fear even though they faced a 0.06% chance of being diagnosed. Enter #8008135 (spells BOOBIES in upside-down calculator numbers), a hashtag social media campaign that directed young girls to a Facebook Messenger chatbot that answered their questions and dispelled myths. Additionally, quizzes, quirky .gifs, and educational games provided a fun learning experience of the facts. H&M distributed T-shirts with the hashtag and sold them in select stores. The organization received $260,000 in donated media to ensure exposure.

Quesion:

1. Can you recall other examples of advertising providing social benefit?

Economic Effects of Advertising

Advertising develops consumers' awareness of products and other communication effects by providing information for their decision making; however, it also affects our economic system. Advertising can encourage consumption and foster economic growth, facilitate entry into markets, and lead to economies of scale, thereby increasing the standard of living. In contrast, critics claim advertising does not provide information adequately, adds to the cost of goods and services, and discourages competition and market entry, thereby leading to industrial concentration and higher prices. To resolve this we turn to the macroeconomic perspective of economists in terms of consumer choice, competition, and product costs and prices.

EFFECTS ON CONSUMER CHOICE

Critics say advertising hampers consumer choice, as large advertisers use their power to limit our options to a few well-advertised brands. Economists argue that advertising is used to achieve (1) **differentiation**, whereby the products or services of large advertisers are perceived as unique or better than competitors', and (2) brand loyalty, which enables large national advertisers to gain control of the market, usually at the expense of smaller brands. Larger companies often charge a higher price and achieve a more dominant position in the market than smaller firms that cannot compete against them and their large advertising budgets. When this occurs, advertising not only restricts the choice alternatives to a few well-known, heavily advertised brands, but also becomes a substitute for competition based on price or product improvements.

Heavily advertised brands dominate the market in certain product categories (e.g., soft drinks). But advertising's defenders claim it generally does not create brand monopolies and reduce the opportunities for new products to be introduced to consumers. In most product categories, a number of different brands are on the store shelves and thousands of new products are introduced every year. The opportunity to advertise gives companies the incentive to develop new brands and improve their existing ones. When a successful new product such as a smart phone is introduced, competitors quickly follow and use advertising to inform consumers about their brand and attempt to convince them it is superior to the original.

EFFECTS ON COMPETITION

Critical economists argue that power in the hands of large firms with huge advertising budgets creates a **barrier to entry**, which makes it difficult for other firms to enter the market. This results in less competition and higher prices. Economists note that smaller firms already in the market find it difficult to compete against the large advertising budgets of the industry leaders and are often driven out of business. Large advertisers clearly enjoy a competitive advantage through **economies of scale** in advertising, particularly with respect to factors such as media costs. Firms such as Procter & Gamble, which spends millions of dollars per year on advertising and promotion, are able to make large media buys at a reduced rate and allocate them to their various products. Large advertisers usually sell more of a product or service, which means they may have lower production costs and can allocate more money to advertising, so they can afford the costly but more efficient media like network television. Their large advertising outlays also give them more opportunity to differentiate their products and develop brand loyalty. To the extent that these factors occur, smaller competitors are at a disadvantage and new competitors are deterred from entering the market.

While advertising may have an anticompetitive effect on a market, there is no clear evidence that advertising alone reduces competition, creates barriers to entry, and thus increases market concentration. Defenders of advertising say it is unrealistic to attribute a firm's market dominance and barriers to entry solely to advertising. Industry leaders often tend to dominate markets because they have superior product quality and the best management and competitive strategies, not simply the biggest advertising budgets. While market entry against large, established competitors is difficult, companies with a quality product at a reasonable price often find a way to break in. Moreover, they usually find that advertising actually facilitates their market entry by making it possible to communicate the benefits and features of their new product or brand to consumers.

EFFECTS ON PRODUCT COSTS AND PRICES

Critics such as consumer advocates argue that advertising increases the prices consumers pay for products and services. First, money spent on brand advertising constitutes an expense that must be covered and the consumer pays for it through higher prices.Second, advertising increases product differentiation by adding perceived value of the product among physically homogeneous products, enabling advertised brands to command a premium price without an increase in quality. For example, the differences in prices between national brands and physically similar private-label brands are evidence of the added value created by advertising. Thus, consumers' willingness to pay more for an advertised national brand rather than purchasing the lower-priced, non-advertised brand is wasteful and irrational.

Proponents of advertising acknowledge that advertising costs are at least partly paid for by consumers. But advertising may help lower the overall cost of a product more than enough to offset its costs. For example, advertising may help firms achieve economies of scale in production and distribution by providing information to and stimulating demand among mass markets. These economies of scale help cut the cost of producing and marketing the product, which can lead to lower prices—if the advertiser chooses to pass the cost savings on to the consumer.

Advertising can also lower prices by making a market more competitive, which usually leads to greater price competition. One researcher concluded that advertising resulted in lower consumer prices and that curtailment of TV advertising would drive up consumer prices.[71] And one economist argued that advertising cannot increase the cost per unit of quality to consumers because, if it did, consumers would not continue to respond positively to advertising.[72] Instead, advertising lowers the costs of information about brand quality, leads to increases in brand quality, and lowers the average price per unit of quality. Finally, advertising is a means to market entry rather than a deterrent and helps stimulate product innovation, which makes markets more competitive and helps keep prices down.

SUMMARIZING ECONOMIC EFFECTS

Albion and Farris suggest that economists' perspectives can be divided into two principal schools of thought that make different assumptions regarding the influence of advertising on the economy.[73] **Figure 19-4** summarizes the main points of the "advertising equals market power" and "advertising equals information" perspectives.

Advertising Equals Market Power The belief that advertising equals market power reflects traditional economic thinking and views advertising as a way to change consumers' tastes, lower their sensitivity to price, and build brand loyalty among buyers of advertised brands. This results in higher profits and market power for large advertisers, reduces competition in the market, and leads to higher prices and fewer choices for consumers. Proponents of this viewpoint generally have negative attitudes regarding the economic impact of advertising.

Figure 19-4 Two schools of thought on advertising's role in the economy

Advertising = Market Power		Advertising = Information
Advertising affects consumer preferences, changes product attributes, and differentiates the product from competitive offerings.	Advertising	Advertising informs consumers about product attributes but does not change the way they value those attributes.
Consumers become brand loyal and perceive fewer substitutes for advertised brands.	Consumer buying behaviour	Consumers become more price sensitive and buy best "value." Only the price–quality relationship affects product elasticity.
Potential entrants must overcome established brand loyalty and spend relatively more on advertising.	Barriers to entry	Advertising makes entry possible because it can communicate product attributes to consumers.
Firms are insulated from market competition and potential rivals; concentration increases, leaving firms with more discretionary power.	Industry structure and market power	Consumers easily compare competitive offerings, which increases rivalry. Efficient firms remain, inefficient leave, and new entrants appear; the effect on concentration is ambiguous.
Firms charge higher prices and are less likely to compete on quality/price dimensions. Innovation may be reduced.	Market conduct	More informed consumers pressure firms to lower prices and improve quality; entrants drive innovation.
Advertisers' excessive profit provides incentive to advertise. Output is restricted compared to perfect competition.	Market performance	Industry prices decrease. Effect on profit due to increased competition and increased efficiency is ambiguous.

Exhibit 19-13 This ad promotes the value of advertising in building strong brands.

Source: American Advertising Federation

Advertising Equals Information The belief that advertising equals information takes a more positive view of advertising's economic effects. This model sees advertising as providing consumers with useful information, increasing their price sensitivity (which moves them toward lower-priced products), and increasing competition in the market. Advertising is viewed as a way to communicate with consumers and tell them about a product and its major features and attributes. More informed and knowledgeable consumers pressure companies to provide high-quality products at lower prices. Efficient firms remain in the market, whereas inefficient firms leave as new entrants appear. Proponents of this model believe the economic effects of advertising are favourable and think it contributes to more efficient and competitive markets. **Exhibit 19-13** shows an ad from the International Advertising Association used to support this positive role of advertising.

A Final Thought The debate over the economic effects of advertising will likely continue; however, the point of view expressed by Leo Burnett many years ago seems relevant today with the growth of mobile devices and other innovations (**Figure 19-5**). While many advertising and marketing experts agree that advertising and promotion play an important role in helping to expand consumer demand for new products, not everyone would agree that this is desirable.

Figure 19-5 The positive economic effects of advertising

To me it means that if we believe to any degree whatsoever in the economic system under which we live, in a high standard of living and in high employment, advertising is the most efficient known way of moving goods in practically every product class.

My proof is that millions of businessmen have chosen advertising over and over again in the operations of their business. Some of their decisions may have been wrong, but they must have thought they were right or they wouldn't go back to be stung twice by the same kind of bee.

It's a pretty safe bet that in the next 10 years many Americans will be using products and devices that no one in this room has even heard of. Judging purely by past performance, American advertising can be relied on to make them known and accepted overnight at the lowest possible prices.

Advertising, of course, makes possible our unparalleled variety of magazines, newspapers, business publications, and radio and television stations.

It must be said that without advertising we would have a far different nation, and one that would be much the poorer—not merely in material commodities, but in the life of the spirit.

— Leo Burnett

Learning Objectives Summary

 Describe the advertising regulation system in Canada.

Various levels of government regulate different aspects of Canadian advertising; however, self-regulation of these laws is quite prominent in Canada. This self-regulation occurs through Ad Standards (AS), a non-profit organization of advertising industry members. AS responds to all complaints with respect to advertising and publishes an annual report that summarizes the complaints it receives each year. AS is also responsible for clearing ads prior to their airing for a number of products. Some of AS's responsibilities have been given to it as the federal government has withdrawn services with the belief that industry is sufficiently responsible.

 Evaluate the ethical perspectives of advertising.

Even though there appears to be sufficient control of advertising, it is a very powerful institution that has been the target of considerable criticism regarding its ethical, social, and economic impact. The criticism of advertising concerns the specific techniques and methods used as well as its effect on societal values, tastes, lifestyles, and behaviour. Critics argue that advertising is deceptive and untruthful; that it is often offensive, irritating, or in poor taste; and that it exploits certain groups. Many people believe advertising should be informative only and advertisers should not use subjective claims, puffery, embellishment, or persuasive techniques.

Advertising often offends consumers by the type of appeal or manner of presentation used; sexually suggestive ads and nudity receive the most criticism. Advertisers say their ads are consistent with contemporary values and lifestyles and are appropriate for the target audiences they are attempting to reach. Advertising to children is an area of particular concern, since critics argue that children lack the experience, knowledge, and ability to process and evaluate persuasive advertising messages rationally.

 Explain the social effects of advertising.

The pervasiveness of advertising and its prevalence in the mass media have led critics to argue that it plays a major role in influencing and transmitting social values. Advertising has been charged with encouraging materialism, manipulating consumers to buy things they do not really want or need, and perpetuating stereotypes through its portrayal of certain groups such as women and visible minorities.

Examine the economic role of advertising and its effects on consumer choice, competition, and product costs and prices.

Advertising has also been scrutinized with regard to its economic effects. The basic economic role of advertising is to give consumers information that helps them make consumption decisions. Some people view advertising as a detrimental force that has a negative effect on competition, product costs, and consumer prices. Economists' perspectives regarding the effects of advertising correspond to two basic schools of thought: the "advertising equals market power" model, and the "advertising equals information" model. Arguments consistent with each perspective were considered in analyzing the economic effects of advertising.

Review Questions

1. Explain why you agree or disagree with the rulings of Ad Standards presented in this chapter regarding the Ford Focus and Kia automobile ads.

2. Evaluate the arguments for and against advertising to children. Do you feel that restrictions are needed for advertising and other forms of promotion targeted to children?

3. Discuss how attitudes toward the use of sex in advertising differ between men and women. Discuss the implications of these attitudinal differences for marketers who are developing ads.

4. Describe the differences between the two major perspectives of the economic impact of advertising: "advertising equals market power" versus "advertising equals information."

Applied Questions

1. Why are the laws for advertising regulation not applied to sponsorship and some other IMC tools?

2. Find the most offensive ad possible and express why it is so offensive. Apply the AS code to determine which guidelines it violates.

3. Explain which position you agree with and why: "Advertising determines Canadian consumers' tastes and values and is responsible for creating a materialistic society," or "Advertising is a reflection of society and mirrors its tastes and values."

4. Do you believe that advertising power has ever restricted your personal choice in buying products?

Endnotes

CHAPTER ONE

1. "AMA Board Approves New Marketing Definition," *Marketing News*, March 1, 1985, p. 1.
2. Richard P. Bagozzi, "Marketing as Exchange," *Journal of Marketing*, 39 (4), October 1975, pp. 32–39.
3. "Mackie Biernacki—Small Size, Big Reach," *Strategy*, January 2019, p. 49.
4. Soonhong Min, Jeffrey W. Overby, and Kun Shin Im, "Relationships Between Desired Attributes, Consequences and Purchase Frequency," *Journal of Consumer Marketing*, 29 (6), 2012, pp. 423–435.
5. Kristin Laird, "Dinner Time Is Prime Time for Maple Leaf Foods," *Marketing Magazine*, June 16, 2011.
6. Melissa Dunne, "Meant for the Road," *Strategy*, October 5, 2018.
7. Mark Burgess, "Designing a Nation," *Strategy*, June 2017, p. 8.
8. Joseph Brean, "World War Pink Comes to Canada," *National Post*, January 27, 2014, p. A1.
9. Jennifer Lee, "Fredericton Deodorant Company Reboots," *Chronicle Herald*, March 1, 2018, p. B2.
10. Kevin Lane Keller, "Conceptualizing, Measuring, and Managing Customer Based Brand Equity," *Journal of Marketing*, 57 (1), January 1993, pp. 1–22.
11. Sreedhar Madhavaram, Vishag Badrinarayanan, and Robert E. McDonald, "Integrated Marketing Communication (IMC) and Brand Identity as Critical Components of Brand Equity Strategy," *Journal of Advertising*, 34 (4), Winter 2005, pp. 69–80.
12. Brand Finance, "Canada 100 2018: The annual report on the most valuable brands in Canada," https://brandfinance.com/knowledge-centre/reports/brand-finance-canada-100-2018/.
13. Ipsos Marketing, "The Most Influential Brands in Canada 2017," https://www.ipsos.com/en-ca/knowledge/consumer-shopper/most-influential-brands-canada-2017.
14. Susan Krashinsky, "Growth in Brand Value of Canadian Firms Slowing," *The Globe and Mail*, May 27, 2014, p. B3.
15. J. Josko Brakus, Bernd H. Schmitt, and Lia Zarantonello, "Brand Experience: What Is It? How Is It Measured? Does It Affect Loyalty?", *Journal of Marketing*, 73 (3), May 2009, pp. 52–68.
16. C. Whan Park, Deborah J. MacInnis, Joseph Priester, Andreas B. Elsingerich, and Dawn Iabucci, "Brand Attachment and Brand Attitude Strength: Conceptual and Empirical Differentiation of Two Critical Brand Equity Drivers," *Journal of Marketing*, 74 (6), November 2010, pp. 1–17.
17. Rajeev Batra, Aaron Ahuvia, and Richard P. Bagozzi, "Brand Love," *Journal of Marketing*, 76 (3), March 2012, pp. 1–16.
18. Justin Dallaire, "How to Drive Brand Love," *Strategy*, January 9, 2018.
19. "All Brands Need Love," *Strategy*, March 2018, p. 32.
20. Emily Wexler, "She the North," *Strategy*, December 2014, p. 26; Rachel Brady, "How the Raptors Redefined Their Brand—and Took Toronto by the Throat," *The Globe and Mail*, October 28, 2014.
21. Melissa Dunne, "Clawing Out a New NBA," *Strategy*, January 2019, p. 38.
22. Paul W. Farris and David J. Reibstein, "How Prices, Ad Expenditures, and Profits Are Linked," *Harvard Business Review*, November–December 1979, pp. 172–84.
23. Tamsin McMahon, "Mortgage Broker's Low Rate Has Downside," *The Globe and Mail*, March 27, 2015, p. B3.
24. Daniel J. Howard and Roger A. Kerin, "Broadening the Scope of Reference Price Advertising Research: A Field Study of Consumer Shopping," *Journal of Marketing*, 70 (4), October 2006, pp. 185–204.
25. Dhruv Grewal, Kent B. Monroe, and R. Krishnan, "The Effects of Price-Comparison Advertising on Buyers' Perceptions of Acquisition Value, Transaction Value, and Behavioral Intentions," *Journal of Marketing*, 62 (2), April 1998, pp. 46–59.
26. Kevin Lane Keller, "Brand Equity Management in a Multichannel, Multimedia Retail Environment," *Journal of Interactive Marketing*, 24 (2), May 2010, pp. 58–70.
27. https://www.ama.org/AboutAMA/Pages/Definition-of-Marketing.aspx
28. V. Kumar and Werner Reinartz, "Creating Customer Value," *Journal of Marketing*, 80 (6), November 2016, pp. 36–68.
29. Philipp E. Boksberger and Lisa Melsen, "Perceived Value: A Critical Examination, Definitions, Concepts and Measure for Service Industry," *Journal of Services Marketing*, 25 (3), 2011, pp. 229–240.
30. Ozgun Atasoy and Carey K. Morewedge, "Digital Goods Are Valued Less Than Physical Goods," *Journal of Consumer Research*, 44 (6), April 2018, pp. 1343–1457.
31. Ralph S. Alexander, ed., *Marketing Definitions* (Chicago: American Marketing Association, 1965), p. 9.
32. Numeris, Weekly Top 30 Programs.
33. "Analysis of the Economics of Canadian Television Programming." Study performed by Nodicity Group Ltd., March 2009.
34. J. Lucy Lee, Jeffrey D. James, and Uy Kyoum Kim, "A Reconceptualization of Brand Image," *International Journal of Business Administration*, 5 (4), 2014, pp. 1–11.
35. Arjun Chaudhuri, "How Brand Reputation Affects the Advertising–Brand Equity Link," *Journal of Advertising Research*, 42 (3), May–June 2002, pp. 33–43.
36. Amit Joshi and Dominique M. Hanssens, "The Direct and Indirect Effects of Advertising Spending on Firm Value," *Journal of Marketing*, 74 (1), January 2010, pp. 20–33.
37. Justin Dallaire, "Belairdirect Goes Beyond the Stadium," *Strategy*, October 12, 2018.
38. Kristin Laird, "Products of the Year," *Marketing Magazine*, May 2014, pp. 42–43.
39. Megan Hayes, "Marketers of the Year: Sandra Sanderson Keeps Shoppers Fabulous," *Strategy*, December 7, 2012.
40. "High Expectations," *Strategy*, June 2017, p. 34.
41. Josh Kolm, "Telus Assembles a Team of Storytellers," *Strategy*, February 21, 2018.
42. Justin Dallaire, "Telus Ramps Up Efforts Against Cyberbullying," *Strategy*, June 18, 2018.
43. Russ Martin, "Influential Partners," *Marketing Magazine*, September 2014.
44. John R. Rossiter and Larry Percy, "How the Roles of Advertising Merely Appear to Have Changed," *International Journal of Advertising*, 32 (3), January 2013, pp. 391–398.
45. Michaela Draganska, Wesley R. Hartmann, and Gena Stanglein, "Internet Versus Television Advertising: A Brand-Building Comparison," *Journal of Marketing Research*, 51 (5), October 2014, pp. 578–590. Issac M. Dinner, Harald J. Van Heerde, and Scott A. Neslin, "Driving Online and Offline Sales: The Cross-Channel Effects of Traditional, Online Display, and Paid Search Advertising," *Journal of Marketing Research*, 51 (5), October 2014, pp. 527–545.
46. Patti Summerfield, "Schneiders Stays True to Tradition," *Strategy*, January 2017.
47. David Brown, "Rogers Media," *Marketing Magazine*, November 14, 2011.
48. Don E. Schultz, "Integrated Marketing Communications: Maybe Definition Is in the Point of View," *Marketing News*, January 18, 1993, p. 17.
49. Don Shultz and Philip Kitchen, "Integrated Marketing Communications in US Advertising Agencies: An Exploratory Study," *Journal of Advertising Research*, 37 (5), September–October 1997, pp. 7–18.
50. Tom Duncan and Sandra E. Moriarty, "A Communication-Based Model for Managing Relationships," *Journal of Marketing*, 62 (2), April 1998, pp. 1–13.
51. Joep P. Cornelissen and Andrew R. Lock, "Theoretical Concept or Management Fashion? Examining the Significance of IMC," *Journal of Advertising Research*, 40 (5), September–October 2000, pp. 7–15.
52. Harlan E. Spotts, David R. Lambert, and Mary L. Joyce, "Marketing Déjà Vu: The Discovery of Integrated Marketing Communications," *Journal of Marketing Education*, 20 (3), December 1998, pp. 210–218.
53. Don E. Schultz, "IMC Receives More Appropriate Definition," *Marketing News*, September 15, 2004, pp. 8–9.
54. Dong Hwan Lee and Chan Wook Park, "Conceptualization and Measurement of Multidimensionality of Integrated Marketing

Communications," *Journal of Advertising Research, 47* (3), September 2007, pp. 222–236.

55. Mike Reid, Sandra Luxton, and Felix Mavondo, "The Relationship Between Integrated Marketing Communication, Market Orientation, and Brand Orientation," *Journal of Advertising, 34* (4), Winter 2005, pp. 11–23.

56. George Low, "Correlates of Integrated Marketing Communications," *Journal of Advertising Research, 40* (3), January–February 2000, pp. 27–39.

57. Philip J. Kitchen, Joanne Brignell, Tao Li, and Graham Spickett Jones, "The Emergence of IMC: A Theoretical Perspective," *Journal of Advertising Research, 44* (1), March 2004, pp. 19–30.

58. Mike Reid, "Performance Auditing of Integrated Marketing Communication (IMC) Actions and Outcome," *Journal of Advertising, 34* (4), Winter 2005, pp. 41–54.

59. Sandra Luxton, Mike Reid, and Felix Mavondo, "Integrated Marketing Communication Capability and Brand Performance," *Journal of Advertising, 44* (1), Winter 2015, pp. 37–46.

60. Mart Ots and Gergely Nyilasy, "IMC: Why Does It Fail?" *Journal of Advertising Research, 54* (2) June 2015, pp. 132–145.

61. Yoram Wind and Catherine Findiesen Hays, "Of the Beyond Advertising Paradigm," *Journal of Advertising Research, 45* (2), June 2016, pp. 142–158.

62. Rajeev Bata and Kevin Lane Keller, "Integrating Marketing Communications: New Findings, New Lessons, and New Ideas," *Journal of Marketing, 80* (6), November 2016, pp. 122–145.

63. Adrian Payne and Pennie Flow, "Strategic Framework for Customer Relationship Management," *Journal of Marketing, 69* (4), October 2005, pp. 167–176.

64. Jonathan R. Capulsky and Michael J. Wolfe, "Relationship Marketing: Positioning for the Future," *Journal of Business Strategy, 11* (4), July–August 1991, pp. 16–26.

65. Jennifer Horn, "Gamification Is Everywhere," *Strategy,* June 2015, p. 16; Tanya Kostiw, "Getting in on the Action," *Strategy,* June 2015, p. 20; Jennifer Horn, "Lucile Bousquet Shows Her Game Face," *Strategy,* December 2013/January 2014, p. 47; Megan Haynes, "Ubisoft Taps the Everyday Hacktivist," *Strategy,* September 2013, p. 22; "Ubisoft Shifts Its Focus to Fans on Campus," *Strategy,* April 2013, p. 16.

66. Susan Krashinsky, "McCain Aims to Bring Warmth Back to the Frozen Food Aisle," *The Globe and Mail,* August 6, 2015.

67. Kristin Laird, "Warming Up a Brand," *Marketing,* September 2014, pp. 8–9.

68. Eve Lazarus, "Tourist Contraction," *Marketing Magazine,* November 28, 2011.

69. Cassies.ca, http://cassies.ca/Entry/viewcase/17506

70. Michel Wedel and P.K. Kannan, "Marketing Analytics for Data-Rich Environments," *Journal of Marketing, 80* (6), November 2016, pp. 97–121.

CHAPTER TWO

1. Alvin J. Silk, "Build It, Buy It or Both? Rethinking the Sourcing of Advertising Services," *International Journal of Marketing Studies, 8* (1), February 2016, pp. 1–13.

2. Sharon Horsky, Steven C. Michael, and Alvin J. Silk, "The Internalization of Advertising Services: An Inter-Industry Analysis," *Review of Marketing Science, 10* (1), 2012, pp. 1–33.

3. Val Maloney, "How Saje Struck Oil," *Strategy,* October 2017, p. 35.

4. M. Louise Ripley, "What Kind of Companies Take Their Advertising In-House?" *Journal of Advertising Research, 31* (5), October/November 1991, pp. 73–80.

5. https://acaweb.ca/en/resource/searching-for-a-marketing-communications-agency-partner/

6. Russ Martin, "An Absolutely Great Year," *Marketing Magazine,* January/February 2014, pp. 18–19, 21–22; "Prayer Is Not a Content Strategy," *Marketing Magazine,* January/February 2014, pp. 23–25; David Brown, "Sid Lee vs. The World," *Marketing Magazine,* January 16, 2012; Nicholas Van Praet, "Status Quo Sucks for Petite Sid Lee," *National Post,* February 24, 2012.

7. Susan Krashinsky, "The Animals Will Stay, but Telus's Ad Business Is Changing Hands," *The Globe and Mail,* June 27, 2014.

8. Megan Haynes, "DDB's Partner Quest," *Strategy,* November 2014, p. A.48.

9. Jennifer Horn, "2014 Agency of the Year," *Strategy,* November 2014, p. 21; Tanya Kostiw, "Participation Is King," *Strategy,* June 2015, p. 31; Jennifer Horn, "Old Brands, New Tricks," *Strategy,* June 2015, p. 26; "Grand Prix Gold Idea Canadian Tire Tests the Limit," *Strategy,* May 2015, p. 21.

10. http://strategyonline.ca/2018/04/20/the-2018-agency-family-tree/

11. Susan Krashinsky, "Global Firm Havas Looks to Double Its Size in Canada," *The Globe and Mail,* December 16, 2014, p. B5.

12. Alvin J. Silk and Charles King III, "How Concentrated Is the U.S. Advertising and Marketing Services Industry? Myth Versus Reality," *Journal of Current Issues & Research in Advertising, 34* (1), 2013, pp. 166–193.

13. Susan Krashinsky, "Ad Agency Young & Rubicam to Operate Under Taxi Canada Name," *The Globe and Mail,* July 6, 2015.

14. Melinda Mattos, "Canadian Agencies Go Global," *Strategy,* June 3, 2011, p. 8; David Brown, "Sid Lee vs. The World," *Marketing Magazine,* January 16, 2012; Bertrand Marotte, "Sid Lee's Texas Office Builds on Its Global Ambitions," *The Globe and Mail,* May 5, 2011.

15. David Parker, "Ad Agency Expands Ties With Travel Alberta," *Calgary Herald,* August 30, 2018, p. A13.

16. Megan Hayes, "What Does It Take to Brand an Agency," *Strategy,* March 2018, p. 14.

17. David Ebner, "Old-School WPP Grapples With a New Class of Advertising Heavyweights," *The Globe and Mail,* September 13, 2018.

18. Tanya Kostiw, "John St.'s Appetite for Acceleration," *Strategy,* November 2014, p. A.28.

19. Jon Steel, *Truth, Lies & Advertising: The Art of Account Planning* (New York: Wiley, 1998).

20. Megan Hayes, "Inside Agencies' Best Laid Plans," *Strategy,* March 2017, p. 30.

21. "Rethink and Develop," *Strategy,* March 2017, p. 24.

22. Susan Krashinsky, "Two Ad Agencies Become One," *The Globe and Mail,* July 16, 2012, p. B3.

23. Jennifer Horn, "From A to Zulu," *Strategy,* November 2014, p. A.42.

24. Josh Kolm, "Planning for Success at PHD," *Strategy,* November 2014, p. A.44.

25. Val Maloney, "OMD Turns Up the Heat on Tech," *Strategy,* November 2014, p. A.32.

26. Tanya Kostiw, "Narrative Fashions Its Own Storyline," *Strategy,* November 2014, p. A.46.

27. Val Maloney, "MEC's Ground-Breaking Year," *Strategy,* November 2014, p. A.52.

28. Simon Houpt, "Beyond Advertising," *Strategy,* June 3, 2011, p. 39.

29. Susan Krashinsky, "What's an Ad Worth? How Canada's Mad Men and Women Get Paid," *Globe and Mail,* August 22, 2013.

30. Susan Krashinsky, "What's an Ad Worth? How Canada's Mad Men and Women Get Paid," *Globe and Mail,* August 22, 2013.

31. Susan Krashinsky, "What's an Ad Worth? How Canada's Mad Men and Women Get Paid," *Globe and Mail,* August 22, 2013.

32. George Nguyen, "Saying No to Pitches," *Strategy,* April 2014, p. 10.

33. https://acaweb.ca/en/resource/improving-the-marketing-communications-value-chain/

34. Susan Krashinsky, "What's an Ad Worth? How Canada's Mad Men and Women Get Paid," *Globe and Mail,* August 22, 2013.

35. Fred Beard, "Marketing Client Role Ambiguity as a Source of Dissatisfaction in Client–Ad Agency Relationships," *Journal of Advertising Research, 36* (5), September/October 1996, pp. 9–20; Paul Michell, Harold Cataquet, and Stephen Hague, "Establishing the Causes of Disaffection in Agency–Client Relations," *Journal of Advertising Research, 32* (2), March–April 1992, pp. 41–48; Peter Doyle, Marcel Corstiens, and Paul Michell, "Signals of Vulnerability in Agency–Client Relations," *Journal of Marketing, 44* (4), Fall 1980, pp. 18–23; Daniel B. Wackman, Charles Salmon, and Caryn C. Salmon, "Developing an Advertising Agency–Client Relationship," *Journal of Advertising Research, 26* (6), December 1986/January 1987, pp. 21–29.

36. Mukund S. Kulkarni, Premal P. Vora, and Terence A. Brown, "Firing Advertising Agencies," *Journal of Advertising, 32* (3), Fall 2003, pp. 77–86.

37. Chris Powell, "The Beer Necessities," *Strategy,* May 2017, p. 39.

38. Matthew Chung, "Veritas Expands Its Influence," *Strategy,* November 2014, p. A.54.

39. Russ Martin, "Porsche Canada Selects Red Urban and Canadian AOR," *Marketing Magazine,* March 17, 2014.

40. www.Lg2boutique.com.

41. Val Maloney, "Media's New Seat at the Table," *Strategy*, June 2017, p. 38.

42. Jeff Fraser, "Good Friends, Big Goals and a Little Extra Flair," *Marketing Magazine*, February/March, 2015, pp. 26–28, 30; Matthew Chung, "TJ Flood Scores an All-Star Strategy," *Strategy*, December 2014, p. 23; Matthew Chung, "Creating the Next Generation," *Strategy*, December 2014, p. 52.

43. Danny Kucharsky, "Worldly Experience," *Marketing Magazine*, July 2014, pp. 8–9.

44. Emily Wexler, "North Strategic Does It Their Way," *Strategy*, November 2014, p. A.36.

45. Emily Wexler, "PR AOY Gold Cases," *Strategy*, November 2014, p. A.38.

46. Megan Haynes, "Think Like an Agency, Act Like Lg2," *Strategy*, November 2014, p. A.25.

47. Harmeet Singh, "Cara's Quest for Relevance," *Strategy*, August 2017, p. 10.

48. Josh Kolm, "The Agile Storyteller," *Strategy*, June 2017, p. 18.

49. Justin Dallaire, "In the Kitchen With Bob Park," *Strategy*, April 2018, p. 10.

50. Philip J. Kitchen and Don E. Schultz, "A Multi-Country Comparison of the Drive for IMC," *Journal of Advertising Research, 39* (1), January/February 1999, pp. 21–38; William N. Swain, "Perceptions of IMC After a Decade of Development: Who's at the Wheel and How Can We Measure Success?" *Journal of Advertising Research, 44* (1), March 2004, pp. 46–67.

51. David N. McArthur and Tom Griffin, "A Marketing Management View of Integrated Marketing Communications," *Journal of Advertising Research, 37* (5), September/October 1997, pp. 19–26.

52. http://www.ana.net/content/show/id/enhancing-relationships.

53. Megan Haynes, "The Creative Wild West," *Strategy*, June 2014, p. 16.

54. Marlene S. Neill and Erin Schauster, "Playing Nice in the Sandbox: Is Collaboration Among Advertising and Public Relations Agencies the Same as Integration?" *Journal of Current Issues and Research in Advertising, 39* (2), 2018, pp. 140–159.

55. Jennifer Horn, "The State of the Marketing Landscape," *Strategy*, January 2019, p. 30.

56. Jennifer Horn, "A Snapshot of the Agency Landscape," *Strategy*, March 2018, p. 30.

CHAPTER THREE

1. David Court, Dave Elzinga, Susan Mulder, and Ole Jorgen Vetvik, "The Consumer Decision Journey," http://www.mckinsey.com/insights/marketing_sales/the_consumer_decision_journey.

2. Katherine N. Lemon and Peter C. Verhoef, "Understanding Customer Experience Throughout the Customer Journey," *Journal of Marketing, 80* (6), November 2016, pp. 69–96.

3. Venkatesh Shankar, Mirella Kleijnen, Suresh Ramanathan, Ross Rizley, Steve Holland, and Shawn Morrissey, "Mobile Shopper Marketing: Key Issues, Current Insights, and Future Research Avenues," *Journal of Interactive Marketing, 34* (2), May 2016, pp. 37–48.

4. Ho Kim and Dominique M. Hanssens, "Advertising and Word of Mouth Effects on Pre-launch Consumer Interest and Initial Sales of Experience Products," *Journal of Interactive Marketing, 37* (1), February 2017, pp. 57–74.

5. Mingyung Kim, Jeeyeon Kim, Jeonghye Choi, and Minakshi Trivedi, "Mobile Shopping Through Applications: Understanding Application Possession and Mobile Purchase," *Journal of Interactive Marketing, 39* (3), August 2017, pp. 55–68.

6. Manjit S. Yadav, Kristine de Valck, Thorsten Hennig-Thurau, Donna L. Hoffman, and Martin Spann, "Social Commerce: A Contingency Framework for Assessing Marketing Potential," *Journal of Interactive Marketing, 27* (4), November 2013, pp. 311–323.

7. A. H. Maslow, "'Higher' and 'Lower' Needs," *Journal of Psychology, 25* (1948), pp. 433–436.

8. "Investing in Commerce," *Strategy*, January 2019, p. 46.

9. For a historic review of memory and consumer behaviour, see James R. Bettman, "Memory Factors in Consumer Choice: A Review," *Journal of Marketing, 43* (2), Spring 1979, pp. 37–53.

10. Dhruv Grewal, Carl-Philip Ahlborm, Lauren Beielspacher, Stephanie M. Noble, and Jens Nordfalt, "In-Store Mobile Phone Use and Customer Shopping Behavior: Evidence From the Field," *Journal of Marketing 82* (4), July 2018, pp. 102–126.

11. David Thomas, "Getting Social With Automobiles," *Marketing Magazine*, August 2014, pp. 18–19.

12. Amar Cheema and Purushottam Papatla, "Relative Importance of Online Versus Offline Information for Internet Purchases: Product Category and Internet Experience Effects," *Journal of Business Research, 63* (9/10), Spring 2010, pp. 979–985.

13. Todd Powers, Dorothy Advincula, Marnila S. Austin, Stacy Graiko, and Jasper Snyder, "Digital and Social Media in the Purchase Decision Process," *Journal of Advertising Research, 52* (4), December 2012, pp. 479–489.

14. Mark Burgess, "Preparing for Brands That Talk," *Strategy*, October 2017, p. 12.

15. Megan Haynes, "Birks Regains Its Lustre," *Strategy*, December 2014, p. 14.

16. Manjit S. Yadav, Kristine de Valck, Thorsten Hennig-Thurau, Donna L. Hoffman, and Martin Spann, "Social Commerce: A Contingency Framework for Assessing Marketing Potential," *Journal of Interactive Marketing, 27* (4), November 2013, pp. 311–323.

17. Susan Krashinsky, "Dove's Beauty Campaign," *Globe and Mail*, April 9, 2015; Kristin Laird, "The Real Impact of Real Beauty," *Marketing Magazine*, September 2014, pp. 20–23.

18. Jonathan Paul, "Digital Hits the Aisles," *Strategy*, March 1, 2011.

19. Manjit S. Yadav, Kristine de Valck, Thorsten Hennig-Thurau, Donna L. Hoffman, and Martin Spann, "Social Commerce: A Contingency Framework for Assessing Marketing Potential," *Journal of Interactive Marketing, 27* (4), November 2013, pp. 311–323.

20. Richard L. Oliver, *Satisfaction: A Behavioral Perspective on the Consumer* (New York: McGraw-Hill, 1997).

21. John A. Howard and Jagdish N. Sheth, *The Theory of Consumer Behavior* (New York: John Wiley & Sons, 1969).

22. Lyman E. Ostlund, *Role Theory and Group Dynamics in Consumer Behavior: Theoretical Sources*, ed. Scott Ward and Thomas S. Robertson (Englewood Cliffs, NJ: Prentice Hall, 1973), pp. 230–275.

23. Jagdish N. Sheth, "A Theory of Family Buying Decisions," in *Models of Buying Behavior*, ed. Jagdish N. Sheth (New York: Harper & Row, 1974), pp. 17–33.

24. Zachary Anesbury, Maxwell Winchester, and Rachel Kennedy, "Brand User Profiles Seldom Change and Seldom Differ," *Marketing Letters, 28* (4), December 2017, pp. 523–535.

25. Iris Vilnai-Yavetz and Sigal Tifferet, "A Picture Is Worth a Thousand Words: Segmenting Consumers by Facebook Profile Images," *Journal of Interactive Marketing, 32* (4), November 2015, pp. 53–69.

26. "Mass Majority," *Strategy*, January 2018, p. 64.

27. Jeremy Freed, "How Luxury Automakers Are Luring Millennials," *The Globe and Mail*, November 30, 2018, p. D1.

28. Robert Fulford, "From Gen X to Gen Z: The Absurd Alphabetification of Society," *National Post*, June 21, 2014, p. A.16.

29. David Booth, "The New Harley-Davidson: We Are Everyone," *National Post*, March 9, 2012, p. DT2.

30. Megan Haynes, "Brands Tap Into Foodie Culture," *Strategy*, May 2015, p. 12.

31. Michael R. Solomon, *Consumer Behavior: Buying, Having, and Being*, 12th ed. (Pearson Prentice Hall, 2017).

32. Justin Dallaire, "Slashing Through Cultural Trends," *Strategy*, November 2018, p. 8.

33. Chris Daniels, "The Visible Majority," *Marketing Magazine*, March 12, 2012.

34. For an excellent discussion of social class and consumer behaviour, see Richard P. Coleman, "The Continuing Significance of Social Class to Marketing," *Journal of Consumer Research, 10* (3), December 1983, pp. 265–280.

35. Susan Robertson Krashinsky, "Beer Makers Shift Ad Efforts to Tap Female Consumers," *The Globe and Mail*, September 2, 2018, p. B1.

36. Russell Belk, "Situational Variables and Consumer Behavior," *Journal of Consumer Research, 2* (3), December 1975, pp. 157–164.

37. Larry Percy and Richard Rosenbaum-Elliot, *Strategic Advertising Management*, 4th ed. (Oxford University Press, 2012). The first OUP edition (2001) included Rossiter as an author.

38. Harmeet Singh, "Activia Starts the Year in Sync," *Strategy,* January 18, 2017.
39. John Rossiter and Larry Percy, *Advertising Communications and Promotion Management* (McGraw-Hill, 1996). An updated version is Larry Percy and Richard Rosenbaum-Elliot, *Strategic Advertising Management,* 4th ed. (Oxford University Press, 2012). The first OUP edition (2001) included Rossiter as an author.
40. Susan Krashinsky, "Losing Loyalty," *The Globe and Mail,* June 6, 2014, p. B.5.
41. Stephen Beatty, "How to Win Back Your Customers, Toyota-Style," *Marketing Magazine,* May 16, 2011, pp. 22–23.
42. Susan Krashinsky, "RIM's Marketing Challenge: Revive the CrackBerry Addiction," *The Globe and Mail,* January 25, 2012, p. B1.
43. Thomas J. Reynolds and Carol B. Phillips, "In Search of True Brand Equity Metrics: All Market Share Ain't Created Equal," *Journal of Advertising Research,* 45 (2), June 2005, pp. 171–186.
44. Susan Krashinsky, "Loblaw Targets Foodies in Ad Overhaul," *The Globe and Mail,* September 18, 2014, p. B.4.
45. Catherine Phillips, "RBC Still Wants to Help Canadians Get Insurance," *Strategy,* April 27, 2018.
46. Justin Dallaire, "Mini-Wheats Fights the Cold With Hot Milk," *Strategy,* January 2018.
47. Megan Hayes, "Marie-Claudel Lalonde's Winning Odds," *Strategy,* January 2018, p. 29.
48. Megan Hayes, "Andrea Graham's Good-Proof Strategy," *Strategy,* January 2017.
49. Megan Hayes, "A Robo-Advisor's Human Touch," *Strategy,* October 2017, p. 20.
50. Justin Dallaire, "Koho's Gaming Approach to Fintech," *Strategy,* July 2018, p. 10.
51. James Peltier, John A. Schibrowsky, Don E. Shultz and Debra Zahay "Interactive IMC: The Relational–Transactional Continuum and the Synergistic Use of Customer Data," *Journal of Advertising Research,* 46 (2), June 2006, pp. 146–159.

CHAPTER FOUR

1. Wilbur Schram, *The Process and Effects of Mass Communications* (Urbana: University of Illinois Press, 1955).
2. Russ Martin, "Stand Up and Say Something," *Marketing Magazine,* February/March 29, 2015; Tanya Kostiw, "Normalizing Today's Normal," *Strategy,* April 2015, p. 16; Tanya Kostiw, "Cheerios' Anti-Diet Mission," *Strategy,* July 2015, p. 9.
3. David G. Mick, "Consumer Research and Semiotics: Exploring the Morphology of Signs, Symbols, and Significance," *Journal of Consumer Research, 13* (2), September 1986, pp. 196–213; Edward F. McQuarrie and David Glen Mick, "Figures of Rhetoric in Advertising Language," *Journal of Consumer Research, 22* (4), March 1996, pp. 424–438.
4. Megan Hayes, "Brand Storytelling Gets Seriously Tech-ified," *Strategy,* August 29, 2012.
5. Chris Powell, "Subaru Canada Sizzles With New Campaign," *Marketing Magazine,* July 6, 2012; Jeromy Lloyd, "2012 Marketers of the Year Shortlist: Subaru," *Marketing Magazine,* November 14, 2012; Alicia Androich, "Holy Holograms! *The Grid* Gets Special Cover Treatment," *Marketing Magazine,* June 20, 2012.
6. Emily Jackson, "Shopper Marketing Techs Up," *Strategy,* August 29, 2012.
7. Gian M. Fulgoni and Andrew Lipsman, "Digital Word of Mouth and Its Offline Amplification," *Journal of Advertising Research,* 55 (1), March 2015, pp. 18–21; Dee T. Allsop, Bryce R. Bassett, and James A. Hoskins, "Word-of-Mouth Research: Principles and Applications," *Journal of Advertising Research,* 47 (4), December 2007, pp. 398–411; Barry L. Bayus, "Word of Mouth: The Indirect Effect of Marketing Efforts," *Journal of Advertising Research,* 25 (3), June/July 1985, pp. 31–39; Robert E. Smith and Christine A. Vogt, "The Effects of Integrating Advertising and Negative Word-of-Mouth Communications on Message Processing and Response," *Journal of Consumer Psychology,* 4 (2), 1995, pp. 133–151.
8. Kate Niederhoffer, Rob Mooth, David Wiesenfeld, and Jonathon Gordon, "The Origin and Impact of CPG New-Product Buzz: Emerging Trends and Implications," *Journal of Advertising Research,* 47 (4), December 2007, pp. 420–426.

9. Tralee Pearce, "Word of Mom: Publicity Money Can't Buy," *The Globe and Mail,* November 18, 2011, p. L2.
10. Michael Trusov, Anand V. Bodapati, and Randolph E. Bucklin, "Determining Influential Users in Internet Social Networks," *Journal of Marketing Research,* 47 (3), August 2010, pp. 643–658.
11. Tao Sun, Seounmi Youn, Guohua Wu, and Mana Kuntaraporn, "Online Word-of-Mouth (or Mouse): An Exploration of Its Antecedents and Consequences," *Journal of Computer Mediated Communication,* 11 (4), July 2006, pp. 1104–1127.
12. Pranjal Gupta and Judy Harris, "How e-WOM Recommendations Influence Product Consideration and Quality of Choice: A Motivation to Process Information Perspective," *Journal of Business Research,* 63 (9/10), September 2010, pp. 1041–1049.
13. Emily Wexler, "Dove's Online Song and Dance," *Strategy,* April 1, 2011, p. 10.
14. John E. Hogan, Katherine N. Lemon, and Barak Libai, "Quantifying the Ripple: Word-of-Mouth and Advertising Effectiveness," *Journal of Advertising Research,* 44 (3), September 2004, pp. 271–280.
15. Jeffrey Graham and William Havlena, "Finding the Missing Link: Advertising's Impact on Word of Mouth, Web Searches, and Site Visits," *Journal of Advertising Research,* 47 (4), December 2007, pp. 427–435.
16. Ed Keller and Brad Fay, "The Role of Advertising in Word-of-Mouth," *Journal of Advertising Research,* 49 (2), June 2009, pp. 154–163.
17. Ed Keller and Brad Fay, "Word-of-Mouth Advocacy," *Journal of Advertising Research,* 52 (4), December 2012, pp. 459–464.
18. Robert Allen King, Pradeep Racherla, and Victoria D. Bush, "What We Know and Don't Know About Online Word-of-Mouth: A Review and Synthesis of the Literature," *Journal of Interactive Marketing,* 28 (3), August 2014, pp. 167–183.
19. Megan Hayes, "Volkswagen Drives Into the Mainstream," *Strategy,* April 2014.
20. Simon Houpt, "Budding Filmmakers Need Not Apply," *The Globe and Mail,* July 14, 2011.
21. Colin Campbell, Leyland F. Pitt, Michael Parent, and Pierre R. Berthon, "Understanding Consumer Conversations Around Ads in a Web 2.0 World," *Journal of Advertising,* 40 (1), Spring 2011, pp. 87–102.
22. Tim Dolan, "The Problem With Dropping the D-word," *Strategy,* January 4, 2019.
23. E. K. Strong, *The Psychology of Selling* (New York: McGraw-Hill, 1925), p. 9.
24. Jonathan Paul, "Value Targeting: Top Youth Brands' Niche Connection Plans," *Strategy,* April 1, 2011, p. 34.
25. Robert J. Lavidge and Gary A. Steiner, "A Model for Predictive Measurements of Advertising Effectiveness," *Journal of Marketing,* 24 (4), October 1961, pp. 59–62.
26. Jonathan Paul, "Value Targeting: Top Youth Brands' Niche Connection Plans," *Strategy,* April 1, 2011, p. 34.
27. William J. McGuire, "An Information Processing Model of Advertising Effectiveness," in *Behavioral and Management Science in Marketing,* ed. Harry J. Davis and Alvin J. Silk (New York: Ronald Press, 1978), pp. 156–180.
28. "Canada's Most Trusted Brands in 2011," *Marketing Magazine,* May 16, 2011, pp. 17–21.
29. Judith L. Zaichkowsky, "Conceptualizing Involvement," *Journal of Advertising,* 15 (2), January 1986, pp. 4–14; Judith L. Zaichkowsky, "The Personal Involvement Inventory: Reduction, Revision, and Application to Advertising," *Journal of Advertising,* 23 (4), December 1994, pp. 59–70.
30. Michael L. Ray, "Communication and the Hierarchy of Effects," in *New Models for Mass Communication Research,* ed. P. Clarke (Beverly Hills, CA: Sage, 1973), pp. 147–175.
31. DeAnna S. Kempf and Russell N. Laczniak, "Advertising's Influence on Subsequent Product Trial Processing," *Journal of Advertising,* 30 (3), Fall 2001, pp. 27–38.
32. Herbert E. Krugman, "The Impact of Television Advertising: Learning Without Involvement," *Public Opinion Quarterly,* 29 (3), Fall 1965, pp. 349–356.
33. Scott A. Hawkins and Stephen J. Hoch, "Low-Involvement Learning: Memory Without Evaluation," *Journal of Consumer Research,* 19 (2), September 1992, pp. 212–225.

34. Harmeet Singh, "Walmart's Refresh," *Strategy*, May 28, 2015.
35. William M. Weilbacher, "Point of View: Does Advertising Cause a 'Hierarchy of Effects'?" *Journal of Advertising Research, 41* (6), November/ December 2001, pp. 19–26; Thomas E. Barry, "In Defense of the Hierarchy of Effects: A Rejoinder to Weilbacher," *Journal of Advertising Research, 42* (3), May/June 2002, pp. 44–47; William M. Weilbacher, "Weilbacher Comments on 'In Defense of the Hierarchy of Effects'," *Journal of Advertising Research, 42* (3), May/ June 2002, pp. 48–49; William M. Weilbacher, "How Advertising Affects Consumers," *Journal of Advertising Research, 43* (2), June 2003, pp. 231–234.
36. Demetrios Vakratsas and Tim Ambler, "How Advertising Works: What Do We Really Know?" *Journal of Marketing, 63* (1), January 1999, pp. 26–43.
37. Anthony A. Greenwald, "Cognitive Learning, Cognitive Response to Persuasion and Attitude Change," in *Psychological Foundations of Attitudes,* ed. A. G. Greenwald, T. C. Brock, and T. W. Ostrom (New York: Academic Press, 1968); Peter L. Wright, "The Cognitive Processes Mediating Acceptance of Advertising," *Journal of Marketing Research, 10* (1), February 1973, pp. 53–62; Brian Wansink, Michael L. Ray, and Rajeev Batra, "Increasing Cognitive Response Sensitivity," *Journal of Advertising, 23* (2), June 1994, pp. 65–76.
38. Melissa Dunne, "Sharon Macleod Bridges to Next Gen Man," *Strategy*, January 2019, p. 16.
39. Peter Wright, "Message Evoked Thoughts, Persuasion Research Using Thought Verbalizations," *Journal of Consumer Research, 7* (2), September 1980, pp. 151–175.
40. Morris Holbrook and Rajeev Batra, "Assessing the Role of Emotions as Mediators of Consumer Responses to Advertising," *Journal of Consumer Research, 14* (3), December 1987, pp. 404–420.
41. Raffi Chowdhury, Douglas Olson, and John Pracejuc, "Affective Responses to Images in Print Advertising," *Journal of Advertising, 37* (3), Fall 2008, pp. 7–18.
42. Gordon W. Allport, "Attitudes," in *Handbook of Social Psychology*, ed. C. M. Murchison (Winchester, MA: Clark University Press, 1935), p. 810.
43. Martin Fishbein and Icek Ajzen, *Predicting and Changing Behaviour: The Reasoned Action Approach* (New York: Psychology Press, 2010).
44. Scott B. Mackenzie, Richard J. Lutz, and George E. Belch, "The Role of Attitude Toward the Ad as a Mediator of Advertising Effectiveness: A Test of Competing Explanations," *Journal of Marketing Research, 23* (2), May 1986, pp. 130–143; Rajeev Batra and Michael L. Ray, "Affective Responses Mediating Acceptance of Advertising," *Journal of Consumer Research, 13* (2), September 1986, pp. 234–249.
45. Tim Ambler and Tom Burne, "The Impact of Affect on Memory of Advertising," *Journal of Advertising Research, 39* (3), March/April 1999, pp. 25–34.
46. Abhilasha Mehta, "Advertising Attitudes and Advertising Effectiveness," *Journal of Advertising Research, 40* (3), May–June 2000, pp. 67–72.
47. David J. Moore and William D. Harris, "Affect Intensity and the Consumer's Attitude Toward High Impact Emotional Advertising Appeals," *Journal of Advertising, 25* (2), Summer 1996, pp. 37–50; Andrew A. Mitchell and Jerry C. Olson, "Are Product Attribute Beliefs the Only Mediator of Advertising Effects on Brand Attitude?" *Journal of Marketing Research, 18* (3), August 1981, pp. 318–332.
48. David J. Moore, William D. Harris, and Hong C. Chen, "Affect Intensity: An Individual Difference Response to Advertising Appeals," *Journal of Consumer Research, 22* (2), September 1995, pp. 154–164; Julie Edell and Marian C. Burke, "The Power of Feelings in Understanding Advertising Effects," *Journal of Consumer Research, 14* (3), December 1987, pp. 421–433.
49. Richard E. Petty and John T. Cacioppo, "Central and Peripheral Routes to Persuasion: Application to Advertising," in *Advertising and Consumer Psychology*, ed. Larry Percy and Arch Woodside (Lexington, MA: Lexington Books, 1983), pp. 3–23.
50. Gerald J. Gorn, "The Effects of Music in Advertising on Choice: A Classical Conditioning Approach," *Journal of Marketing, 46* (1), Winter 1982, pp. 94–101; James J. Kellaris, Anthony D. Cox, and Dena Cox, "The Effect of Background Music on Ad Processing: A Contingency Explanation," *Journal of Marketing, 57* (4), Fall 1993, p. 114.
51. Richard E. Petty, John T. Cacioppo, and David Schumann, "Central and Peripheral Routes to Advertising Effectiveness: The Moderating Role of Involvement," *Journal of Consumer Research, 10* (2), September 1983, pp. 135–146.
52. Deborah J. MacInnis and Bernard J. Jaworski, "Information Processing From Advertisements: Toward an Integrative Framework," *Journal of Marketing, 53* (4), October 1989, pp. 1–23.
53. Demetrios Vakratsas and Tim Ambler, "How Advertising Works: What Do We Really Know?" *Journal of Marketing, 63* (1), January 1999, pp. 26–43.
54. John Rossiter and Larry Percy, *Advertising Communications and Promotion Management* (McGraw-Hill, 1996). An updated version is Larry Percy and Richard Rosenbaum-Elliot, *Strategic Advertising Management,* 4th ed. (Oxford University Press, 2012). The first OUP edition (2001) included Rossiter as an author.
55. Stephen D. Rappaport, "Lessons From Online Practice: New Advertising Models," *Journal of Advertising Research, 47* (2), June 2007, pp. 135–141.
56. Martin Eisend and Farid Tarrahi, "The Effectiveness of Advertising: A Meta-Meta Analysis of Advertising Inputs and Outcomes," *Journal of Advertising, 45* (4), October 2016, pp. 519–531.
57. Figure 4-7 is a shorter adaptation from William J. McGuire, "An Information Processing Model of Advertising Effectiveness," in *Behavioral and Management Science in Marketing*, ed. Harry J. Davis and Alvin J. Silk (New York: Ronald Press, 1978), pp. 156–180.

CHAPTER FIVE

1. http://cassies.ca/content/caselibrary/winners/2011_Hellmanns.pdf.
2. Hollie Shaw, "Data Overload: Marketers Not Ready for Digital Influx," *National Post*, October 28, 2011, p. FP7.
3. Donald S. Tull, "The Carry-Over Effect of Advertising," *Journal of Marketing, 29* (2), April 1965, pp. 46–53.
4. Darral G. Clarke, "Econometric Measurement of the Duration of Advertising Effect on Sales," *Journal of Marketing Research, 23* (4), November 1976, pp. 345–357.
5. Gerard J. Tellis, *Effective Advertising* (Thousand Oaks, California: Sage Publications Inc., 2004).
6. Jennifer Holt, "Cause Action Awards 2015," *Strategy*, April 2015, p. 22.
7. Russell H. Colley, *Defining Advertising Goals for Measured Advertising Results* (New York: Association of National Advertisers, 1961).
8. "Amex Creates a Content Funnel," *Strategy*, March 2017, p. 17.
9. Justin Dallaire, "Breaking Bread With Andrea Hunt," *Strategy*, January 2018, p. 26.
10. Stewart H. Britt, "Are So-Called Successful Advertising Campaigns Really Successful?" *Journal of Advertising Research, 9* (2), June 1969, pp. 3–9.
11. Steven W. Hartley and Charles H. Patti, "Evaluating Business-to-Business Advertising: A Comparison of Objectives and Results," *Journal of Advertising Research, 28* (2), April/May 1988, pp. 21–27.
12. Study cited in Robert F. Lauterborn, "How to Know If Your Advertising Is Working," *Journal of Advertising Research, 25* (1), February/March 1985, pp. RC 9–11.
13. John Rossiter and Larry Percy, *Advertising Communications and Promotion Management* (McGraw-Hill, 1996). An updated version is Larry Percy and Richard Rosenbaum-Elliot, *Strategic Advertising Management,* 4th ed. (Oxford University Press, 2012). The first OUP edition (2001) included Rossiter as an author.
14. Russ Martin, "Boston Pizza Promises to Turn Its Customers Into Fans," *Marketing Magazine*, February 20, 2015; "Boston Pizza's Epic Pizzaburger Launch," *Strategy*, February/March 2014; Tanya Kostiw, "Boston Pizza's Big 5-0," *Strategy*, April 2014; Susan Krashinsky, "Boston Pizza Ad Makes Man, Woman and Child a Fan," *Globe and Mail*, February 26, 2015.
15. Jennifer Horn, "Connie Morrison Breaks Bread With Skeptics," *Strategy*, December 2014.
16. Susan Krashinsky, "To Catch Coke, Pepsi Dusts Off an Old Trick," *The Globe and Mail*, May 17, 2012, p. B3.
17. Eric Lam, "Curtain Still Rises," *National Post*, June 4, 2011, p. FP6.
18. Alicia Androich, "Around and Around We Go," *Marketing Magazine*, June 4, 2012.

19. Matthew Chung, "TJ Flood Scores an All-Star Strategy," *Strategy*, December 19, 2014.
20. Michelle Warren, "Engagement Marketing: The Back-to-School Edition," *Marketing Magazine*, September 12, 2011, pp. 40–43.
21. Brian Wansink and Michael Ray, "Estimating an Advertisement's Impact on One's Consumption of a Brand," *Journal of Advertising Research*, 40 (6), November–December 2000.
22. Susan Krashinsky, "Natural Selection: McDonald's, Coke Hit by Healthy Habits," *The Globe and Mail*, October 22, 2014, p. B1.
23. Kelly Vaughn, Virginia Bell, and Jenni Romaniuk, "Can Brand Users Really Remember Advertising More Than Non-Users?" *Journal of Advertising Research*, 56 (3), September 2016, pp. 311–319.
24. Frank Harrison, "Digging Deeper Into the Empirical Generalizations of Recall," *Journal of Advertising Research*, 53 (2), June 2103, pp. 181–185.
25. Kristin Laird, "Acing the Test," *Marketing Magazine*, January/February 2014.
26. http://cassies.ca/entry/viewcase/7111.
27. http://cassies.ca/content/caselibrary/winners/2011_Activia.pdf.
28. Kristin Laird, "Everything You Want in a Drug Store," *Marketing Magazine*, December 2012.
29. Jeremy Cato, "Mazda Needs the BMW Blueprint," *The Globe and Mail*, March 9, 2012, p. D10.

CHAPTER SIX

1. Susan Krashinsky, "Air Canada Unveils a Global Brand Makeover," *The Globe and Mail*, May 19, 2014, p. B1.
2. Harmeet Singh, "Sephora Earns Its Stripes," *Strategy*, May 2017, p. 35.
3. Megan Haynes, "Birks Regains Its Lustre," *Strategy*, December 2014, p. A14.
4. Charles Blankson, Stavros P. Kalafatis, Julian Ming-Sung, and Costas Hadjicharalambous, "Impact of Positioning Strategies on Corporate Performance," *Journal of Advertising Research*, 48 (1), March 2008, pp. 106–122; Charles Blankson and Stavros P. Kalafatis, "Congruence Between Positioning and Brand Advertising," *Journal of Advertising Research*, 47 (1), March 2007, pp. 79–94.
5. Frank Alpert and M. Kim Saxton, "Can Multiple New-Product Messages Attract Different Consumer Segments," *Journal of Advertising Research*, 55 (3), September 2015, pp. 307–321.
6. Jack Trout, "Branding Can't Exist Without Positioning," *Advertising Age*, March 14, 2005, p. 25.
7. Al Ries and Jack Trout, *Positioning: The Battle for Your Mind*, McGraw-Hill, 2001.
8. John Rossiter and Larry Percy, *Advertising Communications and Promotion Management* (McGraw Hill, 1996).
9. Larry Percy and Richard Elliot, *Strategic Advertising Management*, 4th ed. (Oxford University Press, 2012); David Aaker and Christine Moorman, *Strategic Market Management*, 11th ed. (Wiley 2017).
10. Larry Percy and Richard Elliot, *Strategic Advertising Management*, 4th ed. (Oxford University Press, 2012); Orville Walker, Jr., and John Mullins, *Marketing Strategy: A Decision-Focused Approach*, 8th ed. (McGraw-Hill Irwin, 2014).
11. Jose Maurao da Costa Hernandez, Scott A. Wright, and Filipe Feminiano Rodriques, "Attributes Versus Benefits: The Role of Construal Levels and Appeal Type on the Persuasiveness of Marketing Messages," *Journal of Advertising*, 44 (3), July 2015, pp. 243–253.
12. Hollie Shaw, "Sinking Roots in Canada," *National Post*, June 10, 2011, p. FP12.
13. Chris Powell, "Reebok Gets Fired Up in New Hockey Campaign," *Marketing Magazine*, February 5, 2013.
14. http://cassies.ca/winners/2011/cassies.ca/winners/2011Winners/2011_winners_Activia.html.
15. Matthew Chung, "Samsung Builds Up Its Street Cred," *Strategy*, October 2013; Susan Krashinsky, "Samsung Lets Your Avatar Do the Waiting," *The Globe and Mail*, March 27, 2015, p. B5; Jungah Lee, "Samsung to Target Smart Homes," *National Post*, January 5, 2015, p. FP 1.
16. Justin Dallaire, "Becel Promotes Spontaneous Acts of Baking During Holdiays," *Strategy*, December 21, 2018.

17. Susan Krashinsky, ""Nestlé Urges Workaholics to Take a Break," *The Globe and Mail*, March 10, 2014.
18. Brian Wansink and Jennifer Marie Gilmore, "New Uses That Revitalize Old Brands," *Journal of Advertising Research*, 39 (2), April 1999, pp. 90–98.
19. Paul Brent, "Craft Brewers Carve Out a Niche," *National Post*, June 29, 2011, p. AL7; Tanya Kostiw, "Cracking the Craft Beer Category," *Strategy*, July 2014, p. 12.
20. Josh Kolm, "Anheuser–Busch's New Brews," *Strategy*, May 2015, p. A11.
21. "Blizzard Menu Ever," *Strategy*, May 2015, p. A 41.
22. Chris Powell, "Time for a Marketing Makeover at Canada's Big Banks?" *Marketing Magazine*, August, 2014, pp. 20–24.
23. Stephen A. Spiller and Lena Belogolova, "On Consumer Beliefs About Quality and Taste," *Journal of Consumer Research*, 43 (6), April 2017, pp. 970–991.
24. Praveen K. Kopalle, Robert J. Fisher, Bharat L. Sud, and Kersi Antia, "The Effects of Advertised Quality Emphasis and Objective Quality on Sales," *Journal of Marketing*, 81 (2), March 2017, pp. 114–126.
25. Hollie Shaw, "Loblaw's Recipe to Brand Building," *National Post*, April 17, 2014, p. FP. 7.
26. Harmeet Singh, "SodaStream Launches First Canadian Campaign," *Strategy*, October 8, 2015; Justin Dallaire, "SodaStream's Holiday Spot Backs Sustainable Message," *Strategy*, November 16, 2018.
27. Josh Kolm, "Advil Displays Its Feats of Strength," *Strategy*, January 6, 2017; Justin Dallaire, "Advil Shows Brute Strength of New Formulation," *Strategy*, November 1, 2018.
28. Megan Haynes, "Cracker Barrel's Cheesy Repositioning," *Strategy*, May 1, 2015; Susan Krashinsky, "Cracker Barrel Ads Aim to Solidify Reputation as Big Cheese of Quality," *The Globe and Mail*, April 24, 2015.
29. Melissa Dunne, "Anne-Marie Laberge Takes BRP on Ride," *Strategy*, January 2019, p. 23.
30. Russ Martin, "McDonald's Rolls Out the Welcome Mat With New Platform," *Marketing Magazine*, March 3, 2015; Susan Krashinsky, "McDonald's Canada Welcomes Customers With Candid Ad Campaign," *The Globe and Mail*, March, 3, 2015; Nicholas Misketi, "McDonald's Rebrands as Common Ground," *National Post*, March 23, 2015.
31. For a review of multiattribute models, see William L. Wilkie and Edgar A. Pessemier, "Issues in Marketing's Use of Multiattribute Models," *Journal of Marketing Research*, 10 (4), November 1983, pp. 428–441.
32. David Thomas, "Tims in Transition," *Marketing Magazine*, April 2014.
33. Joel Rubinson and Markus Pfeiffer, "Brand Key Performance Indicators as a Force for Brand Equity Management," *Journal of Advertising Research*, 45 (3), June 2005, pp. 187–197.
34. Harmeet Singh, "A&W Stays Rooted in Real," *Strategy*, October 2017, p. 30; "A&W Makes Things Better," *Strategy*, February 12, 2016.
35. Jennifer Horn, "CIBC—Then and Now," *Strategy*, October 2017, p. 52.
36. Based on a case study available at www.cassies.ca.
37. Based on a case study available at www.cassies.ca.
38. Susan Krashinsky, "The Food Industry's 'Real' Message," *The Globe and Mail*, February 23, 2012.
39. Megan Haynes, "Bringing Soup Strategy to a Boil," *Strategy*, January 2017.
40. Josh Kolm, "Telus Hears You Scream," *Strategy*, November 2015.
41. Harmeet Singh, "Telus Goes Deeper Into Choose Happy," *Strategy*, March 2017.
42. Chris Powell, "Van Houtte Explores Coffee Culture in New Video Series," *Marketing Magazine*, March 21, 2013.
43. Kristin Laird, "Cassies Target Newfoundland Tourism Campaign," *Marketing Magazine*, January 24, 2012.
44. Hollie Shaw, "'Wellthy' Trending: Brands Such as Adidas Link Good Health to Status," *National Post Magazine*, April 27, 2012, p. FP6.
45. Susan Krashinsky, "KD's New Pitch," *The Globe and Mail*, July 2014, p. B3.
46. Stefania Moretti, "An Empire State of Mind," *Canadian Business*, March 12, 2013.

CHAPTER SEVEN

1. www.topadexec.com.
2. Jaafar El-Murad and Douglas C. West, "The Definition and Measurement of Creativity: What Do We Know?" *Journal of Advertising Research, 44* (2), June 2004, pp. 188–201.
3. Robert E. Smith, Scott B. MacKenzie, Xiaojing Yang, Laura Buchholz, William K. Darley, and Xiaojing Yang, "Modeling the Determinants and Effects of Creativity in Advertising," *Marketing Science, 26* (6), November–December 2007, pp. 819–833.
4. Robert E. Smith and Xiaojing Yang, "Toward a General Theory of Creativity in Advertising: Examining the Role of Divergence," *Marketing Theory, 4* (1/2), June 2004, pp. 29–55.
5. Visit http://www.absolutad.com to see examples of the campaign.
6. Jeff Cioletti, "In a Changing World, There's Only One Absolut," *Beverage World,* July 2007, pp. 20–25.
7. Emma Hall, "Absolut Taps Into Past to Create a Better Tomorrow and Fight Today's Rivals," *Ad Age,* July 6, 2017.
8. www.absolut.com.
9. Sheila L. Sasser and Scott Koslow, "Desperately Seeking Advertising Creativity," *Journal of Advertising, 37* (4), Winter 2008, pp. 5–19.
10. Leonard N. Reid, Karen Whitehall, and Denise E. DeLorme, "Top-Level Agency Creatives Look at Advertising Creativity Then and Now," *Journal of Advertising, 27* (2), Summer 1998, pp. 1–16.
11. Thomas Bernardin, Paul Kemp-Robertson, David W. Stewart, Yan Cheng, Heather Wan, John R. Rossiter, Sunil Erevelles, Robert Roundtree, George M. Zinkhan, and Nobuyuki Fukawa, "Envisioning the Future of Advertising Creativity Research," *Journal of Advertising, 37* (4), Winter 2008, pp. 131–149.
12. Daniel W. Baack, Rick T. Wilson, and Brian D. Till, "Creativity and Memory Effects," *Journal of Advertising, 37* (4), Winter 2008, pp. 85–94; Brian D. Till and Daniel Baack, "Recall and Persuasion," *Journal of Advertising, 34* (3), Fall 2005, pp. 47–57.
13. Elizabeth C. Hirschman, "Role-Based Models of Advertising Creation and Production," *Journal of Advertising, 18* (4), December 1989, pp. 42–53.
14. Edith G. Smit, Lex Van Meurs, and Peter C. Neijens, "Effects of Advertising Likeability: A-Year Perspective," *Journal of Advertising Research, 46* (1), March 2006, pp. 73–83.
15. Karolien Poel and Siegfried Dewitte, "Getting a Line on Print Ads," *Journal of Advertising, 37* (4), Winter 2008, pp. 63–74.
16. Micael Dahlen, Sara Rosengren, and Fredrick Torn, "Advertising Creativity Matters," *Journal of Advertising Research, 48* (3), September 2008, pp. 19–26.
17. Charles Young, "Creative Differences Between Copywriters and Art Directors," *Journal of Advertising Research, 40* (3), May–June 2000, pp. 19–26.
18. Alisa White and Bruce L. Smith, "Assessing Advertising Creativity Using the Creative Product Semantic Scale," *Journal of Advertising Research, 41* (6), November–December 2001, pp. 27–34; Douglas C. West, Arthur J. Kover, and Alber Caruana, "Practitioner and Customer Views of Advertising Creativity," *Journal of Advertising, 37* (4), Winter 2008, pp. 35–45.
19. Robert E. Smith, Jiemiao Chen, and Xiaojing Yang, "The Impact of Advertising Creativity on the Hierarchy of Effects," *Journal of Advertising, 37* (4), Winter 2008, pp. 47–61.
20. Smith, MacKenzie, Yang, Buchholz, Darley, and Yang, "Modeling the Determinants and Effects of Creativity in Advertising."
21. Swee Hoon Ang, Yih Hwai Lee, and Siew Meng Leong, "The Ad Creativity Cube: Conceptualization and Initial Validation," *Journal of the Academy of Marketing Science, 35* (2), Summer 2007, pp. 220–232; Arthur J. Kover, Stephen M. Goldenberg, and William L. James, "Creativity vs. Effectiveness? An Integrative Classification for Advertising," *Journal of Advertising Research, 35* (6), November/December 1995, pp. 29–38.
22. Smith, MacKenzie, Yang, Buchholz, Darley, and Yang, "Modeling the Determinants and Effects of Creativity in Advertising."
23. David Ogilvy, *Confessions of an Advertising Man* (New York: Atheneum, 1963); Hanley Norins, *The Compleat Copywriter* (New York: McGraw-Hill, 1966).
24. Hank Sneiden, *Advertising Pure and Simple* (New York: ANACOM, 1977).
25. Scott Koslow, Sheila L. Sasser, and Edward A. Riordan, "Do Marketers Get the Advertising They Need or the Advertising They Deserve?" *Journal of Advertising, 35* (3), Fall 2006, pp. 81–101.
26. Kasey Windels and Mark Wilson Stuhlfaut, "Confined Creativity: The Influence of Creative Code Intensity on Risk Taking in Advertising Agencies," *Journal of Current Issues & Research in Advertising, 35* (2), 2014, pp. 147–166.
27. James Webb Young, *A Technique for Producing Ideas,* 3rd ed. (Chicago: Crain Books, 1975), p. 42.
28. W. Glenn Griffin, "From Performance to Mastery: Development Models of the Creative Process," *Journal of Advertising, 37* (4), Winter 2008, pp. 95–108.
29. Arthur J. Kover, "Copywriters' Implicit Theories of Communication: An Exploration," *Journal of Consumer Research, 21* (4), March 1995, pp. 596–611.
30. Sasser and Koslow, "Desperately Seeking Advertising Creativity."
31. Jon Steel, *Truth, Lies and Advertising: The Art of Account Planning* (Wiley, 1998).
32. Eric Haley, Ronald Taylor, and Margaret Morrison, "How Advertising Creatives Define Excellent Planning," *Journal of Current Issues & Research in Advertising, 35* (2), 2014, pp. 167–189.
33. Mark Childs, "The Brief is Dead. Long Live the Brief," *Strategy,* May 30, 2012.
34. Thomas Kenny, "The Human Problem," *Strategy,* August 25, 2015.
35. Chris Powell, "Molson's Travelling Beer Fridge Comes Home for Canada Day," *Marketing Magazine,* June 23, 2014; Susan Krashinsky, "Cheers to a Winning Ad Campaign," *The Globe and Mail,* February 20, 2015, p. B7; Russ Martin, "Molson Brings Back 'I Am Canadian' for Canada Day," *Marketing Magazine,* June 24, 2013; Susan Krashinsky, "Molson's Newest Red Beer Fridge Touts Canada's Multicultural Side," *The Globe and Mail,* June 25, 2015; Susan Krashinsky, "Molson's Takes Online Beer Fridge Ads to Hockey Airwaves—and Points Beyond," *The Globe and Mail,* December 19, 2013.
36. Susan Krashinsky, "For Tough Times, A Sobering Sell," *The Globe and Mail,* January 26, 2012, p. B3; Hollie Shaw, "Need Your Bank Say More?" *National Post,* February 10, 2012, p. FP12.
37. John O'Toole, *The Trouble With Advertising,* 2nd ed. (New York: Random House, 1985), p. 131.
38. Harvey Schachter, "Don't Sell a Brand. Tell a Story," *The Globe and Mail,* March 16, 2015, p. B5.
39. Rosser Reeves, *Reality in Advertising* (New York: Knopf, 1961), pp. 47, 48.
40. Chun-Tuan Chang, Yuan-Ciao Wu, Yu-Kang Lee, and Xing-Yu Chu, "Right Metaphor, Right Place: Choosing a Visual Metaphor on Product Type and Consumer Differences," *International Journal of Advertising, 37* (2), 2018, pp. 309–336.
41. Susan E. Morgan and Tome Reichert, "The Message Is in the Metaphor: Assessing the Comprehension of Metaphors in Advertisements," *Journal of Advertising, 28* (4), Winter 1999, pp. 1–12; Barbara J. Phillips and Edward F. McQuarrie, "Impact of Advertising Metaphors on Consumer Belief," *Journal of Advertising, 38* (1), Spring 2009, pp. 49–61.
42. Margo van Mulken, Andreu van Hooft, and Ulrike Nederstigt, "Finding the Tipping Point: Visual Metaphor and Conceptual Complexity in Advertising," *Journal of Advertising, 43* (4), October 2014, pp. 333–343.
43. Martin Mayer, *Madison Avenue, U.S.A.* (New York: Pocket Books, 1958).
44. Eunjin Kim, S. Ratneshwar, and Ester Thorson, "Why Narrative Ads Work: An Integrated Process Explanation," *Journal of Advertising, 46* (2), April 2017, pp. 238–296.
45. Susan Krashinsky, "An Edge-of-Your-Seat Approach to Ads," *The Globe and Mail,* March 13, 2015, p. B6.
46. Susan Krashinsky, "Sport Chek Feeds Off Raptors' 'We the North' Campaign," *The Globe and Mail,* January 19, 2015, p. B3.
47. Susan Krashinsky, "SickKids Hopes Intimacy Will Drive Charity," *The Globe and Mail,* November 8, 2014, p. A7.
48. Al Ries and Jack Trout, *Positioning: The Battle for Your Mind* (McGraw-Hill, 2001).
49. "Top Shops: How Canada's Production Partners Are Crafting New Brand Narratives," *Strategy,* April 2018, p. 36.
50. Josh Kolm, "BioSteel Goes Mass," *Strategy,* November 21, 2014; John Lorinc, "Goodbye Gatorade: How BioSteel Is (Very Quietly) Taking Over the NHL," *Canadian Business,* April 2, 2015; Susan Krashinsky, "Drink Maker Tickled Pink With Start Endorsements," *The Globe and Mail,* May 15, 2014, p. B12.

51. Timothy R. V. Foster, "The Art & Science of the Advertising Slogan," 2001, www.adslogans.co.uk.

52. Justin Dallaire, "WestJet Rebrands to Reflect Global Ambitions," *Strategy*, October 2018.

53. Melissa Dunne, "Steam Whistle Steams Ahead With New Packaging," *Strategy*, September 2018.

54. Josh Kolm, "Rogers Launches New Company-wide Brand Platform," *Strategy*, May 2018.

55. Chiranjeev Kohli, Sunil Thomas, and Rajneesh Suri, "Are You in Good Hands? Slogan Recall: What Really Matters," *Journal of Advertising Research, 53* (2), March 2013, pp. 31–42.

56. "CASSIES Gold: A&W Makes Things Better," *Strategy*, February 12, 2016; Harmeet Singh, "2017 Brands of the Year: A&W Stays Rooted in Real," *Strategy*, September 26, 2017; Justin Dallaire, "A&W CEO and Marketer to Receive ACA Gold Medal," *Strategy*, September 13, 2018.

57. Josh Kolm, "Telus Puts Canadian Ahead of Its Products," *Strategy*, December 10, 2014; Susan Krashinsky, "The Animals Will Stay, But Telus' Ad Business Is Changing Hands," *The Globe and Mail*, June 27, 2014; Megan Haynes, "Telus Names The&Partnership AOR," *Strategy* June 27, 2014.

58. Josh Kolm, "Going Hands-On With House of Vans," *Strategy*, September 21, 2018.

59. "Cassies Gold: Nissan Conquers All Conditions," *Strategy*, February 2017.

60. Michael Adams, *Fire and Ice* (Penguin, 2003).

61. http://www.environicsinstitute.org/uploads/news/michael%20 adams%20fire%20and%20ice%20revisited%20-%20eag%20user%20 conference%20keynote%20-%20presentation%20nov%204-2013.pdf.

62. Susan Krashinsky, "Maytag Comes Up With a New Canadian Spin Cycle," *The Globe and Mail*, March 2012, p. B6.

63. William L. Wilkie and Paul W. Farris, "Comparative Advertising: Problems and Potential," *Journal of Marketing, 39* (4), October 1975, pp. 7–15.

64. Fred Beard, "Comparative Television Advertising in the United States: A Thirty-Year Update," *Journal of Current Issues & Research in Advertising, 37* (2), 2016, pp. 183–195.

65. For a review of comparative advertising studies, see Cornelia Pechmann and David W. Stewart, "The Psychology of Comparative Advertising," in *Attention, Attitude and Affect in Response to Advertising*, eds. E. M. Clark, T. C. Brock, and D. W. Stewart (Hillsdale, NJ: Lawrence Erlbaum, 1994), pp. 79–96; Thomas S. Barry, "Comparative Advertising: What Have We Learned in Two Decades?" *Journal of Advertising Research, 33* (2), March–April 1993, pp. 19–29.

66. Darrel D. Muehling, Russell N. Laczniak, and Kristine R. Ehrich, "Consumers' Response to Positive and Negative Comparative Advertisements: The Moderating Effect of Current Brand Usage," *Journal of Current Issues and Research in Advertising, 34* (2), pp. 229–246.

67. Fred Beard, "Practitioner Views of Comparative Advertising," *Journal of Advertising Research, 53* (3), September 2013, pp. 313–323.

68. Stuart J. Agres, "Emotion in Advertising: An Agency Point of View," in *Emotion in Advertising: Theoretical and Practical Explanations*, eds. Stuart J. Agres, Julie A. Edell, and Tony M. Dubitsky (Westport, CT: Quorom Books, 1991).

69. Susan Krashinsky, "Google Puts Fizz Back in Classic Coke Ad," *The Globe and Mail*, April 13, 2012, p. B6.

70. Susan Krashinsky, "Getting Emotional," *The Globe and Mail*, May 23, 2014, p. B7.

71. Hamish Pringle and Peter Field, *Brand Immortality, How Brands Can Live Long and Prosper* (London: Kogan Page Limited), 2009.

72. Susan Krashinsky, "Food Makers Put Their Faith in Nostalgia," *The Globe and Mail*, April 3, 2015, p. B4.

73. Susan Krashinsky, "A New Generation of Moms Meets an Old Favourite," *The Globe and Mail*, April 3, 2018, p. B7.

74. Edward Kamp and Deborah J. MacInnis, "Characteristics of Portrayed Emotions in Commercials: When Does What Is Shown in Ads Affect Viewers?" *Journal of Advertising Research, 35* (6), November/ December 1995, pp. 19–28.

75. For a review of research on the effect of mood states on consumer behaviour, see Meryl Paula Gardner, "Mood States and Consumer Behavior: A Critical Review," *Journal of Consumer Research, 12* (3), December 1985, pp. 281–300.

76. Justin Dallaire, "Air Canada Taps the Emotion of Flying Home for the Holidays," *Strategy*, December 20, 2018.

77. Dacher Keltner and Jennifer S. Lerner, "Emotion," *Handbook of Social Psychology*, eds. Susan T. Fiske, Daniel T. Gilbert, and Gardner Lindzey (John Wiley & Sons, 2010).

78. Susan Krashinsky, "Tugging at Our Glowing Heart Strings," *The Globe and Mail*, January 3, 2014, p. B3.

79. Michael L. Ray and William L. Wilkie, "Fear: The Potential of an Appeal Neglected by Marketing," *Journal of Marketing, 34* (1), January 1970, pp. 54–62.

80. Brian Sternthal and C. Samuel Craig, "Fear Appeals Revisited and Revised," *Journal of Consumer Research, 1* (3), December 1974, pp. 22–34.

81. Punam Anand Keller and Lauren Goldberg Block, "Increasing the Persuasiveness of Fear Appeals: The Effect of Arousal and Elaboration," *Journal of Consumer Research, 22* (4), March 1996, pp. 448–460.

82. John F. Tanner, Jr., James B. Hunt, and David R. Eppright, "The Protection Motivation Model: A Normative Mode of Fear Appeals," *Journal of Marketing, 55* (3), July 1991, p. 45.

83. Herbert Jack Rotfeld, "The Textbook Effect: Conventional Wisdom, Myth and Error in Marketing," *Journal of Marketing, 64* (2), April 2000, pp. 122–127.

84. Deepa Venkatesa, "Fisherman's Friend Is Telling a Few Tall Tales," *Strategy*, November 5, 2018.

85. Martin Eisend, "How Humor in Advertising Works: A Meta-analytic Test of Alternative Models," *Marketing Letters, 22*, 2001, pp. 115–132.

86. For a discussion of the use of humour in advertising, see C. Samuel Craig and Brian Sternthal, "Humor in Advertising," *Journal of Marketing, 37* (2), October 1973, pp. 12–18.

87. Harlan E. Spotts, Marc G. Weinberger, and Amy L. Parsons, "Assessing the Use and Impact of Humour on Advertising Effectiveness: A Contingency Approach," *Journal of Advertising, 26* (3), Fall 1997, pp. 17–32.

88. Yong Zhang, "Response to Humorous Advertising: The Moderating Effect of Need for Cognition," *Journal of Advertising, 25* (1), Spring 1996, pp. 15–32; Marc G. Weinberger and Charles S. Gulas, "The Impact of Humor in Advertising: A Review," *Journal of Advertising, 21* (4), December 1992, pp. 35–59.

89. Marc G. Weinberger and Leland Campbell, "The Use of Humor in Radio Advertising," *Journal of Advertising Research, 30* (6), December 1990–January 1991, pp. 44–52.

90. Thomas J. Madden and Marc C. Weinberger, "Humor in Advertising: A Practitioner View," *Journal of Advertising Research, 24* (4), August/ September 1984, pp. 23–26.

91. David Ogilvy and Joel Raphaelson, "Research on Advertising Techniques That Work and Don't Work," *Harvard Business Review*, July/August 1982, p. 18.

92. Josh Kolm, "Chevy Sparks Interest in the Connected Car," *Strategy*, January 14, 2016.

93. Herbert C. Kelman, "Processes of Opinion Change," *Public Opinion Quarterly, 25* (1), Spring 1961, pp. 57–78.

94. Chanthika Pornpitakpan, "The Persuasiveness of Source Credibility: A Critical Review of Five Decades' Evidence," *Journal of Applied Social Psychology, 34* (2), 2004, pp. 243–281.

95. Brian Sternthal, Ruby Dholakia, and Clark Leavitt, "The Persuasive Effects of Source Credibility: Tests of Cognitive Response," *Journal of Consumer Research, 4* (4), March 1978, pp. 252–260.

96. Robert R. Harmon and Kenneth A. Coney, "The Persuasive Effects of Source Credibility in Buy and Lease Situations," *Journal of Marketing Research, 19* (2), May 1982, pp. 255–260.

97. Roobina Ohanian, "The Impact of Celebrity Spokespersons' Image on Consumers' Intention to Purchase," *Journal of Advertising Research, 31* (1), February/March 1991, pp. 46–54.

98. Erick Reidenback and Robert Pitts, "Not All CEOs Are Created Equal as Advertising Spokespersons: Evaluating the Effective CEO Spokesperson," *Journal of Advertising, 15* (1), 1986, pp. 35–50.

99. Andy Holloway, "Frontman as Pitchman," *National Post*, November 2018, p. A 7.

100. Chanthika Pornpitakpan, "The Persuasiveness of Source Credibility: A Critical Review of Five Decades' Evidence," *Journal of Applied Social Psychology, 34* (2), 2004, pp. 243–281.

101. H. C. Triandis, *Attitudes and Attitude Change* (New York: Wiley, 1971).
102. J. Mills and J. Jellison, "Effect on Opinion Change Similarity Between the Communicator and the Audience He Addresses," *Journal of Personality and Social Psychology, 9* (2), June 1968, pp. 153–156.
103. Harmeet Singh, "Mattel's Girl Power," *Strategy,* April 2015, p. A.8.
104. For an excellent review of these studies, see Marilyn Y. Jones, Andrea J. S. Stanaland, and Betsy D. Gelb, "Beefcake and Cheesecake: Insights for Advertisers," *Journal of Advertising, 27* (2), Summer 1998, pp. 32–51; W. B. Joseph, "The Credibility of Physically Attractive Communicators," *Journal of Advertising, 11* (3), October 1982, pp. 13–23.
105. Michael Solomon, Richard Ashmore, and Laura Longo, "The Beauty Match-Up Hypothesis: Congruence Between Types of Beauty and Product Images in Advertising," *Journal of Advertising, 21* (4), December 1992, pp. 23–34; M. J. Baker and Gilbert A. Churchill, Jr., "The Impact of Physically Attractive Models on Advertising Evaluations," *Journal of Marketing Research, 14* (4), November 1977, pp. 538–555.
106. Kristin Laird, "Karlie Kloss to Be the Face of Joe Fresh/Flare Partnership," *Marketing Magazine,* August 5, 2015; Katie Underwood, "Behind the Brand: Joe Fresh," *Chatelaine,* January 16, 2015.
107. Robert W. Chestnut, C. C. La Chance, and A. Lubitz, "The Decorative Female Model: Sexual Stimuli and the Recognition of the Advertisements," *Journal of Advertising, 6* (4), Fall 1977, pp. 11–14; Leonard N. Reid and Lawrence C. Soley, "Decorative Models and Readership of Magazine Ads," *Journal of Advertising Research, 23* (2), April/May 1983, pp. 27–32.
108. Amanda B. Bower, "Highly Attractive Models in Advertising and the Women Who Loathe Them: The Implications of Negative Affect for Spokesperson Effectiveness," *Journal of Advertising, 30* (3), Fall 2001, pp. 51–63; Amanda B. Bower and Stacy Landreth, "Is Beauty Best? Highly Versus Normally Attractive Models in Advertising," *Journal of Advertising, 30* (1), Spring 2001, pp. 1–12.
109. Kristin Laird, "The Real Impact of Real Beauty," *Marketing Magazine,* September 2014, pp. 20–23.
110. Susan Krashinsky, "Dove Beauty Campaign Loses Its Glow," *The Globe and Mail,* April 10, 2015, p. B6.
111. George E. Belch and Michael A. Belch, "A Content Analysis Study of the Use of Celebrity Endorsers in Magazine Advertising," *International Journal of Advertising, 32 (3),* August 2013, pp. 369–389.
112. Johannes Knoll and Jorg Matthes, "The Effectiveness of Celebrity Endorsements: A Meta-Analysis," *Journal of the Academy of Marketing Science, 45* (1), January 2017, pp. 55–75.
113. Lars Bergkvist and Kris Qiang Zhou, "Celebrity Endorsements: A Literature Review and Research Agenda," *International Journal of Advertising, 35* (4), 2016, pp. 642–663.
114. B. Zafer Erdogan, Michael J. Baker, and Stephen Tagg, "Selecting Celebrity Endorsers: The Practitioner's Perspective," *Journal of Advertising Research, 41* (3), May–June 2001, pp. 39–48; B. Zafer Erdogan and Tanya Drollinger, "Endorsement Practice: How Agencies Select Spokespeople," *Journal of Advertising Research, 48* (4), December 2008, pp. 573–582.
115. Morgan Campbell, "Sponsorship Spat Another Chip for Stroman," *Toronto Star,* January 2018, p. S3.
116. Justin Dallaire, "Jill Schoolenberg's Slam Dunk," *Strategy,* January 2009, p. A 27.
117. Jasmina Illicic and Cynthia M. Webster, "Eclipsing: When Celebrities Overshadow the Brand," *Psychology and Marketing, Vol 31 (11),* November 2014, pp. 1040–1050.
118. Susan Krashinsky, "The Negotiator William Shatner's Alter Ego Comes to Canada," *The Globe and Mail,* September 14, 2014, p. B5.
119. Valerie Folkes, "Recent Attribution Research in Consumer Behavior: A Review and New Directions," *Journal of Consumer Research, 14* (4), March 1988, pp. 8–65.
120. Charles Atkin and M. Block, "Effectiveness of Celebrity Endorsers," *Journal of Advertising Research, 23* (1), February/March 1983, pp. 57–61.
121. Clinton Amos, Gary Holmes, and David Strutton, "Exploring the Relationship Between Celebrity Endorser Effects and Advertising Effectiveness," *International Journal of Advertising, 27* (2), May 2008, pp. 209–234.
122. Michael A. Kamins, "An Investigation Into the 'Match-Up' Hypothesis in Celebrity Advertising," *Journal of Advertising, 19* (1), Spring 1990, pp. 4–13.
123. Grant McCracken, "Who Is the Celebrity Endorser? Cultural Foundations of the Endorsement Process," *Journal of Consumer Research, 16* (3), December 1989, pp. 310–321.

CHAPTER EIGHT

1. Gerald J. Gorn and Charles B. Weinberg, "The Impact of Comparative Advertising on Perception and Attitude: Some Positive Findings," *Journal of Consumer Research, 11* (2), September 1984, pp. 719–727.
2. Kristin Laird, "Scotiabank Redefines Richer Campaign," *Marketing Magazine,* January 23, 2012.
3. David Brown, "Big Data Made Beautiful," *Marketing Magazine,* April/May 2015.
4. Judith A. Garretson and Scot Burton, "The Role of Spokescharacters as Advertisement and Package Cues in Integrated Marketing Communications," *Journal of Marketing, 69* (4), October 2005, pp. 118–132.
5. Russ Martin, "Shock Top and Anomaly Toronto Head to the Super Bowl," *Marketing Magazine,* January 28, 2016; Russ Martin, "Shock Top Surprises Consumers With Talking Beer," *Marketing Magazine,* July 9, 2014.
6. Susan Krashinsky, "The Maytag Man Made for 2014," *The Globe and Mail,* January 9, 2014, p. B3.
7. Harmeet Singh, "CIBC's Strategy to Stand Out," *Strategy,* May 25, 2015.
8. "Juniper Park—The Disruption Agency," *Strategy,* June 2017, p. 54.
9. Barbara B. Stern, "Classical and Vignette Television Advertising: Structural Models, Formal Analysis, and Consumer Effects," *Journal of Consumer Research, 20* (4), March 1994, pp. 601–615; John Deighton, Daniel Romer, and Josh McQueen, "Using Drama to Persuade," *Journal of Consumer Research, 15* (3), December 1989, pp. 335–343.
10. Susan Krashinsky, "Christmas Comes Early for Apple's Marketing Team," *The Globe and Mail,* August 19, 2014, p. B3.
11. "BBDO Pushes Skittles to Top of Cheese-o-Meter," *National Post,* March 30, 2012, p. FP14.
12. Susan Krashinsky, "Creative Ad Campaign Gives Boston Pizza a Boost," *The Globe and Mail,* April 9, 2012, p. B4.
13. Paul van Kuilenbury, Menno D.T. de Jong, and Thomas J.L. van Rompay, "That Was Funny, But What Was the Brand Again?" *International Journal of Advertising, 30* (5), October 2011, pp. 795–814.
14. Herbert E. Krugman, "On Application of Learning Theory to TV Copy Testing," *Public Opinion Quarterly, 26* (4), December 1962, pp. 626–639.
15. Susan Krashinsky, "An Edge-of-Your-Seat Approach to Ads," *The Globe and Mail,* March 13, 2013, p. B6.
16. William E. Baker, Heather Honea, and Cristel Antonia Russell, "Do Not Wait to Reveal the Brand Name: The Effect of Brand-Name Placement on Television Advertising Effectiveness," *Journal of Advertising, 33* (3), Fall 2004, pp. 77–85.
17. C. I. Hovland and W. Mandell, "An Experimental Comparison of Conclusion Drawing by the Communicator and by the Audience," *Journal of Abnormal and Social Psychology, 47* (3), July 1952, pp. 581–588.
18. Alan G. Sawyer and Daniel J. Howard, "Effects of Omitting Conclusions in Advertisements to Involved and Uninvolved Audiences," *Journal of Marketing Research, 28* (4), November 1991, pp. 467–474.
19. George E. Belch, "The Effects of Message Modality on One- and Two-Sided Advertising Messages," in *Advances in Consumer Research, 10,* eds. Richard P. Bagozzi and Alice M. Tybout (Ann Arbor, MI: Association for Consumer Research, 1983), pp. 21–26.
20. Martin Eisend, "Two-Sided Advertising: A Meta-Analysis," *International Journal of Research in Marketing, 23* (2), June 2006, pp. 187–199.
21. Susan Krashinsky, "For Buckley's, It's All About Being Frank," *The Globe and Mail,* April 11, 2011, p. B7.

22. Alan G. Sawyer, "The Effects of Repetition of Refutational and Supportive Advertising Appeals," *Journal of Marketing Research, 10* (1), February 1973, pp. 23–37; George J. Szybillo and Richard Heslin, "Resistance to Persuasion: Inoculation Theory in a Marketing Context," *Journal of Marketing Research, 10* (4), November 1973, pp. 396–403.

23. Andrew A. Mitchell, "The Effect of Verbal and Visual Components of Advertisements on Brand Attitudes and Attitude Toward the Advertisement," *Journal of Consumer Research, 13* (1), June 1986, pp. 12–24; Julie A. Edell and Richard Staelin, "The Information Processing of Pictures in Advertisements," *Journal of Consumer Research, 10* (1), June 1983, pp. 45–60; Elizabeth C. Hirschmann, "The Effects of Verbal and Pictorial Advertising Stimuli on Aesthetic, Utilitarian and Familiarity Perceptions," *Journal of Advertising, 15* (2), 1986, pp. 27–34.

24. Jolita Kisielius and Brian Sternthal, "Detecting and Explaining Vividness Effects in Attitudinal Judgments," *Journal of Marketing Research, 21* (1), February 1984, pp. 54–64.

25. H. Rao Unnava and Robert E. Burnkrant, "An Imagery-Processing View of the Role of Pictures in Print Advertisements," *Journal of Marketing Research, 28* (2), May 1991, pp. 226–231.

26. Susan E. Heckler and Terry L. Childers, "The Role of Expectancy and Relevancy in Memory for Verbal and Visual Information: What Is Incongruency?" *Journal of Consumer Research, 18* (4), March 1992, pp. 475–492.

27. Michael J. Houston, Terry L. Childers, and Susan E. Heckler, "Picture–Word Consistency and the Elaborative Processing of Advertisements," *Journal of Marketing Research, 24* (4), November 1987, pp. 359–369.

28. Robert Meeds and Olan Farnall, "Comparing Visual Attention Allocated to Thematic, Attribute and Benefit Sentences in Advertising Copy Blocks: An Eye-Tracking Approach," *Journal of Current Issues and Research in Advertising, 39* (2), 2018, pp. 101–119.

29. Surendra N. Singh, V. Parker Lessig, Dongwook Kim, Reetina Gupta, and Mary Ann Hocutt, "Does Your Ad Have Too Many Pictures?" *Journal of Advertising Research, 40* (1/2), January–April 2000, pp. 11–27.

30. Jungsil Choi and Duane W. Myer, "The Effect of Product Positioning in a Comparison Table on Consumers' Evaluation of a Sponsor," *Marketing Letters, 23* (1), March 2012, pp. 367–380.

31. Susan Krashinsky, "As Seen on TV, A Lot," *The Globe and Mail,* June 29, 2012, p. B5.

32. Tsai Chen and Hsiang-Ming Lee, "Why Do We Share? The Impact of Viral Videos Dramatized to Sell," *Journal of Advertising Research, 54* (3), September 2014, pp. 292–303.

33. Chris Powell, "From Social to Summits: Why #Likeagirl Is Unstoppable," *Marketing Magazine,* August 10, 2015; Susan Krashinsky, "Taking the Advertising World on Like a Girl," *The Globe and Mail,* July 4, 2015, p. B6; Susan Krashinsky, "P&G's Super Bowl Risk Pays Off," *The Globe and Mail,* February 3, 2015, p. B7; Susan Krashinsky, "Throw Run Fight Swing Punch Like a Girl," *The Globe and Mail,* July 4, 2014.

34. Thales Teixeira, Rosalind Picard, and Rana el Kaliouby, "Why, When, and How Much to Entertain Consumers in Advertisements? A Web-Based Facial Tracking Field Study," *Marketing Science, 33* (6), November–December 2014, pp. 809–827.

35. Alicia Androich, "Microsoft Releases Results for NUads Format," *Marketing Magazine,* January 8, 2013; Rebecca Harris, "Subway Tries Interactive TV With Microsoft XBOX Ad," *Marketing Magazine,* September 26, 2012.

36. Debora V. Thompson and Prashant Malaviya, "Consumer-Generated Ads: Does Awareness of Advertising Co-Creation Help or Hurt Persuasion?" *Journal of Marketing, 77* (3), May 2013, pp. 33–47.

37. Susan Krashinsky, "Humour Virus Infects Online Advertising," *The Globe and Mail,* April 1, 2015, p. B4; Susan Krashinsky, "The Anti Advertising Campaign," *The Globe and Mail,* August 29, 2014, p. B5; Susan Krashinsky, "Bold Charities Learn New Tricks—Prank Ads," *The Globe and Mail,* January 9, 2015, p. B6.

38. David Allan, "A Content Analysis of Music Placement in Prime-Time Advertising," *Journal of Advertising Research, 48* (3), September 2008, pp. 404–414.

39. Russell I. Haley, Jack Richardson, and Beth Baldwin, "The Effects of Nonverbal Communications in Television Advertising," *Journal of Advertising Research, 24* (4), August–September 1984, pp. 11–18.

40. Gerald J. Gorn, "The Effects of Music in Advertising on Choice Behavior: A Classical Conditioning Approach," *Journal of Marketing, 46* (1), Winter 1982, pp. 94–100.

41. Steve Oakes, "Evaluating Empirical Research Into Music in Advertising: A Congruity Perspective," *Journal of Advertising Research, 47* (1), March 2007, pp. 38–50.

42. Susan Krashinsky, "Changing Their Tune," *The Globe and Mail,* July 13, 2012, p. B6.

43. Chris Powell, "Kijiji Puts the Raps on New Campaign," *Marketing Magazine,* October 7, 2015.

44. Linda M. Scott, "Understanding Jingles and Needledrop: A Rhetorical Approach to Music in Advertising," *Journal of Consumer Research, 17* (2), September 1990, pp. 223–236.

45. Jeromy Lloyd, "Swiss Chalet Blasts Back From the Past," *Marketing Magazine,* September 23, 2009.

46. Simon Houpt, "Poutine, Pussycats and Political Messages," *The Globe and Mail,* March 25, 2011, p. B6.

47. John Rossiter and Larry Percy, *Advertising Communications and Promotion Management* (McGraw-Hill, 1996). John Rossiter, Larry Percy, Robert J. Donovan *Journal of Advertising Research, 31* (5), October/November 1991, pp. 11–21.

48. Jenni Romaniuk, "The Efficacy of Brand-Execution Tactics in TV Advertising, Brand Placements, and Internet Advertising, " *Journal of Advertising Research, 49* (2), June 2009, pp. 143–150.

49. www.cassies.ca.

CHAPTER NINE

1. Spike Cramphorn, "What Advertising Testing Might Have Been, If We Had Only Known," *Journal of Advertising Research, 44* (2), June 2004, pp. 1–2.

2. John R. Rossiter, "Methodological Guidelines for Advertising Research," *Journal of Advertising, 46* (1), January 2017, pp. 71–82.

3. John R. Rossiter and Larry Percy, *Advertising Communications and Promotion Management,* (New York: McGraw-Hill), 1996; John R. Rossiter and Stven Bellman, *Marketing Communications,* (Sydney: Pearson), 2005.

4. http://cassies.ca/entry/viewcase/53938.

5. http://cassies.ca/entry/viewcase/53422.

6. Thomas J. Reynolds and Charles Gengler, "A Strategic Framework for Assessing Advertising: The Animatic vs. Finished Issue," *Journal of Advertising Research, 31* (5), October/November 1991, pp. 61–71.

7. Ye Hu, Leonard Lodish, Abba Krieger, and Babk Hayati, "An Update of Real-World TV Advertising Tests," *Journal of Advertising Research, 49* (2), June 2009, pp. 201–206.

8. Rumen Pozharliev, Willem J.M.I. Verbek, and Richard P. Bagozii, "Social Consumer Neuroscience: Neurophysiological Measures of Advertising in a Social Context," *Journal of Advertising, 46* (3), July 2017, pp. 351–362.

9. Paul J. Watson and Robert J. Gatchel, "Autonomic Measures of Advertising," *Journal of Advertising Research, 19* (3), June 1979, pp. 15–26.

10. Priscilla A. LaBarbera and Joel D. Tucciarone, "GSR Reconsidered: A Behavior-Based Approach to Evaluating and Improving the Sales Potency of Advertising," *Journal of Advertising Research, 35* (5), September/October 1995, pp. 33–40.

11. Flemming Hansen, "Hemispheric Lateralization: Implications for Understanding Consumer Behavior," *Journal of Consumer Research, 8* (1), June 1988, pp. 23–36.

12. Jan Stapel, "Recall and Recognition: A Very Close Relationship," *Journal of Advertising Research, 38* (4), July/August 1998, pp. 41–45.

13. Hubert A. Zielske, "Does Day-After Recall Penalize 'Feeling Ads'?" *Journal of Advertising Research, 22* (1), February/March 1982, pp. 19–22.

14. Arthur J. Kover, "Why Copywriters Don't Like Advertising Research—And What Kind of Research Might They Accept," *Journal of Advertising Research, 36* (2), March/April 1996, pp. RC8–RC10.

15. John Philip Jones, "Single-Source Research Begins to Fulfill Its Promise," *Journal of Advertising Research, 35* (3), May/June 1995, pp. 9–16.
16. James F. Donius, "Marketing Tracking: A Strategic Reassessment and Planning Tool," *Journal of Advertising Research, 25* (1), February/March 1985, pp. 15–19.
17. "Positioning Advertising Copy-Testing," *Journal of Advertising, 11* (4), December 1982, pp. 3–29.
18. Russell I. Haley and Allan L. Baldinger, "The ARF Copy Research Validity Project," *Journal of Advertising Research, 31* (2), April/May 1991, pp. 11–32.

CHAPTER TEN

1. Emily Jackson, "Federal Digital Advertising Tops TV for the First Time," *National Post*, February 12, 2018.
2. Demetrios Vakratsas and Zhenfeng Ma, "A Look at the Long-Run Effectiveness of Multimedia Advertising and Its Implications for Budget Allocation Decisions," *Journal of Advertising Research, 45* (2), June 2005, pp. 241–254.
3. Shrihari Sridhar, Frank Germann, Charles Kang, and Rajdeep Grewal, "Relating Online, Regional, and National Advertising to Firm Value," *Journal of Marketing, 80* (4), July 2016, pp. 39–55.
4. Jasper Snyder, "Advertising Across Platforms: Conditions for Multimedia Campaigns," *Journal of Advertising Research, 56* (4), December 2016, pp. 352–367.
5. David Berkowitz, Arthur Allaway, and Giles d'Souza, "The Impact of Differential Lag Effects on the Allocation of Advertising Budgets Across Media," *Journal of Advertising Research, 41* (2), March/April 2001, pp. 27–36.
6. Christine Kohler, Murali K. Mantrala, Sonke Albers, and Vamsi K. Kanuri, "A Meta-Analysis of Marketing Communication Carryover Effects," *Journal of Marketing Research, 54* (6), December 2017, pp. 990–1008.
7. Phillippe Aurier and Anne Borz-Giroux, "Modeling Advertising Impact at Campaign Level: Empirical Generalizations Relative to Long-Term Advertising Profit Contribution and Its Antecedents," *Marketing Letters, 25* (2), June 2014, pp. 193–206.
8. William A. Cook and Vijay S. Talluri, "How the Pursuit of ROMI Is Changing Marketing Management," *Journal of Advertising Research, 44* (3), September 2004, pp. 244–254; Joan Fitzgerald, "Evaluating Return on Investment of Multimedia Advertising With a Single-Source Panel: A Retail Case Study," *Journal of Advertising Research, 44* (3), September 2004, pp. 262–270.
9. Jonathan Paul, "Adidas Goes All In," *Strategy*, April 1, 2011, p. 12.
10. Gian Fulgoni, "Are You Targeting Too Much?" *Journal of Advertising Research, 58* (1), March 2018, pp. 8–11.
11. Jenni Romaniuk, Virginia Beal, and Mark Uncles, "Achieving Reach in a Multi-Media Environment," *Journal of Advertising Research, 53* (2), June 2013, pp. 221–230.
12. "Canada Increases Budget for Advertising to U.S. Tourists," *The Globe and Mail*, April 2, 2014, p. S2.
13. Kristin Laird, "Agencies Collaborate to Make Sport Chek More Inspiring," *Marketing Magazine*, August 29, 2012.
14. Michael J. Naples, *Effective Frequency: The Relationship Between Frequency and Advertising Effectiveness* (New York: Association of National Advertisers, 1979).
15. Susanne Schmidt and Martin Eisend, "Advertising Repetition: A Meta-Analysis on Effective Frequency in Advertising," *Journal of Advertising, 44* (4), October 2015, pp. 415–428.
16. Joseph W. Ostrow, "Setting Frequency Levels: An Art or a Science?" *Journal of Advertising Research, 24* (4), August/September 1984, pp. 9–11.
17. Hugh M. Cannon, John D. Leckenby, and Avery Abernethy, "Beyond Effective Frequency: Evaluating Media Schedules Using Frequency Value Planning," *Journal of Advertising Research, 42* (6), November–December 2002, pp. 33–47.
18. William Havlena, Robert Cardarelli, and Michelle De Montigny, "Quantifying the Isolated and Synergistic Effects of Exposure Frequency for TV, Print, and Internet Advertising," *Journal of Advertising Research, 47* (3), September 2007, pp. 215–221.
19. David A. Aaker and Phillip K. Brown, "Evaluating Vehicle Source Effects," *Journal of Advertising Research, 12* (4), August 1972, pp. 11–16.

20. Sara Rosengren and Micael Dahlen, "Judging a Magazine by Its Advertising," *Journal of Advertising Research, 53* (1), March 2013, pp. 61–70.
21. Jennifer Horn, "AToMiC Awards: Brands Join the Band," *Strategy*, May 29, 2013.
22. Max Kilger and Ellen Romer, "Do Measures of Media Engagement Correlate With Product Purchase Likelihood?" *Journal of Advertising Research, 47* (3), September 2007, pp. 313–325.
23. Kazuya Kusumot, "Affinity-Based Media Selection: Magazine Selection for Brand Message Absorption," *Journal of Advertising Research, 42* (4), July–August 2002, pp. 54–65.
24. Susan Krashinsky, "Why Google Is Wooing Canada's Ad Agencies," *The Globe and Mail*, January 24, 2014, p. B5.
25. Yunjae Cheong, Federico de Gregorio, and Kihan Kim, "Advertising Spending Efficiency Among Top U.S. Advertisers From 1985 to 2012: Overspending or Smart Managing?" *Journal of Advertising, 43* (4), 2014, pp. 344–358.
26. George S. Low and Jakki Mohr, "Setting Advertising and Promotion Budgets in Multi-Brand Companies," *Journal of Advertising Research, 39* (1), January/February 1999, pp. 667–678.
27. Jody Harri and Kimberly A. Taylor, "The Case for Greater Agency Involvement in Strategic Partnerships," *Journal of Advertising Research, 43* (4), December 2003, pp. 346–352.
28. Frank M. Bass, "A Simultaneous Equation Regression Study of Advertising and Sales of Cigarettes," *Journal of Marketing Research, 6* (3), August 1969, p. 291; David A. Aaker and James M. Carman, "Are You Overadvertising?" *Journal of Advertising Research, 22* (4), August/September 1982, pp. 57–70.
29. Julian A. Simon and Johan Arndt, "The Shape of the Advertising Response Function," *Journal of Advertising Research, 20* (4), August 1980, pp. 11–28.
30. Douglas West, John B. Ford, and Paul W. Farris, "How Corporate Cultures Drive Advertising and Promotion Budgets," *Journal of Advertising Research, 54* (2), June 2014, pp. 149–162.
31. Boonghee Yoo and Rujirutana Mandhachitara, "Estimating Advertising Effects on Sales in a Competitive Setting," *Journal of Advertising Research, 43* (3), August 2003, pp. 310–320.

CHAPTER ELEVEN

1. John Doyle, "Watch How You Want: TV Is Still the Future," *The Globe and Mail*, May 21, 2012, p. R3.
2. Leslie A. Wood and David F. Poltrack, "Measuring the Long-Term Effects of Television Advertising," *Journal of Advertising Research, 55* (2) June 2015, pp. 123–131.
3. Ye Hu, Leonard Lodish, Abba Krieger, and Babk Hayati, "An Update of Real-World TV Advertising Tests," *Journal of Advertising Research, 49* (2), June 2009, pp. 201–206.
4. Gian M. Fulgoni, "Measuring Television in the Programmatic Age," *Journal of Advertising Research, 57* (1), March 2017, pp. 10–14.
5. TV Basics 2019, pp. 24–28, ThinkTV.
6. Susan Krashinsky and Eric Atkins, "How Do We Watch Hockey," *The Globe and Mail*, February 5, 2014, p. B.5; Susan Krashinsky, "Rogers Ramps Up NHL Ad Buys," *The Globe and Mail*, July 7, 2014, p. B.3; James Bradshaw, "A Whole New Ball Game," *The Globe and Mail*, October 4, 2014, p. S.1.
7. Val Maloney and Bree Rody-Mantha, "Lean Into Fall TV," *Strategy*, August 2017, p. A17.
8. https://thinktv.ca/research/advertising-revenue-by-media/.
9. Mathew Chung, "The Battle's On," *Marketing*, July 2014.
10. Chris Powell, "Tetley Introduces *Pitch Perfect* Campaign," *Marketing Magazine*, December 4, 2015.
11. Susan Krashinsky Robertson, "Court Fights to Hockey Nights," *The Globe and Mail*, December 12, 2018.
12. Hollie Shaw, "Yum, Yum: Loblaw Cooks Up Some Branding Subtleties," *National Post*, December 2, 2011, p. FP12.
13. Jim Kiriakakis, "Branded Entertainment Is Not an Ad," *Strategy*, July 2014.
14. Val Maloney, "The New Partners," *Strategy*, July 2014.
15. Harmeet Singh, "BMO's CMO Effect," *Strategy*, January 2017. https://www.bellmedia.ca/the-lede/press/a-record-number-of-partners-join-ctvs-the-amazing-race-canada-for-season-7/

16. Siva K. Balasubramanian, James A. Karrh, and Hemant Patwardhan, "Audience Response to Product Placements," *Journal of Advertising, 35* (3), Fall 2006, pp. 115–141.

17. Michael Belch and Cristel A. Russell, "A Managerial Investigation Into the Product Placement Industry," *Journal of Advertising Research, 45* (1), March 2005, pp. 73–92.

18. Ekaterina V. Karniouchina, Can Uslay, and Grigori Erenburg, "Do Marketing Media Have Life Cycles? The Case of Product Placement in Movies," *Journal of Marketing, 75* (3), May 2011, pp. 27–48.

19. Chris Powell, "Shaw Announces Brand Sponsors for Home Show to Win," *Marketing Magazine,* September 17, 2016.

20. https://www.nielsen.com/us/en/solutions/capabilities/brandedintegrationintel.html.

21. Carrie La Ferle and Steven M. Edwards, "Product Placement," *Journal of Advertising, 35* (4), Winter 2006, pp. 65–89.

22. Christine M. Kowalczyk and Marla B. Royne, "Are Products More Real on Reality Shows? An Exploratory Study on Product Placement in Reality Television Programming," *Journal of Current Issues and Research in Advertising, 33* (2), 2012, pp. 248–266.

23. Harsha Gangadharbatla and Terry Daugherty, "Advertising Versus Product Placements: How Consumers Assess the Value of Each," *Journal of Current Issues in Research of Advertising, 34* (2), 2013, pp. 21–38.

24. Davit Davtyan, Kristin Stewart, and Isabella Cunningham, "Comparing Brand Placements and Advertisements on Brand Recall and Recognition," *Journal of Advertising Research, 56* (3), September 2016, pp. 299–310.

25. Val Maloney, "Prime Time Face Off," *Strategy,* July 2014; "Shaw Media Gets Dramatic," *Strategy,* July 2014.

26. Emily Wexler, "The Little Orphan That Could," *Strategy,* July 2014.

27. Simon Houpt, "Where Did the Kids Go?" *The Globe and Mail,* June 16, 2012, p. R12.

28. Robert J. Kent, "Second-by-Second Looks at the Television Commercial Audience," *Journal of Advertising Research, 42* (1), January–February 2002, pp. 71–78.

29. Kristin Laird, "Don't Touch That Dial," *Marketing Magazine,* March 2014.

30. John Doyle, "In Praise of Commercials, Sort Of," *The Globe and Mail,* July 25, 2012, p. R3.

31. Darrell Cole, "Oxford Firm's Ads Go National," *Chronicle-Herald,* March 27, 2018, p. B1.

32. TV Basics 2019, ThinkTV.

33. Susan Krashinsky, "Why Most Super Bowl Ads Get Stopped at the Border," *The Globe and Mail,* February 3, 2012, p. B8.

34. Kate Lynch and Horst Stipp, "Examination of Qualitative Viewing Factors of Optimal Advertising Strategies," *Journal of Advertising Research, 39* (3), May–June 1999, pp. 7–16.

35. Justin Dallaire, "Newfoundland and Labrador Wants Travelers to Create Their Own Stories," *Strategy,* March 2019.

36. Fred K. Beard, "Comparative Television Advertising in the United States: A Thirty-Year Update," *Journal of Current Issues & Research in Advertising, 37* (2) pp. 183–195.

37. Yiting Deng and Carl F. Mela, "TV Viewing and Advertising Targeting," *Journal of Marketing Research, 55* (1), February 2018, pp. 99–118.

38. John J. Cronin, "In-Home Observations of Commercial Zapping Behavior," *Journal of Current Issues and Research in Advertising, 17* (2), Fall 1995, pp. 69–75.

39. Paul Surgi Speck and Michael T. Elliot, "Predictors of Advertising Avoidance in Print and Broadcast Media," *Journal of Advertising, 26* (3), Fall 1997, pp. 61–76.

40. Carrie Heeter and Bradley S. Greenberg, "Profiling the Zappers," *Journal of Advertising Research, 25* (2), April/May 1985, pp. 9–12; Fred S. Zufryden, James H. Pedrick, and Avu Sandaralingham, "Zapping and Its Impact on Brand Purchase Behavior," *Journal of Advertising Research, 33* (1), January/February 1993, pp. 58–66.

41. Lex van Meurs, "Zapp! A Study on Switching Behavior During Commercial Breaks," *Journal of Advertising Research, 38* (1), January/February 1998, pp. 43–53.

42. Alan Ching Biu Tse and Rub P w. Lee, "Zapping Behaviour During Commercial Breaks," *Journal of Advertising Research, 41* (3), May/June 2001, pp. 25–29.

43. TV Basics 2019, ThinkTV.

44. Kenneth C. Wilbur, "How the Digital Video Recorder (DVR) Changes Traditional Television Advertising," *Journal of Advertising, 37* (1), Spring 2008, pp. 143–149.

45. Cristel Antonia Russell and Christopher P. Puto, "Rethinking Television Audience Measures: An Exploration Into the Construct of Audience Connectedness," *Marketing Letters, 10* (4), August 1999, pp. 393–407.

46. Claire M. Segijin, Hilde A.M. Voorveld, and Edith G. Smit, "The Underlying Mechanisms of Multiscreening Effects," *Journal of Advertising, 45* (4), 2016, pp. 391–402.

47. Claire M. Segijin, Hilde A.M. Voorveld, and Edith G. Smit, "How Related Multiscreening Could Positively Affect Advertising Outcomes," *Journal of Advertising, 46* (4), October 2017, pp. 455–472.

48. Snezhanka Kazakova, Verolien Cauberghe, Liselot Hudders, and Christophe Labyt, "The Impact of Media Multitasking on the Cognitive and Attitudinal Responses to Television Commercials: The Moderating Role of the Type of Advertising Appeal," *Journal of Advertising, 45* (4), 2016, pp. 403–416.

49. Linda F. Alwitt and Parul R. Prabhaker, "Identifying Who Dislikes Television Advertising: Not by Demographics Alone," *Journal of Advertising Research, 32* (5), September–October 1992, pp. 30–42.

50. Banwari Mittal, "Public Assessment of TV Advertising: Faint Praise and Harsh Criticism," *Journal of Advertising Research, 34* (1), January–February 1994, pp. 35–53; Ernest F. Larkin, "Consumer Perceptions of the Media and Their Advertising Content," *Journal of Advertising, 8* (2), Spring 1979, pp. 5–7.

51. Lucy L. Henke, "Young Children's Perceptions of Cigarette Brand Advertising Symbols: Awareness, Affect, and Target Market Identification," *Journal of Advertising, 24* (4), Winter 1995, pp. 13–28.

52. ThinkTV.ca.

53. CRTC Communications Monitoring Report 2018.

54. Media Technology Monitor, Radio, Anglo, May 2018.

55. Media Technology Monitor, Streaming Audio, 2017, p. 10.

56. Lorraine Sommerfeld, "Big Brother Is in the Car Monitoring Your Habits," *National Post,* October 12, 2018.

57. Radioconnects.ca, Radio Connects to Consumers, 2018.

58. Avery Abernethy, "Differences Between Advertising and Program Exposure for Car Radio Listening," *Journal of Advertising Research, 31* (2), April/May 1991, pp. 33–42.

CHAPTER TWELVE

1. Herbert E. Krugman, "The Measurement of Advertising Involvement," *Public Opinion Quarterly, 30* (4), Winter 1966–67, pp. 583–596.

2. Media Digest 2015–2016, pp. 119, 137.

3. Magazines Canada, A Comparison of Canada and USA 2014, p. 9.

4. Chris Powell, "Alliance for Audited Media to Measure Multi-Platform Media," *Marketing Magazine,* February 3, 2016.

5. Chris Powell, "Magazines Canada Wants Canadians to Share the Love," *Marketing Magazine,* March 1, 2016.

6. https://www.cardonline.ca/listings/magazine/7777.

7. Magazines Canada, Consumer Magazine Fact Book 2015, p. 32.

8. Magazines Canada, Consumer Magazine Fact Book 2015, p. 30.

9. http://cardonline.ca/listings/14345.jsf.

10. http://cardonline.ca/listings/13639.jsf; Media Digest, Canadian Media Director's Council, 2012–2013, p. 70.

11. Alica Androich, "Canada's Magazines Aren't Doomed," *Marketing Magazine,* May 16, 2011, pp. 26–29, 31–32.

12. Doug Bennet, "How Many City Magazines Does Toronto Actually Need?" *Marketing Magazine,* May 16, 2011.

13. Magazines Canada, Consumer Magazine Fact Book 2015, p. 32.

14. Magazines Canada, Consumer Magazine Fact Book 2015, p. 49.

15. Magazines Canada, Consumer Magazine Fact Book 2015, p. 25.

16. Magazines Canada, Consumer Magazine Fact Book 2012, p. 48.

17. Magazines Canada, Consumer Magazine Fact Book 2012, p. 45.

18. "Crunch," *Marketing Magazine,* May 16, 2011, p. 46.

19. Tom Gierasimczuk, "Where the Young Readers Are," *Marketing Magazine,* May 16, 2011, p. 30.

20. Magazines Canada, Consumer Magazine Fact Book 2015, page 21.

21. Magazines Canada, Consumer Magazine Fact Book 2015, p. 38.

22. Magazines Canada, Consumer Magazine Fact Book 2012, p. 38.

23. Magazines Canada, Consumer Magazine Fact Book 2012, p. 39.
24. News Media Canada, Snapshop Fact Sheet, 2016.
25. News Media Canada, 2019 Ownership Groups.
26. Konrad Yakabuski, "*La Presse*'s Risky Media Experiment Has Begun," *The Globe and Mail*, July 18, 2018; Tim Shufelt, "*La Presse* Move to Non-Profit Status Faces Resistance in Quebec Legislature," *The Globe and Mail*, June 14, 2018.
27. Chris Powell, "Paper Tigers," *Marketing Magazine*, January/February 2014.
28. Chris Powell, "Custom Takes Off," *Marketing Magazine*, June 4, 2012.
29. "*The Globe*'s Recipe for Killer Custom Content," *Strategy*, December 2014.
30. Marina Strauss, "Canadian Tire on Top of Digital Game," *The Globe and Mail*, May 9, 2014, p. B.9.
31. Jason Dubroy, "In Defence of the Flyer," *Strategy*, May 2015.
32. "*Globe and Mail*'s Aggressive Video Push Pays Off in Upscale Audience," *Strategy*, July 2014.
33. Newspapers Canada, Connecting to Canadians With Community Newspapers 2013.
34. Chris Powell, "Postmedia Announces Strategic Partnership With Mogo," *Marketing Magazine*, January 25, 2016.
35. Emily Jackson, "Postmedia's Digital Ad Revenues Rise for Sixth Straight Quarter," *National Post*, July 11, 2018.
36. Mark Sweney, "U.K. Papers Get Boost on Social Media Backlash," *National Post*, August 4, 2018, p. FP2.
37. Magazines Canada, Consumer Magazine Fact Book 2012, pp. 59, 60.
38. Magazines Canada, Consumer Magazine Fact Book 2012, pp. 73, 74.

CHAPTER THIRTEEN

1. Mukesh Bhargava and Naveen Donthu, "Sales Response to Outdoor Advertising," *Journal of Advertising Research*, 39 (4), August 1999, pp. 7–18.
2. Rae Ann Fera, "Apotek: Interactive Billboard," *Marketing Magazine*, May 2014.
3. Charles R. Taylor, George R. Franke, and Hae-Kyong Bang, "Use and Effectiveness of Billboards," *Journal of Advertising*, 35 (4), Winter 2006, pp. 21–34.
4. George R. Franke and Charles R. Taylor, "Public Perceptions of Billboards: A Meta-Analysis," *Journal of Advertising*, 46 (3), 2017, pp. 395–410.
5. Steffi Frison, Marnik G. Dekimpe, Christophe Croux, and Peter DeMaeyer, "Billboard and Cinema Advertising: Missed Opportunity or Spoiled Arms?" *International Journal of Research in Marketing*, 31 (4), December 2014, pp. 425–433.
6. Jack Lakey, "Street Furniture Good Deal for City," *Toronto Star*, May 24, 2018, p. GT3.
7. "Guerrilla Street Cred," *Strategy*, October 2017, p. 40.
8. Lex Van Meurs and Mandy Aristoff, "Split-Second Recognition: What Makes Outdoor Advertising Work?" *Journal of Advertising Research*, 49 (1), March 2009, pp. 82–92.
9. Chris Powell, "Toronto Transit Shelters Forecast Savings at Mark's," *Marketing Magazine*, February 4, 2015.
10. David Brown, "Pattison Debuts Flexity Streetcar Ad for Volvo," *Marketing Magazine*, March 16, 2016.
11. Brenda Bous, "Telus Gives B.C. Bus Commuters Free Wi-Fi," *Marketing Magazine*, August 21, 2014.
12. Jeromy Lloyd, "In-Flight Magazine Smack-Down," *Marketing Magazine*, November 28, 2011, p. 15.
13. Cineplex Annual Report 2017.
14. Chris Powell, "Cineplex Gets Its Game Face On," *Marketing Magazine*, January 12, 2016.
15. Joanna Phillips and Stephanie M. Noble, "Simply Captivating: Understanding Consumers' Attitudes Toward the Cinema as an Advertising Medium," *Journal of Advertising*, 36 (10), Spring 2007, pp. 81–94.
16. Rick T. Wilson and Brian D. Till, "Airport Advertising Effectiveness," *Journal of Advertising*, 37 (1), Spring 2008, pp. 59–72.
17. Theras Wood, "See Me, Touch Me, Feel Me," *Strategy*, June 3, 2011, p. 34.
18. Susan Krashinsky, "Targeted Ads to Be Shown at Health-Care Facilities," *The Globe and Mail*, February 18, 2015, p. B.7.
19. Jeff Fraser, "Big Digital Wants to Make Event Signage Beautiful," *Marketing Magazine*, April 20, 2015.
20. "Newad Brings Digital Precision to Indoor OOH," *Strategy*, October 2018, p. A61.

CHAPTER FOURTEEN

1. Robert C. Blattberg and Scott A. Neslin, *Sales Promotion: Concepts, Methods and Strategies*, (Englewood Cliffs, New Jersey, Prentice Hall, 1990).
2. Pierre Chandon, Brian Wansink, and Gilles Laurent, "A Benefit Congruency Framework of Sales Promotion Effectiveness," *Journal of Marketing*, 64 (4), October 2000, pp. 65–81.
3. Esmeralda Crespo-Amendros and Salvador Del Barrio-Garcia, "The Quality of Inter-User Recall," *Journal of Advertising Research*, 54 (1), March 2014, pp. 56–70.
4. Judith A. Garretson and Scot Burton, "Highly Coupon and Sales Prone Consumers: Benefits Beyond Price Savings," *Journal of Advertising Research*, 43 (3), June 2003, pp. 162–172.
5. Scott A. Nielsen, John Quelch, and Caroline Henderson, "Consumer Promotions and the Acceleration of Product Purchases," in *Research on Sales Promotion: Collected Papers*, ed. Katherine E. Jocz (Cambridge, MA: Marketing Science Institute, 1984).
6. Melinda Mattos, "Nivea Pops Up for 100th Anniversary," *Strategy*, May 1, 2011, p. 10.
7. Leonard M. Lodish and Carl F. Mela, "If Brands Are Built Over Years, Why Are They Managed Over Quarters?" *Harvard Business Review*, July–August 2007, pp. 104–112.
8. Robert C. Blattberg and Scott A. Neslin, *Sales Promotion: Concepts, Methods and Strategies* (Englewood Cliffs, New Jersey, Prentice Hall, 1990).
9. Michael L. Rothschild and William C. Gaidis, "Behavioural Learning Theory: Its Relevance to Marketing and Promotions," *Journal of Marketing*, 45 (2), Spring 1981, pp. 70–78.
10. Devon DelVecchio, H. Shanker Krishnan, and Daniel C. Smith, "Cents or Percent? The Effects of Promotion Framing on Price Expectation and Choice," *Journal of Marketing*, 71, July 2007, pp. 158–170.
11. Sandeep Arora, Frenkel ter Hofstede, and Vijay Mahajan, "The Implications of Offering Free Versions for the Performance of Paid Mobile Apps," *Journal of Marketing*, 81 (6), November 2017, pp. 62–78.
12. Carrie Heilman, Kyryl Lakishyk, and Sonya Radas, "An Empirical Investigation of In-Store Sampling Promotions," *British Food Journal*, 113 (10), 2011, pp. 1252–1266.
13. Suzanne Dansereau, "How Some Canadian Entrepreneurs Are Using Red Carpet Celebrity Events as a Powerful Marketing Tool," *National Post*, February 22, 2015.
14. J. Jeffrey Inman and Leigh McAlister, "Do Coupon Expiration Dates Affect Consumer Behavior?" *Journal of Marketing Research*, 31 (3), August 1994, pp. 423–428.
15. Juliano Laran and Michael Tsiros, "An Investigation of the Effectiveness of Uncertainty in Marketing Promotions Involving Free Gifts," *Journal of Marketing*, 77 (2), March 2013, pp. 112–123.
16. Alec Minnema, Tammo H.A. Bijmolt, and Marielle C. Non, "The Impact of Instant Reward Programs and Bonus Premiums on Consumer Purchase Behavior," *International Journal of Research in Marketing*, 34, 2107, pp. 194–211.
17. Jacob Serebrin, "Class-Action Suit Targets McDonald's in Quebec Over Advertising to Kids," *Montreal Gazette*, November 15, 2018, p. A1.
18. Gerard P. Prendergast, Derek T. Y. Poon, Alex S. L. Tsang, and Ting Yan Fan, "Predicting Deal Proneness," *Journal of Advertising Research*, 48 (2), June 2008, pp. 287–296.
19. Susan Krashinsky, "Sticky Symbols," *The Globe and Mail*, October 17, 2014.
20. Susan Krashinsky, "What's in a Name? Sales, Coke Hopes," *The Globe and Mail*, July 1, 2014, p. B5.
21. Ty Henderson and Neeraj Arora, "Promoting Brands Across Categories With a Social Cause: Implementing Effective Embedded Premium Programs," *Journal of Marketing*, 74 (6), November 2010, pp. 41–60.
22. "Rolling Up a Winner," *Strategy*, May 2014; Rebecca Harris, "Tim Hortons Enhances 'Roll Up the Rim' Ahead of Q4," *Marketing Magazine*, February 18, 2014.

23. Aleksandra Sagan, "Tim Hortons to Revamp Roll-Up-the-Rim Contest After Coffee Shop Sales Slow," *National Post*, April 29, 2019.

24. Josh Kolm, "Keeping the Momentum," *Strategy*, January 2018, p. A33.

25. "The Holistic Thinker," *Strategy*, June 2017, p. A17.

26. Brenda Pritchard and Susan Vogt, *Advertising and Marketing Law in Canada*, Fifth Edition (LexisNexis, Butterworths, 2015).

27. Drew Hasselback, "Canadian Online Coupon Startup Checkout51 Bought by News Corp Unit," *National Post*, July 2015.

28. David Friend, "Canadian Grocery App SnapSaves Sells to Deals Site Groupon," *The Globe and Mail*, June 23, 2014.

29. Peter Tat, William A. Cunningham III, and Emin Babakus, "Consumer Perceptions of Rebates," *Journal of Advertising Research, 28* (4), August/September 1988, pp. 45–50.

30. Haipeng Chen, Howard Marmorstein, Michael Tsiros, and Akshay R. Rao, "When More Is Less: The Impact of Base Value Neglect on Consumer Preferences for Bonus Packs Over Price Discounts," *Journal of Marketing, 76* (4), July 2012, pp. 64–77.

31. Fengyan Cai, Rajesh Bagchi, and Dinesh K. Gauri, "Boomerang Effects of Low Price Discounts: How Low Price Discounts Affect Purchase Propensity," *Journal of Consumer Research, 42*, February, pp. 804–816.

32. Felix Zoellner, "The Impact of Different Price-Promotion Types on Sales and Brand Perception," *Journal of Advertising Research, 55* (3), September 2015, pp. 270–283.

33. Marina Strauss and Jeff Gray, "Mattress Discounts at Sears, Hudson Bay Under Review," *The Globe and Mail*, February 23, 2015, p. B1.

34. Edward A. Blair and E. Lair Landon, "The Effects of Reference Prices in Retail Advertisements," *Journal of Marketing, 45* (2), Spring 1981, pp. 61–69.

35. Lia Zarantonello and Bernd H. Schmitt, "The Impact of Event Marketing on Brand Equity," *International Journal of Advertising, 32* (2), January 2013, pp. 255–280.

36. Rae Ann Fera, "Get the Most Out of VR," *Marketing Magazine*, January 2015.

37. Josh Kolm, "The Frightening Reality of VR," *Strategy*, March 2017, 2017, p. A10.

38. Josh Kolm, "Experience-Based Retail," *Strategy*, May 2017, p. A6.

39. "The Builder of Common Ground," *Strategy*, June 2017, p. A19.

40. Sneh Duggal, "How Auto Brands Are Driving The New Retail," *Strategy*, January 2018, p. A12.

41. Pierre Chandon, J. Wesley Hutchinson, Eric T. Bradlow, and Scott H. Young, "Does In-Store Marketing Work? Effects of the Number and Position of Shelf Facings on Brand Attention and Evaluation at the Point of Purchase," *Journal of Marketing, 73*, November 2009, pp. 1–17.

42. Josh Kolm, "Pushing Protein Snacks," *Strategy*, October 2018, p. A8.

43. William L. Wilkie, Debra M. Desrochers, and Gregory T. Gundlach, "Marketing Research and Public Policy: The Case of Slotting Fees," *Journal of Public Policy and Marketing, 21* (2), Fall 2002, pp. 275–288.

44. Paul N. Bloom, Gregory T. Gundlach, and Joseph P. Cannon, "Slotting Allowances and Fees: Schools of Thought and Views of Practicing Managers," *Journal of Marketing, 64* (2), April 2000, pp. 92–108.

45. http://www.popai.com/engage/docs/Media-Topline-Final.pdf

46. Marina Strauss, "The Fight to Set Prices," *The Globe and Mail*, March 7, 2014, p. B1.

47. Scot Burton, Donald R. Lichtenstein, and Richard G. Netemeyer, "Exposure to Sales Flyers and Increased Purchases in Retail Supermarkets," *Journal of Advertising Research, 39* (5), September–October 1999, pp. 7–14.

48. http://www.ceir.org/ceir-breaking-news-2015-exhibition-industry-census-now-available

49. Srinath Gopalakrishna, Gary L. Lilien, Jerome D. Williams, and Ian K. Sequeria, "Do Trade Shows Pay Off?" *Journal of Marketing, 38* (3), July 1995, pp. 75–83.

50. https://www.grrreatestbeard.ca/en/.

51. Priya Raghubir and Kim Corfman, "When Do Price Promotions Affect Pretrial Brand Evaluations?" *Journal of Marketing Research, 36* (2), May 1999, pp. 211–222.

52. Elizabeth Gardener and Minakshi Trivedi, "A Communications Framework to Evaluate Sales Promotion Strategies," *Journal of Advertising Research, 38* (3), May/June 1998, pp. 67–71.

CHAPTER FIFTEEN

1. Mary Teresa Bitti, "The New Mad Men: PR's Makeover," *National Post*, December 29, 2014, p. FP.7.

2. John Heinzl, "Tims v. Mickey D's," *The Globe and Mail*, November 30, 2011, p. B15.

3. Scott M. Cutlip, Allen H. Center, and Glen M. Broom, *Effective Public Relations*, 11th ed. (Prentice Hall, 2012).

4. Josh Kolm, "Visa's Infinite Social Push at TIFF," *Strategy*, September 8, 2014; Susan Krashinsky, "TIFF Gives Sponsors the Hollywood Treatment," *The Globe and Mail*, September 12, 2014; Josh Kolm, "Going Bigger With Activations: TIFF's Repeat Sponsors," *Strategy*, September 8, 2014.

5. Tanya Kostiw, "Battle Strategies for Besieged Brands," *Strategy*, April 28, 2014.

6. Susan Krashinsky, "Marriage Proposal Video a Boon for Tim Hortons," *The Globe and Mail*, May 29, 2014.

7. "Home Depot Keeps It Close to Home," *Strategy*, April 2015.

8. Simon Houpt, "BMO Finds Fertile Sponsorship Ground on the Soccer Pitch," *The Globe and Mail*, March 31, 2011.

9. http://www.marketwired.com/press-release/have-a-heart-this-valentines-day-at-boston-pizza-1988608.htm, February 4, 2015.

10. Melinda Mattos, "Bringing CSR Into Focus," *Strategy*, May 1, 2011, p. 20.

11. Wing Sze Tang, "Selling Eco Creed," *Marketing Magazine*, April 2014.

12. https://www.canada.ca/en/services/health/campaigns/vision-healthy-canada/healthy-eating/meetings-correspondence.html

13. Josh Kolm, "Planet Fitness Spreads Kindness With Snapchat," *Strategy*, September 27, 2018.

14. Susan Krashinsky, "Fantasy Cars for Real-Life Drivers," *The Globe and Mail*, February 17, 2012, p. B6.

15. Thomas L. Harris, "How MPR Adds Value to Integrated Marketing Communications," *Public Relations Quarterly, 38* (2), Summer 1993, pp. 13–18.

16. http://www.ikea.com/ms/en_CA/about_ikea/press_room/press_release/national/sleep_newsrelease.html.

17. "Toyota Launches Ad Blitz to Reassure Customers," *Marketing Magazine*, February 1, 2010; "*Marketing*'s Q&A: Toyota Boss Talks Brand Re-Building After Massive Recall," *Marketing Magazine*, February 2, 2010; "Toyota Canada Launches Campaign to Distance Itself From U.S. Problems," *Marketing Magazine*, February 23, 2010.

18. Jennifer Horn, "Cause + Action Awards 2014," *Strategy*, May 2014, p. A24.

19. Mark Weiner, "Marketing PR Revolution," *Communication World*, January/February 2005, pp. 1–5.

20. Walter K. Lindenmann, "An Effectiveness Yardstick to Measure Public Relations Success," *Public Relations Quarterly, 38* (1), Spring 1993, pp. 7–10.

21. http://www.multivu.com/players/English/7782651-fairmont-luxury-insights/.

22. James McLeod, "Uber Aims to Reinvent as All-in-One Platform," *National Post*, September 14, 2018.

23. Justin Dallaire, "Canadian Tire Tops Google as Most Admired Company," *Strategy*, April 1, 2019.

24. Justin Dallaire, "MEC, Canadian Tire Most Reputable Brands for CSR," *Strategy*, October 26, 2018.

25. Josh Kolm, "Cause Engagement by the Numbers," *Strategy*, April 2015, p. A9.

26. Bree Rody-Mantha, "Manulife Becomes Title Sponsor for Ride for Heart," *Media in Canada*, November 7, 2017.

27. Carey Toane, "For the Creative Good," *Strategy*, June 3, 2011, p. 24; Emily Wexler, "Cadbury Cycles Change," *Strategy*, May 1, 2011, p. 28.

28. Mathew Chung, "Cadbury's Light-Generating Bikes," *Strategy*, June 2014, p. 8.

29. Justin Dallaire, "Cadbury Bicycle Factory Turns 10," *Strategy*, April 26, 2018.

30. Jennifer Horn, "Cause + Action Awards 2015," *Strategy*, April 2015, p. A22.

31. Phillip Haid, "Stop Telling Me to Be Good," *Strategy*, April 2015, p. A48.

32. "Beyond Tears and Victimhood," *Strategy*, June 2017, p. 22.

33. IEG's Guide to Sponsorship accessed at www.sponsorship.com.

34. T. Bettina Cornwall, Donald P. Roy, and Edward A. Steinard II, "Exploring Managers' Perceptions of the Impact of Sponsorship on Brand Equity," *Journal of Advertising, 30* (2), Summer 2001, pp. 41–51.
35. Kirk L. Wakefield, Karen Becker-Olsen, and T. Bettina Cornwell, "I Spy a Sponsor," *Journal of Advertising, 36* (4), Winter 2007, pp. 61–74.
36. Julie A. Ruth and Bernard L. Simonin, "Brought to You by Brand A and Brand B," *Journal of Advertising, 32* (3), Fall 2003, pp. 19–30; Julie A. Ruth and Bernard L. Simonin, "The Power of Numbers," *Journal of Advertising, 35* (4), Winter 2006, pp. 7–20.
37. Merel Walraven, Tammo H. A. Bijmolt, and Ruun H. Koning, "Dynamic Effects of Sponsoring: How Sponsorship Awareness Develops Over Time," *Journal of Advertising, 43* (2), Summer 2014, pp. 142–154.
38. David M. Woisetschlager, Christof Backhaus, and T. Bettina Cornwell, "Inferring Corporate Motives: How Deal Characteristics Shape Sponsorship Perceptions," *Journal of Marketing, 81,* September 2017, pp. 121–141.
39. Reinhard Grohs, "Drivers of Brand Image Improvements in Sports Event Sponsorship," *International Journal of Advertising, 35* (3), May 2016, pp. 391–420.
40. Norm O'Reilly and Elisa Beselt, Canadian Sponsorship Landscape Study, 2017.
41. http://www.sponsorshipmarketing.ca.
42. Susan Krashinsky, "Planes, Trains, and Banking Machines," *The Globe and Mail,* February 13, 2015, p. B4.
43. Krafthockeyvill.ca; https://www.sponsorshipmarketing.ca/sma_past-winners.html.
44. Rachel Brady, "Lowry Embraces the North With Sport Chek Sponsorship," *The Globe and Mail,* February 10, 2015.
45. Susan Krashinsky, "MLB, NHL, NFL and NBA: Pepsi's Pro-Sport Domination," *The Globe and Mail,* April 14, 2015.
46. Susan Krashinsky, "Olympic Committee Looks to Force the North Face Out of the Village," *The Globe and Mail,* January 17, 2014, p. B1.
47. Susan Krashinsky, "Olympic Committee Takes Issue With Labatt Hockey Ad," *The Globe and Mail,* February 10, 2014, p. B5.
48. Angeline G. Close and Russell Lacey, "How the Anticipation Can Be as Great as the Experience: Explaining Event Sponsorship Exhibit Outcomes via Affective Forecasting," *Journal of Current Issues & Research in Advertising, 35* (2), 2014, pp. 209–224.
49. Francois A. Carrillat, Alain D'Astous, and Marie-Pier Charette Couture, "How Corporate Sponsors Can Optimize the Impact of Their Message Content," *Journal of Advertising Research, 55* (3), September 2015, pp. 255–269.
50. Bettina Cornwell and Isabelle Maignan, "An International Review of Sponsorship Research," *Journal of Advertising, 27* (1), Spring 1998, pp. 1–21.
51. Michel Tuan Pham, "The Evaluation of Sponsorship Effectiveness: A Model and Some Methodological Considerations," *Gestion 2000, 8* (4), July–August 1991, pp. 47–65.
52. Bill Harvey, Stu Gray, and Gerald Despain, "Measuring the Effectiveness of True Sponsorship," *Journal of Advertising Research, 46* (4), December 2006, pp. 398–409.
53. Jennifer Horn, "Cause + Action Awards 2015," *Strategy,* April 2015, p. A22.
54. Jennifer Horn, "Cause + Action Awards 2014," *Strategy,* May 2014, p. A24.

CHAPTER SIXTEEN

1. Bob Stone and Ron Jacobs, *Successful Direct Marketing Methods* (New York, McGraw-Hill, 2010).
2. Jeff Fraser, "Leads Can Now Sign Up for More Info Within Facebook Ads," *Marketing Magazine,* October 13, 2015.
3. Erin Anderssen, "You Can Run From Big Data. . .," *The Globe and Mail,* October 3, 2014, p. L1.
4. Susan Krashinsky, "Big Data Rewards Come With Tricky Set of Risks," *The Globe and Mail,* November 3, 2014, p. B3.
5. Rebecca Harris, "Knowing What They'll Do Next," *Marketing Magazine,* October 2014, pp. 12–13.
6. Sarah Dobson, "Knorr Says 'Frozen' Doesn't Have to Be a Bad Word," *Marketing Magazine,* April 11, 2006; Canadian Marketing Association Awards Magazine, November 16, 2007.
7. Rebecca Harris, "Knowing What They'll Do Next," *Marketing Magazine,* October 2014, pp. 12–13.
8. Phillip Schmitt, Bernd Skiera, and Christophe Van den Bulte, "Referral Programs and Customer Value," *Journal of Marketing, 75* (1), January 2011, pp. 46–59.
9. Susan Krashinsky, "AMEX, Pearson Team Up on Perks," *The Globe and Mail,* June 18, 2012, p. B3.
10. Stan Maklan, Simon Knox, and Joe Peppard, "Why CRM Fails—and How to Fix it," *National Post,* October 25, 2011, p. FE7.
11. Mark Tungate, "It's Not Just Coffee, It's a Lifestyle," *Marketing Magazine,* June 29, 2014.
12. The Goldstein Group, "Acquisition Marketing in a Multi-Channel World: The Resilient Principles of Successful Direct Mail." Report published at www.canadapost.ca.
13. Bree Rody-Mantha, "Direct Mail Revenue Drops for Canada Post," *Media in Canada,* May 3, 2017.
14. "Breaking Through the Noise," White Paper published at www.canadapost.ca.
15. Goldstein Group, "Acquisition Marketing in a Multi-Channel World."
16. Chris Powell, "Canadian Tire Launches 'The Canadian Way' Catalogue Online," *Marketing Magazine,* April 10, 2013.
17. "Canadian Tire's Digital Catalogues, ," *Strategy,* March 4, 2014.
18. "Canadian Tire Takes Its Canadianness to Digital," *Strategy,* February 19, 2015.
19. "Ikea Breathes Inspiration Into Catalogue Pages," *Strategy,* February 19, 2015.
20. Kristin Laird, "IKEA's Mobile-Enabled Catalogue Goes Live in Canada," *Marketing Magazine,* August 13, 2012.
21. Val Maloney, "Ikea Promotes Its Pages," *Strategy,* August 29, 2013.
22. Xi (Alan) Zhang, V. Kumar, and Koray Cosguner, "Dynamically Managing a Profitable Email Marketing Program," *Journal of Marketing Research, 54* (6), December 2017, pp. 851–866.
23. Susan Krashinsky, "The Cost of a World With No Spam," *The Globe and Mail,* June 20 2014, p. B4.
24. Alicia Androich, "The Loyalty Treatment," *Marketing Magazine,* December 3, 2012, pp. 33–39.
25. Brett A.S. Martin, Joel Van Durme, Mika Raulas, and Marko Merisavo, "E-mail Advertising: Exploratory Insights From Finland," *Journal of Advertising Research, 43* (3), September 2003, pp. 293–300.
26. Joseph E. Phelps, Regina Lewis, Lynne Mobilio, David Perry, and Niranjan Raman, "Viral Marketing or Electronic Word-of-Mouth Advertising: Examining Consumer Responses and Motivations to Pass Along Email," *Journal of Advertising Research, 44* (4), December 2004, pp. 333–348.
27. Mandeep Singh, Siva K. Balasubramanian, and Goutan Chakraborty, "A Comparative Analysis of Three Communication Formats: Advertising, Infomercial, and Direct Experience," *Journal of Advertising, 29* (4), Winter 2000, pp. 59–75.
28. www.theshoppingchannel.com.
29. https://www.the-cma.org/regulatory/code-of-ethics.
30. https://crtc.gc.ca/eng/phone/telemarketing/.
31. Josh Kolm, "Are Loyalty Programs the Fifth P of Marketing?" *Strategy,* April 27, 2016.
32. Yuping Liu, "The Long-Term Impact of Loyalty Programs on Consumer Purchase Behavior and Loyalty," *Journal of Marketing, 71* (4), October 2007, pp. 19–35.
33. Hye-Young Kim, Ji Young Lee, Dooyoung Choi, Juanjuan Wu, and Kim K. P. Johnson, "Perceived Benefits of Retail Loyalty Programs: Their Effects on Program Loyalty and Customer Loyalty," *Journal of Relationship Marketing, 12* (2), June 2013, pp. 95–113.
34. Yuping Liu-Thompkins and Leona Tam, "Not All Repeat Customers Are the Same: Designing Effective Cross-Selling Promotion on the Basis of Attitudinal Loyalty and Habit," *Journal of Marketing, 77* (5), September 2013, pp. 21–36.
35. Tammo Bijmolt, Matilda Dorotic, and Peter Verhoef, "Loyalty Programs: Generalizations on Their Adoption, Effectiveness and Design," *Foundations and Trends in Marketing, 5* (4), 2010, pp. 197–258.
36. www.airmiles.ca.
37. Kristin Laird, "Canadian Tire Introduces Enhanced Loyalty Program," *Marketing Magazine,* September 9, 2014; Francine Kopun,

"Canadian Tire Launches New Loyalty Program," *Toronto Star*, September 9, 2014; Linda Nguyen, "Canadian Tire to Roll Out New Digital Loyalty Program," *The Globe and Mail*, September 9, 2014.

38. Catherine Phillips, "Canadian Tire to Launch New Rewards Program," *Strategy*, April 11, 2018.

39. Bond Loyalty Report, 2019. Report published at www.bondbrandloyalty.com.

40. Bond Loyalty Report, 2015. Report published at www.bondbrandloyalty.com.

41. Matt Semansky, "Threats and Opportunities in the Loyalty Game," *Marketing Magazine*, March 28, 2011, pp. 26–27.

42. Jeromy Lloyd, "Cheers to SAQ's CRM Success," *Strategy*, October 2017, p. A 26.

43. Alicia Androich, "Scene Gamifies, Gets Mobile to Keep Movie Buffs Loyal," *Marketing Magazine*, December 22, 2011.

44. Deepa Venkatesan, "Cineplex Rolls Out Scene Gold Paid Loyalty Tier," *Strategy*, November 9, 2018.

45. Alicia Androich, "The Loyalty Treatment," *Marketing Magazine*, December 3, 2012.

46. Rebecca Harris, "Why Starbucks Is Winning at Loyalty," *Marketing Magazine*, July 28, 2015.

47. Goldstein Group, "Acquisition Marketing in a Multi-Channel World."

CHAPTER SEVENTEEN

1. Chang Hoan Cho and Hyoung Koo Khang, "The State of Internet-Related Research in Communications, Marketing, and Advertising: 1994–2003," *Journal of Advertising*, 35 (3), Fall 2006, pp. 143–163.

2. Juran Kim and Sally J. McMillan, "Evaluation of Internet Advertising Research," *Journal of Advertising*, 37 (1), Spring 2008, pp. 99–112.

3. Cate Riegner, "Word of Mouth on the Web: The Impact of Web 2.0 on Consumer Purchase Decisions," *Journal of Advertising Research*, 47 (4), December 2007, pp. 436–447.

4. Kelly Steele, "J.P. Wiser's Ad Campaign Asks for Friendship Toasts," *The Windsor Star*, July 20, 2018, p. A 4.

5. Nigel Hollis, "Ten Years of Learning on How Online Advertising Builds Brands," *Journal of Advertising Research*, 45 (2), June 2005, pp. 255–268.

6. Rebecca Harris, "Mazda Accelerates In-Cinema Gaming With Cineplex, JWT," *Strategy*, November 2013; Jennifer Horn, "B!G Bronze; JWT and Mazda Reinvent the Test Drive," *Strategy* October 30, 2014.

7. Michelle Dipardo, "Coors Light Wants to Save You From an Average Summer," *Marketing Magazine*, July 4, 2014; Michelle Dipardo, "What Happens Now With Coors Light Search and Rescue?" *Marketing Magazine*, July 8, 2014.

8. Grace J. Johnson, Gordon C. Bruner II, and Anand Kumar, "Interactivity and Its Facets Revisited," *Journal of Advertising*, 35 (4), Winter 2006, pp. 35–52.

9. Maria Sicilia, Salvador Ruiz, and Jose L. Munuera, "Effects of Interactivity in a Web Site," *Journal of Advertising*, 34 (3), Fall 2005, pp. 31–45; Alex Wang, "Advertising Engagement: A Driver of Message Involvement on Message Effects," *Journal of Advertising Research*, 46 (4), December 2006, pp. 355–368.

10. Qimei Chen and William Wells, "Attitude Toward the Site," *Journal of Advertising Research*, 39 (5), September–October 1999, pp. 27–38; Qimei Chen, Sandra J. Clifford, and William Wells, "Attitude Toward the Site II: New Information," *Journal of Advertising Research*, 42 (2), March–April 2002, pp. 33–45.

11. Gary L. Geissler, George M. Zinkhan, and Richard T. Watson, "The Influence of Home Page Complexity on Consumer Attention, Attitudes, and Purchase Intent," *Journal of Advertising*, 35 (2), Summer 2006, pp. 69–80.

12. Micael Dahlen, Alexandra Rasch, and Sara Rosengren, "Love at First Site? A Study of Website Advertising Effectiveness," *Journal of Advertising Research*, 43 (1), March 2003, pp. 25–33.

13. Julie S. Stevenson, Gordon Bruner II, and Anand Kumar, "Webpage Background and Viewer Attitudes," *Journal of Advertising Research*, 40 (1/2), January–April 2000, pp. 29–34; Gordon Bruner II and Anand Kumar, "Web Commercials and Advertising Hierarchy-of-Effects," *Journal of Advertising Research*, 40 (1/2), January–April 2000, pp. 35–42.

14. Guda van Noort, Hilde A.M. Voorveld, and Eva A. van Reijmersdal, "Interactivity in Brand Web Sites: Cognitive, Affective, and Behavioural Responses Explained by Consumers' Online Flow Experience," *Journal of Interactive Marketing*, 26 (4), November 2012, pp. 223–234.

15. Susan Krashinsky, "The Wild, Wacky, Weird World of Webby Advertising," *The Globe and Mail*, April 2, 2012, B7.

16. Canadian Internet Advertising Revenue Survey, IAB Canada, December 2018.

17. Teresa Wright, "Government of Canada, Spending Tens of Millions on Ads, Boosted Posts," *Chronicle-Herald*, May 23, 2018, p. A 11.

18. Joe Plummer, Steve Rappaport, Taddy Hall, and Robert Barocci, *The Online Advertising Playbook*, 2007 (John Wiley & Sons, Hoboken, NJ).

19. Susan Krashinsky Robertson, "Moneris Links Digital Ads to Offline Sales as Data Collection Faces Greater Scrutiny," *The Globe and Mail*, November 5, 2018, p. B 1.

20. Susan Krashinsky, "Canadians Open to Selling Their Online Data, Microsoft Finds," *The Globe and Mail*, January 30, 2014, p. B.4; Susan Krashinsky, "Google Broke Canada's Privacy Laws With Targeted Health Ads, Watchdog Says," *The Globe and Mail*, January 15, 2014, p. A.1; Susan Krashinsky, "Advertisers Scramble to Reassure Public After Google Ruling," *The Globe and Mail*, January 17, 2014, p. B.1.

21. Spencer Soper and Mark Bergen, "The Most Valuable Space on the Web," *National Post*, January 20, 2018, p. FP 10.

22. https://www.statista.com/statistics/282989/canada-largest-advertisers/.

23. https://www.wordstream.com/blog/ws/2016/02/29/google-adwords-industry-benchmarks.

24. Chang-Hoan Cho, Jung-Gyo Lee, and Marye Tharp, "Different Forced-Exposure Levels to Banner Advertisements," *Journal of Advertising Research*, 41 (4), July–August 2001, pp. 45–56.

25. Prem N. Shamdasani, Andrea J. S. Stanaland, and Juliana Tan, "Location, Location, Location: Insights for Advertising Placement on the Web," *Journal of Advertising Research*, 41 (4), July–August 2001, pp. 7–21; Wenyu Dou, Randy Lim, and Sixian Yang, "How Smart Are 'Smart Banners'?" *Journal of Advertising Research*, 41 (4), July–August 2001, pp. 31–43.

26. Micael Dahlen, "Banner Advertisement Through a New Lens," *Journal of Advertising Research*, 41 (4), July–August 2001, pp. 21–30; Lara Laobschat, Ernst C. Osinga, and Werner J Reinartz, "What Happens Online Stays Online? Segment-Specific Online and Offline Effects of Banner Advertisements," *Journal of Marketing Research*, 54 (6), December 2017, pp. 901–913.

27. Kelli S. Burns and Richard J. Lutz, "The Function of Format: Consumer Responses to Six On-line Advertising Formats," *Journal of Advertising*, 35 (1) Spring 2006, pp. 53–63.

28. Norris I. Bruce, B.P.S. Murthi, and Ram C. Rao, "A Dynamic Model for Digital Advertising: The Effects of Creative Format, Message Content, and Targeting on Engagement," *Journal of Marketing Research*, 54 (2), April 2017, pp. 202–218; Robert S. Moore, Claire Allison Stammerjohan, and Robin A. Coulter, "Banner Advertiser–Web Site Context Congruity and Color Effects on Attention and Attitudes," *Journal of Advertising*, 34 (2) Summer 2005, pp. 71–84; Ritu Lohtia, Naveen Donthu, and Edmund K. Hershberger, "The Impact of Content and Design Elements on Banner Advertising Click-Through Rates," *Journal of Advertising Research*, 43 (4), December 2003, pp. 410–418.

29. Peter J. Danaher and Guy W. Mullarkey, "Factors Affecting Online Advertising Recall: A Study of Students," *Journal of Advertising Research*, 43 (3), September 2003, pp. 252–267; Idil Yaveroglu and Naveen Donthu, "Advertising Repetition and Placement Issues in On-Line Environment," *Journal of Advertising*, 37 (2), Summer 2008, pp. 31–43.

30. Shawn D. Baron, Caryn Brouwer, and Amaya Garbayo, "A Model for Delivering Branding Value Through High-Impact Digital Advertising," *Journal of Advertising Research*, 54 (3), September 2014, pp. 286–291.

31. Chris Powell, "It's About Real Time," *Marketing Magazine*, August 13, 2012, pp. 36–41; David Brown, "Exchange Is Good," *Marketing Magazine*, November 14, 2011; "Ad Networks vs. Ad Exchanges: How They Stack Up," OpenX Whitepaper, July 2010; "Digging Into the Data," *Marketing Magazine*, November/December 2014.

32. Gian M. Fulgoni, "Fraud in Digital Advertising: A Multibillion-Dollar Black Hole," *Journal of Advertising* Research, 53 (6), June 2016, pp. 122–125.

33. Benjamin Edelman, "What Makes Advertisers Vulnerable to Cheaters, And How They Can Protect Themselves," *Journal of Advertising Research,* 54 (2), June 2014, pp. 127–132.

34. Oliver J. Rutz, Garrett P. Sonnier, and Michael Trusov, "A New Method to Aid Copy Testing of Paid Search Text Advertisements," *Journal of Marketing Research,* 54 (6), December 2017, pp. 885–900.

35. Hans Haans, Neomie Raassens, Roel van Hout, "Search Engine Advertisements: The Impact of Advertising Statements on Click-Through and Conversion Rates," *Marketing Letters,* 24, 2013, pp. 151–163.

36. https://support.google.com/google-ads.

37. https://www.wordstream.com/blog/ws/2016/02/29/google-adwords-industry-benchmarks.

38. Jeffrey P. Dotson, Ruixue Rachel Fan, Elea McDonnell Feit, Jeffrey D. Oldman, and Yi-Hirsh Yeh, "Brand Attitudes and Seach Engine Queries," *Journal of Interactive Marketing,* 37, 2017, pp. 105–116.

39. Michel Laroche, Isar Kiani, Nectarios Economakis, and Marie-Odile Richard, "Effects of Multi-Channel Marketing on Consumers' Online Search Behaviour," *Journal of Advertising Research,* 53 (4), December 2013, pp. 431–443.

40. Chris Powell, "Cross-Screen Video Advertising on the Rise; Videology," *Marketing Magazine,* March 2, 2016.

41. Ellen Himelfarb, "Selling Through Short Film," *The Globe and Mail,* January 27, 2018, p. 8.

42. Alicia Androich, "The Future Is Data," *Marketing Magazine,* August 13, 2012, p. 14.

43. Kendall Goodrich, Shu Z. Schiller, Dennis Galletta, "Consumer Reactions to Intrusiveness of Online-Video Advertisements," *Journal of Advertising Research,* 55 (1), March 2015, pp. 37–50.

44. Hao Li and Hui-Yi Lo, "Do You Recognize Its Brand? The Effectiveness of Online In-Stream Video Advertisements," *Journal of Advertising,* 44 (3), Fall 2015, pp. 208–218.

45. Colin Campbell, Frauke Mattison Thompson, Pamela E. Grimm, and Karen Robson, "Understanding Why Consumers Don't Skip Pre-Roll Video Ads," *Journal of Advertising,* 46 (3), Fall 2017, pp. 411–423.

46. Daniel Belanche, Carlos Flavian, and Alfredo Perez-Rueda, "Understanding Interactive Online Advertising: Congruence and Product Involvement in Highly and Lowly Arousing, Skippable Video Ads," *Journal of Interactive Marketing,* 37, 2017, pp. 75–88.

47. Daniel M. Haygood, "A Status Report on Podcast Advertising," *Journal of Advertising Research,* 47 (4), December 2007, pp. 518–523.

48. Kristin Laird, "What Men Want," *Marketing Magazine,* April 2014.

49. https://www.spotifyforbrands.com/en-CA/.

50. Venkatesh Shankar and Sridhar Balasubramanian, "Mobile Marketing: A Synthesis and Prognosis," *Journal of Interactive Marketing,* 23 (2), May 2009, pp. 118–129.

51. Venkatesh Shankar, Mirella Kleijnen, Suresh Ramanathan, Ross Rizley, Steve Holland, and Shawn Morrissey, "Mobile Shopper Marketing: Key Issues, Current Insights and Future Research Activities," *Journal of Interactive Marketing,* 34, 2016, pp. 37–48.

52. Paul E. Ketelaar, Stefan F. Bernritter, Jonathan van't Riet, Arief Ernst Huhn, Thabo J. van Woudenberg, Barbara C.N. Muller, and Loes Janssen, "Disentangling Location-Based Advertising: The Effects of Location Congruency and Medium Type on Consumers' Ad Attention and Brand Choice," *International Journal of Advertising,* 36 (2), March 2017, pp. 356–367.

53. Nathalie Atkinson, "Online Shopping Is Harder Than Ever," *The Globe and Mail,* December 15, 2018, p. 6.

54. Yaknv Bart, Andrew T. Stephen, and Miklos Sarvary, "Which Products Are Best Suited to Mobile Advertising? A Field Study of Mobile Display Advertising Effects on Consumer Attitudes and Intentions," *Journal of Marketing Research,* 51 (3), June 2014, pp. 270–285.

55. Dhruv Grewal, Yakov Bart, Martin Spann, and Peter Pal Zubcsek, "Mobile Advertising: A Framework and Research Agenda," *Journal of Interactive Marketing,* 34, 2016, pp. 3–14.

56. Susan Krashinsky, "Inside Oreo's Olympics War Room," *The Globe and Mail,* February 21, 2014, p. B.5.

57. Susan Krashinsky, "An Ad for Every Flavour," *The Globe and Mail,* April 25, 2014, p. B.5.

58. Jonathan Paul, "It's Still All About Location, Location, Location," *Strategy,* February 1, 2011, p. 20.

59. Simon Houpt, "It's All Fun and Games—Until Someone Bonds With a Brand," *The Globe and Mail,* January 2, 2011, p. B1.

60. Matt Semansky, "Location-Based Marketing for the Rest of Us," *Marketing Magazine,* August 1, 2011, pp. 16–21.

61. Alicia Androich, "Ready to Get More Social With Your TV?" *Marketing Magazine,* April 12, 2013.

62. Jameson Berkow, "No Magic Formula," *National Post,* January 17, 2011; Marina Strauss and Omar El Akkad, "A Handheld Way Retailers Are Fighting Online Store Wars," *The Globe and Mail,* December 20, 2011.

63. Steven Bellman, Robert F. Potter, Shiree Treleaven-Hassard, Jennifer A. Robinson, and Duane Varan, "The Effectiveness of Branded Mobile Phone Apps," *Journal of Interactive Marketing,* 25 (4), November 2011, pp. 191–200.

64. Chris Daniels, "Rewards for the Mobile Masses," *Marketing Magazine,* August 29, 2011, pp. 51–53.

65. Grant Buckler, "From Your Smartphone to the Big Screen," *The Globe and Mail,* November 23, 2011, p. B18.

66. Jacque Natel and Yasha Sekhavat, "The Impact of SMS Advertising on Members of a Virtual Community," *Journal of Advertising Research,* 48 (3), September 2008, pp. 363–374.

67. Christian Pescher, Phillipp Reichhart, and Martin Spann, "Consumer Decision-Making Processes in Mobile Viral Marketing Campaigns," *Journal of Interactive Marketing,* 28 (1), February 2014, pp. 43–54.

68. Subdh Bhat, Michael Bevans, and Sanjit Sengupta, "Measuring Users' Web Activity to Evaluate and Enhance Advertising Effectiveness," *Journal of Advertising,* 31 (3), Fall 2002, pp. 97–106.

69. Stephen D. Rappaport, *The Digital Metrics Field Guide,* The Advertising Research Foundation, 2014.

70. Stephen D. Rappaport, "Lessons Learned From *A Field Guide to Digital Metrics,*" *Journal of Advertising Research,* 54 (1), March 2014, pp. 110–118.

71. Benjamin Edelman, "Pitfalls and Fraud in Online Advertising Metrics," *Journal of Advertising Research,* 54 (2), June 2014, pp. 127–132.

72. Stephanie Flosi, Gian Fulgoni, and Andrea Vollman, "If an Advertisement Runs Online and No One Sees It, Is It Still an Ad?," *Journal of Advertising Research,* 53 (2), June 2013, pp. 192–199.

73. Alexa Bezjian-Avery, "New Media Interactive Advertising vs. Traditional Advertising," *Journal of Advertising Research,* 38 (4), August 1998, pp. 23–32; John Eighmey, "Profiling User Responses to Commercial Websites," *Journal of Advertising Research,* 37 (3), May–June 1997, p. 66.

74. http://iabcanada.com/files/IABCanada_CMOST_TetleyRedTeaReport_FINAL_English.pdf.

75. Kay Peters, Yubo Chen, Andreas M. Kaplan, Bjorn Ognibeni, and Koen Pauwels, "Social Media Metrics—A Framework and Guidelines for Managing Social Media," *Journal of Interactive Marketing,* 27 (4), November 2013, pp. 281–298.

76. Sung-Joon Yoon and Joo-Ho Kim, "Is the Internet More Effective Than Traditional Media? Factors Affecting the Choice of Media," *Journal of Advertising Research,* 41 (6), November–December 2001, pp. 53–60.

77. Katherine Gallagher, K. Dale Foster, and Jeffrey Parsons, "The Medium Is Not the Message: Advertising Effectiveness and Content Evaluation in Print and on the Web," *Journal of Advertising Research,* 41 (4), July–August 2001, pp. 57–70; Katherine Gallagher, Jeffrey Parsons, and K. Dale Foster, "A Tale of Two Studies: Replicating 'Advertising Effectiveness and Content Evaluation in Print and on the Web'," *Journal of Advertising Research,* 41 (4), July–August 2001, pp. 71–81.

78. Johanna S. Ilfeld and Russell S. Winer, "Generating Website Traffic," *Journal of Advertising Research,* 42 (5), September–October 2002, pp. 49–61.

79. Yumiin Chang and Esther Thorson, "Television and Web Advertising Synergies," *Journal of Advertising,* 33 (2), Summer 2004, pp. 75–84.

80. Ali M. Kanso and Richard Alan Nelson, "Internet and Magazine Advertising: Integrated Partnerships or Not?" *Journal of Advertising Research,* 44 (4), December 2004, pp. 317–326.

81. Robert Davis and Laszlo Sajtos, "Measuring Consumer Interactivity in Response to Campaigns Coupling Mobile and Television Media," *Journal of Advertising Research*, 48 (3), September 2008; Randolph J. Trappey III and Arch G. Woodside, "Consumer Responses to Interactive Advertising Campaigns Coupling Short-Message-Service Direct Marketing and TV Commercials," *Journal of Advertising Research*, 45 (4), December 2005, pp. 382–401.

CHAPTER EIGHTEEN

1. Andreas M. Kaplan and Michael Haenlein, "Users of the World, Unite! The Challenges and Opportunities of Social Media," *Business Horizons*, 2010, 53 (1), January 2011, pp. 59–68.
2. Rebecca A. VanMeter, Douglas B. Grisaffe, and Lawrence B. Chonko, "Of Likes and Pins: The Effects of Consumers' Attachment to Social Media," *Journal of Interactive Marketing*, 32 (4), November 2015, pp. 70–88.
3. Daniel G. Muntinga, Marjolein Moorman, and Edith G. Smit, "Introducing COBRAs: Exploring Motivations for Brand-Related Social Media Use," *International Journal of Advertising*, 30 (1), January 2011, pp. 13–46.
4. Bruno Schivinski, George Christodoulides, and Dariusz Dabrowski, "Measuring Consumers' Engagement With Brand-Related Social-Media," *Journal of Advertising Research*, 56 (1), March 2016, pp. 64–80.
5. Iryna Pentina, Veronique Guilloux, and Anca Cristina Micu, "Exploring Social Media Engagement Behaviours in the Context of Luxury Brands," *Journal of Advertising*, 47 (1), January 2018, pp. 55–69.
6. Shelly Rogers and Esther Thorson, "Special Issue Introduction: Digital Engagement With Advertising," *Journal of Advertising*, 47 (1), January 2018, pp. 1–3.
7. Shu-Chuan Chu and Juran Kim, "The Current State of Knowledge on Electronic Word-of-Mouth in Advertising Research," *International Journal of Advertising*, 37 (1), 2018, pp. 1–13.
8. Ya You, Gaultham G. Vadakkepatt, and Amit M. Joshi, "A Meta-Analysis of Electronic Word-of-Mouth Elasticity," *Journal of Marketing*, 79 (2), March 2015, pp. 19–39.
9. Ana Babic Rosario, Francesca Sotgiu, Kristine De Valck, and Tammo H. A. Bijmolt, "The Effect of Electronic Word of Mouth on Sales: A Meta-Analytic Review of Platform, Product, and Metric Factors," *Journal of Marketing Research*, 53 (3), June 2016, pp. 297–318.
10. Yongjun Sung, Eunice Kim, and Sejung Marina Choi, "#Me and Brands: Understanding Brand-Selfie Posters on Social Media," *International Journal of Advertising*, 37 (1), January 2018, pp. 14–28.
11. Jiye Shin, Heeju Chae, and Eunju Ko, "The Power of e-WOM Using the Hashtag: Focusing on SNS Advertising of SPA Brands," *International Journal of Advertising*, 37 (1), January 2018, pp. 71–85.
12. Andrew N. Smith, Eileen Fischer, and Chen Yongjian, "How Does Brand-Related User-Generated Content Differ Across YouTube, Facebook and Twitter," *Journal of Interactive Marketing*, 26 (2), May 2012, pp. 102–113.
13. Simon Houpt, "The Tweet Taste of Success," *The Globe and Mail*, September 6, 2012, p.B9.
14. Colin Campbell, Justin Cohen, and Junzhao, "Advertisements Just Aren't Advertisements Anymore," *Journal of Advertising Research*, 54 (1), March 2014, pp. c7–10.
15. All summary statistics for social media are sourced from Statistica, Social Networking in Canada.
16. Lisette de Vries, Sonja Gensler, and Peter S. H. Leeflang, "Effects of Traditional Advertising and Social Messages on Brand-Building Metrics and Customer Acquisition," *Journal of Marketing*, 81 (5), September 2017, pp. 1–15.
17. Susan Krashinsky, "An Ad for Every Flavour," *The Globe and Mail*, April 25, 2014, p. B.5.
18. Eilene Zimmerman, "Facebook Goes Toe-to-Toe With Google on Ads," *National Post*, January 27, 2014, p. FP8.
19. Karen Nelson-Field, Erica Riebe, and Byron Sharp, "More Mutter About Clutter," *Journal of Advertising Research*, 53 (2), June 2013, pp. 186–191.
20. Susan Krashinsky, "Mobile Ads Fuel Facebook Revenue Surge," *The Globe and Mail*, July 24, 2014, p. B.8.

21. Susan Krashinsky, "Will the Video Platform Kill the TV Spot?" *The Globe and Mail*, October 24, 2014, p. B.6.
22. Jon D. Morris, Yunmi Choi, and Ilyoung Ju, "Are Social Marketing and Advertising Communications (SMACS) Meaningful?: A Survey of Facebook User Emotional Responses, Source Credibility, Personal Relevance, and Perceived Intrusiveness," *Journal of Critical Issues & Research in Advertising*, 37 (2), 2016, pp. 165–182.
23. Benjamin Rosenthal and Eliane P. Z. Brito, "How Virtual Brand Community Traces May Increase Fan Engagement in Brand Pages," *Business Horizons*, 60, 2017, pp. 375–384.
24. http://fbrep.com//SMB/Pages_Product_Guide.pdf.
25. Lisette de Vries, Sonja Gensler, and Peter S.H. Leeflang, "Popularity of Brand Posts on Brand Fan Pages: An Investigation of the Effects of Social Media Marketing," *Journal of Interactive Marketing*, 26 (2), May 2012, pp. 83–91.
26. Elaine Wallace, Isabel Buil, Leslie de Chernatony, and Michael Hogan, "Who Likes You and Why? A Typology of Facebook Fans," *Journal of Advertising Research*, 54 (1), March 2014, pp. 92–109.
27. Camiel J. Beukeboom, Peter Kerkhof, and Metten de Vries, "Does a Virtual Like Cause Actual Liking? How Following a Brand's Facebook Updates Enhances Brand Evaluations and Purchase Intention," *Journal of Interactive Marketing*, 32 (4), November 2015, pp. 26–36.
28. Tania Yuki, "What Makes Brands' Social Content Shareable on Facebook?" *Journal of Advertising Research*, 55 (4), December 2015, pp. 458–470.
29. Malte Brettel, Jens-Schristan Reich, Jose M Gavilanes, and Tessa C. Flatten, "What Drives Advertising Success on Facebook? An Advertising-Effectiveness Model," *Journal of Advertising Research*, 55 (2) June 2015, pp. 162–175.
30. Hollie Shaw, "Catering to the Kraft Dinner Cult," *National Post*, March 23, 2012, p. FP12.
31. https://business.twitter.com.
32. https://business.twitter.com/.
33. http://searchenginewatch.com/article/2190651/Twitter-Advertising-Guide.
34. "Where's the Party?" *Marketing Magazine*, October 10, 2011, p. 31.
35. Kristin Laird, "Accelerating Social Media," *Marketing Magazine*, October 10, 2011, pp. 28–29.
36. Kristin Laird, "The Very Necessary Twitter Guide for Canadian Marketers," *Marketing Magazine*, October 10, 2011, pp. 24–27.
37. Russ Martin, "Quality Over Quantity," *Marketing Magazine*, November/December 2014.
38. Claire Brownell, "Engaged vs. Edgy; Brands Walk the Fine Line in Retweet Game," *National Post*, January 26, 2015.
39. Rebecca Harris, "The Blitz Begins for Tomorrow's Fans," *Marketing Magazine*, November/December 2014, pp. 9–10.
40. "Who Should Own a Client's Social Media Duties?" *Marketing Magazine*, February 28, 2011, pp. 30–31.
41. Matthew Braga, "To Go Mainstream, Twitter Needs to Kill the Stream," *National Post*, February 8, 2014, p. FP3.
42. Omar El Akkad, "Different Circles," *The Globe and Mail*, November 26, 2014.
43. Russ Martin, "How Samsung Is Using Twitter's New Conversational Ads," *Marketing Magazine*, January 13, 2016.
44. Shiyang Gong, Juanjuna Zhang, Ping Zhao, and Xuping Jiang, "Tweeting as a Marketing Tool: A Field Experiment in the TV Industry," *Journal of Marketing Research*, 54 (6), December 2017, pp. 833–850.
45. Mikyoung Kim and Doori Song, "When Brand-Related UGC Induces Effectiveness on Social Media: The Role of Content Sponsorship and Content Type," *International Journal of Advertising*, 37 (1), January 2018, pp. 105–124.
46. Yuchi Zhang, Wendy W. Moe, and David A. Schweidel, "Modeling the Role of Message Content and Influencers in Social Media Rebroadcasting," *International Journal of Research in Marketing*, 34 (1), March 2017, pp. 100–119.
47. Xia Liu, Alvin C. Burns, Yingjian Hou, "An Investigation of Brand-Related User-Generated Content on Twitter," *Journal of Advertising*, 46 (2), June 2017, pp. 236–247.
48. Theo Araujo, Peter Neijens, and Rens Vliegenthart, "What Motivates Consumers to Re-Tweet Brand Content?" *Journal of Advertising Research*, 55 (3), September 2015, pp. 284–295.

49. Ivor Tossell and John Lorinc, "Social Media Superstars," *The Globe and Mail*, April 25, 2012, p. 11.

50. Megan Haynes, "Risky Business," *Strategy*, June 2015; Susan Krashinsky, "Schick Launches YouTube Web Series to Reach Younger Consumers," *The Globe and Mail*, March 25, 2015.

51. David French, "Product Placement for the Digital Age," *Chronicle-Herald*, January 18, 2018, p. B 4.

52. Simon Houpt, "What Makes a Video Go Viral?" *The Globe and Mail*, May 26, 2011.

53. Susan Krashinsky, "Lululemon Ad Pokes Fun at Own Customers—and Goes Viral," *The Globe and Mail*, January 13, 2012, p. B5.

54. Angeliki Nikolinakou and Karen Whitehill King, "Viral Video Ads: Examining Motivation Triggers to Sharing," *Journal of Current Issues & Research in Advertising*, 39 (2), 2018, pp. 120–139.

55. Jason Y. C. Ho and Melanie Dempsey, "Viral Marketing: Motivations to Forward Online Content," *Journal of Business Research, 63*, 2010, pp. 1000–1006.

56. Jinsong Huang, Song Su, Liuning Zhou, and Xi Liu, "Attitude to the Viral Ad: Expanding Traditional Advertising Models to Interactive Advertising," *Journal of Interactive Marketing*, 27 (4), December 2013, pp. 36–46.

57. Yuping Liu-Thomkins, "Seeding Viral Content," *Journal of Advertising Research, 52* (4), December 2012, pp. 465–478.

58. Susan Krashinsky, "Brand-Building, One Instagram Post at a Time," *The Globe and Mail*, November 10, 2014, p. B.3.

59. Rae Ann Fera, "Mazda; The Long Drive Home," *Marketing Magazine*, July 2014.

60. http://www.blogto.com/blogto-mediakit.pdf.

61. Chris Koentges, "The Hypest of the Hyperlocal," *Marketing Magazine*, June 4, 2012, pp. 21–22.

62. http://en.wikipedia.org/wiki/Wikipedia:Advertisements.

63. https://s3.amazonaws.com/answ-img/AnswersMediaKit_20130201.pdf.

64. Megan Haynes, "Reddit Knows What Canadians Want," *Strategy*, July 2014, p. 10.

65. Kristin Laird, "Pinterest Rate," *Marketing Magazine*, April 9, 2012, pp. 8–10.

66. http://business.pinterest.com/case-study-sephora/.

67. "Lord & Taylor Settles Charges of Deceptive Instagram Posts," *Marketing Magazine*, March 15, 2016;Susan Krashinsky, "Ad Watchdog Warns Against Disguised Marketing Attempt," *The Globe and Mail*, March 26, 2015, p. B.4.

68. Sarah Deshaies, "Quebec's YouTube Stars Uploading Their Lives," *Montreal Gazette*, January 13, 2018, p. D1.

69. http://adstandards.ca/wp-content/uploads/2019/02/Influencer-Marketing-Steering-Committee-Disclosure-Guidelines-Jan-2019.pdf.

70. Megan Hayes, "Long Live the Digital Beauty Regime," *Strategy*, November 2018, p. A 10.

71. "Budweiser's Tit-for-Tat Strategy," *Strategy*, March 2017, p. A 19.

72. James McLeod, "Forget the Kardashians: Meet the New Breed of Influencers Tapping Social Media's Gold Rush," *National Post*, September 29, 2018, p. FP 1.

73. Josh Kolm, "Bigger Isn't Always Better," *Strategy*, March 2018, p. A 6.

74. "Tangerine Taps Influencers," *Strategy*, March 2017, p. A 18.

CHAPTER NINETEEN

1. Brenda Pritchard and Susan Vogt, *Advertising and Marketing Law in Canada*, Fifth Edition (LexisNexis, 2015).

2. A Guide to the Amendments of the *Competition Act*, Competition Bureau Canada, April 22, 2009.

3. Greg Keenan and Jeff Gray, "Competition Bureau Raps Avis, Budget for Misleading Prices," *The Globe and Mail*, March 12, 2015, p. B.1.

4. Aleksandra Sagan, "Competition Bureau Takes on Tickemaster," *Chronicle-Herald*, January 26, 2018, p. B 3.

5. Jean-Francois Ouellet, "Vachon's Igor Crossed the Line in Quebec," *National Post*, March 10, 2009, p. FP13.

6. https://adstandards.ca/.

7. https://adstandards.ca/wp-content/uploads/2018/06/Ad-Standards-2018-Consumer-Research.pdf.

8. https://adstandards.ca/interpretation-guidelines/.

9. https://adstandards.ca/about/childrens-advertising-initiative/.

10. https://adstandards.ca/wp-content/uploads/2018/11/Ad-Standards-CAI-Report-2017-EN.pdf.

11. Carly Weeks, "Critics Fight Proposed Bill Banning Junk-Food Ads," *The Globe and Mail*, June 30, 2018, p. A 9.

12. Joanne Laucius, "Kids Bombarded With Ads Via Social Media Websites," *The Ottawa Citizen*, October 30, 2018, p. A 3.

13. Matt Semansky, "Bell Ignores ASC Ruling," *Marketing Magazine*, February 23, 2009.

14. https://adstandards.ca/wp-content/uploads/2019/04/AdStandards-2019-Complaints-Report-EN.pdf.

15. http://adstandards.ca/en/standards/complaints_report/2001ascReportEn.pdf, accessed December 12, 2007.

16. http://www.adstandards.com/en/-standards/adComplaintsReports.asp?periodquarter =1&periodyear=2007, accessed December 12, 2007.

17. David Brown, "Kia Gets the Goat," *Marketing Magazine*, February 27, 2007.

18. http://www.adstandards.com/en/Standards/adComplaintsReports.asp?periodquarter=2&periodyear=2007.

19. http://www.adstandards.com/en/standards/adComplaintsReports.asp?periodquarter=2&periodyear=2008.

20. Stephanie O'Donohoe, "Attitudes to Advertising: A Review of British and American Research," *International Journal of Advertising*, 14 (3), Fall 1995, pp. 245–261.

21. Banwari Mittal, "Public Assessment of TV Advertising: Faint Praise and Harsh Criticism," *Journal of Advertising Research*, 34 (1), January–February 1994, pp. 35–53.

22. Sharon Shavitt, Pamela Lowery, and James Haefner, "Public Attitudes Toward Advertising; More Favorable Than You Might Think," *Journal of Advertising Research*, 38 (4), July/August 1998, pp. 7–22.

23. https://adstandards.ca/wp-content/uploads/2018/06/Ad-Standards-2018-Consumer-Research.pdf.

24. Gita Venkataramini Johar, "Consumer Involvement and Deception From Implied Advertising Claims," *Journal of Marketing Research, 32* (3), August 1995, pp. 267–279; J. Edward Russo, Barbara L. Metcalf, and Debra Stephens, "Identifying Misleading Advertising," *Journal of Consumer Research, 8* (2), September 1981, pp. 119–131.

25. Ivan L. Preston, *The Great American Blow-Up: Puffery in Advertising and Selling* (Madison: University of Wisconsin Press, 1975), p. 3.

26. Josh Kolm, "Smirnoff Comes Down to Earth," *Strategy*, February 2, 2015.

27. Kim Bhasin, "Estée Lauder CEO Says Sorry for Deception," *Telegraph-Journal*, May 5, 2018, p. A 20.

28. Shelby D. Hunt, "Informational vs. Persuasive Advertising: An Appraisal," *Journal of Advertising, 5* (3), Summer 1976, pp. 5–8.

29. Mittal, "Public Assessment of TV Advertising: Faint Praise and Harsh Criticism"; J. C. Andrews, "The Dimensionality of Beliefs Toward Advertising in General," *Journal of Advertising, 18* (1), March 1989, pp. 26–35; Shavitt, Lowery, and Haefner, "Public Attitudes Toward Advertising; More Favorable Than You Might Think."

30. David A. Aaker and Donald E. Bruzzone, "Causes of Irritation in Advertising," *Journal of Marketing, 49* (2), Spring 1985, pp. 47–57.

31. Stephen A. Greyser, "Irritation in Advertising," *Journal of Advertising Research, 13* (1), February 1973, pp. 3–10.

32. Jen Zoratti, "Weight Watchers' Free Plan Sends Teens Bad Message," *Winnipeg Free Press*, March 6, 2018.

33. Tom Reichert, Courtney Carpenter Childers, and Leonard N. Reid, "How Sex in Advertising Varies by Product Category: An Analysis of Three Decades of Visual Sexual Imagery in Magazine Advertising," *Journal of Current Issues and Research in Advertising, 33* (1), 2012, pp. 1–19.

34. John G. Wirtz, Johnny V. Sparks, and Thais M. Zimbres, "The Effect of Exposure to Sexual Appeals in Advertisements on Memory, Attitude, and Purchase Intention: A Meta-Analytic Review," *International Journal of Advertising, 37* (2), pp. 168–198.

35. https://adstandards.ca/wp-content/uploads/2018/06/Ad-Standards-2018-Consumer-Research.pdf.

36. Becca Clarkson, "Vancouver YWCA Aims to Clean Up Overly Sexual Advertisements," *The Globe and Mail*, May 2, 2018, p. A 9.

37. Scott Ward, Daniel B. Wackman, and Ellen Wartella, *How Children Learn to Buy: The Development of Consumer Information Processing Skills* (Beverly Hills, CA: Sage, 1979).

38. Thomas S. Robertson and John R. Rossiter, "Children and Commercial Persuasion: An Attribution Theory Analysis,"

Journal of Consumer Research, 1 (1), June 1974, pp. 13–20; Scott Ward and Daniel B. Wackman, "Children's Information Processing of Television Advertising," in *New Models for Communications Research*, eds. G. Kline and P. Clark (Beverly Hills, CA: Sage, 1974), pp. 81–119.

39. Merrie Brucks, Gary M. Armstrong, and Marvin E. Goldberg, "Children's Use of Cognitive Defenses Against Television Advertising: A Cognitive Response Approach," *Journal of Consumer Research, 14* (4), March 1988, pp. 471–482.

40. For a discussion on consumer socialization, see Scott Ward, "Consumer Socialization," *Journal of Consumer Research, 1* (2), September 1974, pp. 1–14.

41. Tamara F. Mangleburg and Terry Bristol, "Socialization and Adolescents' Skepticism Toward Advertising," *Journal of Advertising, 27* (3), Fall 1998, pp. 11–21.

42. Robert E. Hite and Randy Eck, "Advertising to Children: Attitudes of Business vs. Consumers," *Journal of Advertising Research, 27* (5), October/ November 1987, pp. 40–53; Ann D. Walsh, Russell N. Laczniak, and Les Carlson, "Mothers' Preferences for Regulating Children's Television," *Journal of Advertising, 27* (3), Fall 1998, pp. 23–36.

43. Dakshana Bascaramurty, "The Fine Line Between a Pokémon Ad and Entertainment," *The Globe and Mail*, November 15, 2011, p. L1.

44. Joanna Pachner and Alicia Androich, "Kids in Play," *Marketing Magazine*, March 14, 2011, pp. 27–28, 30–31.

45. Kate Hammer, "Advertising on School TV Screens Raises Alarm?" *The Globe and Mail*, March 9, 2011, p. A14.

46. Morris B. Holbrook, "Mirror Mirror On the Wall, What's Unfair in the Reflections on Advertising," *Journal of Marketing, 51* (3), July 1987, pp. 95–103.

47. Stephen Fox, *The Mirror Makers: A History of American Advertising and Its Creators* (New York: Morrow, 1984), p. 330.

48. Richard W. Pollay, "The Distorted Mirror: Reflections on the Unintended Consequences of Advertising," *Journal of Marketing, 50* (2), April 1986, p. 33.

49. Hunt, "Informational vs. Persuasive Advertising."

50. Alice E. Courtney and Thomas W. Whipple, *Sex Stereotyping in Advertising* (Lexington, MA: Lexington Books, 1984).

51. Daniel J. Brett and Joanne Cantor, "The Portrayal of Men and Women in U.S. Television Commercials: A Recent Content Analysis and Trends of 15 Years," *Sex Roles, 18* (9/10), 1998, pp. 595–608; John B. Ford and Michael La Tour, "Contemporary Perspectives of Female Role Portrayals in Advertising," *Journal of Current Issues and Research in Advertising, 28* (1), Spring 1996, pp. 81–93.

52. Beverly A. Browne, "Gender Stereotypes in Advertising on Children's Television in the 1990s: A Cross-National Analysis," *Journal of Advertising, 27* (1), Spring 1998, pp. 83–96.

53. Richard H. Kolbe, "Gender Roles in Children's Advertising: A Longitudinal Content Analysis," in *Current Issues and Research in Advertising*, ed. James H. Leigh and Claude R. Martin, Jr. (Ann Arbor: University of Michigan, 1991), pp. 197–206.

54. Steven M. Kates and Glenda Shaw-Garlock, "The Ever Entangling Web: A Study of Ideologies and Discourses in Advertising to Women," *Journal of Advertising, 28* (2), Summer 1999, pp. 33–49.

55. Basil Englis, Michael Solomon, and Richard Ashmore, "Beauty Before the Eyes of Beholders: The Cultural Encoding of Beauty Types in Magazine Advertising and Music Television," *Journal of Advertising, 23* (2), June 1994, pp. 49–64.

56. Stacy Landreh Grau and Yorgos C. Zotos, "Gender Stereotypes in Advertising: A Review of Current Research," *International Journal of Advertising, 35* (5), pp. 761–770.

57. Leonidis Hatzithoumas, Christina Boutsouki, and Paschalina Ziamou, "A Longitudinal Analysis of the Changing Roles of Gender in Advertising: A Content Analysis of Super Bowl Comercials," *International Journal of Advertising, 35* (5), 2016, pp. 888–906.

58. Susan Krashinsky, "Time to Adapt Ads for Modern Men," *The Globe and Mail*, July 9, 2014, p. B.8.

59. Robert E. Wilkes and Humberto Valencia, "Hispanics and Blacks in Television Commercials," *Journal of Advertising, 18* (1), Spring 1989, pp. 19–25.

60. Julia Bristor, Renee Gravois Lee, and Michelle Hunt, "Race and Ideology: African American Images in Television Advertising," *Journal of Public Policy and Marketing, 14* (1), Spring 1995, pp. 48–59.

61. Corliss Green, "Ethnic Evaluations of Advertising: Interaction Effects of Strength of Ethnic Identification, Media Placement, and Degree of Racial Composition," *Journal of Advertising, 28* (1), Spring 1999, pp. 49–64.

62. Charles R. Taylor and Barbara B. Stern, "Asian-Americans: Television Advertising and the 'Model Minority' Stereotype," *Journal of Advertising, 26* (2), Summer 1997, pp. 47–61.

63. Amy Yee, "Casino Ads Shouldn't Target East Asians," *The Ottawa Citizen*, September 5, 2018, p. A 10.

64. Susan Krashinsky, "The Mismatch of Race in TV Ads," *The Globe and Mail*, May 7, 2014, B.4; https://www12.statcan.gc.ca/nhs-enm/2011/ as-sa/99-010-x/99-010-x2011001-eng.cfm.

65. Tanya Kostiw, "Normalizing Today's Normal," *Strategy*, April 2015, p. A.16.

66. Jake Edmisto, "Outfitter Apologizes for Whitewashing the Outdoors," *National Post*, October 24, 2018, p. A 1.

67. Jef I. Richards and John H. Murphy, II, "Economic Censorship and Free Speech: The Circle of Communication Between Advertisers, Media and Consumers," *Journal of Current Issues and Research in Advertising, 18* (1), Spring 1996, pp. 21–33.

68. Lawrence C. Soley and Robert L. Craig, "Advertising Pressure on Newspapers: A Survey," *Journal of Advertising, 21* (4), December 1992, pp. 1–10.

69. Randy W. Elder, Ruth A. Shults, David A. Sleet, James L. Nichols, Robert S. Thompson, and Warda Rajab, "Effectiveness of Mass Media Campaigns for Reducing Drinking and Driving and Alcohol-Involved Crashes," *American Journal of Preventative Medicine, 27* (1), July 2004, pp. 57–65.

70. Deepa Venkatesan, "CNIB Gives Used Smartphones a Second, Accessible Life," *Strategy*, September 24, 2018.

71. Robert L. Steiner, "Does Advertising Lower Consumer Price?" *Journal of Marketing, 37* (4), October 1973, pp. 19–26.

72. James M. Ferguson, "Comments On 'The Impact of Advertising on the Price of Consumer Products,'" *Journal of Marketing, 46* (1), Winter 1982, pp. 102–105.

73. Paul W. Farris and Mark S. Albion, "The Impact of Advertising on the Price of Consumer Products," *Journal of Marketing, 44* (3), Summer 1980, pp. 17–35.

Chapter Sources

CHAPTER 1

RBC's IMC Goes Younger Sources: Josh Kolm, "2018 Brands of the Year: RBC Banks on the Next Generation," *Strategy*, October 2018; Josh Kolm, "RBC Takes a Lighthearted Approach in Latest Campaign," *Strategy*, September 2018; Catherine Phillips, "RBC Still Wants to Help Canadians Get Insurance," *Strategy*, April 2018; Josh Kolm, "RBC Helps Youth Prepare for the Future of Work," *Strategy*, March 2018.

Figure 1-2 Best Canadian brands Source: Based on data from Best Canadian Brands 2014, Interbrand.

Figure 1-3 The top 10 most valuable Canadian brands Source: Based on data from The Most Valuable Canadian Brands of 2018, The Brand Finance Group.

IMC PERSPECTIVE 1-1 Sources: Megan Hayes, "Branding Agropur," *Strategy*, July 2018, p. 50; Justin Dallaire, "Iögo Proteine Energizes the Umlaut," *Strategy*, March 2018; "Designing for a Masterbrand: The New IOGO," *Strategy*; cassies.ca; Rebecca Harris, "Iögo Unveils New Brand Image," *Canadian Grocer*, December 2016; Josh Kolm, "Iögo Shows Off Its New Look," *Strategy*, December 2016.

IMC PERSPECTIVE 1-2 Sources: Justin Dallaire, "Chevrolet Drives the Canadian Dream," *Strategy*, October 2018, p. 28; "Chevrolet Spark Launch," *Strategy*, Promo Awards 2017; Josh Kolm, "Chevrolet Pursues the Canadian Dream," *Strategy*, May 2017; David Gianatasio, "What Is the Canadian Dream?" *Adweek*, June 2017.

CHAPTER 2

Cossette Scores a Hat Trick Sources: "Cossette the Consumer-Centric Shop," *Strategy*, June 2017, p. 60; Chris Powell, "Cossette's Got Global Goals," *Strategy*, March 2018, p. 22; Justin Dallaire, "Cossette vs. Everyone," *Strategy*, November 2018, p. 24; Justin Dallaire, "Antoinette Benoit's Golden Strategy," *Strategy*, January 2019, p. 20: Jennifer Horn, "Cannes 2018: The Outdoor Winner," *Strategy*, June 2018; Cossette: 2018 Strategy Agency of the Year.

Figure 2-1 Largest international marketing communication firms http://strategyonline.ca/2018/04/20/the-2018-agency-family-tree/

IMC PERSPECTIVE 2-1 Sources: "Zulu Alpha Kilo: The Feisty Independent," *Strategy*, May 2017, p. 48; "Zulu Alpha Kilo: Inside the Box Creativity," *Strategy*, June 2017, p. 52; "Zulu Alpha Kilo: The Global Indie," *Strategy*, January 2018, p. 48; Catherine Phillips, "Zulu! Alpha! Kilo!" *Strategy*, July 2018; Josh Kolm, "Zulu Alpha Kilo's Big Design Ideas," *Strategy*, November 2018, p. 34.

IMC PERSPECTIVE 2-2 Sources: "No Fixed Address," *Strategy*, January 2018, p. 52; "Central Station," *Strategy*, January 2018, p. 54; "Cleansheet," *Strategy*, January 2018, p. 56; "CO-OP," *Strategy*, January 2018, p. 58; "The Adaptive Indie," *Strategy*, January 2018, p. 63; "Jacknife," *Strategy*, January 2018, p. 67; "Majestic," *Strategy*, January 2018, p. 68; "Gravity Partners," *Strategy*, January 2018, p. 70;

CHAPTER 3

Ikea's Beautiful Possibilities Sources: "2018 AToMiC Awards," *Strategy*, April 2018; Jennifer Horn, "Ikea Comes Full Circle," *Strategy*, October 2018, p. 24; Susan Krashinsky, "Ikea's New Canadian Ad Reflects Strategic Shirt," *The Globe and Mail*, September 10, 2018; Josh Kolm, "Check It Out: Ikea Ain't Afraid of No Ghosts," *Strategy*, October 31, 2018; Justin Dallaire, "Ikea's Holiday Campaign Taps the Magic of Old Furniture," *Strategy*, November 2018.

IMC PERSPECTIVE 3-1 Sources: 2018 Strategy Awards, *Strategy*, 2018; 2018 AToMiC Awards, *Strategy*, 2018; 2018 Media Innovation Awards, *Strategy*, 2018; Melissa Dunne, "Strategy Awards: Connecting With Canadians," *Strategy*, September 2018.

IMC PERSPECTIVE 3-2 Sources: "Camp Jefferson Gets Fanatical About Growth," *Strategy*, June 2017, p. 62; "CASSIES Bronze: Koodo Tackles Phone Bill Shock," *Strategy*, February 2018; Cassies.ca.

CHAPTER 4

Harley-Davidson Rides to 100 Sources: Jeromy Lloyd, "Harley-Davidson Faces a New Open Road," *Strategy*, March 2017; "2018 Design Agency of the Year," *Strategy*, 2018; "2018 Strategy Awards," *Strategy*, 2018.

IMC PERSPECTIVE 4-1 Sources: Justin Dallaire, "No Frills Finds Pride in Being a Hauler," *Strategy*, May 2018; Melissa Dunne, "The Discount Grocer With Swagger," *Strategy*, November 2018; "Agency of the Year: Loblaw Companies Limited," *Strategy*, 2018.

IMC PERSPECTIVE 4-2 Sources: "Knowing Your Brand DNA," *Strategy*, June 2017; "Leaving the Zoo to Understand the Tiger," *Strategy*, March 2017, p. 27; "2018 AToMiC Awards," *Strategy*, 2018.

CHAPTER 5

Who Is the Real GOAT? Sources: Jeromy Lloyd, "How Canada's New Candy Giant Will Move Forward," *Strategy*, January 2018; Melissa Dunne, "2018 Strategy Awards: Getting People Talking," *Strategy*, September 2018; Josh Kolm, "The Candy Man Can," *Strategy*, January, 2017; 2018 Strategy Awards.

IMC PERSPECTIVE 5-1 Sources: Melissa Dunne, "Never Forget Your Roots," *Strategy*, September 2018; Deepa Venkatesan, "Mark's Shows Its Appreciation for Down Time," *Strategy*, September 2018; Mark Burgess, "Marking Territory, From Work Wear to Casual," *Strategy*, March 2017, p. 58; 2018 Strategy Awards.

IMC PERSPECTIVE 5-2 Sources: Bree Rody-Mantha, "Tourisme Montréal Says Change Is Good," *Strategy*, January 2018; Josh Kolm, "Tourisme Montréal Apologizes in Advance," *Strategy*, December 2016; Catherine Phillips, "Tourisme Montréal Goes for the Young at Heart," *Strategy*, May 2018; 2018 Strategy Awards.

CHAPTER 6

Hugs From Huggies Sources: Jennifer Horn, "Embracing," *Strategy*, May 1, 2018; "2017 Strategy Awards: Huggies Leaves No Baby Unhugged," *Strategy*, November 10, 2017; 2018 Shopper Innovation & Activation Awards; Megan Hayes, "It Came From Canada," *Strategy*, January 2018; cassies.ca.

IMC PERSPECTIVE 6-1 Sources: "CASSIES Silver: Nissan Plugs Rogue in Hostile Terrain," *Strategy*, February 21, 2018; Justin Dallaire, "Nissan Shifts Gears to Conquer the Everyday," *Strategy*, April 27, 2018; Josh Kolm, "Nissan Doesn't Play It Safe," *Strategy*, October 2017, p. 22; cassies.ca.

IMC PERSPECTIVE 6-2 Sources: Jennifer Horn, "What's Going On at Kraft Heinz," *Strategy*, May 2017, p. 12; Megan Hayes, "Is Honesty a Brand's Best Policy," *Strategy*, April 10, 2017; Harmeet Singh, "Kraft Heinz Brings Back a Classico," *Strategy*, September 20, 2018; "CASSIES Bronze: Classico Is Second Best," *Strategy*, February 21, 2018; cassies.ca.

Figure 6-13 Critical analysis guiding repositioning decisions Summarized from cases located on Cassies.ca.

CHAPTER 7

#EatTogether for Wellness Sources: Justin Dallaire, "PC Praises Little Moments in Latest Eat Together Push," *Strategy*, January 4, 2019; Josh Kolm, "PC Takes Aim at the Solitary Desk Lunch," *Strategy*, January 8, 2018; Josh Kolm, "PC Gets the Country to #EatTogether," *Strategy*, January 10, 2017; Justin Dallaire, "Why PC Shifted Its Eat Together Conversation," *Strategy*, July 17, 2018.

IMC PERSPECTIVE 7-1 Sources: Sonya Fatah, "Why Cineplex Has a New Brand Platform," *Media in Canada*, December 16, 2015; Susan Krashinsky, "Cineplex Amps Up the Feel-Good Factor With Animated Short," *The Globe and Mail*, December 15, 2016; 2017 Shopper Innovation & Activation Awards; 2017 Promo Awards; Chris Powell, "Cineplex Elevates the Magic of Film," *Strategy*, December 2016.

Figure 7-3 Basis for emotional appeals Based on Dacher Keltner and Jennifer S. Lerner, "Emotion," *Handbook of Social Psychology,* ed. Susan T. Fiske, Daniel T. Gilbers, and Gardner Lindzey, 2010, John Wiley & Sons.

IMC PERSPECTIVE 7-2 Sources: Justin Dallaire, "Interac Takes On a New World," *Strategy,* October 2, 2017; Justin Dallaire, "Interac's Holiday Push for Alternative Payment Methods," *Strategy,* November 28, 2017; Catherine Phillips, "Interac Shows All the Different Ways to Tap," *Strategy,* May 4, 2018; 2017 Promo Awards; 2016 Promo Awards; 2015 Promo Awards; 2018 AToMiC Awards.

CHAPTER 8

Gain's Romantic Fragrance Sources: "CASSIES Gold: Gaining Cents With Scents," *Strategy,* February 2018; "2017 Strategy Awards," *Strategy,* November 2017; 2017 Strategy Awards; cassies.ca.

IMC PERSPECTIVE 8-1 Sources: 2017 Shopper Innovation & Activation Awards; "CASSIES Gold: Love Is in the Doritos Chip Bouquet," *Strategy,* February 2017; 2017 AToMiC Awards; Josh Kolm, "Doritos Ketchup Is the New Rose," *Strategy,* February 2016.

IMC PERSPECTIVE 8-2 Sources: 2018 Strategy Awards; Melissa Dunne, "It Doesn't Taste Awful . . . and It Works," *Strategy,* September 2018; cassies.ca; https://buckleyscanada.tumblr.com.

CHAPTER 9

Ad Effectiveness Measurement Sources: Thales Teixeira, "How to Profit From Lean Advertising," *Harvard Business Review,* June 2013, pp. 23–25; Wes Nichols, "Advertising Analytics 2.0," *Harvard Business Review,* March 2013, pp. 60–68; Werner Reinartz and Peter Saffert, "Creativity in Advertising," *Harvard Business Review,* June 2013, pp. 106–112.

IMC PERSPECTIVE 9-1 Sources: Diana Lucaci, "Emotion vs Logic: How Do You Decide," *Strategy,* March 4, 2014; "Nothing More Than Feelings," *The Economist,* December 7, 2013; Sarah Evans and Joy Hackenbracht, "Implicit Measurement of Emotion Improves Utility of Concept Testing," *Alert Magazine,* Fourth Quarter 2014.

IMC PERSPECTIVE 9-2 Sources: Mark Burgess, "Montreal Firm Takes Neuro-Marketing Online," *Strategy,* January 27, 2016; Jeff Fraser, "Neuro-Marketing Start-Up Plans Brain Experiment of DX3," *Marketing Magazine,* March 10, 2015; Hollie Shaw, "Looking Inside Your Brain," *National Post,* April 18, 2015, p. FP6; Susan Krashinsky, "Neuro-Marketing Takes Aim at the Mind," *Globe and Mail,* March 6, 2015, p. B7.

CHAPTER 10

Disruption in Canadian Media Sources: Toby Sanger, "It's Time to Level the Digital Playing Field," *Toronto Star,* February 16, 2018, p. A17; Daniel Bernhard, "Tax Rules Helping to Kill Canadian Media," *The Ottawa Citizen,* April 2, 2018; Bill Curry, "Google Says Sales-Tax Decision Is Up to the Government," *The Globe and Mail,* May 11, 2018; Susan Krashinsky, "Facebook to Collect GST on Some Ads Starting Mid 2019," *The Globe and Mail,* August 30, 2018; Emily Jackson, "Deductions for Foreign Online Ads in Crosshairs," *National Post,* August 23, 2018.

Figure 10-1 Net advertising revenues ($ millions) Sources: Television & Radio: CRTC; Newspaper: News Media Canada; Magazine: Magazines Canada & Ad Dynamics; Internet: IAB Canada; Out-of-home: Estimate based on Ad Dynamics; ThinkTV. Internet ad revenue for TV and newspaper is counted within Internet media. TV and newspaper totals include online/mobile ads shown in their respective media.

IMC PERSPECTIVE 10-1 Sources: Patti Summerfield, "Media AOY Gold: Touché Builds on Tech and Talent," *Strategy,* November 5, 2018; Melissa Dunne, "Media AOY Silver: OMD Canada Amps Up Solution Arsenal," *Strategy,* November 5, 2018; Patti Summerfield, "Media AOY Bronze: PHD Canada Digs Deep Into Data," *Strategy,* November 5, 2018; Bree Rody-Mantha, "Media AOY Bronze: Cossette Media Plays the Long Game," *Strategy,* November 5, 2018.

IMC PERSPECTIVE 10-2 Sources: AToMiC Awards 2019: Paralympic; AToMiC Awards 2019: McDonald's; AToMiC Awards 2019: Harley-Davidson; AToMiC Awards 2019: Tourism Ottawa; AToMiC Awards 2019: Fountain Tire; AToMiC Awards 2019: Tobasco.

Figure 10-29 Summary of examples of target and media choices Source: Cassies.ca

Figure 10-30 Summary of Budweiser's Red Lights IMC Plan Source: Cassies.ca

CHAPTER 11

Broadcast Industry in Transition Sources: Susan Krashinsky Robertson, "An Industry Under Threat," *The Globe and Mail,* August 25, 2018, p. B6; Chris Powell, "What's Next in the Digital Revolution," *Strategy,* August 2017, p. A28; Emily Jackson, "Much Ado About," *National Post,* March 10, 2018, p. FP5; Emily Jackson, "BCE Steps Up Game on Crave Rebrand," *National Post,* November 5, 2018, p. FP1; Susan Robertson Krashinsky, "Bell Media, Lions Gate Partnership to Launch Starz Channel in Canada," *The Globe and Mail,* January 24, p. B5.

Figure 11-2 Weekly hours watched, network TV, fall 2018 Data computed from TV Basics 2019 pp. 24–28, ThinkTV

Figure 11-4 Weekly hours watched, specialty TV, fall 2018 Data from TV Basics 2019, pp. 29–31, ThinkTV

Figure 11-8 Weekly hours watched by age, fall 2018 Data from TV Basics 2019, p. 24, ThinkTV.

Figure 11-14 Profile of TV My Way viewers MTM TV My Way 2018, Anglo.

IMC PERSPECTIVE 11-1 Sources: Susan Krashinsky, "Don't Blame Us for Super Bowl Signal Swap," *The Globe and Mail,* January 25, 2014, p. B3; Susan Krashinsky, "CRTC Clears the Way for U.S. Super Bowl Ads," *The Globe and Mail,* January 30, 2015, p. A6; Terence Corcoran, "Super Bowl Ads No Victory," *National Post,* January 30, 2015, p. A1; James Bradshaw, "Bell, CRTC Clash Over Super Bowl Call," *The Globe and Mail,* February 3, 2015, p. B6; Emily Jackson, "Super Bowl Numbers Well Below Simsub Days," *National Post,* February 6, 2018, p. FP10; Michael Lewis, "Bell Media Puts Game Face On," *Toronto Star,* February 2, 2018, p. B1; Christine Dobby, "Top Court Declines Bell's Request to Show Canadian Ads During Super Bowl," *The Globe and Mail,* January 27, 2018, p. B5; Susan Krashinsky Robertson, "Trade Deal Overturns CRTC Decision on Super Bowl Ads," *The Globe and Mail,* October 2, 2018, p. B7.

IMC PERSPECTIVE 11-2 Sources: "What's in It for the Buyers?" *Strategy,* July 2018, p. A38; Susan Krashinsky Robertson, "Corus Testing New Advertising Technology," *The Globe and Mail,* October 20, 2018, p. B23; Susan Krashinsky Robertson, "Corus Grapples With Decline in TV Ads," *The Globe and Mail,* January 2018, p. B2; Bree Rody-Mantha, "What's All the Complaining About?" *Strategy,* August 2017, p. A32; Bree Rody-Mantha, "Complaining and Explaining," *Strategy,* July 2018, p. A40.

CHAPTER 12

Creative Print Ads Source: https://marketingawards.strategyonline.ca/winners/winner/2018/

IMC PERSPECTIVE 12-1 Sources: Chris Powell, "Digital Magazine Readership Tops 5 Million," *Marketing Magazine,* November 18, 2015; Magazines Canada Reader-and-Buyer Study, 2017; Bree Rody-Mantha, "Many Magazine Readers Still Opt for Print," *Media in Canada,* October 22, 2018; Bree Rody-Mantha, "*Sharp* Magazine Is Still All About Print," *Media in Canada,* May 3, 2017.

Figure 12-7 Daily newspaper circulation by publisher ©News Media Canada, Snapshot Fact Sheet, 2016.

IMC PERSPECTIVE 12-2 Sources: Stuart Thomson, "Ottawa's $600M in Funding for Media a Turning Point," *National Post,* November 22, 2018, p. A5; Susan Krashinsky, "Ottawa's Plan to Subsidize Media Lauded," *The Globe and Mail,* November 23, 2018, p. B3; Susan Krashinsky, "Budget Media Provisions Disappointing, Industry Says," *The Globe and Mail,* March 1, 2018, p. B3; Daniel Lebanc, "Media Lobby Eyes Provincial Help as Ottawa Signals Limited Support," *The Globe and Mail,* February 26, 2018, p. A4; Daniel Leblanc, "Ottawa Opens Door to Charitable Status for News Agencies," *The Globe and Mail,* February 28, 2018, p. B7.

CHAPTER 13

Billboards Go Digital Sources: "JUICE Mobile Technology to Provide the Missing Link Between Mobile and OOH Media," *Strategy*, September 2014; "Astral-Out-of-Home Drives Campaign Success With Digital Technology and New Formats," *Strategy*, September 2014; "The New OOH Front: Dynamic, Interactive and Immediate," *Strategy*, September 2014; Chris Powell, "Digital Puts the Awe Into OOH," *Marketing Magazine*, May 2014; Chris Powell, "Digital Outdoor Gets Noticed," *Marketing Magazine*, June 10, 2015; Chris Powell, "The McSnow Report," *Marketing Magazine*, February 17, 2016; "Astral's Creative Approach to Innovation," *Strategy*, October 2018, p. A59; https://carteblancheforcreatives.ca.

Figure 13-2 Consumer responses to digital outdoor ads, % agreement with statements Source: COMMB, Shoppers' Attitudes of Digital OOH.

IMC PERSPECTIVE 13-1 Sources: "Quebecor Transit Shelters Are Upping Interactivity That Grabs Consumer Attention," *Strategy*, September 2014; "Street and the City," *Strategy*, October 2017, p. A47; https://quebecor.solutions/en/plateformes/affichage.

IMC PERSPECTIVE 13-2 Sources: Susan Krashinsky, "Small Screen Strategy, Big Ambition," *The Globe and Mail*, March 25, 2014, p. B3; Jim Middlemiss, "Navigating Digital Media World," *National Post*, June 20, 2014, p. SR2; Shane Schick, "Cineplex Urges Busy Canadians to Make Time for Entertainment," *Marketing Magazine*, December 17, 2015; Cineplex Media Kit 2019; Susan Krashinsky Robertson, "Cineplex Revenue Gets a Lift as Company Eyes Opportunities Beyond Theatres," *Strategy*, August 11, 2018, p. B3.

CHAPTER 14

Budweiser's Red Light Is a Winner Sources: "CASSIES Gold: Bud's Strategy to Own the Goal," *Strategy*, February 21, 2018; Megan Hayes, "It Came From Canada," *Strategy*, January 5, 2018; Chris Powell, "Real World Meets Social Content," *Strategy*, May 14, 2018; Susan Krashinsky Robertson, "A Bright Idea Goes Global," *The Globe and Mail*, January 19, 2018, p. B10; Josh Kolm, "Budweiser's Premium Approach to Celebrating Goals," *Strategy*, January 22, 2018; *Strategy* Media Innovation Award 2017.

IMC PERSPECTIVE 14-1 Sources: Catherine Phillips, "Taco Bells Sends Fans to Texas," *Strategy*, May 17, 2018; Deepa Venkantesan, "Air Canada Vacations Gets New Immersive Look," *Strategy*, September 18, 2018; Josh Kolm, "Would You Trade Two Hours for a Trip to the Yukon," *Strategy*, February 15, 2019; Christopher Lombardo, "Happy Planet Puts on a Smiling Face," *Strategy*, April 17, 2019; "CIL Paints," *Strategy*, February 22, 2017.

IMC PERSPECTIVE 14-2 Sources: "CASSIES Bronze: Coke Bottles Shareable Music," *Strategy*, February 22, 2017; Jeromy Lloyd, "Successful Play a Coke Enjoys Second Summer Launch," *Strategy*, May 4, 2017; Shopper Innovation Award 2017, *Strategy*. Shopper Innovation Award 2018, *Strategy*.

CHAPTER 15

Bell Let's Talk Heals Sources: Emily Jackson, "Why BCE's Let's Talk Keeps Working," *National Post*, February 3, 2018, p. FP4; Josh Kolm, "How Bell Is Keeping the Momentum Going for Let's Talk," *Strategy*, January 25, 2017; Jeromy Lloyd, "Which Causes Remain Key to Canadians?" *Strategy*, October 17, 2017; Justin Dallaire, "Bell Broadens the Let's Talk Conversation," *Strategy*, January 8, 2018; Justin Dallaire, "Bell Let's Talk Finds New Ways to Grow the Discussion," *Strategy*, January 10, 2019.

IMC PERSPECTIVE 15-1 Sources: Kevin Libin, "Treason at Timmies," *National Post*, January 12, 2018, p. FP7; Susan Krashinsky Robertson, "Public Outcry Puts Tim's Brand in Hot Water," *The Globe and Mail*, January 20, 2018, p. B1; Marina Strauss, "Tim Hortons Names New Head Amid Tensions With Franchisees," *The Globe and Mail*, March 9, 2018, p. B1; Hollie Shaw, "Franchisee Ire Greets Tims Makeover," *National Post*, March 28, 2018, p. FP1; Tara Deschamps, "Tim Hortons President Commits to Better Relationship With Franchisee," *The Globe and Mail*, May 11, 2018, p. B3; Marina Strauss, "Tim Hortons Franchisee Group Threatens Protests Over Licence Renewal Dispute," *The Globe and Mail*, June 1, 2018, p. B1; Salmaan Farooqui, "U.S. Tim Hortons Franchise Group Sues RBI," *The Globe and Mail*, July 25, 2018, p. B3; Marina Strauss, "Tim Hortons Serves Up New Initiatives to Spur Sales," *The Globe and Mail*, August 2, 2018, p. B1; Marina Strauss, "Tim Hortons' Dissident Group Vows to Continue Fight," *The Globe and Mail*, September 25, 2018, p. B1; Susan Krashinsky Robertson, "Tim Hortons Returns to 'True Story' Marketing Roots in Effort to Win Back Customers," *The Globe and Mail*, November 29, 2018, p. B1.

IMC PERSPECTIVE 15-2 Sources: Rebecca Harris, "Which Sponsorship Partners Are Tops With Canadians," *Marketing Magazine*, July 7, 2015; Chris Powell, "Tim Hortons Among the Top Sports Sponsor Brands," *Marketing Magazine*, July 8, 2015; Chris Powell, "Ahead in the Game," *Marketing Magazine*, November/December, 2014; Shane McNeil, "Sponsorship Works," *BNN Bloomberg*, April 12, 2019; James Bradshaw, "Game On: Scotiabank Embarks on $800 Million Naming Rights Venture at Air Canada Centre," *The Globe and Mail*, July 2, 2018; James Bradshaw, "TD Bank, Toronto Blue Jays Poised to Strike Expanded Sponsorship Deal," *The Globe and Mail*, August 7, 2018.

CHAPTER 16

Loyalty Program Shakeup Sources: Josh Kolm, "RBC and WestJet to Launch New Loyalty Program," *Strategy*, June 13, 2018; Justin Dallaire, "How Air Miles Plans to Win Loyalty," *Strategy*, April 24, 2018; Justin Dallaire, "Consumers Happiest With Small Rewards," *Strategy*, March 14, 2018; Josh Kolm, "Experience Using a Loyalty Program a Bigger Driver Than Rewards," *Strategy*, April 30, 2019; Sean Claessen, "Banking on Enterprise Loyalty," *Strategy*, June 14, 2018; Josh Kolm, "Focus Is the Future of Loyalty," *Strategy*, December 11, 2018.

Figure 16-3 Reasons why Canadians receive email messages Source: Based on data from ExactTarget, "Subscribers, Fans & Followers #21: The Digital North," June 13, 2013.

IMC PERSPECTIVE 16-1 Sources: Josh Kolm, "Loblaw to Merge PC Plus and Optimum Programs," *Strategy*, November 8, 2017; Justin Dallaire, "Loblaw Enlists Eagle Eye to Enhance PC Optimum," *Strategy*, February 14, 2018; Josh Kolm, "Loblaw's Optimum-ized Digital Ad Approach," *Strategy*, May 6, 2019; Justin Dallaire, "Esso Drops Aeroplan for PC Optimum," *Strategy*, March 14, 2018; Hollie Shaw, "Shoppers Optimum Goes Digital," *National Post*, May 28, 2015.

CHAPTER 17

Internet Media Display Ads Sources: Josh Kolm, "Quesada Partners With Beyond Meat," *Strategy*, February 26, 2019; Josh Kolm, "Leon's Launches Stylish Campaign With New AOR," *Strategy*, May 17, 2019; Josh Kolm, "Schick Shows a More Positive Version of Locker Room Talk," *Strategy*, March 29, 2019; Christopher Lombardo, "Danone Starts a Yogurt Revolution," *Strategy*, June 6, 2019.

DIGITAL AND SOCIAL MEDIA PERSPECTIVE 17-2 Sources: Christopher Lombardo, "Mobile Strategies at Retail," *Strategy*, May 29, 2019; Josh Kolm, "Cirque du Soleil Combines Print and AR," *Strategy*, March 28, 2019; Justin Dallaire, "Loblaw Expands Food Waste Reduction Program," *Strategy*, June 14, 2019; Josh Kolm, "7-Eleven Tries to Catch 'em All," *Strategy*, May 9, 2019; Melissa Dunne, "Helping Tourists Find Icebergs Near Newfoundland and Labrador," *Strategy*, April 25, 2019.

Figure 17-12 Ad impressions by type of Internet media Based on data from Ad impressions by type of Internet media. Source: comScore, Digital Future in Focus, Canada 2015, page 47.

Figure 17-24 Retail shopping activities via smart phone app and browser Based on data from Retail activities via smartphone app and browser. Source: comScore, Digital Future in Focus, Canada 2015, page 25.

CHAPTER 18

Facebook Faced Issues Sources: Tamsin McMahon, "The Long Road to Fixing Facebook," *The Globe and Mail*, March 10, 2018; Selina Wang, "Facebook Changes Could Mean Less Time Spent on Site," *National Post*, January 13, 2018; Susan Krashinsky Robertson, "Canadians' Trust in Facebook Takes a Dive, New Survey Says," *The Globe and Mail*, March 29, 2018; Tamsin McMahon, "Facebook User Growth Slows Amid Privacy Concerns," *The Globe and Mail*, October 31, 2018; Dylan Robertson, "Feds Paid Facebook for Energy Campaign," *Winnipeg Free Press*, April 19, 2018.

Figure 18-11 YouTube and Internet video viewing by age, fall 2018, anglophones 18+ Media Technology Monitor

Figure 18-12 YouTube video view by age, fall 2016, anglophones 18+ Media Technology Monitor

Figure 18-14 YouTube subscriber statistics Source: Compiled by observation on June 4, 2013, May 21, 2016, and June 27, 2019.

DIGITAL AND SOCIAL MEDIA PERSPECTIVE 18-1 Sources: Azzura Lalani, "The Doctor Is Instagramming," *Toronto Star*, February 5, 2018, p. E1; Janna Zitter Appleby, "Would You Like Pics With That?" *The Globe and Mail*, March 10, 2018, p. 8; Melissa Dunne, "How to Tailor Your Strategy to Gen Z," *Strategy*, January 2019, p. A8; "Opera Stars Embrace Instagram," *The Globe and Mail*, October 20, 2018, p. R3; Melissa Dunne, "Yorkdale Dreams Up Insta-Worthy Spaces," *Strategy*, June 25, 2019.

DIGITAL AND SOCIAL MEDIA PERSPECTIVE 18-2 Sources: Bree Rody-Mantha, "Goldfish Go," *Strategy*, March 29, 2019; Melissa Dunne, "Social Engagements: How Snapchat Creates Connections With AR," *Strategy*, March 28, 2019; "The Agency A List: Critical Mass," *Strategy*, May 5, 2019; "The Agency A List: Mindshare," *Strategy*, May 5, 2019; Melissa Dunne, "McDonald's Uses Snapchat to Promote McDelivery," *Strategy*, June 28, 2019; Melissa Dunne, "IGA Brings Tattoos to Life With AR," *Strategy*, June 6, 2019.

CHAPTER 19

No Stopping SickKids VS Sources: Harmeet Singh, "Building the New SickKids," *Strategy*, January 2018, p. A23; Sneh Duggal, "Brands Join SickKids' Fight," *Strategy*, March 2018; http://cassies.ca/entry/viewcase/53983; Strategy Awards, *Strategy*, 2018.

Figure 19-1 Advertising and marketing law in Canada Source: Adapted from *Advertising and Marketing Law in Canada*, Brenda Pritchard and Susan Vogt, LexisNexis, Butterworths, 2006.

Figure 19-2 Summary of annual complaints from Ad Standards Sources: https://adstandards.ca/wp-content/uploads/2019/04/AdStandards-2019-Complaints-Report-EN.pdf; https://adstandards.ca/wp-content/uploads/2018/08/2017adComplaintsReport.pdf; https://adstandards.ca/wp-content/uploads/2018/04/2016adComplaintsReport.pdf

Figure 19-3 Advertising principles of the Association of Canadian Advertisers Based on the Association of Canadian Advertisers, www.aca-online.com.

ETHICAL PERSPECTIVE 19-1 Sources: Aleesha Harris, "American Apparel Plans to Keep It Real," *Vancouver Sun*, November 24, 2018, p. F3; Tara Deschamps, "American Apparel to Launch Comeback With Online Store and a Canadian Owner," *The Globe and Mail*, October 30, 2018, p. B6; Justin Dallaire, "American Apparel Shifts to Inclusive Messaging," *Strategy*, October 9, 2018; Lucy Lau, "American Apparel Rises From the Dead With Online Shop and Vancouver-Shot Lookbook," www.straight.com, October 22, 2018; Nicholas Mizera, "American Apparel Doesn't Deserve a Second Chance in Canada," www.huffingtonpost.ca, October 19, 2018.

ETHICAL PERSPECTIVE 19-2 Sources: Megan Haynes, "Rethink Rejigs the Non-Profit Model," *Strategy*, October 2017, p. A24; Harmeet Singh, "Rethink Breast Cancer Reinvents the Hotline," *Strategy*, September 26, 2017; AToMiC Awards, *Strategy*, 2017.

Figure 19-5 The positive economic effects of advertising Source: These excerpts are from a speech given by Leo Burnett on the American Association of Advertising Agencies' 50th anniversary, April 20, 1967.

Name and Company Index

Note: *f* following a number indicates a figure. Boldface indicates pages on which terms are defined. Cross-references may refer to entries in the Subject Index.

3G Capital, 384
5-hour Energy, 133
7-Eleven, 443
9-1-1, 274
14-Day Challenge (Activia), 66
18K925, 162
24 Hours, 307

A

A&W, 4, 139–140, 141, 158, 167
Abercrombie and Fitch, 490
About, 469
Absolut, 33, 155, 226
Academy Awards, 271, 352
AC/DC, 176
A-Class, 62
Activia, 14, 66, 118, 133
Acura, 404
Ad Age (formerly *Advertising Age*), 36, 160
Ad Standards (AS), 482–487
    gender portrayal complaints to, 495
    on advertising to children, 483, 486–487, 492
    on sexual appeals, 490
    on social media engagement activities, 472
    product type complaints to, 488
Adams, Michael, 168
AdChoices, 428
Adidas, 33, 35, 57, 143, 239
Advertising Age (now *Ad Age*), 36, 160
Advertising Research Foundation (ARF), 54, 229, 444
Advertising Standards Canada, 425, 426*f*, 458
Advil, 136, 196
Adweek, 160
Aero, 129
Aeroplan, 399, 411, 412
African-Americans, 495
Air Canada
    brand name, 5
    emotional appeals, 173
    market positioning strategy, 126
    Marketel and, 33
    on Instagram, 466
    PR activities, 391
    sales promotions, 346
    WestJet and, 167, 291, 329
Air France, 126
Air Miles, 399, 409–410, 411, 412, 442

Air Wick, 16
Air Yukon, 346
Airbnb, 302
Alberta Beef, 297
Alberta Gaming and Liquor Commission, 496
Albion, Mark S., 499
Alcon, 188
Alegría (Cirque du Soleil), 443
Alfa Romeo, 423
"All I Do Is Win" (song), 139
"All In" (Adidas), 143, 239
Alliance for Audited Media (AAM), 298, 309
Alliance of Canadian Cinema, Television and Radio Artists (ACTRA), 267
Always, 33, 200
Amazing Race, The, 55, 272, 274
Amazon, 7, 429
American Apparel, 490–491
American Association of Advertising Agencies, 15
American Express
    brand positioning strategy, 134
    celebrity endorsements, 181, 182, 183
    direct marketing, 402
    hierarchy of effects model and, 108
American Marketing Association (AMA), 4, 8
American Music Awards, 352
ANA (Association of National Advertisers), 40, 41, 47
Anand Keller, Punam, 174
Anderson, Tracy, 45
Annalect, 39
Anomaly, 190
Answers, 469
Apple
    brand equity, 7
    brand positioning strategy, 128, 134, 136
    category need, 116
    creative execution style, 192
Aritzia, 143
Armani, 297
Armstrong, Neil, 295
Arrowhead, 176
AS. *See* Ad Standards (AS)
Asian-Americans, 495
Aspen Marketing Services, 343
Assassin's Creed, 17
Association des professionels de la communication et du marketing, 169
Association of Canadian Advertisers
    advertising agencies and, 33, 41
    advertising principles of, 488, 489*f*

Digital Advertising Alliance of Canada and, 428
    role in measuring TV audiences, 274
Association of Creative Communications Agencies, 169
Association of National Advertisers (ANA), 40, 41, 47
Astral, 319, 321–322, 324, 331
Astro, 14
AToMiC awards, 251, 388
Auto Trader, 438, 485–486
Aveeno, 144
Aventura (CIBC), 190
Avis, 481
Axe, 334, 358

B

Baby Post, The (blog), 473
"Back in Black" (song), 176
Bacon Ranch Naked Chicken Chalupa, 345–346
Baja Blast, 468
Balloon for Ben, A (Cineplex), 36, 157
"Banking Can Be This Comfortable" (TD Canada Trust), 135
"Banking That Fits Your Life" (CIBC), 190
Bannon, Véronique, 373
Barbie, 179
Barrett and Welsh, 295
Baruchel, Jay, 3
BBDO, 34*f*
BCE, 267
"Be in the Black" (Interac), 35, 36
"Be Super" (Mattel), 179
Bear Mountain Resort, 405
Beau's, 24
"Beautiful Possibilities" (IKEA), 51
Beauty, 303
"Beauty on a Small Budget" (CIL), 345
Bebe, 165, 191
Becel, 134, 387, 446
Beckham, David, 181
Beckham, Odell, Jr., 219
Beer Store, The, 297
Beirness, Kate, 224
Belairdirect, 9–10, 446
Bell
    advertising expenditures, 431
    billboards, 319
    brand positioning strategy, 142
    Circo de Bakuza and, 45
    Competition Bureau fines, 472
    Data-Enhanced TV, 285
    distribution channels, 8
    Koodo and, 70
    PR activities, 373, 379

Bell—*Cont.*
  radio advertising, 291
  radio stations owned by, 286
  response to transition in broadcast
      media, 267
  Rogers's complaint against, 484
  Super Bowl ads and, 281
  Zulu Alpha Kilo and, 35–36
Bell Canada Act, 480
Bella and Jack Bring Back the Bees
  (Bourgeois), 88
Ben and Jerry's, 458
Benjamin Moore, 273
Bensimon and Byrne, 39
Best Buy, 114, 406
Best Deodorant in the World, The, 6
Better Business Bureau, 484
"Better Starts Now" (Citizen Watch
  Company), 76–77
Beyond Meat Burritos, 419
Bicycle Factory (Cadbury's), 387–388
Bier Market, 46
Big Bang Theory, The, 274
Big Brothers Big Sisters, 378, 458
"Big Play, The" (Canadian Tire), 106, 388
Big Rock, 35
Billboard, 157
Billy Bishop Airport, 479
BioSteel, 166–167, 181
BioWare, 460
Birks, 55, 127
Bixi, 387
BlackBerry, 66–67, 464
Block, Lauren Goldberg, 174
Blogger, 468, 469
BlogTO, 469
Bluetooth, 323
Blumes, Mark, 103
BMO, 272, 378, 391
BMW
  advertising creativity, 154
  brand attitude, 119
  buyer decision stages and, 149
  Internet media use, 425
  PHD and, 239
  sales promotions, 361
  storytelling, 166
Bombardier, 137, 238
Boomer and Echo (blog), 473
Bose, 400
Boston Bruins, 391
Boston Celtics, 391
Boston Pizza, 111, 192, 378
Bourgeois, Paulette, 88
Boys and Girls Clubs, 379
Brainsights, 224
Brand Development Index (BDI), **243,** 244*f*
Brand Finance, 7
Brand Immortality, 172
Breitling, 181

Briatico, Isabella, 361
Broadcast Code for Advertising to Children,
  481, 486, 492
Broadcasting Act, 480
BT, 180
Buckley, Frank, 195, 196
Buckley's Mixture, 195, 196
Budget, 481
Budweiser, 44, 144, 473. *See also* Red
  Light (Budweiser)
Bugatchi, 297
Buick, 219
Bündchen, Gisele, 32, 90
Burnett, Leo, 165, 500, 501*f*
Burrell, Ty, 187
Burt's Bees, 139–140
Buzzfeed, 452

C
C&B Advertising, 35
Cadbury's, 387–388
Calgary Co-op, 35
California almonds, 115
Calvin Klein, 303, 483, 484
Camp Day (Tim Hortons), 373
"Campaign for Real Beauty" (Dove), 56,
  146, 160, 180
Campbell's, 141, 361, 378
Canada 150, 153
Canada Goose, 423
Canada Post, 18, 401, 403, 404
Canadian Advertising Foundation
  (CAF), 401
Canadian Advertising Rates and Data
  (CARD)
  magazines, 296, 297, 298,
      299–300, 301
  media generally, 254
  newspapers, 309
  outdoor media, 322
  radio, 286
Canadian Advertising Success Stories
  (CASSIES), 102, 143, 169, 213, 405
Canadian Architect, 297
Canadian Association of
  Broadcasters, 274, 486
Canadian Association of Pediatric Health
  Centres, 125
Canadian Association of Plastic
  Surgeons, 467–468
Canadian Blood Services, 10
Canadian Breast Cancer Foundation, 394
Canadian Broadcast Standards Council,
  484, 485
Canadian Broadcasting Act, 267
Canadian Business, 297
Canadian Cancer Society, 403
Canadian Children's Food and Beverage
  Advertising Initiative (CAI), 483,
  489, 492

Canadian Club, 458
Canadian Code of Advertising
  Standards, 482–483, 485, 489*f*
Canadian Community Newspapers
  Association (CCNA), 310
Canadian Cosmetic, Toiletry and
  Fragrance Association, 486
"Canadian Dream" (Chevrolet), 21, 22
Canadian Football League (CFL), 9–10,
  390–391, 462
Canadian Gardening, 250
Canadian Geographic, 303, 304
Canadian Grocer, 297
Canadian Hockey League, 391
Canadian House and Home, 300
Canadian Lawyer, 297
Canadian Living, 252*f,* 282, 300, 303
Canadian Marketing Association (CMA),
  378, 401, 408, 428
Canadian Media Fund, 267
Canadian Media Producers
  Association, 267
Canadian National Institute for the
  Blind (CNIB), 497
Canadian National Railway, 5
Canadian Newspaper Association
  (CNA), 310
Canadian Olympic Committee (COC),
  391, 393
Canadian Out of Home Marketing and
  Measurement Bureau (COMMB),
  324–325
Canadian Paralympic Committee, 251
Canadian Radio-television and
  Telecommunications Commission
  (CRTC)
  code for alcohol advertising, 486
  complaints made via, 484
  number of radio stations listed
      by, 286
  number of TV commercials permitted
      by, 284
  on gender portrayals in
      advertising, 483
  Super Bowl ads and, 280–281, 480
Canadian Standards Association, 483
Canadian Tire
  as most admired company, 386*f*
  brand recognition, 118
  catalogues, 405
  loyalty program, 399, 410
  Mark's, 104
  PR activities, 373, 388, 391
  preprinted inserts, 309
  shopping objectives, 114
  Touché and, 43
  TSN and, 272, 388
  "We All Play for Canada," 44, 106
Canadian Tourism Commission, 68, 69,
  144, 147, 243

Cannes Lions
    advertising effectiveness measurement and, 213
    Chipotle, 190
    IKEA, 51
    Mars, 456
    Procter & Gamble, 200
    SickKids, 31, 441
    Skittles, 192
    Titanium Lion, 170
Canon, 166
Caramilk, 129
CARD. *See* Canadian Advertising Rates and Data (CARD)
Carex Mini-Storage, 295
Carey, Mariah, 93
Cashmere, 144, 145, 357
Casio, 94
CASSIES. *See* Canadian Advertising Success Stories (CASSIES)
Category Development Index (CDI), **243**, 244*f*
CBC
    as national TV network, 269*f*, 270
    Canadian Tire and, 43
    Hockey Night in Canada on, 271
    radio, 480
    visible minorities in ads on, 496
Center for Exhibition Industry Research, 366
Central Station, 44
CFL (Canadian Football League), 9–10, 390–391, 462
Chanel, 90, 179
Charles-Bruneau Foundation, 471
Charmin, 144
Chatelaine, 252*f*, 300
Chatime, 119
Cheer, 250
Cheerios, 77–78, 87–88, 496
Cheetos, 201, 351
Cheil, 134
Chevrolet
    "Canadian Dream," 21, 22
    emotional appeals, 172
    functional benefits of Sonic, 55
    product placement, 272
    teaser advertising, 176
Chill, 297
Chipotle, 190
"Choose Beautiful" (Dove), 56, 180
"Choose Happy" (Koodo), 69, 142
CIBC
    brand positioning strategy, 140
    personality symbol, 190
    PR activities, 373, 389, 390, 391, 394
CIL, 345
Cineplex
    A Balloon for Ben and *Lily and the Snowman*, 36, 157

information processing model and, 84
loyalty program, 113, 399, 412
Mazda and, 423
place-based advertising at, 332–333
President's Choice and, 153
Zulu Alpha Kilo and, 35
Circle K, 362
Circo de Bakuza, 45
Cirque du Soleil, 33, 45, 443, 461
Citizen Watch Company, 76–77
City of Toronto, 322
CityLine, 180
Citytv, 14, 269*f*
Claritas, 63
Clarkson, Kelly, 76–77
Classico, 138–139, 218
Cleansheet, 44
"Club" (Nespresso), 403
Coach, 78
Coast to Coast Monopoly (McDonald's), 238–239
Coca-Cola
    AIDA model and, 84
    brand loyalty, 57
    brand symbol, 77
    category need, 117
    emotional appeals, 172
    Internet media use, 442
    Pepsi and, 68, 112, 349–350
    sales promotions, 349–350, 355–356
Code for Broadcast Advertising of Alcoholic Beverages, 486
Coffee Crisp, 129
Coke. *See* Coca-Cola
COMMB (Canadian Out of Home Marketing and Measurement Bureau), 324–325
"Common Ground" (Harley-Davidson), 75
Competition Act, 472, 481
Competition Bureau, 360, 472, 481, 483
ConAgra, 362
Confessions of an Advertising Man (Ogilvy), 164–165
"Conquer All Conditions" (Nissan), 131, 132
Consumer Drug Advertising Guidelines, 486
Consumer Protection Act of Quebec, 481
Consumer Reports, 54
Consumer Response Council and Appeal Panel, 485
Contagious Magazine, 156
"Conversation" (Scotiabank), 189
Cooking Channel, 278
CO-OP, 44
Coors. *See* Molson Coors
Coors Banquet, 357–358
Coors Light, 119, 144, 424
Copeland, Misty, 32
Corby, 117–118

Cornetto, 172
Corona, 80
Corus, 267, 282, 285
Cosmopolitan TV, 282
Cossette (Vision7), 31, 34, 239, 479
Costco, 81, 402
Cottonelle, 144, 145
Country Music Television, 358
Couponclick.ca, 355
Coupons.com, 355
"Cover" (Coca-Cola), 84
Cracker Barrel, 136–137
Craigslist, 51
Crankworx, 393
Crave, 267, 269
"Crave More" (Loblaw), 67
Crest, 421
CRTC. *See* Canadian Radio-television and Telecommunications Commission (CRTC)
CRTC Act, 480
CTV
    as content streamer, 429
    as national network, 269*f*
    Canadian content on, 267
    network advertising online and, 271
    Super Bowl ads and, 280–281
    TV video ads on, 436
    visible minorities in ads on, 496
Curél, 301
Customer Lifetime Value (CLTV), **408**

D

DAGMAR (Designing Advertising Goals for Measured Results), **106**–107, 110, 228
Dairy Farmers of Canada, 10
Dairy Queen (DQ), 135, 485
"Dance of the Sugar Plum Fairy" (song), 176
Danone, 14, 134, 419
Dare, 10–11
"DareTO" (BMW), 166
Dasani, 203–204, 218
Data-Enhanced TV, 285
DDB, 33, 34*f*, 430
De Grasse, Andre, 181
DeGroote School of Business, 154
Delicious, 470
Dempster's, 272
Denny's, 462
Dentsu, 34*f*
Denver Hayes, 103
Detroit Red Wings, 153
Diageo Canada, 487–488
"Dig It! Get It!" (Cheer), 250
Digital Advertising Alliance of Canada, 428
"Discover Another Side" (Walmart), 87
Discovery Channel, 166, 467

D'Italiano, 110
Dollar Shave Club, 465
Domino's Pizza, 201
Doritos, 24, 25f, 193
Dos Equis, 191
Dove
  Always and, 200
  brand repositioning strategy, 144, 146
  "Campaign for Real Beauty," 56, 146,
    160, 180
  Cossette and, 31
  creative execution style, 188
  market position, 127
  personal communication and, 79
  sales promotions, 367, 368
  source credibility in ads for, 178
  support arguments and, 90
  website, 424
Dr. Who, 274
Drake, 7
"Dreams of Life" (speech), 153
Droga5, 32
Duchene, Matt, 133
Dundas Square, 322
Dunn, Melanie, 31

E

Eastgaard, Bridget, 473
"Eat Real. Eat Local" (Hellmann's), 102
Ecco, 172
Egg Farmers of Canada, 31
Egg Farmers of Ontario, 197
Egg McMuffin, 144, 145
Ehm, Erica, 469
Electronic Arts, 17
Elle, 179, 282
EM Stats Card, 275
Energy Star Canada, 451
Enhanced Data (Rogers), 285
Environics, 63, 168, 301
Epoch Times, 307
EQ3, 419
Esquire, 305
Esso, 399, 411
Estée Lauder, 488
ET Canada, 350
Everyday Gourmet (Campbell's), 361
"Evolution" (Dove), 31, 56
Excel (gum), 101
Exclaim!, 300
"Expect More" (Telus), 142
Expedia, 110
"Extraordinary, Authentic Nourishment
  for All" (Campbell's), 378

F

"Fabulous 50" (Shoppers Drug Mart), 10
Facebook. *See also* consumers' online
  brand-related activities (COBRAs):
  Facebook

Adidas on, 239
advertising revenue and, 233, 431, 451
apps and, 441
as media vehicle, 429f
as non-personal channel, 78
as outlet for receiver's response, 82
as paid, owned, and earned media, 18,
  457–460
as threat to advertising agencies, 35
Axe on, 334
brand equity, 7
Campbell's and, 378
Canadian Paralympic Committee
  and, 251
Canadian Tire on, 43, 272
Cheer on, 250
Cineplex on, 157
Cirque du Soleil on, 461
databases and, 400
Doritos on, 193
Fashion on, 303
Gain on, 187
Harley-Davidson on, 63
influencers on, 473
issues faced by, 451
magazines on, 305
Mars on, 456
media class of, 452
newspaper ad revenues and, 313
overview of Internet marketing
  via, 12
Pinterest *vs.,* 470
post-testing and, 225
Rethink Breast Cancer on, 498
shopping objectives and, 114
strategic use of, 474
Taco Bell on, 346
Ubisoft on, 17
use of augmented reality in, 471–472
user-generated content on, 455
Valentine on, 46
Fairmont Hotels, 382
Farris, Paul W., 499
Fashion, 303
Febreze, 324
Federal Trade Commission, 472
Fey, Tina, 182, 183
FGL, 45
Fiat Chrysler, 431
Fido, 70, 403
FiftyPlus, 300
"Find Yourself" (Newfoundland and
  Labrador Tourism), 143
"Finger Cooking with Bill"
  (Boston Pizza), 111
Firefly, 228
First Watch, 463
Fisher-Price, 201
Fisherman's Friend, 175
Flare, 180, 303

"Flatties and Drummies" (Boston Pizza),
  111, 192
Florence K, 373
Fluevog. *See* John Fluevog
"Fly Over Montréal" (Tourisme
  Montréal), 116
"Fly the Flag" (Air Canada), 173
"Follow the Arches" (McDonald's), 31
"Follow You, Follow Me" (song), 157
Food & Drink, 297
Food and Drugs Act and Regulations,
  486, 487
Food Basics, 81
Food Network, 272, 278
Foot Locker, 101, 239
Ford, 132, 431, 461, 471, 485
Fountain Tire, 239, 251
Fox, Stephen, 493
Frank and Oak, 437, 441
Freebies (Groupon), 359
"Fresh Air" (Newfoundland and
  Labrador Tourism), 205
FreshCo, 39
"Front of the Line" (American
  Express), 402
Frosted Flakes, 367, 368
Fruitsations, 140
"Future Launch" (RBC), 3

G

G&R, 222
Gain, 67, 187
Galaxy, 45, 134
Gallup & Robinson Magazine Impact
  Research Service (MIRS), 226
Game of Thrones (exhibit), 361
Garnier, 415
Gatorade, 181
GE Appliances, 46
Gear Fit, 45
General Electric, 10
General Mills, 31, 77–78, 87–88
General Motors (GM), 288, 431
Generation X, 62
Genesis (band), 157
Gillette, 188, 347
Giovinco, Sebastian, 5
Give-A-Care, 497
Glamour, 179
Global Responsibility Annual Report
  (Starbucks), 23
Global TV, 269f, 278, 496
Globe, 137
Globe and Mail, The
  as national newspaper, 308
  costs of advertising in, 252f
  high-quality reproduction in, 314
  readership, 310
  special ads in, 309
  Wente's article in, 485

GM (General Motors), 288, 431
"GOAT" (Wrigley Canada), 101
GoDaddy, 181
Goldfish, 471
Golf Canada, 250
Golf Sportwagon, 59
Golf Town, 46
Gongshow Gear, 461
Good Deed Cup, 22
Good Times, 282
GoodLife Fitness, 53, 436
Google
  advertising revenue and, 233
  as most admired company, 386f
  as threat to advertising agencies, 35
  Blogger, 469
  brand equity, 7
  Coca-Cola and, 172
  display ads on, 433
  Google Wallet, 177
  magazine advertising and, 300
  Mars and, 456
  Molson and, 163
  newspaper ad revenues and, 313
  on Buckley's, 196
  paid search ads on, 433, 434
Gossip Girl (TV show), 201
GQ, 305
Grammy Awards, 153
Grassroots, 322
Gravity Partners, 44
Great Canadian Cabin, 163
Great White North Franchisee
  Association (GWNFA), 384–385
Greater Toronto Airport Authority, 389
Greenpeace, 376
Gretzky, Wayne, 341
Grey Cup, 462
Grey's Anatomy, 201, 274
Grid, 78
Groupon, 351, 359
Gr-r-reatest Playoff Beard (Frosted
  Flakes), 367
Guardian, The, 308
Gucci, 142
Guess, 423
Guide to Food Labelling and Advertising, 487
*Guidelines for Cosmetic Advertising and
  Labelling Claims,* 486
Gund, 355
Guylian, 103
GWNFA (Great White North Franchisee
  Association), 384–385

H
H&M, 498
Habitat for Humanity, 134
Haiku, 80
"Hair Action" (Axe), 334
Happy Meal, 355

Happy Planet, 346
Harley-Davidson
  AToMic award, 251
  sales promotions, 10
  storytelling, 166
  target audience, 63
  Zulu Alpha Kilo and, 35, 36, 75
HarperCollins, 441
Harry Rosen, 181, 297, 423
Hart, Kevin, 192
Harvey's, 46, 462
Hauler (No Frills), 81, 141
Havas, 34
Head & Shoulders, 112, 127
Health Canada, 379, 486
Heart & Stroke Foundation, 387
Heavy Construction, 297
Heineken, 6
Heinz, 86
Hellmann's, 102
Herbal Essences, 107, 127, 303
HGTV, 273, 278, 429
Hilton, 137
Hockey Canada, 22, 391, 393
Hockey Canada Foundation
  (HCF), 388
Hockey Day in Canada, 391
Hockey News, The, 300, 306
Hockey Night in Canada
  as media vehicle, 237
  as popular vehicle for
    advertising, 273
  Budweiser and, 341
  Kraft Hockeyville and, 390
  Maytag and, 169
  network advertising online during,
    271–272
Holmes, Jessica, 373
Holmes, Mike, 273, 429
Holt Renfrew, 443
Home Depot, 345, 377, 379, 382
Home to Win, 273
Homemakers, 282
Honda
  brand repositioning strategy, 144, 146
  corporate brand, 149
  Internet media use, 428
  Nissan and, 132
  rational appeals, 170
  standard learning model and, 85
Hospital for Sick Children.
  See SickKids
House of Vans (Vans), 168
HSBC, 155
HTC, 279–280
Huawei, 118, 238, 272
Hudson's Bay, 415, 466, 472
Huggies, 125
Hugo Boss, 297
"Hungry" (Snickers), 253

Hunt, Shelby, 493
Hyman, Zack, 419
Hyundai, 38, 118, 192, 195

I
"I Am Canadian" (Molson), 163
"I Got You Babe" (song), 153
"I know you like the wrong vodka"
  (SVEDKA), 57
"I saw your costume" (SVEDKA), 57
"I Will What I Want" (Under Armour), 32
IAB. *See* Interactive Advertising
  Bureau (IAB)
"Ice Truck" (Canadian Tire), 43
IGA, 471–472
Ignazi, Peter, 31
IKEA
  brand repositioning
    strategy, 144, 147
  Cannes Lion, 51
  catalogues, 405
  Leo Burnett agency and, 33
  PR activities, 380
  Rethink and, 158
  slogan, 6
  video ads, 436
"I'm sorry" (Tourisme Montréal), 115
Indigo, 114
Industry Canada, 481
Infinite (Visa), 375
Infinity, 319
Info Canada, 401
Initiative, 43
Innocean, 38
Insider's Report (President's Choice), 136
Inspire (SAQ), 412
Instagram
  as outlet for receiver's response, 82
  as paid, owned, and earned media,
    18, 466–468
  Doritos on, 193
  engagement with, 466f, 467f
  guidelines for influencers using, 473
  Holt Renfrew and, 443
  IKEA on, 51
  Juicy Fruit on, 101
  Lord & Taylor on, 472
  media class of, 452
  overview of Internet marketing via, 12
  Saje and, 32
  Schick on, 464
  strategic use of, 474
  Taco Bell on, 346
Institute of Communication Agencies
  (ICA), 169
Institute of Communications and
  Advertising, 159–160
Institute of Practitioners in Advertising
  Effectiveness Award, 172
Interac, 35, 36, 176–177, 464

Interactive Advertising Bureau (IAB)
   on display ads, 432
   on Internet advertising revenue, 426,
      427f, 438
   privacy guidelines, 425, 428
   role in measuring Internet advertising,
      444, 445
Interbrand, 6, 135
International Advertising
   Association, 500
International Consumer Electronics
   Show (CES), 366
Interpublic, 34f
Intrawest, 415
Intuit, 142
Iögo, 14–15, 144, 145
iPad, 303
iPhone, 96, 97, 119, 188
Ipsos, 222, 373, 385
Ipsos-ASI Next*Print test, 226
Ipsos-ASI Next*TV test, 227
Ipsos-Reid, 7
IPTV, **268**–269
"It's All Good" (McCain), 118
iTunes, 82, 442
"I've changed" (Tourisme Montréal),
   115–116

J
J. Walter Thompson, 158
Jacknife, 44
Jaguar, 53, 404
Java, 225
J.D. Power & Associates, 383
Jeld-Wen, 273
Jergens, 140, 144
Joe Fresh, 179–180
John Fluevog, 63, 64, 206, 207
John St., 37
Jones Soda, 408, 409
Jonze, Spike, 51
Jos Louis, 481
Journal of Advertising Research, 423
Judgement Free Generation (Planet
   Fitness), 379
JUICE Mobile, 319
Juicy Fruit, 101
Jumpstart (Canadian Tire), 106, 373, 388
Just for Laughs (festival), 45
Just for Laughs (TV show), 201
JWT, 34f, 423

K
Kallax, 51
Kebede, Liya, 179
Keg Steakhouse, The, 5, 46, 198
Kellogg's, 349, 367, 368
Keurig, 399
KFC, 361
Kia, 201, 202, 485

Kijiji, 201, 438
Kim Jong Un, 295
Kimberly-Clark, 144
Kissel, Brett, 104
Kit Kat, 129, 134, 485
KitchenAid, 273
Kleenex, 319
KLM, 126
Kloss, Karlie, 179–180
Knorr, 254, 255f, 401–402
Koho, 68
Koodo, 68, 69–70, 142
Kraft
   brand positioning strategy, 136–137, 143
   emotional appeals, 173
   Internet media use, 422, 460
   PR activities, 390
   sales promotions, 355
Kruger Products, 144, 357
Krugman, Herbert E., 86
Kurt Geiger, 179

L
La Presse, 308
La Savoir (Stella Artois), 361
Labatt, 35, 42, 65, 190
Lambesis, 205
Lands' End, 134
Lee Valley Tools, 405
"Legends" (Nissan), 168
Leger Most Admired Company
   Survey, 386f
Leo Burnett, 33, 156, 165
Leon's, 68, 273, 419
Let's Talk (Bell), 373, 379
Lexus, 303
Lg2 Boutique, 43, 46, 295, 497
Liberté, 425
Lifestyle Selections, 347
"Like a Girl" (Always), 33, 200
Lily and the Snowman (Cineplex), 36, 157
Lindenmann, Walter, 381–382
LinkedIn, 305, 429, 452, 456
Lions. *See* Cannes Lions
Lions Gate, 267
Liquor Control Board of Ontario, 135
Liu-Jo, 179
"Live in Italy" (San Pellegrino), 63
"Live Large" (D'Italiano), 110
"Live with Fire" (Reebok), 133
"Live.Laugh.Learn" (Rethink Breast
   Cancer), 497
Loblaw
   brand positioning strategy, 136
   Internet media use, 443
   loyalty program, 410–411
   No Frills, 81
   source characteristics in ads for,
      178, 179
   target audience, 67

"Locals Know" (Canadian Tourism
   Commission), 147
"Long Live the Home" (IKEA), 51
Lord & Taylor, 472
L'Oréal, 55, 179, 271, 375
Lotto 6/49, 67–68
Loulou, 301
Lowry, Kyle, 392
Lucky Charms, 344
Lululemon, 423, 465
Lyft, 181
Lynx, 358

M
MAC Cosmetics, 423
Mach3, 188
Maclean's, 237, 253, 300, 306, 429
Mad Jack, 44
"Made for Each Other" (song), 201
Magazines Canada, 299
Majestic, 44
Major League Baseball (MLB),
   390–391, 392
Major League Soccer (MLS), 390–391
"Making Your Dreams Come True"
   (Air Canada), 346
Man Cave (Ruffles and Budweiser), 44
"Man I AM, The" (Schick), 419
Manulife, 165, 194, 387, 496
Maple Leaf Foods, 5, 44, 375
Maple Leaf Sports & Entertainment
   (MLSE), 391
Marella, 179
Marketel, 33
Marketing Hall of Legends, 195
Marketing Magazine, 43
Mark's, 103–104, 323
Mars, 129, 456
Martell, Pierre, 464
Martell Home Builders, 464
Maslow, Abraham, 53, 142, 493
mass media, 26, **78**
"Master Roaster Since 1919" (Van
   Houtte), 142
Mattel, 179
Maytag, 169, 190, 273
Mazda, 119, 423, 466
McCain, 21, 23, 118
McCain, Michael, 375
McCracken, Grant, 182
McDonald's
   advertising expenditures, 431
   AToMic award, 251
   behavioural objectives, 113
   billboards, 319
   brand positioning strategy, 137, 148
   brand repositioning strategy, 144,
      145–146
   brand symbol, 77
   Cossette and, 31

DQ and, 135
OMD and, 238–239
on Instagram, 468
on Snapchat, 471
PR activities, 373, 374, 381
pricing, 8
sales promotions, 355, 357
Toronto Raptors and, 7
McGee, Christine, 292
McGraw-Hill, 378
McMaster University, 154
MEC (agency), 39
MEC (Mountain Equipment Co-op), 238, 387, 496
Media Technology Monitor (MTM)
on Facebook engagement, 457*f*, 459, 460*f*
on Instagram engagement, 466*f*, 467*f*
on Internet usage, 420*f*, 421*f*
on Reddit and Pinterest engagement, 470*f*
on smart phone usage, 439*f*, 440*f*
on social media usage, 454–456
on TV My Way, 268, 277*f*
on TV video ads, 436*f*
on Twitter engagement, 460*f*, 462, 463*f*
on video streaming, 435*f*, 441*f*
on YouTube usage and engagement, 463–465
Memorial Cup, 391
Mercedes-Benz, 62, 106
Messi, Lionel, 136
Metro, 307
Michelin, 54
Microsoft, 5, 7, 84, 200, 495
Milestones, 46
Milk West, 430
Millar, TJ, 190
Millward Brown, 222, 228, 423
Mini, 24, 149, 407
Miss Dior, 6
Miss Foxine Jewellery, 352
Mitsubishi, 37
MLB (Major League Baseball), 390–391, 392
MLS (Major League Soccer), 390–391
M&Ms, 456
Modern Family, 187
Moen, 273
Mogo, 311
Molson Coors
apps used by, 441
brand repositioning strategy, 144, 145
Budweiser and, 262, 341
Central Station and, 44
creative strategy, 163
emotional appeals, 173
measuring advertising effectiveness of, 224
on Twitter, 461

PR activities, 392
"Rooftop Rink," 10
Monday Night Football, 274
Monopoly, 357
Montana's, 46
Montreal Jazz Festival, 334
Montréal Scope, 301
More, 282
Moreno, Carlos, 31
MotoMaster Eliminator Ultra AGM, 43
Motor Trend, 54, 383
Mott's, 140
Mountain Dew, 360
Mountain Equipment Co-op (MEC), 238, 387, 496
Mover, Emilie, 201
MsLabelled (Schick), 464
MsLabelled (Tetley), 272
MTM. *See* Media Technology Monitor (MTM)
MTV.ca, 250
"My North" (Sport Chek), 165
My Way Rewards (Subway), 399

N
Narrative PR, 39
National Eat Together Day, 153
National French Fry Day, 468
National Hockey League. *See* NHL (National Hockey League)
National Post, 252*f*, 308, 310–311, 312, 429
Natrel, 225
NBA (National Basketball Association), 101, 390–391, 392. *See also* Toronto Raptors
Nespresso, 403
Nestlé, 134
Netflix, 267, 269, 277
Network Solutions, 494
Neurométric, 224, 225
"Never grow up" (Tourisme Montréal), 116
New Era, 101
Newad, 331
Newcap, 286
Newfoundland and Labrador Tourism
brand attitude, 205
brand positioning strategy, 143
brand repositioning strategy, 144, 147
CASSIE, 169
emotional responses, 279
media type chosen by, 239
News America Marketing, 359
News Media Canada, 310
NFL, 281, 392
NHL (National Hockey League). *See also* Toronto Maple Leafs
apps used by, 441
Boston Pizza and, 111
Budweiser and, 144, 341

Canadian Tire and, 43
Frosted Flakes and, 367
President's Choice and, 153
Reebok and, 133
Rogers's deal with, 270
sponsorship deals with, 390–391, 392
TV, mobile, and, 440
NHL Players Association, 341
Nielsen, 108, 273
Nike
brand loyalty, 65
brand positioning strategy, 135
brand symbol, 77
creative execution style, 190
Jacknife and, 44
Juicy Fruit and, 101
selective attention and, 88–89
SickKids and, 479
storytelling, 166
Toronto Raptors and, 7
Nintendo, 17
Nissan
advertising expenditures, 431
"Conquer All Conditions," 131, 132
creative theme, 168
measuring advertising effectiveness of, 220
non-personal channel and, 78
target audience, 64
use of augmented reality, 472
Nivea, 144, 334, 343–344
nlogic, 276
"No Babies Unhugged" (Huggies), 125
No Fixed Address, 43–44
No Frills, 81–82, 141
Nordstrom, 322
North American Free Trade Agreement, 281
North Face, 393
North Strategic, 45
"Not Vanilla," 251
Nourish, 378
Nourishing Oil Care, 79
NRML, 423
Nuit Blanche, 11
Numeris
frequency and, 247
on radio audience, 287, 288
on TV audience, 271, 274–275, 276, 277, 285
reach and, 246
NUVO, 250, 300
NY Fries, 203

O
Oasis, 324
O.C., The, 201
Office of the Privacy Commissioner, 492
Ogilvy, 34*f*
Ogilvy, David, 164–165, 176

Oh Henry!, 129
Oka, 144, 145
Old Spice, 158, 464
Olympics
    Budweiser and, 341
    Canadian Tire's support of, 106
    Molson and, 163
    North Face and, 393
    Oreo's use of Twitter during, 440
    RBC's support of, 3
    Special Olympics Canada, 391
    sponsorship deals with, 390
OMD, 39, 238–239
Omnicom, 34f, 43, 239, 495
On the Bench, 341
"Onslaught" (Dove), 56
Ontario Craft Brewers Association, 135
O'Pry, Sean, 179
Opti-Free, 188
Optimum (Shoppers Drug Mart), 12, 399, 410–411
Oral-B, 86
Orange Door Project (Home Depot), 379, 382
Oreo, 440
Orphan Black, 274
Oscars, 271, 352
Ostrow, Joseph W., 248
Ottawa Senators, 391
"Our Food. Your Questions" (McDonald's), 137
Outback, 146
OutFront, 324
Oxford Frozen Foods, 278

P
#paid, 473
P&G. *See* Procter & Gamble (P&G)
PACT (Position Advertising Copy Testing), **228,** 229f
Pampers, 125
Pan Am Games, 190
Pantene Pro-V, 127, 128
Parks Canada, 16
Participaction, 22, 387
Passion Flakie, 481
"Patches" (Dove), 56, 180
Pattison, 324, 331, 334
PayPal, 176
PC. *See* President's Choice (PC)
Pearson International Airport, 389, 390, 402
Peek Freans, 347
Pennzoil, 358
Pepsi
    brand positioning strategy, 136
    Coca-Cola and, 68, 112, 349–350
    Majestic and, 44
    PR activities, 392
    sales promotions, 349–350, 360

Petro-Canada, 3, 399
PGA Tour, 171–172
PHD, 239
PHD/Touché, 39. *See also* Touché
PhotoLife, 300
PINK, 5–6
Pinsent, Gordon, 203
Pinterest, 469, 470f, 471
Pitch Perfect, 272
Planet Fitness, 379
"Play a Coke" (Coca-Cola), 349–350
Plum Rewards (Indigo), 114
Point of Purchase Advertising Institute (POPAI), 364f
Pokémon, 443
Pollay, Richard, 493
Porsche, 43, 461
Postmedia, 307f, 309, 311, 314
Powell, Norm, 181
Power Corporation, 308
Prada, 135
Pranked, 201
Pre-Show ads (Cineplex), 333
President's Choice (PC)
    #Eat Together, 153
    brand positioning strategy, 136
    loyalty program, 399, 410–411
    source attractiveness in ads for, 179
    sponsorship advertising, 272
    target audience, 67
Priceline.com, 181
Prime Chicken, 5
PRIZM C2, 63, 413
PRIZMNE, 63
Process Equipment and Control News, 297
Procter & Gamble (P&G)
    advertising expenditures, 431
    Always, 33, 200
    Canadian Living and, 303
    coupon books, 354, 355
    creative theme, 166
    Dove and, 144
    economies of scale at, 499
    Internet media use, 421, 429
    media tactics, 250
    newspaper advertising, 312
    on Facebook, 451
    publicity, 376
Promotional Product Professionals of Canada, 356
Psycho, 70
Publicis, 34f
Pugliese, Dina, 66
Puma, 181

Q
Quaker State, 172
Qualcomm, 365
Quebec Milk Producers, 68, 69, 199, 295
Quebecor, 267, 323–324

Quesada Burritos, 419
Questrade, 44
Quora, 469

R
Radio-Canada, 269f
Radio Connects, 287
Range Rover, 133
Raphaelson, Joel, 176
Ratajkowski, Emily, 219
RateHub.ca, 8
RBC
    and communication function of IMC objectives, 102
    approach to new category users, 67
    billboards, 319
    IMC at, 3
    loyalty program, 399
    North Strategic and, 45
    PR activities, 391
RBI (Restaurant Brands International), 384–385, 431
Reactine, 144, 148
Reader's Digest, 301
"Real Food Movement" (Hellmann's), 102
Reality in Advertising (Reeves), 164
Recipe Unlimited, 46
Recipes to Riches, 272
Red Bull, 166, 171, 422
Red Light (Budweiser)
    as sales promotion, 341, 347
    media budget, 262f
    place-based media advertising, 334
    target audience, 146–147, 393
Red Urban, 43
Reddit, 193, 469, 470f
Reebok, 114, 133
Reese's Peanut Butter Cups, 129
Reeves, Rosser, 164
Relax (IKEA), 380
Replica, 175
Report on Business, 308
Restaurant Brands International (RBI), 384–385, 431
Rethink, 38, 39, 158, 295
Rethink Breast Cancer, 497–498
Reward Zone (Best Buy), 406
Richards, Cabbie, 224
Richardson, Sarah, 273
Ride for Heart, 387, 496
Ride to Conquer Cancer, 189
"Rideauculous," 251
Ries, Al, 128, 129, 166
Road & Track, 54
Roberts, Gary, 419
Rogers
    advertising expenditures, 431
    as participant in promotional process, 14
    complaint about Bell ad, 484

distribution channels, 8
Enhanced Data feature, 285
influence of culture on
    advertising by, 64
Joe Fresh and, 180
logo, 6
NHL's deal with, 270
OMD and, 238
PR activities, 374
radio stations owned by, 286
response to transition in broadcast
    media, 267
Scotiabank and, 391
slogan, 167
Telus's brand positioning strategy
    and, 142
Rolex, 6–7
Rolling Rock, 43
Ronald McDonald House Charities
    (RMHC), 381
Ronaldo, Cristiano, 181–182
"Rooftop Rink" (Molson), 10
Roots, The, 361
Roots Canada, 133
Roper ASW, 225
Rotfeld, Herbert, 175
Rouge Maple, 352
Royale, 144
"RRRoll Up the Rim to Win"
    (Tim Hortons), 357
Ruffles, 44
Run for the Cure (CIBC), 373, 394

S
Saje, 32
"Sama's Lunchbox" (Whirlpool), 436
Samsung
    brand attitude, 119
    brand positioning
        strategy, 128, 134
    creative execution style, 188
    distribution, 8
    North Strategic and, 45
    on Twitter, 462
    PR activities, 387
    product placement, 273
    sales promotions, 361
    SickKids and, 479
San Pellegrino, 63–64, 113, 140, 191
SAQ, 412
Save.ca, 355
SavvyMom (blog), 473
Scarpe di Bianco, 361
Scene (Cineplex), 113, 399, 412
Schick, 419, 464
Schneiders, 14
Scope, 201
Scotiabank
    creative execution style, 189
    loyalty program, 412

PR activities, 11, 391
    "You're Richer Than You Think,"
        163, 189
Scout (blog), 469
Sea-Doo, 5
Seagate Technology, 174–175
SeaKlear, 363, 364
"Search+Rescue" (Coors), 424
Second Cup, 84
"See the Big Picture" (Cineplex), 157
Selection, 301
send+receive, 44
Sensorium (Stella Artois), 361
Sephora, 126, 425, 471
"Share a Coke" (Coca-Cola), 117, 355–356
Sharp, 305
Shatner, William, 115, 181
Shaw, 267
Shell, 410
"Shock Free Data" (Koodo), 69–70
Shock Top, 190
Shoppers Drug Mart
    brand awareness, 118
    "Fabulous 50," 10
    loyalty program, 12, 399, 410–411
    sales promotions, 11
Shopping Channel (TSC), The, 407
Show Time ads (Cineplex), 333
Shred-It, 90
SickKids
    brand repositioning strategy, 144, 147
    Cannes Lion, 31, 441
    creative theme, 165
    "SickKids VS," 31, 479
Sid Lee, 33, 35, 39, 143
Siemens, 92
Singing in the Rain, 79
"Sketches" (Dove), 56
Ski Canada, 297, 299, 300
SkipTheDishes, 471
Skittles, 101, 192, 464
Skyy, 205
Sleep Country Canada, 292
Smalls, Joan, 179
Smart, 67, 68, 111, 126
Smirnoff, 487–488
"Snack Time" (Milk West), 430
"Snap It with Pepsi," 350
Snapchat
    Bell on, 373
    guidelines for influencers using, 473
    Pepsi on, 350
    Planet Fitness on, 379
    target audience reached by, 439
    TV and, 440
    usage statistics, 454f, 455f
    use of augmented reality in, 471
Snapdragon, 365
Snickers, 253
SoBe, 127

SodaStream, 136
"Someday" (RBC), 3
Sony, 17, 250, 332, 469
South by Southwest, 361
Space Channel, 274
Special K, 166
Special Olympics Canada, 391
Splat, 52
Sponsorship Marketing Council of
    Canada, 389
Sport Chek
    Adidas and, 239
    creative theme, 165
    on Instagram, 466
    PR activities, 392
    scheduling decisions, 245
    shopping objectives, 114
Sportsnet, 101, 285
Spotify, 82, 349, 437
Spray and Go, 10
Square, 176
Stanley Cup, 367
Star Wars, 472
Starbucks, 13, 21, 23, 412–413
Starch Ad Readership
    Report, 225–226
Starz, 267
Station 19, 274
Statistics Canada, 401
Steam Whistle Brewing, 167
Steel, Jon, 159
Stella Artois, 361
St-Gelais, Marianne, 66
Strange Talk (band), 250
Strategic Business Insights, 63
Strategy
    annual recognition of outstanding
        ads, 10
    as specialty publication, 308
    categories of awards given by, 170
    Media Agency of the Year award
        from, 238
    on Canadian indie advertising
        agencies, 43
    on Canadian Tire, 405
    on Cossette, 31
    on Leo Burnett agency, 33
    on Lg2, 46
    on North Strategic, 45
    on Taxi, 35
    on Telus, 395
    use in research, 160
Stroman, Marcus, 181
Style at Home, 250
Subaru, 78–79, 144, 146, 167–168
Subway, 200–201, 202, 204, 399
Sun Life, 7, 239, 391, 392
Sunnybrook Hospital, 308
Sun-Rype, 77
Sunwing, 203

Super Bowl
    Always ad during, 200
    Canadian broadcasts of, 280–281, 480
    cognitive and emotional responses to
        ads during, 95
    Labatt ad during, 190
    Oreo's use of Twitter during, 440
Supreme Court of Canada, 281
"Surprisingly Stylish" (Leon's), 419
SVEDKA, 56–57
Swiss Chalet, 6, 46, 202, 355

T
Tabasco, 251
Taco Bell, 24, 25f, 345–346, 468
Tacori, 162
TagHeuer, 34
"Take Care of What You Wear Every
    Day" (Jergens), 140
Talbot, Maxime, 133
Tangerine, 7, 391, 473
Target, 466
Taste Challenge (Pepsi), 112
"Taste the Rainbow" (Wrigley), 101
Tavares, John, 133
Taxi, 33, 35
TaylorMade, 171–172, 297
TD Canada Trust, 11, 135, 144, 147, 391
Team Canada, 106, 341, 388, 393
Ted Bates, 164
Telecommunications Act, 480
Telus
    brand positioning strategy, 142
    Cossette and, 239
    creative theme, 167, 168, 183
    distribution channels, 8
    managerial decision making and, 97
    PR activities, 11, 392, 395
    response to transition in broadcast
        media, 267
    Taxi and, 33
    transit media advertising, 328
Tempur-Pedic, 273
Tesla, 378
Tetley, 144, 148, 272, 445
TFC, 5
ThermaCare, 164
ThinkTV, 276, 280
Thomas Pink, 6
Ticketmaster, 481
Tide, 66–67, 70
Tim Hortons
    brand positioning strategy, 138
    emotional appeals, 173
    jingles, 202
    loyalty program, 402
    McDonald's brand repositioning
        strategy and, 145
    on Twitter, 462
    PR activities, 373, 374, 384–385

publicity, 376
    sales promotions, 357
Timeplay (Cineplex), 333
TimsTV (Cineplex), 333
Toews, Jonathan, 43
Toronto Blue Jays
    Boston Pizza and, 111
    influencers and, 473
    sponsorship of, 285, 391
    TV, mobile, and, 440
    Ubisoft and, 45
Toronto Humane Society, 201
Toronto International Film Festival
    (TIFF), 375, 441
Toronto Life, 301
Toronto Maple Leafs, 43, 153, 419, 479
Toronto Raptors
    celebrity endorsements, 181
    Juicy Fruit and, 101
    media vehicles and, 429f
    sponsorship of, 391, 392
    Sport Chek and, 165
    TV, mobile, and, 439, 440
    "We the North," 7
Touché, 43, 238. *See also* PHD/Touché
Tourism Australia, 296
Tourism BC, 23–24
Tourism Ottawa, 251
Tourism Yukon, 346, 405
Tourisme Montréal, 115–116
Toyota
    Nissan and, 132
    PR activities, 380–381, 386
    product placement, 273
    target audience, 66
    TV advertising, 291
Transcontinental, 282
Travel Alberta, 35, 68, 69, 143, 466
TRESemmé, 127, 128
Triangle Rewards (Canadian Tire),
    399, 410
Trip Advisor, 452
Triumph, 495
Trout, Jack, 128, 129, 166
TrueView, 463
Trump, Donald, 295
Truth, Lies, and Advertising
    (Steel), 159
TSN
    as media vehicle, 429f
    as non-personal channel, 78
    Canadian Tire and, 272, 388
    measuring advertising effectiveness
        of, 224
    Oxford Frozen Foods and, 278
    weekly hours watched, 271f
Tucson, 195
Tumblr, 196, 430, 437, 464, 468
Tuscan Chicken Melt, 200–201
TV My Way, 268f, 269

TVA, 269f, 270
Twitter
    as outlet for receiver's response, 82
    as paid, owned, and earned media,
        18, 456, 461–463
    as personal channel, 79
    Bell on, 373
    Campbell's and, 378
    Canadian Paralympic Committee
        and, 251
    Canadian Tire on, 272
    Doritos on, 193
    engagement with, 460f, 462, 463f
    Fashion on, 303
    Gain on, 187
    guidelines for influencers using, 473
    Juicy Fruit on, 101
    Mars on, 456
    Maytag on, 190
    media class of, 452
    mobile and, 439, 440
    overview of Internet marketing via,
        12, 13
    Pinterest *vs.,* 470
    post-testing and, 225
    Schick on, 464
    shopping objectives and, 114
    Smirnoff on, 488
    Toronto International Film Festival
        and, 375
    user-generated content on, 455
Tylenol, 196

U
Uber, 383, 471
Ubisoft, 17, 45
UEFA Champions League, 45
Ultima Foods, 144
Under Armour, 12, 32
Unilever, 134, 180
United European Football
    League, 389
United Way of Toronto, 291
UP Express, 389
UPS, 197, 198
Upstairs Amy (Walmart), 464
Urban Barn, 419
UrbanMom (blog), 473

V
V8, 128
Vachon, 481–482
Valentine, 46
Valpak, 355
Van Houtte, 142
Vancouver Magazine, 301
Vans, 108, 168
Varilux, 188, 189
Vaseline, 10
Vaz-Oxlade, Gail, 176

Velencoso Segura, Andrés, 179
Veritas, 42
Versace, 179, 297
VIA Rail Canada, 31, 135, 238
Viagra, 494
Victoria's Secret, 5–6
Vimeo, 436
Virgin, 70
Virtual Hair Play Van (Axe), 334
Visa, 176, 375
Vision7 (Cossette), 31, 34, 239, 479
"Vitality" (Activia), 118
Vogue, 179
Volkswagen (VW), 43, 46, 80–81, 172
Volunteer Canada, 379
Volvo, 64, 328, 437

W

W Movies, 282
W Network, 271*f*, 282
Walmart
  apps used by, 443
  award-winning print advertising, 295
  "Discover Another Side," 87
  Loblaw and, 67, 81
  on YouTube, 464
Warped Tour, 334
Watch Dogs, 17
Watts, Alan, 153
Waze, 251
WD-40, 141, 362
"We All Play for Canada" (Canadian
  Tire), 44, 106
"We the North" (Toronto Raptors), 7
Wealthsimple, 68
Weather Network, The, 46, 251
Webby Awards, 425
"Welcome to McDonald's," 137
"We'll Make You a Fan" (Boston
  Pizza), 111
Wendy's, 114
Wente, Margaret, 485
West Elm, 419
Western Bulk Transport, 5

WestJet
  Air Canada and, 167, 291, 329
  prank ads, 201
  product attributes, 5
  Rethink and, 158
Weston, Galen, 272
Weston, Galen, Jr., 178
"What the World Needs Now Is Love"
  (song), 153
"What's for Dinner?" (Knorr), 254, 255*f*
"What's Your Tabitat" (Samsung), 134
Where's Buzz the Bee? (General Mills),
  87–88
Whirlpool, 35, 436
Whistler Ski Resort, 415
White Oaks Resort and Spa, 114
Wikipedia, 469
Wind River, 103
Wiser's, 422
W.K. Buckley Limited, 195
Wonder and Wonder+, 140
WordPress, 468, 469
Workopolis, 438
World Cup, 335, 341
World Juniors, 106, 153, 163, 388
World MasterCard Fashion Week, 462
World's Funniest Commercials, 486
WPP, 34*f*, 35
Wrigley, 101
WWF-Canada, 395

X

Xbox, 84, 111, 200, 334
Xperia Ion, 250

Y

Yahoo, 429*f*, 469
Yelp, 469
Yodel, 136
Yoplait, 144, 145
Young, James Webb, 158
Young & Rubicam, 35
"Your Man Reminder" (Rethink Breast
  Cancer), 497

"You're Richer Than You Think"
  (Scotiabank), 163, 189
YouTube
  Adidas on, 239
  as alternative to Facebook, 451
  as non-personal channel, 78–79
  as paid, owned, and earned media, 18,
    456, 463–466
  Always on, 33
  audio streaming on, 287
  Campbell's and, 378
  Canadian Tire on, 43
  Cineplex on, 157
  D'Italiano on, 110
  Doritos on, 193
  engagement with, 464, 465*f*
  Facebook moves into territory of, 458
  guidelines for influencers using, 473
  infomercials on, 407
  Lg2 and, 46
  Maple Leaf Foods on, 375
  McDonald's on, 239
  media class of, 452
  Milk West on, 430
  overview of Internet marketing via, 12
  popularity of viewing TV commercials
    on, 278
  Porsche on, 461
  Rethink Breast Cancer on, 497
  Skittles on, 192, 464
  Taco Bell on, 346
  Tetley on, 272
  Toronto Humane Society on, 201
  usage statistics, 441*f*
  user-generated content on, 455
  video ads on, 436
YTV, 88
YummyMummyClub.ca, 469
Yves Rocher, 405
YWCA, 490

Z

Zulu Alpha Kilo, 35–36, 38, 75, 385
Zurich Insurance, 393

Subject Index

Note: In subheadings, CPM refers to cost per thousand. *f* following a number indicates a figure. Boldface indicates pages on which terms are defined. Cross-references may refer to entries in the Name and Company Index.

A

ability, 92*f*
absolute cost, **252**
  magazine advertising, 306
  newspaper advertising, 312
  outdoor media, 327
  place-based media, 335
  radio advertising, 289
  transit media, 330
  TV advertising, 282
acceleration tools, 342
acceptance, measuring, 218
account executive, **36**
account planning, **159**
account services, 36
account-specific marketing, **345**
accuracy of PR activities, 384
activities, interests, and opinions (AIOs), 63–64
actors, 200
ad exchange, **433**
ad execution thoughts, 89*f*, **90–91**
ad networks, 433
ad recall, 219, 222, 226–227
ad recognition, 218–219, 225–226
ad to consumer relevance, 155
advergames, 438
advertiser disputes, **484**
advertisers, **13–14**
advertising, **9.** *See also* broadcast media; out-of-home media; print media
  approach to, 3
  as part of promotional mix, 9–10
advertising agencies, 32–42. *See also* creative strategy
  choosing, 32–33, 46–47
  compensating, 39–41
  defined, **14,** 32
  evaluating, 41–42
  full-service agencies, 36–39, 46–47
  industry, 34–36
  media budget setting and, 256
  reasons for loss of clients, 42*f*
  role in implementing IMC plan, 25
advertising awareness, 117, 118
advertising campaign, **163**
advertising creativity, **154–155,** 156–157
advertising cycles, 245

advertising effectiveness. *See* measurements
advertising regulation, 480–487. *See also* Canadian Radio-television and Telecommunications Commission (CRTC)
  Ad Standards, 482–487
  advertising to children, 481–482, 483, 486–487
  Competition Act, 481
  Competition Bureau, 360, 472, 481, 483
  for social media, 472
advocacy advertising, **386–387**
affective responses. *See* emotional responses
affective stage, 83*f*, 85, 87
affiliates, **269–270**
affordable method, **259**
agate line, **310–311**
agencies, media, 238–239. *See also* advertising agencies
agency-of-record (AOR), **33**
AIDA model, **83–84**
airport terminal advertising, 334
alpha activity, **223**
alternative evaluation, 55–56, 120*f*
alternative response hierarchy models, 85–87
animatic, **161,** 162
animatic rough, 221*f*
animation, 189–190
annual reports, 23, 377
appeals. *See* message appeals
apps, 13, 54, 441, 442*f*, 443
AR (augmented reality), 471–472
arbitrary allocation, **259**
association tests, 160*f*
associative process, 93
attention
  magazine advertising, 301, 302*f*
  measuring, 218
  newspaper advertising, 314
  outdoor media, 325
  place-based media, 335
  radio advertising, 290
  transit media, 330
  TV advertising, 279
attitude toward the ad, 89*f*, **91**
attractiveness, **178**–183
attributes, product. *See also* salient attributes
  bundles of, 55
  multiattribute attitude model, 138, 139
  salient, 129, 133, 139–141, 219–220
  ways of communicating, 5

audience. *See also* target audience
  measuring Internet, 444
  measuring TV, 274–276, 285
audience contact, 16, 17*f*
audio ads, 437
audio elements, 201–202
audio logos, 6
audio messages, 202, 203
audio streaming, 287, 288*f*, 437
augmented reality (AR), 471–472
average frequency, **248**
average quarter-hour (AQH) figure, **287**
average quarter-hour rating (AQH RTG), **287**
average quarter-hour share (AQH SHR), **287**
awards. *See also* Canadian Advertising Success Stories (CASSIES); Cannes Lions; *Strategy*
  AToMiC, 251, 388
  fictitious, 111
  Institute of Practitioners in Advertising Effectiveness Award, 172
  received by advertising agencies, 31, 33, 35–36, 43
  Webby, 425

B

backlit posters, **320**
bad taste, 488, 489–491
barrier to entry, **498–499**, 500*f*
behavioural objectives, **23–24**
  direct marketing and, 403–404, 414–415
  in PR plan, 379
  Internet media and, 428
  marketing objectives, target audience, and, 105*f*
  media objectives and, 235
  sales promotion and, 348*f*
  setting, 111–116, 120*f*
  strategic use of out-of-home media and, 336
  usefulness of Rossiter & Percy model in setting, 110
behavioural stage, 83*f*, 85
behavioural targeting, **428**
behaviouristic segmentation, 62*f*, **64**–65, 66–70
benchmark measures, **107**
benefit segmentation, **65**
benefits, product
  brand attitude and, 205–206, 207–208
  brand benefit positioning, 136–137, 146
  end, 131*f*, 133, 145

experiential, 56
functional, 55
performance, 55
salient, 130, 138, 139
segmentation and, 61
ways of communicating, 5
big idea, 164
billboards, 319, 320, 332
bleed pages, **303**
blocking chart, **254,** 255*f*
blogs, 452*f*, **468**–469, 473. *See also*
    Tumblr
body copy, **198**–199
bonus packs, **359**–360
bottom-up budgeting, **258**
bounce-back coupon, **354**
brain waves, 223–225
brand activation, 393
brand attachment, 7
brand attitude
    as communication effect, 95*f*
    brand positioning strategy and,
        137–141
    creative tactics for, 204–208
    defined, 96, **118**
    in cognitive response model, 89*f*, 91
    in elaboration likelihood model, 92*f*,
        93–94
    Internet media and, 424, 425*f*
    measuring, 219–220
    media objectives and, 235
    role in setting communication
        objectives, 118–119
brand awareness
    as communication effect, 95*f*
    creative tactics for, 203–204
    defined, 96, **117**
    Internet media and, 422
    measuring, 219
    media objectives and, 235
    role in setting communication
        objectives, 105–106, 117–118
brand benefit positioning, **136**–137, 146
brand channels on YouTube, 464, 465
brand communication effects, 9
brand equity, **6,** 7*f*, 347, 348*f*, 368
brand experience, 7, 94
brand identity, 5, 6*f*, 384
brand image, 9, 164–165, 423
brand influence, 12–13
brand interaction, 9–10
brand love, 7
brand-loyal customers, **66**–67, 146–147
brand loyalty, **57,** 65, 344
brand names, 131*f*, 134, 145
brand position, **128**–129, 131, 392
brand positioning strategy, 127–143, **128**
    consumer purchase motive, 141–143
    determining, 130–132
    differential advantage, 135–137

extensions, 148–149
    market partition, 130, 131*f*, 133–135
    role in creative themes, 166
    target audience brand attitude,
        137–141
brand proliferation, 344
brand purchase intention, 95*f*, 96,
    119, 220
brand recall, 118, 204, 219
brand recognition, 117–118,
    203–204, 219
brand repeat purchase, 237
brand repositioning strategy, 143–148
brand re-trial objective, **112**
brand re-trial purchase, 111–**112,**
    115–116
brand-switching objective, **112**–113
brand-switching purchase, **112**
brand symbols, 5, 77
brand to consumer relevance, 155
brand trial, 237
brand trial objective, **111**
brand trial purchase, **111**
branded content, 272
branded entertainment, 272
broadcast media. *See also* radio
    advertising; television advertising
    cost per ratings point in, 253*f*
    defined, 78
    post-testing advertising in, 227–228
    pretesting advertising in, 222–225
    tactics of Internet media *vs.,* 429*f*
broadcasters, 285
budget. *See* media budget
bundles of attributes, 55
bundles of benefits. *See* benefits, product
business organizations, 378–379
business publications, 297
business-to-business advertising, 10
bus/train murals, 328
bus/train strips, 328
buyer decision stages. *See* consumer
    decision-making process
buying allowances, 362, 363

c

cable television, **268**–269
Canadian content, 267
Canadian creative themes, 168–170
carryover effect, **104**–105, 235
catalogues, 405
category need, 95*f*, 96, **116**–117, 219, 235
category trial objective, **112**
category trial purchase, **112**
cause-related advertising, **387,** 388*f*
cause-related marketing, **387**
celebrity endorsers, 94, 178, 179–183
central brand positioning strategy,
    135–136, 146
central route to persuasion, **92,** 93–94

CEO spokespeople, 178
channel members, 10
channels
    brand, 464, 465
    direct and indirect, 8
    personal and non-personal, 78–80
children, advertising to, 481–482, 483,
    486–487, 491–492, 494
cinema advertising, 332–333
circulation, 298, 309–310
city zone, **309**–310
civic organizations, 378–379
classical conditioning, **93**
classified advertising, **309,** 438
clearance for advertising, 486–487
click-stream, **428**
click-through rate (CTR), **434**
client services, 36
clients, **14**
clutter
    magazine advertising, 306–307
    newspaper advertising, 314
    outdoor media, 327
    place-based media, 335
    PR activities, 383
    radio advertising, 290
    transit media, 330
    TV advertising, 283, 284
COBRAs. *See* consumers' online brand-
    related activities (COBRAs)
cognitive dissonance, **58**
cognitive response model, 89–91, 94, 229
cognitive responses, **89**
    brand attitude and, 205
    in central route to persuasion, 92
    direct marketing, 413
    Internet media, 424, 425*f*
    magazine advertising, 302, 303
    managerial planning for, 96
    measuring, 218, 220
    message processing and, 95
    newspaper advertising, 312
    outdoor media, 327
    place-based media, 335
    radio advertising, 289
    transit media, 330
    TV advertising, 279
cognitive stage, 83*f*, 85, 87
collaborative projects, 452*f*, 469–471. *See
    also* consumers' online brand-related
    activities (COBRAs)
collateral services, **14**
column width, **310**–311
commercials. *See* radio advertising;
    television advertising
commission system, **40**
common ground, 80
communication, **76**
    importance of IMC objectives to, 102
    Internet media and, 419–426

communication effects. *See also* brand attitude; brand awareness; brand purchase intention; category need
defined, 94, **95**
hierarchy of effects model and, 108, 109*f*
in sales promotions, 368*f*
managerial decision making about, 96–97
measuring, 219–221, 445
communication model measures, 444–445
communication objectives, **23**–24, **105**–110
creative evaluation and, 208
humour appeals and, 175*f*
in direct marketing plan, 404
in PR plan, 379–380
Internet media and, 428
link with marketing and behavioural objectives, 111
media budget and, 260, 261*f*
media objectives and, 235, 237
role in measuring advertising effectiveness, 214, 229
sales promotion and, 348*f*
setting, 116–119, 120*f*
strategic use of broadcast media and, 291
strategic use of out-of-home media and, 336
strategic use of print media and, 314–315
communication process, 76–83. *See also* message; receiver
decoding, 80–82
encoding, 77
feedback, 82, 473
noise, 81, 82
non-personal channel, 78–79
personal channel, 79–80
response, 82, 83–88, 94–96, 107–110
role in measuring advertising effectiveness, 229*f*
source, 76
communication task, **107**
community members, 377–378
community newspapers, 307, 310
company analysis, 21*f*, 23
comparative appeals, 171
comparison advertising, 188
compensation for advertising agencies, 39–41
competition, economic effects on, 498–499, 500*f*
competitive parity method, **260**
competitor analysis, 21*f*, 131
competitors
influencing attribute belief about brands from, 140–141

role in brand repositioning strategy, 144
complaints, 483–486, 495
comprehension and reaction test, **221**
comprehensive post-test measuring, 227
concave-downward response curve, **256**, 257*f*
concept test, **221**
conclusion drawing, 194–195
conditioned response, **93**
conditioned stimulus, **93**
consumer analysis, 21*f*, 22
consumer behaviour, **52**
consumer choice, 498, 500*f*
consumer complaints, **483**–484
consumer decision-making process, 52–60
alternative evaluation, 55–56, 120*f*
brand positioning strategy extensions and, 148–149
group decision making, 59–60
information search, 53–55, 120*f*
need recognition, 52–53, 120*f*
post-purchase evaluation, 58, 120*f*
purchase decision, 57, 120*f*
social media and, 457
strategic use of broadcast media and, 291, 292
strategic use of direct marketing and, 414–415
strategic use of out-of-home media and, 336
strategic use of PR and, 394
strategic use of print media and, 314–315
types of decision making, 58–59
consumer franchise-building (CFB) promotions, **348**
consumer jury, **221**
consumer publications, 296*f*, 297
consumer purchase motives, 141–143, 147–148
consumer sales promotion, **342**, 346–361
as part of promotional mix, 10–11
bonus packs, 359–360
contests and sweepstakes, 357–358
coupons, 346–347, 353–355
event marketing, 360–361
list of types of, 343*f*
objectives, 346–347
premiums, 355–356
price discount, 360
promotional products, 356–357
refunds, 358–359
sampling, 346–347, 351–352
strategy decisions, 347–350
tactics decisions, 350–351
consumer socialization process, **491**–492
consumers. *See* target audience

consumers' online brand-related activities (COBRAs). *See also* collaborative projects
defined, 453
eWOM and, 454
Facebook, 457*f*, 459, 460*f*, 466, 467
Instagram, 466*f*, 467*f*
Reddit and Pinterest, 470*f*
Twitter, 456, 460*f*, 462, 463*f*
YouTube, 456, 464, 465*f*
consuming social media. *See* consumers' online brand-related activities (COBRAs)
consumption, 347
content communities, 452*f*, 463–468. *See also* Instagram; YouTube
contentment, 173*f*
contests, 345–346, **357**–358, 365–366
contextual targeting, **429**
contiguity, 93
continuity, **244**, 245*f*
continuous reinforcement schedule, 348
contributing to social media. *See* consumers' online brand-related activities (COBRAs)
controlled-circulation basis, **297**
cookie, **445**
cooperative advertising, **365**
copy platform. *See* creative brief
copy testing, 222, 227, 228, 229*f*
copywriters, **38**
corporate advertising, **385**–394
cause-related advertising, 387, 388*f*
corporate image advertising, 386–387
corporate reputation, 385–386
McDonald's, 381
sponsorship, 388–394
corporate brands, 149
corporate identity, 384
corporate image advertising, **386**–387
corporate social responsibility (CSR), 3, 87–88, 373, **387**
cost effectiveness, 9
cost efficiency
advertising generally, 9
CPM and, 253, 254*f*
magazine advertising, 306
newspaper advertising, 312
outdoor media, 325
place-based media, 335
radio advertising, 289
transit media, 330
TV advertising, 279, 285
cost per order (CPO), 408
cost per ratings point (CPRP), **253**
cost per thousand (CPM), 9, **252**–253, 254*f*, 285
cost-plus system, **40**–41
costs. *See also* absolute cost; media budget

advertising revenues of different media, 233, 234f
allocation to advertising *vs.* sales promotion, 367
correlation to product price, 8
inconsistent terminologies surrounding, 238
media tactics and, 252–254, 255
of direct marketing, 413
of public relations, 383
paid to influencers, 473
product, 499
role in measuring advertising effectiveness, 214
counterarguments, **90**
coupons, 346–347, 353–355
coverage, **237.** *See also* geographic coverage; target audience coverage
creating social media. *See* consumers' online brand-related activities (COBRAs)
creative boutique, **42–43**
creative brief, **37, 162**
creative evaluation, 208–209
creative execution style, **187–192**
creative services, 38
creative space buys, **303**
creative strategy. *See also* message appeals; source characteristics
account planning, 159
advertising campaigns, 163
challenges, 158
defined, 24, **154**
evaluating, 208–209
planning, 157–163
process behind, 158–159
research, 159–162
role in measuring advertising effectiveness, 214, 215, 216–217
creative tactics, **154,** 186–211
creative execution style, 187–192
design elements, 197–203
evaluating, 208–209, 215
message structure/message design, 77, 193–197
planning model, 203–208
creative theme, **164–170**
campaign slogans, 166–167
Canadian, 168–170
consistency, 167–168, 183
of advertising and sales promotion, 367
origin, 164–166
credibility, **177–178,** 383
cross-media optimization studies (CMOST), 445
cross-ruff coupon, **354**
CSR (corporate social responsibility), 3, 87–88, 373, **387**
culture, **64**

cume, **287**
customer relationship management (CRM), 402–403
customers. *See* target audience

D

daily newspapers, 307
database, **400**–403
database marketing, **400**
day-after-recall (DAR) tests, 227
dayparts, **273–274,** 286
deceptive advertising, 487–488
decision making. *See* consumer decision-making process; managerial decision making
decoding, **80–82**
decorative models, 179
degree of change sought, 107
demographic segmentation, 61f, **62,** 70
demographic selectivity, 300
demonstrations, 188, 189
departmental system, **39**
design elements, 197–203
audio messages, 202, 203
print messages, 197–199
video messages, 200–202
diagnostic copy test, **222**
diary, 275
differential advantage, 135–137, 145–146
differentiation, **498**
digestion, 158
digital creative services, 38
digital media. *See* Internet media; social media
digital newspaper ads, 309
digital video ads, 436, 437
digital video network, **329**
digital/interactive agencies, **45–46**
direct broadcast satellite (DBS), **268–269**
direct channels, 8
direct headlines, **198**
direct mail, 352, 354f, 404, 405f
direct marketing, **11,** 398–417, **400**
as part of promotional mix, 11–12
database use, 400–403
direct-response media, 400, 404–408
Internet media and, 446
limitations, 414
loyalty programs, 399, 408–413
measuring effectiveness of, 408
objectives, 403
strategic use of, 414–415
strengths, 413
target audiences, 401–402, 403
direct-response advertising, **12, 407**
direct-response agencies, **45**
direct-response media, **400,** 404–408
direct selling, 415
direct source, 177
directory ads, 438

display ads, 419, **431–433**
display advertising, **308**
dissonance/attribution model, 85f, **86**
distribution
defined, 8
in consumer sales promotions, 351, 352, 354
marketing decisions about, 4f
trade sales promotions and, 361
divergence, 155, 156
diverting, **363**
door-to-door sampling, 352
dramatization, 192
duplicated reach, **246**

E

earned media, **18**–19
Facebook, 459–460
Instagram, 467
overview, 12–13
Twitter, 456, 462–463
YouTube, 456, 464–466
economic censorship, 496
economic effects of advertising, 498–500, 501f
economies of scale, **499**
educators, 378
effective reach, **248**
effectiveness. *See* measurements
efficiency, measurements and, 214. *See also* cost efficiency
elaboration likelihood model (ELM), **91–94,** 95
electrodermal response (EDR), **223**
electroencephalographic (EEG) measures, 223–225
email, 405–407
embedded premium, **356**
emotional appeals, **172–174,** 176–177, 183f
emotional integration, 173
emotional research, 216–217
emotional responses
brand attitude and, 205, 206, 207–208
direct marketing, 413
in cognitive response model, 91
Internet media, 424, 425f
magazine advertising, 302f, 303
managerial planning for, 96
measuring, 218, 220
message processing and, 95
newspaper advertising, 314
outdoor media, 326
place-based media, 335
radio advertising, 290
transit media, 330
TV advertising, 279
employees and PR activities, 377
encoding, **77**
end benefit, 131f, 133, 145

endorsements, 94, 178, 179–183, 383
engagement, media, 250. *See also* consumers' online brand-related activities (COBRAs)
environment
  brand repositioning strategy and, 144
  media, 209
environmental analysis, 21*f*, 23
esteem needs, 53*f*
ethics, **487**–492
ethnic publications, 297
evaluation of advertising agencies, 41–42. *See also* measurements
evaluative criteria, **55**
event marketing, 360–361
event sampling, 352
event sponsorship, **361**, **389**–394
evoked set, 55
eWOM, **453**–454
exchange, **4**
exclusive, **383**
expenditures. *See* costs
experiential advertising, 334
experiential benefits, **56**
expertise, source, 177–178
exposure. *See also* selective exposure
  direct mail, 405
  frequency and, 247*f*, 248*f*, 249
  Internet media, 444–445
  sales promotions, 368*f*
  sponsorships, 392–393
exposure-based methods, 394
extended problem solving, **59**
extensions, 328
exterior posters, **328**
external audiences, **377**
external search, **54**
eye tracking, **223**

F
familiarity, 178, 180
farm publications, 297
favourable brand switchers, **67**, 147
fear appeals, **174**–175, 489
feature appeals, 170–171
fee arrangements, 40, 41
fee-commission combination, **40,** 41
feedback, **82**, 473
field of experience, **80**
field tests, **215**
financial audit, **41**
finished broadcast ads, 222–225
finished print ads, 221–222
fixed-fee method, **40**, 41
flexibility, 10, 238. *See also* scheduling flexibility
flighting, 244*f*, **245**
focus groups, **160**–161, 216
foreign publications, 298
forward buying, **363**

four Ps, 4
freestanding inserts (FSIs), 354
frequency, **237, 247**
  direct marketing, 413
  factors in determining, 248, 249*f*
  Internet media, 429
  magazine advertising, 306
  newspaper advertising, 312
  outdoor media, 325, 326*f*
  place-based media, 335
  PR activities, 383
  purchase, 113
  radio advertising, 288–289
  trade-off between reach and, 245
  transit media, 330
  TV advertising, 278–279
full-service agency, **36**–39, 46–47
functional benefits, **55**
functional magnetic resonance imaging (fMRI), 224

G
galvanic skin response (GSR), **223**
game, **357**
gatefolds, **302**, 303
gender portrayal guidelines, 483
gender stereotyping, 494–495
general pre-planning input, **160**
geographic coverage
  as part of media strategy, 243–244
  Internet media, 428
  magazine advertising, 301
  newspaper advertising, 311
  outdoor media, 325
  place-based media, 335
  radio advertising, 288
  transit media, 329
  TV advertising, 278
geographic segmentation, 61*f*, **62**
geographic selectivity, 282, 301
geographic split run, 301
gift giving, 59–60
governments, 379
gross ratings point (GRP), **248**, 249, 250*f*, 322
group decision making, 59–60
group system, **39**

H
headline, **197**–198
headliners, 328
hemispheric lateralization, **223**
hierarchy of effects model, 83*f*, **84,** 108–109, 229
hierarchy of needs, **53**, 142, 493
high-definition screens and receivers, 270*f*
high-involvement media, 295
high involvement–informational creative tactics, 204*f*, 206–207
high involvement–transformational creative tactics, 204*f*, 207–208

home shopping, 407
horizontal cooperative advertising, **365**
humour appeals, **175**
humour in execution style, 192–193

I
identification, **179**
illumination, 158
illustrations, 199
image advertising, **164**–165, 205
image building, 383
image transfer, **290**
imagery, 191–192
IMC (integrated marketing communications), **15**. *See also* marketing communication
  at Iögo, 14–15
  audience contact, 16, 17*f*
  evolution, 15
  paid, owned, and earned, 18–19
  purpose, 3
  renewed perspective, 16
IMC plan, **20**
IMC planning, **19**–27
  agency relationships, 46–47
  approach to, 25–27
  assessing marketing communications situation, 20–23
  brand positioning strategy extensions, 148–149
  determining objectives, 23–24
  developing programs, 24, 25*f*
  guidelines for creative evaluation, 208–209
  implementing and controlling, 25
  managerial decision making, 96–97
  media budget allocation, 262
  message and source combinations, 183
  objectives for buyer decision stages, 120–121
  program for measuring advertising effectiveness, 228–229
  reviewing marketing plan, 20
  strategic use of broadcast media, 291–292
  strategic use of direct marketing, 414–415
  strategic use of Internet media, 445–446
  strategic use of out-of-home media, 336
  strategic use of PR, 394–395
  strategic use of print media, 314–315
  strategic use of sales promotion, 366–368
  strategic use of social media, 473–474
  target audience profiles, 70–71, 96
immersion, 158
inbound telemarketing, 407

incentive-based system, **41**
incentives, 342, 348*f*, 350, 365–366
incomplete satisfaction motives, 142
inconsistent terminologies, 238
incubation, 158
in-depth interviews, 160*f*
index number, **242**, 243
indirect channels, **8**
indirect headlines, **198**
indirect methods, **224**
indirect source, 177
individual selectivity, 301
influencers, 462, 469, 472–473, 474
infomercial, **407**
information, advertising as, 500*f*
information–persuasion dichotomy, 493
information processing model, 83*f*, **84**,
    109–110
information search, 53–55, 120*f*
informational motives, **141**, 142, 148,
    204*f*, 205
ingredient-sponsored cooperative
    advertising, **365**
inherent drama, **165**
in-house agency, **32**
ink-jet imaging, **301**
inquiry tests, **225**
inserts, **303**
inside/outside of package coupons, 354
instant coupon, **354**
in-store coupons, 354
in-store sampling, 352
insufficient information, media planning
    challenges and, 237–238
integrated marketing communications.
    See IMC (integrated marketing
    communications)
intellectual stimulation motives, 143
interaction via Internet media, 423–424
interactive ads, 200–201
interactive media, **12**. *See also* Internet
    media; social media
interactivity, **424**
interior door cards, **328**
interior transit cards, **328**
internal audiences, **377**
internal search, **53**
internalization, **178**
Internet, **419**
Internet marketing, 12–13
Internet media, 418–448. *See also* social
    media
  advertising plan, 427–428
  advertising revenue, 233, 234*f*,
      426, 427*f*
  as non-personal vs personal channel,
      78–79
  audio ads, 437
  classified and directory ads, 438
  communication via, 419–426

  coupons, 355
  CPM, 253
  display ads, 419, 431–433
  measuring effectiveness of, 444–445
  mobile media, 438–443
  newspapers, 308
  objectives, 428
  paid search ads, 433–434
  promotional ads, 438
  sampling, 352
  strategic use of, 445–446
  strategy, 428–429
  tactics, 429
  target audience, 428
  target audience coverage, 242
  TV and, 271, 276*f*, 284*f*, 285
  usage statistics, 420*f*, 421*f*
  video ads, 434–437
  word-of-mouth via, 79–80
interpretation guidelines, 483
interviews, 383
investors, 377
involvement
  magazine advertising, 303, 304*f*
  newspaper advertising, 312
  outdoor media, 327
  place-based media, 335
  radio advertising, 290
  transit media, 330
  TV advertising, 283
IP address, **428**

J

jingle, **202**

L

laboratory tests, **215**
layout, **38**, **199**
LEAN ads, 432
learning, measuring, 218
lifestyle, 63, 452
likability, 178, 179–180
limited problem solving, **59**
live-action rough, 221*f*
local advertising, 308
location sampling, 352
logos, 5, 6
long-form ads, 200
low-budget ads, 201
low involvement–informational creative
    tactics, 204*f*, 205–206
low-involvement model, 85*f*, **86**
low involvement–transformational
    creative tactics, 204*f*, 206
loyalty programs, 113, 114, 399, 402,
    408–413

M

magazine advertising, 296–307. *See also*
    print media
  advertising revenue, 234*f*

  circulation, 298
  cost estimates, 252*f*, 253, 254*f*
  coupons, 354
  limitations, 306–307
  media characteristics, 241*f*
  rates, 299*f*, 300
  readership, 299
  sampling, 352
  strategic use of, 314–315
  strengths, 300–306
  types of magazines, 296–298
mailing list, **404**
managerial approaches to media budget,
    258–262
managerial decision making
  IMC planning for, 96–97
  importance of IMC objectives for, 102
  response model for, 94–96
manipulation, 493–494
marginal analysis, **256**, 257
market analysis, 21*f*, 23
market partition, 130, 131*f*, 133–135,
    144–145
market position, **127**
market positioning strategy, **126**–127
market power, 499, 500*f*
marketing. *See also* direct marketing
  defined, 4, 8
  Internet, 12–13
marketing analytics, 25
marketing communication, 4–8. *See*
    also IMC (integrated marketing
    communications)
  assessment, 20–23
  positioning within, 128
marketing communication agency, **34.**
    See also advertising agencies
marketing factors, 248, 249*f*
marketing mix, **4**. *See also* distribution;
    marketing communication; price;
    products
marketing objectives, **23**, **103**–104, 105*f*,
    111, 208
marketing plan, **20**
marketing planning process, 60*f*, 61
marketing public relations (MPR), **380**
materialism, **492**–493
meaning transfer model, 182*f*, 183
measurements, 212–231
  advertising agency performance, 41
  challenges, 213
  direct marketing, 408
  how to measure, 216
  importance in DAGMAR, 107
  importance of IMC objectives for,
      102–103
  Internet media, 444–445
  magazine and newspaper circulation,
      298, 309–310
  media planning and, 238

measurements—*Cont.*
of communication effects, 219–221
of feedback in response process, 109f, 110
of processing, 218–219
outdoor media audience, 324–325
post-testing, 216, 218, 225–228, 229
PR activities, 381f, 382, 393–394
pretesting, 216, 218, 221–225, 229
program for, 228–229
radio audience, 287
reasons for, 214
sales promotions, 345, 368
TV audience, 274–276, 285
what to measure, 215
where to measure, 215
media
commissions from, 40
social effects of advertising on, 496
target audience profiles for, 71
media agencies, 238–239
media budget, 255–262
managerial approaches, 258–262
overview, 255–256
theoretical approaches, 256–258
media buying services, **43**, 285
media characteristics, 240f–241f
media class, **237**
in Internet media, 429f
in social media, 452f, 453, 469
mood created by, 250
media engagement, 250
media environment, 209
media factors, 248, 249f
media image
direct marketing, 414
Internet media, 425, 426f
magazine advertising, 303, 304f
newspaper advertising, 312
outdoor media, 327
place-based media, 335
radio advertising, 290
transit media, 330
TV advertising, 280, 284
media mix, 239–241
media objectives, **235–237**
media organizations, **14**
media planners, 238
media planning, **234–239**
media services, 39
media strategy, 239–250
AToMiC awards and, 251
defined, 24, **235**
geographic coverage, 243–244
media mix, 239–241
media objectives and, 236f, 237
reach and frequency, 245–250
scheduling, 244–245, 428–429
target audience coverage, 242–243
media support, 367

media tactics, **235**, 236f, 237, 250–255
media type, **237**, 429f
media-usage characteristics, 240f
media vehicle, **237**, 250–251, 429f
medium, **237**
message, **77–78**
and source combinations, 183
audio, 202, 203
communication effects of, 95–96
creative evaluation and, 209
in PR activities, 380, 384
measuring effectiveness of (*See* measurements)
print, 197–199
processing of, 88–94, 95
target audience profiles for, 70
video, 200–202
message appeals, **170–177**
emotional, 172–174, 176–177, 183f
fear, 174–175
humour, 175
rational, 170–172, 176–177, 183f
message content, **77**, 380
message development. *See* creative strategy
message factors, 248, 249f
message sidedness, 195–196
message structure/message design, **77**, 193–197
metaphors, 165
microfilm advertising, 200
minimum effective frequency, **248**
mixed approach–avoidance motives, 142
mobile media, 438–443. *See also* Internet media
advertising revenue, 427f
apps, 13, 54, 441, 442f, 443
smart phones, 282f, 420f, 439f, 440f
tablets, 420f, 439–441
mobile signage, **322**
motivation, 92f
motives, **53**. *See also* informational motives; transformational motives
movie theatre advertising, 332–333
multiattribute attitude model, **138**, 139
multiple domains, 10
multi-screening, **283**
murals, **321**
music, 201, 202

N

national advertising, 308
national networks, 269–270
national newspapers, 308
need recognition, **52–53**, 120f
needledrop, **201**
negotiated commission, **40**
network radio, 286
new category users, **67–68**, 147
news appeals, 171

news media, PR and, 378, 381, 382–384. *See also* media
newspaper advertising, 307–314. *See also* print media
advertising revenue, 234f
circulation, 309–310
coupons, 354
CPM, 252f, 253
financial challenges for newspapers, 313
limitations, 313–314
media characteristics, 241f
newspaper supplements, 308
rates, 310–311
readership, 310f
sampling, 352
strategic use of, 315
strengths, 311–312
types of advertising, 308–309
types of newspapers, 307–308
noise, **81**, 82
non-franchise-building (non-FB) promotions, **348**
non-personal channel, **78–79**
normal depletion motives, 142

O

objective and task method, **260**, 261f
objectives. *See also* behavioural objectives; communication objectives
determining IMC plan, 23–24
for buyer decision stages, 120–121
marketing, 23, 103–104, 105f, 111, 208
media, 235–237
sales, 104–105
value of, 102–103
offensive advertising, 488, 489–491
off-invoice allowance, **362**
on-air tests, 222
one-sided message, **195**
one-step approach, **404**
online focus groups, 216
online media. *See* Internet media
on-package sampling, 352
open-rate structure, **311**
operant conditioning, **348**
order of presentation, 193, 194f
organizational structure of advertising agencies, 39
other brand loyals, **68**, 147
other brand switchers, **68**, 147
OTT (over-the-top) service, 269, 276f, 277f, 285
outbound telemarketing, 407
outdoor media, **320–327**
limitations, 327
measuring audience, 324–325
media characteristics, 241f
strategic use of, 336

strengths, 325–326
types, 320–324
out-of-home media. *See also* outdoor media; place-based media; transit media
advertising revenue, 234*f*
defined, 78, **319**
strategic use of, 336
overexposure, 181
overshadowing, 181
over-the-top (OTT) service, 269, 276*f*, 277*f*, 285
owned media, **18**–19
Facebook, 18, 458–459
Instagram, 18, 466, 467–468
overview, 12
Twitter, 18, 456, 461–462
video ads, 435–436
YouTube, 18, 456, 464

P

packaging, 6
paid media, **18**–19
Facebook, 457–458
in definition of advertising, 9
Instagram, 466
overview, 12
Twitter, 456, 461
video ads, 436–437
YouTube, 456, 463–464
paid search, **433**–434
partial or intermittent reinforcement schedule, 348
participants in the promotional process, 13–14
pass-along rate, **253**, 254*f*
pass-along readership, **299**
payout plan, **261**, 262*f*
perceived product differentiation, 85*f*
percentage-of-sales method, **259**–260
perception, **88**
perceptual map, 127*f*
performance benefits, **55**
performance by results (PBR), 41
peripheral route to persuasion, 92*f*, **93**–94
permanents, 321
personal channel, 79–80
personal selling, **13**
personality segmentation, 64
personality symbol, 190–191
personalized marketing mechanism, 409
persuasion, 92*f*, 93–94, 493–494
photomatic rough, 221*f*
physiological measurement methods, 223–225
physiological needs, 53*f*
place. *See* distribution
place-based media, 330–335, **331**, 336
planning services, 37–38

podcasting, **437**
point-of-purchase (POP) displays, 363–365
points-pressure mechanism, 409
popularity appeals, 171–172
portable people meter (PPM), 275
portfolio test, **222**
positioning. *See* brand positioning strategy; market positioning strategy
positioning ads, 386
positron emission tomography (PET), 224
posters, **320**, 332
post-purchase evaluation, 58, 120*f*
post-test, **216**, 218, 225–228, 229
PR. *See* public relations (PR)
prank ads, 201
preferred position rate, **311**
premiums, **355**–356
preprinted inserts, **309**
press conferences, **382**–383
press release, **382**
pretest, **216**, 218, 221–225, 229
price, 4*f*, 7–8, 499, 500
price appeals, 171
price discount, **360**
pride, 173*f*
primacy effect, **194**
prime time, 274
print media. *See also* magazine advertising; newspaper advertising
as non-personal channel, 78
award-winning advertising in, 295
post-testing advertising in, 225–226
pretesting advertising in, 221–222
tactics of Internet media *vs.*, 429
print messages, design elements for, 197–199
problem-avoidance motives, 142
problem-removal motives, 142
processing time
magazine advertising, 303, 304*f*
newspaper advertising, 312
outdoor media, 327
place-based media, 335
radio advertising, 290
transit media, 330
TV advertising, 283
product category, 94, 131*f*, 135, 145
product involvement, 85*f*
product/message thoughts, 89*f*, 90
product placement, 272–**273**
product-specific pre-planning input, **160**
product type and offensive advertising, 488, 489
production of video messages, 202*f*
production services, 38
products. *See also* benefits, product attributes, 5, 55
communications about, 5–7

defined, 5
marketing decisions about, 4*f*
professional advertising, 10
program rating, **275**
programmatic buying, 285
projections, 322
projective techniques, 160*f*
promoted accounts, tweets, and trends, 461
promotion. *See also* marketing communication; sales promotion
approach to, 3
defined, 9
promotional ads, 438
promotional allowances, 362, 363
promotional mix, **9**–15
promotional planning process, 65–66
promotional products, **356**–357
promotional pull strategy, **342**, 343
promotional push strategy, **342**, 343
protection motivation model, 174–175
psychographic segmentation, 62*f*, **63**–64
public relations (PR), **11**, 372–396, **374**
as part of promotional mix, 11
behavioural objectives, 379
Bell's Let's Talk, 373
communication objectives, 379–380
corporate advertising, 381, 385–394
direct-response techniques, 415
effectiveness, 381*f*, 382
Internet media's use with, 446
new role, 374–375
news media and, 378, 381, 382–384
situation analysis, 377
strategic use of, 394–395
strategy, 380–381
tactics, 381
target audiences, 377–379, 383, 392–393
traditional view, 374
vs. publicity, 375–376
public relations firm, **45**
publicity, **11**, 375–376
puffery, **487**
pulsing, 244*f*, **245**
pupillometrics, **223**
purchase amount, 113
purchase decision, 57, 120*f*. *See also* repeat purchase; trial purchase
purchase frequency, 113
purchase intention, 89*f*, **91**
purchase motives, 141–143, 147–148
purchase situation, 65
purchase timing, 113–114
push money, **366**

Q

qualitative audit, **41**
qualitative research, **160**, 216
quantitative research, **160**, 216

R

radio advertising, 286–290. *See also* broadcast media
  advertising revenue, 234*f*
  media characteristics, 240*f*–241*f*
  regulating, 480
  strategic use of, 291–292
ratings point, **275**
rational appeals, **170**–172, 176–177, 183*f*
reach, **237**, **245**
  audience measurement and, 274*f*
  direct marketing, 414
  duplicated *vs.* unduplicated, 246*f*
  gross ratings points and, 248, 249, 250*f*
  Internet media, 429
  magazine advertising, 306
  newspaper advertising, 312
  outdoor media, 325
  pass-along rate and, 253, 254
  place-based media, 335
  radio advertising, 288, 289*f*
  transit media, 330
  TV advertising, 271*f*, 278, 279*f*
readability test, **222**
readers per copy, **253**, **299**
readership, **299**, 310*f*
rebates, **358**–359
recall tests, **226**
receiver, **80**, 83–94
  communication processing by, 88–94
  response by, 83–88
recency effect, **194**
recognition tests, **225**–226
refunds, **358**–359
refutation, **195**
regulation. *See* advertising regulation
relationship marketing, **17**
relative cost, **252**
relevance, 154–155, 156
reminder advertising and appeals, 117, 172
remuneration for advertising agencies, 39–41
repeat consumption, **114**
repeat-consumption objective, **114**–115
repeat purchase, 105, **113**, 347, 348*f*, 349*f*
repeat-purchase objective, **113**–114
repetition, 93
repositioning, 143–148
research, **159**–162, 213, 242. *See also* measurements
research services, 37
response, **82**, 83–88, 94–96, 107–110
retail inventories, 362
retail trading zone, **310**
retention, 84
review websites, 469
rewarded-behaviour mechanism, 409
RFM scoring method, **401**
ROI budgeting method, **260**

Rossiter & Percy (R&P) model
  brand positioning strategy and, 141
  creative tactics and, 203–205
  managerial decision making and, 94, 95
  measuring advertising effectiveness using, 217, 220, 229
  setting objectives using, 108, 110, 116
  target audience and, 66–68
rough test, **221**
routine problem solving, **59**
rule of three, 163
run of paper (ROP), **311**

S

safety needs, 53*f*
sales
  factors influencing relationship between advertising and, 257*f*–258*f*
  media budget and, 259–260
sales objectives, 104–105
sales promotion, **10**, **342**. *See also* consumer sales promotion; trade sales promotion
  as part of promotional mix, 10–11
  direct-response techniques, 415
  interaction via, 424
  Internet media's use with, 446
  planning, 342–346
  strategic use of, 366–368
sales promotion agencies, **44**–45
sales response models, 256, 257*f*
sales training programs, 366
salient attributes, **129**, 133, 139–141, 219–220
salient beliefs, **137**–138
salient benefits, **130**, 138, 139
sampling, 346–347, **351**–352
satisfaction, 58
schedules of reinforcement, **348**
scheduling, 244–245, 428–429
scheduling flexibility
  direct marketing, 413
  magazine advertising, 306
  newspaper advertising, 311–312
  outdoor media, 325
  place-based media, 335
  radio advertising, 288
  transit media, 330
  TV advertising, 278
scientific/technical evidence, 188
script, **202**
search engine optimization (SEO), 434
segmentation, 61–65, 66–70
selective attention, **88**–89
selective binding, **301**
selective comprehension, **89**
selective exposure, **88**. *See also* exposure
  direct marketing, 414
  magazine advertising, 301

  newspaper advertising, 314
  outdoor media, 325
  place-based media, 335
  radio advertising, 290
  transit media, 330
  TV advertising, 282
selective perception, **88**
selective retention, **89**
selectivity, **300**. *See also* target audience selectivity
self-actualization needs, 53*f*
self-liquidating premiums, **356**
sensation, **88**
sensory gratification motives, 143, 148
sexual appeals, 489–491
shaping, **348**, 349*f*
share of audience, **275**
shareholders, 377
shock appeals, 491
shopping behaviour, **114**
shopping mall advertising, 332
shopping objectives, 114
short films, 166
short-term programs, 407
showing, **325**
signal substitution, 480
similarity, 178, 179
simultaneous substitution, 280–281
single-source tracking methods, **227**–228
situation analysis, 20, 21*f*, 377
situations, **65**
skipping, 437
slice-of-life executions, 189
slogan/tagline, 6, **166**–167
slotting allowances, 363
smart phones, 282*f*, 420*f*, 439*f*, 440*f*
smart TV, 276*f*
SMS, 442
social approval motives, 143
social bookmarking sites, 469–471
social class, **64**
social effects of advertising, 492–498
  benefits, 496–498
  manipulation, 493–494
  materialism, 492–493
  on the media, 496
  stereotyping, 494–496
social media. *See also* Facebook; Instagram; Internet media; Snapchat; Twitter; YouTube
  apps and, 443
  as media type, 429*f*
  as personal channel, 79
  blogs, 452*f*, 468–469, 473
  classes of, 452*f*, 453, 469
  collaborative projects, 452*f*, 469–471
  content communities, 452*f*, 463–468
  eWOM, 453–454
  influence of, 462, 469, 472–473, 474
  interaction among TV viewers on, 272*f*

measuring effectiveness of, 445
Milk West on, 430
role in Internet marketing, 12
strategic use of, 473–474
usage statistics, 439f, 440f, 454–456
social media attachment, **452,** 453
social media engagement, **453.** *See also*
consumers' online brand-related
activities (COBRAs)
social needs, 53f
social networking sites, 456–463. *See also*
Facebook; Twitter
as social media class, 452f
earned media, 456, 459–460, 462–463
owned media, 18, 456, 458–459, 461–462
paid media, 456, 457–458, 461
usage statistics, 454, 455f
social TV, **272**
socioeconomic segmentation, 61f–62f
sound effects, 203
source, **76, 177**
source bolsters, **90**
source characteristics, 177–183
attractiveness, 178–183
credibility, 177–178
source derogations, **90**
source-oriented thoughts, 89f, 90
spam, **406**
special ads, 309
special-audience newspapers, 308
special interest group complaints, **484**
specialized marketing communication
services, **14,** 39, 42–46, 47
specialty magazines, 297
specialty networks, 271
spectaculars, **321**
spiffs, 366
split-30s, **284**
split-run tests, **225**
sponsorship, **271**–272
as corporate advertising, 388–394
similarity to marketing, 375
sponsorship ads, 309
spot advertising, **270**
spot radio, 286
S-shaped response function, **257**
standard learning model, **85**
station posters, **328**–329
stereotyping, 494–496
storyboard, **38, 161**–162
storytelling, 166, 176–177, 436
straight sell, 188
strategic marketing plan, **126**
strategy. *See* creative strategy; media
strategy
streaming. *See also* over-the-top (OTT)
service
audio, 287, 288f, 437
radio, 286
video, 435f, 441f

street frames, 322
street media, 320f, 321–322, 323–324
street-level posters, **321**
subcultures, **64**
subheads, **198**
superboards, **321**
superbus, **328,** 329
suppliers, 378
support arguments, **90**
sweepstakes, **357**–358
symbols, 5, 77, 190–191

T
tablets, 420f, 439–441
taglines and slogans, 6, 166–167
target audience, 60–70, **65–66**
brand positioning strategy and, 128,
137–141, 148
brand repositioning strategy and,
146–147
creative evaluation and, 209
for direct marketing, 401–402, 403
for Internet media, 428
for PR activities, 377–379, 383,
392–393
importance in DAGMAR, 107
marketing objectives, behavioural
objectives, and, 105f
marketing planning process and, 60–61
message processing by, 94
options for, 66–70
profile of, 70–71, 96
receptivity to celebrity endorsers, 181
sales promotions to, 344
segmentation variables, 61–65
target audience coverage
direct marketing, 413
Internet media, 242
magazine advertising, 306
media strategy and, 242–243
newspaper advertising, 311
outdoor media, 327
place-based media, 335
radio advertising, 290
transit media, 330
TV advertising, 278
target audience selectivity
direct marketing, 413
magazine advertising, 300–301
newspaper advertising, 314
outdoor media, 327
place-based media, 335
radio advertising, 288
transit media, 330
TV advertising, 282
target CPM (TCPM), **253**
target market, **60,** 65–66, 126
teaser advertising, 176
technical/scientific evidence, 188
telemarketing, **407**–408

television advertising, 268–285. *See also*
broadcast media
advertising revenue, 234f
cost efficiency, 9
cost per ratings point, 253f
delivery of TV services, 268–269
direct marketing via, 407
image transfer, 290
limitations, 281–285
measuring audience, 274–276, 285
media characteristics, 240f
mobile and, 439–441
OTT viewing, 269, 276f, 277f, 285
regulating, 480
role in low-involvement model, 86
strategic use of, 291
strengths, 278–281
time periods and programs, 273–274
transition in, 267
types, 269–273
value of target audience profiles for, 71
video ads, 436
television network, **269**–271
television programs, 273–274
television spots, 407
terminologies, inconsistent, 238
test marketing, 227
testimonials, 189
testing. *See* measurements
testing bias, **215**
theatre tests, 222
time, processing. *See* processing time
time limits set by CRTC, 480
time of day scheduling, **429**
time period, 107, 273–274, 286
timing
consumer sales promotions, 350–351
PR activities, 384
top-down budgeting, **258**
total audience, **299**
tracking measures, 394
tracking studies, **228**
trade advertising, **342**
trade allowances, **362**–363
trade sales promotion, 11, **342,** 343f, 346,
361–366
trade show, **366**
trademarks, 5–6, 77
traditional response hierarchy models,
83–85
traffic department, **38**
transformational motives, **141**–142, 143,
148, 204f, 205
transit exterior, 328f, 329
transit interior, 328f
transit media, 327–330, **328**
media characteristics, 241f
strategic use of, 336
transit shelters, **321**–322, 323–324
transit station, 328f, 329

trial purchase, 105, 346–347, 348*f*, 349*f*
trial purchase objectives, 111–113
trivisions, 321
trustworthiness, source, 177–178
two-sided message, **195**–196
two-step approach, **404**

U

unduplicated reach, **246**
unique selling proposition (USP), **164**
untruthful advertising, 487–488
usage imagery, 191–192
usage rates, behaviouristic segmentation and, 65
usage situation, 65, 131*f*, 134, 145
user imagery, 191–192
user positioning, **137,** 146
user status, behaviouristic segmentation and, 65

V

value, communications about, 8
values and lifestyles (VALS), 63
vehicle source effect, **250**
verbal elements, 202, 203
verbal/visual balance, 196–197
verification, 158
vertical cooperative advertising, **365**
video ads, 434–437
video matrix walls, 329
video messages, 200–202
video streaming, 435*f*, 441*f*
visible minorities, 495–496
visual elements, 199
visual logos, 6
visual/verbal balance, 196–197
voiceover, **201**

W

wall banners, **321**
want, **52**
waste coverage, **242**
website communication, 422–424
website strategy, 424–425
websites, **422**
wikis, 469
wild postings, 322
women, portrayals of, 483, 494–495
word-of-mouth (WOM) communication, 79–80, 114, 453–454
World Wide Web (WWW), **419.** *See also* Internet media

Z

zapping, **282**
zipping, **282**